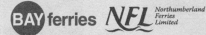

QUÉBEC REGION

HÔTEL CLARION

(418) 653-4901
1 800 463-5241
WWW.CLARIONQUEBEC.COM

LE SAGUENAY REGION

HÔTEL LA SAGUENÉENNE

(418) 545-8326
1 800 461-8390
WWW.LASAGUENEENNE.COM

LAURENTIANS REGION

HÔTEL MONT GABRIEL

(450) 229-3547
1 800 668-5253
WWW.MONTGABRIEL.COM

MONTRÉAL REGION

LE NOUVEL HÔTEL & SPA

(514) 931-8841
1 800 363-6063
WWW.LENOUVELHOTEL.COM

LE MERIDIEN VERSAILLES

(514) 933-8111
1 888 933-8111
WWW.LEMERIDIENVERSAILLESHOTEL.COM

HÔTEL MARITIME PLAZA

(514) 932-1411
1 800 363-6255
WWW.HOTELMARITIME.COM

HÔTEL TRAVELODGE

(514) 874-9090
1 800 363-6535
WWW.TRAVELDOGEMONTREALCENTRE.COM

CHÂTEAU VERSAILLES

(514) 933-3611
1 888 933-8111
WWW.CHATEAUVERSAILLESMONTREAL.COM

TIDAN

GROUPE HÔTELIER ET IMMOBILIER
HOSPITALITY & REAL ESTATE GROUP

www.tidanhotels.com
1-877-768-4326

Atlantic Provinces & Québec

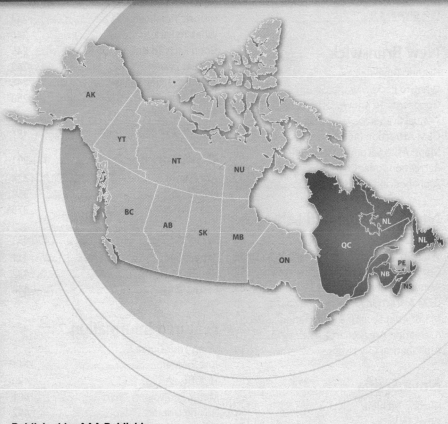

Published by AAA Publishing
1000 AAA Drive, Heathrow, FL 32746-5063
Copyright AAA 2012, All rights reserved

Advertising Rate and Circulation Information: (407) 444-8280

Printed in the USA by Quad/Graphics

This book is printed on paper certified by third-party standards for sustainably managed forestry and production.

 Printed on recyclable paper.
Please recycle whenever possible.

Stock #4604

CONTENTS

Attractions, hotels, restaurants and other travel experience information are all grouped under the alphabetical listing of the city in which those experiences are physically located—or the nearest recognized city.

Our New Look!

USING YOUR
GUIDE
PAGE 5

We've taken the travel series members use more than any other trip planning resource and made it even better, from the inside out.

Discover a colorful twist on your favorite features plus new additions that make the 2012 series our richest, most robust TourBook® edition yet.

Easier to use
- Lighter to carry
- Improved readability
- Reorganized A to Z by city

Easier to navigate
- Mini tables of contents
- Page cross-referencing
- Quick-reference indexes

Easier to travel
- Navigable Atlas maps
- More destination photos
- Recommendations from AAA travel experts

Turn inside. It's a better guide — just for members.

A to Z City Listings

Cities and places are listed alphabetically within each state or province. Attractions, hotels and restaurants are listed once — under the city in which they are physically located.

Cities that are considered part of a larger destination city or area have an expanded city header. The header identifies the larger region and cross-references pages that contain shared trip planning resources:

- Destination map – outline map of the cities that comprise a destination city or area
- Attraction spotting map – regional street map marked with attraction locations
- Hotel/restaurant spotting map and index – regional street map numbered with hotel and restaurant locations identified in an accompanying index

Cities that are not considered part of a larger destination city or area but have a significant number of listings may have these resources within the individual city section:

- Attraction spotting map
- Hotel/restaurant spotting map and index

About Listed Establishments

AAA/CAA Approved attractions, hotels and restaurants are listed on the basis of merit alone after careful evaluation and approval by full-time, professionally trained AAA/CAA inspectors. An establishment's decision to advertise in the TourBook guide has no bearing on its evaluation or rating; nor does inclusion of advertising imply AAA endorsement of products and services.

Information in this guide was believed accurate at the time of publication. However, since changes inevitably occur between annual editions, please contact your AAA travel professional or visit AAA.com to confirm prices and schedules.

Location Abbreviations

Directions are from the center of town unless otherwise specified, using these highway abbreviations:

Bus. Rte.=business route
CR=county road
FM=farm to market

FR=forest road
Hwy.=Canadian highway
I=interstate highway
LR=legislative route
R.R.=rural route
SR/PR=state or provincial route
US=federal highway

Atlas Section

The Atlas Section provides navigable road maps from the AAA Road Atlas series. The overview map displays the entire coverage area. Corresponding, numbered detail maps offer a closer view for route planning and navigation.

Mobile Tags

Look for codes like this Microsoft Tag in the ads and restaurant listings to access special online offers, menus, videos and more.

To use Microsoft Tags:

- Download the free Tag Reader app to your smartphone at http://gettag.mobi
- Start scanning Tags.
- Link to featured content.

Some advertisers use codes other than Microsoft Tags. In those cases, please note any accompanying text that indicates where to download the required reader.

Attraction Listings

 ATTRACTION NAME, 3 mi. n. off SR 20A (Main Ave.), consists of 250 acres with Olmsted-designed gardens, a 205-foot marble and coquina bell tower and a Mediterranean-style mansion. One of the state's oldest attractions, the tower and gardens were dedicated to the American people in 1929 by President Calvin Coolidge on behalf of their founder, a Dutch immigrant.

Other features include daily concerts from the 60-bell carillon, a nature observatory and Nature Preserve Trail. The visitor center presents art exhibits, an orientation film and exhibits about the family legacy, the carillon and endangered plants and animals found on the property.

Hours: Gardens daily 8-6. Last admission 1 hour before closing. Visitor center daily 9-5. Estate tours are given at noon and 2. Carillon concerts are given at 1 and 3. Phone ahead to confirm schedule. **Cost:** $10; $3 (ages 5-12). Gardens and estate $16; $8 (ages 5-12). **Phone:** (555) 555-5555. 🍴 🎇

AAA/CAA inspectors may designate an attraction of exceptional interest and quality as a GEM — a *Great Experience for Members*®. See GEM Attraction Index (listed on CONTENTS page) for complete list of locations.

Adventure Travel

Activities such as air tours, hiking, skiing and white-water rafting are listed to provide member information and do not imply AAA/CAA endorsement. For your safety, be aware of inherent risks and adhere to all safety instructions.

Cost

Prices are quoted without sales tax in the local currency (U.S. or Canadian dollars). Children under the lowest age specified are admitted free when accompanied by an adult. Most establishments accept credit cards, but a small number require cash, so please call ahead to verify.

Icons

SAVE	Show Your Card & Save member discount
🏕	Camping facilities
🍴	Food on premises
🎇	Recreational activities
🐾	Pets on leash allowed
🎇	Picnicking allowed

District of Columbia only:

🚇 Metro station within 1 mile
Icon is followed by station name and AAA/CAA designated station number

Information-Only Attraction Listings

Bulleted listings, which include the following categories, are listed for informational purposes as a service to members:

- **Gambling establishments** (even if located in a AAA/CAA Approved hotel)
- **Participatory recreational activities** (those requiring physical exertion or special skills)
- **Wineries** that offer tours and tastings

Hotel and Restaurant Listings

1 Diamond Rating – AAA/CAA Approved hotels and restaurants are assigned a rating of one to five Diamonds. Red Diamonds distinguish establishments that participate in the AAA/CAA logo licensing program. For details, see p. 11 or AAA.com/Diamonds.

fyi indicates hotels and restaurants that are not AAA/CAA Approved and Diamond Rated but are listed to provide additional choices for members:

- **Hotels** may be unrated if they are: too new to rate, under construction, under major renovation, not evaluated, do not meet all AAA requirements. Hotels that do not meet all AAA requirements may be included if they offer member value or are the only option; details are noted in the listing.
- **Restaurants** may be unrated if they have not yet been evaluated by AAA.

2 Classification or Cuisine Type – noted immediately below the Diamond Rating

- **Hotel Classifications** indicate the style of operation, overall concept and service level. Subclassifications may also be added. (See p. 12 list.)
- **Restaurant Cuisine Types** identify the food concept from more than 100 categories. If applicable, a classification may also be added. (See p. 13 list.)

3 Dollar Amounts – Quoted without sales tax in the local currency (U.S. or Canadian dollars), rounded up to the nearest dollar. Most establishments accept credit cards, but a small number require cash, so please call ahead to verify.

- **Hotel Rates** indicate the publicly available two-person rate or rate range for a standard room, applicable all year unless effective dates are indicated.
- **Restaurant Prices** represent the minimum and maximum entree cost per person. Exceptions may include one-of-a-kind or special market priced items.

4 Spotting Symbol – Ovals containing numbers correspond with numbered location markings on hotel and restaurant spotting maps.

5 Parking – Unless otherwise noted, parking is free, on-site self parking.

6 Hotel Value Nationwide – Blue boxes highlight everyday member benefits available at all AAA/CAA Approved locations across a hotel chain. (See Just For Members section for details.)

7 Hotel Unit Limited Availability – Unit types, amenities and room features preceded by "some" are available on a limited basis, potentially as few as one.

8 Hotel Terms – Cancellation and minimum stay policies are listed. Unless otherwise noted, most properties offer a full deposit refund with cancellations received at least 48 hours before standard check-in. Properties that require advance payment may not refund the difference for early departures.

9 Hotel Check-in/Check-out – Unless otherwise noted, check-in is after 3 p.m. and check-out is before 10 a.m.

10 Restaurant Dress Code – Unless otherwise noted, dress is casual or dressy casual.

11 Restaurant Menu – Where indicated, menus may be viewed in a secure online environment at AAA.com or, if a mobile tag is provided, via the restaurant's website.

12 Hotel Icons – May be preceded by CALL, FEE and/or SOME UNITS.

Member Information:

SAVE Rate guarantee: discounted standard room rate or lowest public rate available at time of booking for dates of stay.

ECO Eco-certified by government or private organization. Visit AAA.com/eco for details.

☒ Smoke-free premises

Services:

📶 Wireless Internet service on premises

✈ Airport transportation

🐾 Pets allowed (call property for restrictions and fees)

🍴 Restaurant on premises

🍴▸ Restaurant off premises (walking distance)

🍽 Room service for 2 or more meals

HOTEL LISTING

1 **2** **3** **5** **9** **12**

HOTEL NAME

▽▽▽
Hotel
$109-$199

Phone: (555)555-5555 **50**

LOGO **AAA Benefit:** Members save a minimum 5% off the best available rate.

4 **6** **7** **8**

Address: 300 Main St 55555 **Location:** I-275 exit 31 southbound; exit 30 northbound. 1.6 mi w on SR 688 (Oak Rd). **Facility:** 149 units, some efficiencies. 3 stories, interior corridors. **Parking:** on-site (fee). **Terms:** check-in 4 pm, cancellation fee imposed. **Amenities:** video games. **Pool(s):** heated outdoor. **Activities:** whirlpool, exercise room. **Guest Services:** valet and coin laundry. **Free Special Amenities:** newspaper and expanded continental breakfast.

RESTAURANT LISTING

11 **1** **2** **3** **13**

RESTAURANT NAME
Menu on AAA.com

▽▽▽
Continental
$15-$35

Phone: 555/555-5555

AAA Inspector Notes: A romantic aura punctuates the modern and casual dining room, which is accented with floral arrangements and dramatic, freshly cut branches. The seasonal menu centers on Tuscan-American cuisine. The pastry chef's decadent creations are popular. Semi-formal attire. **Bar:** full bar. Address: 26 N Main St 55555 **Location:** SR A1A southbound, 2.7 mi so of jct SR 520.

10

L D

 Full bar

Child care

BIZ Business services

&M Accessible features (Call property for available services and amenities.)

Activities:

Full-service casino

Pool

Health club on premises

Health club off premises

In-Room Amenities:

Pay movies

Refrigerator

Microwave

Coffee maker

AC No air conditioning

No TV

CTV No cable TV

No telephones

13 Restaurant Icons

SAVE Show Your Card & Save member discount

AC No air conditioning

&M Accessible features (Call property for available services and amenities.)

Designated smoking section

B Breakfast

L Lunch

D Dinner

24 Open 24 hours

LATE Open after 11 p.m.

Just For Members

Understanding the Diamond Ratings

Hotel and restaurant evaluations are unscheduled to ensure our professionally trained inspectors encounter the same experience members do.

- When an establishment is Diamond Rated, it means members can expect a good fit with their needs. The inspector assigns a rating that indicates the type of experience to expect.
- While establishments at high levels must offer increasingly complex personalized services, establishments at every level are subject to the same basic requirements for cleanliness, comfort and hospitality. Learn more at AAA.com/Diamonds.

Hotels

Budget-oriented, offering basic comfort and hospitality.

Affordable, with modestly enhanced facilities, decor and amenities.

Distinguished, multi-faceted with enhanced physical attributes, amenities and guest comforts.

Refined, stylish with upscale physical attributes, extensive amenities and high degree of hospitality, service and attention to detail.

Ultimate luxury, sophistication and comfort with extraordinary physical attributes, meticulous personalized service, extensive amenities and impeccable standards of excellence.

What's the difference?

- Red Diamonds mark establishments that participate in the AAA/CAA logo licensing program for increased visibility to members.

- Black Diamonds identify all other AAA/CAA Approved and Diamond Rated establishments.

Restaurants

Simple, familiar specialty food at an economical price. Often self-service, basic surroundings.

Familiar, family-oriented experience. Home-style foods and family favorites, often cooked to order, modestly enhanced and reasonably priced. Relaxed service, casual surroundings.

Fine dining, often adult-oriented. Latest cooking trends and/or traditional cuisine, expanded beverage offerings. Professional service staff and comfortable, well-coordinated ambience.

Distinctive fine-dining, typically expensive. Highly creative chefs, imaginative presentations and fresh, top-quality ingredients. Proficient service staff, upscale surroundings. Wine steward may offer menu-specific knowledge.

Luxurious and consistently world-class. Highly acclaimed chefs, artistic and imaginative menu selections using the finest ingredients. Maitre d' and unobtrusive, expert service staff.

Hotel Classifications

Quality and comfort are usually consistent across each Diamond Rating level, but decor, facilities and service levels vary by classification.

1884 Paxton House Inn
Thomasville, GA

Bed & Breakfast – Typically small-scale, emphasizing personal touches. Individually decorated units may not include televisions, telephones or private bathrooms. Usually a common room and continental or full, hot breakfast.

Greenbrier Valley Resorts at
Cobbly Nob, Gatlinburg, TN

Cabin – Vacation-oriented, typically small-scale, free-standing units with simple construction and basic decor. Often in wooded, rural or waterfront location. Cleaning supplies, utensils and bath linens provided. Check-in may be off site.

Camelot by the Sea
Myrtle Beach, SC

Condominium – Vacation-oriented, commonly for extended stays. Routinely rented through a management company. Generally one or more bedrooms, living room, full kitchen and eating area. Studio units combine sleeping and living areas. Cleaning supplies, utensils and linens provided. Check-in may be off site.

The Dunes on the Waterfront
Ogunquit, ME

Cottage – Vacation-oriented, typically small-scale, freestanding units with homey design and decor. Often in wooded, rural or waterfront location. Cleaning supplies, utensils and linens provided. Check-in may be off site.

The Lodge at Moosehead
Lake, Greenville, ME

Country Inn – Similar to bed and breakfasts but larger scale with spacious public areas and dining facility that serves, at a minimum, breakfast and dinner.

The Grand America Hotel
Salt Lake City, UT

Hotel – Commonly multistory with interior room entrances. Unit styles vary. Public areas determined by overall theme, location and service level, but may include restaurant, shops, fitness center, spa, business center and meeting rooms.

Best Western Plus Sea Island
Inn, Beaufort, SC

Motel – Commonly one- or two-story with exterior room entrances and drive-up parking. Typically one bedroom with bathroom. Limited public areas and facilities.

Lost Valley Ranch
Deckers, CO

Ranch – Typically a working ranch with rustic, Western theme, equestrian activities and various unit styles.

Indian Creek-Alexander
Holiday Homes
Kissimmee, FL

Vacation Rental House – Commonly for extended stays. Typically large scale, freestanding and of varying design. Routinely rented through a management company. Often two or more bedrooms, living room, full kitchen, dining room and multiple bathrooms. Cleaning supplies, utensils and linens supplied. Check-in may be off site.

Hotel Subclassifications

These additional descriptives may be added to the classification for more information:

- **Boutique** – Often thematic and informal, highly personalized experience. May have fashionable, luxurious or quirky style.
- **Casino** – (Identified by listing icon) Extensive gambling facilities such as blackjack, craps, keno and slot machines.
- **Classic** – Landmark property, older than 50 years, renowned style and ambience.
- **Contemporary** – Design and theme reflective of current mainstream tastes and style.
- **Extended Stay** – Predominantly long-term units with full-service kitchens.
- **Historic** – Typically 75 years or older with historic architecture, design, furnishings, public record or acclaim and at least one of the following: maintains integrity of the historical nature, listed on the National Register of Historic Places, designated a National Historic Landmark or located in a National Register Historic District.
- **Resort** – Recreation-oriented, geared to a specific destination experience. Typically offer travel packages, meal plans, themed entertainment and social and recreational programs. Extensive recreational facilities may include spa treatments, golf, tennis,

skiing, fishing or water sports. Larger resorts may offer a variety of unit types.

- **Retro** – Contemporary design and theme that reinterpret styles of a bygone era.
- **Vacation Rental** – Typically a house, condo, cottage or cabin offering space, value and conveniences such as full kitchens and washers/dryers. Located in a resort or popular destination area near major points of interest. May require reservations and off-site check-in. Limited housekeeping services.
- **Vintage** – Design and theme reflective of a bygone era.

Restaurant Classifications

If applicable, in addition to the cuisine type noted under the Diamond Rating, restaurant listings may also include one or both classifications:

- **Classic** – Renowned and landmark operation in business for 25 plus years; unique style and ambience.
- **Historic** – Meets one of the following: Listed on National Register of Historic Places, designated a National Historic Landmark or located in a National Register Historic District.

Service Animals

Under the Americans with Disabilities Act (ADA), U.S. businesses that serve the public must allow people with disabilities to bring their service animals into all areas of the facility where customers are normally allowed to go.

Businesses may ask if an animal is a service animal and what tasks the animal has been trained to perform. Businesses may not ask about the person's disability, require special identification for the animal or request removal of the animal from the premises except in limited cases that require alternate assistance. Businesses may not charge extra fees for service animals, including standard pet fees, but may charge for damage caused by service animals if guests are normally charged for damage they cause.

Call the U.S. Department of Justice ADA Information Line: (800) 514-0301 or TTY (800) 514-0383, or visit ada.gov. Regulations may differ in Canada.

AAA/CAA Approved Hotels

For members, AAA/CAA Approved means quality assured.

- Only properties that meet basic requirements for cleanliness, comfort and hospitality pass inspection.
- Approved hotels receive a Diamond Rating that tells members the type of experience to expect.

Guest Safety

Inspectors view a sampling of rooms during evaluations and, therefore, AAA/CAA cannot guarantee the presence of working locks and operational fire safety equipment in every guest unit.

Member Rates

AAA/CAA members can generally expect to pay no more than the maximum TourBook listed rate for a standard room. Member discounts apply to rates quoted within the rate range and are applicable at the time of booking. Listed rates are usually based on last standard room availability. Within the range, rates may vary by season and room type. Obtain current AAA/CAA member rates and make reservations at AAA.com.

Exceptions

- Rates for properties operating as concessionaires for the U.S. National Park Service are not guaranteed due to governing regulations.
- Special advertised rates and short-term promotional rates below the rate range are not subject to additional member discounts.
- During special events, hotels may temporarily increase room rates, not recognize discounts or modify pricing policies. Special events may include Mardi Gras, the Kentucky Derby (including pre-Derby events), college football games, holidays, holiday periods and state fairs. Although some special events are listed in the TourBook guides and on AAA.com, it's always wise to check in advance with AAA travel professionals for specific dates.

If you are charged more than the maximum TourBook listed rate, question the additional charge. If an exception is not in effect and management refuses to adhere to the published rate, pay for the room and contact AAA/CAA. The amount paid above the stated maximum will be refunded if our investigation indicates an unjustified charge.

Reservations and Cancellations

When making your reservation, identify yourself as a AAA/CAA member and request written confirmation of your room type, rate, dates of stay, and cancellation and refund policies. At registration, show your membership card.

To cancel, contact the hotel or your AAA/CAA club office, depending on how you booked your reservation. Request a cancellation number or proof of cancellation.

If your room is not as specified and you have written confirmation of your reservation for a specific room type, you should be given the option of choosing a different room or receiving a refund. If management refuses to issue a refund, contact AAA/CAA.

Contacting AAA/CAA About Approved Properties

If your visit to a AAA/CAA Approved attraction, hotel or restaurant doesn't meet your expectations, please tell us about it — *during your visit or within 30 days*.

Use the easy online form at AAA.com/TourBookComments to send us the details, and save your receipts and other documentation for reference.

Or, send your written comments to us at: AAA Member Comments, 1000 AAA Dr., Heathrow, FL 32746.

AAA/CAA Preferred Hotels

All AAA/CAA Approved hotels are committed to providing quality, value and member service. In addition, those designated as AAA/CAA Preferred Hotels also offer these extra values at Approved locations nationwide. Valid AAA/CAA membership required.

- **Best AAA/CAA member rates for your dates of stay.**
- **Seasonal promotions and special member offers.** Visit AAA.com to view current offers.
- **Everyday member benefit.** Look for the blue boxes in the TourBook listings to find everyday values offered at all AAA/CAA Approved locations nationwide. Chains and offers valid at time of publication may change without notice.

- **Total satisfaction guarantee.** If you book your stay with AAA/CAA Travel and your stay fails to meet your expectations, you can apply for a full refund. Bring the complaint to the hotel's attention during the stay and request resolution; if the complaint is not resolved by the hotel, ask your AAA/CAA travel agent to request resolution through the AAA/CAA Assured Stay program.

Preferred Hotels

Total Satisfaction Guarantee

Best Western, Best Western Plus and Best Western Premier

Conrad Hotels & Resorts, DoubleTree by Hilton, Embassy Suites, Hampton Inns & Suites, Hilton Hotels & Resorts, Hilton Garden Inns, Hilton Grand Vacations, Home2 Suites, Homewood Suites and Waldorf Astoria Collection

ANdAZ, Grand Hyatt, Hyatt Place, Hyatt Regency, Hyatt Summerfield Suites and Park Hyatt

Autograph Collection by Marriott, Courtyard, EDITION Hotels by Marriott, Fairfield Inn, JW Marriott, Marriott Hotels & Resorts, Renaissance Hotels, Residence Inn, Ritz-Carlton Hotels & Resorts, SpringHill Suites and TownePlace Suites

Aloft, Element, Four Points, Le Meridien, Sheraton, St. Regis Hotels & Resorts, The Luxury Collection, Westin and W Hotels

Show Your Card & Save® Member Discounts

Visit AAA.com/Discounts to find local Show Your Card & Save discounts. Your AAA/CAA club may offer even greater discounts on theme park tickets. Amtrak, Gray Line and theme park discounts may be used for up to six tickets; restaurant savings may be used for up to six patrons. Other restrictions may apply.

ATTRACTIONS

SeaWorld, Busch Gardens, Sesame Place

- Save on admission at the gate, participating AAA/CAA offices or AAA.com/SeaWorld.
- Save 10% on up-close dining; visit Guest Relations for details.

Six Flags

- Save on admission at the gate, participating AAA/CAA offices or AAA.com/SixFlags.
- Save 10% on merchandise of $15 or more at in-park stores.

Universal Orlando Resort and Universal Studios Hollywood

- Save on admission at the gate, participating AAA/CAA offices or AAA.com/Universal.
- Save 10% at select food and merchandise venues in-park and at Universal CityWalk®.

DINING & SHOPPING

Hard Rock Cafe

- Save 10% on food, non-alcoholic beverages and merchandise at all U.S., Canadian and select international locations.

Landry's Seafood House, The Crab House, Chart House, Oceanaire, Saltgrass Steak House, Muer Seafood Restaurants and Aquarium Restaurants

- Save 10% on food and nonalcoholic beverages at all of the above restaurants.
- Save 10% on merchandise at Aquarium and Downtown Aquarium restaurants.

Tanger Outlet Centers

- Save up to 20% on total purchase at select merchants with FREE coupon booklet available with registration at AAA customer service desk.
- After first visit, get $5 gift card for each additional location visited in same calendar year.
- Location information: tangeroutlet.com.

TravelCenters of America/Petro Stopping Centers

- Save 10% at the more than 350 full-service and fast-food restaurants inside participating locations nationwide.

TRANSPORTATION & TOURS

Amtrak

- Save 10% on rail fare booked at least 3 days in advance of travel date at AAA.com/Amtrak.

Gray Line

- Save 10% on sightseeing tours of 1 day or less worldwide at AAA.com/GrayLine.

Hertz

- Save on daily, weekend, weekly and monthly rentals at AAA.com/hertz or 1-800-654-3080.

Campobello Island

New Brunswick

With the Gulf of St. Lawrence and Fundy and Chaleur bays lapping its shores on three sides, New Brunswick has literally been shaped by the sea.

The Bay of Fundy tides, said to be the world's highest, have been known to reach 16 metres (52 ft.), the height of a four-story building. According to a Mi'kmaq legend, a giant whale, angered by the god Glooscap, slammed its powerful tail into the water, causing the tremendous ebb and flow. Although the bay's tidal fluctuations are attributable to science rather than lore, they do create some pretty amazing phenomena.

Take the Hopewell Rocks, near the mouth of the Petitcodiac River at Hopewell Cape. These whimsical sandstone sculptures, carved over centuries by the force of the tides, are topped by fir and spruce outcroppings. At low tide the columns resemble flowerpots and can be explored by merely walking on the beach. At high tide, however, when only the upper portions are visible,

Watch Whales Breaching during the Summer

they appear to be tree-topped islands and can be viewed from lookout points along nature trails or by kayak.

The old Loyalist seaport of Saint John is the site of another astounding event, the Reversing Rapids. At the narrow, rocky gorge where the Saint John River's rapids meet the Bay of Fundy, the bay's immense tides actually overpower the river twice each day, causing the rapids to flow backward.

Caves—created by the enormous pressure of the Fundy tides—can be reached from crescent-shaped beaches near St. Martins. Once a bustling 1800s shipbuilding center, this seaside fishing village is now an access point for the Fundy Trail, which includes a low-speed roadway as well as walking and bicycling trails.

A Whale of a Place

Whales love this place—about 15 species flock to the waters near Grand Manan and Deer islands and just off the coast of St. Andrews to feed on the watery buffet churned up by the bay's tidal currents. If you're visiting between July and September, by all means schedule a whale-watching excursion for an up-close glimpse of these magnificent mammals breaching and frolicking.

For a whale of a gastronomic delight, look no further than the Saint John City Market. There you'll find just-caught salmon, lobster and scallops; fresh produce and baked goods; and the local delicacy known as dulse, sun-dried seaweed gathered from rocks along the Bay of Fundy.

Living by the Sea

You'll get a true feel for the Acadian way of life near the coastal town of Caraquet, where the annual Festival acadien de Caraquet is a treasured link to the past. Caught in a power struggle between France and Great Britain, French-speaking Acadians unwilling to swear allegiance to the British crown were deported in 1755. Many of the exiles returned, however, reestablishing their culture and *joie de vivre*.

Caraquet's Acadian Historical Village preserves the traditions and the humble everyday existence of those people. Restored buildings relocated from throughout the province comprise the settlement, where transportation is by ox-drawn cart and homespun interpreters are engaged in daily chores.

For generations Acadians have relied on the Gulf of St. Lawrence's waters for their livelihood. That bond is illustrated at the New Brunswick Aquarium and Marine Centre in Shippagan; here the region's nautical ties can be examined through exhibits about ships and fishermen, and aquariums teeming with marine life.

Recreation

Water, water, everywhere—Canada's largest Maritime Province has 2,400 kilometres (1,500 mi.) of coastline, making aquatic adventure a prime diversion.

Sea kayaking past the Flower Pot Rocks near the Petitcodiac River's mouth is thrilling, and so is a jet boat ride through the Reversing Rapids in Saint John. Paddle past grey seals in Kouchibouguac Bay, or scuba dive the waters off Deer Island.

Sail away on scenic Passamaquoddy Bay, or head inland and cruise the waters of Mactaquac Lake and the Saint John River. Make a splash at the lagoon in Kouchibouguac National Park, where the swimming is refreshing in summer waters that are 24 degrees Celsius (75 F).

If salmon is your fish of choice, you're in the right place; the Miramichi River is world-famous for fishing out the big one. Jig for bluefin tuna in Chaleur Bay, where record-breaking catches have been made.

For landlubbers, five scenic drives traverse the province, all offering access to numerous recreational activities. The 400-kilometre (250-mi.) River Valley Route, running from St-Jacques to Saint John, is maritime Canada's most picturesque. Bicycling enthusiasts cruise in Edmundston, where 130 kilometres (81 mi.) of trails line the Madawaska River in Petit Témis Interprovincial Park.

North America's oldest mountains can be explored along the Appalachian Range Route. If hiking to Mount Carleton—the Maritimes' highest peak—doesn't take your breath away, the scenery will.

Follow the Miramichi River, a 182-kilometre (113-mi.) route from Miramichi to Fredericton. Toss a line into the salmon-filled waters, stroll past waterfalls and over a suspension footbridge, or canoe down a stretch of this pristine waterway.

For a coastal adventure, tour the 391-kilometre (243-mi.) Fundy Coastal Drive from St. Stephen to Aulac. Spelunkers can get lost in the sandstone caves of St. Martins, while rock climbers can rappel cliffs overlooking the Bay of Fundy.

Fundy National Park of Canada, situated on the bay's coastal cliffs, offers more than 100 kilometres (60 mi.) of hiking trails through wooded valleys and highlands inhabited by American martens, whitetail deer, peregrine falcons and other wildlife.

Autumn is the best time to see migrating birds dining in the bay's rich mud flats. Mary's Point attracts bird-watchers in August, when tens of thousands of sandpipers and other birds flock to shore.

Acadian Historical Village (Village Historique Acadien), Caraquet

Historic Timeline

1534	Jacques Cartier explores the coast of New Brunswick.
1604	The first French settlement in North America is founded on St. Croix Island.
1713	France cedes Acadia to Great Britain in the Treaty of Utrecht.
1755	Acadians who choose neutrality are deported; many find refuge in the interior of New Brunswick.
1785	Populated by Loyalists fleeing the American Revolution, Saint John becomes the first incorporated city in Canada.
1867	New Brunswick enters the Canadian Confederation.
1877	The Great Fire in Saint John leaves some 15,000 people homeless.
1922	Rexton's Bonar Law becomes the only Prime Minister of Britain born outside the United Kingdom.
1969	New Brunswick becomes Canada's first bilingual province.
1997	The Confederation Bridge links Prince Edward Island and New Brunswick.
2001	Hartland Bridge, the world's longest covered bridge, marks its 100th anniversary.

What To Pack

Temperature Averages Maximum/Minimum (Celsius)	JANUARY	FEBRUARY	MARCH	APRIL	MAY	JUNE	JULY	AUGUST	SEPTEMBER	OCTOBER	NOVEMBER	DECEMBER
Dalhousie	-8 / -18	-6 / -17	-1 / -11	6 / -3	14 / 2	20 / 8	23 / 12	22 / 11	17 / 6	10 / 1	2 / -5	-4 / -13
Fredericton	-4 / -16	-3 / -15	3 / -8	9 / -2	17 / 4	23 / 9	26 / 13	24 / 12	19 / 6	13 / 1	6 / -4	-2 / -12
Rexton	-2 / -8	-2 / -9	1 / -6	3 / -2	8 / 1	14 / 5	19 / 10	19 / 11	15 / 8	10 / 4	6 / -2	1 / -4
Sackville	-4 / -14	-3 / -14	2 / -8	7 / -2	16 / 3	21 / 8	24 / 12	23 / 12	18 / 7	12 / 2	6 / -3	-1 / -11
St-Jacques	-6 / -16	-4 / -14	2 / -7	11 / 1	18 / 6	24 / 12	26 / 14	24 / 13	19 / 8	13 / 3	5 / -3	-3 / -12
Saint John	-3 / -14	-3 / -13	2 / -8	8 / -2	14 / 3	19 / 8	22 / 11	22 / 11	17 / 7	12 / 3	6 / -2	-1 / -10

From the records of The Weather Channel Interactive, Inc.

Good Facts To Know

ALCOHOL CONSUMPTION: Legal age 19.

ABOUT THE PROVINCE

POPULATION: 729,997.

AREA: 72,908 sq km (28,150 sq mi.); ranks 11th.

CAPITAL: Fredericton.

HIGHEST POINT: 820 m (2,690 ft.), Mount Carleton.

LOWEST POINT: Sea level, Atlantic Ocean.

TIME ZONE(S): Atlantic. DST.

REGULATIONS

TEEN DRIVING LAWS: For the first 12 months of li-
censure, intermediate license holders under age 21
are prohibited from driving between midnight and 5
a.m. and are not permitted to carry more than 3 passengers, with only 1 passenger in the front seat. The
minimum age for an unrestricted license is 17 years
and 8 months. For more information about New Brunswick driver's license regulations contact (506)
453-3992.

SEAT BELT/CHILD RESTRAINT LAWS: Seat belts
required for driver and all passengers 16 and older.
Children ages 9-15 and at least 36 kilograms (80 lb.)
are required to be in a seat belt or child restraint. Child
restraints required for children under 9 years or under
36 kilograms (80 lb.) or 145 centimetres (4 ft., 9 in.)
tall.

CELL PHONE RESTRICTIONS: All drivers are
banned from text messaging and from using any type
of handheld electronic device, including handheld cell
phones and two-way radios.

HELMETS FOR MOTORCYCLISTS: Required for all
riders.

RADAR DETECTORS: Not permitted.

MOVE OVER LAW: Drivers approaching a stopped
emergency vehicle equipped with at least one flashing
red light must slow down, proceed with caution, and if
possible vacate the lane nearest to the emergency
vehicle.

FIREARMS LAWS: By federal law, all nonresidents
entering Canada with a firearm must declare their
weapon in writing and pay a fee of $25 (Canadian).
Contact the Canadian Firearms Centre at (800)
731-4000 to receive a declaration form or for additional information.

HOLIDAYS

HOLIDAYS: Jan. 1 ▪ Good Friday ▪ Easter Monday
▪ Victoria Day, May 24 or closest prior Mon. ▪ Canada
Day, July 1 ▪ New Brunswick Day, Aug. (1st Mon.)
▪ Labour Day, Sept. (1st Mon.) ▪ Thanksgiving, Oct.
(2nd Mon.) ▪ Remembrance Day, Nov. 11
▪ Christmas, Dec. 25 ▪ Boxing Day, Dec. 26.

MONEY

TAXES: New Brunswick's harmonized sales tax is 13
percent—8 percent provincial tax and 5 percent federal goods and services tax; it is applied to most goods
and services.

VISITOR INFORMATION

INFORMATION CENTERS: Provincial welcome centers provide details about attractions, accommodations, historic sites, parks and events. They are
located at Aulac ▪ Campbellton ▪ Cape Jourimain in
Bayfield ▪ St-Jacques ▪ St. Stephen ▪ and Woodstock. All centers are open daily May 15 through the
second Monday in October. For further information
phone (800) 561-0123.

FURTHER INFORMATION FOR VISITORS:
Department of Tourism and Parks
Centennial Building
Room 613, Floor 6
670 King Street
Fredericton, NB E3B 1G1
Canada
(506) 444-5205

FISHING AND HUNTING REGULATIONS:
Department of Natural Resources
Fish and Wildlife Branch
Hugh John Flemming Forestry Centre
1350 Regent Street
Fredericton, NB E3C 2G6
Canada
(506) 453-3826

INTERPROVINCE FERRY INFORMATION:
Bay Ferries Terminals
170 Digby Ferry Rd.
Saint John, NB E2M 0B2
Canada
(506) 649-7777
(888) 249-7245

New Brunswick Annual Events
Please call ahead to confirm event details.

JANUARY

- New Year's Levee
  Dorchester
  506-379-3030
- Hartland Winter Carnival
  Winterfest / Hartland
  506-375-4222
- Perth-Andover Winter
  Carnival / Perth-Andover
  506-273-4845

FEBRUARY

- International Snowmobilers
  Festival / Edmundston
  207-728-0949
- White Gold Festival
  Miramichi
  506-623-2150
- Winterfest New Brunswick
  Fredericton
  506-474-0096

MARCH

- Moncton Boat Show
  Moncton
  888-454-7469
- St. Patrick's Week
  Celebrations / Saint John
  506-634-7919
- Sugar Bush Weekend
  Prince William
  506-363-4999

APRIL

- Fredericton Wine and Food
  Fest / Fredericton
  506-452-9009
- Salon Du Livre of
  Edmundston Book Fair
  Edmundston
  506-739-2104
- Frye Festival / Moncton
  506-859-4389

MAY

- Gathering of the Scots
  Festival / Perth-Andover
  506-273-6710
- FredKid Fair / Fredericton
  506-454-3310
- Francophone Festival
  Fredericton
  506-453-2731

JUNE

- Minto Coal Mining Festival
  Minto
  506-327-3383
- Shiretown Days Festival
  Dorchester
  506-379-3030
- Apple Blossom Festival
  Memramcook
  506-758-2325

JULY

- Canada's Irish Festival on
  the Miramichi / Miramichi
  506-778-8810
- New Brunswick Highland
  Games and Scottish
  Festival / Fredericton
  506-452-9244
- La Foire Brayonne
  Edmundston
  506-739-6608

AUGUST

- Turner's Victoria Park Arts
  and Crafts Fair / Moncton
  506-386-1200
- Atlantic Seafood Festival
  Moncton
  506-384-8585
- Le Festival Acadien de
  Caraquet / Caraquet
  506-727-2787

SEPTEMBER

- Atlantic International
  Balloon Fiesta / Sussex
  506-432-9444
- Fredericton Exhibition
  Fredericton
  506-458-9819
- Harvest Jazz and Blues
  Festival / Fredericton
  888-622-5837

OCTOBER

- Halloween Haunted House
  Tour / Dorchester
  506-397-6633
- Indulge, New Brunswick's
  Festival of Food and
  Flavours / St. Andrews
  506-529-3556
- Thanksgiving Festival
  Prince William
  506-363-4959

NOVEMBER

- Turner's Christmas at the
  Coliseum / Moncton
  506-855-4197
- St. Andrews by-the-Sea
  Winter Festival: A Season of
  Light and Wonder
  St. Andrews
  506-529-3555
- Victorian Christmas
  Woodstock
  506-325-9049

DECEMBER

- Christmas with the Muses,
  the Brothers Belivo and
  Roland Gauvin / Moncton
  506-856-4379
- Christmas Arts and Crafts
  Show / Fredericton
  506-458-9819
- Living Christmas Tree
  Moncton
  506-857-2293

Hopewell Rocks Ocean Tidal Exploration Site, Hopewell Cape

Flag of New Brunswick

Sainte-Cécile Church of Petite-Rivière-de-l'Île, Lamèque

Confederation Bridge

The World's Largest Lobster, Shediac

Great Experience for Members

AAA editor's picks of exceptional note

Le Pays de la
Sagouine

Roosevelt
Campobello
International Park

New Brunswick
Aquarium and Marine
Centre

Kingsbrae Garden

Bouctouche (D-5)
Irving Eco-Centre, "La dune de Bouctouche" *(See p. 37.)*
Le Pays de la Sagouine *(See p. 37.)*

Campobello Island (F-3)
Roosevelt Campobello International Park *(See p. 38.)*

Caraquet (A-5)
Acadian Historical Village (Village Historique Acadien) *(See p. 39.)*

Fredericton (D-3)
The Beaverbrook Art Gallery *(See p. 44.)*

Fundy National Park of Canada (E-5)
Fundy National Park of Canada *(See p. 49.)*

Hopewell Cape (E-5)
Hopewell Rocks Ocean Tidal Exploration Site *(See p. 52.)*

Kings Landing (D-2)
Kings Landing Historical Settlement *(See p. 53.)*

St. Andrews (F-3)
Kingsbrae Garden *(See p. 68.)*

Saint John (E-4)
New Brunswick Museum *(See p. 73.)*

St. Martins (E-4)
Fundy Trail *(See p. 78.)*

Shippagan (B-5)
New Brunswick Aquarium and Marine Centre *(See p. 80.)*

Enjoy great savings on hotel rates

at AAA.com or CAA.ca

Atlantic Provinces
Atlas Section

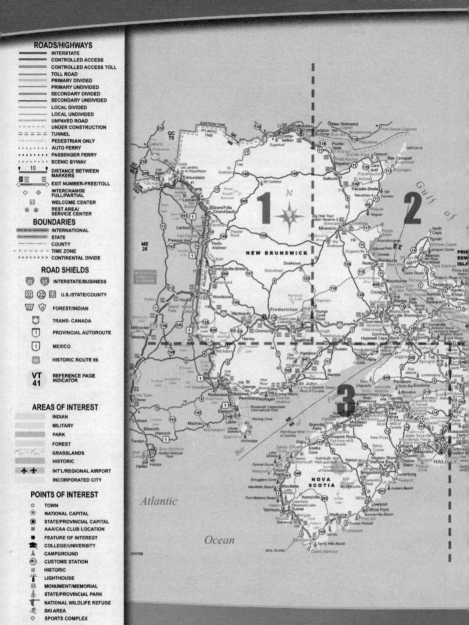

ROADS/HIGHWAYS
- INTERSTATE
- CONTROLLED ACCESS
- CONTROLLED ACCESS TOLL
- TOLL ROAD
- PRIMARY DIVIDED
- PRIMARY UNDIVIDED
- SECONDARY DIVIDED
- SECONDARY UNDIVIDED
- LOCAL DIVIDED
- LOCAL UNDIVIDED
- UNPAVED ROAD
- UNDER CONSTRUCTION
- TUNNEL
- PEDESTRIAN ONLY
- AUTO FERRY
- PASSENGER FERRY
- SCENIC BYWAY
- DISTANCE BETWEEN MARKERS
- EXIT NUMBER-FREE/TOLL
- INTERCHANGE FULL/PARTIAL
- WELCOME CENTER
- REST AREA/ SERVICE CENTER

BOUNDARIES
- INTERNATIONAL
- STATE
- COUNTY
- TIME ZONE
- CONTINENTAL DIVIDE

ROAD SHIELDS
- 95 95 INTERSTATE/BUSINESS
- 22 22 22 U.S./STATE/COUNTY
- 127 FOREST/INDIAN
- TRANS- CANADA
- 1 PROVINCIAL AUTOROUTE
- 1 MEXICO
- 66 HISTORIC ROUTE 66
- VT 41 REFERENCE PAGE INDICATOR

AREAS OF INTEREST
- INDIAN
- MILITARY
- PARK
- FOREST
- GRASSLANDS
- HISTORIC
- INT'L/REGIONAL AIRPORT
- INCORPORATED CITY

POINTS OF INTEREST
- ○ TOWN
- ✷ NATIONAL CAPITAL
- ✪ STATE/PROVINCIAL CAPITAL
- ■ AAA/CAA CLUB LOCATION
- ■ FEATURE OF INTEREST
- 🏛 COLLEGE/UNIVERSITY
- ⚑ CAMPGROUND
- ⊕ CUSTOMS STATION
- ☰ HISTORIC
- 🗼 LIGHTHOUSE
- 🏛 MONUMENT/MEMORIAL
- ⚑ STATE/PROVINCIAL PARK
- ⚑ NATIONAL WILDLIFE REFUGE
- ⛷ SKI AREA
- ○ SPORTS COMPLEX

Including: New Brunswick, Nova Scotia,

Newfoundland and Labrador, Prince Edward Island

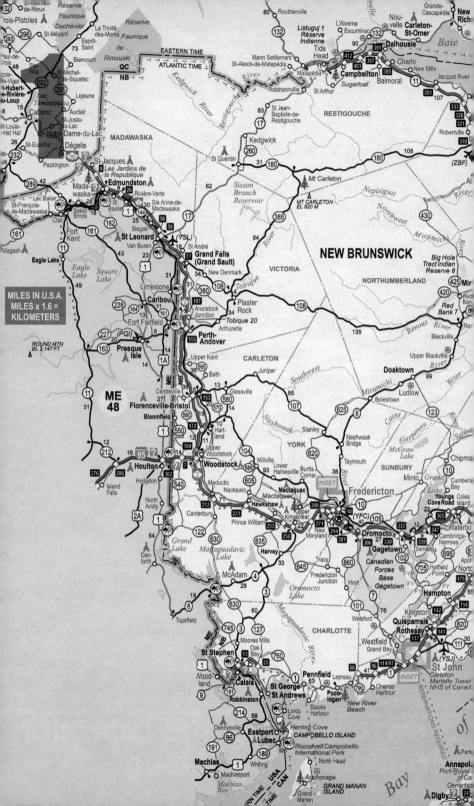

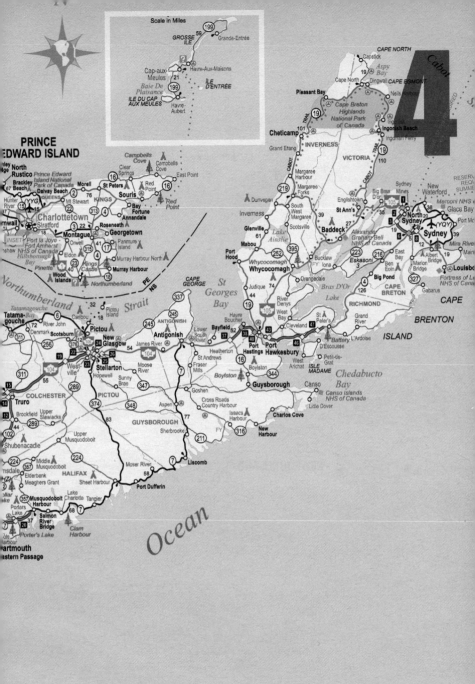

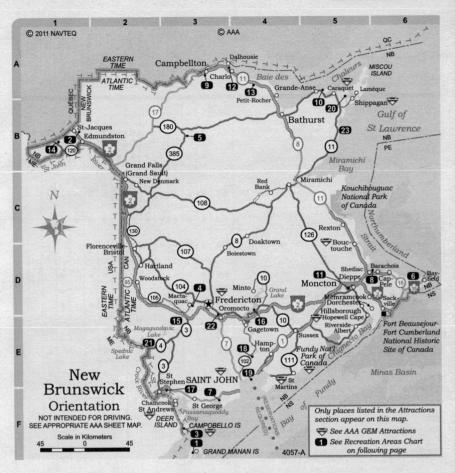

New Brunswick Orientation
NOT INTENDED FOR DRIVING.
SEE APPROPRIATE AAA SHEET MAP.

Scale in Kilometers
45   0   45

Only places listed in the Attractions section appear on this map.

🦅 See AAA GEM Attractions
❶ See Recreation Areas Chart on following page

Safety tip: Keep a current AAA/CAA
Road Atlas in every vehicle

Recreation Areas Chart

The map location numerals in column 2 show an area's location on the preceding map.

	MAP LOCATION	CAMPING	PICNICKING	HIKING TRAILS	BOATING	BOAT RAMP	BOAT RENTAL	FISHING	SWIMMING	PETS ON LEASH	BICYCLE TRAILS	WINTER SPORTS	VISITOR CENTER	LODGE/CABINS	FOOD SERVICE
NATIONAL PARKS *(See place listings.)*															
Fundy (E-5) 206 square kilometres on Hwy. 114, 130 km s.w. of Moncton. Nonmotorized boats only. Bird-watching, cross-country skiing, golf (nine holes), ice skating, snowshoeing, tennis; pool.		•	•	•	•	•	•	•	•	•	•	•	•	•	•
Kouchibouguac (C-5) 238 square kilometres on Rte. 134, n. of Moncton. Canoeing (no motors allowed); bicycle rental.		•	•	•	•	•	•	•	•	•	•	•	•		
PROVINCIAL															
The Anchorage (F-3) 181 hectares on Grand Manan Island, off Hwy. 776 s.w. of Grand Harbour. Beachcombing, kayaking; boardwalk.	❶	•	•	•				•	•	•			•		
de la République (B-1) 44 hectares 8 km n. of Edmundston on Rt. 2. Tennis, volleyball; amphitheater, museum, pool.	❷	•	•	•	•			•	•	•					•
Herring Cove (F-3) 423 hectares on Campobello Island. Interpretive programs. Beachcombing, golf (nine holes), sea kayaking, whale watching; playground.	❸	•	•	•				•	•	•			•	•	
Mactaquac (D-3) 525 hectares 24.5 km w. of Fredericton on Hwy. 105. Cross-country skiing, golf (18 holes), snowmobiling, windsurfing.	❹	•	•	•	•	•		•	•	•		•			•
Mount Carleton (B-3) 17,000 hectares 85 km n.w. of Plaster Rock on Hwy. 385, then on gravel road. Canoeing, cross-country skiing; wilderness.	❺	•	•	•	•			•	•	•		•	•		
Murray Beach (D-6) 26 hectares 16 km n.w. of Cape Tormentine on Hwy. 955. Bird-watching.	❻	•	•	•				•	•	•			•		
New River Beach (F-3) 8 hectares e. of Pennfield off Hwy. 1. Interpretive programs. Volleyball.	❼	•	•	•				•	•	•			•		•
Parlee Beach (D-6) 30 hectares 1.5 km e. of Shediac off Hwy. 15. Amphitheater.	❽	•	•					•	•	•			•		•
Sugarloaf (A-3) 1,142 hectares s.w. of Campbellton on Hwy. 11. Cross-country and downhill skiing, ice skating, snowmobiling, snowshoeing, tennis, volleyball; alpine slide.	❾	•	•	•		•			•	•	•	•	•		•
OTHER															
Caraquet (B-5) 3 hectares 10 km w. of Caraquet on Hwy. 11. Kayaking.	❿	•	•					•	•	•					
Centennial (D-5) 93 hectares 3.4 km w. of Moncton. Biking, cross-country skiing, football, hiking, lawn bowling, skating, tennis, ziplining; lake beach, outdoor splash park. *(See Moncton p. 33.)*	⓫		•	•					•		•	•	•		
Chaleur Beach (A-4) 135 hectares 5 km e. of Dalhousie on Hwy. 11. Windsurfing.	⓬	•	•					•	•	•					
Jacquet River (A-4) 2 hectares 51.5 km n. of Bathurst on Hwy. 11.	⓭	•	•	•	•		•	•	•	•					
Lac Baker (B-1) 5 hectares 3.25 km n.w. of Lac Baker on Hwy. 120. Tennis.	⓮	•		•				•	•	•					
Lake George (E-3) 10 hectares 9.75 km n.w. of Harvey Station via hwys. 3 and 636.	⓯	•	•	•				•	•	•					
Lakeside (E-4) 50 hectares 17.75 km e. of Jemseq.	⓰	•	•	•					•						•
Oak Bay (F-3) 11 hectares 8 km n.e. of St. Stephen on Hwy. 1.	⓱	•	•	•				•	•	•				•	•
Oak Point (E-4) 10 hectares 8 km w. of Evandale off Hwy. 102. Canoeing, kayaking; lighthouse.	⓲	•	•	•				•	•	•			•		
Rockwood (E-4) 870 hectares 2 km. n. of Saint John. Cross-country skiing, golf (18 holes), ice skating; beach, zoo. *(See Saint John p. 74.)*	⓳	•	•	•	•			•	•	•		•	•		
Shippagan (B-5) 20 hectares 3.25 km w. of Shippagan off Hwy. 113.	⓴	•	•	•					•	•					
Spednic Lake (E-2) 347 hectares 20 km w. of McAdam off Hwy. 630. Canoeing.	㉑	•	•	•	•			•	•	•					
Sunbury-Oromocto (E-3) 7 hectares 30 km s.e. of Fredericton off Hwy. 2.	㉒	•	•	•	•			•	•	•					
Val Comeau (B-5) 24 hectares 9.75 km s. of Tracadie-Sheila off Hwy. 11. Bird-watching; beach.	㉓	•	•	•	•	•		•	•	•					

ALMA pop. 301

CAPTAINS INN   Phone: (506)887-2017

Bed & Breakfast
$85-$135

Address: 8602 Main St E4H 1N5 **Location:** On Rt 114; centre. **Facility:** 9 units. 2 stories (no elevator), interior corridors. **Terms:** office hours 7 am-11 pm, 3 day cancellation notice. **Free Special Amenities: local telephone calls and high-speed Internet.**

PARKLAND VILLAGE INN   Phone: 506/887-2313

Boutique Vintage Hotel
$85-$160 7/1-10/21
$75-$150 6/1-6/30

Address: 8601 Main St E4H 1N6 **Location:** Oceanfront. On Rt 114; centre. **Facility:** The pleasant property offers comfortable guest rooms and suites, many offering a splendid view of the Bay of Fundy and Alma's Fisherman's Wharf. 15 units, some two bedrooms. 3 stories (no elevator), interior/exterior corridors. **Terms:** open 6/1-10/21, office hours 8 am-11 pm, cancellation fee imposed. **Dining:** Tides Restaurant, see separate listing. **Activities:** limited beach access. **Free Special Amenities: local telephone calls and high-speed Internet.**

WHERE TO EAT

TIDES RESTAURANT   Phone: 506/887-2313

American
$8-$23

AAA Inspector Notes: This harborfront restaurant offers both indoor and outdoor patio dining overlooking the wonderful Bay of Fundy. Specializing in fresh seafood including lobster, they also serve a fine variety of steak, ribs, chicken and pasta entrees. **Bar:** full bar. **Address:** 8601 Main St E4H 1N6 **Location:** On Rt 114; centre; in Parkland Village Inn. [B] [L] [D]

BARACHOIS (D-6)

Barachois comes from an old French word for "sandbar," appearing dozens of times in Canadian place names. In the Atlantic Provinces, the word has come to mean a salt pond cut off from a larger body of water.

HISTORIC CHURCH OF ST. HENRI-DE-BARACHOIS is at 1350 Rte. 133. Built in 1824, the structure is believed to be the oldest surviving Acadian wooden church in North America. Restored and converted into a museum and cultural center, it houses displays depicting the region's Acadian background. Various cultural activities are presented. **Hours:** Guided 15-minute tours are given on request daily 10-5, mid-June to late Sept. **Cost:** Donations. **Phone:** (506) 532-2976 to verify schedule.

BAS-CARAQUET pop. 1,471

LES CHALETS DE LA PLAGE   Phone: 506/726-8920

Cottage
Rates not provided

Address: 2 rue du Phare E1W 1M9 **Location:** Oceanfront. Jct Rt 11 and 145, 5 mi (8 km) e on Rt 145. **Facility:** These lovely one- and two-story cottages are fully equipped and offer nice decks with barbecues. 17 cottages. 1-2 stories (no elevator), exterior corridors. **Terms:** office hours 8 am-9 pm, check-in 4 pm. **Activities:** beach access, playground. **Guest Services:** coin laundry.

BATHURST (B-4) pop. 12,714
• Restaurants p. 36

Explorer Jacques Cartier reached the Bathurst area and established trade with the local Mi'kmaq Indians in 1534. Nicholas Denys, governor of the Acadian coast and author of one of the first local histories, lived in Bathurst a century later; his memorial is downtown. The city, established in 1826, was named for the then colonial secretary of Great Britain, the Earl of Bathurst.

Now a tourist center on Bathurst Harbour at the mouth of Nepisiguit River, Bathurst also is a city of heavy industries, especially mining and papermaking.

Nearby Youghall Beach Park offers warm-water swimming in the Chaleur and Nepisiguit bays. Boating and fishing are popular pastimes.

Destination Bathurst: 725 College St., 231 CEI Bldg., Bathurst, NB, Canada E2A 4B9. **Phone:** (502) 545-7538 or (866) 540-4877.

ROYAL CANADIAN LEGION WAR MUSEUM is at 575 St. Peter Ave. This museum of the Royal Canadian Legion Branch 18 displays artifacts of the North Shore Regiment and weapons and uniforms from the World Wars. Other exhibits depict the Boer, Korean and Persian Gulf wars. A replica of the Victoria Cross Medal stands in the museum. **Hours:** Mon.-Sat. 9-5, July-Aug.; by appointment rest of year. **Cost:** Donations. **Phone:** (506) 546-3135 or (506) 546-5280.

ATLANTIC HOST HOTEL   Phone: (506)548-3335

Hotel
$110-$160

Address: 1450 Vanier Blvd E2A 4H7 **Location:** Rt 11 exit 310 (Vanier Blvd). **Facility:** 100 units. 2 stories (no elevator), interior corridors. **Parking:** winter plug-ins. **Amenities:** *Some:* high-speed Internet, honor bars. **Dining:** restaurant, see separate listing. **Pool(s):** heated indoor. **Activities:** sauna, whirlpool, cross country skiing, hiking trails, exercise room. *Fee:* snowmobiling. **Guest Services:** valet laundry.

COMFORT INN   Phone: (506)547-8000

Hotel
$90-$100

Address: 1170 St Peter's Ave E2A 2Z9 **Location:** 2.1 mi (3.4 km) n on Rt 134 (St Peter's Ave). Located in a commercial area. **Facility:** 78 units. 2 stories (no elevator), interior corridors. **Terms:** cancellation fee imposed. **Amenities:** *Some:* high-speed Internet.

DANNY'S INN & CONFERENCE CENTRE   Phone: (506)546-6621

Hotel
$89-$159

Address: Rt 134 E2A 3Z2 **Location:** Rt 11 exit 310 (Vanier Blvd) northbound to Rt 134 (St Peter's Ave), 2.5 mi (4 km) n; exit 318 southbound to Rt 134 (St Peter's Ave), 2.3 mi (3.8 km) s. Located in a rural area. **Facility:** 37 units, some efficiencies and kitchens. 1 story, interior/exterior corridors. **Parking:** winter plug-ins. **Amenities:** *Some:* high-speed Internet, honor bars. **Dining:** restaurant, see separate listing. **Pool(s):** heated outdoor. **Activities:** playground, game room. **Guest Services:** valet laundry.

LAKEVIEW INNS & SUITES   Phone: (506)548-4949

Hotel
$104-$192 1/1-5/31
$102-$190 6/1-12/31

Address: 777 St Peter's Ave E2A 2Y9 **Location:** 1.8 mi (3 km) n on Rt 134 (St Peter's Ave). Located in a residential area. **Facility:** 78 units. 3 stories, interior corridors. **Terms:** cancellation fee imposed. **Guest Services:** coin laundry. **Free Special Amenities:** continental breakfast and high-speed Internet.

SAVE ECO Ⅰ↑ CALL &M BIZ 🛜 ✕ 🔒 💬
/ SOME UNITS FEE 🐕 🖨

WHERE TO EAT

ATLANTIC HOST RESTAURANT   Phone: 506/548-3335

American
$9-$22

AAA Inspector Notes: The pleasant, family restaurant features a good variety of seafood, beef, pasta and chicken dishes, as well as fresh sandwiches, salads and soups. The delicious array of rich desserts created by the in-house pastry chef is sure to satisfy the sweet tooth. **Bar:** full bar. **Address:** 1450 Vanier Blvd E2A 4H7 **Location:** Rt 11 exit 310 (Vanier Blvd); in Atlantic Host Hotel.

B L D

DANNY'S   Phone: 506/546-6621

Canadian
$8-$24

AAA Inspector Notes: This attractive dining room and coffee shop with two fireplaces and a patio that's perfect for outdoor dining, is the comfortable setting for an overall good meal. Excellent home-style desserts, tasty seafood, steak, ribs and chicken, are sure to please most any palate. **Bar:** full bar. **Address:** 1223 rue Principale E2A 2Z2 **Location:** Rt 11 exit 310 (Vanier Blvd) northbound to Rt 134 (St Peter's Ave), 2.5 mi (4 km) n; exit 318 southbound to Rt 134 (St Peter's Ave), 2.3 mi (3.8 km) s; in Danny's Inn & Conference Centre. B L D

HOUSE OF LEE   Phone: 506/548-3019

Chinese
$7-$18

AAA Inspector Notes: The spacious restaurant has several dining areas, including a back section that affords a fine view of the harbor. On the menu is a wide variety of Chinese and Canadian cuisine. Another choice is the daily buffet. **Bar:** full bar. **Address:** 315 Main St E2A 1B1 **Location:** Corner of Murray Ave; centre. L D

THE MEGALODON PUB   Phone: 506/547-9893

Canadian
$8-$20

AAA Inspector Notes: In the heart of town, the upbeat sports bar has pool tables and TVs. In addition to classic pub foods, the menu lists popular brick-oven pizzas. Several draft beers are among beverage choices. **Bar:** full bar. **Address:** 100 Main St E2A 1A3 **Location:** At St Peter's Ave. **Parking:** street only. L D

BAYFIELD (D-6) pop. 41

On the eastern tip of the province, Bayfield was the staging area for construction of the Confederation Bridge, built in 1997 to link Borden-Carleton, Prince Edward Island, with Cape Jourimain, New Brunswick, and the mainland. Construction cost $1 billion. The 12.9-kilometre (8-mi.) span is the world's longest over ice-covered waters. A $42.50 toll is charged per private vehicle from Prince Edward Island to Bayfield; there is no toll from Bayfield to Prince Edward Island.

It is believed that centuries before the bridge was built, Mi'kmaq Indians launched their canoes from Cape Jourimain to cross the Northumberland Strait.

In the 19th century, winter crossings were made with iceboats equipped with runners; passengers had to get out and push the boats over frozen stretches.

Cape Jourimain Provincial Visitor Information Centre: 5039 Hwy. 16, P.O. Box 1006, Bayfield, NB, Canada E4M 3Z2. **Phone:** (506) 538-2133.

CAPE JOURIMAIN NATURE CENTRE is off Hwy. 16 exit 51. This 675-hectare (1,668-acre) wildlife area is a major stop-over for migratory birds along the Atlantic flyway. More than 200 species visit or live in the area. The center at the mainland end of the Confederation Bridge includes an exhibit hall, a four-story observation tower, a lighthouse and 13 kilometres (8 mi.) of nature trails.

Time: Allow 1 hour minimum. **Hours:** Daily 8-7, June 12-Aug. 27; 9-6, late May-June 11 and Aug. 28-Oct. 11. **Cost:** $6; $5 (ages 60+); $4 (ages 5-18 and college students with ID); free (ages 0-4); $15 (family, two adults and children). **Phone:** (506) 538-2220 or (866) 538-2220. Ⅱ

BLOOMFIELD

EVELYN'S BED & BREAKFAST   Phone: (506)832-7788

Bed & Breakfast
$99-$119

Address: 374 Rt 121 E5N 4T4 **Location:** Hwy 1 exit 166, follow signs. Located in a rural area. **Facility:** 4 units. 2 stories (no elevator), interior corridors. **Terms:** office hours 7 am-10:30 pm, 7 day cancellation notice-fee imposed. **Pool(s):** heated outdoor. **Activities:** playground.

🏊 🛜 ✕ 🎿 / SOME UNITS 🐕

BOIESTOWN (D-3)

Founded at the junction of the Miramichi and Taxis rivers, Boiestown was named after an American settler from New Hampshire. Thomas Boies ran a lumber mill, one of a half dozen that opened here to take advantage of abundant trees and water power. Boiestown is considered the geographical center of the province.

SAVE **CENTRAL NEW BRUNSWICK WOODMEN'S MUSEUM** is 1.6 km (1 mi.) e. on Hwy. 8. Frontier life in early New Brunswick is depicted at this 6-hectare (15-acre) exhibition area, which chronicles the woods industry and local history with tools, documents, photographs, a restored trapper's cabin, plough and machine sheds, boathouse, fire tower and a man-made lake. Narrated tours aboard the Whooper Train are available. Self-guiding trails also are available. **Time:** Allow 1 hour minimum. **Hours:** Daily 9-5, June 4-Oct. 15. **Cost:** $6; $5 (ages 65+); $3 (ages 6-16); $15 (family); free (ages 0-5 and 97+). **Phone:** (506) 369-7214.

BOUCTOUCHE (D-5) pop. 2,383

François and Charlitte LeBlanc arrived in Bouctouche in 1785, soon followed by other deported Acadian settlers. The area was called "Chebooktoosk," or "big little harbor" by the Mi'kmaq Indians.

Bouctouche was the birthplace of industrialist K.C. Irving, the founding father of one of Canada's biggest conglomerates.

 IRVING ECO-CENTRE, "LA DUNE DE BOUCTOUCHE" is 10 km (6 mi.) n. on Hwy. 475. One of the few remaining sand dunes on the northeast coast of North America is preserved here. The dune extends 12 kilometres (7.5 mi.) across Bouctouche Bay, providing a vital marine habitat. A boardwalk enables visitors to observe the dune's flora and fauna; visitors may also hike a forested nature trail from the dune to the town of Bouctouche. An interpretive center contains interactive displays for all ages.

Ongoing scientific studies are conducted at the site, and bilingual interpreters are available May to November.

Note: Due to severe storm surges in December 2010, only the first 800 metres (2,625 ft.) of the boardwalk past the main facilities are open to visitors. Dogs are not allowed on the grounds; kennel services are available. **Time:** Allow 2 hours minimum. **Hours:** Daily 10-7, late June-Aug. 31; Mon.-Thurs. noon-5, Fri. noon-6, Sat.-Sun. 10-6, mid-May to late June and Sept. 1-early Nov. **Cost:** Free. **Phone:** (506) 743-2600, or (888) 640-3300 in Canada.

KENT MUSEUM is 2.5 km (1.5 mi.) n.e. of Hwy. 11 on Hwy. 475 at 150 du Couvent Rd. This museum occupies a restored three-story Victorian building that served as a convent and educational center 1880-1969. The Gothic Revival chapel and a quilt exhibition are of interest. Exhibits depict Kent's Acadian culture and display the works of local artists. **Hours:** Guided tours Mon.-Sat. 9-5:30, Sun. noon-6, late June-Labour Day; by appointment rest of year. **Cost:** $3; $2 (ages 65+); $1 (students with ID); free (ages 0-5). Cash only. **Phone:** (506) 743-5005.

LE PAYS DE LA SAGOUINE is off Hwy. 11 exit 32A to 57 Acadie St. This island re-creates the Acadian setting and French-speaking characters of Antonine Maillet's story, "Le Pays de la Sagouine." Live performances, children's activities and Acadian food and music are offered throughout the day. Actress Viola Léger has played the part of la Sagouine, the storytelling scrubwoman, for more than 35 years.

All plays and performances on the island are in French; guided tours in English are available. **Time:** Allow 2 hours minimum. **Hours:** Daily 10-4:30, mid-June to early Sept. English tours depart daily at 11 and 1:30. **Cost:** $16; $14 (ages 65+); $13 (students ages 17+ with ID); $11 (ages 5-16); $38 (family). Prices for children's and evening shows vary; phone ahead. **Phone:** (506) 743-1400 or (800) 561-9188.

AUBERGE BOUCTOUCHE INN & SUITES   Phone: 506/743-5003

Hotel
$85-$165

Address: 50 Industrielle St E4S 3H9 **Location:** Rt 11 exit 32A/B. **Facility:** 38 units. 2 stories (no elevator), interior corridors. **Terms:** open 6/1-12/20. **Amenities:** high-speed Internet. **Activities:** exercise room.

LE GITE DE LA SAGOUINE   Phone: 506/743-5554

[fyl] Not evaluated. **Address:** 43 Irving Blvd E4S 3J5 **Location:** On Rt 515; centre. Facilities, services, and decor characterize a mid-scale property.

WHERE TO EAT

RESTAURANT LA SAGOUINE   Phone: 506/743-6606

American
$7-$19

AAA Inspector Notes: Pleasant dining in the heart of town, this country-style restaurant offers a selection of Acadian dishes and seafood cuisine. Nice patio dining is available in season. **Bar:** full bar. **Address:** 43 Irving Blvd E4S 3J5 **Location:** On Rt 515; centre; in Le Gite de la Sagouine. [B] [L] [D]

CAMPBELLTON (A-3) pop. 7,384
• Restaurants p. 38

Campbellton began as a British land grant along the Restigouche River; the first settlers were Scottish. Its early economy focused on a lucrative salmon industry, followed by farming and lumbering eras. In the early 1900s Campbellton became an important railroad center.

Restigouche Theatre, one of New Brunswick's finest, is used for many of Campbellton's cultural activities. Residents and visitors enjoy the ski trails and other recreational facilities of nearby Sugarloaf Provincial Park *(see Recreation Chart)*, which features 304-metre (997-ft.) Sugarloaf Mountain; phone (506) 789-2366. Many hunters and anglers pursuing the riches of the Restigouche and Upsalquitch rivers are outfitted in Campbellton.

Campbellton Provincial Visitor Information Centre: 56 Salmon Blvd., Campbellton, NB, Canada E3N 3H4. **Phone:** (506) 789-2367.

GALERIE RESTIGOUCHE is at 39 Andrew St. This national exhibition center features local, regional, national and international exhibits dealing with art, history, science and nature. The Athol House Room houses a permanent display that chronicles the Mi'kmaq, French, Acadian and Scottish heritage of the Restigouche region. **Hours:** Mon.-Fri. 9-5, Sat.-Sun. 1-5. **Cost:** $1-$2, depending on exhibits. **Phone:** (506) 753-5750.

COMFORT INN   Phone: (506)753-4121

Hotel
$120-$200

Address: 111 Val D'Amour Rd E3N 5B9 **Location:** Hwy 11 exit 415, 0.6 mi (1 km) w. on Sugarloaf St W. **Facility:** 60 units. 2 stories (no elevator), interior/exterior corridors. **Terms:** cancellation fee imposed. **Parking:** winter plug-ins.

HOWARD JOHNSON HOTEL   Phone: (506)753-4133

◆◆◆ ◆◆◆

Hotel

$87-$125

Address: 157 Water St E3N 3H2 Location: Hwy 134; in City Centre Complex. Facility: 66 units. 5 stories, interior corridors. Amenities: high-speed Internet. Dining: 1026 Bar & Grill, see separate listing. Guest Services: valet laundry.

SUPER 8-CAMPBELLTON   Phone: (506)753-8080

◆◆ ◆◆

Hotel

$99-$126

Address: 26 Duke St E3N 2K3 Location: Just s of Roseberry St; jct George and Duke sts; downtown. Facility: 60 units. 3 stories (no elevator), interior/exterior corridors. Pool(s): heated indoor. Activities: sauna, whirlpool, exercise room. Fee: game room. Guest Services: coin laundry.

WHERE TO EAT

1026 BAR & GRILL   Phone: 506/753-3640

◆◆◆ ◆◆◆

Canadian

$8-$20

AAA Inspector Notes: A casual mood pervades this popular sports bar. Guests can choose from daily specials, as well as items on the full menu, which lists steaks, seafood and a variety of finger foods. Bar: full bar. Address: 157 Water St E3N 3H2 Location: Hwy 134; in City Centre Complex; in Howard Johnson Hotel. [B] [L] [D]

CHEZ NIC DINER   Phone: 506/753-7897

◆◆◆ ◆◆◆

Canadian

$6-$16

AAA Inspector Notes: A '50s rock 'n' roll theme lends character to the spacious restaurant, which offers booth, table or soda bar seating. Widely ranging comfort foods are served in ample portions. Bar: full bar. Address: 312 chemin Val D'Amour E3N 4E2 Location: Hwy 11 exit 415, 0.6 mi (1 km) e on Sugarloaf St; in Sugarloaf Mall. [B] [L] [D]

CHINA COAST RESTAURANT   Phone: 506/759-9190

◆◆ ◆◆

Chinese

$8-$18

AAA Inspector Notes: Minimal Oriental decorations color the dining room, where families gather to sample Chinese and Canadian food. Buffets lay out a good variety Wednesday through Friday for lunch and on the weekends for dinner. Bar: full bar. Address: 127 Val D'Amour Rd E3N 3S6 Location: Hwy 11 exit 415, 0.6 mi (1 km) e. [L] [D]

UPPER DECK STEAKHOUSE   Phone: 506/753-2225

◆◆◆ ◆◆◆

Steak

$8-$26

AAA Inspector Notes: The atmosphere is casual and friendly in the steakhouse, which specializes in fine cuts of Alberta beef but also offers a good selection of seafood and Sunday brunch choices. Bar: full bar. Address: 15 Water St E3N 1A6 Location: Centre; adjacent to City Centre Complex. [D]

CAMPOBELLO ISLAND (F-3)

For more than a century, 1767-1881, Campobello Island belonged to the Owen family. The 1835 home of Adm. William F. Owen, who so loved the sea that he reputedly built a quarterdeck on which to pace, is preserved at Deer Point. A picturesque lighthouse stands at East Quoddy Head; whales and porpoises can be seen swimming nearby.

James Roosevelt went to Campobello in 1883 when his son Franklin was 1 year old. From then until 1921, Franklin D. Roosevelt spent most of his summers on the island. A small collection of items relating to the Roosevelt family is among the displays at Campobello Public Library and Museum, in the village of Welshpool; phone (506) 752-7082.

Campobello Chamber of Commerce: 916 Hwy. 774, Welshpool, Campobello Island, NB, Canada E5E 1B1. **Phone:** (506) 752-2233 or (201) 733-2201.

 ROOSEVELT CAMPOBELLO INTERNATIONAL PARK is linked to the mainland by the Franklin D. Roosevelt Memorial Bridge at Lubec, Maine, and also can be reached by ferry from Deer Island from June through September. The centerpiece of the 1,134-hectare (2,802-acre) memorial is a 34-room "cottage" occupied 1905-21 by the soon-to-be president and his family. The house contains original furniture, photographs, toys and other items belonging to the Roosevelts.

The visitor center has one exhibit about the Roosevelts' history and another about the friendship between the U.S. and Canada. A 15-minute film tells the story of the Roosevelts' lives on Campobello Island. The park's natural areas feature scenic drives and walking trails along coves, bogs, beaches and cliffs.

Note: The park is in the Atlantic time zone, 1 hour ahead of the Eastern time zone. Hours listed here are in Eastern daylight time. **Hours:** Grounds, nature areas and trails daily dawn-dusk year-round. Visitor center daily 9-5, Memorial Day weekend-Columbus Day; 9-4, day after Columbus Day-Oct. 31. Cottage daily 9-5, Memorial Day weekend-Columbus Day. Last admission 15 minutes before closing. **Cost:** Donations. **Phone:** (506) 752-2922 or (877) 851-6663. *(See ad p. 74.)*

CAP-PELÉ pop. 2,200

CHALETS DE L'ABOITEAU   Phone: 506/577-2005

[fyi]

Cottage

Did not meet all AAA rating requirements for locking devices in some guest rooms at time of last evaluation on 05/20/2011. Address: 55 Chalets Ln E4N 1R3 Location: Oceanfront. Hwy 15 exit 53, 0.6 mi (1 km) n on Rt 950; in Aboiteau Park. Facilities, services, and decor characterize a mid-scale property.

WHERE TO EAT

FRED'S SEAFOOD RESTAURANT   Phone: 506/577-4269

◆◆ ◆◆

American

$7-$18

AAA Inspector Notes: Popular with the locals, this spacious restaurant has been serving a wide variety of Acadian and Canadian cuisine for more than 30 years. The take-out bar opens seasonally. Bar: full bar. Address: 2270 Acadie Rd E4N 2A5 Location: Hwy 15 exit 53, 0.6 mi (1 km) n on Rt 950. [L] [D]

CARAQUET (A-5) pop. 4,156

Established in 1758 as Capital de l'Acadie, Caraquet is the oldest French settlement in northern

New Brunswick. A monument just west of town honors the area's first Acadian settlers, originally expelled by the British in 1755. The Shrine of Sainte Anne du Bocage overlooks the burial ground of many of these early settlers.

This picturesque and culturally vibrant community is headquarters for a huge fishing fleet. A popular event, the Blessing of the Fleet takes place during the 🌊 Festival acadien de Caraquet in early August.

La Chambre de commerce du Grand Caraquet: 39-1 Boulevard St. Pierre W., Caraquet, NB, Canada E1W 1A5. **Phone:** (506) 727-2931.

ACADIAN HISTORICAL VILLAGE (VILLAGE HISTORIQUE ACADIEN) is 10 km (6 mi.) w. on Hwy. 11. This historic site interprets the lives of the Acadians, New Brunswick's "marsh settlers," from 1770 through the industrial development and modernization of Acadia in 1949. More than 40 authentic Acadian structures, transported to the site and restored, include houses, a chapel, a school, a general store, a printing house, a cobbler's shop, a tinsmith shop, a smithy, a gristmill, a tavern, a covered bridge and the 1910 Château-Albert Hotel. Interpreters in period costumes bring ancestral customs and traditional trades to life.

A visitor center offers an 18-minute slide presentation about Acadian history. **Time:** Allow 2 hours minimum. **Hours:** Daily 10-6, June 10-Sept. 22. Phone ahead to confirm schedule. **Cost:** Admission June 10-Sept. 15 is $16; $14 (ages 65+); $13 (students ages 17+ with ID); $11 (ages 6-16); $38 (family). Admission Sept. 16-Sept. 22 is $8; $5 (students ages 17+ with ID); $4 (ages 6-16); $18 (family). **Phone:** (506) 726-2600 for event schedules or (877) 721-2200.

MUSÉE ACADIEN is off Hwy. 11 at 15 St. Pierre Blvd. E. Historical artifacts depict the general history of the Acadian peninsula. **Hours:** Mon.-Sat. 10-8, Sun. 1-6, July-Aug.; Mon.-Sat. 10-6, Sun. 1-6 in June and Sept. **Cost:** $3; $2 (ages 60+); $1 (students with ID); free (ages 0-12). **Phone:** (506) 726-2682, or (506) 726-2727 in the off-season.

GITE "LE POIRIER" BED & BREAKFAST
Phone: (506)727-4359
Historic Bed & Breakfast
$104-$116
Address: 98 St Pierre Blvd W E1W 1B6 **Location:** On Rt 11; centre. **Facility:** Located in the heart of town, this 1927 house, formerly a judge's residence, is now a tastefully decorated, service-oriented B&B. 5 units. 2 stories (no elevator), interior corridors. **Terms:** office hours 7 am-11 pm, 2-3 night minimum stay - seasonal and/or weekends, 3 day cancellation notice. **Free Special Amenities: full breakfast and high-speed Internet.**
SAVE 🛎️ BIZ 🛜 ✖️

GITE L'ISLE-DU-RANDONNEUR B & B
Phone: 506/727-3877
Bed & Breakfast
Rates not provided
Address: 539 St Pierre Blvd W E1W 1A3 **Location:** 3 mi (5 km) n on Rt 11. **Facility:** Offering a pleasant view of Caraquet Bay, this 1850 home borders a bike trail and is within walking distance of the beach. 4 units, some two bedrooms. 2 stories (no elevator), interior corridors. **Terms:** office hours 7 am-midnight. **Activities:** sauna, whirlpool, hiking trails.
🛜 ✖️ 🔋 / SOME UNITS

SUPER 8
Phone: (506)727-0888
Hotel
$88-$149
Address: 9 Carrefour Ave E1W 1B6 **Location:** Waterfront. Just e of jct Rt 11 and St Pierre Blvd E. **Facility:** 50 units. 3 stories, interior corridors. **Amenities:** high-speed Internet.
Pool(s): heated indoor. **Activities:** whirlpool, waterslide, playground. **Fee:** miniature golf. **Guest Services:** coin laundry.
🛗 CALL 🔋 🏊 🛜 ✖️ 🔋 📶 💻
/ SOME UNITS FEE 🐾

CARAQUETTE FAMILY RESTAURANT
Phone: 506/727-6009

American
$6-$21
AAA Inspector Notes: Bordering the harbor and offering fine views of the Baie des Chaleurs, the family-style restaurant offers a menu of home-style cooking. Included are preparations of fresh seafood, steak, burgers and sandwiches. **Bar:** full bar. **Address:** 89 St. Pierre Blvd E E1W 1B6 **Location:** Jct Rt 11, 1 mi (1.6 km) e on Rt 145.
B L D

L'ORIENTAL RESTAURANT
Phone: 506/726-9000

Chinese
$7-$18
AAA Inspector Notes: Guests will find ample portions of Chinese entrees, Thai and Vietnamese offerings and some Canadian dishes as well as a daily buffet. Plenty of parking surrounds this spot with pleasant, modern decor. **Bar:** full bar. **Address:** 370 St Pierre Blvd W E1W 1A3 **Location:** 2.5 mi (4 km) w on Rt 11.
L D

MITCHAN SUSHI RESTAURANT
Phone: 506/726-1103

Japanese
$16-$24
AAA Inspector Notes: Several pleasant dining sections follow two levels in the converted home. Very well-prepared authentic Japanese cuisine specializes in local fresh seafood selections and some curry dishes. For lunch on the go they offer take-out sushi in the summer months. **Bar:** full bar. **Reservations:** suggested. **Address:** 114 St Pierre Blvd W E1W 1B6 **Location:** On Rt 11; centre. D

CHARLO (A-4) pop. 1,376

Though this small town on Chaleur Bay wasn't incorporated until 1966, Charlo is one of the older settlements in Restigouche County. The first last grant was issued here in 1799; a Catholic parish had been established by 1853.

CHARLO SALMONID ENHANCEMENT CENTRE AND FISH HATCHERY is off Hwy. 11 exit 375, on McPherson St. Speckled trout and Atlantic salmon are bred and raised for release into their natural habitat. **Hours:** Daily 9-4. Phone ahead to confirm schedule. **Cost:** Free. **Phone:** (506) 684-3050.

HERON'S NEST COTTAGES
Phone: 506/684-3766
fyi
Not evaluated. **Address:** 6 Heron Rd E8E 2L1 **Location:** Hwy 11 exit 385, just n to Rt 134. Facilities, services, and decor characterize a mid-scale property.

Visit AAA.com or CAA.ca for one-stop travel planning and reservations

COCAGNE pop. 2,646

COCAGNE MOTEL

Motel
Rates not provided
hours 8 am-midnight.
Phone: 506/576-6657
Address: 1718 Rt 535 E4R 1N6
Location: Rt 11 exit 15, 0.6 mi (1 km)
n. **Facility:** 20 units, some efficiencies.
2 stories (no elevator), exterior
corridors. **Terms:** seasonal, office
Amenities: *Some:* high-speed Internet.

DALHOUSIE (A-3) pop. 3,975

A year-round port at the mouth of the Restigouche River, Dalhousie offers deep-sea fishing and
swimming in the sheltered Chaleur Bay. The Bon
Ami Festival, a 10-day event held in late July, features a parade, fireworks, sporting events and local
arts and crafts exhibits.

RESTIGOUCHE REGIONAL MUSEUM is just off
Hwy. 11 at 115 George St. at Adelaide St. The facility contains an art gallery and a museum with displays about pioneers, farming, commercial fishing
and the Canada Winter Games. **Hours:** Daily 9-5, in
summer; Mon.-Fri. 9-5, Sat.-Sun. 9-1, rest of year.
Cost: Donations. **Phone:** (506) 684-7490.

BEST WESTERN PLUS MANOIR ADELAIDE
Phone: (506)684-5681

Hotel
$109-$119

AAA Benefit: Members
save up to 20%, plus 10%
bonus points with Best
Western Rewards®.

Address: 385 Adelaide St E8C 1B4 **Location:** Centre at
Brunswick St. **Facility:** 49 units. 4 stories, interior corridors.
Amenities: *Some:* high-speed Internet. **Dining:** Le Menuet,
see separate listing. **Guest Services:** coin laundry. **Free
Special Amenities: full breakfast and high-speed
Internet.**

WHERE TO EAT

LE MENUET

Canadian
$8-$24
Phone: 506/684-5681

AAA Inspector Notes: The menu at
this casual spot lists a variety of meat
and seafood dishes, including steak,
salmon, shrimp and trout. Among the
delectable desserts is a tempting
cheesecake. The bilingual servers are
very friendly and offer a casual level of service. **Bar:** full bar.
Address: 385 Adelaide St E8C 1B4 **Location:** Centre at
Brunswick St; in Best Western Plus Manoir Adelaide.

DEER ISLAND (F-3)

Deer Island is at the entrance to Passamaquoddy
Bay, 10 kilometres (6 mi.) by water from St. Andrews
(see place listing p. 67). It can be reached by free
automobile ferry from the mainland south of St.
George at Letete and, during the summer, from
Eastport, Maine; the ferry also runs to Campobello
Island July through August.

Deer Island Point has a 16-hectare (40-acre) park
and beaches. An enormous whirlpool, Old Sow, can

be seen offshore 3 hours before high tide. Currents
rushing through the Western Passage between
Deer Island Point and Dog Island create this whirling
vortex, one of the world's largest. The name comes
from the smaller "piglet" whirlpools that spin away
from their mother. Access to the best lookout is
through a private campground; check with the office
before entering.

DIEPPE (D-5) pop. 18,565, elev. 16m/52'

This suburb of Moncton on the Petitcodiac River
was named in honor of Canadian soldiers killed in
the 1942 raid on Dieppe, France, during World War
II. Marketing itself as an industrial hub, Dieppe is
now one of the fastest-growing cities in New
Brunswick.

Shopping areas: Champlain Place at 477 Paul St.
has more than 160 shops, including Eddie Bauer,
Gap, Tommy Hilfiger and H&M.

CRYSTAL PALACE AMUSEMENT PARK is w. on
Hwy. 15 to exit 10 (Paul St.). This 1.1-hectare (2.8-
acre) entertainment complex includes an indoor
amusement park, an eight-cinema theater and a
hotel. Indoor rides include a roller coaster, a wave
swinger, a climbing wall, an antique carousel, an arcade and a miniature golf course. An outdoor park is
open in summer.

Note: The theater is currently closed for renova-
tions, but the rest of the park remains open. **Hours:**
Daily 10-9, June 24-Aug. 31; Mon.-Thurs. noon-8,
Fri. noon-9, Sat. 10-9, Sun. 10-8, rest of year.
Closed Christmas.

Cost: Admission free. Fees are charged per ride,
attraction and arcade game; phone for ticket and
token prices. Summer all-day pass (includes unlimited access to rides and attractions, except climbing
wall) $23.50; $19.95 (under 48 inches tall); $73.80
(family, four people); $18.45 (each additional family
member). Rest of year all-day pass (includes unlimited access to rides and attractions, except climbing
wall) $20.15; $16.55 (under 48 inches tall); $59.40
(family, four people); $14.85 (each additional family
member). Rates may vary; phone ahead. **Phone:**
(506) 859-4386, or (877) 856-4386 in New Brunswick, Newfoundland and Prince Edward Island.

DOAKTOWN (C-4) pop. 888

Doaktown was named after Squire Robert Doak,
who brought his family from Scotland to New Brunswick in 1815. After settling on a farm in the
Miramichi region, he built a carding mill, grist mill,
saw mill and kiln. As justice of the peace, it is said
he officiated over local marriages for nearly 30
years, and also served as court judge and coroner.

ATLANTIC SALMON MUSEUM is at 263 Main St.
on the Miramichi River. An aquarium, paintings,

prints, publications, sculptures, exotic salmon flies and an audiovisual presentation preserve the history of the area's premier game fish. The museum is dedicated to Atlantic salmon conservation, preservation and promotion. The museum also features a visitor information center. **Hours:** Mon.-Sat. 9-5, May-Oct. (also Sun. 1-5, May 1-Labour Day). **Cost:** $5; $4 (ages 60+); $3 (students with ID); free (ages 0-4); $12 (family, two adults and two children). **Phone:** (506) 365-7787 or (866) 725-6662.

DOAK HISTORIC SITE is at 386 Main St. A house, barn and milk house on the site were built by Squire Robert Doak, who came to New Brunswick from Scotland in 1815 and settled at this site in 1825. Here, he established a carding mill, a gristmill and a sawmill. The house remained in the family until 1979. Original furnishings as well as kitchen and farm tools reflect pioneer life 1830-90. Costumed interpreters carry out such daily chores as gardening, weaving and spinning.

Tours: Guided tours are available. **Time:** Allow 1 hour minimum. **Hours:** Mon.-Sat. 9:30-4:30, mid-June to mid-Sept. **Cost:** Donations. **Phone:** (506) 365-2026. 🖝

THE LEDGES INN   **Phone:** (506)365-1820
◆◆◆◆
Country Inn
$100-$150
Address: 30 Ledges Inn Ln E9C 1A7 **Location:** On Rt 8; centre. Located in a rural area. **Facility:** Most of the well-appointed guest rooms in this comfortable, modern log home overlook a natural setting along the Miramichi River. 10 units. 2 stories (no elevator), interior corridors. **Terms:** office hours 7 am-10 pm, 7 day cancellation notice. **Activities:** *Fee:* canoes, fishing. / SOME UNITS

WHERE TO EAT

VILLAGE FAMILY RESTAURANT   **Phone:** 506/365-4301
◆◆◆
American
$7-$17
AAA Inspector Notes: A very popular family restaurant in the heart of town, this eatery specialize in home-style cooking with daily specials and an on-site bakery. **Address:** 235 Main St E9C 1A9 **Location:** On Rt 8; centre.

 B   L   D

DORCHESTER (D-5) pop. 1,119

Restored to its 1811 appearance, Dorchester's Bell Inn is perhaps the oldest stone building in New Brunswick. Between mid-July and early September, some 2.5 million semipalmated sandpipers—up to 90 percent of the world's population—flock to the nutrient-rich shores of Johnson's Mills, 8 kilometres (5 mi.) south on Hwy. 935.

KEILLOR HOUSE AND ST. JAMES TEXTILE MUSEUM is on Hwy. 106. The 1813 house, built by Yorkshire stonemason John Keillor, exhibits 19th-century furnishings, domestic items and a three-story spiral staircase. Displays include shipbuilding, farming, trade tools and costumes. The St. James Textile Museum is an 1884 church structure housing antique tools, textile equipment, spinning wheels and pedal lathes. Two carriages and a penitentiary collection are displayed in the coach house.

Materials for genealogical research are available by appointment. **Tours:** Guided tours are available. **Hours:** Tues.-Sat. 10-5, Sun. noon-5, mid-June through Labour Day; by appointment rest of year. Phone ahead to confirm schedule. **Cost:** Keillor House or St. James Textile Museum $3; $2 (ages 0-9). **Phone:** (506) 379-6633. 🖝

THE BELL INN RESTAURANT   **Phone:** 506/379-2580
◆◆
American
$7-$15
AAA Inspector Notes: Established in New Brunswick's oldest stone structure, a Provincial historic site built in 1811, this pleasant eatery offers home-style cooking that includes savory chowder and luscious desserts. Historic memorabilia lends an air of authenticity. **Reservations:** suggested. **Address:** 3515 Cape Rd E4K 2X2 **Location:** On Hwy 106; centre. Historic   L   D   🐾

EDMUNDSTON (B-1) pop. 16,643
• Hotels p. 42 • Restaurants p. 42

• Hotels p. 42 • Restaurants p. 42

Edmundston serves as the honorary capital of the Republic of Madawaska, a mythical region evolved from 60 years of disputes over the location of the New Brunswick-Maine boundary. Though the boundary was settled by the Webster-Ashburton Treaty in 1842, residents adopted the unofficial territory, complete with dialect and flag.

Bilingual Edmundston dominates the province's pulp and paper industry. The city also is noted for its hand-loomed fabrics and wood sculpture. Nearby de la République Provincial Park *(see Recreation Chart)* is a cultural and recreational center. On the outskirts of Edmundston, Mont Farlagne provides skiing in winter and spring; phone (888) 837-7669 for snow conditions.

During the summer thousands gather for La Foire Brayonne, a cultural festival featuring internationally acclaimed musicians, local food specialties and crafts.

Edmundston Madawaska Tourism Office: 121 Victoria St., Edmundston, NB E3V 2H5. **Phone:** (506) 737-1850 or (866) 737-6766.

MADAWASKA HISTORICAL MUSEUM is at jct. Hwy. 2 and Hébert Blvd. (exit 18). The museum depicts the cultural life of the Madawaska region since its settlement. A historical display and the Gallerie Colline Art Gallery are featured. **Time:** Allow 30 minutes minimum. **Hours:** Wed.-Thurs. 10-10; Tues. and Fri. 10-5; Sat.-Sun. 1-5, mid-June through Labour Day; Wed.-Thurs. 7-10 p.m., Sun. 1-5, rest of year. Phone ahead to confirm schedule. **Cost:** $3.50; $2 (ages 6-18 and 65+); $7 (family). **Phone:** (506) 737-5282.

AUBERGE LES JARDINS INN

Phone: (506)739-5514

Hotel

$109-$179 6/1-8/31
$89-$139 9/1-5/31

Address: 60 Principale St E7B 1V7 **Location:** Trans-Canada Hwy 2 exit 8. **Facility:** 37 units, some cabins. 2 stories (no elevator), interior/exterior corridors. **Dining:** restaurant, see separate listing. **Pool(s):** outdoor. **Activities:** playground, exercise room. **Guest Services:** coin laundry.

AU NIDAIGLE B&B

Phone: 506/739-7567

Bed & Breakfast

$90-$118 6/1-9/30
$85-$110 10/1-5/31

Address: 1582 Principale St E7C 1N2 **Location:** Trans-Canada Hwy 2 exit 21, just s to Rt 144, then 1.8 mi (3 km) w. **Facility:** The modern-style B&B is situated on acreage in the village area and offers comfortable, well-appointed rooms, some with an air tub and balcony. 5 units. 2 stories (no elevator), interior corridors. **Terms:** 7 day cancellation notice. **Activities:** hiking trails, horseshoes.

BEST WESTERN PLUS EDMUNDSTON HOTEL

Phone: (506)739-0000

Hotel

$140-$170

AAA Benefit: Members save up to 20%, plus 10% bonus points with Best Western Rewards®.

Address: 280 Hebert Blvd E3V 0A3 **Location:** Trans-Canada Hwy 2 exit 18 (Hebert Blvd). **Facility:** 93 units. 4 stories, interior corridors. **Amenities:** high-speed Internet. **Pool(s):** heated indoor. **Activities:** whirlpool, waterslide, exercise room. **Guest Services:** coin laundry. **Free Special Amenities:** full breakfast and high-speed Internet.

CLARION HOTEL & CONFERENCE CENTRE

Phone: 506/739-7321

Hotel

Rates not provided

Address: 100 rue Rice E3V 1T4 **Location:** Trans-Canada Hwy 2 exit 18 (Hebert Blvd), 1 mi (1.6 km) sw, then just w on Church Rd. **Facility:** 102 units. 5 stories, interior corridors. **Dining:** Restaurant La Terrasse, see separate listing. **Pool(s):** heated indoor. **Activities:** sauna, whirlpool. **Free Special Amenities:** continental breakfast and high-speed Internet.

COMFORT INN

Phone: (506)739-8361

Hotel

$80-$180

Address: 5 Bateman Ave E3V 3L1 **Location:** Trans-Canada Hwy 2 exit 18 (Hebert Blvd). **Facility:** 121 units. 2 stories (no elevator), interior corridors. **Parking:** winter plug-ins. **Terms:** cancellation fee imposed. **Amenities:** Some: high-speed Internet. **Activities:** exercise room. **Guest Services:** coin laundry.

DAYS INN EDMUNDSTON

Phone: (506)263-0000

Hotel

$81-$140

Address: 10 rue Mathieu E7C 3E1 **Location:** Trans-Canada Hwy 2 exit 26. **Facility:** 77 units. 2 stories (no elevator), interior corridors. **Activities:** playground. **Guest Services:** coin laundry.

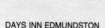

QUALITY INN

Phone: (506)735-5525

Hotel

$72-$135

Address: 919 Canada Rd E3V 3X2 **Location:** Trans-Canada Hwy 2 exit 13B eastbound; exit 13BA westbound. **Facility:** 132 units. 3 stories (no elevator), interior/exterior corridors. **Terms:** cancellation fee imposed. **Dining:** PJ's Bar & Grille, see separate listing. **Pool(s):** heated indoor. **Activities:** sauna, whirlpool, exercise room. **Guest Services:** valet laundry.

WHERE TO EAT

AUBERGE LES JARDINS INN DINING ROOM

Menu on AAA.com

Phone: 506/739-5514

French

$17-$32

AAA Inspector Notes: Country-cottage decor lends to a pleasant, homey atmosphere. The chef offers a fine selection of creative appetizers and entrees, including fresh Atlantic salmon and various fine cuts of meat. Seafood chowder and fine homemade desserts should not be missed. **Bar:** full bar. **Reservations:** required. **Address:** 60 Principale St E7B 1V7 **Location:** Trans-Canada Hwy 2 exit 8; in Auberge Les Jardins Inn.

BEL-AIR RESTAURANT

Phone: 506/735-3329

Canadian

$7-$20

AAA Inspector Notes: This popular family restaurant has a modern theme with a selection of comfortable booths and tables. The menu incorporates several cuisine styles, and portions are ample. **Bar:** full bar. **Address:** 174 Victoria St E3V 2H5 **Location:** Corner of Hebert Blvd; centre.

PJ'S BAR & GRILLE

Phone: 506/735-6434

American

$6-$22

AAA Inspector Notes: This spacious sports bar with its outdoor patio is the place to unwind or catch a favorite game on one of the many TVs. The menu selection is vast with everything from finger foods and Prime steak to seafood and pasta dishes. Service is friendly and relaxed. **Bar:** full bar. **Address:** 919 Canada Rd E3V 3X2 **Location:** Trans-Canada Hwy 2 exit 13B eastbound; exit 13BA westbound; in Quality Inn.

RESTAURANT LA TERRASSE

Phone: 506/739-7321

Canadian

$8-$30

AAA Inspector Notes: Just off the main lobby of the hotel, the pleasant restaurant serves well-prepared steaks and seafood in a relaxing environment. The daily lunch buffet is popular. **Bar:** full bar. **Address:** 100 rue Rice E3V 1T4 **Location:** Trans-Canada Hwy 2 exit 18 (Hebert Blvd), 1 mi (1.6 km) sw, then just w on Church Rd; in Clarion Hotel & Conference Centre.

TAM'S CHINESE RESTAURANT

Phone: 506/735-3349

Chinese

$5-$14

AAA Inspector Notes: Reasonably priced meals and a casual atmosphere mark the small, popular restaurant. A take-out menu is available. **Address:** 261 Victoria St E3V 2H8 **Location:** Trans-Canada Hwy 2 exit 18 (Hebert Blvd), 0.8 mi (1.2 km) s.

FLORENCEVILLE-BRISTOL (D-2)

pop. 1,441

In June 2008, the villages of Bristol and Florenceville merged and became the town of Florenceville-Bristol. On the banks of the Saint John River, Bristol was originally inhabited by the Maliseet

Indians, who called it Shiktehawk. The name was changed to Bristol when the New Brunswick Railway was built there in the 1870s. Florenceville, also on the Saint John River, was originally called Buttermilk Creek; the name was changed in the 1850s in honor of Florence Nightingale.

Home to McCain Foods, reportedly the world's largest producer of french fries, Florenceville-Bristol is known, at least locally, as the French Fry Capital of the World. When hunger strikes, a visit to the café at Potato World Museum *(see attraction listing)* is in order. As you would expect, the menu features many variations of spuds, including potato soup and salad as well as five unusual varieties of french fries.

Off Route 103, the well-preserved, covered Florenceville Bridge was built in 1885 and crosses over the Saint John River. Picnicking near the tranquil river is an enjoyable way to while away an afternoon.

ANDREW AND LAURA McCAIN ART GALLERY is at 8 McCain St. on the lower level of the town's library building. The gallery features contemporary, historical and folk art created by local and regional artists; works are exhibited on a rotating basis. **Time:** Allow 45 minutes minimum. **Hours:** Mon.-Wed. and Fri. 10-4, Thurs. noon-8, Victoria Day weekend-Labour Day; Tues.-Wed. and Fri.-Sat. 10-4, Thurs. noon-8, rest of year. **Cost:** Free. **Phone:** (506) 392-6769.

POTATO WORLD MUSEUM is off Trans-Canada Hwy. exit 153, just e. on Rte. 110 at 385 Centreville Rd. Murals, videos and interactive exhibits trace the history of the potato from its beginnings in South America to the potato industry in New Brunswick. **Tours:** Guided tours are available. **Time:** Allow 1 hour minimum. **Hours:** Mon.-Fri. 9-6, Sat.-Sun. 9-5, June-Aug.; Mon.-Fri. 9-5, Sept. 1 to mid-Oct. **Cost:** $5; $4 (ages 65+); $3 (ages 0-12); $16 (family). Rates may vary; phone ahead. **Phone:** (506) 392-1955. ⊺⊺

FLORENCEVILLE MOTOR INN   **Phone:** (506)392-6053
◈◈◈
Hotel   **Address:** 239 Burnham Rd E7L 1Z1 **Location:** Trans-Canada Hwy 2 exit 153, 2.5 mi (4 km) e on Rt 110 to Rt 130, then 2 mi (3.2 km) s on Rt 130. Located in a quiet rural area. **Facility:**
$100-$109
39 units. 2 stories (no elevator), interior/exterior corridors. **Dining:** Thomas's Table, see separate listing. **Pool(s):** heated indoor.

⊺ ⊻ ⊅ BIZ ⊚ ⊒ / SOME UNITS 🛄 🖼

WHERE TO EAT

BOOTJACKS RESTAURANT   **Phone:** 506/392-6006
◈◈
American   **AAA Inspector Notes:** On the second level of a converted store, the restaurant offers a pleasant country theme with a choice of booth or table seating. The menu offers a selection of burgers, sandwiches, chicken and fish & chips. **Bar:** full bar. **Address:** 331 Main St E7L 3G8 **Location:** Trans-Canada Hwy 2 exit 153; centre. **Parking:** on-site and street. L D
$7-$18

FRESH   **Phone:** 506/392-6000
◈◈◈ ◈◈◈
Canadian   **AAA Inspector Notes:** This tiny, thirty-seat dining room is located in a 1930s passenger rail car at the historic Shogomoc Railway Site in Bristol. The menu changes every six weeks to take advantage of the changing market availability of meat, fish and produce as well as to tap the chef's creative juices. Specialties could include scallops Napoleon, peppered strawberries and greens, fresh fiddlehead ferns, roast salmon, tropical chicken, yogurt cake with red wine poached pears or rhubarb crisp. **Bar:** full bar. **Reservations:** required. **Address:** 9189 Main St E7L 2Y3 **Location:** Jct Rt 130 and 105, 2.5 mi (4 km) n on Rt 105; in Shogomoc Historic Railway Site. **Historic** D
$24-$29

THOMAS'S TABLE   **Phone:** 506/392-6053
◈◈
American   **AAA Inspector Notes:** The large restaurant overlooks hills and farm fields. The menu selection is ample, with selections ranging from burgers and sandwiches to fresh seafood and steaks as well as good seafood chowder. Outdoor seating can be requested in season. **Bar:** full bar. **Address:** 239 Burnham Rd E7L 1Z1 **Location:** Trans-Canada Hwy 2 exit 153, 2.5 mi (4 km) e on Rt 110 to Rt 130, then 2 mi (3.2 km) s on Rt 130; in Florenceville Motor Inn. B L D
$7-$19

FORT BEAUSÉJOUR-FORT CUMBERLAND NATIONAL HISTORIC SITE OF CANADA (E-6)

Fort Beauséjour—Fort Cumberland National Historic Site is 8 kilometres (5 mi.) east of Sackville on Hwy. 2 exit 513A, and 1.5 kilometres (.9 mi.) west of the Nova Scotia border, at 111 Fort Beauséjour Rd.

Built in 1751 in response to the construction of an English fort at Beaubassin a year earlier, Fort Beauséjour defended French interests in the Isthmus of Chignecto. In 1755 a force of New England militia under British command took it after a 2-week siege. That same year, the British initiated the mass deportation of the Acadians at this site.

Renamed Fort Cumberland, the fort withstood an attack by American revolutionaries in 1776. It was manned during the War of 1812 but saw no action, and its military role ceased in 1833.

The visitor center museum contains exhibits of early military and civilian life. Restored stone ruins and grassy ramparts of the star-shaped fort, a cannon exhibit, picnic facilities and outdoor interpretive paintings are on the grounds. Allow 1 hour minimum. Daily 9-5, June 1-Oct. 15. Admission $3.90; $3.40 (ages 65+); $1.90 (ages 6-16); $9.80 (family, two adults and five children). **Cards:** AX, MC, VI. Phone (506) 364-5080.

FREDERICTON (D-3) pop. 47,560
• Hotels p. 46 • Restaurants p. 47
• Attractions map p. 45

One of North America's oldest settlements, Fredericton straddles the broad Saint John River. The area was inhabited by Maliseet Indians thousands of years before European settlement.

Named St. Anne by its French fur-trading founders, the settlement was burned in 1760 by the British in their struggle with the French for control of the continent. Loyalists fleeing the American Revolution revived the settlement in 1783 and renamed it Frederick's Town for the second son of King George III.

New Brunswick became a province in 1784 and Gov. Thomas Carleton made Fredericton the provincial capital in 1785. Today the city is known for its beauty, architecture, heritage and culture.

The former barracks and parade ground of the original military compound on Queen Street now contain a variety of establishments. One is the New Brunswick College of Craft and Design at 457 Queen St.; established in 1938, the school's alumni form the basis of Fredericton's crafts community. The city often is regarded as the pewter capital of Canada because of its many pewtersmiths. Quilters, potters and weavers also are well represented in the area's shops.

In addition to the shops and Saturday morning's Farmers' Market, several downtown landmarks command interest. Historically significant are two cemeteries: The Loyalist Cemetery, near the Saint John River off Waterloo Row, has interesting old tombstones; the Old Burial Ground, along Brunswick Street between York and Regent streets, contains the final resting places of many Loyalists.

A statue of Scottish poet Robert Burns stands on The Green, a grassy promenade along the Saint John River. The Playhouse on Queen Street is the home of Theatre New Brunswick, a touring theatrical company.

Fredericton is at one end of the scenic portion of Hwy. 2, which runs northwest 167 kilometres (104 mi.) along the Saint John River to Woodstock *(see place listing p. 82)*.

More than 85 kilometres (51 mi.) of multi-use trails meander through the city and along the shores of the Saint John and Nashwaak rivers and connect to the Trans Canada Trail System. Bicycle rentals are available during the summer months from Radical Edge, 386 Queen St., phone (506) 459-3478; River Trails Bike Rentals & Tours, on Regent Street, phone (506) 476-7368; and Savage's, 441 King St., phone (506) 457-7452.

In late July Fredericton hosts the ▽ New Brunswick Highland Games Festival on the grounds of the Government House *(see attraction listing)*. This celebration of Scottish culture features Highland dancing, sporting events, clan booths, crafts, food and Celtic entertainment.

Fredericton Tourism: 11 Carleton St., P.O. Box 130, Fredericton, NB, Canada E3B 4Y7. **Phone:** (506) 460-2041 or (888) 888-4768.

Self-guiding tours: The Fredericton Visitor Guide offers a self-guiding walking tour of the city's historic areas and is available at the tourism office; phone (506) 460-2041 or (888) 888-4768.

Shopping areas: Regent Mall, at the top of Regent Street on the south side of Hwy. 8 at exit 6, counts Sears among its 115 stores. Downtown Fredericton has one-of-a-kind shops carrying crafts, fiber arts, jewelry, pewter and other specialty items.

▽ (SAVE) **THE BEAVERBROOK ART GALLERY** is opposite the Legislative Assembly Building at 703 Queen St. A permanent collection of artwork by noted British and Canadian artists includes paintings by 19th-century artist Cornelius Krieghoff and Canadian impressionist James Wilson Morrice. Given to the people of New Brunswick by Lord Beaverbrook in 1959, the gallery displays paintings, sculpture, furniture, porcelain and *objets d'art* dating from the 14th century to the present.

Highlights include late Renaissance paintings, Gobelins and Brussels tapestries and New Brunswick landscape paintings. **Time:** Allow 1 hour minimum. **Hours:** Mon.-Sat. 9-5:30 (also Thurs. 5:30-9), Sun. noon-5:30, June-Dec.; Tues.-Sat. 9-5:30 (also Thurs. 5:30-9), Sun. noon-5:30, rest of year. Closed Jan. 1 and Christmas; phone ahead for other holiday closures. **Cost:** $8; $6 (ages 60+); $3 (ages 6-18 and students with ID); $18 (family, two adults and children ages 6-18); donations (Thurs. after 5:30 p.m.). **Phone:** (506) 458-2028 or (506) 458-0970.

CHRIST CHURCH CATHEDRAL is at 168 Church St. between King and Brunswick sts. Consecrated in 1853, this Anglican cathedral is a replica of St. Mary's Church in Snettisham, Norfolk, England, and exemplifies decorated Gothic architecture. Noon recitals are presented every Friday in July and August. **Tours:** Guided tours are available. **Hours:** Guided tours daily 9-5, July-Aug. Self-guiding tours Mon.-Fri. 9-6, Sat.10-6, Sun. 1-4, rest of year. Phone ahead to confirm schedule. **Cost:** Donations. **Phone:** (506) 450-8500.

FREDERICTON BOTANIC GARDEN is w. of Odell Park with entrances on Prospect St. and Cameron Ct. Established in 1990, this evolving garden will eventually have 12 themed areas. Currently 6 kilometres (4 mi.) of trails wander through a wooded hillside and along a creek past a wide variety of plants and trees, including a collection of azaleas and rhododendrons. **Hours:** Daily dawn-dusk. **Cost:** Free. **Phone:** (506) 452-9269.

FREDERICTON REGION MUSEUM is on Officers' Square at 571 Queen St. Exhibits portray the community from the early First Nations period. Displays illustrate both the province's military and domestic sides of life, ranging from a replica of a World War I trench to a 19-kilogram (42-lb.) Coleman frog. The changing of the guard ceremonies can be seen on Officers' Square in summer.

Hours: Mon.-Sat. 10-5, Sun. noon-5, July 1-early Sept.; Tues.-Sat. 1-4, Apr.-June and early Sept.-Nov. 30; by appointment rest of year. Changing of the guard daily at 11 and 4, July-Aug. (weather permitting). Closed Jan. 1, Christmas and day after Christmas. **Cost:** $5; $2 (students with ID); free (ages 0-5); $10 (family, two adults and children under 18). **Phone:** (506) 455-6041.

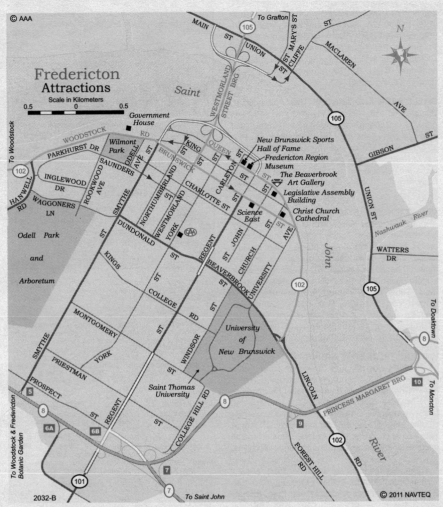

© AAA

Fredericton Attractions

Scale in Kilometers

0.5   0.5

GOVERNMENT HOUSE is at 51 Woodstock Rd. Constructed 1826-28, the restored house is the residence and office of New Brunswick's present lieutenant governor and has been the home of its past governors and lieutenant governors. Antique furnishings from the early 1800s can be seen. Highlights include the reception area, dining and breakfast rooms, library, music room and two conservatories as well as rotating arts and crafts exhibits.

Time: Allow 1 hour minimum. **Hours:** Guided tours Mon.-Sat. 10-4, Sun. noon-4, mid-May through Aug. 31; Mon.-Fri. 10-5, rest of year. Last tour begins 1 hour before closing. **Cost:** Free. **Phone:** (506) 453-2505.

KINGS LANDING HISTORICAL SETTLEMENT—see Kings Landing p. 53.

LEGISLATIVE ASSEMBLY BUILDING is at Queen and St. John sts. The seat of New Brunswick gov-

ernment since 1882, the building features a pair of impressive crystal chandeliers and a self-supporting grand spiral staircase. On permanent display are replicas of Joshua Reynolds' portraits of King George III and Queen Charlotte.

When the House is in session, visitors are welcome to sit in the public galleries; however, they may not take photographs, read books or newspapers, or participate in the proceedings in any way. **Tours:** Guided tours are available. **Time:** Allow 30 minutes minimum. **Hours:** Mon.-Fri. 9-6, Sat.-Sun. 10-5, June 2-Sept. 1; Mon.-Fri. 9-4, rest of year. First tour departs 15 minutes after opening; last tour departs 45 minutes before closing. **Cost:** Free. **Phone:** (506) 453-2527.

NEW BRUNSWICK SPORTS HALL OF FAME is at 503 Queen St. in the Clark Memorial Building. Provincial sports heroes and teams are honored through displays of portraits, photographs and memorabilia, including Olympic medals. **Hours:** Tues.-Sat. 9:30-5, June 1-early Sept.; Wed. 1:30-5:30 (also 6-8 p.m.), Thurs. 4-5:30 (also 6-8 p.m.), Fri. noon-4, Sat. 1-4 or by appointment, rest of year. Closed major holidays. Phone ahead to confirm schedule. **Cost:** $3; $2 (students with ID); $8 (family). **Phone:** (506) 453-3747.

ODELL PARK AND ARBORETUM is bounded by Smythe and Prospect sts., Hanwell Rd. and Waggoners Ln. Walking trails, playgrounds and a picnic area are part of the park, which covers more than 157 hectares (388 acres). The arboretum contains native New Brunswick plants and trees. Local wildlife is protected in the park's game refuge. **Hours:** Daily 8 a.m.-10 p.m. **Cost:** Free. **Phone:** (506) 460-2294.

SAVE **SCIENCE EAST** is at 668 Brunswick St., adjacent to the Boyce farmer's market. "Play, discover and learn" is the motto of this science center, where visitors may go inside a giant kaleidoscope, create tornadoes and participate in more than 150 hands-on exhibits. The center is housed in a former jail built in 1842; the cells display jail artifacts. **Time:** Allow 1 hour, 30 minutes minimum. **Hours:** Mon.-Sat. 10-5, Sun. noon-4, June-Aug.; Mon.-Fri. noon-5, Sat. 10-5, rest of year. **Cost:** $8; $7 (ages 65+); $5 (ages 3-16); $22 (family, two adults and two children). **Phone:** (506) 457-2340.

UNIVERSITY OF NEW BRUNSWICK is on a hill overlooking the city and the Saint John River. Founded in 1785, the university's historic buildings include the 1829 Sir Howard Douglas Hall and the 1851 Brydone Jack Observatory. The Harriet Irving Library preserves rare manuscripts and books, including first editions by Charles Dickens, George Eliot and H.G. Wells. Photographs, films and local documents are displayed at the Provincial Archives.

Tours: Guided tours are available. **Time:** Allow 1 hour minimum. **Hours:** Archives Mon.-Fri. 10-5, Sat. 8:30-5. Closed major holidays. **Cost:** Free. **Phone:** (506) 453-4666, or (506) 453-2122 for the archives.

RECREATIONAL ACTIVITIES

Bicycling

• **River Trails Bike Rentals & Tours** depart from the Lighthouse on the Green at Regent Street. **Hours:** Tours depart daily 10:30-8:30, late June-late Aug.; 10:30-6:30, late May-late June; 10:30-5:30, late Aug. to mid-Sept.; 10:30-5:30, last two weekends in Sept. (weather permitting). **Phone:** (506) 476-7368.

AMSTERDAM INN   **Phone:** (506)474-5050
Hotel
$130-$169
Address: 559 Bishop Dr E3C 2M6 **Location:** Rt 8 exit 6A eastbound; exit 6B westbound, just w of Regent Mall. **Facility:** 50 units. 3 stories, interior corridors. **Terms:** cancellation fee imposed. **Amenities:** high-speed Internet. **Activities:** exercise room.

CARRIAGE HOUSE INN   **Phone:** 506/452-9924
Historic Bed & Breakfast
$119-$129 6/1-9/30
$99-$115 10/1-5/31
Address: 230 University Ave E3B 4H7 **Location:** Just s of George St; centre. **Facility:** Handsome woodwork and other fine details lend a warm ambiance to this 1875 Victorian inn. A variety of rooms styles and sizes are offered. 10 units. 3 stories (no elevator), interior corridors. **Terms:** office hours 7:30 am-10 pm, age restrictions may apply.

CITY MOTEL   **Phone:** 506/450-9900
Hotel
$105-$135 6/1-10/15
$85-$105 10/16-5/31
Address: 1216 Regent St E3B 3Z4 **Location:** Trans-Canada Hwy 2 exit 285A eastbound; exit 285B westbound, 2 mi (3.3 km) n on Rt 101 (Regent St). **Facility:** 55 units. 3 stories (no elevator), interior corridors. **Dining:** Panda Chinese Restaurant, see separate listing. **Activities:** exercise room. **Guest Services:** valet and coin laundry.

THE COLONEL'S IN BED AND BREAKFAST
    Phone: 506/452-2802
Bed & Breakfast
$109-$139 6/1-10/31
$95-$125 11/1-5/31
Address: 843 Union St E3A 3P6 **Location:** On Rt 105, 1.8 mi (3 km) nw of Princess Margaret Bridge. **Facility:** The charming B&B is located on the east side of the Saint John River close to a walking bridge; the well-appointed guest rooms vary in size. 3 units. 3 stories (no elevator), interior/exterior corridors. **Terms:** office hours 6:30 am-10:30 pm. **Guest Services:** coin laundry.

COMFORT INN   **Phone:** (506)453-0800
Hotel
$108-$200
Address: 797 Prospect St E3B 5Y4 **Location:** Trans-Canada Hwy 2 exit 281, 2.5 mi (4 km) ne on Rt 640 (Hanwell Rd). Located in a commercial area. **Facility:** 100 units. 3 stories (no elevator), interior corridors. **Terms:** cancellation fee imposed. **Amenities:** Some: high-speed Internet. **Activities:** exercise room. **Guest Services:** valet and coin laundry.

CROWNE PLAZA FREDERICTON LORD BEAVERBROOK   Phone: (506)455-3371

Hotel
$129-$249

Address: 659 Queen St E3B 5A6 **Location:** Waterfront. Corner of Regent St. **Facility:** 168 units. 7 stories, interior corridors. **Terms:** cancellation fee imposed. **Dining:** James Joyce Irish Pub, The Maverick Room, see separate listings. **Pool(s):** heated indoor. **Activities:** sauna, whirlpool, exercise room. *Fee:* marina. **Guest Services:** valet laundry. **Free Special Amenities: local telephone calls and high-speed Internet.**

CROWNE PLAZA
HOTELS & RESORTS

Fredericton's only downtown hotel on the Saint John River with over 60 years of historic grandeur.

DELTA FREDERICTON   Phone: (506)457-7000

Hotel
$129-$210

Address: 225 Woodstock Rd E3B 2H8 **Location:** Waterfront. 1 mi (1.6 km) n on Rt 102; downtown. **Facility:** 222 units. 7 stories, interior corridors. **Terms:** cancellation fee imposed. **Amenities:** video games (fee), high-speed Internet. **Dining:** Bruno's, see separate listing. **Pool(s):** heated outdoor, heated indoor. **Activities:** sauna, whirlpool, jogging, exercise room. *Fee:* massage. **Guest Services:** valet laundry.

HOWARD JOHNSON PLAZA HOTEL FREDERICTON   Phone: (506)462-4444

Hotel
$77-$107

Address: 958 Prospect St E3B 2T8 **Location:** Rt 8 exit 3 (Hanwell Rd) eastbound; exit 5 (Smythe St) westbound. **Facility:** 113 units, some two bedrooms and kitchens. 2 stories (no elevator), interior/exterior corridors. **Parking:** winter plug-ins. **Terms:** cancellation fee imposed. **Pool(s):** heated outdoor, heated indoor. **Activities:** sauna, whirlpool, exercise room. **Guest Services:** coin laundry.

LAKEVIEW INNS & SUITES-FREDERICTON   Phone: (506)459-0035

Hotel
$107-$140

Address: 665 Prospect St E3B 6B8 **Location:** Rt 8 exit 3 (Hanwell Rd) eastbound; exit 5 (Smythe St) westbound. Located in a commercial area. **Facility:** 97 units. 4 stories, interior corridors. **Activities:** exercise room. **Guest Services:** coin laundry. **Free Special Amenities: expanded continental breakfast and high-speed Internet.**

RAMADA HOTEL FREDERICTON   Phone: (506)460-5500

Hotel
$89-$171

Address: 480 Riverside Dr E3A 8C2 **Location:** On Rt 105; at north end of Princess Margaret Bridge. **Facility:** 114 units. 2 stories (no elevator), interior corridors. **Amenities:** *Some:* high-speed Internet. **Dining:** The Courtyard Restaurant, see separate listing. **Pool(s):** heated indoor. **Activities:** whirlpool, exercise room. *Fee:* golf-9 holes, miniature golf, game room, volleyball. **Guest Services:** valet and coin laundry.

THE VERY BEST-A VICTORIAN B&B   Phone: 506/451-1499

Historic Bed & Breakfast
$119-$139

Address: 806 George St E3B 1K7 **Location:** At Church St. **Facility:** This B&B is in the center of town and offers well-decorated accommodations with modern amenities. 5 units. 2 stories (no elevator), interior corridors. **Terms:** open 6/1-10/31, office hours 7 am-11 pm, age restrictions may apply, cancellation fee imposed. **Pool(s):** heated outdoor. **Activities:** sauna, game room.

WHERE TO EAT

THE BLUE DOOR RESTAURANT & BAR   Phone: 506/455-2583

California
$10-$27

AAA Inspector Notes: One way to classify the fine cuisine at this eatery is a combination of Thai, Indian and West coast dishes with the focus on local-market fresh produce, meat and seafood. **Bar:** full bar. **Reservations:** suggested. **Address:** 100 Regent St E3B 3W4 **Location:** Corner of King and Regent sts. **Parking:** street only.

L D

BREWBAKERS RESTAURANT   Phone: 506/459-0067

American
$9-$26

AAA Inspector Notes: The popular restaurant has the feel of an upbeat pub. The menu is extensive, with offerings ranging from pasta and brick-oven pizzas to fresh seafood and meat entrees. Spacious patio dining is available in season. **Bar:** full bar. **Address:** 546 King St E3B 1E6 **Location:** Between Regent and Carleton sts. **Parking:** on-site (fee).

L D

BRUNO'S   Phone: 506/457-7000

American
$8-$26

AAA Inspector Notes: The restaurant has several dining sections with a bistro decor, and a large patio that borders the Saint John River. The seafood-focused menu lists planked salmon, halibut and excellent chowder. Various meat entrées also are available. **Bar:** full bar. **Address:** 225 Woodstock Rd E3B 2H8 **Location:** 1 mi (1.6 km) n on Rt 102; downtown; in Delta Fredericton.

B L D CALL

CHEZ CORA   Phone: 506/472-2672

Canadian
$6-$13

AAA Inspector Notes: Eggs, omelets, waffles, crepes (sorry, no American-style pancakes here), French toast, fruit platters and all the breakfast meats--that's the specialty here, all day. However, at lunchtime the menu lists a selection of soups, salads, quiches, sandwiches and a dish called the grilled panini crepe. **Address:** 476 Queen St E3B 1B6 **Location:** At Carleton St; centre. **Parking:** on-site (fee).

B L

CHEZ RIZ INDIAN & PAKISTANI CUISINE   Phone: 506/454-9996

Indian
$8-$19

AAA Inspector Notes: This cozy restaurant features rich dark wood accents and pressed-tin walls and ceilings. The buffet lines up well-prepared Indian and Pakistani dishes. **Bar:** full bar. **Address:** 366 Queen St E3B 1B2 **Location:** Just e of Westmoreland St. **Parking:** street only.

L D

THE COURTYARD RESTAURANT   Phone: 506/460-5511

American
$8-$22

AAA Inspector Notes: Decorated with beautiful, hand-painted murals and ceilings depicting Venetian scenes, the spacious restaurant offers booth and table seating. The vast menu is sure to offer something for everyone. Daily specials are prepared for lunch and dinner. **Bar:** full bar. **Address:** 480 Riverside Dr E3B 5E3 **Location:** On Rt 105; at north end of Princess Margaret Bridge; in Ramada Hotel Fredericton. B L D CALL M

DIMITRI'S SOUVLAKI RESTAURANT
Phone: 506/452-8882

Greek
$7-$18

AAA Inspector Notes: The popular restaurant serves distinctive Greek cuisine in a casual atmosphere. Try the classic lamb kebab, chicken brochette or jumbo shrimp. Outdoor seating is a seasonal option. **Bar:** full bar. **Address:** 349 King St E3B 1E4 **Location:** Centre; in Pipers Lane area. **Parking:** on-site (fee). L D

DIPLOMAT RESTAURANT   Phone: 506/454-2400

Chinese
$8-$23

AAA Inspector Notes: In a commercial area adjacent to the Delta Fredericton, this large, popular restaurant satisfies patrons with ample portions of Canadian and Chinese cuisines. Superb desserts are made in house. The staff provides friendly, knowledgeable service with a casual style. **Bar:** full bar. **Address:** 253 Woodstock Rd E3B 2H8 **Location:** 1 mi (1.6 km) n on Rt 102.

B L D 24

EL BURRITO LOCO   Phone: 506/459-5626

Mexican
$11-$23

AAA Inspector Notes: A touch of Puerto Vallarta nestled in the heart of town, the colorfully decorated restaurant prepares Mexican cuisine that patrons can savor on the seasonal patio. Among items on the full menu are quesadillas, chimichangas, burritos and fajitas, in addition to some steak and seafood options. **Bar:** full bar. **Address:** 304 King St E3B 1E3 **Location:** Corner of Westmorland Ave. L D

FRANK'S FINER DINER   Phone: 506/459-0707

American
$6-$15

AAA Inspector Notes: This spacious restaurant offers a 50s theme with booths, tables and a soda counter. The menu includes classic burgers, fish and chips, soups and salads but save room for one of their excellent pies. Keep an eye out for some servers flying around on roller skates. **Address:** 80 Two Nations Crossing E3A 1C9 **Location:** Just e of St. Marys St; opposite Walmart; in north Fredericton. B L D

HILLTOP GRILL & BEVERAGE CO   Phone: 506/458-9057

American
$7-$22

AAA Inspector Notes: A popular spot for an upbeat gathering, the spacious, sports bar-style restaurant offers mainly booth seating. On the menu is a wide variety of satisfying comfort foods, as well as seafood and steaks. **Bar:** full bar. **Address:** 1034 Prospect St E3B 3C1 **Location:** Rt 8 exit 3 (Hanwell Rd) eastbound; exit 5 (Smythe St) westbound. L D

JAMES JOYCE IRISH PUB   Phone: 506/450-9820

Irish
$10-$21

AAA Inspector Notes: Guests can relax in a laid-back pub that has a spacious seasonal patio. On tap is a fine selection of local and imported beers. Examples of splendid Irish-style pub fare include steak and mushroom pie, soda bread with seafood chowder, fish and chips and plenty of finger foods. **Bar:** full bar. **Address:** 659 Queen St E3B 5A6 **Location:** Corner of Regent St; in Crowne Plaza Fredericton Lord Beaverbrook. D

THE LUNAR ROGUE PUB   Phone: 506/450-2065

Canadian
$8-$20

AAA Inspector Notes: The popular landmark nurtures a relaxed atmosphere. Guests can dine inside or out on the patio. Good pub grub, served in ample portions, couples with a fine selection of whistle-whetting beers and single malts. **Bar:** full bar. **Address:** 625 King St E3B 4Y2 **Location:** At Regent St. **Parking:** street only.

L D

THE MAVERICK ROOM   Phone: 506/451-1804

Steak
$24-$35

AAA Inspector Notes: The elegant dining room sports wing-backed chairs. The staff bring you selections of meat to choose your own cut and have it prepared to your specifications. They also offer a selection of fresh seafood and poultry dishes. **Bar:** full bar. **Reservations:** suggested. **Address:** 659 Queen St E3B 5A6 **Location:** Corner of Regent St; in Crowne Plaza Fredericton Lord Beaverbrook. D CALL M

MCGINNIS LANDING RESTAURANT
Phone: 506/458-1212

American
$10-$25

AAA Inspector Notes: Decked out with hardwood floors and hand-painted murals, the roomy, colorful dining room sustains an upbeat atmosphere. On the menu, which boasts an Oriental flair, are fresh seafood and varied meat dishes. **Bar:** full bar. **Address:** 280 King St E3B 1E2 **Location:** At Westmorland St. L D

MEXICALI ROSA'S   Phone: 506/451-0686

Mexican
$10-$31

AAA Inspector Notes: The Mexican cantina makes an excellent choice for family-friendly fun. Old West paintings and murals add color to stucco walls and wooden beams, while a Tex-Mex menu provides a feast of favorites such as fajitas, burritos and some seafood items. Fried ice cream is a sweet treat. **Bar:** full bar. **Address:** 546 King St E3B 1E6 **Location:** At Regent St. **Parking:** street only.

L D

THE PALATE RESTAURANT & CAFE
Phone: 506/450-7911

American
$8-$22

AAA Inspector Notes: The restaurant's menu offers a wide variety of items including fresh seafood and various meats including duck, chicken and lamb. A nice mix of salads and pasta is also available. **Bar:** full bar. **Address:** 462 Queen St E3B 5A6 **Location:** Corner of Queen St and Wilmot Alley. **Parking:** street only.

L D

PANDA CHINESE RESTAURANT   Phone: 506/455-5050

Chinese
$8-$20

AAA Inspector Notes: A friendly and relaxed atmosphere can be found at this casual spot. Offerings include authentic Chinese dishes as well as various combination plates with seafood, duck, chicken and beef. A lunch buffet is available Monday through Friday. **Bar:** full bar. **Address:** 1216 Regent St E3B 3Z4 **Location:** Trans-Canada Hwy 2 exit 285A eastbound; exit 285B westbound, 2 mi (3.3 km) n on Rt 101 (Regent St); in City Motel.

B L D

SMITTY'S   Phone: 506/454-0022

Canadian
$7-$20

AAA Inspector Notes: The family-oriented restaurant satisfies patrons with its ever-popular all-day breakfast items, as well as tasty and wholesome soups and salads at lunchtime. A relaxed mood characterizes the dining space. **Bar:** full bar. **Address:** 1381 Regent St E3C 1A2 **Location:** Centre; at Regent Mall. B L D

SWISS CHALET   Phone: 506/458-8278

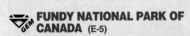

Chicken
$6-$16

AAA Inspector Notes: The popular restaurant is known for its rotisserie chicken and ribs and the tangy Chalet sauce that gives food its special zip. Diners munch on a half or quarter chicken with sides such as steamed vegetables, fries, baked potatoes and salads. Lunch guests often go for the great soup and sandwich combination. Take-out and delivery service are popular options. **Bar:** full bar. **Address:** 961 Prospect St E3B 2T7 **Location:** At Smythe St.

[L] [D]

FUNDY NATIONAL PARK OF CANADA (E-5)

Elevations in the park range from sea level at the Bay of Fundy to 365 metres (1,200 ft.) at Rte. 114 near the Caribou Plains Trail. Refer to CAA/AAA maps for additional elevation information.

Between Moncton and Saint John on Rte. 114, Fundy National Park of Canada overlooks the Bay of Fundy and encompasses 206 square kilometres (80 sq. mi.) of wooded hills and valleys.

When the bay's giant tide recedes, visitors can walk on the sea floor and then follow coastal trails to higher ground for a panoramic view of the water's return. Cliffs rising steeply from the bay vary from the red and khaki of layered sandstone to the gray-green remains of lava flows and granite intrusions. Occasional stream valleys make deep gashes in the cliff walls.

Meadows of wildflowers, rushing waterfalls and placid lakes characterize this wildlife sanctuary and recreation area, which includes more than 100 kilometres (62 mi.) of hiking trails.

General Information and Activities

Fundy National Park of Canada is accessible from the Trans-Canada Hwy. at Penobsquis via Rte. 114, and from Moncton south and then west via Rte. 114. The park, visitor information center and campgrounds are open all year. Most other services operate from the last week in May to mid-October. Some 25 hiking trails offer summer diversion while snowshoeing and cross-country skiing are popular December through March. Park headquarters is at Alma, near the mouth of the Upper Salmon River.

Park interpreters conduct a regular program of nature hikes and illustrated talks. Many self-guiding trails are open all year.

Beaches on the bay include Alma, Cannontown, Herring Cove and Point Wolfe. The park contains a heated salt-water pool, golf course, bowling green and tennis courts. Trout fishing is popular at Bennett Lake, with a daily limit of five fish. The park requires a national park fishing license ($9.80 daily, $34.30 annually), which can be obtained at Bennett Lake or the visitor information center.

Fundy's Acadian forests are home to American martens, Atlantic salmon, moose and whitetail deer as well as peregrine falcons and numerous other species of birds. *See Recreation Chart.*

Note: Although they are accustomed to people, animals should be viewed and photographed with utmost care.

ADMISSION to the park is $7.80; $6.80 (ages 65+); $3.90 (ages 6-16); $19.60 (family, up to seven people, maximum of two adults). Phone (877) 737-3783 for campsite reservations.

PETS are permitted on certain trails and in picnic areas, campgrounds and other parts of the park, but they must be kept on leashes and may not be left unattended.

ADDRESS inquiries to Fundy National Park of Canada, P.O. Box 1001, Alma, NB, Canada E4H 1B4; phone (506) 887-6000.

GAGETOWN (E-4) pop. 719

Gagetown's Loomcrofters demonstrate weaving in a former fur-trading post, one of the oldest buildings on the Saint John River. Built in 1761, it is known as the Blockhouse because rifles and ammunition were stored in its cellar. The Loomcrofters produce tartans, draperies and upholstery materials.

QUEENS COUNTY HERITAGE is at 69 Front St. The museum encompasses three historic sites. Tilley House was the 1818 birthplace of Sir Samuel Leonard Tilley, a father of the Canadian Confederation. Furnishings of the Loyalist and Victorian periods are displayed, many salvaged from older houses in the area. The 1836 Queens County Courthouse, 16 Court House Rd., displays permanent and changing historical exhibits. The 1818 Anthony Flower House, 2270 Lower Cambridge Rd. in Cambridge-Narrows, was home to the 19th-century artist, farmer and community leader and his family. Exhibits and furnishings offer a glimpse at the family's life.

Time: Allow 1 hour minimum. **Hours:** Daily 10-5, mid-June to mid-Sept.; by appointment in May and Oct.-Nov. **Cost:** $3; $5 (for any two sites); $7 (for all three sites); free (ages 0-11). Cash only. **Phone:** (506) 488-2966 for the Tilley House, (506) 488-2483 for the courthouse, or (506) 488-3030 for the Anthony Flower House.

THE CREEK VIEW RESTAURANT   Phone: 506/488-9806

American
$6-$16

AAA Inspector Notes: The quaint restaurant overlooks the village and river and offers pleasant outdoor seating in season. The former 1900s automobile dealership displays turn-of-the-20th-century memorabilia. Tasty country cuisine makes up the full menu. **Bar:** full bar. **Address:** 38 Tilley Rd E5N 1A8 **Location:** Centre. [L] [D]

GRANDE-ANSE (A-5) pop. 758

MUSÉE DES PAPES (POPES' MUSEUM) is on Hwy. 11 at 184 Acadie St. Displays about papal history include a portrait gallery and a finely detailed model of St. Peter's Basilica. Guided tours with an audiovisual presentation are available. **Hours:** Daily 10-6, late June to mid-Aug.; Wed.-Sun. 10-6, mid-Aug. to late Aug. Last tour begins 1 hour before closing. **Cost:** $8; $7 (ages 65+); $4 (ages 12-18); $16 (family). **Phone:** (506) 732-3003.

GRAND FALLS (C-2) pop. 6,133

Grand Falls was a French settlement that became a British military post in 1790. More than 80 percent of its citizens are bilingual, and this is the only town in the Atlantic Provinces with an official name in both languages: the French version is Grand-Sault.

The great horseshoe falls of the Saint John River are considered the largest east of Niagara Falls; the Grand Falls hydroelectric plant provides power to the provincial distribution system. The town is a major shipping point for New Brunswick's seed potato-growing industry, and area farmers supply potatoes to the McCain frozen food plant in Grand Falls, which produces 10 tons of French fries per hour.

Grand Falls District Chamber of Commerce: 131 Pleasant St., Suite 200, Grand Falls, NB, Canada E3Z 1G6. **Phone:** (506) 473-1905.

GRAND FALLS AND GORGE is best viewed from the Malabeam information center on the Ron Turcotte Bridge, which extends from Broadway Boulevard, crossing the Saint John River Gorge. A 23-metre (75.5-ft.) cataract gives Grand Falls its name. On either side of the river, the Malabeam and La Rochelle information centers relate the legend of a young native girl who saved her village by luring a Mohawk tribe over the falls into the gorge. At the La Rochelle center a 250-step stairway leads to Wells-in-Rocks, a series of deep potholes. A pontoon boat ride also is offered (weather and water conditions permitting).

Guided tours are available by appointment; information may be obtained at both information centers. **Hours:** Malabeam center daily 9-9, mid-June to mid-Aug.; 10-7, mid-Aug. through day before Labour Day; 10-5, May 1 to mid-June and Labour Day-Oct. 8. La Rochelle center daily 10-6, June 29-Aug. 31. **Cost:** Park and information centers free. Wells-in-Rocks $5; free (ages 0-12). Guided tour $8; free (ages 0-12). **Parking:** $3. **Phone:** (506) 475-7769 or (877) 475-7769.

GRAND FALLS MUSEUM is at 68 Madawaska Rd., Suite 100. Artifacts, tools, photographs and memorabilia depict the history of the area. An exhibit chronicles Van Morrell's tightrope walk over the falls. **Hours:** Mon.-Sat. 10-4, June 30-Aug. 30. Closed Civic Day. **Cost:** Donations. **Phone:** (506) 473-5265, or (506) 473-5940 in the off-season.

COTE'S BED & BREAKFAST   Phone: (506)473-1415

Bed & Breakfast
$95-$175

Address: 575 Broadway Blvd W E3Z 2L2 **Location:** Trans-Canada Hwy 2 exit 79, follow signs to Main St (downtown), then just w. **Facility:** A quiet residential area on the edge of town shelters this B&B, which has tastefully decorated guest rooms; two suites have a shared deck and hot tub. The owner's dog is on the premises. 4 units. 2 stories (no elevator), interior corridors. **Terms:** age restrictions may apply, 3 day cancellation notice-fee imposed. **Free Special Amenities:** full breakfast and high-speed Internet.

QUALITY INN GRAND FALLS   Phone: (506)473-1300

Hotel
$119-$189

Address: 10039 Rt 144 E3Y 3H5 **Location:** Trans-Canada Hwy 2 exit 75, just w. **Facility:** 100 units, some cabins. 2 stories (no elevator), interior/exterior corridors. **Parking:** winter plug-ins. **Terms:** cancellation fee imposed. **Dining:** Pres-du-Lac Restaurant, see separate listing. **Pool(s):** heated indoor. **Activities:** sauna, whirlpool, paddleboats, putting green, playground, basketball, exercise room. **Guest Services:** coin laundry.

RIVER TRAIL BED & BREAKFAST   Phone: (506)475-8818

Bed & Breakfast
$65-$100

Address: 34 Dominique St E3Y 1A2 **Location:** 0.8 mi (1.2 km) nw on Madawaska Rd, just s on Carrier St; centre. **Facility:** 4 units. 1 story, interior corridors. **Terms:** office hours 7 am-10 pm. **Guest Services:** coin laundry.

WHERE TO EAT

LE GRAND 'SAUT RISTORANTE   Phone: 506/473-3876

Italian
$7-$22

AAA Inspector Notes: In the heart of town, this spacious two-level lodge-style restaurant has a both booth and table seating. Specializing in excellent pizza, this place also serves a good range of pasta, meat and seafood items. **Bar:** full bar. **Address:** 155 Broadway Blvd E3Z 2J8 **Location:** Between Victoria and Church sts.

PRES-DU-LAC RESTAURANT   Phone: 506/473-1300

Canadian
$7-$21

AAA Inspector Notes: Meat and seafood selections fill the menu, which also includes homemade soups and pies and a tasty quiche. Diners can request seating in one of several pleasant dining sections. **Bar:** full bar. **Address:** 10039 Rt 144 E3Y 3H5 **Location:** Trans-Canada Hwy 2 exit 75, just w; in Quality Inn Grand Falls. D

GRAND MANAN ISLAND (F-3) pop. 2,460

Grand Manan lies 15 kilometres (9 mi.) off the coast of Maine in the Bay of Fundy. It is known for its lobster and herring catches and for the preparation of dulse, an edible seaweed. A 1.5-hour boat trip connects the island with Black's Harbour.

Humpback, finback and North Atlantic right whales visit the waters off Grand Manan from mid-July to mid-September; the rare right whales also use the area as a mating ground. Deep-sea excursions and whale-watching trips can be scheduled locally.

Some of the 19 hiking trails that explore the coastline of this island offer visitors the chance to sight seals as well. John J. Audubon made many of his sketches here; more than 275 species of birds have been sighted.

SEA WATCH TOURS leaves from the Seal Cove Pier. Passengers embark on 5-hour whale-watching trips in the Bay of Fundy. Bird-watching tours and excursions to the Machias Seal Island, noted for its puffin colony, also are available. Whale sighting is guaranteed or tour is free. **Hours:** Departures daily at 8 and 1, early July-late Sept. Phone ahead to confirm schedule. **Cost:** $65; $45 (ages 3-12). Reservations are required. **Phone:** (506) 662-8552 or (877) 662-8552.

HAMPTON (E-4) pop. 4,004

The parish of Hampton was established in Kings County in 1795 by Loyalist settlers. By the early 19th century the village on the Kennebecasis River had become a shipbuilding center. The Kings County Courthouse was built on the town square in 1870, and the county jail was moved, block by block, from the former county seat of Kingston. The province's first telephone is thought to have been installed at Hampton.

The 2,000-hectare (4,900-acre) Hampton Marsh, one of the most fertile and productive wetland systems in New Brunswick, is home to waterfowl, marsh birds, eagles, cranes, beavers, otters and moose.

Hampton Visitor Information Centre: 657 Main St., Hampton, NB, Canada E5N 6C6. **Phone:** (506) 832-6111 June-Aug., or (506) 832-6096 rest of year.

KINGS COUNTY MUSEUM is behind the courthouse in the Centennial Building at 27 Centennial Rd. Photographs, documents, clothing, early furniture and pioneer household and farm items are displayed. Of interest is the set of standard weights and

measures sent from the government of England in 1854. A genealogical library is available. The Old Kings County Jail next door houses additional exhibits. **Hours:** Mon.-Fri. 8:30-4:30, June 15-Sept. 30. Tours by appointment rest of year. **Cost:** (includes guided tour) $2; $1 (ages 6-12). **Phone:** (506) 832-6009.

HOLLY'S RESTAURANT   Phone: 506/832-5520

American
$8-$21

AAA Inspector Notes: The selection of country-style cuisine and wonderful desserts are ample in this pleasant restaurant. Patio seating can be requested in season. **Bar:** full bar. **Address:** 454 Main St E5N 6C1 **Location:** Centre; in Hampton Mall. B L D

HARTLAND (D-2) pop. 947

The 391-metre (1,282-ft.) Hartland Covered Bridge, reputedly the world's longest, carries Hwy. 103 across the Saint John River. Bridges were originally covered for protection from the weather. The life expectancy of a regular bridge was perhaps 10 years, while a covered bridge might last a century. There was one drawback in the winter—snow had to be hauled and spread across the floor so that sleds could cross.

With its barn-like roof, a covered bridge eased farm animals' fears of crossing the river. And, of course, the cover of darkness provided an opportunity for young suitors to steal a kiss. Ministers opposed construction of Hartland's "kissing bridge" as a corrupting influence, but they were outvoted. The bridge was completed in 1922.

HARVEY pop. 352

THE LOUGHEED PUB & EATERY   Phone: 506/366-9197

Canadian
$7-$18

AAA Inspector Notes: Nestled in the heart of the village, the neighborhood pub-style restaurant has two dining sections and an outdoor deck. The menu lists typical pub fare, including fish and chips, burgers, sandwiches and snack foods. Live entertainment enhances weekend visits. **Bar:** full bar. **Address:** 3 Hanselpacker Rd E6K 1A1 **Location:** Just n of Rt 3; centre. L D

HAWKSHAW

SUNSET VIEW COTTAGES   Phone: 506/575-2592

Cottage
$90-$120

Address: 45 Hawkshaw Rd E6G 1N8 **Location:** Trans-Canada Hwy 2 exit 231, 1.2 mi (2 km) s on Rt 102. **Facility:** 4 cottages. 1 story, exterior corridors. **Terms:** open 6/1-9/30, office hours 7:30 am-10 pm, 14 day cancellation notice. **Pool(s):** outdoor. **Activities:** boat dock, playground, horseshoes. **Guest Services:** coin laundry.

HILLSBOROUGH (D-5) pop. 1,292

Pennsylvania Germans were the first to immigrate to the west bank of the Petitcodiac River, arriving in 1766 and naming the community Dutch Village. Two decades later the town was renamed to honor an early administrator, Lord Hillsborough.

Clapboard houses along the waterfront road to Moncton *(see place listing p. 56)* evoke images of the 19th century, when wives would pace widow's walks waiting for husbands to sail their ships home to Hillsborough. Mining, primarily of the area's vast gypsum quarries, and farming dominate Hillsborough's economy.

Hillsborough is at the eastern end of the scenic portion of Hwy. 114, which runs 205 kilometres (127 mi.) from Penobsquis, through Fundy National Park and up Chignecto Bay.

NEW BRUNSWICK RAILWAY MUSEUM is on Hwy. 114. The museum houses such train-related memorabilia as lanterns, photographs, antique caboose stoves, velocipedes and motor cars. The rail yard and shop contain two diesel-electric locomotives, a steam crane, a steam engine, coaches, cabooses and maintenance equipment.

Hours: Daily 10-6, late June-Labour Day; Sat. 10-6, June 1-late June and day after Labour Day-Sept. 30. **Cost:** $5; $4 (ages 65+); $3 (ages 6-16); $10 (family, two adults and children ages 0-16). **Phone:** (506) 734-3195.

STEEVES HOUSE MUSEUM is at 40 Mill St. The birthplace and home of one of the fathers of Canadian Confederation has been restored and furnished in the style of the late 19th century. Steeves family artifacts are displayed in the 1812 structure. **Time:** Allow 1 hour minimum. **Hours:** Mon.-Sat. 10-5, Sun. 1-5, mid-June through Labour Day; by appointment rest of year. **Cost:** $3; $2 (ages 7-11); $8 (family). **Phone:** (506) 734-3102, or (506) 734-2363 in the off-season.

HOPEWELL CAPE (E-5)

Richard B. Bennett, the only New Brunswick politician to become prime minister of Canada, was born at Hopewell Hill in 1870. He took office in 1930 as the country's economy faltered and, perhaps unfairly, he shouldered most of the blame for the hardships of the Great Depression. After a landslide defeat for reelection and subsequent conflicts with his fellow Conservatives, Bennett left the country for England, where he served in the House of Lords. He died in 1947 and was buried at his estate in Mickleham, Surrey. He remains the only Canadian prime minister not to be buried on Canadian soil.

ALBERT COUNTY MUSEUM, 3940 Hwy. 114, is housed in a complex of nine buildings that includes a graffiti-covered 1845 jail and a 1904 courthouse. The museum's 22 themed galleries tell the stories of Albert County residents, a diverse group that includes pioneers, artisans, shipbuilders, farmers, an ax murderer and Canada's 11th prime minister, R.B. Bennett. A 20-seat theater shows a film about Prime Minister Bennett's life. **Hours:** Daily 9:30-5:30, Victoria Day-Thanksgiving; by appointment rest of year. Phone ahead to confirm schedule. **Cost:** $6; $5 (ages 60+ and students with ID); free (ages 0-5); $15 (family). **Phone:** (506) 734-2003.

HOPEWELL ROCKS OCEAN TIDAL EXPLORATION SITE is on the Bay of Fundy near the mouth of the Petitcodiac River on Hwy. 114. Ocean tides have carved the Flower Pot Rocks, pillars of sandstone and conglomerate rock with balsam fir and dwarf spruce growing on top. Visitors may walk on the ocean floor below the rocks from 3 hours before low tide until 3 hours after low tide. At high tide, the rocks resemble islands. An interpretive center provides viewing decks and multimedia exhibits about the Bay of Fundy. A shuttle runs from the parking area to the cliff.

Hours: Daily 8-8, late June-late Aug.; 9-7, late Aug.-early Sept.; 9-5, mid-May to late June and early Sept. to mid-Oct. Phone ahead to confirm schedule. **Cost:** $9; $7.75 (ages 65+ and students with ID); free (ages 0-4); $24 (family, two adults and two children). Shuttle $2 each way. Rates may vary; phone ahead. **Phone:** (506) 734-3534, or (877) 734-3429 for information and daily tide tables.

RECREATIONAL ACTIVITIES
Kayaking

• **Baymount Outdoor Adventures Inc.** departs from the kayak building at the lower site of Hopewell Rocks Ocean Tidal Exploration Site. Other activities are offered. **Hours:** Daily 7:30-dusk, early June-Labour Day (weather permitting). **Phone:** (506) 734-2660 or (877) 601-2660.

FAMILY TREASURES INN B & B   Phone: (506)882-2077

Bed & Breakfast
$99-$130 6/1-8/31
$89-$110 9/1-9/30

Address: 4941 Hwy 114 E4H 4K2 **Location:** On Rt 114, 4.8 mi (8 km) w. **Facility:** Just a short drive from the Hopewell Rocks, this pleasant property overlooking Shepody Bay has modern guest rooms, some of which offer gas fireplaces and sun decks. 10 units. 2 stories (no elevator), interior corridors. **Terms:** open 6/1-9/30, office hours 7 am-midnight, 7 day cancellation notice-fee imposed. **Guest Services:** coin laundry. 📶 ⊠ / SOME UNITS 🖵

INNISFREE BED & BREAKFAST   Phone: 506/734-3510

Bed & Breakfast
$99-$139

Address: 4270 Rt 114 E4H 3P4 **Location:** 1 mi (1.6 km) w on Rt 114. Located in a rural area. **Facility:** Gardens enrich this well-appointed B&B within walking distance of Hopewell Rocks Ocean Tidal Exploration Site; a few rooms have a view of the bay. 5 units. 2 stories (no elevator), interior corridors. **Terms:** office hours 7 am-10 pm, age restrictions may apply, 7 day cancellation notice-fee imposed. **Activities:** hiking trails. **Guest Services:** coin laundry. 📶 ⊠ 🅰 🖵

BROADLEAF GUEST RANCH
Menu on AAA.com   Phone: 506/882-2349

American
$6-$21

AAA Inspector Notes: At a guest ranch, this ranch kitchen offers a fine selection of reasonably priced home-style entrées. Portions are ample and service is friendly. **Bar:** full bar. **Reservations:** suggested. **Address:** 5526 Rt 114 E4H 3N5 **Location:** On Rt 114, 7.2 mi (12 km) sw. Ⓑ Ⓛ Ⓓ 🅰

KESWICK RIDGE (D-3) pop. 1,331, elev. 125m/411'

MACTAQUAC HYDROELECTRIC DAM is off the Trans-Canada Hwy. at 451 Hwy. 105. Guided 1-hour tours of the generating station demonstrate how the dam was built and how it operates. **Hours:** Tours daily 9-5, June 1-Labour Day; by appointment rest of year. **Cost:** Free. **Phone:** (506) 462-3800.

KINGS LANDING (D-2)

When the Mactaquac Dam Project was proposed in the 1960s, historians sought a way to save architecturally significant buildings along the Saint John River. The best examples from the Loyalist period were dismantled and relocated from the flood plain to Kings Landing Historical Settlement. Some 70 buildings have been restored.

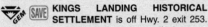 **KINGS LANDING HISTORICAL SETTLEMENT** is off Hwy. 2 exit 253. The 121-hectare (299-acre) site is a meticulous restoration of a typical village in the Saint John River Valley 1820-90. The settlement includes farms, historic houses, mills, a forge, an inn, a printing office, a school, a store and a theater. Staff members in period dress conduct tours and free wagon rides.

Special events include historical reenactments, a fall auction and harvest and Christmas candlelight dinners. An educational program allows children to spend 5 days in the village and dress and live as youngsters did in the 19th century. **Time:** Allow 3 hours minimum. **Hours:** Daily 10-5, May 28-Oct. 10. Phone ahead to confirm schedule. **Cost:** $16; $14 (ages 65+); $13 (students ages 17+ with ID); $11 (ages 6-16); $38 (family, two adults and children ages 6-15). **Phone:** (506) 363-4999.

KOUCHIBOUGUAC NATIONAL PARK OF CANADA (C-5)

> Elevations in the park range from sea level at Northumberland Strait to 30 metres (100 ft.). Refer to CAA/AAA maps for additional elevation information.

Kouchibouguac National Park is entered from hwys. 11 or 134, just south of the village of Kouchibouguac. The park consists of 238 square kilometres (92 sq. mi.) on the central eastern shore. Molded by a whimsical sea, this section of the Maritime Plain is an intricate blend of coastal and inland habitats including rivers, sand dunes, salt marshes, bogs, lagoons, fields and forests and the characteristic flora and fauna of each.

General Information and Activities

The park is open year-round for walking, hiking and winter recreation; the main gate and visitor center are open mid-May to mid-Oct. The Information Centre, 1 kilometre (.6 mi.) east inside the gate, offers a multimedia presentation about the diverse habitats of the park. Information about facilities and such activities as nature walks, evening programs and outdoor presentations also is available. The center is open daily 8-8, mid-June through Labour Day; 9-5, mid-May to mid-June and day after Labour Day-second Mon. in Oct. If the entrance gate kiosk is closed, entry passes may be purchased at the Information Centre.

The St. Louis Kouchibouguacis, Black and Kouchibouguac rivers give the area its Mi'kmaq name—Kouchibouguac (KOOSH-e-boo-gwack), "river of the long tides." These waterways provide a variety of canoe routes to the park's interior. There are beach and woodlands trails, as well as hiking and interpretive self-guiding nature trails that provide access to the park's many habitats. Bicycle, paddleboat, canoe and kayak rentals are available.

Canoeing is a good way to see the waterways and get a close-up view of the park's birdlife and resident seals. Visitors can find grey seals lounging on off-shore sandbars from May through October; bird-watching is best in spring and fall, when shorebirds and waterfowl stop over during their migration.

Primitive campsites are accessible by hiking, canoeing or bicycling. Those intending to use the off-road campgrounds must register at the information center when arriving and leaving.

Anglers need a national park fishing permit ($9.80 daily, $34.30 annually). Kellys Beach provides supervised swimming, a canteen and showers. A 60-kilometre (37-mi.) bicycle trail is said to be one of the best in Atlantic Canada. Cross-country skiing, snowshoeing and tobogganing also are popular.

Trail shelters contain wood stoves and picnic tables; favorite picnic areas within the park are Callanders, La Source and Kellys Beach. *See Recreation Chart.*

ADMISSION to the park is $7.80; $6.80 (ages 65+); $3.90 (ages 6-16); $19.60 (family), mid-June through Labour Day. Admission Apr. 1 to mid-June and day after Labour Day-Nov. 30 is $3.90; $3.15 (ages 65+); $1.90 (ages 6-16); $9.80 (family). Campsites can be reserved in advance.

PETS are permitted only in certain areas. They must be on a leash at all times and may not be left unattended.

ADDRESS correspondence to the Park Superintendent, 186 Hwy. 117, Kouchibouguac National Park of Canada, NB, Canada E4X 2P1; phone (506) 876-2443, or TTY (506) 876-4205.

LAMÈQUE (A-5)

Lamèque Island, off the northeastern coast of the Acadian Peninsula, is reached by drawbridge from Route 313. Each summer, the island hosts the Lamèque International Baroque Music Festival, with performances by top vocalists and instrumentalists. Concerts take place in the 1913 Sainte-Cécile Church of Petite-Rivière-de-l'Île, which is noted for its colorful interior and flawless acoustics; for information phone (506) 344-5846 or (877) 377-8003.

ECOLOGICAL PARK OF THE ACADIAN PENINSULA is 1 km (.6 mi.) e. on Rte. 313 to 65 rue du Ruisseau. Interactive computer kiosks in the nature center educate guests about the Acadian Peninsula's ecological habitats. A boardwalk meanders through an estuary and leads to a 2-kilometre (1.2 mi.) interpretive nature trail. The trail crosses an arboretum with some 30 native species of conifers and deciduous trees. An observation tower provides views of the area.

Time: Allow 2 hours minimum. **Hours:** Daily 10-6, May 22-Sept. 24. **Cost:** $7; $6 (ages 65+); $4 (ages 6-17 and students with ID). **Phone:** (506) 344-3223, or (506) 344-3222 in the off-season.

LOWER NEWCASTLE (C-5)

MacDONALD FARM HISTORIC SITE is 13 km (8 mi.) n.e. on Hwy. 11, on the n. side of the Miramichi River at Bartibog Bridge. The 1815 farmhouse overlooking Miramichi Bay was built by Alexander MacDonald, a Scottish immigrant. Though typical of Georgian stone houses in rural Scotland, it is unusual for New Brunswick. Various outbuildings reflect the ways in which the MacDonald family earned a living. Costumed guides interpret the restored house and working farm and self-guiding nature trails traverse the site.

Hours: Tues.-Sun. 9:30-4:30, June 15-Sept. 1. Phone ahead to confirm schedule. **Cost:** $2.50; $1.50 (ages 6-18 and 55+); $7 (family, two adults and three children). Cash only. **Phone:** (506) 778-6085.

MACTAQUAC (D-3)

Completed in 1968, the Mactaquac Dam Project displaced several thousand residents along the Saint John River. Historically significant buildings were relocated from the flood plain to Kings Landing Historical Settlement *(see place listing p. 53)*. Farms, towns, roads and a railroad line lie submerged beneath the Mactaquac headpond, which extends some 97 kilometres (60 mi.) upriver from the dam.

MACTAQUAC HYDROELECTRIC DAM—see Keswick Ridge p. 53.

ON THE POND COUNTRY RETREAT & SPA
Phone: 506/363-3420

Country Inn
Rates not provided
Address: 20 Rt 615 E6L 1M2 **Location:** From Mactaquac Bridge, 3.6 mi (6 km) w via Rt 105 and 106. Located in a quiet secluded area. **Facility:** Nestled on secluded, riverview grounds, this lodge offers on-site spa service by advance reservation; rooms are well-appointed and comfortably sized. 8 units. 2 stories (no elevator), interior corridors. **Terms:** age restrictions may apply. **Activities:** sauna, beach access, rental canoes, exercise room. *Fee:* massage. 🍴 📶 ✕ 🅿️

MEMRAMCOOK (D-5) pop. 4,638

As Acadians returned to Memramcook in the years following deportation, this region came to be known as *Berceau de l'Acadie,* or "the Cradle of Acadia." The first Acadian college was built here in 1864; Memramcook hosted the first Acadian National Convention in 1881. Most locals (known as "Cookers") speak Chiac, a dialect mixture of Acadian French and English. Early Acadian settlers built dikes to drain the salt marshes; many of these *aboiteaux* are still visible.

MONUMENT LEFEBVRE NATIONAL HISTORIC SITE OF CANADA is off Hwy. 106, next to Memramcook Institute. A 19th-century building commemorates the Acadian renaissance and the site of the first French-language, degree-granting institution in Atlantic Canada, founded in 1864 by Father Camille Lefebvre. A permanent exhibit explores the odyssey of the Acadian people. A restored period theater, noted for its architecture and acoustics, is on the second floor.

Tours: Guided tours are available. **Time:** Allow 1 hour minimum. **Hours:** Daily 9-5, June 1-Oct. 15; Mon.-Sat. 9-5, rest of year. **Cost:** $3.90; $3.40 (ages 65+); $1.90 (ages 6-16); $9.80 (family, two adults and five children). Reservations are required for guided tours during the off-season. **Phone:** (506) 758-9808.

MINTO (D-4) pop. 2,681

The arrival of the railroad in 1904 spurred the growth of Minto, a town originally settled by Loyalists and Irish immigrants. By the early 1910s, Minto was inhabited by Europeans from such countries as Belgium, Italy, Germany and Russia; the immigrants found work in the town's many coal mines. Coal mining is still Minto's main industry.

The Minto Museum and Information Centre, 187 Main St., contains railway and coal-mining artifacts in a renovated train station. A caboose is on the museum grounds; phone (506) 327-3383.

Recreational pursuits revolve around nearby Grand Lake's beaches and harbors and include boating, swimming, camping and fishing. In town, a golf course, parks and a nature trail are available.

THE NEW BRUNSWICK INTERNMENT CAMP MUSEUM is at 420 Pleasant Dr. at jct. Union St. in the Municipal Building. The museum pays tribute to prisoners of war interned at the Fredericton Internment Camp during World War II. Prisoners included German and Italian merchant marines, Jewish refugees and Canadian Nazi sympathizers. More than 600 artifacts are on display in the 186-square-metre (2,000-square-ft.) museum as well as a portion of a reconstructed prisoner's hut and a model of the camp.

Tours: Guided tours are available. **Time:** Allow 30 minutes minimum. **Hours:** Mon.-Fri. 10-5, Sat.-Sun. noon-5, July-Aug.; by appointment rest of year. **Cost:** $1.50; free (ages 0-12); $4 (family). **Phone:** (506) 327-3573.

MIRAMICHI (C-4) pop. 18,129
• Restaurants p. 56

Miramichi was named for its original inhabitants, a Mi'kmaq Indian tribe that prized the river valley for its salmon fishing. Acadian settlers arrived from Nova Scotia in 1757. As immigrants from Ireland, Scotland and New England followed, Miramichi gained a reputation for its commercial fisheries and shipyards, which produced some of the best square-rigged ships in Canada.

Forestry replaced shipbuilding as the area's dominant industry in the late 19th century, and the last commercial cannery closed in 1972, but salmon fishing continues to draw thousands of anglers each year. The modern city of Miramichi was formed in 1995 by the merging of Newcastle, Chatham and eight other villages and districts. The area is home to ♥ Canada's Irish Festival on the Miramichi in mid-July.

BEAUBEARS ISLAND NATIONAL HISTORIC SITE
is reached via boat from the interpretive center at 35 St. Patrick's Dr. The island, uninhabited for more than 100 years, was home to impoverished Acadians expelled from Canada. Remains of slips and foundations are visible. Costumed guides take visitors on history and nature walks, offering details about various shipbuilders, including such important figures as William Davidson, Honourable J. Leonard O'Brien and Peter Mitchell, one of the Fathers of Confederation and the owner of Beaubears Island 1871-93.

The interpretive center features displays about the village of Nelson, shipbuilding on Beaubears Island, the Acadians and the Mi'kmaq who lived along the Miramichi River. **Time:** Allow 1 hour, 30 minutes minimum. **Hours:** Interpretive center Mon.-Sat. 10-8, Sun. noon-8, late June-late Aug.; Mon.-Sat. 10-4, Sun. noon-4, mid-May to late June and late Aug.-early Oct. Boats to the island depart Tues.-Sat. at 2, late June-late Aug. (weather permitting); otherwise by appointment. Phone ahead to confirm schedule. **Cost:** Interpretive center $5; $3.50 (ages 65+ and students with ID); free (ages 0-4). Phone for island tour prices. **Phone:** (506) 622-8526.

HISTORIC BEAVERBROOK HOUSE
is at 518 King George Hwy. Visitors may take a guided tour of the childhood home of William Maxwell Aitken, Lord Beaverbrook. The Victorian-style home was built in 1877. **Time:** Allow 30 minutes minimum. **Hours:** Mon.-Fri. 9-5, mid-June to mid-Aug. **Cost:** $3. **Phone:** (506) 622-5572.

ST. MICHAEL'S MUSEUM AND GENEALOGY CENTRE
is at 10 Howard St. This museum contains historical and religious records and artifacts. The Old St. Michael's rectory, a wooden structure, contains an extensive genealogical collection. **Time:** Allow 30 minutes minimum. **Hours:** Mon.-Fri. 9-5, Sat. 10-4, June-Aug.; Tues.-Sat. 10-4, rest of year. **Cost:** Free. Genealogical searches $30. **Phone:** (506) 778-5152.

W.S. LOGGIE CULTURAL CENTRE
is at 222 Wellington St. Furnished with antiques, the restored 1879 Victorian Second Empire house is characterized by a mansard roof and bay windows. The former residence of William Stewart Loggie now serves as a museum, a meeting center for local organizations and an arts and crafts facility. **Time:** Allow 30 minutes minimum. **Hours:** Daily 10-6, July-Aug. Hours may vary. Phone ahead to confirm schedule. **Cost:** Donations. **Phone:** (506) 773-7645.

HOWARD JOHNSON INN & SUITES MIRAMICHI

Phone: 506/622-0302

◆◆ ◆◆
Hotel
Rates not provided

Address: 1 Jane St E1V 2S6 **Location:** Waterfront. Just s off King George Hwy. **Facility:** 65 units. 2 stories (no elevator), interior corridors. **Dining:** The Wharf Restaurant & Patio, see separate listing. **Pool(s):** indoor. **Activities:** exercise room.

 📶 🛜 ❌ 🛗 💻 / SOME UNITS FEE 🐾 🖼

LAKEVIEW INNS & SUITES

Phone: 506/627-1999

◆◆ ◆◆
Hotel
Rates not provided

Address: 333 King George Hwy E1V 1L2 **Location:** 1.1 mi (1.8 km) w on Rt 8. Located in a commercial area. **Facility:** 60 units. 3 stories, interior corridors. **Amenities:** Some: high-speed Internet. **Guest Services:** coin laundry. **Free Special Amenities:** continental breakfast and high-speed Internet.

SAVE ECO 📶 BIZ 🛜 🛗 💻 / SOME UNITS FEE 🐾 🖼

RODD MIRAMICHI RIVER-A RODD SIGNATURE HOTEL

Phone: (506)773-3111

◆◆ ◆◆
Hotel
$124-$175

Address: 1809 Water St E1N 1B2 **Location:** Waterfront. Hwy 11 exit 120, 0.4 mi (0.6 km) e. **Facility:** 80 units. 3 stories, interior corridors. **Terms:** cancellation fee imposed. **Amenities:** high-speed Internet. **Dining:** The Angler's Reel, see separate listing. **Pool(s):** heated indoor. **Activities:** whirlpool, boat dock, bicycle trails, hiking trails, exercise room. **Guest Services:** valet laundry.

ECO 📶 🍽 CALL 🛗 🛜 ❌ 🛗 💻 / SOME UNITS FEE

CAMPING MIRAMICHI COTTAGES **Phone:** 506/773-6252

Cottage

Did not meet all AAA rating requirements for locking devices in some guest rooms at time of last evaluation on 06/21/2011. **Address:** 116 N Black River Rd E1N 5S4 **Location:** 6 mi (10 km) s on Hwy 11, 0.6 mi (1 km) e. Facilities, services, and decor characterize an economy property.

WHERE TO EAT

THE ANGLER'S REEL **Phone:** 506/773-3111

Canadian
$9-$27

AAA Inspector Notes: Couples settled at tables for two can see the sights of the Miramichi River while sampling fresh seafood, steak and palate-pleasing homemade desserts. The specialty salmon is prepared more than 20 ways. Fresh treats are made in the on-site bakery. The atmosphere is warm and friendly. **Bar:** full bar. **Address:** 1809 Water St E1N 1B2 **Location:** Hwy 11 exit 120, 0.4 mi (0.6 km) e; in Rodd Miramichi River-A Rodd Signature Hotel. B L D CALL &M

KINGSWAY RESTAURANT **Phone:** 506/622-1138

Canadian
$6-$16

AAA Inspector Notes: Serving patrons since 1960, the popular family restaurant presents a menu that lists everything from burgers and hot and cold sandwiches to steaks and seafood. Portions are ample, and parking is plentiful. **Bar:** full bar. **Address:** 367 King George Hwy E1V 1L5 **Location:** Opposite Miramichi Mall. B L D

PORTAGE RESTAURANT **Phone:** 506/773-6447

Canadian
$7-$19

AAA Inspector Notes: A local favorite, this large restaurant has a country feel and hospitable staffers. The menu lists everything from steaks to seafood to various comfort foods and homemade desserts. **Bar:** full bar. **Address:** 191 King St E1N 2P1 **Location:** From Centennial Bridge, 1.8 mi (3 km) s on Rt 11. B L D

TRAN'S PALACE RESTAURANT **Phone:** 506/622-0653

Chinese
$6-$16

AAA Inspector Notes: Basic decor, good food and ample portions are what diners find at the popular restaurant. On the menu is a selection of Chinese, Vietnamese and some Canadian dishes. **Bar:** full bar. **Address:** 224 Pleasant St E1V 1Y5 **Location:** Centre. L D

WELCOME BACK RESTAURANT **Phone:** 506/773-3328

Chinese
$7-$16

AAA Inspector Notes: Serving locals for many years, this pleasant restaurant offers a view of the Miramichi River. A very good selection of Chinese, Szechuan, combination plates and some Canadian dishes are available. **Bar:** full bar. **Address:** 2328 King George Hwy E1V 2Y7 **Location:** Corner of Leroy Ln. L D

THE WHARF RESTAURANT & PATIO

Phone: 506/622-0302

American
$8-$21

AAA Inspector Notes: This popular family restaurant is located on the banks of the Miramichi River and offers patrons a splendid view of the bridge and river activities from the glass atrium or the large deck. A varied menu offers basic comfort foods to fresh seafood, steaks and chicken. The must-try desserts are homemade. **Bar:** full bar. **Address:** 1 Jane St E1V 2S5 **Location:** Just s off King George Hwy; in Howard Johnson Inn & Suites Miramichi. B L D

MISCOU ISLAND (A-6)

Off the northern tip of Lamèque *(see place listing p. 53)*, Miscou Island is a place to relax and watch sea gulls, migratory birds and ships go by. Beaming its warning light since 1856, the picturesque Miscou Island Lighthouse on Route 113 is said to be the oldest in New Brunswick. The lighthouse is open for self-guiding tours May 1 through Thanksgiving weekend. Also along Route 113 is an interpretive boardwalk that loops through a peat bog, allowing visitors a close look at native plants.

MONCTON (D-5) pop. 64,128
• Hotels p. 58 • Restaurants p. 61
• Attractions map p. 57

Moncton began as a settlement of Acadian farmers near the French Fort Beauséjour *(see Fort Beauséjour—Fort Cumberland National Historic Site of Canada p. 43)*. The British, under Lt. Col. Robert Monckton, captured the fort in 1755 and expelled the French. American Loyalists, Scots and Irish incorporated the town in 1855, naming it after Monckton. A clerical error accounts for its present spelling. Shipbuilding and railroads made Moncton the transportation hub of the Maritime Provinces.

Two natural phenomena, Magnetic Hill *(see attraction listing)* and the Tidal Bore, are highlights among city attractions. The Tidal Bore runs up the Petitcodiac River twice daily, causing a small tidal wave ranging in height from 20 to 45 centimetres (8 to 18 in.). The incoming tide moves upstream against the regular flow of water, causing a single river-wide wave. After the bore, the almost empty Petitcodiac River basin rapidly fills with water and, within an hour, the bore passes 28.3 million gallons of water and the water level rises more than 7.5 metres (25 ft.). A good place to observe the bore is at Bore Park, downtown.

Tourism Moncton: 655 Main St. (mid-Oct. to late May), 10 Bendview Ct. (rest of year), Moncton, NB, Canada E1C 1E8. **Phone:** (800) 363-4558.

Self-guiding tours: A walking tour of the historic area begins at City Hall, 655 Main St. Brochures outlining the tour are available on the first floor of the Tourist Information Centre, 10 Bendview Ct.; phone (506) 853-3540.

Shopping areas: Highfield Square, at Highfield and Main streets, has more than 60 shops.

CENTENNIAL PARK is at 811 St. George Blvd. The 93-hectare (230-acre) park features cross-country skiing, skating, hiking and mountain biking trails; an outdoor splash park; a lake beach; football and lawn bowling fields; tennis courts; and a zipline course. A Sherman tank and a CF-100 jet fighter pay tribute to Canada's armed forces; a steam locomotive recalls the railroad's impact on Moncton. *See Recreation Chart.*

Swimming is permitted at Centennial Beach. **Hours:** Daily 8 a.m.-11 p.m. **Cost:** Free. Beach $5;

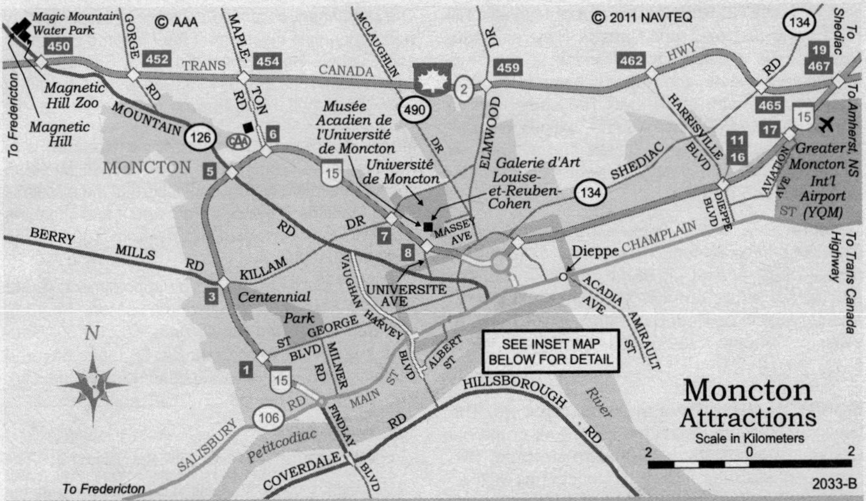

Moncton
Attractions
Scale in Kilometers
2   0   2

2033-B

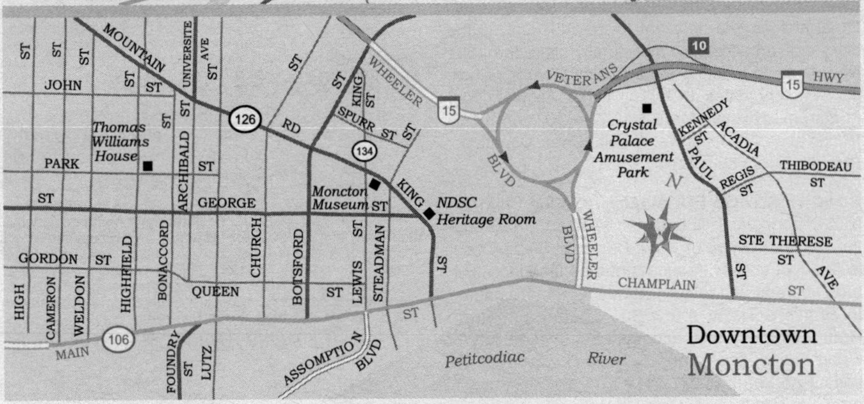

Downtown
Moncton

$4 (ages 13-19 and 60+); $3 (ages 4-12). **Phone:** (506) 853-3516.

LUTZ MOUNTAIN HERITAGE MUSEUM is 1 km (.6 mi.) n. of Magnetic Hill at 3143 Mountain Rd. Built in 1883, the Second Moncton Baptist Church received worshippers until 1974. The building contains pioneer artifacts, a quilt and textile collection, cemetery records dating to 1766 and genealogical materials about families who settled the area. Guided tours are available. **Hours:** Mon.-Sat. 9:30-5:30, mid-June to mid-Sept.; by appointment rest of year. **Cost:** $2; free (ages 0-11); $5 (family). **Phone:** (506) 384-7719, or (506) 384-0903 in the off-season.

MAGIC MOUNTAIN WATER PARK is in Magnetic Hill Park, just off Trans-Canada Hwy. exit 450. The park contains eight waterslides, a wave pool, a children's area with four smaller slides, a lazy river, a splash pad, a whirlpool, two miniature golf courses and an arcade. Entrance is via a three-level steamboat.

Hours: Daily 10-7, early July-late Aug.; 10-6, mid-June to early July and late Aug. to mid-Sept. Phone ahead to confirm schedule. **Cost:** $25.50; $19.50 (children 42-48 inches tall); $14.50 (children under 42 inches tall); $8.50 (ages 60+); free (ages 0-3); $85 (family, four people). Admission after 3 when closing at 7 or after 2:30 when closing at 6 is $17.25; $13.25 (children 42-48 inches tall); $9.75 (children under 42 inches tall); free (ages 0-3). Rates may vary; phone ahead. **Phone:** (506) 857-9283, or (800) 331-9283 in Canada.

MAGNETIC HILL is on a side road next to Magic Mountain Water Park. For an unusual experience, visitors drive "downhill" to a spot indicated by a white post and then, with gears in neutral and brakes released, the car moves backward, coasting "up" the hill. This phenomenon is attributed to an optical illusion from the surrounding hillside sloping away from the road. Attendants are on duty during the main season only.

Parking is available for all vehicle types. **Hours:** Daily dawn-dusk, Victoria Day-Oct. 15. **Cost:** $5 per private vehicle. Free for buses and motorcycles. **Phone:** (506) 858-8841.

MAGNETIC HILL ZOO is part of Magnetic Hill Park, just off Trans-Canada Hwy. exit 450. Visitors drive under a covered bridge to enter this 16-hectare (40-acre) zoo, which is home to 400 animals representing more than 100 species from around the world—lions, jaguars, wolves, zebras, camels, lemurs, monkeys, hawks and pythons. At Old McDonald's Barnyard, children can feed white-tailed deer and goats.

Hours: Daily 9-dusk, Victoria Day-Thanksgiving. **Cost:** Mid-June through Labour Day $12; $10.50 (ages 12-17 and 60+); $8.50 (ages 4-11); $34 (family, two adults and two children); $6.50 (each additional child). Reduced rates offered rest of season. **Phone:** (506) 384-0303 or (506) 877-7720.

MONCTON MUSEUM is at 20 Mountain Rd. The two-story museum blends the stonework of the old City Hall with a stark, bold modern structure. Displays pertain to the history of Moncton as well as traveling exhibits. The Free Meeting House, a national historic site adjacent to the museum, is the city's oldest building. Architecturally plain, the 1821 New England meetinghouse has no steeple or bell; its cemetery dates to 1816. **Time:** Allow 1 hour minimum. **Hours:** Mon.-Sat. 9-4:30, Sun. 1-5. Phone ahead to confirm schedule. **Cost:** Donations. **Phone:** (506) 856-4383.

NDSC HERITAGE ROOM is at 125 King St. in the NDSC Convent. This museum relates the contributions of the Sisters of Notre-Dame-du-Sacré-Coeur to Acadian society in such areas as language, culture, fine arts and religion. Guided tours are offered in English. **Time:** Allow 30 minutes minimum. **Hours:** Mon.-Fri. 9:30-noon and 2-4. Closed Jan. 1, Good Friday, Easter and Christmas. **Cost:** Donations. **Phone:** (506) 857-9414.

THOMAS WILLIAMS HOUSE is at 103 Park St. Built in 1883 by Thomas Williams, an Intercolonial Railroad treasurer, the Victorian-style 12-room house features antiques, memorabilia, three fireplaces and a tearoom. Gardens cover the grounds. **Time:** Allow 1 hour minimum. **Hours:** Tues.-Sun. 10:30-4:30, July-Aug.; by appointment rest of year. Phone ahead to confirm hours. **Cost:** Donations. **Phone:** (506) 857-0590, or (506) 856-4383 in the off-season.

UNIVERSITÉ DE MONCTON is at 165 Massey Ave. Approximately 6,200 students are enrolled at the university, which was founded in 1963 and has campuses in Moncton, Edmundston and Shippagan. With French as its primary study language, the university provides the province's Acadian community with its own academic institution. Guided tours are available by appointment. **Phone:** (506) 858-4000 or (800) 363-8336.

Galerie d'Art Louise-et-Reuben-Cohen is in the Clément-Cormier Bldg. Changing monthly exhibits honor Acadian, Canadian and international artists. The permanent collection consists of contemporary works by artists mainly from the Maritime Provinces and Québec. **Hours:** Mon.-Fri. 10-5, Sat.-Sun. 1-5, June-Sept.; Tues.-Fri. 1-4:30, Sat.-Sun. 1-4, rest of year. **Cost:** Donations. **Phone:** (506) 858-4088.

Musée Acadien de l'Université de Moncton is in the Clément-Cormier Bldg. The Acadian Museum specializes in the history and culture of the Acadians of the Maritime Provinces. Permanent and changing displays depict Acadian history from 1604 to the early 20th century.

Guided tours are offered by appointment. **Time:** Allow 30 minutes minimum. **Hours:** Mon.-Fri. 10-5, Sat.-Sun. 1-5, June-Sept.; Tues.-Fri. 1-4:30, Sat.-Sun. 1-4, rest of year. **Cost:** $4; $2 (ages 60+ and students with ID); free (ages 0-11); $7 (family). **Phone:** (506) 858-4088.

AMSTERDAM INN **Phone:** (506)383-5050
▼▼▼
Hotel
$130-$169 6/1-9/30
$110-$169 10/1-5/31

Address: 2550 Mountain Rd E1G 1B4 **Location:** Trans-Canada Hwy 2 exit 450. **Facility:** 48 units. 2 stories (no elevator), interior corridors. **Terms:** cancellation fee imposed. **Amenities:** high-speed Internet. *Some:* video games. **Guest Services:** valet laundry.

AUBERGE WILD ROSE INN **Phone:** (506)383-9751
▼▼▼
Country Inn
$110-$250

Address: 17 Baseline Rd E1H 1N5 **Location:** Trans-Canada Hwy 2 exit 465, 0.6 mi (1 km) n on Rt 134 (Shediac Rd). Located in a quiet rural area. **Facility:** Bordering a golf course and close to the airport, the inn offers well-appointed rooms, many with a gas fireplace and a double whirlpool tub. 16 units. 2 stories (no elevator), interior corridors. **Activities:** hiking trails, game room, limited exercise equipment. **Guest Services:** complimentary laundry. **Free Special Amenities:** full breakfast and high-speed Internet.

BEST WESTERN PLUS MONCTON
Phone: (506)388-0888
▼▼▼
Hotel
$139-$149

Best Western PLUS

AAA Benefit: Members save up to 20%, plus 10% bonus points with Best Western Rewards®.

Address: 300 Lewisville Rd E1A 5Y4 **Location:** Trans-Canada Hwy 2 exit 459A eastbound, s on Rt 115 to Lewisville Rd, then left; exit 467A westbound, 5 mi (8 km) w on Hwy 15 exit 10. **Facility:** 80 units. 3 stories, interior corridors. **Amenities:** high-speed Internet. **Pool(s):** heated indoor. **Activities:** exercise room. **Guest Services:** valet and coin laundry. **Free Special Amenities:** continental breakfast and high-speed Internet.

CHATEAU MONCTON HOTEL & SUITES AN ASCEND COLLECTION HOTEL **Phone:** (506)870-4444
▼▼▼
Hotel
$132-$229

Address: 100 Main St E1C 1B9 **Location:** Waterfront. Opposite Champlain Place Shopping Centre. Located in a commercial area. **Facility:** 106 units. 5 stories, interior corridors. **Terms:** cancellation fee imposed. **Amenities:** high-speed Internet. **Activities:** exercise room. **Guest Services:** valet laundry. **Free Special Amenities:** expanded continental breakfast and high-speed Internet.

COASTAL INN

Hotel

$119-$154 6/1-9/15
$99-$129 9/16-5/31

Phone: (506)857-9686

Address: 502 Kennedy St E1A 5Y7 **Location:** At Paul St. Opposite Champlain Place Shopping Centre. **Facility:** 104 units, some efficiencies. 2 stories (no elevator), interior/exterior corridors. **Amenities:** *Some:* high-speed Internet. **Dining:** Garden Breeze Restaurant, see separate listing. **Pool(s):** heated indoor. **Activities:** sauna, exercise room. **Guest Services:** coin laundry. **Free Special Amenities:** expanded continental breakfast and high-speed Internet.

COLONIAL INNS

Hotel

Rates not provided

Phone: 506/382-3395

Address: 42 Highfield St E1C 8T6 **Location:** 1 blk n of Main St; centre. Located in a commercial area. **Facility:** 58 units. 2 stories (no elevator), interior/exterior corridors. **Dining:** entertainment. **Pool(s):** heated indoor. **Activities:** sauna, whirlpool. **Guest Services:** valet and coin laundry.

COMFORT INN

Hotel

$99-$275

Phone: (506)384-3175

Address: 2495 Mountain Rd E1G 2W4 **Location:** Trans-Canada Hwy 2 exit 450. **Facility:** 59 units. 2 stories (no elevator), interior corridors. **Terms:** cancellation fee imposed. **Amenities:** high-speed Internet.

COMFORT INN

Hotel

$99-$160

Phone: (506)859-6868

Address: 20 Maplewood Dr E1A 6P9 **Location:** Trans-Canada Hwy 2 exit 459A on Hwy 115 S, left on Rt 134 E (Lewisville Rd). Located in a residential area. **Facility:** 79 units. 2 stories (no elevator), interior corridors. **Parking:** winter plug-ins. **Terms:** cancellation fee imposed. **Amenities:** high-speed Internet.

CROWNE PLAZA MONCTON DOWNTOWN

Phone: (506)854-6340

Hotel

$99-$139

Address: 1005 Main St E1C 1G9 **Location:** At Highfield and Main sts; downtown. **Facility:** 191 units. 9 stories, interior corridors. **Amenities:** video games (fee). **Pool(s):** heated indoor. **Activities:** whirlpool, steamroom, exercise room. **Guest Services:** valet and coin laundry. **Free Special Amenities:** newspaper and high-speed Internet.

CROWNE PLAZA
MONCTON·DOWNTOWN
CENTREVILLE

Bonus Priority Club Rewards points for CAA/AAA members.

▼ See AAA listing p. 60 ▼

Your Family-Friendly Destination!
Votre destination familiale par excellence !

750, rue Main Street
Moncton NB E1C 1E6
506 854-4344
1 800 268-1133

www.deltabeausejour.com

DELTA
BEAUSÉJOUR

Learn about AAA/CAA Diamond Ratings at AAA.com/Diamonds

DELTA BEAUSEJOUR **Phone:** (506)854-4344

Hotel
$209-$329

Address: 750 Main St E1C 1E6 **Location:** Jct Main St and Sommet Ln; downtown. **Facility:** 309 units. 10 stories, interior corridors. **Parking:** on-site (fee). **Terms:** check-in 4 pm. **Amenities:** video games (fee), high-speed Internet. **Dining:** Windjammer Dining Room, see separate listing. **Pool(s):** heated indoor. **Activities:** whirlpool, waterslide, exercise room, spa. **Guest Services:** valet laundry. ***(See ad p. 59.)***

ECO BIZ / SOME UNITS FEE

FUTURE INNS MONCTON HOTEL & CONFERENCE CENTRE **Phone:** (506)852-9600

Hotel
$129-$189 6/1-10/31
$119-$179 11/1-5/31

Address: 40 Lady Ada Blvd E1G 0E3 **Location:** Trans-Canada Hwy 2 exit 454. **Facility:** 129 units. 5 stories, interior corridors. **Amenities:** high-speed Internet. **Dining:** Maverick's Steakhouse & Grill, see separate listing. **Activities:** exercise room. **Guest Services:** valet and coin laundry.

CALL BIZ / SOME UNITS

HAMPTON INN & SUITES MONCTON **Phone:** (506)855-4819

Hotel
$129-$199

AAA Benefit:
Members save up to 10% everyday!

Address: 700 Mapleton Rd E1G 0L7 **Location:** Trans-Canada Hwy 2 exit 454. **Facility:** 127 units. 6 stories, interior corridors. **Terms:** check-in 4 pm, 1-7 night minimum stay, cancellation fee imposed. **Amenities:** high-speed Internet. **Pool(s):** heated indoor. **Activities:** waterslide, exercise room. **Guest Services:** valet laundry. **Free Special Amenities: expanded continental breakfast and high-speed Internet.**

SAVE CALL BIZ / SOME UNITS

Hampton Inn & Suites

"Beautiful Hotel located near all major attractions, shopping and restaurants."

HOLIDAY INN EXPRESS HOTEL & SUITES AIRPORT-DIEPPE **Phone:** (506)388-5050

Hotel
$138-$189 9/2-5/31
$133-$189 6/1-9/1

Address: 425 Adelard Savoie Blvd E1A 7E6 **Location:** Rt 15 exit 11 westbound; exit 16 eastbound. Located in a commercial area. **Facility:** 94 units. 3 stories, interior corridors. **Terms:** check-in 4 pm. **Amenities:** high-speed Internet. **Pool(s):** heated indoor. **Activities:** whirlpool, exercise room. **Guest Services:** valet and coin laundry. **Free Special Amenities: full breakfast and airport transportation.**

SAVE CALL BIZ

HOLIDAY INN EXPRESS HOTEL & SUITES MONCTON **Phone:** (506)384-1050

Hotel
$109-$159

Address: 2515 Mountain Rd E1G 2W4 **Location:** Trans-Canada Hwy 2 exit 450. **Facility:** 151 units. 3 stories, interior/exterior corridors. **Terms:** check-in 4 pm, cancellation fee imposed. **Amenities:** high-speed Internet. **Pool(s):** heated indoor. **Activities:** sauna, whirlpool, exercise room. **Guest Services:** valet and coin laundry. **Free Special Amenities: full breakfast and use of on-premises laundry facilities.**

SAVE ECO CALL / SOME UNITS FEE

HOTEL CASINO NEW BRUNSWICK **Phone:** (506)861-4661

Hotel
$189-$999 6/1-8/31
$149-$999 9/1-5/31

Address: 21 Casino Dr E1G 0R7 **Location:** Trans-Canada Hwy 2 exit 450. **Facility:** Guest will enjoy the modern décor in these large well-appointed guest rooms and spacious suites with balconies. Conveniently attached to the casino and convention center. 126 units. 5 stories, interior corridors. **Terms:** cancellation fee imposed. **Amenities:** high-speed Internet, safes. **Dining:** Moose's Wild Pub, see separate listing. **Pool(s):** heated indoor. **Activities:** whirlpool, exercise room, spa. **Guest Services:** valet laundry. **Free Special Amenities: newspaper and high-speed Internet.** *(See ad p. 61.)*

SAVE CALL BIZ / SOME UNITS FEE

HOTEL ST. JAMES **Phone:** 506/388-4283

Boutique Hotel
$159-$289

Address: 14 Church St E1C 4Y9 **Location:** Corner of Main and Church sts. **Facility:** This quaint boutique hotel in the heart of town features various room types with a modern style and some with a soaker tub. 10 units. 3 stories (no elevator), interior corridors. **Parking:** on-site (fee). **Terms:** cancellation fee imposed. **Amenities:** high-speed Internet, honor bars. **Dining:** St. James Gate, see separate listing.

/ SOME UNITS FEE

HOWARD JOHNSON INN MONCTON **Phone:** (506)384-1734

Motel
$85-$145

Address: 1062 Mountain Rd E1C 2T1 **Location:** Trans-Canada Hwy 2 exit 454 (Mapleton Rd), 1.7 mi (2.8 km) to Rt 126 (Mountain Rd), then just s. Located in a commercial area. **Facility:** 49 units, some efficiencies and kitchens. 2 stories (no elevator), interior/exterior corridors. **Terms:** office hours 7 am-midnight. **Pool(s):** heated indoor.

/ SOME UNITS FEE

MOTEL 6 MONCTON **Phone:** (506)386-6749

Hotel
$75-$120

Address: 2530 Mountain Rd E1G 1B4 **Location:** Trans-Canada Hwy 2 exit 450. **Facility:** 74 units. 3 stories, interior corridors. **Pool(s):** heated indoor. **Activities:** whirlpool, exercise room. **Guest Services:** complimentary laundry. **Free Special Amenities: high-speed Internet and use of on-premises laundry facilities.**

SAVE CALL / SOME UNITS

▼ See AAA listing p. 60 ▼

RAMADA PLAZA CRYSTAL PALACE & CONVENTION CENTRE

Phone: (506)858-8584

Hotel
$123-$261

Address: 499 Paul St E1A 6S5 **Location:** Trans-Canada Hwy 2 exit 459A eastbound, s on Rt 115 to Lewisville Rd, then left; exit 467A westbound, 4.8 mi (8 km) w on Rt 15 to rotary. Located in Crystal Palace Amusement Park. **Facility:** 115 units. 3 stories, interior corridors. **Dining:** McGinnis Landing Restaurant, see separate listing. **Pool(s):** heated indoor. **Activities:** sauna, whirlpool, exercise room. **Guest Services:** valet laundry. **Free Special Amenities: high-speed Internet and airport transportation.**

RESIDENCE INN BY MARRIOTT MONCTON

Phone: (506)854-7100

Extended Stay Hotel
$170-$229

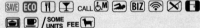
AAA Benefit: AAA hotel discounts of 5% or more.

Address: 600 Main St E1C 0M6 **Location:** At Assomption Blvd. **Facility:** 133 units, some two bedrooms and kitchens. 6 stories, interior corridors. **Parking:** on-site (fee). **Amenities:** high-speed Internet. **Pool(s):** heated indoor. **Activities:** whirlpool, exercise room. **Guest Services:** valet and coin laundry. **Free Special Amenities: full breakfast and high-speed Internet.**

RODD MONCTON

Phone: (506)382-1664

Hotel
$99-$159

Address: 434 Main St E1C 1B9 **Location:** On Rt 106 (Main St) at King St. **Facility:** 97 units. 2-4 stories, interior/exterior corridors. **Parking:** winter plug-ins. **Terms:** cancellation fee imposed. **Amenities:** *Some:* honor bars. **Pool(s):** heated outdoor. **Guest Services:** valet laundry.

SUPER 8 MONCTON/DIEPPE

Phone: (506)858-8880

Hotel
$81-$160

Address: 370 Dieppe Blvd E1A 8H4 **Location:** Hwy 15 exit 16, 0.6 mi (1 km) s. **Facility:** 86 units. 3 stories, interior corridors. **Amenities:** high-speed Internet. **Pool(s):** heated indoor. **Activities:** whirlpool, waterslide, exercise room. **Guest Services:** coin laundry. **Free Special Amenities: continental breakfast and high-speed Internet.**

TRAVELODGE SUITES MONCTON

Phone: 506/852-7000

Hotel
Rates not provided

Address: 2475 Mountain Rd E1G 2J5 **Location:** Trans-Canada Hwy 2 exit 450. Located in a rural area. **Facility:** 75 units. 3 stories, interior corridors. **Activities:** exercise room. **Guest Services:** coin laundry. **Free Special Amenities: full breakfast and high-speed Internet.**

WHERE TO EAT

THE BARNYARD BBQ

Phone: 506/389-9042

Barbecue
$8-$22

AAA Inspector Notes: Grab your cowboy hat and boots and head on over to the Barnyard for a feed of ribs, steaks and chicken wings. An on-site microbrewery offers several tasty thirst quenchers to complement your meal. **Bar:** full bar. **Address:** 131 Mill Rd E1A 6R1 **Location:** 0.4 mi (0.7 km) e of Elmwood Dr. [L] [D]

CAFE ARCHIBALD

European
$7-$17

Phone: 506/853-8819

AAA Inspector Notes: This casual, upbeat bistro, in a commercial location, specializes in fine crepes, pizza, bruschetta and great salads prepared in an open kitchen. The spot is particularly popular with students and artists, who enjoy seasonal dining on the small patio. All meals are prepared as ordered so the wait may be a little longer. **Bar:** beer & wine. **Address:** 221 Mountain Rd E1C 2L5 **Location:** Corner of Archibald St and Mountain Rd.

L D

CHAN'S HOUSE RESTAURANT & TAKE-OUT

Phone: 506/858-0112

Chinese
$8-$17

AAA Inspector Notes: This convenient location is opposite a large shopping center. In addition to a vast menu that includes some Canadian dishes, the restaurant offers daily buffets and take-out. **Bar:** full bar. **Address:** 80 Champlain St E1C 1B9 **Location:** Centre; opposite Champlain Mall. L D

CHEZ CORA

Phone: 506/382-2672

Canadian
$6-$13

AAA Inspector Notes: Eggs, omelets, waffles, crepes (sorry, no American-style pancakes here), French toast, fruit platters and all the breakfast meats--that's the specialty here, all day. However, at lunchtime the menu lists a selection of soups, salads, quiches, sandwiches and a dish called the grilled panini crepe. **Address:** 730 Main St E1C 1E4 **Location:** Centre; adjacent to Delta Beausejour. **Parking:** on-site (fee). B L

FISHERMAN'S PARADISE SEAFOOD & STEAK RESTAURANT

Menu on AAA.com   **Phone: 506/859-4388**

Seafood
$8-$28

AAA Inspector Notes: Spacious dining rooms feature a nautical theme and a friendly staff dressed in early Arcadian attire. Specialties include such fresh seafood dishes as halibut and hearty chowder, as well as a selection of meat entrees, fresh salad and home-style dessert. Service is prompt and courteous. **Bar:** full bar. **Reservations:** suggested. **Address:** 330 Dieppe Blvd E1A 6S4 **Location:** Hwy 15 exit 16, 0.6 mi (1 km) s.

L D

GARDEN BREEZE RESTAURANT   **Phone: 506/855-0564**

Canadian
$7-$20

AAA Inspector Notes: Pleasant staff and home-style cooking is what guests will find at this popular, spacious restaurant. Daily specials along with a senior citizen's menu and a kid's menu also are offered. **Bar:** full bar. **Address:** 500 Kennedy St E1A 5Y7 **Location:** At Paul St; in Coastal Inn. B L D CALL &M

GOLDEN EAGLE RESTAURANT   **Phone: 506/858-8508**

Chinese
$7-$16

AAA Inspector Notes: A popular spot for a good meal, the restaurant specializes in reasonably priced combination plates. Canadian dishes also are available. **Address:** 1590 Mountain Rd E1G 1A4 **Location:** Trans-Canada Hwy 2 exit 450, 2.4 mi (4.2 km) se on Rt 126 (Mountain Rd). L D

GRAFFITI

Phone: 506/382-4299

Mediterranean
$8-$19

AAA Inspector Notes: This popular spot sustains a bustling atmosphere and offers seating on two levels. Many of the well-prepared entrées arrive as a combination plate with Greek salad, potato wedges, vegetables and tasty tzatziki sauce. Gourmet Greek pizza on pita bread is also an option. **Bar:** full bar. **Reservations:** suggested. **Address:** 879 Main St E1C 5J9 **Location:** Just w of Lutz St; centre. **Parking:** on-site (fee). L D

HOUSE OF LAM

Chinese
$9-$21

Phone: 506/384-1101

AAA Inspector Notes: Family run since 1972, this eatery focuses on Szechuan dinners. Sample a variety of dishes from the lunch buffet, served weekdays, and the Sunday dinner buffet. Murals, etched glass and wood dividers decorate the interior of this pleasant restaurant. **Bar:** full bar. **Address:** 957 Mountain Rd E1C 2S4 **Location:** 2.2 mi (3.6 km) nw on Rt 126 (Mountain Rd). L D

JEAN'S RESTAURANT   **Phone: 506/856-8988**

Canadian
$6-$19

AAA Inspector Notes: This conveniently located spot employs casual, friendly servers who wend through the country-themed dining room. Ample choices line the breakfast and lunch menu including the popular all-day breakfast. **Bar:** full bar. **Address:** 1999 Mountain Rd E1G 1B1 **Location:** Trans-Canada Hwy 2 exit 452, 1 mi (1.6 km) s on George Rd. B L D

JUNGLE JIM'S

Phone: 506-386-5467

American
$9-$19

AAA Inspector Notes: Guests can step into a tropical theme at the casual eatery, which employs a friendly staff and nurtures a bustling atmosphere. The menu lines up a wide variety of comfort foods, salads, chicken, beef, seafood and hot wings, all served in ample, flavorful portions. **Bar:** full bar. **Address:** 1134 Mountain Rd E1C 2T3 **Location:** In Rogers Mini Mall. L D

L'IDYLLE

Phone: 506/860-6641

French
$32-$38

AAA Inspector Notes: Regional produce inspires the menu of French cuisine in this charming 1828 converted home. Menu selections include local venison, game birds, pork, fresh seafood and fine local cheeses with a wine list to complement any item. Outdoor dining on the deck is a seasonal option. **Bar:** full bar. **Reservations:** suggested. **Address:** 1788 Amirault St E1A 7S8 **Location:** Jct Champlain Blvd and Rt 106, 3 mi (5 km) s on Rt 106. D

LITTLE LOUIS'

Menu on AAA.com   **Phone: 506/855-2022**

French
$28-$40

AAA Inspector Notes: This restaurant may look deceiving from the exterior but ride the elevator up to the second floor and a fine dining experience awaits. The menu offers a selection of fresh seafood, excellent steaks, pork and game meats to a wonderful six or nine course prix fixe dinner. The atmosphere is relaxed with live jazz several nights a week. Service is professional and friendly. **Bar:** full bar. **Reservations:** suggested. **Address:** 245 Collishaw St E1C 9P9 **Location:** Just w of Vaughan Harvey Blvd. D CALL &M

MAVERICK'S STEAKHOUSE & GRILL

Phone: 506/855-3346

Steak
$9-$31

AAA Inspector Notes: This restaurant offers thoughtful preparations of dry-aged Prime beef, veal and such seafood as lobster, salmon and jumbo shrimp. The wine list is extensive. The atmosphere is relaxed with casual service. **Bar:** full bar. **Address:** 40 Lady Ada Blvd E1C 8P2 **Location:** Trans-Canada Hwy 2 exit 454; in Future Inns Moncton Hotel & Conference Centre.

B L D CALL &M

MCGINNIS LANDING RESTAURANT
Phone: 506/856-6995

American
$8-$23

AAA Inspector Notes: This restaurant offers booth and table seating and prepares menu options ranging from burgers and fish and chips to steak, seafood, stir-fry and various salads. **Bar:** full bar. **Address:** 499 Paul St E1A 6S5 **Location:** Trans-Canada Hwy 2 exit 459A eastbound, s on Rt 115 to Lewisville Rd, then left; exit 467A westbound, 4.8 mi (8 km) w on Rt 15 to rotary; in Ramada Plaza Crystal Palace & Convention Centre.

[B] [L] [D]

MEXICALI ROSA'S
Phone: 506/855-7672

Mexican
$10-$25

AAA Inspector Notes: The Mexican cantina makes an excellent choice for family-friendly fun. Old West paintings and murals add color to stucco walls and wooden beams, while a Tex-Mex menu provides a feast of favorites such as fajitas, burritos and some seafood items. Fried ice cream is a sweet treat. **Bar:** full bar. **Address:** 683 Main St E1C 1E3 **Location:** Between Botsford and Alma sts. **Parking:** on-site (fee).

M.I.C. CANADIAN EATERY AND WHISKEY PUB
Phone: 506/204-2141

Canadian
$9-$23

AAA Inspector Notes: This spacious hockey-oriented restaurant presents a menu that is sure to score. Guests can cross-check the selection, which ranges from cocktails to entrées but should not penalize themselves by skipping dessert. A TV and Xbox awaits guests at each booth. **Bar:** full bar. **Address:** 200 Champlain St E1A 1P1 **Location:** At Acadie St; centre; adjacent to Dieppe City Hall.

[L] [D]

MIKE'S RESTAURANT
Phone: 506/855-6464

American
$6-$16

AAA Inspector Notes: This popular family-friendly restaurant specializes in pizza and hot submarine sandwiches, along with fries, burgers, soup, salads, pasta, grilled meats and seafood. An excellent variety of colorful desserts rounds out the offerings. **Bar:** full bar. **Address:** 30 Mapleton Rd E1C 2T1 **Location:** At Mountain Rd.

[B] [L] [D]

MOOSE'S WILD PUB
Phone: 506/861-4645

American
$10-$22

AAA Inspector Notes: Located in the Casino New Brunswick, patrons to this pub must be 19 years old. This upbeat eatery offers booth and table seating overlooking the active casino. Menu options include a vast array of very well-prepared chowders, salads and finger foods as well as burgers, steak and seafood options. **Bar:** full bar. **Address:** 21 Casino Dr E1G 0R7 **Location:** Trans-Canada Hwy 2 exit 450; in Hotel Casino New Brunswick. [L] [D] CALL [&M]

THE OLD TRIANGLE IRISH ALEHOUSE
Phone: 506/384-7474

Irish
$9-$21

AAA Inspector Notes: Located in the heart of town, this upbeat, spacious Irish pub offers booth and table seating, live music several nights a week and patio dining in season. A menu includes a wide variety of classic pub fare including pizza, a fine selection of salads, chowders and fresh seafood and steak entrees. **Bar:** full bar. **Address:** 751 Main St E1C 1E5 **Location:** At Church St. **Parking:** on-site (fee). [L] [D]

PASTALLI PASTA HOUSE
Phone: 506/383-1050

Italian
$11-$26

AAA Inspector Notes: Several cozy dining sections provide an intimate bistro setting. Patrons can choose from fresh seafood, traditional meats and excellent gourmet pizzas. The homemade desserts are excellent. **Bar:** full bar. **Address:** 611 Main St E1C 1C9 **Location:** Between Lester St and Orange Ln. **Parking:** on-site (fee).

[L] [D] [LATE]

PISCES BY GASTON
Phone: 506/854-0444

Canadian
$9-$27

AAA Inspector Notes: This tastefully decorated, modern restaurant offers an intimate atmosphere with padded high-back booth and table seating. The menu features a selection of fresh seafood and meat entrées, with some hints of Italian, Greek and Spanish cuisine styles. Food is very well-prepared and service is friendly and attentive. **Bar:** full bar. **Reservations:** suggested. **Address:** 300 Main St E1C 1B9 **Location:** Centre; adjacent to Chateau Moncton Hotel & Suites. [L] [D]

PUMP HOUSE BREWERY
Phone: 506/855-2337

American
$8-$19

AAA Inspector Notes: Diners seeking an upbeat, casual place that serves basic, pub-style food and excellent microbrewed beers need look no further. Fine pizzas are baked in a wood-fired oven. **Bar:** full bar. **Address:** 5 Orange Ln E1C 4L6 **Location:** Jct Main St. **Parking:** on-site (fee). [L] [D]

SAIGON THAI RESTAURANT
Phone: 506/869-9996

Thai
$9-$21

AAA Inspector Notes: The pleasant dining room has a casual, friendly atmosphere. Representative of authentic Thai cuisine are preparations of fresh chicken, seafood, beef and curry dishes, in addition to some vegetarian and combination plates. **Bar:** full bar. **Address:** 7 Orange Ln E1C 4L6 **Location:** Jct Main St. **Parking:** on-site (fee). [L] [D]

ST-HUBERT
Phone: 506/858-0053

American
$8-$22

AAA Inspector Notes: The pleasantly decorated family-friendly restaurant serves affordable chicken dinners, ribs, club sandwiches, chicken wings, salads, soups and hot chicken sandwiches. The children's menu includes animal nuggets. **Bar:** full bar. **Address:** 1049 Mountain Rd E1C 2S9 **Location:** Trans-Canada Hwy 2 exit 454, 1.7 mi (2.8 km) s. [L] [D]

ST. JAMES GATE
Phone: 506/388-4283

American
$8-$21

AAA Inspector Notes: The appealing pub-style restaurant has a distinctive cellar decor with comfortable booths and tables. Classic pub fare is served in ample portions and coupled with a good selection of wines and beers on tap. **Bar:** full bar. **Address:** 14 Church St E1C 4Y9 **Location:** Corner of Main and Church sts; in Hotel St. James. **Parking:** street only. [L] [D]

SPORTS ROCK PUB & STEAK HOUSE
Phone: 506/855-6960

American
$9-$24

AAA Inspector Notes: You'll find a bustling atmosphere in this spacious bar with all your favorite sporting events displayed on numerous televisions. The extensive menu features everything from classic pub fare and finger foods to steaks and fresh seafood. **Bar:** full bar. **Address:** 451 Paul St E1H 1N5 **Location:** At Champlain Place Shopping Centre. [B] [L] [D] [24]

SWISS CHALET
Phone: 506/859-8608
Chicken
$6-$16

AAA Inspector Notes: The popular restaurant is known for its rotisserie chicken and ribs and the tangy Chalet sauce that gives food its special zip. Diners munch on a half or quarter chicken with sides such as steamed vegetables, fries, baked potatoes and salads. Lunch guests often go for the great soup and sandwich combination. Take-out and delivery service are popular options. **Bar:** full bar. **Address:** 9 Champlain St E1A 1N4 **Location:** At Champlain Mall. L D

TAJMAHAL FLAVOUR OF INDIA
Phone: 506/854-5557
Indian
$7-$21

AAA Inspector Notes: In the heart of town, this cozy, tastefully decorated restaurant serves a wide array of authentic Indian, Mughlai (Persian influenced) and tandoori dishes, each prepared to order and spiced to the diner's preference. **Bar:** full bar. **Address:** 882 Main St E1C 1G4 **Location:** At Robinson St. **Parking:** street only. L D

VITO'S RESTAURANT
Phone: 506/858-5000
Italian
$8-$20

AAA Inspector Notes: Bordering a bustling street, this spacious restaurant has dining rooms decorated with stonework and mirrors. On the menu are such Italian specialties as fettuccine Alfredo, seafood lasagna, tortellini au gratin and various palate-tempting pizzas. **Bar:** full bar. **Address:** 726 Mountain Rd E1C 2P9 **Location:** Corner of Mountain Rd and Vaughan Harvey Hwy. L D

WINDJAMMER DINING ROOM
Phone: 506/854-4344
Continental
$27-$42

AAA Inspector Notes: This elegant dining room carries out a nautical theme set off by tall ship models and brass porthole aquariums. Formally attired and professional in demeanor, the staff impresses even the most discerning traveler with tableside preparations and presentations of many fresh and creative dishes. The Caesar salad should not be missed. **Bar:** full bar. **Reservations:** suggested. **Address:** 750 Main St E1C 1E6 **Location:** Jct Main St and Sommet Ln; downtown; in Delta Beausejour. **Parking:** on-site (fee) and valet. D

NEW DENMARK (C-2)

The little town of New Denmark claims to be North America's largest Danish colony. Settlers arrived in 1872, lured by promises of 100 acres of "good farming land" from the New Brunswick government. Pamphlets offered weather statistics to dispel the myth of harsh winters, noting that Canadians enjoyed healthier and longer lives than citizens of warmer climates.

NEW DENMARK MEMORIAL MUSEUM is at 6 Main Rd. Founded in 1872, New Denmark was the first Danish settlement in Canada. The museum displays farming and domestic artifacts pertaining to the lives of the settlers. **Hours:** Thurs.-Sun. 9-8, Mon.-Wed. 9-5, mid-June through Labour Day; other times by appointment. **Cost:** Donations. **Phone:** (506) 553-6424, or (506) 553-9931 for appointments.

NIGADOO pop. 983

LA FINE GROBE SUR-MER
Phone: 506/783-3138
French
$17-$26

AAA Inspector Notes: A charming oceanside hideaway, this eatery overlooks picturesque Nepisiguit Bay. Enjoy such savory dishes as crab claws, salmon with sorrel and sauteed scallops either on the outdoor terrace cafe, or in the dining room surrounded by the paintings of local artists. The servers are friendly and attentive. **Bar:** full bar. **Reservations:** suggested. **Address:** 289 Main St E8K 3Y5 **Location:** Hwy 11 exit 321 to Rt 134, 0.5 mi (0.8 km) n; watch for road sign to ocean; from Bathurst, 6.9 mi (11 km) n on Rt 134. D

OROMOCTO (E-3) pop. 8,402

The home of Canadian Forces Base Gagetown, one of the largest military training areas in the British Commonwealth, Oromocto is situated along the Saint John River. Of Maliseet origin, the town's name means "deep water."

Oromocto Tourist Bureau: Waasis and Restigouche rds., Oromocto, NB, Canada E2V 2H1. **Phone:** (506) 446-5010.

NEW BRUNSWICK MILITARY HISTORY MUSEUM is on the military base in Bldg. A-5. Exhibits include uniforms, weapons and other artifacts of the 1800s, the South African War, World Wars I and II, the Korean War, United Nations missions and the present. Military vehicles are in an outdoor display area. **Note:** The museum is closed for renovations until July 1, 2012. **Time:** Allow 1 hour minimum. **Hours:** Mon.-Fri. 8-4, Sat.-Sun. and holidays 10-4. Closed most legal holidays. Phone ahead to confirm schedule. **Cost:** Free. **Phone:** (506) 422-1304.

DAYS INN OROMOCTO
Phone: (506)357-5657
Hotel
$104-$130

Address: 60 Brayson Blvd E2V 4T9 **Location:** Trans-Canada Hwy 2 exit 301 eastbound; exit 303 westbound, just s to Pioneer Ave, then 1 mi (1.6 km) w. **Facility:** 81 units. 3 stories, interior corridors. **Amenities:** Some: high-speed Internet. **Pool(s):** heated indoor. **Activities:** whirlpool, exercise room. **Guest Services:** valet laundry. **Free Special Amenities:** continental breakfast and high-speed internet.

ROBIN'S INN
Phone: 506/446-9077
fyi Not evaluated. **Address:** 42 Chaperral Rd E3B 9Z4 **Location:** Trans-Canada Hwy 2 exit 297. Facilities, services, and decor characterize an economy property.

WHERE TO EAT

JUNGLE JIM'S
Phone: 506/357-0831
Canadian
$8-$19

AAA Inspector Notes: Guests can step into a tropical theme at the casual eatery, which employs a friendly staff and nurtures a bustling atmosphere. The menu lines up a wide variety of comfort foods, salads, chicken, beef, seafood and hot wings, all served in ample, flavorful portions. **Bar:** full bar. **Address:** 2 Gateway Dr E2V 4R3 **Location:** Trans-Canada Hwy 2 exit 303; in Parkview Garden Mall. L D

PENNFIELD pop. 2,322

COMEAU'S SEAFOOD RESTAURANT

Seafood
$7-$16

Phone: 506/755-3011

AAA Inspector Notes: Fresh seafood is served in ample portions. The atmosphere is casual in the two dining sections. Takeout service is available. **Address:** 5025 Hwy 1 E5H 1Y4 **Location:** Centre.

L D

PERTH-ANDOVER pop. 1,797

THE CASTLE INN

Country Inn
Rates not provided

Phone: 506/273-9495

Address: 21 Brentwood Dr E7H 1P1 **Location:** Trans-Canada Hwy 2 exit 115, follow signs over St. John River. **Facility:** With well-appointed rooms and suites, the inn is on a 200-acre wooded estate perched on a hillside overlooking the St. Johns River and township. 13 units. 3 stories (no elevator), interior corridors. **Terms:** office hours 7 am-11 pm. **Dining:** restaurant, see separate listing. **Pool(s):** heated indoor. **Activities:** sauna, whirlpool, steamroom, hiking trails, exercise room. **Free Special Amenities:** continental breakfast.

SAVE   / SOME UNITS FEE

WHERE TO EAT

THE CASTLE INN RESTAURANT   **Phone:** 506/273-9495

Canadian
$20-$27

AAA Inspector Notes: This is a delightful restaurant located in a former mansion overlooking the St. John River. Menu options include fresh salmon, steaks, Castle ribs, lamb chops as well as pasta and lighter fare such as sandwiches and burgers. Patio dining is available in season. **Bar:** full bar. **Reservations:** suggested. **Address:** 21 Brentwood Dr E7H 1P1 **Location:** Trans-Canada Hwy 2 exit 115, follow signs over St. John River; in The Castle Inn.

L D

YORK'S DINING ROOM   **Phone:** 506/273-2847

American
$7-$38

AAA Inspector Notes: In business for more than 70 years, the casual country restaurant overlooks the St. John River. Patrons can sample hearty five-course prix fixe dinners and a la carte lunch items. Arriving with an appetite is a good idea. **Bar:** full bar. **Address:** 1333 Aroostook Rd E7H 1A7 **Location:** Trans-Canada Hwy 2 exit 115, follow signs.

L D

PETIT-ROCHER (A-4)

NEW BRUNSWICK MINING AND MINERALS INTERPRETATION CENTRE is on Hwy. 134 at 397 Rue Principale. The province's mining heritage is honored with exhibitions, educational games and visual projections. Highlights include a simulation of a mine-shaft descent to 975 metres (3,200 ft.). An amusement park is on the grounds. **Hours:** Daily 11-5, June-Aug. **Cost:** $5.25; $4.25 (ages 50+); $3.25 (students with ID); $1 (preschoolers); free (ages 0-2); $12 (family). **Phone:** (506) 542-2672.

Check out
our travel blog at
AAATravelViews.com

POCOLOGAN

BAY BREEZE RESTAURANT   **Phone:** 506/755-3850

Seafood
$6-$16

AAA Inspector Notes: This casual diner offers an array of comfort foods to enjoy while taking in the splendid ocean vista. **Bar:** full bar. **Address:** 6410 Hwy 1 E5J 1E1 **Location:** Centre.

B L D AC

POINTE-VERTE pop. 971

GITE TOUTES SAISONS BED & BREAKFAST

Bed & Breakfast
$149-$169 6/1-9/15
$139-$159 9/16-5/31

Phone: (506)783-3122

Address: 10 rue des Oiseaux E8J 2V6 **Location:** Rt 11 exit 333 to Rt 134, 0.8 mi (1.3 km) nw. **Facility:** All but one of the individually decorated guest rooms in this lovely log home on the Baie des Chaleur offer an ocean view, and two rooms have private balconies. 4 units. 2 stories (no elevator), interior corridors. **Terms:** office hours 7 am-10 pm, 30 day cancellation notice-fee imposed. **Activities:** game room. **Guest Services:** complimentary laundry.

CALL

QUISPAMSIS pop. 15,239

AMSTERDAM INN   **Phone:** (506)849-8050

Hotel
$145-$180 6/1-9/30
$115-$180 10/1-5/31

Address: 114 Millennium Dr E2E 0C6 **Location:** Hwy 1 exit 141. **Facility:** 49 units, some kitchens. 3 stories, interior corridors. **Terms:** cancellation fee imposed. **Amenities:** high-speed Internet. **Pool(s):** heated indoor. **Activities:** exercise room. **Guest Services:** valet laundry.

 / SOME UNITS

RED BANK (C-4)

METEPENAGIAG HERITAGE PARK, 2156 MicMac Rd., traces the 3,000-year-old history of the aboriginal Mi'kmaq culture. Multimedia exhibits in French, English and the native language provide details about history, hunting and fishing techniques, dwellings and modes of travel. Ceramic pottery, archeological finds and a 20-minute video about the Mi'kmaq culture and the Oxbow and Miramichi Rivers also may be seen. Interpretive trails meander along the Oxbow River.

Time: Allow 1 hour minimum. **Hours:** Daily 10-5, May 15-Oct. 31; by appointment rest of year. **Cost:** $8; $6 (ages 6-16 and 65+). **Phone:** (506) 836-6118 or (888) 380-3555.

REXTON (C-5) pop. 862
• Hotels p. 66

Known in 1825 as The Yard, Rexton prospered as a shipyard until cargo-hauling barges, called timber droghers, were replaced by steam-powered ships later that century. The town is the birthplace of Andrew Bonar Law, the only prime minister of Great Britain born outside the British Isles.

BONAR LAW HISTORIC SITE is at jct. hwys. 134 and 116. The 1858 birthplace of Andrew Bonar Law, the only British prime minister born outside Great Britain, is preserved. The original home and barns still stand on this former farm. Also on the grounds are the Richibucto River Museum, which features historical documents, portraits and other artifacts; an interpretive trail; a festival area; and an area for croquet, farmersgolf and other games. Guided tours and special events are offered during the summer. **Hours:** Daily 10-5, mid-June to early Sept. **Cost:** $3. **Phone:** (506) 523-7615, (506) 523-6921 or (877) 731-7007.

JARDINE'S INN   Phone: (506)523-7070

Historic Bed
& Breakfast
$99-$129

Address: 104 Main St E4W 2B3 **Location:** On Rt 134; centre. **Facility:** The quaint property offers comfortable guest rooms with modern amenities. Full breakfasts are delivered to your door. 5 units. 2 stories (no elevator), interior corridors. **Terms:** office hours 8 am-11 pm.

RICHIBUCTO   pop. 1,290

G K'S RESTAURANT   Phone: 506/523-0080

American
$7-$18

AAA Inspector Notes: This family restaurant overlooks the harbor and lobster boats. In addition to specialties of pizza and donairs, it offers a full menu with salads, soups, meats and seafood choices. Patrons can sit on the patio in season and pick up their meals for take-out. **Address:** 9349 Main St E4W 4B6 **Location:** Centre; at the marina. [L] [D]

RIVERSIDE-ALBERT   (E-5) pop. 320

Once known as Hopewell Corner, this village on the Shepody River at the upper reaches of the Bay of Fundy was a 19th-century shipbuilding center. Many homes and buildings from the period survive. The 1904 Riverside Consolidated School, 90 Water St., is the oldest of its kind still in use in New Brunswick; phone (506) 882-3002.

CAPE ENRAGE LIGHTHOUSE is 17 km (11 mi.) s.e. on Hwy. 915, then 6.5 km (4 mi.) e. on Cape Enrage Rd. Built in 1848, this lighthouse on Chignecto Bay is fully automated and operates year-round. Staff live and work at the site. Fossil deposits can be seen along the coastline, where rock-climbing and rappelling are popular. **Time:** Allow 1 hour minimum. **Hours:** Daily 8-8, early May to mid-Oct. **Cost:** Donations. **Phone:** (506) 887-2273 or (888) 423-5454. [≬] [⚘]

LAKEVIEW INN   Phone: (506)882-2245

Bed & Breakfast
$99-$140

Address: 794 Rt 915 E4H 3T4 **Location:** On Rt 915, 6 mi (10 km) w. **Facility:** A Colonial-style exterior dresses up this modern inn offering well-appointed rooms with allergen-free features in a secluded area bordering a lake. 7 units, some houses. 2 stories (no elevator), interior corridors. **Terms:** open 6/1-10/15, office hours 7 am-10 pm, 2 night minimum stay - seasonal and/or weekends, 3 day cancellation notice-fee imposed. **Activities:** canoeing, paddleboats, hiking trails, game room.

CAPE HOUSE RESTAURANT   Phone: 506/887-2273

American
$7-$12

AAA Inspector Notes: Seating on the outdoor deck and in the dining room of the wonderful location at Cape Enrage Lighthouse looks out over the Bay of Fundy. Patrons may enjoy an early dinner. **Bar:** beer & wine. **Address:** 650 Cape Enrage Rd E4H 4Z4 **Location:** 10.6 mi (17 km) w on Rt 114 and 915, 4 mi (6.5 km) e; at Cape Enrage Lighthouse. [L] [D] [✗]

RIVERVIEW   pop. 17,832

THE HOMESTEAD RESTAURANT   Phone: 506/386-1907

American
$6-$16

AAA Inspector Notes: The popular family restaurant is across the river from town and serves a wide variety of home-style items. Ample portions and great desserts keep folks coming back. **Address:** 358 Coverdale Rd E1B 3J5 **Location:** On Rt 114; in Riverview Village. [B] [L] [D]

ROTHESAY   pop. 11,637

SHADOW LAWN INN   Phone: 506/847-7539

Historic
Country Inn
Rates not provided

Address: 3180 Rothesay Rd E2E 5V7 **Location:** Hwy 1 exit 137B eastbound; exit 137A westbound, follow signs for Rothesay Rd and Rt 100, 1 mi (1.6 km) left on Old Hampton Rd (Rt 100), then left on Rt 100. Located in a semi-residential area. **Facility:** Manicured grounds surround this stately Victorian manor house, which offers handsome common areas and varied, well-decorated rooms. 9 units. 2 stories (no elevator), interior corridors. **Terms:** office hours 7 am-11 pm. **Dining:** Side Door Cafe & Patio, see separate listing.

[≬] [⚲] [🛜] [✗] / SOME UNITS [▭] [▱]

BOAZ JAPANESE & KOREAN RESTAURANT
                               Phone: 506/847-4488

Eastern Asian
$8-$20

AAA Inspector Notes: With a bright atmosphere with friendly service, this casual spot offers a wide range of authentic Japanese and some Korean dishes. Food is creative and prepared to order. A small sushi bar allows you to watch the chef in action. Among the dishes served are tempura, sashimi and teriyaki preparations. **Bar:** beer & wine. **Address:** 126 Old Hampton Rd E2E 2N5 **Location:** Just w of Parkdale Ave. [L] [D]

SIDE DOOR CAFE & PATIO   Phone: 506/847-7539

Continental
$12-$32

AAA Inspector Notes: Located in a lovely historic mansion, this restaurant offers several dining areas including patio dining in season. The creative cuisine is predominantly Continental with some French accents. **Bar:** full bar. **Reservations:** required. **Address:** 3180 Rothesay Rd E2E 5V7 **Location:** Hwy 1 exit 137B eastbound; exit 137A westbound, follow signs for Rothesay Rd and Rt 100, 1 mi (1.6 km) left on Old Hampton Rd (Rt 100), then left on Rt 100; in Shadow Lawn Inn. [B] [L] [D]

VITO'S RESTAURANT   Phone: 506/847-4400

♦♦♦ ♦♦♦
Italian
$8-$21

AAA Inspector Notes: This modern restaurant has ample parking. Although this place specializes in pizza and spaghetti, it also prepares chicken, seafood and steaks, as well as fine salads. Spacious patio dining is available in season. Take-out is available. **Bar:** full bar. **Address:** 111 Old Hampton Rd E2E 5V7 **Location:** Just e of Marr St; centre. [L] [D]

SACKVILLE (D-6) pop. 5,411

Pioneer Acadians reclaimed from the sea much of the Sackville area by creating an extensive system of dikes known as *aboiteaux*. During the 18th century Sackville was called Tintamarre, derived from the French name referring to the thundering noise made by geese nesting in the surrounding marshes on a migratory bird route.

A town of firsts, Sackville claims Canada's first Baptist church as well as the first degree conferred upon a woman in the British Empire—the diploma was granted in 1875 at Mount Allison University. The liberal arts college was founded in 1839.

Sackville United Church, an 1876 white-steepled building that features woodwork, curved pews and rose stained-glass windows, houses a collection of photographs and historical items; phone (506) 536-0498. Lillas Fawcett Park on Main Street features a small beach and picnic area; phone (506) 364-4955.

Information Centre: 34 Mallard Dr., Sackville, NB, Canada E4L 4C3. **Phone:** (506) 364-4967.

OWENS ART GALLERY is on the campus of Mount Allison University at 61 York St. With more than 3,000 pieces in its permanent collection, the gallery specializes in contemporary Canadian art and 18th- and 19th-century European paintings, watercolors and prints. **Time:** Allow 1 hour minimum. **Hours:** Mon.-Fri. 10-5, Sat.-Sun. 1-5. Closed major holidays. **Cost:** Donations. **Phone:** (506) 364-2574.

SACKVILLE HARNESS SHOP is at 39 Main St. Open since 1920, the shop preserves the art of handcrafting horse collars and harnesses. **Time:** Allow 30 minutes minimum. **Hours:** Mon.-Fri. 8-5, Sat. 8-noon. Closed major holidays. **Cost:** Free. **Phone:** (506) 536-0642 or (800) 386-4888.

SACKVILLE WATERFOWL PARK is on Main St., adjacent to Mount Allison University. The 22-hectare (55-acre) park, on one of North America's major migratory bird routes, offers 3.5 kilometres (2.2 mi.) of boardwalks and trails with viewing platforms and interpretive signs.

Tours: Guided tours are available. **Hours:** Park open daily dawn-dusk, year-round. Guided tours depart from the Information Centre at 34 Mallard Dr. daily 9-5, May-Aug. **Cost:** Park admission free. Guided tour $6; $4 (ages 6-12 and 50+); $10 (family, two adults and two children). Cash only. Reservations are recommended. **Phone:** (506) 364-4967.

COASTAL INN SACKVILLE   Phone: (506)536-0000

♦♦♦ ♦♦♦
Hotel
$109-$155 6/1-10/7
$99-$135 10/8-5/31

Address: 15 Wright St E4L 4P8 **Location:** Trans-Canada Hwy 2 exit 504. **Facility:** 50 units. 2 stories (no elevator), interior corridors. **Amenities:** high-speed Internet. **Activities:** limited exercise equipment. **Guest Services:** coin laundry.

 / SOME UNITS 🛏 🚪 🖥

MARSHLANDS INN   Phone: 506/536-0170

♦♦♦ ♦♦♦
Historic Country Inn
$94-$225

Address: 55 Bridge St E4L 3N8 **Location:** On Hwy 106; centre. Located in a residential area. **Facility:** In a residential area, this pleasant inn is made up of a main building and a carriage house. Rooms vary from spacious to cozy in size. The carriage house units are more modern. 17 units. 3 stories (no elevator), interior corridors. **Terms:** office hours 7 am-midnight. **Dining:** restaurant, see separate listing. **Free Special Amenities:** newspaper and high-speed Internet.

SAVE 🍴 📶 📶 🚫 / SOME UNITS 🛏 📺

WHERE TO EAT

JOEY'S PIZZA & PASTA   Phone: 506/536-4040

♦♦♦ ♦♦♦
Italian
$8-$18

AAA Inspector Notes: A variety of tasty Italian dishes can be found on the menu at this upbeat eatery where patrons can dine in the lounge or in the dining room. Pizza, served by a friendly staff, is a main draw to this downtown spot. An excellent brunch buffet is offered Monday through Friday. **Bar:** full bar. **Address:** 16 York St E4L 4R2 **Location:** Just w of Main St. **Parking:** street only. [L] [D]

MARSHLANDS INN DINING ROOM   Phone: 506/536-0170

♦♦♦ ♦♦♦
American
$12-$28

AAA Inspector Notes: Quartered in a historic inn, the eatery houses two large dining sections. A menu of regional favorites includes a fine variety of fresh seafood and meat entrees for both lunch and dinner. Also offered are daily specials and fine homemade desserts. **Bar:** full bar. **Reservations:** suggested. **Address:** 55 Bridge St E4L 3N8 **Location:** On Hwy 106; centre; in Marshlands Inn. [B] [L] [D]

PATTERSON'S FAMILY RESTAURANT
    Phone: 506/364-0822

♦♦♦ ♦♦♦
American
$6-$16

AAA Inspector Notes: This diner-style operation serves everything from an all-day breakfast to burger favorites to hearty dinners. Homemade desserts are sure to please, as will the take-out dairy bar. A game room keeps the kids busy while the adults relax over coffee. **Bar:** beer & wine. **Address:** 16 Mallard Dr E4L 4C3 **Location:** Trans-Canada Hwy 2 exit 504. [B] [L] [D]

ST. ANDREWS (F-3) pop. 1,869
• Hotels p. 69 • Restaurants p. 70

St. Andrews is on Passamaquoddy Bay; the tidal variation here is about 8 metres (26 ft.). St. Andrews was settled by United Empire Loyalists in 1783 following the American Revolution. Many of their white clapboard houses were dismantled, barged from Castine, Maine, and reassembled; these houses can still be seen today.

Around the turn of the 20th century St. Andrews-by-the-Sea flourished as Canada's first seaside resort town; the Fairmont Algonquin, a renowned hotel built in 1889, still stands as testament to that era. More than 250 homes in the historic district are 100 to more than 200 years old. The heart of the town still looks much as it did in early photographs.

Town of St. Andrews Visitor Information Centre: 24 Reed Ave., St. Andrews, NB, Canada E5B 1A1. **Phone:** (506) 529-3556.

ATLANTIC SALMON INTERPRETIVE CENTRE is off Hwy. 127E at 24 Chamcook Lake Rd. This complex of post-and-beam buildings features an exhibit hall and an in-stream aquarium with adult Atlantic salmon. Visitors can see the salmon up close through windows. Exhibits include a hall of fame for individuals who have contributed to the conservation of Atlantic salmon. Lectures and guided walks are available. Nature trails along Chamcook Stream are featured.

Hours: Mon.-Sat. 9-5, Sun. noon-5, June-Aug.; by appointment in May and Sept. Phone ahead to confirm schedule. **Cost:** $6; $4 (college students with ID and senior citizens); $3 (children); $15 (family). **Phone:** (506) 529-1038 or (506) 529-1384. ⌂

CHARLOTTE COUNTY ARCHIVES is in the center of town at 123 Frederick St. Housed in the 1832 county jail, the archives present historical documents recounting local history. **Time:** Allow 30 minutes minimum. **Hours:** Mon.-Sat. 9-5, July-Aug.; Mon.-Fri. 9-noon and 1-5 in June and Sept.; Tues.-Fri. 1-4, Apr.-May and Oct.-Nov. **Cost:** Donations. **Phone:** (506) 529-4248.

FUNDY DISCOVERY AQUARIUM, 3.2 km (2 mi.) n.w. on Lower Campus Rd. next to the St. Andrews Biological Station, features the diverse marine life found in the Bay of Fundy. Visitors can view harbor seals, marine invertebrates, sturgeon and other native fish; they also can pet creatures in two touch pools. Special events are offered throughout the year.

Hours: Daily 10-5, May-Sept.; Thurs.-Sun. 10-5, rest of year. Seal feedings at 11 and 4. Phone ahead to confirm schedule. **Cost:** $14; $11.50 (ages 65+); $9.75 (ages 4-17). **Phone:** (506) 529-1215.

FUNDY TIDE RUNNERS WHALE WATCHING AND NATURE TOURS departs from Market Wharf at 16 King St. Two-hour whale-watching trips are offered aboard a 7-metre (24-ft.), rigid-hull Zodiac Hurricane. Finback, humpback and minke whales may be seen, and bald eagles, marine birds, porpoises and seals are regularly sighted.

Hours: Trips depart daily at 10, 1, 4 and 6, July-Aug.; at 10 and 1 in June and Sept.; at 2 in May and Oct. Visitors should arrive 45 minutes prior to departure. **Cost:** $59; $44 (ages 5-12). Fuel surcharge may apply. Ages 0-4 are not permitted. Reservations are recommended. **Phone:** (506) 529-4481.

GREENOCK PRESBYTERIAN CHURCH is at Montague and Edward sts. Capt. Christopher Scott erected the church in 1824. A design of nearly perfect proportions enabled the pulpit and the minister's

and precentor's platforms to be constructed entirely without nails. On the steeple is a hand-carved green oak tree with bright green foliage, the emblem of the town of Greenock (Green Oak), Scotland, Scott's birthplace. **Hours:** Mon.-Sat. 9-noon and 1-4:30, July-Aug. Church service Sun. at 11, May-Oct.; at 9, rest of year. **Phone:** (506) 529-3057.

◆ GEM SAVE **KINGSBRAE GARDEN** is at 220 King St. Overlooking Passamaquoddy Bay, the 11-hectare (27-acre) horticultural garden features more than 50,000 flowers, shrubs and trees. Themed displays include cottage, rose, perennial, knot, ornamental grass, bird and butterfly, fantasy, gravel, culinary herb, edible and wildflower gardens. The Scents and Sensitivity Garden is notable for its raised garden and special flora chosen for the enjoyment of the visually impaired; all signs are in Braille.

Classical music is played throughout the 26 gardens of the .3-hectare (.5-acre) Perennial Garden, which is enclosed by century-old cedar hedges. A woodland trail winds through an old-growth Acadian forest, and a cedar maze leads into a labyrinth. The National Sculpture Competition and Garden mixes floral displays with interesting art pieces. A plant center features unusual plants and shrubs; an art gallery features the works of local artists. Alpacas, goats and peacocks are on-site.

Guided walking tours are available by reservation; motorized carts driven by guides are available for those requiring assistance. **Time:** Allow 1 hour, 30 minutes minimum. **Hours:** Daily 9-6, mid-May through second Sat. in Oct. **Cost:** $14; $10 (ages 7-17 and 60+); $32 (family, two adults and children ages 7-17); free (ages 0-6). Plant center free. Tours $3. **Phone:** (506) 529-3335, ext. 1 or (866) 566-8687. ⌂

MINISTERS ISLAND HISTORIC SITE is 2 km (1.2 mi.) n. on Hwy. 127 to Bar Rd. Named for an Anglican minister who settled here in 1786, the island is the site of Covenhoven, the baronial summer home of Sir William Van Horne, first president of the Canadian Pacific Railway. Guided tours begin with a drive across a sand bar to the island during low tide or aboard a ferry during high tide and continue through the 50-room villa. A spacious livestock barn and a bath house with a tidal swimming pool can be viewed on request.

Visitors must provide their own transportation to the island during low tide. **Hours:** Tours depart daily, May-Oct. Tour times depend on the tides and are available from the Town of St. Andrews Visitor Information Centre, 24 Reed Ave. **Cost:** $15; $10 (students with ID and senior citizens); free (ages 0-6); $25 (per couple). **Phone:** (506) 529-5081 or (877) 386-3922.

ROSS MEMORIAL MUSEUM is at 188 Montague St. at King St. Exhibits in the 1824 Georgian brick house include fine examples of 19th-century New Brunswick and American furniture as well as clocks,

Canadian and American paintings, Oriental rugs and other treasures from the benefactors' world travels. **Time:** Allow 30 minutes minimum. **Hours:** Mon.-Sat. 10-4:30, early June-early Oct. **Cost:** Donations. **Phone:** (506) 529-5124.

ST. ANDREWS BLOCKHOUSE NATIONAL HISTORIC SITE OF CANADA is at 23 Joe's Point Rd. on the waterfront. The fortification was built during the War of 1812 to protect the town from American privateers. Damaged by fire in 1993, the blockhouse has been restored and contains accurate reproductions of artifacts from the 1800s. The beachfront is popular for picnicking. **Hours:** Daily 10-6, June-Aug. **Cost:** Donations. **Phone:** (506) 529-4270, or (506) 636-4011 in the off-season.

SHERIFF ANDREWS HOUSE HISTORIC SITE is at 63 King St. at Queen St. Guides dressed in period costumes offer 20-minute tours of the two-story neoclassical brick home of Elijah Andrews, sheriff of Charlotte County in 1820. **Hours:** Mon.-Sat. 9:30-4:30, mid-June to mid-Sept.; Mon.-Fri. 9:30-4:30, late May to mid-June. **Cost:** Donations. **Phone:** (506) 529-5080.

SUNBURY SHORES ARTS AND NATURE CENTRE INC. is at 139 Water St. The center offers exhibits, courses and workshops focusing on crafts, the visual arts and natural history. A reference library also is on-site. The center owns and maintains a self-guiding walking trail in a nearby woodlot. **Hours:** Tues.-Sat. 9-4:30 (also Mon. 9-4:30, July-Aug.). Phone ahead to confirm schedule. **Cost:** Donations. **Phone:** (506) 529-3386.

TALL SHIP WHALE ADVENTURES is at Market Wharf near the corner of Water and King sts. Passengers board the *Jolly Breeze*—a 72-foot-long square-rigged cutter—for whale-watch excursions into the Bay of Fundy and Passamaquoddy Bay. Built in 1989, the ship is a replica of a tall ship from the early 1900s complete with teak decks. During the cruise, knowledgeable crew members answer questions about local history and wildlife, and children are entertained with planned activities. If weather conditions permit, passengers may assist with the sails or take the helm.

Warm clothing is recommended. **Time:** Allow 3 hours, 30 minutes minimum. **Hours:** Cruises depart daily at 9, 12:45 and 4:30, mid-June through first weekend in Oct. **Cost:** $55; $38 (ages 3-14); $165 (family, two adults and two children). **Phone:** (506) 529-8116 or (866) 529-8116. 🍴

WHALES AND WILDLIFE CATAMARAN STYLE is to the right of Market Wharf at 6 King St. Narrated by marine biologists, the 2.5- to 3-hour sightseeing trips aboard the catamaran M/V *Quoddy Link* frequently offer sightings of finback and minke whales in the early season with the addition of humpback

whales later in the season. Other sightings include seals, porpoises, eagles, an aquaculture site and a herring weir on the Bay of Fundy.

Warm clothing is advised. **Hours:** Cruises depart daily (weather permitting) at 10 and 2 (also at 5:30, July-Aug.), mid-June to mid-Oct. Phone ahead to confirm schedule. **Cost:** $55; $49 (ages 60+); $35 (ages 2-14); $162 (family, two adults and two or more children). Reservations are required. **Phone:** (506) 529-2600 or (877) 688-2600.

THE ALGONQUIN HOTEL & RESORT
Phone: (506)529-8823

Historic Hotel
$159-$569 6/1-10/31
$119-$479 11/1-5/31

Address: 184 Adolphus St E5B 1T7 **Location:** Off Hwy 127. **Facility:** On picturesque landscaped grounds, this is a striking historic hotel with a modern annex section; some rooms offer water views. 234 units. 3-4 stories, interior corridors. **Terms:** check-in 4 pm, 3 day cancellation notice-fee imposed. **Amenities:** *Fee:* video games, high-speed Internet. **Dining:** 3 restaurants, also, The Veranda Restaurant, see separate listing, entertainment. **Pool(s):** heated outdoor. **Activities:** saunas, whirlpool, racquetball court, recreation programs, playground, shuffleboard, volleyball, exercise room. *Fee:* golf-18 holes, miniature golf. **Guest Services:** coin laundry.

ECO 🍴 🍸 🛖 BIZ 🛜 💻
/ SOME UNITS FEE 🐕 🏋 📱 📶

HARRIS HATCH INN
Phone: 506/529-4995

Historic Bed & Breakfast
$75-$150

Address: 142 Queen St E5B 1E2 **Location:** Centre. Located in a residential area. **Facility:** Built in 1840 of bricks baked on-site, this stately home offers spacious, tastefully decorated guest rooms, two with wood-burning fireplaces. 4 units, some kitchens. 1-3 stories (no elevator), interior corridors. **Terms:** office hours 9 am-11 pm, cancellation fee imposed.

🛗 🛜 ✖ 🖋 💻

ROSSMOUNT INN
Phone: (506)529-3351

Country Inn
$85-$140

Address: 4599 Rt 127 E5B 3S7 **Location:** On Hwy 127, 3.8 mi (6.3 km) ne. Located in a rural area. **Facility:** Situated on a hillside overlooking the bay and fields, Rossmount offers fine public areas and a variety of comfortable guest rooms. 18 units. 3 stories (no elevator), interior corridors. **Terms:** open 6/1-1/1 & 5/1-5/31, office hours 8 am-11 pm, cancellation fee imposed. **Dining:** restaurant, see separate listing. **Pool(s):** outdoor. **Activities:** hiking trails. **Free Special Amenities:** local telephone calls and high-speed Internet.

SAVE 🍴 🍸 🛖 🛜 ✖ 🖋

ST. ANDREWS COTTAGES
Phone: 506/529-8555

Cottage
$110-$149

Address: 3889 Rt 127 E5B 2T3 **Location:** On Hwy 127, 1.5 mi (2.5 km) n. **Facility:** These pleasant cottages with covered porches are located in a private wooded setting on the outskirts of town. 6 cottages. 1 story, exterior corridors. **Terms:** open 6/1-10/31 & 4/1-5/31, office hours 9 am-8 pm, 2-4 night minimum stay, 14 day cancellation notice-fee imposed. **Pool(s):** heated outdoor. **Activities:** hiking trails, playground. **Guest Services:** coin laundry.

TARA MANOR INN
Phone: (506)529-3304

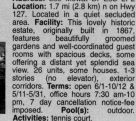

Historic Bed & Breakfast
$99-$169

Address: 559 Mowat Dr E5B 2P2 **Location:** 1.7 mi (2.8 km) n on Hwy 127. Located in a quiet secluded area. **Facility:** This lovely historic estate, originally built in 1867, features beautifully groomed gardens and well-coordinated guest rooms with spacious decks, some offering a distant yet splendid sea view. 26 units, some houses. 1-3 stories (no elevator), exterior corridors. **Terms:** open 6/1-10/12 & 5/11-5/31, office hours 7:30 am-10 pm, 7 day cancellation notice-fee imposed. **Pool(s):** outdoor. **Activities:** tennis court.

(See ad this page.)

TREADWELL INN
Phone: 506/529-1011

Bed & Breakfast
$125-$250 6/1-10/31
$125-$175 11/1-5/31

Address: 129 Water St E5B 1A7 **Location:** Oceanfront. Corner of Edward St. Located in a commercial area. **Facility:** The lawn of this 1820s inn extends to Passamaquoddy Bay. Many rooms offer lovely bay views, and the deluxe suites have whirlpool baths. 7 units. 3 stories (no elevator), interior corridors. **Terms:** office hours 7:30 am-10 pm, 2 night minimum stay - seasonal and/or weekends, 7 day cancellation notice. **Activities:** bicycles.

KINGSBRAE ARMS
Phone: 506/529-1897

[fyi] Not evaluated. **Address:** 219 King St E5B 1Y1 **Location:** Centre; adjacent to Kingsbrae Gardens. Facilities, services, and decor characterize an upscale property.

WHERE TO EAT

THE CLUBHOUSE GRILL
Phone: 506/529-8165

American
$10-$25

AAA Inspector Notes: A picturesque location overlooking the 18th hole and the ocean beyond, diners can sink into one of the comfy wing-back chairs and enjoy the relaxing atmosphere. The menu selection ranges from such comfort foods as sandwiches, wraps and burgers to fresh seafood and steaks-the chowder should not be missed. In season, the covered patio offers an outdoor dining experience. **Bar:** full bar. **Address:** 465 Brandy Cove Rd E5B 1T7 **Location:** Off Rt 127, follow signs to golf course.

L D

THE GABLES RESTAURANT
Phone: 506/529-3440

American
$8-$26

AAA Inspector Notes: In the relaxed atmosphere, guests can sit indoors or outdoors on the spacious treed deck bordering the harbor. A variety of fresh seafood and tasty comfort foods complete the menu. **Bar:** full bar. **Address:** 143 Water St E5B 1A7 **Location:** Centre. **Parking:** street only. L D AC

HARBOUR FRONT RESTAURANT
Phone: 506/529-4887

American
$9-$25

AAA Inspector Notes: Befitting its name, this spacious restaurant is in town on the harborfront. The menu lists a fine selection of fresh seafood and meat dishes. Guests can enjoy sea breezes and lovely harbour views on the spacious outdoor deck. **Bar:** full bar. **Address:** 225 Water St E5B 1B3 **Location:** Between King and Frederick sts; centre. **Parking:** street only. L D AC

▼ See AAA listing this page ▼

THE RED HERRING PUB
Phone: 506/529-8455

American
$8-$20

AAA Inspector Notes: This casual pub and eatery offers indoor and outdoor dining on the deck. A pub menu offering hearty portions of various comfort foods includes fish and chips, lobster rolls, burgers, nachos, wings, soups and salads. Several quality beers are on tap. **Bar:** full bar. **Address:** 211 Water St E5B 1B3 **Location:** Just e of King St; center. [L] [D] [AC]

ROSSMOUNT INN DINING ROOM
Phone: 506/529-3351

Canadian
$20-$29

AAA Inspector Notes: The talented chef/owner at this inn offers fine dining with a European flair. The menu changes regularly and includes a variety of fresh local seafood, meat and produce selections. A live lobster and crab tank are featured. Finish with one of the pastry chef's delightful desserts. **Bar:** full bar. **Reservations:** suggested. **Address:** 4599 Rt 127 E5B 2P2 **Location:** On Hwy 127, 3.8 mi (6.3 km) ne; in Rossmount Inn.

[D] [AC]

THE VERANDA RESTAURANT
Phone: 506/529-8823

American
$14-$36

AAA Inspector Notes: The spacious veranda of this restaurant overlooks the gardens at this landmark establishment. Highlights include a fine chowder and salad buffet that can be combined with an artfully presented and well-prepared main entrees. From fresh seafood, including local lobster, to perfectly cooked steak, every meal is a flavorful event. The young staff offer attentive, friendly service. **Bar:** full bar. **Reservations:** suggested. **Address:** 184 Adolphus St E5B 1T7 **Location:** Off Hwy 127; in The Algonquin Hotel & Resort. **Historic** [B] [D] [AC]

CLAM DIGGER TAKE-OUT
Phone: 506/529-8084

[fyi] Not evaluated. A bounty of deep fried cuisine awaits patrons who venture outside of town to this quaint take-out and dairy bar. Portions are ample and include local fresh seafood, burgers, hand-cut fries and their own secret recipe coleslaw. **Address:** Rt 127 E0G 2X0 **Location:** 2 mi (3.2 km) e.

ST. GEORGE (F-3) pop. 1,309

In 1872 St. George became the site of a granite industry, supplying red granite for such important buildings as a cathedral in Boston and the Parliament buildings in Ottawa.

The town is now known for deer hunting as well as trout and salmon fishing. At St. George the Magaguadavic River flows through a scenic narrow gorge, where a fish ladder helps salmon and other fish navigate the falls. Lake Utopia, a few minutes' drive from St. George, boasts smooth sand beaches as well as plentiful fishing.

St. George Tourist Bureau: 13 Adventure Ln., St. George, NB, Canada E5C 3H9. **Phone:** (506) 755-4327.

THE GRANITE TOWN HOTEL
Phone: 506/755-6415

Hotel
$88-$185

Address: 79 Main St E5C 3J4 **Location:** Hwy 1 exit 56, 1.8 mi (3 km) w. **Facility:** 33 units, some efficiencies. 2 stories (no elevator), interior corridors. **Terms:** cancellation fee imposed. **Free Special Amenities:** continental breakfast and high-speed Internet.

 [SAVE] [wifi] / SOME UNITS [ ] [ ]

WHERE TO EAT

BIRCH GROVE RESTAURANT & TAKE-OUT
Phone: 506/755-3131

American
$7-$16

AAA Inspector Notes: This casual eatery has a country theme and serves a variety of fresh seafood and meat entrees, including hot sandwiches, burgers, fish and chips and steaks. Sweet endings include excellent homemade desserts and offerings from the seasonal take-out dairy bar. **Address:** 34 Brunswick St E5C 1A9 **Location:** Hwy 1 exit 52. [L] [D]

ST-JACQUES (B-1) pop. 1,607

St-Jacques Visitor Information Centre: 17412 Trans-Canada Hwy. 2, St-Jacques, NB, Canada E7B 2J8. **Phone:** (506) 735-2747.

ANTIQUE AUTOMOBILE MUSEUM is off Hwy. 2 exit 8 at entrance to de la République Provincial Park. Vintage cars dating 1905-30 as well as a 1974 Bricklin are displayed. **Hours:** Daily 9-8, early June-early Sept. **Cost:** $4; $3.25 (ages 6-18 and 65+); $10 (family). Cash only. **Phone:** (506) 735-2637.

NEW BRUNSWICK BOTANICAL GARDEN is off Hwy. 2 exit 8 at 15 Principale St. More than 80,000 annual, perennial and alpine plants are displayed in an 8.5-hectare (21-acre) setting. Classical music accompanies visitors as they walk through nine thematic gardens and two arboretums. Guided tours are offered by reservation. **Time:** Allow 1 hour minimum. **Hours:** Daily 9-8, July-Aug.; 9-6 in June and Sept. **Cost:** $14; $12 (ages 65+ and students with ID); $7 (ages 5-17); $30 (family). **Phone:** (506) 737-4444. [TI]

SAINT JOHN (E-4) pop. 68,043
• Hotels p. 75 • Restaurants p. 76
• Attractions map p. 73

Saint John, at the mouth of the Saint John River on the Bay of Fundy, is one of the most active seaports on the Atlantic coast. Its deepwater oil terminals handle some of the world's largest ships.

When Samuel de Champlain entered the estuary of the Saint John River on June 24, 1604, he named the river in honor of the saint whose feast day it was. After the American Revolutionary War several thousand United Empire Loyalists settled in Saint John. In 1785 it became the first incorporated city in Canada.

Restoration of the city's waterfront has blended the area's historic flavor with such modern fixtures as a climate-controlled skywalk, linking the central business district with the waterfront; a trade and convention center; hotels; Brunswick and Market squares shopping complexes; Harbour Station Arena; and the Saint John City Market. Harbour Passage, a series of interconnected waterfront parks, recreation areas and historical heritage sites, provides magnificent views of the harbor and Saint John's working port.

Bay Ferries provides year-round car and passenger service from Saint John to Digby, Nova

Scotia, aboard the *Princess of Acadia*. Reservations for the 3-hour crossing are highly recommended and must be picked up 1 hour prior to sailing time; phone (902) 245-2116 or (888) 249-7245.

The Saint John Firefighters Museum, 24 Sydney St., is housed in an 1840 firehouse and features area artifacts, photographs and fire-related memorabilia from the Great Saint John Fire of 1877; phone (506) 633-1840.

Discover Saint John: P.O. Box 1971, Saint John, NB, Canada E2L 4L1. **Phone:** (506) 658-2990 or (866) 463-8639.

Self-guiding tours: The Loyalist Trail, a 90-minute walking tour through downtown Saint John, retraces the footsteps of the city's Loyalist founders. Prince William's Walk, also about 90 minutes, is through the old commercial district along Prince William, Princess and Germain streets. The Victorian Stroll, a 2-hour tour of the downtown residential area, includes the post-1877 architecture found on King Street E. and Orange and Germain streets. The West Side Walk & Drive explores the historic Conway area.

Brochures outlining these tours are available at the following Visitor Information Centres: on the 11th floor of City Hall; on the first floor of Market Square; at the foot of King Street on Market Square; and at both seasonal city tourist information centers, located at Reversing Rapids and Hwy. 1; phone (866) 463-8639.

Shopping areas: Near the waterfront are Brunswick Square and Market Square, where stores offer clothing, accessories, china, pewter and more. Specialty shops can be found along Prince William, Germain, Canterbury, Charlotte, Union and Princess streets. Saint John's largest shopping complex, McAllister Place, is in the eastern part of the city at the corner of McAllister Drive and Westmoreland Road; the 110 stores include Sears, Sobey's and Zellers.

BARBOUR'S GENERAL STORE is at St. Andrew's Square on King Street opposite City Hall. The restored 19th-century country store contains some 2,000 artifacts, including grocery items, china, farm tools and kitchen utensils. The store's pharmacy stocks more than 300 remedies. Interpreters provide historical information. **Hours:** Daily 9-7, June-Sept.; 9-6, late May-early Oct. **Cost:** Donations. **Phone:** (506) 642-2242, (506) 658-2855 in the off-season or (866) 463-8639.

CARLETON MARTELLO TOWER NATIONAL HISTORIC SITE OF CANADA is off Hwy. 1 exit 120 (Digby Ferry) to 454 Whipple St. Completed in 1815, the circular stone fort served a crucial role in the defense of Saint John and its harbor until 1944. The tower offers a panorama of Canada's oldest incorporated city, including the harbor and the Bay of Fundy. The site includes restored 1866 barracks, a restored 1845 powder magazine and a visitor center with exhibits. An 11-minute audiovisual presentation describes the site's history, from its creation during the War of 1812 to the role it played in World War II.

Time: Allow 30 minutes minimum. **Hours:** Daily 10-5:30, June 1-first weekend in Oct. **Cost:** $3.90; $3.40 (ages 65+); $1.90 (ages 6-16); $9.80 (family of 7, maximum two adults). Rates may vary; phone ahead. **Phone:** (506) 636-4011 or TTY (506) 887-6015.

CHERRY BROOK ZOO is at 901 Foster Thurston Dr. in Rockwood Park. The wooded setting is home to 38 species, including lions, tigers and zebras. In a walk through the Vanished Kingdom Park, visitors can see replicas of animals that have become extinct in the past 200 years. **Hours:** Zoo Mon.-Fri. 10-5, Sat.-Sun. and holidays 10-6 (weather permitting). Last admission 1 hour before closing. Vanished Kingdom Park open May-Oct. Closed Christmas. **Cost:** $10.50; $8.50 (ages 13-17 and senior citizens); $5.50 (ages 3-12); $26.50 (family, two adults and two children). **Phone:** (506) 634-1440.

FORT HOWE LOOKOUT, on Magazine St., was built as a British army fortification in 1777 to protect the vital Saint John River area from American privateers and native unrest. A reconstructed blockhouse overlooks the city, and lookouts offer a magnificent panoramic view of the harbor and city. **Hours:** Daily dawn-dusk, Victoria Day weekend-day before Thanksgiving weekend. **Cost:** Free. **Phone:** (866) 463-8639 for Discover Saint John.

HAYWARD AND WARWICK CHINA MUSEUM is at jct. Princess and Germain sts. at 85 Princess St. Fine china, earthenware and souvenir china manufactured from 1785 to the present are on display. Also featured are exhibits about shipping methods and Foley pottery. **Time:** Allow 30 minutes minimum. **Hours:** Mon.-Sat. 10-5. Closed major holidays. **Cost:** Free. **Phone:** (506) 653-9066 or (888) 653-9066.

HORTICULTURAL GARDENS is at 48 Seely St. and Crown St. Established in 1893, the 1.5-hectare (4-acre) gardens are noted for their floral displays. A monument commemorates local men who fought in World War I. Greenhouses contain a variety of annuals and perennials. **Time:** Allow 30 minutes minimum. **Hours:** Daily 8-4. **Cost:** Free. **Phone:** (506) 657-1773.

IRVING NATURE PARK is off Hwy. 1 exit 119B (Catherwood), .5 km (.3 mi.) s., then 3 km (1.9 mi.) e. on Sand Cove Rd. On a peninsula in the Bay of Fundy, this 243-hectare (600-acre) protected ecosystem includes an Acadian forest, tidal pools, a salt marsh estuary, mud flats, a bog and a barrier beach. Some 250 species of migratory birds have been seen in the area.

A road encircles the park, and eight trails enable visitors to explore on foot or bicycle. An observation tower provides panoramic views. An information

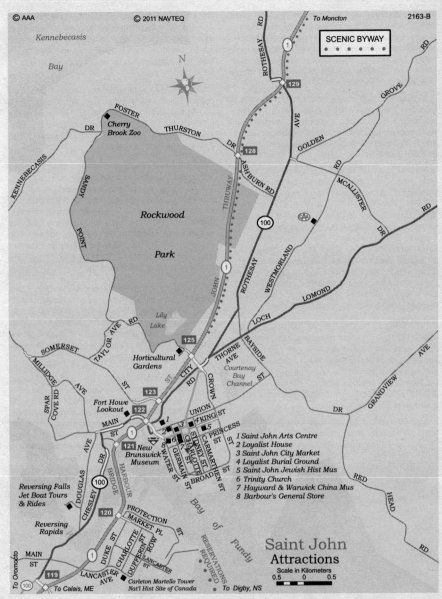

© AAA   © 2011 NAVTEQ   2163-B

Kennebecasis
Bay

SCENIC BYWAY

To Moncton

ROTHESAY RD
129
GROVE RD
FOSTER DR
Cherry Brook Zoo
THURSTON
AVE
GOLDEN
128
ASHBURN RD
MCALLISTER
DR
RD
KENNEBECASIS
SANDY
POINT
Rockwood
Park
100
WESTMORLAND
LOMOND
THRUWAY
RD
JOHN
1
ROTHESAY
LOCH
BAYSIDE
GRANDVIEW AVE
Lily
Lake
125
THORNE AVE
Courtenay
Bay
Channel
SOMERSET
TAYLOR AVE
Horticultural
Gardens
CITY RD
CROWN ST
MILLIDGE AVE
SPAR COVE RD
123
122
Fort Howe
Lookout
MAIN
121
New
Brunswick
Museum
1
UNION
KING ST
PRINCESS
CARMARTHEN ST
RED HEAD RD
Reversing Falls
Jet Boat Tours
& Rides
DOUGLAS
CHESLEY DR
HARBOUR BRIDGE
WATER ST
GERMAIN ST
SYDNEY ST
CHARLOTTE ST
BROADED ST
1 Saint John Arts Centre
2 Loyalist House
3 Saint John City Market
4 Loyalist Burial Ground
5 Saint John Jewish Hist Mus
6 Trinity Church
7 Hayward & Warwick China Mus
8 Barbour's General Store

Reversing
Rapids
100
120
PROTECTION ST
MARKET PL
PRINCE
ROW
DUFFERIN ST
LANCASTER ST
Bay
of
Fundy
RESERVATIONS REQUIRED

Saint John
Attractions
Scale in Kilometers
0.5   0   0.5

MAIN ST
119
1
100
DUKE ST
CHARLOTTE ST
LANCASTER AVE
Carleton Martello Tower
Nat'l Hist Site of Canada
To Oromocto
To Calais, ME   To Digby, NS

---

kiosk is beyond Saints Rest Beach. **Tours:** Guided tours are available. **Hours:** Trails open daily 8-8. Road open May 1-late Oct. **Cost:** Free. **Phone:** (506) 653-7367.

LOYALIST BURIAL GROUND is at Sydney St. and King St. E. Established in 1784, the cemetery once was used as a burial site by United Empire Loyalists. **Hours:** Daily dawn-dusk. **Cost:** Free.

LOYALIST HOUSE is at 120 Union St. at Germain St. The Georgian edifice was built 1810-17 and has

been restored in period. Occupied by the same family for nearly 150 years, the house—the city's oldest unaltered building—survived the Great Fire of 1877. Costumed guides provide historical information about the house and its artifacts. **Hours:** Mon.-Fri. 10-5, May 18-Sept. 15; by appointment rest of year. Last admission 15 minutes before closing. **Cost:** $5; $2 (ages 4-18 and students with ID); $7 (family). **Phone:** (506) 652-3590.

GEM SAVE NEW BRUNSWICK MUSEUM, downtown at 1 Market Sq., relates the natural, industrial and cultural history of the province. Evidence of the area's geological history is seen in the Our Changing Earth gallery; a mastodon skeleton and scorpion fossils are among the highlights. The Hall of Great Whales showcases skeletons and full-scale models of such native whale species as the Right Whale.

Visitors also can view an impressive collection of local and international fine and decorative arts, learn about New Brunswick's shipbuilding heritage and participate in hands-on activities. Historical records are available in the Archives & Research Library at 277 Douglas Ave.

Hours: Museum Mon.-Fri. 9-5 (also Thurs. 5-9), Sat. 10-5, Sun. and holidays noon-5, mid-May through Oct. 31 and during Mar. spring break; Tues.-Fri. 9-5 (also Thurs. 5-9), Sat. 10-5, Sun. and holidays noon-5, rest of year. Archives & Research Library Tues.-Fri. 10-4:30. Closed Jan. 1, Good Friday, Christmas Eve, Christmas, day after Christmas and Dec. 27. **Cost:** Mid-May through Oct. 31 $8; $6 (ages 60+); $4.50 (ages 4-18 and students with ID); $17 (family). Rest of year $7; $5.50 (ages 60+); $4 (ages 4-18 and students with ID); $15 (family). Archives & Research Library free. **Phone:** (506) 643-2300 or (888) 268-9595.

REVERSING FALLS JET BOAT TOURS & RIDES offers sightseeing tours departing from Fallsview Park, 100 Fallsview Ave. A 1-hour narrated boat tour allows passengers to view the Reversing Rapids and whirlpools as well as seals, historic sites, Fort La Tour and Partridge Island. Guides relate the legend of Glooscap, an Indian god who is the guardian of the falls.

Also offered is a 20-minute jet boat thrill ride that takes participants on an accelerated trip through the Reversing Rapids. **Note:** Thrill ride passengers are advised to bring a change of clothing and a towel. This trip is not recommended for pregnant women or those with back problems or other physical impairments. Under 42 inches tall are not permitted on the thrill ride. Children under age 12 must be with an adult.

Time: Allow 1 hour minimum. **Hours:** Trips depart daily 10-dusk, early June-late Sept. **Cost:** Sightseeing tour or thrill ride $43.95; $31.95 (ages 3-12); $135.95 (family, two adults and two children). Reservations are recommended. **Phone:** (506) 634-8987 or (888) 634-8987.

REVERSING RAPIDS is at the mouth of the Saint John River near the foot of Chesley Dr. (Hwy. 100). The reversing "rapids" are created when, at low tide, the river descends into the ocean at the bottom of a 137-metre-wide (449-ft.) gorge. At slack tide the waters are quiet. Then, with the incoming tide, the ocean rises upstream through the chasm. The visitor center at 200 Bridge Rd. offers an excellent view. The phenomenon should be seen at high and low tides to be appreciated fully.

Tide tables are available at CAA Maritimes and tourist bureau offices in Saint John. **Hours:** Visitor center daily 9-7, early June-early Sept.; 9-6, late May-early June and early Sept. to mid-Oct. **Cost:** Visitor center free. **Phone:** (506) 658-2937, (506) 658-2855 during the off-season or (866) 463-8639. ⊞

ROCKWOOD PARK is 2 km (1.2 mi.) n. overlooking Saint John on Mount Pleasant Ave. N. The 870-hectare (2,150-acre) recreational area offers a wide range of year-round outdoor recreation facilities. One of Canada's largest municipal parks, Rockwood contains gardens, nature and riding trails, a large playground, an 18-hole golf course, an arboretum, a

▼ See AAA listing p. 38 ▼

zoo, an aquatic driving range, a camping area and 13 lakes. An interpretation center features exhibits about the park's geology, horticulture and wildlife.

Canoeing, kayaking, sleigh rides, cross-country skiing and ice skating are available. *See Recreation Chart.* Picnicking is permitted; reservations must be made at the interpretation center. **Hours:** Park open daily dawn-dusk. Interpretation center Mon.-Fri. 8:30-4:30. **Cost:** Free. **Phone:** (506) 658-2883, (506) 633-7659 for the riding stables, (506) 634-0090 for the golf course, or (506) 652-4050 for the campground. 🅰️ 🗙

SAINT JOHN ARTS CENTRE is at 20 Hazen Ave. The multi-disciplinary venue serves the community through arts, educational and cultural programming. The building was donated to the community by Andrew Carnegie in 1904. A stained-glass skylight, oak wainscoting, hand-carved fireplace and mosaic tile foyer floor have been restored to their original grandeur. **Hours:** Tues.-Fri. 9-5. Phone ahead to confirm schedule. **Cost:** Donations. **Phone:** (506) 633-4870.

SAINT JOHN BUS TOURS depart from Reversing Rapids, Barbour's General Store or Rockwood Park. Narrated 2-hour bus tours highlight the landmarks of historic Saint John. Passengers can stay on board or exit and re-enter at any of the stops on the tour. **Hours:** Trips depart daily at 9:30, 11:15 and 1, mid-June to early Oct. **Cost:** $20; $5 (ages 6-14). **Phone:** (506) 658-4700.

SAINT JOHN CITY MARKET is at 47 Charlotte St. opposite the n.w. corner of King Sq. The interior of this 1876 building, modeled after an inverted ship's hull, reflects the city's shipbuilding heritage. Described as Canada's oldest charter market, it offers fresh seafood, meat and produce and houses a variety of working artisans, gift shops and eateries. **Time:** Allow 30 minutes minimum. **Hours:** Mon.-Fri. 7:30-6, Sat. 7:30-5. Closed major holidays. **Cost:** Free.

SAINT JOHN JEWISH HISTORICAL MUSEUM is at 91 Leinster St. Considered the only Jewish museum in the Atlantic Provinces, the center features six display areas telling the story of the Saint John Jewish community. Exhibits include a Hebrew school, operational synagogue, a religious display, Jewish artifacts and memorabilia. **Tours:** Guided tours are available. **Time:** Allow 30 minutes minimum. **Hours:** Mon.-Fri. 10-4 (also Sun. 1-4, July-Aug.), late May-late Oct. **Cost:** Donations. **Phone:** (506) 633-1833.

TRINITY CHURCH is at 115 Charlotte St. Built in 1791, the church was destroyed by fire in 1877 and rebuilt in 1880. It contains the Royal Coat of Arms of King George III, which was smuggled out of the Boston State House by Loyalists during the American Revolution. Guided tours are available in the summer. **Hours:** Mon.-Fri. 9-5, July-Aug.; 9-3, rest of year. Phone ahead to confirm schedule. **Cost:** Donations. **Phone:** (506) 693-8558.

BEST WESTERN PLUS SAINT JOHN HOTEL & SUITES
Phone: (506)657-9966

 Hotel $100-$160

 AAA Benefit: Members save up to 20%, plus 10% bonus points with Best Western Rewards®.

Address: 55 Majors Brook Dr E2J 0B2 **Location:** Hwy 1 exit 129 westbound, 1 mi (1.6 km) s on Rt 100 (Rothesay Ave) to McAllister Dr, then just e; exit 128 eastbound, 1 mi (1.6 km) n on Rt 100 (Rothesay Ave), just n to McAllister Dr, then just e. **Facility:** 77 units. 4 stories, interior corridors. **Amenities:** high-speed Internet. **Pool(s):** heated indoor. **Activities:** exercise room. **Guest Services:** coin laundry. **Free Special Amenities: full breakfast and high-speed Internet.**

SAVE 🍽️ CALL 🆓 🚗 BIZ 🛜 🗙 🔌 ▭ / SOME UNITS FEE 🐾 🖻

CHATEAU SAINT JOHN AN ASCEND COLLECTION HOTEL
Phone: (506)644-4444

 Hotel $120-$259

Address: 369 Rockland Rd E2K 3W3 **Location:** Hwy 1 exit 123. **Facility:** 112 units. 6 stories, interior corridors. **Terms:** cancellation fee imposed. **Amenities:** high-speed Internet, safes.

Activities: exercise room. **Guest Services:** valet laundry.

📺 BIZ 🛜 🗙 FEE 🐾 🔌 ▭ / SOME UNITS 🖻

COLONIAL INN SAINT JOHN
Phone: (506)652-3000

 Hotel $114-$130

Address: 175 City Rd E2L 3M9 **Location:** Hwy 1 exit 123. **Facility:** 96 units. 2 stories (no elevator), interior/exterior corridors. **Terms:** cancellation fee imposed. **Pool(s):** heated indoor. **Activities:** sauna, whirlpool, exercise room. **Guest Services:** coin laundry. **Free Special Amenities: local telephone calls and newspaper.**

SAVE 🍽️ 📺 🚗 BIZ 🛜 🔌 / SOME UNITS FEE 🐾

COMFORT INN
Phone: (506)674-1873

 Hotel $114-$140

Address: 1155 Fairville Blvd E2M 5T9 **Location:** Hwy 1 exit 117 westbound; exit 119 eastbound, then left. Located in a commercial area. **Facility:** 59 units. 2 stories (no elevator), interior corridors. **Terms:** cancellation fee imposed. **Amenities:** high-speed Internet.

SAVE ECO 🍽️ FEE 📽️ ▭ / SOME UNITS 🐾 🔌 🖻

DELTA BRUNSWICK
Phone: (506)648-1981

Hotel $99-$199

Address: 39 King St E2L 4W3 **Location:** Centre of downtown; in Brunswick Square Mall. **Facility:** 254 units. 8 stories, interior corridors. **Parking:** on-site (fee). **Terms:** cancellation fee imposed. **Amenities:** video games (fee). Some: high-speed Internet. **Pool(s):** heated indoor. **Activities:** sauna, whirlpool, playground, exercise room. **Guest Services:** valet and coin laundry.

ECO 🍽️ 🧹 📺 🖉 CALL 🆓 🚗 BIZ 🛜 🗙 🔌 🖻 ▭ / SOME UNITS FEE 🐾

ECONO LODGE & SUITES
Phone: (506)635-8700

 Motel $76-$193

Address: 1441 Manawagonish Rd E2M 3X8 **Location:** Hwy 1 exit 119 eastbound, 1.8 mi (3 km) w on Rt 100; exit 117 westbound, 0.3 mi (0.5 km) w on Rt 100. **Facility:** 31 units, some two bedrooms. 2 stories (no elevator), interior/exterior corridors. **Terms:** cancellation fee imposed. **Amenities:** high-speed Internet. **Guest Services:** coin laundry.

🍽️ 🛜 🗙 ▭ / SOME UNITS 🔌 🖻

HAMPTON INN & SUITES
Phone: (506)657-4600

Hotel
$100-$169

AAA Benefit: Members save up to 10% everyday!

Address: 51 Fashion Dr E2J 0A7 **Location:** Hwy 1 exit 129, 1.5 mi (2.4 km) s on Rothesay Ave to Retail Dr; behind Home Depot. **Facility:** 116 units. 4 stories, interior corridors. **Terms:** 1-7 night minimum stay, cancellation fee imposed. **Amenities:** video games (fee), high-speed Internet, safes. **Pool(s):** heated indoor. **Activities:** whirlpool, waterslide, exercise room. **Guest Services:** valet laundry.

HILTON SAINT JOHN
Phone: (506)693-8484

Hotel
$99-$199

AAA Benefit: Members save 5% or more everyday!

Address: 1 Market Square E2L 4Z6 **Location:** Waterfront. Hwy 1 exit 122; at Market Square. Located in a commercial area. **Facility:** 197 units. 10 stories, interior corridors. **Parking:** on-site (fee). **Terms:** 1-7 night minimum stay, cancellation fee imposed. **Amenities:** *Some:* high-speed Internet (fee), safes. **Dining:** The Brigantine Restaurant & Lounge, see separate listing. **Pool(s):** heated indoor. **Activities:** saunas, exercise room. **Guest Services:** valet laundry. **Free Special Amenities:** newspaper and preferred room (subject to availability with advance reservations).

HOLIDAY INN EXPRESS & SUITES
Phone: (506)642-2622

Hotel
$119-$189

Address: 400 Main St/Chesley Dr E2K 4N5 **Location:** 0.6 mi (1 km) w on Hwy 1; north end of Chesley Dr exit 121; off Harbour Bridge. **Facility:** 94 units. 7 stories, interior corridors. **Amenities:** high-speed Internet. **Pool(s):** heated indoor. **Activities:** whirlpool, exercise room. **Guest Services:** valet and coin laundry. **Free Special Amenities:** full breakfast and high-speed Internet.

HOMEPORT HISTORIC INN CIRCA 1858
Phone: (506)672-7255

Historic Bed
& Breakfast
$109-$175

Address: 80 Douglas Ave E2K 1E4 **Location:** Hwy 1 exit 121 eastbound; exit 123 westbound. **Facility:** This appealing hilltop inn offers a variety of tastefully decorated guest units as well as suites with whirlpool baths; some rooms have water views. 10 units, some efficiencies. 2 stories (no elevator), interior corridors. **Terms:** office hours 7 am-10 pm, 4 day cancellation notice.

HOWARD JOHNSON FORT HOWE PLAZA & CONVENTION CENTER
Phone: 506/657-7320

Hotel
Rates not provided

Address: 10 Portland St E2K 4H8 **Location:** Hwy 1 exit 121 eastbound off Harbour Bridge; exit 123 westbound. **Facility:** 133 units. 9 stories, interior corridors. **Pool(s):** heated indoor. **Activities:** whirlpool, exercise room. **Guest Services:** valet laundry. **Free Special Amenities:** local telephone calls and high-speed Internet.

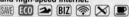

INN ON THE COVE AND SPA
Phone: (506)672-7799

Country Inn
$110-$225

Address: 1371 Sand Cove Rd E2M 4Z9 **Location:** Hwy 1 exit 119A, just s on Bleury St to Sand Cove Rd, then 1.2 mi (2 km) w. **Facility:** Near the Irving Nature Park, this lovely oceanside inn offers tastefully appointed guest rooms with exceptional sea views, some with private balconies. 8 units. 2 stories (no elevator), interior corridors. **Terms:** office hours 8 am-10 pm, 7 day cancellation notice-fee imposed. **Amenities:** high-speed Internet. **Activities:** recreation programs, spa. **Free Special Amenities:** expanded continental breakfast and high-speed Internet.

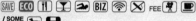

TRAVELODGE SUITES, SAINT JOHN
Phone: 506/635-0400

Hotel
Rates not provided

Address: 1011 Fairville Blvd E2M 5T9 **Location:** Hwy 1 exit 119B eastbound, left on Catherwood Dr, left at lights; exit 119A westbound. Located in a commercial area. **Facility:** 59 units. 3 stories, interior corridors. **Activities:** exercise room. **Guest Services:** coin laundry. **Free Special Amenities:** expanded continental breakfast and high-speed Internet.

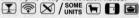

WHERE TO EAT

---

3 MILE STEAKHOUSE & PUB
Phone: 506/657-8325

Steak
$7-$20

AAA Inspector Notes: Popular with sports fans, the steakhouse has numerous TVs and presents a hefty menu with all of the favorite finger foods, as well as steaks, chicken and some seafood entrees, including fish and chips. **Bar:** full bar. **Address:** 1 Golden Grove Rd E2H 1W4 **Location:** At Rothesay Ave. [L] [D]

BIG TIDE BREWING CO.
Phone: 506/214-3311

Canadian
$9-$20

AAA Inspector Notes: There is something for everyone at Saint John's only brew pub. A friendly staff aims to please by dishing up a varied menu alongside excellent beer. **Bar:** full bar. **Address:** 47 Princess St E2L 1M1 **Location:** At Canterbury St; centre. **Parking:** on-site (fee) and street. [L] [D] [LATE]

BILLY'S SEAFOOD RESTAURANT
Phone: 506/672-3474

Seafood
$9-$28

AAA Inspector Notes: In the heart of uptown Saint John, the casually upscale restaurant offers a good selection of fresh seafood dishes and an on-site fish market. Patio dining and jazz music set a relaxing scene in which to feast on lobster, oysters and scallops. **Bar:** full bar. **Address:** 49-51 Charlotte St E2L 2H8 **Location:** Centre; in City Market. **Parking:** on-site (fee). [L] [D]

THE BRIGANTINE RESTAURANT & LOUNGE
Phone: 506/693-8484

American
$8-$28

AAA Inspector Notes: Offering a lovely view of Saint John Harbour, this place invites relaxation over a favorite beverage and classic pub fare. The dinner menu lists a finer selection of meats and fresh seafood. Patio seating is a seasonal option. **Bar:** full bar. **Address:** 1 Market Square E2L 4Z6 **Location:** Hwy 1 exit 122; at Market Square; in Hilton Saint John. **Parking:** on-site (fee).

BRITT'S PUB & EATERY Phone: 506/214-5335

British
$9-$21

AAA Inspector Notes: This pleasant pub offers a variety of well-prepared authentic British fare, including bangers and mash, fish and chips, curry and frites and all-day breakfast. Service is relaxed and friendly. Patio dining is available in season. **Bar:** full bar. **Address:** 42 Princess St E2L 1K2 **Location:** Between Canterbury and Prince William sts; centre. **Parking:** on-site (fee).

[L] [D] [LATE]

CHEZ CORA Phone: 506/634-2672

Canadian
$6-$13

AAA Inspector Notes: Eggs, omelets, waffles, crepes (sorry, no American-style pancakes here), French toast, fruit platters and all the breakfast meats--that's the specialty here, all day. However, at lunchtime the menu lists a selection of soups, salads, quiches, sandwiches and a dish called the grilled panini crepe. **Address:** 39 King St E2L 4W3 **Location:** Centre; in Brunswick Square Mall, Level 3. **Parking:** street only. [B] [L]

CHURCH STREET STEAKHOUSE Phone: 506/648-2374

Steak
$10-$30

AAA Inspector Notes: In the town's old quarter, this restaurant is a fine spot for informal dining in a warm atmosphere. A relaxing decor incorporates rustic elegance with red brick walls and a dark wood-beam ceiling. The specialty is prime cuts of meat, but a selection of well-prepared fresh seafood and a few pasta dishes also are presented. The staff is knowledgeable, friendly and attentive. **Bar:** full bar. **Address:** 10 Grannan's Ln E2L 4S5 **Location:** Corner of Prince William and Church sts; centre. **Parking:** street only. [L] [D]

THE FALLS RESTAURANT Phone: 506/635-1999

American
$8-$25

AAA Inspector Notes: Perched on a rocky ledge overlooking the river and Reversing Falls, guests are offered a splendid view through the large windows. Aged photographs of the falls and environs decorate the walls of the octagon-shaped chandelier room. Atlantic salmon and roast beef are among well-prepared selections. **Bar:** full bar. **Address:** 200 Bridge Rd E2M 7Y9 **Location:** Hwy 1A, 2.5 mi (4 km) sw; at Reversing Falls. [L] [D] [AC]

GRANNAN'S SEAFOOD RESTAURANT Phone: 506/634-1555

Seafood
$9-$25

AAA Inspector Notes: The pleasant, harborside eatery features a casual atmosphere and a bi-level dining room with seasonal patio seating. Including fresh regional seafood, lobsters from a tank and oyster bar preparations, the menu also tempts with pasta and prime rib. **Bar:** full bar. **Address:** 1 Market Square E2L 4Z6 **Location:** Centre; in Market Square. [L] [D]

JADE CITY RESTAURANT Phone: 506/652-1688

Chinese
$8-$18

AAA Inspector Notes: In a convenient mall location, the casual restaurant offers patrons a choice of either booth or table seating. They can choose from the daily buffet, dim sum or selections on the wide menu. **Bar:** full bar. **Address:** 212 McAllister Dr E2J 2S5 **Location:** Centre; in Parkway Mall. [L] [D]

JUNGLE JIM'S Phone: 506/652-5467

Canadian
$8-$19

AAA Inspector Notes: Guests can step into a tropical theme at the casual eatery, which employs a friendly staff and nurtures a bustling atmosphere. The menu lines up a wide variety of comfort foods, salads, chicken, beef, seafood and hot wings, all served in ample, flavorful portions. **Bar:** full bar. **Address:** 87 Prince William St E2L 2B2 **Location:** Centre. **Parking:** on-site (fee) and street. [L] [D]

LEMONGRASS THAI FARE & PEPPERS PUB Phone: 506/657-8424

Thai
$10-$21

AAA Inspector Notes: The pleasant restaurant offers several dining sections and seasonal patio dining. The menu lists a wide variety of well-prepared traditional and creative Thai dishes. **Bar:** full bar. **Address:** 1 Market Square E2L 4Z6 **Location:** Centre; in Market Square. **Parking:** street only. [L] [D] [LATE]

MEDITERRANEAN RESTAURANT Phone: 506/634-3183

American
$7-$18

AAA Inspector Notes: Basic comfort foods ranging from steak and seafood to Greek and Italian dishes are what guests will find on this laid-back restaurant's menu. Family-owned and operated since 1971, the popular spot radiates warmth and friendly charm. The service is pleasant and prompt. **Bar:** full bar. **Address:** 419 Rothesay Rd E2J 2C3 **Location:** Rt 100, 2.5 mi (4 km) ne. [L] [D]

MEXICALI ROSA'S Phone: 506/652-5252

Mexican
$10-$20

AAA Inspector Notes: The Mexican cantina makes an excellent choice for family-friendly fun. Old West paintings and murals add color to stucco walls and wooden beams, while a Tex-Mex menu provides a feast of favorites such as fajitas, burritos and some seafood items. Fried ice cream is a sweet treat. **Bar:** full bar. **Address:** 88 Prince William St E2L 2B3 **Location:** At Princess St; centre. **Parking:** on-site (fee). [L] [D] [LATE] [AC]

SAINT JOHN ALE HOUSE Phone: 506/657-2337

Canadian
$10-$28

AAA Inspector Notes: Overlooking the boardwalk and Saint John Harbour, this spacious historic quarter restaurant has several sections with booth and table seating. The vast menu lists everything from light finger foods to burgers, fish and chips, steaks, fresh seafood and all-day breakfast items. To wash it down, this place offers 29 varieties of beer on tap. **Bar:** full bar. **Address:** 1 Market Square E2L 4Z6 **Location:** Centre; in Market Square. **Parking:** on-site (fee). [L] [D]

STEAMERS LOBSTER COMPANY Phone: 506/648-2325

Seafood
$14-$30

AAA Inspector Notes: The restaurant lives up to its name with lobster, clams and mussels fresh from the tank and into the pots. The atmosphere is upbeat and friendly, with a large patio for seasonal dining. A dinner theater goes on upstairs on Thursday, Friday and Saturday. **Bar:** full bar. **Address:** 110 Water St E2L 4S6 **Location:** Centre; across from cruise ship terminal. **Parking:** street only.

[D] [AC]

SWISS CHALET Phone: 506/657-9477

Chicken
$6-$16

AAA Inspector Notes: The popular restaurant is known for its rotisserie chicken and ribs and the tangy Chalet sauce that gives food its special zip. Diners munch on a half or quarter chicken with sides such as steamed vegetables, fries, baked potatoes and salads. Lunch guests often go for the great soup and sandwich combination. Take-out and delivery service are popular options. **Bar:** full bar. **Address:** 86 Consumer Dr E2J 4Z3 **Location:** At Westmorland Ave.

TACO PICA Phone: 506/633-8492

Mexican
$8-$19

AAA Inspector Notes: A colorful decor and upbeat Latin music infuse this place with energy. The menu offers wonderful authentic Guatemalan, Mexican and Spanish entrees, including such specialties as soft-shell tacos, fajitas and chimichangas. Service is relaxed and friendly. **Bar:** full bar. **Address:** 96 Germain St E2L 4W3 **Location:** Corner of Grannan St. **Parking:** street only. [L] [D]

THANDI Phone: 506/648-2377

International
$11-$25

AAA Inspector Notes: Thandi's is a lovely, bi-level restaurant. The cuisine fuses flavors of East and West. Menu choices range from fresh local seafood, including a fabulous platter, to steaks, pork, chicken and some wonderful, authentic Indian dishes. **Bar:** full bar. **Address:** 33 Canterbury St E2L 2C6 **Location:** Just s of King St.

[L] [D]

VITO'S RESTAURANT Phone: 506/634-3900

Italian
$8-$21

AAA Inspector Notes: This popular, conveniently located restaurant offers two levels of seating. An interesting mix of Italian, Greek and Canadian cuisines, the menu includes pizza, lasagna, chicken souvlaki, sandwiches and baklava. Both booth and table seating overlooking the street are available. A casual level of service is offered at this bustling restaurant. **Bar:** full bar. **Address:** 1 Hazen Ave E2L 3G6 **Location:** Corner of Union St. [L] [D]

VITO'S RESTAURANT Phone: 506/634-1300

Italian
$8-$21

AAA Inspector Notes: This popular, spacious restaurant displays a pleasant, modern decor. On the menu is a wide variety of Italian dishes, including pizza. Take-out orders are accepted. Breakfast is served on Sunday starting at 8 am. **Bar:** full bar. **Address:** 324 Rothesay Ave E2H 2C2 **Location:** Hwy 1 exit 129, 1.2 mi (2 km) w on Rt 100. [L] [D]

VIVALDI'S RESTAURANT Phone: 506/633-1414

Italian
$8-$23

AAA Inspector Notes: Combining a fine blend of Italian and Lebanese specialties, one should add this casually upscale restaurant to their list. On the menu are fine-quality pasta dishes, kebabs, salads, homemade soups, breads and desserts. Lunch is more casual with daily specials. **Bar:** full bar. **Address:** 337 Rothesay Ave E2J 2C3 **Location:** Hwy 1 exit 129, 2 mi (3.3 km) sw on Rt 100.

[L] [D]

ST-LEONARD pop. 1,039

DAIGLE'S MOTEL Phone: (506)423-6351

Hotel
$94-$104 6/1-9/30
$83-$91 10/1-5/31

Address: 68 rue DuPont E7E 1Y1 **Location:** Hwy 17, 0.6 mi (1 km) s of Trans-Canada Hwy 2 exit 58. **Facility:** 50 units. 2 stories (no elevator), exterior corridors. **Parking:** winter plug-ins. **Terms:** office hours 7 am-midnight. **Dining:** restaurant, see separate listing. **Pool(s):** heated outdoor. **Free Special Amenities:** local telephone calls and high-speed Internet.

[SAVE] [🍴] [🏊] [📶] / SOME UNITS FEE [🐾]

WHERE TO EAT

DAIGLE'S DINING ROOM & LOUNGE
  Phone: 506/423-6351

American
$7-$19

AAA Inspector Notes: . Floral arrangements add splashes of color to the casual, family eatery. A widely varied menu offers something for all tastes, from prime rib to scallops to fish 'n' chips. **Bar:** full bar. **Address:** 68 rue DuPont E7E 1Y1 **Location:** Hwy 17, 0.6 mi (1 km) s of Trans-Canada Hwy 2 exit 58; in Daigle's Motel.

[B] [L] [D]

ST. MARTINS (E-4) pop. 386

Settled around 1783, Quaco, as St. Martins first was known, became one of the most prosperous shipbuilding centers in eastern Canada. More than 500 ships were built in a dozen family boatyards during the next 100 years. The era of great sailing ships left its imprint on the town's homes as ship's carpenters decorated them with elaborate architectural details.

Complementing these historic houses are a lighthouse and twin covered bridges. These as well as the rugged setting have made St. Martins a popular scene for photographers and painters.

 FUNDY TRAIL is 10 km (6 mi.) e. off Hwy. 111. This multi-use parkway follows the northern coast of the Bay of Fundy between St. Martins and Fundy National Park of Canada, offering spectacular views of the Quaco Head Lighthouse, Melvin and Pangburn beaches, Fuller Falls and coastal wildlife. A 16-kilometre (10-mi.) low-speed roadway features scenic lookouts; 16 kilometres (10 mi.) of walking and bicycling trails include footpaths to beaches and river estuaries.

At the Big Salmon River Interpretive Centre visitors may cross a suspension foot bridge and see old wharfs and sluices, remnants of the river's lumbering days. The center features a videotape presentation and artifacts related to local history.

Various 2- and 4-hour guided walking tours are available. **Time:** Allow 2 hours minimum. **Hours:** Trail daily 6 a.m.-8 p.m., mid-May to mid-Oct. Interpretive center daily 8-8, mid-May to mid-Oct. **Cost:** $4.50; $4 (ages 65+); $3 (ages 0-12); $16 (family, two adults and two children). Guided walking tours $3.50. **Phone:** (506) 833-2019 or (866) 386-3987.

[🍴] [🏕]

QUACO MUSEUM AND LIBRARY is at 236 Main St. The history and heritage of the St. Martins area is preserved. The museum's main exhibits, which change annually, often deal with shipbuilding—the most important economic and social aspect of the region. Photographs trace the village's growth and show the area's more prominent topographical and geologic features. The archives contain genealogical research material.

Hours: Daily 10-5, July-Aug.; Thurs.-Sun. 1-4 in Sept.; by appointment rest of year. **Cost:** Donations. **Phone:** (506) 833-4740, or (506) 833-2553 in the off-season.

ST. MARTINS COUNTRY INN Phone: (506)833-4534

Country Inn
$105-$175

Address: 303 Main St E5R 1C1 **Location:** Centre. **Facility:** Dating from 1857, this striking Queen Anne mansion with a newer annex offers varied rooms, some with bay views and some with balconies. 16 units. 3 stories (no elevator). **Terms:** open 6/1-10/31 & 5/1-5/31, office hours 7 am-11 pm, 7 day cancellation notice-fee imposed. [🍴] [📶]

TIDAL WATCH INN Phone: (506)833-4772

Country Inn
$110-$225

Address: 16 Beach St E5R 1C7 **Location:** Centre. **Facility:** Well-appointed rooms are featured in both the main inn and a newer annex; many rooms have electric fireplaces. 15 units. 2 stories (no elevator), interior/exterior corridors. **Terms:** open 6/1-10/31 & 5/1-5/31, office hours 8 am-10 pm, 7 day cancellation notice. [🍴] [🍷] [📶] [✕] [💻]

WESTLAN INN

Bed & Breakfast
Rates not provided

Phone: 506/833-2351
Address: 45 Main St E5R 1B4
Location: Just e off Rt 111. **Facility:** A former sea captain's home, the lovely 1844 house features individually decorated rooms; most have a fireplace and a whirlpool bath. 3 units. 2 stories (no elevator), interior corridors. **Terms:** seasonal, office hours 8 am-9 pm.

 / SOME UNITS

WHERE TO EAT

JERE'S FAMILY RESTAURANT & COFFEE SHOP
Phone: 506/833-1997

American
$8-$21

AAA Inspector Notes: A pleasant, country-style family restaurant just a block from the sea, this spot offers a good selection of fresh seafood and meat options, as well as salads, soups and sandwiches. Open at 9 am for late breakfast. **Bar:** full bar. **Address:** 7 Beach St E5R 1C6 **Location:** At Main St; centre. B L D

SAINT-QUENTIN

AUBERGE EVASION DE REVES INN
Phone: 506/235-3551

Motel
Rates not provided

Address: 11 Canada St E8A 1J2 **Location:** Waterfront. 1 mi (1.6 km) w on Rt 17. **Facility:** 14 units. 1 story, interior corridors. **Pool(s):** heated indoor. **Activities:** whirlpool.

 / SOME UNITS

ST. STEPHEN (F-2) pop. 4,780

St. Stephen is on the banks of the tidal St. Croix River, which is the boundary between Canada and the United States; the 7-metre (24-ft.) tides rise and fall twice daily. The International Ferry Point Bridge (Main Street) leads to Calais, Maine, the town's nearest neighbor and closest friend. That friendship hit its acme during the War of 1812, when St. Stephen lent a supply of gunpowder to Calais so that both communities could enjoy Independence Day celebrations rather than engaging in war.

The friendship continues to be obvious during the International Festival in early August, which includes a cross-border parade, entertainment, sporting events and fireworks, typifying the St. Stephen-Calais cooperation.

Chocolate sweetens the spirit of collaboration during the Chocolate Festival in early August. This event, with its chocolate dinners, contests and demonstrations, commemorates the introduction of the chocolate bar, which is reputed to have been created locally at the Ganong Bros. candy factory in 1906; the factory also created the first heart-shaped Valentine's Day candy box.

St. Stephen Provincial Visitor Information Centre: 5 King St., St. Stephen, NB, Canada E3L 2C1. **Phone:** (506) 466-7390.

SAVE **THE CHOCOLATE MUSEUM** is at 73 Milltown Blvd. Highlights include hands-on exhibits, interactive computer displays, a candy-making video, games, and collections of historic chocolate boxes and antique equipment from the candy-making company founded by the Ganong brothers in 1873.

Chocolate samples are available. The Heritage Chocolate Walk is a guided 2- to 3-hour walking tour of the museum and St. Stephen's historic buildings.

Comfortable walking shoes are recommended. **Hours:** Mon.-Sat. 9:30-6:30, Sun. 11-3, July-Aug.; Mon.-Fri. 10-4, Mar.-June and Oct.-Nov. Closed Easter, Victoria Day, Thanksgiving and Remembrance Day. Heritage Chocolate Walk offered late June-Aug. 31. Phone ahead to confirm schedule. **Cost:** Museum $7; $6 (ages 5-21 and 60+); $22 (family, four people). Heritage Chocolate Walk $13; $10 (ages 5-21 and 60+); $5 (ages 0-4); $40 (family, four people). Rates may vary; phone ahead. Reservations are recommended for the Heritage Chocolate Walk. **Phone:** (506) 466-7848.

BLAIR HOUSE HERITAGE INN B&B
Phone: (506)466-2233

Historic Bed
& Breakfast
$94-$119 6/1-10/8
$94-$109 10/9-5/31

Address: 38 Prince William St E3L 1S3 **Location:** Centre. Located in a residential area. **Facility:** First- and second-floor rooms with a view of the river are featured at this pleasant 1850s-era home. 5 units. 2 stories (no elevator), interior corridors. **Terms:** check-in 4 pm, 3 day cancellation notice.

ST. STEPHEN INN
Phone: (506)466-1814

Motel
$55-$130

Address: 99 King St E3L 2C6 **Location:** Just n of Prince William St; centre. **Facility:** 51 units. 2 stories (no elevator), interior/exterior corridors. **Parking:** winter plug-ins.

/ SOME UNITS FEE

WINSOME INN
Phone: (506)466-2130

Motel
$92-$129 6/1-11/20
$92-$110 11/21-5/31

Address: 198 King St E3L 2E2 **Location:** Hwy 1 exit King St, just s on Rt 3. **Facility:** 39 units. 1 story, exterior corridors. **Pool(s):** heated outdoor. **Activities:** playground, volleyball. **Free Special Amenities:** expanded continental breakfast and high-speed Internet.

SAVE / SOME UNITS FEE

WHERE TO EAT

CARMAN'S DINER
Phone: 506/466-3528

Canadian
$6-$15

AAA Inspector Notes: Popular for basic fare at reasonable prices, the restaurant has been around forever. Choices range from sandwiches, burgers and fish and chips to steak and seafood. Parking is plentiful. **Address:** 164 King St E3L 2W9 **Location:** On Hwy 1; centre. B L D

RED ROOSTER COUNTRY RESTAURANT
Phone: 506/466-0018

Canadian
$7-$15

AAA Inspector Notes: Painted murals on the walls contribute to the casual restaurant's early country and Western theme. Home-style cooking includes everything from sandwiches and burgers to steak and seafood. Homemade pies and pastries are a special treat. Service is friendly and relaxed. **Bar:** full bar. **Address:** 5 Old Bay Rd E3L 3W7 **Location:** 1.6 (2.5 km) e on Rt 170.

 B L D

SHEDIAC (D-5) pop. 5,497

Known for its excellent beaches and the warmest water north of Virginia, Shediac claims to be the lobster capital of the world. The 5-day Shediac Lobster Festival takes place in early July and includes a sand sculpture contest at nearby Parlee Beach Provincial Park *(see Recreation Chart)*.

Shediac Visitor Information Bureau: 229 Main St., Shediac, NB, Canada E4P 2A5. **Phone:** (506) 532-7788.

AUBERGE INN THYME
Phone: 506/532-6098

Historic Bed & Breakfast
$95-$150

Address: 310 Main St E4P 2E3 **Location:** Centre. **Facility:** Each guest room is tastefully decorated at this elegant 1912 Victorian mansion; the property has a maximum two person per room policy. 7 units. 2 stories (no elevator), interior corridors. **Terms:** open 6/1-10/30, office hours 9 am-9 pm, 3 day cancellation notice-fee imposed.

GAUDET CHALETS & MOTEL
Phone: 506/533-8877

Motel
Rates not provided

Address: 14 Bellevue Heights E4P 1H2 **Location:** On Rt 133, 1.4 mi (2.4 km) w of Rt 15 exit 37. **Facility:** 46 units, some kitchens and cottages. 1 story, exterior corridors. **Terms:** seasonal, office hours 8 am-10 pm, check-in 4 pm. **Activities:** playground.

MAISON TAIT HOUSE 1911
Phone: (506)532-4233

Historic Country Inn
$189-$229 6/1-9/30
$159-$199 10/1-5/31

Address: 293 Main St E4P 2A8 **Location:** Opposite Town Hall; downtown. **Facility:** A variety of tastefully decorated guest rooms are available, many with an electric fireplace and a few with a soaker tub. 9 units. 2 stories (no elevator), interior corridors. **Terms:** office hours 7 am-11 pm, 2 night minimum stay - seasonal and/or weekends, cancellation fee imposed.

SEELY'S MOTEL
Phone: (506)532-6193

Motel
$80-$185

Address: 21 Bellevue Heights E4P 1G9 **Location:** On Rt 133, 1.5 mi (2.4 km) w of Rt 15 exit 37. **Facility:** 32 units, some efficiencies. 2 stories (no elevator), exterior corridors. **Terms:** 3 day cancellation notice-fee imposed. **Pool(s):** heated indoor. **Guest Services:** coin laundry. **Free Special Amenities:** continental breakfast and high-speed Internet.

WHERE TO EAT

BAYOU RESTAURANT & PUB
Phone: 506/533-9008

Canadian
$8-$18

AAA Inspector Notes: Offerings at the casual pub include quick-serve appetizers, as well as preparations from the full menu. Patio seating is a seasonal option. **Bar:** full bar. **Address:** 607 Main St E4P 8C7 **Location:** Rt 15 exit 37, 1.4 mi (2.4 km) w of Rt 15 on Rt 133.

GABRIELE RESTAURANT
Phone: 506/532-8007

American
$8-$23

AAA Inspector Notes: This spacious restaurant offers a variety of dining options, including several indoor areas as well as open and screened decks. Specializing in seafood, they also offer steak, chicken and pasta dishes. **Bar:** full bar. **Address:** 296 Main St E4P 2E3 **Location:** At Chesley Rd.

THE LOBSTER DECK BAR & GRILL
Phone: 506/351-2010

Seafood
$9-$26

AAA Inspector Notes: This popular restaurant offers relaxed dining indoors or outside on the patio where an evening breeze can be enjoyed. An extensive selection of fresh seafood includes such favorites as the shrimp plate, delicious boiled lobster, fish and chips and various sandwiches and burgers. **Bar:** full bar. **Address:** 312 Main St E4P 2E3 **Location:** Hwy 11 exit 1 northbound, 1.1 mi (1.8 km) e; exit 2A southbound, follow signs to town; centre.

SHIPPAGAN (B-5) pop. 2,872

Of Mi'kmaq origin, the word Shippagan means "passageway for ducks." The town, at the northeastern tip of the Acadian Peninsula, was the site of a Jesuit settlement 1634-62. During that period Nicholas Denys established a trading post that drew Acadian fishermen to the area. Commercial fishing now leads the town's economic concerns. Vast bogs provide major harvests of peat moss.

Municipality of Shippagan: 200 Ave. Hotel De Ville, Shippagan, NB, Canada E8S 1M1. **Phone:** (506) 336-3900.

NEW BRUNSWICK AQUARIUM AND MARINE CENTRE is on Hwy. 113 off Hwy. 11. A modern building sits amid spacious grounds overlooking Chaleur Bay. The center depicts the effect of the sea on life along New Brunswick's northeast coast since the 1500s. Exhibits relate to fishermen, ships and boats; aquariums display more than 100 species of marine life.

A 20-minute audiovisual presentation explains the fishing history of the Gulf of St. Lawrence. The cabin of a reconstructed modern trawler allows visitors to see the array of electronic devices now used in the fishing industry. Educational feeding sessions are held twice daily for the aquarium's harbor seals. **Time:** Allow 2 hours minimum. **Hours:** Daily 10-6, early June-late Sept. **Cost:** $8.50; $6.50 (ages 65+ and students ages 17+ with ID); $5.50 (ages 6-16); $23 (family). **Phone:** (506) 336-3013.

SUSSEX (E-4) pop. 4,241

Sussex is a traditional town at the juncture of Fundy Coastal Scenic Drive and the River Valley Scenic Drive in the heart of Kings County, known for its covered bridges. Covered to protect the flooring and timbers from the effects of sun and rain, the 16 bridges stand throughout the county; more than half are within a 12-kilometre (7-mi.) radius of Sussex. Oldfield, a 30-metre-long (98-ft.) bridge that spans Smiths Creek, was featured on a commemorative 25-cent coin in 1992.

The "kissing bridges," still romantic spots for courting couples, also are popular with the wishful. Local lore says riders' wishes come true if they can hold their breath and lift their feet from the car's floorboards until the car has traveled the span. Maps detailing bridge sites can be obtained from the Sussex and Area Tourist Interpretive Centre off Hwy. 1 exit 195.

Covered Bridge Visitor Information Centre:
11001 Rte. 10, Youngs Cove, NB, Canada E4C
2G5. **Phone:** (506) 362-2632.

ALL SEASONS INN Phone: (506)433-2220

Motel
$69-$139

Address: 1015 Main St E4E 2M6 **Location:** Hwy 1 exit 192 eastbound; exit 198 westbound, left towards Sussex Corner; centre. Located in a quiet rural area. **Facility:** 23 units, some efficiencies. 1 story, exterior corridors. **Parking:** winter plug-ins. **Terms:** 3 day cancellation notice-fee imposed. **Dining:** restaurant, see separate listing.

AMSTERDAM INN & SUITES Phone: (506)432-5050

Hotel
$129-$169

Address: 143 Main St E4E 1S8 **Location:** Hwy 1 exit 192. Opposite Gateway Mall. **Facility:** 31 units. 2 stories (no elevator), interior/exterior corridors. **Terms:** cancellation fee imposed.

FAIRWAY INN Phone: (506)433-3470

Hotel
$125-$175

Address: 216 Roachville Rd E4E 5L6 **Location:** Hwy 1 exit 193. **Facility:** 54 units, some efficiencies. 2 stories (no elevator), interior/exterior corridors. **Terms:** cancellation fee imposed. **Dining:** J J's Diner, see separate listing. **Pool(s):** heated indoor. **Activities:** sauna, whirlpool. **Guest Services:** coin laundry.

PINE CONE MOTEL Phone: 506/433-3958

Motel
Rates not provided

Address: 12808 Rt 114 E4E 5L9 **Location:** Hwy 1 exit 198, 1.2 mi (2 km) e on Rt 114 towards Penobsquis. **Facility:** 20 units. 1 story, exterior corridors. **Terms:** check-in 4 pm.

WHERE TO EAT

ALL SEASONS RESTAURANT Phone: 506/433-2220

Canadian
$7-$17

AAA Inspector Notes: In a spacious log building with fireplaces, this relaxed, family-oriented restaurant delivers a wide range of favorites. Selections include chicken cordon bleu, ribs, lasagna and lobster rolls. Nice music plays in the background. **Bar:** full bar. **Address:** 1015 Main St E4E 2M6 **Location:** Hwy 1 exit 192 eastbound; exit 198 westbound, left towards Sussex Corner; centre; in All Seasons Inn.

BROADWAY CAFE Phone: 506/433-5414

Regional American
$8-$26

AAA Inspector Notes: In a cozy setting of wrought iron and antique mirrors, a menu of creative meat and seafood entrées, excellent homemade bread and rich dessert, awaits your delight. Enjoy a steaming cup of cappuccino or espresso with a slice of white chocolate pecan pie. The service is very casual and unhurried. They also offer a nice patio area for in-season dining. **Bar:** full bar. **Address:** 73 Broad St E4E 2J7 **Location:** Centre; opposite The Old Train Station.

BUCHANAN'S BACKYARD GRILL Phone: 506/433-5446

Canadian
$7-$21

AAA Inspector Notes: This casual eatery serves home-style cooking in a relaxed atmosphere with a choice of booth or table seating. Menu items range from burgers, sandwiches and wraps to fried chicken, steaks and some seafood. **Bar:** full bar. **Address:** 600 Main St E4E 2M5 **Location:** Centre.

CATHY'S CHINESE RESTAURANT Phone: 506/433-4007

Chinese
$8-$17

AAA Inspector Notes: In the heart of town, the cozy restaurant presents a menu of varied Oriental dishes, as well as some Canadian items. **Address:** 612 Main St E4E 7H8 **Location:** Centre. **Parking:** street only.

J J'S DINER Phone: 506/433-3470

Canadian
$7-$21

AAA Inspector Notes: In a handy location bordering the highway, this restaurant has an upbeat atmosphere, thanks in part to its 1950s theme. Patrons can choose either booth or table seating. Menu offerings feature such comfort foods as burgers, fries, soups and sandwiches to fresh seafood and steak. Save room for a slice of one of the homemade pies. **Bar:** full bar. **Address:** 216 Roachville Rd E4E 5L6 **Location:** Hwy 1 exit 193; in Fairway Inn.

THE MASON JAR SPEAK EASY & CABARET Phone: 506/433-6489

American
$8-$22

AAA Inspector Notes: This popular restaurant offers dining on two levels with live music several nights a week. Comfortable booth and table seating can be found in a relaxed atmosphere. The food is well-prepared and the menu selection is ample from finger foods to burgers, sandwiches, fish and chips, fine salads, soups and fresh seafood. Try and save room for the sticky date pudding. **Bar:** full bar. **Address:** 63 Broad St E4E 2J7 **Location:** Opposite The Old Train Station; downtown. **Parking:** street only.

TRACADIE-SHEILA

LE CHATEAU D'ACADIE Phone: 506/395-7565

Bed & Breakfast
$107-$160

Address: 3559 rue Principale E1X 1C9 **Location:** Corner of rue de l'Eglese. **Facility:** Located in the heart of town, the attractive 1939 home offers tastefully decorated guest rooms with modern amenities. 5 units. 2 stories (no elevator), interior corridors. **Terms:** office hours 8 am-11 pm, cancellation fee imposed. **Amenities:** high-speed Internet. **Guest Services:** complimentary laundry.

COMPLEXE LES DEUX RIVIERES Phone: 506/394-4050

[fyi] Not evaluated. **Address:** 100 rue Deux Rivieres E1X 1C9 **Location:** Just e of Rt 11; centre. Facilities, services, and decor characterize a mid-scale property.

WHERE TO EAT

CAPITAINE FRANK FRUITS DE MER RESTAURANT Phone: 506/395-7001

Seafood
$9-$22

AAA Inspector Notes: This is a local favorite specializing in fresh seafood including lobster, shrimp, scallops, haddock and cod. The wonderful seafood chowder should not be missed. For the landlubber, they have burgers, chicken and steaks. Decorated in a nautical theme, this spacious restaurant has comfortable booths along the walls with tables in the center and an option to dine on the patio in season. **Bar:** full bar. **Address:** 3377 Dr Victor LeBlanc Blvd E1X 1A4 **Location:** Corner of Snowball St; center.

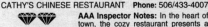

RESTAURANT L'ETOILE DE LA MER
Phone: 506/395-9413

American
$7-$21

AAA Inspector Notes: Located in the heart of town, this pleasant eatery offers a wide range of foods, from homemade soups and salads to burgers, fish and chips, fresh seafood and steaks. Patio dining is a nice option in season. **Bar:** full bar. **Address:** 352 rue du Quai E1X 1A4 **Location:** Corner of Main and Quai sts. B L D

WOODSTOCK (D-2) pop. 5,198

Woodstock is a major border-crossing point with the United States and the oldest incorporated town in New Brunswick. Largely settled by Loyalists after the American Revolution, it is now nestled between the Trans-Canada Hwy. and the Saint John River. The river affords much recreational activity, as do the Trans Canada Trail System and the N.B. Snowmobile Federation Trail.

Woodstock Provincial Visitor Information Centre: 109 Richmond Corner, Tourist Bureau Rd., Woodstock, NB, Canada E7M 4W8. **Phone:** (506) 325-4427.

OLD CARLETON COUNTY COURT HOUSE is 2 km (1.2 mi.) n. on Hwy. 560 via Hwy. 103 at 19 Court St. The court house is restored to its mid-1800s appearance. Highlights include the old jury and prisoner's rooms as well as the main courtroom and the judge's chamber. **Hours:** Tues.-Sat. 10-6, July-Aug.; by appointment rest of year. **Cost:** Donations. **Phone:** (506) 328-9706.

BEST WESTERN PLUS WOODSTOCK HOTEL AND CONFERENCE CENTRE
Phone: (506)328-2378

Hotel
$125-$150

AAA Benefit: Members save up to 20%, plus 10% bonus points with Best Western Rewards®.

Address: 123 Gallop Ct E7M 3P7 **Location:** Trans-Canada Hwy 2 exit 185. **Facility:** 67 units. 3 stories, interior corridors. **Amenities:** high-speed Internet. **Pool(s):** heated indoor. **Activities:** exercise room. **Guest Services:** coin laundry. **Free Special Amenities:** expanded continental breakfast and high-speed Internet.

CANADAS BEST VALUE INN & SUITES
Phone: (506)328-8876

Hotel
$70-$120

Address: 168 Rt 555 E7M 6B5 **Location:** Trans-Canada Hwy 2 exit 188 (Houlton Rd). **Facility:** 50 units. 3 stories (no elevator), interior/exterior corridors. **Parking:** winter plug-ins. **Amenities:** *Some:* high-speed Internet. **Pool(s):** heated outdoor. **Guest Services:** coin laundry.

HOWARD JOHNSON INN
Phone: (506)328-3315

Hotel
$59-$125

Address: 159 Rt 555 exit 188 TCH E7M 6B5 **Location:** Trans-Canada Hwy 2 exit 188 (Houlton Rd). **Facility:** 53 units, some kitchens. 1-2 stories (no elevator), interior/exterior corridors. **Parking:** winter plug-ins. **Terms:** cancellation fee imposed. **Pool(s):** heated indoor. **Activities:** sauna, playground, exercise room. **Guest Services:** coin laundry.

FUSION COFFEE COMPANY
Phone: 506/328-6942

Canadian
$7-$16

AAA Inspector Notes: A quaint and casual bistro with a blackboard menu serving a wide variety of specialty imported coffees and teas. To complement your beverage they offer a delightful array of homemade desserts, sandwiches, wraps and tasty soups. **Bar:** full bar. **Address:** 612 Main St E7M 2C4 **Location:** At King St; centre. B L D

THE RIVERSIDE NEIGHBOURHOOD PUB
Phone: 506/325-2337

American
$6-$18

AAA Inspector Notes: This popular sports pub offers a seasonal patio overlooking the St. John River. A vast array of menu options include steak, seafood, chicken and burgers served in ample portions. **Bar:** full bar. **Address:** 558 Main St E7M 2C3 **Location:** Just e of Broadway St; centre. L D

YOUNGS COVE

MCCREADY'S MOTEL
Phone: 506/362-2916

Motel
Rates not provided

Address: 10995 Rt 10 E4C 2G5 **Location:** Trans-Canada Hwy 2 exit 365, just w at Irving One Stop. Located in a quiet rural area. **Facility:** 10 units. 1 story, exterior corridors. **Parking:** winter plug-ins. **Terms:** office hours 6 am-11 pm. **Dining:** McCready's Restaurant, see separate listing.

MCCREADY'S RESTAURANT
Phone: 506/362-2916

American
$5-$15

AAA Inspector Notes: For casual, home-style cooking, this diner is a convenient stop midway between Fredericton and Moncton. **Address:** 10995 RT 10 E4C 2G5 **Location:** Trans-Canada Hwy 2 exit 365, just w at Irving One Stop; in McCready's Motel. B L D

Complete Vacation Planning

AAA.com/Travel and **CAA.ca/Travel** – everything you need to plan and book your vacations, backed by the travel experts at local AAA/CAA offices.

Gros Morne National Park of Canada

Newfoundland and Labrador

Journey to Newfoundland and Labrador, and a friendly native may ask, "What brings you here?"

Surprisingly, your best response might be "other visitors," for despite its remoteness, Newfoundland and Labrador has long been a crossroads for all sorts of fascinating travelers.

Take icebergs, for example. In spring and early summer, these arctic voyagers parade down "Iceberg Alley" courtesy of the southerly flowing Labrador Current. They've been on the move for thousands of years: first as compacted snow trapped in Greenland's slowly flowing glaciers, then up to 3 years more as seaborne bergs.

By the time they reach Newfoundland and Labrador, most have melted down to house- or car-sized "growlers" and smaller chunks called "bergy bits." Many, however, glide offshore as awesome blue-and-white giants sculpted by wind and waves into fantastic shapes replete with spires, domes and

Watch Ice Formations Travel Down "Iceberg Alley"

arches—invariably evoking images of castles and cathedrals.

With its myriad promontories jutting into the North Atlantic, Newfoundland and Labrador's east coast offers countless spots from which to observe this seasonal procession: Try Long Point, near Twillingate; Notre Dame Bay or St. Anthony.

For a closer encounter, take a boat tour out to the ice. Trips depart from numerous ports, including Newman Sound Wharf in Terra Nova National Park of Canada. From here your chances of spying an itinerant berg are great April through July, but even if you arrive during Iceberg Alley's slack time, the park's scenery won't disappoint.

Icebergs aren't the only behemoths to watch for: Humpback whales tarry along the shoreline from May through August, with some remaining into December. Using binoculars you can spot these migrating mammals from good ol' terra firma, but a nautical jaunt is by far the better choice. What's more, several tour operators double your pleasure by offering combination whale- and bird-watching trips.

Each year about 40 million seabirds pay a visit to the province. At Cape St. Mary's Ecological Reserve, thousands of gannets crowd atop vertigo-inducing cliffs high above the Atlantic. Baccalieu Island teems with millions of storm petrels, and Labrador's Gannet Island supports a multitude of razorbills.

The Atlantic puffin—the provincial bird—is the one most closely identified with Newfoundland and Labrador. Board a sightseeing boat at Bay Bulls or Witless Bay, just south of St. John's, for a tour of the Witless Bay Islands, home to thousands of these orange-beaked, feathered friends.

Doorstep to the New World

Perched at the easternmost edge of North America, Newfoundland and Labrador thrusts into the Atlantic like an outstretched hand welcoming visitors. Evidence at L'Anse aux Meadows National Historic Site of Canada shows that the first Europeans to accept this geographical invitation were 11th-century Norsemen.

Discovered in 1960, eight grassy ridges at the site yielded iron boat nails, proving a Viking settlement had existed there. Today you can step inside one of three re-created Scandinavian-style sod houses like those built at L'Anse aux Meadows a thousand years ago.

Experts believe Newfoundland and Labrador's abundant timber lured Vikings to its shores. No matter what entices you to add your name to the province's lengthy list of visitors, rest assured you'll be in excellent company.

Recreation

Meadows blanketed in wildflowers, waves rolling onto sandy shores or crashing against tall cliffs, cool lakes and rivers—nature presents beautiful backdrops for adventure.

How about dropping a line in a salmon river or trout stream? The Gander and Humber rivers are known for record-size Atlantic salmon; fishing there or in any of the nearly 200 salmon rivers requires a license. On Newfoundland and much of Labrador, licensed fishing guides must accompany non-residents on salmon fishing trips. There are hundreds of other rivers, ponds and lakes where a license is not required that are full of brook trout and Arctic char.

Ice fishing on various frozen lakes and hunting by bow or rifle for moose, caribou and black bears also are popular pastimes.

Don't pass up a trip to beautiful Gros Morne National Park of Canada. Hike Baker's Brook Falls Trail, which terminates in front of the large, multilevel waterfall for which it's named. Or take to the Trout River Pond Trail—it follows the north shore of Trout River Small Pond through a boreal forest into a lush valley, where it meets Trout River Big Pond.

Break out the paddles and go kayaking in the aforementioned ponds. For saltwater adventures, put in along the park's coastline at Trout River and travel north to Bonne Bay—caves and 350-metre-high (1,000-ft.) cliffs accent the shore. A boat tour through Western Brook Pond, a freshwater fjord, also offers splendid views of the countryside.

There's so much water here that it's not surprising to learn that the provincial dog, a furry Newfoundland, has webbed feet. And you'll wish you did, too, when you see all the bays, coves, lakes and ponds perfect for sailing, scuba diving, swimming or windsurfing.

Try white-water rafting or canoeing on the many rivers extending across the province—the Pinware, Eagle and Churchill rivers are ideal for beginners, while rapid-rich Kenamu River is a little rougher.

When the snow falls, head to Terra Nova and Gros Morne national parks of Canada. Each has an extensive system of groomed trails for cross-country skiing and snowshoeing. Trails also are found within two provincial parks: A heated ski chalet at Notre Dame Provincial Park keeps skiers toasty in between treks, and you can ski around a frozen pond at Butter Pot Provincial Park.

When the Snow Starts to Fall, Hit the Slopes

Historic Timeline

1000	Vikings settle along the rugged coastline at L'Anse aux Meadows.
1497	Venetian navigator John Cabot, sailing under the British flag, claims Newfoundland for the Tudor monarchs of England.
1855	Newfoundland becomes completely self-governing.
1866	The first successful transatlantic cable is laid at the tiny town of Heart's Content.
1892	A fire sweeps through St. John's, leaving 11,000 people homeless and causing extensive property damage.
1901	Guglielmo Marconi receives the first transatlantic wireless message in a hospital near Cabot Tower on Signal Hill.
1927	The boundaries of Labrador are defined, granting Newfoundland rights to all of Labrador.
1949	Newfoundland becomes Canada's 10th province.
1992	The once-abundant cod stocks reach an unprecedented low due to decades of overfishing; some 30,000 fishermen are jobless.
1999	Newfoundland celebrates 50 years as a province of Canada with year-long festivities.
2001	The province's name is officially changed from Newfoundland to Newfoundland and Labrador.

What To Pack

Temperature Averages Maximum/Minimum (Celsius)	JANUARY	FEBRUARY	MARCH	APRIL	MAY	JUNE	JULY	AUGUST	SEPTEMBER	OCTOBER	NOVEMBER	DECEMBER
Bonavista	-2 / -8	-2 / -9	1 / -6	3 / -2	8 / 1	14 / 5	19 / 10	19 / 11	15 / 8	10 / 4	6 / -1	1 / -4
Churchill Falls, Labrador	-16 / -27	-14 / -26	-7 / -19	1 / -11	8 / -2	15 / 4	19 / 8	17 / 7	10 / 2	3 / -4	-4 / -13	-14 / -23
Rose Blanche	-2 / -8	-3 / -9	-1 / -6	3 / -2	8 / 2	12 / 6	16 / 11	18 / 12	14 / 8	10 / 4	6 / -2	1 / -5
St. Anthony	-7 / -16	-7 / -16	-3 / -11	1 / -5	6 / -1	12 / 3	17 / 4	16 / 8	12 / 4	1 / -5	-4 / -12	-9 / -13
St. John's	-1 / -8	-2 / -9	1 / -6	4 / -2	10 / 1	16 / 6	20 / 10	19 / 11	16 / 7	11 / 3	6 / -1	1 / -5
Steady Brook	-4 / -14	-4 / -15	1 / -11	6 / -4	12 / 1	18 / 5	23 / 9	21 / 9	16 / 4	10 / 1	4 / -3	-1 / -9

From the records of The Weather Channel Interactive, Inc.

Good Facts To Know

POPULATION: 505,469.

AREA: 370,495 sq km (143,048 sq mi.); ranks 10th.

CAPITAL: St. John's.

HIGHEST POINT: 1,652 m (5,420 ft.), Mount Caubvick, Labrador.

LOWEST POINT: Sea level, Atlantic Ocean.

TIME ZONE(S): Newfoundland is on Newfoundland Standard Time/DST. Labrador is on Atlantic time/DST, except for the south coast (Black Tickle and south), which is on Newfoundland Standard Time. Newfoundland Standard Time is 1.5 hours ahead of Eastern Standard Time. Atlantic Standard Time is 1 hour ahead of Eastern Standard Time.

REGULATIONS

TEEN DRIVING LAWS: Driving is not permitted midnight-5 a.m. unless driver is accompanied by an individual with at least 4 years of driving experience or driver carries proof of work schedule. The number of passengers is restricted to the number of seat belts in the vehicle. The minimum age for an unrestricted driver's license is 17 years and 8 months. Phone (709) 729-6955 for more information about Newfoundland driver's license regulations.

SEAT BELT/CHILD RESTRAINT LAWS: Seat belts required for driver and all passengers. Child restraints required for children under 9 years or under 36 kilograms (80 lb.) or 145 centimetres (4 ft., 9 in.) tall.

CELL PHONE RESTRICTIONS: Drivers are not permitted to use handheld cell phones or engage in text messaging.

HELMETS FOR MOTORCYCLISTS: Required for all riders.

RADAR DETECTORS: Not permitted.

FIREARMS LAWS: By federal law, all nonresidents entering Canada with a firearm must declare their weapon in writing and pay a fee of $25 (Canadian). Contact the Canadian Firearms Centre at (800) 731-4000 to receive a declaration form or additional information.

ALCOHOL CONSUMPTION: Legal age 19.

HOLIDAYS

HOLIDAYS: Jan. 1 ▪ Good Friday ▪ Easter Monday ▪ Victoria Day, May 24 or closest prior Mon. ▪ Canada Day, July 1 ▪ Labour Day, Sept. (1st Mon.) ▪ Thanksgiving, Oct. (2nd Mon.) ▪ Remembrance Day, Nov. 11 ▪ Christmas, Dec. 25 ▪ Boxing Day, Dec. 26.

MONEY

TAXES: Newfoundland and Labrador has a harmonized sales tax comprised of an 8 percent provincial tax and a 5 percent federal goods and services tax (for a total of 13 percent) which is applied to most goods and services.

VISITOR INFORMATION

INFORMATION CENTERS: Provincial visitor centers open daily year-round are located at St. John's International Airport, 9:30 a.m.-midnight ▪ and at Deer Lake Airport, 9:30 a.m.-midnight. Other centers, operated daily from mid-May to mid-Oct., are in Channel-Port-aux-Basques, 6 a.m.-10 p.m. ▪ Argentia, 9-7 (also Mon., Wed. and Sat. 7-11 p.m.) ▪ Deer Lake, 8:30-8 ▪ Notre Dame Junction near Lewisporte, 8:30-8 ▪ Clarenville, 8:30-8 ▪ and Whitbourne, 8:30-8.

FURTHER INFORMATION FOR VISITORS:
Department of Tourism, Culture and Recreation
P.O. Box 8700
St. John's, NL A1B 4J6
Canada
(709) 729-0862
(800) 563-6353

INTERPROVINCE FERRY INFORMATION:
Marine Atlantic Inc.
355 Purves St.
North Sydney, NS B2A 3V2
Canada
(902) 794-5200
(800) 341-7981 for reservations

FERRY SCHEDULES:
The Department of Transportation & Works provides schedules for and information about interprovincial ferry services. For further information phone (709) 729-2300.

Newfoundland and Labrador Annual Events

Please call ahead to confirm event details.

JANUARY

- Suncor Energy Big Band Show / St. John's
  709-722-4441
- Storytelling Circle
  St. John's
  709-685-3444
- Steele N' Steps
  Newfoundland Soiree
  Portugal Cove Cb
  709-754-8687

FEBRUARY

- Wintertainment / Clarenville
  709-466-7937
- Winterlude
  Grand Falls-Windsor
  709-489-0450
- Corner Brook Winter
  Carnival / Corner Brook
  709-632-5343

MARCH

- Cain's Quest Snowmobile
  Endurance Race
  Labrador City
  709-944-6251
- The March Hare Literary
  Festival / Corner Brook
  709-639-9814
- SnoBreak
  Happy Valley-Goose Bay
  709-896-3489

APRIL

- Rotary Music Festival
  St. John's
  709-754-1600
- Newfoundland and Labrador
  Drama Festival
  Grand Falls-Windsor
  709-292-4520
- Easter Games
  Happy Valley-Goose Bay
  709-923-2221

MAY

- Bowl for Kids Sake
  St. John's
  709-368-5437
- Trails, Tales and Tunes
  Festival / Norris Point
  709-458-2896
- Feather and Folk Nature
  Festival / Channel-Port aux
  Basques
  709-639-9260

JUNE

- St. John's Days
  Celebrations / St. John's
  709-754-2489
- The Iceberg Festival
  St. Anthony
  709-454-8888
- Polar Bear Dip
  Labrador City
  709-944-3602

JULY

- The Great Fogo Island Punt
  Race to There and Back
  Fogo
  709-266-1083
- Deer Lake Strawberry
  Festival Days / Deer Lake
  709-635-2031
- Exploits Valley Salmon
  Festival
  Grand Falls-Windsor
  709-489-0407

AUGUST

- Bakeapple Folk Festival
  Forteau
  709-931-2097
- Tuckamore Festival
  St. John's
  709-576-6422
- Brimstone Head Folk
  Festival / Fogo
  709-266-2218

SEPTEMBER

- Rennie's River Duck Race
  St. John's
  709-722-3825
- Gros Morne Theatre
  Festival / Cow Head
  709-639-7238
- Loggers' Sport Festival
  Gambo
  709-674-4222

OCTOBER

- Christmas at the Glacier
  Mount Pearl
  709-745-9627
- Halloween Mardi Gras
  St. John's
  709-753-7822
- Oktoberfest Craft Fair
  Mount Pearl
  709-748-1009

NOVEMBER

- Grand Falls-Windsor Red
  Maple Festival
  Grand Falls-Windsor
  709-489-0450
- Burin Peninsula Crafts Fair
  Marystown
  709-279-1846
- Christmas Parade
  St. John's
  709-726-8244

DECEMBER

- First Night Celebrations
  Mount Pearl
  709-748-1008
- North America's First New
  Year's / St. John's
  709-576-8106
- First Night Celebrations
  Labrador City
  709-944-3602

Inukshuk at Red Bay National Historic Site of Canada, Red Bay

Viking House Reconstruction, L'Anse aux Meadows National Historic Site of Canada

Atlantic Puffin, the Provincial Bird

Signal Hill Tattoo, Signal Hill National Historic Site of Canada

The Capital City of St. John's

Great Experience for Members

AAA editor's picks of exceptional note

Point Amour
Lighthouse

Johnson Geo Centre

The Rooms

Signal Hill National
Historic Site of
Canada

Bell Island (D-5)
Bell Island's Historic Underground #2 Mine
& Museum *(See p. 93.)*

Bonavista (D-5)
Ryan Premises National Historic Site of
Canada *(See p. 94.)*

Ferryland (E-5)
Colony of Avalon *(See p. 98.)*

**Gros Morne National Park of
Canada** (C-2)
Gros Morne National Park of Canada
(See p. 101.)

L'Anse-Amour (B-5)
Point Amour Lighthouse *(See p. 104.)*

**L'Anse aux Meadows National
Historic Site of Canada** (A-3)
L'Anse aux Meadows National Historic Site
of Canada *(See p. 105.)*

St. Bride's (E-4)
Cape St. Mary's Ecological Reserve
(See p. 109.)

St. John's (E-5)
Basilica Cathedral Church and Museum
(See p. 110.)

Johnson Geo Centre *(See p. 111.)*

Railway Coastal Museum *(See p. 111.)*

The Rooms *(See p. 112.)*

**Signal Hill National Historic Site of
Canada** (E-5)
Signal Hill National Historic Site of Canada
(See p. 115.)

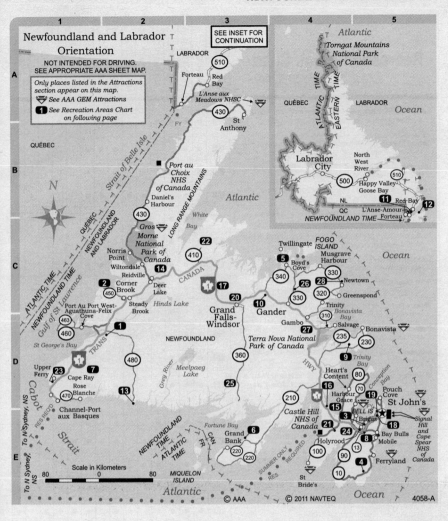

Newfoundland and Labrador
Orientation

NOT INTENDED FOR DRIVING.
SEE APPROPRIATE AAA SHEET MAP.

Only places listed in the Attractions
section appear on this map.
See AAA GEM Attractions
See Recreation Areas Chart
on following page

SEE INSET FOR
CONTINUATION

Recreation Areas Chart The map location numerals in column 2 show an area's location on the preceding map.	MAP LOCATION	CAMPING	PICNICKING	HIKING TRAILS	BOATING	BOAT RAMP	BOAT RENTAL	FISHING	SWIMMING	PETS ON LEASH	BICYCLE TRAILS	WINTER SPORTS	VISITOR CENTER	LODGE/CABINS	FOOD SERVICE
NATIONAL PARKS (See place listings.)														
Gros Morne (C-2) About 1,805 square kilometres.		•	•	•	•			•	•	•			•	•	
Terra Nova (D-4) About 400 square kilometres. Golf.		•	•	•	•	•	•	•	•	•			•		•
Torngat Mountains (A-4) About 9,700 square kilometres.		•		•	•	•			•				•		
PROVINCIAL														
Barachois Pond (D-2) 3,456 hectares 74 km s. of Corner Brook on Hwy. 1. Nature programs.	❶	•	•	•				•	•	•			•	•	
Blow Me Down (C-2) 224 hectares at Lark Harbour via Hwy. 450. Lookout tower, playground.	❷	•	•	•					•	•					

Recreation Areas Chart

The map location numerals in column 2 show an area's location on the preceding map.

	MAP LOCATION	CAMPING	PICNICKING	HIKING TRAILS	BOATING	BOAT RAMP	BOAT RENTAL	FISHING	SWIMMING	PETS ON LEASH	BICYCLE TRAILS	WINTER SPORTS	VISITOR CENTER	LODGE/CABINS	FOOD SERVICE
Butter Pot (E-4) 2,833 hectares 36 km s.w. of St. John's on Hwy. 1. Nature programs. Canoeing, cross-country skiing; playgrounds.	3	•	•	•	•			•	•	•		•	•		
Chance Cove (E-5) 2,068 hectares 43 km s. of Ferryland off Hwy. 10. Scenic. Whale watching.	4	•	•					•	•	•					
Dildo Run (C-4) 327 hectares 17.7 km n.w. of Boyd's Cove on Hwy. 340 on New World Island. Kayaking.	5	•	•	•	•			•		•			•		
Frenchman's Cove (E-3) 51 hectares 24.2 km w. of Marystown on Hwy. 210. Bird-watching, golf.	6	•	•		•	•	•	•	•	•				•	
J.T. Cheeseman (D-1) 182 hectares 11.3 km n.w. of Port aux Basques on Hwy. 1. Bird-watching.	7	•	•	•				•	•	•					
La Manche (E-5) 1,378 hectares 56.2 km s. of St. John's on Hwy. 10. Bird-watching, canoeing.	8	•	•	•	•			•		•					
Lockston Path (D-4) 733 hectares 6.5 km n. of Port Rexton on Hwy. 236. Wildlife viewing.	9	•	•	•	•			•		•					
Notre Dame (C-3) 113 hectares 48.2 km w. of Gander via Hwy. 1. Nature programs. Cross-country skiing; playground.	10	•	•					•	•	•					
Pinware River (B-5) 68 hectares about 10 km n. of L'Anse-au-Loup on Hwy. 510.	11	•	•					•		•					
Pistolet Bay (B-5) 897 hectares 25.7 km n. of St. Anthony on Hwy. 437. Canoeing; playground.	12	•	•	•				•	•	•					
Sandbanks (D-2) 230 hectares 4 km w. of Burgeo on Rte. 480. Bird-watching.	13	•	•	•					•	•					
Sir Richard Squires Memorial (C-2) 1,556 hectares 41.7 km n.e. of Deer Lake on Hwy. 422. Nature programs. Canoeing; playground.	14	•	•	•				•		•			•		
OTHER															
Backside Pond (D-4) 556 hectares 3 km e. of Hopeall on Hwy. 80.	15	•	•	•	•			•	•	•					•
Bellevue Beach (D-4) 75 hectares 11.2 km w. of Bellevue on Hwy. 201. Bird-watching.	16	•	•	•	•	•		•	•	•		•			
Beothuk (C-3) 74 hectares 3.2 km w. of Grand Falls-Windsor on Hwy. 1. Logging exhibit.	17	•	•	•				•	•	•			•		•
Bowring (E-5) 80 hectares at Waterford Bridge Rd. and Cowan Ave. Tennis. *(See St. John's p. 110.)*	18		•	•				•	•	•					•
C.A. Pippy (D-5) 1,343 hectares 1 km n. of St. John's off Hwy. 1. Canoeing, golf. *(See St. John's p. 111.)*	19	•	•	•	•		•	•	•	•					•
Catamaran (C-3) 44 hectares 9.7 km n. of Badger on Hwy. 1. Sailing; indoor pool, playground.	20	•	•		•	•		•		•					•
Fitzgerald's Pond (E-4) 920 hectares 19.2 km n.e. of Dunville on Hwy. 100. Skating, skiing.	21	•	•	•	•			•	•	•					
Flatwater Pond (C-3) 98 hectares 24.2 km s. of Baie Verte on Hwy. 410. Miniature golf; playground.	22	•	•	•	•	•	•	•	•	•	•	•			
Grand Codroy (D-1) 2 hectares 11.2 km n. of Doyles at O'Regans on Hwy. 406. Canoeing.	23	•	•	•				•	•	•					
Gushue's Pond (E-4) 177 hectares 19.2 km w. of Holyrood on Hwy. 1. Canoeing, kayaking; playground.	24	•	•		•			•	•	•			•		
Jipujijkuei Kuespem (D-3) 882 hectares 12 km s. from Head of Bay d'Espoir on Rte. 360. Snowmobiling.	25	•	•		•	•		•	•	•					
Jonathan's Pond (C-4) 440 hectares 19.2 km n. of Gander on Rte. 330. Butterfly habitat.	26	•	•	•	•			•	•	•			•		
Square Pond (D-4) 38 hectares 40.2 km s.e. of Gander on Hwy. 1.	27	•	•	•	•			•	•	•			•		
Windmill Bight (C-4) 73 hectares 111 km n.e. of Gambo on Rte. 330. Beach, playground.	28	•	•	•				•	•	•					

BADGER'S QUAY

BLUE MIST MOTEL   Phone: 709/536-5690
[fyi]   Not evaluated. **Address:** Rt 320 A0G 1B0
Location: On Rt 320 (Main St). Facilities, services, and decor characterize an economy property.

BAY BULLS (E-5)

Bay Bulls derives its name from the French "baie boules," a reference to the dovekie, or bull bird, which winters in Newfoundland and Labrador.

GATHERALL'S PUFFIN AND WHALE WATCH is just off Hwy. 10, following signs to Northside Rd. The 1.5-hour tour ventures to Witless Bay Ecological Reserve, home to the largest seabird colony in North America, afford opportunities to view native wildlife, including Atlantic puffins, murres and kittiwakes. Humpback and minke whales are frequently spotted mid-June to mid-August.

Hours: Up to five departures are offered daily, May-Sept. Passengers should arrive 15 minutes prior to departure. Phone ahead to confirm schedule. **Cost:** $59; $54 (senior citizens); $38 (post-secondary students under age 25 with ID); $21 (ages 9-17); $18 (ages 2-8). Reservations are recommended. **Phone:** (709) 334-2887.

MULLOWNEY'S PUFFIN & WHALE TOURS is off Hwy. 10 on Lower Rd. Passengers can view icebergs, whales and birds from two observation decks aboard the *Mary Vincent.* Fin, humpback and minke whales are some of the species common in the area. Bird species often spotted include Atlantic puffins, guillemots, murres, razorbills and black-legged kittiwakes.

Time: Allow 2 hours, 30 minutes minimum. **Hours:** Tours depart daily at 9:30, noon, 2:30 and 5, May 25-Sept. 15. **Cost:** $55; $50 (senior citizens); $25 (ages 15-18); $20 (ages 6-14). **Phone:** (709) 334-3666 June 1-late Sept., (709) 745-5061 all year, or (877) 783-3467 May 25-Sept. 15. [🍴]

O'BRIEN'S BIRD AND WHALE TOURS, on Hwy. 10, offers 2-hour boat tours to the Bird Islands, home to the Witless Bay Ecological Reserve and one of the largest puffin colonies on North America's east coast. Boat tours cover several islands, where kittiwakes, razorbills, storm petrels and cormorants can be seen. Tours from mid-June to mid-August provide opportunities to view humpback and minke whales.

Hours: Departures daily at 9:30, 11:30, 2 and 4:30, June 15-Aug. 15; at 11:30 and 2, May 1-June 14 and Aug. 16-Sept. 30. **Cost:** $54.95; $49.95 (ages 65+); $42.95 (students with ID); $29.95 (ages 10-17); $24.95 (ages 3-9). Reservations are recommended. **Phone:** (709) 753-4850 or (877) 639-4253. [🍴]

BAY ROBERTS pop. 5,414

JUNGLE JIM'S
◈◈
Canadian
$8-$19

AAA Inspector Notes: Guests can step into a tropical theme at the casual eatery, which employs a friendly staff and nurtures a bustling atmosphere. The menu lines up a wide variety of comfort foods, salads, chicken, beef, seafood and hot wings, all served in ample, flavorful portions. **Bar:** full bar. **Address:** Building 1A, Water St A0A 1G0 **Location:** Jct Conception Bay Hwy; centre. [L] [D]

BELL ISLAND (D-5)

Located in Conception Bay, just a short ferry ride from Portugal Cove, Bell Island is a photographer's dream with picturesque cliffs and a 1939 lighthouse still in operation.

Visitors can bring their automobile aboard the ferry. Picnic areas are available. The ferry departs from Portugal Cove off Hwy. 40; phone (709) 895-6931 or (709) 488-2842.

BELL ISLAND'S HISTORIC UNDERGROUND #2 MINE & MUSEUM is accessed from the Portugal Cove ferry and is just off Main St., following signs. The museum chronicles the 1895-1966 mining industry on Bell Island through many artifacts and photographs. The early years saw surface mining, and then submarine (underground) mining began in 1902 at the No. 2 mine, which is one of six mines that were in operation here.

Before battery packs were available, miners got their lighting from candles, which were worn on their hats or placed into the walls; seal-oil lamps and then carbide lamps. More than half of the ore was loaded by hand with shovels, and horses were used to transport it before automation and conveyor belts came into use. Tools and shovels left behind by miners, remnants of calcium carbide, and a horse stable with a feed box can be seen on the mine tour.

A jacket is recommended, as the temperature inside the mine is a constant 47 F. Hard hats must be worn on the mine tour. **Time:** Allow 1 hour, 30 minutes minimum. **Hours:** Daily 11-7, June-Sept. **Cost:** Museum and tour $10; $8 (ages 60+); $3 (ages 0-11). Museum only $5; $4 (ages 60+); free (ages 0-11). **Phone:** (709) 488-2880, or (709) 488-2938 off-season. [🍴] [▨]

BONAVISTA (D-5) pop. 3,764

John Cabot is thought to have first sighted the New World at Cape Bonavista on June 24, 1497. However, the cape was unoccupied until the 1600s when it became a French fishing station and later a permanent English settlement. Although the British fortified the point in 1696 to deter French aggression, Bonavista was the site of a notable battle in the 18th century. Outfitted with only a few armed ships, a British fishing master and local residents defended the coast from French raiders.

CAPE BONAVISTA LIGHTHOUSE PROVINCIAL HISTORIC SITE

is 6 km (3.5 mi.) n. on Hwy. 230. Built in 1843 to guide mariners bound for Labrador, the lighthouse has been restored to appear as it did during the 1870s. Interpretive displays in the visitor center describe the history of the lighthouse and its keepers. Guides take visitors through the site. A statue of explorer John Cabot stands nearby.

Time: Allow 1 hour minimum. **Hours:** Daily 10-5:30, mid-May to mid-Oct. **Cost:** (Includes admission to The Mockbeggar Plantation Provincial Historic Site) $3; free (ages 0-12 and Sun.). Rates may vary; phone ahead. **Phone:** (709) 468-7444 or (709) 729-0592.

THE MOCKBEGGAR PLANTATION PROVINCIAL HISTORIC SITE,

in the center of town on Mockbeggar Rd., is the former home of F. Gordon Bradley, who served in Parliament and in the federal cabinet in the 1950s. Originally built during the 1870s, the house has been restored to its 1940s appearance. Antiques throughout the house portray the traditional Newfoundland and Labrador lifestyle.

Several outbuildings, including a carpenter's shop and fish store/factory, have been restored. Some are from the late 18th century. **Hours:** Daily 10-5:30, mid-May to mid-Oct. **Cost:** (Includes admission to Cape Bonavista Lighthouse Provincial Historic Site) $3; free (ages 0-12 and Sun.). Rates may vary; phone ahead. **Phone:** (709) 468-7300 or (709) 729-0592.

RYAN PREMISES NATIONAL HISTORIC SITE OF CANADA

is at jct. Ryan's Hill and Old Catalina Rd. This five-building complex served as a major salt fish exporting business in the 19th and 20th centuries.

The site conserves and commemorates four aspects of the East Coast fishery—the inshore, international, Labrador and seal fisheries. Highlights include various interactive and multimedia displays describing the 500-year-old Atlantic fishery heritage. The Bonavista Community Museum houses memorabilia from the local community. An art gallery, interpretive programs and demonstrations of traditional fishing skills also are featured.

Time: Allow 2 hours minimum. **Hours:** Daily 10-6, May 15-Oct. 15. **Cost:** $3.90; $3.40 (ages 66+); $1.90 (ages 6-16); $9.80 (family). **Phone:** (709) 468-1600 in summer, or (709) 468-1601 rest of year.

BOYD'S COVE (C-4) pop. 244

BEOTHUK INTERPRETATION CENTRE, off Hwy. 340, following signs, is the former site of a 17th-century Beothuk community. Visitors can view a videotape presentation, dioramas and artifacts detailing the life of the Beothuk Indians. A 3-kilometre (1.8-mi.) hiking trail leads to the archeological site where the tribe lived from 1650 to 1720; interpretative signs along the way describe the natural area. **Time:** Allow 2 hours minimum. **Hours:**

Daily 10-5:30, mid-May to early Oct. **Cost:** $3. **Phone:** (709) 656-3114 for the center, or (709) 729-0592 for the main office.

BRIGUS (E-5)

HAWTHORNE COTTAGE NATIONAL HISTORIC SITE OF CANADA, off Hwy. 70 at the corner of Irishtown Rd., was the home of Capt. Robert A. Bartlett, who commanded Adm. Robert Peary's ship, *The Roosevelt,* during the first expedition to the North Pole in 1909. The cottage contains period furnishings and photographs from Bartlett's various journeys. **Time:** Allow 1 hour minimum. **Hours:** Cottage daily 9-7, July 1-Labour Day; Wed.-Sun. 9-5, May-June and day after Labour Day to mid-Oct. Phone ahead to confirm schedule. **Cost:** Cottage $4; $3.75 (ages 6-16 and 65+); $10 (family). **Phone:** (709) 528-4004 in summer, or (877) 753-9262 rest of year.

BROOKLYN

ASPEN BY-THE-SEA   **Phone:** 709/467-5219
[fyi]   Not evaluated. **Address:** Main Rd A0C 1V0 **Location:** Rt 234, just off Rt 230; centre. Facilities, services, and decor characterize a mid-scale property.

CAPE RAY (D-1)

CAPE RAY HERITAGE SITE & LIGHTHOUSE MUSEUM is off Hwy. 1 Cape Ray exit, then 4 km (2.5 mi.) n.w. on Hwy. 408. Some 1,800 years ago Dorset Paleoeskimos camped here during their nomadic hunting trip, and artifacts are housed in the museum. In 1856 the first telegraph cable connecting Newfoundland to North America was laid here; the event is commemorated with a plaque. In addition, a lighthouse has been on this site since 1870; the current one was built in 1959. **Time:** Allow 1 hour minimum. **Hours:** Daily 10-8, late June to mid-Sept. Phone ahead to confirm schedule. **Cost:** Donations. **Phone:** (709) 695-2426. 🅷

CAPE SPEAR NATIONAL HISTORIC SITE OF CANADA (E-5)

On the easternmost point of North America, Cape Spear National Historic Site of Canada is known for its lighthouse on a rocky cliff 75 metres (245 ft.) above sea level. The 1835 structure is one of Newfoundland and Labrador's oldest surviving lighthouses. For more than a century it has served as an important approach light to St. John's, 11 kilometres (7 mi.) to the north. During World War II a coastal defense battery at Cape Spear protected St. John's from Nazi submarines.

The lighthouse has been restored and furnished to demonstrate the tradition of lighthouse keepers' work in the province. The site contains World War II gun emplacements and a visitor center with exhibits about lighthouses. The site's scenery attracts hikers, photographers and whale watchers.

Handheld GPS devices that provide visual and audio narration based on the user's location within the site are available at the visitor center; the rental fee is included in the lighthouse admission price.

Grounds daily 24 hours. Lighthouse and visitor center daily 10-6, June 16-Labour Day; Wed.-Sun. 9-5, May 15-June 15 and day after Labour Day-Oct. 15. Site free. Lighthouse $3.90; $3.40 (ages 65+); $1.90 (ages 6-16); $9.80 (family). For further information contact the Historic Sites Manager, Cape Spear National Historic Site of Canada, P.O. Box 1268, St. John's, NL, Canada A1C 5M9. Phone (709) 772-5367.

CARBONEAR   pop. 4,723

FONG'S MOTEL & RESTAURANT   Phone: 709/596-5114
(fyi)   Not evaluated. **Address:** 143 Columbus Dr A1Y 1A6 **Location:** On Hwy 70; centre. Facilities, services, and decor characterize an economy property.

CASTLE HILL NATIONAL HISTORIC SITE OF CANADA (E-4)

At Placentia off Hwy. 100, Castle Hill dates from the 17th century when the French selected the small fishing village of Plaisance as the base of operations for their Newfoundland and Labrador fishing fleet. The Royal Colony of Plaisance was founded at this site in 1662 during the reign of Louis XIV. Fort Royal, a massive fortification, was built atop a prominent hill overlooking the port and the surrounding countryside.

Under the Treaty of Utrecht the area was ceded to the British in 1713. The town was renamed Placentia, and the hill on which the fort stood became known as Castle Hill.

The stabilized ruins of Fort Royal include the remains of the barracks, a powder magazine, guard rooms and a blockhouse. Hiking trails lead visitors to vantage points overlooking Placentia and the Placentia Gut inlet. Displays at the visitor center depict the French and English influence at Placentia.

Allow 30 minutes minimum. Grounds and visitor center open daily 10-6, May 15-Oct. 15. Site free. Exhibit areas $3.90; $3.40 (ages 65+); $1.90 (ages 6-16); $9.80 (family). **Cards:** AX, MC, VI. For further information contact Castle Hill National Historic Site of Canada, P.O. Box 10, Jerseyside, Placentia, NL, Canada A0B 2G0. Phone (709) 227-2401.

CHANNEL-PORT AUX BASQUES
pop. 4,319

HOTEL PORT AUX BASQUES   Phone: (709)695-2171
◇◇ ◇◇
Hotel
$115
Address: 1 Grand Bay Rd A0M 1C0 **Location:** Jct Trans-Canada Hwy 1. **Facility:** 49 units, some efficiencies. 2 stories (no elevator), interior corridors. **Parking:** winter plug-ins. **Activities:** limited exercise equipment. **Guest Services:** coin laundry.

ST. CHRISTOPHER'S HOTEL   Phone: 709/695-7034
◇◇ ◇◇
Hotel
Rates not provided
Address: 146 Caribou Rd A0M 1C0 **Location:** Trans-Canada Hwy 1 exit Port Aux Basques, follow signs 1.2 mi (2 km); downtown. **Facility:** 83 units, some kitchens. 3 stories, interior corridors. **Parking:** winter plug-ins. **Amenities:** high-speed Internet. **Dining:** The Captain's Room, see separate listing. **Activities:** exercise room. **Guest Services:** coin laundry.

WHERE TO EAT

THE CAPTAIN'S ROOM   Phone: 709/695-7034
◇◇ ◇◇
Canadian
$7-$20
AAA Inspector Notes: A friendly crew is on deck in the restaurant, which specializes in seafood. Also on the menu is a decent selection of steaks, poultry and salads. **Bar:** full bar. **Address:** 146 Caribou Rd A0M 1C0 **Location:** Trans-Canada Hwy 1 exit Port Aux Basques, follow signs 1.2 mi (2 km); downtown; in St. Christopher's Hotel. (B) (L) (D)

CHURCHILL FALLS (B-4)
• Restaurants p. 96

CHURCHILL FALLS AND BOWDOIN CANYON are 25 km (16 mi.) w. on Rte. 500. The 77,700-square-kilometre (30,000-sq.-mi.) watershed of the Churchill River drains into a saucer-shaped plateau just above Churchill Falls. At one time the river dropped about 75 metres (245 ft.) over the falls and roared through the steep 8-kilometre-long (5-mi.) canyon where water volumes were measured at 340 cubic metres (12,000 cubic ft.) per second in the winter and 10 times that in the summer.

Because much of the water has been diverted to the town's hydroelectric plant, only a small volume flows, particularly during the summer. A well-maintained trail leads to several viewing areas. **Time:** Allow 1 hour minimum. **Hours:** Daily dawn-dusk. (A)

CHURCHILL FALLS UNDERGROUND POWERHOUSE is on Rte. 500. The site contains the world's second largest underground powerhouse, which resides 305 metres (1,000 ft.) below the ground. Tour guides provide a history of the area, explain the reasons for the dams and dikes and take visitors to the intake ducts and tunnels. Visitors also will see the Administration and Control Building; from here an elevator provides access to the generating station, a very large room with a constant hum from the massive turbines.

Note: Photo ID is required. Hard hats and ear plugs are provided. **Time:** Allow 3 hours minimum. **Hours:** Tours depart daily at 9, 1:30 and 7. Closed major holidays. **Cost:** Free. Ages 0-7 are not permitted. Reservations are required. **Phone:** (709) 925-3335 for the town office.

MIDWAY TRAVEL INN   Phone: 709/925-3211
(fyi)   Not evaluated. **Address:** 2 Ressegieu Dr A0R 1A0 **Location:** Centre; in town complex. Facilities, services, and decor characterize an economy property.

MIDWAY RESTAURANT   Phone: 709/925-3211

Canadian
$7-$18

AAA Inspector Notes: The modern eatery offers a choice of booth or table seating. Seafood and steaks share menu space with a good selection of comfort foods. **Bar:** full bar. **Address:** 2 Ressegieu Dr A0R 1A0 **Location:** Centre; in town complex; in Midway Travel Inn.

B L D

CLARENVILLE pop. 5,274

RESTLAND MOTEL   Phone: 709/466-7636

Hotel
$109-$139

Address: 262 Memorial Dr A5A 1N9 **Location:** Centre. Adjacent to Town Hall. **Facility:** 25 units, some two bedrooms, efficiencies and kitchens. 1-2 stories (no elevator), interior/exterior corridors. **Terms:** cancellation fee imposed.

(icons)

ST. JUDE HOTEL   Phone: (709)466-1717

Hotel
$109-$130

Address: 247 Trans-Canada Hwy A5A 1Y4 **Location:** On Trans-Canada Hwy 1; centre. **Facility:** 63 units. 3 stories, interior corridors. **Amenities:** *Some:* high-speed Internet. **Dining:** Dustabella's Restaurant, see separate listing. **Guest Services:** valet laundry.

(icons)

CLARENVILLE INN   Phone: 709/466-7911

[fyi] Not evaluated. **Address:** 134 Trans-Canada Hwy A5A 1Y3 **Location:** On Trans-Canada Hwy 1; centre. Facilities, services, and decor characterize a mid-scale property.

DUSTABELLA'S RESTAURANT   Phone: 709/466-1717

Canadian
$7-$21

AAA Inspector Notes: A pleasant dining room offers upscale decor within a casual atmosphere. The full menu offers fresh seafood and various meat dishes, including some comfort foods. **Bar:** full bar. **Address:** 247 Trans-Canada Hwy A5A 1Y4 **Location:** On Trans-Canada Hwy 1; centre; in St. Jude Hotel.   B L D

RANDOM SOUND RESTAURANT   Phone: 709/466-7911

Canadian
$7-$20

AAA Inspector Notes: Situated on a hilltop overlooking the harbor, bay and township, the relaxed restaurant offers not only great views but also a bounty in seafood, steaks and comfort foods. **Bar:** full bar. **Address:** 134 Trans-Canada Hwy A5A 1Y3 **Location:** On Trans-Canada Hwy 1; centre; in Clarenville Inn.   B L D

CORNER BROOK (C-2) pop. 20,083

Newfoundland and Labrador's second largest city, Corner Brook is at the mouth of the Humber River, one of the greatest salmon rivers in the world. The Humber was first charted in 1767 by Capt. James Cook, who traveled 24 kilometres (15 mi.) up the river on his expedition to survey the Newfoundland and Labrador coast.

One of Newfoundland and Labrador's first industrial sawmills was built in Corner Brook in 1894, and the city boasts one of the world's largest integrated pulp and paper mills.

The 10-story Government Centre cuts a striking silhouette against Corner Brook's skyline. Also noteworthy is the Arts and Cultural Centre, which contains a theater and art exhibition areas. Margaret Bowater Park, in the heart of town, offers swimming, picnicking and a children's playground.

Northwest from Corner Brook, hwys. 440 and 450 offer scenic drives along the north and south shores of Humber Arm, respectively. On the tip of the southern shore extending into the Bay of Islands, a tower at Blow Me Down Provincial Park *(see Recreation Chart)* offers a view of Guernsey, Tweed and Pearl islands.

Barachois Pond Provincial Park *(see Recreation Chart)* also is in the area and is near Stephenville on Hwy. 1.

Tourist Chalet: 11 Confederation Drive, P.O. Box 475, Corner Brook, NL, Canada A2H 6E6. **Phone:** (709) 639-9792.

CORNER BROOK MUSEUM & ARCHIVES is at 2 West St. The 1925 building was previously used as a courthouse, customs office, post office and telegraph building. Exhibits feature the city's cultural, natural and social history. Local industries showcased include paper, fishing and forestry. Historical photos also are displayed.

Note: At press time the facility was closed indefinitely; phone ahead for updates and to confirm schedule and admission information. **Time:** Allow 1 hour minimum. **Hours:** Daily 9-5, June 30-Aug. 31; Mon.-Fri. 9-4:30, rest of year. Closed Good Friday, Easter Monday, Christmas and day after Christmas. **Cost:** $5; $3 (ages 12-16); free (ages 0-11 with adult). **Phone:** (709) 634-2518.

COMFORT INN   Phone: (709)639-1980

Hotel
$140-$170

Address: 41 Maple Valley Rd A2H 6T2 **Location:** Trans-Canada Hwy 1 exit 5 eastbound; exit 6 westbound, via Confederation Ave. **Facility:** 78 units. 2 stories (no elevator), interior corridors. **Terms:** cancellation fee imposed. **Dining:** Jungle Jim's, see separate listing. **Guest Services:** valet laundry.

(icons)

GLYNMILL INN   Phone: (709)634-5181

Hotel
$121-$205

Address: 1B Cobb Ln A2H 6E6 **Location:** Just w of W Valley Rd; centre. **Facility:** 78 units. 4 stories, interior corridors. **Terms:** cancellation fee imposed. **Amenities:** *Some:* high-speed Internet. **Dining:** The Wine Cellar, see separate listing. **Activities:** hiking trails, exercise room. **Guest Services:** valet laundry.

(icons)

GREENWOOD INN & SUITES-CORNER BROOK   Phone: 709/634-5381

Hotel
Rates not provided

Address: 48 West St A2Z 2Z2 **Location:** At Chestnut St; centre. **Facility:** 102 units. 5 stories, interior corridors. **Amenities:** *Some:* high-speed Internet. **Pool(s):** heated indoor. **Activities:** exercise room. **Guest Services:** coin laundry.

(icons)

MAMATEEK INN

Hotel
Rates not provided

Phone: 709/639-8901
Address: 64 Maple Valley Rd A2H 6G7 **Location:** Trans-Canada Hwy 1 exit 5 eastbound; exit 6 westbound, via Confederation Ave. **Facility:** 55 units. 2 stories (no elevator), interior corridors. **Dining:** restaurant, see separate listing. **Activities:** limited exercise equipment. **Guest Services:** valet laundry.

BELL'S INN

Phone: 709/634-5736
(fyi) Not evaluated. **Address:** 2 Ford's Rd A2H 1S6 **Location:** Corner of St. Marks Ave and Ford's Rd; centre. Facilities, services, and decor characterize a mid-scale property.

WHERE TO EAT

JADE GARDEN RESTAURANT

Chinese
$7-$15

Phone: 709/639-7003
AAA Inspector Notes: With a convenient downtown location, simple decor and casual tone, this eatery offers guests a pleasant experience and a tasty meal. Chinese lanterns light the way as you savor a variety of Cantonese and Szechuan entrees, as well as some Canadian dishes. **Bar:** full bar. **Address:** 82 West St A2H 2Z2 **Location:** Centre. **Parking:** street only. [L] [D]

JENNIFERS-THE UPPER LEVEL RESTAURANT

Phone: 709/632-7979

Canadian
$12-$23

AAA Inspector Notes: In a commercial area, the restaurant displays Old English-style decor in the large, open dining room. The extensive menu includes a selection of fresh seafood, steaks, poultry and ribs, in addition to offerings of comfort food and many value-priced specials. The staff carries out friendly, casual service. **Bar:** full bar. **Address:** 48-50 Broadway A2H 2Z2 **Location:** Jct Caribou Rd. [L] [D]

JUNGLE JIM'S

Canadian
$8-$19

Phone: 709/639-2222
AAA Inspector Notes: Guests can step into a tropical theme at the casual eatery, which employs a friendly staff and nurtures a bustling atmosphere. The menu lines up a wide variety of comfort foods, salads, chicken, beef, seafood and hot wings, all served in ample, flavorful portions. **Bar:** full bar. **Address:** 41 Maple Valley Rd A2H 6T2 **Location:** Trans-Canada Hwy 1 exit 5 eastbound; exit 6 westbound, via Confederation Ave; in Comfort Inn. [L] [D]

MAMATEEK RESTAURANT & PUB

American
$7-$22

Phone: 709/639-2767
AAA Inspector Notes: A fantastic view of the city, ocean and mountains awaits guests at the casual, upbeat eatery. Included in the vast selection on the menu are daily specials and all-day breakfast items. **Bar:** full bar. **Address:** 64 Maple Valley Rd A2H 6G7 **Location:** Trans-Canada Hwy 1 exit 5 eastbound; exit 6 westbound, via Confederation Ave; in Mamateek Inn. [B] [L] [D]

THE WINE CELLAR

Steak
$18-$29

Phone: 709/634-5181
AAA Inspector Notes: As the name might imply, the delightful restaurant is in the basement of a fine hotel. The specialty is beef steaks, but the menu also lists some pork, chicken and a few seafood dishes. A decent wine list is on hand. **Bar:** full bar. **Reservations:** suggested. **Address:** 1B Cobb Ln A2H 6E6 **Location:** Just w of W Valley Rd; centre; in Glynmill Inn. [D]

COW HEAD pop. 493

SHALLOW BAY MOTEL & CABINS

Hotel
$125-$135 6/1-9/30
$105-$115 10/1-5/31

Phone: 709/243-2471
Address: Rt 430 Tr, The Viking Tr A0K 2A0 **Location:** Hwy 430, 2.5 mi (4 km) w towards the ocean, follow signs. **Facility:** 82 units, some cabins. 1-2 stories (no elevator), interior/exterior corridors. **Terms:** cancellation fee imposed. **Dining:** restaurant, see separate listing. **Pool(s):** heated outdoor. **Activities:** sauna, whirlpool, exercise room. **Fee:** miniature golf. **Guest Services:** coin laundry.

WHERE TO EAT

SHALLOW BAY RESTAURANT

Canadian
$7-$20

Phone: 709/243-2471
AAA Inspector Notes: On the waterfront, the spacious family restaurant presents a menu of comfort foods and fresh local seafood. **Bar:** full bar. **Address:** Rt 430 Tr, The Viking Tr A0K 2A0 **Location:** Hwy 430, 2.4 mi (4 km) w towards the ocean, follow signs; in Shallow Bay Motel & Cabins. [B] [L] [D] [🍴]

DANIELS HARBOUR (B-2)

NURSE BENNETT HERITAGE HOUSE is w. off Hwy. 430 on Ingram St. British nurse Myra Grimsley came to Daniels Harbour in 1921. When she married Angus Bennett in 1922, he built this house, out of which she administered medical care. She was the only person to do so along the nearly 200 kilometres (124 mi.) of coastline. She worked mainly out of her kitchen until a medical clinic was added onto the room in the early 1940s.

The house includes period furniture and her medical instruments. **Time:** Allow 30 minutes minimum. **Hours:** Daily 10-6, early June to mid-Sept. **Cost:** $5; $3 (children); $12 (family). **Phone:** (709) 898-2045.

DEER LAKE (C-2) pop. 4,827
• Restaurants p. 98

ROY WHALEN HERITAGE MUSEUM, on Hwy. 1, contains scale models of a logging camp and a hydropower system, early lumberjack tools, photographs, household items, china, cameras, typewriters and local historic newspaper headlines. **Hours:** Daily 9:30-8, mid-June through Aug. 15; 10-5, Aug.16-Dec. 23. Phone ahead to confirm schedule. **Cost:** Free. **Phone:** (709) 635-4440 or (709) 635-8119.

DEER LAKE MOTEL

Hotel
$80-$170

Phone: (709)635-2108
Address: 15 Trans-Canada Hwy 1 A8A 2E5 **Location:** 1 mi (1.6 km) e on Trans-Canada Hwy 1, jct Hwy 430. **Facility:** 55 units. 2 stories (no elevator), interior/exterior corridors. **Dining:** restaurant, see separate listing.
Amenities: Some: high-speed Internet (fee).

WHERE TO EAT

DEER LAKE RESTAURANT   Phone: 709/635-2108

Canadian
$8-$20

AAA Inspector Notes: This eatery offers a casual coffee shop style and serves a variety of home-style entrees, tasty soups, salads and sandwiches. **Bar:** full bar. **Address:** 15 Trans-Canada Hwy 1 A8A 2E5 **Location:** 1 mi (1.6 km) e on Trans-Canada Hwy 1, jct Hwy 430; in Deer Lake Motel. (B) (L) (D)

JUNGLE JIM'S   Phone: 709/635-5054

Canadian
$8-$19

AAA Inspector Notes: Guests can step into a tropical theme at the casual eatery, which employs a friendly staff and nurtures a bustling atmosphere. The menu lines up a wide variety of comfort foods, salads, chicken, beef, seafood and hot wings, all served in ample, flavorful portions. **Bar:** full bar. **Address:** 3 Nicholsville Rd A0K 2E0 **Location:** Off Trans-Canada Hwy 1; centre; in The Driftwood Inn. (L) (D)

DILDO pop. 1,299

INN BY THE BAY & GEORGE HOUSE HERITAGE B&B
      Phone: (709)582-3170

Bed & Breakfast
$109-$179

Address: 78 Front Rd A0B 1P0 **Location:** Hwy 1 exit 28, 7.6 mi (13.5 km) on Rt 80. **Facility:** On a hillside overlooking the harbor and village, the quaint B&B offers pleasant guest rooms in two homes. 10 units. 2 stories (no elevator), interior corridors. **Terms:** open 6/1-10/31 & 5/15-5/31, office hours 7 am-11 pm, 3 day cancellation notice-fee imposed.

EASTPORT pop. 499

SANDY COVE BEACH HOUSEKEEPING CABINS
      Phone: 709/677-3158

(fyi) Not evaluated. **Address:** Barbour Ave A0G 1Z0 **Location:** On Rt 310; on Sandy Cove Beach. Facilities, services, and decor characterize an economy property.

FERRYLAND (E-5) pop. 529

Ferryland is one of the oldest fishing villages in the province. From this area pirate Peter Easton and his crews plundered Spanish treasure fleets and accumulated a fortune during the early 17th century.

In 1621 Sir George Calvert, later the first Lord Baltimore, attempted a settlement in Ferryland, but because of the harsh climate and frequent attacks by the Dutch and French, the venture failed. Lord Baltimore and his family abandoned the site in 1629 and founded a colony in what is now Maryland.

After Easton's time, the colonial wars continued the area's tradition of turbulence. Plaques at the Isle of Bois, a strategic point of defense at the mouth of Ferryland's harbor, mark the sites of two defensive gun batteries used in the mid-18th century against sea attacks.

 COLONY OF AVALON is on Hwy. 10, following signs. In the early 16th century this part of the Avalon Peninsula was visited seasonally by Beothuk Indians and migratory fishermen from England, France, Portugal and Spain. The colony, established in 1621 by Sir George Calvert, was one of several early ventures by the English in the New World and was one of the first in Canada to result in sustained settlement. Deemed as abandoned upon Calvert's departure south to found what is now Maryland, Avalon was granted via royal charter in 1637 to adventurer and merchant Sir David Kirke, who governed the colony until 1651.

At Avalon's several dig sites, visitors can watch archeologists as they carefully unearth such relics as rare coins and gold rings, pottery shards, arrow points, cannonballs and iron spurs as well as foundations of homes occupied by the Calvert and Kirke families. Conservators can be viewed piecing together excavated artifacts within the Conservation Laboratory; the completed objects are displayed at the Interpretation Centre.

In a reproduction of a 17th-century kitchen, interpreters dressed in period costumes relate the customs of Avalon's early residents. Three heritage gardens impart a sense of which herbs and vegetables may have been consumed at the colony in the 1600s.

Tours: Guided tours are available. **Time:** Allow 2 hours minimum. **Hours:** Daily 10-6, mid-May to early Oct. **Cost:** $9.50; $8.50 (ages 65+); $7.50 (students with ID); $24.50 (family, two adults and children ages 0-17). **Phone:** (709) 432-3200 or (877) 326-5669.

FOGO ISLAND (C-4)

Fogo Island, 25 kilometres (15.5 mi.) long by 14 kilometres (8.7 mi.) wide, is off the north central coast and is home to several villages, each with features such as beaches, hiking trails, small museums and historic cemeteries. Fishing has played an important role in the island's history and is evident in the various wharves and fish plants. Fish stages, which are used to house fishing equipment and to process fish, also can be found.

In late July islanders hone their skills during the Great Fogo Island Punt Race to There and Back, the course of which begins at Brimstone Head at the terminal of the canal along Main Street. Participants race flat-bottomed wooden boats, or punts, measuring between 4.1 and 5.3 metres (13.5 and 17.5 ft.) some 16 kilometres (10 mi.) to Change Island and then back.

A nearly 1-hour ferry ride departing from the town of Farewell on the mainland transports passengers to Man O' War Cove near Stag Harbour; phone (709) 627-3492 for ferry information. From there, the town of Tilting is approximately 40 kilometres (24.9 mi.) on Hwy. 334, following signs. The town has the majority of the island's attractions and has been named a National Historic Site. Tilting saw the first Irish settlers in the middle of the 18th century, and eventually that nationality represented the majority of the town's population. Many of today's residents have a strong Irish heritage and speak with a brogue. The old Irish Catholic cemetery contains the graves of early immigrants. For more information about the town, phone (709) 266-1320.

Fogo Island Tourism: P.O. Box 1, Site 5, Fogo Island Central, NL, Canada A0G 2X0. **Phone:** (709) 266-2794 or (709) 266-1320.

FORTEAU (B-5) pop. 448

On the southern Labrador coast, Forteau can be reached by Hwy. 510 from Blanc Sablon, Québec, where a ferry arrives daily in the summer from St. Barbe. The Labrador Straits Museum, west off the L'Anse Amour branch road between Forteau and L'Anse-au-Loup, contains regional artifacts.

GAMBO (D-4) pop. 2,072

The name Gambo is said to derive from the Spanish or Portuguese "Baie de las Gamas" (Bay of the Does), seen on early maps. Gambo was the birthplace of Joseph R. Smallwood, the last father of Canadian Confederation. The Smallwood Sculpture, a 3-metre (10-ft.) bronze statue, stands on the village green.

SMALLWOOD INTERPRETATION CENTRE is on Station Rd. overlooking the Gambo River. The center depicts the life and times of Newfoundland and Labrador political leader Joseph R. Smallwood. Displays include Smallwood's personal effects and items relating to the town's history. **Hours:** Daily 9:30-8. Closed major holidays. **Cost:** $3; $2.50 (ages 66+); free (ages 0-11). **Phone:** (709) 674-4342.

GANDER (C-4) pop. 9,951
• Restaurants p. 100

Because of its low incidence of fog, Gander was chosen as the site of an English air base in the mid-1930s. During World War II Gander became an important base for convoy escort and coastal patrol aircraft as well as a refueling stop for military aircraft crossing the Atlantic.

In Peacekeeper Park, 4 kilometres (2.5 mi.) east on Hwy. 1, stands the Silent Witness Memorial. This statue of an unarmed soldier is a tribute to the 259 members of the 101st U.S. Airborne Division, killed when their plane crashed after refueling at Gander in December 1985. They were on their way home from peacekeeping duties in the Middle East.

Gander International Airport is an important link in transatlantic flying routes; it also is the site of the striking 22-metre (72-ft.) mural "Flight and Its Allegories" by artist Kenneth Lochhead.

Gander enjoys a central spot in one of the finest big-game hunting and salmon-fishing areas of the province. West of Gander across Hwy. 1 is Gander Lake, home of a large number of moose.

The Road to the Shore—hwys. 330, 320 and 1—is a scenic loop drive through coastal communities north and east of Gander.

Cobb's Pond Rotary Park features a 3-kilometre (1.9-mi.) boardwalk that encircles the pond, allowing visitors a closer look at local plants and wildlife. Other nearby parks include Square Pond, Jonathan's Pond and Notre Dame (see Recreation Chart).

Gander Tourism Chalet: 109 Trans-Canada Hwy., Gander, NL, Canada A1V 1P6. **Phone:** (709) 256-6558.

AVIATION DISPLAY, at Gander International Airport, features exhibits about the history of aviation, including plane models and photos of such transatlantic flight pioneers as Charles A. Lindbergh, Amelia Earhart and Capt. Eddie Rickenbacker. **Hours:** Daily 24 hours. **Cost:** Free. **Phone:** (709) 256-6677.

NORTH ATLANTIC AVIATION MUSEUM is at 135 Hwy. 1 near the tourism chalet. Newfoundland and Labrador aviation history is showcased. Many displays pertain to World War II, including Ferry Command and the Newfoundland Airmen's Memorial, a tribute to local aviators who died in that conflict. Visitors can enter a reconstructed DC-3 cockpit and inspect other fighter and bomber aircraft. A Lockheed Hudson Mk II is displayed. More than 2,900 were built, and only eight remain.

Tours: Guided tours are available on request. **Time:** Allow 1 hour, 30 minutes minimum. **Hours:** Daily 9-6, Apr.-Dec.; Mon.-Fri. 9-5, rest of year. **Cost:** $5; $4 (ages 5-15 and 65+); $16 (family, four people). **Phone:** (709) 256-2923.

THOMAS HOWE DEMONSTRATION FOREST, 1 km e. on Hwy. 1, has a 5-kilometre (3.1-mi.) hiking trail and three interpretive walking trails; the forest types and forestry practices of central Newfoundland are showcased. Snowshoeing and cross-country skiing are available when there is enough snow. The forest is named for forest advocate Thomas Howe, the province's first Chief Woods Ranger, who was born in England in 1860 and came to Newfoundland when he was 17. An interpretation center has trees, shrubs and berries as well as a display about Howe.

Tours: Guided tours are available. **Time:** Allow 1 hour minimum. **Hours:** Trails daily dawn-dusk. Interpretive center and tours May-Sept.; phone for schedule. **Cost:** Donations. **Phone:** (709) 256-4693 or (709) 256-4489. ⛺

ALBATROSS HOTEL   **Phone:** (709)256-3956
♦♦♦ ♦
Hotel
$111-$141 1/1-5/31
$108-$138 6/1-12/31   **Address:** Trans-Canada Hwy A1V 1W8 **Location:** On Trans-Canada Hwy 1. **Facility:** 90 units. 3 stories, interior/exterior corridors. **Terms:** cancellation fee imposed. **Amenities:** Some: high-speed Internet. **Dining:** restaurant, see separate listing. **Guest Services:** valet laundry. 🍴 🍸 BIZ 📶 ✖ 🖥 / SOME UNITS 🐾

COMFORT INN   **Phone:** (709)256-3535

Hotel
$144-$154

Address: 112 Trans-Canada Hwy 1 A1V 1P8 **Location:** Centre. **Facility:** 64 units, some efficiencies. 2 stories (no elevator), interior/exterior corridors. **Terms:** cancellation fee imposed. **Dining:** Jungle Jim's, see separate listing. **Activities:** exercise room. **Guest Services:** complimentary laundry.

SINBAD'S HOTEL & SUITES   **Phone:** (709)651-2678

Hotel
$101-$262

Address: 133 Bennett Dr A1V 1W8 **Location:** Centre; opposite Gander Mall. **Facility:** 110 units, some efficiencies. 3 stories, exterior corridors. **Terms:** 1-2 night minimum stay. **Activities:** exercise room. **Guest Services:** coin laundry.

ALBATROSS DINING ROOM   **Phone:** 709/256-3956

American
$7-$22

AAA Inspector Notes: This modern-style dining room serves home-style cooking with limited flair and includes a variety of fresh seafood, steak and Newfoundland specialties. The atmosphere is relaxed and the staff provides friendly casual service. **Bar:** full bar. **Address:** Trans-Canada Hwy A1V 1W8 **Location:** On Trans-Canada Hwy 1; in Albatross Hotel. [B] [L] [D]

BISTRO ON ROE   **Phone:** 709/651-4763

Italian
$9-$24

AAA Inspector Notes: This is a cozy bistro with an owner/chef offering well-prepared prime steaks, seafood and local game meats with a French/Italian-influenced cuisine. **Bar:** full bar. **Address:** 110 Roe Ave A1V 1W8 **Location:** Just e of Cooper Blvd. [D] CALL &M

HIGHLIGHT RESTAURANT   **Phone:** 709/256-3347

Chinese
$7-$16

AAA Inspector Notes: Serving this community for many years, the eatery offers a nice variety of Chinese dishes, various combination plates and a daily buffet. Some Canadian entrees are also available. **Bar:** full bar. **Address:** 77 Elizabeth St A1V 1J9 **Location:** Corner of Airport Blvd; in Town Square Shopping Centre. [L] [D]

JUNGLE JIM'S   **Phone:** 709/651-3444

Canadian
$8-$19

AAA Inspector Notes: Guests can step into a tropical theme at the casual eatery, which employs a friendly staff and nurtures a bustling atmosphere. The menu lines up a wide variety of comfort foods, salads, chicken, beef, seafood and hot wings, all served in ample, flavorful portions. **Bar:** full bar. **Address:** 112 Trans-Canada Hwy 1 A1V 1P8 **Location:** Centre; in Comfort Inn. [L] [D]

GRAND BANK (E-3) pop. 2,580

The fishing community of Grand Bank was named for the renowned Grand Banks, Newfoundland and Labrador's continental shelf that attracted European fishermen to the island as early as the 15th century. These coastal waters still support commercial fishing fleets.

Walking trails around Grand Bank offer a variety of sights. The Marine Hike is about 5 kilometres (3 mi.) and follows the Admiral's Beach shoreline. Nature lovers will enjoy the Nature Trail on Bennett's Hill. Both trails offer a view of the town as well as opportunities to view the native plant and animal life.

Self-guiding tours: Maps of the Heritage Walk, which illustrates the cultural heritage and architecture of Grand Bank, are available at local museums and the Grand Bank Town Hall.

PROVINCIAL SEAMEN'S MUSEUM, 54 Marine Dr., presents Newfoundland and Labrador's seafaring heritage through displays of ship models, photographs and documents relating to the south coast fishing industry. The 1,115-square-metre (12,000-sq.-ft.) building resembles the sails of a schooner and is a memorial to Newfoundlanders who have died at sea; it was originally the Yugoslavian Pavilion for Montréal Expo '67.

Time: Allow 1 hour minimum. **Hours:** Mon.-Sat. 9-4:45, Sun. noon-4:45, late Apr.-early Oct. Phone ahead to confirm schedule. **Cost:** $2.50; $2 (ages 65+ and students with ID); free (ages 0-18). Cash only. **Phone:** (709) 832-1484.

GRAND FALLS-WINDSOR (C-3) pop. 12,738

Since the Harmsworth brothers began producing newsprint for British tabloids in 1909, Grand Falls-Windsor tapped the pulp and paper industry to become one of Newfoundland and Labrador's largest urban centers. In 2009, however, the brothers' century-old newsprint operation shut its doors amid falling world demand for its product. The town's future remains uncertain, but its legacy as a "Garden City" designed by its British founders stands it in good stead.

Beothuk Park contains the Loggers' Life Provincial Museum *(see attraction listing),* a reconstructed turn-of-the-20th-century logging camp furnished with tools of the trade; phone (709) 486-0492. *See Recreation Chart.*

GRAND FALLS FISHWAY—SALMONID INTER-PRETATION CENTRE is s. off Hwy. 1 exit 18, following signs. Exhibits depict the history and life cycle of the Atlantic salmon. A lower-level observatory allows visitors to watch the "King of Fish" fight the current on its way upstream to spawn. **Time:** Allow 1 hour minimum. **Hours:** Daily 8-8, June 15-Sept. 15. **Cost:** $6; $3.50 (ages 11-16); $2.50 (ages 0-10). **Phone:** (709) 489-7350.

LOGGERS' LIFE PROVINCIAL MUSEUM, off Hwy. 1 exit 17, showcases the life of a logger in a recreated 1930s logging camp. Displays about food, tools and social life in the camp can be seen. **Time:** Allow 30 minutes minimum. **Hours:** Mon.-Sat. 9:30-4:45, Sun. and July 1 noon-4:45, mid-May to mid-Sept. **Cost:** $2.50; $2 (senior citizens and students with ID); free (ages 0-18). Cash only. **Phone:** (709) 486-0492.

MOUNT PEYTON HOTEL Phone: 709/489-2251

Hotel
Rates not provided

Address: 214 Lincoln Rd A2A 1P8 **Location:** 0.6 mi (1 km) ne on Trans-Canada Hwy 1. **Facility:** 148 units, some efficiencies. 2 stories (no elevator), interior/exterior corridors. **Dining:** Peyton Corral Steakhouse, see separate listing. **Activities:** exercise room. **Guest Services:** valet and coin laundry.

WHERE TO EAT

JUNGLE JIM'S Phone: 709/489-2939

Canadian
$8-$19

AAA Inspector Notes: Guests can step into a tropical theme at the casual eatery, which employs a friendly staff and nurtures a bustling atmosphere. The menu lines up a wide variety of comfort foods, salads, chicken, beef, seafood and hot wings, all served in ample, flavorful portions. **Bar:** full bar. **Address:** 19 Cromer Ave A2A 2K5 **Location:** Centre; in Exploits Valley Mall. L D

PEYTON CORRAL STEAKHOUSE Phone: 709/489-2251

Steak
$16-$29

AAA Inspector Notes: The restaurant specializes in prime cuts of meat but also prepares a few seafood entrees. The dining room has a Western theme, with a full-size antique carriage at the entrance. **Bar:** full bar. **Reservations:** suggested. **Address:** 214 Lincoln Rd A2A 1P8 **Location:** 0.6 mi (1 km) ne on Trans-Canada Hwy 1; in Mount Peyton Hotel. D

TAI WAN RESTAURANT Phone: 709/489-4222

Chinese
$7-$16

AAA Inspector Notes: Serving its guests for four decades, the eatery is a local landmark. On the menu are combination plates, as well as an ample array of individual dishes and some Canadian cuisine. **Bar:** full bar. **Address:** High St A2A 1P8 **Location:** Centre. **Parking:** street only. L D

GREENSPOND (C-4)

GREENSPOND COURTHOUSE, off Hwy. 320 on Center St., was built in 1899. Museum displays include the original courtroom, jail cells and attendant's quarters. Artifacts reflect the history of the Bonavista North area and include items relating to the fishing and seal-hunting industries. **Hours:** Daily 10-6, July 1-Labour Day; by appointment rest of year. Phone ahead to confirm schedule. **Cost:** Free. **Phone:** (709) 536-3220.

GROS MORNE NATIONAL PARK OF CANADA (C-2)

Elevations in the park range from 230 metres (755 ft.) at Bonne Bay to 806 metres (2,644 ft.) at Gros Morne Mountain. Refer to CAA/AAA maps for additional elevation information.

Seventy kilometres (43 mi.) northwest of Deer Lake on Hwy. 430, Gros Morne National Park of Canada covers some 1,805 square kilometres (695 sq. mi.) in the Long Range Mountains on Newfoundland's western coast. Continental drift created the park's landscape and glacial erosion sculpted it to its present condition. Of the many lakes and fjords,

Western Brook Pond is the most striking, with cliffs rising to 686 metres (2,250 ft.).

Baker's Brook Falls, St. Pauls Inlet, Gros Morne Mountain and the Tablelands on the south side of Bonne Bay also are impressive. Due to its outstanding geology, the park was proclaimed a UNESCO (United Nations Educational, Scientific and Cultural Organization) World Heritage Site in 1987. Other remnants of the area's turbulent geologic past include the volcanic cliffs at Green Gardens, the limestone breccia of Cow Head, bogs and sand dunes.

Though now mostly wilderness, the park area was home to two pre-European cultures, the Maritime Archaic Indians and the Dorset Eskimos, at various times from 2500 B.C. to A.D. 700. Vikings may have visited the park area around A.D. 1000; however, the first confirmed visit by a European was that of Jacques Cartier in 1534.

Typical wildlife includes moose, beavers, snowshoe hare and squirrels. Less frequently sighted are woodland caribou, black bears, foxes and lynx. Whales also are seen in nearby waters. The park boasts 239 species of birds, including gulls, terns, ducks, eagles, warblers and rock ptarmigan. More than half a million pairs of blackpoll warblers breed in the park, making this species the park's most abundant bird.

The area's varied bedrock, soil and elevation have created an environment where diverse plant communities, from seaweeds on the seashore to tundra-like vegetation on the mountain plateau, can exist. Facing the sea along the coast are wind-shaped and stunted balsam fir and white spruce, called tuckamore for their dense, compact form. Peatlands cover most of the coastal plain, while spruce, fir and birch trees cloak the mountain slopes.

General Information and Activities

The park is open all year. The visitor center is open daily 8-8, July 1-Labour Day weekend; daily 9-5, Victoria Day weekend-June 30 and day after Labour Day-Oct. 30; Mon.-Fri. 9-4, May 1-day before Victoria Day weekend. Phone ahead to confirm schedule. The Lobster Cove Head lighthouse and the Broom Point interpretation center both are open daily 10-5:30, mid-May to mid-Oct.

Hwy. 430, the major west coast highway known as the Viking Trail, traverses the park. Hwy. 431 branches off Hwy. 430 to the communities of Woody Point and Trout River.

There are more than 20 hiking trails within the park, ranging from a half-hour stroll down Old Mail Road, 3 kilometres (1.9 mi.) north of Cow Head, to a strenuous 3-day traverse through the Long Range Mountains. Well traveled is the Green Gardens Trail, a walking trail along the coast, 10 kilometres (6 mi.) southwest of Woody Point off Hwy. 431.

In addition to hiking, park activities include camping, picnicking, fishing and cross-country skiing. Overnight back-country camping requires a permit, and fishing is subject to national park regulations; contact the park visitor center or local merchants for details.

Outdoorsy types aren't the only ones drawn to the park. From late May to mid-September arts aficionados gather in Cow Head for the ▽▽ Gros Morne Theatre Festival, which features theatrical performances and traditional Newfoundland music.

The visitor center near Rocky Harbour features a videotape theater, nature exhibits and information about park facilities. Park interpreters conduct hikes and campfire and evening programs from late June through Labour Day. A schedule of interpretive programs is available at all park facilities. *See Recreation Chart.*

ADMISSION to the park mid-May through Oct. 31 is $9.80; $8.30 (ages 65+); $4.90 (ages 6-16); $19.60 (family). Rest of year $7.80; $6.80 (ages 65+); $3.90 (6-16); $15.70 (family).

PETS are permitted in the park but must be restrained at all times. They are not permitted on the top of Gros Morne Mountain or on the Western Brook Pond boat tour.

ADDRESS inquiries to the Superintendent, Gros Morne National Park of Canada, P.O. Box 130, Rocky Harbour, NL, Canada A0K 4N0. Phone (709) 458-2417, (877) 737-3783 for camping, or TTY (866) 787-6221 in Canada for camping in season.

BONTOURS boat tours depart from two locations in and around Gros Morne National Park of Canada; the ticket office is in the Ocean View Motel in Rocky Harbour. The 2-hour Western Brook Pond tour, departing from Western Brook Pond Dock, showcases the Western Brook Pond fjord, the Long Range Mountains, Western Brook Pond, waterfalls and wildlife.

The 2-hour Bonne Bay Discovery tour, departing from Norris Point Dock, features Killdevil, The Tablelands and the Long Range Mountains. The 2-hour Bonne Bay tour, departing from Norris Point Dock, interprets the bay's natural and cultural history.

Note: There is a 3-km (1.9-mi.) walk from the parking lot to the departure location for the Western Brook Pond tour. **Hours:** Tours are offered June-Sept.; phone for schedule. **Cost:** $27-$56; $17-$26 (ages 12-16); $14-$21 (ages 0-11). Passengers taking the Western Brook Pond tour also will need to purchase a national park admission pass. Reservations are recommended. **Phone:** (709) 458-2016 in season or (888) 458-2016.

THE DISCOVERY CENTRE is 4 km (2.5 mi.) w. on Hwy. 431 from Woody Point. Displays in the center educate visitors about the geology, plants, animals and marine mammals of Gros Morne National Park of Canada. Interactive exhibits include models, video programs, artwork and an interpretive garden. A giant 3-D map of the park also is featured.

Time: Allow 1 hour minimum. **Hours:** Daily 9-6 (also Sun. and Wed. 6-9 p.m.), late June-early Sept.; 9-5, mid-May to late June and early Sept. to mid-Oct. **Cost:** Free with park admission. **Phone:** (709) 458-2417.

HAPPY VALLEY-GOOSE BAY (B-5)
pop. 8,700

On Lake Melville in south-central Labrador, Happy Valley-Goose Bay occupies an area known for some of the best fishing in the province. It is accessible by air or boat from Newfoundland.

The area features a variety of trails allowing for such activities as biking and skiing throughout the year. The Happy Valley-Goose Bay Biking and Walking Trail commences in Happy Valley at the lower end of Hamilton River Road and culminates at the Industrial Park on the Canadian side. Birch Brook Nordic Ski Club and Hiking Trails, on Rte. 520 between Goose Bay and North West River, offers 11 groomed trails ranging in length from .5 to 10.4 km. The trails are fit for walking in summer and are arranged for skiing from December through April; phone (709) 896-8560. The Ski Mount Shana facility offers, from December through April, five downhill skiing trails of varying difficulty as well as length, ranging from 305 to 670 metres. A ski lift capable of transporting 44 skiers is on the premises; phone (709) 896-8162 for information.

In early August the ▽▽ Labrador Canoe Regatta is held on Gosling Lake; music and a strongman competition complete the adrenaline-filled experience.

CHERRYWOOD CORPORATE SUITES   **Phone:** 709/896-4000

▽▽ ▽▽
Extended Stay Hotel
Rates not provided

Address: 5 Cherrywood Dr A0P 1C0 **Location:** At Loring Dr. **Facility:** 6 kitchen units, some two bedrooms. 1 story, interior corridors. **Terms:** off-site registration. **Guest Services:** coin laundry.

GOOSE RIVER LODGES   **Phone:** 709/896-2600

▽▽ ▽▽
Cottage
Rates not provided

Address: NW River Rd A0P 1C0 **Location:** Jct Rt 500, 10.6 mi (17 km) nw on Rt 520. **Facility:** 9 cottages. 1 story, exterior corridors. *Bath:* shower only. **Parking:** winter plug-ins.
Activities: hiking trails, playground, horseshoes, volleyball. *Fee:* snowmobiling. **Guest Services:** coin laundry.

HOTEL NORTH   **Phone:** 709/896-9301

▽▽ ▽▽
Hotel
Rates not provided

Address: 25 Loring Dr A0P 1C0 **Location:** Just w of Hamilton River Rd. **Facility:** 54 units, some efficiencies. 1-2 stories (no elevator), interior corridors. **Parking:** winter plug-ins. **Dining:** Mariners Galley, see separate listing.
Activities: exercise room. **Guest Services:** coin laundry.

ROYAL INN & SUITES   **Phone:** 709/896-2456

▽▽ ▽▽
Motel
Rates not provided

Address: 5 Royal Ave A0P 1E0 **Location:** Corner of Tenth St. **Facility:** 37 units, some two bedrooms, efficiencies and kitchens. 2 stories (no elevator), exterior corridors.
Terms: office hours 7 am-11:50 pm. **Amenities:** high-speed Internet. **Guest Services:** coin laundry.

HOTEL NORTH TWO   Phone: 709/896-3398
[fyi]   Not evaluated. **Address:** 382 Hamilton River Rd A0P 1C0 **Location:** Jct Loring Dr. Facilities, services, and decor characterize a mid-scale property.

WHERE TO EAT

BENTLEY'S BEER MARKET   Phone: 709/896-3585

American
$7-$22

AAA Inspector Notes: This spacious, upbeat sports bar is a spot where patrons can unwind and catch up on their favorite game on one of the numerous TVs. Enjoy an array of finger foods or full meals including steak, fresh seafood, pasta and pizza-there certainly is something for everyone. **Bar:** full bar. **Address:** 97 Hamilton River Rd A0P 1E0 **Location:** Center; in Happy Valley area.

[L] [D] CALL[&M]

MARINERS GALLEY   Phone: 709/896-9301

Canadian
$7-$21

AAA Inspector Notes: The pleasant nautical decor includes model ships and a large galleon divider. The menu includes a fine selection of fresh seafood and some chicken and steak selections, as well as basic comfort foods. Servers are friendly and accommodating. **Bar:** full bar. **Address:** 25 Loring Dr A0P 1C0 **Location:** Just w of Hamilton River Rd; in Hotel North. [B] [L] [D]

MIDWAY GARDEN RESTAURANT   Phone: 709/896-5317

Canadian
$6-$20

AAA Inspector Notes: Serving the area for many years, this spacious family-style restaurant offers booth and table seating in a comfortable atmosphere. The menu lists everything from crispy Chester chicken to pizza and burgers. Take-out also is available. **Bar:** full bar. **Address:** 342 Hamilton River Rd A0P 1C0 **Location:** On Rt 520; center; in Goose Bay area. [L] [D]

VALLEY RESTAURANT   Phone: 709/896-7330

Canadian
$5-$12

AAA Inspector Notes: On the menu are home-style preparations and some traditional dishes, including caribou burgers, cod tongues and cod cheeks. Among other choices are daily specials and selections from the all-day breakfast menu. **Bar:** full bar. **Address:** 6 Grand St A0P 1E0 **Location:** Centre. [B] [L] [D]

HARBOUR GRACE (D-5) pop. 3,074

One of Newfoundland and Labrador's oldest and most historic towns, Harbour Grace evolved from the French settlement of Havre de Grace, founded in 1550. English pirate Peter Easton fortified the town in the early 17th century, using it as a base for his renegade band. Harbour Grace steadily developed into Newfoundland and Labrador's second largest town until a series of fires 1814-1944 reversed much of its progress.

With such setbacks on the ground, Harbour Grace turned to the skies to mark its place in history. Beginning in 1919, its runway accommodated such early transatlantic aviators as Wiley Post, who began a flight around the world in 1931, and Amelia Earhart, who took off the following year to become the first woman to make a solo flight across the Atlantic. A statue of Amelia Earhart stands at the intersection of Rte. 70 and Jamie's Way, about 1 kilometre (.6 mi.) west of the airfield she used. The aircraft *Spirit of Harbour Grace* also is displayed at this site.

Among several historic structures in town spared by the seven crippling fires are one of the oldest jails in Canada, one of the oldest Canadian courthouses still in service and St. Paul's Anglican Church, built in 1835.

Harbour Grace Tourist Chalet: P.O. Box 310, Harbour Grace, NL, Canada A0A 2M0. **Phone:** (709) 596-3042.

CONCEPTION BAY MUSEUM, on Water St. in the historic district, is in the 1870 Customs House; the first recorded structure on this site was the 1610 pirate fort of Peter Easton. The museum uses artifacts and period rooms to recount local history, including early transatlantic flight. **Time:** Allow 1 hour minimum. **Hours:** Daily 10-5, June-Sept. **Cost:** $3; $2 (students with ID and children); $1 (ages 66+). **Phone:** (709) 596-5465 Oct.-May.

HEART'S CONTENT (D-4) pop. 418

In 1866 Heart's Content was the focus of one of the greatest technological achievements of the age: the landing of the first successful transatlantic cable. On July 27 the town became the western terminus of the cable that spanned the ocean floor to Valentia, Ireland. Recruited to do the job was the mammoth *Great Eastern*, five times the size of the largest ship afloat at the time.

Other cables were landed in the following decades, and Heart's Content served as a base of Western Union's international cable system until transoceanic telephone cable and satellite communication rendered submarine cable obsolete in the 1960s.

HEART'S CONTENT CABLE STATION PROVINCIAL HISTORIC SITE, 1 km (.6 mi.) n.e. on Hwy. 80 from jct. Hwy 74, consists of the original telegraph buildings and equipment used for the early transatlantic cables to Europe. Interpretive displays explain the station's role in cable history through the 19th and 20th centuries. The station received its first message in 1866 and continued operating until 1965. **Hours:** Daily 10-5:30, Victoria Day weekend-Fri. before Thanksgiving. **Cost:** $3; free (ages 0-12 and Sun.). **Phone:** (709) 583-2160 or (709) 729-0592.

HOLYROOD (E-5) pop. 2,005

Holyrood is a popular summer resort area with coastal scenery and excellent fishing. Nearby streams contain salmon and trout.

SALMONIER NATURE PARK, 12 km (7 mi.) s. of jct. hwys. 1 and 90, is a nature and wildlife preserve. About 40 hectares (100 acres) of the 1,200-hectare (2,965-acre) preserve have been developed for public exhibitions. A boardwalk nature trail links many large enclosures where native mammals and birds—many of which have been rescued and wouldn't survive in the wild—can be seen. The trail is about 3 kilometres (1.9 mi.) long; allow 1 hour minimum for the complete hike.

Trained staff members provide programs that include movies, puppet shows and interpretive theater presentations relating to the province's natural history. **Note:** Though the trail is accessible by stroller and wheelchair, visitors may find it difficult to use wheelchairs that are not power-operated or rugged. **Hours:** Daily 10-6, June 1-Labour Day; 10-4, day after Labour Day-Thanksgiving. **Cost:** Free. **Phone:** (709) 229-7189. 🅰

LABRADOR CITY pop. 8,500

CAROL INN ▼▼▼ ▼▼▼
Hotel
Rates not provided

Phone: 709/944-7736
Address: 215 Drake Ave A2V 2B6 **Location:** Centre. **Facility:** 22 efficiencies. 2 stories (no elevator), interior corridors. **Amenities:** honor bars. **Dining:** Jordan's Family Restaurant, see separate listing. **Guest Services:** coin laundry.

TWO SEASONS INN
Phone: 709/944-2661
[fyi] Not evaluated. **Address:** Avalon Dr A2V 2L3 **Location:** At Drake Ave; centre. Facilities, services, and decor characterize a mid-scale property.

WHERE TO EAT

JORDAN'S FAMILY RESTAURANT **Phone:** 709/944-7772
▼▼▼ ▼▼▼
Canadian
$6-$18

AAA Inspector Notes: The family-style restaurant serves all meals. The menu offers a vast array of comfort foods, including burgers, deep-fried chicken, ribs, fish and chips, pizza and steaks. Service is relaxed and friendly. **Bar:** full bar. **Address:** 215 Drake Ave A2V 2B6 **Location:** Centre; in Carol Inn. Ⓑ Ⓛ Ⓓ

TWO SEASONS RESTAURANT **Phone:** 709/944-2661
▼▼▼ ▼▼▼
Canadian
$6-$18

AAA Inspector Notes: In a convenient location, the restaurant has two dining sections: the more casual front section and the upscale spot in the back. Food is served fresh and in ample portions. **Bar:** full bar. **Address:** Avalon Dr A2V 2L3 **Location:** At Drake Ave; centre; in Two Seasons Inn. Ⓑ Ⓛ Ⓓ

L'ANSE-AMOUR (B-5)

Situated at the southern tip of Labrador, L'Anse-Amour is the site of an ancient burial mound containing artifacts detailing the lives of the Maritime Archaic people some 7,000 years ago. Visitors to the area can view this historic site in addition to exploring the rocky coastline.

Taken from the old French name of L'Anse aux Morts, "Cove of Deaths," L'Anse-Amour has been the site of many shipwrecks, including two Royal Navy vessels. The remnants of the HMS *Raleigh*, which ran aground in 1922, can be seen along the beach.

 POINT AMOUR LIGHTHOUSE is off Hwy. 510 on L'Anse Amour Rd. At a lofty 33 metres (109 ft.), the 1854 Point Amour Lighthouse is the tallest in Atlantic Canada. It was built with locally quarried limestone, and its massive walls are almost 2 metres (6 ft.) thick.

You can climb 132 steps to view a breathtaking panorama of the coastline and the Strait of Belle Isle; if you're lucky you'll spot a whale or an iceberg. There also is a picturesque interpretive walking trail along the shore.

A two-story museum in the lighthouse keeper's home contains a collection of artifacts tracing 4 centuries of maritime history. Guided tours of this building are led by staff dressed in period costumes.

Time: Allow 1 hour minimum. **Hours:** Daily 10-5:30, mid-May to early Oct. **Cost:** $3; free (ages 0-12 and to all Sun.). **Phone:** (709) 927-5825, (709) 729-0592, (709) 931-2013 or (800) 563-6353. 🅰

L'ANSE AU CLAIR pop. 226

NORTHERN LIGHT INN ◆◆◆
Hotel
$109-$129

Phone: 709/931-2332
Address: Rt 510 A0K 3K0 **Location:** Centre. **Facility:** 54 units, some cottages. 2 stories (no elevator), interior corridors. **Amenities:** *Some:* high-speed Internet. **Dining:** Basque Dining Room, see separate listing. **Guest Services:** coin laundry.

WHERE TO EAT

BASQUE DINING ROOM
Phone: 709/931-2332
◆◆◆
Canadian
$6-$20

AAA Inspector Notes: Home-style cooking is what guests expect at the family restaurant. Representative of fresh seafood and meat entrees are some local favorites, including cod tongues and cheeks. Portions are hearty, but it's worth saving room for one of the homemade desserts. **Bar:** full bar. **Address:** Rt 510 A0K 3K0 **Location:** Centre; in Northern Light Inn. Ⓑ Ⓛ Ⓓ

L'ANSE AUX MEADOWS (B-5)

NORSTEAD—A VIKING VILLAGE AND PORT OF TRADE is about 1.5 km (.9 mi.) e. off Hwy. 436, following signs. The site's features have been designed to represent the Viking era (790-1066). A church, blacksmith shop, chieftain's hall and barns are included; *Snorri*, a replica of a Viking ship, also is on the premises. Guides in period costume give interactive demonstrations, allowing visitors to get an idea of what life was like some 1,000 years ago. Dramatic and comedic performances lasting between 1 hour and 70 minutes are offered during the Norstead Theatre Festival.

Time: Allow 1 hour, 30 minutes minimum. **Hours:** Daily 9:30-5:30, early June-late Sept. Norstead Theatre Festival performances Wed.-Mon. at 8 p.m., June-Aug. **Cost:** $10; $8 (ages 66+); $6.50 (ages 6-15); $30 (family). Norstead Theatre Festival performances $20. **Phone:** (709) 623-2828, or (877) 620-2828 in Canada. 🅰

L'ANSE AUX MEADOWS NATIONAL HISTORIC SITE OF CANADA (A-3)

At the tip of Newfoundland's Great Northern Peninsula about 25 kilometres (16 mi.) off Hwy. 430 on Hwy. 436, L'Anse aux Meadows National Historic Site of Canada is the only authenticated Norse site in North America.

According to sagas, the Vikings explored and exploited the resources of the region known as Vinland more than 1,000 years ago. Excavations have disclosed the size and location of the buildings that formed the resource camp. Discoveries include the remains of sod houses, a small forge for smelting iron, several workshops, a bronze cloak pin and a spindle whorl.

Replicas of the Vikings' Scandinavian-type sod houses have been constructed. The visitor reception center has an exhibit detailing the Norse presence in North America. Costumed interpreters explain the function of each building. The Viking site at L'Anse aux Meadows has been declared a World Heritage Site by UNESCO (United Nations Educational, Scientific and Cultural Organization). A walking trail follows the shoreline.

Picnicking is permitted. Guided tours are available. Allow 2 hours minimum. Daily 9-6, June 1 to mid-Oct. Admission $11.70; $10.05 (ages 65+); $5.80 (ages 6-16); $29.40 (family, up to seven members). **Cards:** AX, MC, VI. For information write L'Anse aux Meadows National Historic Site of Canada, P.O. Box 70, St. Lunaire-Griquet, NL, Canada A0K 2X0. Phone (709) 623-2608, or (709) 458-2417 off-season.

MARYSTOWN pop. 5,436

MARYSTOWN HOTEL & CONVENTION CENTRE
Phone: 709/279-1600

[fyi] Not evaluated. **Address:** 76 Ville Marie Dr A0E 2M0 **Location:** Centre. Facilities, services, and decor characterize a mid-scale property.

MOBILE (E-5) pop. 221

MOLLY BAWN WHALE AND PUFFIN TOURS is off Hwy. 10 on Gus O'Reilly Rd. Seabirds and whales can be seen on this 1-hour tour of Witless Bay Ecological Reserve aboard *Molly Bawn II*. Black guillemots, kittiwakes, murres, northern fulmars, puffins and razorbills are frequently sighted. Occasionally dolphins, eagles and icebergs can be seen. **Hours:** Tours depart daily every 90 minutes 10-7, mid-June to early Sept. **Cost:** $30; $25 (ages 6-15 and 65+). **Phone:** (709) 334-2621 May-Sept., or (709) 334-3759 all year.

Find valuable AAA/CAA
member savings
at AAA.com/discounts

THE CAPTAIN'S TABLE RESTAURANT
Phone: 709/334-2278

Seafood
$8-$20

AAA Inspector Notes: The restaurant is a delightful spot to sample great seafood in a relaxing atmosphere. The fish and chips dish is made with fresh cod, and the chowders are a must. Homemade desserts include bumbleberry pie and warm apple dumplings. **Bar:** full bar. **Address:** Rt 10 A0A 3A0 **Location:** Centre.

L D AC

MOUNT PEARL

AROUND THE WORLD RESTAURANT
Phone: 709/368-3494

International
$9-$21

AAA Inspector Notes: As the name might imply, this restaurant offers a wide variety of cuisine options. From basic comfort foods such as burgers, sandwiches, wings and various soups and salads to a few traditional Newfoundland items such as cod tongues and scrunchions to some Mexican, Thai, Italian and Indian options. A fine selection of homemade desserts can be tempting. The decor is basic with booth and table seating and a relaxed atmosphere. **Bar:** full bar. **Address:** Commonwealth Ave A1N 1W8 **Location:** Just n of Smallwood Dr; in Commonwealth Court. B L D

SMITTY'S
Phone: 709/368-8690

Canadian
$7-$20

AAA Inspector Notes: The family-oriented restaurant satisfies patrons with its ever-popular all-day breakfast items, as well as tasty and wholesome soups and salads at lunchtime. A relaxed mood characterizes the dining space. **Bar:** full bar. **Address:** 26 Gibson Dr A1N 5K8 **Location:** Corner of Old Placentia Rd. B L D

MUSGRAVE HARBOUR (C-4) pop. 1,085

Musgrave Harbour lies on the coast of scenic Hamilton Sound where giant icebergs carried south by the Labrador Current are frequently sighted from Hwy. 320. Representative of the region's many maritime associations is the Musgrave Harbour Fisherman's Museum at 4 Marine Dr. It is in a building designed by Sir William Coaker. In 1908 Coaker founded the Fisherman's Protective Union, a political and economic power during World War I.

Sir Frederick Banting Memorial Park, 10 kilometres (6 mi.) east on Hwy. 330, has a playground, miniature golf course, picnic area and hiking trails.

SPINDRIFT-BY-THE-SEA COUNTRY INN
Phone: 709/655-2175

[fyi] Not evaluated. **Address:** 87 Main St A0G 3J0 **Location:** Oceanfront. Rt 330. Facilities, services, and decor characterize a mid-scale property.

NEWTOWN (C-4)

BARBOUR LIVING HERITAGE VILLAGE on Hwy. 330, contains eight restored buildings that once belonged to prosperous merchants and sailors of the Barbour family. The buildings, which date to the late 1800s, are furnished with antiques and contain items brought back from the family's worldwide travels. Evening plays are presented in a restored building once used by the family to salt fish. **Hours:**

One-hour guided tours are given daily 10-6, June-Oct. **Cost:** $7; $6 (ages 60+); $3 (ages 5-18); $15 (family, two adults and children ages 0-18). **Phone:** (709) 536-3220.

NORRIS POINT (C-2) pop. 900

BONNE BAY MARINE STATION is 1.2 km s. on Main St. to the Norris Point Dock, just s. of jct. Clarke's Rd. and Main St. The two-story facility offers 45-minute guided tours during which visitors learn about such Bonne Bay marine plants as algae and plankton as well as crabs and other animals. Interactive touch tanks include sea stars and a variety of fish species. Two-hour boat tours of the bay allow passengers to collect plankton, spot such wildlife as bald eagles and whales and enjoy views of the surrounding Gros Morne National Park. Bay kayaking tours of varying foci and length also are offered.

Time: Allow 1 hour minimum. **Hours:** Tours of the station are offered daily 9-5, late May-Aug. 31; by appointment rest of year. Boat tours depart from the BonTours wharf Mon., Wed. and Fri. at 2, July-Aug. **Cost:** $6.25; $5 (ages 6-17 and 65+); $15 (family, two adults and two children); $3.25 (each additional child with paid family rate). Boat tour $27; $17 (ages 12-16); $62 (family, two adults and two children); $8 (each additional child with paid family rate). Boat tours require a minimum of 10 passengers per departure. **Parking:** Free. **Phone:** (709) 458-2550 or (709) 458-2874.

SUGAR HILL INN   **Phone:** 709/458-2147
[fyi]   Not evaluated. **Address:** Norris Point A0K 3V0 **Location:** Rt 430, 2.5 mi (4 km) s, follow signs. Facilities, services, and decor characterize a mid-scale property.

NORTH WEST RIVER (B-5)

Labrador Heritage Society Museum, on Portage Road, preserves the history of the Labrador people through photographs, manuscripts, book collections and displays; phone (709) 497-8858 or (709) 497-8566.

LABRADOR INTERPRETATION CENTRE is at 2 Portage Rd. Exhibits feature 9,000 years of Labrador's history and cultures. Artifacts include tools and modes of transportation. A theater shows brief films about Labrador and its people. Other highlights are life-size dioramas and a view of the mountain ranges. **Time:** Allow 1 hour minimum. **Hours:** Daily 10-4:30, early June to mid-Sept.; Wed.-Sun. 1-4, rest of year. Closed Armistice Day. Phone ahead to confirm schedule. **Cost:** Free. **Phone:** (709)

497-8566 or (709) 899-1558.

PARADISE   pop. 12,584

WOODSTOCK COLONIAL RESTAURANT
                                Phone: 709/722-6933

Canadian
$10-$26

AAA Inspector Notes: Since 1927, this spacious restaurant has featured a rustic colonial country decor in several dining sections with knickknacks on the walls and along plate racks. Home-style cooking includes a fine variety of fresh seafood and Newfoundland game meat including flipper pie, wild rabbit and venison. The friendly staff provides homey service. **Bar:** full bar. **Reservations:** suggested. **Address:** 1959 Topsail Rd A1W 1Z4 **Location:** Trans-Canada Hwy 1 exit 43, 3 mi (5 km) n. [D]

PORT AU CHOIX   pop. 893

THE SEA ECHO MOTEL   **Phone:** 709/861-3777
[fyi]   Not evaluated. **Address:** Fisher St A0K 4C0 **Location:** Centre. Facilities, services, and decor characterize an economy property.

WHERE TO EAT

THE ANCHOR CAFE   **Phone:** 709/861-3665
American
$7-$18

AAA Inspector Notes: Although this nautically themed family restaurant does not offer ocean views, it does serve the freshest made-to-order seafood and comfort foods, which come in ample portions. A take-out window is available in season. **Bar:** full bar. **Address:** Fisher St A0K 4C0 **Location:** Centre. [L] [D]

PORT AU CHOIX NATIONAL HISTORIC SITE OF CANADA (B-2)

Port au Choix National Historic Site of Canada is 15 kilometres (9 mi.) west of the Port Saunders-Port au Choix turnoff from Hwy. 430. In 1967 a local resident excavating for the construction of a new building discovered human bones, tools and weapons. The discovery led to archeological work that uncovered an ancient burial ground in the area. Scientific testing of the bones and artifacts disclosed that the burial ground was in use between 2300 B.C. and 1200 B.C.; it is said to be one of the largest hunter-gatherer burial grounds in North America.

A visitor center has displays and artifacts from the site's resident Maritime Archaic Indians as well as from the Dorset and Groswater Paleoeskimos, other prehistoric groups that lived along the coast. At each of the archeological sites are interpretive panels describing the site's significance. The nearby Point Riche Lighthouse is a popular spot for picnicking and photography.

Site open daily 24 hours. Visitor center open daily 9-6, June 1 to early Oct. Admission $7.80; $6.55 (ages 65+); $3.90 (ages 6-16); $19.60 (family). For information contact the Superintendent, P.O. Box 140, Port au Choix, NL, Canada A0K 4C0. Phone (709) 861-3522, or (709) 458-2417 off-season.

PORT AU PORT WEST-AGUATHUNA-FELIX COVE (D-1)
pop. 386

OUR LADY OF MERCY CHURCH is on Hwy. 460. After 11 years of construction, the church was consecrated in 1925. The largest wooden structure in the province, its steeple reaches 30 metres (100 ft.). Statues, ornate woodwork and 14 hand-carved stations of the cross made in Italy of Carrara and travertine marble are some of the religious treasures inside. The rectory now houses a museum with such items as religious articles from the church's earlier days and local artifacts.

Time: Allow 1 hour minimum. **Hours:** Daily 10-5, mid-June through Labour Day. **Cost:** Church $3. Museum $2; free (ages 0-11 accompanied by an adult). **Phone:** (709) 648-2632 or (709) 648-2745.

PORT BLANDFORD   pop. 521

TERRA NOVA GOLF RESORT   **Phone:** 709/543-2525

Hotel
Rates not provided
Address: Trans-Canada Hwy 1 A0C 2G0 **Location:** Centre. **Facility:** 83 units, some efficiencies, houses and cottages. 4 stories, interior corridors. **Terms:** seasonal. **Pool(s):** heated outdoor. **Activities:** 2 tennis courts, hiking trails. *Fee:* golf-27 holes. **Guest Services:** complimentary laundry.

TERRA NOVA HOSPITALITY HOME & COTTAGES
Phone: 709/543-2260

[fyi] Not evaluated. **Address:** Trans-Canada Hwy A0C 2G0 **Location:** On Trans-Canada Hwy 1; centre. Facilities, services, and decor characterize a mid-scale property.

PORTLAND CREEK   pop. 91

MOUNTAIN WATERS RESORT   **Phone:** 709/898-2490

[fyi] Not evaluated. **Address:** Viking Trail A0G **Location:** On Rt 430, 3 mi (5 km) n, 1 mi (1.6 km) on gravel entry road. Facilities, services, and decor characterize a mid-scale property.

PORT REXTON   pop. 351

FISHERS' LOFT INN   **Phone:** 709/464-3240
Country Inn
Rates not provided
Address: Mill Rd A0C 2H0 **Location:** On Rt 230; centre. **Facility:** With a wonderful location on a hill overlooking Trinity Bay, three buildings house spacious guest units, some of which boast water views. 21 units. 2 stories (no elevator), interior corridors. **Terms:** seasonal. **Activities:** hiking trails. **Guest Services:** valet laundry.

Safety tip: Keep a current
AAA/CAA Road Atlas
in every vehicle

PORTUGAL COVE CB

THE BEACH HOUSE ROOMS & SUITES
Phone: 709/895-1250

Country Inn
Rates not provided
Address: 38 Beachy Cove Rd A1M 1N3 **Location:** Oceanfront. On Rt 40 (Portugal Cove Rd); centre. **Facility:** On the shoreline overlooking Portugal Cove and Bell Island, this lovely property offers fine accommodation in suites, cottages and guest rooms. 10 units, some kitchens and cottages. 2 stories (no elevator), exterior corridors. **Terms:** office hours 7 am-11 pm. **Amenities:** honor bars. **Dining:** Atlantica Restaurant, see separate listing. **Guest Services:** complimentary laundry.

WHERE TO EAT

ATLANTICA RESTAURANT   **Phone:** 709/895-1250

Regional Canadian
$29-$45
AAA Inspector Notes: This beautiful dining room offers a splendid view of Portugal Cove and Bell Island. Its menu focuses on fresh local seafood and fine cuts of meat, including steak, duck and chicken. All foods are creatively prepared by a highly skilled team, and service is friendly and professional. **Bar:** full bar. **Reservations:** required. **Address:** 38 Beachy Cove Rd A0A 3K0 **Location:** On Rt 40 (Portugal Cove Rd); centre; in The Beach House Rooms & Suites. [D]

PORTUGAL COVE SOUTH (E-4) pop. 222, elev. 10m/36'

MISTAKEN POINT ECOLOGICAL RESERVE is 16 km (10 mi.) s.e. of Portugal Cove South via the Cape Race Lighthouse gravel road. Mistaken Point, appointed its name due to the quandary of navigating its parlous surrounding waters, which is said to have caused more than 50 shipwrecks, once was a sea floor during the late Precambrian age some 575 million years ago. The site preserves an assemblage of fossils from this time, including the imprints of more than 20 species of ancient soft-bodied organisms. Some of these fossils are similar to specimens found in Australia and Russia, lending further credence to the once supercontinent Pangaea.

Visitor access to the reserve's fossils is permitted only by official Newfoundland Parks and Natural Areas guided tours originating at the Edge of Avalon Interpretive Centre on Rte. 10. The center houses a selection of Mistaken Point fossils and provides information about the area. The road heading to the reserve features walking trails and leads to the 1907 Cape Race Lighthouse, which received the wireless distress signals from the *Titanic* after it struck an iceberg in 1912.

Note: Though the gravel road leading to the reserve entrance is rough and rugged, no off-road or all-terrain vehicles, including snowmobiles, are permitted in the reserve. The route taken on the guided tours can be slippery and muddy in places. Visitors are advised to exercise caution and wear sturdy walking shoes or boots. A small stream must be crossed via stepping stones en route to the fossil site. Dress appropriately for cool (and often wet and windy) weather, while taking into consideration the frequent occurrence of fog (156 days per year on average). Allow 3 hours minimum (including travel time from the interpretive center to the trailhead). **Hours:** Guided tours of the reserve depart daily at 1, early May-early Oct. Interpretive center daily 10-7, mid-May to mid-Oct. Lighthouse daily dawn-dusk, year-round. **Cost:** Free. **Phone:** (709) 635-4520 or (709) 438-1100.

POUCH COVE (D-5) pop. 1,756

One of the oldest communities on the Avalon Peninsula, Pouch (POOCH) Cove attracted settlers as early as 1611. Those who settled in the town did so outside the law, since permanent residence in Newfoundland and Labrador was illegal in the 17th and 18th centuries. Pouch Cove's dangerous harbor, however, kept away most ships that threatened discovery.

RATTLING BROOK

WINDAMERE CABINS   **Phone:** 709/268-3863
[fyi]   Not evaluated. **Address:** Rt 391 A0J 1H0 **Location:** 0.6 mi (1 km) s. Facilities, services, and decor characterize an economy property.

RED BAY (B-5) pop. 227

Red Bay is considered to be the site of the first industrial enterprise in North America—production of whale oil for European markets in the 16th century.

RED BAY NATIONAL HISTORIC SITE OF CANADA, on Hwy. 510, displays artifacts from a 16th-century Basque whaling station. A short ferry ride to Saddle Island allows visitors to tour the remnants of the station's structures and a whaler's cemetery. **Hours:** Museum daily 9-6, June 1-Oct. 1. Saddle Island tours daily 9-5, July-Sept. **Cost:** Museum $7.80; $6.55 (ages 66+); $3.90 (ages 6-16); $19.60 (family). Ferry $2; free (ages 0-6). **Phone:** (709) 920-2051 or (709) 920-2142.

REIDVILLE (C-2)

NEWFOUNDLAND INSECTARIUM, Hwy. 1 exit 16, then .5 km (.3 mi.) n. on Hwy. 430, is on 10 hectares (25 acres) bordering the Humber River. Featured are more than 100 live and mounted displays, including spiders, butterflies, beetles and scorpions.

Time: Allow 1 hour minimum. **Hours:** Daily 9-6, July-Aug.; Mon.-Fri. 9-5, Sat.-Sun. noon-5, May-June and Sept.-Oct. **Cost:** $10.50; $9 (senior citizens); $7 (ages 5-14). **Phone:** (709) 635-4545 or (866) 635-5454.

ROCKY HARBOUR pop. 978

FISHERMAN'S LANDING INN   **Phone:** 709/458-2711
Hotel
$129-$189 6/1-9/30
$99-$139 10/1-5/31
Address: 21-29 W Link Rd A0K 4N0 **Location:** Rt 430; first entrance to Rocky Harbour. **Facility:** 40 units. 1 story, interior/exterior corridors. **Terms:** cancellation fee imposed. **Dining:** The Galley Dining Room, see separate listing. **Activities:** whirlpool, exercise room. **Guest Services:** complimentary laundry.

A-1 WILDFLOWERS BED & BREAKFAST
                                Phone: 709/458-3000
[fyi]   Not evaluated. **Address:** 108 Main St N A0K 4N0 **Location:** Rt 430, just s on W Link Rd, just w on Pond Rd, then 0.6 mi (1 km) n. Facilities, services, and decor characterize an economy property.

GROS MORNE CABINS   **Phone:** 709/458-2020
[fyi]   Not evaluated. **Address:** 772 Main St S A0K 4N0 **Location:** Oceanfront. Rt 430, just s on W Link Rd, just w on Pond Rd, then just s. Facilities, services, and decor characterize a mid-scale property.

OCEAN VIEW HOTEL   **Phone:** 709/458-2730
[fyi]   Not evaluated. **Address:** 38-42 Main St A0K 4N0 **Location:** Rt 430, just s on W Link Rd, just w on Pond Rd, then just n. Facilities, services, and decor characterize an economy property.

WHERE TO EAT

THE GALLEY DINING ROOM   **Phone:** 709/458-2711
American
$15-$25
AAA Inspector Notes: This quaint dining room offers fresh seafood and steak options as well as some comfort foods including burgers, sandwiches, soups and chowders. **Bar:** full bar. **Address:** 21-29 W Link Rd A0K 4N0 **Location:** Rt 430 southbound exit to Rocky Harbour; in Fisherman's Landing Inn. [B] [D]

ROSE BLANCHE (D-1)

ROSE BLANCHE LIGHTHOUSE is on Hwy. 470. Local workers built the lighthouse 1871-73 using granite from a nearby quarry. D & T Stevenson, a Scottish company named after the father and uncle of author Robert Louis Stevenson, assisted in the project. The structure was reconstructed in 1999 using most of the original materials. The house is furnished with antiques and some reproduced pieces representative of the 19th century.

Note: The lighthouse is reached via a 10-minute walk along a winding gravel path. The area sometimes is foggy. **Tours:** Guided tours are available. **Time:** Allow 1 hour minimum. **Hours:** Daily 9-9, May-Oct. **Cost:** $3; $2 (ages 6-18); $7 (family). **Phone:** (709) 956-2052, or (709) 956-2903 during the off-season.

ST. ALBANS pop. 1,278

ST. ALBAN'S INN   **Phone:** 709/538-3885
[fyi]   Not evaluated. **Address:** 140 Main St A0H 2E0 **Location:** Centre. Facilities, services, and decor characterize an economy property.

ST. ANTHONY (C-5) pop. 2,442

St. Anthony is the main service center for the northern portion of the Great Northern Peninsula. The Jordi Bonet murals, in the Charles S. Curtis Memorial Hospital, depict scenes from Sir Wilfred Grenfell's life.

GRENFELL INTERPRETATION CENTRE & HISTORIC PROPERTIES is in the center of town on Hwy. 430. The center has displays that highlight the life of Sir Wilfred Grenfell, founder of the Grenfell Hospital Mission to Newfoundland and Labrador. He established the hospital in response to the needs of destitute fishermen in the area and was knighted for his work in 1928. Exhibits at the Dock House Museum detail the impact of fishing on the area; displays show how boats were built and repaired.

At the end of a walking trail is Tea House Hill, the burial site of Grenfell and his wife. A rotunda features ceramic murals depicting life in the province. A park also is on the grounds. **Time:** Allow 2 hours minimum. **Hours:** Daily 9-6, mid-June to late Sept.; otherwise varies. Phone ahead to confirm schedule. **Cost:** (Includes Grenfell House Museum) $10; $8 (ages 60+); $3 (ages 5-18); $22 (family, two adults and children ages 0-11). **Phone:** (709) 454-4010.

Grenfell House Museum is in the center of town on Hwy. 430. The museum was the home of Sir Wilfred Grenfell. Built in the early 1900s, the building now houses artifacts, antiques and exhibits about Grenfell's life and work. **Time:** Allow 1 hour minimum. **Hours:** Tours daily 9-6, mid-June to mid-Sept.; by appointment rest of year. Phone ahead to confirm schedule. **Cost:** Included in Grenfell Interpretation Centre & Historic Properties admission of $10; $8 (ages 60+); $3 (ages 5-18); $22 (family, two adults and children ages 0-11). **Phone:** (709) 454-4010.

NORTHLAND DISCOVERY BOAT TOURS is off Hwy. 430 on West St. Offering excursions aboard a 15-metre (50-ft.) vessel, this tour company takes passengers into Iceberg Alley, where icebergs, dolphins, whales and a variety of birds can be seen. **Time:** Allow 3 hours minimum. **Hours:** Tours depart daily at 9, 1 and 4, late May to mid-Sept. **Cost:** $55; $28 (ages 13-17); $20 (ages 5-12); $10 (ages 2-4). **Phone:** (709) 454-3092 or (877) 632-3747.

ST. BRIDE'S (E-4) pop. 386

CAPE ST. MARY'S ECOLOGICAL RESERVE, 5 km (3 mi.) s. on Hwy. 100, then 16 km (10 mi.) s. on a paved road to the cape, features a wide variety of birds, including gannets, common murres, thick-billed murres, black-legged kittiwakes, razorbills and black guillemots. A 1.4-kilometre (.9 mi.) trail meanders along the coast and leads to Bird Rock, a 100-metre-tall (328-ft.) sandstone bank where the birds congregate; photographic opportunities abound. An interpretive center contains exhibits about seabirds and a scale model of the reserve.

Whales, dolphins, porpoises and seals can be seen during the summer. In spring and fall shorebirds and raptors migrate to the area. Winter brings sea ducks, including harlequins and common eiders.

Note: Stay on the trail and avoid steep slopes and cliff edges. Check with staff about trail conditions before beginning. The area sometimes is windy and foggy. The trail contains areas of loose rock and sometimes is slippery. **Time:** Allow 2 hours, 30 minutes minimum. **Hours:** Reserve daily 24 hours. Interpretive center daily 8-7, mid-June to mid-Sept.; 9-5 in May and Oct. **Cost:** Free. **Phone:** (709) 277-1666, or (709) 635-4520 off-season. 🏕

BIRD ISLAND RESORT   Phone: 709/337-2450
[fyi] Not evaluated. **Address:** Rt 100 A0B 2Z0
      Location: Centre. Facilities, services, and decor characterize an economy property.

WHERE TO EAT

ATLANTICA INN RESTAURANT   Phone: 709/337-2860
[fyi] Not evaluated. Basic favorite dishes are on the menu of the modest restaurant. **Address:** Rt 100 A0B 2Z0 **Location:** Centre.

ST. JOHN'S (E-5) pop. 100,646
• Hotels p. 112 • Restaurants p. 113

One of the oldest cities in North America, St. John's is the capital, principal port and commercial center of the island. It is believed to be named for the feast day of St. John the Baptist, since it was on that day in 1497 that John Cabot discovered Newfoundland and Labrador. The city's perfectly sheltered harbor drew many European explorers and fishermen during the 1500s, until Sir Humphrey Gilbert sailed into the harbor on Aug. 5, 1583, and reaffirmed possession of Newfoundland and Labrador by claiming the land for the British.

St. John's achieved much of its importance because of its geographic position. It is closer to Europe than any other city in North America. From Lester's Field within the city boundaries, Capt. John Alcock and Lt. Arthur Brown flew to Clifden, Ireland, in 1919, completing the first nonstop flight across the Atlantic Ocean in 16 hours.

History is commemorated with several memorials. The Sir Humphrey Gilbert Plaque on Water Street marks the area where Sir Humphrey planted the Royal Standard of Elizabeth I in 1583. Above the plaque is the Provincial War Memorial, honoring Newfoundland and Labrador's war dead. A statue of Gaspar Côrte-Real, on Prince Philip Drive in the city's north end, recognizes the significance of the explorer and his country, Portugal, in Newfoundland and Labrador history.

On King's Bridge Road is the Commissariat House, the Georgian home of the assistant commissary general who was responsible for outfitting the British garrison in town. The 1818-21 house, furnished in period, is most accessible through a walking tour of the city because parking is limited; phone (709) 729-6730 or (709) 729-0592.

Memorial University of Newfoundland was founded in 1925 as a memorial to the province's World War I dead and has achieved a world reputation for cold-ocean research.

Of historical interest northeast of St. John's is Torbay, the 1762 landing site of Lt. Col. William Amherst and his troops. From Torbay, Amherst marched to defeat the French at Signal Hill *(see Signal Hill National Historic Site of Canada p. 115).* Fort Amherst, the first lighthouse in the province, was built by the British Military Garrison in 1810. It is located at the base of the Southside Hills, opposite Signal Hill.

The Arts and Culture Centre on Prince Philip Drive at Allendale Road offers a theater and library; phone (709) 729-3900.

A popular reminder of the city's past is the St. John's Regatta, held on Quidi Vidi Lake the first Wednesday in August; if the weather is unfavorable for rowing, the regatta occurs the next favorable day. Dating from 1825, the regatta is considered one of the oldest continuing sports events in North America; music and games of chance supplement the racing fun.

The East Coast Trail runs south of St. John's along the Avalon Peninsula to Cappahayden, offering hikers an unparalleled view of the Newfoundland and Labrador coast, its historic sites and settlements. When completed, the route will extend 540 kilometres (335 mi.) to Trepassey Bay. Trail segments range in difficulty and walking distance, from 1.5 to 10 hours. Phone (709) 738-4453 for trail guides and information.

The Grand Concourse Walkways comprise a 125-kilometre (78-mi.) system of trails traversing the city as well as nearby Mount Pearl and Paradise. Phone (709) 737-1077 for more information.

During the ⬥ Festival 500 *Sharing the Voices* event in July, local venues host a series of noncompetitive performances showcasing the talents of international choral groups.

The City of St. John's Economic Development, Tourism & Culture: P.O. Box 908, St. John's, NL, Canada A1C 5M2. **Phone:** (709) 576-8106 or (709) 576-8455.

Self-guiding tours: Walking and driving tour information is provided in the St. John's Visitor Guide, available at 348 Water St. and at the airport.

Shopping areas: Water Street, one of the oldest thoroughfares in North America, has been the commercial center of St. John's for more than 400 years. The street is lined with a variety of stores, restaurants and pubs. Duckworth Street, running parallel to Water Street, has an array of boutiques and ethnic restaurants.

ANGLICAN CATHEDRAL OF ST. JOHN THE BAPTIST, Gower St. at Church Hill, is said to be one of the finest examples of ecclesiastical Gothic architecture in North America. Construction began in 1847 and the cornerstone was laid in 1849. After the Great Fire of 1892, restoration efforts continued for 13 years. Sculptured arches and carved furnishings are of interest. **Hours:** Tours daily 10-noon and 2-4, early June-Sept. 30; by appointment rest of year. **Cost:** Free. **Phone:** (709) 726-5677.

AVALON WILDERNESS RESERVE is about 100 km (62 mi.) s. off Hwy. 10 on Horse Chops Rd. The 1,070-square-kilometre (413-sq.-mi.) reserve protects a small number of Avalon caribou (the southernmost woodland caribou herd in the world). With its landscape of barrens, thickets, small forests, bogs, ponds and rivers, the reserve is a good place for canoeing, fishing, hiking, hunting, photography, primitive camping and wildlife observation.

Note: The reserve is in a remote location; there are no facilities, amenities or trail markers within its borders. It is accessed via several rough gravel roads. Informing others of a trip to the reserve and an estimated return date is strongly recommended. Cell phone coverage is intermittent in the area. An entry permit, available at any provincial park office and by mail, must be obtained before visiting. **Hours:** Daily 24 hours. **Cost:** Free. **Phone:** (709) 635-4520 for entry permits and for advice on the best entry points. ⊠ ⛺

BASILICA CATHEDRAL CHURCH AND MUSEUM is at 200 Military Rd. at Harvey Rd. and Bonaventure Ave. The cornerstone for the Basilica Cathedral of St. John the Baptist was laid in 1841 and construction was far enough along in 1850 to allow masses to take place; in 1855 the cathedral was completed and consecrated. Built in the shape of a Latin cross, the church is noted for its statuary, ornate ceiling design and stained glass windows.

Attached to the church is the Basilica Cathedral Museum, housed in an 1859 library that is said to be the oldest public library and reading room in Newfoundland. The museum contains an extensive collection of artifacts, including books, furniture, liturgical garments, paintings and sacred vessels.

Time: Allow 1 hour minimum. **Hours:** Church Mon.-Fri. 8-3, Sat. 10-6:15, Sun. 8-12:30, Oct. 1-late June; Mon.-Fri. 8-5:30, Sun. 8-12:30, rest of year. Museum Mon.-Sat. 10-4, Sun. 1-4, June 15-Sept. 15; by appointment rest of year. Phone ahead to confirm schedule. **Cost:** Church and museum by donation. **Phone:** (709) 754-2170 for the church, or (709) 726-3660 for the museum.

BOWRING PARK, at Waterford Bridge Rd. and Cowan Ave. on the w. end of town, is a traditional English botanical garden with several bronze statues. Many foreign dignitaries have planted trees in the park to mark their visits to the city. Summer activities include swimming, tennis and picnicking, while winter activities include cross-country skiing and tobogganing *(see Recreation Chart)*. An amphitheater plays host to events during the summer. **Hours:** Daily 8 a.m.-10 p.m. **Cost:** Free. **Phone:** (709) 576-8306. ⊠

C.A. PIPPY PARK is on the n. end of town via Hwy. 1 off Allandale Rd., following signs. Designed to integrate the city's modern architecture with surrounding woodlands, steep hillsides, waterways and ponds, the 1,343-hectare (3,317-acre) park contains a 211-site vehicle campground; nine- and 18-hole golf courses overlooking the city; a driving range and a miniature golf course; grand concourse and wilderness trails; and opportunities for fishing and other recreational and cultural pursuits *(see Recreation Chart)*.

Time: Allow 4 hours minimum. **Hours:** Grounds daily dawn-dusk. **Cost:** Grounds free. **Phone:** (709) 737-3655, (709) 737-3669 for the campground or (877) 477-3655. ⛰ ⊠ ⌂

The Fluvarium, in C.A. Pippy Park off Prince Philip Dr., is the only facility in North America with underwater viewing windows that allow visitors to look directly into a stream. There also are exhibits and interpretive programs that focus on freshwater ecology. **Time:** Allow 1 hour, 30 minutes minimum. **Hours:** Mon.-Fri. 9-5, Sat.-Sun. 10-5, July-Aug.; Mon.-Fri. 9-4:30, Sat.-Sun. noon-4:30, rest of year. **Cost:** $7; $5 (ages 60+ and students with ID); $4 (ages 3-13); $20 (family, two adults and two children). **Phone:** (709) 754-3474 or (709) 722-3825. ⏸

Memorial University of Newfoundland Botanical Garden, at 306 Mount Scio Rd. in C.A. Pippy Park, encompasses 44 hectares (110 acres) with a semiformal area and a much larger natural area. The cultivated section features rock, cottage, heritage, rhododendron and vegetable gardens.

The natural area includes most of the major natural habitat types of the Canadian boreal forest biome and features a network of trails. Guided tours are available on request and require a minimum of 10 participants. Visitors must stay on trails and not pick or collect plants and flowers. **Time:** Allow 1 hour, 30 minutes minimum. **Hours:** Daily 10-5, May-Sept.; 10-4, Oct.-Nov. Closed Nov. 11. **Cost:** June-Sept. $6; $4 (ages 60+); $2.50 (ages 6-18). Rest of year $4; $3 (ages 60+); $2 (ages 6-18). First Fri. of the month free. Ages 0-9 must be accompanied by an adult. **Phone:** (709) 864-8590. ⏸

JAMES J. O'MARA PHARMACY MUSEUM, 488 Water St. at Apothecary Hall, is a restored late 1800s drugstore. Displays include late 19th-century pharmacy equipment, scales, medicine bottles, oak store fixtures and an ornate tin ceiling. **Hours:** Daily 10-4:30, early July-late Aug.; by appointment rest of year. Closed major holidays. **Cost:** Free. **Phone:** (709) 753-5877.

JOHNSON GEO CENTRE is at 175 Signal Hill Rd. next to Signal Hill National Historic Site of Canada. The center houses interactive exhibits that describe the earth's geologic history with special attention paid to local rock formations, which are some of the oldest in the world. The mostly underground center is an exhibit itself; constructed in a basin to take advantage of natural rock walls, it is heated by six 152-metre-deep (500-ft.) geothermal wells.

A presentation in the GEO Theatre portrays the immense forces that have shaped the planet; the Steele Earth & Space Theatre shows 2-D and 3-D movies several times daily. Displays about the biology and geology of Signal Hill can be seen along eight outdoor trails.

Time: Allow 2 hours minimum. **Hours:** Mon.-Sat. 9:30-5, Sun. noon-5. Phone for Steele Earth & Space Theatre show times. **Cost:** Center $11.50; $9 (senior citizens and students with ID); $5.50 (ages 5-17); $32 (family, two adults and up to four children ages 5-17). Steele Earth & Space Theatre $9; $6 (ages 3-17). Combination center and Steele Earth & Space Theatre $16; $10 (ages 3-17). **Phone:** (709) 737-7880, or (866) 868-7625 in Canada.

OLD GARRISON CHURCH (ST. THOMAS'), on Military Rd., was built in 1836 and is one of the oldest wooden churches in Newfoundland. First used by the military, the church still displays the Hanoverian coat of arms that was the royal symbol for British troops stationed in St. John's until 1870. The church also has its original 1847 bell, which was cast in London by the same company that cast Big Ben. **Tours:** Guided tours are available. **Time:** Allow 30 minutes minimum. **Hours:** Guided and self-guiding tours Mon.-Fri. 9-2, early June-early Sept. **Phone:** (709) 576-6632.

QUIDI VIDI BATTERY PROVINCIAL HISTORIC SITE is off Quidi Vidi Rd. on Cuckhold's Cove Rd., overlooking Quidi Vidi Village. The site was originally constructed by the French following their capture of St. John's in 1762. British forces rebuilt this small fortification in 1780 and held it until their withdrawal from Newfoundland and Labrador in 1870.

The battery is restored to its 1812 appearance and manned by guides in period uniform. **Note:** The site is closed indefinitely for repairs; phone for more information. **Hours:** Daily 10-5:30, mid-May to mid-Oct.; by appointment rest of year. **Cost:** $3; free (ages 0-12 and Sun.). **Phone:** (709) 729-2977 or (709) 729-0592.

RAILWAY COASTAL MUSEUM is at 495 Water St. Housed in the restored 1903 Newfoundland Railway Station building, the museum features exhibits that describe the history and importance of the Coastal Boat Service and the Newfoundland Railway to the province's isolated fishing communities for news, mail and transportation.

Within two converted railcars are replica interiors of a sleeper car, dining car, kitchen, smoker, coach and mail car. An automated model train passes through detailed reproductions of many of the island's scenic points. A mini-theater shows footage filmed from railways and Coastal Boats servicing Newfoundland's "outports." A 15-metre-wide (50-ft.) mural shows St. John's as it looked in the 1940s.

Time: Allow 1 hour, 30 minutes minimum. **Hours:** Daily 10-5, June 1 to mid-Oct.; Tues.-Sun. 10-5, rest of year. **Cost:** $6; $5 (ages 60+ and students with ID); $4 (ages 6-15); $13 (family, two adults and up to three children). **Phone:** (709) 724-5929, or (866) 600-7245 in Canada.

GEM SAVE THE ROOMS is at 9 Bonaventure Ave. A museum, art gallery and archives make up this attraction dedicated to the history of the province. Along with the permanent collection, temporary and traveling exhibits are featured.

One of the museum exhibits is dedicated to the province's early landscape and its human and animal inhabitants. Another describes Fort Townsend, the original structure on this site. This 18th-century British fort protected Britain's fishing interests. The exhibit also recognizes the importance of the Royal Newfoundland Constabulary, a group that has been a part of the site since 1870.

The art gallery consists of more than 7,000 works, most of which are contemporary pieces by Newfoundland and Labrador artists. Canadian and international artists are represented as well. The archives consists of such topics as architecture, cartography, government and sports and can be researched through a variety of mediums, including manuscripts, film and still images.

Time: Allow 2 hours minimum. **Hours:** Museum and art gallery Mon.-Sat. 10-5 (also Wed. 5-9), Sun. and statutory holidays noon-5, June 1-Oct. 15; Tues.-Sat. 10-5 (also Wed. 5-9), Sun. and statutory holidays noon-5, rest of year. Archives Mon.-Sat. 10-5 (also Wed. 5-9), June 1-Oct. 15; Tues.-Sat. 10-5 (also Wed. 5-9), rest of year. Closed Jan. 1, Good Friday, Armistice Day, Christmas Eve, Christmas and day after Christmas. **Cost:** $7.50; $5 (ages 60+ and students with ID); $4 (ages 6-16); $20 (family, two adults and two children); free (Wed. 6-9 p.m. and first Sat. of the month). Archives $10 (one-time fee on first visit). **Phone:** (709) 757-8000.

ABBA INN (DOWNTOWN)
Phone: (709)754-0058

Bed & Breakfast
$109-$149 6/1-10/15
$69-$89 10/16-5/31

Address: 36 Queens Rd A1C 2A5 **Location:** At Chapel St; centre. **Facility:** 4 units. 3 stories (no elevator), interior corridors. **Parking:** street only. **Terms:** office hours 8 am-11 pm, check-in 3:30 pm, 7 day cancellation notice-fee imposed.

A GOWER STREET HOUSE (DOWNTOWN)
Phone: (709)754-0058

Bed & Breakfast
$99-$149 6/1-10/15
$59-$69 10/16-5/31

Address: 180 Gower St A1C 1P9 **Location:** At Cathedral St; centre. Located in a residential area. **Facility:** 5 units. 3 stories (no elevator), interior corridors. **Bath:** some shared. **Terms:** office hours 8 am-11 pm, 2-4 night minimum stay - seasonal, 14 day cancellation notice-fee imposed.

COMFORT INN AIRPORT
Phone: (709)753-3500

Hotel
$114-$140

Address: 106 Airport Rd A1A 4Y3 **Location:** Trans-Canada Hwy 1 exit 47A, 0.6 mi (1 km) n on Rt 40 (Portugal Cove Rd). **Facility:** 144 units. 2 stories (no elevator), interior corridors. **Terms:** check-in 4 pm, cancellation fee imposed. **Dining:** Clancy's Restaurant, see separate listing. **Activities:** exercise room. **Guest Services:** complimentary and valet laundry.

COURTYARD BY MARRIOTT ST. JOHN'S
Phone: (709)722 6636

Hotel
$159-$219

AAA Benefit:
AAA hotel discounts of 5% or more.

Address: 131 Duckworth St A1C 1E9 **Location:** At Ordnance St. **Facility:** 86 units. 4 stories, interior corridors. **Amenities:** video games (fee), high-speed Internet. **Activities:** exercise room. **Guest Services:** valet and coin laundry.

DELTA ST. JOHN'S HOTEL AND CONFERENCE CENTRE
Phone: 709/739-6404

Hotel
Rates not provided

Address: 120 New Gower St A1C 6K4 **Location:** At Barter's Hill Rd; centre. **Facility:** 403 units. 11 stories, interior corridors. **Parking:** on-site (fee). **Amenities:** high-speed Internet. **Pool(s):** heated indoor. **Activities:** sauna, whirlpool, exercise room. **Guest Services:** valet laundry.

EXTENDED STAY DELUXE ST. JOHN'S - DOWNTOWN
Phone: (709)754-7888

Extended Stay Hotel
$144-$165 6/1-10/31
$124-$145 11/1-5/31

Address: 222 LeMarchant Rd A1C 2H9 **Location:** Corner of Pleasant St. **Facility:** 93 efficiencies. 4 stories, interior corridors. **Terms:** cancellation fee imposed. **Amenities:** high-speed Internet (fee). **Activities:** exercise room. **Guest Services:** coin laundry.

THE GUV'NOR INN
Phone: 709/726-0092

Hotel
$110-$230

Address: 389 Elizabeth Ave A1B 1V1 **Location:** 2 blks n of Freshwater Rd. **Facility:** 37 units. 2 stories (no elevator), interior/exterior corridors. **Terms:** cancellation fee imposed. **Dining:** restaurant, see separate listing. **Activities:** exercise room. **Guest Services:** valet and coin laundry.

HOLIDAY INN ST. JOHN'S-GOVT CENTRE
Phone: (709)722-0506

Hotel
$159-$219

Address: 180 Portugal Cove Rd A1B 2N2 **Location:** Trans-Canada Hwy 1 exit 47A, 0.9 mi (1.4 km) s. **Facility:** 252 units. 5 stories, interior/exterior corridors. **Amenities:** Fee: video games, high-speed Internet. **Pool(s):** heated outdoor. **Activities:** playground, exercise room. **Guest Services:** valet and coin laundry.

LEASIDE MANOR HERITAGE INN Phone: 709/722-0387

▼▼▼▼
Historic Bed & Breakfast
$119-$349 6/1-10/15
$99-$249 10/16-5/31

Address: 39 Topsail Rd A1E 2A6 **Location:** Just s of Water St. Located in a residential area. **Facility:** A stylized roof, Colonial columns and leaded windows add interest to this 1922 Tudor mansion surrounded by manicured grounds. 11 units, some kitchens. 2 stories (no elevator), interior/exterior corridors. **Terms:** office hours 6:30 am-8 pm, age restrictions may apply, 7 day cancellation notice-fee imposed. **Guest Services:** coin laundry.

[BIZ] 🛜 ✕ 🛏 / SOME UNITS 🖥

MCCOUBREY MANOR B & B Phone: 709/722-7577

▼▼▼▼
Historic Bed & Breakfast
Rates not provided

Address: 6-8 Ordnance St A1C 3K7 **Location:** Just n of Duckworth St; centre. Located in a commercial area. **Facility:** This lovely, 1904 Queen Anne-style heritage home in the heart of town offers tastefully decorated rooms and two kitchen suites. 6 units, some kitchens. 2 stories (no elevator), interior/exterior corridors. **Terms:** office hours 8 am-10 pm, age restrictions may apply. **Guest Services:** complimentary laundry.

[🍴] 🛜 ✕ / SOME UNITS 🖥 🖥

MURRAY PREMISES HOTEL Phone: 709/738-7773

▼▼▼▼
Hotel
$159-$369

Address: 5 Becks Cove A1C 6H1 **Location:** At Harbour Dr; centre. Opposite city wharf. **Facility:** 67 units. 4 stories, interior corridors. **Terms:** cancellation fee imposed. **Amenities:** high-speed Internet. **Guest Services:** valet laundry.

[🍴] [BIZ] ✕ 🛏 🖥

QUALITY HOTEL-HARBOURVIEW
Phone: (709)754-7788

▼▼▼
Hotel
$117-$171

Address: 2 Hill-O-Chips A1C 6B1 **Location:** At Cavendish Square; centre. **Facility:** 159 units. 5 stories, interior corridors. **Terms:** cancellation fee imposed. **Amenities:** Some: high-speed Internet. **Dining:** Rumpelstiltskin's, see separate listing. **Activities:** exercise room. **Guest Services:** valet laundry.

[SAVE] [ECO] [🍴] [🍸] [BIZ] 🛜 FEE[🎥] 🖥
/ SOME UNITS 🛏

RAMADA ST. JOHN'S Phone: (709)722-9330

▼▼▼
Hotel
$86-$179

Address: 102 Kenmount Rd A1B 3R2 **Location:** Trans-Canada Hwy 1 exit 45, 1 mi (1.6 km) s on Team Gushue Hwy to Kenmount Rd. **Facility:** 79 units, some kitchens. 4 stories, interior corridors. **Terms:** 3 day cancellation notice. **Dining:** P J Billington's, see separate listing. **Activities:** exercise room. **Guest Services:** valet laundry. **Free Special Amenities:** local telephone calls and high-speed Internet.

[SAVE] [✈] [🍴] [🍸] 🛜 ✕ 🖥 / SOME UNITS 🛏

SHERATON HOTEL NEWFOUNDLAND
Phone: (709)726-4980

▼▼▼▼
Hotel
$125-$318

Ⓢ Sheraton
HOTELS & RESORTS

AAA Benefit: Members get up to 15% off, plus Starwood Preferred Guest® bonuses.

Address: 115 Cavendish Square A1C 3K2 **Location:** At Duckworth and Ordnance sts. **Facility:** 301 units. 9 stories, interior corridors. **Amenities:** video games (fee), high-speed Internet. **Dining:** Oppidan, see separate listing. **Pool(s):** heated indoor. **Activities:** saunas, whirlpool, racquetball court, exercise room. **Guest Services:** valet laundry.

[SAVE] [ECO] [🍴] 🛖 [🏋] [🐾] [🏊] [BIZ] 🛜 ✕
FEE[🎥] 🖥 / SOME UNITS 🛏 🛏

SUPER 8 Phone: (709)739-8888

▼▼▼
Hotel
$122-$135

Address: 175 Higgins Line A1B 4N4 **Location:** Trans-Canada Hwy 1 exit 47A, just s on Rt 40 (Portugal Cove Rd). **Facility:** 81 units. 4 stories, interior corridors. **Terms:** cancellation fee imposed. **Amenities:** high-speed Internet. **Pool(s):** heated indoor. **Activities:** whirlpool, waterslide. **Guest Services:** coin laundry.

[ECO] [🍴] CALL[📞] [🛏M] [🏊] [BIZ] 🛜 FEE[🎥] 🛏 🖥
🖥 / SOME UNITS 🐾

TRAVELLERS INN ST. JOHN'S Phone: 709/722-5540

▼▼▼ ▼▼
Hotel
Rates not provided

Address: 199 Kenmount Rd A1B 3P9 **Location:** Trans-Canada Hwy 1 exit 45, 1 mi (1.6 km) s on Team Gushue Hwy to Kenmount Rd. Located in a commercial area. **Facility:** 88 units. 2 stories (no elevator), interior/exterior corridors. **Amenities:** high-speed Internet. **Pool(s):** heated outdoor.

[ECO] [🍴] [🍸] [🏊] [BIZ] 🛜 🖥
/ SOME UNITS 🐾 [🏋] 🛏 🖥

BANBERRY HOUSE B & B Phone: 709/579-8006

[fyi] Not evaluated. **Address:** 116 Military Rd A1C 2C9 **Location:** Centre; at Rawlins Cross. Facilities, services, and decor characterize a mid-scale property.

CAPITAL HOTEL Phone: 709/738-4480

[fyi] Not evaluated. **Address:** 208 Kenmount Rd A1B 3P9 **Location:** Trans-Canada Hwy 1 exit 45, 4 mi (6.4 km) s on Team Gushue Hwy to Kenmount Rd. Facilities, services, and decor characterize a mid-scale property.

COMPTON HOUSE HERITAGE INN
Phone: 709/739-5789

[fyi] Not evaluated. **Address:** 26 Waterford Bridge Rd A1E 1C6 **Location:** Just s of jct Water St. Facilities, services, and decor characterize a mid-scale property.

WATERFORD MANOR Phone: 709/754-4139

[fyi] Not evaluated. **Address:** 185 Waterford Bridge Rd A1E 1C7 **Location:** 2 mi s of jct Water St. Facilities, services, and decor characterize a mid-scale property.

WINTERHOLME HERITAGE INN Phone: 709/739-7979

[fyi]
Bed & Breakfast

Did not meet all AAA rating requirements for locking devices in some guest rooms at time of last evaluation on 02/24/2011. **Address:** 79 Rennies Mill Rd A1C 3R1 **Location:** At Circular Rd. Facilities, services, and decor characterize a mid-scale property.

WHERE TO EAT

BIANCA'S RESTAURANT Phone: 709-726-9016

▼▼▼▼
Regional Canadian
$13-$32

AAA Inspector Notes: This colorful upscale bistro is located in the heart of the city and through the large plate glass windows you can watch the bustling street scene. The menu features creatively presented fresh seafood, steak, and some game meat prepared in the open style kitchen. To complement the fine cuisine they offer a superb selection of wine. **Bar:** full bar. **Reservations:** suggested. **Address:** 171 Water St A1C 6J9 **Location:** Just n of Bairds Cove Ln; downtown. **Parking:** street only. [L] [D]

THE CELLAR RESTAURANT
Phone: 709/579-8900

Regional Steak
$28-$39

AAA Inspector Notes: Offering two elegant dining areas, the restaurant's first level is an open plan with rich oak paneling and high ceilings, while the cellar offers more intimate, private dining areas amongst the wine racks. The menu features an array of meat and fresh seafood items, and entrees show creative preparation and artful presentation. A fine selection of wine includes many by-the-glass choices, and splendid desserts add the finishing touch to a fine experience. **Bar:** full bar. **Reservations:** suggested. **Address:** 189 Water St A1C 5M5 **Location:** Corner of Baird's Cove Ln. **Parking:** street only.

CHEZ CORA
Phone: 709/722-6720

Canadian
$6-$13

AAA Inspector Notes: Eggs, omelets, waffles, crepes (sorry, no American-style pancakes here), French toast, fruit platters and all the breakfast meats--that's the specialty here, all day. However, at lunchtime the menu lists a selection of soups, salads, quiches, sandwiches and a dish called the grilled panini crepe. **Address:** 215 Water St A1C 6C9 **Location:** Downtown; in Atlantic Place, 2nd Floor. **Parking:** on-site (fee).

CLANCY'S RESTAURANT
Phone: 709/753-3500

American
$9-$25

AAA Inspector Notes: In a convenient location near the airport, this place provides all-day dining in a pub-themed atmosphere with comfortable booths and tables. **Bar:** full bar. **Location:** Trans-Canada Hwy 1 exit 47A, 0.6 mi (1 km) n on Rt 40 (Portugal Cove Rd); in Comfort Inn Airport.

THE GUV'NOR PUB & EATERY
Phone: 709/726-3053

American
$8-$25

AAA Inspector Notes: In the fashion of an Old English Pub, the eatery boasts a relaxed atmosphere. Its menu lists a fine selection of classic pub fare and finger foods as well as a selection of fresh seafood and steaks. Several imported and domestic beers are on tap. **Bar:** full bar. **Address:** 389 Elizabeth Ave A1B 1V1 **Location:** 2 blks n of Freshwater Rd; in The Guv'nor Inn.

INDIA GATE RESTAURANT
Phone: 709/753-6006

Indian
$9-$20

AAA Inspector Notes: An extensive menu offers a wide range of traditional Indian favorites, spiced to order from mild to fiery hot. Exotic Indian music and soft lighting create a serene mood as you sample items from the very good lunch buffet available Monday through Friday. **Bar:** full bar. **Address:** 286 Duckworth St A1C 5W8 **Location:** Corner of Duckworth and Cathedral sts. **Parking:** on-site (fee).

JUNGLE JIM'S

Canadian
$8-$19

For additional information, visit AAA.com

AAA Inspector Notes: Guests can step into a tropical theme at the casual eatery, which employs a friendly staff and nurtures a bustling atmosphere. The menu lines up a wide variety of comfort foods, salads, chicken, beef, seafood and hot wings, all served in ample, flavorful portions. **Bar:** full bar.

LOCATIONS:

Address: 657 Topsail Rd A1E 2E3 **Location:** Just e of Burgeo St. **Phone:** 709/745-6060

Address: 2 Holdsworth Ct, George St A1C 4J7 **Location:** Centre. **Phone:** 709/753-5467

Address: 286 Torbay Rd A1C 6K1 **Location:** Corner of Newfoundland Dr; centre. **Phone:** 709/722-0261

MAGIC WOK EATERY
Phone: 709/753-6907

Chinese
$8-$18

AAA Inspector Notes: The spacious modern restaurant presents a menu of traditional Chinese cuisine, prepared Hong Kong style, and some Canadian dishes. **Bar:** full bar. **Address:** 402-408 Water St A1C 1C9 **Location:** At Princess St; centre.

MEXICALI ROSA'S
Phone: 709/237-8226

Mexican
$10-$20

AAA Inspector Notes: The Mexican cantina makes an excellent choice for family-friendly fun. Old West paintings and murals add color to stucco walls and wooden beams, while a Tex-Mex menu provides a feast of favorites such as fajitas, burritos and some seafood items. Fried ice cream is a sweet treat. **Bar:** full bar. **Address:** 36 George St A1C 1J2 **Location:** At Adelaide St. **Parking:** on-site (fee).

OPPIDAN
Phone: 709/726-4980

Regional American
$14-$38

AAA Inspector Notes: This tastefully-decorated, modern restaurant is on two levels and offers a glimpse of the harbor and Signal Hill through the floor-to-ceiling picture windows. The menu offers an excellent array of fresh local seafood and choice cuts of meat. The seafood chowder should not be missed. Try to save room for one of the tempting desserts. **Bar:** full bar. **Reservations:** suggested, for dinner. **Address:** 115 Cavendish Square A1C 3K2 **Location:** At Duckworth and Ordnance sts; in Sheraton Hotel Newfoundland.

THE PEPPER MILL
Phone: 709/726-7585

Regional Seafood
$10-$28

AAA Inspector Notes: This quaint restaurant specializes in excellent fresh, local seafood including halibut, cod, prawns and mussels. Not to be missed is the signature seafood chowder. They also offer some steak and chicken items for the landlubber. The atmosphere is relaxed and service is very friendly and attentive. **Bar:** full bar. **Reservations:** suggested. **Address:** 178 Water St A1C 1B1 **Location:** Just n of Baird's Cove Ln; downtown. **Parking:** street only.

P J BILLINGTON'S
Phone: 709/722-9330

American
$10-$24

AAA Inspector Notes: This family restaurant features booth and table seating, an ample menu variety and all-day meals. **Bar:** full bar. **Address:** 102 Kenmount Rd A1B 3R2 **Location:** Trans-Canada Hwy 1 exit 45, 1 mi (1.6 km) s on Team Gushue Hwy to Kenmount Rd; in Ramada St. John's.

PORTOBELLO'S RESTAURANT
Phone: 709/579-7050

Italian
$24-$38

AAA Inspector Notes: Wall-to-wall glass provides a splendid view at this spacious, two-level harbor front restaurant. The menu reflects a fine array of Italian dishes with a hint of traditional Newfoundland influence. Creative presentations and excellent wine parings are what guests can expect at this eatery. **Bar:** full bar. **Reservations:** suggested. **Address:** 115 Duckworth St A1C 1E9 **Location:** Corner of Duckworth and Hill O'Chip's sts.

RAYMONDS
Phone: 709/579-5800

Regional Canadian
$30-$45

AAA Inspector Notes: Located in the heart of town, this upscale dining room with a relaxing lounge offers a fine view of the harbor. The exciting and innovative menu focus is on market-fresh Newfoundland and Labrador ingredients including seafood, game meat, Prime steaks and seasonal native berries and vegetables. A tasting menu is very popular with wine pairings. Service is equally flawless, friendly and attentive. Semi-formal attire. **Bar:** full bar. **Reservations:** required. **Address:** 95 Water St A1C 1A5 **Location:** At Cochrane St; centre. **Parking:** street only.

RUMPELSTILTSKIN'S
Phone: 709/579-6000

American
$9-$23

AAA Inspector Notes: The atmosphere is warm and upbeat in the pleasant restaurant, which offers a great view of the harbor from several tables. Among the varied entrees are preparations of steak and seafood. Tempting desserts include the cheesecake and custard. **Bar:** full bar. **Address:** 2 Hill-O-Chips A1C 6B1 **Location:** At Cavendish Square; centre; in Quality Hotel-Harbourview.

B L D

THE SHANGHAI RESTAURANT
Phone: 709/753-2378

Chinese
$10-$30

AAA Inspector Notes: Specializing in Szechuan and Peking cuisine, this ornate restaurant is divided into several pleasant rooms, some with booth seating. The menu offers an ample variety with dishes seasoned to the diner's taste. **Bar:** full bar. **Address:** 210 Water St A1C 1A9 **Location:** At Bairds St; centre. **Parking:** street only.

L D

SUN SUSHI RESTAURANT
Phone: 709/726-8688

Japanese
$8-$19

AAA Inspector Notes: Located in the heart of town, this open-style dining room offers a vast array of tasty Japanese entrees and sushi bar combinations. **Bar:** beer & wine. **Address:** 186 Duckworth St A1C 1G5 **Location:** At Kings Rd; centre. **Parking:** street only.

L D

SWISS CHALET
Phone: 709/753-6030

Chicken
$6-$16

AAA Inspector Notes: The popular restaurant is known for its rotisserie chicken and ribs and the tangy Chalet sauce that gives food its special zip. Diners munch on a half or quarter chicken with sides such as steamed vegetables, fries, baked potatoes and salads. Lunch guests often go for the great soup and sandwich combination. Take-out and delivery service are popular options. **Bar:** full bar. **Address:** 70 Aberdeen Ave A1A 5N6 **Location:** At Stavenger Dr; centre. L D

TAJ MAHAL RESTAURANT
Phone: 709/576-5500

Indian
$8-$20

AAA Inspector Notes: The food at this eatery is hard to beat. Through the kitchen window, guests can view traditional Indian dishes being carefully prepared to patrons' spice comfort zones. **Bar:** full bar. **Address:** 203 Water St A1A 5G6 **Location:** Just s of Baird's Cove Ln; centre. **Parking:** street only. L D

YELLOWBELLY BREWERY & PUBLIC HOUSE
Phone: 709/757-3784

American
$9-$25

AAA Inspector Notes: In an 1860s former warehouse in the historic section of town, the setting of this eatery has lovely stone and brick walls and beamed ceilings. The brew pub offers seating in the casual pub or on the second level, which has an open kitchen. On the menu are choices ranging from wood-fire pizza and gourmet burgers to fresh seafood and steaks. Several fine microbrews are available. **Bar:** full bar. **Address:** 288 Water St A1C 6K4 **Location:** Corner of George and Water sts. **Parking:** street only. L D

ZACHARY'S RESTAURANT
Phone: 709/579-8050

American
$7-$20

AAA Inspector Notes: Conveniently open for all meals, this casual restaurant offers a nice menu selection ranging from burgers and sandwiches to fresh seafood, steak and homemade desserts. **Bar:** full bar. **Address:** 71 Duckworth St A1C 1E6 **Location:** At Kings Bridge Rd. **Parking:** street only. B L D

ST. PAULS pop. 309

GROS MORNE RESORT
Phone: 709/243-2606

[fyi] Not evaluated. **Address:** Cow Head A0K 4Y0 **Location:** On Rt 430; at north end of park. Facilities, services, and decor characterize a mid-scale property.

WHERE TO EAT

THE GROS MORNE RESORT FINE DINING ROOM
Phone: 709/243-2606

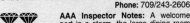

Canadian
$22-$30

AAA Inspector Notes: Overlooking the beautiful St. Paul's Inlet and Gros Morne Mountain Range, this upper level dining room offer the freshest of seafood and meat selections creatively prepared by the talented chef. Service is relaxed and friendly. **Bar:** full bar. **Address:** Rt 430 A0K 4Y0 **Location:** On Rt 430; at north end of park; in Gros Morne Resort. D

GROS MORNE RESORT RESTAURANT
Phone: 709/243-2606

Canadian
$7-$20

AAA Inspector Notes: A welcome port in a storm, the large dining room overlooks the Gros Morne Mountains. The vast menu selection is likely to have something for everyone, from full dinners to lighter fare. Portions are good, and the cooking is home-style. **Bar:** full bar. **Address:** Rt 430 A0K 4Y0 **Location:** On Rt 430; at north end of park; in Gros Morne Resort. B L D

SIGNAL HILL NATIONAL HISTORIC SITE OF CANADA (E-5)

Reached from Duckworth St., Signal Hill rises 160 metres (525 ft.) above the narrow approach to St. John's harbor. Because of its strategic location, the area was the site of many battles between the English and the French for control of Newfoundland and Labrador and its fisheries. The British defeated the French in 1762 in the last battle between the two countries in North America.

Within the site is Cabot Tower, built to commemorate the Diamond Jubilee of Queen Victoria and the 400th anniversary of John Cabot's voyage to Newfoundland and Labrador. A city landmark, the tower contains an exhibit about the history of communications and signaling. In 1901 Guglielmo Marconi received the first transatlantic wireless message in a hospital near Cabot Tower.

Other points of interest are several batteries built during the 18th and 19th centuries, a reconstructed signal mast and 1830s barracks. A visitor center houses an exhibit about the history of Newfoundland and Labrador. A summer tradition since it was first performed as a centennial celebration in 1967, the Signal Hill Tattoo re-enacts military exercises performed by the Royal Newfoundland Regiment of Foot. Steep hiking trails traverse the site's outer reaches. Picnicking is permitted on the grounds.

Handheld GPS devices that provide visual and audio narration based on the user's location within the site are available at the visitor center; the rental fee is included in the price of admission to the exhibits.

Allow 1 hour minimum. Visitor center daily 10-6, June 16-Sept. 7; Thurs.-Mon. 10-6, May 15-June 15 and Sept. 8-Oct. 15; by appointment rest of year. Phone ahead to confirm schedule. Cabot Tower daily 8:30 a.m.-9 p.m., May 15-Labour Day; 8:30-4:30, Apr. 1-May 14 and day after Labour Day-Nov. 15. Signal Hill Tattoo performances Wed.-Thurs. and Sat.-Sun. at 11 and 3, early July to mid-Aug. (weather permitting).

Site free. Exhibits $3.90; $3.40 (ages 65+); $1.90 (ages 6-16); $9.80 (family, maximum two adults and five children); Signal Hill Tattoo performance $5; free (ages 0-5). For more information contact the Area Superintendent, Historic Parks & Sites/Newfoundland, P.O. Box 1268, St. John's, NL, Canada A1C 5M9; phone (709) 772-5367, or (888) 773-8888 in Canada.

STEADY BROOK (C-2)

RECREATIONAL ACTIVITIES
Skiing

- **Marble Mountain Ski Resort** is 10 km (6 mi.) e. on Hwy. 1. **Hours:** Fri.-Mon. 9-4:30 (also Fri. 4:30-9:30), Tues.-Thurs. 10-4:30, Dec.-Apr. **Phone:** (709) 637-7600.

GEORGE'S MOUNTAIN VILLAGE COTTAGES
Phone: 709/639-8168
[fyi] Not evaluated. **Address:** Trans-Canada Hwy A2H 2N2 **Location:** Trans-Canada Hwy 1 exit Marble Mountain, follow signs. Facilities, services, and decor characterize a mid-scale property.

STEPHENVILLE pop. 6,588

HOLIDAY INN STEPHENVILLE   **Phone:** (709)643-6666

Hotel
$133-$143 7/1-5/31
$128-$138 6/1-6/30
Address: 44 Queen St A2N 2M5 **Location:** Centre. Adjoins a shopping mall. **Facility:** 47 units. 2 stories, interior corridors. **Amenities:** *Some:* high-speed Internet. **Dining:** Emile's Pub & Eatery, see separate listing.
Guest Services: valet laundry.

[ECO] [🍴] [Y] [BIZ] [📶] [✕] [☕]
/ SOME UNITS [🐾] [🔒] [🧳]

WHERE TO EAT

EMILE'S PUB & EATERY   **Phone:** 709/643-6666

Canadian
$7-$21
AAA Inspector Notes: Named in honor of the famous local fiddler Emile Benoit, the pleasant restaurant prepares a fine selection of fresh seafood, steaks, ribs, chicken and pasta dishes. A bowl of the wonderful chowder should not be missed. **Bar:** full bar. **Reservations:** suggested. **Address:** 44 Queen St A2N 2M5 **Location:** Centre; in Holiday Inn Stephenville. [B] [L] [D]

SWIFT CURRENT

KILMORY RESORT   **Phone:** 709/549-2410
[fyi] Not evaluated. **Address:** Rt 210 Burin Peninsula Hwy A0E 2W0 **Location:** On Rt 210; centre. Facilities, services, and decor characterize a mid-scale property.

TERRA NOVA NATIONAL PARK OF CANADA (D-4)

Elevations in the park range from sea level at Bonavista Bay to 229 metres (750 ft.) at Blue Hill. Refer to CAA/AAA maps for additional elevation information.

Seventy kilometres (45 mi.) south of Gander and 240 kilometres (150 mi.) north of St. John's on Hwy. 1, Terra Nova National Park of Canada is characterized by bold headlands extending from a rocky, mostly forested interior. Covering more than 400 square kilometres (155 sq. mi.) of the island of Newfoundland's eastern shore, the park is bounded on the south by Clode Sound, bisected by Newman Sound and touched on its northern edge by Alexander Bay.

Numerous lakes, ponds and streams in the park contain eastern brook trout, salmon and Arctic char. Saltwater fishing offers cod, mackerel and herring. Moose, black bears, red foxes, beavers, lynx and various smaller species inhabit the area, which serves as a wildlife refuge.

Such migrating birds as the Arctic tern can be sighted off the coast during the spring and fall. Permanent feathered residents include willow ptarmigan, boreal and black-capped chickadees, bald eagles, ospreys and Canada jays.

General Information and Activities

Terra Nova National Park of Canada is open all year. A visitor center with a marine interpretation center is at Saltons in the middle of the park. Information kiosks are at the campgrounds at Malady Head and Newman Sound.

The visitor center is open daily 10-8, late June-Labour Day. Brochure boxes and the park administration building at Newman Sound provide information October through May.

Roads within the park are open all year. Hwy. 1 traverses the area; the Eastport Hwy. in the north end of the park reaches the Eastport Peninsula. Trails provide approximately 100 kilometres (62 mi.) for hiking. Some of the popular routes include the Southwest Arm Brook Trail, which begins at the Southwest Arm Picnic Area, and the 18-kilometre (11-mi.) Coastal Trail. Some trails become cross-country skiing routes December through March or April.

Back-country camping, picnicking, boating, fishing, swimming and scuba diving are among other activities available. Docks along the park's shoreline provide mooring; a national park permit is needed for freshwater fishing. A park entry permit is required for all park activities; additional permits may be required for camping, docking and fishing. Terra Nova Golf Resort, an 18-hole golf course at the eastern end of the park, operates from May 1 to mid-October.

Lodging, dining and supplies are available in such nearby communities as Musgravetown, Bunyan's Cove, Port Blandford, Terra Nova, Charlottetown,

Glovertown, Traytown and communities on the Eastport Peninsula.

At the Newman Sound Day Use Area there are telescopes for viewing the nearby bird sanctuary; lookout towers are at Ochre Hill and Blue Hill. Guided hikes, outdoor theater presentations and beaver-watching expeditions are conducted by park interpreters late June through Labour Day.

The Saltons Day Use Area features a marine interpretation center, with a touch tank and other displays about marine life. The center is open daily 9-9, mid-May through Labour Day; 9-5, day after Labour Day to mid-Oct. The Day Use Area also features tour boat and sea-kayaking operators. *See Recreation Chart.*

ADMISSION to the park mid-May to mid-Oct. is $5.80; $4.90 (ages 65+); $2.90 (ages 6-16); $14.70 (family, maximum two adults and five children). Rest of year free.

PETS are allowed in the park but must be on a leash or otherwise physically restricted at all times.

ADDRESS inquiries to Superintendent, Terra Nova National Park of Canada, Glovertown, NL, Canada A0G 2L0; phone (709) 533-2801, or (877) 737-3783 in Canada for camping in season.

TORNGAT MOUNTAINS NATIONAL PARK OF CANADA (A-4)

Elevations in the park range from sea level to about 1,652 metres (5,420 ft.) at Mount Caubvick. Refer to CAA/AAA maps for additional elevation information.

Torngat Mountains National Park of Canada encompasses approximately 9,700 square kilometres (3,745 sq. mi.) from northern Labrador south to Saglek Fjord. The eastern and western boundaries are the Labrador Sea and the provincial boundary line with Québec. Inuit had lived on this land for thousands of years; archeological evidence has been found that is nearly 7,000 years old. The Maritime Archaic Indians, Pre-Dorset and Dorset as well as people from the Thule culture are known to have been in this area. Although no one lives here anymore, some Inuit do come to hunt, fish and travel. Visitors may participate in air tours, backcountry skiing, backpacking, boating, camping, cultural exploration, fishing (license required), guided expeditions and tours, hiking, mountain climbing and nature watching. *See Recreation Chart.*

Getting to the national park is difficult. The two access locations are Nain, in Labrador, and Kangiqsualujjuaq, in Québec. Charter transportation is then required. Depending on the weather, air and boat charters are available from Nain, and air charters are available from Kangiqsualujjuaq. Snowmobile charters may be a possibility; phone for information.

Note: Due to the extreme weather conditions often present, the difficult terrain, the wildlife present

and the remoteness of the park, only those very experienced traveling in such conditions should attempt a visit. Visitors should always be prepared in case an emergency extends their trip; wilderness first aid and self-rescue training are recommended skills. This remote wilderness has no roads or lodging facilities; visitors may camp anywhere that is not an archeological site, but camping should be avoided on the coast due to the high concentration of polar bears. Black bears, foxes, wolves and muskoxen are some of the other animals inhabiting the park. Polar bear sightings are quite frequent, and traveling with an armed Inuit guide is recommended since firearms are prohibited in the park for non-Inuit. Visitors must travel with polar bear deterrents and know how to use them. Contact the park office for further information about park conditions and hazards.

Note: All visitors must register as early as possible prior to entering the park as well as notify the office upon the completion of their trip. Registering in person is preferred, but other options are available; phone for details. In addition, all visitors must watch a video about polar bear safety and participate in a safety briefing and orientation, which covers the park's potential hazards as well as risks accompanying recreational activities. The park office is open Mon.-Fri. 8-4:30; closed holidays. The park is open all year, but the most practical time to visit is March through April and July through August, with the best weather often occurring mid-July to mid-August. However, weather conditions can change significantly from year to year. The office is at 17 Sandbanks Rd. in Nain; phone (709) 922-1290, or (888) 922-1290 within Canada. For more information write to Torngat Mountains National Park, Box 471, Nain, NL, Canada A0P 1L0.

TRAYTOWN pop. 302

PINETREE LODGE & CABINS   **Phone:** 709/533-6601
[fyi] Not evaluated. **Address:** Main St A0G 4K0
        Location: On Rt 310. Facilities, services, and decor characterize a mid-scale property.

TRINITY (C-4) pop. 191
• Hotels p. 118 • Restaurants p. 118

Portuguese explorer Gaspar Côrte-Real, the first recorded visitor to Trinity, sailed into its harbor on Trinity Sunday in 1501. The area's first settlers, under the command of Capt. Robert Ward, reportedly arrived in 1558, almost 30 years before Sir Humphrey Gilbert landed at St. John's and claimed Newfoundland for England in 1583.

In the early 1700s Trinity was frequently raided by pirates and captured twice by the French. To defend themselves, the settlers built fortifications, remains of which can be seen along the coast. Another historic structure in town is St. Paul's Church, built in 1892. Dr. John Clinch, who was also a pastor, is buried in the churchyard. During the late 1700s he administered the first Jenner smallpox vaccination in North America.

Because its appearance has changed little since the late 19th century, Trinity also has a lively tourist trade. In the summer popular local activities include fishing, boating and whale watching.

GREEN FAMILY FORGE is on West St. The Green family worked as blacksmiths in town from the mid-18th- to the mid-20th century. The current building, built 1895-1900, now serves as a museum with more than 1,500 artifacts representing several hundred years of blacksmith work. Visitors can watch demonstrations by the blacksmith.

Tours: Guided tours are available. **Time:** Allow 30 minutes minimum. **Hours:** Daily 10-5:30, May 30-Sept. 30. Blacksmith demonstrations are offered Mon.-Fri. **Cost:** (Includes admission to Hiscock House Provincial Historic Site, Lester-Garland House, Mercantile Premises, Trinity Historical Society Museum and Trinity Visitor Centre) $12; free (ages 0-12 and Sun.). **Phone:** (709) 464-3599.

HISCOCK HOUSE PROVINCIAL HISTORIC SITE, on Church St., has been restored to its 1910 appearance. The two-and-a-half-story gable-roofed house represents a typical local merchant's dwelling in rural Newfoundland during the early 20th century. Guides in period costumes conduct tours.

Time: Allow 30 minutes minimum. **Hours:** Daily 10-5:30, mid-May to mid-Oct. **Cost:** (Includes admission to Green Family Forge, Lester-Garland House, Mercantile Premises, Trinity Historical Society Museum and Trinity Visitor Centre) $12; free (ages 0-12 and Sun.). Cash only. **Phone:** (709) 464-2042 or (709) 729-0592.

LESTER-GARLAND HOUSE, on West St., is a 1997 reconstruction of the brick Georgian house that was built on this site in the 1760s for Benjamin Lester, a fish merchant from Poole, England. Lester's grandson, John Bingley Garland, was a later resident and extended the house. The original stone foundations and some of the bricks have been incorporated. Visitors can see some original furnishings as well as the Trinity Historical Society Archives.

Tours: Guided tours are available. **Time:** Allow 30 minutes minimum. **Hours:** Daily 10-5:30, mid-May to mid-Oct. **Cost:** (Includes admission to Green Family Forge, Hiscock House Provincial Historic Site, Mercantile Premises, Trinity Historical Society Museum and Trinity Visitor Centre) $12; free (ages 0-12 and Sun.). **Phone:** (709) 464-3599.

MERCANTILE PREMISES, on West St., overlooks the harbor and is perhaps the oldest wooden structure in the province. It used to serve as a counting house and merchant shop; the office area was built in the 1750s and Benjamin Lester built the shop in 1764. Artifacts from the fishing town are displayed throughout the building.

Tours: Guided tours are available. **Time:** Allow 30 minutes minimum. **Hours:** Daily 10-5:30, mid-May to mid-Oct. **Cost:** (Includes admission to Green Family Forge, Hiscock House Provincial Historic Site, Lester-Garland House, Trinity Historical

Society Museum and Trinity Visitor Centre) $12; free (ages 0-12 and Sun.). Cash only. **Phone:** (709) 464-2042 or (709) 729-0592.

TRINITY HISTORICAL SOCIETY MUSEUM, off Hwy. 239 on Church St., displays more than 2,000 items of local and provincial interest in a saltbox house dating from 1880. Exhibits include 1890s medical supplies, an early 1900s shoemaker's kit and a demonstration about fish barrel construction.

Hours: Daily 10-5:30, mid-May to mid-Oct. **Cost:** (Includes admission to Green Family Forge, Hiscock House Provincial Historic Site, Lester-Garland House, Mercantile Premises and Trinity Visitor Centre) $12; free (ages 0-12 and Sun.). **Phone:** (709) 464-3599.

TRINITY VISITOR CENTRE is on West St. The history of Trinity is presented through displays of illustrations, maps and photographs. **Hours:** Daily 10-5:30, mid-May to mid-Oct. **Cost:** (Includes admission to Green Family Forge, Hiscock House Provincial Historic Site, Lester-Garland House, Mercantile Premises and Trinity Historical Society Museum) $12; free (ages 0-12 and Sun.). Cash only. **Phone:** (709) 464-2042 or (709) 729-0592.

ARTISAN INN AND CAMPBELL HOUSE
Phone: 709/464-3377
[fyi] Not evaluated. **Address:** High St A0C 2S0 **Location:** Centre. Facilities, services, and decor characterize a mid-scale property.

ERIKSEN PREMISES   **Phone:** 709/464-3698
[fyi] Not evaluated. **Address:** West St A0C 2S0 **Location:** Centre. Facilities, services, and decor characterize a mid-scale property.

WHERE TO EAT

HERITAGE TEA ROOM   **Phone:** 709/464-3698

Canadian
$7-$21
AAA Inspector Notes: Hearty portions of down-home cooking mean no diner leaves hungry from the quaint village restaurant. **Bar:** full bar. **Address:** West St A0C 2S0 **Location:** Centre; in Eriksen Premises. **Historic**

TWILLINGATE (C-4) pop. 2,448

Settled about 1700, Twillingate shares the name of the island on which it is built. Named Toulinguet by French fishermen who thought it resembled Point Toulinguet near Brest, France, the island supports a fishing community. Twillingate celebrates its seafaring heritage with the Fish, Fun and Folk Festival, which features fish dinners, dancing, music and craft displays in late July.

The Long Point Lighthouse, just north of Twillingate on Hwy. 340, offers views of the North Atlantic. The vista is especially beautiful at sunset. In June and July icebergs can be seen drifting south from the Arctic.

TWILLINGATE MUSEUM, off Hwy. 340, contains typical furnishings and household items of an average Newfoundland family during the late 19th- and early 20th centuries. Displays feature local handicrafts and maritime artifacts as well as reproductions of Maritime Archaic Indian artifacts. **Time:** Allow 2 hours minimum. **Hours:** Daily 9-5, early May to mid-Oct. Phone ahead to confirm schedule. **Cost:** Donations. **Phone:** (709) 884-2825.

WINERIES

• **Auk Island Winery** is 2 km (1.2 mi.) n. at 29 Durrell St., following signs. **Hours:** Daily 9:30-5:30, in summer; 10-4:30, rest of year. Closed Jan. 1, Easter, Thanksgiving, Christmas Eve, Christmas and day after Christmas. **Phone:** (709) 884-2707 to verify seasonal schedules or (877) 639-4637.

ANCHOR INN MOTEL   **Phone:** 709/884-2777
(fyi) Not evaluated. **Address:** North Side A0G 4M0 **Location:** Oceanfront. On Main St. Facilities, services, and decor characterize an economy property.

HARBOUR LIGHTS INN   **Phone:** 709/884-2763
(fyi) Not evaluated. **Address:** 189 Main St A0G 4M0 **Location:** Overlooking the harbor. Facilities, services, and decor characterize a mid-scale property.

UPPER FERRY (D-1)

CODROY VALLEY WETLANDS INTERPRETATION CENTRE is 5 km (3 mi.) w. of the Trans Canada Hwy. on Rte. 406. The estuary wetlands comprise 925 hectares at the mouth of the Grand Codroy River and provide sanctuary for migratory birds, including large flocks of Canada Goose and Black and Pintail duck, smaller cliques of Greenwinged Teal, American Wigeon and Greater Scaup as well as rarely seen species. The center houses interactive exhibits focusing on concepts of ecosystems and estuaries.

A marked trail along the river offers ideal birdwatching opportunities. Fishing is permitted in the Grand Codroy and the nearby Little Codroy rivers, which are frequented by such fish as Atlantic salmon. **Time:** Allow 1 hour minimum. **Hours:** Wetlands area open daily dawn-dusk. Center generally open daily 9-8, in summer. Phone ahead to confirm schedule. **Cost:** Donations. **Phone:** (709) 955-2109. 🗚

INDOOR WILDLIFE EXHIBIT AND NATURE PARK is off Hwy. 1 Doyles exit, then 3.5 km (2 mi.) w. on Hwy. 406. Bears, birds, caribou, fish and moose are among the more than 300 mounted animals featured in exhibits throughout the museum. A wildlife trail allows visitors to see native wild animals, including a fox and coyote. A petting zoo lets visitors get close to such animals as a llama, mule and goat.

Time: Allow 1 hour, 30 minutes minimum. **Hours:** Daily 10-6, early June-Sept. 30. **Cost:** $7; $5 (ages 0-18); $20 (family). **Phone:** (709) 955-2843.
🍴 🗚

WABUSH

WABUSH HOTEL   **Phone:** 709/282-3221
◈◈◈ ◈◈
Hotel   **Address:** 9 Grenfell St A0R 1B0 **Location:** Centre. **Facility:** 85 units. 3 stories, interior corridors. **Amenities:** high-speed Internet. **Dining:** Grenfell Restaurant, see separate listing. **Activities:** exercise room. **Fee:** massage. **Guest Services:** coin laundry. 🍴 🍸 BIZ 📶 ✕

Rates not provided

WHERE TO EAT

GRENFELL RESTAURANT   **Phone:** 709/282-3221
◈◈◈ ◈◈
Chinese   **AAA Inspector Notes:** Guests are seated in either of two dining sections, one of which is more casual. Those not in the mood for the daily buffet can peruse the full menu of Chinese and Canadian entrees. **Bar:** full bar. **Address:** 9 Grenfell St A0R 1B0 **Location:** Centre; in Wabush Hotel. B L D
$7-$20

Canadian, Chinese & International Cuisine

WILTONDALE

FRONTIER COTTAGES   **Phone:** 709/453-2520
(fyi) Not evaluated. **Address:** Viking Tr A0K 4N0 **Location:** Jct Hwy 430 and 431; entrance to Gros Morne National Park. Facilities, services, and decor characterize a mid-scale property.

Autumn in Nova Scotia

Nova Scotia

Keep your eyes and ears open in breathtaking Nova Scotia—it has plenty of treats for both.

Nature's bounty runs unchecked here. The landscape unfurls along meandering roads. Stretches of rugged coastline harbor history-rich anchorages.

The Bay of Fundy is characterized by dramatic tides, which have been recorded to rise 16 metres (52 feet) at Minas Basin.

Hiking trails lead to hidden surprises such as waterfalls, promontories and cliffs. Many coves and islands in Kejimkujik National Park and National Historic Site of Canada can be reached only by canoe.

And sounds? Crashing waves on sandy beaches lure surfers and serenity seekers to Lawrencetown. The clap of lobster traps being stacked rings out in Pictou. Moose calls break the haunting quiet of marshes. Shorebirds squawking noisily signal fall migration. And musical tradition means Scottish strathspeys, Acadian jigs and Celtic rock.

Minas Basin

Echoes of Scotland

A lively melody screams from a fiddle. Girls in pleated tartan skirts, waistcoats and argyle kneesocks step and kick to a Scottish drum's quick rhythm. Bagpipe music echoes across green valleys.

Scottish King James VI would be proud. In 1621 he granted territory to establish Nova Scotia, Latin for "New Scotland," and many immigrant families remain loyal to their roots.

Scottish Nova Scotians celebrate grandly: Almost every summer Saturday residents frolic at a *ceilidh* (kay-lee), Gaelic for party. Often spontaneous, these get-togethers may happen in kitchens or on front porches—wherever there's a fiddle. They are distinctively Celtic and include traditional singing, step dancing, fiddling concerts or storytelling.

At the Antigonish Highland Games, burly men in kilts throw weights and tall spruce logs. Pipers in Scottish finery—Prince Charlie jackets, sporrans (change purses), kilts, hose and brogues (lace-up shoes)—delight guests with tunes, just like at the first games in the 1860s. And, of course, there's an old-fashioned pipe band competition or Highland dancing to fiddle and piano music.

Nova Scotia has its own plaid, the colors of which are found in nature. Green depicts the three-fourths of the landscape covered in forest, while blue and white represent the rugged, sapphire sea surrounding the country, especially the staggering Bay of Fundy.

A French Flair

Prior to the arrival of the Scots, French settlers claimed the region, naming it Acadia ("peaceful land"). But it didn't stay tranquil long, due to a prolonged conflict between Britain and France for control of the territory.

Numerous sites are reminiscent of Acadia. The 1605 founding of Port-Royal marked the beginning of French colonization in North America: Imagine fur-trading days at Port-Royal National Historic Site of Canada, where steeply pitched roofs and fieldstone chimneys typify Norman-style architecture.

Once an Acadian village, Grand Pré National Historic Site of Canada has an exhibit about England's 1755 deportation of Acadians. Henry Wadsworth Longfellow memorialized the event with his epic poem "Evangeline," which tells of a woman separated from her beloved during the exile. Based on a true story, the poem evolved into an Acadian myth. A statue dedicated to Longfellow and a wishing well named for the heroine are on the grounds. An Acadian flag, similar to the tricolor French banner, tops the site. The flag decorates homes along St. Mary's Bay—the "French Shore"—where many French-speaking Acadian villages remain.

Coastal towns like Digby, Yarmouth and Pubnico evoke an Acadian milieu. Nearby Point de l'Eglise (Church Point) is home to Université Ste-Anne, a French language institute focusing on Acadian cultural studies.

Recreation

You're near water wherever you go in Nova Scotia. With the Atlantic Ocean and an interior speckled with lakes, rivers and streams, water sports make a splash.

Seasoned white-water rafters might tackle the powerful Bay of Fundy, the only place in the world where you paddle upriver. Sheltered ocean inlets tempt sea kayakers, while inland waters attract the tame at heart.

Halifax and Sydney harbors welcome world-class sailors; outfitters provide rentals and lessons. For scuba diving, check out the shipwrecks along Nova Scotia's rocky shores; June through October is best.

Cape Breton Highlands National Park of Canada accommodates short strolls and overnight adventures. The Trans Canada Trail traverses Halifax, New Glasgow, Pictou, Sydney and Tatamagouche and provides hiking, bicycling, horseback riding, cross-country skiing and snowmobiling.

For camping, try Cape Breton Highlands National Park of Canada on the rugged section of Cape Breton Island. It offers hiking, bicycling, fishing and swimming. Canoeing is a great way to explore Kejimkujik National Park and National Historic Site of Canada.

When snow falls, hit Nova Scotia's ski slopes. For snowboarding and snowtubing try Ski Wentworth. Keppoch Mountain near Antigonish offers night skiing. Powder enthusiasts camp overnight in Cape Breton Highlands National Park's ski cabins after a day of cross-country trails or downhill skiing at Cape Smokey. Kejimkujik National Park and National Historic Site of Canada beckons cross-country skiers and snowshoers. Snowmobiling is another wintertime activity.

Anglers are lured to the province's rich fishing grounds. Saltwater enthusiasts charter boats to search for bluefin tuna, shark, cod, halibut and mackerel. Striped bass lurk in tidal estuaries and along Bay of Fundy beaches. Freshwater lakes and rivers have speckled trout, Atlantic salmon, brown trout, American shad, smallmouth bass and yellow perch. Many rivers allow fly fishing only.

Due to Nova Scotia's position on the Atlantic flyway, bird-watching is prime. Cruise along Cape Dauphin to spot rare Atlantic puffins nesting on cliffs. And keep your eyes peeled for humpback, pilot and minke whales; summer is best for viewing these migrating creatures. Outfitters can arrange wildlife-viewing charters.

Port-Royal National Historic Site of Canada

Historic Timeline

1497	Explorer John Cabot claims Cape Breton Island for England.
1534	Jacques Cartier claims the region for France.
1605	French colonization of Acadia begins with the settlement of Port Royal.
1621	King James I grants "New Scotland" (Nova Scotia) to Sir William Alexander.
1755	After France cedes the territory, Acadians who refuse to pledge British loyalty are deported.
1848	Nova Scotia becomes the first Canadian colony to win responsible government.
1901	Guglielmo Marconi sends the first west-east transatlantic wireless message from Glace Bay to Cornwall, England.
1912	Halifax, the closest seaport, becomes the final resting place for many *Titanic* victims.
1917	Some 2,000 people die when a World War I munitions ship explodes in Halifax harbor.
1984	North America's first tidal power plant opens at Annapolis Royal on the Bay of Fundy.
2003	Hurricane Juan, the most damaging storm in a century, makes landfall at Shad Bay.

What To Pack

Temperature Averages Maximum/Minimum (Celsius)	JANUARY	FEBRUARY	MARCH	APRIL	MAY	JUNE	JULY	AUGUST	SEPTEMBER	OCTOBER	NOVEMBER	DECEMBER
Amherst	-4 / -14	-3 / -14	2 / -8	7 / -2	16 / 3	21 / 8	24 / 12	23 / 12	18 / 7	12 / 2	6 / -3	-1 / -11
Halifax	-1 / -9	-1 / -9	3 / -5	8 / -1	13 / 4	18 / 9	22 / 13	22 / 13	18 / 10	13 / 5	8 / 1	2 / -6
Kentville	-1 / -11	-1 / -11	3 / -6	9 / -1	17 / 4	22 / 9	25 / 13	24 / 12	19 / 7	14 / 3	8 / -1	2 / -7
Sydney	-2 / -10	-2 / -11	1 / -7	6 / -2	12 / 2	18 / 7	23 / 12	22 / 12	18 / 8	12 / 4	7 / -2	1 / -6
Truro	-2 / -11	-2 / -11	2 / -6	8 / -1	14 / 4	20 / 9	23 / 13	23 / 13	18 / 9	13 / 4	7 / -1	1 / -7
Yarmouth	1 / -7	0 / -7	3 / -4	8 / 1	13 / 5	17 / 9	20 / 12	21 / 12	18 / 9	13 / 5	8 / 1	3 / -4

From the records of The Weather Channel Interactive, Inc.

Good Facts To Know

ABOUT THE PROVINCE

POPULATION: 913,462.

AREA: 55,284 sq km (21,345 sq mi.); ranks 12th.

CAPITAL: Halifax.

HIGHEST POINT: 532 m (1,745 ft.), White Hill, Cape Breton Island.

LOWEST POINT: Sea level, Atlantic Ocean.

TIME ZONE(S): Atlantic. DST.

GAMBLING

MINIMUM AGE FOR GAMBLING: 19.

REGULATIONS

TEEN DRIVING LAWS: No more than one front-seat passenger is permitted. Driving is not permitted midnight-5 a.m. The minimum age for an unrestricted driver's license is 18 years, 3 months. For more information about Nova Scotia driver's license regulations phone (902) 424-5851.

SEAT BELT/CHILD RESTRAINT LAWS: Seat belts required for driver and all passengers ages 16 and older. Children ages 9-15 and at least 145 centimetres (4 feet, 9 inches) tall are required to be in a child restraint or seat belt. Child restraints are required for children under age 9 and less than 145 centimetres (4 feet, 9 inches) tall.

CELL PHONE RESTRICTIONS: Drivers are not permitted to use hand-held cell phones or engage in text messaging.

HELMETS FOR MOTORCYCLISTS: Required for all riders.

RADAR DETECTORS: Not permitted.

MOVE OVER LAW: Motorist is required to slow down to the speed limit or 60 kph (37 mph), whichever is less, and if possible vacate the lane nearest to the roadside emergency.

FIREARMS LAWS: By federal law, all nonresidents entering Canada with a firearm must declare their weapon in writing and pay a fee of $25 (Canadian). Contact the Canadian Firearms Centre at (800) 731-4000 to receive a declaration form or for additional information.

ALCOHOL CONSUMPTION: Legal age 19.

HOLIDAYS

HOLIDAYS: Jan. 1 ▪ Good Friday ▪ Easter Monday ▪ Victoria Day, May 24 or the closest prior Mon. ▪ Canada Day, July 1 ▪ Natal Day, Aug. (1st Mon.) ▪ Labour Day, Sept. (1st Mon.) ▪ Thanksgiving, Oct. (2nd Mon.) ▪ Remembrance Day, Nov. 11 ▪ Christmas, Dec. 25 ▪ Boxing Day, Dec. 26.

MONEY

TAXES: Nova Scotia has a harmonized sales tax composed of a 10 percent provincial tax and a 5 percent federal goods and services tax (for a total of 15 percent), which is applied to most goods and services.

VISITOR INFORMATION

INFORMATION CENTERS: Provincial visitor centers open year-round are in Halifax at the Halifax International Airport, off Hwy. 102 exit 6 ▪ on the Halifax waterfront at the boardwalk ▪ and in Amherst on Hwy. 104 at the New Brunswick border. The center in Pictou, at jct. Hwy. 106 and Rte. 6, is open May-Dec. ▪ and the center in Port Hastings, off the causeway, is open May-Jan.

Other centers, generally open May-Oct., are found in Yarmouth at 228 Main St. ▪ in Digby on Shore Road ▪ and in Peggy's Cove. Most centers are open 8:30-4:30, with longer hours at some locations during tourist season.

FURTHER INFORMATION FOR VISITORS:
Nova Scotia Department of Tourism, Culture and Heritage
Information and Reservations
P.O. Box 456
1800 Argyle St.
Halifax, NS B3J 2R5
Canada
(902) 424-5000
(800) 565-0000

FISHING AND HUNTING REGULATIONS:
Service Nova Scotia
c/o Department of Natural Resources
FIOPOP Administrator
P.O. Box 698
Halifax, NS B3J 2T9
Canada
(902) 424-5935

INTERPROVINCE FERRY INFORMATION:
Marine Atlantic Inc.
355 Purves St.
North Sydney, NS B2A 3V2
Canada
(902) 794-5200
(800) 341-7981 for reservations

Bay Ferries Ltd.
94 Water St.
P.O. Box 634
Charlottetown, PE C1A 7L3
Canada
(902) 566-3838
(888) 249-7245 for reservations *(See ad opposite inside front cover.)*

Nova Scotia Annual Events

Please call ahead to confirm event details.

JANUARY	FEBRUARY	MARCH
■ Acadia Art Show / Wolfville 902-585-1373 ■ In the Dead of Winter Music Festival / Halifax 902-483-6334 ■ Winter Frolic / New Ross 902-689-2210	■ International Boat Show Halifax 888-454-7469 ■ Carnaval d'Hiver de Pomquet / Antigonish 902-386-2388 ■ Winter Icewine Festival Wolfville 902-492-9291	■ Trek for Tourette / Halifax 902-865-2533 ■ Atlantic Outdoor Sports and RV Show / Halifax 902-827-7469 ■ Cheer Expo Grand Championships / Halifax 250-890-0106

APRIL	MAY	JUNE
■ ViewFinders: International Film Festival for Youth Halifax 902-422-6965 ■ Tartan Day / Pictou 902-485-4563 ■ Halifax Comedy Fest Halifax 902-490-5963	■ Atlantic Band Festival Halifax 877-647-2244 ■ SuperNova Theatre Festival Halifax 902-429-7070 ■ Victoria Day Weekend Annapolis Royal 902-532-7018	■ Shelburne County Lobster Festival / Shelburne 902-637-2903 ■ Greek Fest / Halifax 902-479-1271 ■ Fox Mountain Bluegrass Festival / Berwick 902-543-9732

JULY	AUGUST	SEPTEMBER
■ Antigonish Highland Games Antigonish 902-863-4275 ■ Royal Nova Scotia International Tattoo / Halifax 902-420-1114 ■ Yarmouth Seafest Yarmouth 800-565-0000	■ Western Nova Scotia Exhibition / Yarmouth 902-742-8222 ■ Festival of the Tartans New Glasgow 902-755-1555 ■ Digby Scallop Days Festival Digby 902-245-4531	■ Oktoberfest Tatamagouche 800-895-1177 ■ Atlantic Fringe Festival Halifax 902-435-4837 ■ Canadian Deep Roots Music Festival / Wolfville 902-542-7668

OCTOBER	NOVEMBER	DECEMBER
■ Celtic Colours International Festival / Port Hawkesbury 902-562-6700 ■ Great Scarecrow Festival and Antique Fair Mahone Bay 902-624-6151 ■ Halifax Pop Explosion--Music, Art and Culture Festival / Halifax 888-311-9090	■ Old Fashioned Christmas Sherbrooke 902-522-2400 ■ Berwick Santa Claus Celebrations / Berwick 902-538-8616 ■ Fezziwig Family Christmas Frolic / Wolfville 902-697-2677	■ New Ross Christmas Festival / New Ross 902-689-2663 ■ BT New Year's Eve Halifax 902-490-4729 ■ Pictou Christmas Light-up Pictou 902-458-6057

The Big Fiddle, Sydney Harbour

See Diverse Sea Life on a Boat Tour

Tour Alexander Keith's Nova Scotia Brewery

Take a Tugboat Ride on *Theodore Too*, Halifax

Town of Lunenburg

Great Experience for Members

AAA editor's picks of exceptional note

Fort Anne National
Historic Site of
Canada

Sherbrooke Village

K.C. Irving
Environmental
Science Centre &
Harriet Irving
Botanical Gardens

Alexander Graham
Bell National Historic
Site of Canada

Annapolis Royal (D-1)
Annapolis Royal Historic Gardens
(See p. 130.)

Fort Anne National Historic Site of Canada
(See p. 130.)

Upper Clements Parks *(See p. 130.)*

Baddeck (B-5)
Alexander Graham Bell National Historic Site of Canada *(See p. 132.)*

Cape Breton Highlands National Park of Canada (A-5)
Cape Breton Highlands National Park of Canada *(See p. 137.)*

Fortress of Louisbourg National Historic Site of Canada (B-6)
Fortress of Louisbourg National Historic Site of Canada *(See p. 147.)*

Glace Bay (B-6)
The Miners' Museum *(See p. 148.)*

Grand Pré (C-2)
Grand Pré National Historic Site of Canada *(See p. 148.)*

Granville Ferry (D-1)
North Hills Museum *(See p. 149.)*

Halifax (D-3)
Canadian Museum of Immigration at Pier 21 *(See p. 152.)*

Halifax Citadel National Historic Site of Canada *(See p. 152.)*

Maritime Museum of the Atlantic *(See p. 153.)*

Iona (B-5)
Highland Village Museum *(See p. 172.)*

Lunenburg (D-2)
Fisheries Museum of the Atlantic *(See p. 179.)*

New Ross (D-2)
Ross Farm Museum *(See p. 185.)*

Peggy's Cove (D-3)
Peggy's Cove *(See p. 186.)*

Port-Royal National Historic Site of Canada (C-1)
Port-Royal National Historic Site of Canada *(See p. 189.)*

Sherbrooke (C-4)
Sherbrooke Village *(See p. 192.)*

Shubenacadie (C-3)
Shubenacadie Provincial Wildlife Park *(See p. 193.)*

Stellarton (C-4)
Nova Scotia Museum of Industry *(See p. 194.)*

Wolfville (C-2)
K.C. Irving Environmental Science Centre & Harriet Irving Botanical Gardens *(See p. 201.)*

Yarmouth (E-1)
Yarmouth County Museum and Archives *(See p. 203.)*

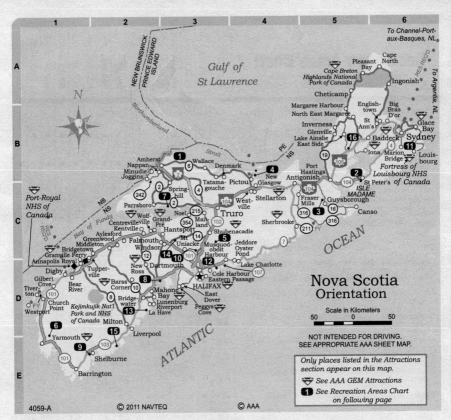

Nova Scotia
Orientation

Scale in Kilometers
50   0   50

NOT INTENDED FOR DRIVING.
SEE APPROPRIATE AAA SHEET MAP.

Only places listed in the Attractions
section appear on this map.

⬇ See AAA GEM Attractions
❶ See Recreation Areas Chart
  on following page

4059-A   © 2011 NAVTEQ   © AAA

Get pet travel tips and enter the photo contest at AAA.com/PetBook

Recreation Areas Chart

The map location numerals in column 2 show an area's location on the preceding map.

	MAP LOCATION	CAMPING	PICNICKING	HIKING TRAILS	BOATING	BOAT RAMP	BOAT RENTAL	FISHING	SWIMMING	PETS ON LEASH	BICYCLE TRAILS	WINTER SPORTS	VISITOR CENTER	LODGE/CABINS	FOOD SERVICE
NATIONAL PARKS *(See place listings.)*															
Cape Breton Highlands (A-5) 950 square kilometres 5 km n.e. of Chéticamp on Cabot Tr.		•	•	•				•	•	•			•	•	
Kejimkujik (D-1) 381 square kilometres in southwestern Nova Scotia off Hwy. 8 at Maitland Bridge. Canoeing, cross-country skiing, snowshoeing.		•	•	•	•	•	•	•	•	•	•	•	•		•
PROVINCIAL															
Amherst Shore (B-3) 328 hectares 6 km e. of Lorneville off Hwy. 366. Beachcombing.	❶	•							•						
Battery (B-5) 46 hectares 1.5 km e. of St. Peter's on Hwy. 4. Lighthouse.	❷	•	•	•				•	•						
Boylston (C-5) 90 hectares 6.5 km n. of Guysborough on Hwy. 16.	❸	•	•	•	•			•		•					
Caribou (B-4) 31 hectares 8 km n. of Pictou off Hwy. 106.	❹	•	•	•				•	•	•					
Dollar Lake (C-3) 1,193 hectares 23 km e. of Halifax via Hwy. 212.	❺	•	•	•	•	•		•	•						•
Ellenwood Lake (D-1) 112 hectares 19.25 km n.e. of Yarmouth on Hwy. 340.	❻	•	•	•	•	•			•						
Five Islands (C-3) 408 hectares 24.25 km e. of Parrsboro off Hwy. 2.	❼	•	•	•				•	•	•					
Graves Island (D-2) 49 hectares 3.25 km e. of Chester off Hwy. 3.	❽	•	•	•					•	•					
The Islands (E-1) 25 hectares 4.75 km w. of Shelburne off Hwy. 3.	❾	•	•	•					•	•					
Laurie (D-3) 28 hectares 40.25 km n. of Halifax on Hwy. 2 on Grand Lake.	❿	•	•	•	•			•	•	•					
Mira (B-6) 86 hectares 22.5 km s.e. of Sydney off Hwy. 22.	⓫		•	•	•			•	•	•					
Porter's Lake (D-3) 86 hectares 19.25 km e. of Dartmouth off Hwy. 7.	⓬		•	•	•	•		•	•	•					
Risser's Beach (D-2) 92 hectares 24 km s. of Bridgewater on Hwy. 331.	⓭	•	•						•	•					•
Smiley's (C-3) 40 hectares 12.75 km e. of Windsor on Hwy. 14.	⓮		•	•				•	•	•					
Thomas Raddall (D-2) 678 hectares near Liverpool off Hwy. 103.	⓯	•	•	•					•			•			•
Whycocomagh (B-5) 205 hectares 151 km e. of Whycocomagh on Hwy. 105.	⓰	•	•	•				•	•	•					

ALEXANDER GRAHAM BELL NATIONAL HISTORIC SITE OF CANADA—See Baddeck p. 132.

AMHERST (B-3) pop. 9,505

As the geographical midpoint of the Atlantic Provinces, Amherst is known for its stately Victorian homes and for its role as Cumberland County's commercial center. Covering some 207 square kilometres (80 sq. mi.), the city is built on high ground above the fertile Tantramar marshes.

CUMBERLAND COUNTY MUSEUM is at 150 Church St. This was the home of Sen. Robert Barry Dickey, a father of confederation. Succeeding generations who resided in the 1838 house include James Dickey, a mayor of Amherst, and Arthur Dickey, a minister of defense for Canada. Exhibits interpret the natural, social and industrial history of Cumberland County. Extensive genealogy archives and gardens also are offered. **Hours:** Tues.-Fri. 9-5, Sat. noon-5. **Cost:** $3; free (ages 0-15); $5 (family). Cash only. **Phone:** (902) 667-2561.

AMHERST WANDLYN MEETING & CONVENTION HOTEL
Phone: (902)667-3331

Hotel
$105-$145

Address: 1539 Southampton Rd B4H 3Z2 **Location:** Trans-Canada Hwy 104 exit 3, 0.6 mi (1 km) w. **Facility:** 88 units. 3 stories (no elevator), interior/exterior corridors. **Parking:** winter plug-ins. **Terms:** cancellation fee imposed. **Amenities:** Some: high-speed Internet. **Dining:** Field & Marsh Dining Room, see separate listing. **Pool(s):** heated indoor. **Activities:** whirlpool, exercise room. **Guest Services:** coin laundry.

COMFORT INN
Phone: (902)667-0404

Hotel
$113-$145

Address: 143 Albion St S B4H 2X2 **Location:** Trans-Canada Hwy 104 exit 4, 1 mi (1.6 km) n on Rt 2. Located in a commercial area. **Facility:** 60 units. 2 stories (no elevator), interior corridors. **Terms:** cancellation fee imposed.

SUPER 8
Phone: (902)660-8888

Hotel
$94-$144

Address: 40 Lord Amherst Dr B4H 4W6 **Location:** Trans-Canada Hwy 104 exit 4. **Facility:** 50 units. 3 stories, interior corridors. **Terms:** cancellation fee imposed. **Amenities:** high-speed Internet, safes. **Pool(s):** heated indoor. **Activities:** whirlpool, waterslide. **Guest Services:** coin laundry.

WHERE TO EAT

DUNCAN'S PUB
Phone: 902/660-3111

Canadian
$8-$22

AAA Inspector Notes: In the heart of town, this relaxing pub offers a fine selection of salads, chowders and classic pub fare, including fresh seafood items. Well-prepared foods are made to order and served in ample portions. **Bar:** full bar. **Address:** 49 Victoria St B4H 1X9 **Location:** At Church St; centre. **Parking:** on-site and street.

FIELD & MARSH DINING ROOM
Phone: 902/667-3331

American
$7-$23

AAA Inspector Notes: The casual decor reflects a pleasant marsh theme that compliments the lovely views of the valley and Tantramar Marsh that can be enjoyed from the dining room's atrium windows. The seasonal menu lays out a fine selection of fresh seafood and meat entrees. Uniformed staff provide friendly, attentive service with a casual flair. **Bar:** full bar. **Address:** 1539 Southampton Rd B4H 3Z2 **Location:** Trans-Canada Hwy 104 exit 3, 0.6 mi (1 km) w; in Amherst Wandlyn Meeting & Convention Hotel.

JUNGLE JIM'S
Phone: 902/661-4414

Canadian
$8-$19

AAA Inspector Notes: Guests can step into a tropical theme at the casual eatery, which employs a friendly staff and nurtures a bustling atmosphere. The menu lines up a wide variety of comfort foods, salads, chicken, beef, seafood and hot wings, all served in ample, flavorful portions. **Bar:** full bar. **Address:** 147 S Albion St B4H 2X2 **Location:** Trans-Canada Hwy 104 exit 4, 0.8 mi (1.3 km) n on Rt 2; in Town Square Mall.

LOON ONN RESTAURANT
Phone: 902/667-1333

Chinese
$7-$15

AAA Inspector Notes: Popular with families, business travelers and young professionals, this restaurant in a commercial area is convenient to major shopping malls. All items are prepared to order, and delightful house specialties include moo goo gai pan, seafood wor bar and Cantonese chow mein. A large, open-style dining room is decorated with vibrant red and natural pine walls, and the service is very casual and friendly. **Bar:** full bar. **Address:** 107 Albion St S B4H 2X2 **Location:** Trans-Canada Hwy 10 exit 4, 1 mi (1.6 km) n on Rt 2.

WEST WINDS RESTAURANT
Phone: 902/661-2314

Canadian
$7-$18

AAA Inspector Notes: Home-cooking and ample portions are what guests will find at this casual restaurant with friendly service. Menu selection includes chowders, salads, sandwiches, burgers, steak and fresh seafood. Take-out service also is offered. **Bar:** beer & wine. **Address:** 34 Hwy 6 B4H 3Z2 **Location:** Trans-Canada Hwy 104 exit 3; adjacent to Esso station.

ANNAPOLIS ROYAL (D-1) pop. 444
• Hotels p. 130 • Restaurants p. 131

In the 1630s the French built Fort Anne on the south shore of the Annapolis Basin. When Great Britain took control in 1710, the name was changed to Annapolis Royal in honor of Queen Anne. Enlarged and altered by the British, the fort successfully withstood repeated French and Indian attacks and sieges in the 1740s. Annapolis Royal was the capital of Nova Scotia from 1710 until Halifax was founded in 1749.

Along the Annapolis Basin shore, the original French dikes hold back the Bay of Fundy tides, which rise from 6 to 9 metres (20 to 30 ft.). The best place for walking along the dikes is at the Annapolis Royal Historic Gardens (see attraction listing). An explanation of the tides' effects on the local environment is provided at the Annapolis Royal Tidal Generating Station (see attraction listing).

St. George Street provides several examples of the town's antiquity. Among the restorations are the

1784 Robertson-McNamara House, the 1817 Runciman House and the 1922 King's Theatre. Paralleling Lower St. George Street, a waterfront walkway offers a fine view of North Mountain and the Annapolis Basin.

Annapolis Royal and District Board of Trade: P.O. Box 2, Annapolis Royal, NS, Canada B0S 1A0. **Phone:** (902) 532-5454.

▼GEM **ANNAPOLIS ROYAL HISTORIC GARDENS** is at 441 St. George St. The 4-hectare (10-acre) park features themed gardens representing different periods in Port Royal's history. Highlights include the Governor's Garden, the Knot Garden, the Rock Garden, the Victorian Garden and a rose collection that includes almost 2,000 bushes representing some 250 varieties.

The Acadian section includes a replicated 1671 thatched-roof house, which provides a glimpse into early settlers' lives. New trends in plant materials and gardening techniques are demonstrated in The Innovative Garden. More than 2 kilometres (1.2 mi.) of paths wind among the gardens and displays. **Time:** Allow 30 minutes minimum. **Hours:** Daily 9-dusk, mid-May to mid-Oct. **Cost:** $7.75; $6.75 (ages 60+ and students with ID); free (ages 0-16 accompanied by an adult). **Phone:** (902) 532-7018.

ANNAPOLIS ROYAL TIDAL GENERATING STATION is on the causeway 1 km (.6 mi.) e. on Hwy. 1. The station, which opened in 1984, is the first and only modern tidal power plant in North America. It produces electricity by harnessing the tidal waters of the Bay of Fundy. An interpretive center features audiovisual presentations, a miniature model and two enclosed observation decks. **Time:** Allow 30 minutes minimum. **Hours:** Daily 10-6, mid-May to mid-Oct. Phone ahead to confirm schedule. **Cost:** Donations. **Phone:** (902) 532-5454.

▼GEM **FORT ANNE NATIONAL HISTORIC SITE OF CANADA** is 1 blk. n. of jct. hwys. 8 and 1. In the 1700s both France and England viewed this as an important site for maintaining control of eastern Canada. The French built four forts on the site before it was seized by the British in 1710. Fort Anne was Nova Scotia's capital until 1749; the last regiment was withdrawn in 1854.

Surviving structures include well-preserved ramparts and bastions, a powder magazine and a storehouse. The Fort Anne Museum features exhibits about the Mi'kmaq, Acadians, planters and Loyalists. The Fort Anne Heritage Tapestry illustrates four centuries of area history. Monuments honor various figures from the fort's history.

Tours: Guided tours are available. **Time:** Allow 1 hour minimum. **Hours:** Museum daily 9-5:30, May 15-Oct. 15; Mon.-Fri. by appointment, rest of year. Grounds daily dawn-dusk, year-round. **Cost:** Museum $3.90; $3.40 (ages 65+); $1.90 (ages 6-16); $9.80 (family, up to seven people with a maximum of two adults). **Phone:** (902) 532-2397 May 15-Oct. 15, or (902) 532-2321 during the off-season.

LOWER ST. GEORGE STREET runs along the waterfront. The oldest section of Annapolis Royal features many historic buildings, including the North Hills Museum *(see attraction listing in nearby Granville Ferry p. 149)*, the Sinclair Inn Museum and the O'Dell House Museum *(see attraction listing).*

Hours: Sinclair Inn Museum Mon.-Sat. 9-5, Sun. 12:30-5, June 1-Sept. 1; Tues.-Sat. 9-5, Sept. 2-Oct. 15. Phone ahead to confirm schedule. **Cost:** Sinclair Inn Museum by donations. Research fee $3. **Phone:** (902) 532-7754.

The O'Dell House Museum is at 136 St. George St. This restored two-story 1869 inn and tavern was built by Cory O'Dell, a Pony Express rider. The museum houses schoolroom artifacts; a Victorian mourning room; a kitchen and parlor; a toy room; and a genealogical research center with information dating back to the Acadian settlers. The second floor is devoted to the area's shipbuilding history.

Time: Allow 1 hour minimum. **Hours:** Daily 9-5, late May-early Sept.; Mon.-Fri. 1-4, rest of year (weather permitting). Phone ahead to confirm schedule. **Cost:** $3; $2 (ages 6-17 and senior citizens); $7 (family). **Phone:** (902) 532-7754.

▼GEM **PORT-ROYAL NATIONAL HISTORIC SITE OF CANADA**—see place listing p. 189.

▼GEM SAVE **UPPER CLEMENTS PARKS** is 6 km (4 mi.) w. at 2931 Hwy. 1. This family theme park offers more than 20 amusement rides and attractions, including a carousel, a roller coaster, water slide and ziplines. Miniature golf, gardens, a haunted house and live entertainment also are featured. A miniature train provides rides around the park.

Time: Allow 4 hours minimum. **Hours:** Theme park open daily 11-7, mid-June to early Sept. Phone ahead to confirm schedule. **Cost:** $25.50 with unlimited rides and activities (with the exception of laser tag and ziplines). Some height and weight restrictions apply. Park only (includes entertainment, train and haunted house) $10; $7 (ages 65+); free (ages 0-2 with adult). Single ride tickets $4. **Phone:** (902) 532-7557 or (888) 248-4567. 🍴 ⊠ 🏕

ANNAPOLIS ROYAL INN **Phone:** (902)532-2323
▼▼ ▼▼
Motel
$120-$150 6/1-10/15
$89-$109 10/16-5/31
Address: 3924 Hwy 1 B0S 1A0 **Location:** 0.6 mi (1 km) w. Located in a rural area. **Facility:** 30 units. 1 story, exterior corridors. **Terms:** office hours 7 am-11 pm, 30 day cancellation notice. **Amenities:** *Some:* high-speed Internet. **Activities:** sauna, whirlpool. **Guest Services:** coin laundry. BIZ 🛜 💻 / SOME UNITS 🐾

GARRISON HOUSE INN **Phone:** (902)532-5750
▼▼▼ ▼▼
Historic
Country Inn
$75-$169
Address: 350 St George St B0S 1A0 **Location:** Jct Rt 1 and 8. Across from Fort Anne National Historic Park. **Facility:** Dating from 1854, the inn is in the heart of town, within walking distance of several attractions. 7 units. 3 stories (no elevator), interior corridors. **Terms:** open 6/1-11/30, office hours 7 am-11 pm, cancellation fee imposed. **Dining:** restaurant, see separate listing.
🍴 🍷 🛜 ⊠ 🚭

HILLSDALE HOUSE INN

Phone: (902)532-2345

Historic Bed
& Breakfast
$85-$160

Address: 519 St George St B0S 1A0 **Location:** Just e of Rt 1; centre. **Facility:** The circa 1856 Hillsdale House is a fine mansion with lovely landscaped grounds and tastefully decorated rooms on three levels as well as in a carriage house. 13 units. 3 stories (no elevator), interior corridors. **Terms:** open 6/1-10/30 & 4/15-5/31, office hours 7 am-10 pm. **Activities:** horseshoes.

THE KING GEORGE INN

Phone: (902)532-5286

Historic Bed
& Breakfast
$80-$160

Address: 548 Upper St George St B0S 1A0 **Location:** Jct Rt 1 and 8, just e on Rt 8. Located in a commercial area. **Facility:** Once a sea captain's home, the inn dates from 1868 and offers some rooms with private decks. Guests should note the property's scent-free policy. 8 units. 2 stories (no elevator), interior corridors. **Terms:** office hours 7 am-11 pm.

WHERE TO EAT

CHARLIE'S PLACE RESTAURANT

Phone: 902-532-2111

Chinese
$7-$18

AAA Inspector Notes: Some of the restaurant's dining sections overlook historic Fort Anne. On the menu are a variety of combination plates, an ample selection of Chinese food and some Canadian dishes. **Bar:** full bar. **Address:** Rt 1 B0S 1A0 **Location:** Rt 1, 0.3 mi (0.5 km) w.

 L D

THE GARRISON HOUSE DINING ROOM

Phone: 902-532-5750

American
$16-$30

AAA Inspector Notes: The charming country inn specializes in lobsters and fresh seafood from the Bay of Fundy and produce from the Annapolis Valley. Eclectic folk art, particularly of fish, and antique mirrors enhance the intimate feel. Homemade pie, cake and torte are delicious. **Bar:** full bar. **Reservations:** suggested. **Address:** 350 St George St B0S 1A0 **Location:** Jct Rt 1 and 8; in Garrison House Inn. D CALL

LEO'S CAFE

Phone: 902-532-7424

American
$8-$14

AAA Inspector Notes: This popular café enables guests to relish the flavors of creative sandwiches, pita wraps, fresh salads and tasty soups and chowders. Homemade desserts quiet a rumbling sweet tooth. Pleasant patio seating is available in season. A peruse through the gift shop might uncover a treasure or keepsake trinket. **Address:** 222 St George St B0S 1A0 **Location:** Centre. **Parking:** street only. B L

YE OLDE TOWNE PUB

Phone: 902-532-2244

American
$8-$20

AAA Inspector Notes: Traditional pub fare--such as fish and chips, steak and kidney pie and steak and eggs--is hearty and flavorful. An interesting selection of draft beer is offered in the 1884 building. The upbeat, friendly atmosphere attracts a bustling tourist trade. **Bar:** full bar. **Address:** 9-11 Church St B0S 1A0 **Location:** Across from town wharf; centre. L D

ANTIGONISH (C-4) pop. 4,236

An abundance of beech nuts—and foraging bears—is thought to have given this area its name, derived from a Mi'kmaq word meaning "the place of broken branches." A group of officers from the Nova Scotia Volunteers received a land grant at Antigonish Harbour in 1784.

A rollicking good time is had each year in early July at the Antigonish Highland Games. Held since 1863, the games are the oldest continuous highland games outside of Scotland. In addition to a tug-of-war contest, a road race, ceilidhs and piping and drumming competitions, visitors can enjoy a concert under the stars, highland dancing, a street fair and a grand parade.

ST. NINIAN CATHEDRAL is at 121 St. Ninian St. Completed in 1874, the cathedral is constructed of local limestone and sandstone in Roman Basilica style. Highlights include impressive hand-painted frescoes, high Gothic ceilings, handsome woodwork and two square towers that rise 38 metres (125 ft.). A painting of St. Ninian, completed in the 1850s, is in the rear of the cathedral. **Hours:** Sun.-Wed. 7 a.m.-8 p.m., Thurs.-Fri. 8-8, July-Aug.; daily 7-7, rest of year. **Cost:** Free. **Phone:** (902) 863-2338.

ANTIGONISH VICTORIAN INN

Phone: 902-863-1103

Historic Bed
& Breakfast
Rates not provided

Address: 149 Main St B2G 2B6 **Location:** Between St. Mary's and Court sts. Located in a commercial area. **Facility:** Located in the heart of town on 5 landscaped acres, this Queen Anne-style mansion offers a variety of tastefully decorated guest rooms and suites. 13 units. 3 stories (no elevator), interior/exterior corridors. **Terms:** office hours 9 am-9 pm, check-in 3:30 pm, age restrictions may apply.

MARITIME INN ANTIGONISH

Phone: (902)863-4001

Hotel
$115-$195

Address: 158 Main St B2G 2B7 **Location:** Between St. Mary's and Court sts; centre. Located in residential area. **Facility:** 32 units, some two bedrooms. 2 stories (no elevator), interior/exterior corridors. **Dining:** Main Street Cafe, see separate listing. **Free Special Amenities:** newspaper and high-speed Internet.

WHERE TO EAT

THE ALCOVE BISTRO & LOUNGE

Phone: 902-863-2248

International
$12-$26

AAA Inspector Notes: This quaint bistro, in the heart of town, offers a very relaxed atmosphere while serving well-prepared comfort foods with a fusion of International flavors including Thai, Italian and Canadian dishes. Using only fresh local seafood and quality meats, they also offer thin-crust pizza, chowders and salads. **Bar:** full bar. **Reservations:** suggested. **Address:** 76 College St B2G 2X8 **Location:** Corner of Main St; opposite Town Hall. **Parking:** street only. L D

GABRIEAU'S BISTRO

Menu on AAA.com

Phone: 902-863-1925

Canadian
$9-$25

AAA Inspector Notes: The cozy bistro is open for all meals. Evening dining is more sophisticated but still reflects a casual atmosphere. The diverse menu offers a fine selection of seafood and meat entrees and an array of excellent homemade desserts. **Bar:** full bar. **Address:** 350 Main St B2G 2C5 **Location:** Corner of Hawthorne St. B L D

LOBSTER TREAT RESTAURANT Phone: 902/863-5465

American
$7-$25

AAA Inspector Notes: This family-run dining room has been serving customers since 1974. Finished in pine and tastefully decorated with local art, it is a cozy spot to unwind. Fresh seafood-with limited selections of steak, chicken and pasta-shares top billing with such sinful desserts as German apple cake. **Bar:** full bar. **Reservations:** suggested. **Address:** 241 Post Rd B2G 2K6 **Location:** 1 mi (1.6 km) w on Trans-Canada Hwy 104. L D

MAIN STREET CAFE Phone: 902/863-4001

American
$8-$25

AAA Inspector Notes: Overlooking the main street, the friendly, family-focused cafe features fresh regional seafood, steaks and pasta dishes. **Bar:** full bar. **Address:** 158 Main St B2G 2B7 **Location:** Between St. Mary's and Court sts; in Maritime Inn Antigonish.

B L D CALL M

AULD'S COVE

COVE MOTEL & RESTAURANT/GIFT SHOP
Phone: 902/747-2700

Motel
$105-$130

Address: 227 Auld's Cove Rd B0H 1P0 **Location:** 0.6 mi (1 km) n off Trans-Canada Hwy 104; 1.9 mi (3 km) w of Canso Cswy. **Facility:** 30 units. 1 story, exterior corridors. **Terms:** open 6/1-10/31 & 5/1-5/31, office hours 7 am-11 pm. **Dining:** restaurant, see separate listing. **Activities:** canoeing, fishing. **Guest Services:** coin laundry.

SAVE [icons] / SOME UNITS

WHERE TO EAT

COVE MOTEL RESTAURANT Phone: 902/747-2700

Seafood
$8-$30

AAA Inspector Notes: An impressive waterfront location offers a fine view of Canso Strait. Enjoy a pleasant nautical decor as you peruse a menu of fresh Nova Scotia seafood like lobster, scallops, mussels and a good selection of fish. Steak, ribs, chicken and pasta entrees are also offered. **Bar:** full bar. **Address:** 227 Auld's Cove Rd B0H 1P0 **Location:** 0.6 mi (1 km) n off Trans-Canada Hwy 104; 1.9 mi (3 km) w of Canso Cswy; in Cove Motel & Restaurant/Gift Shop. B L D CALL M

AYLESFORD (C-2) pop. 829

Aylesford was settled in 1784 by United Empire Loyalists, who named the community for the Fourth Earl of Aylesford, Lord of the Bedchamber to King George III. Here, at the highest point in the Annapolis Valley, the waters of the Annapolis River wind through fertile meadows and fruit orchards.

OAKLAWN FARM ZOO is off Hwy. 101 exit 16, following signs to 1007 Ward Rd. The 20-hectare (50-acre) zoo has one of the largest displays of cats and primates in Atlantic Canada, including a white tiger. Hoofed animals such as deer and goats can be fed by hand. **Time:** Allow 1 hour, 30 minutes minimum. **Hours:** Daily 10-dusk, Easter weekend to mid-Nov. **Cost:** $7; $4 (ages 65+ and students with ID); $3 (ages 3-12). **Phone:** (902) 847-9790.

BADDECK (B-5) pop. 873
• Restaurants p. 134

Baddeck, on the shore of the Bras d'Or Lakes on Cape Breton Island, derives its name from the Mi'kmaq word *abadak,* which means "place with an island near." The nearby island is Kidston's in Baddeck Harbour.

During the era of wooden ships Baddeck's boatyards helped sustain the economy. Today its harbor bustles with yachts and commercial boating traffic. Early on, the town was popularized by American editor and writer Charles Dudley Warner in his "Baddeck and That Sort of Thing." The village attracted many well-known persons who built summer houses in the area. Among those who came was Alexander Graham Bell, drawn because the scenery reminded him of Scotland. The resemblance does not end with the scenery; Gaelic is spoken, and old Highland Scottish customs persist in the local culture.

About 4 kilometres (2.5 mi.) from town is Bell's former summer home, Beinn Bhreagh, Gaelic for "beautiful mountain." His descendants continue to occupy the estate, which is closed to the public. On the property are the graves of Dr. and Mrs. Bell.

A number of scenic routes originate in Baddeck. The Cabot Trail, a road around northern Cape Breton, loops through here and runs through Ingonish *(see place listing p. 171),* Cape North *(see place listing p. 138)* and Chéticamp *(see place listing p. 139).* Other routes lead through the Margaree Valley and to Whycocomagh and Lake Ainslie. Nearby waters are renowned for trout fishing and yachting.

ALEXANDER GRAHAM BELL NATIONAL HISTORIC SITE OF CANADA, at the e. end of the village on Rte. 205, features a large collection of artifacts, photographs and personal mementos commemorating the life and work of inventor Alexander Graham Bell. Displays cover his extraordinary range of interests, including aeronautics, agriculture, genetics, marine engineering, medical science and his work with the hearing impaired.

The main building's striking architectural style is based on the tetrahedron, the geometric form Bell used in designing his passenger-carrying kites. The landscaped grounds offer a view of the Bell estate across Baddeck Bay on the Bras d'Or Lakes.

During July and August the site offers special programs, including kite-building workshops and experiments that Bell and his grandchildren performed with everyday materials as well as presentations about Bell's life and work.

Time: Allow 1 hour minimum. **Hours:** Daily 8:30-6, July 1-Oct. 15; 9-6, in June; 9-5 in May and Oct. 16-31; by appointment rest of year. **Cost:** $7.80; $6.55 (ages 65+); $3.90 (ages 6-16 and students with ID); $19.60 (family). **Phone:** (902) 295-2069.

BRAS D'OR LAKES & WATERSHED INTERPRE-TIVE CENTRE is off Hwy. 105 exit 9, then s. to 532 Chebucto St. Housed in an 1885 stone post office, the museum features exhibits about the history, geology and wildlife of the Bras d'Or Lakes. The center offers brochures and maps of the area, including the best sites for viewing bald eagles. **Time:** Allow 30 minutes minimum. **Hours:** Daily 9-7, June-Aug.; 1-4, in Sept. **Cost:** Donations. **Phone:** (902) 295-1675.

AUBERGE GISELE'S COUNTRY INN
Phone: 902/295-2849

ᐁᐁᐁ
Hotel
Rates not provided

Address: 387 Shore Rd B0E 1B0 **Location:** Trans-Canada Hwy 105 exit 8, 1 mi (1.6 km) e. **Facility:** 78 units, some two bedrooms. 3 stories, exterior corridors. **Terms:** seasonal, office hours 7 am-11 pm. **Dining:** Gisele's Dining Room, see separate listing. **Activities:** sauna, whirlpool. **Guest Services:** coin laundry.

🍴 📶 ⊠ 💻 / SOME UNITS 🛢 🖼

CASTLE MOFFETT
Phone: (902)756-9070

ᐁᐁᐁ
Country Inn
$199-$440

Address: 11980 Trans-Canada Hwy 105 B0E 3M0 **Location:** In Bucklaw area; 11.8 mi (19 km) w of town. **Facility:** A new world castle, the property spans a brook and overlooks Bras d'Or Lakes; roomy quarters have gas fireplaces, four-poster beds and lovely views. 9 units. 3 stories (no elevator), interior corridors. **Terms:** open 6/1-10/30 & 5/1-5/31, office hours 6:30 am-11:30 pm, 14 day cancellation notice-fee imposed. **Activities:** sauna, hiking trails, exercise room. *Fee:* massage. **Free Special Amenities: continental breakfast and high-speed Internet.**

SAVE 🍴 🍷 CALL 🛏M 📶 ⊠ 💻

HUNTER'S MOUNTAIN CHALETS **Phone:** (902)295-3392

ᐁᐁ ᐁ
Cottage
$78-$138

Address: 562 Cabot Tr B0E 1B0 **Location:** Trans-Canada Hwy 105 exit 7, 1.6 mi (2.6 km) n. Located in a quiet area. **Facility:** 12 cottages, some two bedrooms and efficiencies. 1 story, exterior corridors. **Terms:** open 6/1-10/31 & 5/11-5/31, office hours 8:30 am-9 pm, check-in 4 pm, 4 day cancellation notice-fee imposed. **Activities:** playground.

CALL 🛏M 📶 ⊠ 🎿 🎁 🛢 🖼 / SOME UNITS FEE 🐾

INVERARY ON BADDECK BAY **Phone:** 902/295-3500

ᐁᐁᐁ ᐁᐁᐁ
Hotel
$139-$159 6/16-10/31
$99-$129 6/1-6/15

Address: 368 Shore Rd B0E 1B0 **Location:** Trans-Canada Hwy 105 exit 8, 1 mi (1.6 km) e on Rt 205 (Shore Rd). **Facility:** 185 units, some cottages. 1-3 stories (no elevator), interior/exterior corridors. **Terms:** open 6/1-10/31, 3 day cancellation notice. **Dining:** Lakeside Restaurant, see separate listing. **Pool(s):** heated indoor. **Activities:** sauna, whirlpool, rental boats, rental canoes, rental paddleboats, boat dock, 2 tennis courts, rental bicycles, playground, exercise room, spa. *(See ad this page.)*

SAVE 🍴 🍷 CALL 🛏M 🏊 BIZ 📶 ⊠ 💻 / SOME UNITS FEE 🐾 🛢

Learn about
AAA/CAA Diamond Ratings
at AAA.com/Diamonds

▼ *See AAA listing this page* ▼

MCINTYRE'S HOUSEKEEPING COTTAGES
Phone: (902)295-1133

Cottage
$120-$350 6/1-10/18
$80-$300 10/19-5/31

Address: 8908 Hwy 105 B0E 1B0 **Location:** Trans-Canada Hwy 105, 3 mi (5 km) w. **Facility:** 9 units, some houses and cottages. 1 story, exterior corridors. **Terms:** office hours 8 am-10 pm, 4 day cancellation notice-fee imposed. **Activities:** playground.

SILVER DART LODGE & MACNEIL HOUSE
Phone: (902)295-2340

Hotel
$107-$240 7/1-10/17
$99-$216 6/1-6/30

Address: 257 Shore Rd B0E 1B0 **Location:** Trans-Canada Hwy 105 exit 8, 0.6 mi (1 km) e on Rt 205 (Shore Rd). **Facility:** 90 units, some two bedrooms and kitchens. 1-3 stories (no elevator), interior/exterior corridors. **Terms:** open 6/1-10/17. **Dining:** McCurdys Restaurant, see separate listing, entertainment. **Pool(s):** heated outdoor. **Activities:** bicycles, hiking trails, playground, basketball, horseshoes, exercise room. **Guest Services:** coin laundry. **Free Special Amenities:** local telephone calls and high-speed Internet.

THE LYNWOOD INN
Phone: 902/295-1995

[fyi] Not evaluated. **Address:** 23 Shore Rd B0E 1B0 **Location:** Centre. Facilities, services, and decor characterize a mid-scale property.

WHERE TO EAT

BADDECK LOBSTER SUPPERS
Phone: 902/295-3307

Seafood
$28-$30

AAA Inspector Notes: A memorable Nova Scotia experience awaits at this very informal restaurant. Guests order a choice of three entrees, hard-shell Atlantic whole lobster, planked fresh salmon or striploin grilled steak. Then every guest gets unlimited fresh steamed Cape Breton mussels plus a tasty seafood chowder, homemade bread and a choice of dessert all included with the purchase of one of the main entrees. **Bar:** full bar. **Address:** 17 Ross St B0E 1B0 **Location:** Centre. [D] CALL [GM]

BELL BUOY RESTAURANT & SUPPER HOUSE
Menu on AAA.com
Phone: 902/295-2581

Seafood
$9-$30

AAA Inspector Notes: A good selection of wine complements selections of seafood, steak and poultry. If you are a land and sea lover, the combination platters will satisfy any appetite. Most tables have a view of Baddeck Bay. **Bar:** full bar. **Address:** 536 Chebucto St B0E 1B0 **Location:** On Rt 205; centre. [D]

GISELE'S DINING ROOM
Phone: 902/295-2849

American
$22-$28

AAA Inspector Notes: Fine dining in a relaxed atmosphere is what guests can expect. The menu features fresh local seafood, prime cuts of meat and a nice selection of homemade desserts. **Bar:** full bar. **Reservations:** suggested. **Address:** 387 Shore Rd B0E 1B0 **Location:** Trans-Canada Hwy 105 exit 8, 1 mi (1.6 km) e; in Auberge Gisele's Country Inn. [B] [D]

LAKESIDE RESTAURANT
Phone: 902/295-3500

Regional Canadian
$12-$27

AAA Inspector Notes: Near the shoreline, the restaurant affords wonderful ocean views. This place has received the prestigious "Taste of Nova Scotia" designation for its delightful selection of fabulous Cape Breton cuisine, which diners pair with a huge selection of wines, beers and ales. **Bar:** full bar. **Reservations:** suggested. **Address:** 368 Shore Rd B0E 1B0 **Location:** Trans-Canada Hwy 105 exit 8, 1 mi (1.6 km) e on Rt 205 (Shore Rd); in Inverary on Baddeck Bay. [L] [D]

MCCURDYS RESTAURANT
Phone: 902/295-2340

Regional American
$10-$27

AAA Inspector Notes: This pleasant restaurant features great comfort food and wonderful views of the lake from its hilltop location. Patrons can listen to Celtic music every evening while sampling steak, pizza or pasta. **Bar:** full bar. **Address:** 257 Shore Rd (Hwy 205) B0E 1B0 **Location:** Trans-Canada Hwy 105 exit 8, 0.6 mi (1 km) e on Rt 205 (Shore Rd); in Silver Dart Lodge & MacNeil House. [B] [L] [D] CALL [GM]

YELLOW CELLO CAFE
Phone: 902/295-2303

Italian
$8-$20

AAA Inspector Notes: A very popular gathering spot for locals and tourists alike. Fine selection of tasty homemade pizza, pasta and seafood entrées. Peak season offers an option to dine outdoors on the pleasant deck. **Bar:** full bar. **Address:** 525 Chebucto St B0E 1B0 **Location:** Centre. [B] [L] [D] [X]

BARRINGTON (E-1) pop. 7,331

Following the 1755 expulsion of the Acadians, French habitations in the area of what is now Barrington were destroyed. The New Englanders who replaced the Acadians re-established the site in the 1760s.

Reached by causeway from Barrington Passage, nearby Cape Sable Island is a major seafood harvesting center in southern Nova Scotia. The Cape Sable Island boat, renowned for its stability and good handling in shallow water and rough seas, was invented at Clarks Harbour in the early 1900s. Modern motorized adaptations of the boat are used in most seafood-harvesting operations.

The Cape Sable Historical Society Centre and Community Museum, 2402 Hwy. 3, contains local artifacts and genealogical material.

BARRINGTON WOOLEN MILL MUSEUM is at 2368 Hwy. 3 on the Barrington River. This was the last water-powered woolen mill to operate in eastern Canada. Built in 1882, it was in use until 1962. Displays follow the stages in the manufacture of yarn and cloth from raw wool. A mural illustrates the history of farming in Nova Scotia and contains the first tartan created in the province. **Time:** Allow 30 minutes minimum. **Hours:** Mon.-Sat. 9:30-5:30, Sun. 1-5:30, June-Sept. **Cost:** $3; $10 (family). Rates may vary; phone ahead. **Phone:** (902) 637-2185.

OLD MEETING HOUSE MUSEUM is at 2408 Hwy. 3. The 1765 New England-style meetinghouse is said to be Canada's oldest nonconformist house of worship still in existence. Guides in period costume explain the history of the community. Many early townspeople are buried in the adjacent graveyard. **Time:** Allow 30 minutes minimum. **Hours:** Mon.-Sat. 9:30-5:30, Sun. 1-5:30, June-Sept. **Cost:** $3; $10 (family). Rates may vary; phone ahead. **Phone:** (902) 637-2185.

SEAL ISLAND LIGHT MUSEUM is at 2410 Hwy. 3 overlooking the bay. This is a three-story replica of the original Seal Island lighthouse that was built in the early 1800s. The museum houses memorabilia including a lantern and lens used 1907-79. **Time:** Allow 30 minutes minimum. **Hours:** Mon.-Sat. 9:30-5:30, Sun. 1-5:30, June-Sept. **Cost:** $2; free (ages 0-5); $10 (family). Rates may vary; phone ahead. **Phone:** (902) 637-2185.

WEST NOVA SCOTIA MILITARY MUSEUM is at 2401 Hwy. 3 in the old courthouse building. Military artifacts from World Wars I and II include medals, uniforms and weapons as well as photographs. **Time:** Allow 30 minutes minimum. **Hours:** Mon.-Sat. 9:30-5:30, Sun. 1-5:30, July-Aug.; Mon.-Fri. 10-5, in June. **Cost:** Donations. **Phone:** (902) 637-2185.

BARSS CORNER (D-2)

PARKDALE-MAPLEWOOD COMMUNITY MUSEUM is at 3005 Barss Corner Rd. The museum contains agricultural implements, tools, domestic utensils, personal articles and other items from the late 1800s and early 1900s. A research center and heritage garden also are part of the museum. **Hours:** Mon.-Fri. 9-5, May-Oct. (also Sat. 9-5, July-Aug.). Closed Labour Day weekend. **Cost:** Donations. **Phone:** (902) 644-2893 May-Oct., or (902) 644-2375 rest of year.

BAYFIELD

SEA'SCAPE COTTAGES   **Phone:** 902/386-2825

Cottage
$115-$145

Address: 6 Sea Scape Cottage Ln B0H 1R0 **Location:** Waterfront. Trans-Canada Hwy 104 exit 36, 3.2 mi (5.3 km) n on Sunrise Tr, then 1.1 mi (1.8 km) w on Ferry Rd. Located in a quiet secluded area. **Facility:** 8 units, some cabins and cottages. 1 story, exterior corridors. *Bath:* shower only. **Terms:** open 6/1-10/31 & 5/1-5/31, office hours 7 am-9 pm, 30 day cancellation notice-fee imposed. **Activities:** fishing, hiking trails. *Fee:* canoes.

BEAR RIVER (D-1)

An important shipbuilding and milling center at the end of the 19th century, Bear River has retained its pioneer flavor. The village has come to be known as the "Switzerland of Nova Scotia." The Dutch Windmill serves as a tourist bureau and contains a collection of photographs and logging and shipbuilding tools.

Bear River Board of Trade: P.O. Box 235, Bear River, NS, Canada B0S 1B0. **Phone:** (902) 467-3200.

BELLE COTE

ISLAND SUNSET RESORT & SPA   **Phone:** 902/235-2669

 Not evaluated. **Address:** 19 Beach Cove Ln B0E 1C0 **Location:** On Cabot Tr; centre. Facilities, services, and decor characterize a mid-scale property.

BERWICK   pop. 2,454

UNION STREET CAFE & THE WICK PUB
Phone: 902/538-7787

Canadian
$8-$21

AAA Inspector Notes: A local favorite with an upbeat, friendly atmosphere. The cafe and pub are split with the same menu in either section. Ample selections of classic pub fare as well as steaks, seafood, chicken and various great salads. **Bar:** full bar. **Address:** 183 Commercial St B0P 1E0 **Location:** Hwy 101 exit 15, 1 mi (1.6 km) e.

BIG BRAS D'OR (B-6)

Big Bras d'Or, meaning "Arm of Gold" in French, is on Boularderie Island, which is separated from the rest of Cape Breton Island by two narrow channels that connect the virtually tideless Bras d'Or Lake to the Atlantic Ocean.

[SAVE] **BIRD ISLAND BOAT TOURS** departs from Mountain Vista Seaside Cottages and Campground off Hwy. 105 exit 14, then 6.5 km (4 mi.) w. to 1672 Old Rte. 5. This 2.75-hour boat ride to the Bird Islands, Ciboux and Hertford offers a look at seals, eagles and seabirds such as the Atlantic puffin, razorbill auk, great cormorant, double-crested cormorant and kittiwake gull.

Departures require a minimum of four passengers. **Hours:** Tours depart daily at 10 and 1:30, mid-June to late Aug.; at 10 *or* 5:30, mid-May to mid-June; at 10 *or* 4:30, late Aug.-late Sept. (sea conditions permitting). **Cost:** Fare mid-May through July 1 $37; $15 (ages 7-12). Fare July 2-late Sept. $32; $15 (ages 7-12). **Phone:** (902) 674-2384 or (800) 661-6680.

BIG POND

RITA'S TEA ROOM   **Phone:** 902/828-2667

Canadian
$8-$18

AAA Inspector Notes: Run by singer/songwriter Rita MacNeil, the spacious tea room is nestled in the trees opposite the bay. The kitchen prepares lunch and light fare for early dinner service. Patio dining is a pleasant option in season. **Bar:** beer & wine. **Address:** 8077 Hwy 4 B1J 1Z3 **Location:** Centre.

BRIDGETOWN (C-2) pop. 972
• Hotels p. 136

At the head of navigation on the Annapolis River, Bridgetown was once an important shipbuilding center during the "age of sail." Stately Victorian-era houses are a reminder of its seafaring past.

Bridgetown Visitor Information Centre: 232 Granville St., Bridgetown, NS, Canada B0S 1C0. **Phone:** (902) 665-5150.

Self-guiding tours: A brochure outlining walking tours of historic areas is available at the visitor information center.

THE JAMES HOUSE MUSEUM is 1 blk. s. of Hwy. 1 at 12 Queen St. Displays in the 1835 house include a 150th anniversary quilt, period costumes, the Legion Memorial Museum containing military uniforms and memorabilia, and a museum collection that changes every summer. **Hours:** Mon.-Sat. 10-4, May-Sept.; by appointment rest of year. **Cost:** Donations. **Phone:** (902) 665-4530.

BRIDGETOWN MOTOR INN   **Phone:** 902/665-4403

Motel
Rates not provided

Address: 396 Granville St B0S 1C0 **Location:** Hwy 101 exit 20, 0.6 mi (1 km) w on Rt 1. **Facility:** 28 units. 2 stories (no elevator), exterior corridors. **Parking:** winter plug-ins. **Pool(s)** outdoor. **Guest Services:** coin laundry.

BRIDGEWATER (D-2) pop. 7,944

A farming and manufacturing community in the heart of the LaHave River Valley, the town was founded in the early 1800s and was named for the bridge spanning the river. Picturesque drives follow both banks. As an active waterway for commercial and pleasure craft, the river contributes to Bridgewater's importance as a regional economic center.

Shipyards Landing Park offers boat ramps and scenic vistas. The Bridgewater Woodland Gardens contain winding trails punctuated by azaleas and rhododendrons. The gardens also contain a large pond and picnic tables. The town's 8-kilometre (4.8 mi.) Centennial Trail is a hiking and bicycling path that meanders through woods and along the LaHave River.

Bridgewater & Area Chamber of Commerce: 220 North St., Bridgewater, NS, Canada B4V 2V6. **Phone:** (902) 543-4263.

DESBRISAY MUSEUM is .75 km (.5 mi.) s. to 130 Jubilee Rd. on the w. side of the LaHave River. One of Canada's oldest museum collections was started by Judge Mather Byles DesBrisay and opened to the public in 1902. Exhibits focus on the natural, cultural and industrial history of Bridgewater and Lunenburg County. Changing exhibits also are presented.

Time: Allow 1 hour minimum. **Hours:** Tues.-Sat. 9-5, Sun. 1-5, June-Aug.; Wed.-Sun. 1-5, rest of year. Phone ahead to confirm schedule. **Cost:** $3.50; $2.50 (ages 65+); $2 (ages 5-16); $8 (family); free (Sat.). Rates may vary; phone ahead. **Phone:** (902) 543-4033.

WILE CARDING MILL MUSEUM is at 242 Victoria Rd. (Hwy. 325). An 1860 carding mill features original machinery and an operating waterwheel.

Costumed staff demonstrate how to use the machinery. Visitors may hand card wool, use a drop spindle and make a sample of yarn.

Children's programs are offered. **Time:** Allow 30 minutes minimum. **Hours:** Mon.-Sat. 9:30-5:30, Sun. 1-5:30, June-Sept. Phone ahead to confirm schedule. **Cost:** $3.50; $2.25 (ages 65+); $2 (ages 6-17); $8 (family). Rates may vary; phone ahead. **Phone:** (902) 543-8233.

BEST WESTERN PLUS BRIDGEWATER HOTEL & CONVENTION CENTRE   **Phone:** (902)530-0101

Hotel
$120-$170

AAA Benefit: Members save up to 20%, plus 10% bonus points with Best Western Rewards®.

Address: 527 Hwy 10 B4V 7P4 **Location:** Hwy 103 exit 12, just n. **Facility:** 63 units. 3 stories, interior corridors. **Amenities:** high-speed Internet. **Pool(s):** heated indoor. **Activities:** whirlpool, waterslide, exercise room. **Guest Services:** coin laundry. **Free Special Amenities:** full breakfast and high-speed Internet.

THE BRIDGEWATER HOTEL   **Phone:** 902/543-8171

Hotel
Rates not provided

Address: 35 High St B4V 1V8 **Location:** Hwy 103 exit 13, just e. **Facility:** 42 units. 2 stories (no elevator), interior corridors. **Pool(s):** sauna, heated indoor. **Activities:** whirlpool.

COMFORT INN   **Phone:** (902)543-1498

Hotel
$89-$129

Address: 49 North St B4V 2V7 **Location:** Hwy 103 exit 12, 1.1 mi (1.7 km) s on Rt 10. **Facility:** 61 units. 2 stories (no elevator), interior corridors. **Terms:** cancellation fee imposed.

DAYS INN & CONFERENCE CENTRE BRIDGEWATER   **Phone:** (902)543-7131

Hotel
$81-$121

Address: 50 North St B4V 2V6 **Location:** Hwy 103 exit 12, 1.1 mi (1.7 km) s on Rt 10. **Facility:** 70 units. 2 stories (no elevator), interior corridors. **Amenities:** *Some:* high-speed Internet. **Pool(s):** heated indoor. **Activities:** exercise room. **Guest Services:** valet and coin laundry.

WHERE TO EAT

KO'S RESTAURANT   **Phone:** 902/543-6080

Chinese
$8-$17

AAA Inspector Notes: This popular spot overlooks the LaHave River and offers a lovely outdoor deck option in season. The menu boasts a variety of Chinese and Canadian dishes with a decent selection of combination plates. **Bar:** full bar. **Address:** 434 King St B4V 1B2 **Location:** Corner of King and Dufferin sts; centre. **Parking:** street only.

TWO CHEF'S

Canadian
$6-$17

Phone: 902/543-9661
AAA Inspector Notes: The restaurant entices guests with its informal atmosphere, friendly service and diverse menu, which includes several East Indian dishes. **Bar:** full bar. **Address:** 28 Davison Dr B4V 3A2
Location: Centre; in Eastside Plaza. L D

CALEDONIA

MERSEY RIVER CHALETS & NATURE RETREAT
Phone: 902/682-2443
fyi Not evaluated. **Address:** Rt 8 B0T 1B0 **Location:** 1.2 mi (1.8 km) e on gravel entry road, 0.3 mi (0.5 km) n of Kejimkujik National Park, on Rt 8; centre. Facilities, services, and decor characterize a mid-scale property.

CANNING pop. 798

THE FARMHOUSE INN

Historic Bed
& Breakfast
$110-$160

Phone: 902/582-7900
Address: 9757 Main St B0P 1H0
Location: Hwy 101 exit 11, follow signs to town, then 5 mi (8 km) n on Rt 358. **Facility:** With a history that dates to the 1850s, this converted house combines a rich heritage with modern amenities such as whirlpool tubs. 6 units. 2 stories (no elevator), interior/exterior corridors. **Terms:** office hours 8 am-11 pm. 📶 ❌

CANSO (C-5) pop. 911

Canso is one of the oldest fishing communities in the Maritimes. French fishermen came to Canso in the early 1600s because of the abundance of codfish. The town now offers sightseeing and sport fishing.

Town of Canso Tourism and Trade: P.O. Box 189, Canso, NS, Canada B0H 1H0. **Phone:** (902) 366-2525.

CANSO ISLANDS NATIONAL HISTORIC SITE OF CANADA lies .5 km (.3 mi.) off the waterfront. A visitor center on Union Street offers views of Grassy Island Fort National Historic Site. The fort became the object of bitter feuding between the French and British until it was destroyed and abandoned abruptly in 1744. The visitor center features artifacts, dioramas and an audiovisual presentation. A boat ferries visitors to Grassy Island.

Time: Allow 30 minutes minimum. **Hours:** Visitor center open daily 10-6, June 1-Sept. 15. Boats depart according to demand (weather permitting). **Cost:** Visitor center free. Park and boat fare by donation. **Phone:** (902) 366-3136 or (902) 295-2069.

WHITMAN HOUSE MUSEUM is at 1297 Union St. Memorabilia from the C.H. Whitman family is displayed in the 1885 house, which features extensive woodwork, solid brass hardware, antiques and two fireplaces. The house also contains exhibits reflecting Canso's days as an important Western Union communications center. **Tours:** Guided tours are available. **Time:** Allow 1 hour minimum. **Hours:** Daily 9-5, June-Sept.; by appointment rest of year. **Cost:** Donations. **Phone:** (902) 366-2170 or (902) 366-2525.

CAPE BRETON HIGHLANDS NATIONAL PARK OF CANADA (A-5)

Elevations in the park range from sea level to 532 metres (1,745 ft.) at White Hill. Refer to CAA/AAA maps for additional elevation information.

Cape Breton Highlands National Park of Canada has entrances on the Cabot Trail 5 kilometres (3 mi.) northeast of Chéticamp on the west side of the island and at Ingonish Beach on the east. The park is in the northern part of Cape Breton Island. Bounded on the west by the Gulf of St. Lawrence and on the east by the Atlantic Ocean, the park protects 950 square kilometres (366 sq. mi.) of highlands and coastal wilderness. The first national park in the Atlantic provinces, it bears a striking resemblance to coastal regions of Scotland.

Along the western shore, steep hills reaching a height of more than 335 metres (1,100 ft.) rise sharply to a broad plateau covering most of the park area. The eastern shore also is rocky, indented with numerous coves and sandy beaches at the mouths of valleys.

Less frequented by visitors, the interior high plateau of the park is similar to subarctic regions, containing heath bogs, stunted spruce forest and dry, rocky barrens. Along the seacoast headlands the trees are stunted and twisted into grotesque shapes. The rest of the park is covered with a typical Acadian mixed forest of conifers and hardwoods.

The park, a wildlife sanctuary, protects a variety of animals, including black bears, foxes and snowshoe hares. Motorists are advised to drive with care. Moose often are seen along the highways. Among the 200 species of birds are the bald eagle and redtailed hawk. Whale-watching is popular both from land and by boat tours offered in nearby communities.

The Cabot Trail, a circle tour of the eastern and western shores of Cape Breton Island and the picturesque Margaree Valley, winds along the edge of the park's rugged, forested slopes, providing a scenic 300-kilometre (186-mi.) drive.

General Information and Activities

The park is open all year, with full facilities offered mid-May to mid-October. Information centers are maintained at the park's entrances at Chéticamp *(see place listing p. 139)* and Ingonish *(see place listing p. 171)*. The Chéticamp Visitor Centre has a 10-minute slide show about the park and a children's corner. Interpretive events are presented during July and August. An entry permit is required for park use, including Cabot Trail sightseeing.

The park offers a wide range of activities, including camping at its six campgrounds, hiking, swimming, wildlife and bird-watching, tennis, bicycling and fishing. Highland Links, within the park, is a world-class 18-hole golf course. Changing facilities, tennis courts and a picnic area are provided at the Ingonish Beach Day Use Area. The main beach is the only land separating the surf from a quiet freshwater lake; supervised swimming takes place during July and August. Picnic facilities and unsupervised swimming are available at Black Brook, La Bloc, North Bay Beach and Warren Lake.

Pilot whales are a fairly common sight offshore, while minke, finback and humpback whales can be seen periodically as well. Whale-watching and deep sea fishing excursions depart from port towns near the park.

Hiking trails lead from the Cabot Trail to the interior or along the shore. The 25 trails, ranging from short, easy strolls to challenging mountain hikes with panoramic views, are described on the park map. Bicycling is permitted on designated trails only. Fall foliage is at its best from late September to mid-October. Certain park trails are groomed for cross-country skiing in the winter. *See Recreation Chart.*

ADMISSION to the park is $7.80 per day; $6.80 (ages 66+); $3.90 (ages 6-16); $19.60 (family). Annual passes are available.

PETS are permitted in the park except on beaches and the Skyline Trail. They must be on a leash at all times.

ADDRESS inquiries to Cape Breton Highlands National Park of Canada, Ingonish Beach, NS, Canada B0C 1L0. Phone (902) 224-2306, (888) 773-8888 for an information packet or (877) 737-3783 for camping reservations.

CAPE NORTH (A-6)

Cape North, a Cape Breton Island district on Aspy Bay, is the northernmost point on the scenic Cabot Trail. The 19-kilometre (12-mi.) road connecting Cape North with Capstick on St. Lawrence Bay offers ocean and mountain scenery. Cabot Landing, a provincial park with a picnic area and beach on Aspy Bay, is believed to have been the landing site of John Cabot and his son Sebastian. A trail leads to the top of 442-metre (1,450-ft.) Sugar Loaf Mountain.

NORTH HIGHLANDS COMMUNITY MUSEUM is at 29243 Cabot Tr. Pioneer life and northern Cape Breton traditions are depicted through exhibits, artifacts and photographs, a blacksmith's forge and a settler's garden. Events such as the *Titanic* and *Auguste* shipwrecks, construction of the first transatlantic cable and the development of gypsum mining also are explored. Archive and genealogy research are available by appointment.

Visitor information also is available. **Time:** Allow 30 minutes minimum. **Hours:** Daily 10-5, early June to mid-Oct. **Cost:** Donations. **Phone:** (902) 383-2579.

CENTREVILLE (C-2)

Many residents of Cape Sable Island, on which Centreville is found, are descendants of Archelaus

Smith, who was among the tide of New Englanders, mainly from Cape Cod, Mass., who settled Nova Scotia's South Shore in the 1760s. For the next half-century their livelihoods of fishing and shipping were subject to attacks by Yankee privateers.

ARCHELAUS SMITH MUSEUM is 4 km (2.5 mi.) s. to 915 Hwy. 330. The collection includes marine exhibits, local art, artifacts from shipwrecks and displays of handicrafts and household items. Genealogical information is available. **Hours:** Mon.-Sat. 9:30-5:30, Sun. 1:30-5:30, July-Aug. **Cost:** Donations. **Phone:** (902) 745-2642.

BETWEEN THE BUSHES   Phone: 902/582-3648

American
$11-$26

AAA Inspector Notes: In the middle of a pick-your-own blueberry field, the restaurant is casual at lunch and more of a fine-dining spot in the evening. The chefs focus on farm-fresh produce, meats and seafood in nicely presented entrees. Desserts and breads are homemade. **Bar:** full bar. **Address:** 1225 Middle Dyke Rd B0P 1J0 **Location:** Hwy 101 exit 12, 6 mi (10 km) n, follow signs.

L   D

CHARLOS COVE

SEAWIND LANDING COUNTRY INN
                                      Phone: 902/525-2108

Country Inn
$99-$169

Address: 159 Wharf Rd B0H 1T0 **Location:** Oceanfront. Rt 316, 0.5 mi (0.8 km) se on gravel road. Located in a quiet rural setting. **Facility:** In a rural area overlooking Tor Bay, this pet friendly inn offers small but pleasant rooms in the main inn; larger rooms are in the annex building. 14 units. 2 stories (no elevator), interior/exterior corridors. **Terms:** office hours 7 am-10 pm. **Dining:** restaurant, see separate listing. **Guest Services:** complimentary laundry.

WHERE TO EAT

SEAWIND LANDING COUNTRY INN DINING ROOM
                                      Phone: 902/525-2108

Regional American
$22-$29

AAA Inspector Notes: Reservations are strongly suggested at the elegant country inn, which features an ever-changing selection of "country gourmet" food. The chef relies heavily on regional ingredients and infuses dishes with a French flair. Choices might include scallops drenched in vermouth, or fresh Atlantic salmon in season. Dessert hounds should not pass up the delicious wild blueberry cake. Whatever is on the menu, expect outstanding food and good service. **Bar:** full bar. **Reservations:** suggested. **Address:** 159 Wharf Rd B0H 1T0 **Location:** Rt 316, 0.5 mi (0.8 km) se on gravel road; in Seawind Landing Country Inn. B   D   CALL 🖥M   🍴

CHESTER pop. 10,741

MECKLENBURGH INN   Phone: 902/275-4638

Historic Bed
& Breakfast
$105-$155

Address: 78 Queen St B0J 1J0 **Location:** Between Union and Regent sts. **Facility:** This converted circa 1890s house is in the heart of town and offers individually decorated guest rooms. A covered porch and balcony offer a relaxing area to unwind. 4 units. 2 stories (no elevator), interior corridors. **Terms:** open 6/1-1/1 & 5/1-5/31, office hours 8 am-10 pm, 2 night minimum stay - weekends, 14 day cancellation notice-fee imposed.

WINDJAMMER MOTEL   Phone: 902/275-3567

Motel

$75-$85 6/1-9/15
$65-$75 9/16-5/31

Address: 4070 Rt 3 B0J 1J0 **Location:** 0.6 mi (1 km) w. **Facility:** 18 units. 1 story, exterior corridors. **Parking:** winter plug-ins. **Terms:** office hours 7 am-10 pm, cancellation fee imposed.

WHERE TO EAT

THE ROPE LOFT   Phone: 902/275-3430

Seafood
$9-$23

AAA Inspector Notes: This rustic sea shanty has enjoyed the same splendid location overlooking Chester Harbour since 1816. Offering a fine selection of fresh local seafood with an emphasis on regional creations, the menu includes such favorites as fish cakes and chowder. **Bar:** full bar. **Address:** 36 Water St B0J 1J0 **Location:** Off Rt 3; on Front Harbour. **Parking:** street only. **Historic** [L] [D] [AC]

CHESTER BASIN

THE SWORD & ANCHOR BED & BREAKFAST
     Phone: 902/275-2478

Bed & Breakfast
Rates not provided

Address: 5306 Hwy 3 B0J 1K0 **Location:** Centre. **Facility:** 10 units, some two bedrooms, kitchens and cottages. 2 stories (no elevator), interior corridors. **Terms:** seasonal.

WHERE TO EAT

SEASIDE SHANTY & CHOWDER HOUSE
     Phone: 902/275-2246

Canadian
$7-$22

AAA Inspector Notes: The popular spot offers fine dining amid a relaxed atmosphere. Entrees are creatively presented and prepared to order. From fine cuts of meat to salmon, scallops and lobster, there is likely something to tempt anyone's palate. **Bar:** full bar. **Address:** 5315 Rt 3 B0J 1J0 **Location:** Centre; at Marina. [L] [D] [AC]

CHÉTICAMP (A-5)

- Hotels p. 140 • Restaurants p. 140

This thriving shore community is sheltered from the Gulf of St. Lawrence by Chéticamp Island. Farming, rug hooking and fishing for lobster and crab are the basis of the area's economy. Saint-Pierre Church dominates the waterfront. The stone church was built in 1892 under the direction of Father Pierre Fiset. Father Fiset's tomb and the original 1904 Casavant organ are on display; phone (902) 224-2064.

Chéticamp lies on an especially scenic section of the Cabot Trail, which circles the northern tip of Cape Breton Island and passes the western entrance of Cape Breton Highlands National Park of Canada (see place listing p. 137), 5 kilometres (3 mi.) northeast of town.

ACADIAN MUSEUM is at 15067 Main St. (Cabot Trail) near Saint-Pierre Church. Spinning, weaving and rug hooking are demonstrated at this museum, part of the Coopérative Artisanale. Displays include French-Canadian antiques, glassware and rugs dating to the 1900s. Guided tours explain how wool is carded and spun, and visitors are invited to hook their own rug strips. **Hours:** Daily 9:30-5:30, May-Oct. **Cost:** Donations. **Phone:** (902) 224-2170.

CAPTAIN ZODIAC WHALE CRUISE departs from the town center at 14925 Cabot Tr. Whale sightings are guaranteed aboard these fast-moving Zodiac vessels, which travel close to shore for views of pilot and minke whales and farther out to sea for glimpses of humpbacks, dolphins and fin whales.

Passengers are provided with all-weather floatation suits. Zodiac trips are not advised for pregnant women and people with back or neck problems. **Time:** Allow 2 hours minimum. **Hours:** Cruises depart daily at 9, 11, 1, 3 and 5, May 1-Oct. 15 (weather permitting). **Cost:** Fare $39; $19 (ages 0-16). Reservations are required. **Phone:** (902) 224-1088 or (877) 232-2522.

ELIZABETH LeFORT GALLERY is at 15584 Cabot Tr. in Les Trois Pignons building. A collection of tapestries by Acadian artist Dr. Elizabeth LeFort features more than 20 hooked rugs with historic themes. Tapestries of other local artists are displayed as well. **Time:** Allow 30 minutes minimum. **Hours:** Daily 9-7, July-Aug.; daily 9-5, May-June and Sept.-Oct.; Mon.-Fri. by appointment rest of year. **Cost:** $5; $4 (ages 65+); $3.50 (ages 6-18 and college students with ID). **Phone:** (902) 224-2642.

SEASIDE WHALE & NATURE CRUISES departs from Quai Mathieu on the boardwalk. Narrated cruises offer more than a 95-percent chance of whale sightings as well as glimpses of eagles, seabirds and wildlife along the coast of Cape Breton Highlands National Park of Canada (see place listing p. 137). Hydrophones on board enable passengers to hear whale calls.

Minimum of six adults required for the tour. **Time:** Allow 3 hours minimum. **Hours:** Cruises depart three times daily, mid-June to mid-Oct. (weather permitting). **Cost:** $25; $20 (ages 65+); $12 (ages 6-15); $70 (family of four; $10 per extra family member). Reservations are required. **Phone:** (902) 224-2899.

WHALE CRUISERS LTD. departs from Chéticamp Harbour opposite Saint-Pierre Church. On narrated 3-hour cruises, the Whale Cruiser travels the Gulf of St. Lawrence in search of pilot, finback, humpback and minke whales. Passengers have the opportunity to view spectacular scenery, interesting geology and a variety of birds and wildlife found along the shores of Cape Breton Highlands National Park of Canada (see place listing p. 137).

Hours: Tours depart daily at 9, 1 and 5, June 1-Sept. 15; at 9 and 5, May 15-31; at 10 and 4, Sept. 16-Oct. 15. **Cost:** Fare $28; $18 (ages 13-19); $12 (ages 2-12). **Phone:** (902) 224-3376 or (800) 813-3376.

CABOT TRAIL SEA & GOLF CHALETS
Phone: 902/224-1777

◈◈
Cottage
$139-$179

Address: 71 Fraser Doucet Ln B0E 1H0 **Location:** Centre. **Facility:** 13 cottages, some houses. 1 story, exterior corridors. **Terms:** seasonal, office hours 8 am-9 pm, 7 day cancellation notice-fee imposed. **Activities:** playground, basketball, horseshoes, volleyball.

/ SOME UNITS FEE 🐾

LAURIE'S MOTOR INN
Phone: (902)224-2400

◈◈
Hotel
$90-$249

Address: 15456 Laurie Rd B0E 1H0 **Location:** Centre. **Facility:** 56 units, some kitchens and houses. 2 stories (no elevator), interior/exterior corridors. **Terms:** open 6/1-10/31 & 5/1-5/31, office hours 7 am-10 pm, 3 day cancellation notice. **Activities:** playground. **Guest Services:** coin laundry. **Free Special Amenities:** local telephone calls and high-speed Internet.

WHERE TO EAT

LE GABRIEL RESTAURANT & LOUNGE
Phone: 902/224-3685

◈◈
Canadian
$7-$26

AAA Inspector Notes: The relaxing restaurant favors traditional preparations of seafood, like shellfish noodle bake and seafood kebabs. An interesting lighthouse facade adds to the eatery's nautical charm. The butterscotch pie is a delicious dessert choice. **Bar:** full bar. **Address:** 15424 Cabot Tr B0E 1H0 **Location:** Centre. 🇱 🇩

CHURCH POINT (D-1)

When exiled Acadians returned to Nova Scotia to find their homeland occupied, many accepted the British government's offer of 67-hectare (40-acre) lots along St. Mary's Bay, which became known as the "French Shore." In 1891 the Université Sainte-Anne was founded at Pointe de l'Eglise (Church Point) to preserve Acadian culture; it remains the only French-language university in the province.

SAINTE-MARIE (ST. MARY'S) CHURCH MUSEUM is on Hwy. 1. This 1905 Roman Catholic Church is one of the largest wooden churches in North America. The exhibit rooms feature a collection of vestments, religious articles, church furnishings, documents and photographs. One exhibit displays a collection of Madonna statues from around the world. Videos and interpretive panels provide insights into the exhibits. **Hours:** Daily 9-5, mid-May to mid-Oct.; by appointment rest of year. **Cost:** Donations. **Phone:** (902) 769-2832 for the rectory, or (902) 769-2378 for the church.

LE MANOIR SAMSON
Phone: 902/769-2526

◈◈
Motel
$80-$110

Address: 1768 Rt 1 B0W 1M0 **Location:** On Hwy 1; centre. **Facility:** 13 units, some kitchens. 2 stories (no elevator), exterior corridors. **Terms:** open 6/1-9/6 & 5/1-5/31, cancellation fee imposed.

BAIE STE-MARIE OCEAN FRONT COTTAGES
Phone: 902/769-0797

fyi Not evaluated. **Address:** Riverside Rd B0W 1M0 **Location:** Oceanfront. Hwy 101 exit 28, follow signs; 19 mi (30 km) sw of Digby. Facilities, services, and decor characterize a mid-scale property.

COLE HARBOUR (D-3) elev. 40m/130'

COLE HARBOUR HERITAGE FARM MUSEUM is at 471 Poplar Dr. The museum, which consists of several historic buildings, is on a site that has been farmed since the early 1780s. Exhibits include photographs, historic documents, gardens, farm and household equipment, and livestock. The property connects with a walkway that winds through the neighboring parkland.

The 1785 Giles House is a farmhouse filled with late 18th- to early 20th-century household items. Other buildings include a blacksmith shop, three barns and the Harris House which has a tearoom on its Victorian veranda.

Time: Allow 1 hour minimum. **Hours:** Mon.-Sat. 10-4, Sun. and holidays noon-4, May 15-Oct. 15; by appointment rest of year. **Cost:** Donations. **Phone:** (902) 434-0222 for the museum, or (902) 462-0154 for the tea room. 🇹 🅰

DARTMOUTH (D-3)

• **Restaurants p. 143**
• **Attractions map p. 151**
• **Hotels & Restaurants map & index p. 155**

On the eastern shore of Halifax Harbour, Dartmouth is connected to the city of Halifax by two suspension bridges and by ferry. The Angus L. MacDonald Bridge, spanning the harbor, is the fourth longest bridge in the British Commonwealth.

The city is a popular visitor destination and offers many fine restaurants, historic houses, a waterfront boardwalk and interesting attractions. Bedford Institute of Oceanography on Bedford Basin is reputed to be the largest Canadian center for marine research. South of Dartmouth, at Cow Bay and Eastern Passage, is the Canadian Forces Base Shearwater, first built for American seaplanes during World War I.

Dartmouth's 23 lakes once provided the area with ice for summer refrigeration. Today they are the centers of year-round recreation. Lake Banook is the site of a world-class canoe paddling course where international paddling events are staged each year. Lake Micmac often is the setting of water-skiing competitions. In winter, skating and ice hockey are popular pursuits. Scenic beaches include Clam Harbour, Lawrencetown, Martinique and Rainbow Haven.

Self-guiding tours: Brochures outlining self-guiding walking tours of the Halifax-Dartmouth area are available at the visitor information centers in Halifax *(see place listing p. 150).*

Check out
our travel blog at
AAATravelViews.com

(See map & index p. 155.)

BLACK CULTURAL CENTRE FOR NOVA SCOTIA

is at 1149 Main St. Exhibit galleries and a library preserve the art, history and culture of the province's citizens of African descent. Permanent exhibits focus on such themes as settlement by African-American Loyalists and the African-Nova Scotian community. **Hours:** Tues.-Fri. 9-5 (also Sat. 10-3, June-Sept.). **Cost:** $6; $4 (ages 65+ and students with ID); free (ages 0-5); $20 (family, two adults and three children). **Phone:** (902) 434-6223 or (800) 465-0767.

DARTMOUTH HERITAGE MUSEUM, EVERGREEN HISTORIC HOUSE

is at 26 Newcastle St. Panoramic views of Halifax Harbour and a collection of Victorian furnishings are features of this 1867 residence. One of Dartmouth's grand estates, it was built for a prominent local judge and was also the home of Dr. Helen Creighton, noted Nova Scotian folklorist. Children's activities and special events are available throughout the year.

Guided tours available during the summer season. **Hours:** Tues.-Sun. 10-1 and 2-5, June-Aug.; Tues.-Sat. 10-1 and 2-5, rest of year. **Cost:** $2; free (ages 0-12). **Phone:** (902) 464-2301 or (902) 464-2300.

QUAKER HOUSE

is at 57 Ochterloney St. One of the oldest houses in Dartmouth, the 1785 house is representative of the type of prefabricated structures built by the Nantucket Quaker whalers who lived in Dartmouth in the late 1700s. A trunk contains period dress-up clothes for children. A beautiful historic garden is on view. Costumed guides provide tours. **Hours:** Tours are offered Tues.-Sun. 10-1 and 2-5, June-Aug. **Cost:** $2; free (ages 0-12). **Phone:** (902) 464-5823 or (902) 464-2300.

ROYAL CANADIAN LEGION MILITARY MUSEUM

is at 52 King St. The collection includes military uniforms from World Wars I and II as well as the Korean and Boer wars. Separate rooms feature exhibits about the Army, Navy, Air Force, Merchant Navy and Army Medical Corps. Photographs, weapons and a collection of shoulder badges also are displayed.

Hours: Mon., Wed. and Fri. 1-4, June 1-Nov. 11; by appointment rest of year. **Cost:** Donations. Reservations are required 1 week in advance for guided tours. **Phone:** (902) 463-1050.

SHEARWATER AVIATION MUSEUM

is off Hwy. 111, following Hwy. 322 (Pleasant St.) toward Eastern Passage, continuing to the entrance of the Canadian Forces Base Shearwater. The museum, within the grounds of a military base, displays aircraft, photographs, uniforms and memorabilia related to the history of the Canadian air defense forces.

Hours: Mon.-Fri. 10-5, Sat.-Sun. and statutory holidays noon-4, June-Aug.; Tues.-Fri. 10-5, Sat. noon-4, Apr.-May and Sept.-Nov.; by appointment rest of year. Guided 1-hour tours are available by reservation. Closed major holidays. **Cost:** Donations. **Phone:** (902) 720-1083.

BEST WESTERN PLUS DARTMOUTH HOTEL & SUITES   **Phone:** (902)463-2000   [27]

Hotel
$139-$149

AAA Benefit: Members save up to 20%, plus 10% bonus points with Best Western Rewards®.

Address: 15 Spectacle Lake Dr B3B 1X7 **Location:** Hwy 111 exit 3 (Burnside Dr), n to Commodore Dr. **Facility:** 121 units. 4 stories, interior corridors. **Amenities:** high-speed Internet. **Pool(s):** heated indoor. **Activities:** whirlpool, exercise room. **Guest Services:** valet and coin laundry. **Free Special Amenities:** full breakfast and high-speed Internet. *(See ad p. 142.)*

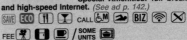

COASTAL INN DARTMOUTH   **Phone:** (902)465-7777   [33]

Extended Stay Hotel
$109-$154 6/1-9/15
$99-$139 9/16-5/31

Address: 379 Windmill Rd B3A 1J6 **Location:** Hwy 111 exit Shannon Park, 1 mi (1.6 km) e on Rt 7. **Facility:** 56 efficiencies. 3 stories, interior corridors. **Activities:** exercise room. **Guest Services:** coin laundry. **Free Special Amenities:** expanded continental breakfast and high-speed Internet.

COMFORT INN   **Phone:** (902)463-9900   [32]

Hotel
$99-$149

Address: 456 Windmill Rd B3A 1J7 **Location:** Hwy 111 exit Shannon Park. Located in a commercial area. **Facility:** 80 units. 2 stories (no elevator), interior corridors. **Amenities:** high-speed Internet.

DAYS INN   **Phone:** (902)465-6555   [29]

Hotel
$89-$125

Address: 20 Highfield Park Dr B3A 4S8 **Location:** From A. Murray MacKay Bridge, 0.8 mi (1.2 km) n on Hwy 111 exit 3 (Burnside Dr). Located in a commercial area. **Facility:** 139 units. 2 stories, interior/exterior corridors. **Terms:** cancellation fee imposed. **Amenities:** high-speed Internet. **Dining:** Favorites Cuisine, see separate listing. **Pool(s):** heated indoor. **Activities:** whirlpool, exercise room. **Guest Services:** valet and coin laundry. **Free Special Amenities:** full breakfast and newspaper.

(See map & index p. 155.)

HAMPTON INN & SUITES BY HILTON- HALIFAX/DARTMOUTH

Phone: 902/406-7700 **26**

Hotel
Rates not provided

AAA Benefit: Members save up to 10% everyday!

Address: 65 Cromarty Dr B3B 0G2 **Location:** Hwy 118 (Lakeview Dr) exit Wright Ave; in Dartmouth Crossing Outlet Mall. **Facility:** 163 units. 7 stories, interior corridors. **Amenities:** high-speed Internet. **Pool(s):** heated indoor. **Activities:** whirlpools, waterslide, bicycles, exercise room. **Guest Services:** valet and coin laundry. **Free Special Amenities: full breakfast and high-speed Internet.** *(See ad p. 142.)*

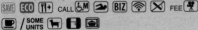

HOLIDAY INN HALIFAX-HARBOURVIEW

Phone: (902)463-1100 **34**

Hotel
$119-$209 6/1-11/15
$109-$199 11/16-5/31

Address: 101 Wyse Rd B3A 1L9 **Location:** Adjacent to Angus L Macdonald Bridge. **Facility:** 196 units. 7 stories, interior corridors. **Parking:** on-site (fee). **Amenities:** *Some:* high-speed Internet. **Pool(s):** heated outdoor. **Activities:** exercise room. **Guest Services:** valet and coin laundry.

PARK PLACE HOTEL & CONFERENCE CENTRE RAMADA PLAZA

Phone: (902)468-8888 **28**

Hotel
$99-$194

Address: 240 Brownlow Ave B3B 1X6 **Location:** From A. Murray MacKay Bridge, 0.7 mi (1.2 km) n on Hwy 111 exit 3 (Burnside Dr). Located in Park Place Centre. **Facility:** 178 units. 5 stories, interior corridors. **Terms:** cancellation fee imposed. **Dining:** The Peppermill Restaurant, see separate listing. **Pool(s):** heated indoor. **Activities:** sauna, whirlpool, waterslide, exercise room. **Guest Services:** valet laundry.

Park Place Hotel & Conference Centre RAMADA PLAZA

**Free Full Hot Breakfast Buffet
Free Parking, Wi-Fi, Local Calls
Near Dartmouth Crossing & MicMac Mall**

QUALITY INN HALIFAX/DARTMOUTH

Phone: (902)469-5850 **30**

Hotel
$85-$125

Address: 313 Prince Albert Rd B2Y 1N3 **Location:** Hwy 111 exit 6A, 1 blk s. **Facility:** 54 units. 4 stories, interior corridors. **Terms:** cancellation fee imposed. **Dining:** Rocco's Ristorante Italiano, see separate listing. **Activities:** exercise room. **Guest Services:** valet and coin laundry. **Free Special Amenities: continental breakfast and high-speed Internet.**

Your hotel provider in Nova Scotia. Four Modern Full-Service Properties here to serve you.

SUPER 8 HOTEL-DARTMOUTH

Phone: (902)463-9520 **35**

Hotel
$77-$166

Address: 65 King St B2Y 4C2 **Location:** Corner of King and Queen sts; centre of downtown. **Facility:** 80 units, some two bedrooms and kitchens. 8 stories, interior corridors. **Parking:** on-site (fee). **Terms:** cancellation fee imposed. **Activities:** exercise room. **Guest Services:** valet and coin laundry.

TRAVELODGE SUITES

Phone: 902/465-4000 **31**

Hotel
Rates not provided

Address: 101 Yorkshire Ave Ext B2Y 3Y2 **Location:** Hwy 111 exit Princess Margaret Blvd; at toll booth for A. Murray MacKay Bridge. **Facility:** 75 units. 3 stories, interior corridors. **Activities:** exercise room. **Guest Services:** valet and coin laundry. **Free Special Amenities: expanded continental breakfast and room upgrade (subject to availability with advance reservations).**

WHERE TO EAT

CHEZ CORA

Phone: 902/433-0079

Canadian
$6-$13

AAA Inspector Notes: Eggs, omelets, waffles, crepes (sorry, no American-style pancakes here), French toast, fruit platters and all the breakfast meats--that's the specialty here, all day. However, at lunchtime the menu lists a selection of soups, salads, quiches, sandwiches and a dish called the grilled panini crepe. **Address:** 644 Portland Centre B2W 6C4 **Location:** Just w of Carver St.

B L

ELA! GREEK TAVERNA

Phone: 902/481-7999 **35**

Greek
$10-$26

AAA Inspector Notes: This stylish taverna offers a bit of a Greek theme. A fine array of innovative Greek dishes including fresh seafood and lamb are offered. Try to save room for one of their delightful desserts. **Bar:** full bar. **Address:** 150 Hector Gate B3B 0E6 **Location:** Hwy 118 (Lakeview Dr) exit Wright Ave; in Dartmouth Crossing Outlet Mall. L D

(See map & index p. 155.)

FAN'S RESTAURANT
Phone: 902/469-9165 **39**

Chinese
$8-$15

AAA Inspector Notes: Well-prepared Northern Chinese cuisine includes such dishes as ginger beef, salt and pepper squid and sweet and sour chicken at this eatery in a small commercial shopping area. Friendly staffers explain entree preparations, especially the dim sum, offered Saturday and Sunday mornings. During the week patrons will find the lunch specials a very good value. **Bar:** full bar. **Address:** 451 Windmill Rd B3A 1J9 **Location:** Hwy 111 exit Shannon Park; across from Comfort Inn. L D

FAVORITES CUISINE
Phone: 902/466-4001 **37**

American
$8-$21

AAA Inspector Notes: The atmosphere is casual and upbeat in this open, airy restaurant, a favorite gathering spot for families. Large-sized portions of such entrees as fajitas and filet mignon are tasty and filling. Chocolate lovers' mouth's water for the brownie-bottom pie. The staff is casual and friendly. **Bar:** full bar. **Address:** 20 Highfield Park Dr B3A 4S8 **Location:** From A. Murray MacKay Bridge, 0.8 mi (1.2 km) n on Hwy 111 exit 3 (Burnside Dr); in Days Inn. B L D

LA PERLA DINING ROOM
Phone: 902/469-3241 **40**

Italian
$13-$34

AAA Inspector Notes: A cozy ambience characterizes this sophisticated dining room, where opera music plays in the background and elegant table settings are spaced amid subtle illumination. The menu centers on well-prepared Northern Italian selections of pasta, veal and seafood. In season, guests enjoy dining alfresco on the balcony overlooking the city and harbor. **Bar:** full bar. **Reservations:** suggested. **Address:** 73 Alderney Dr B2Y 2N7 **Location:** Centre; opposite ferry terminal. **Parking:** on-site (fee). L D

MACASKILL'S WATERFRONT RESTAURANT
Phone: 902/466-3100 **41**

Canadian
$12-$29

AAA Inspector Notes: Several dining areas, as well as the breezy patio, overlook the lovely harbor and city. The romantic setting includes soft candle light and pleasant music. Menu selections include thoughtful preparations of local seafood and meat. Servers are knowledgeable and friendly. **Bar:** full bar. **Reservations:** suggested. **Address:** 88 Alderney Dr B2Y 4J2 **Location:** Jct Portland St; in ferry terminal. **Parking:** on-site (fee). L D

THE PEPPERMILL RESTAURANT
Menu on AAA.com
Phone: 902/468-8888 **36**

American
$8-$28

AAA Inspector Notes: The spacious restaurant prepares a wide variety of entrées, including steaks, seafood and pasta dishes. The splendid lunch buffet is set up weekdays. **Bar:** full bar. **Address:** 240 Brownlow Ave B3B 1X6 **Location:** From A. Murray MacKay Bridge, 0.7 mi (1.2 km) n on Hwy 111 exit 3 (Burnside Dr); in Park Place Hotel & Conference Centre Ramada Plaza.
B L D CALL M

ROCCO'S RISTORANTE ITALIANO
Phone: 902/461-0211 **38**

Italian
$12-$25

AAA Inspector Notes: Nicely decorated in Southern Italian accents, the restaurant is a relaxing spot for fine dining. Creative specialties include fresh pan-fried haddock with lemon juice and tortellini in a creamy tomato-pesto sauce. **Bar:** full bar. **Reservations:** suggested. **Address:** 313 Prince Albert Rd B2Y 1N3 **Location:** Hwy 111 exit 6A, 1 blk s; in Quality Inn Halifax/Dartmouth.
B L D

SMITTY'S
Phone: 902/435-4444

Canadian
$7-$20

AAA Inspector Notes: The family-oriented restaurant satisfies patrons with its ever-popular all-day breakfast items, as well as tasty and wholesome soups and salads at lunchtime. A relaxed mood characterizes the dining space. **Bar:** full bar. **Address:** 107 Main St B2W 1R6 **Location:** Corner of Gordon Ave and Main St. B L D

SUSHI NAMI ROYALE
Phone: 902/481-9081 **34**

Japanese
$10-$21

AAA Inspector Notes: A modern decor can be found here with an open theme great for viewing the chefs in action. The menu selection is vast with soups, salads, endless appetizers and combination plates of sushi, sashimi, teriyaki and even sushi pizza. Service is friendly and relaxed. **Bar:** full bar. **Address:** 149 Hector Ave B3B 0E5 **Location:** Hwy 118 exit Wright Ave; in Dartmouth Crossing Outlet Mall. L D

SWISS CHALET
Phone: 902/462-0906

Chicken
$6-$16

AAA Inspector Notes: The popular restaurant is known for its rotisserie chicken and ribs and the tangy Chalet sauce that gives food its special zip. Diners munch on a half or quarter chicken with sides such as steamed vegetables, fries, baked potatoes and salads. Lunch guests often go for the great soup and sandwich combination. Take-out and delivery service are popular options. **Bar:** full bar. **Address:** 100 Main St B2X 1R5 **Location:** At Tacoma St. L D

DENMARK (B-3)

SUTHERLAND STEAM MILL is off Hwy. 6 on Hwy. 326. The site includes a restored 1894 sash and door factory, sawmill and carriage shop. Throughout its 64 years of operation, the two-story steam mill also manufactured sleighs, sleds and gingerbread trim, examples of which are displayed on the second floor.

Time: Allow 30 minutes minimum. **Hours:** Mon.-Sat. 10-5, Sun. 1-5, June 1-Oct. 15. **Cost:** $3.60; $2.55 (ages 6-17 and 65+); $7.95 (family, two adults and children). **Phone:** (902) 657-3016, or (902) 424-7398 in the off-season.

DIGBY (D-1) pop. 2,092

Digby overlooks the scenic Annapolis Basin and Digby Gut. Some of the highest tides on the planet occur nearby; Fisherman's Wharf is a good spot for viewing the fluctuations that can vary as much as 9.7 metres (32 feet) within 6 hours. The highest tides occur a day or two after the full moon.

The city is named for Sir Robert Digby, a British admiral whose command transported 1,500 Loyalists from New England in 1783. The Admiral's Well, dug in the 19th century, is on the admiral's original property near the entrance to Fisherman's Wharf. John Edison, great-grandfather of Thomas Alva Edison, was among the early settlers, many of whom are buried in the Old Loyalist Graveyard and Trinity Anglican Church Cemetery.

One of the most popular areas in the Atlantic Provinces, Digby is home to one of the largest scallop fleets in the world. It also is gateway to a region of spectacular beauty, Digby Neck and Islands. The narrow ribbon of land known as Digby Neck juts far out into the Bay of Fundy, providing breathtaking views and one of North America's best whale-watching areas.

South on Digby Neck along scenic Rte. 217 is Sandy Cove, a popular spot for painters, photographers, and whale- and bird-watchers. Farther south are the towns of Tiverton (see place listing p. 196) on Long Island and Westport (see place listing p. 199) on Brier Island; both can be reached by car ferry.

Side trips from Digby lead to the village of Bear River (see place listing p. 135), Point Prim on the Bay of Fundy and St. Mary's Bay. Digby is the northern terminus of scenic Hwy. 101, which follows the coast of St. Mary's Bay south to Yarmouth (see place listing p. 203).

Bay Ferries Ltd. provides year-round car and passenger service from Digby to Saint John, New Brunswick, aboard the Princess of Acadia. Reservations for the 3-hour crossing are highly recommended and must be picked up 1 hour prior to sailing time; phone (902) 245-2116, (888) 249-7245 or TTY (902) 626-2561.

Digby Tourism: P.O. Box 579, Digby, NS, Canada B0V 1A0. **Phone:** (902) 245-5714 or (888) 463-4429.

ADMIRAL DIGBY MUSEUM is at 95 Montague Row. The history of Digby County is recounted through a collection of pioneer furnishings, photographs, maps and marine artifacts. **Time:** Allow 30 minutes minimum. **Hours:** Mon.-Sat. 9-5, mid-June to late Aug.; Tues.-Fri. 9-noon and 1-4:30, late Aug. to mid-Oct.; Wed. and Fri. 9-noon and 1-4:30, rest of year. **Cost:** Donations. Research fee $8. **Phone:** (902) 245-6322.

ADMIRAL DIGBY INN & COTTAGES
Phone: (902)245-2531

Hotel
$85-$150

Address: 441 Shore Rd B0V 1A0. **Location:** Hwy 101 exit 26, 1.5 mi (2.5 km) n, follow Saint John Ferry signs, 3 mi (5 km) w on Victoria Rd, just e of ferry terminal. **Facility:** 47 units, some kitchens and cottages. 2 stories (no elevator), exterior corridors. **Terms:** open 6/1-10/30. **Dining:** The Admiralty Room, see separate listing. **Pool(s):** heated indoor. **Guest Services:** coin laundry. **Free Special Amenities:** room upgrade (subject to availability with advance reservations) and high-speed Internet.

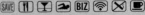
Over the Bay of Fundy to Digby. Welcome to our Family Owned & Friendly, Full Service Inn. GREAT VIEWS!

Admiral Digby

BAYSIDE INN B & B
Phone: 902/245-2247

Bed & Breakfast
$64-$108

Address: 115 Montague Row B0V 1A0. **Location:** Centre. **Facility:** 10 units. 3 stories (no elevator), interior corridors. *Bath:* some shared. **Parking:** on-site and street. **Terms:** open 6/1-10/30 & 4/15-5/31, office hours 8 am-10 pm, 3 day cancellation notice. **Free Special Amenities: high-speed Internet.**

THE BREAKERS BED & BREAKFAST
Phone: 902/245-4643

Bed & Breakfast
$99-$145

Address: 5 Water St B0V 1A0. **Location:** Centre of downtown. **Facility:** Overlooking the harbor, the circa 1853 inn features period decor with an astounding collection of antique furnishings, artwork and collectibles. 3 units. 2 stories (no elevator), interior corridors. **Terms:** open 6/15-10/15, 3 day cancellation notice-fee imposed.

DIGBY PINES GOLF RESORT AND SPA
Phone: (902)245-2511

Historic Hotel
$182-$338

Address: 103 Shore Rd B0V 1A0. **Location:** Hwy 101 exit 26, 1.5 mi (2.5 km) n, follow Saint John Ferry signs, 1.5 mi (2.5 km) w on Victoria Rd, follow signs; 1.2 mi (2 km) e of ferry terminal. **Facility:** Built in 1929, this beautiful Norman-style château-and-cottage complex graces a hillside overlooking the scenic Digby Harbour and Annapolis Basin. 147 units, some cabins and cottages. 1-3 stories, interior/exterior corridors. **Terms:** open 6/1-10/7 & 5/18-5/31, 3 day cancellation notice-fee imposed. **Dining:** Churchill's Restaurant and Lounge, see separate listing. **Pool(s):** heated outdoor. **Activities:** sauna, 2 lighted tennis courts, recreation programs, bicycles, hiking trails, playground, shuffleboard, exercise room, spa. *Fee:* golf-18 holes. **Guest Services:** valet laundry. **Free Special Amenities:** early check-in/late check-out and room upgrade (subject to availability with advance reservations).

DOCKSIDE SUITES
Phone: (902)245-4950

Hotel
$89-$159

Address: 34 Water St B0V 1A0. **Location:** Centre; in Fundy Complex. **Facility:** 6 units, some efficiencies and kitchens. 2 stories, interior/exterior corridors. **Parking:** on-site and street. **Terms:** cancellation fee imposed. **Amenities:** high-speed Internet. **Dining:** Fundy Restaurant & Dockside Bar, see separate listing. **Activities:** boat dock. *Fee:* charter fishing.

HARMONY SUITES AND BED & BREAKFAST
Phone: 902/245-2817

Bed & Breakfast
$69-$135

Address: 111 Montague Row B0V 1A0. **Location:** Centre. Located overlooking harbor. **Facility:** 10 units. 2 stories (no elevator), exterior corridors. **Terms:** cancellation fee imposed. **Amenities:** high-speed Internet. **Free Special Amenities: expanded continental breakfast and high-speed Internet.**

WHERE TO EAT

THE ADMIRALTY ROOM
Phone: 902/245-2531

American
$14-$29

AAA Inspector Notes: This second-story dining room treats guests to a wonderful view of the Annapolis Basin. Included in the array of seafood choices are scallops and lobsters from the tank as well as steak, chicken and burgers. Service is friendly and relaxed. **Bar:** full bar. **Address:** 441 Shore Rd B0V 1A0 **Location:** Hwy 101 exit 26, 1.5 mi (2.5 km) n, follow Saint John Ferry signs, 3 mi (5 km) w on Victoria Rd, just e of ferry terminal; in Admiral Digby Inn & Cottages.

CHURCHILL'S RESTAURANT AND LOUNGE
Phone: 902/245-2511

American
$13-$35

AAA Inspector Notes: High ceilings, pillars and elegant French doors provide a warm and intimate setting that combines with a true culinary experience. An updated look and menu ensures there is something for everyone. Chef Dale Nichols and his culinary team craft creative entrées that are beautifully presented and influenced by local products. The menu also has casual fare including a selection of gourmet burgers, pasta dishes and traditional favorites. **Bar:** full bar. **Reservations:** suggested. **Address:** 103 Shore Rd B0V 1A0 **Location:** Hwy 101 exit 26, 1.5 mi (2.5 km) n, follow Saint John Ferry signs, 1.5 mi (2.5 km) w on Victoria Rd, follow signs; 1.2 mi (2 km) e of ferry terminal; in Digby Pines Golf Resort and Spa.

B L D CALL &M JC

FUNDY RESTAURANT & DOCKSIDE BAR
Phone: 902/245-4950

American
$9-$25

AAA Inspector Notes: The spacious restaurant has several dining sections and affords splendid views of the harbor and scallop fleet. Specializing in fresh local seafood, this place also prepares some steak, chicken and pasta dishes. Large decks provide ample outdoor seating in season. **Bar:** full bar. **Address:** 34 Water St B0V 1A0 **Location:** Centre; in Fundy Complex; in Dockside Suites. **Parking:** on-site and street.

B L D

HOUSE OF WONG
Phone: 902/245-4125

Chinese
$7-$17

AAA Inspector Notes: This spacious restaurant on the water overlooks the harbor and fishing fleet. The menu offers an abundant selection, from fresh seafood to all your favorite Chinese dishes and combination plates. Some Canadian dishes available. **Bar:** full bar. **Address:** 110 Water St B0V 1A0 **Location:** At Birch St.

L D

EAST DOVER (D-3)

RECREATIONAL ACTIVITIES
Kayaking
• **NovaShores Adventures** departs from 283 East Dover Rd. **Hours:** Trips depart daily at 9:30 and 2, May-Oct. **Phone:** (902) 392-2761 or (866) 638-4118.

EASTERN PASSAGE (D-3)

Named for the channel of water running into Halifax Harbour between the mainland and Lawlor and McNabs islands, Eastern Passage was first mentioned on a nautical chart in 1759.

FISHERMAN'S COVE is off Hwy. 322 at 200 Government Wharf Rd. A 1.5 mile boardwalk meanders past a complex of shops, restaurants and a tourist information center. Nature tours, harbor tours and fishing excursions are available. The Marine Interpretive Centre includes aquariums, bird exhibits, photographs and interactive exhibits.

Hours: Daily 24 hours, May-Oct.; Fri.-Sun. 24 hours, Nov. 1-Dec. 23. Information center daily 9-6, May 15-Oct. 15. Marine Interpretive Centre Tues.-Sun. noon-7, June 1-Sept. 1; by appointment rest of year. Shop and restaurant hours vary. **Cost:** Complex free. Marine Interpretive Centre $2. **Phone:**
(902) 465-6093, (902) 465-3661 for the interpretive center, or (902) 465-8009 for the information center.

BOONDOCKS RESTAURANT
Phone: 902/465-3474

Seafood
$9-$24

AAA Inspector Notes: Bordering Fisherman's Cove, the pleasant location is known for its views of the busy harbor. Ample portions of seafood and other meat entrees are nicely presented and served piping hot. The large patio offers comfortable seating in season. **Bar:** full bar. **Address:** 200 Government Wharf Rd B3G 1M7 **Location:** 5.4 mi (9 km) e of Dartmouth on Rt 322; centre.

L D

EAST LAKE AINSLIE (B-5)

The largest natural freshwater lake in Nova Scotia, Lake Ainslie is a popular destination for anglers—and marathon runners who race 42 kilometres (26 mi.) around its shores every September.

THE MacDONALD HOUSE is on Hwy. 395. Overlooking Lake Ainslie, this pioneer farmhouse is furnished with antiques and items that reflect life in rural 1800s Cape Breton. Nearby are two barns with several wagons, buggies and wheeled farm implements. The property also contains hiking trails and a one-room schoolhouse that operated 1926-54.

. **Hours:** Tues.-Sun. 10-5, July-Aug.; by appointment rest of year. **Cost:** $4; 50c (ages 0-15); $8 (family, two adults and school-age children). **Phone:** (902) 258-3317, or (902) 258-2850 in winter.

ENGLISHTOWN (B-6)

The French settlement of Port Dauphin was to have been the capital of Cape Breton Island (Île Royale), but instead Louisbourg was selected as the seat of government in 1718. After the fall of Louisburg 40 years later, many British soldiers settled in the area, and Port Dauphin was renamed Englishtown.

SAVE **DONELDA'S PUFFIN BOAT TOURS** departs from the Englishtown Wharf. Puffins, eagles, razorbill auks, kittiwake gulls, cormorants and grey seals are among the species that may be viewed on these 2.5-hour narrated excursions. Bird checklists are provided.

Dogs are allowed aboard with the permission of other passengers. **Hours:** Tours to see puffins and shorebirds are offered daily at 10, 1:30 and 5:15, July-Aug.; at 10:30 and 1:30, June 7-30; at 11, May 6-June 6. Grey seal and eagle tours depart at 11, late Aug.-late-Sept. **Cost:** Fare $34.50; $32 (ages 61+); $15 (ages 6-12). **Phone:** (902) 929-2563 or (877) 278-3346.

FALMOUTH (C-2) pop. 1,179

Falmouth was one of 14 townships created by Gov. Charles Lawrence in 1759. The land left vacant after the Acadian expulsion was offered free to any New Englander who would relocate to Nova Scotia.

Thousands of farmers from Connecticut, Rhode Island and Massachusetts accepted the offer; they became known in Canada as the New England Planters.

WINERIES

• **Sainte Famille Wines Ltd.** is at jct. Dyke Rd. and Dudley Park Ln. **Hours:** Tastings Mon.-Sat. 9-5, Sun. noon-5, Apr.-Dec.; Mon.-Sat. 9-5, rest of year. Tours are given Mon.-Sat. at 10 and 2, Sun. at 2, May-Oct. **Phone:** (902) 798-8311 or (800) 565-0993.

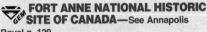

FORT ANNE NATIONAL HISTORIC SITE OF CANADA—See Annapolis Royal p. 129.

FORTRESS OF LOUISBOURG NATIONAL HISTORIC SITE OF CANADA (B-6)

On Cape Breton Island, 35 kilometres (22 mi.) south of Sydney on Hwy. 22 beyond the modern town of Louisbourg, the 6,000-hectare (14,826-acre) Fortress of Louisbourg National Historic Site includes a reconstruction of the massive fortress erected by the French 1720-45 to defend their colonies.

Under the terms of the 1713 Treaty of Utrecht, France was permitted to keep Cape Breton Island (Île Royale) and Prince Edward Island (Isle St. Jean). English Harbour, renamed Louisbourg, was then selected by the French as the most suitable point for an Atlantic stronghold. It served as headquarters for the French fleet and became an important fishing and trading center. Later it was used as the base for French privateers preying on New England shipping.

In 1745, after a 47-day siege, Louisbourg was captured by a volunteer force from New England led by Col. William Pepperell and an English fleet under Commodore Peter Warren. Three years later the colony was returned to France by the Treaty of Aix-la-Chapelle. After being twice blockaded by British fleets during the Seven Years' War, Louisbourg was once again captured in 1758. In 1760 the fortifications were demolished on orders from British prime minister William Pitt.

About one-quarter of colonial Louisbourg has been reconstructed to its 1744 appearance, resulting in one of Canada's largest national historic sites. Costumed guides depicting musicians, fishermen, soldiers, servants and the upper class are on hand to interpret the site. Period stories, dance, music, cooking and gardening are demonstrated. Buildings open include the house of the king's engineer; a fisherman's house; soldiers' barracks; the military bakery; a merchant's house; a civil administrator's house; and the king's bastion, one of the largest buildings in North America at the time. The king's bastion includes the lavishly furnished governor's apartments.

Visitors can sample food in the manner of the 18th century at period restaurants. Picnic areas are located on the park grounds. The park also offers saltwater beaches and fishing. Kennington Cove is within the park and has ocean beaches, picnic areas and scenic views. Lighthouse Point, the location of Canada's first lighthouse, is at the eastern end of the park.

The visitor reception center has an audiovisual presentation, models and exhibits; buses depart from the center at frequent intervals for the 5-minute drive to the reconstructed site.

A Mi'kmaq interpretive trail beginning behind the visitor reception center offers nature, history and culture exhibits as well as a panoramic view of the fortress and coastline along its 5-minute trek. Other trails include a ruins walk at the reconstructed site and an interpretive walk at the Royal Battery.

Comfortable shoes and a sweater are advised. Pets are not permitted. Guided tours are available. Allow a full day minimum. Daily 9-5:30, July-Aug.; 9:30-5, mid-May through June 30 and Sept. 1 to mid-Oct. Facilities are limited mid-May through May 31 and mid-Oct. through Oct. 31. Schedule may vary; phone ahead. Admission June-Sept. $17.60; $14.95 (ages 65+); $8.80 (ages 6-16); $44.10 (family). Admission in May and Oct. $7.30; $6.05 (ages 65+); $3.65 (ages 6-16); $18.10 (family). **Cards:** MC, VI. Phone (902) 733-2280 or TTY (902) 733-3607.

FRASER MILLS (C-4)

FRASER MILLS FISH HATCHERY is on Hwy. 316 following signs. More than half a million trout are raised here annually. Situated on the banks of the South River, the hatchery displays brook, rainbow and brown trout and landlocked Atlantic salmon in several large outdoor tanks. A separate building houses immature trout in various stages of development from fry to fingerling. Early equipment and sports fishery information are displayed in the visitor center. **Time:** Allow 30 minutes minimum. **Hours:** Daily 9-4. **Cost:** Free. **Phone:** (902) 783-2926.

GILBERTS COVE (D-1)

GILBERT COVE LIGHTHOUSE is off Hwy. 1 on Lighthouse Rd. Situated at the end of a prominent point of land, the restored lighthouse offers an excellent view of the sea as well as the village and surrounding countryside. Old photographs of the area are displayed inside. **Time:** Allow 30 minutes minimum. **Hours:** Lighthouse open Mon.-Sat. 10-4, Sun. noon-4, mid-June to mid-Sept.; hours vary in early June and mid-Sept. Grounds daily 24 hours. **Cost:** Free. **Phone:** (902) 837-5584.

GLACE BAY (B-6) pop. 19,968

Since 1720, when French troops dug coal from the cliffs of the town to supply the garrison at Louisbourg, the name Glace Bay has been synonymous with coal. It shares this identity with several other communities along the northeastern corner of Cape Breton Island, where rich seams of bituminous coal extend miles into the Atlantic Ocean.

From Table Head on the outskirts of Glace Bay, Italian inventor Guglielmo Marconi sent the first west-to-east trans-Atlantic wireless message to Cornwall, England, on Dec. 15, 1902. Marconi conducted many radio experiments at his transoceanic wireless station at Table Head, the first on the North American continent.

MARCONI NATIONAL HISTORIC SITE OF CANADA is at 1 Timmerman St. Surrounded by 18-metre-high (60-ft.) cliffs that overlook the Atlantic Ocean, the site depicts Guglielmo Marconi's initiation of the age of telecommunication with the transmission of the world's first official wireless message from this site on Dec. 15, 1902. Also featured is a local amateur radio station. **Time:** Allow 30 minutes minimum. **Hours:** Daily 10-6, June 1-Sept. 15. **Cost:** Free. **Phone:** (902) 295-2069.

THE MINERS' MUSEUM is 1.6 km (1 mi.) w. via Commercial and South sts. to 17 Museum St. Museum exhibits focus on the geology of coal; mining methods, techniques and equipment; and the development of the coal industry. Interactive kiosks provide information about the communities and history of Cape Breton's mining industry.

Retired miners lead guided tours of the underground mine Ocean Deeps Colliery beneath the museum as well as a miners' village with a reconstructed miner's house and company store. During summer months The Men of the Deeps, a choir of working and retired miners, perform at the theater. Videos about mining, an underground garden and art by Jack Lily MacLellan complete the experience.

Visitors must don hard hats and slickers on the mine tour. **Tours:** Guided tours are available. **Hours:** Daily 10-6 (also Tues. 6-7 p.m.), June 1-Labour Day; daily 10-6, day after Labour Day-Oct. 31; Mon.-Fri. 9-4, rest of year. **Cost:** $6; $5 (ages 0-11). Museum and mine tour $12; $10 (ages 0-11); $28 (family, two adults and two children). **Phone:** (902) 849-4522.

GLENVILLE (B-5)

GLENORA DISTILLERY TOURS is 9 km (6 mi.) n. of Mabou on Rte. 19 on Ceilidh Trail. Some 50,000 litres (13,208 gal.) of whiskey are produced annually at the 121-hectare (300-acre) facility, which includes milling, warehouse, bottling and hospitality buildings. North America's first and Canada's only single malt distillery, Glenora also blends and bottles Smuggler's Cove dark rum.

Tastings are offered on guided distillery tours. **Time:** Allow 1 hour minimum. **Hours:** Tours depart daily on the hour 9-5, mid-May through Oct. 31. **Cost:** $7; free (ages 0-16). **Phone:** (902) 258-2662 or (800) 839-0491.

GLENORA INN & DISTILLERY   Phone: 902/258-2662

Hotel
Rates not provided

Address: 13729 Rt 19 B0E 1X0 **Location:** On Rt 19. **Facility:** 15 units, some cottages. 2 stories (no elevator), interior/exterior corridors. **Terms:** seasonal, office hours 7 am-7 pm. **Dining:** restaurant, see separate listing.

WHERE TO EAT

GLENORA DINING ROOM & PUB   Phone: 902/258-2662

Regional American
$10-$35

AAA Inspector Notes: Located in North America's only single malt distillery, the pub is very pleasant in an open, airy concept with cathedral ceilings and large windows overlooking gardens. Celtic music enlivens the atmosphere from mid-June through mid-October. The menu consists of typical pub fare including soups, salads and sandwiches. The single malt whiskey is distilled on the premises. **Bar:** full bar. **Address:** 13729 Rt 19 B0E 1X0 **Location:** On Rt 19; in Glenora Inn & Distillery.

GRAND PRÉ (C-2)

The name Grand Pré, which means "great meadow," refers to the extensive diked lands in the area. Settlers from Port-Royal moved to Grand Pré in the late 17th century and, copying the successful dike and floodgate system used in Port-Royal, reclaimed the rich marine sediment from the Minas Basin. Soon Grand Pré became the largest and most important community in Acadia.

During France's attempt to retake Acadia following the British conquest, French troops made a surprise attack upon British troops in Grand Pré on Feb. 11, 1747. The incident, which claimed nearly 100 lives, helped convince the British administration that the native Acadians should be deported. Grand Pré was the principal scene of the Acadian expulsion in 1755, which was immortalized by Henry Wadsworth Longfellow's poem "Evangeline."

CHURCH OF THE COVENANTER is off Hwy. 101 exit 10 to 1989 Grand Pre Rd. New England planters used hand-hewn boards held by square handmade nails to build this church, which was completed in 1811. It features box pews, sounding boards and a pulpit that reaches halfway to the ceiling. **Time:** Allow 30 minutes minimum. **Hours:** Daily 9-dusk, May-Oct. **Cost:** Free. **Phone:** (902) 542-3796.

GRAND PRÉ NATIONAL HISTORIC SITE OF CANADA is inland from Minas Basin at 2205 Grand-Pre Rd. This site commemorates the town's Acadian settlers who were deported 1755-63 to British colonies throughout North America. The Acadian village that once stood here inspired Henry Wadsworth Longfellow's epic poem "Evangeline."

An interpretation center celebrates 400 years of Acadian culture, beginning with the first French settlement at Port Royal in 1604. A multimedia theater re-creates the difficult conditions of the Acadian expulsion. Other highlights include a memorial church, exhibit hall, art gallery, Evangeline's Well, a statue of the fictional heroine and a bust of Longfellow. As visitors walk clockwise around the statue of Evangeline, her face seems to age.

Time: Allow 30 minutes minimum. **Hours:** Daily 9-6, mid-May to mid-Oct. **Cost:** $7.90; $6.65 (ages 65+); $3.95 (ages 6-16); $19.80 (family, two adults and up to five children). **Phone:** (902) 542-3631, (866) 542-3631 or TTY (902) 532-7472.

WINERIES

• **Domaine de Grand Pré** is 3 km (1.9 mi.) e. on Rte. 1. **Hours:** Tastings Mon.-Sat. 10-6, Sun. 11-6, May-Oct.; Wed.-Sun. 11-5, Nov.-Dec.; Sat. 11-5, Sun. noon-5, rest of year. Tours depart daily at 11, 3 and 5, May-Oct. Closed Jan. 1-2 and Dec. 25-27. Phone ahead to confirm holiday schedule. **Phone:** (902) 542-1753, or (866) 479-4637 in Canada.

EVANGELINE INN & MOTEL   **Phone:** 902/542-2703

Motel
Rates not provided

Address: 11668 Hwy 1 B0P 1M0 **Location:** Hwy 101 exit 10, 1 mi (1.6 km) sw on Rt 1. **Facility:** 18 units. 1 story, exterior corridors. **Terms:** seasonal, office hours 9 am-9 pm. **Amenities:** high-speed Internet. **Dining:** restaurant, see separate listing. **Pool(s):** heated indoor.

WHERE TO EAT

EVANGELINE CAFE   **Phone:** 902/542-2703

American
$6-$12

AAA Inspector Notes: This bright and airy family style restaurant is the place for good home-style cooking with ample portions. A full menu and open for all meals; breakfast does not start until 8 am. **Address:** 11668 Hwy 1 B0P 1M0 **Location:** Hwy 101 exit 10, 1 mi (1.6 km) sw on Rt 1; in Evangeline Inn & Motel. B L D

LE CAVEAU RESTAURANT   **Phone:** 902/542-7177

American
$12-$35

AAA Inspector Notes: A lovely location in a vineyard, the 1826 Georgian-style farmhouse has been converted into a fine restaurant and wine bar. The use of local and homegrown produce is evident in the creative entrees. This place offers a fine selection of its own wines and ciders, as well as imports. A nice patio dining area opens in season. **Bar:** full bar. **Reservations:** suggested. **Address:** 11611 Hwy 1 B0P 1M0 **Location:** On Rt 1, 1.8 mi (3 km) e of Wolfville; Hwy 101 exit 10, 0.6 mi (1 km) w; in Grand-Pre Winery. L D

GRANVILLE FERRY (D-1) pop. 161

A small village on the north side of the Annapolis River, Granville Ferry has many Victorian-style houses and a few that were built in the late 1700s. Iron door hinges in the shape of H's and L's, known as Holy Lord hinges, were brought from New England by settlers to fend off the powers of witchcraft.

NORTH HILLS MUSEUM is off Hwy. 1 on the north shore of the Annapolis River at 5065 Granville Rd. This saltbox-style house, once part of an 18th-century farm, was renovated by R.P. Patterson in the 1960s. It contains a fine Georgian

collection of English mahogany, oak and walnut furnishings, ceramics, glass, silver, 18th-century porcelain and paintings. Guided tours highlight the collection and Acadian history.

Time: Allow 30 minutes minimum. **Hours:** Mon.-Sat. 9:30-5:30, Sun. 1-5:30, June 1 to mid-Oct. **Cost:** $3; $2 (ages 6-17 and 65+); $7 (family). **Phone:** (902) 532-2168.

MOUNTAIN TOP COTTAGES   **Phone:** 902/532-2564

fyi   Not evaluated. **Address:** 888 Parker Mountain Rd B0S 1H0 **Location:** Hwy 1, 2.7 mi (4.5 km) n. Facilities, services, and decor characterize a mid-scale property.

GREENWOOD (C-2)

Settled by British Loyalists who fled America after the Revolutionary War, Greenwood became a market hub for farmers in the Annapolis Valley. In 1940 the Royal Air Force chose Greenwood as the site of its East Coast base, where aviators trained during World War II. Today, 14 Wing Greenwood is home to four Air Force squadrons.

GREENWOOD MILITARY AVIATION MUSEUM is at 20 Ward Rd., Bldg. 151. Exhibits trace the history of the Canadian Air Force at 14 Wing Greenwood from World War II to the present. Argus, Lancaster and Neptune aircraft are displayed. **Time:** Allow 1 hour minimum. **Hours:** Daily 9-5, June-Aug.; Tues.-Sat. 10-4, rest of year. **Cost:** Donations. **Phone:** (902) 765-1494, ext. 5955.

GUYSBOROUGH (C-5) pop. 4,681
• Hotels p. 150

At the head of Chedabucto Bay, the Shiretown of Guysborough was founded in 1636 when French trader Nicholas Denys established a fishing station here. Guysborough is named in honor of Sir Guys Carleton, commander in chief of the British forces in North America and governor general of Canada during the 1780s.

Because of its seaside location, Guysborough provides many choices for water-based recreational activities; possibilities include boating and canoeing. A tourist complex and golf course overlook Mussel Cove and the harbor. Just southeast is a section of the Trans Canada Trail, which has been constructed on an abandoned railroad bed.

Guysborough Regional Development Authority: 46 Main St., P.O. Box 49, Guysborough, NS, Canada B0H 1N0. **Phone:** (902) 533-3731 or (800) 355-3731.

THE OLD COURTHOUSE MUSEUM is 34 km (21 mi.) s. of Hwy. 104 exit 37 on Hwy. 16. This restored 1843 courthouse accommodated county and supreme court sessions for 130 years. Its Gothic-style windows and cedar shingles exemplify mid-19th-century architecture. Exhibits depict an early French fort and the timber industry. Domestic tools and early photographs are featured. Genealogy information is available. A visitor information center is also located in the museum. **Time:** Allow 30 minutes minimum. **Hours:** Mon.-Fri. 9-5, Sat.-Sun. 10-5, June-Sept. **Cost:** Donations. **Phone:** (902) 533-4008.

DESBARRES MANOR INN   **Phone:** (902)533-2099

▼▼▼▼
Historic
Country Inn
$149-$259

Address: 90 Church St B0H 1N0 **Location:** Centre. Located in a residential area. **Facility:** Set in a charming village, this circa 1837 mansion offers richly furnished living rooms and guest units. The dining room and deck overlook a valley. 10 units. 3 stories (no elevator), interior corridors. **Terms:** office hours 7 am-10 pm, 14 day cancellation notice-fee imposed. **Guest Services:** valet laundry. 🍴 🍸 📶 ✉ 🅰

HALIFAX (D-3) pop. 372,679

• Hotels p. 158 • Restaurants p. 168
• Attractions map p. 151
• Hotels & Restaurants map & index p. 155

Because of the harbor that extends inland 26 kilometres (16 mi.), Halifax, the capital of Nova Scotia, was one of the first English settlements in Canada. It was founded in 1749 by Edward Cornwallis, who recognized the site's potential as a naval and military depot. After the British attained supremacy throughout Canada in 1763, Halifax served as the Atlantic headquarters for the Royal Army and Navy.

Until World War I, Halifax's military character was moderated by a civilian shipbuilding industry, which brought considerable wealth to the port economy. During World War I and World War II the city was part of the North American lifeline to war-torn Europe. Halifax still remains the principal naval outpost on Canada's east coast.

This commercial, administrative and military center of Atlantic Canada is distinguished by a blend of modern office towers and restored buildings. Museums, shops and galleries lure locals and visitors to the city's waterfront boardwalk. Theater, symphony performances, live music, cinemas, pubs and cafés combine to create a lively downtown entertainment scene.

Many of the city's historic buildings were constructed by order of Prince Edward, Duke of Kent, Halifax's commander in chief 1794-1800. Princess Lodge, on Bedford Basin, was his primary residence. The prince commissioned the Town Clock on Citadel Hill to discourage tardiness, designing the four-sided tower so that it could be seen anywhere in town.

Halifax Citadel National Historic Site of Canada (see attraction listing p. 152) is one of Canada's most visited attractions. The massive star-shaped fortification, among the best preserved in the country, offers historic re-enactments, museums, a noon gun firing and lofty views of the harbor.

Halifax is fortunate to have anything left to preserve, considering the awesome maritime disaster that shook the city at 9:05 a.m., Dec. 6, 1917. The French munitions ship Mont Blanc collided with the steamer Imo in Halifax Harbour, causing a fire that ignited the volatile cargo of the munitions ship. The ensuing explosion literally blew the Mont Blanc to pieces, heaved the Imo onto the Dartmouth shore and leveled the north end of the city, killing more than 2,000 people. Reminders of the event still mark the city, which commemorates the "Halifax Explosion" every year. Boston, the first city to come to Halifax's aid, receives a Nova Scotian Christmas tree each year.

On April 16, 1912, the crew aboard the cable repair ship Mackay-Bennett set sail from Halifax to retrieve the corpses of 306 Titanic victims. Fairview Lawn Cemetery, 3720 Windsor St., is the resting place for 121 of these individuals, many of whom are unidentified.

The 🍷 Royal Nova Scotia International Tattoo, held in early July, is an extravaganza featuring military music, pageantry and precision drills as well as dance and athletic competitions. Crack military units from around the world perform, and the traditional Naval Gun Run Competition pits Canadian naval teams against one another in a contest that involves dismantling, transporting and reassembling a cannon.

🍷 Alexander Keith's Natal Day Festival celebrates the birthdays of both the Halifax and Dartmouth communities. The festival consists of entertainment, sports activities, family events, breakfasts and fireworks. The civic holiday occurs in the last week of July and first week of August. Street performers entertain visitors during the 🍷 Halifax International Busker Festival. Jugglers, acrobats and musicians are just a few examples of the line-up appearing over the 10-day event held in August.

McNabs Island, in outer Halifax Harbour, lures hikers and picnickers during warm weather. Of historical interest is Fort McNab National Historic Site, which preserves an 1892 fort built to defend the harbor; phone (902) 426-5080. Nearby Lawlor Island is popular with bird-watchers, and stories persist that another harbor island, named Devils Island, is haunted. Ferry service to the islands is available from McNabs Island Ferry; phone (902) 465-4563 or (800) 326-4563.

A variety of tours, including sailing, whale-watching, fishing, golfing, walking and bus excursions, are offered throughout Halifax and the surrounding area; phone Nova Scotia Department of Tourism and Culture at (800) 565-0000. Dartmouth Ferry, the oldest continually running saltwater ferry in North America, crosses the harbor year-round. [SAVE] Gray Line Halifax, (902) 425-9999 or (800) 565-7173, provides excursions highlighting Halifax's historic sites.

Halifax is the site of North America's longest-running market, in operation since 1750. The new Halifax Seaport Farmers' Market, in a sustainable building on the waterfront at 1209 Marginal Rd., Pier 20, has more than 150 vendors selling everything from fresh local produce to meats, bakery items, plants, wine and arts and crafts. The market operates Tuesday through Sunday in summer, Wednesday and Friday through Sunday the rest of

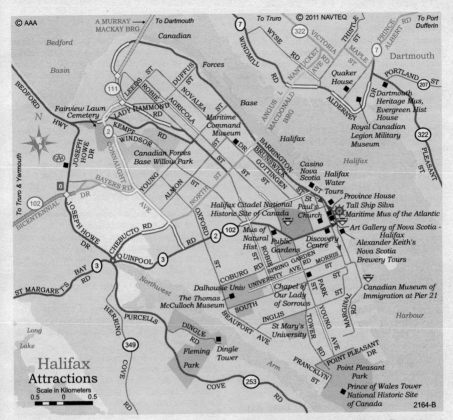

© AAA   A MURRAY →   To Dartmouth
MACKAY BRG
Canadian

To Truro   © 2011 NAVTEQ   To Port Dufferin

Halifax Attractions

Scale in Kilometers
0.5   0   0.5

2164-B

(See map & index p. 155.)

the year. Just a short walk away, the old Halifax Farmer's Market, in an 1800s brewery on Hollis Street, is open Saturday 7-1.

Halifax Waterfront-Nova Scotia Visitor Information Centre: 1655 Lower Water St., Halifax, NS, Canada B3J 1S2. **Phone:** (902) 424-4248.

Self-guiding tours: Brochures detailing tours of the historic and downtown areas of Halifax are available at the visitor information center.

Shopping areas: Halifax Shopping Centre, 7001 Mumford Rd., features some 170 retailers, including Coast Mountain, Pier 1 Imports and Sears. Spring Garden Road, between Barrington and Robie streets, is home to a variety of specialty shops, boutiques and restaurants.

ALEXANDER KEITH'S NOVA SCOTIA BREWERY TOURS is at 1496 Lower Water St. Costumed interpreters depict the history of this restored 19th-century working brewery. Tours include demonstrations of early and modern brewing techniques as well as tastings presented in a tavern setting.

Time: Allow 1 hour minimum. **Hours:** Mon.-Sat. noon-8, Sun. noon-5, June-Oct.; Fri. 5-8, Sat.

noon-8, Sun. noon-5, rest of year. Tours depart every 30 minutes, May-Oct.; every hour on the hour, rest of year. Phone ahead to confirm schedule. **Cost:** $15.95; $13.95 (ages 65+ and military and students with ID); $7.95 (ages 5-18); $41.95 (family, two adults and three children). **Phone:** (902) 455-1474, ext. 222 or (877) 612-1820. 🍴

ART GALLERY OF NOVA SCOTIA– HALIFAX is in the Old Dominion Building at 1723 Hollis St. The gallery showcases historical and contemporary works by international, national and Nova Scotia artists. Of note is an internationally recognized collection of regional folk art.

Time: Allow 30 minutes minimum. **Hours:** Daily 10-5 (also Thurs. 5-9). Guided tours depart daily at 2:30 (also Thurs. at 7). Closed Jan. 1 and Christmas. **Cost:** $12; $10 (ages 60+); $7 (college students with ID); $5 (ages 6-17); $30 (family, two adults and three children). **Phone:** (902) 424-5280. 🍴

ATLANTIC CANADA AVIATION MUSEUM is at 20 Sky Blvd. across Hwy. 102 from Halifax Stanfield International Airport. A comprehensive collection depicts Atlantic Canada's aviation history, beginning with the first powered flight in 1909.

(See map & index p. 155.)

Artifacts include photographs, uniforms, medals, aircraft engines and weapons. A hangar displays flight simulators, home-built aircraft and restored vintage aircraft, including fighter planes, crop dusters, helicopters and rescue aircraft. **Time:** Allow 1 hour minimum. **Hours:** Daily 9-5, mid-May to late Sept.; by appointment rest of year. **Cost:** Donations. **Phone:** (902) 873-3773.

CANADIAN MUSEUM OF IMMIGRA-TION AT PIER 21 is at 1055 Marginal Rd., just n. of Barrington St. The restored historic site tells the stories of 1.5 million immigrants, war brides, displaced people, evacuee children and Canadian military service personnel who passed through its doors 1928-71.

Canada's last remaining ocean immigration shed, Pier 21 delivers a dramatic exploration of a critical part of Canada's heritage through interactive exhibits, multimedia presentations and activities for all ages.

A ship exhibit provides information about the different vessels that carried immigrants across the Atlantic, and a train car exhibit has historical data about those who traveled across the country from Vancouver to Halifax. Canadian visitors are encouraged to add their family's immigration story to the museum's collection.

Tours: Guided tours are available. **Time:** Allow 2 hours minimum. **Hours:** Daily 9:30-5:30, May-Oct.; daily 9:30-5, in Nov.; Mon.-Sat. 10-5, in Apr.; Tues.-Sat. 10-5, rest of year. Closed Jan. 1, Good Friday, Christmas and day after Christmas. **Cost:** $8.60; $7.60 (ages 60+); $6 (students with ID); $5 (ages 6-16); $22 (family, two adults and three children). **Phone:** (902) 425-7770.

CHAPEL OF OUR LADY OF SORROWS is in Holy Cross Cemetery at South and S. Park sts. This small chapel was built in one day—Aug. 31, 1843—by some 2,000 men. A stained-glass window dates from 1661, and the altar carvings are replicas of works made in 1550. **Hours:** Mon.-Fri. 8-4, June-Sept. **Cost:** Free. **Phone:** (902) 865-6663.

DINGLE TOWER is on Dingle Rd. in Fleming Park. Built by Sir Sandford Fleming in 1912, the tower commemorates the 1758 convening of the first elected assembly. It overlooks the Northwest Arm and the western slope of the peninsula. **Time:** Allow 30 minutes minimum. **Hours:** Daily dawn-dusk, May-Sept. **Cost:** Free. **Phone:** (902) 490-4000, (902) 490-4886, (800) 835-6428 in Nova Scotia or TTY (902) 490-6645.

DISCOVERY CENTRE is at 1593 Barrington St. The science center presents changing displays, workshops and shows about science and technology. More than 80 hands-on exhibits feature such topics as bridges, electricity, chemistry, bubbles, health, physics, optical illusions and light and sound.

Time: Allow 1 hour minimum. **Hours:** Mon.-Sat. 10-5, Sun. 1-5. Closed Jan.1, Apr. 2, Nov. 11 and Dec. 25-26. **Cost:** June-Sept. $8.50; $7.50 (ages 60+); $7 (students with ID); $6 (ages 3-18). Admission rest of year $7.50; $6.50 (ages 60+); $6 (students with ID); $5 (ages 3-18). **Phone:** (902) 492-4422.

HALIFAX CITADEL NATIONAL HISTORIC SITE OF CANADA is on Citadel Hill overlooking downtown Halifax. One of the country's best surviving examples of a 19th-century fortification, the current large star-shaped masonry structure is the fourth fort to be built on this site; it was completed in 1856 to defend the city and harbor. It was occupied by the British until 1906 and then by the Canadian military until well after World War II.

Exhibits and restored rooms depict the fort's significance as a key naval station within the British Empire. Interesting features include a musketry gallery and vaulted rooms. The ramparts offer excellent views of Halifax and its harbor. The Army Museum displays military artifacts and uniforms.

Between May and October interpreters dressed as members of the 78th Highlanders regiment re-enact military drills and fire one of the oldest continuous noon guns in the world. Interactive exhibits, audiovisual displays, marching bands and muster parades are available.

Guided tours in French and English are offered in summer. **Time:** Allow 2 hours minimum. **Hours:** Fort and exhibits daily 9-6, July-Aug.; 9-5, May-June and Sept.-Oct. Grounds daily 9-5. **Cost:** June 1-Sept. 15 $11.70; $10.05 (ages 65+); $5.80 (ages 6-16); $29.40 (family, two adults and up to five children). Cost May 7-31 and Sept. 16-Oct. 31 $7.80; $6.55 (ages 65+); $3.90 (ages 6-16); $19.60 (family, two adults and up to five children). Free rest of year. **Parking:** $3.15. **Phone:** (902) 426-5080.

HALIFAX WATER TOURS departs from Cable Wharf. Conducted by Murphy's–The Cable Wharf, 1- and 2-hour sightseeing tours of Halifax Harbour are offered aboard the stern-wheeler *Harbour Queen I.* A narrator points out prominent sights and offers a historical commentary. Nature and whale-watching tours aboard the two-story *Haligonian III* last 2.5 hours. Also available are amphibious Harbour Hopper tours, *Theodore Too* tugboat tours, deep-sea fishing, tall ship excursions, moonlight cruises and ferry service to Fort McNab National Historic Site.

Hours: Sightseeing and nature and whale-watching tours depart daily, mid-May through Sept. 30. Phone ahead to confirm schedule. **Cost:** Sightseeing and nature and whale-watching tour fares $17.99-$33.99; $16.99-$32.99 (ages 65+); $14.99-$19.99 (ages 6-16); $5 (ages 2-5); $56.99-$95.99 (family, two adults and two children ages 0-15). **Phone:** (902) 420-1015.

HARBOUR HOPPER TOURS departs from the parking lot on the n. side of the Maritime Museum of

(See map & index p. 155.)

the Atlantic. Sightseeing tours of Halifax are conducted in Lark V vehicles, boats used by the U.S. military during the Vietnam War that are capable of transportation on both land and water. Refitted for tourism use, the green amphibious vehicles take passengers past sights such as Citadel Hill and the Public Gardens before splashing into the harbor for views of the Halifax and Dartmouth skylines. Guides provide commentary and fun facts about the area during the 1-hour tour.

Time: Allow 1 hour minimum. **Hours:** Departures daily at 10:15, 11:30, 12:45, 2, 3:15, 4:30, 5:45 and 7, May 1-late Oct. (weather permitting). During peak season additional tours may be scheduled. **Cost:** $25.99; $23.99 (ages 65+); $14.99 (ages 6-15); $8.99 (ages 0-5); $70.99 (family, two adults and two children; additional children $9.99). **Phone:** (902) 490-8687.

MARITIME COMMAND MUSEUM is at 2725 Gottingen St. in the Admiralty House. Displays include Royal Canadian Navy artifacts, scale models of ships, weapons, photographs and uniforms of the Canadian Navy. **Time:** Allow 30 minutes minimum. **Hours:** Mon.-Fri. 8:30-3:30. Closed major holidays. **Cost:** Donations. **Phone:** (902) 721-8250.

MARITIME MUSEUM OF THE ATLANTIC is at 1675 Lower Water St. Nova Scotia's rich maritime heritage is presented through such exhibits as *Titanic*: The Unsinkable Ship and Halifax, Shipwreck Treasures of Nova Scotia, Days of Sail, Age of Steam and Halifax Wrecked. The William Robertson & Son Ship Chandlery features hundreds of early-20th-century marine artifacts, supplies and navigational tools. Ship models, figureheads, bells, foghorns and other items are displayed throughout the museum.

Canada's first hydrographic vessel, CSS *Acadia*, is docked at the museum's wharf and may be toured May through October. The HMCS *Sackville*, one of the last remaining corvettes used for convoy escorts during WWII, is docked nearby June through September.

Time: Allow 1 hour minimum. **Hours:** Daily 9:30-5:30 (also Tues. 5:30-8), June-Oct.; Tues.-Sat. 9:30-5 (also Tues. 5-8), Nov.-Apr.; Mon.-Sat. 9:30-5:30 (also Tues. 5:30-8), rest of year. Closed Jan. 1, Good Friday and Dec. 24-26. **Cost:** May-Oct. $8.75; $7.75 (ages 65+ and students with ID); $4.75 (ages 6-17); $22.50 (family, two adults and children ages 0-16). Admission rest of year $4.75; $4 (ages 65+ and students with ID); $2.75 (ages 6-17); $11 (family, two adults and children ages 0-16). Rates may vary; phone ahead. **Phone:** (902) 424-7490.

MOUNT ST. VINCENT UNIVERSITY ART GALLERY is 5 km (3 mi.) w. at 166 Bedford Hwy. on the first floor of the Seton Academic Centre. The gallery offers changing artwork of local, regional, national and international origin; crafts and fine arts; and a permanent collection of paintings, sculptures and ceramics. **Time:** Allow 30 minutes minimum. **Hours:** Tues.-Fri. 11-5, Sat.-Sun. 1-5. **Cost:** Free. **Phone:** (902) 457-6160 or (902) 457-6291.

MUSEUM OF NATURAL HISTORY is off Bell Rd. at 1747 Summer St. n. of the Public Gardens. The province's natural history is presented through exhibits about marine life, geology, fossils, minerals, dinosaurs, birds and mushrooms. The Nature Centre features a bee colony; in summer a butterfly house is filled with exotic winged wonders. The archeology display depicts nearly 11,000 years of human history, while other galleries feature a variety of natural and cultural history exhibits.

Time: Allow 1 hour minimum. **Hours:** Mon.-Sat. 9-5 (also Wed. 5-8), Sun. noon-5, June 1-Oct. 15; Tues.-Sat. 9:30-5 (also Wed. 5-8), Sun. 1-5, rest of year. Closed Jan. 1, Good Friday and Dec. 25-26. **Cost:** $5.75; $5.25 (ages 65+); $3.75 (ages 6-17); $11.50-$16.50 (family, one or two adults and four children). **Phone:** (902) 424-7353.

POINT PLEASANT PARK is at the s. end of the city on Point Pleasant Dr. Commanding a view of the harbor and the Northwest Arm, Point Pleasant contains batteries and forts that served as part of Halifax's defense network until the end of World War II. The 74-hectare (183-acre) park, which was heavily damaged by a hurricane in 2003, features nature trails and walks and a supervised beach.

Motorized vehicles are not permitted on the park grounds. Off-leash areas for pets are available. **Hours:** Daily dawn-dusk. **Cost:** Free. **Phone:** (902) 490-4700.

Prince of Wales Tower National Historic Site of Canada is in Point Pleasant Park. The 1796 tower was built under the direction of the Duke of Kent, father of Queen Victoria. The round stone structure, almost three times as wide as it is high, was the prototype of a new system of coastal defense intended to fend off possible attacks by Napoleon Bonaparte's forces. The tower served as part of Halifax's coastal defense network.

Exhibits portray the tower's history, architectural features and significance as a defensive structure. **Time:** Allow 30 minutes minimum. **Hours:** Tower daily 9-5, July-Aug. Grounds open daily year-round. **Cost:** Free. **Phone:** (902) 426-5080.

PROVINCE HOUSE is at 1726 Hollis St. This example of Georgian architecture is considered the oldest legislative building in Canada. The 1818 house contains portraits and historical relics. Nova Scotia's legislative assembly has met in the building since 1819. Legislative sessions are held in the spring and fall and are open to the public. **Tours:** Guided tours are available. **Time:** Allow 30 minutes minimum. **Hours:** Mon.-Fri. 9-5, Sat.-Sun. and holidays 10-4, July-Aug.; Mon.-Fri. 9-4, rest of year. **Cost:** Free. **Phone:** (902) 424-4661.

(See map & index p. 155.)

PUBLIC GARDENS are bounded by S. Park St., Sackville St., Spring Garden Rd. and Summer St. Covering 7 hectares (17 acres), the gardens opened in 1867. They are considered to be among the finest examples of Victorian gardens in North America. Tree-shaded gravel walks wind among the flower beds, fountains, ponds and shrubs. Concerts and guided tours are available.

Time: Allow 30 minutes minimum. **Hours:** Daily 8-dusk, mid-May to mid-Nov. (weather permitting). Guided tours are given Wed. at 2 and 6, July-Aug.; otherwise by appointment. Concerts are presented Sun. at 2, June-Sept. **Cost:** Free.

ST. PAUL'S CHURCH is at 1749 Argyle St. The 1750 church is said to be the oldest Protestant church in Canada. The walls are covered with interesting tablets depicting men and women from the city's past. The Old Burying Ground, 3 blocks south, contains the graves of some town founders and what is reputed to be the only Crimean War memorial in Canada. **Time:** Allow 30 minutes minimum. **Hours:** Mon.-Sat. 9-4:30, June-Aug.; Mon.-Fri. 9-4:30, rest of year. **Cost:** Donations. **Phone:** (902) 429-2240.

[SAVE] **TALL SHIP** *SILVA* departs from Queen's Wharf at Prince and Lower Water sts. This three-mast schooner offers sailing tours of Halifax and Bedford harbors as well as McNabs Island. Marine animals, including whales, seals and birds, are frequently spotted during the cruises. **Time:** Allow 2 hours minimum. **Hours:** Trips depart daily at noon, 2 and 4, June-Sept. **Cost:** Fare $19.95; $18.95 (ages 60+ and students with ID); $13.95 (ages 6-12); $58.95 (family). **Phone:** (902) 429-9463. [†]

THE THOMAS McCULLOCH MUSEUM is in the Life Science Centre of Dalhousie University at 1355 Oxford St. In addition to an 1833 collection of mounted native birds, the museum displays ceramic mushrooms, marine exhibits and specimens of beetles and butterflies. **Tours:** Guided tours are available. **Hours:** Mon.-Fri. 8:30-4:30. Closed major holidays. **Cost:** Free. **Phone:** (902) 494-3515.

YORK REDOUBT NATIONAL HISTORIC SITE OF CANADA is 13 km (8 mi.) s. on Hwy. 253 (Purcell's Cove Rd.). Established in 1793 on a bluff overlooking Halifax Harbour, this fortification was a key element in the city's defense. York Redoubt served as a training ground for Canadian troops during World War I and as the site of the Plotting Room and Fire Command Post for Halifax defenses during World War II. The site features tunnels, muzzle-loading guns, a panoramic view of the harbor, interpretive panels and walking trails.

Time: Allow 1 hour minimum. **Hours:** Grounds and exhibits daily 8-dusk, June-Oct. Grounds only 8-5, rest of year. **Cost:** Free. **Phone:** (902) 426-5080.

GAMBLING ESTABLISHMENTS
• **Casino Nova Scotia** is at 1983 Upper Water St. **Hours:** Daily 24 hours. Closed major holidays. **Phone:** (902) 425-7777 or (888) 642-6376.

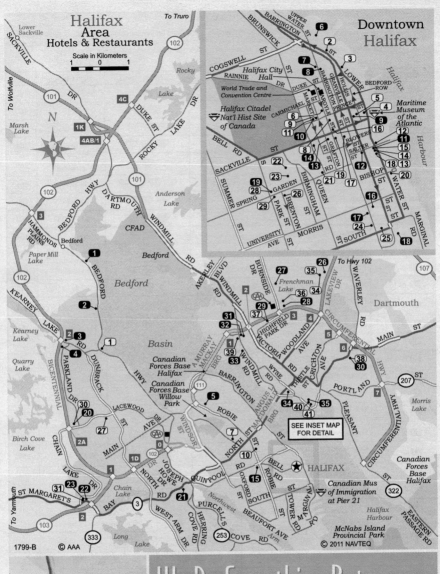

Halifax
Area
Hotels & Restaurants

Scale in Kilometers
1   0   1

Downtown
Halifax

Halifax City Hall
World Trade and Convention Centre
Halifax Citadel Nat'l Hist Site of Canada

Maritime Museum of the Atlantic

SEE INSET MAP FOR DETAIL

1799-B   © AAA
© 2011 NAVTEQ

Halifax Area

This index helps you "spot" where approved hotels and restaurants are located on the corresponding detailed maps. Hotel daily rate range is for comparison only and shows the property's high season. Restaurant rate range is a combination of lunch and/or dinner. Turn to the listing page for more detailed rate information and consult display ads for special promotions.

HALIFAX

Map Page	Hotels	Diamond Rated	High Season	Page
1 p. 155	**Esquire Motel**	▽	$89-$145 [SAVE]	160
2 p. 155	**Comfort Inn Halifax**	▽▽	$79-$149 [SAVE]	160
3 p. 155	**Holiday Inn Express Halifax/Bedford**	▽▽▽	$99-$149 [SAVE]	163
4 p. 155	Quality Inn & Suites Halifax	▽▽▽	$100-$160	164
5 p. 155	Chebucto Inn	▽	Rates not provided	159
6 p. 155	**Halifax Marriott Harbourfront** (See ad p. 162.)	▽▽▽▽	$189-$270 [SAVE]	161
7 p. 155	Delta Halifax	▽▽▽	$115-$209	160
8 p. 155	Delta Barrington	▽▽▽	$139-$239	160
9 p. 155	**Radisson Suite Hotel Halifax**	▽▽▽	$179 [SAVE]	164
10 p. 155	**The Prince George Hotel**	▽▽▽	$179-$279 [SAVE]	164
11 p. 155	Courtyard by Marriott Halifax Downtown	▽▽▽	$116-$269	160
12 p. 155	**Four Points Sheraton Halifax** (See ad p. 161.)	▽▽▽	$120-$210 [SAVE]	160
13 p. 155	**Residence Inn Halifax Downtown** (See ad p. 166.)	▽▽▽	$169-$229 [SAVE]	164
14 p. 155	**Cambridge Suites Hotel**	▽▽▽	$119-$219 [SAVE]	158
15 p. 155	**Atlantica Hotel Halifax** (See ad p. 158.)	▽▽▽	$119-$230 [SAVE]	158
16 p. 155	**The Halliburton** (See ad p. 163.)	▽▽▽	$155-$350 [SAVE]	161
17 p. 155	**Halifax's Waverley Inn** (See ad p. 163.)	▽▽▽	$129-$229 [SAVE]	161
18 p. 155	**The Westin Nova Scotian** (See ad p. 167.)	▽▽▽▽	$139-$395 [SAVE]	164
19 p. 155	**The Lord Nelson Hotel & Suites** (See ad p. 165.)	▽▽▽	$189 [SAVE]	164
20 p. 155	Future Inns Halifax	▽▽	$129-$179	160
21 p. 155	**Best Western Plus Chocolate Lake Hotel** (See ad p. 159.)	▽▽▽	$99-$199 [SAVE]	158
22 p. 155	**Lakeview Inns & Suites**	▽▽	$139-$299 [SAVE]	164
23 p. 155	**Comfort Hotel Halifax**	▽▽▽	$99-$169 [SAVE]	160

Map Page	Restaurants	Diamond Rated	Cuisine	Meal Range	Page
① p. 155	China Town Restaurant	▽▽▽	Chinese	$8-$23	168
② p. 155	44 North Restaurant	▽▽▽	Regional Canadian	$9-$32	168
③ p. 155	Salty's on the Waterfront	▽▽▽	Seafood	$13-$36	170
④ p. 155	McKelvie's Delishes Fishes Dishes	▽▽▽	Seafood	$13-$30	169
⑤ p. 155	Ryan Duffy's	▽▽▽	Steak	$12-$45	170
⑥ p. 155	The Five Fishermen Restaurant & Grill	▽▽▽	Seafood	$12-$40	169
⑦ p. 155	Brooklyn Warehouse	▽▽	Canadian	$9-$20	168
⑧ p. 155	The Press Gang	▽▽▽	Seafood	$23-$39	170
⑨ p. 155	the Wooden Monkey	▽▽	Canadian	$10-$22	170
⑩ p. 155	jane's on the common	▽▽▽	Canadian	$11-$22	169
⑪ p. 155	gio	▽▽▽▽	Regional Canadian	$15-$32	169
⑫ p. 155	Waterfront Warehouse Restaurant & Tug's Pub	▽▽	Canadian	$9-$24	170

Map Page	Restaurants (cont'd)	Diamond Rated	Cuisine	Meal Range	Page
⑬ p. 155	Cheelin Restaurant	▼▼	Chinese	$8-$18	168
⑭ p. 155	Red Stag Tavern	▼▼	Canadian	$9-$22	170
⑮ p. 155	**Cut Contemporary Steakhouse**	▼▼▼	Steak	$29-$49	168
⑯ p. 155	Durty Nelly's Irish Pub	▼▼	Irish	$10-$22	168
⑰ p. 155	Pogue Fado' Irish Public House	▼▼	Irish	$10-$18	169
⑱ p. 155	**da Maurizio Dining Room**	▼▼▼	Italian	$27-$33	168
⑲ p. 155	ela! Greek Taverna	▼▼▼	Greek	$10-$26	168
⑳ p. 155	**The Bicycle Thief**	▼▼▼	International	$21-$35	168
㉑ p. 155	The Fireside Bar/Restaurant	▼▼	Canadian	$9-$24	169
㉒ p. 155	Fid Resto	▼▼▼	International	$12-$29	169
㉓ p. 155	Sushi Nami Royale	▼▼	Japanese	$10-$21	170
㉔ p. 155	Henry House Restaurant and Pub	▼▼	Canadian	$7-$18	169
㉕ p. 155	Cafe Chianti	▼▼▼	Italian	$10-$28	168
㉖ p. 155	il Mercato Ristorante	▼▼	Italian	$10-$24	169
㉗ p. 155	Sushi Nami Royale	▼▼	Japanese	$10-$21	170
㉘ p. 155	**Victory Arms Pub**	▼▼	American	$9-$25	170
㉙ p. 155	**Onyx**	▼▼▼▼	New World	$21-$39	169
㉚ p. 155	Redwood Grill	▼▼	Canadian	$8-$22	170
㉛ p. 155	Canadiana Restaurant & Lounge	▼▼	American	$7-$18	168

DARTMOUTH

Map Page	Hotels	Diamond Rated	High Season	Page
㉖ p. 155	**Hampton Inn & Suites by Hilton- Halifax/ Dartmouth** *(See ad p. 142.)*	▼▼▼	Rates not provided [SAVE]	143
㉗ p. 155	**Best Western Plus Dartmouth Hotel & Suites** *(See ad p. 142.)*	▼▼▼	$139-$149 [SAVE]	141
㉘ p. 155	**Park Place Hotel & Conference Centre Ramada Plaza**	▼▼▼	$99-$194 [SAVE]	143
㉙ p. 155	**Days Inn**	▼▼	$89-$125 [SAVE]	141
㉚ p. 155	**Quality Inn Halifax/Dartmouth**	▼▼	$85-$125 [SAVE]	143
㉛ p. 155	**Travelodge Suites**	▼▼	Rates not provided [SAVE]	143
㉜ p. 155	**Comfort Inn**	▼▼	$99-$149 [SAVE]	141
㉝ p. 155	**Coastal Inn Dartmouth**	▼▼	$109-$154 [SAVE]	141
㉞ p. 155	**Holiday Inn Halifax-Harbourview**	▼▼▼	$119-$209 [SAVE]	143
㉟ p. 155	Super 8 Hotel-Dartmouth	▼▼	$77-$166	143

Map Page	Restaurants	Diamond Rated	Cuisine	Meal Range	Page
㉞ p. 155	Sushi Nami Royale	▼▼	Japanese	$10-$21	144
㉟ p. 155	ela! Greek Taverna	▼▼▼	Greek	$10-$26	143
㊱ p. 155	**The Peppermill Restaurant**	▼▼	American	$8-$28	144
㊲ p. 155	Favorites Cuisine	▼▼	American	$8-$21	144
㊳ p. 155	Rocco's Ristorante Italiano	▼▼▼	Italian	$12-$25	144
㊴ p. 155	Fan's Restaurant	▼▼	Chinese	$8-$15	144
㊵ p. 155	La Perla Dining Room	▼▼▼	Italian	$13-$34	144
㊶ p. 155	MacAskill's Waterfront Restaurant	▼▼▼	Canadian	$12-$29	144

(See map & index p. 155.)

ATLANTICA HOTEL HALIFAX
Phone: (902)423-1161 **15**

Hotel
$119-$230

Address: 1980 Robie St B3H 3G5 **Location:** Jct Quinpool St. Opposite the Commons. **Facility:** 230 units. 15 stories, interior corridors. **Parking:** on-site (fee). **Terms:** cancellation fee imposed. **Amenities:** high-speed Internet. **Pool(s):** heated indoor. **Activities:** sauna, whirlpool, exercise room. **Guest Services:** valet and coin laundry. **Free Special Amenities:** local telephone calls and high-speed Internet. *(See ad this page.)*

SAVE ECO [Y] [Y] [→] [BIZ]
[icons] FEE [icons] / SOME UNITS [icons]

BEST WESTERN PLUS CHOCOLATE LAKE HOTEL
Phone: (902)477-5611 **21**

Hotel
$99-$199

AAA Benefit: Members save up to 20%, plus 10% bonus points with Best Western Rewards®.

Address: 20 St. Margaret's Bay Rd B3N 1J4 **Location:** Waterfront. 0.4 mi (0.7 km) e of Armdale Rotary. **Facility:** 142 units. 3-9 stories, interior/exterior corridors. **Amenities:** video games (fee), high-speed Internet. **Pool(s):** heated indoor. **Activities:** whirlpool, exercise room. *Fee:* game room. **Guest Services:** valet and coin laundry. **Free Special Amenities: full breakfast and high-speed Internet.** *(See ad p. 159.)*

SAVE ECO [Y] [Y] CALL [icons] [→] [BIZ] [icons] [X]
[icons] [icons] / SOME UNITS [icons] [icons]

Find valuable AAA/CAA
member savings
at AAA.com/discounts

CAMBRIDGE SUITES HOTEL
Phone: (902)420-0555 **14**

Hotel
$119-$219

Address: 1583 Brunswick St B3J 3P5 **Location:** Corner of Brunswick and Sackville sts. **Facility:** 200 units, some efficiencies. 6 stories, interior corridors. **Parking:** on-site (fee). **Terms:** cancellation fee imposed. **Amenities:** video games (fee), high-speed Internet. **Activities:** sauna, whirlpool, exercise room. **Guest Services:** valet and coin laundry. **Free Special Amenities: continental breakfast and high-speed Internet.**

SAVE ECO [Y] [Y] CALL [icons] [BIZ] [icons] [X] FEE [icons]
[icons] [icons] [icons] / SOME UNITS [icons]

▼ See AAA listing this page ▼

(See map & index p. 155.)

CHEBUCTO INN

Hotel
Rates not provided
exterior corridors.

Phone: 902/453-4330
Address: 6151 Lady Hammond Rd
B3K 2R9 **Location:** Jct Hwy 111 and
Rt 2 (Bedford Hwy), 0.4 mi (0.7 km) e.
Located in a residential area. **Facility:**
31 units. 2 stories (no elevator),

▼ See AAA listing p. 158 ▼

(See map & index p. 155.)

COMFORT HOTEL HALIFAX

Phone: (902)405-4555   **23**

Hotel
$99-$169

Address: 88 Chain Lake Dr B3S 1A2 **Location:** Hwy 102 exit 2A eastbound; Hwy 103 exit 2. Located in Bayers Lake Business Park. **Facility:** 73 units. 4 stories, interior corridors. **Terms:** cancellation fee imposed. **Amenities:** high-speed Internet, safes. **Dining:** Canadiana Restaurant & Lounge, see separate listing. **Pool(s):** heated indoor. **Activities:** sauna, exercise room. **Guest Services:** coin laundry. **Free Special Amenities:** full breakfast and high-speed Internet.

COMFORT INN HALIFAX

Phone: (902)443-0303   **2**

Hotel
$79-$149

Address: 560 Bedford Hwy B3M 2L8 **Location:** On Rt 2 (Bedford Hwy), 6 mi (9.6 km) w. **Facility:** 63 units, some efficiencies and kitchens. 3 stories, interior corridors. **Terms:** cancellation fee imposed. **Amenities:** *Some:* high-speed Internet. **Pool(s):** heated indoor. **Activities:** exercise room. **Guest Services:** coin laundry. **Free Special Amenities:** expanded continental breakfast and high-speed Internet.

COURTYARD BY MARRIOTT HALIFAX DOWNTOWN

Phone: (902)428-1900   **11**

Hotel
$116-$269

AAA Benefit:
AAA hotel discounts of 5% or more.

Address: 5120 Salter St B3J 0A1 **Location:** At Lower Water St; centre. **Facility:** 125 units. 8 stories, interior corridors. **Parking:** valet only. **Amenities:** high-speed Internet. **Dining:** Cut Contemporary Steakhouse, see separate listing. **Pool(s):** heated indoor. **Activities:** whirlpool, exercise room, spa. **Guest Services:** valet and coin laundry.

DELTA BARRINGTON

Phone: (902)429-7410   **8**

Hotel
$139-$239

Address: 1875 Barrington St B3J 3L6 **Location:** Between Cogswell and Duke sts. **Facility:** 200 units. 3 stories, interior corridors. **Parking:** valet only. **Terms:** cancellation fee imposed. **Amenities:** *Fee:* video games, high-speed Internet. *Some:* honor bars. **Pool(s):** heated indoor. **Activities:** saunas, exercise room. *Fee:* massage. **Guest Services:** valet laundry.

DELTA HALIFAX

Phone: (902)425-6700   **7**

Hotel
$115-$209

Address: 1990 Barrington St B3J 1P2 **Location:** Corner of Cogswell and Barrington sts. Located in Scotia Square. **Facility:** 296 units, some two bedrooms. 8 stories, interior corridors. **Parking:** on-site (fee) and valet. **Terms:** cancellation fee imposed. **Amenities:** high-speed Internet (fee). **Pool(s):** heated indoor. **Activities:** saunas, whirlpool, exercise room. *Fee:* massage. **Guest Services:** valet laundry.

ESQUIRE MOTEL

Phone: 902/835-3367   **1**

Motel
$89-$145 6/1-10/15
$69-$135 10/16-5/31

Address: 771 Bedford Hwy B4A 1A1 **Location:** Hwy 102 exit 4A, 3.3 mi (5.3 km) e on Rt 2 (Bedford Hwy). **Facility:** 28 units. 1 story, exterior corridors. **Parking:** winter plug-ins. **Terms:** office hours 7 am-midnight, cancellation fee imposed. **Pool(s):** outdoor. **Free Special Amenities:** room upgrade (subject to availability with advance reservations) and high-speed Internet.

FOUR POINTS SHERATON HALIFAX

Phone: (902)423-4444   **12**

Hotel
$120-$210

FOUR POINTS BY SHERATON **AAA Benefit:** Members get up to 15% off, plus Starwood Preferred Guest® bonuses.

Address: 1496 Hollis St B3J 3Z1 **Location:** Between Salter and Bishop sts. **Facility:** 177 units. 6 stories, interior corridors. **Parking:** on-site (fee). **Terms:** cancellation fee imposed. **Amenities:** high-speed Internet. **Pool(s):** heated indoor. **Activities:** whirlpool, exercise room. **Guest Services:** valet laundry. **Free Special Amenities:** newspaper and high-speed Internet.
(See ad p. 161.)

FUTURE INNS HALIFAX

Phone: (902)443-4333   **20**

Hotel
$129-$179 6/1-9/30
$119-$169 10/1-5/31

Address: 30 Fairfax Dr B3S 1P1 **Location:** Hwy 102 exit 2A. Adjacent to Bayers Lake Business Park. **Facility:** 132 units. 4 stories, interior corridors. **Terms:** cancellation fee imposed. **Amenities:** high-speed Internet. **Dining:** Redwood Grill, see separate listing. **Activities:** exercise room. **Guest Services:** valet and coin laundry.

(See map & index p. 155.)

HALIFAX MARRIOTT HARBOURFRONT
Phone: (902)421-1700   **6**

Hotel
$189-$270

Marriott HOTELS & RESORTS   **AAA Benefit:** AAA hotel discounts of 5% or more.

Address: 1919 Upper Water St B3J 3J5 **Location:** Adjacent to historic properties and Casino Nova Scotia. Located in a commercial area. **Facility:** Views of the waterfront and city are offered from many of the nicely-appointed rooms at this sophisticated hotel adjacent to the harbor. 352 units, some two bedrooms. 6 stories, interior corridors. **Parking:** on-site (fee) and valet. **Amenities:** high-speed Internet (fee). *Some:* safes. **Dining:** 44 North Restaurant, see separate listing. **Pool(s):** heated indoor. **Activities:** whirlpool, exercise room, spa. **Guest Services:** valet laundry. *(See ad p. 162.)*

SAVE ECO ⫪ ⊻ CALL ⟨&M⟩ ⋙ BIZ 🛜 ✕ FEE 🎦 ▯ / SOME UNITS FEE 🐾 ▤ ▦

HALIFAX'S WAVERLEY INN
Phone: (902)423-9346   **17**

Historic Hotel
$129-$229 6/1-10/31
$109-$199 11/1-5/31

Address: 1266 Barrington St B3J 1Y5 **Location:** Between Harvey and Morris sts. Located 2 blks from Via Rail Station. **Facility:** Built in 1866, the inn offers many accommodations furnished with antiques; rooms vary in size and are individually decorated. 34 units. 3 stories (no elevator), interior corridors. **Guest Services:** valet laundry. **Free Special Amenities:** expanded continental breakfast and high-speed Internet.
(See ad p. 163.)

SAVE ⫪+ BIZ 🛜 ✕ / SOME UNITS ▤

THE HALLIBURTON
Phone: (902)420-0658   **16**

Historic Hotel
$155-$350 6/1-10/31
$130-$250 11/1-5/31

Address: 5184 Morris St B3J 1B3 **Location:** Between Barrington and Hollis sts. Located by Dalhousie Tech University. **Facility:** Antiques furnish many of the guest rooms in this property's terraced buildings, which offer a variety of rooms and suites. 29 units. 3 stories (no elevator), interior corridors. **Terms:** cancellation fee imposed. **Guest Services:** valet laundry. **Free Special Amenities:** expanded continental breakfast and high-speed Internet.
(See ad p. 163.)

SAVE ECO ⫪ ⊻ BIZ 🛜
✕ ▯

HILTON GARDEN INN HALIFAX AIRPORT
Phone: (902)873-1400

Hotel
$129-$199

 Hilton Garden Inn™   **AAA Benefit:** Unparalleled hospitality at a special Member rate.

Address: 200 Pratt & Whitney Dr B2T 0A2 **Location:** Hwy 102 exit 5A, 0.8 mi (1.2 km) e, then just n. **Facility:** 145 units. 5 stories, interior corridors. **Terms:** 1-7 night minimum stay, cancellation fee imposed. **Amenities:** video games (fee), high-speed Internet. **Pool(s):** heated indoor. **Activities:** whirlpool, exercise room. **Guest Services:** valet and coin laundry.

SAVE ✈ ⫪ ⊻ CALL ⟨&M⟩ ⋙ BIZ 🛜 ✕ FEE 🎦 ▤ ▦ ▯

HOLIDAY INN EXPRESS HALIFAX AIRPORT
Phone: (902)576-7600

Hotel
$139-$199

Address: 180 Pratt & Whitney Dr B2T 0A2 **Location:** Hwy 102 exit 5A, 0.8 mi (1.2 km) e, then just n. **Facility:** 119 units. 4 stories, interior corridors. **Pool(s):** heated indoor. **Activities:** exercise room. **Guest Services:** valet and coin laundry.

SAVE ⫪+ CALL ⟨&M⟩ ⋙ BIZ 🛜 ✕ FEE 🎦 ▤ ▦ ▯ / SOME UNITS 🐾

▼ See AAA listing p. 160 ▼

▼ See AAA listing p. 161 ▼

(See map & index p. 155.)

HOLIDAY INN EXPRESS HALIFAX/BEDFORD
Phone: (902)445-1100

Hotel
$99-$149

Address: 133 Kearney Lake Rd B3M 4P3 **Location:** Hwy 102 exit 2. Located in a residential area. **Facility:** 98 units. 3 stories, interior corridors. **Amenities:** high-speed Internet. **Pool(s):** heated indoor. **Activities:** whirlpool, exercise room. **Guest Services:** valet and coin laundry. **Free Special Amenities:** expanded continental breakfast and high-speed Internet.

INN ON THE LAKE, AN ASCEND COLLECTION HOTEL
Phone: (902)861-3480

Hotel
$117-$320

Address: 3009 Hwy 2 B2T 1J5 **Location:** Hwy 102 exit 5. **Facility:** 39 units, some three bedrooms. 3 stories (no elevator), interior corridors. **Terms:** cancellation fee imposed. **Amenities:** Some: high-speed Internet. **Dining:** Encore Traditional Cuisine, see separate listing. **Pool(s):** outdoor. **Activities:** canoeing, paddleboats, 2 tennis courts.

▼ See AAA listing p. 161 ▼

▼ See AAA listing p. 161 ▼

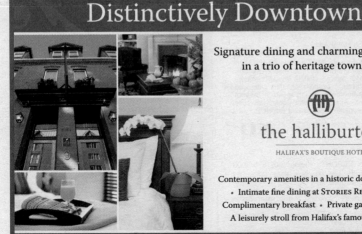

(See map & index p. 155.)

LAKEVIEW INNS & SUITES   Phone: (902)450-3020   22

Hotel
$139-$299

Address: 98 Chain Lake Dr B3S 1A2 **Location:** Hwy 102 exit 2A eastbound; Hwy 103 exit 2. Located in Bayers Lake Business Park. **Facility:** 65 units. 3 stories, interior corridors. **Pool(s):** indoor. **Activities:** limited exercise equipment. **Guest Services:** valet and coin laundry. **Free Special Amenities: expanded continental breakfast and high-speed Internet.**

SAVE ECO [+] CALL M 2 BIZ 🤝 X 目 🖼
🖥 / SOME UNITS FEE 🐾

THE LORD NELSON HOTEL & SUITES   Phone: (902)423-6331   19

Historic Hotel
$189 6/1-10/31
$129 11/1-5/31

Address: 1515 S Park St B3J 2L2 **Location:** Corner of Park St and Spring Garden Rd. **Facility:** Opposite the Halifax Public Gardens, the grand 1927 hotel was expanded in the 1970s; the average to spacious rooms are tastefully decorated. 261 units. 8 stories, interior corridors. **Parking:** on-site (fee) and valet. **Terms:** 3 day cancellation notice-fee imposed. **Amenities:** high-speed Internet. *Some:* safes. **Dining:** Victory Arms Pub, see separate listing. **Activities:** exercise room. **Guest Services:** valet and coin laundry, area transportation-downtown. **Free Special Amenities: local telephone calls and newspaper.** *(See ad p. 165.)*

SAVE ECO [+] Y CALL M BIZ 🤝 X 🖥
/ SOME UNITS 🐾 目 🖼

THE PRINCE GEORGE HOTEL
Phone: (902)425-1986   10

Hotel
$179-$279 6/1-10/31
$149-$259 11/1-5/31

Address: 1725 Market St B3J 3N9 **Location:** Between Prince and Carmichael sts. Next to World Trade Centre. **Facility:** This full-service downtown hotel, close to the Citadel, offers rooms and suites with city or waterfront views. 203 units. 6 stories, interior corridors. **Parking:** on-site (fee) and valet. **Terms:** cancellation fee imposed. **Amenities:** high-speed Internet. **Dining:** gio, see separate listing. **Pool(s):** heated indoor. **Activities:** sauna, whirlpool, exercise room. **Guest Services:** valet laundry. **Free Special Amenities: local telephone calls and high-speed Internet.**

SAVE ECO FEE [+] Y CALL M 2 BIZ 🤝
X FEE 目 🖥 / SOME UNITS FEE 🐾

QUALITY INN & SUITES HALIFAX
Phone: (902)444-6700   4

Hotel
$100-$160

Address: 980 Parkland Dr B3M 4Y7 **Location:** Hwy 102 exit 2. **Facility:** 113 units. 5 stories, interior corridors. **Terms:** cancellation fee imposed. **Amenities:** high-speed Internet. **Pool(s):** heated indoor. **Activities:** whirlpool, waterslide, exercise room, spa. *Fee:* game room. **Guest Services:** valet and coin laundry.

ECO [+] CALL M 2 BIZ 🤝 X FEE 目
🖼 🖥 / SOME UNITS 🐾

QUALITY INN HALIFAX AIRPORT   Phone: (902)873-3000

Hotel
$109-$170

Address: 60 Sky Blvd B2T 1K3 **Location:** Hwy 102 exit 6. **Facility:** 156 units. 3 stories (no elevator), interior corridors. **Terms:** cancellation fee imposed. **Pool(s):** heated outdoor, heated indoor. **Activities:** whirlpool, horseshoes, volleyball, exercise room. **Guest Services:** coin laundry.

ECO [+] Y 2 BIZ 🤝 X 🖥
/ SOME UNITS 🐾 目 🖼

RADISSON SUITE HOTEL HALIFAX
Phone: (902)429-7233   9

Hotel
$179 6/1-10/31
$139 11/1-5/31

Address: 1649 Hollis St B3J 1V8 **Location:** Between Sackville and Prince sts. **Facility:** 104 units. 8 stories, interior corridors. **Parking:** valet only. **Amenities:** high-speed Internet. **Dining:** Ryan Duffy's, see separate listing. **Pool(s):** heated indoor. **Activities:** saunas, whirlpool, exercise room. **Guest Services:** valet and coin laundry.

SAVE ECO [+] Y 2 BIZ 🤝 X 目 🖼 🖥

RESIDENCE INN HALIFAX DOWNTOWN
Phone: (902)422-0493   13

Extended Stay Hotel
$169-$229

AAA Benefit: AAA hotel discounts of 5% or more.

Address: 1599 Grafton St B3J 2C3 **Location:** Corner of Sackville St. **Facility:** 92 units, some two bedrooms, efficiencies and kitchens. 6 stories, interior corridors. **Parking:** on-site (fee). **Amenities:** high-speed Internet. **Activities:** exercise room. **Guest Services:** valet and coin laundry. **Free Special Amenities: full breakfast and high-speed Internet.** *(See ad p. 166.)*

SAVE ECO [+] CALL M BIZ 🤝 X FEE 🐾 目
🖼 🖥 / SOME UNITS FEE 🐾

STARDUST MOTEL TIMBERLEA   Phone: 902/876-2301

Motel
Rates not provided

Address: 1791 St. Margaret's Bay Rd B3T 1B8 **Location:** Waterfront. Hwy 103 exit 2A, 3 mi (5 km) w on Rt 3; in Timberlea. **Facility:** 21 units. 2 stories (no elevator), exterior corridors. **Terms:** office hours 7 am-midnight.

[+] 🤝 X / SOME UNITS 目 🖼

THE WESTIN NOVA SCOTIAN
Phone: (902)421-1000   18

Classic Historic Hotel
$139-$395

WESTIN
HOTELS & RESORTS

AAA Benefit: Enjoy up to 15% off your next stay, plus Starwood Preferred Guest® bonuses.

Address: 1181 Hollis St B3H 2P6 **Location:** Between Barrington and Lower Water sts. **Facility:** This circa 1931 grand hotel with lovely public areas overlooks the Halifax waterfront and cruise ship terminal; guest rooms vary in size and decor. 310 units. 9-11 stories, interior corridors. **Parking:** on-site (fee) and valet. **Terms:** cancellation fee imposed. **Amenities:** high-speed Internet (fee), safes, honor bars. **Pool(s):** heated indoor. **Activities:** whirlpool, tennis court, exercise room, spa. **Guest Services:** valet laundry, area transportation-downtown. **Free Special Amenities: local transportation and children's activities.** *(See ad p. 167.)*

SAVE ECO [+] 🐾 Y CALL M 2 BIZ 🤝 X
FEE 🐾 🖥 / SOME UNITS 🐾

(See map & index p. 155.)

▼ See AAA listing p. 164 ▼

(See map & index p. 155.)

(See map & index p. 155.)

▼ See AAA listing p. 164 ▼

Halifax's new downtown

Located next to shopping, entertainment & great restaurants

THE WESTIN
NOVA SCOTIAN
HALIFAX

1181 Hollis St.
1.877.993.7846

thewestinnovascotian.com

Get the free mobile app at
http://gettag.mobi

Are we meeting your travel needs?

If your visit to an establishment listed in a AAA TourBook guide doesn't meet your expectations, tell us about it.

Complete an easy online form at
AAA.com/TourBookComments.

(See map & index p. 155.)

WHERE TO EAT

44 NORTH RESTAURANT   Phone: 902/421-1700   ②

Regional Canadian
$9-$32

AAA Inspector Notes: Affording one of the city's finest harbor views, this spacious dining room has two levels designed to showcase the sights. The menu reflects the ocean location with a splendid array of fresh seafood. For meat lovers, there is a selection of choice cuts. **Bar:** full bar. **Reservations:** suggested. **Address:** 1919 Upper Water St B3J 3J5 **Location:** Adjacent to historic properties and Casino Nova Scotia; in Halifax Marriott Harbourfront. **Parking:** on-site (fee) and valet. [B] [L] [D] CALL ⑤M

THE BICYCLE THIEF
Menu on AAA.com   Phone: 902/425-7993   ⑳

International
$21-$35

AAA Inspector Notes: This delightful waterfront restaurant overlooks Halifax Harbor with patio seating open in summer. A bustling atmosphere can be found here with friendly servers quick to bring out a fine assortment of creative Italian and Canadian dishes. **Bar:** full bar. **Reservations:** suggested. **Address:** 1475 Lower Water St B3J 3Z2 **Location:** Between Bishop and Salter sts; at Bishop's Landing Complex. **Parking:** on-site (fee).

[L] [D] CALL ⑤M

BROOKLYN WAREHOUSE   Phone: 902/446-8181   ⑦
Canadian
$9-$20

AAA Inspector Notes: Located in the North End, this colourful and casual bistro offers a warm and friendly atmosphere. The menu includes a wonderful variety of salads, sandwiches, fish and chips and an excellent Brooklyn burger complete with cheddar, bacon and red-pepper mayonnaise. Save room for one of their decadent desserts. **Bar:** full bar. **Address:** 2795 Windsor St B3K 5E3 **Location:** Corner of Almon St; opposite Halifax Forum. **Parking:** street only. [L] [D]

CAFE CHIANTI   Phone: 902/423-7471   ㉕
Italian
$10-$28

AAA Inspector Notes: The extensive menu at this eatery lists selections of pasta, seafood, beef and chicken, with several vegetarian choices. Goulash and stroganoff are among Eastern European specialties. An attractive dining room is decorated with murals and vases, soft lighting and music. Wine list is excellent. **Bar:** full bar. **Reservations:** suggested. **Address:** 1241 Barrington St B3J 1Y2 **Location:** Between Morris and South sts. **Parking:** street only.

[L] [D]

CANADIANA RESTAURANT & LOUNGE
Phone: 902/450-1286   ㉛
American
$7-$18

AAA Inspector Notes: Patrons can choose either booth or table seating at this large, family-oriented restaurant. The varied menu swings from burgers and pizza to fresh seafood, steak and pasta as well as all-day breakfast. **Bar:** full bar. **Address:** 15 Lakelands Blvd B0J 1Z2 **Location:** Hwy 102 exit 2A eastbound; Hwy 103 exit 2; in Comfort Hotel Halifax. [B] [L] [D]

CHEELIN RESTAURANT   Phone: 902/422-2252   ⑬

Chinese
$8-$18

AAA Inspector Notes: Menu choices focus on Beijing and Szechuan cuisine--such as sweet and sour chicken and beef with broccoli. Attractive table settings add to the ambience of the comfortable dining area. **Bar:** full bar. **Address:** 1496 Lower Water St B3J 1R9 **Location:** Centre; in Brewery Market. **Parking:** on-site (fee).

[L] [D]

CHEZ CORA

Canadian
$6-$13

AAA Inspector Notes: Eggs, omelets, waffles, crepes (sorry, no American-style pancakes here), French toast, fruit platters and all the breakfast meats--that's the specialty here, all day. However, at lunchtime the menu lists a selection of soups, salads, quiches, sandwiches and a dish called the grilled panini crepe. [B] [L]

LOCATIONS:
Address: 1535 Dresden Row B3J 3T1 **Location:** Just off Spring Garden Rd. **Phone:** 902/490-2672

Address: 287 Lacewood Dr B3M 3Y7 **Location:** Just e of Dunbrack St. **Phone:** 902/457-2672

Address: 1475 Bedford Hwy, Suite 107 B4A 3Z5 **Location:** Just e of Union St. **Phone:** 902/832-5252

CHINA TOWN RESTAURANT   Phone: 902/443-2444   ①
Chinese
$8-$23

AAA Inspector Notes: Diners can appreciate views of the waterfront marina on the shore of Bedford Basin from booths and tables in the spacious restaurant. The menu blends Chinese, Peking, Szechuan and Cantonese cuisine. **Bar:** full bar. **Address:** 381 Bedford Hwy B3M 2L3 **Location:** 5 mi (8 km) w on Rt 2 (Bedford Hwy) exit Birch Cove-Kearney Lake from Bicentennial Dr. [L] [D]

CUT CONTEMPORARY STEAKHOUSE
Phone: 902/429-5120   ⑮

Steak
$29-$49

AAA Inspector Notes: This sophisticated steakhouse offers a fine selection of USDA Prime beef carefully prepared and aged in house to preserve the flavors. Menu selections include porterhouse, New York strip loin, Kobe rib-eye and filet mignon as well as some chicken and seafood items. Premium wines and liqueurs complement the menu offerings. Downstairs is the more casual Urban Grill which offers a daily lunch and dinner. **Bar:** full bar. **Reservations:** suggested. **Address:** 5120 Salter St B3J 0A1 **Location:** At Lower Water St; centre; in Courtyard by Marriott Halifax Downtown. **Parking:** valet and street only.

[D] CALL ⑤M

DA MAURIZIO DINING ROOM
Phone: 902/423-0859   ⑱
Italian
$27-$33

AAA Inspector Notes: The upscale, highly acclaimed restaurant offers elegant decor and a sophisticated atmosphere. Fresh seafood, prime meats and pasta are the basis for a menu of creative, flavorful cuisine. **Bar:** full bar. **Reservations:** suggested. **Address:** 1496 Lower Water St B3J 1R7 **Location:** Between Salter and Bishops sts; in Brewery Market. **Parking:** on-site (fee). [D]

DURTY NELLY'S IRISH PUB
Phone: 902/406-7640   ⑯

Irish
$10-$22

AAA Inspector Notes: Built in Ireland and shipped across the Atlantic, this authentic Irish pub was reconstructed piece by piece in Nova Scotia. Three large dining sections of varying themes are offered. The menu features various pub snacks to full entrees including Guinness-braised lamb, Kilkenny fish and chips, Jameson-lacquered ribs, salmon or haddock with colcannon. **Bar:** full bar. **Address:** 5221 Sackville St B3J 3P8 **Location:** Corner of Argyle St. **Parking:** on-site (fee). [L] [D]

ELA! GREEK TAVERNA   Phone: 902/492-7999   ⑲

Greek
$10-$26

AAA Inspector Notes: A delightful Greek setting awaits patrons who venture into the stylish taverna. From the open-style kitchen comes an array of Greek dishes coupled with a fine wine list. Save room for one of the splendid desserts. **Bar:** full bar. **Address:** 1565 Argyle St B3J 2B2 **Location:** At Blowers St. **Parking:** street only.

[L] [D]

For additional information, visit AAA.com

(See map & index p. 155.)

ENCORE TRADITIONAL CUISINE   Phone: 902/861-3480

American
$8-$29

AAA Inspector Notes: The attractive Victorian-style inn, appointed with antiques, looks out at scenic Lake Thomas. Couples favor the restaurant for special occasions. Planked salmon is served with smoked tomato chutney. Death by chocolate is a deliciously decadent dessert. **Bar:** full bar. **Reservations:** suggested. **Address:** 3009 Hwy 2 B2T 1J5 **Location:** Hwy 102 exit 5; in Inn on the Lake.

B   L   D

FID RESTO   Phone: 902/422-9162   22

International
$12-$29

AAA Inspector Notes: A delightful restaurant and true to its name, Fid manages to splice a blend of Asian and French cuisine in a most colorful and creative style. The superb wine list pleases even the most discriminating wine buff. **Bar:** full bar. **Address:** 1569 Dresden Row B3N 1H6 **Location:** Between Artillery Pl and Sackville St. **Parking:** street only.   L   D

THE FIRESIDE BAR/RESTAURANT
Phone: 902/423-5995   21

Canadian
$9-$24

AAA Inspector Notes: Various cozy sections of this popular restaurant allow patrons to unwind. Menu highlights include tarragon chicken crepes, dilled salmon and fiery pork chops. **Bar:** full bar. **Address:** 1500 Brunswick St B3J 3X9 **Location:** Corner of Spring Garden Rd. **Parking:** street only.   L   D   LATE

THE FIVE FISHERMEN RESTAURANT & GRILL
Phone: 902/422-4421   6

Seafood
$12-$40

AAA Inspector Notes: The all-you-can-eat salad and mussel bar is a big attraction at this moderately upscale restaurant, which is inside an 1816 building appointed with nautical decor. Delicious entrées include Cajun-blackened halibut and creative daily specials. The more casual grill is open for lunch and dinner. The restaurant has been in business since 1974. **Bar:** full bar. **Reservations:** suggested. **Address:** 1740 Argyle St B3J 2W1 **Location:** Corner of George St. **Parking:** street only.   L   D

GIO   Phone: 902/425-1987   11

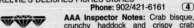

Regional Canadian
$15-$32

AAA Inspector Notes: Comfortable leather seats or padded banquettes and an upscale bar area characterize this chic restaurant featuring stylish lighting, unique glass sculptures and an open concept. Presenting an innovative contemporary cuisine with an Asian influence, talented chefs make the most of living by the sea with focus on fresh seafood, regional meats and some exotic items. **Bar:** full bar. **Reservations:** suggested. **Address:** 1725 Market St B3J 3N9 **Location:** Between Prince and Carmichael sts; in The Prince George Hotel. **Parking:** on-site (fee) and valet.   L   D   CALL ㊐M

HENRY HOUSE RESTAURANT AND PUB
Phone: 902/423-5660   24

Canadian
$7-$18

AAA Inspector Notes: Set in the 1830s Henry House, this historic restaurant is decorated with granite, wood beams, twin fireplaces and pub-style furnishings. On a menu of mostly basic fare are such specialties as fish and chips, smoked salmon fettuccine and Mediterranean meatloaf. Home-brewed ales are fitting accompaniments. The service is very relaxed and friendly. **Address:** 1222 Barrington St B3J 1Y4 **Location:** Between Morris and South sts. **Historic**   L   D   ㊏

IL MERCATO RISTORANTE
Phone: 902/422-2866   26

Italian
$10-$24

AAA Inspector Notes: The colorful bistro, with its bustling atmosphere, prepares a fine selection of gourmet delights: pasta, fresh seafood and meat entrees, as well as thin-crust pizza. Save room for an excellent dessert from the showcase. **Bar:** full bar. **Address:** 5650 Spring Garden Rd B3J 3M7 **Location:** Between S Park St and Dresden Row. **Parking:** street only.

L   D   CALL ㊐M

JANE'S ON THE COMMON   Phone: 902/431-5683   10

Canadian
$11-$22

AAA Inspector Notes: This bustling little spot, opposite the park, serves wonderful chowders, soups and salads as well as specialty sandwiches and seafood. The atmosphere is unhurried and very friendly. **Bar:** full bar. **Address:** 2394 Robie St B3K 4M7 **Location:** At Cunard St; opposite Common. **Parking:** street only.   B   L   D

JUNGLE JIM'S   Phone: 902/450-5468

Canadian
$8-$19

AAA Inspector Notes: Guests can step into a tropical theme at the casual eatery, which employs a friendly staff and nurtures a bustling atmosphere. The menu lines up a wide variety of comfort foods, salads, chicken, beef, seafood and hot wings, all served in ample, flavorful portions. **Bar:** full bar. **Address:** 189 Chain Lake Dr B3S 1G9 **Location:** In Bayers Lake Business Park.   L   D

MCKELVIE'S DELISHES FISHES DISHES
Phone: 902/421-6161   4

Seafood
$13-$30

AAA Inspector Notes: Crab bisque, crunchy haddock and crispy crab cakes are representative of tastefully prepared menu choices. In a refurbished fire station, the restaurant bustles with activity. All desserts, including pleasing ice creams and sorbets, are homemade. **Bar:** full bar. **Reservations:** suggested. **Address:** 1680 Lower Water St B3J 2Y3 **Location:** Between Prince and Sackville sts. **Parking:** street only.   L   D

MEXICALI ROSA'S   Phone: 902/422-7672

Mexican
$10-$31

AAA Inspector Notes: The Mexican cantina makes an excellent choice for family-friendly fun. Old West paintings and murals add color to stucco walls and wooden beams, while a Tex-Mex menu provides a feast of favorites such as fajitas, burritos and some seafood items. Fried ice cream is a sweet treat. **Bar:** full bar. **Address:** 5472 Spring Garden Rd B3J 1H5 **Location:** At Dresden Rd; centre. **Parking:** on-site (fee).   L   D

ONYX   *Menu on AAA.com*   Phone: 902/428-5680   29

New World
$21-$39

AAA Inspector Notes: More than 150 wines and various special drinks quench parched palates at this chic, sophisticated wine and martini bar. The talented chef changes the two- and three-course prix fixe menus regularly, but remains steadfast in a focus on eye-catching presentation. The desserts should not be missed. **Bar:** full bar. **Reservations:** suggested. **Address:** 5680 Spring Garden Rd B3J 1H5 **Location:** At S Park St. **Parking:** street only.   D   CALL ㊐M

POGUE FADO' IRISH PUBLIC HOUSE
Phone: 902/429-6222   17

Irish
$10-$18

AAA Inspector Notes: Folks find a touch of the blarney in the upbeat Irish-themed pub. Traditional Irish fare and basic comfort foods pair with a good selection of imported and domestic draft beers. **Bar:** full bar. **Address:** 1581 Barrington St B3J 1Z7 **Location:** Between Blowers and Sackville sts. **Parking:** street only.

L   D   ㊏

(See map & index p. 155.)

THE PRESS GANG Phone: 902/423-8816

Seafood
$23-$39

AAA Inspector Notes: Candlelight enhances this distinctive setting-amid 250-year-old exposed stone walls, pillars and wooden beams. Although the menu centers on fresh seafood, it also lists organic meats, fine chowders and items from the raw oyster bar. **Bar:** full bar. **Reservations:** suggested. **Address:** 5218 Prince St B3J 3X4 **Location:** Corner of Prince and Argyle sts; centre. **Parking:** on-site (fee). D

RED STAG TAVERN Phone: 902/422-0275   14

Canadian
$9-$22

AAA Inspector Notes: Located next to Alexander Keith's Brewery, kilt clad servers happily serve your favorite brew in a classic pub setting. **Bar:** full bar. **Address:** 1496 Lower Water St B3J 1R9 **Location:** Centre; in Brewery Market. **Parking:** street only. L D

REDWOOD GRILL Phone: 902/446-4243 30

Canadian
$8-$22

AAA Inspector Notes: Booths and tables alike contribute to the modern, contemporary decor. In addition to comfort foods, such as burgers, pizza and fish and chips, the menu lists fresh seafood, steaks and creatively prepared pasta dishes. **Bar:** full bar. **Address:** 30 Fairfax Dr B3S 1P1 **Location:** Hwy 102 exit 2A; in Future Inns Halifax. B L D

RYAN DUFFY'S Phone: 902/421-1116   5

Steak
$12-$45

AAA Inspector Notes: An upscale yet comfortable decor and atmosphere is offered at this eatery, decorated in rich red and black with soft lighting. They offer a selection of fine in-house, dry-aged grade AAA beef and fresh seafood options. Pleasant competent service. **Bar:** full bar. **Address:** 1650 Bedford Row B3J 1T2 **Location:** Between Sackville and Prince sts; in Radisson Suite Hotel Halifax. **Parking:** on-site (fee). B L D

SALTY'S ON THE WATERFRONT Phone: 902/423-6818 3

Seafood
$13-$36

AAA Inspector Notes: Overlooking the harbor, the popular restaurant has a fine-dining space upstairs, a more casual, booth-filled area on the first floor and a spacious dining deck. Fresh-off-the-boat fish is prepared with quality ingredients and attractively presented. An irresistible array of homemade desserts tempts the sweet tooth. **Bar:** full bar. **Reservations:** suggested, for upstairs. **Address:** 1869 Upper Water St B3J 1S9 **Location:** On waterfront; in historic property. **Parking:** on-site (fee). L D

SMITTY'S Phone: 902/429-1148

Canadian
$7-$20

AAA Inspector Notes: The family-oriented restaurant satisfies patrons with its ever-popular all-day breakfast items, as well as tasty and wholesome soups and salads at lunchtime. A relaxed mood characterizes the dining space. **Bar:** full bar. **Address:** 1490 Martello St B3H 4K8 **Location:** Between Spring Garden Rd and College St. **Parking:** on-site (fee). B L D

SUSHI NAMI ROYALE Phone: 902/457-3874   27

Japanese
$10-$21

AAA Inspector Notes: A modern decor can be found here with an open theme great for viewing the chefs in action. The menu selection is vast with soups, salads, endless appetizers and combination plates of sushi, sashimi, teriyaki and even sushi pizza. Service is friendly and relaxed. **Bar:** full bar. **Address:** 278 Lacewood Dr B3M 3N8 **Location:** Corner of Dunbar St; at Clayton Park. L D

SUSHI NAMI ROYALE Phone: 902/422-9020 23

Japanese
$10-$21

AAA Inspector Notes: A modern decor can be found here with an open theme great for viewing the chefs in action. The menu selection is vast with soups, salads, endless appetizers and combination plates of sushi, sashimi, teriyaki and even sushi pizza. Service is friendly and relaxed. **Bar:** full bar. **Address:** 1535 Dresden Row B3J 3T1 **Location:** Corner of Artillery Pl. **Parking:** on-site (fee). L D

SWISS CHALET Phone: 902/454-4226

Chicken
$6-$16

AAA Inspector Notes: The popular restaurant is known for its rotisserie chicken and ribs and the tangy Chalet sauce that gives food its special zip. Diners munch on a half or quarter chicken with sides such as steamed vegetables, fries, baked potatoes and salads. Lunch guests often go for the great soup and sandwich combination. Take-out and delivery service are popular options. **Bar:** full bar. **Address:** 3462 Kempt Rd B3K 4X7 **Location:** At Young St. L D

VICTORY ARMS PUB
Menu on AAA.com Phone: 902/420-9781 28

American
$9-$25

AAA Inspector Notes: The delightful English-style pub nurtures a relaxing atmosphere. Guests can couple well-prepared, traditional pub entrees, a quality steak or fresh seafood with a favorite beverage for a meal that won't disappoint. **Bar:** full bar. **Location:** Corner of Park St and Spring Garden Rd; centre; in The Lord Nelson Hotel & Suites. **Parking:** on-site (fee). B L D

WATERFRONT WAREHOUSE RESTAURANT & TUG'S PUB Phone: 902/425-7610 12

Canadian
$9-$24

AAA Inspector Notes: A pleasant nautical theme weaves through the large, converted warehouse, boat shed and seasonal patio. Ample portions of a wide variety of foods are served with aromatic, warm bread. **Bar:** full bar. **Address:** 1549 Lower Water St B3J 1S2 **Location:** At Salter St. **Parking:** on-site (fee). L D AC

THE WOODEN MONKEY Phone: 902/444-3844 9

Canadian
$10-$22

AAA Inspector Notes: Step in to a relaxing atmosphere in this two-story restaurant which focuses on healthy dining for all tastes. They offer environmentally friendly produce, meats and seafood with a selection of gluten-free and vegetarian dishes, pizza, soups and salads. Enjoy an excellent variety of beer on tap, fine wines by the bottle or glass and decadent desserts including the signature dessert chocolate tofu pie. **Bar:** full bar. **Address:** 1707 Grafton St B3J 3N9 **Location:** Corner of Prince St. **Parking:** on-site (fee). L D

HANTSPORT (C-3) pop. 1,191

Although one of Canada's smallest towns when it was incorporated in 1895, Hantsport became an important shipbuilding port. The prosperity of that era is evident today in the town's many stately Victorian homes. The mighty Bay of Fundy tides can be seen at Hantsport's wharf or at nearby Fundy Centennial Park.

Hantsport Visitor Information Centre: 2 Willow St., Hantsport, NS, Canada B0P 1P0. **Phone:** (902) 684-9302.

CHURCHILL HOUSE AND THE MARINE MEMORIAL ROOM is on Main St. This 1860 Victorian house belonged to a prominent shipbuilding family. Restored rooms feature hand-painted wallcoverings, imported crystal chandeliers and original woodwork. Shipyard artifacts and models of locally built ships are displayed throughout the house. **Time:** Allow 30 minutes minimum. **Hours:** Tues.-Sat. 9-4, July-Aug. **Cost:** Donations. **Phone:** (902) 684-9302, or (902) 684-3200 in the off-season.

HUBBARDS

DAUPHINEE INN   **Phone:** 902/857-1790

Country Inn
$99-$195

Address: 167 Shore Club Rd B0J 1T0 **Location:** Rt 103 exit 6, 1.4 mi (2.4 km) e on Rt 3, then 0.5 mi (0.8 km) s. Located in a quiet area. **Facility:** At this attractive inn adjacent to a marina on Hubbards Cove, guests enjoy views of the harbor while relaxing on a large sun deck. 6 units. 3 stories (no elevator), interior corridors. **Terms:** open 6/1-10/24, office hours 8 am-10 pm, check-in 4 pm, cancellation fee imposed. **Dining:** restaurant, see separate listing. **Activities:** fishing, bicycles. *Fee:* boat dock.

WHERE TO EAT

DAUPHINEE INN DINING ROOM   **Phone:** 902/857-1790

American
$17-$32

AAA Inspector Notes: A picturesque setting overlooking Hubbards Cove. The Dauphinee offers fine dining on upper floor with focus on fresh seafood. A pub with deck on lower floor offers comfort foods. **Bar:** full bar. **Address:** 167 Shore Club Rd B0J 1T0 **Location:** Rt 103 exit 6, 1.4 mi (2.4 km) e on Rt 3, then 0.5 mi (0.8 km) s; in Dauphinee Inn. [D]

SHORE CLUB LOBSTER SUPPERS   **Phone:** 902/857-9555

Seafood
$25-$38

AAA Inspector Notes: In a former dance hall, the spacious restaurant offers an all-you-can-eat self-serve salad and mussel bar, as well as a choice of lobster or beef dinner and dessert. **Bar:** full bar. **Reservations:** suggested. **Address:** 250 Shore Club Rd B0J 1T0 **Location:** Rt 103 exit 6, 1.4 mi (2.4 km) e on Rt 3, then 0.6 mi (1 km) s. [D]

INGONISH (A-6)

The Portuguese settled around Ingonish in the 1520s, followed by the French. During most of the 17th century Port d'Orleans, as Ingonish was known, was a thriving French center, second only to Louisbourg. It was abandoned after Louisbourg was destroyed by the British.

Ingonish is a year-round resort town offering coastal scenery. Rocky parapets punctuate the shore between numerous coves. A scenic stretch of the Cabot Trail circles the northern peninsula of Cape Breton Island. Just south at Ingonish Beach is the eastern entrance to Cape Breton Highlands National Park of Canada *(see place listing p. 137).*

INGONISH BEACH

KELTIC LODGE RESORT & SPA   **Phone:** (902)285-2880

Hotel
$155-$345

Address: Middle Head Peninsula B0C 1L0 **Location:** In Cape Breton Highlands National Park; off Cabot Tr. Located in a quiet area. **Facility:** 105 units, some two bedrooms and cottages. 1-3 stories (no elevator), interior/exterior corridors. **Terms:** open 6/1-10/21, 3 day cancellation notice-fee imposed. **Dining:** Purple Thistle Dining Room, see separate listing, entertainment. **Pool(s):** heated outdoor. **Activities:** beach access, hiking trails, game room, exercise room, spa. *Fee:* golf-18 holes, bicycles. **Guest Services:** valet laundry. **Free Special Amenities:** full breakfast and high-speed Internet.

LANTERN HILL & HOLLOW   **Phone:** 902/285-2010

Cottage
$175-$260

Address: 36845 Cabot Tr B0C 1L0 **Location:** Oceanfront. 2 mi (4.2 km) n of park gate. **Facility:** These lovely, large cottages (all with decks and BBQs) and three tastefully decorated guest rooms occupy a scenic setting bordering a sandy beach. 9 units, some cottages. 1-2 stories (no elevator), interior/exterior corridors. **Terms:** open 6/1-10/15 & 5/25-5/31, office hours 8 am-9 pm, 3 day cancellation notice. **Activities:** limited beach access.

WHERE TO EAT

MAIN STREET RESTAURANT & BAKERY   **Phone:** 902/285-2225

American
$7-$23

AAA Inspector Notes: This restaurant/bakery offers a full menu for breakfast, lunch and dinner. Guests will find classic sandwiches, salads, a variety of pastas and entrees and, of course, lobster. Dinner service includes a selection of enticing daily specials. Since the spot has its own bakery, diners can count on some good, homemade sweets as well. If the weather cooperates, diners can opt for a seat on the recently expanded patio. **Bar:** full bar. **Address:** 37764 Cabot Tr B0C 1L0 **Location:** 0.6 mi (1 km) s of park gate. [B] [L] [D]

PURPLE THISTLE DINING ROOM   **Phone:** 902/285-2880

American
$20-$42

AAA Inspector Notes: This elegant, spacious dining room offers lovely views of the ocean and hills and may bring back memories of a bygone era to some diners. The menu specializes in the bountiful, fresh local seafood but a selection of meat dishes are an option. Complete the experience with one of the tantalizing homemade desserts. The staff provides friendly, attentive service. Semi-formal attire. **Bar:** full bar. **Reservations:** suggested. **Address:** Middle Head Peninsula B0C 1L0 **Location:** In Cape Breton Highlands National Park; off Cabot Tr; in Keltic Lodge Resort & Spa. [B] [D] CALL

INGONISH FERRY

THE CASTLE ROCK COUNTRY INN   **Phone:** 902/285-2700

[fyi] Not evaluated. **Address:** 39339 Cabot Tr B0C 1L0 **Location:** Northern slope of Cape Smokey Mountain. Facilities, services, and decor characterize a mid-scale property.

INVERNESS (B-5) pop. 1,464

Settled by immigrants from Invernesshire, Scotland, Inverness has been a coal-mining center since 1865. Most of the residents trace their lineage to the town's original Scottish Highlanders. Several scenic drives, including Hwy. 19 along Cape Breton Island's western shore, are accessible.

INVERNESS MINERS MUSEUM is at 62 Lower Railway St. Exhibits and artifacts in eight rooms focus on the city's pioneering, coal mining and railroad history. An extensive fossil collection and coal pit model also are featured. **Time:** Allow 30 minutes minimum. **Hours:** Daily 9-6, mid-June to mid-Oct.; by appointment rest of year. **Cost:** $5; $3 (ages 60+ and students with ID); free (ages 0-12). Cash only. **Phone:** (902) 258-3822 or (902) 258-3000.

IONA (B-5)

HIGHLAND VILLAGE MUSEUM is at 4119 Hwy. 223. This 17-hectare (43-acre) living-history center depicts Nova Scotia's Scottish Gaelic heritage from the late 18th through early 20th centuries. Gaelic-speaking costumed interpreters present craft and cultural demonstrations including fiddle music and Gaelic song. They also staff 11 buildings, including an 1830s log house and barn, an 1874 church, a 1900s blacksmith shop, a one-room schoolhouse, and a general store stocked with goods. Rare barnyard animals roam the grounds. A visitor center contains an orientation video and a genealogy room.

The museum's hillside location provides a beautiful view of the Bras d'Or Lakes. Living history programs for children allow them to dress in pioneer clothes and pretend to be a young Gael. Workshops and holiday programs are presented throughout the year.

Note: The tour includes walking up a hill, on stairs and on gravel paths. Comfortable walking shoes are recommended. **Time:** Allow 1 hour minimum. **Hours:** Village daily 9:30-5:30, June 1 to mid-Oct. Visitor center daily 9:30-5:30, June 1 to mid-Oct.; Mon-Fri 9-5, rest of year. Genealogy assistance by appointment. **Cost:** $9; $7 (ages 65+); $4 (ages 6-17); $22 (family, two adults and two children). **Phone:** (902) 725-2272 or (866) 442-3542.

ISLE MADAME (C-6)

Lying off the southern coast of Cape Breton Island, Isle Madame is across the Lennox Passage Bridge at the junction of hwys. 104 and 320. Named after the queen of France by Acadian settlers after the fall of Louisbourg in 1758, this 44-square-kilometre (17-sq.-mi.) island has beaches, rocky coves, picnic areas and picturesque fishing villages.

The island village of Arichat is one of the oldest communities in Nova Scotia. Highlights in Arichat include the LeNoir Forge Museum, a restored French stone blacksmith shop; phone (902) 226-9364.

JEDDORE OYSTER POND (D-4)

Jeddore Oyster Pond is part of a community of quiet hamlets on Nova Scotia's eastern shore. A large lumber industry, based chiefly on pulpwood, once supported the Jeddore district.

FISHERMAN'S LIFE MUSEUM is at 58 Navy Pool Loop Rd. The coastal life of the early 1900s is recreated in the house where Ervin and Ethelda Myers and their 13 daughters once lived. The museum includes a vegetable garden, a barn with livestock, a chicken coop, a woodshed, a dairy, and a fish shed at the wharf. Cooking and other domestic chores of the era are demonstrated.

Tours: Guided tours are available. **Time:** Allow 30 minutes minimum. **Hours:** Daily 10-5, June 1-Oct. 15. **Cost:** $3.60; $2.55 (ages 6-17 and 65+); $7.95 (family, two adults and children). **Phone:** (902) 889-2053 June 1-Oct. 15, or (902) 424-7398 rest of year.

JOGGINS (B-2)

Joggins is known for its fossil fields and 30-metre-high (100-ft.) cliffs where fossilized trees and plants are visible. Coal may have been mined in the area as early as 1650. Commercial mining began in 1854 with construction of a loading wharf and a narrow-gauge railway. The Joggins Mine closed in 1927, and the once thriving town would never recover from a catastrophic fire a year later.

JOGGINS FOSSIL CLIFFS is at 100 Main St. The fossils embedded in the 15 kilometres (9 mi.) of coastal cliffs along the Bay of Fundy contain an important record of life during the Coal Age 300 million years ago. A sizable collection of carboniferous fossils found at this UNESCO World Heritage Site includes plants and rare insects as well as reptile and amphibian footprints. The Joggins Fossil Centre, on the site of an old coal mine overlooking the cliffs, is the repository for these specimens.

Time: Allow 30 minutes minimum. **Hours:** Daily 9:30-5:30, Apr.-Oct.; by appointment rest of year. **Cost:** $8; $6 (ages 5-18, ages 65+ and students with ID); $20 (family of three); $25 (family of four or five). **Phone:** (902) 251-2727 or (888) 932-9766.

KEJIMKUJIK NATIONAL PARK AND NATIONAL HISTORIC SITE OF CANADA (D-1)

Elevations in the park range from 91 metres (300 ft.) at Lake George to 168 metres (550 ft.) near Fire Tower. Refer to CAA/AAA maps for additional elevation information.

Off Hwy. 8 at Maitland Bridge, Kejimkujik (ke-jim-KOO-jik) National Park and National Historic Site encompasses 381 square kilometres (147 sq. mi.) in the southwestern region of Nova Scotia. The park's gently rolling landscape is broken by numerous lakes connected by rivers. Kejimkujik Lake, the park's namesake and largest lake, has many hidden coves and islands. Hundreds of years before the arrival of the first Europeans in Canada, this lake and its surroundings were the home of nomadic Mi'kmaq people.

Kejimkujik Drive (Hwy. 8) follows a series of rivers and lakes which the Mi'kmaq, traveling in canoes, used as a "highway" for more than 1,000 years. Kejimkujik National Park is at the center of the drive, with Annapolis Royal and Liverpool at opposite ends. The route meanders past forested hills, sawmills and Christmas tree plantations.

A mixture of hardwoods and conifers covers low oval-shaped hills that were carved long ago by glaciers. Wildlife includes black bears, white-tailed deer, barred owls, pileated woodpeckers, beavers, bobcats and such water birds as the common loon. A few rare bird species, such as the scarlet tanager and great crested flycatcher, also live in the park's woods. Its wetlands have the largest population of reptiles and amphibians in the Atlantic Provinces.

Canoeing along the connected waterways of the park is one of the best ways to explore its natural beauty. Self-guiding hiking trails are another means for exploration; interpretive signs along the way explain the trail's features. Fall is an especially good time to explore, as the woodlands transform into their autumn colors.

Kejimkujik Seaside is the portion of the park on the wild and isolated stretch of coastline along Nova Scotia's Atlantic shore. Off Hwy. 103, 25 kilometres (16 mi.) southwest of Liverpool, this part of the park features glacier-carved headlands, expansive white beaches and rocky coves. The area also is known for its abundant wildlife. Picnicking is available at the St. Catherines River entrance, an area that also features viewing platforms and two nature trails with interpretive signs. Seals and shore birds are plentiful. Separate admission fees apply.

General Information and Activities

The park is open all year. Full services are available mid-June through Labour Day. A summer interpretive program includes exhibits, demonstrations, outdoor theater presentations and guided nature hikes. Back-country campsites are available along the park's canoe routes and hiking trails; for detailed camping information contact the park's visitor center.

Summer brings a wide range of programs and activities. A supervised swimming beach is at Merrymakedge. Canoes, kayaks, rowboats, paddleboats and bicycles can be rented daily at Jakes Landing mid-May to mid-October. Winter activities include cross-country skiing, winter camping and snowshoeing. Picnic lunches can be enjoyed within the comfort of one of the park's warm-up shelters.

The visitor center is open daily 8:30-8, mid-June through Labour Day; daily 8:30-4:30, Jan. 1 to mid-June and day after Labour Day-Oct. 31; Mon.-Fri. 8:30-4:30, rest of year. Service areas are outside the park boundaries. *See Recreation Chart.*

ADMISSION to the park mid-May through Oct. 31 is $5.80; $4.90 (ages 65+); $2.90 (ages 6-16); $14.70

(family). Free rest of year. Admission to Kejimkujik Seaside mid-June to mid-Oct. $3.90; $3.40 (ages 65+); $1.90 (ages 6-16); $9.80 (family). Free rest of year. **Cards:** AX, MC, VI.

PETS are permitted in the park, but they must remain on a leash at all times and are not permitted on the beaches.

ADDRESS inquiries to the Superintendent, Kejimkujik National Park and National Historic Site of Canada, P.O. Box 236, Maitland Bridge, NS, Canada B0T 1B0. Phone (902) 682-2772.

KEMPT

THE WHITMAN INN	Phone: (902)682-2226

Country Inn
$69-$125

Address: 12389 Hwy 8 B0T 1B0 **Location:** On Rt 8, 2.4 mi (4 km) s of Kejimkujik National Park. Located in a quiet secluded area. **Facility:** 9 units, some two bedrooms and kitchens. 2 stories (no elevator), interior corridors. **Terms:** office hours 8 am-10 pm, cancellation fee imposed. **Pool(s):** heated indoor. **Activities:** game room.

KEMPTVILLE

TROUT POINT LODGE	Phone: 902/761-2142

Country Inn
Rates not provided

Address: 189 Trout Point Rd B0W 1Y0 **Location:** 6.6 mi (11 km) e on Rt 203, 2.1 mi (3.5 km) n on gravel entry road. **Facility:** Built of logs and granite, the lodge is on 200 acres at Trout Point, which is adjacent to a large wilderness area bordered by a scenic river system. 12 units, some cottages. 3 stories (no elevator), exterior corridors. **Terms:** seasonal, office hours 8 am-11 pm. **Activities:** sauna, whirlpool, canoeing, bicycles, hiking trails. *Fee:* massage.

KENTVILLE (C-2) pop. 5,815
• Hotels p. 174 • Restaurants p. 174

Kentville elected its first female mayor in 1946 at a time when not all women in Canada had the right to vote. Gladys Porter would go on to become the first woman elected to the Nova Scotia Legislative Assembly.

KINGS COUNTY MUSEUM is at 37 Cornwallis St. The 1903-80 Kings County courthouse now serves as a resource center for the cultural and natural history of Kings County. The museum, which features a national commemorative exhibit about the New England planters, also contains county genealogical information. **Hours:** Mon.-Sat. 9-4, July-Aug.; Mon.-Fri. 9-4, mid-Mar. through June 30 and Sept. 1 to mid-Dec. **Cost:** Donations. Archives $3. **Phone:** (902) 678-6237.

ALLEN'S MOTEL

Phone: 902/678-2683

Motel

$70-$150

Address: 384 Park St B4N 1M9 **Location:** Hwy 101 exit 14, 1.8 mi (3 km) e on Rt 1. **Facility:** 12 units, some kitchens and cottages. 2 stories (no elevator), exterior corridors. **Terms:** open 6/1-12/1 & 4/1-5/31, office hours 7:30 am-10 pm. **Amenities:** high-speed Internet. **Guest Services:** coin laundry. **Free Special Amenities:** local telephone calls and high-speed Internet. [SAVE] [X] [▣] / SOME UNITS 🛏 🖼

SUN VALLEY MOTEL

Phone: 902/678-7368

Motel

Rates not provided

Address: 843 Park St B4N 3V7 **Location:** Hwy 101 exit 14, 0.5 mi (0.8 km) e on Rt 1. **Facility:** 13 units, some efficiencies. 1 story, exterior corridors. **Terms:** office hours 7:30 am-10:30 pm. **Activities:** playground.

📶 [🍴] [☎] 🛏 🖼 [▣] / SOME UNITS FEE 🐾

WHERE TO EAT

KAI-WING RESTAURANT

Phone: 902/679-6599

Chinese

$8-$18

AAA Inspector Notes: On the edge of town in a commercial area bordering the highway, the comfortable restaurant offers a wide variety of well-prepared Oriental and Canadian entrees. All dishes are fresh and prepared to order, and the service is casual, friendly and attentive. **Bar:** full bar. **Address:** 7299 Hwy 1 B4R 1B9 **Location:** Hwy 101 exit 14, just e. [L] [D]

KING'S ARMS PUB

Phone: 902/678-0066

Canadian

$8-$21

AAA Inspector Notes: In the heart of town, the pleasant English-style pub has thick, solid-wood tables and a large brick fireplace to enhance its Old World feel. The menu centers on fresh seafood and meat entrees, in addition to pub staples served in hearty portions. The lovely patio invites seasonal relaxation. **Bar:** full bar. **Address:** 390 Main St B4N 1K5 **Location:** Centre. **Parking:** street only. [L] [D]

PADDY'S BREWPUB & ROSIE'S RESTAURANT

Phone: 902/678-3199

Canadian

$7-$20

AAA Inspector Notes: Patrons can choose either the pub section or the restaurant for well-prepared seafood and steaks, as well as some traditional pub favorites and daily specials. **Bar:** full bar. **Address:** 42 Aberdeen St B4N 1M9 **Location:** At Webster St; centre. **Parking:** street only. [L] [D]

KINGSTON

BEST WESTERN AURORA INN

Phone: (902)765-3306

Hotel

$135-$140

AAA Benefit: Members save up to 20%, plus 10% bonus points with Best Western Rewards®.

Address: 831 Main St B0P 1R0 **Location:** Hwy 101 exit 17 to Rt 1, follow signs. **Facility:** 23 units, some two bedrooms. 1 story, exterior corridors. **Guest Services:** coin laundry. **Free Special Amenities:** expanded continental breakfast and newspaper.

[SAVE] [🍴] [🛗] [📶] [X] [▣] / SOME UNITS FEE [🐾] 🛏 🖼

LaHAVE (D-2)

Artists have long been drawn to the romantic coastal scenery around LaHave, one of the oldest settlements in Canada. Arriving in 1604, Pierre de Monts named the site Cap de la Havre, meaning "the harbor."

FORT POINT MUSEUM is at 100 Fort Point Rd. (Hwy. 331). A lighthouse contains the museum for Fort Sainte-Marie-de-Grâce National Historic Site, which commemorates both the first landing of permanent settlers under Issac de Razilly, lieutenant general of Acadia, and the first capital of New France in Acadia.

Historical artifacts document those early settlements and the subsequent history of the area. The lighthouse offers majestic views of the surrounding bays and countryside. **Time:** Allow 1 hour minimum. **Hours:** Daily 10-5, June 1-Labour Day; by appointment rest of year. **Cost:** Donations. **Phone:** (902) 688-1632. 🎫

LaHAVE ISLANDS HERITAGE MARINE MUSEUM is off Hwy. 331 at Crescent Beach to 100 LaHave Islands Rd. The former LaHave Islands United Church displays fishing memorabilia and relics illustrating local history back to the first settlers' arrival in the 1780s. Visitors can see a more-than-60-year-old, 8-metre (27-ft.) Bush Island boat that has been fully restored. **Time:** Allow 1 hour minimum. **Hours:** Daily 10-5, June 1-Labour Day; by appointment rest of year. **Cost:** Donations. **Phone:** (902) 688-2973 or (902) 688-2170.

LAKE CHARLOTTE (D-4)

MEMORY LANE HERITAGE VILLAGE is off Hwy. 7 following signs to 5435 Clam Harbour Rd. Costumed interpreters offer guided tours of this village, re-creating the sights and sounds of a typical Eastern Shore community from the 1940-50s era. Buildings include a restored store, church, school, icehouse, Esso garage and homestead, which are furnished in period detail.

Time: Allow 2 hours minimum. **Hours:** Daily 11-4, June 15-Sept. 15; by appointment rest of year. **Cost:** $6; $4 (ages 12-17, ages 60+ and students with ID); $16 (family, two adults and three children). **Phone:** (902) 845-1937, or (877) 287-0697 in Canada. 🍴

LISCOMB

LISCOMBE LODGE RESORT & CONFERENCE CENTRE
Phone: (902)779-2307

▼▼ ▼▼
Resort Hotel
$139-$209

Address: 2884 Hwy 7 (RR 1) B0J 2A0 **Location:** On Hwy 7. **Facility:** This picturesque lodge, situated in a wooded area overlooking the river, offers a variety of cottages and lodge rooms. 68 units, some houses. 1-2 stories (no elevator), interior/exterior corridors. **Terms:** open 6/1-10/15 & 5/21-5/31, 3 day cancellation notice-fee imposed. **Dining:** Riverside Dining Room, see separate listing. **Pool(s):** heated indoor. **Activities:** sauna, whirlpools, canoeing, paddleboats, tennis court, recreation programs in summer, bicycles, playground, horseshoes, shuffleboard, exercise room. *Fee:* boat dock, game room. **Guest Services:** coin laundry. **Free Special Amenities:** high-speed Internet.

SAVE 🛎 🍽 Ⓨ CALL 🄼 🛶 ✕ 📺 ▢
/ SOME UNITS 🐾 🦮 🦽 🛗

WHERE TO EAT

RIVERSIDE DINING ROOM   **Phone:** 902/779-2307

▼▼▼▼
American
$10-$30

AAA Inspector Notes: Pleasant location bordering the Liscomb River, the restaurant features a charming and rustic atmosphere. The menu offers a wide range of seafood and meat options, including planked salmon and fine desserts. **Bar:** full bar. **Reservations:** suggested. **Address:** 2884 Hwy 7 (RR 1) B0J 2A0 **Location:** On Hwy 7; in Liscombe Lodge Resort & Conference Centre.

Ⓑ Ⓛ Ⓓ CALL 🄼 🦽

LITTLE BROOK

CHATEAU D'LA BAIE B & B   **Phone:** 902/769-3113

▼▼▼▼
Bed & Breakfast
$95-$129

Address: 959 Rt 1 B0W 1Z0 **Location:** Oceanfront. Hwy 101 exit 29 to Rt 1. **Facility:** The beautiful 1920s home is nestled on the shore of St. Mary's Bay; spacious rooms and public areas are tastefully furnished with period antiques. 7 units. 2 stories (no elevator), interior corridors. **Terms:** cancellation fee imposed. 📶 / SOME UNITS 🦽

LIVERPOOL (D-2) pop. 2,759
• Hotels p. 176 • Restaurants p. 177

Like its English namesake, Liverpool is at the mouth of the Mersey River. Samuel de Champlain landed at the site in 1604, but it was not until 1759 that 70 families from Connecticut established a town.

Fort Point, at Fort Point Lighthouse Park, was built in the 1700s. One of its cairns commemorates the arrival of Champlain while another honors Liverpool's privateers. Visitors can climb the stairs of the park's 1855 lighthouse, which also houses an interpretive center.

Region of Queens Department of Economic Development: P.O. Box 1264, Liverpool, NS, Canada B0T 1K0. **Phone:** (902) 354-5741 or (800) 655-5741.

SAVE **HANK SNOW HOME TOWN MUSEUM** is off Hwy. 103 exit 19 to 148 Bristol Ave. A large collection of personal memorabilia belonged to country music legend Hank Snow, who was born in nearby Brooklyn. Items on display include awards, photographs, clothing and Snow's 1947 Cadillac convertible. The center also is home to the Nova Scotia Country Music Hall of Fame. A country music library and archives are available. **Time:** Allow 1 hour minimum. **Hours:** Mon.-Sat. 9-5, Sun. noon-5, mid-May to mid-Oct.; Mon.-Fri. 9-5, rest of year. **Cost:** $5; $4 (ages 55+); free (ages 0-12). **Phone:** (902) 354-4675 or (888) 450-5525.

PERKINS HOUSE MUSEUM is at 105 Main St. This 1766 Connecticut-style house was built by Col. Simeon Perkins, noted Nova Scotian merchant, colonel, judge, legislator and diarist. **Time:** Allow 30 minutes minimum. **Hours:** Mon.-Sat. 9:30-5:30, Sun. 1-5:30, June 1-Oct. 15. **Cost:** $4 (includes admission to the Queens County Museum and Exhibit Centre); free (ages 0-5); $9 (family, two adults and two children). **Phone:** (902) 354-4058.

QUEENS COUNTY MUSEUM AND EXHIBIT CENTRE is next to the Perkins House Museum at 109 Main St. Artifacts, photographs and documents relate the history of Queens County. Exhibits highlight the Mi'kmaq Indians, privateers and area forests. Col. Simeon Perkins' original diary gives an account of the colonial town between 1766 and the War of 1812. The Thomas Raddall Research Centre contains a library and genealogical data.

Time: Allow 30 minutes minimum. **Hours:** Mon.-Sat. 9:30-noon and 1-5:30, Sun. 1-5:30, June 1-Oct. 15; Mon.-Sat. 9-noon and 1-5, rest of year. **Cost:** $4 (includes admission to Perkins House Museum); $9 (family, two adults and two children). **Phone:** (902) 354-4058.

ROSSIGNOL CULTURAL CENTRE is at 205 Church St. This 2.2-square metre (24,000-sq. ft.) center features a variety of museums, galleries, libraries and wildlife exhibits and a cultural village. Far-ranging collections include folk art, antique apothecary items, outhouses, hunting and fishing artifacts, scrimshaw, bronzes, historic photographs and mounted animals from around the world.

Time: Allow 1 hour minimum. **Hours:** Mon.-Sat. 10-5:30, mid-May to mid-Oct. (also Sun. noon-5:30, July-Aug.). **Cost:** $5 (includes admission to Sherman Hines Museum of Photography); $4 (ages 65+); $3 (ages 6-18). **Phone:** (902) 354-3067.

SHERMAN HINES MUSEUM OF PHOTOGRAPHY is at 219 Main St. The 1902 town hall houses an extensive collection of antique stereoscopes, tripods, picture albums, cameras and other vintage paraphernalia. The museum also features galleries of contemporary photography, photographic fine arts and holograms. A photography research library is available.

Time: Allow 1 hour minimum. **Hours:** Mon.-Sat. 10-5:30, May 15-Oct. 15. (also Sun. noon-5:30, July-Aug.). **Cost:** $5 (includes admission to Rossignol Cultural Centre); $4 (ages 65+ and students with ID). **Phone:** (902) 354-2667.

BEST WESTERN PLUS LIVERPOOL HOTEL & CONFERENCE CENTRE   Phone: (902)354-2377

Hotel

$130-$140

AAA Benefit: Members save up to 20%, plus 10% bonus points with Best Western Rewards®.

Address: 63 Queens Place Dr B0T 1K0 **Location:** Hwy 103 exit 19, just e. **Facility:** 65 units. 3 stories, interior corridors. **Amenities:** high-speed Internet. **Pool(s):** heated indoor. **Activities:** exercise room. **Guest Services:** coin laundry. **Free Special Amenities: full breakfast and high-speed Internet.** (See ad this page.)

SAVE ECO (TI) (Y) CALL (M) (BIZ) (wifi) (X) (icons) / SOME UNITS FEE (icons)

LANE'S PRIVATEER INN   Phone: 902/354-3456

Hotel

$95-$142 6/1-10/31
$85-$120 11/1-5/31

Address: 27 Bristol Ave B0T 1K0 **Location:** Waterfront. Hwy 103 exit 19, 1.2 mi (2 km) se on Rt 8 and 3. **Facility:** 27 units. 3 stories (no elevator), interior/exterior corridors. **Terms:** cancellation fee imposed. **Dining:** restaurant, see separate listing. **Free Special Amenities: full breakfast and high-speed Internet.**

SAVE (TI) (Y) (wifi) (X) / SOME UNITS (icons)

▼ See AAA listing this page ▼

Create complete trip routings and custom maps
with the TripTik® Travel Planner on AAA.com or CAA.ca

GOLDEN POND RESTAURANT   Phone: 902/354-5186

Chinese
$7-$18

AAA Inspector Notes: Offering a wide variety of Chinese and Canadian dishes, this spacious restaurant overlooks the Mersey River. Patrons may enjoy patio dining in season. **Bar:** full bar. **Address:** 73 Henry Hensey Dr B0T 1K0 **Location:** Just w of Market St. ⓁⒹ

LANE'S PRIVATEER RESTAURANT
    Phone: 902/354-3456

Canadian
$10-$24

AAA Inspector Notes: This quaint restaurant, decorated with local artwork, is located in the original section of an inn dating back to 1798. The menu offers a nice selection of fresh seafood, steak and daily specials. Seasonal patio dining overlooking the Mersey River also is an option. **Bar:** full bar. **Address:** 27 Bristol Ave B0T 1K0 **Location:** Centre; in Lane's Privateer Inn.
ⒷⓁⒹ

LORNEVILLE

AMHERST SHORE COUNTRY INN
    Phone: (902)661-4800

Country Inn
$109-$199 6/1-10/31
$99-$169 12/1-5/31

Address: RR 2, 5091 Rt 366 B4H 3X9 **Location:** Oceanfront. On Rt 366; centre. Located in a quiet rural area. **Facility:** Gas fireplaces warm the varied rooms and duplex suites at this country inn, which overlooks Northumberland Strait; open weekends only 12/4-4/30. 8 units. 2 stories (no elevator), interior/exterior corridors. **Terms:** open 6/1-10/31 & 12/1-5/31, office hours 9 am-10:30 pm, 7 day cancellation notice-fee imposed. **Activities:** limited beach access, hiking trails.
(See ad this page.)

/ SOME UNITS 🍽️ 📺

▼ See AAA listing this page ▼

LOUISBOURG (B-6)

The first French settlers arrived in Louisbourg Harbour in 1713. Seventeen years later the most formidable French military establishment on the Atlantic was under construction on the southwestern arm of the harbor. The fortress town, surrounded by a masonry and packed-earth wall almost 3.2 kilometres (2 mi.) long, served until 1758 as the governmental, commercial and military center of the French colony that included Cape Breton and Prince Edward islands.

With the development of the coal-mining industry on Cape Breton Island during the 19th century, Louisbourg took on a new role as a shipping center, connected to numerous coal mines by a network of small railroads. Fishing and tourism fuel Louisbourg's economy. The picturesque Havenside district and the town's many wharves, sailing vessels and shore facilities provide an excellent perspective of Louisbourg's fishing industry.

Near the harbor are the ruins of one of the oldest lighthouses in North America. Built 1730-33 by order of Louis XV, the Louisbourg Lighthouse was damaged by fire during the British siege of Louisbourg in 1758. A small exhibit pavilion marks the site. Nightly performances of Cape Breton music, drama, dance and comedy are presented mid-June through October at the Louisbourg Playhouse; phone (902) 733-2996 or (888) 733-2787.

 FORTRESS OF LOUISBOURG NATIONAL HISTORIC SITE OF CANADA—see place listing p. 147.

SYDNEY AND LOUISBURG RAILWAY MUSEUM is at 7336 Main St. This restored 1895 railway station contains the stationmaster's office and several exhibit rooms with displays and models devoted to the history of railway technology and marine shipping. Period coach cars, a freight car, a tanker and a caboose are adjacent to the museum.

A working model of the S & L Railway main line also is displayed in the original 1895 freight shed. A tourist information office is on the premises. **Hours:** Daily 9-6, July-Aug.; 9-5 in June and Sept. **Cost:** Donations. **Phone:** (902) 733-2720.

CRANBERRY COVE INN   Phone: 902/733-2171

Historic Bed & Breakfast
$105-$160

Address: 12 Wolfe St B1C 2J2 **Location:** Centre. Located in a residential area near fountain. **Facility:** Each guest room at this bright pink turn-of-the-20th-century home has a distinctive theme; four have fireplaces. 7 units. 3 stories (no elevator), interior corridors. **Terms:** open 6/1-10/31, office hours 8 am-10 pm, 3 day cancellation notice-fee imposed.

LOUISBOURG HARBOUR INN   Phone: (902)733-3222

Historic Bed & Breakfast
$110-$180

Address: 9 Lower Warren St B1C 1G6 **Location:** Centre. **Facility:** This century-old converted sea captain's house has nicely-appointed rooms, most of which offer an ocean view. 8 units. 3 stories (no elevator), interior corridors. **Terms:** open 6/7-10/15, office hours 8 am-8 pm, 3 day cancellation notice.

POINT OF VIEW SUITES & RV PARK LTD   Phone: 902/733-2080

Motel
Rates not provided

Address: 15 Commercial St Ext B1C 2J4 **Location:** Waterfront. 0.6 mi (1 km) e on Rt 22. Located in campground towards the Fortress. **Facility:** 19 units, some two bedrooms and kitchens. 2 stories (no elevator), exterior corridors. **Terms:** seasonal, office hours 8 am-9 pm. **Activities:** fishing. **Guest Services:** coin laundry.

WHERE TO EAT

LOBSTER KETTLE RESTAURANT   Phone: 902/733-2723

Seafood
$9-$25

AAA Inspector Notes: A popular spot with tourists, the harborside restaurant prepares a variety of seafood, including lobster and crab in season. The serve-yourself salad bar is a great accompaniment to any meal, and servings are generous. **Bar:** full bar. **Address:** 41 Commercial St B1C 1B5 **Location:** Just s off Main St at Strathcona St; along waterfront.

LOWER ARGYLE

YE OLDE ARGYLER LODGE   Phone: (902)643-2500

Country Inn
$100-$215

Address: Rt 3 B0W 1W0 **Location:** Oceanfront. Hwy 103 exit 32, 4.5 mi (7.5 km) e. **Facility:** Located at a peaceful location overlooking the ocean and harbor, the inn features well-appointed guest rooms; some units offer views of the harbor. 6 units. 2 stories (no elevator), interior corridors. **Terms:** open 6/1-10/31, office hours 7 am-10 pm, 3 day cancellation notice-fee imposed. **Dining:** restaurant, see separate listing. **Activities:** boat dock. **Guest Services:** coin laundry. **Free Special Amenities:** full breakfast and high-speed Internet.

WHERE TO EAT

YE OLDE ARGYLER DINING ROOM   Phone: 902/643-2500

American
$7-$32

AAA Inspector Notes: The quaint dining room offers a lovely oceanfront view through large picture windows. The menu features fresh local seafood, ribs, steak and chicken, and items off a salad and mussel bar accompany the entrees. Service is friendly, yet casual, which suits the environment. **Bar:** full bar. **Reservations:** suggested. **Address:** Rt 3 B0W 1W0 **Location:** Hwy 103 exit 32, 4.5 mi (7.5 km) e; in Ye Olde Argyler Lodge.

LOWER SACKVILLE

SWISS CHALET   Phone: 902/864-1886

Chicken
$6-$16

AAA Inspector Notes: The popular restaurant is known for its rotisserie chicken and ribs and the tangy Chalet sauce that gives food its special zip. Diners munch on a half or quarter chicken with sides such as steamed vegetables, fries, baked potatoes and salads. Lunch guests often go for the great soup and sandwich combination. Take-out and delivery service are popular options. **Bar:** full bar. **Address:** 560 Sackville Dr B4C 2S2 **Location:** At Cross Rd; centre.

LUNENBURG (D-2) pop. 2,317
• Restaurants p. 180

Once the site of an Indian encampment and later a French fishing harbor, the Lunenburg area was granted by Oliver Cromwell to Charles de La Tour in 1656. Families from Hanover as well as French, German and Swiss immigrants, founded the town and cleared farmland 1751-53.

Old Town Lunenburg—now a UNESCO World Heritage Site—has been called "the best surviving example of a planned British colonial settlement in North America." On the spit of land between front and back bays, the town was laid out in a rectangular grid with narrow streets and garden plots.

Among Old Town's many preserved 18th-century buildings are some of the earliest churches in Canada. St. John's Church, established in 1754 by royal charter, ministered to the Hanoverians, Indians, French and English. The 1776 Zion Evangelical Lutheran Church holds the St. Antoine Marie bell from Louisbourg. Also of historical interest is a monument that commemorates the sacking of the town on July 1, 1782, when a fleet from Boston plundered stores, shops and houses.

Lunenburg is said to be one of the greatest fishing ports on the continent and was home to the *Bluenose*, the undefeated champion of the North Atlantic fishing fleet and the winner of four international schooner races from 1921 to 1931; her likeness is on the Canadian dime.

Tours of Lunenburg's harbor depart from the wharf behind the dory shop. Summer deep-sea fishing, whale-watching and lobster cruises depart daily from the Fisheries Museum of the Atlantic *(see attraction listing)*; reservations are advised.

A few kilometres south of Hwy. 3 is the village of Blue Rocks, named for the bluish hue of the surrounding rocks and ledges.

Historic Lunenburg is the backdrop for the Lunenburg Folk Harbour Festival in early August, which features music from top-notch performers.

Lunenburg Visitor Information Centre: 11 Blockhouse Hill Rd., Lunenburg, NS, Canada B0J 2C0. **Phone:** (902) 634-8100 or (888) 615-8305.

Self-guiding tours: A walking tour map of Old Town Lunenburg is available from the visitor information center.

FISHERIES MUSEUM OF THE ATLANTIC is at 68 Bluenose Dr. The complex includes two historic ships and five waterfront buildings. The fishing schooner *Theresa E. Connor* is outfitted as a working ship, and visitors can inspect her decks and gear. Adjacent is the dragger *Cape Sable*, a steel-hulled trawler. Visitors are welcome below deck on both ships.

The buildings contain an aquarium with native freshwater and saltwater fish, displays of ship models and sea artifacts, exhibits depicting the story of rumrunning and the history of the *Bluenose,* and a theater presenting a variety of films about fishing and local history. The Fishermen's Memorial Room honors local fishermen and vessels lost at sea.

There also are three floors of exhibits, including the Banks Fishery Age of Sail Gallery, Sea Monsters exhibit and a boat-building shop. **Tours:** Guided tours are available. **Time:** Allow 2 hours minimum. **Hours:** Tues.-Sat. 9:30-7, Sun.-Mon. 9:30-5:30, July-Aug.; daily 9:30-5:30, May-June and Sept.-Oct.; Mon.-Fri. 9:30-4, rest of year. Hours may vary. Closed major holidays. Phone ahead to confirm schedule. **Cost:** mid-May to mid-Oct. $10; $7 (ages 60+); $3 (ages 6-17); $22 (family). Admission rest of year $4; free (ages 0-5). **Phone:** (902) 634-4794 or (866) 579-4909. [T] [A]

▼ See AAA listing p. 199 ▼

BRIGANTINE INN & SUITES
Phone: (902)634-3300

Hotel
$70-$180 6/1-10/27
$70-$135 5/1-5/31

Address: 82 Montague St B0J 2C0 **Location:** Corner of King St. Opposite the harbour. **Facility:** 15 units, some kitchens. 3 stories (no elevator), interior corridors. **Parking:** street only. **Terms:** open 6/1-10/27 & 5/1-5/31, office hours 8 am-10 pm. **Amenities:** high-speed Internet. **Dining:** Grand Banker Bar & Grill, see separate listing. **Free Special Amenities: local telephone calls and high-speed Internet.**

THE HOMEPORT MOTEL
Phone: 902/634-8234

Motel
Rates not provided

Address: 167 Victoria Rd B0J 2C0 **Location:** 0.6 mi (1 km) w on Rt 3. **Facility:** 15 units, some two bedrooms and kitchens. 1 story, exterior corridors. **Terms:** seasonal, office hours 7 am-11 pm. **Guest Services:** coin laundry.

KAULBACH HOUSE HISTORIC INN
Phone: 902/634-8818

Historic Bed
& Breakfast
$99-$169

Address: 75 Pelham St B0J 2C0 **Location:** Centre. **Facility:** This restored, in-town hotel dates from around 1880; lovely guest rooms vary in size and style, with some having compact baths. 6 units. 3 stories (no elevator), interior corridors. *Bath:* shower only. **Terms:** open 6/1-10/31 & 5/1-5/31, office hours 7 am-9 pm, check-in 4 pm, 14 day cancellation notice-fee imposed.

LUNENBURG ARMS HOTEL & SPA
Phone: (902)640-4040

Boutique Hotel
$129-$299

Address: 94 Pelham St B0J 2C0 **Location:** Corner of Pelham and Duke sts; centre. **Facility:** The hotel offers attractive, well-appointed guest rooms, many offering views of the harbour; restaurants and shops are within walking distance. 24 units. 3 stories, interior corridors. **Terms:** office hours 8 am-10 pm, cancellation fee imposed. **Amenities:** high-speed Internet. **Dining:** Tin Fish Casual Fine Dining, see separate listing. **Activities:** spa.

THE LUNENBURG INN
Phone: (902)634-3963

Historic Bed
& Breakfast
$124-$189 6/1-11/30
$109-$144 4/1-5/31

Address: 26 Dufferin St B0J 2C0 **Location:** At Faukland St; centre. **Facility:** A large sun deck at this 1893 Victorian home overlooks the town; rooms are tastefully appointed and very well maintained. 7 units. 3 stories (no elevator), interior corridors. **Terms:** open 6/1-11/30 & 4/1-5/31, office hours 7 am-10 pm, cancellation fee imposed.

THE MARINER KING HISTORIC INN
Phone: (902)634-8509

Boutique Hotel
$115-$318

Address: 15 King St B0J 2C0 **Location:** At Lincoln St. **Facility:** Comprised of three historic buildings, this downtown property offers tastefully decorated units with well-appointed, modern amenities. 14 units. 2-3 stories (no elevator), interior corridors. **Parking:** street only. **Terms:** office hours 8 am-10 pm. **Amenities:** safes, honor bars. **Activities:** limited exercise equipment. **Free Special Amenities: full breakfast and high-speed Internet.**

SPINNAKER INN
Phone: (902)634-8973

Country Inn
$110-$175 6/1-10/31
$99-$140 11/1-5/31

Address: 126 Montague St B0J 2C0 **Location:** Centre. **Facility:** 4 efficiencies. 3 stories (no elevator), interior corridors. **Parking:** street only. **Terms:** office hours 7:30 am-11 pm, 3 day cancellation notice-fee imposed. **Amenities:** *Some:* high-speed Internet. **Guest Services:** complimentary laundry.

THE RUMRUNNER INN
Phone: (902)634-9200

fyi Not evaluated. **Address:** 66-70 Montague St B0J 2C0 **Location:** Centre. Facilities, services, and decor characterize a mid-scale property.

WHERE TO EAT

FLEUR DE SEL RESTAURANT
Menu on AAA.com
Phone: 902/640-2121

French
$24-$45

AAA Inspector Notes: In the heart of the historic town, the pleasant, cozy gem sustains a casual elegance with help from a decor that incorporates butter yellow and white accents. A fair-weather option is to dine on the lovely garden patio. The chef creates wonderful dishes using fresh regional ingredients; specialties include butter-poached lobster, pan-seared Lunenburg scallops, grilled beef tenderloin and duck breast. The decadent desserts shouldn't be overlooked. **Bar:** full bar. **Reservations:** suggested. **Address:** 53 Montague St B0J 2C0 **Location:** Jct Lower St. **Parking:** street only. [D]

GRAND BANKER BAR & GRILL
Phone: 902/634-3300

American
$9-$20

AAA Inspector Notes: Views of the harbor are splendid from this casual eatery. The staff is upbeat and attentive. Menu selections range from comfort foods to steak, chicken and fresh seafood dinners. Farm-fresh, high-quality and local ingredients are used. **Bar:** full bar. **Address:** 82 Montague St B0J 2C0 **Location:** Corner of King St; in Brigantine Inn & Suites. **Parking:** street only.

MAGNOLIA'S GRILL
Phone: 902/634-3287

Canadian
$8-$20

AAA Inspector Notes: In the heart of town lies this cozy gem. A chalkboard menu lists a selection of fine homemade comfort foods and desserts. A bustling atmosphere and staff provide friendly, casual service. **Bar:** full bar. **Address:** 128 Montague St B0J 2C0 **Location:** Centre. **Parking:** street only. [L] [D]

OLD FISH FACTORY RESTAURANT & ICE HOUSE BAR
Phone: 902/634-3333

Seafood
$9-$26

AAA Inspector Notes: The nautically-themed dining room affords a splendid view of Lunenburg Harbour. The pleasant, knowledgeable staff aptly explains preparations of fresh Atlantic seafood, including lobster, mussels and salmon. Outside seating is available on a wharf. **Bar:** full bar. **Address:** 68 Bluenose Dr B0J 2C0 **Location:** In Fisheries Museum of the Atlantic. **Parking:** on-site and street. [L] [D]

TIN FISH CASUAL FINE DINING
Phone: 902/640-4040

American
$10-$26

AAA Inspector Notes: The restaurant offers a lively colourful decor and well-prepared, beautifully presented food. Choices include seafood dishes--such as fresh salmon, halibut and lobster--as well as chicken, lamb and steaks. If weather permits, patio dining is available. **Bar:** full bar. **Address:** 94 Pelham St B0J 2C0 **Location:** Corner of Pelham and Duke sts; centre; in Lunenburg Arms Hotel & Spa.

TRATTORIA DELLA NONNA RISTORANTE & PIZZERIA
Phone: 902-640-3112

Italian
$13-$29

AAA Inspector Notes: The friendly, knowledgeable staff work as a team to keep up at the busy pace at this popular spot. A touch of Italy can be found here with a nice selection of creatively prepared fine Italian dishes along with gourmet wood-fired pizza. During peak season, an upbeat, bustling atmosphere prevails. **Bar:** full bar. **Reservations:** suggested. **Address:** 9 King St B0J 2C0 **Location:** Corner of Montague St. **Parking:** on-site (fee). D

Wood fired pizza, seafood dishes, pasta extraordinaire

MABOU

THE MULL CAFE & DELI
Phone: 902-945-2244

American
$7-$23

AAA Inspector Notes: This pleasant roadside diner featuring all the usual favorites including sandwiches and burgers for lunch and more hearty fare for dinner. Try one their homemade desserts. **Bar:** full bar. **Address:** 11630 Rt 19 B0E 1X0 **Location:** Centre. L D

MAHONE BAY (D-2) pop. 904

The quaint seacoast village of Mahone Bay offers art, craft and antiques shops and a picturesque shoreline consisting of stones and boulders. Captain Ephraim Cook, who came to the area to start a shipbuilding industry, settled the town in 1754.

The Three Churches, which have stood on the bay since the mid-1800s, are renowned landmarks that greet visitors as they enter the community. Cape Cod, Georgian and Victorian-style houses also still stand. Bayview Cemetery contains the tombs of many of Mahone Bay's original settlers.

Mahone Bay Chamber of Commerce: P.O. Box 59, Mahone Bay, NS, Canada B0J 2E0. **Phone:** (902) 624-6151 or (888) 624-6151.

MAHONE BAY SETTLERS MUSEUM & CULTURAL CENTRE is at 578 Main St. This community museum is set in an 1870s house and features ceramics produced locally before 1950. The museum also houses displays about the area's settlement during the 1750s, the local shipyards and seasonal exhibits. **Hours:** Mon.-Sat. 10-5, Sun. 1-5, June-Sept. **Cost:** Donations. **Phone:** (902) 624-6263.

AMBER ROSE INN
Phone: 902/624-1060

Bed & Breakfast
$125-$135

Address: 319 Main St B0J 2E0 **Location:** Centre. **Facility:** The quaint property, built in 1875 as a general store, now houses three spacious, tastefully-decorated guest rooms. 3 units. 2 stories (no elevator), interior corridors. **Parking:** no self-parking. **Terms:** seasonal, office hours 7 am-11 pm, 3 day cancellation notice-fee imposed.

BAYVIEW PINES COUNTRY INN
Phone: 902/624-9970

Historic Bed & Breakfast
$100-$165

Address: 678 Oakland Rd B0J 2E0 **Location:** Hwy 103 exit 10, 1.2 mi (2 km) w on Rt 3 to Kedy's Landing, 3.6 mi (6 km) e of Mahone Bay. Located in a quiet rural area. **Facility:** Bay views are featured from most of the units at this country-style inn on quiet, expansive grounds. Located in the main inn or an annex, guest rooms range in size from small to spacious. 10 units, some two bedrooms and kitchens. 2 stories (no elevator), interior/exterior corridors. **Terms:** open 6/1-10/31 & 5/1-5/31, 5 day cancellation notice. **Activities:** boat ramp, hiking trails.

FISHERMAN'S DAUGHTER BED & BREAKFAST
Phone: 902/624-0483

Historic Bed & Breakfast
$115-$145

Address: 97 Edgewater St B0J 2E0 **Location:** On Rt 3; centre. **Facility:** This lovingly restored 1840 heritage property is bordered by two churches and overlooks the picturesque Mahone Bay. 4 units. 2 stories (no elevator), interior corridors. **Terms:** seasonal, check-in 4 pm, cancellation fee imposed.

WHERE TO EAT

MUG & ANCHOR PUB
Phone: 902/624-6378

American
$8-$20

AAA Inspector Notes: The spacious, rustic pub, which has a large seasonal deck, overlooks the harbor. A fine selection of draft beers accompanies a variety of seafood, chicken and steak. **Bar:** full bar. **Address:** Rt 3 B0J 2E0 **Location:** Centre; in Mader's Wharf. L D

SALTSPRAY CAFE
Phone: 902/624-0457

American
$8-$16

AAA Inspector Notes: A new location boasts views of a small creek from the outdoor deck of this casual eatery, which specializes in fresh local seafood. Great chowders, lobster rolls and homemade desserts line the menu. **Bar:** full bar. **Address:** 436 S Main St B0J 2E0 **Location:** On Rt 3; centre. L D CALL

MAITLAND (C-3)

Originally called *Menesatung*, an Indian word meaning "healing waters," the area was renamed in 1828 for Sir Peregrine Maitland, lieutenant governor of Nova Scotia. Settlers were attracted to the area by the proximity of forests with trees large enough for ship timbers.

LAWRENCE HOUSE MUSEUM is at 8660 Hwy. 215. This was the home of shipbuilder William Lawrence, who built what was said to be the largest wooden-hulled, full-rigged ship in Canada. The 1870 Victorian house contains furnishings and memorabilia of the Lawrence family and has two formal Victorian parlors overlooking the shipyard. Photographs, exhibits and tours feature Lawrence's era of shipbuilding, including an exhibit depicting the community of Maitland, a scale model of the "great ship" and 23 period rooms.

Time: Allow 30 minutes minimum. **Hours:** Mon.-Sat. 10-5, Sun. 1-5, June 1-Oct. 15. **Cost:** $3.60; $2.55 (ages 6-17 and 65+); $7.95 (family, two adults and children). **Phone:** (902) 261-2628.

MARGAREE HARBOUR (B-5)

Margaree Harbour is the northern terminus for the Ceilidh (kay-lee) Trail, Hwy. 19. Beginning at the Canso Causeway at Port Hastings *(see place listing p. 189)*, the Ceilidh Trail skirts the western shore of Cape Breton Island and provides access to many beaches before joining the Cabot Trail at Margaree Harbour, which also has a beach.

MARION BRIDGE (B-6)

SAVE **TWO RIVERS WILDLIFE PARK** is 10 km (6 mi.) w. of Rte. 327. Moose, red deer, cougars, barred owls, American bald eagles, beavers and arctic foxes are among the North American wildlife on display. A pond offers refuge to waterfowl, including swans, geese and ducks. Miniature donkeys, a Shetland pony, pygmy goats, rabbits and a llama are presented in a petting zoo. Hiking, swimming and wagon rides are available in summer. Cross-country skiing, ice fishing, ice skating and sleigh rides are available in winter.

Time: Allow 1 hour, 30 minutes minimum. **Hours:** Daily 10-7, mid-June through Labour Day; 10-5, mid-Apr. to mid-June and day after Labour Day-late Oct.; 10-4, rest of year. Closed Christmas. **Cost:** $6; $4 (ages 5-17 and 55+); $20 (family, two adults and two children). **Phone:** (902) 727-2483.

MAVILLETTE

CAPE VIEW MOTEL & COTTAGES   **Phone:** 902/645-2258

Motel
Rates not provided

Address: 124 John Doucette Rd B0W 2Y0 **Location:** Rt 1, 19.2 mi (32 km) ne of Yarmouth; centre. **Facility:** 15 units, some efficiencies and cottages. 1 story, exterior corridors. **Terms:** seasonal, office hours 7:30 am-10 pm. **Activities:** beach access.

WHERE TO EAT

CAPE VIEW RESTAURANT   **Phone:** 902/645-2519

American
$8-$24

AAA Inspector Notes: The spacious restaurant affords a splendid view of the ocean and Mavillette Beach. On the vast menu are selections of fresh seafood, steaks and various comfort foods, as well as some Acadian dishes, such as rappie pie. Guests can request seating on the patio in season. **Bar:** full bar. **Address:** 157 John Doucette Rd B0W 1L0 **Location:** Rt 1, 19.2 mi (32 km) ne of Yarmouth; centre. ⨃ ⨃ ⨃

METEGHAN RIVER

AU HAVRE DU CAPITAINE HOTEL   **Phone:** 902/769-2001

Hotel
$75-$129 6/1-9/30
$60-$129 10/1-5/31

Address: 9118 Rt 1 B0W 2L0 **Location:** Hwy 101 exit 29 southbound; exit 31 northbound, follow signs. **Facility:** 18 units. 2 stories (no elevator), interior/exterior corridors. **Terms:** cancellation fee imposed. **Dining:** L'Auberge Au Havre du Capitaine Restaurant, see separate listing. ⨃ ⨃ ⨃ ⨃

WHERE TO EAT

L'AUBERGE AU HAVRE DU CAPITAINE RESTAURANT
Phone: 902/769-2001

Canadian
$7-$21

AAA Inspector Notes: A down home, relaxing Acadian experience is what guests can expect at this very popular restaurant. Typically during peak season guests may be entertained by local musicians. The menu specializes in fresh local seafood and wonderful Acadian cuisine. **Bar:** full bar. **Address:** 9118 Rt 1 B0W 2L0 **Location:** Hwy 101 exit 29 southbound; exit 31 northbound, follow signs; in Au Havre du Capitaine Hotel. B L D

MIDDLETON (C-2) pop. 1,829

Middleton, in the heart of the Annapolis Valley, is a prosperous pastoral town. Holy Trinity Church, at the west end of town, is one of five 200-year-old Loyalist churches remaining in Nova Scotia. Keeping time at the town hall is an unusual water clock, which is powered by water flowing through carefully calibrated tubes.

Middleton Tourist Bureau: P.O. Box 907, Middleton, NS, Canada B0S 1P0. **Phone:** (902) 825-4100.

ANNAPOLIS VALLEY MACDONALD MUSEUM is at 21 School St. Devoted to the culture and natural history of the Annapolis Valley, the museum displays antique clocks and watches, local historical artifacts, a re-created classroom and general store, an art gallery, a genealogical research library, and a greenhouse with a natural history exhibit.

Time: Allow 30 minutes minimum. **Hours:** Mon.-Sat. 9-4:30, Sun. 1-4:30, June 15-Sept. 30; Mon.-Fri. 10:30-4:30, rest of year. **Cost:** $3; free (ages 0-12); $6 (family, two adults and children ages 13-18). **Phone:** (902) 825-6116.

CENTURY FARM INN   **Phone:** 902/825-6989

Historic Bed
& Breakfast
$85-$110

Address: 10 Main St B0S 1P0 **Location:** Hwy 101 exit 18, 0.6 mi (1 km) s on Brooklyn St, then just w on Rt 1. Located in a quiet rural setting. **Facility:** Pleasant rooms of varying size are offered in this 1886 farmhouse on 110 acres; surrounding fields border a brook and the Annapolis River. 4 units. 2 stories (no elevator), interior corridors. **Terms:** office hours 10 am-10 pm, age restrictions may apply, 3 day cancellation notice. **Activities:** fishing, cross country skiing, hiking trails. **Guest Services:** coin laundry. ⨃ ⨃

FALCOURT INN   **Phone:** (902)825-3399

Historic
Country Inn
$130-$220

Address: 8979 Hwy 201, RR 3 B0S 1P0 **Location:** Hwy 101 exit 18 or 18A to Hwy 1, take Hwy 1 to Rt 10, 1.8 mi (3 km) s to Rt 201, then 0.6 mi (1 km) e. Located in a quiet rural area. **Facility:** The well-appointed rooms and cozy two-bedroom cottage at this former fishing lodge look out onto the scenic countryside along a meandering river. 12 units, some houses and cottages. 2 stories (no elevator), interior/exterior corridors. **Dining:** The Perfect Pear & Clubhouse Lounge, see separate listing. **Activities:** hiking trails. **Fee:** fishing. **Guest Services:** coin laundry. ⨃ ⨃ ⨃ ⨃

MID-VALLEY MOTEL

Phone: 902/825-3433

♦♦♦♦

Motel

Rates not provided

Address: 121 Main St B0S 1P0 **Location:** Hwy 101 exit 18, 0.6 mi (1 km) w on Rt 1. **Facility:** 57 units, some efficiencies and kitchens. 1 story, exterior corridors. **Terms:** office hours 8 am-2 am. **Pool(s):** outdoor. **Activities:** playground. **Guest Services:** coin laundry.

WHERE TO EAT

THE BIG SCOOP RESTAURANT

Phone: 902/825-4526

♦♦ ♦♦

American

$6-$18

AAA Inspector Notes: This spacious, family-style restaurant offers a wide range of menu options including home-style turkey dinners, fresh haddock, burgers, fish and chips, sandwiches, soups and salads. Wonderful homemade desserts and soft ice cream are good meal enders. Patio dining and a take-out bar are available in season. **Bar:** full bar. **Address:** Rt 1 B0S 1P0 **Location:** 1 mi (1.6 km) e on Rt 1. [L] [D] CALL [&M]

PASTA JAX & RIBS

Phone: 902/825-6099

♦♦ ♦♦

Italian

$7-$22

AAA Inspector Notes: A very popular restaurant with two dining options: Dine in the eclectic restaurant with works by local artists or in the pub. The menu is the same and features fresh seafood and various pasta dishes as well as steaks, sandwiches and burgers. **Bar:** full bar. **Address:** 300 Main St B0S 1P0 **Location:** At Commercial St. [L] [D]

THE PERFECT PEAR & CLUBHOUSE LOUNGE

Phone: 902/825-3399

♦♦ ♦♦ ♦♦

Canadian

$16-$30

AAA Inspector Notes: Sophisticated menu offerings include escargot, rack of lamb, pan-fried haddock and sirloin steak. A stone fireplace, beamed ceilings and oak paneling give the dining room--which overlooks the Nictaux River--the rustic aura of a 1920s fishing lodge. **Bar:** full bar. **Address:** 8979 Hwy 201, RR 3 B0S 1P0 **Location:** Hwy 101 exit 18 or 18A to Hwy 1, take Hwy 1 to Rt 10, 1.8 mi (3 km) s to Rt 201, then 0.6 mi (1 km) e; in Falcourt Inn. [D] [⋈]

MILTON (D-2) pop. 1,057

MILTON BLACKSMITH SHOP MUSEUM is off Hwy. 103 exit 19, then 2 km (1.2 mi.) n. on Hwy. 8 to 351 West St. The current building dates to 1903, although the site has long been used as a blacksmith shop. Antique tools, an anvil, a forge and a collection of historic town photographs are displayed. **Time:** Allow 1 hour minimum. **Hours:** Mon.-Fri. 10-5, Sun. 1-5, June-Aug.; Mon.-Fri. 10-4, in Sept. **Cost:** $1; free (ages 0-17). **Phone:** (902) 350-0268. [⊞]

MINUDIE (B-2)

J.F.W. DesBarres received the land grant to Minudie in 1764. The DesBarres estate, which included a grindstone quarry, was later purchased by Amos Seaman, wealthy owner of a shipping and trading company. For his shrewd development of the quarry, Seaman became known as the "grindstone king." His grand mansion fell into ruin after his death, but the 1863 Universalist Church he commissioned is still in use.

AMOS SEAMAN SCHOOL MUSEUM is in the center of town at 5554 Barronsfield Rd. The museum features one of the province's oldest one-room schoolhouses as well as local artifacts. **Hours:** Daily 10-6, July-Aug. **Cost:** Free. **Phone:** (902) 251-2289.

MOOSE RIVER

TIDAL RIVER RIDGE COTTAGES   **Phone:** 902/254-3333

[fyi] Not evaluated. **Address:** Rt 2 B0M 1N0 **Location:** On Rt 2, 7.8 mi (13 km) e of Parrsboro; centre. Facilities, services, and decor characterize a mid-scale property.

MOUNT UNIACKE (C-3)

Mount Uniacke was named by Richard John Uniacke, an aristocratic Irish adventurer who became attorney general of Nova Scotia in 1797. Serving in the post for the remainder of his life, Uniacke was responsible for a revision of the laws of the province. He chose to build his estate in this area because of the land's resemblance to his ancestral home in Ireland.

UNIACKE ESTATE MUSEUM PARK is off Hwy. 101 at exit 3 to Rte. 1. Built 1813-15 for Attorney General Richard John Uniacke, this 376-hectare (930-acre) Georgian-style expansive county estate contains original furnishings and treasured possessions. The estate has seven walking trails featuring a variety of wildlife and outdoor exhibits.

Time: Allow 30 minutes minimum. **Hours:** Mon.-Sat. 9:30-5:30, Sun. 11-5:30, June 1-Oct. 15. Trails daily dawn-dusk, year-round. **Cost:** $3.60; $2.55 (ages 6-17 and 65+); $7.95 (family, two adults and children). **Phone:** (902) 866-2560 or (902) 866-0032.

MUSQUODOBOIT HARBOUR (D-3)

An Indian word for "rolling out in foam," Musquodoboit is known appropriately as a sport fishing center. The Musquodoboit River offers salmon and trout fishing. In the fall, hunting is popular in the Musquodoboit Valley. Lumbering further supplements the town's economy.

Antigonish-Eastern Shore Tourist Association: 9042 Hwy. 7, Musquodoboit Harbour, NS, Canada B0J 2L0. **Phone:** (902) 889-2362.

MUSQUODOBOIT RAILWAY MUSEUM is on Hwy. 7 in the center of town. A restored 1916 station of the Canadian National Railway houses a large collection of Nova Scotian railway memorabilia and photographs. Equipment and rolling stock, including a rail snowplow, diesel engine, flat car, caboose and smoker/baggage car, are on the grounds. A tourist information bureau also is on-site. **Hours:** Daily 9-4, June-Aug.; Sat.-Sun. 9-4, in Sept. Information office daily 9-6, June-Aug.; Thurs.-Sun. 10-4 in May and Sept. **Cost:** Donations. **Phone:** (902) 889-2689. [⊞]

ELEPHANT'S NEST BED & BREAKFAST
Phone: 902/827-3891

Bed & Breakfast
$110-$150 6/1-10/20
$110 10/21-12/31

Address: 127 Pleasant Dr B0J 1N0 **Location:** Waterfront. Jct Hwy 107 and 7, 1.8 mi (3 km) w, follow signs. Located in a rural, residential area. **Facility:** Situated on the shores of a spring-fed lake, this cozy, waterfront B&B offers well-appointed rooms, lovely gardens and various water activities. 3 units. 2 stories (no elevator), interior corridors. **Terms:** open 6/1-12/31, office hours 6 am-11 pm, check-in 4 pm, 3 day cancellation notice-fee imposed. **Activities:** whirlpool, canoeing, paddleboats.

NAPPAN (B-2)

NAPPAN RESEARCH FARM is 6 km (4 mi.) s. on Hwy. 2, then 5 km (3 mi.) w. on Hwy. 302. The 223-hectare (551-acre) farm was established in 1887 for specialized agricultural and livestock research. Cattle are raised on the farm. Plants grown include forage crops and cereal grains. The farm also has a 2-hectare (5-acre) wetland demonstration site with nature trails. **Time:** Allow 1 hour minimum. **Hours:** Mon.-Fri. 8:30-4:30. Closed major holidays. **Cost:** Free. **Phone:** (902) 667-3826. 🎦

NEW GLASGOW (C-4) pop. 9,455

On the banks of the East River, New Glasgow is at a site marked as a large Indian village on a map by French traveler and historian Pierre François Xavier de Charlevoix. The discovery of coal in 1798 in Pictou County led to the town's founding in 1875. New Glasgow was named for the Scottish hometown of the area's first settler, James Carmichael.

The Samson Trail, 2.5 kilometres (1.5 mi.) along the New Glasgow riverfront, is named for the "Samson" locomotive. Considered to be the oldest steam locomotive in Canada, it once worked the Foord coal seam near Stellarton (*see place listing p. 193*).

A legend lingers of three Scottish bachelors who made a trip to Halifax to seek out and marry lassies who had recently arrived by boat. Today many in the county claim to be descendants of the trio.

Pictou County Tourist Association: 980 E. River Rd., New Glasgow, NS, Canada B2H 3S8. **Phone:** (902) 752-6383.

CARMICHAEL-STEWART HOUSE MUSEUM is .5 km (.3 mi.) e. at 86 Temperance St. Displays include china, pioneer artifacts, an extensive period clothing collection and glass items from three glass factories that once operated nearby. **Hours:** Mon.-Sat. 9:30-4:30, early June to mid-Sept. **Cost:** Donations. **Phone:** (902) 752-5583.

COMFORT INN
Phone: (902)755-6450

Hotel
$110-$150

Address: 740 Westville Rd B2H 2J8 **Location:** On Hwy 289, just e of jct Trans-Canada Hwy 104 exit 23. Opposite shopping mall. **Facility:** 62 units. 2 stories (no elevator), interior corridors. **Terms:** cancellation fee imposed. **Amenities:** *Some:* high-speed Internet. **Guest Services:** valet laundry.

COUNTRY INN & SUITES BY CARLSON
Phone: (902)928-1333

Hotel
$127-$137 1/1-5/31
$124-$134 6/1-12/31

Address: 700 Westville Rd B2H 2J8 **Location:** On Hwy 289, just e of jct Trans-Canada Hwy 104 exit 23. Opposite shopping mall. **Facility:** 65 units. 3 stories, interior corridors. **Activities:** exercise room. **Guest Services:** coin laundry.

WHERE TO EAT

CROFTER'S STEAK & SEAFOOD   **Phone: 902/755-3383**

American
$15-$22

AAA Inspector Notes: A popular spot with the locals, this restaurant seats patrons in two dining sections decorated with historical photographs and artifacts of early Nova Scotia. On the menu is a good selection of seafood and meat entrées served in ample portions. **Bar:** full bar. **Address:** 565 Stellarton Rd B2H 1M7 **Location:** Trans-Canada Hwy 104 exit 24, 0.6 mi (1 km) n on Rt 374. Ⓛ Ⓓ

THE DOCK FOOD, SPIRITS, ALES   Phone: 902/752-0884

Canadian
$8-$21

AAA Inspector Notes: This traditional Irish pub is in one of the oldest commercial buildings in Nova Scotia. A warm, friendly atmosphere prevails inside the 1845 stone building. A fine selection of beers complements offerings from the full pub menu. **Bar:** full bar. **Address:** 130 George St B2H 2K6 **Location:** Jct River Rd and George St; centre. **Parking:** on-site (fee). Ⓛ Ⓓ

SWISS CHALET   **Phone: 902/752-5013**

Chicken
$6-$16

AAA Inspector Notes: The popular restaurant is known for its rotisserie chicken and ribs and the tangy Chalet sauce that gives food its special zip. Diners munch on a half or quarter chicken with sides such as steamed vegetables, fries, baked potatoes and salads. Lunch guests often go for the great soup and sandwich combination. Take-out and delivery service are popular options. **Bar:** full bar. **Address:** 660 Westville Rd B2S 2J8 **Location:** Jct Western Ave. Ⓛ Ⓓ

NEW HARBOUR

LONELY ROCK SEASIDE BUNGALOWS
Phone: (902)387-2668

Cottage
$90-$230

Address: 150 New Harbour Rd B0H 1T0 **Location:** Rt 316, 0.4 mi (0.7 km) s. Located in a rural area. **Facility:** Bordered on one side by the ocean, the property enjoys a secluded setting; offered are one-, two- and three-bedroom deluxe cottages with decks. 6 cottages. 1 story, exterior corridors. **Terms:** office hours 7 am-10 pm, 3 night minimum stay - seasonal, 14 day cancellation notice-fee imposed. **Activities:** canoeing, playground.

NEW MINAS

JUNGLE JIM'S   **Phone: 902/681-5467**

Canadian
$8-$19

AAA Inspector Notes: Guests can step into a tropical theme at the casual eatery, which employs a friendly staff and nurtures a bustling atmosphere. The menu lines up a wide variety of comfort foods, salads, chicken, beef, seafood and hot wings, all served in ample, flavorful portions. **Bar:** full bar. **Address:** 9049 Commercial St B4N 5A4 **Location:** Centre; in New Minas Court. Ⓛ Ⓓ

SMITTY'S
◆◆◆
Canadian
$7-$20

Phone: 902/681-8291
AAA Inspector Notes: The family-oriented restaurant satisfies patrons with its ever-popular all-day breakfast items, as well as tasty and wholesome soups and salads at lunchtime. A relaxed mood characterizes the dining space. **Bar:** full bar. **Address:** 5494 Prospect Rd B4N 3K8 **Location:** Hwy 101 exit 12, just n. B L D

SWISS CHALET
◆◆◆
Chicken
$6-$16

Phone: 902/681-1761
AAA Inspector Notes: The popular restaurant is known for its rotisserie chicken and ribs and the tangy Chalet sauce that gives food its special zip. Diners munch on a half or quarter chicken with sides such as steamed vegetables, fries, baked potatoes and salads. Lunch guests often pay for the great soup and sandwich combination. Take-out and delivery service are popular options. **Bar:** full bar. **Address:** 9275 Commercial St B4N 3G2 **Location:** Commercial Street Plaza; centre. L D

NEW ROSS (D-2)

At the request of the Earl of Dalhousie, governor of Nova Scotia, the lumbering center of New Ross was established in 1816 by Capt. William Ross and 172 former soldiers of the Nova Scotia Fencibles. Anxious to settle the interior uplands of the province, the governor rewarded one enterprising settler with a piano that four soldiers delivered from Chester, 24 kilometres (15 mi.) away.

 SAVE **ROSS FARM MUSEUM** is at 4568 Hwy. 12. This living-history museum depicts Nova Scotia's agricultural heritage through the story of the Ross family, who farmed the land 1816-1970. Costumed interpreters demonstrate daily activities on the farm, which is home to heritage breeds of cattle, horses, sheep, pigs and chickens that were common in the 19th century.

The museum changes with the seasons: in spring lambs and piglets are born, chickens begin laying eggs and the ground is prepared and planted. In summer interpreters tend gardens, process wool and, most importantly, get the hay in. Butter is made Wednesdays and Saturdays, and visitors are invited to milk the cow daily at 4:30.

During the fall harvest, produce matures and canning and pickling begin. Jams and jellies are made throughout the season as fruits and berries are available.

Time: Allow 2 hours minimum. **Hours:** Daily 9:30-5:30, May-Oct.; Wed.-Sun. 9:30-4:30, rest of year. Closed Jan. 1-2 and Dec. 22-31. **Cost:** $6; $5 (ages 65+); $2 (ages 6-17); $15 (family, two adults and school-age children); free (Sun. 9:30-11). **Phone:** (902) 689-2210 or (877) 689-2210. ⊞

NOEL (C-3)

BURNTCOAT HEAD PARK AND INTERPRETIVE CENTRE is 5 km (3 mi.) n. of jct. hwys. 215 and 354 at 611 Burntcoat Rd. The 1.2-hectare (3-acre) park overlooks the Bay of Fundy. What is thought to be the world's highest recorded tide—16 metres (52.6

feet)—was observed here in 1960. A wooden lighthouse containing history displays is open in summer. Walking trails lead to the rocky shore and offer scenic views of Cobequid Bay. Video presentations allow for viewing of the tides and area history.

Time: Allow 1 hour minimum. **Hours:** Park open daily 10-6, May-Oct. Lighthouse 10-6, mid-May to late Aug. **Cost:** Donations. **Phone:** (902) 369-2529. ⊞

NORTH EAST MARGAREE (B-5)

North East Margaree lies within the pastoral Margaree Valley on Cape Breton Island. Some of Canada's best salmon waters are found at the Forks, Brook, Seal and Hatchery pools along the Margaree River.

MARGAREE SALMON MUSEUM is just off the Cabot Trail following signs to 60 E. Big Interval Rd. Displays include fishing and poaching equipment and an aquarium as well as books, pictures and articles relating to angling. One exhibit depicts the life cycle of the Atlantic salmon. **Phone:** (902) 248-2848.

NORTH SYDNEY

CLANSMAN MOTEL
◆◆◆
Motel
$89-$125

Phone: (902)794-7226
Address: 9 Baird St B2A 0A9 **Location:** Hwy 125 exit 2, just e on King St. **Facility:** 46 units, some cottages. 2 stories (no elevator), interior/exterior corridors. **Parking:** winter plug-ins. **Dining:** restaurant, see separate listing. **Pool(s):** heated outdoor. **Activities:** playground, horseshoes. **Guest Services:** coin laundry. **Free Special Amenities:** local telephone calls and high-speed Internet.

SAVE ◀▮▶ ⊤ CALL &M ⊇ 🛜 ⊟ ▣ ▯ / SOME UNITS 🐕

NORTH STAR INN
◆◆
Hotel
Rates not provided

Phone: 902/794-8581
Address: 39 Forrest St B2A 3B1 **Location:** Trans-Canada Hwy 105 exit 21; at ferry terminal. **Facility:** 101 units. 2 stories, interior corridors. **Pool(s):** heated indoor. **Activities:** whirlpool.

◀▮▶ ⊤ CALL &M ⊇ 🛜 ▣ / SOME UNITS ⊟ ▣

WHERE TO EAT

CLANSMAN RESTAURANT
◆◆
Canadian
$7-$20

Phone: 902/794-7226
AAA Inspector Notes: Home-style cooking is the focus of the warm, homey restaurant. Once a favorite with area miners, the delicious poor man's pudding blends cake, sauce, brown sugar and coconut and tops the mixture with ice cream or whipped topping. **Bar:** full bar. **Address:** 9 Baird St B2A 3M3 **Location:** Hwy 125 exit 2, just e on King St; in Clansman Motel. B L D CALL &M

PARRSBORO (C-2) pop. 1,401
• Hotels p. 186 • Restaurants p. 186

On the north shore of Minas Basin, Parrsboro has a history rich in Indian and pirate legends. Glooscap, a Mi'kmaq man-god, mighty warrior and magician, reputedly once roamed the area. Deno, an Italian pirate, is said to have entombed the daughter of a British naval captain in a cave at Black Point.

In 1776 a settlement took root on Partridge Island around a ferry terminus. Ferry service between Partridge Island and the Annapolis Valley proved to be a valuable transportation link and continued until World War II. The fertile land around the harbor at the mouth of the Parrsboro River prompted the island's population to eventually shift to the mainland community of Mill Village, renamed Parrsboro in 1784 after John Parr, Nova Scotia's governor general.

Twice daily the Bay of Fundy tides rise and fall between 12 and 15 metres (39 and 49 ft.) in the harbor. Good areas for viewing this phenomenon are Glooscap Park, Partridge Island and Parrsboro Wharf at First Beach. Among the area's other attractions are amethysts, agates, other semiprecious stones and rare fossils. A scenic drive winds along the shore of Minas Basin between Parrsboro and Advocate.

On the waterfront an old ferry that once traversed the bay to Kingsport is now the home of Parrsboro's resident theater company. The Ship's Company Theatre, 18 Lower Main St., offers productions in summer; phone (902) 254-3000 or (800) 565-7469 for ticket information.

Town of Parrsboro: 4030 Eastern Ave., P.O. Box 400, Parrsboro, NS, Canada B0M 1S0. **Phone:** (902) 254-2036.

[SAVE] **FUNDY GEOLOGICAL MUSEUM** is in the center of town, following signs to 162 Two Islands Rd. The museum examines the planet's origins and early life through displays of Triassic and Jurassic fossils excavated from nearby Minas Basin. Other exhibits highlight minerals, rockhounding and a collection of Nova Scotian minerals.

Time: Allow 1 hour minimum. **Hours:** Daily 9:30-5:30, June 1-Oct. 15; hours vary rest of year. Phone ahead to confirm schedule. **Cost:** $6.25; $5 (ages 65+ and college students with ID); $3.50 (ages 6-17); $15 (family, two adults and school-age children). Rates may vary; phone ahead. **Phone:** (902) 254-3814 or (866) 856-3466.

OTTAWA HOUSE BY-THE-SEA MUSEUM is 6 km (4 mi.) s.e. via Main St. at 1155 Whitehall Rd. This sole remnant of the original Partridge Island settlement was built as an inn in the late 1700s by James Ratchford, a prominent trader. Sir Charles Tupper, prime minister of Canada in 1896, bought Ottawa House as his summer retreat and hosted many visiting dignitaries here.

Museum exhibits include maritime artifacts, a collection of shipbuilding tools, and photographs of vessels launched from local shipyards. **Hours:** Daily 10-6, June 1-Sept. 15. **Cost:** $2; free (ages 0-11). **Phone:** (902) 254-2376 June 1-Sept. 15, or (902) 392-2051 rest of year.

GILLESPIE HOUSE INN **Phone:** 902-254-3196

Historic Bed & Breakfast
$99-$139

Address: 358 Main St B0M 1S0 **Location:** On Rt 2; centre. **Facility:** An Old World ambience enhances guest rooms at this pleasant 1890s home, where guests may relax on the spacious sun porch or in one of the parlors. 7 units. 2 stories (no elevator), interior corridors. **Terms:** open 6/1-10/31 & 5/1-5/31, cancellation fee imposed.

[SAVE] [Y+] CALL [&M] [wifi] [X] [K] [N] [☎] / SOME UNITS FEE [pet]

THE MAPLE INN BED & BREAKFAST **Phone:** (902)254-3735

Historic Bed & Breakfast
$85-$210

Address: 2358 Western Ave B0M 1S0 **Location:** Centre. **Facility:** The historic inn's parlor areas and guest rooms are tastefully decorated; on the top floor is a spacious two-bedroom suite. 8 units, some two bedrooms. 3 stories (no elevator), interior corridors. **Terms:** open 6/1-10/28 & 5/3-5/31, office hours 7 am-10 pm, 5 day cancellation notice-fee imposed. [Y+] [wifi] [X] [K]

THE PARRSBORO MANSION INN **Phone:** (902)254-2585

Bed & Breakfast
$130-$160

Address: 3916 Eastern Ave B0M 1S0 **Location:** On Rt 2; centre. **Facility:** Acreage surrounds this pleasant property offering spacious, tastefully decorated guest rooms in the main home and in an attached annex wing. 4 units. 2 stories (no elevator), interior corridors. **Terms:** open 6/15-10/15, 7 day cancellation notice. **Pool(s):** heated outdoor. **Guest Services:** coin laundry.

[Y+] [bowl] [wifi] [X] / SOME UNITS [K]

THE SUNSHINE INN **Phone:** 902-254-3135

Motel
$89-$175

Address: Rt 2 B0M 1S0 **Location:** 2 mi (3.2 km) n. Located in a rural area. **Facility:** 15 units, some cottages. 1 story, exterior corridors. **Terms:** open 6/1-10/31 & 5/1-5/31, office hours 6 am-10:30 pm, cancellation fee imposed. **Activities:** fishing, hiking trails, playground.

[wifi] [Z] [fridge] / SOME UNITS FEE [pet] [K] [microwave]

WHERE TO EAT

GLOOSCAP FAMILY RESTAURANT & LOUNGE **Phone:** 902-254-3488

American
$7-$18

AAA Inspector Notes: The popular family restaurant offers a choice of seating in the main restaurant, in the lounge or on the outdoor deck. Comfort foods include some seafood and steak items, in addition to delicious homemade desserts. **Bar:** full bar. **Address:** 758 Upper Main St B0M 1S0 **Location:** 0.8 mi (1.2 km) n on Rt 2. [L] [D]

PEGGY'S COVE (D-3)

Peggy's Cove is one of several fishing villages built around the snug harbors of the craggy south coast. Huge granite boulders are scattered throughout the village. An old lighthouse standing on a massive granite ledge and fishing boats moored along weatherworn wharves are a part of the atmosphere that makes this cove well-known among artists and photographers. The lighthouse also serves as the post office during the summer. The Marine Studio, built about 1875 as a fish shed, displays works by local artists.

William E. Garth Memorial Park, off Hwy. 333, features a monument dedicated to Canadian fishermen. Carved on the face of a granite outcropping, it depicts fishermen, their families and a guardian angel with outstretched wings.

PICTOU (B-4) pop. 3,813
• Restaurants p. 188

Sent by the Philadelphia Co. in 1767, six families from Pennsylvania and Maryland settled Pictou, formerly the site of an ancient Indian village. The Dutch cargo ship *Hector* arrived in 1773 bearing 179 passengers from the Scottish Highlands, the first of thousands to emigrate from Scotland to Canada in the next century. As the main port of entry, Pictou became known as "the birthplace of New Scotland."

Three rivers empty into the harbor, making Pictou one of Nova Scotia's largest lobster fisheries as well as an active shipbuilding center.

Hector Festival is a re-enactment of the *Hector* settlers' landing, and pipe bands; Highland dancing and parades are featured at various locations during the 5-day event.

GROHMANN KNIVES OUTLET is at 116 Water St. Guided tours of its knife production factory are offered. Minimum of four adults required for the tour. **Time:** Allow 30 minutes minimum. **Hours:** Mon.-Fri. 9-5. Tours are given Mon.-Fri. 9-3:30. Weekend and evening hours may vary. Phone ahead to confirm schedule. **Cost:** Free. **Phone:** (902) 485-4224 or (888) 756-4837.

HECTOR EXHIBIT CENTRE & ARCHIVES is off Hwy. 106 at 86 Haliburton Rd. Changing exhibits reflect the history, heritage, culture and art of the people of Pictou County. Genealogy information also is available. **Time:** Allow 30 minutes minimum. **Hours:** Mon.-Sat. 9:30-5:30, Sun. 1-5:30, June 1 to mid-Sept.; by appointment rest of year. **Cost:** $5 (includes admission to McCulloch House Museum); $16 (family). Research fee $5. **Phone:** (902) 485-4563.

HECTOR HERITAGE QUAY is downtown on the waterfront. Anchored in the harbor is a full-scale replica of the *Hector*, the three-masted Dutch sailing ship that brought the first Scottish immigrants to Nova Scotia in 1773. Costumed interpreters depict the history.

Tours: Guided tours are available. **Hours:** Mon.-Sat. 9-5 (also Tues.-Thurs. 5-7, July-Aug.), Sun. 10-5, Victoria Day weekend to mid-Oct. Phone ahead to confirm schedule. **Cost:** $7; $5 (ages 13-18, ages 61+ and students with ID); $2 (ages 6-12); $15 (family, two adults and two children). Rates may vary; phone ahead. **Phone:** (902) 485-4371. 🅣🅗

LOCH BROOM LOG CHURCH is off Hwy. 104 exit 19 to Rte. 376 following signs. This simple country log church is a replica of Pictou County's first house

of worship, built in 1787. Like the original, the interior features rough wooden benches and a candle chandelier. The church is in a placid setting overlooking the river. **Time:** Allow 30 minutes minimum. **Hours:** Tues.-Sat. 11-6, Sun. noon-6, July-Aug. Hours may vary. Phone ahead to confirm schedule. **Cost:** Donations. **Phone:** (902) 485-4891. 🅣🅗

McCULLOCH HOUSE MUSEUM is at 100 Old Haliburton Rd.; visitors should check in at the Hector Exhibit Centre & Archives just in front of the museum. This early 19th-century Scottish-style house was the home of Dr. Thomas McCulloch, his wife Isabella and their family. Dr. McCulloch was a reverend, a naturalist and a proponent of equal access to education.

His large collection of bird specimens can be seen on the first floor of the house, along with exhibits about the history of Pictou; family possessions, including Dr. McCulloch's desk; and details about the reverend's educational pursuits. A number of the exhibits have interactive elements. A staff member provides information about Dr. McCulloch and the Pictou area and is available to answer any questions.

Tours: Guided tours are available. **Time:** Allow 1 hour minimum. **Hours:** Mon.-Sat. 10-5, Sun. 1-5, June 1-Oct. 15. Closed major holidays. **Cost:** $5 (includes the Hector Exhibit Centre & Archives); $16 (family). **Phone:** (902) 485-4563.

NORTHUMBERLAND FISHERIES MUSEUM AND HERITAGE ASSOCIATION is off Hwy. 106 to 71 Front St. A restored 1904 railroad station contains some 2,000 artifacts related to the fishing industry of the Northumberland Strait. The collection includes an original fisherman's bunkhouse, fishing gear, restored boat engines, a cannery display, model boats, live rare lobsters and a gallery of vintage photographs. Visitors can see a fully operational lobster hatchery, and a replica lighthouse and interpretive panels about the fishing industry and maritime culture are available along the Pictou waterfront.

Tours: Guided tours are available. **Time:** Allow 30 minutes minimum. **Hours:** Mon.-Sat. 10-5, Sun. noon-5, in July; Mon.-Sat. 9-5, in Aug.; Mon.-Fri. 9-5 in June and Sept. **Cost:** $5; $3 (students with ID and senior citizens); free (ages 0-6); $10 (family). **Phone:** (902) 485-4972. 🅣🅗

AUBERGE WALKER INN   **Phone:** 902/485-1433

Historic Bed & Breakfast
$55-$149

Address: 78 Coleraine St B0K 1H0 **Location:** Between Water and Front sts; centre. **Facility:** Views of the waterfront enhance some rooms at this inn dating from 1865. 11 units, some efficiencies. 4 stories (no elevator), interior corridors. **Terms:** seasonal, 3 day cancellation notice-fee imposed.

📶 🛜 ✖ / SOME UNITS 🅐🅒

BRAESIDE COUNTRY INN
Phone: (902)485-5046

Historic Country Inn

$75-$165 6/1-9/30
$75-$145 10/1-5/31

Address: 126 Front St B0K 1H0 **Location:** Between Chapel and Welsford sts; centre. Several of the 1938 inn's comfortable, individually decorated accommodations overlook the harbor; some rooms are compact, perfect for one guest. 18 units. 3 stories (no elevator), interior corridors. **Terms:** office hours 7:30 am-10 pm, 3 day cancellation notice-fee imposed. **Dining:** restaurant, see separate listing. **Guest Services:** coin laundry, area transportation-within 9 mi (15 km).

CARIBOU RIVER COTTAGE
Phone: 902/485-6352

Cottage

Rates not provided

Address: 1308 Shore Rd B0K 1H0 **Location:** From PEI ferry terminal, 2.7 mi (4.5 km) w on Three Brooks Rd to Shore Rd. **Facility:** 4 cottages. 1 story, exterior corridors. **Activities:** canoeing, bicycles, hiking trails. **Guest Services:** coin laundry.

CONSULATE INN
Phone: 902/485-4554

Bed & Breakfast

$75-$159

Address: 157 Water St B0K 1H0 **Location:** Waterfront. Corner of Willow and Water sts; centre. **Facility:** This 1810 stone home sits on expansive grounds bordering the waterway and offers a variety of rooms; some units with water views. 11 units, some cottages. 2 stories (no elevator), interior/exterior corridors. **Terms:** age restrictions may apply, cancellation fee imposed.

THE CUSTOMS HOUSE INN
Phone: 902/485-4546

Historic Bed & Breakfast

Rates not provided

Address: 38 Depot St B0K 1H0 **Location:** Jct Front St, towards water; centre. **Facility:** The former Customs House is a sturdy structure of brick and stone and dates from 1870; some of the guest rooms offer great waterfront views. 8 units. 2 stories (no elevator), interior corridors. **Amenities:** high-speed Internet.

PICTOU LODGE BEACH RESORT
Phone: (902)485-4322

Resort Hotel

$89-$499

Address: 172 Lodge Rd B0K 1H0 **Location:** 4.3 mi (7 km) nw on Braeshore Rd; midway between Pictou and PEI ferry terminal at Caribou. Located in a quiet area. **Facility:** On the shores of beautiful Northumberland Strait, this 1925 resort offers a wide variety of accommodations, including rustic log cottages, modern motel rooms and two-bedroom oceanfront cottages. 63 units, some two bedrooms, three bedrooms, efficiencies and kitchens. 1 story, exterior corridors. **Terms:** open 6/1-1/2 & 5/11-5/31, 3 day cancellation notice-fee imposed. **Amenities:** Some: high-speed Internet. **Dining:** restaurant, see separate listing. **Pool(s):** heated outdoor. **Activities:** canoeing, paddleboats, putting green, bicycles, hiking trails, jogging, playground, game room, horseshoes, volleyball, limited exercise equipment. **Guest Services:** coin laundry. **Free Special Amenities:** local telephone calls and high-speed Internet.

WILLOW HOUSE INN
Phone: 902/485-5740

Historic Bed & Breakfast

$80-$120 6/1-10/15
$60-$110 10/16-5/31

Address: 11 Willow St B0K 1H0 **Location:** Corner of Willow and Church sts; centre. **Facility:** Said to have been built by the town's first mayor, this restored 1840 home offers individually decorated rooms. 6 units, some two bedrooms. 3 stories (no elevator), interior corridors.

WHERE TO EAT

BRAESIDE COUNTRY INN DINING ROOM
Phone: 902/485-5046

Canadian

$19-$29

AAA Inspector Notes: Well-prepared seafood and meat specialties include rack of lamb, prime rib of beef and fresh local seafood. Displays of china and glass decorate the attractive dining room. **Bar:** full bar. **Reservations:** suggested. **Address:** 126 Front St B0K 1H0 **Location:** Between Chapel and Welsford sts; centre; in Braeside Country Inn.

MRS. MACGREGOR'S TEA ROOM & RESTAURANT
Phone: 902/382-1878

American

$6-$20

AAA Inspector Notes: A lovely tea room located in the downtown area, the eatery serves an array of tasty lunch items as well as homemade desserts. Reservations are recommended 24 hours prior for afternoon tea service. **Bar:** beer & wine. **Address:** 59 Water St B0K 1H0 **Location:** Between Market St and Carrols Ln. **Parking:** street only.

PICTOU LODGE BEACHFRONT RESORT
Phone: 902/485-4322

American

$8-$30

AAA Inspector Notes: The historic dining room features attractive log construction and a large stone fireplace. Guests can enjoy a pre-dinner beverage or post-dinner dessert in the comfortable lounge or on the spacious deck overlooking the ocean. The menu touts a bountiful selection of fresh local seafood and some fine meat dishes. Homemade baked goods are outstanding. **Bar:** full bar. **Reservations:** suggested. **Address:** 172 Lodge Rd B0K 1H0 **Location:** 4.3 mi (7 km) nw on Braeshore Rd; midway between Pictou and PEI ferry terminal at Caribou; in Pictou Lodge Beachfront Resort. **Historic**

PIPER'S LANDING COUNTRY DINING
Phone: 902/485-1200

American

$16-$28

AAA Inspector Notes: Beautiful views of the water can be enjoyed from several sections in the charming, bayfront restaurant. A creative home-style flair flavors traditional fresh seafood and meat entrees, as well as some pasta dishes. It's hard to choose from a list of fine desserts. **Bar:** full bar. **Reservations:** suggested. **Address:** Hwy 376 B0K 1H0 **Location:** Pictou Rotary, 1.8 mi (3 km) w.

SETTLER'S SALT WATER CAFE
Phone: 902/485-2558

Seafood

$6-$21

AAA Inspector Notes: Located right at the water's edge overlooking the harbor, this bustling sea shack is a popular place for visitors and locals alike. Quick, friendly servers deliver a variety of salads, burgers, wraps, seafood entrees and the top seller, fish and chips. Guests can choose a lobster from a tank at the front of the restaurant. The covered patio is the most coveted spot at this seat-yourself, pub-style cafe. **Bar:** full bar. **Address:** 67 Caladh Ave B0K 1H0 **Location:** Just w of Hector Heritage Quay; on waterfront. **Parking:** street only.

PLEASANT BAY (A-5)

This fishing community on the west coast of Cape Breton Island was settled by Scottish immigrants in 1828. The town often marked its history by extraordinary events, such as the "Year of the Flour," when flour barrels washed ashore from a floundering ship in 1874. Two other years were marked by similar good fortune—fresh butter tins and barrels of rum.

WHALE INTERPRETIVE CENTRE is off Cabot Trail at 104 Harbour Rd. Displays describe 16 whale species found off Cape Breton, with life-size and scale models, recorded whale calls and interactive exhibits. A 10-minute videotape presentation chronicles the history of whaling, and a touch tank contains saltwater creatures in a landscaped marine environment. The center also serves as an outlet for dozens of whale-watch and eco-tour companies that operate along the Cabot Trail coastline.

Time: Allow 30 minutes minimum. **Hours:** Daily 9-5, June 1-Oct. 15. **Cost:** $5; $4 (ages 6-18 and 55+); $16 (family, two adults and two children). **Phone:** (902) 224-1411.

RUSTY ANCHOR RESTAURANT   **Phone:** 902/224-1313

Seafood
$9-$23

AAA Inspector Notes: From a spot overlooking Pleasant Bay, diners can savor fresh local seafood, including boiled lobster and crab. The popular restaurant's spacious deck affords splendid views. **Bar:** full bar. **Address:** 23197 Cabot Trail Rd B0E 2P0 **Location:** Centre.

[B] [L] [D] [✗]

PORT DUFFERIN

MARQUIS OF DUFFERIN SEASIDE INN
                                  Phone: (902)654-2696

Motel
$94

Address: 25658 Hwy 7, RR 1 B0J 2R0 **Location:** On Hwy 7. Located in a quiet rural area. **Facility:** 9 units. 1 story, exterior corridors. **Terms:** open 6/15-9/30, office hours 8 am-8 pm, cancellation fee imposed. **Activities:** canoeing, boat dock, fishing, bicycles. [✗] [✗] [✗] [✗] /SOME UNITS [✗]

PORT HASTINGS (C-5)

Opened in 1955, the 1,370-metre (4,500-ft.) Canso Causeway *(see attraction listing)* at Port Hastings prevents ice from entering the Strait of Canso from the north, thus providing a navigable harbor 16 kilometres (10 mi.) long year-round. Overlooking the strait and St. Georges Bay is 260-metre (850-ft.) Creignish Mountain.

Highlights of local history are the focus of the Port Hastings Historical Museum and Archives on Church Street in the village of Hastings.

CANSO CAUSEWAY crosses the Strait of Canso and links Cape Breton Island with the mainland. Said to be the world's deepest causeway, it reaches a depth of 65 metres (213 ft.) and is 244 metres (800 ft.) wide at the base. An estimated 10 million tons of rock were used in its construction. The causeway prevents ice from entering the Strait of Canso. A navigation lock allows the passage of oceangoing traffic.

ECONO LODGE MACPUFFIN   **Phone:** (902)625-0621

Motel
$90-$140

Address: 373 Hwy 4 B9A 1M8 **Location:** 1 mi (1.6 km) n on Hwy 4; 1 mi (1.6 km) s of Canso Cswy. **Facility:** 32 units. 1-2 stories (no elevator), exterior corridors. **Terms:** cancellation fee imposed. **Pool(s):** heated indoor. **Activities:** limited exercise equipment. **Guest Services:** coin laundry.

[✗] CALL [✗] [✗] [✗] [✗] [✗] /SOME UNITS [✗]

PORT HAWKESBURY pop. 3,517

MARITIME INN PORT HAWKESBURY
                                  Phone: (902)625-0320

Hotel
$117-$199

Address: 717 Reeves St B9A 2S2 **Location:** 4.2 mi (6.4 km) e of Canso Cswy on Hwy 4; opposite shopping centre. **Facility:** 73 units, some two bedrooms. 3 stories (no elevator), interior/exterior corridors. **Terms:** cancellation fee imposed. **Dining:** Miller's Café, Tap & Grill, see separate listing. **Pool(s):** outdoor, heated indoor. **Activities:** sauna, exercise room. **Guest Services:** coin laundry. **Free Special Amenities:** newspaper and high-speed internet.

[SAVE] [✗] [✗] [✗] [BIZ] [✗] [✗] [✗] / SOME UNITS [✗] [✗]

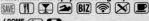
WHERE TO EAT

MILLER'S CAFÉ, TAP & GRILL   **Phone:** 902/625-0320

American
$9-$25

AAA Inspector Notes: A relaxed pub atmosphere and friendly staff go hand in hand at this spot. From typical pub comfort foods to such fresh catches as haddock and halibut are offered. Tempting desserts are made on the premises. **Bar:** full bar. **Reservations:** suggested. **Address:** 717 Reeves St B9A 2S2 **Location:** 4.2 mi (6.4 km) e of Canso Cswy on Hwy 4; opposite shopping centre; in Maritime Inn Port Hawkesbury. [L] [D]

ROSE GARDEN CHINESE RESTAURANT
                                  Phone: 902/625-5600

Chinese
$7-$16

AAA Inspector Notes: Booth and table seating is available in the basic dining rooms. Offerings at the casual restaurant include ample portions of quality food, including a large selection of combination plates and a popular buffet. **Bar:** full bar. **Address:** 708 Reeves St, Unit 2 B9A 2S1 **Location:** 4.2 mi (6.4 km) e of Canso Cswy on Hwy 4. [L] [D]

PORT HOOD

HAUS TREUBURG COUNTRY INN & COTTAGES
                                  Phone: (902)787-2116

Country Inn
$105-$210

Address: 175 Main St B0E 2W0 **Location:** Centre. **Facility:** 7 units, some cottages. 2 stories (no elevator), interior/exterior corridors. **Terms:** open 6/1-12/31, office hours 7 am-11 pm, 7 day cancellation notice-fee imposed. **Activities:** limited beach access.

[✗] [✗] [✗] [✗] / SOME UNITS [✗] [✗] [✗] [✗]

PORT-ROYAL NATIONAL HISTORIC SITE OF CANADA (C-1)

Off Hwy. 1 on the north shore of the Annapolis River opposite Goat Island, the historic site is a reconstruction of Port-Royal, one of the oldest European settlements in Canada and one of the first French settlements in North America.

In 1604 French explorer Samuel de Champlain named the harbor. The next year the colonists who survived the terrible winter of 1604 on Dochet's Island (St. Croix Island), where 35 out of 79 people died of scurvy, founded the Port-Royal colony.

In 1613 English captain Samuel Argall led an expedition from Virginia and captured the Port-Royal Habitation. The attackers pillaged and burned the buildings and destroyed all French markings.

The Port-Royal settlement spawned several significant accomplishments before it was destroyed, however. The colonists grew one of the first cereal crops in Canada and built one of the country's earliest water mills.

Canada's first European play, "Le Théâtre de Neptune," was written and produced in Port-Royal by Marc Lescarbot, and Champlain established North America's first recorded social club, "L'Ordre de Bon Temps" (Order of the Good Time) in 1606. Visitors to Nova Scotia can join this historic order free at Nova Scotia provincial tourist information centers by pledging to "have a good time, remember us pleasantly, think of us kindly and come back again."

Port-Royal Habitation has been rebuilt near what is believed to have been the original site, using Champlain's plan and studies of early 17th-century French architecture. The settlement, protected by a palisade and a cannon platform, centers on a courtyard in the style of a 17th-century French farm. The buildings include a governor's residence, gentleman's quarters, chapel, guardroom, kitchen, bakery, blacksmith shop, living quarters, an artisan's workshop and a common room.

All timber framing has been joined together without spikes or nails. The buildings are furnished with early 17th-century reproductions, and guides are dressed in period costume. Allow 30 minutes minimum. Daily 9-6, July-Aug; 9-5:30, May 15-June 30 and Sept. 1-Oct. 15. Admission $3.90; $3.40 (ages 65+); $1.90 (ages 6-16); $9.80 (family). Phone (902) 532-2898 or (902) 532-2321 in the off-season.

QUEENSLAND

SURFSIDE INN

Historic
Country Inn
Rates not provided

Phone: 902/857-2417
Address: 9609 St Margarets Bay Rd B0J 1T0 **Location:** Hwy 103 exit 6, follow signs on Rt 3. **Facility:** A nice beach is opposite this inn, which offers a deck, a dining area, some bay view rooms and some rooms with whirlpool tubs. 8 units. 2 stories (no elevator), interior corridors. **Terms:** office hours 8 am-9 pm.

RIVERPORT (D-2)

Settled by German immigrants in 1754, this harbor community at the mouth of the LaHave River was first known as Ritcey's Cove. In 1861 the town supported a thousand miners searching for gold in the local sea caves. Fire destroyed the town in 1920.

THE OVENS NATURAL PARK is on Hwy. 332. A cliffside nature trail leads to the sea caves or "ovens." A museum contains pictures, tools and memorabilia from the area's 1861 gold rush. Gold panning is offered. Live music is provided Tuesday through Saturday in July and August by Steve Chapin, the brother of singer Harry Chapin. Guided kayak tours are available.

Time: Allow 1 hour minimum. **Hours:** Mon.-Fri. 9-8, Sat.-Sun. 9-9, July-Aug.; daily 9-5, May 15-31; daily 9-6 in June and Sept. **Cost:** Park $8; $4 (ages 5-11 and 65+). **Phone:** (902) 766-4621.

ST. ANN'S (B-6)

A large portion of New Zealand's Scottish population can trace its roots to St. Ann's, the departure point for a steady migration of about 900 residents. The exodus, which lasted 8 years, began in 1851 when the Rev. Norman MacLeod and 130 residents sailed from St. Ann's Harbour for Australia. Disappointed with conditions in Australia, the party moved in 1854 to New Zealand, where they found their promised land at Waipu.

Despite the loss of almost half its population during the 1850s, St. Ann's remains the heart of Cape Breton's Gaelic community. The lore of the clans was embodied in the figure of Angus McAskill, the Scottish giant who lived and died at St. Ann's. Residents of St. Ann's still recount tales of McAskill's great strength and appetite.

THE GAELIC COLLEGE OF CELTIC ARTS AND CRAFTS is 1.5 km (.9 mi.) n. off Hwy. 105 exit 11 to 51779 Cabot Tr. The only institution of its kind in North America, the Gaelic College was founded in 1938. On Wednesday nights in July and August a traditional *ceilidh* (kay-lee) features Gaelic singing, piping, fiddle music and dancing. **Phone:** (902) 295-3411.

Gaelic College Craft Center, on the campus of The Gaelic College of Celtic Arts and Crafts, displays clan tartans and other handcrafted Celtic items. **Hours:** Daily 8:30-8, May-Sept. **Cost:** Free. **Phone:** (902) 295-3441.

Great Hall of the Clans Museum, on the campus of The Gaelic College of Celtic Arts and Crafts, depicts the history and culture of Scotland from its early days to the present and includes a brief account of the Great Migration from the Highlands. Interactive exhibits show the relationship between music, dance, song, stories and crafts of Nova Scotia Gaels. **Hours:** Daily 9-5, July-Aug.; Mon.-Fri. 9-5, May-June and in Sept. **Cost:** $7; $5.50 (students with ID); $20 (family, two adults and two children). **Phone:** (902) 295-3441.

THE LOBSTER GALLEY RESTAURANT

Seafood
$9-$35

Phone: 902/295-3100
AAA Inspector Notes: Bordering St. Ann's Harbour, this restaurant is a lovely place to enjoy ocean scenes and a good variety of fresh local seafood. The specialty is lobster, which diners select from large tanks. A nautical theme prevails in all three informal dining areas. **Bar:** full bar. **Address:** 51943 Cabot Tr B0E 1B0 **Location:** Hwy 105 exit 11, 5 mi (8 km) e of Baddeck.

ST. PETER'S (B-5)

St. Peter's, named San Pedro by its Portuguese founders, was a fishing base 1521-27. In the next century Nicholas Denys developed the area's fishing grounds and timber resources and established a fur-trading post protected by a fort. Successively renamed St. Pierre and Port Toulouse, the port remained a French stronghold until 1745, when the British plundered the community and burned four schooners at anchor.

The French returned and undertook the enormous task of building a road from the post to Louisbourg. This connection proved fatal, however, and Port Toulouse tumbled with the final fall of Louisbourg in 1758. Renamed St. Peter's, the town boasted Fort Granville, built in 1793 under the leadership of Lieutenant Colonel Moore. The remains of Fort Granville's ramparts still are visible at Battery Provincial Park (see Recreation Chart).

The Mi'kmaq Indians once carried their canoes across the St. Peter's Canal on Hwy. 4. An interpretive exhibit explains the operation of the tidal lock system. The canal area, now a national historic site, is a popular spot for picnicking, fishing and watching vessels pass between the Atlantic Ocean and Bras d'Or Lake.

The Acadian Pioneers' Museum, 8 kilometres (5 mi.) west in River Bourgeois, presents exhibits that depict Acadian customs and shipbuilding 1870-1930.

NICOLAS DENYS MUSEUM is .75 km (.5 mi.) e. off Hwy. 4. Articles pertain to the man who built St. Peter's in the 1650s. **Time:** Allow 1 hour minimum. **Hours:** Daily 9-5, June-Sept. **Cost:** Donations. **Phone:** (902) 535-2379.

SCOTSBURN

STONEHAME LODGE & CHALETS   **Phone:** 902/485-3468

Cottage
$85-$240

Address: 310 Fitzpatrick Mountain Rd B0K 1R0 **Location:** Rt 256, 7.5 mi (12 km) w of Pictou via Rt 376, last 1.2 mi (2 km) on gravel entry road. Located in a quiet secluded area on top of a mountain. **Facility:** Set on a scenic mountaintop, the property offers sweeping views from the cottages, motel section or the main lodge. 27 units, some cottages. 2 stories (no elevator), exterior corridors. **Terms:** office hours 7 am-10 pm, 14 day cancellation notice. **Pool(s):** heated outdoor. **Activities:** whirlpool, cross country skiing, snowmobiling, tobogganing, hiking trails, horseshoes. **Guest Services:** coin laundry.

SHELBURNE (E-1) pop. 1,879
• Hotels p. 192 • Restaurants p. 192

The shipbuilding center of Shelburne was founded in 1783 by Loyalists who fled the United States at the close of the Revolutionary War. By 1784 the number of refugees had grown to such an extent that Shelburne's population exceeded that of both Montréal and Québec. Eventually adverse economic conditions and the government's inability to supply free land and provisions to all the refugees caused thousands of Loyalists to seek homes elsewhere.

A number of trophy-winning yachts have been built in Shelburne. Shelburne native Donald MacKay, an American shipbuilder noted for the remarkably sleek clippers he produced in Boston, learned his trade in Shelburne shipyards early in the 19th century. Just outside town, The Islands Provincial Park affords picnicking and camping opportunities (see Recreation Chart).

BLACK LOYALIST HERITAGE SOCIETY HISTORICAL SITE AND MUSEUM is w. on Hwy. 103 to exit 26, then 5 km (3 mi.) w. on Hwy. 3 to 104 Old Birchtown Rd. in Birchtown village. About 30,000 Loyalists fled the United States during the American Revolution; among them were 3,500 of African descent. Many of these black Loyalists settled in Birchtown.

A museum in the 1830 Black Loyalist Schoolhouse has a well-documented history of the black Loyalists' arrival in Nova Scotia, the struggle that many endured working for Nova Scotians and newly arrived white Loyalists. The museum's historical artifacts, photographs and period clothing help depict the province's black Loyalists and their descendants.

A trail leads past a pit house, an A-frame structure made of logs with a fire pit in the center, that is representative of the homes of the early black Loyalists. The trail continues to the coast where burial grounds can be found.

Tours: Guided tours are available. **Time:** Allow 1 hour minimum. **Hours:** Museum Tues.-Sun. 11-5, Mon. by appointment, June-Aug.; by appointment rest of year. Historical site open year-round. **Cost:** $3; free (ages 0-12). **Phone:** (902) 875-1310 or (888) 354-0772.

J.C. WILLIAMS DORY SHOP MUSEUM is at 11 Dock St. Built and operated as a two-story waterside dory factory 1880-1970, this museum features interpretive displays about the processes involved in building these small fishing boats. **Time:** Allow 1 hour minimum. **Hours:** Daily 9:30-5:30, June-Sept. **Cost:** $3; free (ages 0-15). Combination admission with the Muir-Cox Shipbuilding Interpretive Centre, Ross-Thomson House Museum and Shelburne County Museum $8. **Phone:** (902) 875-3141 in the off-season.

MUIR-COX SHIPBUILDING INTERPRETIVE CENTRE is at the s. end of Dock St. along the waterfront. Exhibits depict the history and tradition of one of the oldest boat-building operations in Atlantic Canada. The shipyard, which operated 1820-1984, produced barques, fishing boats, schooners and yachts. The center is housed in a restored yacht shed and features boatbuilding demonstrations, photographs and artifacts.

Time: Allow 30 minutes minimum. **Hours:** Daily 9:30-5:30, June-Sept. **Cost:** $3; free (ages 0-15). Combination admission with the J.C. Williams Dory Shop Museum, Ross-Thomson House Museum and the Shelburne County Museum $8. **Phone:** (902) 875-2483.

ROSS-THOMSON HOUSE MUSEUM is at 9 Charlotte Ln. Thought to be the only surviving 18th-century store in Nova Scotia, the 1785 building features vintage merchandise and is furnished in the sparsely elegant style of the period. A militia room is upstairs. A Loyalist garden is planted with heirloom varieties of herbs, vegetables and flowers.

Hours: Daily 9:30-5:30, June 1 to mid-Oct. **Cost:** $3; free (ages 0-15). Combination admission with the J.C. Williams Dory Shop Museum, Muir-Cox Shipbuilding Interpretive Centre and Shelburne County Museum $8. **Phone:** (902) 875-3141.

SHELBURNE COUNTY MUSEUM is at Dock St. and Maiden Ln. The museum houses a 1740 fire engine, said to be the oldest in Canada. Maritime and shipbuilding artifacts also are displayed. Permanent and changing exhibits depict the history of the county.

Time: Allow 30 minutes minimum. **Hours:** Daily 9:30-5:30, June 1 to mid-Oct.; Mon.-Fri. 10-noon and 2-5, rest of year. **Cost:** $3; free (ages 0-15). Combination admission with the J.C. Williams Dory Shop Museum, Muir-Cox Shipbuilding Interpretive Centre and Ross-Thomson House Museum $8. **Phone:** (902) 875-3219.

THE COOPER'S INN   **Phone:** 902/875-4656

Historic Bed & Breakfast
$100-$185

Address: 36 Dock St B0T 1W0 **Location:** Hwy 103 exit 26, 1.5 mi (2.5 km) e on Rt 3, follow one way to Dock St. Located in historic district. **Facility:** A lovely suite on the top floor is the crowning glory of this pre-1800s converted home, which offers some rooms with water views. 8 units. 3 stories (no elevator), interior/exterior corridors. **Terms:** open 6/1-10/10, office hours 8 am-10 pm, cancellation fee imposed.

MACKENZIE'S MOTEL, COTTAGES, AND SUITES
Phone: 902/875-2842

Motel
$75-$160 6/1-10/15
$70-$150 10/16-5/31

Address: 260 Water St B0T 1W0 **Location:** Hwy 103 exit 26, 1 mi (1.6 km) e on Rt 3. Located in a commercial area. **Facility:** 15 units, some kitchens and cottages. 1 story, exterior corridors. **Terms:** office hours 8 am-11 pm, cancellation fee imposed. **Pool(s):** heated outdoor.

WILDWOOD MOTEL   **Phone:** (902)875-2964

Motel
$75-$90

Address: Minto St B0T 1W0 **Location:** Hwy 103 exit 26, 1.1 mi (1.8 km) e on Rt 3. Located in a residential area. **Facility:** 20 units. 1 story, exterior corridors. **Terms:** office hours 7 am-11 pm, cancellation fee imposed.

Learn about
AAA/CAA Diamond Ratings
at AAA.com/Diamonds

WHERE TO EAT

CHARLOTTE LANE CAFE & CRAFTS
Phone: 902/875-3314

Continental
$8-$29

AAA Inspector Notes: Well-prepared, creative entrees, such as garlic shrimp linguine and lobster and scallop brandy gratin, make up a menu full of interesting choices. The mid-1800s home is loaded with character, from its old wood floors to its wrought-iron light fixtures. Patio dining is available in season. **Bar:** full bar. **Reservations:** suggested, for dinner. **Address:** 13 Charlotte Ln B0T 1W0 **Location:** Between John St and Maiden Ln; centre. **Parking:** street only. **Historic** L D AC

LUONG'S RESTAURANT   **Phone:** 902/875-1300

Chinese
$7-$18

AAA Inspector Notes: The popular restaurant prepares a wide selection of Chinese and Canadian cuisine, including some Szechuan dishes and combination plates. **Bar:** full bar. **Address:** 165 Water St B0T 1W0 **Location:** Centre. **Parking:** street only. L D

ROSE AND GRIFFON PUB & EATERY
Phone: 902/875-3333

American
$10-$22

AAA Inspector Notes: A rustic decor can be found at this pub-style restaurant with its spacious wooden booths and tables. The ample portions include a variety of fresh seafood and meat dishes including daily specials. **Bar:** full bar. **Address:** 160 Water St B0T 1W0 **Location:** Corner of King St. B L D

SOPHIA'S CAFE   **Phone:** 902/875-1148

American
$6-$16

AAA Inspector Notes: The atmosphere is casual at this favorite, where locals come for mile-high pie and excellent seafood and lobster chowders as well as an all-day breakfast menu. **Bar:** beer & wine. **Address:** 115 King St B0T 1W0 **Location:** Centre; in Shelburne Mall. B L D

SHERBROOKE (C-4)

Charles de Sainte-Etienne La Giraudiere, a French fur trader, built a post on the St. Mary's River at what became the village of Sherbrooke in 1655. Access to the area was by water, and a flourishing trade took advantage of the local natural resources. In 1861 gold was discovered, and the town boomed for 20 years. The village is a center for hunters and anglers.

SHERBROOKE VILLAGE is on Hwy. 7 (Nova Scotia's Marine Drive). Costumed interpreters demonstrate skills, crafts and household chores at this restoration of an 1860s lumbering and mining town. The McDonald Brothers' Sawmill operates daily, and a hands-on history program is available. Other highlights include horse-drawn wagon rides, a nature center and evening concerts.

Thirty-two buildings comprise the village, including a blacksmith shop, general store, tearoom, craft workshops, boat-building shop and ambrotype photography studio. **Time:** Allow 2 hours minimum. **Hours:** Daily 9:30-5, June 1-Oct. 15. **Cost:** $10; $8 (ages 65+); $4.25 (ages 6-16); $27.50 (family). **Phone:** (902) 522-2400 or (888) 743-7845.

SHUBENACADIE (C-3) pop. 886

Meaning "place where wild potatoes grow," Shubenacadie (shoo-ben-ack-a-dee) is in a district that has always been the home of the Mi'kmaq Indians of central Nova Scotia. In 1737 Abbé le Loutre, sent by the Society of Foreign Missions, established their headquarters and built an Indian mass house; the cemetery still is visible.

Pottery crafted by Mi'kmaq Indians from Shubenacadie clay has been discovered throughout the province. A local industry still uses the clay. Dairying and lumbering also are historically associated with the area.

SHUBENACADIE PROVINCIAL WILDLIFE PARK is off Hwy. 102 exit 11, then s. on Hwy. 2 to 149 Creighton Rd. The park consists of 20 hectares (49 acres) of natural woodland with a large variety of animals and birds, most native to Nova Scotia or North America. More than 3 dozen species of ducks and geese live in the park, while hundreds of others come to nest or rest while migrating.

The Creighton Forest Environment Centre, housed in three buildings, contains photographs and interactive exhibits, including a working beehive, describing wildlife and their habitat. Displays enhanced by sound effects portray environments as a forest community. The Ducks Unlimited Greenwing Legacy Interpretive Centre provides displays about waterfowl and wetlands and their importance in the environment. A 5-hectare (12-acre) picnic area with tables, shelters, running water and a large playground is on the premises. Guided tours of two wetland trails are available.

Time: Allow 1 hour minimum. **Hours:** Park and environment and interpretive centers daily 9-7, May 15-Oct. 15; Sat.-Sun. 9-3, rest of year (weather permitting). Closed Christmas. **Cost:** May 15-Oct. 15 $4.25; $1.75 (ages 6-17); $11 (family, two adults and three children). Admission rest of year $2.50; $1.50 (ages 6-17); $7.75 (family, two adults and three children). Children must be with an adult. **Phone:** (902) 758-2040.

SMITHS COVE

BIRCH VILLA COTTAGES   **Phone:** (902)245-4945

Cottage
$89-$174
Address: RR 1 B0S 1S0 **Location:** Hwy 101 exit 25 eastbound; exit 24 westbound. **Facility:** 13 units, some cottages. 1 story, exterior corridors. **Terms:** open 6/1-10/1, office hours 8 am-10 pm, 2 night minimum stay - seasonal, 7 day cancellation notice-fee imposed. **Pool(s):** heated outdoor. **Activities:** playground. **Guest Services:** coin laundry.

Check out our travel blog at AAATravelViews.com

HARBOURVIEW INN   **Phone:** (902)245-5686

Bed & Breakfast
$119-$179
Address: 25 Harbourview Rd B0S 1S0 **Location:** Hwy 101 exit 25 eastbound; exit 24 westbound. **Facility:** Several verandas at this lovely circa 1899 property create the perfect spot to relax and enjoy your getaway. The inn's comfortable guest rooms, each with a DVD player, vary in size and style. 13 units, some two bedrooms. 1-2 stories (no elevator), interior/exterior corridors. **Terms:** open 6/1-10/15 & 5/15-5/31, office hours 7 am-10 pm, 7 day cancellation notice-fee imposed. **Pool(s):** outdoor. **Activities:** beach access, tennis court, hiking trails, playground, shuffleboard. **Guest Services:** valet laundry. **Free Special Amenities: full breakfast and high-speed Internet.**

HEDLEY HOUSE INN BY THE SEA   **Phone:** 902/245-2500

Motel
Rates not provided
Address: RR 1 B0S 1S0 **Location:** Oceanfront. Hwy 101 exit 25 eastbound; exit 24 westbound. **Facility:** 14 units, some efficiencies. 1 story, exterior corridors. **Terms:** seasonal, office hours 8 am-8:30 pm.

SPRINGHILL (C-3) pop. 3,941

A 6-metre (20-ft.) monument topped by a statue of a miner stands on Main Street as a memorial to the hundreds of workers who have died in mishaps since mining began in Springhill in 1872. Despite the great promise manifested in the Number 2 mine, said to be the deepest in Canada, Springhill's mining industry was plagued with a series of tragic accidents that finally prompted the closure of the mines in 1958.

Even after two fires completely devastated its business district, the indomitable town refused to die. Springhill was awarded a gold medal from the Carnegie Hero Fund Commission for its courage in the face of disaster. Recovery has followed development of a diversified industrial base.

ANNE MURRAY CENTRE is at 36 Main St. This museum chronicles the life and career of singer Anne Murray, Springhill's favorite daughter. Awards, costumes, memorabilia and photographs are featured. **Time:** Allow 1 hour minimum. **Hours:** Daily 9-4:30, mid-May to mid-Oct.; by appointment rest of year. **Cost:** $6; $5 (ages 7-17 and 56+); $18 (family, maximum of three adults). **Phone:** (902) 597-8614.

SPRINGHILL MINERS' MUSEUM is 1 km (.6 mi.) s.w. off Hwy. 2 at 145 Black River Rd. The museum offers exhibits about the history of coal mining in Springhill. Experienced miners conduct tours of the mine. Protective wear and plastic bags are provided for those wishing to dig coal. **Time:** Allow 30 minutes minimum. **Hours:** Daily 9-5, mid-May to mid-Oct. **Cost:** $5.50; $4.75 (ages 7-18 and 61+); $3.50 (ages 3-6). **Phone:** (902) 597-3449.

STELLARTON (C-4) pop. 4,717
• Hotels p. 194 • Restaurants p. 194

While coal fueled the growth of Stellarton, the Sobeys put food on miners' tables. J.W. Sobey started a meat delivery service in 1907, and his son persuaded him to open a small grocery store in 1924. Their family business would expand to more than 1,300 supermarkets across the country. Sobeys, now one of Canada's largest food distributors, is still headquartered in Stellarton.

 NOVA SCOTIA MUSEUM OF IN-DUSTRY is at 147 N. Foord St. The museum is, appropriately enough, on the site where industrialization first took place in Nova Scotia: In the 1820s the General Mining Co. began mining coal here using newly developed methods, such as steam engines, brought from Great Britain. Two of Canada's oldest steam locomotives, "Samson" and "Albion," are among the more than 37,000 artifacts displayed at the museum.

Hands-on exhibits demonstrate bottle making, loom mills and steam and water power. Early household appliances and a collection of Nova Scotia glass also are displayed. Modern industries such as forestry, hairstyling, munitions and tourism are explored and the Shaping the Future Gallery takes a look at what lies ahead.

Hours: Mon.-Sat. 9-5, Sun. 10-5, July-Oct.; Mon.-Sat. 9-5, Sun. 1-5, May-June; Mon.-Fri. 9-5, rest of year. Closed Jan. 1, Good Friday, Victoria Day, Thanksgiving and Dec. 25-26. **Cost:** $8.15; $4.85 (ages 65+); $3.60 (ages 6-17); $16.80 (family, two adults and school-age children). **Phone:** (902) 755-5425.

HOLIDAY INN EXPRESS STELLARTON-NEW GLASGOW
Phone: (902)755-1020

Hotel
$129-$169

Address: 86 Lawrence Blvd B0K 1S0 **Location:** Hwy 104 exit 24, just s, then 0.6 mi (1 km) w. **Facility:** 125 units. 4 stories, interior corridors. **Parking:** winter plug-ins. **Amenities:** high-speed Internet. **Pool(s):** heated indoor. **Activities:** whirlpool, waterslide, exercise room. **Guest Services:** valet and coin laundry. **Free Special Amenities:** full breakfast and high-speed Internet.

WHERE TO EAT

JUNGLE JIM'S
Phone: 902/695-5467
▼▼▼
Canadian
$8-$19

AAA Inspector Notes: Guests can step into a tropical theme at the casual eatery, which employs a friendly staff and nurtures a bustling atmosphere. The menu lines up a wide variety of comfort foods, salads, chicken, beef, seafood and hot wings, all served in ample, flavorful portions. **Bar:** full bar. **Address:** 127 N Foord St B0K 1S0 **Location:** Trans-Canada Hwy 104 exit 24, just n. L D

SUMMERVILLE

QUARTERDECK BEACHSIDE VILLAS
Phone: 902/683-2998
(fyi) Not evaluated. **Address:** 7499 Rt 3 B0N 2K0 **Location:** Oceanfront. Hwy 103 exit 20, 0.3 mi (0.5 km) n. Facilities, services, and decor characterize a mid-scale property.

SYDNEY (B-6)

Colonists from New York and New Hampshire settled Sydney, Nova Scotia's third-largest city, beginning in 1785. Known as Spanish Bay, Sydney was renamed in honor of England's colonial secretary, Lord Sydney. The city was the capital of the Cape Breton colony 1785-1820, before the island was annexed by Nova Scotia. The area attracted a large number of Scottish settlers in the early 1800s, and with the opening of the coal mines and a steel plant at the turn of the 20th century, a large number of Eastern European settlers arrived, helping to account for the city's diverse ethnic population.

Sydney, on scenic Sydney Harbour, is an important seaport and the commercial capital of picturesque Cape Breton Island. The University College of Cape Breton also is in the city.

Sydney and Area Chamber of Commerce: P.O. Box 131, Sydney, NS, Canada B1P 6G9. **Phone:** (902) 564-6453.

CAPE BRETON CENTRE FOR HERITAGE AND SCIENCE is in the Lyceum Building at 225 George St. Permanent and changing historical exhibits focus on the Cape Breton area. Local exhibits are presented in the summer. **Time:** Allow 30 minutes minimum. **Hours:** Mon.-Fri. 9-5, June-Aug.; Mon. 1-4, Tues.-Fri. 10-4, rest of year. **Cost:** Donations. **Phone:** (902) 539-1572.

COSSIT HOUSE MUSEUM is at 75 Charlotte St. This is one of the oldest houses in Sydney. Built in 1787 by the Rev. Ranna Cossit, the first Anglican minister assigned to permanent duty in Cape Breton, the house is restored to its late 18th-century appearance and has period furnishings. **Time:** Allow 30 minutes minimum. **Hours:** Mon.-Sat. 9-5, Sun. 1-5, June 1-Oct. 15. **Cost:** $2; $1 (ages 6-17 and 65+); $5 (family). **Phone:** (902) 539-7973.

THE JOST HOUSE is at 54 Charlotte St. The 1786 two-story dwelling depicts 2 centuries of regional history. Highlights include an 18th-century kitchen, Victorian antiques, an apothecary display and a maritime exhibit. **Tours:** Guided tours are available. **Time:** Allow 1 hour minimum. **Hours:** Mon.-Sat. 9-5, June-Aug.; Mon.-Sat. 10-4, Sept.-Oct. **Cost:** $2; $1 (ages 10-17 and 65+); $5 (family, two adults and two children). **Phone:** (902) 539-0366.

SAINT PATRICK'S MUSEUM is at the n. end of the Government Wharf at 89 Esplanade St. Built in 1828, this is said to be the oldest Roman Catholic church on Cape Breton Island. It contains exhibits about the history of Sydney and the surrounding area. **Hours:** Daily 9-5:30, June-Aug.; by appointment rest of year. **Cost:** Donations. **Phone:** (902) 562-8237 or (902) 539-1572.

GAMBLING ESTABLISHMENTS
• **Casino Nova Scotia** is at 525 George St. **Hours:** Mon.-Wed. 10 a.m.-4 a.m., Thurs.-Sun. daily 24 hours. Closed Good Friday, Easter, Nov. 11 and Dec. 25. **Phone:** (902) 563-7777 or (888) 642-6376.

A CHARMING VICTORIAN BED & BREAKFAST
Phone: 902/564-0921

Bed & Breakfast
$110-$125 6/1-10/31
$90-$125 11/1-5/31

Address: 115 George St B1P 1H9 **Location:** At Pleasant St; centre. **Facility:** The turn-of-the-century home is in the heart of the historic district; individually decorated guest rooms are tasteful and comfortable. 3 units. 2 stories (no elevator), interior corridors. **Terms:** office hours 7 am-11 pm, check-in 4 pm, 3 day cancellation notice. **Free Special Amenities: full breakfast and high-speed Internet.**

CAMBRIDGE SUITES HOTEL
Phone: (902)562-6500

Hotel
$111-$220

Address: 380 Esplanade B1P 1B1 **Location:** Hwy 4, 3.1 mi (5 km) e of jct Hwy 125 exit 6E; downtown. **Facility:** 147 units, some efficiencies. 8 stories, interior corridors. **Parking:** on-site (fee). **Terms:** 30 day cancellation notice-fee imposed. **Amenities:** *Fee:* video games, high-speed Internet. *Some:* safes, honor bars. **Dining:** Trio Restaurant, see separate listing. **Activities:** sauna, whirlpool, exercise room. **Guest Services:** coin laundry. **Free Special Amenities: expanded continental breakfast and high-speed Internet.**

COMFORT INN
Phone: (902)562-0200

Hotel
$111-$163

Address: 368 Kings Rd B1S 1A8 **Location:** Hwy 4, 2.1 mi (3.5 km) e of jct Hwy 125 exit 6E. Located in a commercial area. **Facility:** 61 units. 2 stories (no elevator), interior corridors. **Terms:** cancellation fee imposed.

DAYS INN SYDNEY
Phone: (902)539-6750

Hotel
$98-$158

Address: 480 Kings Rd B1S 1A8 **Location:** Hwy 4, 1.7 mi (2.8 km) e of jct Hwy 125 exit 6E. **Facility:** 163 units. 3 stories (no elevator), interior corridors. **Pool(s):** heated indoor. **Activities:** sauna, whirlpool, exercise room. **Guest Services:** coin laundry. **Free Special Amenities: continental breakfast and high-speed Internet.**

DELTA SYDNEY
Phone: 902/562-7500

Hotel
Rates not provided

Address: 300 Esplanade B1P 1A7 **Location:** At Prince St; centre. **Facility:** 152 units. 8 stories, interior corridors. **Amenities:** video games (fee). **Dining:** Highland Mermaid Restaurant, see separate listing. **Pool(s):** heated indoor. **Activities:** sauna, whirlpool, waterslide, exercise room. **Guest Services:** valet laundry.

QUALITY INN SYDNEY
Phone: (902)539-8101

Hotel
$95-$135

Address: 560 Kings Rd B1S 1B8 **Location:** Hwy 4, 2 mi (3.3 km) e of jct Hwy 125. **Facility:** 70 units. 3 stories (no elevator), interior corridors. **Terms:** cancellation fee imposed. **Pool(s):** heated indoor. **Activities:** exercise room. **Guest Services:** coin laundry. **Free Special Amenities: local telephone calls and newspaper.**

GEORGE & COTTAGE BED AND BREAKFAST
Phone: 902/567-6782

[fyi] Not evaluated. **Address:** 808 George St B1P 1L6 **Location:** At Cottage Rd; centre. Facilities, services, and decor characterize a mid-scale property.

 WHERE TO EAT

ALLEGRO GRILL & DELI
Phone: 902/562-1623

Canadian
$8-$25

AAA Inspector Notes: This wonderful grill in the heart of town offers great soups, salads and sandwiches for lunch and a creative menu for dinner which includes various seafood and meat entrees created with flair by the owner/chef. Delightful desserts are sure to please. **Bar:** full bar. **Address:** 222 Charlotte St B1P 1C5 **Location:** Between Dorchester and Pitt sts. **Parking:** on-site (fee).

DON CHERRY'S
Phone: 902/539-5343

Canadian
$7-$19

AAA Inspector Notes: This hockey-oriented restaurant presents a menu that is sure to score. Guest's can cross-check the selections which range from light appetizers to full entrees, but should not penalize themselves by skipping dessert. **Bar:** full bar. **Address:** 1290 Kings Rd B1S 1E2 **Location:** Hwy 125 exit 6; in Value Check Plaza.

GOVERNORS PUB & EATERY
Phone: 902/562-7646

Canadian
$7-$22

AAA Inspector Notes: Some sections of the late-19th-century former mayor's house overlook the harbor. On the menu are seafood, beef and chicken entrées as well as lighter pub fare. Homemade desserts are worth saving room for. Diners can request seating on the deck overlooking the harbor or venture upstairs to the pub. **Bar:** full bar. **Address:** 233 Esplanade St B1P 1A6 **Location:** Hwy 4, 3.3 mi (5.5 km) e of Hwy 125 exit 6E; centre.

HIGHLAND MERMAID RESTAURANT
Phone: 902/562-7500

Canadian
$12-$25

AAA Inspector Notes: This eatery offers a lovely view of Sydney Harbour. The menu selection is vast with Mediterranean-influenced dishes which include seafood, meats, pasta and pizza options served in ample portions. The service is friendly and relaxed. **Bar:** full bar. **Address:** 300 Esplanade B1P 1A7 **Location:** At Prince St; centre; in Delta Sydney.

PEKING RESTAURANT
Phone: 902/539-7775

Chinese
$8-$21

AAA Inspector Notes: Traditional choices--such as beef with broccoli, lo mein and sweet and sour pork--are served in plentiful portions. Illuminated photographs of China, as well as other Oriental appointments, decorate the slightly fancy, and peacefully quiet, dining rooms. **Bar:** full bar. **Address:** 355 Charlotte St B1P 1E1 **Location:** Between Prince and Wentworth sts. **Parking:** street only.

SMITTY'S
Phone: 902/539-0979

Canadian
$7-$20

AAA Inspector Notes: The family-oriented restaurant satisfies patrons with its ever-popular all-day breakfast items, as well as tasty and wholesome soups and salads at lunchtime. A relaxed mood characterizes the dining space. **Bar:** full bar. **Address:** 272 B Prince St B1P 5N6 **Location:** In Sydney Shopping Centre.

SWISS CHALET

Chicken
$6-$16

Phone: 902/562-3232

AAA Inspector Notes: The popular restaurant is known for its rotisserie chicken and ribs and the tangy Chalet sauce that gives food its special zip. Diners munch on a half or quarter chicken with sides such as steamed vegetables, fries, baked potatoes and salads. Lunch guests often go for the great soup and sandwich combination. Take-out and delivery service are popular options. **Bar:** full bar. **Address:** 482 Grand Lake Rd B1P 5S8 **Location:** Jct Hwy 125.

[L] [D]

TRIO RESTAURANT

Canadian
$9-$24

Phone: 902/563-7009

AAA Inspector Notes: This contemporary restaurant has the energized feel of a lively bistro. Diverse menu offerings include chicken stir-fry, stuffed haddock, tortellini, pork tenderloin and rack of lamb. The seafood chowder should not be missed. **Bar:** full bar. **Address:** 380 Esplanade B1P 1B1 **Location:** Hwy 4 3.1 mi (5 km) e of jct Hwy 125 exit 6E; downtown; in Cambridge Suites Hotel. [L] [D]

TATAMAGOUCHE (B-3) pop. 689

At the mouth of the French and Waugh rivers, Tatamagouche is named for an Indian word meaning "meeting place of the waters." The original French settlement came to an abrupt end in 1755, when a detachment of New Englanders destroyed Tatamagouche and two schooners bound for the Louisbourg fortress with supplies.

Following the close of the Seven Years' War, a second attempt at settlement was directed by Col. Joseph Frederick Walsh Desbarres, a French Huguenot who received a land grant along the French and Waugh rivers. Nothing remains of the village he built, although many residents of Tatamagouche trace their lineage to these first Huguenot settlers.

One notable resident was Anna Swan, born in 1846. The 240-centimetre-tall (8-ft.) woman toured with P.T. Barnum's "Greatest Show on Earth" for several years.

The Fraser Culture Centre on Main Street contains maritime art, North Shore archives, the Tatamagouche Visitor Information Centre and a room devoted to Anna Swan and her husband; phone (902) 657-3285.

Tatamagouche Visitor Information Centre: 362 Main St., Tatamagouche, NS, Canada B0K 1V0. **Phone:** (902) 657-3285.

BALMORAL GRIST MILL MUSEUM is 5 km (3 mi.) s. off Hwy. 311 on Hwy. 256. Built in 1874, this is thought to be the oldest operational gristmill in Nova Scotia. Visitors can see flour being ground and examine the mill's unique Scottish oat-drying kiln. **Time:** Allow 30 minutes minimum. **Hours:** Mon.-Sat. 10-5, Sun. 1-5, June 1-Oct. 15. **Cost:** $3.60; $2.55 (ages 6-17 and 65+); $7.95 (family, maximum of two adults). **Phone:** (902) 657-3016, or (902) 424-7398 in the off-season.

CREAMERY SQUARE HERITAGE CENTRE is at 39 Creamery Rd. The main building, which served as a creamery 1925-92, now houses the Anna Swan Museum; The Creamery Exhibit, which tells the story of the historic creamery; The Brule Fossil Collection, featuring a re-creation of creatures that

roamed the Walchia forest during the Permian period; The Sunrise Trail Museum; and The North Shore Archives.

Time: Allow 1 hour minimum. **Hours:** Mon.-Sat. 10-8, Sun. noon-5, late June-late Aug.; Mon.-Fri. 2-5 or by appointment, Sat. 10-5, Sun. noon-5, Victoria Day weekend-late June. **Cost:** $5; $4 (ages 55+); free (ages 0-11). **Phone:** (902) 657-3449.

Anna Swan Museum is at 39 Creamery Rd. in the Creamery Square Heritage Centre. Born near Tatamagouche, Anna Swan (1846-88) grew to a height of almost 2.5 metres (8 ft.). The museum tells her story through exhibits depicting her early childhood, career, wedding to an equally tall Englishman and her medical condition.

Hours: Mon.-Sat. 10-8, Sun. noon-5, late June-late Aug.; Mon.-Fri. 2-5 or by appointment, Sat. 10-5, Sun. noon-5, Victoria Day weekend-late June. **Cost:** Included with admission to Creamery Square Heritage Centre. **Phone:** (902) 657-3449.

Sunrise Trail Museum is at 39 Creamery Rd. in the Creamery Square Heritage Centre. Permanent exhibits pertain to North Shore Indians, shipbuilding, Acadians at Tatamagouche and early agriculture. **Hours:** Mon.-Sat. 10-8, Sun. noon-5, late June-late Aug.; Mon.-Fri. 2-5 or by appointment, Sat. 10-5, Sun. noon-5, Victoria Day weekend-late June. **Cost:** Included with admission to Creamery Square Heritage Centre. **Phone:** (902) 657-3500.

CHOWDER HOUSE ON MAIN

American
$8-$20

Phone: 902/657-2223

AAA Inspector Notes: This is the place for chowder lovers. Choices include a wide variety of fresh, homemade chowders including seafood, clam, salmon, corn and veggie to name a few. They also offer a selection of sandwiches, burgers, fish and chips, and fine desserts. Patio dining is an option in season. **Bar:** full bar. **Address:** 223 Main St B0K 1V0 **Location:** Centre. **Parking:** street only. [B] [L] [D]

TIVERTON (D-1)

Tiverton is on the northern tip of Long Island, which is just off Digby Neck, a narrow peninsula jutting beyond Digby *(see place listing p. 144)* into the Bay of Fundy. Tiverton's main industry is fishing; lobsters are caught during the winter season. A variety of seabirds and whales can be seen during boat charters and whale cruises, which are available in summer.

Balancing Rock, located on the eastern shore, is a natural landmark situated along a scenic trail. The Island Museum and Visitor Information Centre houses historical memorabilia and exhibits depicting the area's heritage; phone (902) 839-2853.

TRURO (C-3) pop. 11,765
• Restaurants p. 198

Once a large community of Acadian farmers, Truro was later settled by the Scottish and English. Their descendants operate extensive dairy farms in the vicinity. The Nova Scotia Agricultural College, across the Salmon River at Bible Hill, opened in 1905.

Bible Hill also is the site of harness racing on Sundays year-round at Nova Scotia Provincial Exhibition Raceway; phone (902) 893-8075.

Note: Policies concerning admittance of children to pari-mutuel betting facilities vary. Phone for information.

Victoria Park, 400 hectares (1,000 acres) of woodlands interspersed with numerous springs and two waterfalls, has hiking trails, picnic facilities, a swimming pool, tennis courts and other recreational facilities.

The tidal bore is a natural phenomenon of the Salmon River's changing flow. Unlike typical tides that advance gradually, here the water rushes into the river in strong currents or even waves. A viewing area is just off Hwy. 102 exit 14 at the end of Tidal Bore Road. A timetable for the bore is available from the chamber of commerce.

Truro and District Chamber of Commerce: 605 Prince St., Truro, NS, Canada B2N 1G2. **Phone:** (902) 895-6328.

COLCHESTER HISTORICAL MUSEUM is at 29 Young St. Changing exhibits and displays pertain to the human and natural history of Colchester County. Permanent exhibits include maps, photographs, cemetery records and historical documents. The museum also has a research library specializing in genealogy and community histories. **Time:** Allow 1 hour minimum. **Hours:** Mon.-Fri. 10-5, Sat. 1-4, June-Aug.; Tues.-Fri. 10-noon and 1-4, Sat. 1-4, rest of year. **Cost:** $2; $1 (ages 6-16 and students with ID). **Phone:** (902) 895-6284.

LITTLE WHITE SCHOOLHOUSE MUSEUM is on the campus of Nova Scotia Community College at

20 Arthur St. The 1871 one-room schoolhouse contains antique school desks, books and various artifacts. An archive includes old textbooks, educational publications, school records and photographs of former students. **Time:** Allow 30 minutes minimum. **Hours:** Mon.-Fri. 10-5, June-Aug.; Tues. 9-noon or by appointment rest of year. **Cost:** Donations. **Phone:** (902) 895-5170.

BAKER'S CHEST TEAROOM AND BED & BREAKFAST
Phone: 902/893-4824

Bed & Breakfast
$100-$120

Address: 53 Farnham Rd B2N 2X6 **Location:** Hwy 102 exit 14A, 3 mi (4.6 km) e to Main St. **Facility:** Tastefully decorated guest rooms and public areas, including an attractive tearoom serving lunch, comprise this century-old home on the edge of town. 4 units. 2 stories (no elevator), interior corridors. **Terms:** office hours 7 am-11 pm. **Pool(s):** outdoor. **Activities:** whirlpool, exercise room. **Guest Services:** coin laundry.

BEST WESTERN PLUS GLENGARRY HOTEL
Phone: (902)893-4311

Hotel
$125-$155

AAA Benefit: Members save up to 20%, plus 10% bonus points with Best Western Rewards®.

Address: 150 Willow St B2N 4Z6 **Location:** 0.6 mi (1 km) se on Hwy 2. **Facility:** 92 units. 3 stories, interior/exterior corridors. **Parking:** winter plug-ins. **Amenities:** *Some:* high-speed Internet. **Dining:** Glengarry Dining Room, see separate listing. **Pool(s):** outdoor, heated indoor. **Activities:** whirlpool. **Guest Services:** valet laundry. **Free Special Amenities:** local telephone calls and high-speed Internet. *(See ad this page.)*

▼ See AAA listing this page ▼

COMFORT INN
Hotel
$81-$119

Phone: (902)893-0330
Address: 12 Meadow Dr B2N 5V4
Location: Hwy 102 exit 14. Located in a commercial area. **Facility:** 80 units. 2 stories (no elevator), interior corridors. **Terms:** cancellation fee imposed.

HOLIDAY INN HOTEL & CONFERENCE CENTRE TRURO
Phone: (902)895-1651
Hotel
$99-$159

Address: 437 Prince St B2N 1E6
Location: Just e of Willow St; centre. **Facility:** 114 units, some efficiencies. 4 stories, interior corridors. **Parking:** winter plug-ins. **Terms:** cancellation fee imposed. **Amenities:** high-speed Internet. **Pool(s):** heated indoor. **Activities:** whirlpool, exercise room. **Guest Services:** valet and coin laundry.

SUPER 8
Hotel
$99-$136

Phone: (902)895-8884
Address: 85 Treaty Tr B2N 5A9
Location: Hwy 102 exit 13A. **Facility:** 50 units. 3 stories, interior corridors. **Amenities:** high-speed Internet, safes. **Pool(s):** heated indoor. **Activities:** whirlpool, waterslide. **Guest Services:** coin laundry.

TULIPS AND THISTLE BED & BREAKFAST
Phone: (902)895-6141
Bed & Breakfast
$100-$125

Address: 913 Pictou Rd B6L 2N1
Location: Hwy 104 westbound exit 17, 0.6 mi (1 km) e on Rt 4 (Pictou Rd); eastbound 1.3 mi (2 km) e on Rt 4 (Pictou Rd). **Facility:** On the outskirts of town in a pleasant country setting, this modern home offers spacious gathering areas and a variety of individually decorated guest rooms, which range in size from cozy to spacious. 4 units. 2 stories (no elevator), interior corridors. **Terms:** check-in 4 pm, 3 day cancellation notice. **Guest Services:** coin laundry. **Free Special Amenities:** full breakfast and high-speed Internet.

IRWIN LAKE CHALETS
Phone: 902/673-2219
[fyi] Not evaluated. **Address:** Loch Haven Ln B2N 5B6 **Location:** Waterfront. Hwy 102 exit 14, 3 mi (5 km) s on Rt 236, 1.8 mi (3 km) w on gravel entry road. Facilities, services, and decor characterize a mid-scale property.

WHERE TO EAT

CHOW FAMILY RESTAURANT
Chinese
$7-$20

Phone: 902/895-9256
AAA Inspector Notes: The interesting menu dabbles in Canadian, Chinese and Polynesian cuisine. One dining area carries out an Oriental theme, while another has a Polynesian feel. The patio is relaxed and cozy. Servers show good menu knowledge and follow-up skills. **Bar:** full bar. **Address:** 344 Prince St B2N 1E6 **Location:** Just s of Juniper St. L D

FRANK & GINO'S GRILL AND PASTA HOUSE
Phone: 902/895-2165
Italian
$8-$20

AAA Inspector Notes: An upbeat, bustling atmosphere is what guests will find at the popular eatery. Diners can relax in a booth or at a table while perusing a menu of well-prepared pasta, pizza and meat dishes, as well as tasty focaccia. **Bar:** full bar. **Address:** 286 Robie St B2N 1L3 **Location:** Corner of Robie and Juniper sts. L D

GLENGARRY DINING ROOM
Canadian
$7-$20

Phone: 902/893-4311
AAA Inspector Notes: Patrons can relax in the bright atrium of the casual and contemporary dining room. The daily lunch buffet is a nice complement to a menu of seafood, beef and chicken choices. Homemade seafood casserole is flavorful, as are the fresh-baked biscuits and pies. **Bar:** full bar. **Address:** 150 Willow St B2N 4Z8 **Location:** 0.6 mi (1 km) se on Hwy 2; in Best Western Plus Glengarry Hotel. B L D

JUNGLE JIM'S
Canadian
$8-$19

Phone: 902/895-5467
AAA Inspector Notes: Guests can step into a tropical theme at the casual eatery, which employs a friendly staff and nurtures a bustling atmosphere. The menu lines up a wide variety of comfort foods, salads, chicken, beef, seafood and hot wings, all served in ample, flavorful portions. **Bar:** full bar. **Address:** 245 Robie St B2N 5N6 **Location:** Centre; in Truro Mall. L D

MURPHY'S FAMOUS FISH & CHIP RESTAURANT
Phone: 902/895-1275
Seafood
$8-$17

AAA Inspector Notes: English-style seafood, such as the signature fish and chips, is the specialty at this bustling, friendly restaurant with a homey, relaxed atmosphere. Portions are ample and flavors are fresh. **Address:** 88 Esplanade St B2N 2K3 **Location:** Centre; adjacent to rail station. L D

SALTSCAPES RESTAURANT & GENERAL STORE
Phone: 902/843-6700
American
$7-$20

AAA Inspector Notes: Guests can take a stroll through the fine gift shop before heading to the spacious dining area of this family spot. With a casual, county decor, the walls of the eatery are adorned with antique kitchen utensils. The walls is where the antiques stay as the staff in the modern kitchen churn out hearty portions of home-style cooking. **Bar:** full bar. **Address:** 25 Treaty Tr B2N 5A9 **Location:** Hwy 102 exit 13A. L D CALL

SMITTY'S
Canadian
$7-$20

Phone: 902/843-0843
AAA Inspector Notes: The family-oriented restaurant satisfies patrons with its ever-popular all-day breakfast items, as well as tasty and wholesome soups and salads at lunchtime. A relaxed mood characterizes the dining space. **Bar:** full bar. **Address:** 64 Robie St B2N 5C1 **Location:** Hwy 102 exit 14, 0.6 mi (1 km) e. B L D

SWISS CHALET
Chicken
$6-$16

Phone: 902/895-6699
AAA Inspector Notes: The popular restaurant is known for its rotisserie chicken and ribs and the tangy Chalet sauce that gives food its special zip. Diners munch on a half or quarter chicken with sides such as steamed vegetables, fries, baked potatoes and salads. Lunch specials often go for the great soup and sandwich combination. Take-out and delivery service are popular options. **Bar:** full bar. **Address:** 79 Robie St B2N 1K8 **Location:** Hwy 102 exit 14, 0.6 mi (1 km) e. L D

THE WOODEN HOG & RED BIRD LOUNGE
Phone: 902/895-0779
American
$7-$18

AAA Inspector Notes: A friendly, relaxed atmosphere envelops the delightful café. The lighter menu lists tasty soups, salads, nachos and sandwiches, while full meals include fresh halibut, poached salmon, fettuccine primavera and chicken cordon bleu. **Bar:** full bar. **Address:** 627 Prince St B2N 1G2 **Location:** Corner of Louise and Prince sts. L D

TUPPERVILLE (C-1)

Tupperville is in the fertile orchard country of the Annapolis Valley, farmed by the Acadians as early as 1630. At nearby Bloody Creek, British soldiers from Annapolis Royal were massacred by the French and Indians in 1711 and 1757. Despite the area's violent history, Col. James Delancy, leader of the pro-British raids around New York during the American Revolution, settled at this site after being banished from the United States in 1783. It was also home to Sir Charles Tupper, a 19th-century provincial prime minister.

TUPPERVILLE SCHOOL MUSEUM is at 2663 Hwy. 201. This 1858 one-room schoolhouse contains century-old desks, books, a potbellied stove, a school bell and other furnishings. The museum also contains photographs of former students and community members as well as the works of woodcarver Louis Jeremy. **Time:** Allow 30 minutes minimum. **Hours:** Daily 10-5, July 1-Labour Day; Wed.-Sun. 10-5, in June; by appointment rest of year. **Cost:** Donations. **Phone:** (902) 665-2427, or (902) 665-4815 in the off-season. ⊞

TUSKET

MARCO'S GRILL & PASTA HOUSE   **Phone:** 902/648-0253

Italian
$7-$20

AAA Inspector Notes: Not far from Yarmouth, the restaurant is worth the drive for well-prepared seafood, pasta and fine chowders. Homemade desserts shouldn't be missed. **Bar:** full bar. **Address:** 237 Gavel Rd B0W 3M0 **Location:** Hwy 103 exit 33, just w. Ⓛ Ⓓ

WALLACE (B-3)

WINERIES

• **Jost Vineyards** is 5 km (3.1 mi.) e. on Rte. 6 to 48 Vintage Ln. **Hours:** Tastings daily 9-6, June 15-Sept. 15; daily 9-5, May 1-June 14 and Sept. 16-Dec. 23; Mon.-Sat. 9-5, rest of year. Tours are given daily at noon and 3, mid-June to mid-Sept. **Phone:** (902) 257-2636 or (800) 565-4567.

FOX HARB'R GOLF RESORT & SPA
                          Phone: (902)257-1801

Resort Hotel
$225-$425

Address: 1337 Fox Harbour Rd B0K 1Y0 **Location:** Oceanfront. Hwy 6, 3.6 mi (6 km) w, 3.6 mi (6 km) n on Ferry Rd, then 1.2 mi (2 km) e. **Facility:** Spacious guest rooms, each sporting an upscale decor with several amenities, are located in 12 manor-style buildings located away from the main lodge. 82 units, some houses. 2 stories (no elevator), interior corridors. **Terms:** open 6/1-12/31 & 5/1-5/31, 3 day cancellation notice-fee imposed. **Amenities:** high-speed Internet, honor bars. **Dining:** 2 restaurants. **Pool(s):** heated indoor. **Activities:** saunas, whirlpools, beach access, marina, 4 tennis courts, cross country skiing, recreation programs, bicycles, hiking trails, volleyball, exercise room, spa. *Fee:* boats, sailboats, fishing, charter fishing, golf-27 holes. **Guest Services:** valet laundry, area transportation-within 10 mi (17 km). **Free Special Amenities:** local telephone calls and newspaper.

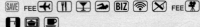

WESTERN SHORE

ATLANTICA HOTEL & MARINA OAK ISLAND
                          Phone: (902)627-2600

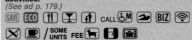

Resort Hotel
$109-$169

Address: 36 Treasure Dr B0J 3M0 **Location:** Hwy 103 exit 9 or 10, follow signs on Rt 3; 6 mi (10 km) e of Mahone Bay. **Facility:** Overlooking the bay and marina, this pleasant resort offers deluxe oceanfront chalets as well as traditional rooms, some with a deck or balcony. 120 units, some cottages and condominiums. 3 stories, interior corridors. **Terms:** cancellation fee imposed. **Amenities:** *Some:* high-speed Internet. **Dining:** La Vista Dining Room, see separate listing. **Pool(s):** heated outdoor, heated indoor, whirlpool, miniature golf, tennis court, playground, horseshoes, shuffleboard, exercise room, spa. *Fee:* marina. **Guest Services:** coin laundry. **Free Special Amenities:** high-speed Internet and children's activities.
(See ad p. 179.)

SAVE ECO ⏹ ⏹ ⏹ CALL ⏹ ⏹ BIZ ⏹
⏹ ⏹ / SOME UNITS FEE ⏹ ⏹ ⏹

WHERE TO EAT

LA VISTA DINING ROOM   **Phone:** 902/627-2600

American
$9-$25

AAA Inspector Notes: A bounty of food awaits at La Vista, the portions are very generous as is the superb view of the marina and bay from the spacious dining room. Evening buffet in season. **Bar:** full bar. **Address:** 36 Treasure Dr B0J 3M0 **Location:** Hwy 103 exit 9 or 10, follow signs on Rt 3; 6 mi (10 km) e of Mahone Bay; in Atlantica Hotel & Marina Oak Island. Ⓑ Ⓛ Ⓓ

WESTPORT (D-1) pop. 249

Westport is on Brier Island, Nova Scotia's westernmost point. The town is a 1-hour drive and two ferry trips from Digby *(see place listing p. 144)* via lovely Digby Neck and Long Island. The island's three lighthouses guide ships through the surrounding treacherous waters. Two of them, the Grand Passage Light (Northern Light) and the Brier Island Light (Western Light), can be reached by car.

Westport was the childhood home of Joshua Slocum, who in 1898 became the first person to sail around the world alone. A plaque honoring Slocum is part of a small memorial on the island's eastern edge within sight of the Peters Island Lighthouse.

Brier Island's location in the sea-life-rich Bay of Fundy and its position on bird migration routes makes it a prime spot to view the area's abundant wildlife. Seals and porpoises as well as minke, humpback, finback and right whales are among the marine mammals visitors can see. Whale-watch and bird-watching cruises depart from Westport spring through fall.

BRIER ISLAND WHALE AND SEABIRD CRUISES depart from Brier Island, which is reached via Hwy. 217 and two car ferries from Digby Neck. The ferry connections must be timed to avoid a delay in crossing. Cruises into the Bay of Fundy offer sightings and behavioral observations of various species of whales, dolphins, porpoises and seabirds. All cruises are narrated by experienced naturalists. The partially enclosed MV *Mega Nova* carries 50 passengers, while the 12-passenger Zodiac *Cetacean* is open-air.

Warm clothing is necessary. Zodiac cruises are not recommended for ages 0-5, expectant mothers or individuals with back problems. **Hours:** Three- to 5-hour cruises aboard the MV *Mega Nova* depart daily at 9:30, 1:30 and 5:30, July-Aug.; at 9:30 and 1:30, early June-June 30 and Sept. 1 to mid-Oct. (weather permitting). Two- to 2.5-hour cruises aboard the *Cetacean* depart daily at 10:30, 1 and 3:30, May 15 to mid-Oct. (during peak season, additional cruises may be offered).

Cost: *Mega Nova* fare $49; $41 (students with ID and senior citizens); $27 (ages 6-12); $21 (ages 0-5). *Cetacean* fare $55; $50 (students with ID and senior citizens); $45 (ages 6-12). Reservations are recommended. **Phone:** (902) 839-2995 or (800) 656-3660.

MARINER CRUISES WHALE & SEABIRD TOURS departs from Brier Island, reached via Hwy. 217W and car ferries from Digby Neck and Long Island. Two-and-a-half to 4-hour whale and seabird tours in the Bay of Fundy are conducted by a naturalist. Visitors may spot several species of whales, including humpbacks, fin and minke as well as porpoises, dolphins, seals and various seabirds.

Warm clothing is advised. **Hours:** Daily 8-8, June 12-Oct. 15. **Cost:** Fare $49; $41 (ages 65+ and students with ID); $27 (ages 4-12). **Phone:** (902) 839-2346 or (800) 239-2189. [TI]

WESTVILLE (C-4) pop. 3,805

[SAVE] **MAGIC VALLEY** is 9 km (6 mi.) w. off Hwy. 104 exit 20. The park includes Storybook Village and Old MacDonald's Farm. Pedal and bumper boats, miniature golf, park rides, train rides, a pool and waterslide complex also are featured. **Hours:** Daily 11-6, July 1-Labour Day (weather permitting). **Cost:** Park rides (includes all rides except miniature golf and water activities) $16.95; free (ages 0-2); $63.95 (family, two adults and two children). Park only $8. Individual rides $1.50-$3.50. **Phone:** (902) 396-4467. [TI]

Explore the Travel Guides
on AAA.com/Travel or
CAA.ca/Travel

WHYCOCOMAGH

KELTIC QUAY BAYFRONT LODGE & COTTAGES
Phone: 902/756-1122

Cottage
$199-$299 6/1-10/31
$149-$249 11/1-5/31

Address: 90 Main St B0E 3M0 **Location:** Just se off Trans-Canada Hwy 105; centre. **Facility:** Set in a quiet spot on the Bras d'Or Lakes, the property offers pleasant, spacious and well-equipped duplex cottages with splendid views of the bay. 11 cottages. 2 stories (no elevator), exterior corridors. **Terms:** office hours 8 am-10 pm, check-in 4 pm, 3 day cancellation notice-fee imposed. **Amenities:** high-speed Internet. **Activities:** rental boats, canoeing, paddleboats, horseshoes, shuffleboard.

[icons] / SOME UNITS FEE [icon]

WHERE TO EAT

VI'S RESTAURANT
Phone: 902/756-2338

American
$6-$15

AAA Inspector Notes: This family-run, casual diner has been faithfully serving customers since 1957. Home-style cooking includes full breakfast, lunch and dinner options. **Bar:** full bar. **Address:** General Delivery B0E 3M0
Location: Trans-Canada Hwy 105 exit 5. [B] [L] [D]

WINDSOR (C-3) pop. 3,709

A popular base for exploring the Annapolis Valley, Windsor is at the confluence of the Avon and St. Croix rivers. The town's original Acadian settlers reclaimed thousands of hectares from the sea by building several kilometres of dikes. During the mid-18th century the area was resettled by Loyalists and planters from New England and Imperial troops garrisoned at Fort Edward.

The phenomenal tidal fluctuations at Windsor average about 12 metres (40 ft.) each day. For the best times and viewing locations, contact the Windsor-West Hants Visitor Information Centre, off Hwy. 1 exit 6; phone (902) 798-2690.

Of historic interest is King's-Edgehill School, one of the oldest educational institutions in the British Commonwealth. Home to a respected touring company of puppeteers, the Mermaid Theatre of Nova Scotia, 132 Gerrish St., allows visitors to view puppets and stages from previous shows or watch new ones being created; phone (902) 798-5841. Windsor also claims the title of "Birthplace of Hockey" thanks to 19th-century author Thomas Chandler Haliburton, who described an early form of the game being played at Long Pond.

Town of Windsor: P.O. Box 158, Windsor, NS, Canada B0N 2T0. **Phone:** (902) 798-2275.

FORT EDWARD NATIONAL HISTORIC SITE OF CANADA is off King St. on Fort Edward St. The blockhouse and earthworks are all that remain of Fort Edward, built in 1750 by British Maj. Charles Lawrence. Many Acadian families were detained here after the 1755 deportation. Garrisoned by Imperial troops for more than a century, Fort Edward was an important base during the Seven Years' War, the American Revolution and the War of 1812. Canadian and American forces trained at the fort during World War I. A 1.2-kilometre (.7 mi.) trail surrounds the earthworks.

Time: Allow 30 minutes minimum. **Hours:** Fort daily 10-5, mid-June through Labour Day. Grounds daily dawn-dusk, year-round. **Cost:** Free. **Phone:** (902) 798-2639 mid June through Aug. 31, or (902) 532-2321 during the off-season.

HALIBURTON HOUSE MUSEUM is .75 km (.5 mi.) w. on Clifton Ave. This was the estate of Judge Thomas C. Haliburton, Canada's first internationally famous author. The 1836 villa features Victorian furnishings as well as Haliburton's desk. **Time:** Allow 1 hour minimum. **Hours:** Mon.-Sat. 10-5, Sun. 1-5, June 1-Oct. 15. **Cost:** $3.60; $2.55 (ages 6-17 and 65+); $7.95 (family). **Phone:** (902) 798-2915.

SHAND HOUSE MUSEUM is off Hwy. 101, .75 km (.5 mi.) s. on Avon St. The 1890 Victorian house with gingerbread trim contains original period furniture as well as all the conveniences of 1890, including central heating, closets, electric lighting and indoor plumbing. **Time:** Allow 30 minutes minimum. **Hours:** Mon.-Sat. 10-5, Sun. 1-5, June 1-Oct. 15. **Cost:** $3.60; $2.55 (ages 6-17 and 65+); $7.95 (family, two adults and two children). **Phone:** (902) 798-8213.

WEST HANTS HISTORICAL SOCIETY MUSEUM is at 281 King St. Home furnishings, housewares, clothing, toys, maritime objects, books and musical instruments reflect daily provincial life. A genealogy research library is available. **Time:** Allow 1 hour minimum. **Hours:** Tues.-Sat. 9-5, mid-June to late Aug.; Wed. 9-5, rest of year. **Cost:** Donations. Research fee $4. **Phone:** (902) 798-4706.

WINDSOR HOCKEY HERITAGE CENTRE is at 128 Gerrish St. Exhibits trace the development of the sport of ice hockey from its origins around 1800 to the present. Displays include hockey sticks carved by Mi'kmaq Indians, wooden pucks cut from tree branches, early hockey nets and Acme Club Spring Skates that clamped to boot or shoe bottoms. **Time:** Allow 30 minutes minimum. **Hours:** Tues.-Fri. 10-5, May-Oct; Tues.-Wed. and Fri. 10-5 and by appointment rest of year. **Cost:** Donations. **Phone:** (902) 798-1800.

SUPER 8   Phone: (902)792-8888
▼▼▼▼   **Address:** 63 Cole Dr B0N 2T0
Hotel   **Location:** Hwy 101 exit 5A, just s.
$51-$136   **Facility:** 66 units. 3 stories, interior corridors. **Terms:** cancellation fee imposed. **Amenities:** high-speed Internet. *Some:* video games. **Pool(s):** heated indoor. **Activities:** whirlpool, waterslide, exercise room. **Guest Services:** coin laundry.
[ECO] [↕] CALL [⌂] [⇄] [BIZ] [📶] [✕] [▯] [▣] [▢]
/ SOME UNITS FEE [🐾]

WHERE TO EAT

COCOA PESTO BISTRO   Phone: 902/472-3300
▼▼▼ ◆◆◆   **AAA Inspector Notes:** This splendid 1850s home located in the heart of town evokes a relaxed atmosphere both indoors and out. The menu lists various seafood and meat dishes including salmon, haddock, chicken and steaks, all prepared with local ingredients and various forms of cooking: Meats are smoked, slow-cooked, steamed or flash fried. **Bar:** full bar. **Address:** 494 King St B0N 2T0 **Location:** Corner of Albert St; centre. [L] [D]
Canadian
$9-$24

THE SPITFIRE ARMS ALEHOUSE   Phone: 902/792-1460
▼▼▼ ◆◆   **AAA Inspector Notes:** This classic English-style pub is decorated in a theme recalling the famous Spitfire fighter plane. A bounty of beers is on tap to assist in washing down well-prepared pub fare, including wraps, burgers, fish and chips, meat pies, stir-fries and ploughman's lunches. **Bar:** full bar. **Address:** 29 Water St B0N 2T0 **Location:** Hwy 101 exit 6, just e to King St. **Parking:** street only. [L] [D]
British
$8-$20

WOLFVILLE (C-2) pop. 3,772
• Hotels p. 202 • Restaurants p. 203

Wolfville was resettled by New Englanders following the expulsion of the Acadians in 1755. It is the home of Acadia University, founded in 1838 by the Nova Scotia Baptist Educational Society.

The closest town to Grand Pré *(see place listing p. 148)*, Wolfville is a popular base for exploring the historic region associated with the Acadian deportation. Several old Acadian settlements lie along the Gasperau River and are accessible from Gaspereau Avenue in town.

K.C. IRVING ENVIRONMENTAL SCIENCE CENTRE & HARRIET IRVING BOTANICAL GARDENS is off University Ave. on the campus of Acadia University. The 2-hectare (6-acre) botanical gardens contain nine habitats from the Acadia Forest region, including a sand barrens, a coniferous woodland and a marsh. Interpretive signs provide details about native plants and endangered species. A glassed-in winter garden and a medicinal and food garden also are on the grounds.

The science center features greenhouses, a conservatory and botanical laboratories. Nature trails and picnic areas are available. **Time:** Allow 1 hour, 30 minutes minimum. **Hours:** Gardens daily 7:30 a.m.-dusk (weather permitting). Science center daily 8 a.m.-10 p.m. **Cost:** Free. **Phone:** (902) 585-5242.

PRESCOTT HOUSE MUSEUM is off Hwy. 101 exit 11, 1.5 km (.9 mi.) n. of Greenwich on Hwy. 358, then 4 km (2.5 mi.) e. to 1633 Starrs Point Rd. Built by Charles Ramage Prescott, merchant, legislator and pioneer horticulturist, the 1800s Georgian house features gardens and is known for its collections of oriental rugs and samplers.

Time: Allow 30 minutes minimum. **Hours:** Mon.-Sat. 10-5, Sun. 1-5, June 1-Oct. 15. **Cost:** $3.60; $2.55 (ages 6-17 and 65+); $7.95 (family, two adults and children). **Phone:** (902) 542-3984 June 1-Oct.15, or (902) 424-7398 rest of year.

RANDALL HOUSE MUSEUM is at 259 Main St. The museum, set in a Georgian period farmhouse, displays historical artifacts from the New England planters who settled in the area after the expulsion of the Acadians in 1760. Other exhibits chronicle regional history up to present times. **Hours:** Tues.-Sat. 10-5, Sun. 1:30-5, early June to mid-Sept. Afternoon tea is served Fri. 2-4. **Cost:** $2; free (ages 0-11). **Phone:** (902) 542-9775. 🍴

BLOMIDON INN   Phone: (902)542-2291

Historic
Country Inn

$139-$269 6/1-12/18
$129-$249 12/28-5/31

Address: 195 Main St B4P 1C3 **Location:** On Rt 1. Located in a residential area. **Facility:** Meticulously landscaped gardens surround this 19th-century sea captain's mansion; guest rooms vary in size, style and furnishings. 33 units, some kitchens and cottages. 3 stories (no elevator), interior corridors. **Terms:** open 6/1-12/18 & 12/28-5/31, office hours 6:30 am-1 am, cancellation fee imposed. **Amenities:** high-speed Internet. **Dining:** restaurant, see separate listing. **Activities:** tennis court.
(See ad this page.)

SAVE 🍴 🛎 📶 ✕

/ SOME UNITS 🏢 📷

TATTINGSTONE INN   Phone: 902/542-7696

Historic Bed
& Breakfast

$118-$188 6/1-10/27
$108-$188 10/28-5/31

Address: 620 Main St B4P 1E8 **Location:** 0.4 mi (0.6 km) w on Rt 1. Located in a residential area. **Facility:** Well-coordinated decor is accented with artwork and antiques to bring a charming ambience to this 1877 inn and carriage house. 9 units. 2 stories (no elevator), interior/exterior corridors. **Terms:** office hours 8 am-9 pm, cancellation fee imposed. **Pool(s):** heated outdoor. **Guest Services:** valet laundry.

SAVE 🍴 ⛛ 🐟 📶 ✕ / SOME UNITS 🐾

VICTORIA'S HISTORIC INN   Phone: 902/542-5744

Historic Bed
& Breakfast

$128-$245 6/1-10/31
$108-$245 11/1-5/31

Address: 600 Main St B4P 1E8 **Location:** 0.4 mi (0.6 km) w on Rt 1. Located in a commercial-residential area. **Facility:** Built in 1893, the mansion offers a variety of well-appointed guest rooms and suites in a main inn and a carriage house. 16 units. 3 stories (no elevator), interior/exterior corridors. **Terms:** office hours 7 am-11 pm. 📶 ✕

▼ See AAA listing this page ▼

WHERE TO EAT

ACTON'S GRILL & CAFE   Phone: 902/542-7525

Canadian
$11-$27

AAA Inspector Notes: For many years, the restaurant has attracted patrons with its creative cuisine. A relaxed bistro-style atmosphere and a menu of varied fresh seafood, choice meats and pasta dishes are the main draws. Finish with a decadent dessert, cappuccino or espresso. **Bar:** full bar. **Reservations:** suggested. **Address:** 406 Main St B4P 1C9 **Location:** On Rt 1; centre.

L D

THE BLOMIDON INN DINING ROOM
Phone: 902/542-2291

American
$9-$28

AAA Inspector Notes: A renowned wine list complements creative regional cuisine, including preparations of fresh seafood from the Bay of Fundy. The romantic inn restaurant, which has the ambience of a Victorian manor house, is a favorite spot for special occasions. **Bar:** full bar. **Address:** 195 Main St B4P 1C3 **Location:** On Rt 1; in Blomidon Inn. L D

PADDY'S BREWPUB & ROSIE'S RESTAURANT
Phone: 902/542-0059

American
$7-$21

AAA Inspector Notes: Guests can opt for seating in one of two sections: the casual, upbeat pub or the quieter dining room. Both offer the same menu items and friendly casual service. Food selection is good, from fresh seafood to burgers to pizza, and a brewmaster creates a fine variety of handcrafted ales on site. **Bar:** full bar. **Address:** 460 Main St B4P 1E2 **Location:** Centre; at Elm Ave. L D

TEMPEST WORLD CUISINE   Phone: 902/542-0588

Fusion
$12-$28

AAA Inspector Notes: This attractive dining room is open and airy with large picture windows. Guests enjoy the additional option of dining on the patio in season. The cuisine is varied with focus on creatively prepared meat, fresh seafood and local produce. **Bar:** full bar. **Reservations:** suggested. **Address:** 117 Front St B4P 1A5 **Location:** Just down from corner of Main St and Central Ave; centre.
Historic L D

YARMOUTH (E-1) pop. 7,162
• Hotels p. 204 • Restaurants p. 204

Yarmouth was founded in 1651 by French colonists, who subsequently were expelled by the British in 1755. The area was settled by New Englanders in 1761 and later by returning Acadians and Loyalists. An important shipbuilding and shipping town during the days of sail, Yarmouth prospered during the 19th century. Figuring prominently in the city's economy was the Killam Brothers Shipping Office, 90 Water St., which managed sailing fleets for more than 200 years. Now a museum, its 19th-century furnishings and ledgers tell the story of the era; phone (902) 742-5539.

Yarmouth lies at the end of two scenic routes: Hwy. 1, which follows St. Mary's Bay north to Digby *(see place listing p. 144)*, and Hwy. 3, which heads east to Shelburne *(see place listing p. 191)*.

Yarmouth Chamber of Commerce: P.O. Box 532, Yarmouth, NS, Canada B5A 4B4. **Phone:** (902) 742-3074.

Self-guiding tours: A tourist information center at Main and Forest streets in front of the ferry terminal provides brochures outlining a self-guiding walking tour of various points of interest, including the city's Georgian and Italianate houses. The center also provides additional information about ferry service; phone (902) 742-6639.

ARGYLE TOWNSHIP COURT HOUSE & GAOL is 15 km (9 mi.) s. on Rte. 3 (Lighthouse Rte.) in Tusket. Built 1803-05, the courthouse remained in use until 1945. Guided tours of the old jail, courtroom, judge's chamber and jail keeper's quarters are available. Genealogical archives contain Argyle and Yarmouth County records and provincial census data from 1770-1891.

Time: Allow 30 minutes minimum. **Hours:** Daily 9-5, July-Aug.; Mon.-Fri. 9-noon and 1-4, May-June and Sept.-Oct. **Cost:** $2; free (ages 0-9); $4 (family). Research fee $5; $3 (half-day). **Phone:** (902) 648-2493.

ART GALLERY OF NOVA SCOTIA–YARMOUTH is at 341 Main St. A permanent collection with a focus on Nova Scotia folk art is on display. Historical, contemporary, works on paper, ceramics and temporary exhibits also may be seen. **Time:** Allow 1 hour minimum. **Hours:** Thurs.-Sun. noon-5. **Cost:** Donations. **Phone:** (902) 749-2248.

FIREFIGHTERS MUSEUM OF NOVA SCOTIA is at 451 Main St. Vintage firefighting equipment includes horse-drawn steamers and hand-drawn, hand-operated pumpers. Photographs, leather hoses, lanterns and buckets also are on display. A library is available on site.

Time: Allow 1 hour minimum. **Hours:** Mon.-Sat. 9-5, Sun. 10-5, July-Aug.; Mon.-Sat. 9-5 in June and Sept. 1 to mid-Oct.; Mon.-Fri. 9-4, Sat. 1-4, rest of year. **Cost:** $3; $2.50 (ages 65+); $1.50 (ages 6-17); $6 (family). **Phone:** (902) 742-5525.

 YARMOUTH COUNTY MUSEUM AND ARCHIVES is at 22 Collins St. Housed in a granite church, the museum contains one of Canada's largest collections of ships portraits. Also featured are ships models, a lens from the Yarmouth lighthouse, costumes, a 1921 electric car, and a collection of tools, glass, china, toys and household items.

Another highlight is a stone bearing a mysterious runic inscription that is linked to Norse explorations of around A.D. 1000. Five period rooms are offered. Archives contain historical documents, photographs and genealogical records.

Time: Allow 30 minutes minimum. **Hours:** Museum open Mon.-Sat. 9-5, mid-May to mid-Oct.; Tues.-Sat. 2-5, rest of year. Archive hours vary; phone ahead. **Cost:** Museum $3; $2.50 (ages 60+); $1 (ages 15-18); 50c (ages 6-14); $6 (family, two adults and school-age children). Combination ticket with Pelton-Fuller House $5; $4 (ages 60+); $2 (ages 15-18); $1 (ages 6-14); $10 (family, two adults and school-age children). Archives $5; $1 (students with ID). **Phone:** (902) 742-5539.

Pelton-Fuller House is at 20 Collins St. This 1895 Victorian house served as the summer retreat for businessman Alfred Fuller, the original Fuller Brush man. Antiques and collections as well as some of Mr. Fuller's brushes are displayed; visitors also may stroll through the gardens.

Time: Allow 30 minutes minimum. **Hours:** Guided tours are given Mon.-Sat. 10-4, June-Oct.; by appointment rest of year. **Cost:** $3; $2.50 (ages 60+); $1 (ages 15-18); 50c (ages 6-14); $6 (family, two adults and school-age children). Combination ticket with Yarmouth County Museum and Archives $5; $4 (ages 60+); $2 (ages 15-18); $1 (ages 6-14); $10 (family, two adults and school-age children). **Phone:** (902) 742-5539.

BEST WESTERN MERMAID
Phone: (902)742-7821

Motel
$99-$140

AAA Benefit: Members save up to 20%, plus 10% bonus points with Best Western Rewards®.

Address: 545 Main St B5A 1J6 **Location:** Corner of Main St and Starrs Rd. Located near downtown. **Facility:** 45 units, some efficiencies. 2 stories (no elevator), exterior corridors. **Amenities:** high-speed Internet. **Pool(s):** heated outdoor. **Guest Services:** coin laundry. **Free Special Amenities:** continental breakfast and high-speed Internet.

/ SOME UNITS FEE

COMFORT INN
Phone: (902)742-1119

Hotel
$101-$138

Address: 96 Starrs Rd B5A 2T5 **Location:** Jct Hwy 101 E and 3. Adjacent to mall. **Facility:** 79 units. 2 stories (no elevator), interior corridors. **Terms:** cancellation fee imposed.

/ SOME UNITS

LAKELAWN MOTEL
Phone: (902)742-3588

Motel
$59-$79

Address: 641 Main St B5A 1K2 **Location:** 0.6 mi (1 km) n on Hwy 1. **Facility:** 30 units. 2 stories (no elevator), interior/exterior corridors. **Terms:** office hours 7 am-11 pm.

/ SOME UNITS FEE

RODD GRAND YARMOUTH
Phone: (902)742-2446

Hotel
$111-$151

Address: 417 Main St B5A 4B2 **Location:** Corner of Grand St. **Facility:** 138 units. 7 stories, interior corridors. **Terms:** cancellation fee imposed. **Dining:** Haley's Restaurant & Lounge, see separate listing. **Pool(s):** heated indoor. **Activities:** sauna, whirlpool, exercise room. **Guest Services:** valet laundry.

/ SOME UNITS

VOYAGEUR MOTEL
Phone: 902/742-7157

Motel
$104-$189 6/1-10/1
$79-$169 10/2-5/31

Address: RR 1 B5A 4A5 **Location:** 3 mi (4.8 km) ne on Hwy 1. **Facility:** 17 units. 1 story, exterior corridors. **Terms:** office hours 6:30 am-midnight, 3 day cancellation notice. **Activities:** hiking trails, jogging. **Guest Services:** coin laundry. / SOME UNITS FEE

WHERE TO EAT

THE AUSTRIAN INN
Phone: 902/742-6202

Austrian
$7-$30

AAA Inspector Notes: Representative of menu choices are Wiener schnitzel, pork cordon bleu, chicken Oscar and plenty of Canadian-style steak and seafood entrees. The quiet dining room is a pleasant place for a romantic, candlelit dinner. Soft music plays in the background. **Bar:** full bar. **Reservations:** suggested. **Address:** Hwy 1 B5A 4A5 **Location:** 2.6 mi (4.4 km) ne on Hwy 1. L D

HALEY'S RESTAURANT & LOUNGE
Phone: 902/742-2446

Canadian
$8-$22

AAA Inspector Notes: This sports bar offers booth and table seating in a relaxed atmosphere. The menu offers a wide range of choices from fresh seafood, steaks and chicken entrées to such comfort foods as burgers, clubhouse sandwiches and chowders. **Bar:** full bar. **Address:** 417 Main St B5A 4B2 **Location:** Corner of Grand St; in Rodd Grand Yarmouth. L D

JUNGLE JIM'S
Phone: 902/742-9708

Canadian
$7-$19

AAA Inspector Notes: Guests can step into a tropical theme at the casual eatery, which employs a friendly staff and nurtures a bustling atmosphere. The menu lines up a wide variety of comfort foods, salads, chicken, beef, seafood and hot wings, all served in ample, flavorful portions. **Bar:** full bar. **Address:** 95 Starrs Rd B5A 2T6 **Location:** Jct Hwy 101 E and 3; opposite mall. L D

LOTUS GARDEN RESTAURANT
Phone: 902/742-1688

Chinese
$7-$17

AAA Inspector Notes: A popular spot with the local crowd, this restaurant presents a vast menu that lists a good mix of combination plates and some Canadian cuisine. **Bar:** full bar. **Address:** 67 Starrs Rd B5A 3K7 **Location:** Corner of Pleasant St. L D

RUDDER'S SEAFOOD RESTAURANT & BREW PUB
Phone: 902/742-7311

Canadian
$8-$24

AAA Inspector Notes: Overlooking Killam's Marina, the restaurant has seating on two levels as well as a spacious deck for seasonal dining. Specializing in seafood, the menu also includes such pub fare as steaks, chicken and burgers. Boiled lobster suppers are another option. Live entertainment on weekends and Wednesday night karaoke can get pretty lively. **Bar:** full bar. **Address:** 96 Water St B5A 4P9 **Location:** At Killam's Wharf; close to ferry terminal; centre. L D

Coastal Village of French River

Prince Edward Island

From charming Charlottetown, "Canada's birthplace"—to lively Orwell, where Celtic traditions thrive—to the shops in which Mi'kmaq Indians still display their wares, Prince Edward Island presents a character deeply steeped in the past.

Quiet communities—such as Cavendish, described in Lucy Maud Montgomery's "Anne of Green Gables"—move at a leisurely pace that reflects an earlier time.

Vivid natural tapestries are woven from the vibrant greens of pastures, rich rusts of sandstone cliffs and deep, glistening blues of rolling ocean waves. In autumn, shades of apricot-orange, scarlet red and brilliant gold decorate the landscape. Tides wash the sands of secluded, relaxing beaches.

When Anne, the quirky, red-headed orphan in the classic novel "Anne of Green Gables," first came to the island, she believed it to be as lovely "as anything she ever dreamed...."

What did she see? Country lanes shaded

Green Gables Heritage Place, Cavendish

by moss-draped trees. Surf-carved rocks. The sea, cobalt blue and sparkling in the sun. Apple and cherry trees sprinkled with blossoms. Dandelions dotting grassy fields. And lilac trees, limbs heavy with aromatic purple flowers.

It's easy to see why author Lucy Maud Montgomery used Cavendish, her childhood home, as a model for the fictional hamlet of Avonlea, where she set "Anne of Green Gables," numerous sequels and other novels. Fans flock to Cavendish to visit the restored Green Gables House. Originally a cottage belonging to the author's cousins, it's more popularly recognized as Anne's home base for dreaming up shenanigans.

The author's love of nature and this unspoiled maritime island was apparent in her tribute to the pastoral area she called home and the easygoing lifestyle of its residents. Bordering Cavendish, Prince Edward Island National Park is a veritable delight. Beaches, freshwater ponds, saltwater marshes, woodlands and historical landmarks appeal to nature lovers.

Taking it Easy

Other areas on the island that aren't specifically featured in Montgomery's stories nevertheless exhibit a similar unhurried, relaxed mood.

Make yourself at home in one of numerous

cottages, country inns or bed and breakfasts; the island boasts a wide variety of graceful properties in idyllic settings, where unwinding is the most important thing on the "to do" list.

Set out for a stroll along the coast—with so many public beaches, you won't have to go far to squish white (or red) sand between your toes. Acquaint yourself with the countryside on a lighthouse hunt—more than 50 dot the coast. En route amid rolling hills are roadside stands offering homegrown fruits and cafés filled with the aroma of just-baked scones.

In Charlottetown, brick government buildings, Victorian houses and shingled taverns on Great George, King and Water streets have been restored. Tour Province House, site of meetings in 1864 that led to Canada's confederation 3 years later. Or peruse quaint shops selling works created by local artists and craftspeople in Olde Charlottetown and Peake's Wharf.

Bagpipe and fiddle music celebrates Summerside's Celtic heritage, while museums depict Acadian culture, fox breeding and shipbuilding. Watch sailboats dock from the waterfront boardwalk or fill a basket with yummy jams and jellies at the town's farmers market.

Then snuggle under a blanket woven at an island woolen mill and crack the spine on one of Lucy Maud Montgomery's popular tales.

Recreation

The island makes up for its lack of deep-wilderness recreation areas with a variety of well-maintained outdoor playgrounds. You can enjoy golf May through October on the rolling greens of more than 30 parklike courses tucked about, most within an hour's drive of Charlottetown. Eighteen-hole venues include championship Brudenell River; Dundarave, Brudenell's companion course; and the course at Summerside, challenging to any skill level.

Well-maintained Belvedere, just a putt or two away from downtown Charlottetown, is one of Canada's oldest courses. Also steeped in tradition is Green Gables, off Hwy. 6 on the northern shore; this redesigned jewel has been an ocean-side favorite since 1939. Tournament-caliber greens include Mill River, north of O'Leary, and the celebrated Links at Crowbush Cove, which offers spectacular views of the Gulf of St. Lawrence from its vantage point just off Hwy. 350 near Lakeside.

With no part of the province more than 16 kilometres (10 mi.) from the ocean or an inlet, fishing, swimming and sea kayaking are close at hand. Prince Edward Island National Park preserves an elongated section of the northern seashore from New London Bay to Tracadie Bay and offers year-round ocean access.

In addition to camping, provincial parks on the island's perimeter are ideal for beachcombing and clamming. The beach at Cedar Dunes, south of West Point off Lady Slipper Drive, is flanked by cedar trees. Lord Selkirk Park's activity center caters to families; it's west of Eldon off Kings Byway Drive. Cabot Beach, off Blue Heron Drive, overlooks Malpeque Bay.

Part of the Trans Canada Trail, the Confederation Trail bicycling and hiking path traverses the 280-kilometre-long (174-mi.) province, following an abandoned railway bed that roughly parallels Hwy. 2. The western section extends from Tignish, near land's end at North Cape, to Kensington. Whether you pedal your own wheels, rent a mountain bike from a local outfitter or indulge in a customized, guided tour with van support, you'll find this an easy ride. The route shifts from pastoral fields to scenic rivers to wooded parcels; in between, the route is dotted with trailside shelters.

Great George Street, Charlottetown

Historic Timeline

1534	Jacques Cartier is the first European to land on the island, later named Île Saint-Jean.
1720	The French establish a capital at Port La Joye near present-day Charlottetown.
1758	Britain gains control of the island and deports Acadian settlers.
1799	The island is renamed for Queen Victoria's father, Prince Edward, Duke of Kent.
1803	Lord Selkirk establishes a colony of 800 Scottish Highlanders at Belfast.
1864	The "Fathers of Confederation" meet at Charlottetown to discuss a Canadian union.
1873	Prince Edward Island becomes Canada's seventh province—and its smallest.
1874	Lucy Maud Montgomery, author of "Anne of Green Gables," is born in Clifton (now New London).
1993	Catherine Callbeck, Canada's first female premier, is elected.
1997	The Confederation Bridge links Prince Edward Island to the mainland.
2000	The Council of Atlantic Premiers is formed to promote the interests of Prince Edward Island and three other provinces.

What To Pack

Temperature Averages Maximum/Minimum (Celsius)	JANUARY	FEBRUARY	MARCH	APRIL	MAY	JUNE	JULY	AUGUST	SEPTEMBER	OCTOBER	NOVEMBER	DECEMBER
Alberton	-4 / -12	-4 / -12	1 / -7	6 / -2	13 / 4	19 / 10	23 / 14	22 / 14	18 / 9	12 / 4	6 / -1	-1 / -8
Charlottetown	-4 / -12	-4 / -13	1 / -8	6 / -2	13 / 3	19 / 9	23 / 13	22 / 13	18 / 9	12 / 4	6 / -1	-1 / -8
Montague	-3 / -12	-4 / -12	1 / -7	6 / -1	13 / 4	19 / 10	23 / 14	22 / 14	18 / 9	12 / 5	6 / -1	-1 / -7
Mount Stewart	-4 / -12	-4 / -13	1 / -8	6 / -2	13 / 3	19 / 9	23 / 13	22 / 13	18 / 9	12 / 4	6 / -1	-1 / -8
O'Leary	-4 / -12	-4 / -12	1 / -7	6 / -2	13 / 4	19 / 10	23 / 14	22 / 14	18 / 9	12 / 4	6 / -1	-1 / -8
Summerside	-4 / -12	-4 / -12	1 / -7	6 / -2	13 / 4	19 / 10	23 / 14	22 / 14	18 / 9	12 / 4	6 / -1	-1 / -8

From the records of The Weather Channel Interactive, Inc.

Good Facts To Know

ABOUT THE PROVINCE

POPULATION: 135,294.

AREA: 5,656 sq km (2,184 sq mi.); ranks 13th.

CAPITAL: Charlottetown.

HIGHEST POINT: 152 m (499 ft.), Queens County.

LOWEST POINT: Sea level, Atlantic Ocean.

TIME ZONE(S): Atlantic. DST.

GAMBLING

MINIMUM AGE FOR GAMBLING: 19.

REGULATIONS

TEEN DRIVING LAWS: For the first year there is a maximum of three passengers, either all from the immediate family of the driver or two from the immediate family and one additional passenger. Minimum age for an unrestricted driver's license is 17. For more information about Prince Edward Island driver's license regulations phone (902) 368-5200.

SEAT BELT/CHILD RESTRAINT LAWS: Seat belts required for driver and all passengers 16 and older. Children ages 10 through 15 and at least 18 kilograms (40 lbs.) are required to be in a child restraint or seat belt; child restraints are required for children under age 10 and under 145 centimetres (4 feet, 9 inches) tall.

CELL PHONE RESTRICTIONS: All drivers are prohibited from the use of handheld electronic devices and text messaging while driving.

HELMETS FOR MOTORCYCLISTS: Required for all riders.

RADAR DETECTORS: Not permitted.

MOVE OVER LAW: Requires motorist to slow down half the posted speed limit, and if possible vacate the lane nearest to a stopped emergency vehicle with its lights engaged.

FIREARMS LAWS: By federal law, all nonresidents entering Canada with a firearm must declare their weapon in writing and pay a fee of $25 (Canadian). Contact the Canadian Firearms Program at (800) 731-4000 to receive a declaration form and additional information.

ALCOHOL CONSUMPTION: Legal age 19.

HOLIDAYS

HOLIDAYS: Jan. 1 ▪ Islander Day, Feb. (3rd Mon.) ▪ Good Friday ▪ Easter Monday ▪ Victoria Day, May 24 or closest prior Mon. ▪ Canada Day, July 1 ▪ Natal Day, Aug. (1st Mon.) ▪ Labour Day, Sept. (1st Mon.) ▪ Thanksgiving, Oct. (2nd Mon.) ▪ Remembrance Day, Nov. 11 ▪ Christmas, Dec. 25 ▪ Boxing Day, Dec. 26.

MONEY

TAXES: The federal Goods and Service Tax is 5 percent. Prince Edward Island's provincial sales tax is 10 percent.

VISITOR INFORMATION

INFORMATION CENTERS: Prince Edward Island has one provincial information center on the mainland at Caribou, Nova Scotia. The island has visitor information centers at Gateway Village in Borden-Carleton ▪ Cavendish ▪ Charlottetown ▪ Mount Pleasant ▪ Souris ▪ Summerside ▪ and Wood Islands. The Charlottetown center is open year-round. The Borden-Carleton location is open March through November. The others are open mid-May to mid-October.

FURTHER INFORMATION FOR VISITORS:
Charlottetown Visitor Center
P.O. Box 2000
Charlottetown, PE C1A 7N8
Canada
(800) 463-4734

FISHING AND HUNTING REGULATIONS:
Dept. of Environment, Energy and Forestry
P.O. Box 2000
Charlottetown, PE C1A 7N8
Canada
(902) 368-5000

INTERPROVINCE FERRY INFORMATION:
Northumberland Ferries & Bay Ferries Ltd.
94 Water St.
P.O. Box 634
Charlottetown, PE C1A 7L3
Canada
(902) 566-3838
(877) 635-7245

Traversier C.T.M.A. Ferry
435 Chemin Avila Arseneau
Cap-Aux-Meules, QC G4T 1J3
Canada
(418) 986-3278
(888) 986-3278

Prince Edward Island Annual Events

Please call ahead to confirm event details.

JANUARY

- Music PEI Week and Awards Gala Charlottetown 902-894-6734
- WinterTide Holiday Festival Charlottetown 902-629-4023
- Robbie Burns Concert Charlottetown 902-566-2082

FEBRUARY

- WinterDine / Charlottetown 902-368-8636
- Jack Frost Children's WinterFest / Charlottetown 800-955-1864
- Stratford Winter Carnival Stratford 902-569-2535

MARCH

- St Patrick's Day Bash Charlottetown 902-892-6992
- Bluegrass Old Country Jamboree / Summerside 902-439-2344
- St. Patrick's Day Fun Run Charlottetown 902-368-4110

APRIL

- PEI Guitar Festival Charlottetown 902-368-4413
- Tartan Day / Charlottetown 902-659-2060
- Voices of Spring Charlottetown 902-628-6135

MAY

- East Prince Music Festival Summerside 902-368-2348
- Savour Food and Wine Show / Charlottetown 902-370-3997
- Ceilis at the Irish Hall Charlottetown 902-368-7083

JUNE

- Summerside Highland Gathering and Event in the Tent / Summerside 902-436-5377
- Tignish Irish Moss Festival Tignish 902-882-2476
- DierseCity / Charlottetown 902-628-6009

JULY

- Stratford Strawberry Festival Stratford 902-569-1995
- Cavendish Beach Music Festival / Cavendish 888-311-9090
- P.E.I. Potato Blossom Festival / O'Leary 902-859-4722

AUGUST

- West Prince Red Clay Bluegrass and Old-Time Music Festival / Tignish 902-853-2107
- Old Home Week Charlottetown 902-629-6623
- Community Harvest Festival Kensington 902-836-3509

SEPTEMBER

- Eastern Kings Exhibition Souris 902-687-2784
- Island Storytelling Festival Summerside 902-432-1296
- PEI International Shellfish Festival / Charlottetown 902-892-4455

OCTOBER

- Tuesday Night Ceilidh Georgetown 902-652-2053
- Prince Edward Island Marathon / Charlottetown 902-569-8692
- Haunted Mansion Halloween Nights of Fear! Kensington 902-836-3336

NOVEMBER

- Downtown Summerside Christmas Parade Summerside 902-436-7546
- Souris Christmas Parade Festival / Souris 902-687-2157, ext. 0
- Charlottetown Christmas Parade / Charlottetown 902-566-5548

DECEMBER

- Souris Christmas Parade Souris 902-687-2157
- New Year's Eve Family Party / Summerside 902-432-1282
- A Green Gables Christmas Cavendish 902-963-7874

Potato Field

Bottle Houses, Cap-Egmont

East Point Lighthouse,
East Point

Malpeque Harbor

Elmira Railway Museum, Elmira

Great Experience for Members

AAA editor's picks of exceptional note

Confederation Centre
of the Arts

Province House
National Historic Site

Orwell Corner Historic
Village

Prince Edward Island
National Park of
Canada

Cavendish (B-3)

Avonlea Village of Anne of Green Gables
(See p. 216.)

Green Gables Heritage Place *(See p. 217.)*

Charlottetown (B-4)

Confederation Centre of the Arts *(See p. 220.)*

Founders' Hall *(See p. 220.)*

Province House National Historic Site
(See p. 221.)

North Cape (A-1)

North Cape, Nature & Technology in Perfect Harmony *(See p. 232.)*

Orwell (B-5)

Orwell Corner Historic Village *(See p. 233.)*

Prince Edward Island National Park of Canada (B-4)

Prince Edward Island National Park of Canada *(See p. 234.)*

Summerside (B-2)

Wyatt Heritage Properties *(See p. 237.)*

Enjoy great savings on hotel rates at AAA.com or CAA.ca

© AAA

Prince Edward Island
Orientation

NOT INTENDED FOR DRIVING.
SEE APPROPRIATE AAA SHEET MAP.

Scale in Kilometers

25   0   25

To Cape-aux-Meules, QC

North Cape

Tignish

Alberton

Woodstock

O'Leary

West Point

Cap-Egmont

Mont Carmel

Bideford
Port Hill

Malpeque

Miscouche

SUMMERSIDE

Kensington

Park Corner

New London

New Glasgow

Stanley Bridge

Rustico

Cavendish

Prince Edward Island National Park of Canada

Gulf of St Lawrence

CHARLOTTETOWN

Bonshaw

Port La Joye-Fort Amherst NHS of Canada

Hillsborough Bay

Mt Stewart

Georgetown

Montague
Orwell

Eldon

Murray Harbour

Wood Islands

Cardigan Bay

East Point

Elmira

Souris

Northumberland

PRINCE EDWARD ISLAND

NEW BRUNSWICK

Strait

NEW BRUNSWICK

NOVA SCOTIA

PRINCE EDWARD ISLAND

NOVA SCOTIA

N

Only places listed in the Attractions section appear on this map.
⬇ *See AAA GEM Attractions*
1 *See Recreation Areas Chart on following page*

© 2011 NAVTEQ

4061-A

Recreation Areas Chart

The map location numerals in column 2 show an area's location on the preceding map.

	MAP LOCATION	CAMPING	PICNICKING	HIKING TRAILS	BOATING	BOAT RAMP	BOAT RENTAL	FISHING	SWIMMING	PETS ON LEASH	BICYCLE TRAILS	WINTER SPORTS	VISITOR CENTER	LODGE/CABINS	FOOD SERVICE
NATIONAL PARKS *(See place listings.)*															
Prince Edward Island (B-4) 26 square kilometres. Cross-country skiing, ice-skating, windsurfing; beaches.		•	•	•	•	•		•	•	•	•	•	•	•	•
PROVINCIAL															
Brudenell River (B-5) 563 hectares 3 mi. w. of Georgetown on Hwy. 3. Golf (36 holes), horseback riding, horseshoes, lawn bowling, tennis, windsurfing; boat tours, canoe rental, heated pool, interpretive programs, playground, sea kayak rental.	**1**	•	•	•	•		•	•	•	•	•		•	•	•
Cabot Beach (B-3) 138 hectares 16 km n.w. of Kensington off Hwy. 20. Nature programs. Disc golf, supervised swimming, windsurfing; playground, recreation programs.	**2**							•	•	•	•		•		
Cedar Dunes (B-1) 57 hectares 24.25 km s.w. of O'Leary on Hwy. 14 at West Point. Nature programs. Supervised swimming, windsurfing; lighthouse museum, playground. *(See West Point p. 240.)*	**3**	•	•	•				•	•	•				•	•
Green Park (B-2) 94 hectares on Hwy. 12. Disc golf, windsurfing; playground, river beach. *(See Port Hill p. 234.)*	**4**	•	•		•	•		•	•					•	•
Jacques Cartier (A-1) 11 hectares 6.5 km n. of Alberton on Cape Kildare. Beach volleyball, supervised swimming, windsurfing; children's programs, full-time naturalist, playground.	**5**	•	•					•	•	•					
Linkletter (B-2) 29 hectares 4 mi. (6.5 km) w. of Summerside via Hwy. 11. Windsurfing, playground.	**6**	•	•		•			•	•						•
Lord Selkirk (B-5) 60 hectares, 1 mi (1.6 km) e. of Eldon on Hwy. 1. Clamming, golf (9 holes), miniature golf, windsurfing; beach, playground, pool.	**7**	•	•						•	•					
Mill River (A-1) 183 hectares at St. Anthony on Hwy. 136 off Hwy. 2. Cross-country skiing, golf (18 holes), tennis, volleyball, windsurfing; canoe and kayak rentals, interpretive and recreation programs, playgrounds.	**8**	•		•			•			•	•		•		
Northumberland (C-5) 30 hectares 3 km e. of Wood Islands ferry. Bird-watching, supervised swimming; family programs, nature trails.	**9**							•	•	•				•	
Panmure Island (B-5) 35 hectares n. of Gaspereaux on Hwy. 347 off Hwy. 17. Supervised swimming; bike rentals, lighthouse tours, playground, recreational programs.	**10**	•	•		•			•	•	•	•				•
Red Point (A-6) 7 hectares, 8 mi (12.75 km) n.e. of Souris on Hwy. 16. Supervised swimming; beach, organized recreational activities, playground.	**11**	•			•				•	•					
Wood Islands (C-5) 12 hectares at the Wood Islands Ferry Terminal. Clamming; playground.	**12**		•		•	•		•	•	•					•

ALBERTON (A-1) pop. 1,081

Alberton's name was changed from Cascumpec in honor of Albert Edward, Prince of Wales, who visited the island in 1860. Just outside the community a plaque commemorates the founding of the silver fox fur industry in Alberton.

ALBERTON MUSEUM is on Hwy. 12 at 457 Church St. Furnished rooms in this restored 1878 courthouse include farm implements, photographs, a military display, exhibits about harness racer Joe O'Brien and items relating to the silver fox fur industry. Island genealogical research materials and welcome center information are available. **Hours:** Mon.-Sat. 9:30-5:30, Sun. by appointment, mid-June through August 31; Mon.-Fri. 9:30-5:30, in Sept.; by appointment rest of year. **Cost:** Donations. **Phone:** (902) 853-4048, or (902) 853-3372 in the off-season.

BRIARWOOD INN, COTTAGES & LODGE
Phone: 902/853-2518

◆◆◆ ◆◆◆
Motel
$79-$125 6/1-9/15
$60-$99 9/16-5/31

Address: 253 Matthews Ln C0B 1B0 **Location:** Waterfront. 1.9 mi (3 km) e on Rt 12. **Facility:** 25 units, some two bedrooms, kitchens and cottages. 1-2 stories (no elevator), interior/exterior corridors. **Bath:** some shared. **Terms:** office hours 7 am-11 pm, 30 day cancellation notice-fee imposed. **Activities:** playground. **Guest Services:** coin laundry.

🛜 ⊠ 🐾 / SOME UNITS FEE 🐶 🍴 🖥 🖵

NORTHPORT PIER INN
Phone: 902/853-4520

◆◆◆
Hotel
$125-$172

Address: 298 Rt 152 C0B 1B0 **Location:** Oceanfront. 1.8 mi (3 km) s on Rt 152. **Facility:** 14 units. 2 stories (no elevator), interior/exterior corridors. **Terms:** open 6/1-9/30, 7 day cancellation notice-fee imposed. **Activities:** playground.

🍴 CALL ♿ 🛜 ⊠ / SOME UNITS 🍴 🖥

WHERE TO EAT

THE BOAT SHOP STEAK & SEAFOOD
Phone: 902/853-4510

◆◆◆
American
$9-$28

AAA Inspector Notes: A splendid ocean view awaits visitors to the converted boat building shop, on the pier overlooking Northport Harbour and Cascumpec Bay. The contemporary menu specializes in seafood dishes made from local ingredients. Patio seating is available. **Bar:** full bar. **Address:** 296 Harbourview Dr C0B 1B0 **Location:** 1.8 mi (3 km) s on Rt 152 (Northport Rd); adjacent to pier; centre. [B] [L] [D]

ANNANDALE

THE INN AT SPRY POINT
Phone: (902)583-2400

◆◆◆
Bed & Breakfast
$159-$299

Address: 222 Ark Ln C0A 2B0 **Location:** Off Rt 310, 2.6 mi (4.3 km) e on Spry Point Rd, follow signs. Located in a quiet secluded area. **Facility:** On 80 acres at the tip of a peninsula, this handsome inn captures broad views of the ocean and beaches; many rooms have private balconies. 15 units. 2 stories (no elevator), interior/exterior corridors. **Terms:** open 6/24-9/16, office hours 7 am-11 pm, 8 day cancellation notice-fee imposed. **Activities:** hiking trails.

🍸 CALL ♿ BIZ 🛜 ⊠ 🎿

BAY FORTUNE

THE INN AT BAY FORTUNE
Phone: (902)687-3745

◆◆◆
Country Inn
$135-$335

Address: 758 Rt 310 C0A 2B0 **Location:** Jct Hwy 2, 1.2 mi (2 km) s on Rt 310; 7.2 mi (12 km) w of Souris. Located in a rural quiet area. **Facility:** Overlooking Bay Fortune, the inn offers an array of tastefully decorated rooms, many featuring wood or gas fireplaces and balconies or decks. 17 units. 1-4 stories (no elevator), interior/exterior corridors. **Terms:** open 6/1-10/6 & 5/25-5/31, office hours 7 am-11:30 pm, 8 day cancellation notice-fee imposed. **Dining:** restaurant, see separate listing. **Free Special Amenities:** full breakfast and local telephone calls.

SAVE 🍴 🍸 BIZ 🛜 ⊠

WHERE TO EAT

THE INN AT BAY FORTUNE
Phone: 902/687-3745

◆◆◆ ◆◆◆
Regional Canadian
$27-$38

AAA Inspector Notes: In a wonderful location overlooking Bay Fortune, the restaurant serves lovingly prepared, creative, contemporary cuisine. An open kitchen provides an opportunity to observe the chef in action. The menu is rich in traditional dishes that use fresh local produce, meats and seafood. Much of the produce comes from the property's extensive organic gardens. Guests can choose from seating on the enclosed verandah overlooking the bay, or in the relaxed main dining room. **Bar:** full bar. **Reservations:** suggested. **Address:** 758 Rt 310 C0A 2B0 **Location:** Jct Hwy 2, 1.2 mi (2 km) s on Rt 310, 7.2 mi (12 km) w of Souris. [D] 🎿

SHELTERED HARBOUR CAFE
Phone: 902/687-1997

◆◆◆
American
$7-$18

AAA Inspector Notes: A popular port in a storm, this casual restaurant does not overlook any water but the food is great with a home-style flavor. Open for all meals and serving ample portions. Noted for their seafood and chowders. **Bar:** full bar. **Address:** 2065 Rt 2 C0A 2B0 **Location:** On Rt 2; in Abel's Corner Ultramar and Convenience. [B] [L] [D] CALL ♿

BEDEQUE

HISTORIC MAPLETHORPE BED AND BREAKFAST
Phone: (902)887-2909

◆◆◆
Country Inn
$100-$160 6/1-9/15
$85-$125 9/16-5/31

Address: 2123 Hwy 112 C0B 1C0 **Location:** On Rt 112; centre. **Facility:** 5 units, some two bedrooms and kitchens. 2 stories (no elevator), interior corridors. **Terms:** office hours 7 am-11 pm, 7 day cancellation notice-fee imposed. **Activities:** bicycles.

🍴 🍸 🛜 ⊠ / SOME UNITS 🍴 🖥

BIDEFORD (B-2)

BIDEFORD PARSONAGE MUSEUM is at 784 Bideford Rd. (Rte. 166). Originally built as a private residence for Thomas H. Pope, an accountant and a telegraph operator, this 1878 house later became a parsonage and a manse for the Methodist Church and United Church, respectively. From 1894 to 1895 it was Canadian author Lucy Maud Montgomery's home while she taught at the local school.

The yellow Victorian house with white trim has been restored and still has its original flooring. Period pieces are displayed throughout, including furniture, books, photographs and Victorian dresses.

The tour includes the foyer; living room (where many weddings were performed); pantry; parson's room; and Lucy Maud Montgomery's room, which has a lovely view. **Tours:** Guided tours are available. **Time:** Allow 30 minutes minimum. **Hours:** Daily 9-5, June-Sept. (also Wed. 5-7:30, July-Aug.). **Cost:** $5; $2.50 (ages 7-18); a family rate is available. **Phone:** (902) 831-3133 or (902) 831-2817.

BONSHAW (B-3)

W.W. Irving named this settlement after Bonshaw Tower in his native Dumfries, Scotland. The scenic drive between Borden and Churchill on Hwy. 1 runs through Bonshaw, providing exceptional sightseeing by car.

CAR LIFE MUSEUM is on Hwy. 1. The museum features a collection of restored antique cars dating from 1898, farm machinery from the early 1800s and farm tractors of the early 1900s. Highlights include a 1959 Cadillac owned by Elvis Presley. **Hours:** Daily 10-5, July-Aug.; 10-4 in June and Sept. 1 to mid-Sept. **Cost:** $6; $5.50 (senior citizens); $2.50 (ages 6-14). **Phone:** (902) 675-3555, or (902) 629-9777 in the off-season.

BRACKLEY BEACH

BRACKLEY BEACH NORTH WINDS INN & SUITES
            Phone: (902)672-2245

Motel
$69-$179

Address: 3828 Portage Rd C1E 1Z3 **Location:** Jct Rt 6 and 15. **Facility:** 66 units, some kitchens. 2 stories (no elevator), exterior corridors. **Terms:** office hours 7 am-midnight, 14 day cancellation notice-fee imposed. **Pool(s):** heated indoor. **Activities:** sauna, whirlpool, rental bicycles, playground, exercise room. **Guest Services:** coin laundry. *(See ad starting on p. 224.)*

[ⓘ] CALL [&M] [🛒] [BIZ] [📶] [✕] [🗎] [🖼] [▭]

WHERE TO EAT

THE DUNES CAFE & STUDIO GALLERY
            Phone: 902/672-1883

Canadian
$12-$34

AAA Inspector Notes: Dine in or out at this pleasant gem which has a large art gallery overlooking a delightful water garden and the distant sand dunes. The menu is varied, with the focus on fresh local seafood and produce all creatively presented on their own handmade pottery. Although ample portions are likely to fill diners up, they should try to save room to sample one of the sumptuous desserts. **Bar:** full bar. **Reservations:** suggested. **Address:** Rt 15 C1E 1Z3 **Location:** Jct Rt 6 and 15, 0.6 mi (1 km) n.

[L] [D] CALL [&M] [AC]

BROOKVALE (B-3)

RECREATIONAL ACTIVITIES

Winter Activities

- **Brookvale Winter Activity Park** is at 2018 Rte. 13 (Alpine entrance); Nordic entrance is at 1800 Rte. 13. **Hours:** Wed. and Fri. 1:30-9:30, Sat.-Sun. 9-5:30, Thurs. 5:30-9:30, mid-Dec. to mid-Mar. (weather permitting). Phone ahead to confirm schedule. **Phone:** (902) 658-7861, or (902) 658-7866 for Nordic/Cross-Country Centre.

CAP-EGMONT (B-2)

The Egmont Bay coastline features red sandstone cliffs with such rock formations as The Horse. Although rumors suggest that pirates' treasure might be buried nearby, fresh fish and lobsters are the cape's most commonly found riches.

BOTTLE HOUSES are at 6891 Hwy. 11 (North Cape Coastal Drive). Three fanciful buildings are made of more than 25,000 glass bottles of various shapes and sizes. Visitors can walk through a chapel, a six-gabled house and another structure—all built with bottles. The surrounding grounds feature a Garden Interpretation Center set up in a replica of the Cap Egmont Lighthouse, rock gardens and more than 70 varieties of flowers.

Time: Allow 30 minutes minimum. **Hours:** Daily 9-6, mid-May to early Oct. (also 6-8 p.m., July-Aug.). **Cost:** $6.50; $6 (ages 60+ and students with ID); $2 (ages 6-16); $16 (family, two adults and children). **Phone:** (902) 854-2987, or (902) 854-2254 in the off-season.

CAVENDISH (B-3)

• Restaurants p. 219

Cavendish was affectionately described in Lucy Maud Montgomery's popular works "Anne of Green Gables" and "Anne of Avonlea." Maud, as she preferred to be called, came to Cavendish when she was 21 months old to live with her maternal grandparents after her mother died. The author, who died in Toronto in 1942, is buried in Cavendish Cemetery.

In the waters off Cavendish rest the remains of the *Marco Polo*, a wooden sailing ship that established a world speed record in 1852 when it sailed from Liverpool, England, to Melbourne, Australia. The vessel ran aground and broke up in an 1883 gale.

The north shore is noted for its scenic beaches, many of which are operated by Prince Edward Island National Park *(see place listing p. 234)*. A long-established tradition of community lobster dinners distinguishes this part of the province. The feasts pack throngs of people into community halls, particularly around New Glasgow and St. Ann.

AVONLEA VILLAGE OF ANNE OF GREEN GABLES is 1.6 km (1 mi.) w. of Hwy. 13 on Hwy. 6. The schoolhouse where Lucy Maud Montgomery taught in 1896 and the church she attended are preserved on the site, which features costumed interpreters, live theater with characters from "Anne of Green Gables," musical shows, puppet shows and a chocolate factory. Visitors can attend a period county fair complete with games and a pig race, attend four concerts, take island dance lessons and play period children's games.

Also on the grounds are the Clifton Manse, a fishing shanty and gardens. Horse and wagon rides are available. Some bilingual service is available. **Time:** Allow 3 hours minimum. **Hours:** Daily 10-5, mid-June through Labour Day; 10-4, day after Labour Day to mid-Sept. (with limited programs offered). **Cost:** (valid for 2 days) $19.05; $17.31 (ages 66+); $15.48 (ages 3-18); $64.93 (family, two adults and all dependent children ages 0-17). Admission day after Labour Day to mid-Sept. $8; free (ages 0-11). **Phone:** (902) 963-3050. 🏕

GREEN GABLES HERITAGE PLACE is w. of Hwy. 13 on Hwy. 6 at 8619 Cavendish Rd., part of Lucy Maud Montgomery's Cavendish National Historic Site. Immortalized in Lucy Maud Montgomery's "Anne of Green Gables," the site is affiliated with Prince Edward Island National Park (see place listing p. 234).

The farm was the home of David Jr. and Margaret Macneill, cousins of Montgomery's grandfather. The house is furnished in late 19th-century style, and outbuildings have been restored to the Victorian period. The Haunted Woods and Balsam Hollow walking trails, as described in the book, are on the grounds. A visitor center features an audiovisual presentation and exhibits about Montgomery's life; bilingual guide services are available.

Hours: Daily 9-5, May-Oct. Phone for schedule rest of year. **Cost:** $7.80; $6.55 (ages 65+); $3.90 (ages 6-16); $19.60 (family). A combination ticket with The Site of Lucy Maud Montgomery's Cavendish Home is available. **Phone:** (902) 963-7874. 🍴

RIPLEY'S BELIEVE IT OR NOT! ODDITORIUM is 1.4 km (.9 mi.) w. on Hwy. 6 at Cranberry Village. Fourteen galleries with collections of unusual objects provide visitors with experiences such as standing next to a 10-foot-tall robot, seeing a shrunken head or touching a piece of the Berlin Wall. Optical illusions and video presentations round off the experience.

Time: Allow 1 hour minimum. **Hours:** Daily 9 a.m.-9:30 p.m., July-Aug.; 9:30-4:30 in June and Sept. Last admission 1 hour before closing. Phone ahead to confirm schedule. **Cost:** $11.99; $9.99 (senior citizens); $7.49 (ages 6-15); $32.99 (family). **Phone:** (902) 963-2242, or (902) 962-2022 in the off-season.

SAVE **SANDSPIT** is 2 km (1.2 mi.) w. of Hwy. 13 on Hwy. 6. This amusement park offers rides and old-fashioned carnival games. Visitors can try the Cyclone roller coaster, Can-Am race cars, bumper boats, miniature golf, an antique-style carousel and more. A children's play area is included. **Hours:** Daily 10 a.m.-11 p.m., mid-July to mid-Aug.; 10-10, mid-Aug. through Labour Day; 9-3:30, mid-June to mid-July. **Cost:** Park free. Rides $3-$10. Daily pass $22.50; $18.50 (children 36-47 inches tall); $12.50 (under 36 inches tall); $82 (family of four). **Phone:** (902) 963-2626. 🍴 🏕

SAVE **SHINING WATERS FAMILY FUN PARK** is 1.6 km (1 mi.) w. on Hwy. 6 from jct. Hwy. 13. This 36-acre amusement park has a petting farm, walking trails through a streamside forest, a Storybook Land, paddleboat rides, two inner tube slides, five other waterslides and a wading pool. **Time:**

Allow 4 hours minimum. **Hours:** Daily 10-7, July 1-Aug. 21; 10-6, June 16-30 and Aug. 22-Sept. 5. **Cost:** $19.50; $16.50 (children 42-47 inches tall); $13.50 (children 36-41 inches tall). **Phone:** (902) 963-3939 or (877) 963-3939. 🍴 🏕

THE SITE OF LUCY MAUD MONTGOMERY'S CAVENDISH HOME, on Hwy. 6 at 8523 Cavendish Rd., .4 km (.2 mi.) e. of jct. Hwy. 13, is part of Lucy Maud Montgomery's Cavendish National Historic Site. This is the homestead where the author wrote "Anne of Green Gables" and lived for half of her life. The site captures the essence of the Cavendish Montgomery knew and loved. Although the old farmhouse and buildings no longer exist, the property includes gardens and exhibits as well as signs containing quotes from Montgomery's journal to help visitors understand her life on this farm.

Hours: Daily 9-5, mid-May to mid-Oct. (also 5-6, July-Aug.). **Cost:** $3; $1 (ages 0-15). A combination ticket with Green Gables Heritage Place is available. **Phone:** (902) 963-2231.

WAX WORLD OF THE STARS is 1.4 km (.9 mi.) w. on Hwy. 6. Wax displays of the famous feature such film, TV, music and sports personalities as Julia Roberts, Jim Carrey, Shrek and Michael Jordan as well as royal personages. Exhibits include memorabilia, sound effects and videos. Visitors are permitted to take photographs.

Time: Allow 1 hour minimum. **Hours:** Daily 9 a.m.-8:30 p.m., July-Aug.; 9:30-4:30 in June and Sept. Last admission 1 hour before closing. Phone ahead to confirm schedule. **Cost:** $11.99; $9.99 (ages 65+); $7.49 (ages 6-12); $32.99 (family, two adults and two children). **Phone:** (902) 963-3444, or (902) 962-2022 in the off-season.

BAY VISTA MOTEL
Phone: 902/963-2225

Motel
$59-$135

Address: 9517 Cavendish Rd C0A 1E0 **Location:** Jct Rt 13, 2.8 mi (4.8 km) w on Rt 6. Located in a quiet rural area. **Facility:** 32 units, some efficiencies and cottages. 1 story, exterior corridors. **Terms:** open 6/1-9/30, office hours 7:30 am-10:30 pm, cancellation fee imposed. **Amenities:** high-speed Internet. **Pool(s):** heated outdoor. **Activities:** playground. **Guest Services:** coin laundry.

CAVENDISH BEACH COTTAGES
Phone: 902/963-2025

Cottage
$119-$215

Address: RR 2 Hunter River C0A 1E0 **Location:** 1.1 mi (1.9 km) ne of jct Rt 6 and 13, on Gulf Shore Rd; free access to property through park. Located in PEI National Park. **Facility:** 13 cottages. 1 story, exterior corridors. **Terms:** open 6/1-10/5 & 5/10-5/31, office hours 8 am-9 pm, 10 day cancellation notice-fee imposed. **Activities:** limited beach access, playground. **Guest Services:** coin laundry.

CAVENDISH BOSOM BUDDIES COTTAGES & SUITES
Phone: 902/963-3449

Cottage
$90-$300

Address: RR 1 C0A 1N0 **Location:** Jct Rt 6 and 13, 0.4 mi (0.7 km) e on Rt 6. **Facility:** 17 units, some cottages. 1-2 stories (no elevator), exterior corridors. **Terms:** open 6/1-10/16 & 5/1-5/31, office hours 8 am-10 pm, 3 night minimum stay - seasonal and/or weekends, 14 day cancellation notice-fee imposed. **Activities:** playground. **Guest Services:** coin laundry.

Visit AAA.com or CAA.ca
for one-stop travel
planning and reservations

CAVENDISH MAPLES COTTAGES
Phone: (902)963-2818

Cottage
$79-$319

Address: 73 Avonlea Blvd C0A 1M0 **Location:** Jct Rt 6 and 13, 1.5 mi (2.5 km) w on Rt 6. **Facility:** Guests will find a variety of well-appointed cottages nestled among mature trees; a gas grill is available on the deck of each unit. 22 cottages. 1 story, exterior corridors. **Terms:** open 6/1-10/15 & 5/15-5/31, office hours 9 am-9 pm, 3-5 night minimum stay - seasonal, 30 day cancellation notice-fee imposed. **Pool(s):** heated outdoor. **Activities:** whirlpool, playground, game room, horseshoes, volleyball. **Guest Services:** coin laundry. **Free Special Amenities:** local telephone calls and high-speed internet.

KINDRED SPIRITS COUNTRY INN & COTTAGES
Phone: 902/963-2434

Bed & Breakfast
$65-$450

Address: Memory Ln, Rt 6 C0A 1N0 **Location:** Jct Rt 13, 0.5 mi (0.8 km) w. **Facility:** Varying in size, guest rooms are situated in the main inn and annex section; six cottages feature a private hot tub on a large deck. 46 units, some cottages. 2 stories (no elevator), interior/exterior corridors. **Terms:** open 6/1-10/21 & 5/15-5/31, office hours 7 am-11 pm, 30 day cancellation notice-fee imposed. **Pool(s):** heated outdoor. **Activities:** whirlpool, rental bicycles, playground, game room, exercise room. **Guest Services:** coin laundry. **Free Special Amenities:** full breakfast and high-speed Internet.
(See ad starting on p. 224.)

LAKEVIEW LODGE & COTTAGES
Phone: 902/963-2436

Cottage
$52-$401

Address: Hwy 6 C0A 1N0 **Location:** Jct Rt 13, 0.6 mi (1 km) w. Located in a quiet area; adjacent to Green Gables Golf Course. **Facility:** 36 units, some efficiencies and cottages. 1 story, exterior corridors. **Terms:** open 6/1-9/30, office hours 7 am-10 pm, 30 day cancellation notice-fee imposed. **Amenities:** *Some:* high-speed Internet. **Pool(s):** heated outdoor. **Activities:** whirlpool, playground, horseshoes. **Guest Services:** coin laundry.

▼ See AAA listing p. 230 ▼

MARCO POLO INN

Phone: (902)963-2352

Bed & Breakfast
$85-$115

Address: Rt 13 C0A 1N0 **Location:** 0.6 mi (1 km) s. **Facility:** 6 units. 2 stories (no elevator), interior/exterior corridors. **Terms:** open 6/1-9/16 & 5/28-5/31, office hours 7 am-11 pm, 7 day cancellation notice-fee imposed. 📶 ☒

SILVERWOOD MOTEL

Phone: 902/963-2439

Motel
Rates not provided

Address: Cavendish Beach Resort C0A 1N0 **Location:** Jct Rt 6, 1 mi (1.6 km) w of jct Rt 13. **Facility:** 45 units, some two bedrooms and efficiencies. 2 stories (no elevator), interior/exterior corridors. **Terms:** seasonal, office hours 8 am-11 pm. **Pool(s):** heated outdoor. **Activities:** playground.

🍴 🏊 📶 ☒ 🛏 🖼

SUNDANCE COTTAGES

Phone: (902)963-2149

Cottage
$85-$300

Address: 34 Mac Coubrey Ln C0A 1N0 **Location:** Jct Rt 13, 0.4 mi (0.6 km) e on Rt 6. **Facility:** On spacious grounds with distant ocean views, Sundance offers a selection of cottages varying in quality and style; all include a deck and grill. 23 cottages. 1 story, exterior corridors. **Terms:** open 6/1-10/18 & 5/6-5/31, office hours 8 am-10:30 pm, 14 day cancellation notice-fee imposed. **Pool(s):** heated outdoor. **Activities:** whirlpool, bicycles, playground. **Guest Services:** coin laundry. **Free Special Amenities:** local telephone calls and high-speed Internet. *(See ad starting on p. 224.)*

SAVE 🏊 📶 ☒ 🛏 🖼 / SOME UNITS FEE 🐾

SWEPT AWAY COTTAGES

Phone: 902/963-2929

Cottage
$89-$285

Address: 40 Simpson Mill Rd C0A 1N0 **Location:** Jct Rt 13, 2.4 mi (4 km) w on Rt 6. **Facility:** Located on a hill on spacious grounds, the property offers a variety of cottages, from one level units to deluxe two story cottages with jetted tubs. 16 units, some houses and cottages. 2 stories (no elevator), exterior corridors. **Terms:** open 6/1-10/25 & 5/3-5/31, office hours 8 am-10 pm, 2 night minimum stay - seasonal, 30 day cancellation notice-fee imposed. **Pool(s):** heated outdoor. **Activities:** sauna, whirlpool, playground, game room, exercise room. **Guest Services:** coin laundry.

🏊 📶 ☒ 🛏 🖼

WHERE TO EAT

CHEZ YVONNE'S RESTAURANT & BAKERY

Phone: 902/963-2070.

American
$8-$20

AAA Inspector Notes: In the heart of town, this family-run business has been serving the public since 1979. Tasty home-style cooking complements the wonderful pies and pastries produced in the on-site bakery. Deck seating is a seasonal option. **Bar:** full bar. **Address:** 8947 Rt 6 C0A 1N0 **Location:** 1 mi (1.6 km) w of jct Rt 13. B L D

RACHAEL'S RISTORANTE

Phone: 902/963-3227

Italian
$9-$24

AAA Inspector Notes: Located in the heart of town, this spacious two-story restaurant also offers a large outdoor deck. The menu selection ranges from sandwiches to tasty brick oven pizza and pasta dishes. **Bar:** full bar. **Address:** Rt 6 C0A 1N0 **Location:** Jct Rt 6 and 13. B L D

CHARLOTTETOWN (B-4) pop. 32,174
• Hotels p. 222 • Restaurants p. 226

Settled as a French fortified post called Port La Joye in 1720, Charlottetown was named after Queen Charlotte, consort to George III, after Prince Edward Island was ceded to Britain. In 1764 it became the capital of the province, a position it retains. In 1864 the Fathers of Confederation convened in the town to consider a political-economic union that resulted in the formation of Canada 3 years later.

Presently Charlottetown is a commercial and educational center. Despite its 21st-century character, the city still evokes the feeling of a colonial seaport. Quaint sections include Great George Street and Peake's Wharf, a restored waterfront area now housing craft shops, boutiques, restaurants, a hotel and convention center.

Charlottetown owes much of its charm to William and Robert Harris, brothers who were major creative forces both on the island and in Canada during the late 1800s and early 1900s. Robert, the painter, is noted for his portrayal of the 1864 Confederation meetings; William, the architect, is known for his Gothic-style churches, public buildings and houses. The combined efforts of the brothers can be seen in the All Souls' Chapel of St. Peter's Cathedral.

The Charlottetown Festival is held at the Confederation Centre of the Arts *(see attraction listing)* from mid-June to early October. The festival features such original Canadian musical productions as "Anne of Green Gables—The Musical." Other productions also are performed on the Mainstage and in other theaters. Charlottetown Summer-Fest runs several days from late June to early July in celebration of Canada Day; there are children's activities, a petting zoo, a custom-made Cirque du Soleil performance, buskers' shows, fireworks and a 10-hour concert. The Prince Edward Island International Shellfish Festival, held in mid-September, is a celebration of the island's shellfish industry bringing together great food, music and cooking competitions.

Tourism Charlottetown's Walk & Sea Visitor Centre: 6 Prince St., Charlottetown, PE, Canada C1A 4P5. **Phone:** (902) 368-4444, (800) 955-1864 or (800) 463-4734.

Self-guiding tours: Walking tours with a historical focus, including waterfront and Victoria park walks, are described in a free brochure called "Historic Charlottetown," available at Tourism Charlottetown's Walk & Sea Visitor Centre at Founders' Hall, 6 Prince St. A more ambitious tour is the 177-kilometre (110-mi.) Blue Heron Scenic Drive, which begins and ends in Charlottetown and encircles all of Queens County.

Shopping areas: The Charlottetown Mall on University Avenue features numerous shops. The Confederation Court Mall, downtown on Queen Street, offers shopping opportunities in its more than 75 stores. Craft, gift and specialty shops at Peake's Wharf on the waterfront are open May through October.

ABEGWEIT SIGHTSEEING TOURS departs from Charlottetown Hotel at 157 Nassau St.; hotel/motel pickup is available with at least 1-hour notice.

Seven-hour tours of the North Shore, the South Shore and sites from "Anne of Green Gables" include stops at several attractions along the way. **Hours:** Tours depart daily at 10:30, June-Sept.; by appointment rest of year. **Cost:** (includes admission fees to visited attractions) $80; $40 (ages 0-11). **Phone:** (902) 894-9966.

ARDGOWAN NATIONAL HISTORIC SITE is at 2 Palmers Ln. at jct. Mt. Edward Rd. Ardgowan was the home of W.H. Pope, one of Prince Edward Island's Fathers of Confederation. It is an example of the cottage orné (picturesque cottage) architectural style. Visitors may stroll the grounds to see the period gardens and birds that frequent the site. **Hours:** Daily dawn-dusk. **Cost:** Free. **Phone:** (902) 566-7050. ⛔

BEACONSFIELD HISTORIC HOUSE is at 2 Kent St. This 25-room residence was designed in 1877 for James Peake, a wealthy shipbuilder. Restored and furnished in Victorian style, the house features imported chandeliers, marble fireplaces, gas lights and central heating. The veranda and gardens offer a fine view of the harbor. **Hours:** Daily 10-5, June-Aug.; Mon.-Tues. and Thurs.-Fri. noon-4, rest of year. **Cost:** $4.50; $3.50 (students with ID); free (ages 0-6 except for special events); $12.50 (family). **Phone:** (902) 368-6603.

CONFEDERATION CENTRE OF THE ARTS is downtown at jct. Grafton and Queen sts. Canada's national memorial to the Fathers of Confederation, this arts and culture center is recognized for its musical theater and choral productions, art exhibitions and heritage programs. The center houses the Homburg Theatre and several other theaters, a public library and an outdoor amphitheater. The Mack Theatre, part of the complex, is on the corner of University Avenue and Grafton Street.

The center's art gallery has a permanent collection that includes more than 15,000 works of Canadian historical and contemporary art. Featured are works by Canada's foremost portrait artist, Robert Harris, and the original manuscript for Lucy Maud Montgomery's "Anne of Green Gables." The center also hosts the Charlottetown Festival's comedy, dramatic and musical productions from mid-June to early October.

Hours: Art gallery open daily 9-5, mid-May to mid-Aug.; Wed.-Sat. 11-5, Sun. 1-5, rest of year. Musical productions are offered at the outdoor amphitheater Mon.-Sat. at noon, July-Aug. Closed major holidays. Phone ahead to confirm schedule.

Cost: Gallery admission by donation. Outdoor musical productions free. Ticket prices for the Charlottetown Festival range from $20-$58. Reservations are recommended for all ticketed events. **Phone:** (902) 628-1864 for the box office, (902) 566-1267 for the box office, or (800) 565-0278 for information about programs, ticket prices and reservations.

COWS CREAMERY FACTORY TOURS, 397 Capital Dr. (Hwy. 1) at the North River Causeway, lets visitors see how the company's ice cream, cheddar cheese and T-shirts are produced. A theater shows a film highlighting the company's history, and the tour guide explains the production processes as visitors look through windows to the production areas. Afterward ice cream samples are offered.

Guests must wear a cap during the factory portion of the tour. **Time:** Allow 45 minutes minimum. **Hours:** Tours depart daily every half-hour 10-4, mid-May to late Sept.; by appointment rest of year. Phone ahead to confirm schedule. **Cost:** $6; $4 (ages 3-12). A family rate is available. **Phone:** (902) 370-3155.

EMERALD ISLE CARRIAGE TOURS horse-drawn trolley wagon tours depart from Founders' Hall at 6 Prince St.; pickup is offered for horse-drawn carriage tours. A 30-minute carriage tour points out the highlights of the city's downtown—historic buildings as well as boutiques and outdoor restaurants. The 1-hour trolley and 1-hour carriage tour each include those sights as well as Victoria Park and additional historic houses and gardens in Charlottetown's oldest residential area. All include narration about Charlottetown's founding fathers.

Hours: Trolley tours depart daily at 11, 12:30 and 3, June-Oct. Carriage tours are available daily 10-10. Phone ahead to confirm schedule. **Cost:** Trolley tour $20; $12 (ages 5-14). One-hour carriage tour $100 (per carriage). Thirty-minute carriage tour $60 (per carriage). Reservations are recommended for trolley tours and required for carriage tours. **Phone:** (902) 394-3780.

FOUNDERS' HALL is at 6 Prince St. at Confederation Landing. Built to commemorate Canada's birthplace, Founders' Hall focuses on the historic meetings of the Fathers of Confederation in 1864. Visitors don audio headsets, with narration available in English and French, as they move through the Time Travel Tunnel, where multimedia displays and interactive exhibits depict Canada's evolution as a country.

The Hall of Delegates includes life-size statues and holovisual portrayals of the founding fathers. The Road of the Provinces reflects each new part of the country at the time it joined Confederation.

Time: Allow 1 hour, 30 minutes minimum. **Hours:** Daily 8:30-8, July-Aug.; 9-4:30, rest of year. Phone ahead to confirm schedule. **Cost:** $9.50; $8.50 (ages 60+ and students; $6.25 (ages 6-12). Combination ticket with Confederation Players Walking Tour $10. **Phone:** (902) 368-1864 or (800) 955-1864.

Confederation Players Walking Tour departs from Founders' Hall. Costumed interpreters take visitors on a guided walking tour through the streets of

Charlottetown. Trips include the 1-hour Historic Great George Street tour and the 90-minute The Ghostly Realm tour.

Hours: Historic Great George Street tour departs daily at 11 and 3:30 (in English), mid-June through Aug. 31 (also available in French at 3, mid-June to mid-Aug.). The Ghostly Realm tour departs Mon.-Sat. at 7:30 p.m., mid-June through Aug. 31. **Cost:** $12.50; $7.50 (ages 0-12). Combination ticket with Founders' Hall $10. **Phone:** (902) 368-1864.

GOVERNMENT HOUSE is at 1 Terry Fox Dr. Built in 1834, the Georgian-style house comprises two stories. Highlights include an impressive stairway, eight Doric columns that support the gallery and, in the dining room, a mahogany table that seats 24. The house is the private living quarters of the Lieutenant Governor.

A brochure with a self-guiding walking tour is available at the gatehouse. **Tours:** Guided tours are available. **Time:** Allow 30 minutes minimum. **Hours:** Grounds open daily dawn-dusk. House open Mon.-Fri. 10-3:30, July-Aug. House tours are given on the half-hour. **Cost:** Donations. **Phone:** (902) 368-5480.

[SAVE] **GRAY LINE TOURS BY PRINCE EDWARD TOURS** departs from Founders' Hall at 6 Prince St. The 4-hour Island Drive & Anne of Green Gables Tour offers brief stops at quaint villages and points of interest along the north shore. The 7-hour Island's Finest Tour continues to include French River and Lake of Shining Waters. The Big Pink City Tour covers city highlights from a pink double-decker bus in a little over an hour. A 1.5- to 2-hour cruise in Charlottetown Harbour provides scenic views, a look at local wildlife and information about the lobster industry. Other tours also are offered. A 2-hour seal-watching cruise departing from Murray River (9441 Main St.) is offered as well.

Hours: Island Drive & Anne of Green Gables Tour departs Tues.-Wed., Fri. and Sun. at 11:30, May-Oct. Island's Finest Tour departs Mon., Thurs. and Sat. at 9:30, May-Oct. Big Pink City Tour departs daily at 11, 1 and 2:30, June-Sept. Charlottetown Harbour cruise departs daily at 10, 1 and 3:30, July 31-Aug. 31; one daily departure (phone for time), Sept. 1-late Oct.. Murray River cruise departs Sat.-Thurs. at 10, 1 and 3:30, Fri. at 10 and 1, July-Aug.; daily at 1, early June-late June and in Sept. Phone for other tour schedules and to confirm all schedules. Phone ahead to confirm schedule.

Cost: Island Drive & Anne of Green Gables Tour (includes admission fees) $50; $35 (ages 0-12); $135 (family, two adults and two children). Island's Finest Tour (includes admission fees) $70; $55 (ages 0-12); $175 (family). Big Pink City Tour $19; $5 (children); $43 (family). Either cruise $38; $18.50 (ages 5-13). Phone for other tour fees. Reservations are required. **Phone:** (902) 566-5259 or (877) 286-6532.

HARBOUR HIPPO TOURS tours depart from 2 Prince St. at the Lower Prince St. wharf, next to Founders' Hall. Sightseeing tours aboard an amphibious vehicle afford a tour of Charlottetown's historic streets as well as a ride in Charlottetown Harbour; the view from the water provides a nice vantage point of the city. The friendly guides share historical events about the city and Prince Edward Island.

Hours: Tours are typically offered daily every 1.5 to 2 hours 10:30-5, June 1 to mid-Sept. Departure times vary and may be delayed by weather. Phone ahead to confirm schedule. **Cost:** $24; $19 (ages 66+); $16 (ages 5-17). A family rate is available. **Phone:** (902) 628-8687.

[GEM] **PROVINCE HOUSE NATIONAL HISTORIC SITE** is at Richmond and Great George sts. next to the Confederation Centre of the Arts. The stately, three-story building was the site of the 1864 Charlottetown Conference, a meeting among representatives from Britain's North American colonies that ultimately led to the creation of Canada in 1867. Today it's both a historic landmark and the current seat of Prince Edward Island's legislature. You'll recognize the Greek Revival sandstone building, completed in 1847, by its four large columns supporting a classical triangular pediment.

Inside, the restored Confederation Chamber is where the conference was held. Here you'll find historic documents and photographs as well as original furnishings from the 1840s. White-washed walls, heavy red drapes, large meeting tables swathed in green fabric, mahogany bookcases and desks, and brass chandeliers with glass globe shades characterize the decor in this part of the building. On the other side of the building, the Legislative Assembly chamber has a similar 19th-century feel although actively in use today.

You can wander among the history displays on your own; bilingual guides are on hand to answer questions. During the summer, a troupe of performers dressed in period costumes reenact vignettes dramatizing the meetings that took place here. Those history-making events are further portrayed in a 17-minute film titled "A Great Dream." **Hours:** Daily 8:30-5, June 1-second Mon. in Oct.; Mon.-Fri. 9-5, rest of year. **Cost:** $3.40. **Phone:** (902) 566-7626.

ST. DUNSTAN'S BASILICA is at 45 Great George St. The basilica, built in 1916, is the fourth Roman Catholic church to occupy this site. Built in the form of a Gothic cross, its triple spires are a Charlottetown landmark. A rose window from Germany is above the main altar. Fan vaulting and marble details highlight the church's interior. **Time:** Allow 30 minutes minimum. **Hours:** Daily 8-4. Phone ahead to confirm schedule. **Cost:** Donations. **Phone:** (902) 894-3486.

GAMBLING ESTABLISHMENTS

- **Red Shores Racetrack & Casino at Charlottetown Driving Park** is at 21 Exhibition Dr. **Hours:**

Casino open Fri.-Sat. 11 a.m.-2 a.m., Mon.-Thurs. 11 a.m.-midnight, Sun. noon-midnight. Harness racing takes place seasonally; the busiest times are May-Aug. Phone ahead to confirm schedule. **Phone:** (902) 620-4222 or (877) 620-4222.

BEST WESTERN CHARLOTTETOWN

Phone: (902)892-2461

 Hotel
$117-$185

 AAA Benefit: Members save up to 20%, plus 10% bonus points with Best Western Rewards®.

Address: 238 Grafton St C1A 1L5 **Location:** Between Hillsborough and Weymouth sts; centre. **Facility:** 146 units, some efficiencies. 2-4 stories, interior corridors. **Parking:** winter plug-ins. **Amenities:** high-speed Internet. **Pool(s):** heated indoor. **Activities:** sauna, game room, exercise room. **Guest Services:** coin laundry. **Free Special Amenities:** expanded continental breakfast and high-speed Internet.

COMFORT INN

Phone: 902/566-4424

Hotel
Rates not provided

Address: 112 Trans-Canada Hwy 1 C1E 1E7 **Location:** Trans-Canada Hwy 1, 2.8 mi (4.5 km) w. Located in a commercial area. **Facility:** 80 units. 2 stories (no elevator), interior corridors. **Amenities:** high-speed Internet.

DELTA PRINCE EDWARD

Phone: (902)566-2222

Hotel
$123-$339

Address: 18 Queen St C1A 8B9 **Location:** At Water and Queen sts. Located at harborfront. **Facility:** 211 units. 10 stories, interior corridors. **Parking:** on-site (fee). **Terms:** cancellation fee imposed. **Amenities:** video games (fee), high-speed Internet. **Dining:** Selkirk Restaurant, see separate listing. **Pool(s):** heated indoor. **Activities:** saunas, whirlpool, exercise room, spa. *Fee:* game room. **Guest Services:** valet and coin laundry. *(See ad this page.)*

DUNDEE ARMS

Phone: (902)892-2496

Country Inn
$175-$280 6/1-9/30
$140-$250 10/1-5/31

Address: 200 Pownal St C1A 3W8 **Location:** At Fitzroy St; centre. **Facility:** The main inn is circa 1903 Victorian-style with pleasant, well-appointed units; an additional two-story annex section offers comfortable modern units. 22 units. 3 stories (no elevator), interior/exterior corridors. **Terms:** office hours 7 am-11 pm, 3 day cancellation notice-fee imposed. **Dining:** Griffon Dining Room, see separate listing. **Guest Services:** valet laundry. **Free Special Amenities:** newspaper and high-speed Internet.

▼ See AAA listing this page ▼

ECONO LODGE

Motel

$90-$160

Phone: (902)368-1110
Address: 20 Lower Malpeque Rd C1A 7J9 **Location:** Jct Trans-Canada Hwy 1 and Lower Malpeque Rd, 2.8 mi (4.5 km) w. **Facility:** 63 units, some efficiencies. 2 stories (no elevator), interior/exterior corridors. **Terms:** cancellation fee imposed. **Pool(s):** heated outdoor. **Activities:** whirlpool. **Guest Services:** coin laundry.

THE ELMWOOD HERITAGE INN

Historic Bed & Breakfast

$149-$275 6/1-9/30
$99-$199 10/1-5/31

Phone: (902)368-3310
Address: 121 N River Rd C1A 3K7 **Location:** Centre; entrance opposite Green St. Located in a residential area. **Facility:** This pleasant Victorian mansion on a quiet secluded acre offers tastefully appointed guest rooms and suites, some with a fireplace and whirlpool tub. 8 units, some kitchens. 3 stories (no elevator), interior corridors. **Terms:** open 6/1-9/30 & 10/1-5/31, office hours 7 am-10 pm, 14 day cancellation notice-fee imposed. **Guest Services:** complimentary and valet laundry. **Free Special Amenities: full breakfast and room upgrade (subject to availability with advance reservations).**
(See ad starting on p. 224.)

FITZROY HALL

Historic Bed & Breakfast

$110-$300

Phone: 902/368-2077
Address: 45 Fitzroy St C1A 1R4 **Location:** Corner of Fitzroy and Pownal sts. Located in a historic residential area. **Facility:** Guest rooms at this stately 1872 Victorian mansion are large and tastefully decorated, and some are suite-style rooms with private decks. 8 units. 3 stories (no elevator), interior corridors. **Terms:** office hours 7 am-10 pm, 30 day cancellation notice-fee imposed. **Guest Services:** valet laundry. **Free Special Amenities: full breakfast and high-speed Internet.**
(See ad starting on p. 224.)

GARDEN GATE INN

Motel

$89-$98 6/1-9/7
$75-$85 9/8-5/31

Phone: 902/892-3411
Address: 639 University Ave C1E 1E5 **Location:** 2.1 mi (3.5 km) w on Trans-Canada Hwy 1. **Facility:** 19 units, some two bedrooms, efficiencies and kitchens. 1 story, interior/exterior corridors. **Terms:** office hours 7:30 am-11 pm, 3 day cancellation notice. **Free Special Amenities: local telephone calls and high-speed Internet.**

THE GREAT GEORGE

Hotel

$219-$899 6/1-10/31
$175-$899 11/1-5/31

Phone: (902)892-0606
Address: 58 Great George St C1A 4K3 **Location:** Corner of Dorchester St. Located in a historic area. **Facility:** 54 units, some efficiencies and kitchens. 4 stories, interior corridors. **Terms:** cancellation fee imposed. **Amenities:** high-speed Internet. **Activities:** exercise room. **Guest Services:** valet and coin laundry.

HILLHURST INN

Historic Bed & Breakfast

$99-$245

Phone: 902/894-8004
Address: 181 Fitzroy St C1A 1S3 **Location:** At Hillsborough St; centre. Located in a residential area. **Facility:** Featuring distinctive oak and beech woodwork in common areas, the 1897 Georgian Revival home has guest rooms in varied size and decor; one is compact. 9 units. 3 stories (no elevator), interior corridors. **Terms:** office hours 7 am-10 pm, 14 day cancellation notice-fee imposed.
(See ad starting on p. 224.)

HOLIDAY INN EXPRESS HOTEL & SUITES CHARLOTTETOWN

Hotel

$159-$189 6/1-9/30
$129-$149 10/1-5/31

Phone: (902)892-1201
Address: 200 Capital Dr C1E 2E8 **Location:** On Trans-Canada Hwy 1, 3 mi (5 km) w. **Facility:** 133 units. 3 stories, interior corridors. **Terms:** cancellation fee imposed. **Amenities:** video games (fee), high-speed Internet. **Pool(s):** heated indoor. **Activities:** whirlpool, exercise room. **Guest Services:** valet and coin laundry.

THE HOTEL ON POWNAL

Hotel

$153-$204 6/1-10/31
$132-$173 11/1-5/31

Phone: (902)892-1217
Address: 146 Pownal St C1A 3W6 **Location:** Corner of Kent St; downtown. **Facility:** 45 units, some kitchens. 2 stories (no elevator), interior/exterior corridors. **Terms:** cancellation fee imposed. **Guest Services:** coin laundry.

QUALITY INN ON THE HILL

Hotel

Rates not provided

Phone: 902/894-8572
Address: 150 Euston St C1A 1W5 **Location:** Just e of University Ave. **Facility:** 73 units. 3-5 stories, interior corridors. **Guest Services:** valet laundry.

RODD CHARLOTTETOWN-A RODD SIGNATURE HOTEL

Classic Historic Hotel

$125-$247

Phone: (902)894-7371
Address: 75 Kent St C1A 7K4 **Location:** Corner of Kent and Pownal sts. **Facility:** This classic hotel built in 1931 features woodwork with a coat-of-arms motif; the guest rooms reflect an older charm and vary in size. 115 units. 5 stories, interior corridors. **Terms:** cancellation fee imposed. **Amenities:** high-speed Internet. **Dining:** Chambers Restaurant & Bar, see separate listing. **Pool(s):** heated indoor. **Activities:** sauna, whirlpool, limited exercise equipment. **Guest Services:** valet laundry.
(See ad starting on p. 224.)

RODD ROYALTY

Hotel

$125-$195

Phone: (902)894-8566
Address: Intersection Hwy 1 & 2 C1A 8C2 **Location:** 2.5 mi (4 km) w on Trans-Canada Hwy 1. Located in a commercial area. **Facility:** 118 units. 1-3 stories, interior/exterior corridors. **Terms:** cancellation fee imposed. **Pool(s):** heated indoor. **Activities:** waterslide, exercise room. **Guest Services:** valet laundry. *(See ad starting on p. 224.)*

SHIPWRIGHT INN

Historic Bed & Breakfast

$99-$299

Phone: (902)368-1905
Address: 51 Fitzroy St C1A 1R4 **Location:** Just e of Pownal St. Located in a residential area. **Facility:** Pleasant grounds surround the attractive 1860 Victorian home; five of its well-appointed rooms feature a gas fireplace. 9 units. 2 stories (no elevator), interior corridors. **Terms:** office hours 7 am-10 pm, age restrictions may apply, 14 day cancellation notice-fee imposed. **Guest Services:** valet laundry. **Free Special Amenities: full breakfast and high-speed Internet.** *(See ad starting on p. 224.)*

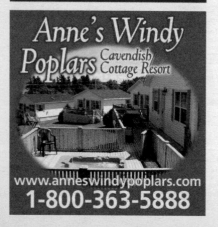
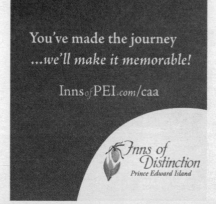

There's an undiscovered haven where beaches are only 15 minutes away from any starting point. An escape where dining on the freshest saltwater delicacies is commonplace and memories that will last forever are around every corner. **That's our island. That's Prince Edward Island.**

Start your adventure today at **tourismPEI.com/aaa**

or by calling **1.800.463.4PEI**

FAIRHOLM INN & CARRIAGE HOUSE
Phone: 902/892-5022

[fyi] Not evaluated. **Address:** 230 Prince St C1A 4S1 **Location:** Corner of Prince and Fitzroy sts. Facilities, services, and decor characterize a mid-scale property.

WHERE TO EAT

CANTON CAFE
Phone: 902/892-2527

Chinese
$8-$19

AAA Inspector Notes: Popular local restaurant established in 1970. Menu features a wide variety of well-prepared Cantonese and Szechuan dishes prepared to your own taste. Service is relaxed but competent. **Bar:** full bar. **Address:** 73 Queen St C1A 4A8 **Location:** Corner of Dorchester St. **Parking:** street only. [L] [D]

CHAMBERS RESTAURANT & BAR   **Phone:** 902/894-7371

Canadian
$10-$28

AAA Inspector Notes: The elegant dining room is decorated in rich, floral wallpaper with wood trim and brass chandeliers. The menu selection is ample with a focus on prime cuts of beef and fresh local seafood. **Bar:** full bar. **Reservations:** suggested. **Address:** 75 Kent St C1A 7K4 **Location:** Corner of Kent and Pownal sts; in Rodd Charlottetown-A Rodd Signature Hotel. [B] [L] [D]

THE CHURCHILL ARMS PUB
Phone: 902/367-3450

English
$8-$18

AAA Inspector Notes: The delightfully cozy pub serves authentic English-style pub foods with a decent selection of imported beers on tap. **Bar:** full bar. **Address:** 75 Queen St C1A 4A8 **Location:** Corner of Dorchester St. **Parking:** street only. [L] [D]

CLADDAGH OYSTER HOUSE
Phone: 902/892-9661

Canadian
$21-$32

AAA Inspector Notes: The restored exterior of this chic restaurant belies its contemporary decor, complete with a rich red and black color scheme and a lovely waterfall. The menu offers a wide variety of fresh seafood including oysters, mussels and selections from a fresh lobster tank, plus island beef, chicken and some pasta dishes. All of the mouthwatering desserts are made in house. Uniformed servers are very pleasant and knowledgeable. **Bar:** full bar. **Reservations:** suggested. **Address:** 131 Sydney St C1A 1G5 **Location:** Just off corner of Queen and Sydney sts. **Parking:** street only. [D]

FISHBONES OYSTER BAR & SEAFOOD GRILL
Phone: 902/628-6569

Seafood
$13-$24

AAA Inspector Notes: Located in the heart of the city at Victoria Row, the upbeat restaurant offers live jazz performances in peak season. The menu specializes in fresh seafood, including offerings from a raw oyster bar, as well as a good selection of pub and finger foods. **Bar:** full bar. **Address:** 136 Richmond St C1A 1H9 **Location:** At Queen St. **Parking:** street only. [L] [D]

THE GAHAN HOUSE BREWERY   **Phone:** 902/626-2337

Canadian
$9-$20

AAA Inspector Notes: The island's only brewery restaurant brews a wide variety of handcrafted ales the old-fashioned way with no preservatives. Friendly servers contribute to the relaxing, casual atmosphere. Guests can request patio seating in season. **Bar:** full bar. **Address:** 126 Sydney St C1A 1G5 **Location:** At Queen St. **Parking:** street only. [L] [D]

GLOBE WORLD FLAVOURS
Phone: 902/370-4040

International
$12-$28

AAA Inspector Notes: Guests can dine, drink and dance the night away at is vibrant nightclub/restaurant. Prior to it turning into an evening hot spot (typically at 11 pm), diners can enjoy various creative dishes which include crispy orange beef, Moroccan salmon, Shanghai chicken and peppered island tenderloin. Guests may also opt for the lounge menu which has a selection of well-prepared comfort foods. A popular outdoor patio is available in season. **Bar:** full bar. **Address:** 132 Richmond St C1E 1E5 **Location:** At Queen St; on Victoria Row. **Parking:** street only. [L] [D] [LATE]

GRIFFON DINING ROOM
Phone: 902/892-2496

Canadian
$9-$27

AAA Inspector Notes: Enjoy fine dining in the relaxed atmosphere of this 1903 Victorian home. Attentive servers deliver menu offerings of nicely presented fresh seafood and varied meat entrees, including some preparations of game. Seasonal patio dining is a casual option at the Hearth and Cricket Pub. **Bar:** full bar. **Reservations:** suggested. **Address:** 200 Pownal St C1A 3W8 **Location:** At Fitzroy St; centre; in Dundee Arms. **Historic** [B] [L] [D]

HUNTER'S ALE HOUSE
Phone: 902/367-4040

Canadian
$7-$21

AAA Inspector Notes: This upbeat pub-style restaurant offers outdoor dining in season. The menu ranges from fresh seafood and steaks to burgers, sandwiches, fine chowders and salads. Portions are ample and desserts are made on the premises. **Bar:** full bar. **Address:** 185 Kent St C1A 8S9 **Location:** Corner of Prince and Kent sts. **Parking:** street only. [L] [D]

LOBSTER ON THE WHARF
Phone: 902/368-2888

Seafood
$10-$32

AAA Inspector Notes: A casual atmosphere is the focus of the spacious harborfront restaurant, which has two levels and an outdoor deck. Although lobster is the specialty, the menu also includes clams, mussels, oysters and scallops for seafood lovers and steaks and chicken for those who prefer meat. **Bar:** full bar. **Address:** 2 Prince Street Wharf C1A 4P5 **Location:** Centre; at Confederation Landing Park. [L] [D]

LUCY MAUD DINING ROOM
Phone: 902/894-6868

Canadian
$13-$29

AAA Inspector Notes: In The Culinary Institute of Canada, this restaurant has its services provided by students. Views from the large plate-glass windows, and table appointments are elegant. Seasonal game selections stand out on a menu of creatively presented seafood and meat preparations. The young staff is very friendly and attentive. **Bar:** full bar. **Reservations:** suggested. **Address:** 4 Sydney St C1A 1E9 **Location:** At Rochford St; centre; in The Culinary Institute of Canada. [L] [D]

THE MERCHANTMAN PUB
Phone: 902/892-9150

Canadian
$9-$25

AAA Inspector Notes: Original brick and wood-beam ceilings enhance the warm, friendly ambience of the casual, neighborhood eatery. Pub foods are available all day, while evening selections center on heartier selections, including well-seasoned Thai and Cajun specialties. **Bar:** full bar. **Address:** 23 Queen St C1A 4A2 **Location:** Corner of Queen and Water sts; centre. **Parking:** street only. [L] [D]

OFF BROADWAY RESTAURANT & 42ND STREET LOUNGE
Phone: 902/566-4620

Canadian
$11-$28

AAA Inspector Notes: Cozy atmosphere, all booth seating with brick and wood-beam interior, and high pine dividers, enhances the restored 1870s building. The Saturday and Sunday brunch draws a good crowd. The menu lists appetizers, crepes, steak and seafood, plus a tempting assortment of homemade desserts. **Bar:** full bar. **Reservations:** suggested. **Address:** 125 Sydney St C1A 1G5 **Location:** Just off corner of Queen and Sydney sts. **Parking:** street only. **Historic** [L] [D]

THE OLD TRIANGLE IRISH ALEHOUSE
Phone: 902/892-5200

Irish
$11-$21

AAA Inspector Notes: The menu offers everything from classic Irish pub fare to Canadian preparations of steak and seafood, all of which couple with a good selection of beers on tap, at this upbeat Irish-style pub, which has booth and table seating. **Bar:** full bar. **Address:** 89 University Ave C1A 4L1 **Location:** Corner of Fitzroy St. **Parking:** on-site (fee). [L] [D]

OUTRIDERS COOKHOUSE
Phone: 902/894-8889

Canadian
$7-$17

AAA Inspector Notes: This is a casual eatery on the edge of town. Their specialty is barbecue ribs but they also offer a selection of steaks, chicken and some seafood dishes. **Bar:** full bar. **Address:** 345 Mt. Edward Rd C1A 8C2 **Location:** Just n of Arterial Hwy 2.

[L] [D] [LATE]

PAPA JOE'S RESTAURANT & LOUNGE
Phone: 902/566-5070

Canadian
$7-$17

AAA Inspector Notes: The cheerful, family-friendly roadside restaurant presents a diverse menu that features fresh seafood and steaks, as well as sandwiches, burgers and a selection of Lebanese dishes. **Bar:** full bar. **Address:** 345 University Ave C1A 4M8 **Location:** Corner of University Ave and Pond St. [L] [D]

THE PILOT HOUSE FINE FOOD & SPIRITS
Phone: 902/894-4800

Canadian
$9-$30

AAA Inspector Notes: An upbeat atmosphere and friendly casual service are what guests find at this popular watering hole. The menu lists a good selection of very well-prepared fresh seafood and meat entrees. **Bar:** full bar. **Address:** 70 Grafton St C1A 1K7 **Location:** Just w of Queen St. **Parking:** street only. [L] [D]

RUM RUNNERS
Phone: 902/892-2207

American
$7-$19

AAA Inspector Notes: A friendly, pub-style atmosphere prevails at the upbeat restaurant. Patrons can order from the full menu or the lighter pub menu. A European-style sidewalk cafe opens seasonally. **Bar:** full bar. **Address:** 73 Water St C1A 1A5 **Location:** Corner of Queen and Water sts. **Parking:** street only. [L] [D]

Get pet travel tips
and enter the photo contest
at AAA.com/PetBook

SELKIRK RESTAURANT
Phone: 902/894-1208

Canadian
$10-$30

AAA Inspector Notes: This elegant lobby dining room opens to the main lobby of the hotel and features a waterfall to offset the lobby noise. Soft lighting and comfortable winged-back chairs set the stage for a romantic mood. The menu offers creative fresh seafood and meats including their tasty seafood chowder or sample the delightful seafood platter for two. They also have a fine selection of steak, pork and prime rib to satisfy the meat lover. The staff is knowledgeable and friendly. **Bar:** full bar. **Reservations:** suggested. **Address:** 18 Queen St C1A 8B9 **Location:** At Water and Queen sts; in Delta Prince Edward. **Parking:** on-site (fee). [B] [L] [D]

Culinary creations use fresh PEI produce

SHADDY'S MEDITERRANEAN CUISINE
Phone: 902/368-8886

Mediterranean
$8-$20

AAA Inspector Notes: A local landmark in the heart of town, this restaurant serves a wide variety of Canadian and Lebanese entrées. Among choices are great sandwiches, burgers, fresh seafood, souvlaki, shish taouk and seasonal lobster as well as a gluten-free menu. The patio opens seasonally. **Bar:** full bar. **Address:** 44 University Ave C1A 4K6 **Location:** At Kent St; centre. **Parking:** street only. [B] [L] [D]

SIMS CORNER STEAKHOUSE & WINE BAR
Phone: 902/894-7467

Steak
$12-$35

AAA Inspector Notes: This upscale, trendy steakhouse in the heart of town has a casual atmosphere. Specializing in prime quality cuts of meat and some seafood dishes. The staff are friendly and professional. **Bar:** full bar. **Address:** 86 Queen St C1A 1G5 **Location:** Corner of Sydney St. **Parking:** street only. [L] [D]

SIRENELLA RISTORANTE
Phone: 902/628-2271

Italian
$10-$25

AAA Inspector Notes: The cozy restaurant is a trendy spot for comfortable dining or a cup of delicious gourmet coffee. Decorative lighting and candles soften the mood in the dining room. Outdoor dining is popular during the summer months. **Bar:** full bar. **Address:** 83 Water St C1A 1A5 **Location:** Centre; adjacent to Prince Edward Hotel. [L] [D]

SMITTY'S
Phone: 902/892-5752

Canadian
$7-$20

AAA Inspector Notes: The family-oriented restaurant satisfies patrons with its ever-popular all-day breakfast items, as well as tasty and wholesome soups and salads at lunchtime. A relaxed mood characterizes the dining space. **Bar:** full bar. **Address:** 449 University Ave C1A 8K3 **Location:** In University Plaza. [B] [L] [D]

SWISS CHALET
Phone: 902/894-7440

Chicken
$6-$16

AAA Inspector Notes: The popular restaurant is known for its rotisserie chicken and ribs and the tangy Chalet sauce that gives food its special zip. Diners munch on a half or quarter chicken with sides such as steamed vegetables, fries, baked potatoes and salads. Lunch guests often go for the great soup and sandwich combination. Take-out and delivery service are popular options. **Bar:** full bar. **Address:** 359 University Ave C1A 4M9 **Location:** At Summer St. [L] [D]

CLEAR SPRINGS

JOHNSON SHORE INN
Phone: 902/687-1340

[fyi] Not evaluated. **Address:** RR 3, Rt 16 C0A 2B0 **Location:** Oceanfront. Jct Rt 16 and 305, 0.6 mi (1 km) w on Rt 16, 1 mi (1.5 km) n on dirt entry road. Facilities, services, and decor characterize a mid-scale property.

CORNWALL pop. 4,677

FIREDANCE COUNTRY INN B & B
Phone: (902)675-3471

Bed & Breakfast
$88-$175

Address: 35 Firedance Ridge RR 2 C0A 1H0 **Location:** Hwy 1 to New Haven, 4 mi (6 km) s on Rt 9, follow signs to St. Catherines. **Facility:** The inn occupies a lovely, rural location overlooking farm fields and the Clyde River; some rooms have water views or soaker tubs. 6 units. 3 stories (no elevator), interior/exterior corridors. **Terms:** office hours 8 am-10 pm, 14 day cancellation notice-fee imposed.
(See ad starting on p. 224.)

 CALL

HOWARD JOHNSON HOTEL
Phone: (902)566-2211

Hotel
$80-$131

Address: 100 Trans-Canada Hwy C0A 1H0 **Location:** On Hwy 1, 4.3 mi (7 km) w of Charlottetown. Located in a quiet rural area. **Facility:** 58 units, some two bedrooms. 2 stories (no elevator), interior/exterior corridors. **Pool(s):** heated indoor. **Activities:** sauna. **Guest Services:** coin laundry.

SUNNY KING MOTEL
Phone: 902/566-2209

Motel
$54-$116

Address: 3 Centennial Dr C0A 1H0 **Location:** On Hwy 1; centre. **Facility:** 25 units, some efficiencies and kitchens. 2 stories (no elevator), exterior corridors. **Parking:** winter plug-ins. **Terms:** office hours 8 am-11 pm, 3 day cancellation notice-fee imposed. **Pool(s):** outdoor. **Guest Services:** coin laundry.

SUPER 8
Phone: (902)892-7900

Hotel
$114-$127

Address: 15 York Point Rd C0A 1H0 **Location:** On Hwy 1, 3.7 mi (6 km) w of Charlottetown. **Facility:** 62 units. 2 stories (no elevator), interior corridors. **Terms:** cancellation fee imposed. **Amenities:** *Some:* high-speed Internet. **Pool(s):** heated indoor. **Activities:** whirlpool, exercise room. **Guest Services:** coin laundry.

MAGGIE'S FAMILY RESTAURANT
Phone: 902/892-7772

Canadian
$6-$17

AAA Inspector Notes: This family-style, spacious restaurant offers booth and table seating with a country theme. Many items on the vast menu are homemade including a selection of pies and cakes. **Bar:** full bar. **Address:** 11 York Point Rd C0A 1H0 **Location:** On Hwy 1, 3.7 mi (6 km) w of Charlottetown. [B] [L] [D]

Create complete trip routings and custom maps with the TripTik® Travel Planner on AAA.com or CAA.ca

DALVAY BEACH

DALVAY BY-THE-SEA HERITAGE INN
Phone: (902)672-2048

Historic Country Inn
$189-$399

Address: 16 Cottage Cres PEI National Pkwy C0A 1P0 **Location:** Off Rt 6; at east end of PEI National Park. **Facility:** A wonderful historic inn located in the park and bordering a pond. A variety of room styles and sizes and some deluxe cottages with decks. 33 units, some cottages. 1-3 stories (no elevator), interior/exterior corridors. **Terms:** open 6/1-10/15, office hours 8 am-11 pm, 15 day cancellation notice-fee imposed. **Dining:** restaurant, see separate listing. **Activities:** beach access, canoeing, 2 tennis courts, rental bicycles, hiking trails, playground, horseshoes. **Guest Services:** coin laundry. *(See ad starting on p. 224.)*

DALVAY BY-THE-SEA DINING ROOM
Menu on AAA.com **Phone:** 902/672-2048

Eastern Canadian
$12-$36

AAA Inspector Notes: This elegant dining room is in the historic 1895 Dalvay Mansion. On the menu are fresh local seafood and traditional meat selections. Breakfast, lunch and afternoon tea (from 2 pm to 4 pm) are served in a more casual service style than dinner. The sticky date pudding for dessert should not be missed. **Bar:** full bar. **Reservations:** suggested. **Address:** 16 Cottage Cres PEI National Pkwy C0A 1P0 **Location:** Off Rt 6; at east end of PEI National Park; in Dalvay by-the-Sea Heritage Inn. *(See ad starting on p. 224.)*

[B] [L] [D] CALL

EAST POINT (A-6)

EAST POINT LIGHTHOUSE is off Hwy. 16 following signs, at the n.e. tip of the island. The 20-metre (67-ft.) octagonal tower was constructed in 1867 at the point where the Gulf of St. Lawrence and Northumberland Strait meet. Interpretive displays and scenic views from the top of the tower can be seen on guided tours of the structure.

Time: Allow 1 hour, 30 minutes minimum. **Hours:** Daily 10-6, June 16-Labour Day. Guided tours depart as needed; last tour begins 30 minutes before closing. Hours are extended during the high season. Phone ahead to confirm schedule. **Cost:** $5; $4 (ages 13-17 and 55+); $2 (ages 6-12); $12 (family). **Phone:** (902) 357-2106, or (902) 357-2420 in the off-season.

ELDON (B-5)

Led by Lord Selkirk, 800 Highlanders settled the area around Eldon and Belfast in 1803. Lord Selkirk Provincial Park *(see Recreation Chart)*, on the opposite side of Hwy. 1, overlooks Orwell Bay. Skirting the coastline, the Trans-Canada Highway continues southeast to Wood Islands *(see place listing p. 240)*, where Northumberland Ferries & Bay Ferries Ltd. regularly departs for a 75-minute trip to Caribou, Nova Scotia; phone (877) 635-7245 for information. For further information about the park phone (902) 659-7221.

ELMIRA (A-6)

At its peak, the railway system linking Prince Edward Island to the mainland included 121 stations along 400 kilometres (250 mi.) of track. The circuitous route connected almost every village on the island, ending at the Elmira station. Today, the depot marks the eastern terminus of the Confederation Trail, a 280-kilometre-long (174-mile) biking, hiking and snowmobile path that roughly parallels Hwy. 2 and covers the island from tip to tip.

ELMIRA RAILWAY MUSEUM is at 457 Elmira Rd. Containing one of the largest model railway collections in Canada, the station features exhibits that recount the history of railroading on Prince Edward Island. Photographs and maps highlight the island's rail stations with their varied architecture. Artifacts displayed include the station's telegraph equipment, fare books and schedules. Visitors can ride the PEI Miniature Railway.

Time: Allow 30 minutes minimum. **Hours:** Daily 9-5, July 1-Sept. 4; Mon.-Fri. 9-5, Sept. 5-28. **Cost:** $4; $3 (students with ID); $11 (family). Miniature train ride $5; $3.50 (children); $13.50 (family). **Phone:** (902) 357-7234, or (902) 368-6600 in the off-season. 🎠

FRENCH RIVER

THE BEACH HOUSE INN   **Phone:** 902/886-2145
▼▼◆▼▼
Bed & Breakfast   **Address:** Cape Rd C0B 1M0
$79-$189   **Location:** Just off Rt 20; centre. Located in rural area. **Facility:** In a secluded area a short stroll from the beach, this quaint property has an artsy style and offers individually decorated guest rooms and cottages. 9 units, some cottages. 2 stories (no elevator), interior/exterior corridors. **Terms:** open 6/1-10/31, office hours 9 am-9 pm, 14 day cancellation notice-fee imposed. **Activities:** limited beach access, bicycles.
🛜 ✕ 🏋 / SOME UNITS FEE 🐾 🛁 🖥 ▭

GEORGETOWN (B-5) pop. 634

The first town built near what is now Georgetown did not survive its infancy. Soon after French immigrant Jean-Pierre de Roma and his followers built dwellings, storehouses, wharves and bridges at nearby Brudenell Point in the early 1740s, some of the settlers defected and field mice ruined the crops. In 1745 a group of New Englanders burned the settlement, causing de Roma and his family to flee to Québec.

The town, re-established across the Brudenell River from the point, has since become a primary harbor and deepwater port. The principal local industry is shipbuilding. A rock causeway links the Georgetown shore with Brudenell Island, a former 1750s Scottish cemetery.

King's Playhouse is on Hwy. 3 at 65 Grafton St. The summer theater presents professional repertory productions in a 300-seat 1983 playhouse that is a reproduction of the town hall. Concerts, Tuesday night Ceilidhs and a Wednesday farmers market (4-8 p.m.) are held as well. The box office opens daily at 1; phone (902) 652-2053, or (888) 346-5666 (within Canada).

THE GEORGETOWN INN   **Phone:** (902)652-2511

Historic
Country Inn   **Address:** 62 Richmond St C0A 1L0
$85-$155   **Location:** Centre. **Facility:** Now a cozy inn, this 1840 building has formerly served as a mercantile store, a post office, a bank, a Masonic lodge and a hardware store. 8 units. 3 stories (no elevator), interior corridors. **Terms:** office hours 7 am-10 pm, 5 day cancellation notice-fee imposed. **Dining:** restaurant, see separate listing. 🍴 BIZ 🛜 ✕

WHERE TO EAT

GEORGETOWN INN DINING ROOM
                        Phone: 902/652-2511

Canadian   **AAA Inspector Notes:** The casual
$16-$25   restaurant occupies an 1840s shipbuilder's home. The owner/chef's focus is on fresh island produce, meats and seafood in pleasing dishes such as lobster pot pie, grilled halibut, strip loin steak or pork chops. **Bar:** full bar. **Reservations:** suggested. **Address:** 62 Richmond St C0A 1L0 **Location:** Corner of Kent St; in The Georgetown Inn. D

KENSINGTON (B-3) pop. 1,485
• Restaurants p. 230

Prior to the opening of the Prince Edward Island Railway in 1870, Kensington was called Barrett's Cross after a Mrs. Barrett who ran an inn at the crossroads of what are now highways 2, 6, 20 and 101.

Kensington and Area Chamber of Commerce: P.O. Box 234, Kensington, PE, Canada C0B 1M0. **Phone:** (902) 836-3209.

HAUNTED MANSION is on Hwy. 2 at 81 Victoria St. W., opposite the Royal Canadian Legion Home. A Tudor-style building, inhabited by the "Mad Doctor," houses a series of spooky rooms and cellars devoted to frightening those who dare enter. The adjacent Secret Water Gardens include waterfalls, fountains, streams and pools. A small animal farm and children's play areas also are on the grounds. **Time:** Allow 1 hour minimum. **Hours:** Daily 9-7, July-Aug.; 10-5, in June and Sept. Phone for Oct. schedule. **Cost:** $13; $8 (ages 6-16). **Phone:** (902) 836-3336.

VETERANS MEMORIAL MILITARY MUSEUM is at 86 Victoria St. W., next to the Kensington Royal Canadian Legion. Dedicated to those who served during wartime, the two-story museum displays dioramas and artifacts such as diaries, arms, uniforms, medals and photographs from Prince Edward Island military personnel. **Time:** Allow 30 minutes minimum. **Hours:** Mon.-Sat. 11-1, July-Sept.; by appointment, Oct.-Nov. Phone ahead to confirm schedule. **Cost:** Donations. **Phone:** (902) 836-3600.

FROSTY TREAT DAIRY BAR   Phone: 902/836-3000

American
$6-$13

AAA Inspector Notes: The popular take-out spot serves fried clams, fish and chips, burgers and a bounty of ice cream flavors. **Address:** 109 Victoria St W C0B 1M0 **Location:** On Rt 2; centre.

L D AC

THE HOME PLACE RESTAURANT   Phone: 902/836-5686

Canadian
$12-$25

AAA Inspector Notes: The restaurant has several dining locations, from the quaint dining room with a delightful lounge to seasonal outdoor dining on the deck. The menu offers a wide variety of well-prepared seafood and meat dishes, including fresh oysters and mussels as well as tasty homemade desserts. **Bar:** full bar. **Address:** 21 Victoria St E C0B 1M0 **Location:** Just e on Rt 6; in The Home Place Inn.

D

LOTUS GARDEN RESTAURANT   Phone: 902/836-5055

Chinese
$6-$16

AAA Inspector Notes: This spacious, open-style restaurant offers a wide variety of Chinese and American cuisine, including various combination plates and a Saturday buffet. Portions are ample. **Bar:** full bar. **Address:** 31 Broadway St C0B 1M0 **Location:** On Rt 2; centre; in Save Easy Mall.

L D

MALPEQUE (B-2)

Malpeque is known for the remarkable Malpeque oyster. Deemed "the tastiest oyster in the world" at a 1900 Paris exhibition, the species almost completely died out in 1917 from cancer. Miraculously, the hardy oyster overcame the disease and proliferated. One of few creatures known to have conquered cancer on its own, the Malpeque oyster has been the subject of medical research and testing for many years.

At the Malpeque wharf, visitors can arrange deep-sea and tuna fishing expeditions. Fine beach and recreation facilities are available at nearby *Cabot Beach Provincial Park (see Recreation Chart)*.

KEIR MEMORIAL MUSEUM is on Hwy. 20 at Malpeque Corner. The museum, built in 1927, was once a Presbyterian church. It now portrays themes that best describe the occupations of the people of the community with artifacts gifted or loaned to the museum by local residents. The museum chronicles the Malpeque oyster harvest, early farming, fishing, trade, commerce and the community's cultural and religious life. Displays include a Victorian kitchen, a weaving room, a typical country schoolroom and an 1887 horse-drawn hearse.

Tours: Guided tours are available. **Time:** Allow 30 minutes minimum. **Hours:** Mon.-Fri. 9-5, Sat.-Sun. 1-5, July 1-Labour Day. **Cost:** $2; $1 (ages 5-12); $5 (family). **Phone:** (902) 836-3054, or (902) 836-5613 in the off-season.

MAYFIELD

CAVENDISH GATEWAY RESORT BY CLARION COLLECTION   Phone: 902/963-2213

Hotel
Rates not provided

Address: 6596 Rt 13 C0A 1N0 **Location:** On Rt 13, 3.6 mi (6 km) w of Cavendish; centre. **Facility:** 54 units, some kitchens and cottages. 3 stories (no elevator), interior/exterior corridors. **Terms:** seasonal. **Pool(s):** heated indoor. **Activities:** tennis court. *Fee:* game room. **Guest Services:** coin laundry. *(See ad p. 218.)*

BIZ X

/SOME UNITS FEE AC

MISCOUCHE (B-2) pop. 769, elev. 18m/59'

ACADIAN MUSEUM OF PRINCE EDWARD ISLAND is 8 km (5 mi.) w. on Hwy. 2. The museum collection includes farming, woodworking, shoe-making and blacksmith tools and many other items of Acadian life and culture. An audiovisual presentation is shown at the start of the tour. Acadian genealogical research materials are available.

Time: Allow 1 hour minimum. **Hours:** Daily 9:30-5, July-Aug.; Mon.-Fri. 9:30-5, Sun. 1-4, rest of year. **Cost:** $4.50; $3.50 (students with ID); free (ages 0-5 except during special events); $12.50 (family). **Phone:** (902) 432-2880.

MONTAGUE (B-5) pop. 1,802

One of the largest towns on Prince Edward Island, Montague was named in the 1760s for George Brudenell, the Earl of Cardigan and Duke of Montague. Montague serves as a port and commercial center. Nearby on Hwy. 4 is Buffaloland Provincial Park, where herds of North American bison and white deer can be seen.

GARDEN OF THE GULF MUSEUM is at 564 Main St. Exhibits include 19th-century farm and cooking implements, a pictorial history exhibit and a themed display, which changes every year. **Hours:** Mon.-Sat. 9-5, July-Aug.; Mon.-Fri. 9-5 in June and Sept. **Cost:** $3; free (ages 0-11). Cash only. **Phone:** (902) 838-2467 or (902) 838-2820.

GILLIS' DRIVE-IN RESTAURANT   Phone: 902/838-2031

Canadian
$6-$12

AAA Inspector Notes: Guests can step back in time at the popular '50s-style drive-in. Leaving the lights on indicates curb service is desired, but the option to dine inside also is available. On the menu are fish, beef and chicken burgers, fish and chips and fine items from the dairy bar. **Address:** Rt 4 C0A 1R0 **Location:** On Rt 4, 0.6 mi (1 km) n.

L D AC

WINDOWS ON THE WATER CAFE   Phone: 902/838-2080

Canadian
$12-$25

AAA Inspector Notes: Overlooking the picturesque river and marina, this casual restaurant delivers well-prepared and well-presented specialties using local purveyors for fresh produce, meats and, of course, seafood including lobster. Sweet temptations beckon from the dessert tray. A wrap-around deck is popular in season. The young servers provide friendly, relaxed service. **Bar:** full bar. **Reservations:** suggested. **Address:** 106 Sackville St C0A 1R0 **Location:** At Main St.

L D

MONT-CARMEL (B-2)

A handful of Acadian families who left Malpeque in 1812 founded the parish of Mont-Carmel. These settlers had to clear new land to create their village, as their ancestors were forced to do during the Acadian deportations of 1758. Many years later, in the mid-1960s, Mont-Carmel's residents used their Acadian heritage to promote tourism as a replacement for their faltering fishing trade.

NOTRE-DAME-DU-MONT-CARMEL CHURCH (OUR LADY OF MONT-CARMEL ACADIAN CHURCH) is on Hwy. 11 just e. of jct. Hwy. 124. Overlooking the Northumberland Strait, the brick church features a Gothic interior and two steeples. The symmetrical facade and rounded vaults of the 1898 church suggest the homeland of the island's Acadian settlers. An old graveyard is next to the church. **Time:** Allow 30 minutes minimum. **Hours:** Daily 9-6. Phone ahead to confirm schedule. **Cost:** Donations. **Phone:** (902) 854-2208.

MORELL pop. 306

RODD CROWBUSH GOLF & BEACH RESORT
                    Phone: (902)961-5600

Resort Hotel
$180-$246

Address: Rt 350 Lakeside C0A 1S0 **Location:** 3 mi (5 km) w on Rt 2, follow signs. **Facility:** Located on the eastern shore, this resort offers a great opportunity for relaxation in standard hotel rooms, suites, or in townhouse-styled cottages. 81 units, some cottages. 2-3 stories, interior/exterior corridors. **Terms:** seasonal, 3 day cancellation notice-fee imposed. **Dining:** David's at Crowbush, see separate listing. **Pool(s):** heated indoor. **Activities:** sauna, whirlpool, beach access, 2 lighted tennis courts, exercise room, spa. *Fee:* golf-18 holes. **Guest Services:** valet and coin laundry. *(See ad starting on p. 224.)*

WHERE TO EAT

DAVID'S AT CROWBUSH
                  Phone: 902/961-5600

American
$25-$38

AAA Inspector Notes: The pleasant dining room overlooks the fifth fairway at the Links at Crowbush Cove. In addition to specialties of fresh local island seafood, the menu lists prime cuts of meat and homemade desserts. **Bar:** full bar. **Reservations:** suggested. **Address:** Rt 350 Lakeside C0A 1S0 **Location:** 3 mi (5 km) w on Rt 2, follow signs; in Rodd Crowbush Golf & Beach Resort.

MOUNT STEWART (B-4) pop. 261

HILLSBOROUGH RIVER ECO-CENTRE is at 104 Main St. The center houses a museum display about the river's historical, cultural and environmental importance and use as a transportation route. Outdoor trails showcase the indigenous bird and plant species found in the vicinity. **Time:** Allow 30 minutes minimum. **Hours:** Daily 10-6, July 1-early Sept.; phone for reduced spring and fall hours. Phone ahead to confirm schedule. **Cost:** Donations. **Phone:** (902) 676-2050, or (902) 676-2881 in the off-season.

MURRAY HARBOUR (C-5) pop. 358

Murray Harbour, once known as Eskwader, or "the fishing place," by the Mi'kmaq Indians, is one of several busy seaports that line the harbor of the same name. A number of fresh seafood outlets occupy the area. Deep-sea or tuna fishing expeditions depart daily from the wharf in nearby Murray River.

CAPE BEAR LIGHTHOUSE AND MARCONI MUSEUM is 6 km (4 mi.) e. on Hwy. 18. Overlooking the Northumberland Strait, the lighthouse has guided vessels since 1881. Visitors are permitted to climb to the top of the lighthouse. A replica of the Marconi station that stood beside the lighthouse 1905-22 also is on-site. The museum features maritime artifacts, audiovisual displays, archival photographs and artwork. This is said to be one of the first Canadian land dispatch centers to hear the distress signals from the sinking *Titanic*.

Tours: Guided tours are available. **Time:** Allow 30 minutes minimum. **Hours:** Daily 10-6, June-Sept. Phone ahead to confirm schedule. **Cost:** $3.50; $1.50 (ages 6-15); $7.50 (family). Cash only. **Phone:** (902) 962-2917.

FOX RIVER COTTAGES
                  Phone: 902/962-2881

Cottage
$85-$140

Address: 239 Machon Point Rd C0A 1V0 **Location:** Oceanfront. Rt 18, 0.6 mi (1 km) se. **Facility:** 3 cottages. 1 story, exterior corridors. **Terms:** open 6/1-10/15 & 5/20-5/31, 30 day cancellation notice-fee imposed. **Activities:** limited beach access, canoeing. **Guest Services:** complimentary and valet laundry.

NEW GLASGOW (B-3)

NEW GLASGOW GARDENS OF HOPE is just e. of Hwy. 13 at 2841 New Glasgow Rd. on the grounds of the Prince Edward Island Preserve Co. Twelve acres of landscaped water and flower gardens overlook the Clyde River. Nearly 2 kilometres (1.2 mi.) of trails wend past gardens and sculptures. **Time:** Allow 1 hour minimum. **Hours:** Daily 8:30 a.m.-dusk. **Cost:** Donations. **Phone:** (902) 964-4300 or (800) 565-5267.

NEW GLASGOW LOBSTER SUPPERS
                  Phone: 902/964-2870

Seafood
$20-$39

AAA Inspector Notes: Serving guests since 1958, this restaurant is known for its lobster pound, which contains 20,000 pounds of the tasty bottom-dwellers. Fittingly, the menu features lots of delicious lobster dinners, which are served with all-you-can-eat chowder, mussels, salad and tempting homemade desserts. **Bar:** full bar. **Address:** 604 Rt 258 C0A 1N0 **Location:** Off Rt 13, jct Rt 224 and 258; 5.8 mi (9.6 km) s of Cavendish.

THE OLDE GLASGOW MILL RESTAURANT

Phone: 902-964-3313

▽▼▽ ▽▼▽
Canadian
$18-$30

AAA Inspector Notes: This restored 1896 feed mill is located in a charming area bordering the Tidal River Clyde and hills. You can dine on two levels and both offer a nice view. They feature creative preparations of fresh seafood, meat and pasta. Finish with one of their excellent desserts over a special coffee. **Bar:** full bar. **Reservations:** suggested. **Address:** Rt 13 C0A 1N0 **Location:** Just w of Rt 224; centre. D

PRINCE EDWARD ISLAND PRESERVE COMPANY RESTAURANT

Phone: 902-964-4300

▽▼▽ ▽▼▽
Canadian
$9-$21

AAA Inspector Notes: Overlooking the picturesque Clyde River, this casual restaurant prepares home-style potato pie, fish cakes, lobster sandwiches and excellent desserts. Cathedral ceilings, hardwood floors and stenciled walls enhance the appeal of the dining room. Service is pleasant and attentive. After eating, guests can peruse the preserves factory and gift shops. **Bar:** beer & wine. **Reservations:** suggested. **Address:** 2841 New Glasgow Rd C0A 1N0 **Location:** Off Rt 13; jct Rt 224 and 258. L D

NEW LONDON (B-3)

Lobster suppers began in 1964 when the parish of St. Ann sponsored the dinners to raise money. They have since become immensely popular and are held in several area communities. St. Ann's Church and the New London Lions Club sponsor lobster suppers from late June to late September; phone (902) 621-0635.

LUCY MAUD MONTGOMERY BIRTHPLACE is at 6461 Hwy. 20 at New London Corner. Memorabilia of the author, whose works include "Anne of Green Gables," includes the author's personal scrapbooks and her wedding shoes and veil as well as a replica of her wedding dress. **Hours:** Daily 9-5, mid-May to mid-Oct. **Cost:** $4; 50c (ages 6-12). **Phone:** (902) 886-2099.

NORTH CAPE (A-1)

The northernmost point on Prince Edward Island, North Cape was originally called Cap du Sauvage by explorer Jacques Cartier. In 1534 his vessel was beckoned by an Indian standing on the shore, but when it arrived the Indian was gone. Also gone are the hundreds of walrus that inhabited nearby Seacow Pond before they were killed by early inhabitants.

 NORTH CAPE, NATURE & TECHNOLOGY IN PERFECT HARMONY is on Hwy. 12 at the n.w. tip of the island. The site includes the 1866 North Cape Lighthouse, an interpretive center, a wind test facility and a commercial wind farm. At low tide, visitors can walk out to the longest natural rock reef in North America to view sea life and, weather permitting, the harvesting of Irish moss. The Black Marsh Nature Trail leads through an open bog area, interpreting the area's history, local fishing and coastal ecology.

Towering windmills and turbines generate energy at the Wind Energy Institute of Canada, Canada's national research center devoted to studying how wind can be harnessed as a power supply. The North Cape Interpretive Centre features an aquarium as well as displays and a videotape presentation about the Wind Energy Institute of Canada. Exhibits about North Cape history and Atlantic Canada's first wind farm also are showcased.

Time: Allow 1 hour, 30 minutes minimum. **Hours:** Daily 9-8, July-Aug.; 10-6, May-June and Sept. 1-second Mon. in Oct. Phone ahead to confirm schedule. **Cost:** $5; $4 (ages 56+); $3 (students with ID); free (ages 0-7 with adult); $13 (family). **Phone:** (902) 882-2991.

WIND & REEF SEAFOOD RESTAURANT

Phone: 902/882-3535

▽▼▽ ▽▼▽
Seafood
$9-$25

AAA Inspector Notes: At the northern tip of the island, the restaurant overlooks the ocean, reef and wind turbines. On the menu is a fine variety of fresh seafood, including chowders and lobster. **Bar:** full bar. **Address:** Rt 12 C0B 2B0 **Location:** In Interpretive Centre. L D

NORTH RUSTICO pop. 599

GULF VIEW COTTAGES

Phone: 902/963-2052

◇◇ ◇◇
Cottage
$95-$160

Address: 36 MacNeill Ln, Gulf Shore Rd C0A 1X0 **Location:** In PEI National Park. **Facility:** 15 cottages. 1 story, exterior corridors. **Terms:** open 6/1-10/12 & 5/24-5/31, office hours 7 am-11 pm, 14 day cancellation notice-fee imposed. **Activities:** playground. **Guest Services:** coin laundry.

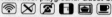

ST. LAWRENCE MOTEL

Phone: (902)963-2053

▽▼▽
Motel
$52-$168

Address: 351 Gulf Shore Pkwy W C0A 1N0 **Location:** On RR 2. Located in PEI National Park. **Facility:** 16 units, some two bedrooms and kitchens. 1 story, exterior corridors. **Terms:** open 6/1-9/30 & 5/18-5/31, office hours 8 am-10 pm, 14 day cancellation notice-fee imposed. **Pool(s):** heated outdoor. **Activities:** playground, game room. **Guest Services:** coin laundry.

SAINT NICHOLAS MOTEL

Phone: 902/963-2898

▽▼▽
Motel
$65-$85

Address: RR 3 Hunter River C0A 1N0 **Location:** Just w on Rt 6. Located in a quiet rural setting. **Facility:** 18 units. 1 story, exterior corridors. **Terms:** open 6/1-10/15 & 5/15-5/31, office hours 7 am-11 pm, cancellation fee imposed. **Amenities:** high-speed Internet.

WHERE TO EAT

BY THE BAY FAMILY RESTAURANT

Phone: 902/963-2290

▽▼▽ ▽▼▽
American
$8-$20

AAA Inspector Notes: In the heart of North Rustico, this casual restaurant offers ample portions of home-style cooking. Some menu items include the popular fish and chips, burgers, sandwiches, soups, salads and some Italian dishes. **Bar:** full bar. **Address:** 7207 Main St C0A 1X0 **Location:** On Rt 6; just s of Harbourview Dr.

FISHERMAN'S WHARF LOBSTER SUPPERS & RESTAURANT   Phone: 902/963-2669

♦♦♦   **AAA Inspector Notes:** This spacious
restaurant is a favorite for lobster
Seafood   suppers, which include lobster in the
$8-$30   shell, steamed mussels, seafood
chowder and the all-you-can-eat salad
bar. Steak, ham and scallops also are
offered. Baked goods are fresh and tasty. The service is
friendly. **Bar:** full bar. **Address:** Main St (Rt 6) C0A 1X0
Location: Centre. [L] [D] CALL [&M]

THE PEARL CAFE   Phone: 902/963-2111

♦♦♦   **AAA Inspector Notes:** A unique cafe
with casual, friendly service, the eatery
Canadian   places a focus on preparing quality
$22-$32   food using fresh local produce, dairy
products, seafood and meats. All
foods are prepared from scratch,
which may take a little extra time. **Bar:** full bar.
Reservations: suggested. **Address:** 7792 Cavendish Rd
C0A 1X0 **Location:** 2 mi (3.2 km) w on Rt 6.
[D] CALL [&M] [X]

O'LEARY (B-1) pop. 861

O'Leary was named for an Irish settler who arrived on Prince Edward Island in 1837. The town's
location on the island railway line made it a center
for trade and industry. Fishing and agriculture—
particularly potato production—are mainstays of the
local economy.

PRINCE EDWARD ISLAND POTATO MUSEUM is
off Hwy. 142 at jct. Parkview Dr. and Dewar Ln. Visitors are greeted by a 4-metre (14-ft.) sculptured fi-
berglass spud. The importance of the potato is
depicted through industry displays and a collection
of farm equipment. The complex includes a community museum, a historic schoolhouse, a chapel and
a log barn.

Time: Allow 1 hour minimum. **Hours:** Mon.-Sat.
9-5, Sun. 1-5, May 15-Oct. 15. **Cost:** $6; $14
(family). **Phone:** (902) 859-2039, or (902) 853-2312
in the off-season. [⊞]

ORWELL (B-5)

Founded in the late 1700s by Scottish, Irish and
British Loyalist settlers, Orwell was named for Sir
Francis Orwell, England's Minister of Plantations.

A notable Orwellian was Sir Andrew Macphail, a
talented man whose occupations included medicine,
education, journalism and agriculture. Macphail, a
physician and medical professor at McGill University
in Montréal, wrote "The Master's Wife," the story of
local Scottish immigrants. He also was the first
editor of the *Canadian Medical Journal.* His agricultural research led him to develop new strains of potato plants, a boost for one of the province's most
important crops.

Besides potatoes, strawberries are an important
local crop. Also held periodically are ceilidhs (KAY-
lees), Old World community music festivals.

▼ **ORWELL CORNER HISTORIC VILLAGE** is
GEM off Hwy. 1, following signs. Visitors to this restored small rural crossroads village of the late

1890s can tour a period home, general store,
church, community hall, post office, smithy, shingle
mill and barns. The shopkeeper's home is outfitted
with such items as a cast-iron stove, horsehair sofa,
pump organ, 1820s loom and spinning wheels.

The barns house chickens, goats, pigs and
sheep. Carts, wagons, farm machinery and tools
from the late 19th century are displayed. The vintage farm equipment in the PEI Agricultural Heritage
Museum helps tell the story of European agriculture
on the island from the 17th century to 1950.

Hours: Daily 9:30-5, July 1-Sept. 4; Mon.-Fri.
9-4:30, May 24-June 30 and Sept. 6-Oct. 7. **Cost:**
$7.50; $5 (students with ID); $20 (family, two adults
and two children). **Phone:** (902) 651-8585.

SIR ANDREW MACPHAIL HOMESTEAD is off
Hwy. 1 at 271 Macphail Park Rd., just beyond the
Orwell Corner Historic Village. Built in 1850, the 65-
hectare (160-acre) homestead features the restored
Macphail home, antiques, gardens, a playhouse and
many nature trails. Special events are held. Guided
tours lasting about 45 minutes are available. **Time:**
Allow 1 hour minimum. **Hours:** Wed.-Sat. 10-6,
June 1-Nov. 15. **Cost:** Donations. **Phone:** (902)
651-2789. [↑↓]

PARK CORNER (B-3)

Park Corner was settled in 1775 by James
Townsend and his family. Townsend, whose descendants include Lucy Maud Montgomery, named the
town after his former home in Berkshire, England.

The shore north of Park Corner is graced by
gently sloping sand dunes. Sprouting from the
dunes is marram grass, whose long roots mesh beneath the dunes and anchor them. While the grass
can withstand the salty breezes, it cannot withstand
being walked on. Once the grass has been
trampled, the sand dunes shift and large holes
called blowouts form, stifling the marram grass and
disrupting the otherwise stable shoreline.

[SAVE] **ANNE OF GREEN GABLES MUSEUM** is at
4542 Hwy. 20. The Anne of Green Gables Museum at the beautiful Campbell Homestead is dedicated to the life and works of Lucy Maud
Montgomery, author of "Anne of Green Gables."
The house was built in 1872 by her aunt and uncle,
and the scenery at the site inspired the places she
wrote about, like the Lake of Shining Waters. She
was married July 5, 1911, in the parlor.

A bookcase with glass doors brings to mind
Anne's enchanted bookcase description from the
novel. There also is a collection of the author's be-
longings, including a patchwork quilt. Visitors can
take a carriage ride led by a gentleman resembling
her character of Matthew. The peaceful route
traverses the grounds with its gardens and lake;
longer trips venture farther out and may include
silver birch tree stands, rolling hills, fields and farms,
and a beautiful beach.

Time: Allow 30 minutes minimum. **Hours:** Daily 9-5, July-Aug.; 10-4, mid-May through June 30 and Sept. 1 to mid-Oct. Phone ahead to confirm schedule. **Cost:** $5; $1 (ages 6-18). Short carriage ride $4; $1.50 (children). Carriage ride (for up to five people); $55 (30-minute ride); $90 (1-hour ride). Reservations are required for carriage rides. **Phone:** (902) 886-2884 (Sat.-Sun.), or (800) 665-2663 (Mon.-Fri.).

LUCY MAUD MONTGOMERY HERITAGE MUSEUM is on Hwy. 20. This was the home of Senator Donald Montgomery, author Lucy Maud Montgomery's grandfather. Built in 1879 and still owned by the Montgomery family, the home features family antiques and memorabilia from the author's nine novels.

Tours: Guided tours are available. **Hours:** Daily 10-6, June-Sept. Phone ahead to confirm schedule. **Cost:** $3.50; free (ages 0-12). **Phone:** (902) 886-2752.

PORT HILL (B-2)

Port Hill and Bideford are neighboring towns named by English settlers for two similarly situated towns in Devonshire, England.

GREEN PARK SHIPBUILDING MUSEUM AND HISTORIC YEO HOUSE are on Hwy. 12 near Tyne Valley, in Green Park. The museum traces the history of shipbuilding on Prince Edward Island, where some 4,500 vessels set sail in the 19th century. Costumed guides conduct tours of the 1865 Yeo House, once home to the island's wealthiest shipbuilder. An interpretive center features historical displays about the Yeo family business. *(See Recreation Chart.)*

Time: Allow 2 hours minimum. **Hours:** Daily 9-5, July-Aug. Hours are reduced in June and Sept.; phone ahead to confirm. **Cost:** $5; $3.50 (students with ID); $13.50 (family); free (ages 0-6 except during special events). **Phone:** (902) 831-7947, or (902) 368-6600 in the off-season. 🅷

PORT LA JOYE—FORT AMHERST NATIONAL HISTORIC SITE OF CANADA (C-4)

Port La Joye—Fort Amherst National Historic Site of Canada is west of Charlottetown on Hwy. 1, then southeast on Hwy. 19 to Rocky Point. The site consists of 89 hectares (220 acres) of woods and rolling grasslands overlooking Hillsborough Bay and Charlottetown Harbour where the French built their first European-style settlement in 1720.

The English took the area in 1758 and constructed Fort Amherst, which quickly fell into disrepair after 1768 when the official military presence was withdrawn; only the earthworks remain. A visitor center offers an interpretive display. Guide service and picnic facilities are available. Grounds open daily 24 hours, June-Oct. Visitor center open daily 9-5, July-Aug. Admission $3.90; $3.40 (ages 65+);

$1.90 (ages 6-16); $9.80 (family, two adults and five children). Phone (902) 675-2220 or (902) 566-7626.

▽ PRINCE EDWARD ISLAND NATIONAL PARK OF CANADA (B-4)

Elevations in the park range from sea level to 49 metres (160 ft.). Refer to CAA/AAA maps for additional elevation information.

Prince Edward Island National Park of Canada can be reached from six entrances along hwys. 6, 13, 15 and 25. With an area of about 26 square kilometres (10 sq. mi.), the park extends 40 kilometres (25 mi.) along the island's northern shore along the Gulf of St. Lawrence. It offers long stretches of sandy beaches, sweeping sand dunes, ponds and woodlands, and salt marshes that abound with waterfowl and shore birds, including the great blue heron.

Many years of wind and wave erosion have carved the park's sand dunes, beaches and red sandstone cliffs. Greenwich, east on Hwy. 2 to Hwy. 313 at St. Peters, shelters a rare and relatively undisturbed parabolic dune, a migrating wave of sand that has swept through forests, leaving skeletal trees in its wake. Sharp-eyed hikers may glimpse a variety of wildlife throughout the park, including the red fox.

General Information and Activities

The park is open daily. Camping is available at Cavendish and Stanhope from mid-June to mid-October; there is a camping fee. Vehicles (including motorcycles and minibikes) must stay on designated roadways and are not allowed on the sand dunes, beaches or trails.

Prince Edward Island's north shore offers an abundance of water sports and recreational activities in July and August. Lifeguards supervise beaches at Brackley, Cavendish, Cavendish Campground, Greenwich, North Rustico, Ross' Lane and Stanhope Lane. Anglers can charter boats at nearby harbors for deep-sea fishing. A national park fishing license is required to fish in the ponds and streams within the park. A number of small lakes and ponds have brook trout, but motorboats are not permitted on these ponds.

The park also has facilities for golf and tennis. For cyclists and hikers, an array of multiuse trails crisscross the park, including a paved trail that runs along the scenic Gulf Shore Parkway. A regular schedule of interpretive activities is offered daily July through August.

Two visitor centers offer park information daily mid-May to early September—one at the intersection of hwys. 6 and 13, the second at the intersection of hwys. 15 and 6. *See Recreation Chart.*

ADMISSION early June-Labour Day $7.80; $6.80 (ages 65+); $3.90 (ages 6-16); $19.60 (family, two adults and five children). Admission is free rest of year. Seasonal passes are also available.

PETS are allowed in most areas except as posted. Animals must be leashed or otherwise physically restrained at all times and are not permitted at beaches or in public buildings.

ADDRESS inquiries to Parks Canada, 2 Palmers Ln., Charlottetown, PE, Canada C1A 5V8. Phone (902) 672-6350, (877) 737-3783 for reservations or TTY (902) 566-7061.

GREENWICH INTERPRETATION CENTRE, jct. hwys. 2 and 313, includes interactive displays about the peninsula's fragile ecosystem and archeological significance. Visitors can take part in hands-on learning opportunities and view "Wind, Sea and Sand," a 12-minute multimedia presentation about Greenwich's geographic history.

Time: Allow 1 hour minimum. **Hours:** Daily 10-6, early July-early Sept.; 10-5, June 1-late June and early Sept.-Sept. 30. Phone ahead to confirm schedule. **Cost:** included with national park admission early June-Labour Day of $7.80; $6.80 (ages 65+); $3.90 (ages 6-16); $19.60 (family, two adults and five children). Admission rest of year free. **Phone:** (902) 961-2514. [⛔] [⛲]

ROLLO BAY

ROLLO BAY INN   **Phone:** 902/687-3550
♦♦♦
Hotel   **Address:** 1067 Lower Rollo Bay Rd
Rates not provided   C0A 2B0 **Location:** 2.5 mi (4 km) w
                       on Hwy 2. Located in a rural area.
                       Facility: 20 units, some efficiencies, 2
                       stories (no elevator), interior/exterior
corridors. [BIZ] [📶] [✕] / SOME UNITS [📶] [📷]

ROSENEATH

BRUDENELL CHALETS   **Phone:** 902/652-2900
♦♦♦♦
Cottage   **Address:** 1068 Georgetown Rd C0A
Rates not provided   1L0 **Location:** Jct Rt 4 and 3, 4 mi (6
                       km) e on Rt 3. Located in a quiet rural
                       area. **Facility:** A choice of cottages, all
                       with gas grills and screened porches,
is offered at this pleasant property. 15 cottages. 1 story, exterior corridors. **Terms:** seasonal, office hours 8 am-10 pm, check-in 4 pm. **Pool(s):** heated outdoor. **Activities:** rental bicycles, playground, basketball, horseshoes, volleyball. **Guest Services:** complimentary laundry.
 [🍴] [🛏] [BIZ] [📶] [✕] [📷] [📷] [📺] / SOME UNITS [🐾]

Download eTourBook guides for ereaders and smartphones at AAA.com/ebooks

---

RODD BRUDENELL RIVER-A RODD SIGNATURE RESORT   **Phone:** 902/652-2332

♦♦♦/♦♦♦   **Address:** 86 Dewars Ln, Rt 3 C0A
Resort Hotel   1L0 **Location:** Jct Rt 4, 3.3 mi (5.5
$110-$189   km) e. Located in Brudenell River
               Provincial Park. **Facility:** Avid golfers
               will enjoy this resort located on
spacious manicured grounds overlooking lovely golf courses and Brudenell River. Choose from hotel rooms and fully or semi-equipped cottages. 131 units, some cottages. 1-3 stories, interior/exterior corridors. **Terms:** seasonal, 3 day cancellation notice-fee imposed. **Dining:** Club 19-Fun Food Drink, see separate listing. **Activities:** sauna, whirlpool, rental canoes, 2 lighted tennis courts, rental bicycles, hiking trails, playground, exercise room, spa. **Fee:** boat dock, golf-46 holes, horseback riding. **Guest Services:** valet laundry.
(See ad starting on p. 224.)
[🍴] [🍸] CALL [&M] [🛶] [📶] [📷]
/ SOME UNITS FEE [🐾] [📷] [📷] [📷]

ROSENEATH COUNTRY INN BED & BREAKFAST
                                Phone: 902/838-4590
♦♦♦
Historic Bed   **Address:** 135 Dewars Rd C0A 1G0
& Breakfast   **Location:** Off Rt 4, follow signs.
               Located in a quiet rural area. **Facility:**
$110-$120 6/1-10/31   Gardens, a veranda and a tranquil
$80-$90 11/1-5/31   riverfront setting distinguish this 1868
               farmhouse-turned-bed and breakfast.
               4 units, some two bedrooms. 2 stories
(no elevator), interior corridors. **Terms:** 14 day cancellation notice-fee imposed. **Activities:** bicycles, hiking trails. **Guest Services:** coin laundry. [📶] [✕] [MC] [W]

WHERE TO EAT

CLUB 19-FUN FOOD DRINK   **Phone:** 902/652-2332

♦♦♦   **AAA Inspector Notes:** In a lovely
American   location overlooking the golf course,
$9-$19   the casual, pub-style restaurant offers
            a wide selection of Canadian fare for
            breakfast, lunch or dinner. Patio dining
            is a nice option in season. **Bar:** full
bar. **Address:** Rt 3 C0A 1G0 **Location:** Jct Rt 4, 3.3 mi (5.5 km) e; in Rodd Brudenell River-A Rodd Signature Resort.
[B] [L] [D] CALL [&M]

RUSTICO (B-3)

Trail rides through the fields and woods bordering scenic Rustico Bay are offered by area outfitters mid-June through Labour Day.

FARMERS' BANK OF RUSTICO MUSEUM AND DOUCET HOUSE is on Hwy. 243 next to St. Augustine's Church. Opened in 1864 and operated until 1894, the bank was important in the establishment of credit unions in Canada. The Farmers' Bank exhibit offers information about the founding of the bank by Pere Georges-Antoine Belcourt. The site also traces the history of Acadians in this area; the Doucet House was built about 1772 and may be the oldest Acadian dwelling in the province. Interpretive programs are offered.

Time: Allow 1 hour minimum. **Hours:** Mon.-Sat. 9:30-5:30, Sun. 1-5, June-Sept.; by appointment rest of year. **Cost:** $4; $3 (senior citizens); $2 (students with ID); $8 (family, two adults and two children ages 0-12; $1.50 per extra child). Cash only. **Phone:** (902) 963-3168, or (902) 963-2304 in the off-season.

ST. ANN

ST. ANN'S CHURCH LOBSTER SUPPERS
Phone: 902/621-0635

Seafood
$21-$42

AAA Inspector Notes: Since 1964, the restaurant has delivered fine, flavorful lobster dinners accompanied by salad, chowder, mussels, dessert and coffee. The congenial atmosphere is welcoming to families. The professional staff provides courteous, attentive service. **Bar:** full bar. **Address:** Rt 224 C0A 1N0 **Location:** On Rt 224; midway between Stanley Bridge and Hunter River. (D)

ST. PETERS

THE INN AT ST. PETERS
Phone: (902)961-2135

Country Inn
$150-$270

Address: 1668 Greenwich Rd C0A 2A0 **Location:** Jct Rt 16 and 313, 0.6 mi (1 km) w on Rt 313. **Facility:** A splendid bay and garden view can be enjoyed from private decks at the inn's spacious, tastefully decorated guest rooms. 16 units. 1 story, exterior corridors. **Terms:** seasonal, office hours 8 am-10 pm, 2 night minimum stay - seasonal, 7 day cancellation notice-fee imposed. **Dining:** restaurant, see separate listing. **Activities:** bicycles.

WHERE TO EAT

THE INN AT ST. PETERS DINING ROOM
Phone: 902/961-2135

American
$26-$35

AAA Inspector Notes: The bright and airy dining room affords splendid views of St. Peters Bay and the landscaped grounds. Service is attentive yet relaxed. Fine ingredients, fresh local produce, seafood, meats and the chef's skill merge to create a memorable meal. **Bar:** full bar. **Reservations:** suggested. **Address:** 1668 Greenwich Rd C0A 2A0 **Location:** Jct Rt 16 and 313, 0.6 mi (1 km) w on Rt 313; in The Inn at St. Peters. (D) CALL

RICK'S FISH'N'CHIPS & SEAFOOD HOUSE
Phone: 902/961-3438

American
$6-$13

AAA Inspector Notes: The popular seafood take-out bar offers indoor and outdoor seating. Portions are ample, and the French fries are hand-cut on site. **Bar:** beer & wine. **Address:** Rt 2 C0A 2A0 **Location:** Jct Rt 2 and 16; centre. (L) (D)

SOURIS (B-6) pop. 1,232

Ships bringing provisions to Prince Edward Island during its early settlement also brought mice, which proliferated at such an amazing rate that the French settlers named their town after them. Souris also gained recognition through American playwright Elmer Harris, who used the town as the setting for his 1940 play "Johnny Belinda," which ran for 320 consecutive performances in New York. The film version was shot in Fort Bragg, Calif.

Some of the island's finest white sand beaches lie between Souris and Bothwell. In town, the beach is accessible from a small park off Hwy. 2. Red Point Provincial Park *(see Recreation Chart)* also has an excellent beach and developed recreational facilities.

Local waters support industry as well as recreation. Souris has a large fishing and lobster industry. Ferry service to Québec's Magdalen Islands in the Gulf of St. Lawrence is available April through January; phone Traversier C.T.M.A. Ferry at (418) 986-3278, or (888) 986-3278.

BASIN HEAD FISHERIES MUSEUM is 12 km (8 mi.) e. on Hwy. 16, on a bluff overlooking the Northumberland Straight. The museum showcases the island's historic inshore fishery. The ways of inshore fishing are reflected in boat gear, photographs and dioramas. There is a cannery, and a boardwalk offers access to a white "singing" sands beach and playground.

Time: Allow 1 hour minimum. **Hours:** Daily 9-5, June 1-late Sept. Phone ahead early and late in the season to verify the site is open. **Cost:** $4; $3.50 (students with ID); $11.50 (family). **Phone:** (902) 357-7233, or (902) 368-6600 in the off-season.

BLUEFIN RESTAURANT
Phone: 902/687-3271

American
$6-$19

AAA Inspector Notes: This spacious, country-style diner has booth seating and pleasant servers. Well-prepared home-style cooking includes fresh breads and pastries baked daily. **Bar:** full bar. **Address:** 10 Federal Ave C0A 2B0 **Location:** Just s of Main St; centre. (B) (L) (D)

SOUTH RUSTICO

BARACHOIS INN
Phone: 902/963-2194

(fyi) Not evaluated. **Address:** 2193 Church Rd C1A 7M4 **Location:** On Rt 143; centre. Facilities, services, and decor characterize a mid-scale property.

STANLEY BRIDGE (B-3)

Stanley Bridge, a resort community southwest of Cavendish, is noted for its picturesque inlets and fine inland fishing on the Stanley and Trout rivers. Tuna boat charters can be arranged at the Stanley Bridge wharf.

STANLEY BRIDGE MARINE AQUARIUM AND MANOR OF BIRDS is off Hwy. 6 at 32 Campbellton Rd. The facility features an aquarium with native fish and touch tanks; Irish moss and interpretive shellfish exhibits; and mounted fur-bearing animals, butterflies and more than 700 birds. **Time:** Allow 30 minutes minimum. **Hours:** Daily 9:30-8, June-Aug.; 9:30-5, Sept.-Oct. **Cost:** $7.25; $5.75 (ages 5-14). **Phone:** (902) 886-3355.

INN AT THE PIER

▼▼▼
Country Inn
Rates not provided

Phone: 902/886-3126
Address: 9796 Cavendish Rd C0A 1E0 **Location:** Rt 6, 3.6 mi (6 km) w of Cavendish; centre. **Facility:** Situated on the shores of New London Bay and overlooking the distant sand dunes, this modern inn offers a variety of room styles and suites, some with ocean views and a patio or deck. 18 units. 2 stories (no elevator), interior/exterior corridors. **Terms:** seasonal, office hours 7 am-11 pm, check-in 4 pm. **Pool(s):** heated outdoor. **Activities:** whirlpool, boat dock, rental bicycles. **Guest Services:** coin laundry.
(See ad starting on p. 224.)

🍴 🍸 🛥 BIZ 🛜 ✕ 💻
/ SOME UNITS FEE 🐾 🛗 🖼

WHERE TO EAT

CARR'S OYSTER BAR RESTAURANT & LOUNGE
Phone: 902/886-3355

▼▼
Seafood
$10-$30

AAA Inspector Notes: On the harborfront, the restaurant focuses its menu on fresh seafood but also prepares such comfort foods as burgers and sandwiches. Patrons of this casual spot can relax either indoors or out on the deck. **Bar:** full bar. **Address:** Campbellton Rd C0A 1E0 **Location:** At Rt 6 and 238.

L D 🅰Ⓒ

STRATFORD pop. 7,083

SOUTHPORT MOTEL
Phone: 902/569-2287
[fyi] Not evaluated. **Address:** 20 Stratford Rd C1B 1T5 **Location:** Trans-Canada Hwy 1, just s on Stratford Rd, then 1.2 mi (2 km) e of Charlottetown over bridge. Facilities, services, and decor characterize an economy property.

SUMMERSIDE (B-2) pop. 14,500
• Hotels p. 238 • Restaurants p. 238

Often referred to as Prince Edward Island's western capital, Summerside lies on the narrow strip of land that connects Prince and Queens counties. Supposedly warmer than its neighboring towns on the north shore, the city is considered to be on the "summer side" of the island.

Summerside boasts neat residential streets lined with stately wood-frame houses that resemble châteaus. Murals on various buildings depict the town's history, including a 400-square-foot mural at Fire Hall, 248 Fitzroy St., portraying the Great Fire of 1906. Its public wharf serves the large ocean-going vessels that carry Prince Edward Island potatoes to ports worldwide.

Summerside marks the beginning of the North Cape Coastal Drive, a 300-kilometre (186-mi.) scenic drive linking the communities of western Prince Edward Island. The drive shows off the most rugged portion of the island's coastline, including red sandstone cliffs at the island's northern tip as well as the picturesque fishing villages and farm communities along the way.

The College of Piping and Celtic Performing Arts of Canada puts on the 🐟 Highland Storm late June through late August on their Summerside campus. Performers include pipers, drummers and Highland and step dancers along with fiddlers and singers. Phone (902) 436-5377 or (877) 224-7473.

Summerside Visitor Destination Centre: Spinnakers Landing, 150 Harbour Dr., Summerside, PE, Canada C1N 5P1. **Phone:** (902) 888-8364 or (877) 734-2382.

Shopping areas: Spinnakers Landing, on the waterfront, features several shops, boutiques, entertainment and eateries. Also on the waterfront are Waterfront Place and Summerside Mall. County Fair Mall is nearby.

BISHOP'S FOUNDRY MUSEUM, 101 Water St. at jct. Autumn St., once operated as Bishop's Foundry and Thomas Hall Manufacturing Co. Ltd., which employed four generations of metal workers. The former machine shop displays lathes, gadgets and tools. **Time:** Allow 30 minutes minimum. **Hours:** Mon.-Sat. 10-5, mid-June to early Sept.; by appointment rest of year. **Cost:** Donations. **Phone:** (902) 432-1296.

EPTEK ART & CULTURE CENTRE is at 130 Harbour Dr. on the waterfront. History and the fine arts are the focus of changing exhibits originating in local and other Canadian communities. **Time:** Allow 30 minutes minimum. **Hours:** Mon.-Sat. 9-6, Sun. noon-6, July-Aug; Tues.-Fri. 10-4, Sun. noon-4, rest of year. **Cost:** Donations. **Phone:** (902) 888-8373.

INTERNATIONAL FOX MUSEUM & HALL OF FAME is at 33 Summer St. in the 1911 Historic Armoury Building. The attraction offers a guided tour and an interactive display relating the history of fox farming. In the late 1800s the elusive silver fox was first successfully raised in captivity on Prince Edward Island. This led to an industry with high stakes, secrecy, adventure and intrigue. Fox farming became a worldwide industry thanks to the local breeding stock.

Gallery 33, an art gallery with changing exhibits, is housed on the top floor. **Hours:** Mon.-Sat. 10-5, late June-early Sept.; Mon.-Fri. by appointment rest of year. Phone ahead to confirm schedule. **Cost:** Donations. **Phone:** (902) 432-7916, or (902) 432-1296 in the off-season.

PRINCE EDWARD ISLAND SPORTS HALL OF FAME AND MUSEUM is at 124 Harbour Dr. in the Wyatt Centre. The facility features displays and information about the accomplishments of the many men and women who have been inducted into the hall of fame. **Time:** Allow 30 minutes minimum. **Hours:** Mon. and Fri. 10-5:30, Tues. and Thurs. 10-8, Wed. noon-5:30, July-Aug. **Cost:** Donations. **Phone:** (902) 436-0423.

🔺 **WYATT HERITAGE PROPERTIES,** at 75-85 Spring St., and 205 Prince St., comprises three buildings. The MacNaught History Centre and Archives (75 Spring St.) is a genealogical resource with information about all of Prince Edward Island, and it also features changing historical exhibits.

The 1867 Wyatt House Museum (85 Spring St.) was the home of Wanda Lefurgey Wyatt until her death in 1998, at the age of 102. The house has been restored and displays many historically significant artifacts. Guided tours give visitors a glimpse into the life of the Lefurgey and Wyatt families.

The Lefurgey Cultural Centre (205 Prince St.), an 1867 shipbuilder's house, now serves as an arts and crafts center. This historic home offers art classes, studio space, music and performing arts classes and children's programming. Free summer concerts are held in the Spring Street common area every Wednesday evening July through August.

Time: Allow 1 hour minimum. **Hours:** History center and archives open Tues.-Sat. 10-5 (also Tues. 6-9 p.m.), all year. Wyatt house tours depart Mon.-Sat. on the hour 10-5, June 1-late Sept.; by appointment rest of year. Last tour begins 1 hour before closing. Cultural center open year-round; phone for schedule. Concerts held Wed. at 6:30, July-Aug. **Cost:** $7; $5.50 (ages 61+ and students with ID). **Phone:** (902) 432-1296.

CAIRNS MOTEL
Phone: 902/436-5841

Motel
$49-$90

Address: 721 Water St E C1N 4J2 **Location:** 1.3 mi (2.1 km) e on Hwy 11. **Facility:** 20 units. 1 story, exterior corridors. **Parking:** winter plug-ins. **Terms:** open 6/1-11/1, office hours 7:30 am-10 pm. **Activities:** bicycle trails. **Guest Services:** coin laundry.

CLARK'S SUNNY ISLE MOTEL
Phone: 902/436-5665

Motel
$47-$83

Address: 720 Water St E C1N 4J1 **Location:** 1.4 mi (2.4 km) e on Hwy 11. **Facility:** 21 units. 1 story, exterior corridors. **Terms:** open 6/1-10/31 & 5/1-5/31.

ECONO LODGE
Phone: 902/436-9100

Hotel
Rates not provided

Address: 80 All Weather Hwy C1N 4P3 **Location:** Jct Hwy 1A and 2, 3.1 mi (5 km) w on Hwy 2. Located in a rural area. **Facility:** 40 units, some efficiencies. 1 story, interior corridors. **Pool(s):** heated indoor.

LOYALIST COUNTRY INN, A LAKEVIEW RESORT
Phone: (902)436-3333

Hotel
$149-$249 6/1-9/30
$89-$199 10/1-5/31

Address: 195 Harbour Dr C1N 5R1 **Location:** Centre of downtown. **Facility:** 82 units. 3 stories, interior corridors. **Dining:** Crown & Anchor Tavern, Prince William Dining Room, see separate listings. **Pool(s):** heated indoor. **Activities:** sauna, exercise room. **Fee:** bicycles. **Guest Services:** valet laundry. **Free Special Amenities:** local telephone calls and high-speed Internet.

SLEMON PARK HOTEL & CONFERENCE CENTRE
Phone: (902)432-1780

Hotel
$113-$143 1/1-5/31
$110-$140 6/1-12/31

Address: 12 Redwood Ave C0B 1T0 **Location:** On Rt 2, 3 mi (5 km) w at Summerside Airport. **Facility:** 88 units, some two bedrooms and efficiencies. 2 stories (no elevator), interior corridors. **Terms:** cancellation fee imposed. **Amenities:** high-speed Internet. **Activities:** jogging, basketball, game room, volleyball, exercise room. **Guest Services:** coin laundry. **Free Special Amenities:** continental breakfast and high-speed Internet.

SILVER FOX INN
Phone: (902)436-1664

[fyi] Not evaluated. **Address:** 61 Granville St C1N 2Z3 **Location:** Corner of Belmont St. Facilities, services, and decor characterize a mid-scale property.

WHERE TO EAT

BROTHERS 2 RESTAURANT PUB & DINNER THEATRE
Phone: 902/436-9654

Canadian
$9-$23

AAA Inspector Notes: The atmosphere is casual and upbeat in this spacious pub-style restaurant which includes a seasonal dinner theater. The restaurant delivers such delicious selections as pizza and preparations of pasta, seafood and steak. Decorated in a pub style with wood and brass accents, seating is at booths or tables. The uniformed staff is very friendly and the service is casual and attentive. **Bar:** full bar. **Address:** 618 Water St E C1N 4K2 **Location:** 1 mi (1.6 km) e on Hwy 11. [L] [D]

CHINA STAR RESTAURANT
Phone: 902/888-3228

Chinese
$8-$18

AAA Inspector Notes: Guests are seated in either of two pleasant dining sections to browse the menu of Cantonese and Szechuan entrees, including combination plates and daily lunch specials. **Bar:** full bar. **Address:** 265 Water St C1N 1K8 **Location:** At Summer St; centre. **Parking:** street only. [L] [D]

CROWN & ANCHOR TAVERN
Phone: 902/436-3333

American
$7-$21

AAA Inspector Notes: A nice port in a storm, the restaurant offers guests casual, friendly service and a menu that centers on traditional pub fare. Among offerings are fish and chips, burgers and stir-fries. **Bar:** full bar. **Address:** 195 Harbour Dr C1N 5R1 **Location:** Centre of downtown; in Loyalist Country Inn, a Lakeview Resort. [L] [D]

GENTLEMAN JIM'S RESTAURANT   Phone: 902/888-2647

American
$7-$21

AAA Inspector Notes: A homey country theme weaves through this casual, family-oriented restaurant. Seafood chowder and rib steak represent traditional surf and turf fare. The coconut cream pie delights the taste buds. **Bar:** full bar. **Address:** 480 Granville St N C1N 4K6 **Location:** Across from County Fair Mall; centre.

L D

GRANVILLE ST DINER   Phone: 902/724-3043

American
$5-$12

AAA Inspector Notes: This spacious, modern diner offers booth and table seating with a relaxed family atmosphere. The menu selection is vast with numerous comfort foods, daily specials and full breakfast menu anytime. Service is casual and friendly. **Address:** 519 Granville St C1N 5J4 **Location:** Just s of Hwy 2 exit Granville St; adjacent to Walmart. B L D

PRINCE WILLIAM DINING ROOM   Phone: 902/436-3333

Canadian
$10-$28

AAA Inspector Notes: In the evening, soft candlelight enhances the elegant atmosphere of the attractive dining room. The menu includes fresh local seafood, prime cuts of meat and some pasta dishes. Service is relaxed and friendly. **Bar:** full bar. **Address:** 195 Harbour Dr C1N 5R1 **Location:** Centre of downtown; in Loyalist Country Inn, a Lakeview Resort. B L D

STARLITE DINER AND DAIRY BAR

Phone: 902/436-9075

American
$6-$14

AAA Inspector Notes: Patrons experience a flashback to the '50s in this upbeat, rock 'n roll diner. Great hamburgers, seafood platters and sandwiches ground the menu. Shakes and floats have satisfied sugar cravings since 1959. This commercial location borders the highway. **Bar:** beer & wine. **Address:** 810 Water St E C1N 4J6 **Location:** Jct Hwy 1A and 11. B L D

TIGNISH (A-1) pop. 758

Tignish was founded in 1799 by eight Acadian families who came by open boat from Malpeque. Twelve years later they were joined by Irish settlers. The community's first priest noted that the blending of French and English language and culture did not go easily at first, though the two groups eventually forged a peaceful coexistence.

A convent was built in 1868 for the sisters of the Congregation de Notre Dame, who came from Montréal to teach. The private girls' school was opened to the public 50 years later and continued to serve as an educational facility until 1966. Scholars debate about the origin of the town's name, attributing it to both Mi'kmaq and Irish sources.

ST. SIMON AND ST. JUDE CATHOLIC CHURCH is at Church and Maple sts. The red brick church houses the Tignish Pipe Organ, built in 1882 by Louis Mitchell. The 1,118-pipe organ has been used to help celebrate many of Tignish's historical events, including its bicentennial in 1999. **Hours:** Daily 8-7. Tours are available Mon.-Fri. 8:30-4:30. Organ recitals are offered July 1 to mid-Aug. **Cost:** Free. **Phone:** (902) 882-2049 for organ recital times.

TIGNISH HERITAGE INN & GARDENS

Phone: 902/882-2491

Bed & Breakfast
$85-$135

Address: 206 Maple St C0B 2B0 **Location:** Adjacent to St Simon and St Jude Church; centre. **Facility:** 17 units. 3 stories (no elevator), interior corridors. **Terms:** open 6/1-10/15 & 5/15-5/31, office hours 7 am-11 pm, cancellation fee imposed. **Guest Services:** coin laundry. [icons]

DRIFTWOOD COUNTRY COTTAGES

Phone: 902/882-2617

fyi Not evaluated. **Address:** Hwy 12 C0B 2B0 **Location:** Oceanfront. 2.5 mi (4 km) n. Facilities, services, and decor characterize a mid-scale property.

WHERE TO EAT

COUSIN'S VILLAGE FISHER RESTAURANT

Phone: 902/882-5670

American
$6-$19

AAA Inspector Notes: This popular family restaurant serves all meals. Service is casual and friendly. Menu varies from sandwiches and burgers to steak and seafood. Portions are ample and desserts are homemade. **Bar:** full bar. **Address:** 276 Phillips St C0B 2B0 **Location:** 0.6 mi (1 km) s on Rt 2. L D

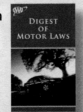

WEST POINT (B-1)

WEST POINT LIGHTHOUSE MUSEUM is off Hwy. 14 at 364 Cedar Dunes Park Rd. in Cedar Dunes Provincial Park. Built in 1875, the light was manned continuously until 1963. The beacon and its attached dwelling have been restored, and a museum includes exhibits and memorabilia documenting the history of the island's lighthouses. Accommodation rentals are available. **Hours:** Museum open daily 10-8, late May-early Oct. **Cost:** $3.50; $3 (senior citizens); $2 (ages 0-11); $8 (family). **Phone:** (902) 859-3605.

WEST POINT LIGHTHOUSE   **Phone:** 902/859-3605
 Not evaluated. **Address:** RR 2 ouest C0B 1V0 **Location:** Oceanfront. On Rt 14; centre. Facilities, services, and decor characterize a mid-scale property.

WOOD ISLANDS (C-5)

WOOD ISLANDS LIGHTHOUSE & INTERPRETIVE MUSEUM is off Hwy. 1, 1 km (.6 mi.) s. of the ferry terminal via Lighthouse Rd. This lovely lighthouse stands at the southernmost point on Prince Edward Island. Built in 1876, it still operates while also functioning as a museum that depicts the area's maritime heritage. Displays chronicle the history of early 20th-century rum running and the history of the island's ferry service to Nova Scotia; exhibit rooms include a re-created lighthouse keeper's quarters. Climb to the top of the beacon tower for a 360-degree view that takes in shoreline cliffs and Northumberland Strait.

Tours: Guided tours are available. **Time:** Allow 1 hour minimum. **Hours:** Daily 9:30-6, mid-June to mid-Sept. Last admission 30 minutes before closing. **Cost:** $5.99; $4.99 (ages 65+); $3 (ages 6-13); $14 (family, two adults and two children ages 0-13). **Phone:** (902) 962-3110. ⊞

MEADOW LODGE MOTEL   **Phone:** 902/962-2022
▼ **Address:** Trans-Canada Hwy 1, Civic 313 C0A 1B0 **Location:** 1 mi (1.6 km) nw of Wood Islands ferry terminal. **Facility:** 18 units, some two bedrooms and kitchens. 1 story, exterior corridors. **Terms:** seasonal, office hours 7 am-11 pm.
Motel
Rates not provided
⊠ 🐾 🔇 / SOME UNITS 🐾

WOODSTOCK (B-1)

MILL RIVER FUN PARK is 1 km (.6 mi.) w. of Hwy. 136 on Hwy. 2. The park offers adult and children's waterslides, other water rides, bumper boats and miniature golf. **Hours:** Daily 11-7, July 1-Labour Day weekend. **Cost:** $9; free (ages 0-5). **Phone:** (902) 859-3915, (902) 859-8790 in the off-season or (877) 445-4938. ⊞

RODD MILL RIVER   **Phone:** (902)859-3555

Resort Hotel
$100-$156
Address: Rt 136 C0B 1V0 **Location:** On Rt 136, just e of jct Rt 2. Located in Mill River Provincial Park. **Facility:** This large hotel offers a variety of room styles, some overlooking the lovely golf course, and a fine selection of recreational facilities. 90 units, some two bedrooms and kitchens. 3 stories (no elevator), interior corridors. **Terms:** seasonal, check-in 4 pm, 3 day cancellation notice-fee imposed. **Dining:** The Hernewood Dining Room, see separate listing. **Pool(s):** heated indoor. **Activities:** sauna, whirlpool, waterslide, rental canoes, marina, 4 tennis courts (2 lighted), racquetball courts, cross country skiing, ice skating, tobogganing, recreation programs, rental bicycles, hiking trails, playground, exercise room. **Fee:** golf-18 holes, massage. **Guest Services:** valet laundry.
(See ad starting on p. 224.)
🅿 🍽 🏠 🏊 📶 BIZ 🛜 ✕ 🖥
/ SOME UNITS 🐾 🔥

WHERE TO EAT

THE HERNEWOOD DINING ROOM
          Phone: 902/859-3555
American
$7-$22
AAA Inspector Notes: This delightful location overlooks the golf course and the views are particularly good from the seasonal deck. The menu outlines a fine selection of fresh seafood and meat entrées, all served in ample portions. The waitstaff are friendly and offer attentive service. **Bar:** full bar. **Address:** Rt 136 C0B 1V0 **Location:** On Rt 136, just e of jct Rt 2; in Rodd Mill River.
B L D

AAA Travel Information
In Print, Online and On The Go

**Get AAA's reliable travel information
just the way you want it.**

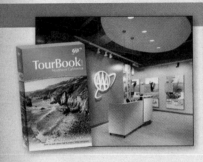

- **TourBook® Guides** - Printed guidebooks available at AAA/CAA offices
- **Travel Guides** - Online destination content available at AAA.com and CAA.ca
- **eTourBook℠ Guides** - eReader travel guides available at AAA.com/ebooks

Create and save trips online with TripTik® Travel Planner and
use them on the go with the TripTik Mobile app.

- **TripTik Travel Planner** - Online trip planning at AAA.com and CAA.ca
- **TripTik Mobile** - Travel app details at AAA.com/mobile

Changing of the Guard, Québec

Québec

"Parlez-vous français?"

In Québec, the answer will most likely be a resounding "*Oui!*" But if your French is limited to menu items, don't worry. Many Québécers can converse in English, especially in Montréal and Québec City. Besides, visitors don't need to speak a word of French to enjoy what Canada's largest province has to offer.

For instance, even if you don't know that *château* means castle, one look at medieval-style Fairmont Le Château Frontenac's turrets soaring above Québec City's historic Lower Town will give you an idea. Skiers enjoy the *neige* of the Laurentian Highlands whether or not they know the Gallic word for snow, and a crunchy *pomme* from an orchard in the rustic Eastern Townships region tastes delicious no matter what it's named.

Can't recall an appropriate French adjective to describe the majestic headlands rising from the sea at Forillon National Park of Canada? A simple "wow" will suffice. All you

Stained Glass Detail, Basilica of Notre-Dame, Montréal

really need to remember is that Québec means beautiful in any language.

Aesthetically Fruitful

To see firsthand what are arguably the province's most stunning examples, look to its churches and sanctuaries. An awe-inspiring, neo-Gothic edifice, Montréal's Basilica of Notre-Dame took 5 years to build and houses a 10-bell carillon, massive pipe organ and 11,240-kilogram (12-ton) bell. The striking Ste-Anne-de-Beaupré Shrine in Ste-Anne-de-Beaupré includes splendid mosaics and hundreds of stained-glass panels, while an octagonal design lends to the Shrine of Notre-Dame-du-Cap's appeal in Trois-Rivières.

Also remarkable is Québec's main Parliament Building, an 1886 Second Empire-style building boasting four wings and an impressive fountain at its main entrance.

As landscape architecture goes, Montréal's Mont-Royal Park—designed by Frederick Law Olmsted—skillfully blends form and function, and more than 22,000 plant varieties flourish in the breathtaking Montréal Botanical Garden. In Grand-Métis, Reford Gardens is known for its artfully arranged primroses and blue poppies.

On a considerably smaller scale, painters, sketchers and sculptors unleash their flights of fancy in various media. Many splendid works by Canadian artists are among those at the Montréal Museum of Contemporary Art. An important collection of Canadian painting resides at the Montréal Museum of Fine Arts. To appreciate Québécois art from the French Colonial period to the present, visit the National Museum of Fine Arts of Québec in the capital city.

Native crafts are the focus not only of the Québec Handicraft Show in Montréal, but also of such facilities as Museum of the Early Canadians in St-Jean-Port-Joli.

Music, too, is central to the lives of many Québécers, including pop superstar Céline Dion, born in Charlemagne. Melodic sounds fill the air at such Montréal events as the International Music Competition; the Franco-Folies of Montréal; and the Montréal International Jazz Festival, which welcomes some of the world's most renowned performers.

Québec Tourist Regions

For the purposes of providing tourism information, the province of Québec divides itself into 20 regions. The **northern regions** are Abitibi-Témiscamingue, Saguenay-Lac-St-Jean, Côte-Nord (Manicouagan and Duplessis), Baie-James. The **southern regions** are Eastern Townships, Montréal, Laval, Montérégie. The **eastern regions** are Québec, Charlevoix, Gaspésie, Îles de la Madeleine, Chaudière-Appalaches (south shore of Québec), Bas-St-Laurent. The **western regions** are Laurentides and Outaouais. The **central regions** are Lanaudière, Mauricie, Centre-du-Québec.

Recreation

The terrain of Québec's 38-plus parks and wildlife reserves varies from craggy peaks at Mont-Tremblant to nearly impenetrable forests in La Mauricie National Park of Canada. Some 6,000 kilometres (3,750 mi.) of coastline allow you to explore such treasures as the Gaspé Peninsula, the Saguenay Fjord, and the innumerable lakes and rivers of La Vérendrye Wildlife Reserve.

Camping is marvelous year-round in Mont-Tremblant National Park, where horseback riding through scenic valleys and pine-scented forests is a whinnying idea.

In winter, ice fishing shacks spring up on frozen lakes and rivers, including St-Pierre and Deux-Montagnes lakes, the Saguenay Fjord and Ste-Anne-de-la-Pérade, near Trois-Rivières. You'll catch redfish, cod and turbot in the Saguenay, and rainbow and speckled trout in the Laurentians.

The Laurentian and Appalachian mountain ranges beckon downhill skiers with more than 800 trails and 80 resorts, including Gray Rocks, Mont-Blanc, Mont-Gabriel, Mont-St-Sauveur, Ski Chantecler and Tremblant. Only minutes from Québec City are the 50 trails of Mont-Ste-Anne and the night-skiing facilities of Stoneham. The Charlevoix region and Appalachian range also offer plenty of opportunities for both downhill and cross-country ski adventures.

Joseph-Armand Bombardier of Québec invented the snowmobile in 1922 and marketed the single-passenger Ski-Doo in 1960—and mobile mania has been riding rampant over the province ever since. Popular access points for snowmobiling along portions of the multipurpose Trans Canada Trail include Gatineau, Mont-Laurier and Montréal.

Gatineau, Mont Ste-Anne and Gaspésie parks and Laurentides Wildlife Reserve have networks for cross-country skiing that range from 150 to 300 kilometres (95 to 185 mi.). Linear Park is a network of 200 kilometres (130 mi.) of well-groomed trails between St-Jérôme and Mont-Laurier.

Québec City's Plains of Abraham, part of Battlefields Park, also offers excellent cross-country skiing and snowshoeing. In warmer weather, Montréalers flock to Mont-Royal Park for its network of bike paths, while the Route Verte is an accessible and expanding provincial network of bike paths.

Anse-Blanchette, Forillon National Park of Canada

Historic Timeline

1534	Jacques Cartier claims the area around the Gulf of St. Lawrence for King François I of France.
1608	Samuel de Champlain establishes the first European settlement near present-day Québec City.
1759	Great Britain gains control of New France, formalized under the 1763 Treaty of Paris.
1896	Sir Wilfrid Laurier becomes Canada's first French-Canadian prime minister.
1943	British, Canadian and U.S. government leaders attend a top-secret military conference in Québec City.
1959	Inauguration of the St. Lawrence Seaway takes place.
1968	The separatist Parti Québécois is founded by René Lévesque.
1976	Montréal hosts the Summer Olympic Games.
1985	The historic district of Québec City is named a UNESCO World Heritage Site.
1998	An ice storm paralyzes large portions of Québec and Ontario.
2000	The multipurpose recreational Trans Canada Trail, which will span 22,000 kilometres (13,670 mi.) when completed, opens.

What To Pack

Temperature Averages Maximum/Minimum (Celsius)

	JANUARY	FEBRUARY	MARCH	APRIL	MAY	JUNE	JULY	AUGUST	SEPTEMBER	OCTOBER	NOVEMBER	DECEMBER
Gatineau	-7/-16	-5/-14	2/-7	11/1	18/7	23/12	26/15	24/14	19/9	13/3	4/-2	-4/-11
Montréal	-6/-16	-4/-14	2/-7	11/1	18/6	24/12	26/14	24/13	19/8	13/3	5/-3	-3/-12
Québec	-8/-18	-6/-16	0/-9	8/-2	17/4	22/10	24/13	23/12	18/7	11/2	3/-4	-5/-13
St-Félicien	-11/-21	-9/-19	-2/-12	7/-3	15/3	21/9	23/12	22/11	16/6	9/1	1/-6	-8/-17
Sept-Îles	-9/-20	-8/-18	-2/-12	4/-4	10/1	16/7	19/11	18/9	13/4	7/-1	1/-7	-7/-16
Val-d'Or	-11/-23	-9/-22	-2/-15	7/-5	16/2	21/7	23/11	21/9	16/5	9/-1	0/-8	-8/-18

From the records of The Weather Channel Interactive, Inc.

Good Facts To Know

ABOUT THE PROVINCE

POPULATION: 7,546,131.

AREA: 1,356,367 sq km (523,696 sq mi.); ranks 2nd.

CAPITAL: Québec.

HIGHEST POINT: 1,622 m (5,321 ft.), Mont-d'Iberville.

LOWEST POINT: Sea level, Gulf of St. Lawrence.

TIME ZONE(S): Eastern. DST in Canada begins in the early morning of the first Sunday in April and ends in the early morning of the last Sunday in October.

GAMBLING

MINIMUM AGE FOR GAMBLING: 18.

REGULATIONS

TEEN DRIVING LAWS: Minimum age for an unrestricted driver's license is 18 years and 8 months. Phone (800) 361-7620 for more information about Québec driver's license regulations.

SEAT BELT/CHILD RESTRAINT LAWS: Seat belts are required for driver and all passengers. Children whose seated height is under 63 centimetres (25 in.) are required to be in a child restraint.

CELL PHONE RESTRICTIONS: Drivers are not permitted to use handheld cell phones.

HELMETS FOR MOTORCYCLISTS: Required for all riders.

RADAR DETECTORS: Not permitted.

FIREARMS LAWS: By federal law, all nonresidents entering Canada with a firearm must declare their weapon in writing and pay a fee of $25 (Canadian). Contact the Canadian Firearms Centre at (800) 731-4000 to receive a declaration form or for additional information.

ALCOHOL CONSUMPTION: Legal age 18.

HOLIDAYS

HOLIDAYS: Jan. 1 ▪ Good Friday ▪ Easter Monday ▪ Victoria Day, May 24 (if a Mon.) or the closest prior Mon. ▪ St-Jean-Baptiste Day, June 24 ▪ Canada Day, July 1 ▪ Labour Day, Sept. (1st Mon.) ▪ Thanksgiving, Oct. (2nd Mon.) ▪ Christmas, Dec. 25.

MONEY

TAXES: The federal Goods and Service Tax is 5 percent. Québec's provincial sales tax is 8.5 percent on goods and services.

VISITOR INFORMATION

INFORMATION CENTERS: Travel information is distributed free daily at provincial information centers in Dégelis ▪ Lacolle ▪ Montréal ▪ Québec ▪ Rigaud ▪ Rivière-Beaudette ▪ and Stanstead. The Montréal and Québec offices, which are open year-round, are closed Jan. 1 and Christmas. **Note:** Schedules are subject to change. Phone Tourisme Québec at (877) 266-5687 to confirm hours.

FURTHER INFORMATION FOR VISITORS:
Tourisme Québec
P.O. Box 979
Montréal, QC H3C 2W3
Canada
(514) 873-2015
(877) 266-5687 (in Canada)

RECREATION INFORMATION:
SÉPAQ
Place de la Cité
Tour Cominar
2640 boul. Laurier, Suite 250
Québec, QC G1V 5C2
Canada
(800) 665-6527

Québec Annual Events

Please call ahead to confirm event details.

JANUARY	FEBRUARY	MARCH
■ Montreal International Auto Show / Montréal 514-331-6571 ■ The Snow Fest / Montréal 514-872-6120 ■ Wildside Festival / Montréal 514-288-3161	■ Snowflake Kingdom--Winterlude Gatineau 819-243-3383 ■ Quebec Winter Carnival Québec 418-626-3716 ■ Winter Carnival / Chicoutimi 418-698-3888	■ Beauceron Maple Festival St-Georges 418-227-4642 ■ St. Patrick's Parade Montréal 514-993-7997 ■ International Festival of Films on Art / Montréal 514-874-1637

APRIL	MAY	JUNE
■ Jazz and Blues Heritage Festival / Chicoutimi 418-549-7111 ■ Quebec City Gastronomy Festival / Québec 418-683-4150 ■ Quebec International Book Fair / Québec 418-692-0010	■ Victoriaville International Contemporary Music Festival / Victoriaville 819-752-7912 ■ Quebec Symphony Orchestra Festival Sherbrooke 819-823-7229 ■ Montreal Chamber Music Festival / Montréal 514-489-7444	■ Grand Prix of Canada Weekend / Montréal 888-205-3315 ■ Montreal International Jazz Festival / Montréal 514-871-1881 ■ Montreal French Music Madness / Montréal 514-876-8989

JULY	AUGUST	SEPTEMBER
■ World Culture Festival Drummondville 819-472-1184 ■ Quebec City Summer Festival / Québec 888-992-5200 ■ Festival Just for Laughs Montréal 514-845-2322	■ Expo Quebec / Québec 418-691-3976 ■ New France Festival Québec 418-694-3311 ■ Casino du Lac-Leamy Sound of Light / Gatineau 888-429-3389	■ International Garden Festival / Grand-Métis 418-775-2222 ■ Hot Air Balloon Festival Gatineau 819-243-2331 ■ Bell Challenge / Québec 418-627-3343

OCTOBER	NOVEMBER	DECEMBER
■ National Pet Show Québec 514-761-5086 ■ Fall Rhapsody / Chelsea 819-827-2020 ■ Snow Goose Festival St-Joachim-de-Montmorency 418-827-4052	■ Montreal Book Fair Montréal 514-845-2365 ■ Cinemania Film Festival Montréal 514-878-0082 ■ National Pet Show Montréal 514-761-5086	■ Christmas in the Park Montréal 514-281-8942 ■ Quebec City Celebrates Christmas / Québec 418-692-6635 ■ Christmas at the Garden Montréal 514-872-1400

Cosmodôme/Canada Space
Camp, Laval

Louis XIV Bust at Place-Royale,
Québec

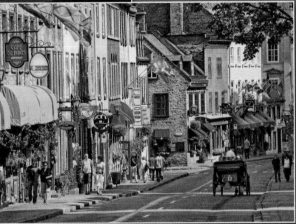

Rue St-Louis, Québec

Île du Pot à l'Eau-de-Vie
Lighthouse, Rivière-du-Loup

Montréal Museum of Fine Arts, Montréal

Great Experience for Members

AAA editor's picks of exceptional note

Canadian Museum of
Civilization

Ste-Anne-de-Beaupré
Shrine

Parliament Building

Reford Gardens

Chambly (F-7)
Fort Chambly National Historic Site
(See p. 272.)

Chelsea (E-3)
Gatineau Park *(See p. 273.)*

Forillon National Park of Canada (B-9)
Forillon National Park of Canada *(See p. 283.)*

**Fort Lennox National Historic
Site (F-8)**
Fort Lennox National Historic Site
(See p. 284.)

Gatineau (E-3)
Canadian Museum of Civilization *(See p. 285.)*

Granby (F-8)
Granby Zoo *(See p. 288.)*

Grand-Métis (C-7)
Reford Gardens *(See p. 289.)*

Hemmingford (F-7)
Parc Safari *(See p. 289.)*

La Baie (C-6)
Saguenay Cruises *(See p. 292.)*

**La Mauricie National Park of
Canada (D-4)**
La Mauricie National Park of Canada
(See p. 296.)

Laval (E-7)
Cosmodôme/Canada Space Camp
(See p. 299.)

Lévis (A-1)
Lévis Forts National Historic Site *(See p. 302.)*

Miguasha (C-8)
Miguasha National Park *(See p. 307.)*

**Mingan Archipelago National Park
Reserve of Canada (A-9)**
Mingan Archipelago National Park Reserve of
Canada *(See p. 307.)*

Montebello (E-3)
Parc Oméga *(See p. 308.)*

Montmagny (D-6)
Grosse Île and the Irish Memorial National
Historic Site *(See p. 309.)*

Montréal (F-7)
Basilica of Notre-Dame *(See p. 329.)*

Château Ramezay—Historic Site and Museum
of Montréal *(See p. 329.)*

Lachine Rapids Jet Boat Tours *(See p. 332.)*

McCord Museum of Canadian History
(See p. 327.)

Montréal Biodôme *(See p. 331.)*

Montréal Botanical Garden *(See p. 327.)*

Montréal Museum of Fine Arts *(See p. 328.)*

Mont-Royal Park *(See p. 328.)*

Old Montréal *(See p. 329.)*

Olympic Park *(See p. 331.)*

Pointe-à-Callière, Montréal Museum of
Archaeology and History *(See p. 330.)*

St. Joseph's Oratory *(See p. 331.)*

The Stewart Museum at the Old Fort
(See p. 327.)

Percé (C-9)
Île Bonaventure and Percé Rock National
Park *(See p. 400.)*

Québec (B-2)
Artillery Park Heritage Site *(See p. 412.)*

Battlefields Park *(See p. 415.)*

The Citadel *(See p. 413.)*

Dufferin Terrace *(See p. 413.)*

Laurentides Wildlife Reserve *(See p. 416.)*

Montmorency Falls Park *(See p. 416.)*

Museum of Civilization *(See p. 416.)*

Museum of French America *(See p. 414.)*

National Museum of Fine Arts of Québec
(See p. 416.)

Our Lady of Victories Church *(See p. 417.)*

Parliament Building *(See p. 417.)*

Place-Royale *(See p. 417.)*

Québec Aquarium *(See p. 417.)*

Québec City Cruises *(See p. 418.)*

Rimouski (C-7)
Pointe-au-Père Maritime Historic Site—
Museum of the Sea *(See p. 453.)*

Rivière-Éternité (C-6)
Saguenay Fjord National Park *(See p. 456.)*
Saguenay-St. Lawrence Marine Park *(See p. 456.)*

Roberval (C-5)
Val-Jalbert Historic Village *(See p. 456.)*

St-Constant (F-7)
Exporail, The Canadian Railway Museum *(See p. 458.)*

St-Félicien (C-5)
St-Félicien Wild Animal Zoo *(See p. 459.)*

St-Joachim-de-Montmorency (A-2)
Cap Tourmente National Wildlife Area *(See p. 464.)*

Ste-Anne-de-Beaupré (A-2)
Canyon Ste-Anne *(See p. 469.)*
Ste-Anne-de-Beaupré Shrine *(See p. 469.)*

Ste-Anne-des-Monts (B-8)
Gaspésie National Park *(See p. 470.)*

Shawinigan (E-5)
City of Energy *(See p. 474.)*

Trois-Rivières (E-5)
Shrine of Notre-Dame-du-Cap *(See p. 481.)*
Forges of St. Maurice National Historic Site of Canada *(See p. 481.)*

Val-d'Or (C-2)
The City of Gold *(See p. 483.)*

Québec
Atlas Section

ROADS/HIGHWAYS

- INTERSTATE
- CONTROLLED ACCESS
- CONTROLLED ACCESS TOLL
- TOLL ROAD
- PRIMARY DIVIDED
- PRIMARY UNDIVIDED
- SECONDARY DIVIDED
- SECONDARY UNDIVIDED
- LOCAL DIVIDED
- LOCAL UNDIVIDED
- UNPAVED ROAD
- UNDER CONSTRUCTION
- TUNNEL
- PEDESTRIAN ONLY
- AUTO FERRY
- PASSENGER FERRY
- SCENIC BYWAY
- **10** DISTANCE BETWEEN MARKERS
- EXIT NUMBER-FREE/TOLL
- INTERCHANGE FULL/PARTIAL
- WELCOME CENTER
- REST AREA/ SERVICE CENTER

BOUNDARIES

- INTERNATIONAL
- STATE
- COUNTY
- TIME ZONE
- CONTINENTAL DIVIDE

ROAD SHIELDS

- INTERSTATE/BUSINESS
- U.S./STATE/COUNTY
- FOREST/INDIAN
- TRANS- CANADA
- PROVINCIAL AUTOROUTE
- MEXICO
- HISTORIC ROUTE 66
- **VT 41** REFERENCE PAGE INDICATOR

AREAS OF INTEREST

- INDIAN
- MILITARY
- PARK
- FOREST
- GRASSLANDS
- HISTORIC
- INT'L/REGIONAL AIRPORT
- INCORPORATED CITY

POINTS OF INTEREST

- o TOWN
- NATIONAL CAPITAL
- STATE/PROVINCIAL CAPITAL
- AAA/CAA CLUB LOCATION
- FEATURE OF INTEREST
- COLLEGE/UNIVERSITY
- CAMPGROUND
- CUSTOMS STATION
- HISTORIC
- LIGHTHOUSE
- MONUMENT/MEMORIAL
- STATE/PROVINCIAL PARK
- NATIONAL WILDLIFE REFUGE
- SKI AREA
- SPORTS COMPLEX

CITIES/TOWNS are color-coded by size, showing where to find AAA Approved and Diamond rated lodgings or restaurants listed in the AAA TourBook guides and on AAA.com:

- RED - major destinations and capitals; many listings
- Black - destinations; some listings
- Grey - no listings

WESTER

Kilometers 40   20
Miles 40
ONE INCH EQUALS APPROXIMATE

La Sarre
Lake Abitibi
Roquemaure
Parc National d'Aiguebelle
Amos
Duparquet
Mont-Brun
Lac Parent
Lac Preissac
Rouyn-Noranda
Cadillac
196
113
Mont-beillard
Malartic
Dubuisson
Val-d'Or
391
Réservoir Grand
Réserve Faunique
17
Lac du Quinze
Angliers
St-Eugène-de-Guigues
Lac Simard
Decelles
Lac Victoria
227
Réservoir Cabonga
Fort Témiscamingue National Historic Site of Canada
Vérendrye
Réservoir Baskatong
Lac Kipawa
Lac Dumoine
63
533
Mattawa
Montcerf Lytton
Mont-Lauri
Maniwaki
St-Aimé-du-Lac-des-Îles
3
Stonecliffe
Messines
Réserve Faunique de Papineau-
Gracefield
105
309
157
ER074B
4
Labelle
Val-Des-Bois
269
Petawawa
148
Fort-Coulonge
301
Otter Lake
Pembroke
58
Foresters Falls
Shawville
105
Wakefield
Round Lake Centre
58
60
Cobden
148
Chelsea
Barry's Bay
60
Eganville
41
Renfrew
132
Gatineau
62
41
Arnprior
29
OTTAWA
53
Limoges
28
Almonte
416
ON 73
Kemptville
Smiths Falls
31
62
41
Perth
43

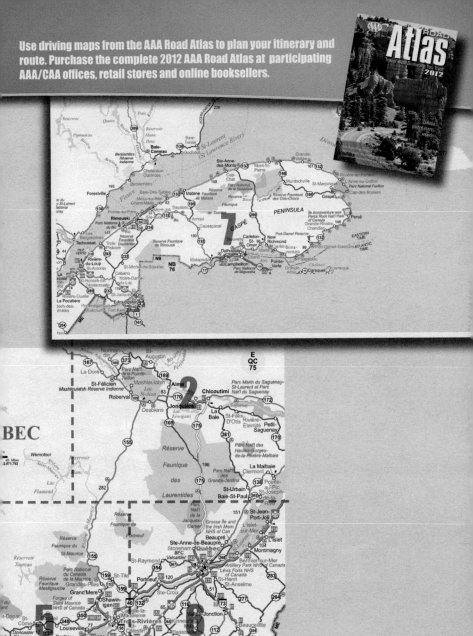

QUÉBEC

1:1,584,000
Scale in Kilometers

25 0 25

25 0 25
Scale in Miles

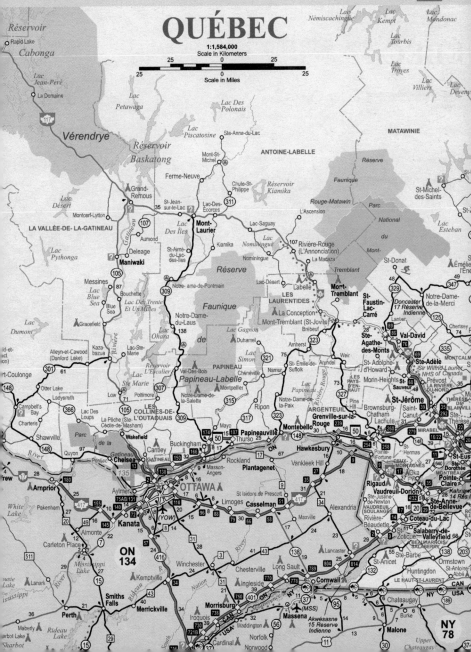

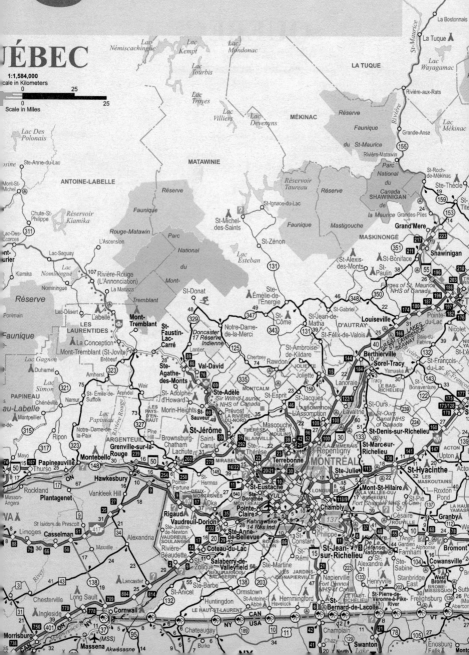

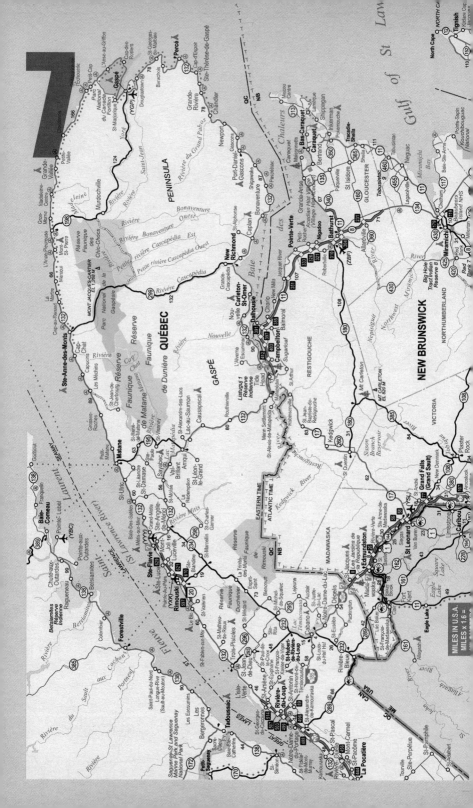

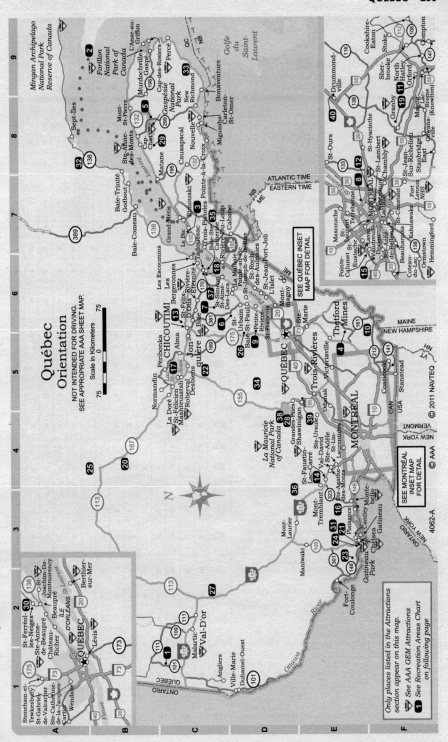

Québec
Orientation

NOT INTENDED FOR DRIVING.
SEE APPROPRIATE AAA SHEET MAP.

Scale in Kilometers

75   0   75

Only places listed in the Attractions
section appear on this map.

See AAA GEM Attractions

See Recreation Areas Chart
on following page

© 2011 NAVTEQ

© AAA

4062-A

Recreation Areas Chart

The map location numerals in column 2 show an area's location on the preceding map.

	MAP LOCATION	CAMPING	PICNICKING	HIKING TRAILS	BOATING	BOAT RAMP	BOAT RENTAL	FISHING	SWIMMING	PETS ON LEASH	BICYCLE TRAILS	WINTER SPORTS	VISITOR CENTER	LODGE/CABINS	FOOD SERVICE
NATIONAL PARKS *(See place listings.)*															
Forillon (B-9) 244 sq. km 20 km n.e. of Gaspé via Hwy. 132.		•	•	•	•	•		•	•	•	•	•	•	•	•
La Mauricie (D-4) 536 sq. km n. of Trois-Rivières via Hwy. 55 Exit 226.		•	•	•	•	•	•	•	•		•	•	•	•	•
Mingan Archipelago (A-9) 110 sq. km 870 km e. of Québec via Hwy. 138.		•	•	•	•								•		
PROVINCIAL															
Aiguebelle National (C-1) 268 sq. km 50 km n.e. of Rouyn-Noranda via Hwy. 101. Nature programs. Snowshoeing; equipment rentals.	❶	•	•	•	•	•	•	•	•			•	•	•	
Anticosti National (B-9) 572 sq. km. 35 km from Longue-Pointe-de-Mingan. Horseback riding; bicycle and kayak rentals.	❷	•	•	•				•	•					•	
Bic National (C-7) 33 sq. km s. of Le Bic via Hwy. 132. Kayaking; yurts. *(See Le Bic p. 301.)*	❸	•	•	•	•	•	•				•	•	•	•	•
Frontenac National (E-5) 155 sq. km 120 km s. of Québec via Hwys. 73 and 112. Nature programs. Canoe camping, kayaking.	❹	•	•	•	•	•	•	•	•				•		
Gaspésie National (B-8) 802 sq. km 40 km s. of Ste-Anne-des-Monts via Hwy. 299. Nature programs. Canoeing, cross-country and telemark skiing, snowshoeing. *(See Ste-Anne-des-Monts p. 470.)*	❺	•	•	•	•	•	•	•				•	•	•	•
Grands-Jardins National (C-6) 310 sq. km 20 km n. of St-Urbain via Hwy. 381. Canoeing, cross-country skiing, kayaking. *(See St-Urbain p. 467.)*	❻	•	•	•	•		•	•				•	•	•	•
Hautes-Gorges-de-la-Rivière-Malbaie National (C-6) 224 sq. km 26 km n. of St-Aimé-des-Lacs via rue Principale. *(See St-Aimé-des-Lacs p. 457.)*	❼	•	•	•	•			•	•			•		•	•
Îles-de-Boucherville National (E-7) 10 km e. of Montréal Hwy. 25 via the Louis-Hyppolite Lafontaine Tunnel-Bridge. Canoeing, kayaking, snowshoeing; interpretive programs.	❽		•	•				•			•	•	•		•
Jacques-Cartier National (D-5) 670 sq. km 40 km n.w. of Québec via Hwy. 175. Nature programs. Canoeing, kayaking, rafting, snowshoeing. *(See Québec p. 415.)*	❾	•	•	•	•		•	•				•	•	•	•
Mont-Mégantic National (F-6) 10 km from Notre-Dame-des-Bois.	❿	•	•	•							•	•	•		
Mont-Orford National (F-9) 58 sq. km n. of Orford on Hwy. 10. Canoeing, cross-country skiing, snowshoeing; huts. *(See Orford p. 398.)*	⓫	•	•	•	•	•	•	•	•		•	•	•		
Mont-St-Bruno National (E-8) 6 sq. km 20 km e. of Montréal via Hwys. 20 and 30.	⓬		•	•							•	•	•		•
Monts-Valin National (C-6) 17 km n.e. of Chicoutimi.	⓭	•	•	•	•			•	•			•	•	•	
Mont-Tremblant National (E-4) 1,510 sq. km 23 km e. of Hwy. 117N. Nature programs. Backcountry hiking, canoeing and canoe camping, cross-country skiing with huts, snowshoeing. *(See Mont-Tremblant p. 392.)*	⓮	•	•	•	•	•	•	•	•		•	•	•	•	•
Oka National (E-6) 23.7 sq. km 1.5 km e. of Oka on Hwy. 344. Nature programs. Canoeing, cross-country skiing, snowshoeing, windsurfing.	⓯	•	•	•	•	•	•	•	•		•	•	•	•	•
Plaisance National (E-3) 28 sq. km 55 km e. of Gatineau via Hwy. 148E. Canoeing.	⓰	•	•	•	•	•	•	•			•	•	•	•	
Pointe-Taillon National (C-5) 92 sq. km s. of Péribonka off Hwy. 169.	⓱	•	•	•		•		•	•		•		•		
Saguenay Fjord National (C-6) 300 sq. km accessible via Hwy. 170. Backcountry skiing, ice fishing, snowshoeing. *(See Rivière-Éternité p. 456.)*	⓲	•	•	•								•	•		•
Yamaska National (F-8) 13 sq. km 15 km n.e. of Granby via Hwy. 112. Cross-country skiing, snowshoeing, windsurfing. Food Service in summer only.	⓳	•	•	•	•	•	•	•	•		•	•	•		•
OTHER															
Ashuapmushuan Wildlife Reserve (B-4) 4,487 sq. km n.w. of St-Félicien on Hwy. 167. Canoeing, fishing, hunting. *(See St-Félicien p. 459.)*	⓴	•	•	•	•			•	•					•	•

Recreation Areas Chart

The map location numerals in column 2 show an area's location on the preceding map.

	MAP LOCATION	CAMPING	PICNICKING	HIKING TRAILS	BOATING	BOAT RAMP	BOAT RENTAL	FISHING	SWIMMING	PETS ON LEASH	BICYCLE TRAILS	WINTER SPORTS	VISITOR CENTER	LODGE/CABINS	FOOD SERVICE
Gatineau Park (E-3) 36,300 hectares n. of Gatineau between the Gatineau and Ottawa rivers via hwys. 5, 105, 148 and 366. *(See Chelsea p. 273.)*	21	•	•	•	•			•	•	•	•	•			•
Lac la Pêche Sector C (C-5) Canoeing.	22	•	•		•	•	•	•	•						
Lac Philippe (E-3) Cross-country skiing, snowshoeing.	23	•	•	•	•	•	•	•	•			•	•		•
Parkway Sector (E-3) Alpine and cross-country skiing, snowshoeing.	24		•	•	•			•	•	•	•	•	•		•
Lacs-Albanel-Mistassini-et-Waconichi Wildlife Reserve (B-4) 25,285 sq. km 32 km n. of Chibougamau. Canoeing.	25	•											•	•	
Laurentides Wildlife Reserve (D-5) 7,861 sq. km in the Laurentian Mountains, 60 km n.w. of Québec via Hwy. 175. Canoeing, cross-country skiing, snowmobiling, snowshoeing; nature trails. *(See Québec p. 416.)*	26	•	•		•		•	•		•		•	•	•	•
La Vérendrye Wildlife Reserve (C-2) 12,589 sq. km 60 km n.w. of Mont-Laurier on Hwy. 117. Canoeing, hunting; snowmobile trails. *(See Mont-Laurier p. 308.)*	27	•	•		•		•	•	•	•			•	•	
Mastigouche Wildlife Reserve (D-4) 1,534 sq. km 85 km n.w. of Trois-Rivières off Hwy. 349. Canoeing, hunting, snowmobiling.	28	•	•	•	•		•	•	•	•				•	
Matane Wildlife Reserve (C-8) 1,282 sq. km 40 km s.e. of Matane.	29	•	•	•	•		•	•	•	•				•	
Mont-Ste-Anne (A-2) 64 sq. km n.w. of Beaupré on Hwy. 360E. Golf. *(See Beaupré p. 265.)*	30							•	•	•	•	•	•	•	•
Papineau-Labelle Wildlife Reserve (E-3) 1,628 sq. km 82 km n. of Gatineau via Hwys. 50 and 309. Cross-country skiing, hunting.	31	•	•	•	•			•						•	
Port-Cartier/Sept-Îles Wildlife Reserve (A-8) 6,423 sq. km 27 km n. of Port Cartier. Canoeing.	32	•			•		•	•	•	•				•	
Port-Daniel Reserve (C-9) 64 sq. km 8 km n. of Port Daniel.	33	•	•	•			•	•	•	•					
Portneuf Wildlife Reserve (D-5) 775 sq. km 5 km n. of Rivière-à-Pierre. Canoeing, cross-country skiing, mountain climbing, snowmobiling, snowshoeing.	34	•	•	•	•	•	•	•	•	•				•	
Rimouski Wildlife Reserve (C-7) 774 sq. km 68 km s.e. of Rimouski.	35	•	•		•		•	•		•				•	
Rouge-Matawin Wildlife Reserve (D-3) 1,394 sq. km 26 km w. of St-Michel-des-Saints via Hwy. 131. Canoeing and canoe camping, hunting, snowmobiling. Food Service in winter only.	36	•	•		•			•					•	•	•
Saguenay-St. Lawrence Marine Park (C-6) 1,245 sq. km accessible via hwys. 138, 170, 172 and 132. Bird-watching, ice fishing, kayaking, scuba diving. *(See Rivière-Éternité p. 456.)*	37	•	•	•				•		•			•		•
St-Maurice Wildlife Reserve (D-4) 784 sq. km 48.25 km n. of Grand-Mère. Canoeing.	38	•	•		•		•	•	•	•				•	•
Shawinigan-Falls (E-4) between Shawinigan and Shawinigan-Sud on Hwy. 157. Cross-country skiing.	39	•	•	•	•			•		•				•	
Voltigeurs (E-8) 3 sq. km 2 km e. of Drummondville off Autoroute 20 exit 181 following signs. *(See Drummondville p. 281.)*	40	•	•					•	•	•			•		•

ALMA (C-5) pop. 29,998

Alma is at the junction of the Saguenay River and lac St-Jean. Called Piekouagami, meaning "flat lake," by the Montagnais Indians, lac St-Jean was discovered by Jesuit missionary Father Jean de Quen in 1647. This vast lake, 49 kilometres (31 mi.) long and 29 kilometres (18 mi.) wide, is surrounded by agricultural land known for its blueberries.

Two-hour cruises on lac St-Jean are offered by Dam-en-Terre Tourist Complex (Complexe touristique de la Dam-en-Terre) aboard the NV La Tournée, which departs from 1385 ch. de la Marina Dam-en-Terre. Also available at the complex are a marina, a beach, cottages, summer theater and opportunities for camping; phone (418) 668-3016 or (888) 289-3016.

Alma Tourist Information Bureau: 1682 av. du Pont Nord, Alma, QC, Canada G8B 5G3. **Phone:** (418) 668-3611, or (877) 668-3611 in Canada.

THE ODYSSEY OF THE BUILDERS THEME PARK (L'Odyssée des Bâtisseurs Parc Thématique) is off Hwy. 169 at 1671 av. du Pont Nord. This site explores the importance of water in the economic and social development of the region. Explored in depth is the construction of the Isle-Maligne hydroelectric plant and its dam. In summer, a 360-degree multimedia show is presented in a converted water tower housing a theater and an observatory.

Time: Allow 2 hours minimum. **Hours:** Daily 9-5, mid-June through Sept. 30; Mon.-Fri. 9-4, rest of year. **Cost:** $14; $13 (ages 60+); $7 (ages 6-17). **Phone:** (418) 668-2606 or (866) 668-2606.

COMFORT INN

Phone: (418)668-9221

Hotel
$119-$124

Address: 870 ave du Pont S G8B 2V8 **Location:** On Hwy 169; centre. **Facility:** 60 units. 2 stories (no elevator), interior corridors. **Parking:** winter plug-ins. **Terms:** cancellation fee imposed. **Guest Services:** valet laundry.

HOTEL UNIVERSEL

Phone: (418)668-5261

Hotel
$129-$289

Address: 1000 boul des Cascades G8B 3G4 **Location:** Centre. **Facility:** 71 units. 4 stories, interior corridors. **Terms:** check-in 4 pm, cancellation fee imposed. **Dining:** Restaurant Le Bordelais, see separate listing. **Pool(s):** heated indoor. **Activities:** whirlpool, snowmobiling, bicycles, exercise room, spa. *Fee:* steamroom. **Guest Services:** valet laundry. **Free Special Amenities: local telephone calls and high-speed Internet.**

WHERE TO EAT

CHEZ MARIO TREMBLAY-BAR-RESTAURANT

Phone: 418/668-7231

Steak
$10-$28

AAA Inspector Notes: This popular restaurant and bar--co-owned by former pro hockey player and coach Mario Tremblay--serves up great pub fare, including AAA Alberta steaks, seafood, ribs, chicken and pizza. Try the delicious house-prepared sugar pie. A display of Montreal Canadiens memorabilia adorns the walls. **Bar:** full bar. **Address:** 534 ave Collard ouest G9B 1N2 **Location:** Just s of rue St-Joseph; centre.

RESTAURANT LE BORDELAIS

Phone: 418/668-7419

French
$14-$36

AAA Inspector Notes: The comfortable hotel restaurant offers something for everyone on a varied menu listing fine French cuisine, Canadian-Chinese food, lighter pub-style dishes and children's meals. Interesting selections include guinea fowl, beef filet, stuffed chicken, Charlevoix veal, magret of duck, lamb and a fresh fish of the day. **Bar:** full bar. **Reservations:** suggested. **Address:** 1000 boul des Cascades G8B 3G4 **Location:** Centre; in Hotel Universel.

RESTO ROBERTO

Phone: 418/662-2191

Italian
$8-$27

AAA Inspector Notes: This family-friendly pizzeria has a comfortable, casual decor, and its varied menu is sure to please everyone. In addition to gourmet and traditional pizza, the menu lists egg rolls, French onion soup, chicken cooked over charcoal, burgers, ribs, combination platters, pasta dishes, coquilles St. Jacques, fish and chips, smoked meat, club sandwiches, fajitas and hot submarine sandwiches. **Bar:** full bar. **Address:** 11 rue Scott est G8B 1B6 **Location:** On Hwy 169.

AMOS pop. 12,584

AMOSPHERE COMPLEXE HOTELIER
Phone: (819)732-7777

◆◆◆
Hotel
$93-$120

Address: 1031 Rt 111 est J9T 1N2 **Location:** Centre. **Facility:** 42 units. 2 stories (no elevator), interior/exterior corridors. **Parking:** winter plug-ins. **Amenities:** high-speed Internet. *Some:* safes, honor bars. **Activities:** whirlpools, snowmobiling, bicycles, exercise room. **Guest Services:** valet and coin laundry. **Free Special Amenities:** local telephone calls and high-speed Internet.

SAVE ⏍ BIZ 📶 / SOME UNITS 🐾 📶 🖥

ANGLIERS (C-1) pop. 308

T.E. DRAPER, 11 rue T.E. Draper at the waterfront, plied the river floating wood 1929-72 for Canadian International Paper. A video presentation, a guided warehouse tour and a visit aboard the tugboat provide insights into mid-20th-century logging techniques. The warehouse contains displays about logging camps and machinery. Tour narration in English is available. **Time:** Allow 1 hour minimum. **Hours:** Tours daily 10-6, June 24-Labour Day. Last tour begins 1 hour before closing. **Cost:** $5; $4 (ages 60+); $1.50 (ages 6-11). Cash only. **Phone:** (819) 949-4431.

ANJOU

- **Hotels & Restaurants map & index p. 342**
- **Part of Montréal area — see map p. 312**

QUALITY HOTEL EAST   **Phone:** (514)493-6363 **15**

◆◆◆
Hotel
$90-$250

Address: 8100 ave Neuville H1J 2T2 **Location:** Hwy 40 exit 78, just n on boul Langelier, 0.4 mi (0.7 km) e on rue Jarry, then s. **Facility:** 157 units. 9 stories, interior corridors. **Parking:** winter plug-ins. **Terms:** cancellation fee imposed. **Amenities:** high-speed Internet. **Guest Services:** valet laundry.

SAVE ECO ⏍ Y ♿ BIZ 📶 FEE 🐾 🖥 / SOME UNITS FEE 🐾 FEE 📶 FEE 🖥

WHERE TO EAT

IL PAZZESCO   **Phone:** 514/353-3801 **44**

◆◆◆
Italian
$14-$35

AAA Inspector Notes: For casually upscale dining and a great variety of pasta, seafood and meat, this is the place. A large mural depicting musicians adorns the wall, and servers are friendly and prompt. **Address:** 7031 rue Jarry est H1J 1G3 **Location:** Hwy 40 est exit 78, just n to rue Jarry, then 0.4 mi (0.7 km) e. L D

Safety tip: Keep a current
AAA/CAA Road Atlas
in every vehicle

AYER'S CLIFF pop. 1,096

AUBERGE RIPPLECOVE & SPA   **Phone:** (819)838-4296

◆◆◆
Country Inn
$155-$558

Address: 700 Ripplecove Rd J0B 1C0 **Location:** Hwy 55 exit 21, 5 mi (8 km) s on Rt 141. **Facility:** An interesting mix of traditional and contemporary styles characterize this upscale lakefront inn surrounded by well-tended lawns and gardens. 33 units, some houses and cottages. 3 stories (no elevator), interior corridors. **Parking:** winter plug-ins. **Terms:** check-in 4 pm, age restrictions may apply, 7 day cancellation notice. **Amenities:** *Some:* honor bars. **Dining:** restaurant, see separate listing. **Pool(s):** 2 heated outdoor. **Activities:** whirlpool, canoeing, paddleboats, boat dock, fishing, lighted tennis court, cross country skiing, snowmobiling, ice skating, bicycles, spa. **Guest Services:** valet laundry.

SAVE ⏍ 🏊 BIZ 📶 ✕ / SOME UNITS 📶 🖥 📖

WHERE TO EAT

AUBERGE RIPPLECOVE INN DINING ROOM
Menu on AAA.com   **Phone:** 819/838-4296

◆◆◆
French
$15-$48

AAA Inspector Notes: Overlooking Lake Massawippi, this upscale dining room and outdoor terrace are favorite spots for an elegant, sophisticated experience. The innovative menu includes such artfully presented selections as veal tenderloin, Eastern Townships duck, leg of Quebec lamb, fresh fish, grilled filet mignon, tiger shrimp, beef tartar and house-smoked salmon. Live music is offered on most nights. The service is friendly and refined. Semi-formal attire. **Bar:** full bar. **Reservations:** suggested. **Address:** 700 Ripplecove Rd J0B 1C0 **Location:** Hwy 55 exit 21, 5 mi (8 km) s on Rt 141; in Auberge Ripplecove & Spa. B L D

BAIE-COMEAU (B-7) pop. 22,554
- **Hotels p. 264 • Restaurants p. 264**

Baie-Comeau began as a pulp and newsprint milling town. Publisher Robert R. McCormick, who needed paper for his Chicago and New York newspapers, established the mill in 1937. McCormick is memorialized in a downtown statue that depicts him exploring the area by canoe.

A ferry service operates from 14 Rte. Maritime in Baie-Comeau to Matane. Advance reservations are required; phone (418) 294-8593, or (877) 562-6560 for reservations.

Manicouagan Tourist Association: 337 boul. La Salle, Suite 304, Baie-Comeau, QC, Canada G4Z 2Z1. **Phone:** (418) 294-2876, or (888) 463-5319 in Québec.

MANICOUAGAN 2 AND MANICOUAGAN 5 HYDROELECTRIC DAMS AND INSTALLATIONS (Installations de Production d'Électricité de Manicouagan 2 et de Manicouagan 5), 22 km (14 mi.) and 214 km (133 mi.) n. on Hwy. 389, respectively, are among the world's largest hydroelectric power dams, each capable of producing more than 1 million watts.

Manic 2 has a 70-metre (230-ft.) waterfall and a 518-square-kilometre (200-sq.-mi.) reservoir. The Manic 5, Barrage Daniel-Johnson, which has a 2,000-square-kilometre (772-sq.-mi.) reservoir and a

150-metre (490-ft.) waterfall, is the largest arch and buttress type dam in the world.

Note: Photo ID is required to tour the facility. Tour narration in English is offered. **Time:** Allow 1 hour, 30 minutes minimum. **Hours:** Both separate 90-minute guided tours of each installation are offered daily at 9:30, 11:30, 1:30 and 3:30, late June-Aug. 31. **Cost:** Free. **Phone:** (866) 526-2642.

COMFORT INN

Hotel
$125-$175

Phone: (418)589-8252
Address: 745 boul Lafleche G5C 1C6 **Location:** On Rt 138. **Facility:** 61 units. 2 stories (no elevator), interior corridors. **Parking:** winter plug-ins. **Terms:** cancellation fee imposed. **Guest Services:** valet laundry.

ECONO LODGE BAIE-COMEAU

Motel
Rates not provided

Phone: 418/589-7835
Address: 1060 boul Lafleche G5C 2W9 **Location:** On Rt 138; centre. **Facility:** 39 units. 1 story, exterior corridors. **Parking:** winter plug-ins. **Terms:** office hours 6 am-10:30 pm, check-in 4 pm. **Amenities:** high-speed Internet. **Guest Services:** valet laundry.

HOTEL LE MANOIR

Hotel
$115-$125

Phone: (418)296-3391
Address: 8 ave Cabot G4Z 1L8 **Location:** Rt 138, 2.6 mi (4.4 km) e, follow signs. **Facility:** 60 units. 3 stories, interior corridors. **Parking:** winter plug-ins. **Terms:** 30 day cancellation notice. **Amenities:** honor bars. *Some:* safes. **Dining:** restaurant, see separate listing. **Activities:** beach access, lighted tennis court, snowmobiling, exercise room. **Guest Services:** valet laundry.

L'AUBERGE LE PETIT CHÂTEAU

Country Inn
Rates not provided

Phone: 418/295-3100
Address: 2370 boul Lafleche G5C 1E4 **Location:** On Rt 138. **Facility:** This contemporary-style property has good-size rooms and a comfortable parlor near the lobby. 12 units. 2 stories (no elevator), interior corridors. **Parking:** winter plug-ins. **Terms:** office hours 7 am-11 pm, check-in 4 pm.

HOTEL LE MANOIR DINING ROOM

French
$14-$36

Phone: 418/296-3391
AAA Inspector Notes: This large, oval-shaped dining room has a high, beamed ceiling and large windows overlooking the St. Lawrence River. Table settings are elegant, and many boast lovely riverfront views. The menu of Quebec regional cuisine includes chicken "supreme," sweetbreads, lamb, braised salmon, fresh halibut, grilled beef, duck confit and surf and turf. **Bar:** full bar. **Address:** 8 ave Cabot G4Z 1L8 **Location:** Rt 138, 2.8 mi (4.4 km) e, follow signs; in Hotel Le Manoir.

BAIE-ST-PAUL (D-6) pop. 7,288

In a narrow river valley that opens on the St. Lawrence River, Baie-St-Paul has been a source of inspiration for generations of Canadian painters. Houses built in the early 1800s line the narrow streets of the town, which boasts numerous art galleries. The Baie-St-Paul Museum of Contemporary Art (Musée d'art contemporain de Baie-St-Paul), 23 rue Ambroise-Fafard, displays the works of noted Canadian artists; phone (418) 435-3681.

In the surrounding mountains a number of outlooks, such as the Cap-aux-Corbeaux and rang Ste-Catherine, provide a panorama of the bay and Isle-aux-Coudres *(see place listing p. 291)*, which lie opposite the village in the St. Lawrence River.

Baie-St-Paul Tourism Office: 444 boul. Mgr-De Laval, Baie-St-Paul, QC, Canada G3Z 2V3. **Phone:** (418) 435-4160 or (800) 667-2276.

GRANDS-JARDINS NATIONAL PARK—see St-Urbain p. 467.

AUBERGE LA PIGNORONDE

Country Inn
$70-$250

Phone: 418/435-5505
Address: 750 boul Mgr-de-Laval G3Z 2V5 **Location:** Rt 138, 0.8 mi (1.3 km) w of jct Rt 362. **Facility:** 28 units. 3 stories (no elevator), interior corridors. **Terms:** open 6/1-10/9 & 12/9-5/31, office hours 7 am-11 pm, 15 day cancellation notice-fee imposed. **Pool(s):** heated indoor. **Activities:** hiking trails, shuffleboard. **Guest Services:** valet laundry, area transportation. **Free Special Amenities:** local telephone calls and high-speed Internet.

▼ *See AAA listing p. 265* ▼

AUBERGE LE CORMORAN & BELLE PLAGE
Phone: (418)435-3321

Country Inn
$79-$149 6/1-10/11
$74-$129 10/12-5/31

Address: 192 rue Ste-Anne G3Z 1P8 **Location:** 1.1 mi (1.8 km) s on rue Ste-Anne from jct Rt 362. Located in a quiet area. **Facility:** 37 units. 2 stories (no elevator), interior corridors. **Parking:** winter plug-ins. **Terms:** 7 day cancellation notice-fee imposed. **Pool(s):** heated outdoor. **Activities:** Fee: boat dock, massage. **Guest Services:** valet laundry.

AUX PORTES DU SOLEIL
Phone: 418/435-3540

Motel
$68-$134

Address: 29 rue de la Lumiere G3Z 1Y7 **Location:** On Rt 362, 0.5 mi (0.8 km) s of jct Rt 138. **Facility:** 16 units, some two bedrooms. 1 story, exterior corridors. **Parking:** winter plug-ins. **Terms:** seasonal, cancellation fee imposed. **Activities:** whirlpool. Fee: massage. **Guest Services:** coin laundry.

HOTEL BAIE-SAINT-PAUL
Phone: 418/435-3683

Hotel
Rates not provided

Address: 911 boul Mgr-de-Laval G3Z 1A1 **Location:** On Rt 138, 0.3 mi (0.5 km) e of Rt 362. **Facility:** 62 units. 2 stories, interior corridors. **Parking:** winter plug-ins. **Activities:** snowmobiling, exercise room, spa.

L'ESTAMPILLES
Phone: (418)435-2533

Country Inn
$140-$210

Address: 24 ch Cap-aux-Corbeaux nord G3Z 1A7 **Location:** Hwy 362, just n. **Facility:** 11 units. 2 stories (no elevator), interior corridors. **Parking:** winter plug-ins. **Terms:** seasonal, check-in 4 pm, 3 day cancellation notice-fee imposed. **Dining:** Restaurant L'estampilles, see separate listing. **Activities:** sauna, whirlpool, snowmobiling. Fee: massage. *(See ad p. 264.)*

WHERE TO EAT

AU PIERRE-NARCISSE RESTAURANT-BAR
Phone: 418/435-2056

Canadian
$8-$30

AAA Inspector Notes: The casual eatery is in a cozy inn that has been operated by the same family for generations. Wholesome food tops a menu that includes pasta, burgers, steak, fish, ribs, pizza, salad and steaks. **Bar:** full bar. **Reservations:** suggested. **Address:** 41 rue Ambroise-Fafard G3Z 2J2 **Location:** Just w of rue Ste-Anne; centre. L D

CHEZ MON AMI ALEX
Phone: 418/435-2255

Mediterranean
$15-$30

AAA Inspector Notes: Country inn charm punctuates the comfortable stone-walled dining room in a quaint village. The chef blends interesting flavors in creative preparations of Mediterranean-influenced regional food, including meat favorites, fresh fish and other seafood. **Bar:** full bar. **Reservations:** suggested. **Address:** 23 rue St-Jean-Baptiste G3Z 1M2 **Location:** Centre; in Auberge La Maison Otis. D

RESTAURANT L'ESTAMPILLES
Phone: 418/435-2533

French
$12-$40

AAA Inspector Notes: This upscale contemporary country inn is an ideal setting for a romantic dinner of fine food prepared by an accomplished French chef. Seating is offered in the upscale dining room or, in summer, on the veranda. Choose from such menu items as house-smoked or roasted salmon, sweet breads, rack of lamb or duck filet. You'll want to sample one of the artfully presented desserts. Friendly servers are able to discuss, with ease, the carefully selected wine list options. **Bar:** full bar. **Reservations:** suggested. **Address:** 24 chemin Cap-aux-Corbeaux Nord G3Z 1A7 **Location:** Hwy 362, just n; in L'estampilles. B D

BAIE-STE-CATHERINE (C-6) pop. 227

At the confluence of the Saguenay and St. Lawrence rivers, this small town is the home base for several whale-watching cruise companies. From May through early October Croisières AML offers daily 3-hour and 6.5-hour cruises (weather permitting); phone (800) 563-4643. There is no guarantee that whales will be sighted, though often several are. A free ferry service connects Baie-Ste-Catherine to Tadoussac *(see place listing p. 478)*; phone (418) 235-4395 for schedule.

POINTE-NOIRE INTERPRETATION AND OBSERVATION CENTRE (Centre d'interprétation et d'observation de Pointe-Noire), on Rte. 138, is part of the Saguenay-St. Lawrence Marine Park *(see attraction listing p. 456)*. Visitors can observe marine mammals, especially beluga whales, and birds at the confluence of the St. Lawrence estuary and the Saguenay Fjord. Educational activities conducted by naturalists are available.

Hours: Daily 10-5, mid-June through Labour Day; Fri.-Sun. 10-5, day after Labour Day-second Mon. in Oct. **Cost:** $5.80; $4.90 (senior citizens); $2.90 (ages 6-16); $14.70 (family). **Phone:** (418) 237-4383, (418) 235-4703 or (888) 773-8888.

BAIE-TRINITÉ (B-7) pop. 526

POINTE-DES-MONTS HISTORIC LIGHTHOUSE (Phare de Pointe-des-Monts) is 5 km (3 mi.) w. on Hwy. 138, then 11 km (7 mi.) s. following signs. Two iron cannons, fired to warn ships during times of heavy fog, are near the 1830 lighthouse. A staircase leads to the top of the lighthouse, which affords an excellent view.

The Pointe-des-Monts Historic Lighthouse Corp. has displays pertaining to a lighthouse keeper's lifestyle, navigation and shipwrecks off Pointe-des-Monts. Whales and many species of waterfowl can be seen. **Time:** Allow 30 minutes minimum. **Hours:** Daily 9-5, mid-June to mid-Sept. **Cost:** $8. **Phone:** (418) 939-2400.

BEAUHARNOIS (F-7) pop. 11,918, elev. 37m/124'
• Part of Montréal area — see map p. 312

BEAUHARNOIS GENERATING STATION (Centrale Hydroelectrique de Beauharnois) is 10 km (6.5 mi.) w. on Rte. 132 at 80 rue Edgar-Hebert in the sector of Melocheville. The facility is one of the world's largest hydroelectric power stations. Exhibits are on display in the interpretation center. The 90-minute guided tour includes a chance to view the 38 turbine generating units in the 1-kilometre (.6-mi.) building.

Note: Photo ID is required. **Hours:** Tours are given daily at 9:30, 11:15, 1 and 2:45, mid-May through Labour Day. **Cost:** Free. **Phone:** (800) 365-5229.

BEAUPRÉ (A-2) pop. 3,006
- Hotels p. 266 • Restaurants p. 266
- Part of Québec area — see map p. 405

MONT-STE-ANNE, on Hwy. 360E, is a popular year-round recreation area. Alpine skiing and snowboarding are available on 66 trails, with a vertical drop of 625 metres (2,050 ft.). Dog sledding, ice canyoning and paragliding also are offered. In addition to natural snowfall, an extensive snowmaking system ensures the trails are blanketed by snow all winter. In summer visitors enjoy mountain biking, hiking, camping and golf as well as the gondola lift, which provides a panorama of mountains, valleys, and rivers. *See Recreation Chart.*

Hours: Grounds daily dawn-dusk, year-round. Gondola daily 10:30-4, June-Oct.; otherwise varies. Phone ahead to confirm schedule. **Cost:** Grounds $5.27. Gondola $17.56; $40.37 (family, four people). **Phone:** (418) 827-4561 or (888) 827-4579.

CHALETS MONT STE-ANNE   **Phone:** (418)827-5776

▼▽◆▽▼
Condominium
$200-$285 12/1-5/31
$160-$200 6/1-11/30

Address: 1 rue Beau Soleil G0A 1E0 **Location:** On Hwy 138, 2.3 mi (3.7 km) e on Hwy 360, then just w on Beau Mont. **Facility:** These attractive and comfortable one- to five-bedroom condos are at the base of a popular and scenic ski hill. 41 condominiums, some two and three bedrooms. 2 stories (no elevator), exterior corridors. **Terms:** check-in 6 pm, 2 night minimum stay, 45 day cancellation notice-fee imposed. **Activities:** snowmobiling, hiking trails. *Fee:* downhill & cross country skiing. **Guest Services:** complimentary laundry.

HÉBERGEMENT MONT STE-ANNE

Phone: 418/827-2002

▼▽◆▽▼
Condominium
Rates not provided

Address: 1000 boul du Beau-Pre G0A 1E0 **Location:** Hwy 138 E exit 360. **Facility:** These large, upscale condos are located at the foot of the ski hill and are equipped with fireplaces. Heated indoor parking is available. 60 units, some two bedrooms, efficiencies and kitchens. 5 stories, interior corridors. **Terms:** office hours 8 am-10 pm, check-in 4 pm. **Activities:** ice skating, rental bicycles, hiking trails. *Fee:* downhill & cross country skiing. **Guest Services:** coin laundry.

WHERE TO EAT

LE BEAU REGARD   **Phone:** 418/827-5211

▼▽◆▽▼
French
$16-$34

AAA Inspector Notes: An upscale ski resort is the setting for this elegant yet casual dining room. The menu features fine French-influenced regional cuisine, including guinea fowl, pork, lamb, beef, smoked trout, deer, sweetbreads, snow crab and fresh fish. **Bar:** full bar. **Reservations:** suggested. **Address:** 500 boul Beau-Pre G0A 1E0 **Location:** Hwy 360, 2.3 mi (3.7 km) ne from jct Hwy 138; in Chateau Mont Sainte-Anne. B D

BECANCOUR pop. 11,134

AUBERGE GODEFROY   **Phone:** (819)233-2200

Hotel
$153-$171

Address: 17575 boul Becancour G9H 1A5 **Location:** Hwy 55 exit 176 southbound, 0.6 mi (1 km) n on boul Port Royal, then 0.3 mi (0.5 km) e; exit northbound, 0.5 mi (0.8 km) n on ave Godefroy. **Facility:** 71 units. 3 stories, interior corridors. **Parking:** winter plug-ins. **Terms:** check-in 4 pm. **Amenities:** honor bars. **Dining:** Le Godefroy, see separate listing. **Pool(s):** heated outdoor, heated indoor. **Activities:** saunas, whirlpools, steamrooms, snowmobiling, bicycles, hiking trails, horseshoes, volleyball, exercise room, spa. **Guest Services:** valet laundry.

WHERE TO EAT

LE GODEFROY   **Phone:** 819/233-2200

▼▽◆▽▼
French
$14-$36

AAA Inspector Notes: This high-ceiling, elegant dining room, overlooking scenic grounds, is known for its fine regional cuisine, a popular Sunday brunch and its lunch buffets. Menu items include regional fish and seafood, poultry, beef, pork, sweetbreads and an eight-course evening tasting menu. **Bar:** full bar. **Reservations:** suggested. **Address:** 17575 boul Becancour G9H 1A5 **Location:** Hwy 55 exit 176 southbound, 0.6 mi (1 km) n on boul Port Royal, then 0.3 mi (0.5 km) e; exit northbound, 0.5 mi (0.8 km) n on ave Godefroy; in Auberge Godefroy. B L D

BELOEIL pop. 18,927
- Part of Montréal area — see map p. 312

HOSTELLERIE RIVE GAUCHE   **Phone:** 450/467-4477

▼▽◆▽▼
Hotel
$115-$145

Address: 1810 boul Richelieu J3G 4S4 **Location:** Hwy 20 exit 112, 0.6 mi (1 km) s on rue Serge-Pepin, then just sw on Rt 223, follow signs. **Facility:** 22 units. 4 stories, interior corridors. **Parking:** winter plug-ins. **Terms:** check-in 4 pm, cancellation fee imposed. **Dining:** restaurant, see separate listing. **Activities:** snowmobiling. *Fee:* massage. **Guest Services:** valet laundry. **Free Special Amenities:** local telephone calls and high-speed Internet.

WHERE TO EAT

RESTAURANT RIVE GAUCHE   **Phone:** 450/467-4477

▼▽◆▽▼
French
$13-$35

AAA Inspector Notes: This restaurant offers splendid views of the Richelieu River and Mont-St-Hilaire from the dining room and seasonal terrace. The chef makes use of the abundant high-quality regional produce. Select from Atlantic salmon, guinea fowl, Boileau-region deer, snow crab, scallops and foie gras. The tasting menu can be paired with a selection of wine by the glass from the excellent wine list. The sit-down multi-course Sunday brunch draws a very good crowd. **Bar:** full bar. **Reservations:** suggested. **Address:** 1810 boul Richelieu J3G 4S4 **Location:** Hwy 20 exit 112, 0.6 mi (1 km) s on rue Serge-Pepin, then just sw on Rt 223, follow signs; in Hostellerie Rive Gauche. B L D

BERTHIER-SUR-MER (A-2) pop. 1,239, elev. 11m/35'

LACHANCE CRUISES (Croisières Lachance), 110 de la Marina, offers narrated cruises to Grosse Île and the Irish Memorial National Historic Site *(see attraction listing p. 309)*. Also available is a nature and culture cruise on the archipelago that includes a stop and a guided tour on Isle-aux-Grues. Special cruises are offered seasonally; tours highlight the Loto-Québec International Fireworks Competition, concerts at Grosse Île, or the colony of razorbills that settles in the eastern tip of the archipelago each spring.

Hours: Bilingual cruises and tours are available May-Oct. Departure times vary; phone ahead. Cruises board 30-45 minutes before departure. **Cost:** Grosse Île cruise $49.50; $28 (ages 6-16). Archipelago nature and culture cruise $46; $26 (ages 6-16). Prices for special seasonal cruises vary. Reservations are recommended. **Phone:** (418) 259-2140 or (888) 476-7734.

BERTHIERVILLE pop. 4,007

ST-HUBERT

Canadian
$8-$22

Phone: 450/836-1777

AAA Inspector Notes: The pleasantly decorated family-friendly restaurant serves affordable chicken dinners, ribs, club sandwiches, chicken wings, salads, soups and hot chicken sandwiches. The children's menu includes animal nuggets. **Bar:** full bar. **Address:** 1091 ave Gilles-Villeneuve J0K 1A0 **Location:** Hwy 40 exit 144. L D

BOISCHATEL

• Hotels & Restaurants map & index p. 429
• Part of Québec area — see map p. 405

ECONO LODGE MONTMORENCY

Hotel
$75-$145

Phone: (418)822-4777 33

Address: 5490 boul Ste-Anne G0A 1H0 **Location:** On Hwy 138. **Facility:** 32 units. 2 stories (no elevator), interior corridors. **Parking:** winter plug-ins. **Terms:** cancellation fee imposed. **Activities:** sauna. **Guest Services:** coin laundry. **Free Special Amenities:** continental breakfast and high-speed Internet.

SAVE TI+ BIZ 🛜 ✕
/ SOME UNITS FEE 🐕 FEE 🛎 FEE 🖥

BONAVENTURE (C-9) pop. 2,673

A seaside resort, Bonaventure was founded in 1760 by 12 Acadian families who were among those expelled from Nova Scotia by the British in 1755. The climate and conditions of the region are favorable for agriculture.

Bonaventure Tourist Information Bureau: 97A av. Port-Royal, Bonaventure, QC, Canada G0C 1E0. **Phone:** (418) 534-4014.

ACADIAN HISTORICAL MUSEUM OF QUÉBEC

(Musée acadien du Québec), on Hwy. 132 at 95 av. Port-Royal, has handicrafts, antiques and artifacts depicting the region's Acadian legacy. Guided tours are available; narration in English is offered. **Time:** Allow 1 hour minimum. **Hours:** Daily 9-6, June 24-Labour Day; daily 9-5, day after Labour Day-second Mon. in Oct.; Mon.-Fri. 9-noon and 1-4, Sun. 1-4:30, rest of year. **Cost:** $8.25; $6.25 (ages 60+); $5.25 (students with ID); $13.25 (family, one adult and two children). **Phone:** (418) 534-4000.

BOUCHERVILLE pop. 39,062

• Restaurants p. 269
• Hotels & Restaurants map & index p. 342
• Part of Montréal area — see map p. 312

COMFORT INN

Motel
$98-$135

Phone: (450)641-2880 18

Address: 96 boul de Mortagne J4B 5M7 **Location:** Hwy 20 exit 92, just n. **Facility:** 100 units. 2 stories (no elevator), interior corridors. **Parking:** winter plug-ins. **Terms:** cancellation fee imposed. **Amenities:** high-speed Internet. **Guest Services:** valet laundry.

ECO TI+ BIZ 🛜 FEE 🐾 🖥

HOTEL MORTAGNE

Hotel
$139-$269

Phone: (450)655-9966 20

Address: 1228 rue Nobel J4B 5H1 **Location:** Hwy 20 exit 93 eastbound; exit 92 westbound, take overpass to south side, then just s. **Facility:** 130 units. 6 stories, interior corridors. **Terms:** check-in 4 pm, 2 night minimum stay - seasonal and/or weekends, cancellation fee imposed. **Amenities:** high-speed Internet, safes. **Dining:** Restaurant Sens, see separate listing. **Pool(s):** heated indoor. **Activities:** sauna, whirlpool, exercise room, spa. **Guest Services:** valet laundry. **Free Special Amenities:** local telephone calls and high-speed Internet.

(See ad p. 268.)

SAVE ECO TI Y CALL 🔊 🛄 BIZ 🛜 ✕
FEE 🐾 🛏 🖥 / SOME UNITS 🖥

HOTEL WELCOMINNS

Hotel
$125-$195

Phone: (450)449-1011 19

Address: 1195 rue Ampere J4B 7M6 **Location:** Hwy 20 exit 92, just n. **Facility:** 116 units. 3 stories, interior/exterior corridors. **Parking:** winter plug-ins. **Amenities:** video games (fee), high-speed Internet. *Some:* safes. **Pool(s):** heated indoor. **Activities:** sauna, whirlpool, limited exercise equipment. **Guest Services:** valet and coin laundry. **Free Special Amenities:** expanded continental breakfast and high-speed Internet.

(See ad p. 268.)

SAVE TI+ 🛄 BIZ 🛜 ✕
FEE 🐾 🛏 🖥

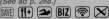

Visit AAA.com or CAA.ca for one-stop
travel planning and reservations

(See map & index p. 342.)

WHERE TO EAT

BISTRO LE TIRE-BOUCHON
Phone: 450/449-6112 (47)

French
$15-$28

AAA Inspector Notes: Bistro-style cuisine includes selections from many regions of France. Confit of peppered duck is served with roasted potatoes and julienne carrots. Among other house specialties are veal, salmon and terrine foie gras. Rich woods, warm fabrics and elegant table settings give the dining room an air of sophistication. **Bar:** full bar. **Reservations:** suggested. **Address:** 141-K boul de Mortagne J4B 6G4 **Location:** Hwy 20 exit 92, just n; in Place de Mortagne. [L] [D]

MADISONS NEW YORK GRILL & BAR
Phone: 450/449-1221 (49)

Steak
$10-$35

AAA Inspector Notes: The casual pub and steakhouse has comfortable chairs and private leather-upholstered booths. Its grill menu lists fresh seafood, filet mignon, rib steaks, milk-fed veal, roast beef, ribs, grilled chicken, burgers, giant shrimp, shrimp cocktail, salmon salad, Caesar salad and a choice of sandwiches, including club, crab and red tuna. **Bar:** full bar. **Address:** 1190 rue Volta J4B 7A2 **Location:** Hwy 20 exit 92. [L] [D]

RESTAURANT SENS
Phone: 450/655-4939 (48)

French
$15-$28

AAA Inspector Notes: Those who enjoy a casually elegant restaurant lounge may find this stylish hotel bistro-bar the ideal place to gather. Enjoy before dinner drinks at the bar or on the seasonal terrace and then move to a table for some upscale bistro fare attractively presented. The menu boasts Angus beef steak (or a burger from the bistro menu), lamb shank, fresh fish, pasta of the day, scallops and salads. In summer, an outdoor grill is fired up. **Bar:** full bar. **Reservations:** suggested. **Address:** 1228 rue Nobel J4B 5H1 **Location:** Hwy 20 exit 93 eastbound; exit 92 westbound, take overpass to south side, then just s; in Hotel Mortagne. [B] [L] [D] CALL [&M]

ST-HUBERT
Phone: 450/449-9366

Canadian
$8-$22

AAA Inspector Notes: The pleasantly decorated family-friendly restaurant serves affordable chicken dinners, ribs, club sandwiches, chicken wings, salads, soups and hot chicken sandwiches. The children's menu includes animal nuggets. **Bar:** full bar. **Address:** 500 rue Albanel J4B 2Z6 **Location:** Hwy 132 exit Montarville. [L] [D]

BROMONT pop. 6,049

AUBERGE CHATEAU-BROMONT
Phone: (450)534-3133

Hotel
$99-$159

Address: 95 rue Montmorency J2L 2J1 **Location:** Hwy 10 exit 78, 1.8 mi (2.8 km) w on boul Bromont, then just n on rue Champlain; in Station Touristique Bromont. **Facility:** 40 units. 3 stories (no elevator), interior corridors. **Terms:** check-in 4 pm, cancellation fee imposed. **Dining:** Restaurant de l'Auberge, see separate listing. **Pool(s):** heated outdoor. **Activities:** whirlpool, lighted tennis court, game room, exercise room. **Guest Services:** valet laundry, area transportation-ski slopes, water park & Hotel Château-Bromont.

/ SOME UNITS FEE

HOTEL BROMONT
Phone: 450/534-3790

Hotel
$119-$189 6/6-5/31
$98-$188 6/1-6/5

Address: 125 boul Bromont J2L 2K7 **Location:** Hwy 10 exit 78, 1.6 mi (2.7 km) s. **Facility:** 41 units, some efficiencies. 3 stories (no elevator), interior/exterior corridors. **Terms:** 2 night minimum stay - seasonal and/or weekends, cancellation fee imposed. **Amenities:** high-speed Internet. **Pool(s):** heated indoor. **Activities:** whirlpool. **Guest Services:** valet laundry.

HOTEL CHÂTEAU-BROMONT
Phone: (450)534-3433

Hotel
$150-$300

Address: 90 rue Stanstead J2L 1K6 **Location:** Hwy 10 exit 78, 1.8 mi (2.9 km) s on boul Bromont, then 0.8 mi (1.2 km) w on rue Champlain (toward ski hill). **Facility:** 164 units. 3 stories, interior corridors. **Parking:** winter plug-ins. **Terms:** check-in 4 pm, 2 night minimum stay - seasonal and/or weekends, cancellation fee imposed. **Amenities:** video games (fee), safes, honor bars. **Dining:** Restaurant Quatre Canards, see separate listing. **Pool(s):** heated outdoor, heated indoor. **Activities:** whirlpools, steamrooms, racquetball court, exercise room, spa. **Guest Services:** valet laundry, area transportation-ski slopes, golf & water park.

/ SOME UNITS

LE ST-MARTIN BROMONT HOTEL & SUITES
Phone: (450)534-0044

Hotel
$169-$400

Address: 111 boul du Carrefour J2L 3L1 **Location:** Hwy 10 exit 78. **Facility:** 70 units. 3 stories, interior corridors. **Amenities:** high-speed Internet, honor bars. *Some:* safes. **Pool(s):** heated outdoor. **Activities:** whirlpool, exercise room. **Guest Services:** valet laundry.

/ SOME UNITS FEE

WHERE TO EAT

GOLDEN PUB
Phone: 450/534-1575

Canadian
$8-$19

AAA Inspector Notes: This lively Irish pub-restaurant has a seasonal terrace with a great view of the Bromont ski hill. Inside there is a pub section and a separate dining area open to all ages. Menu offerings include roast beef, mussels and fries, shrimps, burgers, sausages, pizza, salads, sandwiches, chicken wings, French onion soup and pies made in house. **Bar:** full bar. **Address:** 201 rue Champlain J2L 3B2 **Location:** Hwy 10 exit 78, 1.6 mi (2.7 km) s. [L] [D] [LATE]

MICRO-BRASSERIE BROUEMONT RESTAURANT
Phone: 450/534-0001

Canadian
$9-$20

AAA Inspector Notes: Microbrewed beers are served in the casual atmosphere of the rural village eatery. A fireplace keeps the dining room cozy during the ski season, and a terrace opens seasonally. The menu lists sandwiches, soups, grilled chicken, steaks, sausage and burgers. **Bar:** full bar. **Reservations:** required. **Address:** 107 boul Bromont J2L 2K7 **Location:** Hwy 10 exit 78, 1.4 mi (2.3 km) s. [L] [D]

RESTAURANT DE L'AUBERGE
Phone: 450/534-3133

Italian
$15-$35

AAA Inspector Notes: Fine Italian cuisine is served in this laid-back hotel restaurant, which offers great mountain views. The menu focuses on well-prepared Italian dishes that are attractively presented. The seasonal terrace is popular in summer. **Bar:** full bar. **Address:** 95 rue Montmorency J2L 2J1 **Location:** Hwy 10 exit 78, 1.8 mi (2.8 km) w on boul Bromont, then just n on rue Champlain; in Station Touristique Bromont; in Auberge Chateau-Bromont.

[B] [L] [D]

RESTAURANT QUATRE CANARDS

Phone: 450/534-3433

French
$21-$50

AAA Inspector Notes: The comfortable, well-appointed hotel restaurant presents a varied menu of fine French cuisine that makes use of quality regional produce. Specialties include Lake Brome duck, loin of deer, marinated trout and yellow perch filets, salmon tournedos, rack of lamb, Charlevoix veal and steamed lobster. **Bar:** full bar. **Reservations:** suggested. **Address:** 90 rue Stanstead J2L 1K6 **Location:** Hwy 10 exit 78, 1.8 mi (2.9 km) s on boul Bromont, then 0.8 mi (1.2 km) w on rue Champlain (toward ski hill); in Hotel Château-Bromont. B L D

REST-O-BAR L'ÉTRIER

Phone: 450/534-3562

Steak
$10-$45

AAA Inspector Notes: Overlooking nearby ski hills, this casual eatery, named for the French word for "stirrup," has a rustic country decor with wood walls and a fireplace. Live music is performed most weekends, and the terrace opens seasonally. Steak and seafood top a menu that includes AAA Angus filet mignon, snow crab ravioli, guinea fowl breast, pork chops and walleye. **Bar:** full bar. **Address:** 547 rue Shefford (CP 86) J2L 1B9 **Location:** Hwy 10 exit 78, 0.3 mi (0.5 km) s on boul Bromont, then just e. B L D

ST-HUBERT

Phone: 450/534-0223

Canadian
$8-$22

AAA Inspector Notes: The pleasantly decorated family-friendly restaurant serves affordable chicken dinners, ribs, club sandwiches, chicken wings, salads, soups and hot chicken sandwiches. The children's menu includes animal nuggets. **Bar:** full bar. **Address:** 8 boul De Bromont J2L 1A9 **Location:** Hwy 10 exit 78. L D

BROSSARD pop. 71,154

- Hotels & Restaurants map & index p. 342
- Part of Montréal area — see map p. 312

ALT HOTEL QUARTIER DIX 30

Phone: 450/443-1030 **54**

Hotel
Rates not provided

Address: 6500 boul de Rome J4Y 0B6 **Location:** Jct Hwy 10 and 30, just w on Hwy 30 exit boul de Rome; in Quartier Dix 30 Mall. **Facility:** 158 units. 14 stories, interior corridors. **Amenities:** high-speed Internet. *Some:* video games. **Guest Services:** valet laundry.

BEST WESTERN PLUS BROSSARD

Phone: (450)466-6756 **51**

Hotel
$126-$180

 AAA Benefit: Members save up to 20%, plus 10% bonus points with Best Western Rewards®.

Address: 7746 boul Taschereau J4X 1C2 **Location:** Rt 134 0.8 mi (1.3 km) w of Hwy 10 exit boul Taschereau ouest. Located in a commercial area. **Facility:** 114 units. 2 stories, interior corridors. **Parking:** winter plug-ins. **Terms:** cancellation fee imposed. **Pool(s):** heated indoor. **Activities:** sauna, exercise room. **Guest Services:** coin laundry. **Free Special Amenities:** expanded continental breakfast and high-speed Internet.

COMFORT INN

Phone: (450)678-9350 **52**

Hotel
$90-$210

Address: 7863 boul Taschereau J4Y 1A4 **Location:** Rt 134, 0.9 mi (1.5 km) w of Hwy 10 exit boul Taschereau ouest. **Facility:** 100 units. 2 stories, interior corridors. **Parking:** winter plug-ins. **Terms:** cancellation fee imposed. **Amenities:** high-speed Internet. **Guest Services:** valet laundry.

ECONO LODGE MONTREAL - BROSSARD

Phone: (450)466-2186 **53**

Motel
$87-$200

Address: 8350 boul Taschereau J4X 1C2 **Location:** Rt 134, 1.4 mi (2.3 km) w of Hwy 10 exit boul Taschereau ouest. **Facility:** 73 units, some efficiencies. 2-3 stories (no elevator), interior/exterior corridors. **Parking:** winter plug-ins. **Terms:** check-in 4 pm, cancellation fee imposed. **Amenities:** *Some:* high-speed Internet.

HOTEL BROSSARD

Phone: 514/890-1000 **50**

Hotel
Rates not provided

Address: 7365 boul Marie-Victorin J4W 1A6 **Location:** On Hwy 132, 0.3 mi (0.5 km) w of Pont Champlain. **Facility:** 125 units, some kitchens. 3 stories, interior corridors. **Amenities:** high-speed Internet. **Activities:** *Fee:* massage. **Guest Services:** valet laundry.

QUALITY INN & SUITES

Phone: (450)671-7213 **49**

Hotel
$116-$161

Address: 6680 boul Taschereau J4W 1M8 **Location:** Rt 134, 0.3 mi (0.4 km) e of jct Hwy 10 exit boul Taschereau est. Located in a commercial area. **Facility:** 100 units. 3 stories, interior corridors. **Terms:** cancellation fee imposed. **Pool(s):** heated indoor. **Amenities:** high-speed Internet. **Activities:** exercise room. *Fee:* massage. **Guest Services:** valet and coin laundry. **Free Special Amenities:** full breakfast and high-speed Internet.

WHERE TO EAT

CHEZ CORA

Phone: 450/672-7371

Canadian
$6-$13

AAA Inspector Notes: Eggs, omelets, waffles, crepes (sorry, no American-style pancakes here), French toast, fruit platters and all the breakfast meats--that's the specialty here, all day. However, at lunchtime the menu lists a selection of soups, salads, quiches, sandwiches and a dish called the grilled panini crepe. **Address:** 3 Place du Commerce J4W 2Z6 **Location:** Hwy 10 exit boul Taschereau, just e. B L

L'AUROCHS ANGUS STEAKHOUSE

Phone: 450/445-1031 **84**

Steak
$24-$95

AAA Inspector Notes: In an upscale suburban shopping mall, this luxurious steakhouse serves Certified Angus Beef steaks, fish and seafood. Guests can sample fine wines and sink back into padded leather seats as well-attired servers meet their needs. The mall offers street parking in front of the restaurant or complimentary indoor parking nearby. **Bar:** full bar. **Address:** 9395 boul Leduc, Suite 5 J4Y 0A5 **Location:** Jct Hwy 10 and 30, just w on Hwy 30 exit boul de Rome; in Quartier Dix 30 Mall. **Parking:** street only. L D

(See map & index p. 342.)

LES 3 BRASSEURS

Phone: 450/676-7215   (83)

Canadian
$9-$21

AAA Inspector Notes: This lively brew pub specializes in home-brewed beers, beer cocktails and a pizza-like dish called flammekueche (flamm for short). Hailing from Alsace, France, this dish features a thin-baked crust topped with such tasty ingredients as Quebec cheese, bacon, onions, sour cream, feta cheese, smoked meat and pesto. The menu also lists salads, sandwich wraps, French onion soup, croque monsieur, baby back ribs and steak. Patrons can view brewery equipment through a glass wall. **Bar:** full bar. **Reservations:** required. **Address:** 9316 boul Leduc J4Y 0B3 **Location:** Jct Hwy 10 and 30, just w on Hwy 30 exit boul de Rome; in Quartier Dix 30 Mall. (L) (D) (LATE)

RESTAURANT CUMULUS   Phone: 450/678-1038   (82)

Canadian
$13-$29

AAA Inspector Notes: This casually upscale dining room located in a suburban shopping mall serves up such great comfort foods as fish and chips, roast pork, pizza, pasta, mussels and steak and fries as well as seafood, chicken and items off a children's menu. Guests are seated at comfortable padded chairs or leather booths with upscale marble table tops. The high ceilings, ornate lighting and decorative pillars and moldings give this space a glamorous feel. **Bar:** full bar. **Address:** 9330 boul Leduc J4Y 0B3 **Location:** Jct Hwy 10 and 30, just w on Hwy 30 exit boul de Rome; in Quartier Dix 30 Mall. (L) (D)

ROUGE BISTRO & GRILL ORIENTAL
Phone: 450/676-8886   (85)

Asian
$12-$25

AAA Inspector Notes: This contemporary, suburban restaurant boasts a stylish decor centered around Asian-style statue replicas and a varied menu that offers Chinese, Thai, Malaysian and Mongolian dishes. Select from a menu divided between dishes originating from the sea, sky, land or garden, with a level of spiciness indicated on the hot and spicy selections. Sample noodles, Hunan dumplings, giant Thai shrimp, Cantonese chow mein, General Tao chicken, Mongolian beef, broccoli with oyster sauce and red curry duck. **Bar:** full bar. **Address:** 6000 boul de Rome, Suite 60 J4Y 0B6 **Location:** Jct Hwy 10 and 30, just w on Hwy 30 exit boul de Rome; in Quartier Dix 30 Mall.
(L) (D)

ST-HUBERT

Phone: 450/676-7910

Canadian
$8-$22

AAA Inspector Notes: The pleasantly decorated family-friendly restaurant serves affordable chicken dinners, ribs, club sandwiches, chicken wings, salads, soups and hot chicken sandwiches. The children's menu includes animal nuggets. **Bar:** full bar. **Address:** 6325 boul Taschereau J4Z 1A5 **Location:** Hwy 10 exit boul Taschereau, then e. (L) (D)

CABANO (D-7) pop. 3,199

FORT INGALL is 2 km (1.2 mi.) n. of Hwy. 185 at 81 ch. Caldwell (Hwy. 232). The original of this reconstructed fort on the shores of lac Témiscouata, built in 1839 to protect the vital portage between Québec and Halifax, Nova Scotia, was occupied during the border conflict between Maine and Canada.

Guided tours are available; narration in English is offered. **Time:** Allow 1 hour, 30 minutes minimum. **Hours:** Daily 9-5, June-Sept.; 10-4 in May and Oct. **Cost:** $9; $7 (ages 6-12, ages 66+ and students with ID); $20 (family). **Phone:** (418) 854-2375 or (866) 242-2437. (⛰) (🏕)

CANTLEY (E-3) pop. 7,926, elev. 181m/593'

MONT CASCADES WATERPARK (Parc aquatique Station Mont Cascades) is 7 km (4.3 mi.) w. on Hwy. 307 to 448 Mont Cascades Rd. A downhill ski area in the winter, the Mont Cascades site features a water park that keeps summer visitors well-entertained. Highlights include speed slides, raft rides, activity pools and children's rides.

Time: Allow a full day. **Hours:** Water park daily 10-6, mid-June through Labour Day. **Cost:** Water park $26; $19 (under 122 centimetres or 48 inches tall and nonparticipants). Water park after 2 p.m. $23; $17 (under 122 centimetres or 48 inches tall and nonparticipants). **Phone:** (819) 827-0301. (🍴)

RECREATIONAL ACTIVITIES
Skiing

- **Mont Cascades** is 7 km (4.3 mi.) w. on Hwy. 307 to 448 Mont Cascades Rd. **Hours:** Mon.-Fri. 10-10, Sat.-Sun. 8:30 a.m.-10 p.m., late Nov.-early Apr. Phone ahead to confirm schedule. **Phone:** (819) 827-0301.

CAP-CHAT (B-8) pop. 2,777

The Cap-Chat takes its name from a rock 1 kilometre (.6 mi.) west of town that resembles a crouching cat (chat). Safari Anticosti offers 2-day/1 night ecotours June 24 through August 31. Write Safari Anticosti, 208B, Notre-Dame Est, C.P. 398, Cap-Chat, QC, Canada G0J 1E0; phone (418) 786-5788.

THE AEOLIAN OF CAP-CHAT (Éole Cap-Chat) is 2 km (1.2 mi.) w. on Hwy. 132, following signs. The Aeolian of Cap-Chat, said to be the tallest (110 m, 360 ft.) and most powerful (4 megawatts) vertical axis windmill in the world, is named for Aeolus, the Greek god of the winds. Like the Aeolian harp, a box with strings that sound when wind passes over them, the Aeolian of Cap-Chat makes a resonant sound when the wind strikes it.

Guided tours of the Nordais wind park are available. **Time:** Allow 1 hour, 30 minutes minimum. **Hours:** Daily 9-5, June-Sept. **Cost:** $14; $13 (ages 65+ and students with ID); $8 (ages 6-17); $35 (family, two adults and children). **Phone:** (418) 786-5719 or (418) 763-9935.

CAP-DES-ROSIERS (B-9)

CAP-DES-ROSIERS LIGHTHOUSE NATIONAL HISTORIC SITE (Lieu historique national du Phare de Cap-des-Rosiers) is on Rte. 132 at the n.e. tip of the Gaspé Peninsula. From this point a messenger was dispatched in 1759, in one of the decisive battles of the Seven Years' War, to warn Québec of the impending arrival of British general James Wolfe's fleet.

The 1858 lighthouse, fog signal and radio beacon are still in operation. The structure is 34 metres (112 ft.) tall and the light is 41 metres (135 ft.) above the high-water line. **Tours:** Guided tours are available.

Hours: Daily 10-7, mid-June through Sept. 30. **Cost:** Free. Guided tour $2.50; $5 (family). **Phone:** (418) 892-5577.

CARLETON-ST-OMER (C-8)

A popular seaside resort community, Carleton was settled by Acadians who eluded exile to Louisiana. The town's name was originally Tracadièche, a Micmac Indian word meaning "place of many herons." It was changed to Carleton in honor of Guy Carleton, governor general of Canada during the late 18th century.

The arts have a secure role in Carleton-St-Omer. Galleries display the work of area artists. A work of art itself, the St-Joseph-de-Carleton Church, on boulevard Perron, contains paintings, silverware and vestments acquired in 1800. Productions by the Moluque Theatre are offered Tuesday through Saturday evenings from mid-July to late August.

Preserved fossils are found at Miguasha National Park *(see attraction listing p. 307),* southwest via Hwy. 132. The park contains the Escuminac Geological Formation, which represents a paleoecosystem of the Devonian period, 370 million years ago. These fossils illustrate the transition from aquatic vertebrates to land vertebrates, making the park an important paleontological site.

Carleton Tourist Information Bureau: 629 boul. Perron, Carleton-St-Omer, QC, Canada G0C 1J0. **Phone:** (418) 364-3544.

MONT ST-JOSEPH'S NOTRE-DAME ORATORY (Oratoire Notre-Dame-du-Mont-St-Joseph), reached by car or bus, is a chapel at the summit of Mont St-Joseph. At 555 metres (1,820 ft.), it offers one of the best views of the Baie des Chaleurs. **Hours:** Daily 9-7, June 23-Labour Day; 9-5, day after Labour Day to mid-Sept. **Cost:** $4.75; $3.75 (students with ID and senior citizens); $11.75 (family). **Phone:** (418) 364-2256.

CAUSAPSCAL (C-8) pop. 2,458

At the confluence of the salmon-filled Causapscal and Matapédia rivers, Causapscal serves as a lumber and fishing center on the Gaspé Peninsula. On the edge of town, tall conical chimneys mark the sawing complexes where wood processing residues are burned.

Scenic points of interest in the Causapscal area include 40-metre-high (131-ft.) Philomène Falls (Chutes à Philomène), 16 kilometres (10 mi.) north off Hwy. 132, and a covered bridge over the Matapédia River just south of town. Even though the last 10 kilometres (6 mi.) of road to the river at the falls is not very good, the spot is a favorite of fly fishermen.

Causapscal Tourist Information Bureau: 48 rue St-Jacques Sud, Causapscal, QC, Canada G0J 1J0. **Phone:** (418) 756-6048.

MATAMAJAW HISTORICAL SITE (Site historique Matamajaw), 53 C St-Jacques Sud, is the restored former facility of the Matamajaw Salmon Fishing Club, founded in the early 1900s by a group of businessmen who bought the 1870 estate of a British lord. The club operated for more than 60 years. Exhibits include a man-made salmon pool.

Time: Allow 30 minutes minimum. **Hours:** Tues.-Sun. 9:30-4:30, early June to mid-Sept. Phone ahead to confirm schedule. **Cost:** $7; $6 (ages 66+ and students with ID); free (ages 0-5); $20 (family). **Phone:** (418) 756-5999.

CHAMBLY (F-7) pop. 22,608
- **Part of Montréal area — see map p. 312**

FORT CHAMBLY NATIONAL HISTORIC SITE (Lieu historique national du Fort-Chambly) is off Hwy. 10 exit 22 at 2 rue de Richelieu at jct. av. Bourgogne and rue Langevin, at the foot of the Richelieu River Rapids. This 1-hectare (2.5-acre) park contains one of several forts built here by the French. In 1665 Jacques de Chambly constructed a wooden fort on this site to subdue the Iroquois. Two other wooden forts followed before the French built a stone fort on the site to prevent a British invasion.

Taken by English troops in 1760, the fort was invaded by American troops in 1775 during the American Revolution and again in 1812 during the war with the United States. A British garrison occupied the fort sporadically during the 19th century until its final abandonment in 1860.

The restored fort has appears as it did in 1750 when the Compagnie franche de la Marine was garrisoned here. Interpretive center displays explain the living conditions of the French garrison.

Time: Allow 1 hour, 30 minutes minimum. **Hours:** Daily 10-5, June-Aug.; Wed.-Sun. 10-5, Apr.-May and Sept.-Oct. **Cost:** $5.65; $4.90 (ages 65+); $2.90 (ages 6-16 and students with ID); $14.20 (family). **Phone:** (450) 658-1585 or (888) 773-8888.

| FOURQUET FOURCHETTE | **Phone:** 450/447-6370 |

Quebec
$11-$35

AAA Inspector Notes: Adjacent to historic Fort Chambly, this relaxed family restaurant is furnished in decor typical of early settler dwellings. Traditional Quebec cuisine can be sampled from an a la carte menu that features seafood, game, meat and chicken delicacies. Many microbrewed beers are available. **Bar:** beer only. **Reservations:** suggested. **Address:** 1887 Bourgogne Ave J3L 1Y8 **Location:** Adjacent to Fort Chambly. L D

CHÂTEAU-RICHER (A-2) pop. 3,563
- **Part of Québec area — see map p. 405**

Settled in 1640, Château-Richer was established as a parish in 1678 by Bishop de Laval, the first bishop of New France. De Laval reportedly named the village after the priory of Château-Richer in

France. There also is a legend that one of the town's settlers named Richer established a shelter in a huge tree trunk. The townspeople ridiculed him by calling his habitat Château Richer, a name later assumed by the parish.

Primarily an agricultural community, the town has a number of area roadside stands selling summer vegetables and maple syrup as well as bread baked in two old stone ovens that stand near the highway.

ALBERT GILLES COPPER ART MUSEUM, 7450 boul. Ste-Anne, displays the copper artwork of renowned artisan Albert Gilles. Born in France in 1895, Gilles immigrated to the United States in the 1930s but eventually settled in Québec. Prior to his death in 1979, Gilles' clients included such famous figures as Roy and Walt Disney, Mae West, Fredric March and Constance Bennett; he also was commissioned to prepare copper works for Pope Pius XII and for churches throughout North America. The museum displays decorative and religious works showcasing the *repoussé* technique and also describes copper extraction and its practical uses.

Time: Allow 30 minutes minimum. **Hours:** Daily 9-4, Sat.-Sun. 1-4, Nov.-Jan.; Mon.-Fri. 8:30-5, May-Oct.; Mon.-Fri. 9-4, rest of year. Closed Jan. 1 and Christmas. **Cost:** Free. **Phone:** (418) 824-4224.

BEE AND HONEY MUSEUM (Musée de l'Abeille—Économusée du Miel), 4 km (2.5 mi.) w. on Hwy. 138 to 8862 boul. Ste-Anne, features interpretive exhibits about bees and the production of honey. While learning about the insects and the sweet liquid they produce, visitors observe the bees at work in a glass beehive. In summer the Bee Safari features a humorous presentation about the tiny workers. Honey and honey wine tastings also are offered.

Time: Allow 1 hour minimum. **Hours:** Daily 9-6, late June-Labour Day; daily 9-5, late Mar.-late June and day after Labour Day to mid-Oct.; daily 11-5, mid- to late Oct.; Fri.-Sun. 11-5, early Jan.-late Mar. and late Oct. to mid-Dec. Phone ahead to confirm schedule. **Cost:** Admission free. Fees may be charged for individual activities. **Phone:** (418) 824-4411.

CÔTE-DE-BEAUPRÉ INTERPRETATION CENTRE (Centre d'interprétation de la Côte-de-Beaupré) is at 7976 av. Royale. The center provides information about the geography, heritage and socioeconomic development of the Côte-de-Beaupré region, where 170 pioneer families settled in the 17th century. Displays include documents, maps, sketches and photographs. On the ground level are archeological pits affording views of convent ruins from the 17th and 19th centuries.

Time: Allow 30 minutes minimum. **Hours:** Daily 9:30-4:30, mid-May through Labour Day; Mon.-Fri. 9:30-4:30, rest of year. **Cost:** $6; $5 (ages 66+); $4 (students with ID); free (ages 0-16 and to all Mon.). **Phone:** (418) 824-3677, or (877) 824-3677 in Canada.

PETIT-PRÉ MILL (Moulin du Petit-Pré) is at 7007 av. Royale. Costumed bilingual interpreters demonstrate 18th-century milling practices at this stone-walled historic building. The mill, believed to be the oldest commercial flour mill in North America, grounds wheat and buckwheat into flour by means of a large water wheel. **Time:** Allow 1 hour minimum. **Hours:** Daily 9-5, mid-Apr. to mid-Oct. **Cost:** $6.50; $5.50 (ages 64+ and students with ID); $3 (ages 6-12); $15 (family, two adults and two children). **Phone:** (418) 824-7007. 🍽 🛆

WINERIES

- **Moulin du Petit Pré Vineyards** (Vignoble du Moulin du Petit Pré) is at 7021 av. Royale. **Hours:** Mon.-Fri. 11-6, May 1-Dec. 1; by appointment rest of year. **Cost:** June 1 to mid-Oct. $5; free (students with ID). Rest of season free. **Phone:** (418) 824-7077.

AUBERGE BAKER

Country Inn
$79-$150

Phone: (418)666-5509
Address: 8790 ave Royale G0A 1N0
Location: 3 mi (5 km) e, just off Hwy 138 via private road. **Facility:** 8 units, some houses and cottages. 2 stories (no elevator), interior/exterior corridors. **Parking:** winter plug-ins. **Terms:** 14 day cancellation notice. **Dining:** restaurant, see separate listing. **Activities:** snowmobiling. 🍽 📶 ✖ / SOME UNITS 🛆

WHERE TO EAT

RESTAURANT BAKER
Menu on AAA.com

Regional French
$13-$47

Phone: 418/824-4478
AAA Inspector Notes: The cozy, circa 1840 farmhouse is appointed with country-style decor and has a laid-back atmosphere. Preparations of game are the specialty on a menu of traditional Quebecois and fine French cuisine that also includes duck confit, blood sausage ("boudin noir"), lamb and veal. **Bar:** full bar. **Reservations:** suggested. **Address:** 8790 ave Royale G0A 1N0 **Location:** 3 mi (5 km) e, just off Hwy 138 via private road; in Auberge Baker. **Historic** Ⓑ Ⓛ Ⓓ

CHELSEA (E-3) pop. 6,703, elev. 109m/357'
• Restaurants p. 274

GATINEAU PARK (Parc de la Gatineau) is just n. between the Gatineau and Ottawa rivers. Hwys. 5, 105, 148 and 366 provide access from Gatineau to the park's recreation areas. The park encompasses about 36,100 hectares (89,205 acres) of the rocky, wooded Laurentian Mountains.

In the southern section the scenic Gatineau Parkway links the lac des Fées and lac Meech areas. Along with a bicycle path, the route provides access to picnic grounds and lookouts. Farther north the lac Philippe area offers fine beaches and fringe areas. In the northwestern section, the lac La Pêche area provides more wilderness, a beach and canoe-camping facilities.

Lacs Meech, La Pêche and Philippe provide bass fishing. Alpine skiing is available at Camp Fortune. There are 200 kilometres (125 mi.) of cross-country ski trails with day-use and overnight shelters. In summer ski trails are hiking and mountain biking trails.

Anglers must have a valid Québec fishing license. **Hours:** Park open daily 24 hours. Visitor center open daily 9-5; noon-5, Christmas. **Cost:** Park admission free. Access fee for the beach, boat ramp areas and picnic areas at lacs Meech, La Pêche and Philippe mid-June through Labour Day $9 (per private vehicle). Access fee for the cross-country ski network $12; $8 (ages 13-17, ages 60+ and students with ID); $25 (family, two adults and three children). **Phone:** (819) 827-2020 or (800) 465-1867.

Mackenzie King Estate, Scott Rd. to Old Chelsea Rd. to Gatineau Pkwy. following signs, was a summer residence of three-time prime minister William Lyon Mackenzie King. The first floor is now a tearoom. Historical interpreters and audiovisual presentations give an overview of the 1921-48 era during Canada's longest-governing prime minister. Presentations are available in English. The formal gardens are restored and gardener-historians describe King's gardening techniques.

Tours: Guided tours are available. **Time:** Allow 1 hour, 30 minutes minimum. **Hours:** Mon.-Fri. 11-5, Sat.-Sun. 10-6, mid-May to mid-Oct. **Cost:** $8 (per private vehicle). **Phone:** (819) 827-2020.

RESTAURANT LES FOUGÈRES
Menu on AAA.com   **Phone:** 819/827-8942
French
$13-$40
AAA Inspector Notes: This relaxed and elegant country dining room treats patrons to superb food pairings on a menu that includes fresh fish, Prince Edward Island scallops, shrimp, grain-fed chicken, sweetbreads, lamb and venison. The service is refined. Connected to the restaurant is the owner's gourmet and gift shop where house-prepared frozen meat pies, jams and chutneys are among the items for sale. **Bar:** full bar. **Reservations:** suggested. **Address:** 783 Rt 105 J9B 1P1 **Location:** On Rt 105, 1.2 mi (2 km) n of Old Chelsea. [L] [D]

CHICOUTIMI (C-6)

A regional trade center, Chicoutimi is at the farthest point of deepwater navigation on the scenic Saguenay River, which flows 160 kilometres (100 mi.) east from lac St-Jean to the St. Lawrence River.

The Saguenay begins as a series of rapids tumbling out of the lake. The river then passes Chicoutimi's aluminum smelters, slices through the sheer, 400-metre-high (1,312-ft.) cliffs of Saguenay Fjord National Park *(see attraction listing p. 456)* and finally empties into a section of the St. Lawrence River, where various species of whales feed. Sightseeing cruises are available during the summer months.

Many of Chicoutimi's galleries contain local arts and crafts. St. Francis Xavier Cathedral (Cathédrale de St-François-Xavier), at Bégin and Racine streets, is known for its stained-glass windows. Nearby lakes and forests provide hunting and fishing opportunities.

In 2002 Chicoutimi amalgamated with Saguenay and is now one of the city's three boroughs, along with Jonquière and La Baie *(see place listings).*

Chicoutimi Tourist Information Bureau: 295 rue Racine Est, C.P. 8266, Chicoutimi, QC, Canada G7H 5B7. **Phone:** (418) 698-3167 or (800) 463-6565.

Self-guiding tours: Maps detailing self-guiding tours of the downtown area are in the guidebooks available at the tourist information bureau.

Shopping areas: Place du Royaume and Place Saguenay on boulevard Talbot together have 330 stores, including Sears.

THE PULPMILL OF CHICOUTIMI REGIONAL MUSEUM AND HISTORICAL SITE (La Pulperie de Chicoutimi lieu historique et musée) is 1 km (.6 mi.) s.w. of Pont Dubuc, following signs to 300 rue Dubuc. On the grounds are the remains of the Chicoutimi Pulp Co., founded in 1896, a regional museum and two restored stone buildings of architectural distinction. Also here is the former home of noted folk artist Arthur Villeneuve, who began his career by painting his house with scenes of his life and regional history. The interpretive center offers interactive displays dealing with history.

Guided tours are available; reservations are required for narration in English. Self-guiding audio tours are available for a fee. **Time:** Allow 2 hours minimum. **Hours:** Historic site and museum daily 9-6, June 23-Labour Day; museum only Wed.-Sun. 10-4, rest of year. Closed Jan. 1, Christmas Eve, Christmas and Dec. 31. Last admission 1 hour before closing, June 23-Labour Day. Phone ahead to confirm schedule.

Cost: Grounds free. Museum $12; $9.50 (ages 65+); $6.50 (students with ID); $4 (ages 5-17); $28 (family, two adults and two children, $2 for each additional child); $25 (family, two adults and one child). Prices may vary. **Phone:** (418) 698-3100 or (877) 998-3100.

SAFETY VILLAGE (Village de la Sécurité) is 5 km (3 mi.) n. via Pont Dubuc, following signs to 200 rue Pinel. At this miniaturized town, the buildings, cars and streets have been scaled down to a child's perspective. Animated activities and theatrical plays educate young visitors about responsibility. Kids also learn how to respond to various emergency situations.

Time: Allow 1 hour minimum. **Hours:** Daily 9:30-5:30, mid-June to late Aug.; otherwise by appointment. Last admission 2 hours, 30 minutes before closing. Phone ahead to confirm schedule. **Cost:** $8 (ages 2-14); $6 (adults). **Phone:** (418) 545-6925 or (888) 595-6925.

COMFORT INN

Hotel
$89-$127

Phone: (418)693-8686

Address: 1595 boul Talbot G7H 4C3 **Location:** Jct Rt 170, 1.8 mi (2.8 km) n. **Facility:** 80 units. 2 stories, interior corridors. **Parking:** winter plug-ins. **Terms:** 4 night minimum stay, cancellation fee imposed. **Guest Services:** valet laundry.

HOTEL LA SAGUENÉENNE

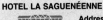

Hotel
$99-$172

Phone: (418)545-8326

Address: 250 des Sagueneens G7H 3A4 **Location:** Just w of jct Rt 175 (boul Talbot); in Saguenay sector. Located in a commercial area. **Facility:** 118 units. 4 stories, interior corridors. **Parking:** winter plug-ins. **Amenities:** safes. **Pool(s):** heated indoor. **Activities:** sauna, whirlpools, lifeguard on duty, snowmobiling, exercise room. **Guest Services:** valet laundry. **Free Special Amenities:** local telephone calls and high-speed Internet.

(See ad opposite title page.)

LE MONTAGNAIS-HOTEL & CENTRE DE CONGRÈS

Phone: 418/543-1521

Hotel
$115-$140 6/1-8/21
$115-$130 8/22-5/31

Address: 1080 boul Talbot G7H 3B6 **Location:** On Rt 175. **Facility:** 296 units. 2-6 stories, interior/exterior corridors. **Parking:** winter plug-ins. **Amenities:** high-speed Internet. *Some:* safes. **Dining:** 2 restaurants. **Pool(s):** heated outdoor, heated indoor. **Activities:** saunas, whirlpools, steamroom, waterslide, lifeguard on duty, playground, shuffleboard, exercise room, spa. *Fee:* game room. **Guest Services:** valet laundry.

WHERE TO EAT

INTERNATIONAL CAFÉ

International
$9-$27

Phone: 418/690-5129

AAA Inspector Notes: This lively bistro-pub offers an internationally inspired menu of creatively presented comfort foods such as beef or lamb burgers, tartares, tempura shrimp, fajitas, pasta, risotto, Thai food, General Tao chicken and foie gras. The ambience is relaxed and the decor decidedly exotic. **Bar:** full bar. **Address:** 460 rue Racine est G7H 1T7 **Location:** Corner of rue Begin; centre; in Hotel Chicoutimi.

LA BOUGRESSE

French
$12-$35

Phone: 418/543-3178

AAA Inspector Notes: Wholesome, reasonably priced food-such as Quebec veal, steak and fries, sweetbreads, mussels, lamb and filet mignon-is the restaurant's clear strength. The stylish contemporary bistro boasts a lively atmosphere. Service is pleasant and professional. **Bar:** full bar. **Reservations:** suggested. **Address:** 260 rue Riverin G7H 4R4 **Location:** Corner of rue Hotel Dieu; centre.

ST-HUBERT

Canadian
$8-$22

Phone: 418/545-4104

AAA Inspector Notes: The pleasantly decorated family-friendly restaurant serves affordable chicken dinners, ribs, club sandwiches, chicken wings, salads, soups and hot chicken sandwiches. The children's menu includes animal nuggets. **Bar:** full bar. **Address:** 939 boul Talbot G7H 4B5 **Location:** Centre.

SCORES ROTISSERIE

Canadian
$8-$20

Phone: 418/543-3000

AAA Inspector Notes: Those for whom cholesterol isn't a concern should consider a side dish of poutine--a greasily good Quebec specialty of french fries, melted cheese curds and gravy--with their preference among Scores Rotisserie's favorites, which include rotisserie chicken dishes, baby back ribs, sandwiches and preparations from the all-you-can-eat soup and salad bar. Although lemon pie, cakes and brownies beckon for dessert, another Quebec staple, tarte au sucre ("sugar pie"), merits extra consideration. **Bar:** full bar. **Address:** 1870 boul Talbot G7H 7Y2 **Location:** Centre.

COATICOOK (F-5) pop. 9,204

The banks of the Coaticook River were first settled about 1750 by the Abenaki Indians, who named the site Koatikeku, or "river of the land of the pines." The town of Coaticook, incorporated in 1888, is a center of light manufacturing and area industries and services.

Coaticook Tourist Information Bureau: 137 rue Michaud, Coaticook, QC, Canada J1A 1A9. **Phone:** (819) 849-6669 or (866) 665-6669.

COATICOOK RIVER GORGE PARK (Parc de la Gorge de Coaticook) is at 135 rue Michaud. A 3.5-kilometre (2 mi.) trail with wooden steps and a suspension bridge parallels the preglacial gorge with cliffs rising to 50 metres (164 ft.). A playground also is on-site.

Note: The steep terrain may be difficult for some to negotiate. Nonslip walking shoes are required. Guided tours in English are available. **Hours:** Tours are offered daily 9-7, June 24-day before Labour Day; 10-5, first weekend in May-June 23 and Labour Day-last week in Oct. **Cost:** $7.50; $4.50 (ages 6-15). Reservations are required for guided tours. **Phone:** (819) 849-2331.

COMPTON (F-9) pop. 3,047

LOUIS S. ST. LAURENT NATIONAL HISTORIC SITE (Lieu historique national Louis-S.-St-Laurent) is at 6790 Rte. Louis S. St. Laurent (Hwy. 147). The site consists of the house in which Louis S. St. Laurent, prime minister of Canada 1948-57, was born, and his father's general store, where audiotapes recreate the passionate political discussions that often took place there. Visitors glimpse the atmosphere of the rural way of life in the early 20th century. A sound and light show recalls St. Laurent's career as a lawyer and politician.

Time: Allow 1 hour, 30 minutes minimum. **Hours:** Daily 10-5, mid-May to late Aug.; daily 10-noon and 1-5, late Aug.-late Sept.; Sat.-Sun. 10-noon and 1-5, late Sept. to mid-Oct. **Cost:** $3.90; $3.40 (ages 66+); $1.90 (ages 6-16); $9.80 (family). **Phone:** (819) 835-5448 or (888) 773-8888.

COOKSHIRE-EATON (F-9) pop. 5,004

COMPTON COUNTY HISTORICAL SOCIETY MUSEUM (Musée de la Société d'histoire du Comté de Compton), at 374 RR 253, is housed in a former

Congregational church built in 1841 and the Eaton Academy. The church displays local artifacts and period furniture; the schoolhouse contains agricultural equipment and utensils. An archive stores books about the history of the Eastern Townships. **Time:** Allow 1 hour, 30 minutes minimum. **Hours:** Wed.-Fri. 1-5, June-Aug.; Sat.-Sun. 1-5, in Sept. **Cost:** $5; $4 (senior citizens); $3 (ages 6-17). **Phone:** (819) 875-5256.

COTEAU-DU-LAC (F-6) pop. 6,346

A resort community on the St. Lawrence River, Coteau-du-Lac is in an agricultural region known for its dairy and pig farms. Not far from the river is a small hill *(coteau)* on which a church was built—hence the town's name.

COTEAU-DU-LAC NATIONAL HISTORIC SITE (Lieu historique national de Coteau-du-Lac) is 1.5 km (.9 mi.) s. off Hwy. 20 exit 17, then 2 km (1.2 mi.) s. on rue Principale to 308 A ch. du Fleuve. This was the location of Canada's first lock canal, built in 1779. During the War of 1812, a British military post was built here; it defended the site until the mid-19th century. Of interest are the remaining canal and fortifications foundations as well as a reconstructed octagonal blockhouse that contains historical items.

Guided tours are available; narration in English is offered. **Hours:** Daily 10-5, May 24-early Sept.; Sat.-Sun. 10-5, early Sept.-early Oct. **Cost:** $3.90; $3.40 (ages 66+); $1.90 (ages 6-16); $9.80 (family). **Phone:** (450) 763-5631 or (888) 773-8888.

CHEZ LES DE VILLEMURE   **Phone:** 450/763-5743

French
$17-$39

AAA Inspector Notes: Decorated with flowers, fireplaces and wood accents, the cozy restaurant exudes a warm, country-style ambience. Interesting regional preparations of ostrich, bison, duck, deer and veal liver combine with fresh fish, roast beef and steak dishes on the diverse menu. The family-run restaurant has been in operation since 1946. **Bar:** full bar. **Reservations:** suggested. **Address:** 7 rue Principale J0P 1B0 **Location:** Hwy 20 exit 17, 0.6 mi (1 km) s. **Parking:** street only. D

CÔTE ST-LUC pop. 31,395

• **Hotels & Restaurants map & index p. 342**
• **Part of Montréal area — see map p. 312**

ERNIE & ELLIE'S RESTAURANT
   Phone: 514/344-4444   88

Kosher
$8-$25

AAA Inspector Notes: In a shopping mall, this glatt kosher restaurant prepares kosher Chinese dishes, rib steaks, roasted chicken, chicken soup, ribs, sandwiches, split franks, grilled fish and burgers. This place closes for Sabbath observance. Take-out service is available. **Bar:** full bar. **Reservations:** suggested. **Address:** 6900 Decarie boul H3X 2T8 **Location:** Just e of Hwy 15 (Decarie Expwy); corner of Vezina; in Decor Decarie Shopping Mall. L D

COWANSVILLE (F-8) pop. 12,182, elev. 126m/416'

WINERIES

• **Les Diurnes Vineyard** (Vignoble Les Diurnes) is 1.7 km (1.1 mi.) w. on rue de la Rivière, just s.w.

toward boul. Jean-Jacques Bertrand, .5 km (.3 mi.) s. on boul. Jean-Jacques Bertrand, 1.2 km (.8 mi.) w. on rue Beaumont, then just n. to 205 Montée Lebeau. Guided tours are available by appointment. **Hours:** Mon.-Fri. 10-6, May-Oct.; by appointment rest of year. **Phone:** (450) 263-1526.

AUBERGE DES CARREFOURS   **Phone:** 450/263-7331

Hotel
Rates not provided

Address: 111 Place Jean-Jacques Bertrand J2K 3R5 **Location:** Hwy 10 exit 68, 9.9 mi (15.9 km) s on Rt 139. **Facility:** 32 units. 3 stories (no elevator); interior corridors. **Amenities:** high-speed Internet. **Dining:** Restaurant des Chefs, see separate listing. **Guest Services:** valet laundry.

WHERE TO EAT

RESTAURANT DES CHEFS   **Phone:** 450/263-7331

Canadian
$8-$36

AAA Inspector Notes: The cozy and rustic wood-paneled interior is in keeping with the hotel restaurant's rural surroundings. When it's cold outside, the fireplace adds to the ambience. The menu focuses on popular comfort foods, including Angus roast beef, sandwiches, pasta dishes, steak and seafood. Buffets are offered on some days. **Bar:** full bar. **Address:** 111 Place Jean-Jacques-Bertrand J2K 3R5 **Location:** Hwy 10 exit 68, 9.9 mi (15.9 km) s on Rt 139; in Auberge des Carrefours. B L D

DANVILLE pop. 4,041

RESTAURANT LE TEMPS DES CERISES
   Phone: 819/839-2818

Regional French
$12-$27

AAA Inspector Notes: In a renovated rural church, this informal dining room serves creative regional cuisine and delicious desserts. **Bar:** full bar. **Address:** 79 rue du Carmel J0A 1A0 **Location:** 0.4 mi (0.7 km) s on rue Daniel-Johnson from jct Rt 116, then just w; centre. L D

DESBIENS (C-5) pop. 1,074

THE MÉTABETCHOUANE HISTORICAL AND ARCHAEOLOGICAL CENTRE (Centre d'histoire et d'archéologie de la Métabetchouane), 234 rue Hébert, relates the story of the first encounter between the area's indigenous peoples and French explorers and trappers. On the grounds are replicas of the 1847 Hudson's Bay Co. trading post, a chapel and a historic powder magazine.

Guided tours are available; reservations are required for narration in English. **Time:** Allow 1 hour minimum. **Hours:** Daily 10-5, June 24-Labour Day. **Cost:** $7; $3 (ages 4-12). **Phone:** (418) 346-5341.

THE HOLE OF THE FAIRY CAVE (Caverne Trou de la fée) is 5.5 km (3.5 mi.) w. on 7th av. Docents lead guided tours of the site's impressive underground cavern. Visitors also can traverse gravel walking trails to view two impressive sets of waterfalls and the ruins of a 1922 concrete river dam.

Note: Visitors to the cavern must be physically agile and not inhibited by claustrophobia, as the cavern has narrow and rocky passages, and 101 steep steps that descend 68 metres (228 ft.). Bats and mice live in the cave and may be encountered during the tour. The underground temperature remains a damp 4-6 degrees Celsius (39-43 degrees Fahrenheit); warm clothing and comfortable walking shoes are recommended. Tour narration in English is available by reservation.

Time: Allow 3 hours minimum. **Hours:** Daily 9-7, mid-June to mid-Aug.; 10-6, mid-Aug. through Sept. 30; 10-6 (hiking only), Oct. 1-8. Last admission 2 hours before closing. **Cost:** Park admission and cave tour $18; $11 (ages 4-11). Park admission only $12; $6 (ages 4-11). Under 4 are not permitted in the cave. Cash only. **Phone:** (418) 346-1242.

DOLLARD-DES-ORMEAUX pop. 48,930
- Hotels & Restaurants map & index p. 342
- Part of Montréal area — see map p. 312

ABIE'S SMOKED MEAT & STEAK
Phone: 514/626-2243

Deli
$8-$18

AAA Inspector Notes: This suburban deli is known for its Montreal-style smoked meat, as well as a variety of classic deli favorites including potato latkes, matzo ball soup, chopped liver and rib steaks. **Bar:** beer only. **Address:** 3980 boul St-Jean H9G 1X1 **Location:** Hwy 40 exit 52, 0.9 mi (1.4 km) n. [L] [D]

BATON ROUGE
Phone: 514/626-6440

American
$10-$35

AAA Inspector Notes: This one offers an intimate setting with a casual steakhouse ambiance. Offerings include their signature BBQ pork ribs, fresh grilled fish, chicken, meal-sized salads, pasta, burgers and sandwiches. But the main attraction remains the aged AAA grade steaks and the slow-roasted prime rib of beef. **Bar:** full bar. **Reservations:** required. **Address:** 3839 boul St-Jean H9G 1X2 **Location:** Hwy 40 exit 52, 0.8 mi (1.3 km) n.

DUNNS FAMOUS DELICATESSEN
Phone: 514/472-0049

Deli
$7-$27

AAA Inspector Notes: This popular deli franchise brings to the suburbs the smoked meat made famous at the original downtown Montreal restaurant. Among specialties are rib steaks, Montreal-style smoked meat on rye, matzo ball soup and hearty breakfasts. The family-friendly setting features classic deli booth seating and friendly service. **Bar:** full bar. **Address:** 3360 boul des Sources H9B 1Z9 **Location:** Hwy 40 exit 55 (boul des Sources), 0.4 mi (0.6 km) n. [L] [D] [LATE]

MADISONS NEW YORK GRILL & BAR
Phone: 514/421-9292

Steak
$10-$30

AAA Inspector Notes: This lively suburban Montreal pub and steakhouse has comfortable chairs and private leather-upholstered booths. The grill menu offers fresh seafood, filet mignon, rib steaks, milk-fed veal, roast beef, ribs, grilled chicken, burgers and giant shrimp as well as shrimp cocktail, salmon salad, Caesar salad and a choice of sandwiches, including club, crab or red tuna. **Bar:** full bar. **Address:** 11590 boul de Salaberry H9B 2R8 **Location:** Hwy 40 exit 55 (boul des Sources), 0.6 mi (1 km) nw, then just sw. [L] [D]

RESTAURANT AIKAWA
Phone: 514/684-4333

Japanese
$12-$26

AAA Inspector Notes: This chic sushi bar offers an extensive choice of sushi, sashimi and sushi maki menu items and many flavorful eye-catching specialty dishes, including a few dessert sushi selections. Delivery and take out are available. **Bar:** full bar. **Address:** 55 ave Brunswick H9B 1P7 **Location:** Hwy 40 exit 55 (boul des Sources), just n, then just e; in Promenades des Sources. [L] [D]

SCORES ROTISSERIE
Phone: 514/626-6060

Canadian
$8-$20

AAA Inspector Notes: Those for whom cholesterol isn't a concern should consider a side dish of poutine--a greasily good Quebec specialty of french fries, melted cheese curds and gravy--with their preference among Scores Rotisserie's favorites, which include rotisserie chicken dishes, baby back ribs, sandwiches and preparations from the all-you-can-eat soup and salad bar. Although lemon pie, cakes and brownies beckon for dessert, another Quebec staple, tarte au sucre ("sugar pie"), merits extra consideration. **Bar:** full bar. **Reservations:** required. **Address:** 3612 boul St-Jean H9G 1X1 **Location:** Hwy 40 exit 52 (St-Jean nord), 0.6 mi (1 km) n. [L] [D]

DORVAL pop. 17,600
- Restaurants p. 281
- Hotels & Restaurants map & index p. 342
- Part of Montréal area — see map p. 312

ALOFT MONTREAL AIRPORT

Phone: (514)633-0900 **64**

Hotel
$99-$229

 AAA Benefit: Enjoy the new twist, get up to 15% off + Starwood Preferred Guest® bonuses.

Address: 500 ave McMillan H9P 0A2 **Location:** Just n of Hwy 520 on north side service road at airport entrance. **Facility:** 136 units. 5 stories, interior corridors. *Bath:* shower only. **Parking:** on-site (fee), winter plug-ins. **Terms:** cancellation fee imposed. **Amenities:** high-speed Internet, safes. **Pool(s):** heated indoor. **Activities:** exercise room. **Guest Services:** valet and coin laundry, area transportation-Dorval train station. **Free Special Amenities:** high-speed Internet and airport transportation. *(See ad this page.)*

BEST WESTERN PLUS MONTREAL AIRPORT HOTEL

Phone: (514)631-4811 **65**

Hotel
$130-$140

AAA Benefit: Members save up to 20%, plus 10% bonus points with Best Western Rewards®.

Address: 13000 Cote de Liesse H9P 1B8 **Location:** Jct Hwy 20 and 520, follow signs for Montreal-Pierre Elliott Trudeau International Airport. **Facility:** 173 units. 3 stories, interior corridors. **Parking:** winter plug-ins. **Dining:** 2 restaurants. **Pool(s):** heated indoor. **Activities:** exercise room, spa. *Fee:* sauna. **Guest Services:** valet and coin laundry, area transportation-Dorval train station. **Free Special Amenities:** local telephone calls and high-speed Internet.

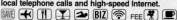

COMFORT INN DORVAL

Phone: (514)636-3391 **61**

Hotel
$95-$225

Address: 340 ave Michel-Jasmin H9P 1C1 **Location:** Hwy 520 exit 2 eastbound; exit 1 westbound, just e along service road to ave Marshall, follow to ave Michel-Jasmin. **Facility:** 97 units. 2 stories, interior corridors. **Parking:** winter plug-ins. **Terms:** cancellation fee imposed. **Amenities:** high-speed Internet. **Guest Services:** valet and coin laundry.

▼ See AAA listing this page ▼

Simply Reliable

The Diamond Ratings in this TourBook guide are backed by our expert, in-person evaluations, whether the hotel or restaurant is no-frills, moderate or upscale.

Learn more at **AAA.com/Diamonds**

(See map & index p. 342.)

HAMPTON INN & SUITES BY HILTON MONTREAL (DORVAL)
Phone: 514/633-8243   60

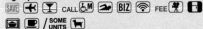

▽▽▽▽
Hotel
Rates not provided

AAA Benefit: Members save up to 10% everyday!

Address: 1900 Rt Transcanadienne (Hwy 40) H9P 2N4 **Location:** Hwy 40 exit 55, 0.5 mi (0.8 km) e of boul des Sources on south side service road. **Facility:** 143 units. 4 stories, interior corridors. **Parking:** winter plug-ins. **Amenities:** high-speed Internet. **Pool(s):** heated indoor. **Activities:** exercise room. **Guest Services:** valet and coin laundry, area transportation-Dorval train station. **Free Special Amenities:** expanded continental breakfast and high-speed Internet.

[SAVE] [↦] [Y] CALL [&M] [↝] [BIZ] [�] FEE [📹] [🛏] / SOME UNITS [🐕]

MARRIOTT FAIRFIELD INN & SUITES AEROPORT DE MONTREAL AIRPORT
Phone: (514)631-2424   66

▽▽▽▽
Hotel
$107-$143

FAIRFIELD INN & SUITES Marriott
AAA Benefit: AAA hotel discounts of 5% or more.

Address: 700 ave Michel-Jasmin H9P 1C5 **Location:** Jct Hwy 20 and 520, follow signs for airport. **Facility:** 162 units. 9 stories, interior corridors. **Parking:** on-site (fee), winter plug-ins. **Amenities:** high-speed Internet. *Some:* safes. **Pool(s):** heated indoor. **Activities:** exercise room. **Guest Services:** valet and coin laundry, area transportation-Dorval train station. **Free Special Amenities:** expanded continental breakfast and airport transportation.

[SAVE] [↦] [Y|] [Y] CALL [&M] [↝] [BIZ] [⌐globe] [✗]
FEE [📹] [🛏] / SOME UNITS [🐕] [🛏]

▼ See AAA listing p. 281 ▼

LET YOUR EXPECTATIONS SOAR

10% Off
single/double
Based on Availability, for AAA Members only

- Guestrooms equipped with a small fridge and coffee & tea
- Indoor pool, whirlpool, spa and gym
- Bijou Bar, café illy, 24-hour in-room dining
- 20 minutes to downtown
- Inside Montréal Airport

MONTREAL AIRPORT MARRIOTT
Marriott 800 Place
Leigh Capreol Dorval, QC H4Y 0A4 CAN
Phone 514.636.6700
www.montrealairportmarriott.com

Marriott.
MONTRÉAL AIRPORT

For information or to make reservations,
call 1-866-580-6279 or visit
www.montrealairportmarriott.com.

Four Diamond
▽▽▽▽
Award

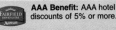

▼ See AAA listing p. 281 ▼

Sunday Mornings are Better when Shared

Sheraton
Montreal Airport
HOTEL

Located less than 2 minutes from Montréal's Pierre Elliott Trudeau Int'l Airport by 24 hour complimentary shuttle. Just a short drive to the West Island business district, 2 minutes from the Via Rail train station and only a 20 minutes drive to downtown Montreal. This airport hotel features 470 guest rooms, an in/outdoor saltwater swimming pool, a fully equipped gym and spa and even yoga. Fully renovated property.

Scan to get Closer to us and see our special offers.

Get the free mobile app at
http://gettag.mobi

10%
Discount

Based on availability

Book at Sheraton.com/AAA or call 1 866 961 3779

spg*
Starwood
Preferred
Guest

Show Your Card & Save

Plan. Map. Go.

TripTik® Travel Planner

Where premier mapping technology meets complete travel information. Only on AAA.com and CAA.ca.

(See map & index p. 342.)

MONTREAL AIRPORT MARRIOTT
Phone: (514)636-6700   **62**

Hotel
$149-$359

Marriott HOTELS & RESORTS
AAA Benefit: AAA hotel discounts of 5% or more.

Address: 800 Place Leigh Capreol H4Y 0A4 **Location:** Jct Hwy 20 and 520, 0.6 mi (1 km) n; in Montreal-Pierre Elliott Trudeau International Airport. **Facility:** Located at the airport, guests enjoy peace and quiet thanks for soundproof windows at this luxury hotel. 279 units. 9 stories, interior corridors. **Parking:** on-site (fee) and valet. **Amenities:** high-speed Internet (fee), safes. **Dining:** Bijou Resto-Bar, see separate listing. **Pool(s):** heated indoor. **Activities:** whirlpool, exercise room, spa. **Guest Services:** valet and coin laundry. *(See ad p. 279.)*

QUALITY INN & SUITES AEROPORT MONTREAL-TRUDEAU
Phone: (514)631-4537   **67**

Hotel
$80-$143

Address: 1010 chemin Herron H9S 1B3 **Location:** Hwy 20 exit 54 westbound, just s on boul Fenelon to ave Dumont, follow to chemin Herron; exit 56 eastbound, 1.1 mi (1.7 km) along service road. **Facility:** 108 units, some efficiencies. 2-3 stories, interior corridors. **Amenities:** video games (fee). **Activities:** saunas, whirlpool, exercise room. **Guest Services:** valet and coin laundry, area transportation-within 3 mi (5 km) & train station. **Free Special Amenities:** expanded continental breakfast and high-speed Internet.

THE SHERATON MONTREAL AIRPORT HOTEL
Phone: (514)631-2411   **63**

Hotel
$169-$249

Ⓢ **Sheraton** HOTELS & RESORTS
AAA Benefit: Members get up to 15% off, plus Starwood Preferred Guest® bonuses.

Address: 12505 boul Cote-de-Liesse H9P 1B7 **Location:** Just n of Hwy 520 on north side service road at airport entrance. **Facility:** This large, oval-shape convention hotel offers very good-size rooms with stylish décor and luxurious bedding, and the windows block out most of the airport noise. 465 units, some two bedrooms. 2-4 stories, interior corridors. **Parking:** on-site (fee). **Terms:** 30 night minimum stay, cancellation fee imposed. **Amenities:** high-speed Internet, safes. **Dining:** Eclipse, see separate listing. **Pool(s):** heated indoor/outdoor. **Activities:** saunas, whirlpool, steamroom, exercise room, spa. **Guest Services:** valet laundry. *(See ad p. 280.)*

Get pet travel tips
and enter the photo contest
at AAA.com/PetBook

WHERE TO EAT

BIJOU RESTO-BAR   **Phone:** 514/828-5117   **105**

French
$15-$35

AAA Inspector Notes: Glass-globe chandeliers and a glass-walled wine cellar give this upscale airport dining room a contemporary feel. Guests move easily from drinks in the adjacent lobby bar to a comfortable, yet casual, dinner of contemporary regional cuisine. **Bar:** full bar. **Reservations:** suggested. **Address:** 800 Place Leigh Capreol H4Y 0A4 **Location:** Jct Hwy 20 and 520, 0.6 mi (1 km) n; in Montreal-Pierre Elliott Trudeau International Airport; in Montreal Airport Marriott. **Parking:** on-site (fee) and valet.

B L D LATE CALL 🖐M

ECLIPSE   **Phone:** 514/631-2411

Continental
$16-$35

Bar: full bar. **Address:** 12505 boul Cote-de-Liesse H9P 1B7 **Location:** Just n of Hwy 520 on north side service road at airport entrance; in The Sheraton Montreal Airport Hotel.

B L D CALL 🖐M

SCORES ROTISSERIE   **Phone:** 514/636-6060

Canadian
$8-$20

AAA Inspector Notes: Those for whom cholesterol isn't a concern should consider a side dish of poutine--a greasily good Quebec specialty of french fries, melted cheese curds and gravy--with their preference among Scores Rotisserie's favorites, which include rotisserie chicken dishes, baby back ribs, sandwiches and preparations from the all-you-can-eat soup and salad bar. Although lemon pie, cakes and brownies beckon for dessert, another Quebec staple, tarte au sucre ("sugar pie"), merits extra consideration. **Bar:** full bar. **Reservations:** required. **Address:** 444 ave Dorval H9S 3H7 **Location:** Hwy 20 exit 55, just s. L D

DRUMMONDVILLE (E-8) pop. 67,392
• Hotels p. 282 • Restaurants p. 283

Founded in 1815, Drummondville took the name of Sir Gordon Drummond, then lieutenant-governor of Upper Canada. Electric power dams on the St-François River and the Hemming Rapids spurred the town's industrial growth.

Drummondville Tourism Bureau: 1350 rue Michaud, Drummondville, QC, Canada J2C 2Z5. **Phone:** (819) 477-5529 or (877) 235-9569.

PIONEER VILLAGE (Village Québécois d'Antan) is 5 km (3 mi.) e. off Autoroute 20 exit 181, following signs to 1425 rue Montplaisir. The living-history village contains 70 buildings dating 1810-1910. The buildings are furnished in period. Costumed interpreters demonstrate the trades and crafts of colonial Québec.

Note: All descriptions and interpretations are in French. **Hours:** Daily 10-5:30, June-Aug.; Fri.-Sun. 10-5:30, in Sept. **Cost:** Admission in 2011 was $23.95; $21.95 (ages 65+); $17.95 (students with ID); $13.95 (ages 4-12); $59.95 (family). Phone ahead for 2012 prices. **Phone:** (877) 710-0267.

VOLTIGEURS CAMPING (Camping des Voltigeurs) is 2 km (1.2 mi.) e. off Autoroute 20 exit 181, following signs to 575 rue Montplaisir. Named after the Québec regiment that defeated an invading American army in the War of 1812, Voltigeurs Park overlooks the St-François River. The recreation complex includes 290 campsites, playgrounds, volleyball and basketball facilities, and a swimming pool. Accessible nearby are 5 kilometres (3 mi.) of bicycle trails. *See Recreation Chart.*

Hours: Park open daily dawn-dusk. Reception desk and campground open daily 8 a.m.-11 p.m., late May-early Sept. **Cost:** A camping fee is charged. **Phone:** (819) 477-1360.

BEST WESTERN PLUS HOTEL UNIVERSEL DRUMMONDVILLE   **Phone:** (819)478-4971

Hotel
$99-$220

AAA Benefit: Members save up to 20%, plus 10% bonus points with Best Western Rewards®.

Address: 915 rue Hains J2C 3A1 **Location:** Hwy 20 exit 177, just s on boul St-Joseph. **Facility:** 115 units. 4 stories, interior corridors. **Parking:** winter plug-ins. **Terms:** check-in 4 pm. **Dining:** Restaurant La Verriere, see separate listing. **Pool(s):** heated indoor. **Activities:** whirlpool. *Fee:* massage. **Guest Services:** valet laundry. **Free Special Amenities:** local telephone calls and high-speed Internet. *(See ad this page.)*

COMFORT INN   **Phone:** (819)477-4000

Hotel
$72-$135

Address: 1055 rue Hains J2C 6G6 **Location:** Hwy 20 exit 177, 0.3 mi (0.5 km) s on boul St-Joseph, then just w. **Facility:** 59 units. 2 stories (no elevator), interior corridors. **Parking:** winter plug-ins. **Terms:** cancellation fee imposed. **Amenities:** high-speed Internet. **Guest Services:** valet laundry.

HOTEL & SUITES LE DAUPHIN   **Phone:** (819)478-4141

Hotel
$99-$150

Address: 600 boul St-Joseph J2C 2C1 **Location:** Hwy 20 exit 177, 0.8 mi (1.3 km) s. **Facility:** 120 units, some kitchens. 1-2 stories, interior/exterior corridors. **Parking:** winter plug-ins. **Terms:** check-in 4 pm. **Amenities:** high-speed Internet. **Pool(s):** heated indoor. **Activities:** exercise room, spa. **Guest Services:** valet and coin laundry.

QUALITY SUITES   **Phone:** (819)472-2700

Hotel
$100-$169

Address: 2125 rue Canadien J2C 7V8 **Location:** Hwy 20 exit 175, just s. **Facility:** 71 units. 4 stories, interior corridors. **Terms:** cancellation fee imposed. **Amenities:** high-speed Internet. **Pool(s):** heated indoor. **Activities:** whirlpool, exercise room. **Guest Services:** valet and coin laundry.

Complete Vacation Planning

AAA.com/Travel and **CAA.ca/Travel** – everything you need to plan and book your vacations, backed by the travel experts at local AAA/CAA offices.

WHERE TO EAT

RESTAURANT LA VERRIERE   **Phone:** 819/478-4971

French
$10-$24

AAA Inspector Notes: This casually elegant hotel restaurant offers a menu of regional French cuisine including filet mignon, frogs' legs, breast of chicken, veal, duck, crab legs, wild game and pasta. A lighter menu is offered at lunch time. **Bar:** full bar. **Address:** 915 rue Hains J2C 3A1 **Location:** Hwy 20 exit 177, just s on boul St-Joseph, then just e; in Best Western Plus Universel. *(See ad p. 282.)* [B] [L] [D]

RESTAURANT NORMANDIN   **Phone:** 819/472-7522

Canadian
$7-$13

AAA Inspector Notes: The family restaurant prepares affordable comfort foods that include roasted chicken, hot chicken sandwiches, pasta, burgers and fries. Take-out service, a children's menu and cutely decorated desserts are among other offerings. **Address:** 130 boul St-Joseph J2C 2A8 **Location:** On Hwy 143. [B] [L] [D]

ST-HUBERT   **Phone:** 819/477-6622

Canadian
$8-$22

AAA Inspector Notes: The pleasantly decorated family-friendly restaurant serves affordable chicken dinners, ribs, club sandwiches, chicken wings, salads, soups and hot chicken sandwiches. The children's menu includes animal nuggets. **Bar:** full bar. **Address:** 125 boul St-Joseph J2C 2A5 **Location:** Hwy 20 exit 177. [L] [D]

SCORES ROTISSERIE   **Phone:** 819/478-5455

Barbecue
$7-$20

AAA Inspector Notes: Those for whom cholesterol isn't a concern should consider a side dish of poutine--a greasily good Quebec specialty of french fries, melted cheese curds and gravy--with their preference among Scores Rotisserie's favorites, which include rotisserie chicken dishes, baby back ribs, sandwiches and preparations from the all-you-can-eat soup and salad bar. Although lemon pie, cakes and brownies beckon for dessert, another Quebec staple, tarte au sucre ("sugar pie"), merits extra consideration. **Bar:** full bar. **Address:** 120 boul St-Joseph J2C 8J5 **Location:** Hwy 20 exit 177, just s. [L] [D]

DUHAMEL-OUEST (D-1) pop. 870

FORT TÉMISCAMINGUE NATIONAL HISTORIC SITE (Lieu historique national du Fort-Témiscamingue) is 6 km (4 mi.) s. via Hwy. 101 at 834 ch. du Vieux-Fort. Visitors learn about the site at the narrows of lac Témiscamingue, which was critical to Algonquin Indians and later to Europeans, who built a fur-trading post here about 1720. While the post operated for nearly 200 years, only the fort's chimneys and cemeteries remain visible today. Costumed docents re-create the past on the Discovery Trail, which features replica Hudson's Bay Co. buildings. An interpretation center with interactive displays also is on-site. The Enchanted Forest is composed of strangely shaped eastern cedars.

Guided tours are available; narration in English is offered. **Time:** Allow 1 hour, 30 minutes minimum. **Hours:** Daily 9-5, mid-June through Labour Day. **Cost:** $4.90; $4.15 (ages 66+ and students with ID); $2.90 (ages 6-16); $11.70 (family). Reservations are recommended for guided tours. **Phone:** (819) 629-3222 or (888) 773-8888. [icons]

FORESTVILLE pop. 3,543

ECONO LODGE   **Phone:** 418/587-2278

Motel
Rates not provided

Address: 5 Rt 138 est G0T 1E0 **Location:** On Rt 138; centre. **Facility:** 55 units. 1 story, interior/exterior corridors. **Parking:** winter plug-ins. **Terms:** check-in 4 pm. **Dining:** Le Danube Bleu, see separate listing. **Guest Services:** valet laundry. [icons] / SOME UNITS [icons]

WHERE TO EAT

LE DANUBE BLEU   **Phone:** 418/587-2278

[diamonds]
Seafood
$8-$30

AAA Inspector Notes: The house specialty catamaran combines cod, sole, halibut, crab, shrimp and scallops in a visually appealing dish. Steak, pasta, seafood sandwiches and fried or roasted chicken round out the menu. A salad bar is offered. The diner has been family-run since 1956, and the adjacent upscale lounge is a popular nightlife spot. **Bar:** full bar. **Address:** 5 Rt 138 est G0T 1E0 **Location:** On Rt 138; centre; in Econo Lodge. [B] [L] [D]

FORILLON NATIONAL PARK OF CANADA (B-9)

Elevations in the park range from sea level at the Gulf of St. Lawrence to 553 metres (1,750 ft.) in the center of the park at a series of four lakes. Refer to AAA/CAA maps for additional elevation information.

Forillon National Park of Canada (Parc national du Canada Forillon) encompasses 244 square kilometres (95 sq. mi.) on the northeast tip of the Gaspé Peninsula and is accessible from Gaspé via Hwy. 132 E. Jagged seaside cliffs, capes, pebbled beach coves, fir covered highlands and ocean terraced lowlands typify park scenery. Of sedimentary origin, geologic formations contain rocks ranging in age from the Ordovician to the Devonian periods.

White-tailed deer, moose, black bears, foxes, beavers, minks and porcupines can be seen from the many hiking trails. The cliffs and headlands are home to colonies of seabirds, including double-crested cormorants, black-legged kittiwakes, black guillemots, razorbills and other marine bird species; during spring and fall many species of migrating birds rest there. Grey and harbor seals bask on offshore rocks, and seven species of whales cavort in the park's bays.

General Information and Activities

The interpretation center near Cap-des-Rosiers offers exhibits and films. Naturalists offer interpretive activities in French; some programs are given in English. Three campgrounds are available, and cross-country skiing, snowshoeing and dog sledding are popular winter pursuits.

The park is open year-round. The interpretation center near Cap-des-Rosiers is open daily 10-5, June 1 to mid-Oct. Reception and information centers at Penouille and L'Anse-au-Griffon are open daily, June 1-Labour Day. Hours vary; phone ahead. *See Recreation Chart.*

ADMISSION to the park is $7.80; $6.80 (ages 66+); $3.90 (ages 6-16); $19.60 (family). Reduced rates are offered off-season. The daily camping fee is $25.50, or $29.40 for a site with electricity.

ADDRESS inquiries to the Park Superintendent, Forillon National Park of Canada, 122 boul. Gaspé, Gaspé, QC, Canada G4X 1A9; phone (418) 368-5505, (888) 773-8888, or (877) 737-3783 for campsite reservations.

FORT-COULONGE (E-2) pop. 1,369

COULONGE WATERFALLS PARK AND ADVENTURE PARK (Parc des Chutes Coulonge et parc d'aventure) is accessible via Hwy. 148, following signs to 100 Promenade du Parc des Chutes. The small site includes a 48-metre (157-ft.) waterfall, a 762-metre (2,500-ft.) canyon and a 1-kilometre (0.6-mi.) walking trail. The Adventure Park features a variety of zipline adventures, including eight tree-to-tree ziplines and a children's obstacle course, and the VIA Ferrata rock climbing trail.

Time: Allow 1 hour, 30 minutes minimum. **Hours:** Grounds daily 10-5, May 1 to mid-Oct. Phone ahead to confirm schedule. **Cost:** Grounds $7; $5 (ages 12-16 and 65+); $4 (ages 4-11); $20 (family). Prices for zipline courses vary, and reservations are required. **Phone:** (819) 683-2770.

FORT LENNOX NATIONAL HISTORIC SITE (F-8)

The 81-hectare (200-acre) Fort Lennox National Historic Site (Lieu historique national du Fort-Lennox) is accessible via St-Paul-de-l'Île-aux-Noix, about 19 km (12 mi.) s. of St-Jean-sur-Richelieu. The well-preserved buildings of Fort Lennox, one of the largest forts built in Canada, sit at the south end of Île aux Noix on the Richelieu River. The island is reached by ferry, which departs from the visitor center on the mainland every 30 minutes on the quarter-hour.

The first fortifications were begun by the French in 1759 during the Seven Years' War to resist the advance of the British, who captured and destroyed the fort the following year. In 1775 the island was occupied by American troops under generals Richard Montgomery and Philip Schuyler. After the Americans evacuated the island in 1776, the British built stronger fortifications. During the War of 1812, the British established a shipyard and the island became a naval base.

Between 1819 and 1829 a new fort was constructed; the complex was named for Charles Lennox, Duke of Richmond. The fort was garrisoned for many years, but the British finally abandoned it in 1870. Among the massive stone buildings are the officers' quarters, guardhouse, powder magazine,

barracks and commissary. Narrated tours are available. Picnicking is permitted.

Daily 10-5, mid-May through Labour Day; Sat.-Sun. 10-6, day after Labour Day to mid-Oct. Phone ahead to confirm schedule. Admission $7.80; $6.70 (ages 66+); $3.90 (ages 6-16); $19.50 (family). Prices may vary. Phone (450) 291-5700 or (888) 773-8888.

GASPÉ (B-9) pop. 14,819

At the eastern extremity of the Gaspé Peninsula, the town of Gaspé adjoins the mouth of the York River and overlooks an immense natural harbor. Explorer Jacques Cartier sailed into this bay in 1534 with two ships, and upon landing erected a cross claiming Canada for France. The word Gaspé is derived from the Micmac Indian word *gespeg,* meaning "land's end."

Commemorating the French explorer's landing is the Jacques Cartier Monument, 2 kilometres (1.2 mi.) north on Hwy. 132, across from The Museum of Gaspésie *(see attraction listing).* Six slabs shaped like dolmens recall Cartier's Breton heritage and depict the events of his landing; phone (418) 368-1534.

Gaspé lies along the scenic portion of Hwy. 132, which follows the tip of the Gaspé Peninsula from Ste-Anne-des-Monts on the northern coast to Grand-Rivière on the southern coast.

Gaspé Tourist Information Bureau: 27 York Est, Gaspé, QC, Canada G4X 2K9. **Phone:** (418) 368-6335.

THE MUSEUM OF GASPÉSIE (Musée de la Gaspésie), 80 boul. de Gaspé, presents exhibits about the history of the region and works by local artists. On-site are an archive center, an impressive source of Gaspésian cultural and genealogical information, and a monument dedicated to Jacques Cartier. Audio guides describing the historical interpretation trail on the grounds are available for rent.

Guided tours are available if requested a minimum of 1 week in advance. **Time:** Allow 30 minutes minimum. **Hours:** Daily 9-5, June-Oct.; Mon.-Fri. 9-noon and 1-5, Sat. 1-5, rest of year. **Cost:** $8.50; $6.50 (ages 12-18 and 65+); $14.25 (family). **Phone:** (418) 368-1534.

MOTEL ADAMS   **Phone:** (418)368-2244

Motel
$88-$154

Address: 20 rue Adams G4X 2R8 **Location:** Corner of rue Jacques Cartier; centre. **Facility:** 96 units. 2 stories (no elevator), interior/exterior corridors. **Parking:** winter plug-ins. **Terms:** check-in 4 pm, 3 day cancellation notice. **Dining:** Adams Restaurant, see separate listing. **Guest Services:** coin laundry. 🍽 📶 ✉ 🛗 💻

WHERE TO EAT

ADAMS RESTAURANT
Menu on AAA.com

▽▽ ▽▽
Canadian
$8-$25

Phone: 418/368-4949

AAA Inspector Notes: This family-run diner serves a variety of wholesome meals at great prices. Menu items include fresh fish, other seafood, hamburgers, pasta, salads and sandwiches. House-prepared pies are a wise choice for dessert. **Bar:** full bar. **Address:** 20 rue Adams G4X 2R8 **Location:** Corner of rue Jacques Cartier; centre; in Motel Adams. B L D

GASPÉ PENINSULA (C-8)

Approaching the Gaspé Peninsula on his 1534 first voyage to North America, Jacques Cartier enjoyed one of the most spectacular views on the continent: sheer cliffs battered by the sea, clouds of seabirds and craggy mountains covered with forests.

Bounded by the Gulf of St. Lawrence to the northeast, the St. Lawrence River and Cap-Chat to the north and Matapédia and the Baie des Chaleurs to the south, the Gaspé is circled by an 885-kilometre (553-mi.) section of Hwy. 132.

French-Canadian fishermen have molded the history of the peninsula's rugged north shore; villages shelter in the coves and display their catches drying on *vigneau* racks. Acadian, Basque, Loyalist and Micmac Indian communities as well as fashionable resorts give the south shore a cosmopolitan flavor.

Forming a 1,268-metre-high (4,160-ft.) backdrop, the Chic-Chocs Mountains of the peninsula's interior shelter herds of moose and rare woodland caribou inside Gaspésie National Park *(see attraction listing p. 470)*. At the northeastern tip of the peninsula, the Chic-Chocs meet the sea in Forillon National Park of Canada *(see place listing p. 283)*.

Towns listed individually on the Gaspé Peninsula are Bonaventure, Cap-Chat, Causapscal, Gaspé, Grand-Métis, Murdochville, Percé, Pointe-à-la-Croix and Ste-Anne-des-Monts. Another town worth visiting is New-Carlisle, a picturesque Loyalist village.

GATINEAU (E-3) pop. 242,124
• Restaurants p. 287

Part of the National Capital Region, Gatineau is one of the oldest settlements in the area. In 1800 Philemon Wright arrived from Woburn, Mass., with his family and a number of townspeople and soon established the timber trade that sustained the region for more than a century. The E.B. Eddy Co., a pulp and paper products factory integral to the city's main industry, was built then.

Several parks offer recreational facilities and picnic areas. The city also offers an array of cultural activities as well as such special events as the ▽ Casino du Lac-Leamy Sound of Light, a musical fireworks show and competition held in August. The Wings Over Gatineau air show and the Gatineau Hot Air Balloon Festival both take place in September.

Outaouais Tourism: 103 rue Laurier, Gatineau, QC, Canada J8X 3V8. **Phone:** (819) 778-2222 or (800) 265-7822.

Shopping areas: Three shopping malls serve the Gatineau area. Les Galeries de Hull, 320 boul. St-Joseph, has 70 stores; Les Promenades de l'Outaouais, 1100 boul. Maloney Ouest, has 200 stores; and Place du Centre, 200 Promenade du Portage, has 60 stores.

▽ **CANADIAN MUSEUM OF CIVILIZATION**
(Musée canadien des civilisations) is at 100 rue Laurier. The museum, located directly across the Ottawa River from the Parliament Buildings, illustrates Canada's history from the continent's prehistoric beginnings through successive periods of migration, native settlement, exploration, fur trading, immigration and the modern era.

Life-size reconstructions such as a West Coast native village and other historic sites present a dramatic interpretation of the country's past. Other highlights include the Canadian Children's Museum, the Canadian Postal Museum and an IMAX theater.

Hours: Mon.-Fri. 9-6 (also Thurs.-Fri. 6-8 p.m.), Sat.-Sun. 9:30-6, July 1-Labour Day; Mon.-Fri. 9-6 (also Thurs. 6-8 p.m.), Sat.-Sun. 9:30-6, May-June and Labour Day-second Mon. in Oct.; Mon.-Fri. 9-5 (also Thurs. 5-8), Sat.-Sun. 9:30-5, rest of year. The IMAX schedule does not always correspond with museum schedule; phone ahead for show times. Closed Christmas.

Cost: Museum admission $12. One IMAX film $10; $8 (ages 3-12); $30 (family, two adults and three children). Combination ticket (includes museum admission and one IMAX film) $18; $15 (ages 65+ and students with ID); $12 (ages 3-12). Other combination tickets are available. Prices may vary. **Phone:** (819) 776-7000, (819) 776-7010 for show times, (800) 555-5621 or TTY (819) 776-7003. ⊞

▽ **GATINEAU PARK**—see Chelsea p. 273.

GAMBLING ESTABLISHMENTS

• **Casino du Lac-Leamy** is at 1 boul. du Casino. **Hours:** Daily 24 hours. **Phone:** (819) 772-2100 or (800) 665-2274.

BEST WESTERN PLUS GATINEAU-OTTAWA

Phone: (819)770-8550

▽▽▽ ▽▽
Hotel
$109-$199

AAA Benefit: Members save up to 20%, plus 10% bonus points with Best Western Rewards®.

Address: 131 rue Laurier J8X 3W3 **Location:** Between rue St-Laurent and St-Etienne, just e of Alexandria Bridge; in Hull sector. **Facility:** 133 units, some kitchens. 9 stories, interior corridors. **Parking:** on-site (fee). **Terms:** check-in 4 pm. **Pool(s):** heated indoor. **Activities:** exercise room. **Guest Services:** valet laundry. **Free Special Amenities:** local telephone calls and high-speed Internet.

SAVE ECO ⫿⫿ 🍸 🛏 BIZ 🛜 ✕ 🖥
/ SOME UNITS FEE 🗄 FEE 🖵

CHÂTEAU CARTIER

Phone: (819)778-0000

Resort Hotel
$129-$229

Address: 1170 chemin Aylmer J9H 7L3 **Location:** On Rt 148, 0.6 mi (1 km) w of Champlain Bridge; in Aylmer sector. **Facility:** The resort features a spa and extensive recreational facilities, including a golf course bordering the river. Guest rooms are very spacious and feature luxurious bedding. 129 units. 6 stories, interior corridors. **Terms:** check-in 4 pm, cancellation fee imposed. **Amenities:** safes. **Dining:** Ekko de Brasil, see separate listing. **Pool(s):** heated indoor. **Activities:** saunas, steamrooms, racquetball courts, cross country skiing, ice skating, tobogganing, rental bicycles, hiking trails, volleyball, exercise room, spa. *Fee:* golf-18 holes. **Guest Services:** valet laundry. **Free Special Amenities:** local telephone calls and high-speed Internet.

CLARION HOTEL & CONFERENCE CENTRE

Phone: (819)568-5252

Hotel
$105-$130

Address: 111 rue Bellehumeur J8T 6K5 **Location:** Hwy 50 exit 139, 1 mi (1.6 km) se on boul Maloney ouest (Hwy 148), then just sw. **Facility:** 116 units. 2 stories (no elevator), interior corridors. **Parking:** winter plug-ins. **Terms:** cancellation fee imposed. **Amenities:** *Some:* safes, honor bars. **Pool(s):** heated outdoor. **Activities:** spa. *Fee:* saunas, exercise room. **Guest Services:** valet laundry. **Free Special Amenities:** continental breakfast and children's activities.

COMFORT INN GATINEAU

Phone: (819)243-6010

Hotel
$117-$161

Address: 630 boul La Gappe J8T 7S8 **Location:** Hwy 50 exit 140, 1.1 mi (1.9 km) e. **Facility:** 80 units. 2 stories (no elevator), interior corridors. **Parking:** winter plug-ins. **Terms:** check-in 4 pm, cancellation fee imposed. **Amenities:** high-speed Internet. **Guest Services:** valet laundry.

FOUR POINTS BY SHERATON HOTEL & CONFERENCE CENTRE GATINEAU-OTTAWA

Phone: (819)778-6111

Hotel
$99-$240

FOUR POINTS BY SHERATON **AAA Benefit:** Members get up to 15% off, plus Starwood Preferred Guest® bonuses.

Address: 35 rue Laurier J8X 4E9 **Location:** Corner of rue Victoria; across from Canadian Museum of Civilization; in Hull sector. **Facility:** 201 units. 9 stories, interior corridors. **Parking:** on-site (fee). **Terms:** cancellation fee imposed. **Amenities:** video games (fee), high-speed Internet. **Pool(s):** heated indoor. **Activities:** exercise room. **Guest Services:** valet laundry. **Free Special Amenities:** local telephone calls and high-speed Internet.

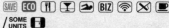

HILTON LAC-LEAMY

Phone: 819/790-6444

Hotel
Rates not provided

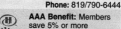 **AAA Benefit:** Members save 5% or more everyday!

Address: 3 boul du Casino J8Y 6X4 **Location:** In Casino du Lac Leamy; in Hull sector. **Facility:** In addition to impressive banquet rooms, this upscale casino hotel has elegant guest rooms with marble baths and one or two beds. 349 units. 20 stories, interior corridors. **Parking:** on-site and valet. **Terms:** check-in 4 pm. **Amenities:** safes, honor bars. *Fee:* video games, high-speed Internet. **Dining:** 4 restaurants, also, Le Baccara, see separate listing, entertainment. **Pool(s):** heated outdoor, heated indoor. **Activities:** sauna, whirlpools, steamrooms, boat dock, 2 lighted tennis courts, cross country skiing, rental bicycles, hiking trails, game room, horseshoes, shuffleboard, volleyball, exercise room, spa. **Guest Services:** valet laundry. **Free Special Amenities:** newspaper.

HOLIDAY INN PLAZA LA CHAUDIÈRE GATINEAU-OTTAWA

Phone: (819)778-3880

Hotel
$129-$159

Address: 2 rue Montcalm J8X 4B4 **Location:** 0.5 mi (0.8 km) w of Portage Bridge at Rt 148 and rue Montcalm; in Hull sector. **Facility:** 232 units, some kitchens. 14 stories, interior corridors. **Parking:** on-site (fee) and street. **Amenities:** safes. *Some:* high-speed Internet. **Pool(s):** heated indoor. **Activities:** saunas, whirlpool, exercise room. **Guest Services:** valet laundry. **Free Special Amenities:** local telephone calls and high-speed Internet.

HOTEL LES SUITES VICTORIA

Phone: (819)777-8899

Hotel
$110-$225

Address: 1 rue Victoria J8X 1Z6 **Location:** 0.3 mi (0.5 km) n of one Laurier from Portage Bridge, just n; in Hull sector. **Facility:** 39 units, some efficiencies and kitchens. 3 stories, interior corridors. **Terms:** check-in 4 pm, cancellation fee imposed. **Amenities:** high-speed Internet. **Guest Services:** valet and coin laundry.

RAMADA PLAZA MANOIR DU CASINO

Phone: (819)777-7538

Hotel
$99-$217

Address: 75 rue d'Edmonton J8Y 6W9 **Location:** Hwy 5 exit 3 (boul du Casino), follow signs; in Hull sector. **Facility:** 174 units. 3 stories, interior corridors. **Parking:** winter plug-ins. **Terms:** check-in 4 pm, cancellation fee imposed. **Amenities:** high-speed Internet. *Some:* safes. **Pool(s):** heated indoor. **Activities:** saunas, whirlpool, limited exercise equipment, spa. **Guest Services:** valet laundry. **Free Special Amenities:** expanded continental breakfast and high-speed Internet.

WHERE TO EAT

CHEZ CORA

Canadian
$7-$13
Phone: 819/771-3561
AAA Inspector Notes: Eggs, omelets, waffles, crepes (sorry, no American-style pancakes here), French toast, fruit platters and all the breakfast meats--that's the specialty here, all day. However, at lunchtime the menu lists a selection of soups, salads, quiches, sandwiches and a dish called the grilled panini crepe. **Address:** 1 rue Gamelin J8Y 1V4 **Location:** Corner of rue St-Joseph; center; in Hull sector. [B] [L]

DELI CHENOY'S

Deli
$10-$25
Phone: 819/561-3354
AAA Inspector Notes: A popular spot for movie-goers, this convenient family deli specializes in Montreal-style smoked meat sandwiches, steaks, seafood and cheesecake. **Bar:** full bar. **Address:** 120 boul de l'Hôpital J8T 8M2 **Location:** Just s of boul Maloney ouest.
[B] [L] [D] [LATE]

EKKO DE BRASIL

Brazilian
$38-$43
Phone: 819/776-7969
AAA Inspector Notes: This restaurant and pub is the ideal place to dine after a day of golf or other outdoor activity while visiting the upscale resort. Guests might start with a drink in the pub before moving into the casual, comfortable dining room. For a fixed price, the menu offers all-you-can-eat Brazilian-style grilled meats cut tableside, in addition to a hot and cold buffet. Be sure to ask about weekend show times for the live Brazilian dancers and their Mardi Gras inspired performance. **Bar:** full bar. **Address:** 1170 chemin Aylmer J9H 5E1 **Location:** On Rt 148, 0.6 mi (1 km) w of Champlain Bridge; in Aylmer sector; in Chateau Cartier. [D]

LE BACCARA
Menu on AAA.com

French
$30-$63
Phone: 819/772-6210
AAA Inspector Notes: Nestled atop Casino du Lac-Leamy, this adult-only dining room has a bank of oversized windows that afford a view of the Ottawa skyline. Custom table settings, fine crystal stemware, an impressive art collection and intuitive service make this a favorite place for special occasions. As guests pass the open kitchen, they can watch the detailed attention given to food preparation. Adding to the experience are contemporary French cuisines and, on some nights, the soothing sounds of a harpist. Semi-formal attire. **Bar:** full bar. **Reservations:** suggested. **Address:** 1 boul du Casino J8Y 6W3 **Location:** In Casino du Lac-Leamy; in Hull sector; in Hilton Lac-Leamy. **Parking:** on-site and valet. [D]

MAISON SAMORN
Thai
$10-$20
Phone: 819/595-0232
AAA Inspector Notes: Thai cuisine is served in a cozy, informal dining room. Among specialties are jumbo shrimp, pad thai, fried rice with seafood, salmon in red curry and a choice of soups. **Bar:** full bar. **Address:** 53 rue Kent J8X 3J9 **Location:** Corner of rue Victoria; in Hull sector. [L] [D]

PAPAYE VERTE
Thai
$11-$20
Phone: 819/777-0404
AAA Inspector Notes: Classic Thai cuisine is served in cozy, upscale dining rooms facing the Museum of Civilization. The menu features Thai soups, meat and seafood dishes, stir-fries, curries and noodle and rice dishes. Combination dish specials are offered daily. The seasonal terrace is popular in summer. **Bar:** full bar. **Address:** 69 rue Laurier J8X 3V7 **Location:** Corner of rue Papineau; in Hull sector; facing Canadian Museum of Civilization. [L] [D]

RESTAURANT LE TARTUFFE

Regional French
$19-$45
Phone: 819/776-6424
AAA Inspector Notes: The vintage Victorian home serves fine regional cuisine, including creative preparations of grilled salmon, braised corn-fed chicken, roasted Barbarie duck breast, stuffed rabbit, roasted red deer, grilled veal chops, Alberta beef and rack of lamb. **Reservations:** suggested. **Address:** 133 Notre-Dame-de-L'Ile J8X 3T2 **Location:** Corner of rue Papineau. **Parking:** street only. [L]

RISTORANTE FIORENTINA

Italian
$15-$27
Phone: 819/770-7273
AAA Inspector Notes: The cozy 1896 Victorian-style home houses several comfortable dining rooms where guests can relax and enjoy a wide variety of home-style dishes. **Bar:** full bar. **Address:** 189 boul St-Joseph J8Y 3X2 **Location:** Just ne of rue Montcalm; in Hull sector. [L] [D]

ST-HUBERT
Canadian
$8-$22
Phone: 819/643-4419
AAA Inspector Notes: The pleasantly decorated family-friendly restaurant serves affordable chicken dinners, ribs, club sandwiches, chicken wings, salads, soups and hot chicken sandwiches. The children's menu includes animal nuggets. **Bar:** full bar. **Address:** 357 boul Maloney ouest J8P 3W1 **Location:** Center. [L] [D]

STERLING GRILLADES & FRUITS DE MER/STEAKHOUSE & SEAFOOD

Steak
$18-$45
Phone: 819/568-8788
AAA Inspector Notes: This vintage waterfront home houses a stylish and contemporary steak and seafood restaurant. Guests can start with a serving of beef tartare, oysters on the half shell, caviar, smoked salmon or duck foie gras terrine. Main courses include clams, snow crab, grilled lobster, fresh fish, veal rib chops, filet mignon, porterhouse or rib steak. **Bar:** full bar. **Address:** 835 rue Jacques-Cartier J8T 2W3 **Location:** Hwy 50 exit 139, 0.6 mi (1 km) se on boul Maloney ouest (Rt 148), then 1.3 mi (2.1 km) sw on Greber Blvd. [L] [D]

GODBOUT (B-7) pop. 361

A fishing village on the North Shore of the Gulf of St. Lawrence, Godbout was the site of an early Hudson's Bay fur-trading post. It is now known among anglers for the salmon fishing opportunities it affords. A ferry service runs between Godbout and Matane; phone (418) 568-7575 for schedules and fares.

AMERINDIAN AND INUIT MUSEUM OF GODBOUT (Musée Amerindian et Inuit de Godbout), 134 rue Pascal-Comeau, presents a collection of recent Indian and Inuit sculpture, small pottery and other artifacts. Visitors can observe artists at work. Artists' schedules vary; phone ahead. **Hours:** Museum open daily 9-9, mid-June to late Sept. **Cost:** $5; $2.50 (ages 5-15). **Phone:** (418) 568-7306.

GRANBY (F-8) pop. 47,637
• Hotels p. 288 • Restaurants p. 288

Situated along the Yamaska River and Lac Boivin, Granby is a growing commercial hub boasting several multipurpose recreational trails, golf courses and parks. While bicycling is among the area's most popular outdoor activities, fishing, cross-country skiing and inline skating also can be enjoyed.

Additionally, the city is well-known for its public art displays and fountains, which include a fountain carved and dug in rock on boulevard Leclerc; "Vision commune," a sculpture by Roger Lapalme in Du Millénaire Park on rue Principale; and a Wallace fountain, symbol of Paris, in Isabel Park at rue Dufferin and boulevard Leclerc.

Tourism Granby: 111 rue Denison Est, Granby, QC, Canada J2G 4C4. **Phone:** (450) 372-7056 or (800) 567-7273.

 GRANBY ZOO (Zoo de Granby), off Autoroute 10 exit 68 or 74 following signs to 1050 boul. David-Bouchard. Visitors observe about 2,000 animals representing nearly 270 species, including African elephants, Amur tigers, gorillas, giraffes and snow leopards. Zookeepers and naturalist guides offer various presentations that describe animal life. The zoo also features an amusement park with such rides as bumper cars, a carousel and a Ferris wheel.

Alcoholic beverages, glass containers and pets are not permitted. **Time:** Allow 3 hours minimum. **Hours:** Opens daily at 10, mid-Feb. to early Mar.; early June-Labour Day and late Dec.-early Jan.; Sat.-Sun. at 10, early Jan. to mid-Feb. and day after Labour Day-second Mon. in Oct.; otherwise varies. Phone ahead for closing times and to confirm all schedules.

Cost: Victoria Day weekend-late Aug. (includes Amazoo Yoplait Water Park) $18.99; $15.99 (ages 65+); $11.99 (ages 3-12); $49.99 (family, two adults and two children). Admission rest of season (zoo only) varies. Two-day combination passes also are available. Under 13 must be with an adult. **Phone:** (877) 472-6299.

Amazoo Yoplait Water Park (Parc aquatique Amazoo Yoplait) is off Autoroute 10 exit 68 or 74 following signs to 1050 boul. David-Bouchard. This water park contains two large wave pools, a lazy river ride and water games; the water is heated.

Alcoholic beverages, glass containers and pets are not permitted. **Hours:** Open daily, Victoria Day weekend-late Aug. Hours vary; phone ahead. **Cost:** (includes Granby Zoo) $18.99; $15.99 (ages 66+); $11.99 (ages 3-12); $49.99 (family, two adults and two children). Prices may vary. Two-day combination passes also are available. **Phone:** (877) 472-6299.

NATURE INTERPRETATION CENTRE OF LAC BOIVIN (Centre d'interprétation de la nature du du lac Boivin), 700 rue Drummond, is a park offering more than 9 kilometres (6 mi.) of hiking trails and an observation tower overlooking marsh and swamp. Explanatory signs identify different flora and fauna along the trails. **Note:** Interpretive displays are in French. **Time:** Allow 1 hour, 30 minutes minimum.

Hours: Trails daily dawn-dusk. Visitor center Mon.-Fri. 8:30-4:30, Sat.-Sun. 9-5. Closed Jan. 1, Christmas and day after Christmas. **Cost:** Free. **Phone:** (450) 375-3861.

HOTEL CASTEL & SPA CONFORT

Phone: (450)378-9071

▼▼ ▲▲▼
Hotel
$110-$143 6/1-10/11
$99-$132 10/12-5/31

Address: 901 rue Principale J2G 2Z5 **Location:** On Rt 112, 0.6 mi (1 km) e of jct Rt 139; Hwy 10 exit 68. **Facility:** 136 units. 5 stories, interior corridors. **Parking:** winter plug-ins. **Terms:** check-in 4 pm. **Dining:** 2 restaurants, also, Restaurant La Rotonde, see separate listing. **Pool(s):** heated outdoor. **Activities:** whirlpools, playground, shuffleboard, exercise room, spa. **Guest Services:** valet laundry.

 / SOME UNITS

ST-CHRISTOPHE HOTEL BOUTIQUE & SPA, AN ASCEND COLLECTION HOTEL   **Phone:** 450/405-4782

▼▼ ▲▲▼
Hotel
Rates not provided

Address: 255 rue Denison est J2H 2R4 **Location:** On Rt 112; centre. **Facility:** 50 units. 5 stories, interior corridors. **Amenities:** high-speed Internet, safes. **Pool(s):** heated indoor. **Activities:** whirlpool, spa. **Guest Services:** valet laundry. **Free Special Amenities:** expanded continental breakfast and high-speed Internet.

WHERE TO EAT

CHEZ CORA   **Phone:** 450/375-6199

▼▼ ▲▼
Canadian
$6-$13

AAA Inspector Notes: Eggs, omelets, waffles, crepes (sorry, no American-style pancakes here), French toast, fruit platters and all the breakfast meats--that's the specialty here, all day. However, at lunchtime the menu lists a selection of soups, salads, quiches, sandwiches and a dish called the grilled panini crepe. **Address:** 15 rue Simonds nord J2J 2P5 **Location:** Centre; in Les Galeries Granby.

B L

RESTAURANT LA ROTONDE   **Phone:** 450/378-9071

▼▼ ▲▲▼
French
$23-$35

AAA Inspector Notes: The wood-beamed rotunda ceiling frames this traditionally elegant dining room that highlights some high-quality, regional produce, including Quebec pork, tenderloin veal, elk bavette, Canadian walleye, guinea fowl, butterfly shrimp and beef tenderloin. Main ingredients and sauces are enhanced with some excellent local honey, cheese and wine products, as well as fine seasonal vegetables. Wine pairings are offered along with tasting menus. **Bar:** full bar. **Reservations:** required. **Address:** 901 rue Principale J2G 2Z5 **Location:** On Rt 112, 0.6 mi (1 km) e of jct Rt 139; Hwy 10 exit 68; in Hotel Castel & Spa Confort. D CALL M

RESTO-PUB LE MACINTOSH   **Phone:** 450/776-1044

▼▼ ▲▼
Canadian
$10-$25

AAA Inspector Notes: Either in the lively bar room or informal dining areas, this popular pub pleases with a variety of comfort foods, including burgers, steak, pasta, sandwiches and salads. A variety of beers is available on tap. **Bar:** full bar. **Address:** 12 rue Principale J2G 2T4 **Location:** On Rt 112, corner of boul Mountain; centre. L D

ST-HUBERT   **Phone:** 450/378-4656

▼▼ ▲▼
Canadian
$8-$22

AAA Inspector Notes: The pleasantly decorated family-friendly restaurant serves affordable chicken dinners, ribs, club sandwiches, chicken wings, salads, soups and hot chicken sandwiches. The children's menu includes animal nuggets. **Bar:** full bar. **Address:** 940 rue Principale J2G 2Z4 **Location:** On Rt 112; centre. L D

GRANDES-BERGERONNES—See Les Bergeronnes p. 301.

GRANDES-PILES (D-5) pop. 350, elev. 122m/400'

THE LUMBERJACK'S MUSEUM (Le Musée du Bûcheron), 780 5th av., is a restored lumberjack village with 22 buildings that chronicles the timber trade 1850-1950. Pit saws, fire towers, charcoal kilns and wood shops are on the grounds. Guided tours are available; narration in English is offered. **Time:** Allow 1 hour minimum. **Hours:** Daily 9-5, May 15-Oct. 15. **Cost:** $13; $11.50 (ages 65+ and students with ID); $5.70 (ages 6-12); $34 (family). **Phone:** (819) 538-6947.

GRAND-MÉRE

AUBERGE LE FLORÈS   Phone: 819/538-9340

Country Inn
Rates not provided

Address: 4291 50ieme Ave G9T 1A6 **Location:** Hwy 55 N exit 220, follow signs. **Facility:** In a rural setting, the cozy cottage offers country-elegant guest rooms, fine dining, well-kept grounds and a health club. 34 units. 2 stories (no elevator), interior corridors. **Pool(s):** heated outdoor. **Activities:** lifeguard on duty, snowmobiling, exercise room, spa. *Fee:* saunas, whirlpools.

[icons] / SOME UNITS

AUBERGE SANTÈ LAC DES NEIGES
    Phone: 819/533-4518

Country Inn
Rates not provided

Address: 100 Lac des Neiges G9T 5K5 **Location:** Hwy 55 exit 220, follow signs. Located in a quiet area. **Facility:** 11 units. 2 stories (no elevator), interior corridors. **Parking:** winter plug-ins. **Terms:** age restrictions may apply. **Pool(s):** heated indoor. **Activities:** sauna, whirlpool, limited beach access, boating, canoeing, paddleboats, fishing, cross country skiing, ice skating, hiking trails, spa.

[icons] / SOME UNITS

GRAND-MÉTIS (C-7) pop. 268

Until the construction in 1929 of boulevard Perron (Hwy. 132) around the land's perimeter, Grand-Métis was an isolated village on the Gaspé Peninsula. At the turn of the 20th century, Grand-Métis was the favorite salmon and summer vacation spot of the wealthy Sir George Stephen (Lord Mount Stephen), the first president of the Canadian Pacific Railway.

REFORD GARDENS (Jardins de Métis) is n.e. on Hwy. 132, following signs. Once the summer fishing camp of Sir George Stephen (Lord Mount Stephen), the estate was given in 1918 to Stephen's niece, Elsie Reford, who transformed the property into one of eastern Canada's most beautiful gardens.

Paths lead through formal and natural beds that display more than 3,000 species of trees, flowers and shrubs. Colorful rhododendrons and crab apples highlight the gardens in early summer and give way to thousands of lilies, roses and blue poppies in mid- and late summer. Built in 1887, Estevan Lodge houses a museum with exhibitions about the history of the gardens and summer life along the Métis River. Held from late June to early October,

the [icon] International Garden Festival (Festival international de jardins) is a showcase for innovative landscape design.

Time: Allow 2 hours minimum. **Hours:** Daily 8:30-8, July-Aug.; 8:30-6, early June-June 30 and Sept. 1-early Oct. Last admission 2 hours before closing, July-Aug.; 1 hour before closing, rest of season. **Cost:** $17; $16 (ages 65+); $15 (students with ID); $9 (ages 14-18). **Phone:** (418) 775-2222.

GRENVILLE-SUR-LA-ROUGE pop. 1,315

HÔTEL DU LAC CARLING   Phone: 450/533-9211

Resort Hotel
Rates not provided

Address: 2255 Rt 327 nord J0V 1B0 **Location:** 3.1 mi (5 km) n. **Facility:** Manicured grounds and upscale common areas inspired by European-style châteaux bring an atmosphere of luxury to this hotel. Amenities include a marble-bottom pool, tennis courts and golf course. 100 units. 3 stories, interior corridors. **Parking:** winter plug-ins. **Amenities:** safes. **Dining:** Restaurant L'If, see separate listing. **Pool(s):** heated indoor. **Activities:** saunas, whirlpools, boating, canoeing, paddleboats, fishing, 2 lighted indoor tennis courts, racquetball court, cross country skiing, snowmobiling, ice skating, tobogganing, bicycles, hiking trails, horseback riding, sports court, exercise room, spa. *Fee:* golf-18 holes. **Guest Services:** valet laundry. **Free Special Amenities:** full breakfast and high-speed Internet.

[SAVE] [icons] [BIZ] [icons]
/ SOME UNITS FEE [icons]

WHERE TO EAT

RESTAURANT L'IF   Phone: 450/533-9211

French
$12-$31

AAA Inspector Notes: In an upscale hotel adjacent to a golf course, this elegant dining room makes its mark with fine regional cuisine, including filet of trout, pan-fried scallops, oven-roasted, free-range chicken breast, braised lamb shank, pan-fried beef tenderloin, pan-fried Barbarie duck and Boileau deer. **Bar:** full bar. **Reservations:** required. **Address:** 2255 Rt 327 nord J0V 1B0 **Location:** 3.1 mi (5 km) n; in Hotel du Lac Carling. [B] [L] [D]

HEMMINGFORD (F-7) pop. 1,763

Like many other villages across the Québec countryside, Hemmingford's origins were as a mission and parish. With the extension of the Canadian National Railway through town, it became a trading site for the surrounding rural region. Today 1 million apple trees, a cider mill and winemakers characterize the region.

PARC SAFARI, 8 km (5 mi.) w. on Hwy. 202 off Autoroute 15 exit 6, is a 200-acre family-oriented park with a zoological theme. The animal area includes a drive-through wildlife park highlighting more than 800 animals from five continents; the Deer Trail; carnivores, including lions and tigers, which are viewable via an observatory and a tunneled glass walkway; a pedestrian bridge spanning the primates' habitat; and Afrika Terrace, where giraffes get up close and personal with visitors.

The amusement area offers mechanical rides and miniature golf. Nairobi Park is a play zone for young children. The on-site water park has tube rides and lake and beach areas. In addition live shows are presented on three stages.

Time: Allow 4 hours minimum. **Hours:** Daily 10-7, late June-late Aug. and Labour Day weekend-Labour Day; daily 10-4, mid-May to late June, late Aug.-day before Labour Day weekend and day after Labour Day to mid-Sept.; Fri.-Sat. 10-4, mid-Sept. to early Oct. Phone ahead to confirm schedule. **Cost:** $34; $21 (ages 3-17). Prices for individual activities vary. **Phone:** (450) 247-2727.

ÎLE D'ORLÉANS (A-2)
- **Hotels & Restaurants map & index p. 429**
- **Part of Québec area — see map p. 405**

Île d'Orléans (Orleans Island), in the St. Lawrence River and reached by bridge from Hwy. 138, contains churches built by the French. Continuously inhabited since the 17th century, the island was originally called Île de Bacchus after the Roman god of wine and revelry because of the number of wild grapes that grew in the vicinity.

The early 18th-century churches, along with mills and houses of the same period, create an atmosphere reminiscent of old France. The 1717-19 St-Pierre and the 1743-48 Ste-Famille retain much of their original decor. Today Île d'Orléans also is known for fruit and vegetable production as well as for handicrafts.

THE AÏEUX HOUSE (La Maison de nos Aïeux) is at 3907 ch. Royal on Île d'Orléans in the village of Ste-Famille. Built in the early 20th century, this former presbytery today shelters a Québec genealogy center. Historical exhibits are on display, as is a contoured scale model of the island that illustrates the borders between the rolling farmlands. Next to The Aïeux House, a scenic riverfront park features a memorial sculpture commemorating Île d'Orléans' founding French-Canadian families.

Time: Allow 1 hour minimum. **Hours:** Daily 10-6, late June-Labour Day; Mon.-Fri. 10-4, mid-Feb. to late June and day after Labour Day to mid-Dec. **Cost:** $4; free (ages 0-12). Combination ticket with The Drouin House $7. Cash only. **Phone:** (418) 829-0330.

THE DROUIN HOUSE (La Maison Drouin) is at 4700 ch. Royal on Île d'Orléans in the village of Ste-Famille. Docents lead tours of the 1730 farmhouse, which the Drouin family, the home's third inhabitants, occupied until 1984. Interesting features include the original roof framing with retention pins, handmade wrought nails, a stone hearth and a bread oven.

Time: Allow 30 minutes minimum. **Hours:** Daily 10-6, late June-Labour Day; 1-5, day after Labour Day-day before Thanksgiving. Phone ahead to confirm schedule. **Cost:** $4; free (ages 0-12). Combination ticket with The Aïeux House $7. Cash only. **Phone:** (418) 829-0330.

MAUVIDE-GENEST MANOR (Manoir Mauvide-Genest) is at 1451 ch. Royal on Île d'Orléans in the village of St-Jean. This mid-18th-century stone manor was built by a respected French surgeon and businessman named Jean Mauvide, who, at one time, operated Île d'Orléans' four mills and served as seigneur for half the island.

Descriptive panels detail the history of the house and the vicinity. An attractive New France-style garden also is on the grounds. Led by staff members in period costume, guided tours of the manor are available in either English or French. **Note:** Although an elevator is available, the property is only partially handicap accessible; it lacks a reserved parking spot and level walkways and some areas are not easily accessible by wheelchair.

Time: Allow 30 minutes minimum. **Hours:** Daily 10-5, May 1-early Sept.; by appointment rest of year. **Cost:** $6; $5 (ages 55+); $4 (ages 6-12); $20 (family). Guided tour additional $2; free (ages 0-12 and 55+). Cash only. **Phone:** (418) 829-2630.

ST. LAWRENCE MARITIME PARK (Parc maritime de St-Laurent) is on Île d'Orléans in the village of St-Laurent at 120 ch. de la Chalouperie. The park is on the site of a former shipyard where wood- and steel-hull ships and boats were constructed between 1908 and 1967, a period when shipbuilding was the island's primary industry.

A guided tour explains the shipbuilding process. Visitors see riverfront workshops and the dock from which the finished boats were launched. An interpretation center also is available. **Time:** Allow 1 hour minimum. **Hours:** Daily 10-5, late June-Labour Day; Sat.-Sun. 10-5, day after Labour Day-Oct. 31. **Cost:** $4; free (ages 0-12). **Phone:** (418) 828-9672.

AUBERGE CHAUMONOT   **Phone:** 418/829-2735

Country Inn
Rates not provided

Address: 425 chemin Royal G0A 3S0 **Location:** On Rt 368; in municipality of St-Francois. **Facility:** 8 units. 3 stories (no elevator), interior corridors. **Terms:** seasonal.

AUBERGE LA GOELICHE   **Phone:** (418)828-2248   **30**

Country Inn
$109/$279

Address: 22 chemin du Quai G0A 4C0 **Location:** 3.1 mi (5 km) w on Rt 368 from bridge, follow signs; in municipality of Ste-Petronille. **Facility:** Most of this contemporary country inn's upscale, individually decorated rooms overlook the St. Lawrence River. 19 units, some two bedrooms and kitchens. 2 stories (no elevator), interior corridors. **Terms:** 30 day cancellation notice-fee imposed. **Amenities:** honor bars. **Pool(s):** outdoor. **Activities:** cross country skiing. **Guest Services:** valet laundry.

(See map & index p. 429.)

WHERE TO EAT

LE MOULIN DE SAINT-LAURENT   Phone: 418/829-3888

French
$14-$32

AAA Inspector Notes: The 18th-century flour mill boasts stone walls, attractive plants and flowers, a cozy summer terrace and pleasant views of a nearby waterfall. Smoked fish, chicken liver pate and game terrine top a menu that also features breast of chicken, salmon, scallops, quail, filet mignon, lamb and veal. Belgian waffles satisfy for dessert. A lighter lunch menu is available. **Bar:** full bar. **Reservations:** suggested. **Address:** 754 chemin Royal G0A 3Z0 **Location:** On Rt 368, 7.5 mi (12 km) se of Île d'Orleans bridge; in municipality of St-Laurent. **Historic**

ÎLES DE LA MADELEINE

The Îles de la Madeleine (Magdalen Islands) are 215 kilometres (134 mi.) east of the Gaspé Peninsula in the Gulf of St. Lawrence. The 96-kilometre-long (60-mi.) archipelago encompasses about a dozen islands and several islets. First visited by Jacques Cartier in 1534, the islands were settled in 1755 by Acadians expelled from Nova Scotia.

Most Madelinots are fishermen who live in small port communities that dot the islands. The culture and heritage of the people are captured in the exhibits at the Museum of the Sea (Musée de la Mer) in Havre-Aubert; phone (418) 937-5711.

Colonies of birds, representing more than 50 species, inhabit the islands during migration periods. A large bird sanctuary, Île Rocher-aux-Oiseaux, can be visited by boat through arrangements with local fishermen in Grande-Entrée; phone (418) 986-2245.

The islands are accessible by boat from Montréal as well as Souris, Prince Edward Island. Daily air service is available from Charlottetown, Prince Edward Island; Moncton, New Brunswick; and Montréal and Gaspé.

Îles de la Madeleine Tourist Information Bureau: 128 ch. Principal, Cap-aux-Meules, QC, Canada G4T 1C5. **Phone:** (418) 986-2245 or (877) 624-4437.

ISLE-AUX-COUDRES (D-6)

Isle-aux-Coudres can be reached by a ferry that departs daily from the village of St-Joseph-de-la-Rive, which is just off Hwy. 362; phone (418) 438-2743 for schedule and fare information. The scenic island, in Charlevoix County on the north shore of the St. Lawrence River, was first visited in 1535 by Jacques Cartier, who named it for the abundance of hazelnut trees found there.

Now visited for its rugged, tree-shrouded beauty and tranquil charm, the island is a center for artisans who make textiles, including Québec rag rugs (cata-lognes), table mats and bed covers.

THE MILLS OF ISLE-AUX-COUDRES—MUSEUM OF FLOUR MILLING (Les Moulins de l'Isle-aux-Coudres—Économusée de la Meunerie) is on the Rouge River, following signs to 36 ch. du Moulin.

The site consists of a restored 1825 watermill and 1836 windmill that took turns grinding flour, depending on which source of energy was more abundant.

Today guides conduct milling demonstrations, and the buildings as well as the miller's house and forge contain displays about 19th-century rural life. The welcome center also offers exhibitions of popular art. Guided tours are available; narration is in French. **Time:** Allow 45 minutes minimum. **Hours:** Daily 9:30-5:30, mid-May to mid-Oct. **Cost:** $9; $5 (ages 6-18); $20 (family). Prices may vary; phone ahead. **Phone:** (418) 438-2184.

HOTEL MOTEL LA ROCHE PLEUREUSE

Phone: 418/438-2734

Hotel
Rates not provided

Address: 2901 chemin des Coudriers G0A 2A0 **Location:** On Île aux Coudres, 4.8 mi (8 km) e of ferry dock, follow signs; in la Baleine sector; access by ferry boat. **Facility:** 87 units. 1-2 stories, interior/exterior corridors. **Terms:** seasonal. **Dining:** entertainment. **Pool(s):** heated outdoor. **Activities:** lighted tennis court, recreation programs in summer, rental bicycles, shuffleboard, spa. **Guest Services:** valet laundry.

JONQUIÈRE (C-5)

• Restaurants p. 292

Two modernistic churches in Jonquière reflect the province's revival of religious architecture during the 1960s. The St-Raphaël Church (Église St-Raphaël), 2381 St-Jean-Baptiste, has no walls; instead, the copper roof rises 19.4 metres (64 ft.) from the ground, supporting itself and enclosing the space. The Our Lady of Fatima Church (Église Notre-Dame-de-Fatima), 3635 Notre-Dame, is shaped like an Indian tepee.

In 2002 Jonquière amalgamated with Saguenay and is now one of the city's three boroughs, along with Chicoutimi and La Baie (see place listings p. 274 and p. 292).

Jonquière Tourist Information Office: Convention Center, 3919 boul. Harvey, Jonquière, QC, Canada G7X 0L4. **Phone:** (418) 698-3167, or (800) 463-6565 in Canada.

HOLIDAY INN SAGUENAY CONVENTION CENTRE

Phone: (418)548-3124

Hotel
$123-$137

Address: 2675 boul du Royaume G7S 5B8 **Location:** Hwy 70 exit 39, just ne, follow signs. Next to a mall. **Facility:** 155 units. 10 stories, interior corridors. **Parking:** winter plug-ins. **Dining:** Restaurant Côte Jardin, see separate listing. **Pool(s):** heated outdoor. **Activities:** snowmobiling, exercise room, spa. **Fee:** steamroom. **Guest Services:** valet and coin laundry.

WHERE TO EAT

RESTAURANT CÔTE JARDIN   Phone: 418/548-3124

French
$10-$26

AAA Inspector Notes: This casual hotel dining room offers a reliable menu of steak, seafood, fresh fish, pasta and chicken. Service is friendly. **Bar:** full bar. **Reservations:** suggested. **Address:** 2675 boul du Royaume G7S 5B8 **Location:** Hwy 70 exit 39, just ne, follow signs; in Holiday Inn Saguenay Convention Centre.

[B] [L] [D]

RESTAURANT LE BERGERAC   Phone: 418/542-6263

New French
$16-$36

AAA Inspector Notes: The intimate, turn-of-the-20th-century house is appointed with country-style decor, and its atmosphere is relaxed. Three-to-five-course table d'hote menus lay out innovative meat, fish and game specialties prepared by the chef/owner. The wine list is impressive. **Bar:** full bar. **Reservations:** suggested, for dinner. **Address:** 3919 rue St-Jean G7X 3J5 **Location:** Hwy 170 W, 1.3 mi (2 km) s on boul Harvey, 0.3 mi (0.4 km) e on rue St-Dominique, just n on rue St-Thomas, then just w on rue St-Simon; behind hardware store. [L] [D]

ST-HUBERT   Phone: 418/542-0363

Canadian
$8-$22

AAA Inspector Notes: The pleasantly decorated family-friendly restaurant serves affordable chicken dinners, ribs, club sandwiches, chicken wings, salads, soups and hot chicken sandwiches. The children's menu includes animal nuggets. **Bar:** full bar. **Address:** 3657 boul Harvey G7X 3A9 **Location:** Centre. [L] [D]

KAHNAWAKE (F-7)

• Part of Montréal area — see map p. 312

In 1670-71 a French and Indian village was founded at La Prairie by French Jesuits. The native population moved farther up the St. Lawrence beginning in 1676 and finally established a settlement in Kahnawake, meaning "by the rapids," in 1716. The village served as a refuge for Iroquois converts to Christianity. The reservation has no street names or numbers.

ST. FRANCIS XAVIER MISSION AND SHRINE OF KATERI TEKAKWITHA (Mission St-François-Xavier et Sanctuaire de Kateri Tekakwitha) is at the center of the village on Route de l'Église. The church houses the tomb of Iroquois maiden Kateri Tekakwitha, who has been beatified by the Vatican and is expected to become the first North American Indian saint. A small museum contains material relating to Blessed Kateri as well as paintings and other artifacts. **Time:** Allow 30 minutes minimum. **Hours:** Mon.-Fri. 10-noon and 1-4, Sat.-Sun. 10-4. **Cost:** Donations. **Phone:** (450) 632-6030.

Explore the Travel Guides
on AAA.com/Travel or
CAA.ca/Travel

KIRKLAND

• Hotels & Restaurants map & index p. 342
• Part of Montréal area — see map p. 312

LE STEAK FRITES ST-PAUL   Phone: 514/505-0808   [108]

Steak
$21-$40

AAA Inspector Notes: The lively and informal bistro specializes in certified AAA-grade steak and all-you-can-eat thin, matchstick fries. The menu is rounded out with such classics as duck confit, smoked salmon, grilled shrimp, salmon fillet and a surf and turf option. For dessert, try the traditional crème brûlée or chocolate covered profiteroles. In typical French bistro fashion, the daily menu is written on a chalkboard. As this is a bring-your-own-wine restaurant, no alcohol is sold on the premises. **Reservations:** suggested. **Address:** 16977 Rte Transcanadienne H9H 5J1 **Location:** Hwy 40 exit 50, then just n on boul St-Charles; in Centre Piazza Azzurri. [L] [D]

MADISONS NEW YORK GRILL & BAR   Phone: 514/426-9111   [109]

Steak
$10-$30

AAA Inspector Notes: This lively, suburban pub and steakhouse has comfortable chairs and private leather-upholstered booths. The grill menu offers fresh seafood, filet mignon, rib steaks, milk-fed veal, roast beef, ribs, grilled chicken, burgers and giant shrimp as well as shrimp cocktail, salmon salad, Caesar salad and a choice of sandwiches, including club, crab or red tuna. **Bar:** full bar. **Reservations:** required. **Address:** 3000 rue Jean-Yves H9J 2R6 **Location:** Hwy 40 exit 49, then just nw. [L] [D] CALL [LM]

ST-HUBERT   Phone: 514/695-2064

Canadian
$8-$22

AAA Inspector Notes: The pleasantly decorated family-friendly restaurant serves affordable chicken dinners, ribs, club sandwiches, chicken wings, salads, soups and hot chicken sandwiches. The children's menu includes animal nuggets. **Bar:** full bar. **Address:** 2939 boul St-Charles H9H 3B5 **Location:** Between Hwy 20 and 40. [L] [D]

LA BAIE (C-6) pop. 18,793, elev. 22m/75'

SAGUENAY CRUISES (Les Croisières du Fjord) departs from the Bagotville Wharf in La Baie. Offering views of stunning natural surroundings, the narrated sightseeing trips explore the Saguenay River and fjord. After a 1.5-hour stopover in Ste-Rose-du-Nord, the journey continues to Cap Trinité, where the 9-metre-high (30-ft.), white pine Statue de Notre-Dame-du-Saguenay was erected in 1881.

Cruises departing from Ste-Rose-du-Nord, Baie-Éternité, L'Anse-St-Jean and Tadoussac also are available. Inquire about weather policies **Time:** Allow a full day. **Hours:** Departures require a minimum of 20 passengers. Cruises depart La Baie daily at 10 and return at 5:30, July 1-early Sept. Schedules for cruises departing from other ports vary. **Cost:** $50; $25 (ages 5-14). Reservations are required. **Phone:** (418) 543-7630 or (800) 363-7248.

AUBERGE DES 21   Phone: 418/697-2121

Country Inn
$150-$225 6/1-10/31
$99-$175 11/1-5/31

Address: 621 rue Mars G7B 4N1 **Location:** Just e via rue Bagot (Hwy 170 E). **Facility:** This contemporary country inn offers a well-equipped spa and upscale guest rooms, some with views of the bay. A few luxury units have an oversize tub and separate shower stall. 31 units, some two bedrooms. 2 stories (no elevator), interior corridors. **Parking:** winter plug-ins. **Amenities:** Some: high-speed Internet. **Dining:** Restaurant Le Doyen, see separate listing. **Pool(s):** heated outdoor. **Activities:** lifeguard on duty, bicycles, spa. **Guest Services:** valet laundry.

AUBERGE DES BATTURES   Phone: (418)544-8234

Country Inn
$115-$230 6/1-9/30
$92-$189 10/1-5/31

Address: 6295 boul de la Grande Baie sud G7B 3P6 **Location:** 4.5 mi (7.5 km) e on Rt 170 E; jct Rt 381 S. **Facility:** Perched on a small hilltop, the cozy inn features small to spacious guest rooms, each with quality furnishings and a private balcony or terrace. 32 units. 3 stories, interior/exterior corridors. **Terms:** office hours 6:30 am-10:30 pm, 7 day cancellation notice-fee imposed. **Dining:** Restaurant Les Outardes, see separate listing. **Activities:** snowmobiling, game room, exercise room. Fee: massage. **Guest Services:** valet laundry. **Free Special Amenities:** local telephone calls and high-speed Internet.

WHERE TO EAT

RESTAURANT LE DOYEN   Phone: 418/697-2121

Regional French
$15-$28

AAA Inspector Notes: Overlooking the beautiful Saguenay River, the elegant dining room is decorated in a contemporary style. Attentive service and pleasantly presented dishes make for a memorable dining experience at the upscale country inn. Menu highlights include terrine of guinea fowl, rabbit, grilled veal, caribou, Atlantic salmon and smoked trout. **Bar:** full bar. **Reservations:** suggested. **Address:** 621 rue Mars G7B 4N1 **Location:** Just e via rue Bagot (Hwy 170 E); in Auberge des 21. B L D

RESTAURANT LES OUTARDES   Phone: 418/544-8234

French
$25-$40

AAA Inspector Notes: Through large windows, this casually elegant dining room offers guests panoramic views of the bay. The menu features fine regional produce along with smoked salmon, cod, scallops, pike, shrimp, wild game and regional cheeses. The main dining room has hardwood floors and a cozy fireplace. **Bar:** full bar. **Address:** 6295 boul de la Grande-Baie sud G7B 3P6 **Location:** 4.5 mi (7.5 km) e on Rt 170 E; jct Rt 381 S; in Auberge Des Battures. B D

LAC-BEAUPORT pop. 6,081
• Part of Québec area — see map p. 405

AUBERGE QUATRE TEMPS   Phone: 418/849-4486

Country Inn
$79-$179

Address: 161 chemin Tour du Lac G3B 0T5 **Location:** Hwy 73 N exit 157, 4.1 mi (6.5 km) e on boul du Lac. **Facility:** On the shores of scenic Lac Beauport, this upscale lodging offers rooms with balconies, as well as a few one-bedroom suites with exterior entrances. 31 units, some efficiencies. 3 stories (no elevator), interior/exterior corridors. **Parking:** winter plug-ins. **Terms:** cancellation fee imposed. **Pool(s):** heated outdoor, heated indoor. **Activities:** sauna, whirlpool, limited beach access, rental paddleboats, cross country skiing, snowmobiling, ice skating, hiking trails, volleyball, spa. **Guest Services:** valet laundry.

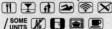

WHERE TO EAT

ARCHIBALD MICROBRASSERIE   Phone: 418/841-2224

Canadian
$12-$31

AAA Inspector Notes: Resembling a rustic hunting lodge, the restaurant's wood-beamed interior is adorned with a hanging canoe and a stuffed animal above the bar. Preservative-free beers are brewed on the premises and a menu of pub food includes burgers, Angus beef, ribs, mussels in beer sauce, duck, veal liver, lamb, gourmet pizza, fish, salad and pasta. The seasonal terrace is a good place to enjoy the rural scenery. **Bar:** full bar. **Address:** 1021 boul du Lac G0A 2C0 **Location:** Hwy 73 N exit 157, 2 mi (3.3 km) e. L D

LAC-BROME (KNOWLTON) (F-8)
pop. 5,629
• Restaurants p. 294

At the foot of Mont Brome and on the shores of lac Brome, the country resort of Lac-Brome is known for its Victorian Swiss chalet-style villas along the lake. Recreational activities include tennis, golf, fishing and water sports. The area also is noted for its duck breeding, with the Brome Lake Duck Festival (Canard en fête) occurring in September.

BROME COUNTY HISTORICAL MUSEUM (Musée de la Société d'histoire du comté de Brome), in the sector of Knowlton at 130 rue Lakeside, comprises five buildings, including a general store and the old Knowlton Academy, built in 1854. The buildings contain displays of Victorian and Indian items, military memorabilia, farm tools, embroidery and weaving.

The World War I Fokker D.VII biplane, part of German war reparations to Canada, is the only one known to have the original camouflage-fabric covering intact. **Time:** Allow 1 hour, 30 minutes minimum. **Hours:** Mon.-Sat. 10-4:30, Sun. 11-4:30, mid-May through second Mon. in Oct. **Cost:** $5; $3 (ages 66+); $2.50 (ages 6-15). **Phone:** (450) 243-6782.

AUBERGE KNOWLTON   Phone: 450/242-6886

Country Inn
$130-$160

Address: 286 chemin Knowlton J0E 1V0 **Location:** Corner of Hwy 104 and Rt 243; centre. **Facility:** In the heart of a lively Victorian village, this remodeled inn offers warm hospitality and pleasantly decorated rooms. 12 units. 3 stories (no elevator), interior corridors. **Terms:** office hours 8 am-9 pm. **Dining:** Le Relais Restaurant-Bistro, see separate listing.

AUBERGE LAKEVIEW INN   Phone: (450)243-6183

Historic
Country Inn
$150-$240 6/1-10/31
$125-$230 11/1-5/31

Address: 50 rue Victoria J0E 1V0 **Location:** Centre. **Facility:** The small but charming rooms in this restored 1874 Victorian inn are furnished with reproduction period pieces. A few deluxe studios include a whirlpool tub. 28 units. 3 stories (no elevator), interior corridors. **Terms:** 14 day cancellation notice-fee imposed. **Dining:** restaurant, see separate listing. **Pool(s):** heated outdoor. **Activities:** exercise room. Fee: massage. **Free Special Amenities:** newspaper and early check-in/late check-out.

AUBERGE QUILLIAMS INN

Phone: (450)243-0404

Country Inn
$159-$350

Address: 572 chemin Lakeside J0E 1R0 **Location:** Hwy 10 exit 90, 3.1 mi (4.9 km) s on Rt 243. **Facility:** Private balconies adjoin all rooms at this contemporary country inn, which overlooks a scenic lake. Some rooms feature a fireplace. 38 units, some efficiencies. 3 stories (no elevator), interior corridors. **Terms:** check-in 4 pm, 3 day cancellation notice-fee imposed. **Amenities:** safes, honor bars. **Dining:** Restaurant Auberge Quilliams, see separate listing. **Pool(s):** heated outdoor, heated indoor. **Activities:** sauna, whirlpool, beach access, canoeing, fishing, cross country skiing, exercise room, spa. **Free Special Amenities:** continental breakfast and high-speed Internet.

THE AUBERGE LAKEVIEW INN DINING ROOM
Menu on AAA.com   Phone: 450/243-6183

French
$25-$70

AAA Inspector Notes: Staffers in smart attire serve French and international cuisine in this elegant, 19th-century-style dining room. Local produce wakes up the flavors in creative preparations of meat, fish and poultry as well as the house specialty, Brome Lake duck. **Bar:** full bar. **Reservations:** suggested. **Address:** 50 rue Victoria J0E 1V0 **Location:** Centre; in Auberge Lakeview Inn. D

LE RELAIS RESTAURANT-BISTRO   Phone: 450/242-2232

Canadian
$10-$32

AAA Inspector Notes: Regional cuisine and some pub foods are prepared at this charming country town's relaxed hotel bistro. On the varied menu are French onion soup, mussels, salmon, fish and chips, fried clams, roast chicken, steak and sandwiches. Ask about the daily special. The freshly baked pies or carrot cake are worth trying for dessert. **Bar:** full bar. **Reservations:** suggested. **Address:** 286 chemin Knowlton J0E 1V0 **Location:** Corner of Hwy 104 and Rt 243; centre; in Auberge Knowlton. B L D

RESTAURANT AUBERGE QUILLIAMS

Phone: 450/243-0404

French
$15-$39

AAA Inspector Notes: In an upscale Eastern Townships inn, the sophisticated restaurant emphasizes quality regional produce in such preparations as Brome Lake duck, striped sea bass, rabbit, Angus beef, pan-seared ostrich, yellowfin tuna, veal and rack of lamb. Visitors may view the vast wine cellar with its own wine tasting area and private dining room. A lighter bistro menu is available Sunday through Thursday. **Bar:** full bar. **Reservations:** suggested. **Address:** 572 chemin Lakeside J0E 1R0 **Location:** Hwy 10 exit 90, 3.1 mi (4.9 km) s on Rt 243; in Auberge Quilliams Inn. B L D

Visit AAA.com or CAA.ca

for one-stop travel

planning and reservations

LACHINE (F-7)
• Hotels & Restaurants map & index p. 342
• Part of Montréal area — see map p. 312

SAVE **THE FUR TRADE AT LACHINE NATIONAL HISTORIC SITE** (Lieu historique national du Commerce-de-la-Fourrure-à-Lachine), 1255 boul. St-Joseph at 12th av., is in a stone warehouse built in 1803 for the storage of pelts. It was first used by the North West Co. then owned by the Hudson's Bay Co. Displays portray Lachine's and Montréal's roles in the fur trade. Events are held Saturday and Sunday afternoons during the summer.

Hours: Daily 9:30-5, mid-May to mid-Oct.; Mon.-Fri. 9:30-5, early Apr. to mid-May. **Cost:** $3.90; $3.40 (ages 65+); $1.90 (ages 6-16); $9.80 (family, two adults and children). **Phone:** (514) 637-7433.

LACHINE CANAL NATIONAL HISTORIC SITE (Lieu historique national Canal-de-Lachine) runs 13.4 km (8 mi.) s.w. from the Old Port in Montréal, through LaSalle to lac St-Louis at Lachine. Dollier de Casson first had the idea to build a canal between Lachine and Montréal in 1680. Construction on the canal began in 1689 but ended with Casson's death in 1701. In the early 19th century, immigration and trade expansion made linking Lachine and Montréal a necessity, and the waterway was completed in 1825.

Closed in 1970, the canal reopened in 2002 for recreational use. A 12-kilometre (7.5-mi.) multipurpose path, hiking trails and picnic areas line the channel, creating many distinctive urban green spaces.

The visitor center at Lock No. 5 at Lachine has free exhibits about the canal's history. From mid-May to mid-October, interpretive boat tours are offered at the Atwater Quay; reservations are required. Kayak and bicycle rentals are available in the Atwater-Charlevoix sector. **Hours:** Canal grounds open daily dawn-11 p.m. Canal open to pleasure boats daily, mid-May to mid-Oct. Visitor center open Mon.-Fri. 9-5, mid-May through Sept. 30. **Cost:** Grounds free. Fees may be charged for services. **Phone:** (514) 283-6054 or (888) 773-8888.

SAVE **LACHINE MUSEUM** (Musée de Lachine), 1 ch. du Musée, is on the site of one of oldest fur trading posts in the area. Artwork and archeological displays are exhibited within a complex of buildings built between 1669 and 1671. Included in the museum's collections are paintings, 19th-century furniture and a variety of relics relating the history of the post. A sculpture garden featuring 50 works also is on the grounds.

Guided tours are available; narration in English is offered. **Time:** Allow 30 minutes minimum. **Hours:** Wed.-Sun. 11:30-4:30 (also Tues. 11:30-4:30, in summer), Apr. 1 to mid-Nov. **Cost:** Free. **Phone:** (514) 634-3478.

(See map & index p. 342.)

HOLIDAY INN EXPRESS HOTEL & SUITES MONTREAL AEROPORT

Hotel
$140-$165

Phone: (514)422-8080 **57**
Address: 10888 Cote-de-Liesse H8T 1A6 **Location:** Jct Hwy 520 and 54ieme Ave; from Hwy 20 exit 58, 0.9 mi (1.4 km) n to 54ieme Ave, then just ne. **Facility:** 154 units. 6 stories, interior corridors. **Terms:** 3 day cancellation notice. **Amenities:** high-speed Internet. **Pool(s):** heated indoor. **Activities:** sauna, whirlpool, exercise room. *Fee:* massage. **Guest Services:** valet and coin laundry, area transportation-within 6 mi (10 km) & Dorval train station. **Free Special Amenities:** full breakfast and airport transportation.

SAVE ECO ✈ ¶✚ 🏊 BIZ 🛜 ✕ FEE 👤
📠 🔺 💳

Built in '08. Modern looking wood floors in all rooms. FREE Hot Breakfast, Wi-Fi, Shuttle & Parking.

WHERE TO EAT

12 BAR GRILL

▽▽ ▽▽
Canadian
$7-$28

Phone: 514/637-1212 **100**
AAA Inspector Notes: This brasserie-style bar and restaurant is a great place to grab a pitcher of draft beer and enjoy inexpensive pub food, including prime quality steaks, burgers, pasta and chicken. Le Douze (French for Number 12) is named for the jersey number of retired Montreal Canadiens hockey star Yvan Cournoyer, who once owned the restaurant. **Bar:** full bar. **Reservations:** required. **Address:** 625 32ieme Ave H8T 3G6 **Location:** Hwy 20 exit 32 ave, 0.3 mi (0.5 km) s. B L D

RESTAURANT TOPAZE

▽▽ ▽▽
Steak
$9-$28

Phone: 514/634-7044 **101**
AAA Inspector Notes: This suburban, waterfront restaurant and bar overlooks a pretty park and serves a varied menu of steaks, seafood, burgers, pasta and salad. Terrace seating is ideal during the warm summer months. **Bar:** full bar. **Address:** 2166 rue St-Joseph H8S 2N7 **Location:** Just e of 25ieme Ave; on the riverfront. L D

RISTORANTE IL FORNETTO

▽▽▽ ▽▽
Italian
$12-$30

Phone: 514/637-5253 **102**
AAA Inspector Notes: This suburban lakefront restaurant prepares affordable wood-oven-baked pizza, salads and dishes of fresh pasta, fish, meat and seafood. An excellent espresso finishes the meal with style. **Bar:** full bar. **Reservations:** suggested. **Address:** 1900 boul St-Joseph H8S 2N5 **Location:** Corner of 19th Ave; lakefront. **Parking:** street only. L D

LA DORÉ (C-4) pop. 1,454

THE PIONEERS MILL (Moulin des Pionniers), 4201 rue des Peupliers, is the site of an 1889 sawmill. Other highlights include an interpretation center, a 1904 farmhouse, and mountain biking and hiking trails past the site's 21 species of trees. **Hours:** Daily 9:30-5, early June to mid-Oct. **Cost:** $12; $9 (ages 66+); $8 (students with ID); free (ages 0-11); $25 (family, two adults and children). **Phone:** (418) 256-8242 or (886) 272-8242. ¶

LA MALBAIE (D-6) pop. 8,959

• Restaurants p. 296

La Malbaie is a popular summer resort along the St. Lawrence River. Samuel de Champlain chose the town's name, which means "bad bay," because of the rugged, perilous shoreline found there. An artists' colony, the town has several small galleries and craft shops open during the summer.

Charlevoix Tourist Information Bureau: 495 boul. de Comporté, La Malbaie, QC, Canada G5A 3E7. **Phone:** (418) 665-4454 or (800) 667-2276.

CHARLEVOIX MUSEUM—see Pointe-au-Pic p. 402.

GAMBLING ESTABLISHMENTS

• **Casino de Charlevoix** is at 183 rue Richelieu. **Hours:** Sun.-Thurs. 9 a.m.-2 a.m., Fri.-Sat. 9 a.m.-3 a.m., late June-Labour Day; Sun.-Thurs. 10 a.m.-1 a.m., Fri.-Sat. 10 a.m.-3 a.m., early Apr.-late June and day after Labour Day-late Oct.; Mon.-Thurs. 11 a.m.-midnight, Fri.-Sat. 10 a.m.-3 a.m., Sun. 10 a.m.-midnight, rest of year. Phone ahead to confirm schedule. **Phone:** (418) 665-5300 or (800) 665-2274.

AUBERGE FLEURS DE LUNE

▽▽ ▽▽
Bed & Breakfast
$94-$230

Phone: (418)665-1090
Address: 301 rue St-Raphael G5A 2N6 **Location:** Rt 138; in Cap-a-L'Aigle sector (entrance from Rt 138). **Facility:** 10 units, some cottages. 2 stories (no elevator), interior/exterior corridors. *Bath:* some shared. **Parking:** winter plug-ins. **Terms:** 2 night minimum stay - seasonal. **Guest Services:** valet laundry.

🛜 ✕ 🎿 🏊 / SOME UNITS 📺 🔺 💳

ECONO LODGE

▽▽ ▽▽
Hotel
Rates not provided

Phone: 418/665-3733
Address: 625 boul de Comporté G5A 1T1 **Location:** On Rt 362, just w of jct Rt 138. **Facility:** 17 units. 3 stories (no elevator), interior corridors. **Parking:** winter plug-ins. **Dining:** Restaurant Le Plaza, see separate listing.

¶✚ 🛜 FEE 👤 🔺 💳

FAIRMONT LE MANOIR RICHELIEU

Phone: (418)665-3703

Classic Historic Resort Hotel

$139-$279

Address: 181 rue Richelieu G5A 1X7 **Location:** On Rt 362, 2.6 mi (4.1 km) w of jct Rt 138. Adjacent to a casino. **Facility:** This full-service, family-friendly riverfront resort is adjacent to a casino and golf course, and the on-site recreational facilities are extensive. 405 units. 5 stories, interior corridors. **Parking:** on-site and valet. **Terms:** check-in 4 pm, cancellation fee imposed. **Amenities:** safes, honor bars. **Fee:** video games, high-speed Internet. **Dining:** 4 restaurants, also, Le Charlevoix, see separate listing, entertainment. **Pool(s):** 2 heated outdoor, heated indoor. **Activities:** sauna, whirlpools, steamroom, 3 lighted tennis courts, ice skating, recreation programs, hiking trails, shuffleboard, volleyball, exercise room, spa. **Fee:** charter fishing, golf-27 holes, miniature golf, snowmobiling, bicycles. **Guest Services:** valet laundry. **Free Special Amenities: high-speed Internet and children's activities.**

The Castle on the cliff, Fairmont Le Manoir Richelieu your luxury hotel in the region of Charlevoix

LA MAISON DES BERGES DU SAINT-LAURENT

Phone: 418/665-2742

Historic Country Inn

Rates not provided

Address: 830 rue Richelieu G5A 2X3 **Location:** Just off Rt 362, 1.8 mi (2.9 km) w of jct Rt 138; in Pointe-au-Pic sector. **Facility:** Overlooking the riverfront road, this cozy village cottage has pleasant, well-maintained guest rooms, four of which afford river views. 8 units. 3 stories (no elevator), interior corridors.

LA PINSONNIÈRE

Phone: (418)665-4431

Country Inn

$295-$495 6/1-10/31
$295-$445 11/1-5/31

Address: 124 rue St-Raphael G5A 1X9 **Location:** Just off Rt 138, follow signs; in Cap-a-L'Aigle sector. **Facility:** Manicured grounds surround this riverfront estate, which features spacious, luxurious rooms with therapeutic or jetted tubs and fireplaces. 17 units, some two bedrooms. 2 stories (no elevator), interior corridors. **Terms:** check-in 4 pm, 2 night minimum stay - weekends, 15 day cancellation notice-fee imposed. **Amenities:** safes, honor bars. **Some:** high-speed Internet. **Dining:** restaurant, see separate listing. **Pool(s):** heated indoor. **Activities:** sauna, tennis court, cross country skiing, snowmobiling. **Fee:** massage. **Guest Services:** valet laundry.

Create complete trip routings
and custom maps with the
TripTik® Travel Planner
on AAA.com or CAA.ca

WHERE TO EAT

LE CHARLEVOIX

Phone: 418/665-3703

French

$36-$49

AAA Inspector Notes: In a classic luxury hotel, this upscale restaurant showcases the finest in regional cuisine and makes creative use of fresh local ingredients. An effort is made to seek out organic and sustainable produce, when available. Menu items may include roasted shrimp, organic salmon, Dover sole, lobster in Sortilege liqueur, black Angus beef tenderloin, slow-cooked veal fillet, rack of lamb, stuffed deer fillet and duck breast. Most tables afford memorable views of the river and manicured grounds. **Bar:** full bar. **Address:** 181 rue Richelieu G5A 1X7 **Location:** Rt 362, 2.6 mi (4.1 km) w of jct Rt 138; in Fairmont Le Manoir Richelieu. **Parking:** on-site and valet.

RESTAURANT DE LA PINSONNIÈRE

Phone: 418/665-4431

French

$12-$52

AAA Inspector Notes: Grilled scallops, halibut, Quebec lamb and pork, milk-fed veal, roast squab, duck and Atlantic salmon are representative of the haute Quebecois cuisine with some Asian influences. The wine list is extensive and live music is offered most nights in the elegant, comfortable dining room, which affords lovely river views. During summer, the terrace is a cozy place for light lunches. **Bar:** full bar. **Reservations:** required. **Address:** 124 rue St-Raphael G5A 1X9 **Location:** Just off Rt 138, follow signs; in Cap-a-L'Aigle sector; in La Pinsonnière.

RESTAURANT L'ALLEGRO

Phone: 418/665-2595

Italian

$11-$34

AAA Inspector Notes: This cheerful, lively corner bistro-with its sunny summer terrace-is a favorite spot for affordably-priced pasta and pizza. Prices include the gratuity. Opening hours may vary depending on the season. **Bar:** full bar. **Reservations:** suggested. **Address:** 990 rue Richelieu G5A 2X3 **Location:** Centre; in Pointe-au-Pic sector.

RESTAURANT LE PLAZA

Phone: 418/665-3733

Canadian

$11-$39

AAA Inspector Notes: This bay front, family-friendly eatery specializes in grilled meats, fish, seafood, brochettes, pizza and fondues. A children's menu is available. Alcohol is not sold on the premises, but guests are free to bring in their own wine or beer. **Address:** 625 boul de Comporté G5A 1T1 **Location:** On Rt 362, just w of jct Rt 138; in Econo Lodge.

LA MAURICIE NATIONAL PARK OF CANADA (D-4)

Elevations in the park range from 98 metres (320 ft.) along the St. Maurice River to 457 metres (1,500 ft.) at an area near Lake Houle. Refer to AAA/CAA maps for additional elevation information.

North of Trois-Rivières, halfway between Montréal and Québec and accessible from Hwy. 55, La Mauricie National Park of Canada (Parc national du Canada de la Mauricie) is an unspoiled area in the Laurentian Mountains that occupies 536 square kilometres (206 sq. mi.) in the St. Maurice Valley. The park overlies bedrock dating from the Precambrian era, which began about 980 million years ago.

During the last ice age, glaciers scored the land and left rolling hills. Terraces along the St. Maurice

River once formed the beaches of the postglacial Champlain Sea. Two main valleys are marked by chains of narrow lakes.

Of the more than 193 bird species that have been observed, 116 nest in the park. Mammals include moose, black bears, wolves and red foxes. Picnicking, camping, canoeing, swimming and fishing are popular pastimes in summer; winter brings cross-country skiing, snowshoeing and winter camping.

Park open mid-May to mid-Oct. and late Dec.-Mar. 31. Hours vary; phone ahead. Admission $7.80; $6.80 (ages 65+); $3.90 (ages 6-16); $19.60 (family). Prices may vary, and an extra fee may be charged for individual activities. For more information contact the Park Superintendent, La Mauricie National Park of Canada, 702 5th St., P.O. Box 160, Main Station, Shawinigan, QC, Canada G9N 6T9; phone (819) 538-3232 or (888) 773-8888, or (877) 737-3783 for camping reservations. *See Recreation Chart.*

L'ANCIENNE-LORETTE pop. 16,516
• Hotels & Restaurants map & index p. 429
• Part of Québec area — see map p. 405

CHÂTEAU REPOTEL   Phone: (418)872-1111   37

Hotel
$93-$150
Address: 6555 boul Wilfrid-Hamel G2E 5W3 **Location:** Jct boul Duplessis and Wilfrid-Hamel (Hwy 138). **Facility:** 100 units. 4 stories, interior corridors. **Parking:** on-site (fee), winter plug-ins. **Amenities:** *Some:* honor bars. **Guest Services:** valet laundry. 🛎 🛜 / SOME UNITS 🅿

COMFORT INN   Phone: (418)872-5900   39
Hotel
$80-$120
Address: 1255 boul Duplessis G2G 2B4 **Location:** Jct boul Duplessis and Wilfrid-Hamel (Hwy 138). **Facility:** 59 units. 2 stories (no elevator), interior corridors. **Parking:** winter plug-ins.
Terms: cancellation fee imposed. **Guest Services:** valet laundry.
 🛎 🛜 🖥 / SOME UNITS FEE 🐾 FEE 🅿 FEE 🖼

HOTEL & SUITES LE TIMES   Phone: (418)877-7788   36
Hotel
$149-$169 6/1-9/30
$139-$159 10/1-5/31
Address: 6515 boul Wilfrid-Hamel G2E 5W3 **Location:** Just e of autoroute 540 (boul Duplessis). **Facility:** 111 units. 5 stories, interior corridors. **Parking:** winter plug-ins. **Terms:** cancellation fee imposed.
Amenities: high-speed Internet. *Some:* safes. **Pool(s):** heated indoor. **Activities:** exercise room. **Fee:** massage. **Guest Services:** valet and coin laundry.
🛎 🏊 BIZ 🛜 ✕ / SOME UNITS 🅿 🖼 🖥

HOTEL MUST   Phone: 418/380-6878   38
Hotel
$115-$305
Address: 1345 route de l'Aeroport G2G 1G5 **Location:** Corner of boul Wilfrid-Hamel. **Facility:** 179 units. 7 stories, interior corridors. **Terms:** check-in 4 pm. **Amenities:** high-speed Internet, safes. **Pool(s):** heated indoor. **Activities:** sauna, whirlpool, waterslide, lifeguard on duty, exercise room. **Guest Services:** valet and coin laundry.
 🍴 🍸 CALL 🎦 🏊 BIZ 🛜 ✕ FEE 🐾
🅿 🖼 🖥

WHERE TO EAT

CAGE AUX SPORTS   Phone: 418/872-3000

Canadian
$8-$22
AAA Inspector Notes: This popular Quebec chain of sports bars presents a menu of pub foods, including ribs, chicken, burgers, salads, crispy fries, pasta and tasty desserts. Guests might begin the meal with a basket of freshly popped popcorn as they check out the sports memorabilia. Children are welcomed. **Bar:** full bar. **Address:** 6476 boul Wilfrid-Hamel ouest G2E 2J1 **Location:** Just e of boul Duplessis. 🅛 🅓

L'ANSE-AU-GRIFFON (B-9)

LeBOUTILLIER MANOR (Manoir LeBoutillier), on Hwy. 132 at 578 boul. Griffon, was the fishing post of merchant and legislator John LeBoutillier during the mid-19th century. The building faces the harbor, where LeBoutillier could oversee his fishing fleets. Exhibits depict the commercial development of the region's fishing industry. **Tours:** Guided tours are available. **Hours:** Daily 9-5, mid-June to early Oct. Last admission 30 minutes before closing. **Cost:** $7; $5 (ages 66+ and students with ID); free (ages 0-11); $16 (family). **Phone:** (418) 892-5150.

LA POCATIERE pop. 4,575

MOTEL LE POCATOIS   Phone: 418/856-1688
Motel
$109-$189
Address: 235 Rt 132 G0R 1Z0 **Location:** Hwy 20 exit 439, 0.5 mi (0.8 km) s. **Facility:** 21 units. 2 stories, interior/exterior corridors. **Parking:** winter plug-ins. **Guest Services:** valet laundry.
🍴 🍸 🛜 🖥 🖼 / SOME UNITS 🐾

LASALLE (F-7) elev. 7m/26'
• Part of Montréal area — see map p. 312

LACHINE RAPIDS EXCURSIONS (Les Excursions Rapides de Lachine), 8912 boul. LaSalle, provides guided trips aboard specially designed jet boats. Lasting 1 hour and 15 minutes, the high-speed adventure offers visitors an up-close encounter with the St. Lawrence River's rumbling rapids. Whitewater rafting excursions, kayak and raft rentals, and kitesurfing courses also are available.

Hours: Jet boat tours depart several times daily 9-6, May 1-Sept. 1. **Cost:** Jet boat trip $51; $40 (ages 13-18); $30 (ages 8-12); $127 (family, two adults and two children). White-water rafting excursion $41; $35 (ages 13-18); $24 (ages 6-12); $104 (family, two adults and two children). Reservations are required. **Phone:** (514) 767-2230 or (800) 324-7238.

LAURENTIAN HIGHLANDS

The Laurentian Mountain region, *Les Laurentides* in French, is part of Québec's vast wilderness of dense forests, glacial lakes and rivers stretching northwest of the populous St. Lawrence Valley. The land's inhospitableness caused many settlers to leave Québec in the 19th century, but not Roman Catholic priest François-Xavier-Antoine Labelle.

As proof of his faith, Father Labelle created 20 new parishes in the Laurentian wilderness just northwest of Montréal, promising his parishioners that one day strangers would flock to the area and scatter gold by the handful. When Father Labelle began his efforts, there were barely a dozen communities north of St-Jérôme, and gold was nowhere apparent.

If he returned today, Labelle would find his prophecy fulfilled in the 19 ski resorts that line Hwy. 117 from St-Jérôme to Mont-Tremblant. The mountains and lakes that once provided foresters and farmers with their livelihoods are now the backbone of a resort area devoted principally to skiing.

Herman "Jack Rabbit" Johannssen loved touring the region and created the Maple Leaf Trail, which linked Prévost with Mont-Tremblant; only part of the trail remains today.

Improvising with lines, tackles and an automobile engine, Alex Foster laid the cornerstone for alpine skiing by building Canada's first ski tow and laying out a slalom run in Prévost in the 1930s.

From a simple rope tow and slalom run have come the more than 350 ski runs that now dot the mountainsides as well as the many trails connecting various communities.

The Laurentians are more than a ski resort; they also are a retreat from the nearby urban centers. The tranquility of the area has encouraged painters, musicians, artisans and writers to settle in Ste-Adèle, Val-David and other such villages.

During the summer, works are displayed in numerous theaters, craft fairs and folklore festivals. The region also is known for its spectacular fall foliage from mid-September to mid-October.

Mont-Tremblant National Park *(see attraction listing p. 392)* has hundreds of trails from which to view the park's many lakes, waterfalls and wildlife.

Towns in the Laurentian Highlands listed individually are Mont-Tremblant, St-Jérôme, St-Sauveur, Ste-Adèle, Ste-Agathe-des-Monts and Val-David.

LAVAL (E-7) pop. 368,709

- **Restaurants p. 300**
- **Hotels & Restaurants map & index p. 342**
- **Part of Montréal area — see map p. 312**

Granted to the Jesuits in 1636, Île Jésus—an island surrounded by the Mille-Îles and Prairies rivers and lac des Deux-Montagnes—was almost exclusively used as farmland for more than 2 centuries. In the early 1900s, the slowly urbanizing Île Jésus became a popular destination for vacationers visiting from Montréal, just south across the Rivière des Prairies. Over time a speckled landscape of villages began to emerge, and 14 separate municipalities on the island amalgamated to form the city of Laval in 1965.

While you'll certainly encounter modern communities in Laval, the area still is known for its charming rural landscapes. Many local farmers sell the fruits (such as strawberries, raspberries and apples) of their labor in the vicinity. Several agricultural operations welcome visitors who delight in picking their own produce, including Chez Vaillancourt, 3155 av. des Perron, (450) 622-6429 or (450) 625-3006, open May through October; Ferme D. et M. Sauriol,

▼ See AAA listing p. 467 ▼

(See map & index p. 342.)

3150 boul. des Mille-Îles, (450) 666-6564, open mid-June to mid-October; and Ferme F. Turcot et Fils, 7209 av. des Perron, (450) 622-6872, open June through October.

Continue nibbling at the 440 Public Market (Marché Public 440) on Hwy. 440, home to a variety of specialty food vendors. With the market offering everything from gourmet cheeses to fine chocolates, you're certain to find a few goodies to bring home (though it's doubtful such delectable treats will make it that far). Sample a snack or two while browsing the stores, but try not to spoil your appetite! With on-site eateries serving up sushi, deli fare, pizza, steaks and seafood, the market (open Wed. and Sat. 9-6, Thurs.-Fri. 9-9) is a convenient munching spot for indecisive diners.

In addition many of the former municipalities now comprising Laval afford ample shopping opportunities. Such neighborhoods as Old Ste-Rose (Vieux-Ste-Rose) and Old St-Vincent-de-Paul (Vieux-St-Vincent-de-Paul) boast quaint streets lined by clothing boutiques, arts and crafts shops, cafés and antique dealers. In pastoral Old Ste-Dorothée (Vieux-Ste-Dorothée) the province's largest concentration of flower producers will enchant you with vibrant, fragrant displays of merchandise.

Chock-full of green space, Laval beckons nature lovers. One of the area's largest natural expanses is Mille-Îles River Park (Parc de la Rivière-des-Mille-Îles), which is part of a protected wildlife sanctuary. Explore marshes and forested islands teeming with life on a solo kayak trip along the river, or board a rabaska canoe for a narrated group tour of the archipelago. Located at 345 boul. Ste-Rose, the park is open daily from mid-May to mid-October; phone (450) 622-1020.

The Nature Centre (Centre de la Nature), 901 av. du Parc, is a 50-hectare (123-acre) urban park frequented year-round by such outdoor enthusiasts as hikers, kayakers and rock climbers. Also on the grounds are a small farm inhabited by barnyard animals, an observatory, and a greenhouse sheltering tropical plants; phone (450) 662-4942.

An exhilarating way to take in Laval's many parks and wooded expanses is to traverse the Route Verte, a vast network of bike paths crisscrossing Québec. From Montréal, the trail cuts across the center of Île Jésus; it also runs along the lower half of the island's northern shore. For those who prefer to travel by foot, hiking trails abound in Laval. Five kilometres (3 mi.) of trails are available at Papineau Woods (Bois Papineau), 3235 boul. St-Martin Est, while a 4-kilometre (2.5-mi.) pedestrian pathway highlights the scenic beauty of the Park of the Meadows (Parc des Prairies).

Laval Tourism: 2900 boul. St-Martin Ouest, Laval, QC, Canada H7T 2J2. Phone: (450) 682-5522 or (877) 465-2825.

COSMODÔME/CANADA SPACE CAMP is off Hwy. 15 exit 8, .5 km (.3 mi.) w. on boul. St-Martin, .8 km (.5 mi.) n. on boul. Pierre Péladeau, and .2 km (.1 mi.) on av. du Cosmodôme. The Cosmodôme is a science center devoted to the science and technologies of space flight. Visitors choose from three interactive "missions"; during each 60-minute educational experience, participants must make decisions as if they were interplanetary explorers, engineers or space station workers.

A space camp also is offered; phone ahead for details. Tours: Guided tours are available. Time: Allow 2 hours minimum. Hours: Cosmodôme daily 9-5, late June-Labour Day; Tues.-Sun. 10-5, rest of year. Cost: One 60-minute mission and permanent exhibition $15; $12 (students with ID); $10 (ages 60+); $40 (family); free (ages 0-6). Other combination tickets are available. Prices may vary. Phone: (450) 978-3600 or (800) 565-2267.

LAVAL CHILDREN'S MUSEUM (Musée pour Enfants de Laval) is 1 km (.6 mi.) n. of Hwy. 440 exit 19 at 3805 boul. Curé-Labelle. Two levels of themed play rooms are featured at the museum, which is geared toward children ages 2 through 8. With interactive displays highlighting the day-to-day skills needed in various trades, young visitors can emulate such working professionals as veterinarians, police officers, firefighters and construction workers. Time: Allow 2 hours minimum. Hours: Daily 9-5 (also Fri.-Sun. 5-6). Cost: $13.29 (ages 18 mo.-17 yr.); $7.10 (adults). Phone: (450) 681-4333.

WATER INTERPRETATION CENTRE (Centre d'interprétation de l'eau) is at 12 rue Hotte. The center's exhibits detail the intricacies of water, the resource's importance to and impact on the environment, and society's endeavor to use it responsibly and preserve it for future generations.

Note: Text contained within the center's exhibits is displayed in French only. Tours: Guided tours are available. Time: Allow 45 minutes minimum. Hours: Tues.-Sun. noon-5, mid-May to mid-Oct.; Wed. and Sun. noon-5, rest of year. Closed Jan. 1, Christmas Eve, Christmas and day after Christmas. Cost: $7; $5 (ages 60+); $4 (students with ID); free (ages 0-8); $15 (family). Phone: (450) 963-6463. 🎫

COMFORT INN
Hotel
$118-$173

Phone: (450)686-0600 27
Address: 2055 Autoroute des Laurentides H7S 1Z6 Location: Hwy 15 exit 8 (boul St-Martin), e on boul St-Martin, 0.4 mi (0.7 km) n on boul Le Corbusier, then just w on boul Tessier.
Facility: 120 units. 2 stories (no elevator), interior corridors. Parking: winter plug-ins. Terms: cancellation fee imposed. Guest Services: valet laundry.

SAVE ECO 🍽 🍸 BIZ 📶 FEE 🐾 ▭
/SOME UNITS FEE 🛏 FEE 🔌 FEE 🖼

(See map & index p. 342.)

ECONO LODGE
Phone: 450/681-6411 **30**

Hotel

Rates not provided

Address: 1981 boul Cure-Labelle H7T 1L4 **Location:** Hwy 15 exit 8 (boul St-Martin) northbound; exit 10 southbound 1.3 mi (2 km) w on boul St-Martin ouest, then 0.3 mi (0.5 km) n. Located in a commercial area. **Facility:** 75 units. 2 stories (no elevator), interior/exterior corridors. **Parking:** winter plug-ins. **Terms:** check-in 4 pm. **Pool(s):** outdoor.

HAMPTON INN & SUITES-LAVAL
Phone: (450)687-0010 **31**

Hotel

$119-$149

AAA Benefit: Members save up to 10% everyday!

Address: 1961 boul Cure-Labelle H7T 1L4 **Location:** Hwy 15 exit 8 (boul St-Martin) northbound; exit 10 southbound 1.4 mi (2.3 km) w on boul St-Martin ouest, then just n. **Facility:** 104 units. 5 stories, interior corridors. **Terms:** 1-7 night minimum stay, cancellation fee imposed. **Amenities:** video games (fee), high-speed Internet. **Pool(s):** heated indoor. **Activities:** exercise room. **Guest Services:** valet and coin laundry. **Free Special Amenities: expanded continental breakfast and high-speed Internet.**

HOLIDAY INN LAVAL MONTREAL
Phone: (450)682-9000 **26**

Hotel

$109-$229

Address: 2900 boul Le Carrefour H7T 2K9 **Location:** Hwy 15 exit 10, follow signs. Adjacent to shopping centre. **Facility:** 176 units. 6 stories, interior corridors. **Terms:** cancellation fee imposed. **Amenities:** high-speed Internet. **Dining:** Cage aux Sports, see separate listing. **Pool(s):** heated indoor. **Activities:** exercise room. **Guest Services:** valet and coin laundry. **Free Special Amenities: high-speed Internet and use of on-premises laundry facilities.**

HOTEL CHÂTEAUNEUF LAVAL
Phone: (450)681-9000 **23**

Hotel

$100-$199

Address: 3655 Autoroute des Laurentides H7L 3H7 **Location:** Hwy 15 exit 10, just n on east side service road. **Facility:** 70 units. 3 stories, interior corridors. **Amenities:** high-speed Internet. **Pool(s):** heated indoor. **Guest Services:** valet laundry. **Free Special Amenities: local telephone calls and high-speed Internet.**

HOTEL HILTON MONTREAL-LAVAL
Phone: 450/682-2225 **25**

Hotel

Rates not provided

AAA Benefit: Members save 5% or more everyday!

Address: 2225 Autoroute des Laurentides H7S 1Z6 **Location:** Hwy 15 exit 8 (boul St-Martin) northbound; exit 10 southbound. **Facility:** 169 units. 10 stories, interior corridors. **Amenities:** high-speed Internet (fee), honor bars. **Pool(s):** heated indoor. **Activities:** whirlpool, exercise room. **Guest Services:** valet laundry.

LE ST-MARTIN HOTEL & SUITES
Phone: (450)902-3000 **29**

Hotel

$129-$369

Address: 1400 rue Maurice-Gauvin H7S 2P1 **Location:** Hwy 15 exit 8 (boul St-Martin) northbound; exit 10 southbound just e. **Facility:** 116 units, some kitchens. 3-6 stories, interior corridors. **Parking:** winter plug-ins. **Amenities:** high-speed Internet, honor bars. **Activities:** whirlpools, exercise room. **Guest Services:** valet laundry. **Free Special Amenities: expanded continental breakfast and high-speed Internet.**

QUALITY SUITES LAVAL
Phone: (450)686-6777 **28**

Hotel

$128-$188

Address: 2035 Autoroute des Laurentides H7S 1Z6 **Location:** Hwy 15 exit 8 (boul St-Martin), 0.4 mi (0.7 km) n on boul Le Corbusier, then just w on boul Tessier. **Facility:** 115 units. 3 stories, interior corridors. **Parking:** winter plug-ins. **Terms:** cancellation fee imposed. **Amenities:** high-speed Internet. **Guest Services:** valet laundry.

SHERATON LAVAL HOTEL
Phone: (450)687-2440 **24**

Hotel

$129-$269

AAA Benefit: Members get up to 15% off, plus Starwood Preferred Guest® bonuses.

Address: 2440 Autoroute des Laurentides H7T 1X5 **Location:** Hwy 15 exit 10. **Facility:** This posh hotel is near a major shopping center and offers spacious, luxurious guest rooms. 244 units. 7 stories, interior corridors. **Amenities:** high-speed Internet (fee), honor bars. *Some:* safes. **Pool(s):** heated indoor. **Activities:** sauna, whirlpool, steamroom, exercise room, spa. **Guest Services:** valet laundry.

WHERE TO EAT

BATON ROUGE
Phone: 450/681-9902

American

$10-$35

AAA Inspector Notes: This one offers an intimate setting with a casual steakhouse ambiance. Offerings include their signature BBQ pork ribs, fresh grilled fish, chicken, meal-sized salads, pasta, burgers and sandwiches. But the main attraction remains the aged AAA grade steaks and the slow-roasted prime rib of beef. **Bar:** full bar. **Address:** 3035 boul Le Carrefour H7T 1C8 **Location:** Hwy 15 exit 10, then just w; in Carrefour Laval Shopping Centre. [L] [D]

CAGE AUX SPORTS
Phone: 450/688-8244

Canadian

$8-$22

AAA Inspector Notes: This popular Quebec chain of sports bars presents a menu of pub foods, including ribs, chicken, burgers, salads, crispy fries, pasta and tasty desserts. Guests might begin the meal with a basket of freshly popped popcorn as they check out the sports memorabilia. Children are welcomed. **Bar:** full bar. **Address:** 2900 boul Le Carrefour H7T 2K9 **Location:** Hwy 15 exit 10, follow signs; in Holiday Inn Laval Montreal. [L] [D] [LATE]

(See map & index p. 342.)

COMMENSAL VEGETARIAN RESTAURANT
                              Phone: 450/978-9124

Vegetarian
$9-$15

AAA Inspector Notes: An upscale self-service buffet features an extensive selection of creative hot and cold items, such as leek pot pie, sweet potato kasha and lasagna, plus a variety of desserts, everything of which is exclusively vegetarian. The pleasant, contemporary surroundings change often as new paintings are displayed. **Bar:** beer & wine. **Address:** 3180 boul St-Martin ouest H7T 1A1 **Location:** Hwy 15 exit 9 northbound; exit 10 southbound, 0.3 mi (0.5 km) w. L D

LE TIRE-BOUCHON BISTRO PARISIEN
                         Phone: 450/681-1228   53

French
$15-$30

AAA Inspector Notes: A great selection of wines by the glass and classic French bistro dishes add joie de vivre to this inviting eatery in a popular mall. The menu offers duck confit salad, crab cakes, foie gras terrine, Toulouse sausages, steak frites, blood sausage, filet mignon, sweetbreads, stuffed caribou, mussels and salmon or beef tartare. **Bar:** full bar. **Reservations:** required. **Address:** 2930 ave Pierre-Peladeau H7T 3B3 **Location:** Hwy 15 exit 8, 0.3 mi (0.4 km) w on boul St-Martin ouest, just n; in Centropolis Mall. L D

RESTAURANT LE SAINT-CHRISTOPHE
                              Phone: 450/622-7963   52

French
$48-$62

AAA Inspector Notes: Traditional fine French cuisine is presented in the elegant parlors of a 1912 red-brick home. Service is friendly and attentive. A seasonal terrace faces lovely gardens. The four- or five-course tasting menu features such specialties as foie gras, quail breast and leg, braised salmon, cassoulet (in winter months), roasted sweetbreads and filet mignon. An impressive selection of cheese is offered nightly as well as refined wine service. **Bar:** full bar. **Reservations:** suggested. **Address:** 94 boul Ste-Rose est H7L 1K4 **Location:** Hwy 15 exit 16, 1.7 mi (2.7 km) e. **Historic** D

RISTORANTE TERRACINA   Phone: 450/973-4143   54

Italian
$13-$28

AAA Inspector Notes: This casually elegant restaurant specializes in traditional Italian cuisine, with an excellent variety of pastas, seafood and meats, including osso buco, calamari and fish. **Bar:** full bar. **Address:** 2070 boul Cure-Labelle H7T 1V6 **Location:** Hwy 15 exit 8 (boul St-Martin) northbound; exit 10 southbound 1.5 mi (2.5 km) w on boul St-Martin ouest, then just n. L D

ST-HUBERT   Phone: 450/687-4170

Canadian
$8-$22

AAA Inspector Notes: The pleasantly decorated family-friendly restaurant serves affordable chicken dinners, ribs, club sandwiches, chicken wings, salads, soups and hot chicken sandwiches. The children's menu includes animal nuggets. **Bar:** full bar. **Address:** 3325 boul St-Martin ouest H7N 5B5 **Location:** Hwy 15 exit boul St-Martin. L D

LE BIC (C-7)

BIC NATIONAL PARK (Parc national du Bic), s. via Hwy. 132, preserves some of the tidal coastline along the St. Lawrence River. Its inlets, marshes and wooded hills are home to a variety of marine life and thousands of eider ducks and seals. The Rivière-du-Sud-Ouest Visitors Centre is at the park's main entrance.

Hiking and bicycle trails traverse the park; snowshoeing and kayaking also are popular activities. *See Recreation Chart.* Pets are not permitted. **Hours:** Rivière-du-Sud-Ouest Visitors Centre open daily, late May-early Oct. Hours vary; phone ahead. **Cost:** $6; $2.75 (ages 6-17); $12 (family, two adults and children); $8.75 (family, one adult and children). Prices may vary. **Phone:** (418) 736-5035 or (800) 665-6527. ▲ ⑪ ⌧ ⌂

LES BERGERONNES (C-6) pop. 600, elev. 32m/105'

CAP-DE-BON-DÉSIR INTERPRETATION AND OBSERVATION CENTRE (Centre d'interprétation et d'observation du Cap-de-Bon-Désir) is at 13 ch. de Cap-de-Bon-Désir and is part of the Saguenay-St. Lawrence Marine Park *(see attraction listing p. 456).* Landlubbers can view the diverse marine wildlife of the St. Lawrence estuary. On-site naturalists conduct various interpretation activities and are available to answer visitors' questions.

English narration is available. **Hours:** Daily 9-6, mid-June through Labour Day; 9-5, day after Labour Day to mid-Oct. **Cost:** $7.80; $6.80 (ages 65+); $3.90 (ages 6-16); $19.60 (family). **Phone:** (418) 232-6751, (418) 235-4703 or (888) 773-8888. ⌂

LES EBOULEMENTS pop. 1,264

AUBERGE LE SUROUET   Phone: 418/635-1401

Country Inn
$110

Address: 195 rue du Village G0A 2M0 **Location:** On Rt 362. **Facility:** An art gallery is on the grounds of this inn, which offers some rooms with fireplaces and balconies. The countryside setting is enchanting. 5 units. 2 stories (no elevator), interior corridors. **Parking:** winter plug-ins. **Terms:** open 6/1-10/31. **Dining:** Restaurant le Surouet, see separate listing. ⑪ ⌂ ⌧ ▢ / SOME UNITS ⌧

WHERE TO EAT

RESTAURANT LE SUROUET   Phone: 418/635-1401

French
$13-$25

AAA Inspector Notes: Fine, regional ingredients flavor the dishes of French bistro cuisine at this relaxed restaurant set in a pleasant country inn. Stop in for anything from a light luncheon to a complete multi-course prix fixe dinner, including such classics as and fries, chicken breast, burgers, pizza and pasta. The terrace is a nice spot for after-dinner drinks, and patrons are welcomed to browse the on-site artisan shop and mini-art gallery. **Bar:** full bar. **Reservations:** suggested. **Address:** 195 rue du Village G0A 2M0 **Location:** On Rt 362; in Auberge Le Surouet. B L D ⌧

LES ESCOUMINS (C-6)

MARINE ENVIRONMENT DISCOVERY CENTRE (Centre de découverte du milieu marin) is at 41 rue des Pilotes. Part of the Saguenay-St. Lawrence Marine Park *(see attraction listing p. 456),* the facility features displays about the marine life of the St.

Lawrence estuary and explores its underwater mysteries. Visitors can glimpse marine mammals from the shore or take part in a variety of interpretive and interactive activities, including broadcast diving.

Time: Allow 1 hour, 30 minutes minimum. **Hours:** Daily 9-6, mid-June through Labour Day; Fri.-Sun. 9-6, day after Labour Day to mid-Oct. **Cost:** $7.80; $6.80 (senior citizens); $3.90 (ages 6-16); $19.60 (family). Prices for interpretive activities vary. **Phone:** (418) 233-4414 or (888) 773-8888.

LÉVIS (A-1)
- **Hotels & Restaurants map & index p. 429**
- **Part of Québec area — see map p. 405**

LÉVIS FORTS NATIONAL HISTORIC SITE (Lieu historique national des Forts-de-Lévis) is on the s. shore of the St. Lawrence River, .5 km (.3 mi.) n. of jct. rue Mgr Ignace Bourget and Hwy. 132. One of three British detached forts built 1865-72 on the heights of Pointe-Lévy, Fort No. 1 was meant to protect the city of Québec from an invasion by the United States following the American Civil War.

The Treaty of Washington between the United States and England, signed in 1871, settled the disagreements between the two countries. Consequently none of the forts ever housed a garrison.

Tours highlight 19th-century military architecture, cannons, the powder magazine, vaulted caponiers, the shooting gallery and massive terrepleins.

The restored Fort No. 1 offers both guided and self-guiding tours that are available in English. **Time:** Allow 2 hours minimum. **Hours:** Daily 10-5, early May-late Aug.; Sat.-Sun. 10-5, last weekend in Sept. Phone ahead to confirm schedule. **Cost:** $3.90; $3.40 (ages 66+); $1.90 (ages 6-16); $9.80

(family). **Phone:** (418) 835-5182 or (888) 773-8888.

COMFORT INN   Phone: (418)835-5605 **45**

Hotel
$85-$145

Address: 10 du Vallon est G6V 9J3 **Location:** Hwy 20 exit 325S eastbound; exit 325 westbound. **Facility:** 99 units. 2 stories (no elevator), interior corridors. **Parking:** winter plug-ins. **Terms:** cancellation fee imposed. **Guest Services:** valet laundry.

COMFORT INN & SUITES RIVE-SUD QUEBEC
Phone: 418/836-3336 **46**

Hotel
Rates not provided

Address: 495 Rte-du-Pont G7A 2N9 **Location:** on Rt 116; in St-Nicolas sector. **Facility:** 77 units. 4 stories, interior corridors. **Parking:** winter plug-ins. **Amenities:** high-speed Internet. **Pool(s):** heated indoor. **Activities:** whirlpool, exercise room. **Guest Services:** valet and coin laundry.

FOUR POINTS BY SHERATON LEVIS CONVENTION CENTRE   Phone: (418)838-0025 **42**

Hotel
$100-$210

FOUR POINTS BY SHERATON **AAA Benefit:** Members get up to 15% off, plus Starwood Preferred Guest® bonuses.

Address: 5800 rue J. B. Michaud G6V 0B3 **Location:** Hwy 20 exit 325N, 0.3 mi (0.5 km) n on Rte du President-Kennedy. **Facility:** 150 units. 10 stories, interior corridors. **Dining:** Cosmos Café, see separate listing. **Activities:** whirlpool, exercise room. **Guest Services:** valet laundry. **Free Special Amenities:** high-speed Internet. *(See ad this page.)*

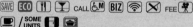

▼ See AAA listing this page ▼

(See map & index p. 429.)

HOTEL KENNEDY
Phone: 418/837-0233 **44**

Hotel
$90-$190

Address: 129 Rte du President-Kennedy G6V 6C8 **Location:** Hwy 20 exit 325N, just n. **Facility:** 37 units, some efficiencies. 2 stories, interior/exterior corridors. **Amenities:** high-speed Internet. **Guest Services:** valet laundry.

 / SOME UNITS FEE

QUALITY INN & SUITES LEVIS
Phone: (418)833-1212 **43**

Hotel
$109-$189

Address: 5800 rue des Arpents G6V 0B5 **Location:** Hwy 20 exit 325, just ne. **Facility:** 96 units. 4 stories, interior corridors. **Terms:** cancellation fee imposed. **Amenities:** high-speed Internet. Some: safes. **Pool(s):** heated indoor. **Activities:** exercise room. **Guest Services:** valet and coin laundry.

WHERE TO EAT

CHEZ CORA
Phone: 418/838-1444

Canadian
$6-$13

AAA Inspector Notes: Eggs, omelets, waffles, crepes (sorry, no American-style pancakes here), French toast, fruit platters and all the breakfast meats--that's the specialty here, all day. However, at lunchtime the menu lists a selection of soups, salads, quiches, sandwiches and a dish called the grilled panini crepe. **Address:** 79 Rte du President-Kennedy G6V 4Z6 **Location:** On Rte 132; centre.

B L

COSMOS CAFÉ
Phone: 418/830-8888 **28**

Continental
$9-$22

AAA Inspector Notes: This stylish hotel café and bar features wholesome foods including twelve choices of pasta, French onion soup, poutine, burgers, smoked salmon, cheese platters, pizza, gourmet hot dogs, salads, grilled chicken, veal parmigiana and filet mignon. A large breakfast menu also is available. After dark, the fiber-optic lighting system continuously changes the room's color scheme. **Bar:** full bar. **Reservations:** suggested. **Address:** 5700 rue J. B. Michaud G6V 0B3 **Location:** Hwy 20 exit 325N, 0.3 mi (0.5 km) n on Rte du President-Kennedy; in Four Points by Sheraton Levis Convention Centre. B L D CALL M

RESTAURANT L'INTIMISTE
Phone: 418/838-2711 **27**

French
$10-$38

AAA Inspector Notes: This comfortable, upscale dining room in Old Levis presents a menu of grilled pork, salmon filet, breast of duck, lamb, sweetbreads, flambeed scallops and red deer. The ferry boat dock for trips into Old Quebec is a short drive away. **Bar:** full bar. **Reservations:** suggested. **Address:** 35 ave Begin G6V 4B8 **Location:** Just e of boul Alphonse-Desjardins; in Old Levis. **Parking:** street only. L D

RESTAURANT MUSTANG BILL PIZZA
Phone: 418/831-0613 **29**

Canadian
$6-$20

AAA Inspector Notes: This family-friendly restaurant serves a variety of popular comfort foods, including pizza, club sandwiches, burgers, smoked meat, pasta and onion rings. For dessert try the house-prepared pies. Take-out and delivery are available. **Bar:** full bar. **Address:** 231 Rte du Pont G7A 2T6 **Location:** On Rt 116, just s of Rt 132; in St-Nicholas sector. L D

RESTAURANT NORMANDIN
Phone: 418/839-5861

Canadian
$6-$12

AAA Inspector Notes: The family restaurant prepares affordable comfort foods that include roasted chicken, hot chicken sandwiches, pasta, burgers and fries. Take-out service, a children's menu and cutely decorated desserts are among other offerings. **Bar:** full bar. **Address:** 2080 boul de la Rive-Sud G6W 2S6 **Location:** On Hwy 132; in St-Romuald sector. B L D

ST-HUBERT
Phone: 418/835-1234

Canadian
$8-$22

AAA Inspector Notes: The pleasantly decorated family-friendly restaurant serves affordable chicken dinners, ribs, club sandwiches, chicken wings, salads, soups and hot chicken sandwiches. The children's menu includes animal nuggets. **Bar:** full bar. **Address:** 49 C Rte du President-Kennedy G6V 4Z1 **Location:** Centre. L D

L'ILE-PERROT pop. 9,927
• Hotels & Restaurants map & index p. 342
• Part of Montréal area — see map p. 312

SMOKE MEAT PETE
Phone: 514/425-6068 **122**

Canadian
$8-$23

AAA Inspector Notes: Fans of this diner say you "can't beat Pete's meat." The house specialty is Montreal-style smoked meat but the varied menu includes other deli and fast-food favorites like grilled steaks, latkes and burgers. The seasonal terrace is popular in summer. Live blues music performed nightly from Thursday to Saturday. **Bar:** beer & wine. **Address:** 283 1ere ave J7V 5A1 **Location:** Hwy 20 exit boul Perrot, just se. B L D LATE

ZENTO SUSHI
Phone: 514/425-0302

Japanese
$14-$30

AAA Inspector Notes: Located in a suburban strip mall, this stylishly decorated restaurant serves up a wide assortment of freshly prepared sushi, sashimi and maki as well as a variety of popular Japanese dishes. **Bar:** full bar. **Address:** 475 boul Grand, Unit 12 J7V 4X4 **Location:** Hwy 20 exit boul Don-Quichotte, just s. L D

L'ISLET (D-6) pop. 3,840
• Hotels p. 304 • Restaurants p. 304

Located alongside the St. Lawrence River, the city of L'Islet merged with the villages of L'Islet-sur-Mer and St-Eugène to form the current municipality in 2000. L'Islet-sur-Mer has produced seafarers for more than 3 centuries; as a result, it is known locally as *la patrie des marins*, meaning "the sailor's homeland." Native Capt. J.E. Bernier took possession of the Arctic islands in the name of Canada on July 1, 1909. A plaque on Melville Island commemorates the event.

Of interest is the 1768 Notre-Dame-de-Bon-Secours Church (Église Notre-Dame-de-Bon-Secours) at 15 rue des Pionniers Est (Hwy. 132). The church has a wealth of decorative objects, including artwork by silversmith François Ranvoyzé and wood sculptor Médard Bourgault.

MARITIME MUSEUM OF QUÉBEC (Musée Maritime du Québec) is off Hwy. 20 exit 400 at 55 ch. des Pionniers Est (Hwy. 132). Housed in a former convent built in 1877, the museum describes the history of navigation on the St. Lawrence River.

Models, sailing ships, wooden boats and exhibits about Capt. J.E. Bernier's Arctic exploration are offered. Located behind the museum, Hydro-Québec Park, home to the ice breaker *Ernest Lapointe* and the hydrofoil *Bras d'Or 400*, features walking trails, interpretive displays and splendid views of the St. Lawrence River.

Hours: Museum daily 9-6, late June-Labour Day; 10-5, late May-late June and day after Labour Day-Thanksgiving; by appointment rest of year. The *Ernest Lapointe* and the *Bras d'Or 400* are generally open daily 10-4, in summer; phone ahead to confirm schedules. **Cost:** $10; $9 (senior citizens); $8 (students with ID); $5 (ages 6-12); $25 (family). **Phone:** (418) 247-5001.

AUBERGE DES GLACIS   Phone: 418/247-7486

Historic Country Inn
$60-$100 1/11-5/31
$57-$95 6/1-1/10

Address: 46 Rt de la Tortue G0R 1X0 **Location:** 2.1 mi (3.3 km) e on chemin Lamartine est from jct Rt 285, then 0.3 mi (0.5 km) n. Located in a quiet area. **Facility:** Built in 1841, the restored stone flour mill is in a clearing near a river. A small private lake, a terrace and fine dining await guests. 16 units. 3 stories (no elevator), interior corridors. **Terms:** office hours 7 am-11 pm, 7 day cancellation notice-fee imposed. **Dining:** Restaurant Auberge Des Glacis, see separate listing. **Activities:** cross country skiing, snowmobiling, bicycles, hiking trails. *Fee:* massage. **Free Special Amenities:** expanded continental breakfast and high-speed Internet.

WHERE TO EAT

RESTAURANT AUBERGE DES GLACIS
                              Phone: 418/247-7486

French
$20-$55

AAA Inspector Notes: Hardwood floors, stained glass, a wood-burning stove and stone walls and a wood-beamed ceiling (dating back to 1841) frame this country elegant dining room. The menu boasts dozens of local produce suppliers of meat, vegetables, cheese and wine. The house specialty is the French dish quenelle-pureed meat reformed into a mound, lightly breaded and baked until the exterior coating rises up into a wafer-thin pastry. The menu also features filet mignon, scallops, fresh fish and pan-seared foie gras. **Bar:** full bar. **Reservations:** suggested. **Address:** 46 Rt de la Tortue G0R 1X0 **Location:** 2.1 mi (3.3 km) e on chemin Lamartine est from jct Rt 285, then 0.3 mi (0.5 km) n; in Auberge Des Glacis. **Historic**

LONGUEUIL pop. 128,016
• Hotels & Restaurants map & index p. 342
• Part of Montréal area — see map p. 312

HOLIDAY INN MONTREAL-LONGUEUIL
                         Phone: (450)646-8100   **35**

Hotel
$119-$129

Address: 900 rue St-Charles est J4H 3Y2 **Location:** Rt 132 exit 11. **Facility:** 142 units. 6 stories, interior corridors. **Amenities:** *Some:* high-speed Internet. **Pool(s):** heated indoor. **Activities:** whirlpool, exercise room. **Guest Services:** valet laundry.

HOTEL DAUPHIN MONTREAL LONGUEUIL
                         Phone: (450)646-0110   **36**

Hotel
$99-$149

Address: 1055 rue St-Laurent ouest J4K 1E1 **Location:** Rt 132 exit 8 (Metro Longueuil), 0.3 mi (0.5 km) se on Place Charles-Lemoyne. **Facility:** 80 units. 6 stories, interior corridors. **Parking:** winter plug-ins. **Amenities:** high-speed Internet, safes. **Activities:** exercise room. **Guest Services:** valet and coin laundry.

(See map & index p. 342.)

HOTEL GOUVERNEUR ILE-CHARRON

Phone: (450)651-6510   **34**

Hotel
$99-$169

Address: 2405 rue Ile-Charron J4G 1R6 **Location:** Hwy 25 S exit 1 (Ile-Charron), just e. **Facility:** 125 units. 6 stories, interior corridors. **Terms:** cancellation fee imposed. **Amenities:** video games (fee). *Some:* honor bars. **Pool(s):** heated outdoor. **Activities:** boat dock, volleyball, exercise room. **Guest Services:** valet laundry.

[SAVE] [icons] [BIZ] [wifi]
FEE [icons] / SOME UNITS FEE [icon]

MOTEL LA SIESTA

Phone: (450)671-7555   **38**

Motel
$85-$169 6/1-11/30
$75-$169 12/1-5/31

Address: 3179 boul Taschereau est J4V 2H4 **Location:** Jct Hwy 10 exit 8E, then 2.8 mi (4.4 km) e on Rt 134; in Greenfield Park sector. Located in a busy commercial area. **Facility:** 49 units. 2 stories, exterior corridors. **Parking:** winter plug-ins. **Amenities:** high-speed Internet. **Guest Services:** valet and coin laundry. **Free Special Amenities:** full breakfast and high-speed Internet.
(See ad p. 304.)

[SAVE] [icons] [wifi] [icon]

SANDMAN HOTEL MONTREAL-LONGUEUIL

Phone: (450)670-3030   **37**

Hotel
$129-$179

Address: 999 de Serigny J4K 2T1 **Location:** Rt 132 exit 7, 0.5 mi (0.8 km) n on boul Lafayette. Adjacent to Longueuil Metro Station. **Facility:** 214 units. 17 stories, interior corridors. **Terms:** 3 night minimum stay, cancellation fee imposed. **Amenities:** high-speed Internet. **Pool(s):** heated indoor. **Activities:** sauna, exercise room. **Guest Services:** valet laundry.

[ECO] [icons] CALL [icons] [BIZ] [wifi] FEE [icons]
/ SOME UNITS FEE [icon]

WHERE TO EAT

COMMENSAL VEGETARIAN RESTAURANT

Phone: 450/676-1749

Vegetarian
$8-$14

AAA Inspector Notes: An upscale self-service buffet features an extensive selection of creative hot and cold items, such as leek pot pie, sweet potato kasha and lasagna, plus a variety of desserts, everything of which is exclusively vegetarian. The pleasant, contemporary surroundings change often as new paintings are displayed. **Bar:** beer & wine. **Address:** 4817 boul Taschereau est J4V 2J1 **Location:** Rt 134 (boul Taschereau), corner of ave Auguste; in Greenfield Park sector. [L] [D]

ST-HUBERT

Phone: 450/646-4447

Canadian
$8-$22

AAA Inspector Notes: The pleasantly decorated family-friendly restaurant serves affordable chicken dinners, ribs, club sandwiches, chicken wings, salads, soups and hot chicken sandwiches. The children's menu includes animal nuggets. **Bar:** full bar. **Address:** 825 rue St-Laurent ouest J4K 2V1 **Location:** Centre; in Place Longueuil. [L] [D]

LOUISEVILLE   pop. 7,433

GITE DU CARREFOUR ET MAISON HISTORIQUE J.L.L. HAMELIN

Phone: (819)228-4932

Historic Bed & Breakfast
$65-$95

Address: 11 ave St-Laurent ouest J5V 1J3 **Location:** On Rt 138; Hwy 40 exit 174 westbound; exit 166 eastbound; centre. Located in a rural area. **Facility:** Built in 1898 in neo-Queen Anne style, this architectural standout is furnished with high-quality antiques, ornate mirrors, impressive artwork, crystal chandeliers and lovely rugs. 5 units. 2 stories (no elevator), interior corridors. *Bath:* some shared. **Parking:** winter plug-ins. **Terms:** 15 day cancellation notice-fee imposed. **Guest Services:** complimentary laundry.

[icons] / SOME UNITS [icon]

MAGOG   (F-9) pop. 14,283

• Restaurants p. 306

Magog was founded in 1799 by British Loyalists who left the United States after the American Revolutionary War. It is named for nearby lac Memphrémagog, which is the Abenaki Indian word for "vast expanse of water." The lake as well as the area's rivers, streams and mountains has made Magog a popular vacation resort, offering fishing, hiking, and water and winter sports.

In Ste-Catherine-de-Hatley the Île-du-Marais Nature Trail is reached by a causeway into lac Magog. The trail offers a self-guiding hike around the island April through October. More than 226 species of birds use the island as a nesting ground.

Memphre Tourist Information Bureau: 55 rue Cabana, Magog, QC, Canada J1X 2C4. **Phone:** (819) 843-2744 or (800) 267-2744.

MONT-ORFORD NATIONAL PARK—see Orford p. 398.

AUBERGE DU MONT-ORFORD

Phone: 819/868-0669

Hotel
$99-$130

Address: 3159 rue Principale ouest J1X 0J6 **Location:** Hwy 10 exit 115 S, follow signs to Rt 112 ouest (Eastman), then 0.6 mi (1 km) w. **Facility:** 22 kitchen units. 2 stories (no elevator), interior corridors. **Terms:** office hours 8 am-9 pm, 2 night minimum stay - seasonal and/or weekends, 5 day cancellation notice-fee imposed. **Amenities:** high-speed Internet. *Some:* video games. **Activities:** whirlpool, playground, exercise room.

[icons] [wifi] [icons] [icon] [icon] [icon]

HOTEL & SPA ÉTOILE SUR LE LAC

Phone: (819)843-6521

Hotel
$170-$405

Address: 1200 rue Principale ouest J1X 2B8 **Location:** Hwy 10 exit 115 S, 2.5 mi (4 km) e on Rt 112. **Facility:** 60 units, some two bedrooms and kitchens. 5-6 stories, interior corridors. **Terms:** cancellation fee imposed. **Amenities:** high-speed Internet. **Pool(s):** heated outdoor. **Activities:** sauna, ice skating, spa. **Fee:** bicycles.

WHERE TO EAT

PIZZERIA ORFORD

Phone: 819/843-6554

Italian
$9-$25

AAA Inspector Notes: This casual eatery, family-operated since 1969, offers an excellent variety of pizza and pasta, as well as barbecue chicken, smoked meat sandwiches, hot subs and a full breakfast menu. The Italian buffet is popular at lunchtime and in the evening. **Bar:** full bar. **Address:** 176 rue Principale ouest J1X 2A5 **Location:** On Rt 112, just e of rue Merry; centre. **Parking:** street only.

B L D

ST-HUBERT

Phone: 819/847-3366

Canadian
$8-$22

AAA Inspector Notes: The pleasantly decorated family-friendly restaurant serves affordable chicken dinners, ribs, club sandwiches, chicken wings, salads, soups and hot chicken sandwiches. The children's menu includes animal nuggets. **Bar:** full bar. **Address:** 1615 chemin Riviere-aux-Cerises J1X 3W3 **Location:** Hwy 10 exit 118.

L D

MALARTIC (C-2) pop. 3,640

MALARTIC MINERALOGICAL MUSEUM (Musée minéralogique de Malartic), 1 blk. s. of Hwy. 117 at 650 rue de la Paix, offers exhibits about mining operations and geology, and a multimedia presentation about geological landscape conversion. Guided tours are available; narration in English is offered. **Time:** Allow 1 hour minimum. **Hours:** Daily 9-5, June 1-Sept. 15; Mon.-Fri. 9-5, Sat.-Sun. by appointment, rest of year. **Cost:** $6; $4.50 (ages 56+ and students with ID); $3 (ages 5-12); $15 (family, two adults and two children). **Phone:** (819) 757-4677.

MANIWAKI (E-3) pop. 4,102, elev. 182m/600'

HISTORY OF FOREST FIRE PREVENTION INTERPRETATION CENTRE (Centre d'interprétation de l'historique de la protection de la forêt contre le feu) is at 8 rue Comeau. A granite Second Empire-style edifice built in 1887 by Irish immigrant Charles Logue houses the interpretation center. Displays detail the history of forest fire protection and prevention efforts in Maniwaki, a region in which forestry is a major industry.

At a re-created forest fire command post, visitors learn about the tracking and assessment of forest fires as well as how such tactical resources as helicopters and other aircraft are mobilized. In addition visitors can climb a 24-metre-tall (80-ft.) reproduction forest fire observation tower. An on-site art gallery hosts traveling exhibitions. Narrated tours of a

tugboat once used to transport timber along the Baskatong Reservoir can be arranged at the interpretation center.

Time: Allow 1 hour, 30 minutes minimum. **Hours:** Interpretation center Tues.-Sun. 10-5, May 1 to mid-Oct.; by appointment rest of year. Tugboat tours are given Wed.-Sun. at 10 and 2. **Cost:** Interpretation center or tower $5; $3 (ages 6-17). Combination ticket $8; $5 (ages 6-17). Guided tugboat tour free. **Phone:** (819) 449-7999.

CHÂTEAU LOGUE HOTEL GOLF RESORT

Phone: (819)449-4848

Resort Hotel
$95-$129

Address: 12 rue Comeau J9E 2R8 **Location:** On Rt 107, 0.6 mi (1 km) ne of Rt 105. **Facility:** This contemporary mini-resort includes an 1887 stone manor featuring meeting space and a forestry museum. Guest rooms are very good sized. 51 units. 3 stories, interior corridors. **Parking:** winter plug-ins. **Terms:** check-in 4 pm, cancellation fee imposed. **Dining:** Le Poste De Traite-Trading Post, see separate listing. **Pool(s):** heated indoor. **Activities:** sauna, whirlpool, canoeing, boat dock, fishing, cross country skiing, snowmobiling, bicycles, hiking trails, exercise room. **Fee:** golf-9 holes, massage. **Guest Services:** valet laundry.

WHERE TO EAT

LE POSTE DE TRAITE-TRADING POST

Phone: 819/449-4848

Quebec
$7-$38

AAA Inspector Notes: The restaurant entrance is decorated like a vintage trading post-a job once fulfilled by the adjacent 1887 stone heritage building and inn. Wagon wheels, rural artwork and a wood ceiling complete the cozy country decor. Representative of fine regional cuisine are pork tenderloin, rack of lamb, grilled New York strip steak, black pepper steak, breast of duck with liver pate, red deer, sliced caribou, chicken supreme, pasta, fresh fish and seafood. A lighter pub menu is offered, as well. **Bar:** full bar. **Reservations:** suggested. **Address:** 12 rue Comeau J9E 2R8 **Location:** On Rt 107, 0.6 mi (1 km) ne of Rt 105; in Chateau Logue Golf Resort.

B L D

MASCOUCHE (E-7) pop. 33,764
• Part of Montréal area — see map p. 312

MOORE GARDENS (Les Jardins Moore) is off Hwy. 25 at exit 28, then 3.8 km (2.3 mi.) w. on ch. Ste-Marie to 1455 ch. Pincourt. This 2.2-hectare (5.5-acre) display garden is a riot of color provided by 120 species of perennials and masses of annuals on the banks of the Mascouche River. The garden planning area emphasizes eco-friendly methods. A small museum honors the garden's founder, W.D. Moore. **Time:** Allow 2 hours minimum. **Hours:** Daily 9:30-5:30, June 24-Labour Day. **Cost:** $5; $2 (ages 8-17). **Phone:** (450) 474-0588.

MASHTEUIATSH (C-5) elev. 107m/350'

THE NATIVE MUSEUM OF MASHTEUIATSH (Le Musée Amérindien de Mashteuiatsh), 1787 rue Amishk, is dedicated to preserving the history and culture of the First Nations peoples who first inhabited the Saguenay-Lac-St-Jean region. The Ilnuatsh, as they are known, are represented through archeology, art and hand crafts. Educational films highlight the traditional Montagnais lifestyle.

Time: Allow 1 hour minimum. **Hours:** Daily 9-6, May 15-Oct. 15; Mon.-Thurs. 9-noon and 1-4, Fri. 9-noon and 1-3, rest of year. Closed major holidays. **Cost:** $10; $8.50 (ages 65+ and students with ID); $6 (ages 6-12); free (ages 0-5); $28 (family, four persons). **Phone:** (418) 275-4842 or (888) 875-4842.

MATANE (C-7) pop. 14,742

A fishing community at the confluence of the Matane and St. Lawrence rivers, Matane is the outfitting point for salmon fishing in the Matane Wildlife Reserve (Réserve faunique de Matane) *(see Recreation Chart)*. Matane fishermen also harvest halibut, cod and shrimp from the St. Lawrence River. Visitors can observe salmon fishing downtown along the Matane River; in season migrating salmon leap across the Mathieu-D'Amours Dam.

A ferry service from Matane runs to Baie-Comeau and Godbout in Québec's northlands; reservations are required. Phone (418) 562-2500 or (877) 562-6560 for schedules and fares.

Matane Tourist Office: 968 av. du Phare Ouest, Matane, QC, Canada G4W 1V7. **Phone:** (418) 562-1065 or (877) 762-8263.

RESTAURANT LE VIEUX RAFIOT **Phone:** 418/562-8080

▼▼ ▼▼
Seafood
$10-$30

AAA Inspector Notes: A nautical theme punctuates the decor of this casual pub and restaurant, which specializes in seafood, including Matane shrimp, sole, mussels, crab and lobster. Also on the menu are chicken, ribs, pasta, thin-crust pizzas and salads. The seasonal terrace is popular in summer. **Bar:** full bar. **Address:** 1415 ave du Phare ouest G4W 3M6 **Location:** On Rt 132; centre. [L] [D]

MIGUASHA (C-8)

MIGUASHA NATIONAL PARK (Parc national de Miguasha), 231 Rte. Miguasha Ouest, 6 km (4 mi.) s. of jct. Hwy. 132, is a UNESCO World Heritage Site. First discovered here in 1842, many well-preserved fossils were removed from this site until the late 20th century. A preservation park was created in 1985 to protect and enhance the Escuminac Formation—a paleoecosystem of the Devonian period dating 378 million years ago. These fossils illustrate a very important event in the course of evolution—the transition from aquatic vertebrates to land vertebrates.

Fossils are exhibited in the Museum of Natural History. The 1.9-kilometre (1.2-mi.) Evolution of Life trail features interpretive panels, picnic areas and views of the estuary. **Note:** Digging is strictly forbidden. Pets are not permitted. **Hours:** Museum daily 9-5, June 1-early Oct.; Mon.-Fri. 8:30-4:30, rest of year. **Cost:** Park admission $6; $2.75 (ages 6-17); $12 (family, two adults and children); $8.75 (family, one adult and children). Museum $9.50; $4.75 (ages 6-17); $23.75 (family, two adults and children); $14.25 (family, one adult and children). Prices may vary. **Phone:** (418) 794-2475 or (800) 665-6527. [🍴] [🏕]

MINGAN ARCHIPELAGO NATIONAL PARK RESERVE OF CANADA (A-9)

Elevations in the park range from sea level at the Gulf of St. Lawrence to 46 metres (150 ft.) on some of the islands within the reserve. Refer to AAA/CAA maps for additional elevation information.

Mingan Archipelago National Park Reserve of Canada (Réserve de parc national du Canada de l'Archipel-de-Mingan) consists of a group of 1,000 islands off the north shore of the St. Lawrence Gulf and is accessible by boat from Longue-Pointe-de-Mingan and Havre-St-Pierre. The archipelago, which is north of Anticosti Island (Île d'Anticosti) in the Jacques Cartier Strait, stretches about 150 kilometres (93 mi.) and was formed mostly from sedimentary rock. Erosion by the sea has resulted in spectacular rock formations; the monoliths are the most popular.

The islands support a variety of plant life and an abundant waterfowl population. The cold waters surrounding the islands harbor whales, seals and other marine creatures.

General Information and Activities

The park can be reached by air or, for those traveling by car, via Hwy. 138E. From Québec City, it is approximately 870 kilometres (540 mi.) to Havre-St-Pierre, where the highway ends. Boats depart Havre-St-Pierre for the islands from June to September; reservations are required.

Popular recreational activities include boating, sea kayaking, scuba diving and fishing. Boating season lasts from June to September. In addition, the islands' interesting topography and other features make for excellent wilderness camping. **Note:** Campers are advised to take extra provisions and water, and to allow extra time to return, because the unpredictable sea can cause delays.

Information about park interpretation programs may be obtained at the Havre-St-Pierre visitor center, 1010 Promenade des Anciens, (418) 538-3285, and at the Longue-Pointe-de-Mingan visitor center, 625 rue du Centre, (418) 949-2126.

ADMISSION to the park is $5.80; $4.90 (ages 65+); $2.90 (ages 6-16); $14.70 (family, seven persons with a maximum of two adults). A permit is required for wilderness camping; the fee is $15.70. Fees are charged by private transporters authorized by Parks Canada to offer boat service to the islands. These fees vary depending on the destination and the type of service provided. Reservations are required for boat trips. The park website has a list of transportation providers with phone numbers and links.

ADDRESS inquiries to Mingan Archipelago National Park Reserve of Canada, Administrative Office, c/o

Visitors Services, 1340 rue de la Digue, Havre-St-Pierre, QC, Canada G0G 1P0. Phone (418) 538-3331, or (888) 773-8888 for general park information. *See Recreation Chart.*

MONTEBELLO (E-3) pop. 987

MANOIR PAPINEAU NATIONAL HISTORIC SITE (Lieu historique national du Manoir Papineau) is at 500 Notre-Dame and is accessible via the Montebello Tourist Information Office on Hwy. 148. Prominent political figure Louis-Joseph Papineau built the three-story manor house on the wooded north bank of the Ottawa River in 1850. The restored structure is furnished in period with original décor. A small stone chapel on the grounds contains the tombs of Papineau and other family members. Two other historical buildings are open to the public.

Guided tours are available in French and English. **Time:** Allow 1 hour minimum. **Hours:** Daily 10-5, mid-May to early Sept.; Sat.-Sun. 10-5, early Sept. to mid-Oct. **Cost:** $7.80; $6.55 (ages 66+); $3.90 (ages 6-16); $19.60 (family). **Phone:** (819) 423-6965 or (888) 773-8888.

PARC OMÉGA, 4 km (2.5 mi.) n. on Hwy. 323, is a 12-kilometre (7.5-mi.) drive-through 890-hectare (2,200-acre) wildlife park with free-roaming large and small native creatures. Inhabitants include beaver; wild boar; buffalo; fallow, red and white-tailed deer; duck; elk; goose; wapiti; raccoons; reindeer; bears; foxes; and wolves. Also on-site are a small farm with barnyard animals as well as walking and hiking trails along which visitors may encounter fauna. During the summer a birds of prey show is presented.

Pets are not permitted. **Time:** Allow 1 hour minimum. **Hours:** Daily 9-6, June-Oct.; 10-5, rest of year. Birds of prey show given at noon, 2 and 4, late June-Labour Day. Last admission 1 hour before closing. **Cost:** June-Oct. $19; $18 (senior citizens); $14 (ages 6-15); $8 (ages 2-5). Rest of year $15; $14 (senior citizens); $11 (ages 6-15); $6 (ages 2-5). **Phone:** (819) 423-5487.

AUBERGE MONTEBELLO Phone: 819/423-0001

Hotel

$169-$209 6/1-10/31
$149-$189 11/1-5/31

Address: 676 rue Notre-Dame J0V 1L0 **Location:** On Rt 148; centre. **Facility:** 44 units. 4 stories (no elevator), interior corridors. **Terms:** cancellation fee imposed. **Amenities:** *Some:* high-speed Internet. **Pool(s):** heated outdoor. **Activities:** sauna, whirlpool, bicycles, playground, horseshoes, exercise room, spa. *Fee:* boat dock.

WHERE TO EAT

AUX CHANTIGNOLES Phone: 819/423-6341

French
$16-$50

AAA Inspector Notes: Within the charming and luxurious Chateau Montebello, this dining room presents a menu of fine regional cuisine, much of it French-influenced. A well-presented breakfast buffet is served daily. Reservations are a must, especially in high-season. The quieter, window-lined tables overlooking the well-tended grounds are highly coveted by couples, while families with young children may feel more comfortable in the more informal interior dining area. **Bar:** full bar. **Address:** 392 rue Notre-Dame J0V 1L0 **Location:** On Rt 148; in Fairmont Le Chateau Montebello.

MONT-LAURIER (D-3) pop. 7,365

Named after Sir Wilfrid Laurier, Canada's prime minister 1896-1911, Mont-Laurier is at the foot of Mont Sir Wilfrid. The town is a shipping and trading center for the surrounding dairy and lumber industries and is popular with fishing and hunting enthusiasts.

Mont-Laurier Chamber of Commerce: 445 rue du Pont, Mont-Laurier, QC, Canada J9L 2R8. **Phone:** (819) 623-3642.

LA VÉRENDRYE WILDLIFE RESERVE (Réserve faunique La Vérendrye), 60 km (37 mi.) n.w. on Hwy. 117, covers 12,589 square kilometres (4,861 sq. mi.), with approximately 2,200 square kilometres (849 sq. mi.) suitable for canoe trips and wilderness camping. Fishing is excellent. The reserve is a game sanctuary; motorists should be alert for animals

crossing the roadway. *See Recreation Chart.*
Hours: Sat.-Wed. 7-7, Thurs. 7 a.m.-9 p.m., Fri. 7 a.m.-10 p.m., mid-May to mid-Sept. **Cost:** Free. **Phone:** (819) 438-2017 or (819) 736-7431.

BEST WESTERN PLUS HOTEL MONT-LAURIER
Phone: 819/623-5252

Hotel
Rates not provided

AAA Benefit: Members save up to 20%, plus 10% bonus points with Best Western Rewards®.

Address: 1231 boul A-Paquette J9L 1M6 **Location:** On Rt 117; centre. **Facility:** 39 units. 2 stories, interior/exterior corridors. **Parking:** winter plug-ins. **Pool(s):** heated indoor. **Activities:** snowmobiling, exercise room. **Guest Services:** valet laundry. **Free Special Amenities: expanded continental breakfast and high-speed Internet.**

COMFORT INN
Phone: (819)623-6465

Hotel
$114-$129

Address: 700 boul A-Paquette J9L 1L4 **Location:** On Hwy 117; centre. **Facility:** 49 units. 2 stories (no elevator), interior/exterior corridors. **Parking:** winter plug-ins. **Terms:** check-in 4 pm, cancellation fee imposed. **Dining:** Cage aux Sports, see separate listing. **Activities:** sauna, whirlpool, snowmobiling, exercise room. *Fee:* massage. **Guest Services:** valet laundry.

QUALITY INN MONT-LAURIER
Phone: 819/623-3555

Hotel
Rates not provided

Address: 111 boul A-Paquette J9L 1J2 **Location:** On Rt 117; centre. **Facility:** 50 units. 3 stories, interior/exterior corridors. **Parking:** winter plug-ins. **Pool(s):** heated indoor. **Activities:** snowmobiling, game room, exercise room. **Guest Services:** valet and coin laundry.

WHERE TO EAT

CAGE AUX SPORTS
Phone: 819/623-6435

Canadian
$8-$22

AAA Inspector Notes: This popular Quebec chain of sports bars presents a menu of pub foods, including ribs, chicken, burgers, salads, crispy fries, pasta and tasty desserts. Guests might begin the meal with a basket of freshly popped popcorn as they check out the sports memorabilia. Children are welcomed. **Bar:** full bar. **Address:** 700 boul A-Paquette J9L 1L4 **Location:** On Hwy 117; centre; in Comfort Inn. [B] [L] [D]

PLACE MONT-LAURIER PIZZERIA
Phone: 819/623-2597

Italian
$6-$21

AAA Inspector Notes: The menu lists simple, well-prepared comfort foods, including many traditional Greek and Italian dishes. Pizza, pasta, brochettes, seafood, steak and roast chicken are among choices. The decor reflects the style of a modern diner, with lots of greenery and large windows. **Bar:** full bar. **Reservations:** suggested. **Address:** 457 boul A-Paquette J9L 1K7 **Location:** On Hwy 117; centre. [L] [D] [LATE]

MONTMAGNY (D-6) pop. 11,353
• Hotels p. 310 • Restaurants p. 310

One of the earliest towns along the south shore of the St. Lawrence River, Montmagny is the commercial center for a fertile valley region. Wheat fields and 18th-century villages dot the landscape south of Montmagny before giving way to hilly country crossed by rivers and snowmobile and cross-country skiing trails.

A stopping point on a natural migratory route, Montmagny plays host to thousands of snow geese in spring and fall. Known as "the Snow Goose Capital," the city offers cultural and athletic activities during the Snow Goose Festival in October.

The Couillard-Dupuis Manor (Manoir Couillard-Dupuis), 301 boul. Taché Est, is a stone edifice built in 1789 that now houses the Accordion Museum (Musée de l'Accordéon); phone (418) 248-7927. A ferry links Montmagny with Isle-aux-Grues *(see attraction listing)*, which features a number of historical structures.

Montmagny Tourism Information Bureau: 45 av. du Quai, C.P. 71, Montmagny, QC, Canada G5V 3S3. **Phone:** (418) 248-9196 or (800) 463-5643.

GROSSE ÎLE AND THE IRISH MEMORIAL NATIONAL HISTORIC SITE (Lieu historique national de la Grosse-Île-et-le-Mémorial-des-Irlandais) is in the St. Lawrence River and is reached by cruises from Berthier-sur-Mer, Québec City and Baie de Beauport. The island was once known as Quarantine Station because of the great number of immigrants who were quarantined here during the period 1832-1937. More than 4 million immigrants passed through the Québec City port during this period.

A Celtic cross on the summit of the island's western section commemorates the Great Famine and the tragic events of 1847 on Grosse Île, when 100,000 mostly Irish immigrants arrived—thousands of them died of typhus fever and are buried in Grosse Île's Irish cemetery. Today more than 25 historic buildings are on the island; many are being restored. Guided tours include a visit to the disinfection building, a 60-minute walking tour and a 60-minute tram tour; narration in English is available.

Private watercraft are not permitted to dock on the island. **Time:** Allow 4 hours minimum. **Hours:** Site open early May to mid-Oct. Durations of trips and length of stay on the island vary. Some departures require a minimum number of persons; phone ahead. Carriers depart daily, mid-June through Labour Day; by appointment early May to mid-June and day after Labour Day to mid-Oct. Guided tours are offered mid-May to mid-Oct. (weather permitting). **Cost:** The park tour fee is included in the carriers' packages. Package cruise rates $50-$80. **Phone:** (418) 234-8841.

ISLE-AUX-GRUES (Crane Island), on the St. Lawrence River and reached by ferry from Montmagny, is the largest of the 21 islands in the archipelago and the only one inhabited throughout the year. Bicycling and guided tours of historical buildings are offered. Tour narration in English is available. **Hours:** Ferry runs daily, Apr.-Dec. Phone ahead to confirm schedule. **Cost:** Free. **Phone:** (418) 241-5117 for ferry information.

MANOIR DES ÉRABLES 1814   **Phone:** (418)248-0100

Country Inn
$115-$265 6/1-10/31
$99-$250 11/1-5/31

Address: 220 boul Tache est (Rt 132) G5V 1G5 **Location:** Hwy 20 exit 376, 1.4 mi (2.2 km) e on Rt 228, 0.9 mi (1.5 km) e. **Facility:** On the grounds are a Victorian-style building that dates to 1814, a stone manor house and a nine-room motel. 24 units. 3 stories (no elevator), interior/exterior corridors. **Terms:** office hours 7 am-10 pm, check-in 4 pm, 10 day cancellation notice-fee imposed. **Dining:** Manoir Des Érables 1814 Dining Room, see separate listing. **Pool(s):** heated outdoor. **Activities:** snowmobiling, bicycles, spa.

WHERE TO EAT

MANOIR DES ÉRABLES 1814 DINING ROOM
Menu on AAA.com   **Phone:** 418/248-0100

Quebec
$18-$58

AAA Inspector Notes: Built in 1814, the lovely Victorian-style manor exudes charm and sophistication. The gastronomic menu highlights fine Quebecois cuisine and features roasted salmon, grilled tuna, larded sturgeon, quail or guinea fowl, stuffed rabbit, walleye filet, veal chops and beef sirloin. Appetizers include game terrine, marinated salmon and smoked sturgeon. An excellent selection of wines and cheeses is offered. **Bar:** full bar. **Reservations:** suggested. **Address:** 220 boul Tache est (Rt 132) G5V 1G5 **Location:** Hwy 20 exit 376, 1.4 mi (2.2 km) e on Rt 228, 0.9 mi (1.5 km) e; in Manoir des Érables 1814. B D

RESTAURANT NORMANDIN   **Phone:** 418/248-3667

Canadian
$7-$13

AAA Inspector Notes: The family restaurant prepares affordable comfort foods that include roasted chicken, hot chicken sandwiches, pasta, burgers and fries. Take-out service, a children's menu and cutely decorated desserts are among other offerings. **Address:** 25 boul Tache est (Rt 132) G5V 1B6 **Location:** On Hwy 132. B L D LATE

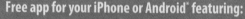

Plan. Map. Go.
TripTik® Travel Planner

Where premier mapping technology meets complete travel information. Only on AAA.com and CAA.ca.

Montréal

Then & Now

You're at a party. The hostess is French and the *hors-d'oeuvres* and decor have a European flair. A five-course meal with French wine graces the elegant table. Hushed *tête-à-têtes*, however, are in English. On the coffee table are the *Times* of New York and the *Times* of London, and through the windows rows of prim Victorian homes evoke a British architectural legacy.

You're in bilingual, multicultural Montréal, where two societies live side by side. This coexistence, however, is defined by linguistic tensions sparking endless political battles.

Looking for gold for King François I, French explorer Jacques Cartier set out in 1534 to find a shortcut to the Orient. His geography a tad off, he came instead upon an island in the St. Lawrence River he called Mont Royal. In 1611 Samuel de Champlain arrived at that island and established a fur-trading post.

Following intense fighting with the Iroquois, in 1716, the French built a wall roughly following the boundaries of today's Old Montréal. Decades of prosperity behind the wall ended when the English began seeking a North American foothold. The 1763 Treaty of Paris ceded all of Canada to the British, ending French control. Surprisingly, British governors were accepting of the culture and guaranteed use of the French language and Roman Catholic religion. Nevertheless, local demographics underwent a radical change.

The 1800s saw Montréal's city limits expand. The old city walls were demolished, and by the 1900s the Canadian Pacific Railway boom fueled a building frenzy. Mansions were constructed and the harbor became an architectural showpiece.

As Montréal basked in its Golden Age, ethnic neighborhoods sprang up as the population exploded with Irish, Chinese, Greek and Italian emigrants. Hungarian bakeries, Portuguese gift shops and a commercial mix along diverse *"La Main"* (boulevard St-Laurent) echo this influx.

With economic inequality increasing, the gap between the French and English widened. Canada's economic focus shifted from St. Lawrence River ports toward Toronto and the Great Lakes. As a result, after World War II Québec was an isolated province where the church dictated public policy. The "Quiet Revolution" reawakened the masses and unveiled the Montréal visitors see today.

Many believed a culturally French Québec should not have to endure a federalist government that didn't protect its uniqueness. Talk turned to separatism, and the liberated Québécois acted to effect religious, political and social reform.

After Parti Québécois came into power in 1976, French was voted the official language. Over the next 2 decades the fight for sovereignty continued, though voters twice turned it down.

Sunset over Place Jacques-Cartier

(Continued on p. 313.)

Destination Montréal

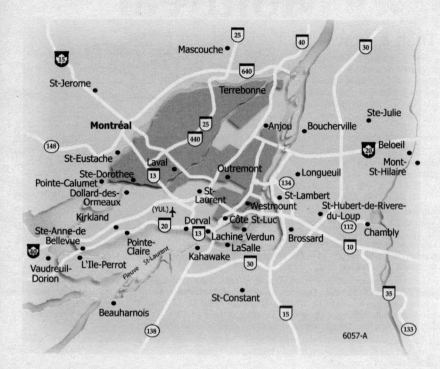

This map shows cities in the Montréal vicinity where you will find attractions, hotels and restaurants. Cities are listed alphabetically in this book on the following pages.

Fast Facts

ABOUT THE CITY

POP: 1,620,693 ■ **ELEV:** 15 m/49 ft.

MONEY

SALES TAX: Canada levies a 5 percent Goods and Service Tax. Québec's provincial sales tax is 8.5 percent on goods and services. The Montréal area hotel room occupancy tax is 3.5 percent per night.

WHOM TO CALL

EMERGENCY: 911

POLICE (non-emergency): (514) 280-2000

TEMPERATURE: (514) 283-4006

HOSPITALS: Maisonneuve-Rosemont Hospital (Hôpital Maisonneuve-Rosemont), (514) 252-3400 ■ Montréal General Hospital (Hôpital général de Montréal), (514) 934-1934 ■ St. Mary's Hospital Center (Centre hospitalier de St-Mary), (514) 345-3511.

WHERE TO LOOK AND LISTEN

NEWSPAPERS: Four major papers serve the city. *The Gazette* is printed in English; *La Presse, Le Devoir* and *Le Journal de Montréal* are in French. All the papers carry daily events columns. The weekly *Montréal Mirror* tabloid as well as the daily *Metro* and *24H* free newspapers also carry events columns. The Sunday newspapers are *Le Journal de Montréal* and *The Gazette*.

RADIO: The Montréal radio station CBC (940 AM and 88.5 and 93.5 FM) is programmed by the Canadian Broadcasting Corp. ■ CJAD (800 AM) also offers news broadcasts in English.

VISITOR INFORMATION

Tourisme Montréal Infotouriste Centre: 1255 rue Peel, Suite 100, Montréal, QC, Canada H3B 4V4. **Phone:** (514) 873-2015 or (800) 363-7777.
Walk-in centers are at 1001 rue du Square-Dorchester, between rues Peel and Metcalfe, and in Old Montréal at Place Jacques-Cartier, 174 rue Notre-Dame Est.

TRANSPORTATION

AIR TRAVEL: Montréal-Pierre Elliott Trudeau International Airport (YUL), formerly Montréal-Dorval Airport, 22 kilometres (14 mi.) west of downtown in Dorval, handles commercial flights. *See Arriving, Air Travel.*

RENTAL CARS: Nearly all major rental-car companies serve Montréal, and desks are inside airline terminals at the Montréal-Pierre Elliott Trudeau International Airport. *See Arriving, Air Travel.*

RAIL SERVICE: Amtrak, (800) 872-7245, and VIA Rail Canada, (514) 989-2626, operate from Central Station, 895 de la Gauchetière beneath Queen Elizabeth Hotel. As part of the underground city, Central Station is connected to the Métro subway and to Windsor Station, at rues Peel and de la Gauchetière.

BUSES: Greyhound Lines Inc. and Adirondacks Trailways run to New York City. Orléans Montréal operates within Québec. Terminus Voyageur station serves Canada and the United States. Voyageur buses link Ontario cities.

TAXIS: Cabs are plentiful in Montréal, and you should have no problem hailing one in the city. Taxis are metered, and fares generally are fixed at $3.30 to start, plus $1.60 for each kilometre (.6 mi.) traveled as well as 60c for every waiting minute. Major companies are Diamond, (514) 273-6331 ■ and Taxi Co-op, (514) 725-9885.

PUBLIC TRANSPORTATION: Société de transport de Montréal (STM) provides bus, Métro (subway) and commuter train service throughout greater Montréal. *See Getting Around, Public Transportation.*

BOATS: Large vessels put in at Montréal's docks. Port d'escale du Vieux-Port de Montréal (Bassin Jacques Cartier), 333 rue de la Commune Ouest, charges $2.60 per hour for vessels 5.8 metres (19 ft.) or less in length, or $5.25 per hour for vessels measuring 6 to 30 metres (20 to 99 ft.). Rates may be increased on weekends; phone (514) 283-5414 to verify pricing.

(Continued from p. 311.)

Today the "two solitudes" described by Canadian novelist Hugh McLennan in 1945 have created parallel communities. While most residents are bilingual, Francophones and Anglophones rarely interact. Perhaps the greatest tension is that each group knows it is a vulnerable minority—the French a distinct minority within Canada, and Anglophones a distinct minority within Montréal. Squabbling persists mainly among politicians, and Montréalers are generally content to leave it that way.

Although Montréal is bilingual, it is a *multi*cultural city. Recent immigration again has changed the city's face as newcomers from Asia, Africa, the Antilles and the Near East make Montréal their home.

Loyalty to its Gallic roots gives Montréal its individuality. But it's not just sidewalk cafés and croissants that make the city *très* cosmopolitan. Montréal is grand boulevards and twisting alleys, Gothic cathedrals and vast beer halls, Bohemian artists and *haute couture,* and considerable *joie de vivre.*

Must Do: AAA Editor's Picks

- Orient yourself. The **streets in Montréal** are laid out in the traditional east-west grid, in this case parallel to the St. Lawrence River. The river, though, takes an unfortunate northwest swing at Montréal, resulting in the east-west streets actually running north-south.

- Stop and catch a whiff of the roses, as well as the lilacs, that float on breezes during spring and summer at the showcase ❧ **Montréal Botanical Garden** (Jardin botanique de Montréal), said to be one of the continent's finest. Especially delightful are the **Chinese Garden** (Jardin de Chine) with its miniature trees, lake and pavilions, and the **Japanese Garden and Pavilion** (Jardin et Pavillon japonais), known for its koi ponds, bridges and bonsai collection.

- Try a **smoked meat sandwich** for a true taste of Montréal. Similar to a pastrami or corned beef sandwich, Montréal smoked meat is beef rubbed with spices, then marinated and smoked, sliced thin, piled between two slices of rye bread and typically served with fries, coleslaw and a pickle.

- Inspired by his enormous neo-Gothic masterpiece, the architect of the awe-inspiring ❧ **Basilica of Notre-Dame** (Basilique Notre-Dame) converted to Catholicism in order to be buried beneath it. The interior of the church, built 1824-29, was hand-carved in wood and is resplendent with gold leaf and stained-glass windows.

- Clip-clop through the narrow, cobblestone streets of ❧ **Old Montréal** (Vieux-Montréal) in a horse-drawn *calèche* (carriage), a tour akin to time traveling to the early 18th century.

- Escape from the rush of the city to the serenity and greenness of ❧ **Mont-Royal Park** (Parc du Mont-Royal), whose signature mountain was climbed in 1535 by Jacques Cartier, the French explorer who searched in vain for a "northwest passage" from the Atlantic to the Pacific Ocean.

- Stand on the site that was Montréal's birthplace at ❧ **Pointe-à-Callière, Montréal Museum of Archaeology and History** (Pointe-à-Callière, Musée d'archéologie et d'histoire de Montréal), where a multimedia presentation about the city's history is presented in a theater overlooking archeological ruins.

- Visit four ecosystems—a tropical rain forest, the marine environment of the St. Lawrence, a Laurentian forest and the frigid polar world—in one day at the ❧ **Montréal Biodôme** (Biodôme de Montréal). The combination zoo/aquarium/garden, part of ❧ **Olympic Park** (Parc Olympique), is in the former velodrome from the 1976 Summer Games.

- Honor the memory and deeds of St. André Bessette, a humble caretaker known for his ability to heal the infirm, at ❧ **St. Joseph's Oratory** (L'Oratoire St-Joseph). It was André's greatest wish to build a shrine to his patron saint, and his small wooden chapel grew to become a grand basilica crowned by a huge copper dome.

- Put on comfortable shoes before exploring the 29-kilometre (18-mi.) network of pedestrian walkways that constitutes **Underground Montréal**, a subterranean maze of shops, offices, theaters, restaurants and subway stations designed to help residents cope with the city's harsh winters.

- Learn a few **words or phrases in French** and slip them into your conversations with locals. They'll appreciate your effort and you'll learn there's more to the language than *cul de sac, croissant* and *bonjour.*

- Hold on tight and prepare to be soaked (despite the provided ponchos, hats and footwear) as your boat jumps waves and surges upstream through the rapids of the St. Lawrence River on ❧ **Lachine Rapids Jet Boat Tours** (Le voyage Saute-Moutons sur les Rapides de Lachine); don't forget to bring a change of clothes.

Chinese Garden, Montréal Botanical Garden

Montréal 1-day Itinerary

AAA editors suggest these activities for a great short vacation experience. Those staying in the area for a longer visit can access a 3-day itinerary at AAA.com/TravelGuide.

Morning

- In ▒ **Old Montréal** (Vieux-Montréal) gas lamps, cobblestone streets and 18th- and 19th-century buildings repurposed as chic boutique hotels exude Old World charm. Stroll through the narrow streets on the island in the St. Lawrence River where explorers Jacques Cartier and Samuel de Champlain landed in 1535 and 1611. Shops, galleries and restaurants now line the historic area's main thoroughfare, rue St-Paul, and shopkeepers welcome you with a friendly *"Bonjour,"* followed by a charmingly accented "Hello."

- The ▒ **Basilica of Notre-Dame** (Basilique Notre-Dame) isn't hard to find; the huge church's twin spires are a Montréal landmark. Its interior—dark, hushed and ornately gilded—is in stark contrast to the bustle of the busy street outside its massive doors. Opposite the basilica is the **Place d'Armes**, a square dedicated to the city's founder, where you'll find a row of horse-drawn carriages waiting to board passengers for a tour of the historic district.

- Nearby is ▒ **Château Ramezay—Historic Site and Museum of Montréal** (Château Ramezay—Musée et site historique de Montréal), built as the residence of Claude de Ramezay, an early 18th-century French governor. The castle-like building is now a museum exploring Montréal's early history, with exhibits dating as far back as its Amerindian days. A small garden in the rear has plantings reminiscent of the governor's era.

Afternoon

- Almost just around the corner is **Place Jacques-Cartier**, technically a public square but really more like a wide, sloping pedestrian mall. This lively gathering spot is filled with open-air sidewalk cafes and, in summer, street performers, musicians and flower vendors. A monument honors Lord Nelson's victory over Napoleon Bonaparte at Trafalgar.

- The square is a good place for lunch, or try the nearby **Chez l'épicier Restaurant Bar à Vin**. The name translates to "the grocery," which is fitting since the menus are printed on brown paper bags, and the eatery has an area with shelves stocked with gourmet products. Comfort food prepared with a creative Québécois twist might include snail shepherd's pie or parsnip soup.

- After lunch, walk through the **Old Port** (Vieux-Port) area, a broad promenade along the St. Lawrence River. You'll join bicyclists, joggers and inline skaters taking in the views and enjoying the parklike expanse. Near the far end is ▒ **Pointe-à-Callière, Montréal Museum of Archaeology and History** (Pointe-à-Callière, Musée d'archéologie et d'histoire de Montréal). Despite its contemporary exterior, this museum is all

Go Shopping at the Bonsecours Market

about the past—in fact, it was built on top of the remains of Ville-Marie, the earliest European colony. After viewing a multimedia presentation about Montréal's history, visitors descend underground to an archeological dig which has unearthed part of the old city wall and the city's first Catholic cemetery.

- An alternative, especially if you're traveling with children, is the **Montréal Science Centre** (Centre des sciences de Montréal), which is just before the archeology museum. Easily identifiable by the bright red sculpture of molecules in front, the museum has an IMAX theater and lots of hands-on activities involving science and technology. Exhibits encourage exploration of science's daily uses, finding solutions to environmental disasters and the creation of a news report.

Evening

- After relaxing a bit, head back to Old Montréal to the Bonsecours Market (Marché Bonsecours), an impressive domed neoclassical building on rue St-Paul. This mid-19th-century edifice, built as a public market, still draws shoppers, who come now to scour its upscale boutiques for items handmade by Canadian craftspeople.

- Nearby is **La Menara**, where a dinner reservation transports you to an exotic Moroccan oasis. Meals are served in a canopied tent draped in vivid red fabrics and feature a choice of such North African favorites as couscous and tajines.

- End your day in Old Montréal with a stroll around the romantically lit historic district, stopping to window-shop at boutiques and art galleries and possibly at a bakery or candy shop for a delectable confection.

Arriving
By Car

The major highway route from the United States is I-87, which becomes Autoroute 15; I-87 enters Canada from northeastern New York. Autoroute 10 enters the city from the Eastern Townships and Vermont. From the east across the Champlain Bridge, Autoroute 20 allows controlled access to the downtown areas, and Autoroute 40 proceeds along the north shore of the St. Lawrence River. The Montréal Laurentian Autoroute, Hwy. 15, arrives from the north, while Autoroute 40 enters Montréal from the west.

Air Travel

Montréal-Pierre Elliott Trudeau International Airport (YUL), formerly Montréal-Dorval Airport, 22 kilometres (14 mi.) west of downtown in Dorval, handles commercial flights. Terminal exit signs direct travelers to Hwy. 20, which becomes Hwy. 720 (Autoroute Ville-Marie). From here, the exits to rues Guy, Atwater and de la Montagne provide access to downtown and Old Montréal.

Taxis to downtown average $35 from Montréal-Trudeau. Station Aérobus, (800) 465-1213, serves the airport. The 747 Express Bus operates 24 hours daily and provides transportation between Montréal's central transit station (Berri-UQAM) and the airport. The fare, which includes a 24-hour pass for the city's bus and subway network, is $7; only coins are accepted for payment aboard the 747.

Nearly all major rental-car companies serve Montréal, and desks are inside airline terminals at Montréal-Trudeau. Be prepared for a high provincial

The Jacques-Cartier Bridge over the St. Lawrence River

tax on car rentals and an extra charge for insurance coverage. For the best prices, reservations should be made several weeks in advance, especially during peak seasons. Local AAA/CAA clubs can provide this assistance or additional information. Hertz, (514) 842-8537, (800) 263-0600 in Canada for English speakers, (800) 263-0678 in Canada for French speakers, or (800) 654-3131 outside Canada, offers discounts to AAA/CAA members.

Getting Around
Street System

Montréal can be a tricky place to navigate until you fully understand its odd layout. The city is on an island in the St. Lawrence River, which generally flows west to east from the Great Lakes to the Atlantic Ocean. The banks of the St. Lawrence are known as the north shore and south shore, even though the river flows almost due north where it meets Montréal. Consequently, the streets that run parallel to the river are labeled from boulevard St-Laurent east-west, even though they actually run north-south; those perpendicular to the water, though nearly east-west, are labeled north-south.

Though it makes for an odd sensation at sunrise, it is easiest to orient yourself as if the harbor were to your south. Accordingly, the principal east-west streets downtown include boulevard René-Lévesque, rue Ste-Catherine, boulevard de Maisonneuve and rue Sherbrooke. The main downtown arteries running north-south include rue Crescent, rue McGill, rue St-Denis and boulevard St-Laurent.

In Old Montréal, rues St-Jacques, Notre-Dame, St-Paul and de la Commune are the main thoroughfares running parallel to the south shore. Avenues du Mont-Royal and Laurier are the major streets north of the downtown area, near Mont-Royal Park.

Boulevard St-Laurent is the dividing point between east and west (*est* and *ouest*) in Montréal. North-south streets do not have an equivalent dividing line, but numbers start at the south shore and climb with the topography. Even-numbered addresses are on the south and west sides of streets, odd-numbered addresses on the north and east sides.

Expressways in Québec are called autoroutes, and two such highways provide quick routes around the city. Canada's premier highway, the Trans-Canada, forks when it reaches Montréal, with Autoroute 40 crossing the northern side east to west and Autoroute 20 traveling along the south side. Though always well-patrolled, neither route is well-maintained. Both may have limited access.

Avenues De Lorimier and Papineau merge south of rue Ontario as the Jacques-Cartier Bridge, which crosses the St. Lawrence River to the islands of Ste-Hélène and Notre-Dame.

Drivers should be aware that right turns on red lights are illegal in Montréal.

Parking

Most major downtown office buildings, shopping centers and hotels have underground parking; Place d'Youville, the Montréal World Trade Centre, Place Jacques-Cartier and Quai de l'Horloge all have lots. There is metered street parking in most commercial areas though parking generally is prohibited on main arteries during rush hours, 7-9 a.m. and 4-6 p.m. Regulations are posted on white signs throughout the city. Rates vary from lot to lot, but normally range $3-$5 per hour or $8-$15 per day. For further information, phone (514) 868-3737.

Public Transportation

Société de transport de Montréal (STM) provides clean, safe and comfortable bus, Métro (subway) and commuter train service throughout greater Montréal. Tickets are good for both bus and Métro. Transfer tickets are valid in any direction for the next 90 minutes; request one when you pay your fare. Buses on major routes operate through the night. Depending on which line, the last departure for each of the Métro lines varies (12:15 a.m.-12:50 a.m.) Monday through Friday; final departures on Saturday and Sunday nights are offered from 12:15 a.m. to as late as 1:30 a.m. Service for all lines resumes at 5:30 a.m.

Tickets are sold at subway stations for $2.75 each or in strips of six for $12.75. For short visits, the best deal is a 1-day tourist pass for $9 or a 3-day pass for $17. A monthly pass can be purchased for $65 up to 10 days before the month for which it is valid. A 7-day pass is $20. Métro tickets are good on buses, but if you don't have a ticket, you must have exact change.

Murals, sculpture, stained-glass windows, enameled frescoes and ceramics adorn the 68 Métro stations. Artistic themes range from city history to the abstract.

Note: In this TourBook, attraction listings often include the nearest Métro (M:) station or stations. Consult a transit map to determine which train line is nearest and most direct. Pick up a free STM guide and commuter train schedule at ticket booths; phone (514) 786-4636 or (514) 280-5308.

Shopping

Montréal's stores reflect the city's cosmopolitan nature and its French heritage. The city is considered Canada's *haute couture* capital, not only for the number of stores but also for their variety. Wares range from imported designer labels to local handicrafts.

Antiques

The best concentrations of antique dealers are along **rue Notre-Dame Ouest**, between rue Guy and avenue Atwater, and on St-Paul in Old Montréal. A cluster of restored graystones scattered up and down both sides of the street houses a dozen or more shops with various quaint treasures. Discriminating collectors may want to venture to the west end of **rue Sherbrooke**, where exquisite mahogany, Royal Crown Derby china and popular old china and silver patterns can be had for a price. Antique dealers in **Westmount** also cater to a more discriminating clientele. Bargain-hunters should visit rue

Montréal's Métro Service

Notre-Dame shops, where the prices often are negotiable.

Malls

What began in 1962 as a simple shopping center beneath Place Ville-Marie is now an underground maze of walkways stretching 30 kilometres (18.6 mi.) and embracing 2,000 shops, 200 restaurants and 30 theaters. Subterranean promenades and the Métro connect the clusters of buildings. Most of Montréal's spectacular shopping malls have found a home in Underground Montréal. Many malls begin underground and reach upward to several floors above ground.

Shops in the underground generally are open Mon.-Wed. 10-6, Thurs.-Fri. 10-9, Sat. 10-5, Sun. 11-5. Most are closed holidays.

Place Ville-Marie, with its shop-lined corridors centered on a sculpted fountain, was the first of these subterranean centers to be built. Known to locals as PVM (pronounced pay-vay-em), the complex teems with trendy boutiques.

Other shopping clusters have since been added, including **Centre Eaton, Les Cours Mont-Royal, Place Bonaventure, Place Montréal Trust** and **Les Promenades de la Cathédrale.**

In Place Montréal Trust, underground at the corner of rue Ste-Catherine and avenue McGill College, bright atria and cascading fountains link innovative architecture and glass walls. Directly beneath Christ Church Cathedral at 625 rue Ste-Catherine Ouest, Les Promenades de la Cathédrale has shops on two levels. Place Bonaventure, at rues de la Gauchetière and University, links some 100 shops with the Bonaventure Hilton International.

A modern restoration of the Hôtel Mont-Royal resulted in Les Cours Mont-Royal, a three-story mall at 1455 rue Peel. Centre Eaton, 705 rue Ste-Catherine, is anchored by Les Ailes de la Mode department store.

Complexe Desjardins, a partially underground marvel of waterfalls, fountains, trees and hanging vines, comprises lanes of shops connected to four tall office towers and the Hotel Wyndham.

These underground marketplaces present an almost endless array of merchandise, from everyday items to luxury articles. Just browsing can be as pleasurable as shopping, for the window displays are interesting.

Markets

Open-air **Jean-Talon Market** on avenue Casgrain and **Atwater Market**, an indoor bazaar near the Lachine Canal at 138 Atwater Ave., both feature merchants offering such goods as fresh fruits and vegetables, flowers and pastries.

Outlets

Hordes of Montréalers shop right off the factory rack in the **Chabanel Fashion District**, on rue Chabanel, west of rue St-Laurent. A solid row of towering garment factories and fashion wholesalers provides everything a bargain hunter could want. Most showrooms are open to the public only on Saturday, when serious shoppers storm the place for deals on jeans, lingerie, sweaters, leather accessories, bathing suits and the like. On Sunday morning, head for **Old Montréal**, where a similar scene takes place at numerous clothes discounters that congregate along rue Notre-Dame east of rue McGill.

Have Coffee and a Pastry on Rue St-Denis

Specialty Districts

Most of Montréal's big department stores were founded when Scottish, Irish and English families dominated the city's commerce, so the names remain noticeably Anglophone—Holt Renfrew, Ogilvy and The Bay. The main branches of Ogilvy and The Bay, dazzling emporiums, stretch along **rue Ste-Catherine**, where the city's traditional downtown shopping street comprises myriad shops in the blocks between rues Guy and Carré Phillips.

Rue Sherbrooke, 2 blocks north of rue Ste-Catherine, is the center of high fashion, represented by the venerable Holt Renfrew, exclusive art galleries and such haute couture boutiques as Ralph Lauren and Yves St-Laurent. Holt Renfrew also has a small branch across the street from the Ritz-Carlton Montréal on rue Sherbrooke. For local creations there are a number of boutiques along rues Laurier, St-Denis, St-Hubert and St-Laurent.

Running south off Sherbrooke, the businesses housed in quaint Victorian-style town houses along **rue Crescent** and **rue de la Montagne** are popular for shopping. Those looking for the best in exotic coffees and avant-garde bookstores won't want to miss **rue St-Denis**, where cafés and restaurants spill out into the streets to accommodate shoppers taking a break for pasta or pastries. Other shops along this street offer an array of items for the home. La Main (boulevard St-Laurent) is a hodgepodge of ethnic eateries and gift shops. Begin at the intersection of avenue Viger and head north.

In Old Montréal, handmade crafts fashioned by Canadian artisans steal the show. Visitors typically start accumulating distinctive mementos at **Bonsecours Market** (Marché Bonsecours)—the striking domed neoclassical building at the eastern end of rue St-Paul is hard to pass up. Fifteen upscale boutiques and eateries are housed in the mid-19th-century edifice, which also presents contemporary art exhibitions.

Near the intersection of **rue de la Gauchetière**, the Chinese community offers its wares. Mah-jongg sets, jade carvings, silk saris and delicate brocades are among the items that can be found along the way. The smells of deli meats and sausages mingle where the Hungarians and Polish Jews congregate several blocks up near rue Sherbrooke. Still farther north, clothing and ceramics stores operated by Portuguese emigrants occupy the area that the Greek community once embraced. The ice cream parlors and pastry shops in **Little Italy**, near rue Jean-Talon, offer shoppers a place to refuel before making their way back along the street.

Shops along rue Laurier, in the posh French neighborhood of **Outremont**, have built a reputation for staying on the cutting edge of European trends, whether it be in clothes, food or home furnishings. A selection of boutiques and local stores similar in quality to those on Laurier can be found along **avenue Greene** in nearby Westmount. This smaller area is less frequented by tourists, so it is usually easier to find parking.

Outside the downtown area are a number of suburban shopping malls offering many of the same attractions as their urban counterparts. They include **Carrefour Laval**, hwys. 15 and 440 in Laval; **Centre Fairview Pointe-Claire**, Hwy. 40 and boulevard St-John in Pointe-Claire; **Centre Rockland**, Hwy. 40 and boulevard L'Acadie in Mont-Royal; and **Les Galeries d'Anjou**, Hwys. 40 and 25 in Ville d'Anjou.

Big Events

A hub on the international film festival circuit, Montréal welcomes a remarkable variety of programs each year.

The granddaddy is the **Montréal World Film Festival** (Festival des Films du Monde de Montréal), a competition similar to those held at Cannes and Venice. Staged from late August to early September, the event occupies various theaters throughout the area. Other significant festivals include the **International Festival of Films on Art** (Festival International du Film sur l'Art) in March; and the 9-day **Montréal Fringe Festival** in June.

Premier sporting events include the 65-kilometre (40-mi.) **Tour de l'Île de Montréal**, which brings 45,000 cyclists to the city in early June; the July **Valleyfield International Regatta**, said to be the largest speedboat event in North America; and Canada's international tennis championships, the **Rogers Cup** (Coupe Rogers), in August.

The city's other events cover a broad spectrum. Each new year gets off to a frosty start with the ice sculptures and competitive winter sports of the **Snow Festival** (Fête des Neiges) at the end of January. The weeklong event keeps the city entertained with costume balls, giant ice slides and all varieties of winter fun.

Starting in late February, the **Montréal High Lights Festival** (Festival Montréal en Lumière) includes fireworks, a food and wine circuit, an underground footrace, live music and an all-night party.

The **Montréal International Music Competition** (Concours Musical International de Montréal), held at the Place des Arts, begins in mid-May and runs into the first week of June. This competition is divided into strings, piano and voice categories. June marks the beginning of the **Loto-Québec International Fireworks Competition** (L'International des Feux Loto-Québec), which typically ends in early August.

The **FrancoFolies of Montréal** (Les FrancoFolies de Montréal), which showcases the talents of more than 1,000 French-language performers from around the world, is held in June. The **St-Jean-Baptiste Celebration** on June 24 is an official holiday honoring the patron saint of French Canadians. Bonfires, fireworks, dancing and music are among the day's events and activities.

The ☙ **Montréal International Jazz Festival** (Festival International de Jazz de Montréal), during which the world's foremost jazz artists participate in concerts, takes place from late June to early July. The ☙ **Just for Laughs Festival** (Festival Juste

Just for Laughs Festival

pour rire) in July is a program of comedy acts from around the world. Performers are both established comedians and newcomers. Many acts perform in the Latin Quarter on rue St-Denis and are free; admission is charged for others taking place in theatres. Some acts are in French and some are presented in English.

Finally, December ushers in the **Québec Handicraft Show** and scores of Christmas festivities.

Sports & Rec

While sunshine and rising temperatures in the summer months permit a wide range of recreational activities, naturally, winter sports predominate in a city where the weather swings between cool and frigid most of the year. Few would argue with the assertion that Canadians are perhaps the best hockey players in the world and that Canadian hockey fans are the most loyal and discriminating sports fans anywhere. Indeed, hockey *belongs* to Canada. And although no sport is likely to match hockey on Montréal's popularity scale, a handful of other professional sports ably compete to fill gaps on the entertainment bill.

Football The **Montréal Alouettes** (Larks) play in the Canadian Football League from mid-June to mid-November at **Percival Molson Stadium**; phone (514) 871-2255.

Hockey Near the end of the 19th century two enterprising students at McGill University are said to have invented not only the puck but the general rules of the game of hockey as it is known today. By the time the National Hockey League (NHL) was formed in 1917, the 8-year-old **Montréal Canadiens** franchise already was the pride of Montréal. The club won five consecutive Stanley Cup titles from 1956-60, an epic streak dramatized as a metaphor for Québécois pride in Rick Salutin's play "Les Canadiens."

The Canadiens have taken possession of the Stanley Cup a record 24 times. The team has garnered enough NHL title banners to intimidate even the most formidable opponent and has achieved an impressive presence in the Hockey Hall of Fame in Toronto. Among the former players honored there are such legends as Maurice "Rocket" and younger brother Henri Richard, Jean Béliveau and Guy Lafleur. Home games during the regular season are played at **Centre Bell** from October through March, with playoffs starting in April and ending in June; phone (514) 932-2582.

Horse Racing Harness racing is the ticket at **Hippodrome de Montréal**, 7440 boul. Décarie. International events in the trotting circuit are held at the track. Races are scheduled year-round; phone (514) 739-2741. Public transportation is recommended, as traffic is heavy.

Note: Policies vary concerning admittance of children to pari-mutuel betting facilities. Phone for information.

Soccer The **Montréal Impact** is the city's North American Soccer League franchise. The team plays from mid-April to mid-September. Its home, **Saputo Stadium** (Stade Saputo), is located at 4750 rue Sherbrooke Est at Olympic Park; phone (514) 328-3668.

Bicycling Montréal's extensive network of bicycle paths covers nearly 450 kilometres (280 mi.) of the

See the Montréal Canadiens Play at Centre Bell

island. The paths are open from April 1 to mid-November. Bicycling maps are available at most sporting goods stores and *Infotouriste* centers; phone (514) 873-2015.

The 12-kilometre (7.5-mi.) **Lachine Canal path** runs along the old canal and offers a view of the Lachine Rapids between René-Lévesque and St-Louis parks. This path is illuminated at night. **Old Port's** waterfront views, though more placid, also make it popular; the 2.4-kilometre (1.5-mi.) path is perfect for a quick trip. **Maisonneuve Park** (Parc Maisonneuve) offers a well-maintained track that winds past the Montréal Botanical Garden and a golf course. For those with more time and energy, the **St. Lawrence Seaway** route, 16 kilometres (10 mi.) long, lets bicyclists follow the narrow part of the seaway.

Though there are no designated paths, **Jean-Drapeau Park** (Parc Jean-Drapeau), spread over **Île Notre-Dame** and **Île Ste-Hélène**, also is a prime spot for exploring on two wheels. Bicyclists should keep in mind that the islands often are slightly cooler and more windy than downtown.

One caveat about pedaling around the city: Montréal residents are notorious for wild driving, so it is highly recommended that bicyclists wear helmets and pay close attention to road signs. Moreover, traffic lights for cyclists are popping up everywhere in Montréal, given the popularity of this means of transport. Vélo-Québec, 1251 rue Rachel Est (Maison des Cyclistes), provides brochures, guidebooks and path information; phone (514) 521-8356. For those without their own wheels, La Cordée, 2159 rue Ste-Catherine Est, and Vélo Adventures in Old Port have rentals. In addition BIXI, a public bicycle-sharing service that made its debut in 2009, offers rental bicycles at some 400 self-service stations May through November. The first 30 minutes of BIXI service are free; phone (514) 789-2494 or (877) 820-2453.

Fishing Its abundance of lakes and rivers makes Montréal a popular place with those who enjoy fishing. Anglers must obtain a provincial license, which is available at most sporting goods stores. The Ministry of Environment and Société de la Faune et des Parcs du Québec provides information about fishing areas; phone (800) 561-1616 in Canada.

Hardier souls may prefer the challenge of ice fishing, in which groups huddle around a hole in the ice inside a traditional Québécois ice-fishing shack. Muskie, perch and pike are typical catches.

Golf Several golf courses are easily accessible from downtown Montréal. The following courses are among the many in the city that offer at least 18 holes and are open to the public, weather permitting, from late April to mid-October: Club de Golf Atlantide Inc., (514) 425-2000, 2201 Don Quichotte in Île Perrot; Club de Golf Beaconsfield, (514) 695-0832, 49 av. Golf in Pointe-Claire; Club de Golf Chantecler, (450) 229-3742, 2520 ch. Du Club in Ste-Adèle; Club de Golf Le Parcours du Cerf, (450)

448-2373, 2500 boul. Fernand-Lafontaine in Longueuil; Club de Golf Vaudreuil Inc., (450) 455-2731, 1126 St-Antoine in Vaudreuil-Dorion; and Golf Dorval, (514) 631-6624, 2000 Reverchon in Dorval.

For information about courses and tournaments contact the Association de golf du Québec, 4545, Pierre-de-Coubertin, C.P. 1000, Succursale M, Montréal, QC, Canada H1V 3R2; phone (514) 252-3345.

Hiking With a landmark such as **Mont Royal**, the city obviously has a preferred site for scenic hikes. Beginning at the Mont-Royal Métro stop, well-marked trails ascend to two lookout points and provide views from the main chalet at **Mont-Royal Park**.

Jogging and Walking Montréal's myriad parks prove popular with joggers and walkers alike. Those who prefer level and forgiving terrain should follow Lachine Canal or negotiate a park, such as **Lafontaine** or Maisonneuve. Mont-Royal Park, with its uphill climbs and natural terrain, is more challenging, but the view makes the extra effort worthwhile.

Tennis Most of Montréal's 390-plus municipal courts are open to the public at no charge or for a small fee. The **Claude-Robillard Sports Complex** (Complexe sportif Claude-Robillard), along with the **Jeanne-Mance**, **Kent**, Lafontaine and **Somerled** community parks offer courts. Area clubs include **Uniprix Stadium** (Stade Uniprix) in Montréal, 285 rue Faillon Ouest, (514) 273-1234; **Tennis Île-des-Soeurs** in Île-des-Soeurs, 300 ch. du Golf, (514) 766-1208; and **Tennis Longueuil** in Longueuil, 550 Curé-Poirier Ouest, (450) 679-6131.

Water Sports Although most of the water around Montréal is too polluted for swimming, taking a dip is popular at pools scattered around the city. About 50 indoor pools are available. The indoor Olympic-size pool at **Olympic Park** is open to the public for a small admission fee; phone (514) 252-8687. Public indoor pools also are at the **Cégep du Vieux Montréal**, a college at 255 rue Ontario Est, and at the Claude-Robillard Sports Complex (Complexe sportif Claude-Robillard), 1000 rue Émile-Journault. Both locations charge a nominal fee. Several large outdoor pools are near the Métro stop near Jean-Drapeau Park (Parc Jean-Drapeau); phone (514) 872-7708. A fee is charged.

Island hop to Île Notre-Dame for the city's only beach. Artificial **Jean-Drapeau Beach Park** (Plage du Parc Jean-Drapeau) is the former **Regatta Lake** from Expo 67. The water comes from the Lachine Rapids and is treated to make it safe for swimming. Locals flock here in the summer months to picnic and bask in the sun before winter strikes again.

Winter Sports A city fanatical about hockey is certain to have a wealth of places for ice-skating. Montréal offers more than 275 outdoor rinks. The most popular is at the Old Port of Montréal **Bassin Bon Secours**; another favorite is the rink at lac des Castors.

Speed demons will be interested in tobogganing and ice sliding when the city freezes over. The best

Visit the Indoor Pool at Olympic Park

toboggan runs are in Mont-Royal Park and on the hills around **lac des Castors**.

The thick blanket of snow that covers Montréal makes the city and its environs prime skiing venues. Mont-Royal has excellent trails for cross-country enthusiasts, and it's possible to ski in several other city parks when the powder gets deep. Cross-country skiers and snowshoers frequent the ecology trail at Maisonneuve Park (Parc Maisonneuve) next to the Montréal Botanical Garden *(see attraction listing p. 327)*.

Cross-country trails and rental equipment are available at Détour Nature, (514) 271-6046, and La poubelle du ski, (514) 384-1315.

Serious downhill skiers need only make a short road trip to the nearby **Laurentians** and **Eastern Townships** for the fabulous runs at Bromont, Owl's Head, Orford, Sutton or Mont-Tremblant.

Some of these areas have dog sledding, sleigh rides and snowmobiling available. In fact the inventor of the snowmobile—Joseph Bombardier—was born in the Eastern Townships in the town of Valcourt, which markets itself as "the snowmobile capital of the world." For more information phone Ski East (Association Touristique des Cantons-de-l'Est) at (819) 564-8989 or the Association Touristique des Laurentides (ATL) at (450) 436-8532.

Performing Arts

With its distinctly European tastes and modern air, Montréal would seem a hotbed of innovative performing arts. But the cultural scene here actually is new. It wasn't until the 1960s that theater, cinema and dance hit the city with full force. Today French-language productions are presented at about 20 theaters around town, and the city is hailed within the province for its provocative avant-garde cinema.

Dance The **Grand Canadian Ballet of Montréal** (Les Grands Ballets Canadiens de Montréal), performing both classical and modern repertory at **Place des Arts**, has attracted enthusiastic audiences for 50 years. The troupe has toured internationally and has featured the works of many new Canadian composers and choreographers. Its December production of "The Nutcracker" is a big seasonal event in Montréal; phone (514) 842-2112 or (866) 842-2112 for the box office.

Another longtime company is **Les Sortilèges National Folklore Ensemble** (L'Ensemble national de folklore Les Sortilèges). The group of 20 dancers has performed Québécois and other folk dances in colorful costumes for more than 40 years. They entertain in various halls around the city; check the local papers or phone (514) 522-5955.

Film Montréal is host to many film festivals *(see event listings p. 319)*. **Cinéma du Parc**, 3575 av. du Parc, shows specialized and offbeat fare.

Music The world-renowned **Montréal Symphony Orchestra** (Orchestre symphonique de Montréal) performs during its regular season at **L'Adresse symphonique** on the eastern edge of Place des Arts, but locals recommend attending one of the performances at the **Basilica of Notre-Dame** (Basilique Notre-Dame) *(see attraction listing p. 329)* on rue Notre-Dame. Performances usually begin between 6:30 p.m. and 8 p.m.; phone (514) 842-2925.

Enjoy Ballet or Opera at Place des Arts

At the Montréal Museum of Fine Arts (Musée des beaux-arts de Montréal) *(see attraction listing p. 328)* on Sherbrooke St. W., musical performances by ensembles and solo artists take place regularly at the **Bourgie Concert Hall,** housed in a 19th-century church; phone (514) 285-2000, ext. 4, or (800) 899-6873.

The **Metropolitan Orchestra** (Orchestre Métropolitain) promotes classical music while preparing new generations of musicians. The orchestra's regular season performances are at the **Maisonneuve Theatre** in Place des Arts; phone (514) 842-2112 or (866) 842-2112 for the box office.

Opera Founded in 1980, the **Opera of Montréal** (L'Opéra de Montréal) is a young assemblage that stages six productions, both traditional and lesser-known, annually at Place des Arts. All operas are presented with English and French subtitles. The company's season runs from September through June; phone the box office at (514) 842-2112 or (866) 842-2112.

Theater Montréal's most extraordinary theatrical event is perhaps **Cirque du Soleil** (the name means "Circus of the Sun"). The modern, extravagant affair, which was founded in the city in 1984, is a circus without animals. The performers' kaleidoscopic shows—which include a mix of theatrical gymnastics, vertical pole-walking, music and fantastic special effects—captivate audiences of all ages. Having already achieved cult status on its American tours, the troupe stunned European audiences during its debut visit in 1996; phone (514) 522-2324 for performance dates and admission costs.

The Old Stock Exchange building at 453 rue St-François-Xavier now is home to the **Centaur Theatre**, (514) 288-3161, Montréal's primary venue for English-language drama and musicals. Centaur's seven-play lineup has included contemporary Canadian dramas and Broadway hits. The **Yiddish Theater**, founded in 1937, stages two plays a year in Yiddish. Each runs for 4 weeks or longer, usually in June and November, at the **Segal Centre for Performing Arts**, 5170 ch. de la Côte-Ste-Catherine; phone (514) 739-2301 for schedule information.

At least 10 major French theater companies in the city stage productions stretching from classics to farce. **Théâtre de Quat'Sous**, 100 av. des Pins Est; **Théâtre du Nouveau Monde**, 84 rue Ste-Catherine Ouest; and **Théâtre d'Aujourd'hui**, 3900 rue St-Denis, offer eclectic French fare from September through May. **Théâtre du Rideau Vert**, 4664 rue St-Denis, unveils mostly French classics and modern works by Québec playwrights year-round. The **Compagnie Jean Duceppe**, at 175 rue Ste-Catherine Ouest in the Métro Place des Arts, presents contemporary works examining society and mores; phone (514) 842-2112 or (866) 842-2112.

Open-air theater draws crowds during the summer to Lafontaine Park and Île Ste-Hélène. The **Repercussion Theatre** puts on Shakespearean productions at various Montréal parks; phone (514) 931-2644.

INSIDER INFO:

Driving in La Métropole

In bilingual Montréal, international driving symbols are in use, as they are throughout the province *(see the AAA/CAA Atlantic Provinces and Québec Map)*. Prohibitory information is presented in signs with a white-centered red circle with a red diagonal slash. Mandatory information, such as seat belt usage, is presented in signs with a white-centered green circle. Radar detectors are not permitted. **Note:** Québec uses the 24-hour clock, e.g., 1730 is 5:30 p.m.

Below are French/English equivalents of some of the more common driving directions and information appearing on signs.

GENERAL INFORMATION

Nord	North
Sud	South
Est	East
Ouest	West
Lun.	Mon.
Mar.	Tues.
Mer.	Wed.
Jeu.	Thurs.
Ven.	Fri.
Sam.	Sat.
Dim.	Sun.

SIGNS

ARRÊT	STOP
Accotement Mou	Soft Shoulder
Arrét Interdit	No Stopping
Cul-de-sac	Dead End
Débarcadére	Loading Zone
Demi-tour Interdit	No U Turn
Dépassement Interdit	No Passing
Déviation	Bypass
École	School
Fin	End
Glissant	Slippery
Lentement	Slow
Pas de Virage à Gauche	No Left Turn
Pas de Virage à Droite	No Right Turn
Passage à Niveau	Railroad Crossing
Reculez	Back Up
Rétrécissement	Road Narrows
Route à Chaussées Séparées	Divided Highway
Sens Unique	One Way
Stationnement	Parking
Stationnement Interdit	No Parking
Vitesse	Speed
Voie Réservée	Reserved Lane

Montréal Museums Pass

The Montréal Museums Pass provides access to more than 30 major Montréal museums and attractions in the city for a period of 3 consecutive days, with public transportation services (unlimited access to the bus and Métro system) included.

Sam Colbey of the Grand Canadian Ballet of Montréal

Included in the pass are Avataq Cultural Institute; Bibliothèque et Archives nationales du Québec; The Biosphère; Canadian Centre for Architecture; The Château Dufresne Museum; Château Ramezay—Historic Site and Museum of Montréal; Cinémathèque québécoise; Cité historia, musée d'histoire du Sault-au-Récollet; Darling Foundry; DHC/ART Foundation for Contemporary Art; Exhibition Centre la-Prison-des-Patriotes; The Fur Trade at Lachine National Historic Site; Lachine Museum; McCord Museum of Canadian History; Montréal Biodôme; Montréal Botanical Garden; Montréal History Centre; The Montréal Holocaust Memorial Centre; Montréal Insectarium; Montréal Museum of Contemporary Art; Montréal Museum of Fine Arts; Montréal Science Centre; Museum of Hospitallers of the Hospital of Montréal; Museum of the Proud People: Montréal Museum of Industrial and Working-Class History; The Museum of Québec Masters and Artisans; Notre-Dame-de-Bon-Secours Chapel and Marguerite Bourgeoys Museum; Pointe-à-Callière, Montréal Museum of Archaeology and History; The Redpath Museum; St. Gabriel House; Sir George-Étienne Cartier National Historic Site; Stewart Hall Art Gallery; and The Stewart Museum at the Old Fort.

The pass sells for $65 (taxes included), or $60 without the Société de transport de Montréal (STM) public transit card. There is no senior citizen or student/child discount. The pass can be purchased from most member institutions; downtown at the Montréal Infotouriste Centre at the Travelprice agency counter, 1255 rue Peel, Suite 100; in Old Montréal at the Infotouriste Centre at 174 rue Notre-Dame Est; at the La Vitrine discount ticket outlet,

145 rue Ste-Catherine Ouest; and from some major hotels. For more information phone (514) 845-6873, or (514) 873-2015 or (877) 266-5687 for Tourisme Québec.

ATTRACTIONS

ANGRIGNON PARK (Parc Angrignon), 3400 boul. des Trinitaires (M: Angrignon), covers 107 hectares (264 acres). Cross-country skiing and ice-skating are popular activities in winter. **Cost:** Free. 🎁

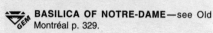

BASILICA OF NOTRE-DAME—see Old Montréal p. 329.

BMO FINANCIAL GROUP MUSEUM (Musée de BMO Groupe financier) is at 129 rue St-Jacques (M: Place d'Armes), adjacent to the BMO Bank of Montréal's main branch—an impressive neoclassic structure built in 1847—and the corporation's head office.

Paraphernalia related to banking, including old coins, paper bills and checks, is on display within a re-creation of an early 19th-century cashier's office. A collection of mechanical piggy banks is featured, along with photographs and other items chronicling the history of Canada's oldest banking institution. **Time:** Allow 1 hour minimum. **Hours:** Mon.-Fri. 10-4. Closed non-banking days. **Cost:** Free. **Phone:** (514) 877-6810.

[SAVE] **CANADIAN CENTRE FOR ARCHITECTURE** (Centre Canadien d'Architecture), 1920 rue Baile (M: Guy-Concordia), is an international research center and museum. Its extensive collections advance knowledge, promote public understanding, and widen thought and debate on the art of architecture, its history, theory, practice and role in society.

Facing the facility from the south side of boulevard René-Lévesque is a sculpture garden that evokes the history of architecture as well as the city that surrounds the site. **Hours:** Wed.-Sun. 11-6 (also Thurs. 6-9 p.m.). **Cost:** $10; $7 (ages 65+); $5 (students with ID); $3 (ages 6-12); free (ages 0-5 and to all Thurs. 5:30-9 p.m.). **Phone:** (514) 939-7026.

[SAVE] **THE CHÂTEAU DUFRESNE MUSEUM** (Le Musée du Château Dufresne) is at 2929 av. Jeanne-d'Arc. This Beaux Arts-style mansion, built 1915-18, features ceiling and wall murals by artist Guido Nincheri; imported Italian marble stairs; and friezes and varied woods. Temporary exhibits are displayed, and a manicured seasonal garden is on the grounds.

Guided tours are available by reservation. **Time:** Allow 1 hour minimum. **Hours:** Wed.-Sun. 10-5. Closed Jan. 1 and Christmas. **Cost:** $7; $6 (ages 64+ and students with ID); $3.50 (ages 6-12); $16 (family, two adults and two children ages 0-11, or one adult and three children ages 0-11). Guided tour $5. **Phone:** (514) 259-9201. 🎁

CHÂTEAU RAMEZAY—HISTORIC SITE AND MUSEUM OF MONTRÉAL—see Old Montréal p. 329.

CHRIST CHURCH CATHEDRAL (Anglican), 635 rue Ste-Catherine Ouest, between Union and University (M: McGill), is Gothic in style. Completed in 1859, it is a copy of a 14th-century English church. In partnership with local property developers, an underground shopping mall and meeting and activity rooms for the church were constructed beneath the cathedral. Concerts are offered periodically throughout the year. **Time:** Allow 30 minutes minimum. **Hours:** Sun.-Fri. 9-5:30, Sat. 11:30-5. **Cost:** Free. **Phone:** (514) 843-6577.

THE FUR TRADE AT LACHINE NATIONAL HISTORIC SITE—see Lachine p. 294.

THE GOVERNOR'S FEAST—see Old Montréal p. 329.

GRANDE BIBLIOTHÈQUE, 475 boul. de Maisonneuve Est (M: Berri-UQAM), is a major public library and the province's largest cultural institution. Offered in French and English, 90-minute guided tours describe the collections—part of Québec's national archives—housed on-site as well as the library's history and mission. The contemporary building houses more than 4 million documents, including 1 million books. A variety of cultural presentations, such as art exhibits, literary events and live performances, are held here periodically.

Self-guiding audio tours in French or English are available. **Time:** Allow 1 hour minimum. **Hours:** Library open Tues.-Fri. 10-10, Sat.-Sun. 10-6. Reservations are required for guided tours. Closed major holidays. **Cost:** Free. **Phone:** (514) 873-1100, or (800) 363-9028 outside Montréal. 🍽

ÎLE NOTRE-DAME (Notre Dame Island) is next to Île Ste-Hélène in the St. Lawrence River (M: Jean-Drapeau). Summer facilities include a floral park, a beach and an inline skating and bicycling path on the Gilles Villeneuve circuit. Winter offerings are a long ice-skating path and cross-country ski trails.

From the last week of January to the middle of February, the more than 125 activities and exhibits of the Fête des Neiges, or "Snow Festival," include snow and ice sculptures, dog sledding and a tube slide. **Time:** Allow 4 hours minimum. **Hours:** Island accessible daily 6 a.m.-11 p.m. **Cost:** Free. **Parking:** $13. **Phone:** (514) 872-6120.

ÎLE STE-HÉLÈNE (St. Helen's Island) is in the middle of the St. Lawrence River and reached via the Jacques-Cartier Bridge or the Cité du Havre (M: Jean-Drapeau). Jean-Drapeau Park (Parc Jean-Drapeau) enables visitors to walk or bike (rentals are available at the Métro station) past sculptures

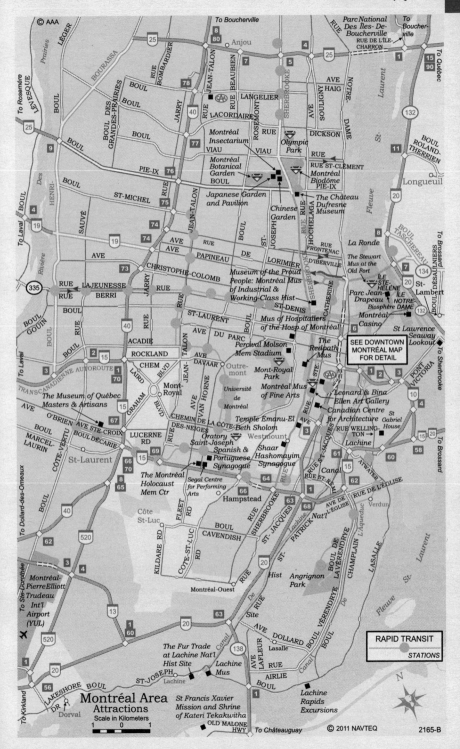

© AAA

To Boucherville

Parc National
Des Îles-De-
Boucherville
RUE DE L'ÎLE-
CHARRON

To
Boucher-
ville

Anjou

To Québec

Montréal
Insectarium

Montréal
Botanical
Garden

Olympic
Park

RUE ST-CLÉMENT

Montréal
Biodôme

The Château
Dufresne
Museum

Japanese Garden
and Pavilion

Chinese
Garden

Longueuil

La Ronde

The Stewart
Mus at the
Old Fort

Museum of the Proud
People: Montréal Mus
of Industrial &
Working-Class Hist

Parc Jean-
Drapeau

Biosphère

Mus of Hospitallers
of the Hosp of Montréal

Montréal
Casino

St Lawrence
Seaway
Lookout

Percival Molson
Mem Stadium

The
Redpath
Mus

SEE DOWNTOWN
MONTRÉAL MAP
FOR DETAIL

The Museum of Québec
Masters & Artisans

Mont-Royal
Park

Mont-
Royal

Université
de
Montréal

Mont-Royal Mus
of Fine Arts

Leonard & Bina
Ellen Art Gallery

Canadian Centre
for Architecture

St
Gabriel
House

Temple Emanu-El-
Beth Sholom

Oratory
Saint-Joseph

Westmount

Lachine

Spanish &
Portuguese
Synagogue

Shaar
Hashomayim
Synagogue

St-Laurent

The Montréal
Holocaust
Mem Ctr

Segal Centre
for Performing
Arts

Hampstead

Canal

Côte
St-Luc

Nat'l

Verdun

Montréal-
Pierre Elliott
Trudeau
Int'l
Airport
(YUL)

Montréal-Ouest

Angrignon
Park

The Fur Trade
at Lachine Nat'l
Hist Site

Lachine
Mus

Lachine

Lachine
Rapids
Excursions

Montréal Area
Attractions
Scale in Kilometers

St Francis Xavier
Mission and Shrine
of Kateri Tekakwitha

Dorval

To Châteauguay

RAPID TRANSIT

STATIONS

© 2011 NAVTEQ

2165-B

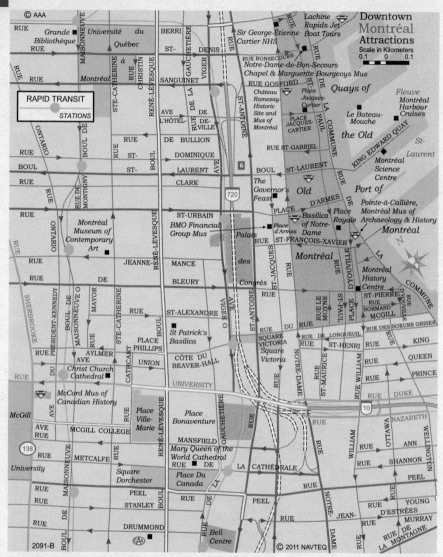

© AAA

Downtown Montréal Attractions

Scale in Kilometers
0.1   0   0.1

RAPID TRANSIT
STATIONS

© 2011 NAVTEQ

and buildings from Expo 67, a rose garden and historic sites such as an 1822 powder magazine and a military cemetery.

In the center of the island is Hélène-de-Champlain Park (Parc Hélène-de-Champlain), a landscaped area with picnic facilities; on the east end is the amusement park La Ronde. **Time:** Allow 4 hours minimum. **Hours:** Island accessible daily 6 a.m.-11 p.m. **Cost:** Free. **Parking:** $13. **Phone:** (514) 872-6120.

SAVE **Biosphère** is at 160 ch. du Tour de l'Isle on Île Ste-Hélène (M: Jean-Drapeau). This geodesic structure, the largest building of its kind in the world, reproduces more than three-fourths of a sphere and

was originally constructed to house the U.S. pavilion at Expo 67. Inside, a museum features interactive exhibits and live presentations delving into environmental issues, including those pertaining to the atmosphere as well as to natural resources and their consumption.

Tours: Guided tours are available. **Time:** Allow 1 hour minimum. **Hours:** Daily 10-6, June-Oct.; Tues.-Sun. 10-6, rest of year. Closed Jan. 1, Christmas and day after Christmas. **Cost:** $12; $8 (ages 64+ and students with ID); free (ages 0-17). Admission with proof of arrival via foot, bicycle, hybrid vehicle or public transit $9; $6 (ages 64+ and students with ID); free (ages 0-17). **Phone:** (514) 283-5000.

La Ronde, on Île Ste-Hélène at 22 ch. Macdonald (M: Jean-Drapeau), is an amusement park with more than 40 attractions and rides. It includes such roller coasters as ENDÔR - L'attaque, a suspended coaster built in part above Lac des Dauphins; the Goliath, which is more than 53 metres (175 ft.) high; and the Vampire, a suspended looping coaster. Au Pays de Ribambelle is geared toward pint-sized visitors.

Hours: Opens daily at 10:30, mid-May to early Sept.; opens select days at noon, early Sept.-late Oct. Phone ahead for closing times and to confirm schedule. **Cost:** All-inclusive $44.99; $32.50 (ages 61+ and children under 137 centimetres or 54 inches tall); free (ages 0-2). Prices may vary. **Phone:** (514) 397-2000.

The Stewart Museum at the Old Fort (Le Musée Stewart au Vieux Fort) is on Île Ste-Hélène at 20 ch. du Tour de l'Isle in Jean-Drapeau Park (M: Jean-Drapeau). The museum's permanent exhibition, History and Memory, chronicles more than 5 centuries of history through interactive displays and a collection of nearly 500 objects, documents and rare books. Such topics as navigation, maritime trade, New France residents' day-to-day life, and the history and heritage of Île Ste-Hélène are explored.

The museum is housed in the Old Fort, erected 1820-24 by the British military. In summer, interpretive programs are conducted by La Compagnie Franche de la Marine and the Olde 78th Fraser Highlanders. **Tours:** Guided tours are available. **Hours:** Wed.-Sun. 11-5. Closed Jan. 1 and Christmas. **Cost:** $13; $10 (students with ID and senior citizens); free (ages 0-6). **Phone:** (514) 861-6701.

LACHINE CANAL NATIONAL HISTORIC SITE— see Lachine p. 294.

LACHINE MUSEUM—see Lachine p. 294.

LEONARD & BINA ELLEN ART GALLERY (Galerie Leonard & Bina Ellen) is at 1400 boul. de Maisonneuve Ouest, on the ground floor of Concordia University's McConnell Library Building (M: Guy-Concordia). Comprising nearly 1,700 works of art, the gallery's permanent collection includes paintings, sculptures, prints and photographs. Contemporary art is the focus of the museum, with an emphasis on the post-1960s period. A wide range of pieces by 20th-century Canadian artists are displayed.

Temporary exhibitions occur regularly. **Time:** Allow 1 hour minimum. **Hours:** Tues.-Fri. noon-6, Sat. noon-5, Sept.-June. Closed major holidays. **Cost:** Free. **Phone:** (514) 848-2424, ext. 4778. [¶]

MARY QUEEN OF THE WORLD CATHEDRAL (Cathédrale Marie-Reine-du-Monde), bounded by rues Cathédrale and Mansfield on boul. René-Lévesque (M: Bonaventure or Peel), was built 1870-94. The Roman Catholic cathedral, a one-third

scale replica of St. Peter's in Rome, contains a collection of paintings by Québec artist George Delfosse. **Time:** Allow 30 minutes minimum. **Hours:** Mon.-Fri. 7-6, Sat. 7:30-6, Sun. 8:30-6. **Cost:** Free. **Phone:** (514) 866-1661.

McCORD MUSEUM OF CANADIAN HISTORY (Musée McCord d'histoire canadienne), across from McGill University at 690 Sherbrooke St. W. (M: McGill), has exhibits about the history of Canada dating from the 18th century to the present. In addition to a library and archives, collections dealing with costumes and textiles, decorative arts, archeology and ethnology, paintings, prints and drawings, and photographs by noted photographer William Notman are presented. Changing exhibits also are offered.

Note: Wheelchair access is on the west side of the museum, at 2175 Victoria St. Food is available Tues.-Sun. 11:30-2. **Hours:** Museum open Sat.-Mon. 10-5, Tues.-Fri. 10-6, in summer; Tues.-Fri. 10-6, Sat.-Sun. and Mon. holidays 10-5, rest of year. Archives open by appointment only. Closed Jan. 1, Christmas and day after Christmas. **Cost:** $12; $9 (ages 66+); $6 (students with ID); $4 (ages 6-12); $22 (family). **Phone:** (514) 398-7100 or (514) 398-7100, ext. 249.

MONTRÉAL BIODÔME—see Olympic Park p. 331.

MONTRÉAL BOTANICAL GARDEN (Jardin botanique de Montréal) is at 4101 rue Sherbrooke Est (M: Pie-IX). Founded in 1931 by botanist Frère Marie-Victorin, the internationally recognized 75-hectare (180-acre) site showcases nearly 23,000 plant species and cultivars, 10 exhibition greenhouses and about 30 thematic gardens.

Visitors can discover different aromas, sounds and textures while blindfolded in the Courtyard of Senses; share a cup of matcha with friends at the Japanese Garden and Pavilion *(see attraction listing)*; or learn about the bond between Amerindian and Inuit peoples and the plant world at the First Nations Garden. In addition, changing exhibits and special events are offered throughout the year.

Time: Allow 2 hours, 30 minutes minimum. **Hours:** Opens daily at 9, mid-May through Oct. 31; Tues.-Sun. at 9, rest of year. Closing times vary; phone ahead. Closed Christmas Eve and Christmas. **Cost:** May 15-Oct. 31 $16.50; $12.50 (ages 65+ and students with ID); $8.25 (ages 5-17); $2.50 (ages 2-4). Rest of year $14; $10.50 (ages 65+ and students with ID); $7 (ages 5-17); $2 (ages 2-4). Prices may vary. **Phone:** (514) 872-1400. [¶]

Chinese Garden (Jardin de Chine) is at the Montréal Botanical Garden at 4101 rue Sherbrooke Est (M: Pie-IX). The 2.5-hectare (6-acre) Ming Dynasty style garden features plants and trees native to Canada and southern China, including a courtyard with penjings (miniature trees). Other highlights include a 9-metre (30-ft.) waterfall and an ornamental pond. Changing art exhibits are displayed. The garden celebrates The Magic of Lanterns, a show featuring Chinese silk lanterns, mid-September through October 31. **Hours:** Garden open May-Oct. **Cost:** Included with Montréal Botanical Garden admission.

Japanese Garden and Pavilion (Jardin et Pavillon japonais) is at the Montréal Botanical Garden at 4101 rue Sherbrooke Est (M: Pie-IX). The 2.5-hectare (6-acre) site contains native Canadian plants arranged in traditional Japanese style, with koi ponds, streams and bridges. Among the designs are a stone garden, bonsai courtyard and the tea garden, which leads to the tea ceremony room. The contemporary Japanese pavilion provides a glimpse into the culture of Japan. **Hours:** Open May-Oct. **Cost:** Included with Montréal Botanical Garden admission.

SAVE **Montréal Insectarium** (Insectarium de Montréal) is at the Montréal Botanical Garden at 4101 rue Sherbrooke Est (M: Pie-IX). The facility features collections of both live and mounted specimens as well as interactive displays. In the We are the Insects exhibition, visitors learn about insects' universe—from their behaviors to their impact on the environment. **Hours:** Opens daily at 9, mid-May through Oct. 31; Tues.-Sun. at 9, rest of year. Closing times vary; phone ahead. **Cost:** Included with Montréal Botanical Garden admission.

SAVE **MONTRÉAL HISTORY CENTRE** (Centre d'histoire de Montréal), 335 Place d'Youville (M: Square-Victoria), is in a late 19th-century fire hall. Exhibits depict the events behind the history and development of Montréal. Audiovisual presentations re-create the sound and landscapes of various periods in the city's long and rich history. **Time:** Allow 1 hour minimum. **Hours:** Tues.-Sun. 10-5, late Jan.-early Dec. Closed major holidays. Phone ahead to confirm schedule. **Cost:** $6; $5 (ages 55+); $4 (students with ID); $15 (family). **Phone:** (514) 872-3207.

SAVE **THE MONTRÉAL HOLOCAUST MEMORIAL CENTRE** (Le Centre commémoratif de l'Holocauste à Montréal), 1 Carré Cummings Square (5151 ch. de la Côte-Ste-Catherine) (M: Côte-Ste-Catherine), educates visitors about the systematic extermination of Jews and other groups the Nazis deemed undesirable during World War II.

The permanent collection comprises 6,000 original artifacts, photographs and documents, many of which were donated by Holocaust survivors who later made Montréal their home. Also featured are archival film footage, eyewitness testimonies and a memorial flame.

Time: Allow 1 hour minimum. **Hours:** Mon.-Thurs. 10-5 (also Wed. 5-9), Fri. and Sun. 10-4. Closed Jewish and statutory holidays. Phone ahead to confirm schedule. **Cost:** $8; $5 (students with ID). Under 14 must be with an adult. **Phone:** (514) 345-2605.

SAVE **MONTRÉAL MUSEUM OF CONTEMPORARY ART** (Musée d'art contemporain de Montréal), next to the Place des Arts at 185 rue Ste-Catherine Ouest (M: Place-des-Arts), displays works by Canadian and foreign contemporary artists from its collection of more than 7,000 pieces. Works date from 1940 to the present. A sculpture garden also is on the premises.

Time: Allow 1 hour minimum. **Hours:** Tues.-Sun. and Mon. holidays 11-6 (also Wed. 6-9 p.m.). Phone ahead to confirm schedule. **Cost:** $12; $10 (ages 60+); $8 (students with ID); free (ages 0-11 and to all Wed. 5-9 p.m.); $24 (family). **Phone:** (514) 847-6226. [T]

GEM SAVE **MONTRÉAL MUSEUM OF FINE ARTS** (Musée des beaux-arts de Montréal) encompasses three pavilions at 1379, 1380 and 1339 Sherbrooke St. W. (M: Guy-Concordia or Peel). Founded in 1860, this was one of the first public art galleries in Canada. The museum offers exhibitions from an extensive holding, some 33,000 objects representing the main trends in art from antiquity to the present day, and impressive temporary exhibitions.

Added in 2011, the Claire and Marc Bourgie Pavilion of Québec and Canadian Art chronicles six historical periods through its 600-piece collection. The Bourgie Concert Hall features performances presented by the Arte Musica Foundation, in residence at the museum. **Hours:** Tues.-Fri. 11-5 (also Wed.-Fri. 5-9), Sat.-Sun. 10-5. **Cost:** Permanent collection free. Special exhibitions $15; $12 (ages 65+); $9 (ages 13-25); free (ages 0-12 with adult); $30 (family, two adults and two children, or one adult and three children); $7.50 (to all Wed. 5-9 p.m.). **Phone:** (514) 285-2000 or (800) 899-6873.

MONTRÉAL SCIENCE CENTRE—see Old Montréal p. 330.

GEM **MONT-ROYAL PARK** (Parc du Mont-Royal) is on the highest summit of Mont Royal (M: Mont-Royal), with an entrance at 1260 ch. Remembrance. The lighted cross at the top commemorates the promise made by Paul de Chomedey, Sieur de Maisonneuve to erect a cross if the colony was spared during the flood of Dec. 25, 1642. The first cross was erected in 1643.

The 1858 Smith House, at the park entrance, is a reception and interpretation center offering visitor services year-round, including downloadable podcasts for self-guiding tours and several guided walking tours. The Kondiaronk Lookout near a chalet built in 1932 offers a panorama of Montréal and the St. Lawrence River.

The park is traversed by trails used by summer joggers and winter skiers. Beaver Lake is a haven for skaters in the winter. A pavilion at Beaver Lake offers seasonal rental of pedal-boats, snow-tubes, cross-country skis, snowshoes and skates. **Hours:** Park open daily 6 a.m.-midnight. Smith House open daily 9-5. Phone ahead to confirm schedule. **Cost:** Free. **Phone:** (514) 843-8240. ⬛

SAVE **MUSEUM OF HOSPITALLERS OF THE HOSPITAL OF MONTRÉAL** (Musée des Hospitalières de l'Hôtel-Dieu de Montréal) is at 201 av. des Pins Ouest. Exhibits detail the history of the Hospitallers of St. Joseph, nursing sisters who arrived in the city in 1659. The once-cloistered group staffed the city's first hospital, l'Hôtel-Dieu de Montréal, which was established by early Catholic settlers and remains in use. A 17th-century staircase imported from France is among the museum's some 20,000 artifacts.

Additional displays focus on the origins of early medicine, medical procedures pioneered in Montréal and the founding of the city's nursing school. Guided tours are available by appointment.

Time: Allow 1 hour, 30 minutes minimum. **Hours:** Tues.-Fri. 10-5, Sat.-Sun. 1-5, mid-June to mid-Oct.; Wed.-Sun. 1-5, rest of year. Tours of the grounds' garden are available Sun. in summer; phone ahead to verify availability. **Cost:** $6; $5 (students with ID); free (ages 0-12). A fee may be charged for guided tours. **Phone:** (514) 849-2919.

MUSEUM OF THE PROUD PEOPLE: MONTRÉAL MUSEUM OF INDUSTRIAL AND WORKING-CLASS HISTORY (Écomusée du Fier Monde: Musée d'Histoire Industrielle et Ouvrière de Montréal) is at 2050 Amherst St. Housed in a restored 1920s building, the museum offers a permanent exhibit showcasing the effects of the Industrial Revolution on the Centre-Sud, one of Montréal's oldest working-class neighborhoods.

The building once was the site of the Généreux public bath, which the city's low-income and often exploited workers and their families used prior to the inclusion of baths and showers in modern homes. Additional displays focus on the quality of life at the time and the endeavors undertaken to improve it and the neighborhood's safety conditions.

Guided tours are available by appointment. **Time:** Allow 1 hour minimum. **Hours:** Wed. 11-8, Thurs.-Fri. 9:30-4, Sat.-Sun. 10:30-5. **Cost:** $6; $4 (ages 64+ and students with ID); free (ages 0-6). **Phone:** (514) 528-8444.

THE MUSEUM OF QUÉBEC MASTERS AND ARTISANS—see St-Laurent p. 464.

NOTRE-DAME-DE-BON-SECOURS CHAPEL AND MARGUERITE BOURGEOYS MUSEUM—see Old Montréal p. 330.

NOTRE DAME ISLAND—see Île Notre-Dame p. 324.

OLD MONTRÉAL (Vieux-Montréal), bounded by the river and rues des Soeurs-Grises, Notre-Dame and St-Hubert (M: Place-d'Armes, Square-Victoria or Champ-de-Mars), is a 38-hectare (94-acre) historic area with some buildings dating the 17th century. Government offices, courthouses, shipping interests and the financial district occupy the site of Ville-Marie, the original settlement.

In House of the Mother d'Youville (Maison de mère d'Youville), residence and headquarters of the Sisters of Charity of Montréal ("Grey Nuns of Montréal"), visitors can view artifacts of Montréal's early history and tour rooms in which Marguerite d'Youville lived and died; reservations are required.

The Old City is best seen by walking along rues Notre-Dame, Bonsecours and St-Paul. A brochure with a map outlining a self-guiding tour of the area is available from Tourisme Montréal (*see Fast Facts*).

Hours: The Old Montréal tourism office at 174 rue Notre-Dame Est is open daily 9-7, Apr.-Oct.; Wed.-Sun. 9-5, rest of year. Closed Jan. 1 and Christmas. Phone ahead to confirm schedule. **Phone:** (514) 873-2015 for Tourisme Montréal, or (514) 842-9411 for Maison de mère d'Youville reservations.

Basilica of Notre-Dame (Basilique Notre-Dame), on the Place d'Armes at 110 rue Notre-Dame Ouest, is among the most magnificent of French-Canadian churches and is one of the largest churches in North America. Stained-glass windows depict religious scenes and the history of the original parish. Guided 20-minute tours are offered. An evening sound and light show "And Then There was Light" is offered.

Hours: Basilica Mon.-Fri. 8-4:30, Sat. 8-4, Sun. 12:30-4. Sound and light show schedule varies. Phone ahead to confirm schedule. **Cost:** (includes guided tour) $5; $4 (ages 7-17). Sound and light show $10; $9 (ages 60+); $5 (ages 1-17). **Phone:** (514) 842-2925 or (866) 842-2925.

SAVE **Château Ramezay—Historic Site and Museum of Montréal** (Château Ramezay—Musée et site historique de Montréal), 280 Notre-Dame Est (M: Champ-de-Mars), was built in the early 18th century for Claude de Ramezay, the acting governor of New France 1714-16 and the governor of Montréal for nearly 2 decades. The museum traces the history of the city and the province from pre-contact Amerindian times through the early 20th century.

The property has been meticulously restored and includes a small, 18th-century rear garden with multilingual interpretive panels describing the estate's flowers, fruits and vegetables, and medicinal plants. **Hours:** Daily 10-6, June 1-Thanksgiving; Tues.-Sun. 10-4:30, rest of year. Closed Jan. 1, Christmas Eve, Christmas and Dec. 31. **Cost:** $10; $8 (ages 65+); $7 (students with ID); $5 (ages 5-17); $22 (family). **Phone:** (514) 861-3708.

The Governor's Feast (Le Festin du Gouverneur) is presented in Old Montréal's Restaurant Le Vauquelin, 52 rue St-Jacques Ouest. Visitors are the nobles to whom maidens and vassals serve meals, while other minions entertain during the 2-hour, 17th-century bilingual festal feast in New France. **Hours:**

Dinner show presented nightly at 6:30 (also at 9, Nov.-Dec.). Shows may be cancelled if demand is low; phone ahead to confirm schedule. **Cost:** $42.95; $39.50 (students with ID). Reservations are recommended. **Phone:** (514) 879-1141.

SAVE **Montréal Science Centre** (Centre des sciences de Montréal) is at jct. boul. St-Laurent and rue de la Commune Ouest (M: Place d'Armes). This hands-on, learning center presents science and technology in such a way as to make learning fun. Eye-catching, high-tech interactive displays cover such topics as robotics, health and communications. The IMAX-TELUS Theatre also is in the center.

Time: Allow 3 hours minimum. **Hours:** Museum Mon.-Sat. 10-9, Sun. 10-6, mid-May through Labour Day; Mon.-Fri. 9-4, Sat.-Sun. 10-5, rest of year. IMAX films are screened daily every 50 minutes beginning at 10. IMAX schedule may vary; phone ahead. Closed Jan. 1 and Christmas.

Cost: Exhibits or one IMAX film $11.50; $10.50 (ages 13-17 and 61+); $8.50 (ages 4-12); $36.50 (family, two adults and two children, or one adult and three children; $6.50 for each additional child). Combination ticket (includes exhibits and one IMAX film) $19; $17 (ages 13-17 and 61+); $14 (ages 4-12); $60.50 (family, two adults and two children, or one adult and three children; $9.50 for each additional child). Other combination tickets are available. **Phone:** (514) 496-4724 or (877) 496-4724.

SAVE **Notre-Dame-de-Bon-Secours Chapel and Marguerite Bourgeoys Museum** (Chapelle Notre-Dame-de-Bon-Secours et Musée Marguerite-Bourgeoys) is at 400 rue St-Paul Est (M: Champs-de-Mars). The remains of Marguerite Bourgeoys, founder of the first uncloistered congregation of women in the New World, are under the left side altar.

Artifacts, some as old as 2,000 years, relate the story of Montréal. The museum also has the highest lookout point accessible to the public in Old Montréal and provides breathtaking panoramas of the river and the harbor. The archeological site under the nave of the present chapel displays the foundation of the 17th-century chapel.

Visits to the archeological site are restricted to groups of 10 people or less and require a guide. **Time:** Allow 30 minutes minimum. **Hours:** Tues.-Sun. 10-5:30, May 1 to mid-Oct.; Tues.-Sun. 11-3:30, Mar.-Apr. and mid-Oct. to mid-Jan. **Cost:** Museum $10; $7 (ages 65+ and students with ID); $5 (ages 6-12). Archeological site tour (includes museum) $12; $22 (family, maximum two adults). Reservations are recommended for archeological site tours. **Phone:** (514) 282-8670.

Place d'Armes, adjoining rue St-Jacques, is the old financial center of Montréal. Here stands the monument to Paul de Chomedey, Sieur de Maisonneuve, founder of the city in 1642.

Place Jacques-Cartier, on the slope from Champs-de-Mars to the waterfront, contains the Nelson monument, erected in 1809 to honor Lord Horatio Nelson's victory at Trafalgar. Artists, musicians, jugglers, and acrobats perform in the square during the summer. Flower markets, cafés and historic buildings also are highlights of the area.

Place Royale, bounded by rues St-Paul and de la Commune, is the city's oldest public square. Dating back to 1657, it was originally the marketing center of the settlement.

GEM SAVE **Pointe-à-Callière, Montréal Museum of Archaeology and History** (Pointe-à-Callière, Musée d'archéologie et d'histoire de Montréal), 350 Place Royale, is built atop actual remains of the original European settlement. A multimedia show unfolds the history of Montréal, followed by an underground archeological tour. Highlights include the first Catholic cemetery, remains of the vaulted Little St-Pierre River, and an early Montréal sewer system and fortifications. A virtual installation depicting an 18th-century marketplace also is presented.

Hours: Mon.-Fri. 10-6, Sat.-Sun. 11-6, June 24-Labour Day; Tues.-Fri. 10-5, Sat.-Sun. 11-5, rest of year. **Cost:** $14; $10 (ages 65+); $8 (students with ID); $6 (ages 6-12); $30 (family). Prices may vary; phone ahead. **Phone:** (514) 872-9150. [**Ⅱ**]

Quays of the Old Port of Montréal (Quais du Vieux-Port de Montréal) is on the waterfront in Old Montréal with entrances on boul. St-Laurent and rues de la Commune and Berri. This outdoor urban recreation, entertainment and cultural site is a federal park. The Old Port offers events, shows and recreational activities. Facilities include restaurants, boutiques and a free observation deck atop the Clock Tower. **Hours:** Park open daily 10 a.m.-1 a.m.; most activities take place May 15-Sept. 30. **Cost:** Park admission free. **Phone:** (514) 496-7678.

SAVE **Sir George-Étienne Cartier National Historic Site** (Lieu historique national de Sir-George-Étienne-Cartier), 458 rue Notre-Dame Est, consists of two adjoining buildings, each a former residence of Sir George-Étienne Cartier. A 19th-century lawyer, businessman and political leader, Cartier helped shape many of Québec's and Canada's institutions.

The west house has been carefully restored to its Victorian style and illustrates the lifestyle of the upper-middle class to which Cartier belonged. The east house presents modern exhibits that highlight Cartier's achievements in a period of major changes.

Hours: Daily 10-5:30, late June-early Sept.; Wed.-Sun. 10-5, early Apr.-late June and early Sept.-late Dec. Phone ahead to confirm schedule. **Cost:** $3.90; $3.40 (ages 65+); $1.90 (ages 6-16); $9.80 (family). **Phone:** (514) 283-2282 or (888) 773-8888.

GEM SAVE OLYMPIC PARK (Parc Olympique), 46 hectares (114 acres) in the eastern part of the city, with an entrance at 4545 av. Pierre-de-Coubertin (M: Pie-IX or Viau), was host to the 1976 Summer Olympics. A major highlight of the park is the 165-metre-high (541-ft.) Montréal Tower. An observatory at the top of the tower offers 80-kilometre (50-mi.) views of the Montréal region. It is reached by a funicular that takes visitors to the top via a cable system along the back of the structure. All activities begin at the Tourist Hall located at the base of the Montréal Tower.

Guided tours of the Olympic Stadium and of the Sports Centre are offered daily. **Hours:** Cable car rides to the observatory daily 9-7, mid-June to early Sept.; 9-5, mid-Feb. to mid-June and early Sept.-early Jan. Closed early Jan. to mid-Feb. for annual maintenance. Guided tour schedule varies; phone ahead. **Cost:** Cable car fare in 2011 was $15.25; $11.50 (ages 65+ and students with ID); $7.65 (ages 5-17). Guided tour fee in 2011 was $8.25; $6.20 (ages 65+ and students with ID); $4.15 (ages 5-17). Combination ticket price in 2011 was $20; $15 (ages 65+ and students with ID); $10 (ages 5-17). Phone ahead for 2012 prices. **Phone:** (514) 252-4737 or (877) 997-0919.

GEM SAVE Montréal Biodôme (Biodôme de Montréal) is at 4777 av. Pierre-de-Coubertin in Olympic Park (M: Viau). Four ecosystems are explored through re-creations of their natural habitats: a tropical forest, a Laurentian forest, the St. Lawrence marine environment and the polar regions. Interpreters are stationed at various points in the habitats to provide explanations.

The Tropical Forest contains more than 1,000 fish, amphibians, reptiles, birds and mammals. In the Laurentian Forest a coniferous forest and impressive rock formations surround a beaver lake. Scarce vegetation, a rich variety of wildlife and a granite basin holding 2.5 million litres (660,430 U.S. gallons) of saltwater are the hallmarks of the Marine Environment of the St. Lawrence River. The Polar World illustrates the dramatic—and distinct—landscapes and fauna of the Arctic and Antarctic.

Time: Allow 2 hours minimum. **Hours:** Daily 9-5, mid-Feb. to mid-Sept.; Tues.-Sun. 9-5, rest of year. Open statutory holidays. **Cost:** $16.50; $12.50 (ages 65+ and students with ID); $8.25 (ages 5-17); $2.50 (ages 2-4). **Parking:** $10. **Phone:** (514) 868-3000.

SAVE THE REDPATH MUSEUM (Le Musée Redpath) is at 859 Sherbrooke St. W., between McTavish and University on the McGill University campus (M: Peel or McGill). When erected in 1882, this was Canada's first building designed to be a museum. The themes of the permanent exhibits include paleontology, ethnology, archeology; minerals and gems; and Québec fauna. **Hours:** Mon.-Fri. 9-5, Sun. noon-5. Closed major holidays. **Cost:** Donations. **Phone:** (514) 398-4094.

SAVE ST. GABRIEL HOUSE (Maison St-Gabriel), 2146 Place Dublin (M: Charlevoix and bus 57), was purchased in 1668 by Marguerite Bourgeoys, the founder of the Congrégation de Notre-Dame de Montréal, and is a fine example of traditional Québec architecture. Converted into a museum in 1966, it showcases aspects of rural life in the 17th century and the experience of the King's Wards. Its garden has been re-created in the spirit of New France.

Hours: Guided tours are given Tues.-Sun. 11-6, mid-June through Labour Day; Tues.-Sun. 1-5, mid-Jan. to mid-June and day after Labour Day to mid-Dec.; by appointment rest of year. **Cost:** $10; $8 (ages 65+); $5 (students with ID); $3 (ages 6-12); $20 (family). **Phone:** (514) 935-8136.

ST. HELEN'S ISLAND—see Île Ste-Hélène p. 324.

GEM ST. JOSEPH'S ORATORY (L'Oratoire St-Joseph), 3800 ch. Queen Mary (M: Côte-des-Neiges or Snowdon), is one of the world's largest basilicas and one of the city's most important religious shrines. It was begun in 1904 and the basilica was completed in 1967. The oratory was the dream of Holy Cross Brother André Bessette, who had a simple wooden chapel on the site. During his service there from 1904 (when he was 59 years old) until his death in 1937, Brother André was known as a healer, invoking cures for hundreds through prayer to his patron saint, St. Joseph.

Brother André was canonized in 2010; his tomb is beside the church. Other highlights include the original chapel, built 1904-10, and a French-made, 56-bell carillon. **Hours:** Church open daily 6 a.m.-9:30 p.m. The carillon plays Wed.-Fri. at noon and 3, Sat. at noon and 2:30, Sun. at 12:15 and 2:30. The chapel and the basilica close at 5:30, Nov.-Apr. **Cost:** Donations. **Parking:** $5. **Phone:** (514) 733-8211 or (877) 672-8647.

ST. LAWRENCE SEAWAY LOOKOUT—see St-Lambert p. 464.

ST. PATRICK'S BASILICA (Basilique St-Patrick), 460 boul. René-Lévesque Ouest (M: Square-Victoria), is a religious center for English-speaking Catholics. Gothic panels, paintings and stations of the cross decorate the interior. **Hours:** Daily 9-6. **Cost:** Free. **Phone:** (514) 866-7379.

SEGAL CENTRE FOR PERFORMING ARTS (Le Centre Segal des arts de la scène), 5170 ch. de la Côte-Ste-Catherine (M: Côte-Ste-Catherine), presents changing exhibits of Canadian and international contemporary art. **Hours:** Mon.-Thurs. 8:30-6 (also Mon.-Thurs. 6-10 p.m., Sept.-June), Fri. 8:30-4:30, Sun. 10-5. **Cost:** Free. **Phone:** (514) 739-2301.

SHAAR HASHOMAYIM SYNAGOGUE—see Westmount p. 486.

SIR GEORGE-ÉTIENNE CARTIER NATIONAL HISTORIC SITE—see Old Montréal p. 330.

SPANISH AND PORTUGUESE SYNAGOGUE (Synagogue Espagnole et Portugaise), 4894 av. St-Kevin (M: Côte-Ste-Catherine), is the oldest Orthodox Jewish congregation in Canada. The 1958 synagogue is the third site the congregation has occupied since it was founded in 1768. **Hours:** Open by appointment Mon.-Thurs. 9-5, Fri. 9-1, Sun. 9-noon. **Cost:** Free. **Phone:** (514) 737-3695.

TEMPLE EMANU-EL BETH SHOLOM—see Westmount p. 486.

GAMBLING ESTABLISHMENTS

- **Montréal Casino** is at 1 av. du Casino. **Hours:** Daily 24 hours. **Phone:** (514) 392-2746 or (800) 665-2274.

Sightseeing
Boat Tours

LACHINE RAPIDS JET BOAT TOURS (Le voyage Saute-Moutons sur les Rapides de Lachine) departs from the s. end of rue Berri at the Clock Tower Basin in Montréal's Old Port (M: Champ-de-Mars). The 1-hour trip travels upstream on the St. Lawrence through the historic Lachine Rapids. These once-unnavigable waterways accounted for Montréal's strategic location.

The 1,350-horsepower, flatbottom boats negotiate whirlpools as well as waves up to 3 metres (10 ft.) high. Although rain ponchos, hats and plastic footwear are provided, a change of clothes is recommended. Under 6 are not permitted. **Hours:** Trips depart daily at 10, noon, 2, 4, and 6, May 1 to mid-Oct. **Cost:** $65; $60 (ages 66+); $55 (ages 13-18); $45 (ages 6-12). Reservations are required. **Phone:** (514) 284-9607.

LE BATEAU-MOUCHE departs from the Jacques-Cartier Pier at the foot of Place Jacques-Cartier (M: Champs-de-Mars). The glass-roofed, Paris-style riverboat offers narrated tours on the St. Lawrence River near Île Ste-Hélène and Île Notre-Dame. Available to visitors are three 1-hour cruises and one 90-minute cruise; the tours provide good views of the waterfront and skyline. A 3.5-hour dinner cruise also is offered; reservations are required.

Tour narration in English is available. **Hours:** One-hour cruises depart daily at 11, 2:30 and 4, mid-May to mid-Oct. Ninety-minute cruises depart daily at 12:30, mid-May to mid-Oct. Boarding is 30 minutes before departure. **Cost:** One-hour cruise $24; $22 (ages 65+ and students with ID); $12 (ages 6-16); $48 (family). Ninety-minute cruise $28; $26 (ages 65+ and students with ID); $12 (ages 6-16); $56 (family). Prices may vary; phone ahead. **Phone:** (514) 849-9952 or (800) 361-9952.

MONTRÉAL HARBOUR CRUISES (Croisières AML) departs from the Quai King-Edward Pier in Montréal's Old Port (M: Champ-de-Mars). Sightseeing tours traverse Montréal Harbour and the St. Lawrence River and circle the Boucherville Islands. Available to sightseers are two 90-minute cruises and one 1-hour cruise; also offered are a 4-hour fireworks trip available in June and July, weekend brunch cruises and a 4-hour dinner-dance cruise.

Hours: Sightseeing cruises depart daily at 11:30 (90 minutes), 2 (90 minutes) and 4 (1 hour), early May to mid-Oct. **Cost:** Ninety-minute sightseeing cruise $29; $17 (ages 60+ and students with ID); $16 (ages 6-16). One-hour sightseeing cruise $25; $23 (ages 60+ and students with ID); $13 (ages 6-16). Family rates are available. Prices may vary. Reservations are required. **Parking:** $15. **Phone:** (514) 842-3871 or (800) 563-4643.

Bus and Carriage Tours

Visitors to Montréal have a wide choice of tour itineraries and prices. SAVE Gray Line de Montréal, (514) 934-1222, offers local tours. Also, *calèches*, or horse-drawn carriages, circulate around the city.

A flexible way to see the city is by taxi. Guides who ride in your automobile also are available. The competency and fees of all guides are regulated by law. They must hold a certificate from the School of Tourism of Montréal, wear an official city badge and produce a valid tourist guide license.

SAVE **GRAY LINE HOP-ON/HOP-OFF DOUBLE DECKER TOURS** departs from the Infotouriste Centre at 1255 rue Peel and takes visitors on a narrated sightseeing tour of the downtown area. Bilingual drivers detail Montréal's history in English and French. Additional specialized guided tours are available May through October; schedules and prices vary.

Hours: Downtown area narrated sightseeing tours depart daily at 10, noon, 1 and 3. Phone ahead to confirm schedule. **Cost:** (valid for unlimited daily round-trips, mid May through second Mon. in Oct.) $40; $36 (ages 65+ and students with ID); $28 (ages 5-11). Prices may vary. **Phone:** (514) 398-9769.

Driving Tours

Although multilane divided highways provide fast transit between Montréal and the rest of Québec, older roads that follow the same route—Hwy. 132 on the south shore of the river and Hwy. 138 on the north—offer scenic alternatives. These roads, which follow the courses of original 18th-century roads, wind through small villages and towns with the best examples of Québec's domestic and ecclesiastical architecture.

Beyond the towns, the roads pass through farmland divided in parallel strips, each with its own access to the river—remnants of a system laid out under seigneurial ownership during French colonial times.

In summer the farms beckon motorists to stop and pick raspberries; roadside stands offer *frites* (french fries), vegetables and baked goods, and shops sell hand-carved whirligigs or homemade *catalognes* (rag rugs). In short, these old highways offer an introduction to a resilient and singular culture.

Walking Tours

Brochures outlining self-guiding walking tours of Old Montréal with explanations of its architecture can be obtained at the Infotouriste Centre at 174 Notre-Dame Est and at the information kiosk at 1001 rue du Square-Dorchester.

Costumed guides from Guidatour lead a variety of walking tours. Narration in English is available. Tours depart from the front of the Basilica of Notre-Dame; phone (514) 844-4021.

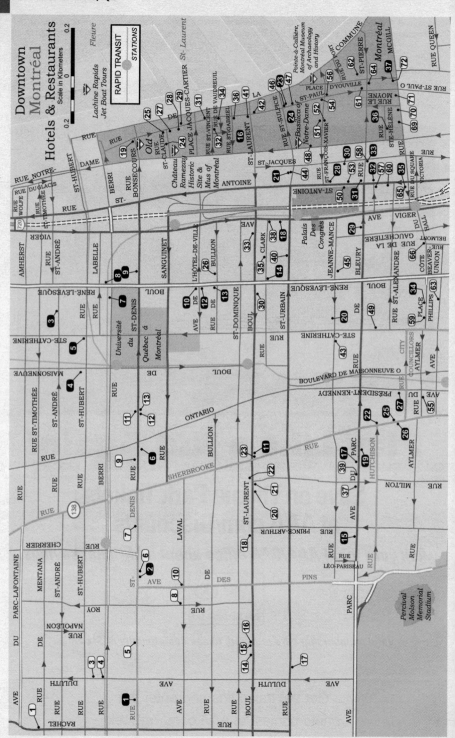

Downtown
Montréal
Hotels & Restaurants

Scale in Kilometers

0.2   0   0.2

Lachine Rapids
Jet Boat Tours

RAPID TRANSIT
STATIONS

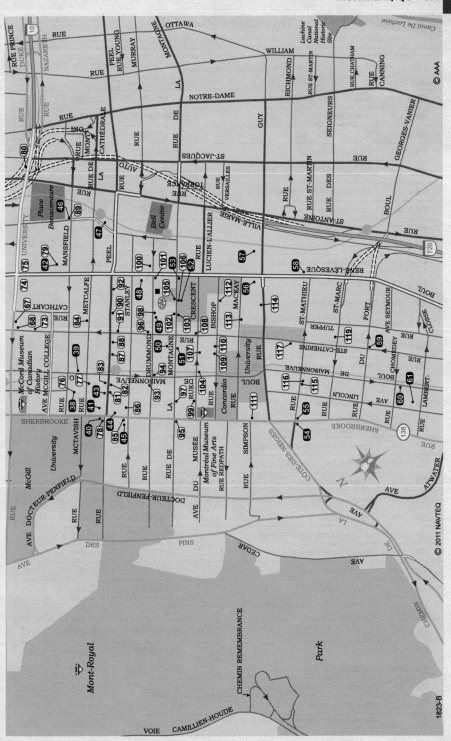

© 2011 NAVTEQ

1823-B

Downtown Montreal

This index helps you "spot" where approved hotels and restaurants are located on the corresponding detailed maps. Hotel daily rate range is for comparison only and shows the property's high season. Restaurant rate range is a combination of lunch and/or dinner. Turn to the listing page for more detailed rate information and consult display ads for special promotions.

DOWNTOWN MONTREAL

Map Page	Hotels	Diamond Rated	High Season	Page
❶ p. 334	**Anne Ma Soeur Anne Hotel-Studio**	◈◈	$90-$155 SAVE	350
❷ p. 334	Hotel Kutuma	◈◈◈	$135-$400	357
❸ p. 334	Hotel Manoir des Alpes	◈◈	$80-$130	362
❹ p. 334	**Auberge Le Pomerol**	◈◈	$115-$200 SAVE	350
❺ p. 334	**Hotel Gouverneur Place Dupuis** *(See ad p. 359.)*	◈◈◈	$125-$399 SAVE	357
❻ p. 334	**Auberge Le Jardin d'Antoine**	◈◈	$107-$172 SAVE	350
❼ p. 334	Hotel Lord Berri	◈◈	$119-$156	362
❽ p. 334	Hotel Le Roberval	◈◈	$119-$169	362
❾ p. 334	Hotel Les Suites Labelle	◈◈	$129-$169	362
❿ p. 334	**Days Inn Montreal Downtown** *(See ad p. 352.)*	◈◈◈	$81-$369 SAVE	353
⓫ p. 334	Opus Hotel Montreal	◈◈◈	Rates not provided	371
⓬ p. 334	**Candlewood Suites** *(See ad p. 350.)*	◈◈◈	$99-$169 SAVE	353
⓭ p. 334	**Holiday Inn Express Hotel & Suites Montreal Centre-Ville** *(See ad p. 356.)*	◈◈◈	$107-$300 SAVE	356
⓮ p. 334	**Hotel Travelodge Montreal Centre** *(See ad opposite title page.)*	◈◈	$76-$242 SAVE	365
⓯ p. 334	**New Residence Hall/McGill University**	◈◈◈	$89-$149 SAVE	371
⓰ p. 334	Marriott SpringHill Suites	◈◈◈	$134-$209	371
⓱ p. 334	Parc Suites Hotel	◈◈◈	Rates not provided	371
⓲ p. 334	**Holiday Inn Select Montreal Centre-Ville Downtown** *(See ad p. 357.)*	◈◈◈	$119-$229 SAVE	356
⓳ p. 334	**Quality Hotel Downtown Montreal**	◈◈	$89-$365 SAVE	374
⓴ p. 334	**Hyatt Regency Montreal** *(See ad p. 349.)*	◈◈◈	$89-$529 SAVE	365
㉑ p. 334	**Hôtel Place d'Armes**	◈◈◈◈	$199-$1500 SAVE	364
㉒ p. 334	**Hilton Garden Inn Montreal Centre-Ville**	◈◈◈	$209-$299 SAVE	353
㉓ p. 334	Hôtel Nelligan	◈◈◈◈	$169-$1299	364
㉔ p. 334	**Le Saint-Sulpice Hôtel Montréal**	◈◈◈	$239-$539 SAVE	368
㉕ p. 334	**Holiday Inn Montreal-Midtown**	◈◈◈	$119-$149 SAVE	356
㉖ p. 334	**L'Appartement Hotel**	◈◈	$127-$245 SAVE	365
㉗ p. 334	**Delta Montreal**	◈◈◈	$175-$322 SAVE	353
㉘ p. 334	**Embassy Suites Montreal par/by Hilton** *(See ad p. 354.)*	◈◈◈	$149-$579 SAVE	353
㉙ p. 334	Hotel Le Dauphin Montreal Downtown Convention Centre	◈◈◈	$142-$295	362
㉚ p. 334	LHotel	◈◈◈	$195-$485	368
㉛ p. 334	**Le Westin Montréal**	◈◈◈◈	$159-$329 SAVE	368
㉜ p. 334	**InterContinental Montréal** *(See ad p. 366.)*	◈◈◈◈	$179-$289 SAVE	365
㉝ p. 334	**Hôtel Le St-James** *(See ad p. 363.)*	◈◈◈◈	$320-$625 SAVE	362
㉞ p. 334	**Le Square Phillips Hotel & Suites** *(See ad p. 369.)*	◈◈◈	$145-$369 SAVE	368

DOWNTOWN MONTREAL (cont'd)

Map Page	Hotels (cont'd)	Diamond Rated	High Season	Page
35 p. 334	**W Montréal** *(See ad p. 373.)*	◆◆◆◆	$169-$799 [SAVE]	375
36 p. 334	**Hotel Gault** *(See ad p. 359.)*	◆◆◆	$300-$720 [SAVE]	357
37 p. 334	Hotel St-Paul	◆◆◆	Rates not provided	364
38 p. 334	Hôtel Le Germain Montréal	◆◆◆◆	Rates not provided	362
39 p. 334	**Le St-Martin Centre-Ville Hôtel Particulier** *(See ad p. 370.)*	◆◆◆	$175-$535 [SAVE]	368
40 p. 334	**Best Western Ville-Marie Hotel & Suites**	◆◆◆	$110-$426 [SAVE]	350
41 p. 334	**Hôtel Omni Mont-Royal**	◆◆◆◆	$179-$279 [SAVE]	364
42 p. 334	**Fairmont The Queen Elizabeth**	◆◆◆◆	Rates not provided [SAVE]	353
43 p. 334	**Residence Inn by Marriott Montreal-Downtown** *(See ad p. 373.)*	◆◆◆	$169-$229 [SAVE]	374
44 p. 334	**Hotel Le Cantlie Suites** *(See ad p. 361.)*	◆◆◆	$139-$499 [SAVE]	362
45 p. 334	**Sofitel Montréal Le Carré Doré** *(See ad p. 374.)*	◆◆◆◆	$180-$350 [SAVE]	374
46 p. 334	**Hilton Montréal Bonaventure** *(See ad p. 355.)*	◆◆◆◆	$190-$625 [SAVE]	356
47 p. 334	**Marriott Montréal Château Champlain**	◆◆◆◆	$159-$599 [SAVE]	368
48 p. 334	**Le Centre Sheraton** *(See ad p. 367.)*	◆◆◆◆	$144-$699 [SAVE]	365
49 p. 334	**Best Western Plus Montreal Downtown-Hotel Europa**	◆◆◆	$99-$189 [SAVE]	350
50 p. 334	**Loews Hôtel Vogue** *(See ad p. 371.)*	◆◆◆◆	$152-$764 [SAVE]	368
51 p. 334	**Hotel de la Montagne**	◆◆◆	$179-$299 [SAVE]	357
52 p. 334	Novotel Montreal Centre *(See ad p. 372.)*	◆◆◆	$119-$499	371
53 p. 334	**Hôtel Le Crystal**	◆◆◆◆	$209-$2499 [SAVE]	362
54 p. 334	**Château Versailles Hotel** *(See ad opposite title page.)*	◆◆◆	Rates not provided [SAVE]	353
55 p. 334	**Le Meridien Versailles-Montreal** *(See ad opposite title page.)*	◆◆◆	$149-$509 [SAVE]	365
56 p. 334	**Hotel Maritime Plaza** *(See ad opposite title page.)*	◆◆◆	$100-$600 [SAVE]	362
57 p. 334	Hôtel Espresso Montréal Centre-Ville/Downtown	◆◆◆	$99-$169	357
58 p. 334	**Le Nouvel Hotel & Spa** *(See ad opposite title page.)*	◆◆◆	$109-$499 [SAVE]	365
59 p. 334	**Hotel du Fort** *(See ad p. 358.)*	◆◆◆	$105-$299 [SAVE]	357
60 p. 334	La Tour Belvedere Apartment Hotel	◆◆	Rates not provided	365
61 p. 334	**Residence Inn by Marriott Montreal Westmount**	◆◆◆	$179-$199 [SAVE]	374

Map Page	Restaurants	Diamond Rated	Cuisine	Meal Range	Page
1 p. 334	**La Fonderie**	◆◆	Fondue	$22-$32	379
3 p. 334	Restaurant Au Pied de Cochon	◆◆◆	Quebec	$14-$46	383
4 p. 334	Khyber Pass Cuisine Afghane	◆◆	Afghan	$14-$18	379
5 p. 334	L'Express	◆◆	French	$14-$25	381
6 p. 334	Le Nil Bleu Restaurant	◆◆◆	Ethiopian	$10-$18	380
7 p. 334	**Restaurant de l'Institut**	◆◆◆	Quebec	$15-$32	383
8 p. 334	Pintxo cuisine espagnole	◆◆	Basque	$16-$28	383
9 p. 334	L'Amère à Boire	◆◆	International	$10-$18	379
10 p. 334	Laloux	◆◆◆	French	$22-$28	379

Map Page	Restaurants (cont'd)	Diamond Rated	Cuisine	Meal Range	Page
⑪ p. 334	Restaurant Fou d'Asie	◆◆	Asian	$10-$26	383
⑫ p. 334	Zyng Nouillerie	◆◆	Asian	$9-$14	386
⑬ p. 334	**Commensal Vegetarian Restaurant**	◇◇	Vegetarian	$8-$14	377
⑭ p. 334	Moishe's Steak House	◆◆◆	Steak	$28-$54	382
⑮ p. 334	Coco Rico	◆	Portuguese	$6-$10	377
⑯ p. 334	Schwartz's Montreal Hebrew Delicatessen	◆	Deli	$6-$20	385
⑰ p. 334	Café Santropol	◆◆	Coffee/Tea	$8-$13	376
⑱ p. 334	Maestro S.V.P.	◆◆◆	Seafood	$10-$45	382
⑲ p. 334	Restaurant Les Filles du Roy	◆◆◆	French	$25-$55	384
⑳ p. 334	Buonanotte	◆◆◆	Italian	$17-$49	376
㉑ p. 334	Wood 35 Restaurant & Bar	◆◆◆	Italian	$17-$32	386
㉒ p. 334	Globe Restaurant	◆◆◆	International	$16-$38	378
㉓ p. 334	Koko Restaurant	◆◆◆	Mediterranean	$14-$32	379
㉔ p. 334	Le Club Chasse et Peche	◆◆◆	French	$15-$38	380
㉕ p. 334	Chez l'épicier Restaurant Bar à Vin	◆◆◆	French	$14-$40	377
㉖ p. 334	Restaurant le Piémontais	◆◆◆	Italian	$17-$42	384
㉗ p. 334	Restaurant L'Autre Version	◆◆◆	Mediterranean	$15-$40	384
㉘ p. 334	L'Usine de Spaghetti du Vieux-Montreal	◆◆	Italian	$12-$25	382
㉙ p. 334	La Menara	◆◆◆	Moroccan	$40	379
㉚ p. 334	Deer Garden Jardin du Cerf	◆◆	Chinese	$7-$14	377
㉛ p. 334	Chez Queux	◆◆◆	French	$25-$36	377
㉜ p. 334	Galiano's Pasta & Bar	◆◆	Italian	$11-$32	378
㉝ p. 334	Pho Cali Restaurant	◆◆	Vietnamese	$6-$10	383
㉞ p. 334	Les 3 Brasseurs	◆◆	Canadian	$9-$21	381
㉟ p. 334	La Maison V.I.P.	◆◆	Chinese	$9-$15	379
㊱ p. 334	Vieux-Port Steakhouse	◆◆◆	Steak	$14-$45	385
㊲ p. 334	El Gitano	◆◆	Spanish	$13-$32	378
㊳ p. 334	Chez Chine	◆◆◆	Chinese	$10-$45	377
㊴ p. 334	Chez Gautier	◆◆◆	French	$10-$35	377
㊵ p. 334	La Maison Kam Fung	◆◆	Chinese	$9-$18	379
㊶ p. 334	Crêperie Chez Suzette	◆◆	French	$9-$27	377
㊷ p. 334	Le Steak frites St-Paul	◆◆	Steak	$12-$39	381
㊸ p. 334	**Brasserie T!**	◇◇◇	French	$17-$25	376
㊹ p. 334	Aix Cuisine Du Terroir	◆◆◆	French	$18-$39	375
㊺ p. 334	Le Latini	◆◆◆	Italian	$14-$40	380
㊻ p. 334	Restaurant Verses	◆◆◆	French	$14-$40	384
㊼ p. 334	Méchant Boeuf Bar-Brasserie	◆◆	French	$15-$25	382
㊽ p. 334	Tatami Sushi Bar	◆◆	Asian	$12-$30	385
㊾ p. 334	**Osco!**	◇◇◇	French	$21-$39	383
㊿ p. 334	Fourquet Fourchette du Palais	◆◆	Quebec	$12-$34	378

Map Page	Restaurants (cont'd)	Diamond Rated	Cuisine	Meal Range	Page
51 p. 334	Bonaparte	▽▽▽	French	$16-$36	375
52 p. 334	Casa de Mateo	▽▽	Mexican	$15-$23	376
53 p. 334	Gazette	▽▽▽	Continental	$16-$29	378
54 p. 334	Santos Café & Lounge	▽▽	Canadian	$15-$20	385
55 p. 334	House of Jazz/Maison de Jazz	▽▽	American	$10-$30	379
56 p. 334	Stash Café	▽▽	Polish	$12-$18	385
57 p. 334	**Restaurant Toqué!**	▽▽▽▽▽	French	$25-$48	384
58 p. 334	**Restaurant XO**	▽▽▽▽	French	$18-$40	384
59 p. 334	Soupebol	▽▽	Asian	$7-$15	385
60 p. 334	Le Steak frites St-Paul	▽▽	Steak	$11-$39	381
61 p. 334	Les Pyrenées Restaurant	▽▽▽	Basque	$9-$37	381
62 p. 334	**Gibby's**	▽▽▽	Steak	$28-$48	378
63 p. 334	Restaurant Julien	▽▽▽	French	$20-$36	384
64 p. 334	Restaurant La Gargote	▽▽	French	$16-$33	384
65 p. 334	Otto Ristorante-Bar *(See ad p. 373.)*	▽▽▽	Mediterranean	$25-$42	383
66 p. 334	Briskets Montreal/Salon Krausmann	▽	Canadian	$8-$17	376
67 p. 334	Restaurant Bofinger Barbeque Smokehouse	▽	Barbecue	$7-$15	383
68 p. 334	Guido & Angelina	▽▽	Italian	$11-$35	378
69 p. 334	Boris Bistro	▽▽	French	$17-$24	376
70 p. 334	Brit & Chips	▽▽	English	$8-$15	376
71 p. 334	Holder Restaurant-Bar	▽▽	French	$16-$32	378
72 p. 334	Restaurant Vauvert	▽▽▽	French	$17-$42	384
73 p. 334	Les 3 Brasseurs	▽▽	Canadian	$9-$21	381
74 p. 334	Le Restaurant Club Lounge 737	▽▽▽	French	$14-$46	381
75 p. 334	Vargas Steakhouse Bar Sushi	▽▽▽	Sushi	$14-$50	385
76 p. 334	**Laurie Raphaël/Montréal Restaurant/Boutique**	▽▽▽▽	Quebec	$26-$35	380
77 p. 334	Restaurant Sho-dan Concept Japonais	▽▽	Japanese	$12-$28	384
78 p. 334	Zawedeh Restaurant	▽▽	Lebanese	$10-$35	386
79 p. 334	**The Beaver Club**	▽▽▽▽	French	$28-$48	375
80 p. 334	Le Tour de Ville	▽▽▽	French	$36-$55	381
81 p. 334	Cavalli Ristorante-Bar	▽▽▽	Italian	$26-$44	377
82 p. 334	L'Entrecôte Saint-Jean	▽▽	French	$19-$24	380
83 p. 334	L'Orchidee Chine Restaurant Chinois	▽▽▽	Chinese	$13-$30	382
84 p. 334	Dunns Famous Delicatessen	▽▽	Deli	$11-$24	378
85 p. 334	Renoir	▽▽▽	French	$20-$48	383
86 p. 334	Le Taj Restaurant	▽▽	Indian	$12-$25	381
87 p. 334	Ferreira Café	▽▽▽	Portuguese	$24-$40	378
88 p. 334	Carlos and Pepes	▽▽	Mexican	$7-$19	376
89 p. 334	Le Castillon	▽▽▽	Continental	$10-$34	380

Map Page	Restaurants (cont'd)	Diamond Rated	Cuisine	Meal Range	Page
90 p. 334	Café Republique Restaurant Bar	▼▼	French	$13-$29	376
91 p. 334	Reuben's Deli & Steak	▼▼	Deli	$7-$26	384
92 p. 334	Le Piment Rouge	▼▼▼	Chinese	$20-$35	380
93 p. 334	M:brgr	▼▼	Burgers	$14-$40	382
94 p. 334	Le Pois Penché Brasserie Parisienne	▼▼▼	French	$18-$40	380
95 p. 334	Café Holt	▼▼	Coffee/Tea	$17-$22	376
96 p. 334	Mister Steer	▼▼	American	$8-$25	382
97 p. 334	Jardin Sakura	▼▼	Japanese	$15-$40	379
98 p. 334	Ristorante Le Medusa	▼▼▼	Italian	$15-$35	385
99 p. 334	Troika Restaurant	▼▼▼	Russian	$25-$40	385
100 p. 334	Decca 77 Restaurant	▼▼▼	French	$18-$45	377
101 p. 334	La Queue de Cheval Bar & Steakhouse	▼▼▼	Steak	$27-$60	380
102 p. 334	Restaurant Européa	▼▼▼▼	French	$20-$45	383
103 p. 334	Rosalie Restaurant	▼▼▼	French	$14-$35	385
104 p. 334	Newtown Restaurant	▼▼▼	Mediterranean	$30-$42	382
105 p. 334	Il Campari Centro	▼▼▼	Italian	$17-$42	379
106 p. 334	L'Ô sur la Montagne	▼▼▼	Canadian	$12-$23	382
107 p. 334	Wienstein and Gavinos Pasta Bar Factory Co Ltd	▼▼	Italian	$11-$32	386
108 p. 334	Les 3 Brasseurs	▼▼	Canadian	$9-$21	381
109 p. 334	Le Milsa Rotisserie Brésilienne	▼▼	Brazilian	$25-$30	380
110 p. 334	Mesa 14	▼▼	Mexican	$12-$25	382
111 p. 334	Bice Ristorante	▼▼	Italian	$26-$48	375
112 p. 334	Bishoku Japanese Restaurant	▼▼	Japanese	$10-$30	375
113 p. 334	La Baguette D'Ivoire	▼▼	Asian	$10-$15	379
114 p. 334	Chez La Mere Michel	▼▼▼	Traditional French	$26-$40	377
115 p. 334	Au Bistro Gourmet	▼▼	French	$11-$35	375
116 p. 334	Restaurant La Pizzella	▼▼▼	Italian	$16-$45	384
117 p. 334	3 Amigos Resto-Bar	▼▼	Mexican	$7-$20	375
119 p. 334	Alpenhaus Restaurant	▼▼	Swiss	$18-$35	375

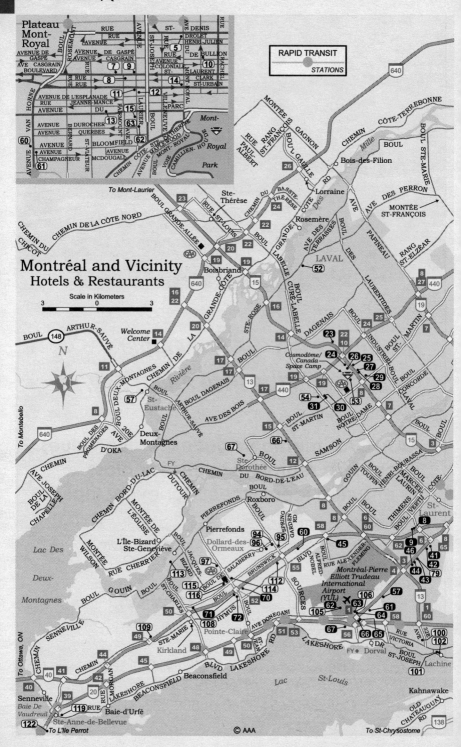

Plateau Mont-Royal

Montréal and Vicinity
Hotels & Restaurants

Scale in Kilometers

RAPID TRANSIT
STATIONS

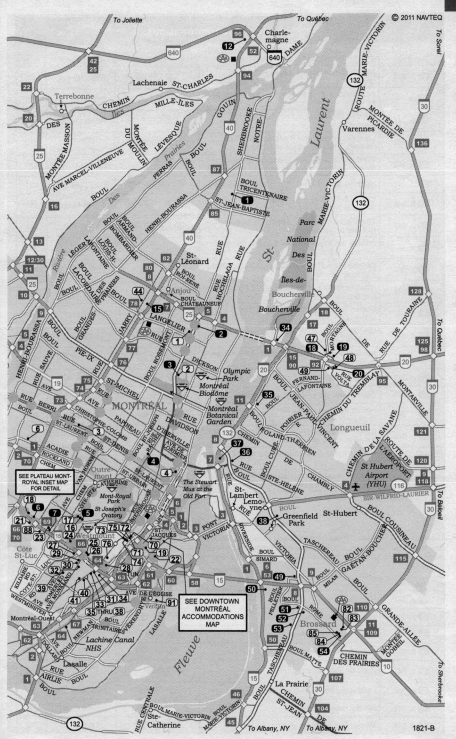

© 2011 NAVTEQ

To Joliette
To Québec
To Sorel

Charlemagne

Terrebonne
Lachenaie ST-CHARLES

To Quebec

Varennes

MONTÉE DE PICARDIE

St-Léonard

Anjou

Parc National Des Iles-de-Boucherville

Boucherville

Olympic Park
Montréal Biodôme
Montréal Botanical Garden

MONTRÉAL

Longueuil

SEE PLATEAU MONT-ROYAL INSET MAP FOR DETAIL

Outremont

The Stewart Mus at the Old Fort

Mont-Royal Park
St Joseph's Oratory

St-Lambert Lemoyne

Greenfield Park

St-Hubert

St Hubert Airport (YHU)

Westmount

Côte St-Luc

Côte St-Luc

Brossard

Montréal-Ouest

SEE DOWNTOWN MONTRÉAL ACCOMMODATIONS MAP

Lachine Canal NHS

Lasalle

La Prairie

Ste-Catherine

To Albany, NY
To Albany, NY

To Sherbrooke

1821-B

✈ Airport Accommodations

Map Page	MONTRÉAL-PIERRE ELLIOTT TRUDEAU INTERNATIONAL AIRPORT	Diamond Rated	High Season	Page
64 p. 342	Aloft Montreal Airport, 0.8 mi (1.2 km) to terminal	▼▼▼	$99-$229 [SAVE]	278
65 p. 342	Best Western Plus Montreal Airport Hotel, 0.6 mi (1 km) s of terminal	▼▼▼	$130-$140 [SAVE]	278
61 p. 342	Comfort Inn Dorval, 0.9 mi (1.5 km) s of terminal	▼▼	$95-$225 [SAVE]	278
60 p. 342	Hampton Inn & Suites by Hilton Montreal (Dorval), 6 mi (10 km) nw of terminal	▼▼▼	Rates not provided [SAVE]	279
66 p. 342	Marriott Fairfield Inn & Suites Aeroport de Montreal Airport, 0.6 mi (1 km) s of terminal	▼▼▼	$107-$143 [SAVE]	279
62 p. 342	Montreal Airport Marriott, in airport terminal	▼▼▼▼	$149-$359 [SAVE]	281
67 p. 342	Quality Inn & Suites Aeroport Montreal-Trudeau, 0.8 mi (1.2 km) s of terminal	▼▼	$80-$143 [SAVE]	281
63 p. 342	The Sheraton Montreal Airport Hotel, 0.3 mi (0.5 km) to terminal	▼▼▼▼	$169-$249 [SAVE]	281
57 p. 342	Holiday Inn Express Hotel & Suites Montreal Aeroport, 0.8 mi (1.3 km) se of terminal	▼▼▼	$140-$165 [SAVE]	295
42 p. 342	Crowne Plaza Montreal Airport, 3.3 mi (5.5 km) e of terminal	▼▼▼	$119-$189 [SAVE]	465
46 p. 342	Hilton Garden Inn Montreal Airport, 2.1 mi (3.5 km) e of terminal	▼▼▼	$131-$176	465
9 p. 342	Marriott Courtyard Montreal Airport, 3 mi (5 km) ne of terminal	▼▼▼	$122-$199	387
8 p. 342	Marriott Residence Inn Montreal Airport, 3 mi (5 km) from terminal	▼▼▼	$128-$209	387
45 p. 342	Novotel Montreal Airport, 5.9 mi (9.5 km) from terminal	▼▼▼	$129-$329 [SAVE]	465
44 p. 342	Quality Hotel Dorval, 2.1 mi (3.5 km) e of terminal	▼▼▼	$127-$195	465
72 p. 342	Comfort Inn, 4.8 mi (8 km) e of terminal	▼▼	$85-$135 [SAVE]	402
71 p. 342	Holiday Inn Pointe-Claire Montreal Aeroport, 4.8 mi (8 km) e of terminal	▼▼▼	$139-$259	402
70 p. 342	Quality Suites Montreal Aeroport, Pointe-Claire, 4.8 mi (8 km) e of terminal	▼▼▼	$124-$169 [SAVE]	402
41 p. 342	Holiday Inn Montreal-Airport, 3.3 mi (5.5 km) e of terminal	▼▼▼	$199-$229 [SAVE]	465
43 p. 342	Park Inn Hotel & Suites Montreal Airport, 2.1 mi (3.4 km) e of terminal	▼▼	$89-$249 [SAVE]	465

Montreal and Vicinity

This index helps you "spot" where approved hotels and restaurants are located on the corresponding detailed maps. Hotel daily rate range is for comparison only and shows the property's high season. Restaurant rate range is a combination of lunch and/or dinner. Turn to the listing page for more detailed rate information and consult display ads for special promotions.

MONTRÉAL

Map Page	Hotels	Diamond Rated	High Season	Page
1 p. 342	Hotel Le Prestige	▼▼	$96-$150	386
2 p. 342	Auberge Royal Versailles Hotel	▼▼▼	$110-$180 [SAVE]	386
3 p. 342	Hotel Universel Montreal (See ad p. 364.)	▼▼▼	$127-$149 [SAVE]	386
4 p. 342	Auberge de la Fontaine	▼▼▼	$139-$193 [SAVE]	386
5 p. 342	Hotel Terrasse Royale	▼▼	Rates not provided	386
6 p. 342	Hotel Ruby Foo's (See ad p. 360.)	▼▼▼	$149-$229 [SAVE]	386
7 p. 342	Quality Hotel Midtown	▼▼	$99-$159 [SAVE]	387
8 p. 342	Marriott Residence Inn Montreal Airport	▼▼▼	$128-$209	387

MONTRÉAL (cont'd)

Map Page	Hotels (cont'd)		Diamond Rated	High Season	Page
⑨ p. 342	Marriott Courtyard Montreal Airport		▽▽▽	$122-$199	387

Map Page	Restaurants	Diamond Rated	Cuisine	Meal Range	Page
① p. 342	Ristorante La Dora	▽▽	Italian	$9-$23	391
② p. 342	Le Stadium Club Restaurant & Bar	▽▽	Italian	$11-$32	389
③ p. 342	Tapeo-Bar a Tapas	▽▽	Spanish	$6-$17	391
④ p. 342	Kitchenette	▽▽▽	French	$14-$35	389
⑤ p. 342	La Binerie Mont-Royal	▽	Quebec	$5-$11	389
⑥ p. 342	Dunns Famous Delicatessen	▽▽	Deli	$7-$27	388
⑦ p. 342	Soy	▽▽	Asian	$10-$18	391
⑧ p. 342	Wilensky's Light Lunch Inc	▽	Deli	$5-$10	391
⑨ p. 342	Thai Grill	▽▽▽	Thai	$16-$32	391
⑩ p. 342	Restaurant Chez Doval	▽▽	Portuguese	$9-$20	390
⑪ p. 342	La Chronique	▽▽▽▽	International	$25-$42	389
⑫ p. 342	Restaurant Juni	▽▽▽	Japanese	$21-$35	390
⑬ p. 342	Milos Restaurant	▽▽▽	Greek	$22-$35	389
⑭ p. 342	Beauty's Luncheonette	▽▽	Canadian	$10-$30	388
⑮ p. 342	Laurier Gordon Ramsay	▽▽	Canadian	$13-$28	389
⑯ p. 342	Cracovie Restaurant Polonais	▽▽	Polish	$15-$25	388
⑰ p. 342	Pizzafiore	▽▽	Italian	$8-$18	390
⑱ p. 342	Rib 'n Reef Steakhouse & Cigar Lounge	▽▽▽	Steak	$29-$62	390
⑲ p. 342	Restaurant Joe Beef Montreal	▽▽▽	French	$25-$50	390
㉑ p. 342	Gibeau Orange Julep	▽	Canadian	$6-$10	388
㉒ p. 342	Restaurant & Taverne Magnan	▽▽	Steak	$9-$31	390
㉓ p. 342	Le Grill Midtown	▽	Kosher	$6-$16	389
㉔ p. 342	Chez Benny	▽	Kosher	$6-$17	388
㉕ p. 342	Quartier Perse	▽▽	Iranian	$16-$30	390
㉖ p. 342	Lezvos West	▽▽▽	Mediterranean	$12-$22	389
㉗ p. 342	Cote St-Luc Bar-B-Q	▽▽	Chicken	$9-$23	388
㉘ p. 342	Tehran Restaurant	▽▽	Middle Eastern	$14-$23	391
㉙ p. 342	Monkland Tavern	▽▽	California	$10-$26	390
㉚ p. 342	Saint-Viateur Bagel & Café	▽▽	Deli	$7-$15	391
㉛ p. 342	Chalet Bar-B-Q Rotisserie	▽▽	Barbecue	$6-$11	388
㉜ p. 342	Le Maistre	▽▽▽	French	$20-$26	389
㉝ p. 342	Restaurant Bofinger Barbeque Smokehouse	▽	Barbecue	$8-$20	390
㉞ p. 342	Restaurant Momesso	▽	Deli	$5-$15	390
㉟ p. 342	B & M Restaurant	▽▽	Canadian	$8-$34	388
㊱ p. 342	Asean Garden	▽▽	Asian	$10-$19	388
㊲ p. 342	La Louisiane	▽▽	Cajun	$13-$30	389
㊳ p. 342	Alex H. Restaurant	▽▽	Italian	$18-$30	388

Map Page	Restaurants (cont'd)	Diamond Rated	Cuisine	Meal Range	Page
㊴ p. 342	B & M Restaurant	♦♦	Canadian	$8-$34	388
㊵ p. 342	Le Coin d'Asie	♦♦	Asian	$8-$20	389
㊶ p. 342	Restaurant Ganges	♦♦♦	Indian	$8-$14	390

TERREBONNE

Map Page	Hotel	Diamond Rated	High Season	Page
⓬ p. 342	Super 8 Hotel Lachenaie Terrebonne	♦♦♦	$105-$162	479

ANJOU

Map Page	Hotel	Diamond Rated	High Season	Page
⓯ p. 342	**Quality Hotel East**	♦♦	$90-$250 [SAVE]	263

Map Page	Restaurant	Diamond Rated	Cuisine	Meal Range	Page
㊹ p. 342	Il Pazzesco	♦♦♦	Italian	$14-$35	263

BOUCHERVILLE

Map Page	Hotels	Diamond Rated	High Season	Page
⓲ p. 342	Comfort Inn	♦♦	$98-$135	267
⓳ p. 342	**Hotel WelcomINNS** *(See ad p. 268.)*	♦♦♦	$125-$195 [SAVE]	267
⓴ p. 342	**Hotel Mortagne** *(See ad p. 268.)*	♦♦♦	$139-$269 [SAVE]	267

Map Page	Restaurants	Diamond Rated	Cuisine	Meal Range	Page
㊼ p. 342	Bistro Le Tire-Bouchon	♦♦♦	French	$15-$28	269
㊽ p. 342	Restaurant Sens	♦♦♦	French	$15-$28	269
㊾ p. 342	Madisons New York Grill & Bar	♦♦	Steak	$10-$35	269

LAVAL

Map Page	Hotels	Diamond Rated	High Season	Page
㉓ p. 342	**Hotel Châteauneuf Laval**	♦♦♦	$100-$199 [SAVE]	300
㉔ p. 342	**Sheraton Laval Hotel**	♦♦♦♦	$129-$269 [SAVE]	300
㉕ p. 342	**Hotel Hilton Montreal-Laval**	♦♦♦	Rates not provided [SAVE]	300
㉖ p. 342	**Holiday Inn Laval Montreal**	♦♦♦	$109-$229 [SAVE]	300
㉗ p. 342	**Comfort Inn**	♦♦	$118-$173 [SAVE]	299
㉘ p. 342	**Quality Suites Laval**	♦♦	$128-$188 [SAVE]	300
㉙ p. 342	**Le St-Martin Hotel & Suites**	♦♦♦	$129-$369 [SAVE]	300
㉚ p. 342	Econo Lodge	♦♦	Rates not provided	300
㉛ p. 342	**Hampton Inn & Suites-Laval**	♦♦♦	$119-$149 [SAVE]	300

Map Page	Restaurants	Diamond Rated	Cuisine	Meal Range	Page
㊲ p. 342	Restaurant Le Saint-Christophe	♦♦♦♦	French	$48-$62	301
㊳ p. 342	Le Tire-Bouchon Bistro Parisien	♦♦♦	French	$15-$30	301
㊴ p. 342	Ristorante Terracina	♦♦	Italian	$13-$28	301

LONGUEUIL

Map Page	Hotels	Diamond Rated	High Season	Page
㉞ p. 342	**Hotel Gouverneur Ile-Charron**	♦♦♦	$99-$169 [SAVE]	305
㉟ p. 342	Holiday Inn Montreal-Longueuil	♦♦♦	$119-$129	304
㊱ p. 342	Hotel Dauphin Montreal Longueuil	♦♦♦	$99-$149	304
㊲ p. 342	Sandman Hotel Montreal-Longueuil	♦♦♦	$129-$179	305
㊳ p. 342	**Motel La Siesta** *(See ad p. 304.)*	♦♦	$85-$169 [SAVE]	305

ST-LAURENT

Map Page	Hotels	Diamond Rated	High Season	Page
41 p. 342	**Holiday Inn Montreal-Airport**	◈◈◈	$199-$229 (SAVE)	465
42 p. 342	**Crowne Plaza Montreal Airport**	◈◈◈	$119-$189 (SAVE)	465
43 p. 342	**Park Inn Hotel & Suites Montreal Airport** (See ad p. 387.)	◈◈	$89-$249 (SAVE)	465
44 p. 342	Quality Hotel Dorval	◈◈◈	$127-$195	465
45 p. 342	**Novotel Montreal Airport** (See ad p. 372.)	◈◈◈	$129-$329 (SAVE)	465
46 p. 342	Hilton Garden Inn Montreal Airport	◈◈◈	$131-$176	465

Map Page	Restaurant	Diamond Rated	Cuisine	Meal Range	Page
79 p. 342	Ristorante Venezia	◈◈	Italian	$10-$34	465

BROSSARD

Map Page	Hotels	Diamond Rated	High Season	Page
49 p. 342	**Quality Inn & Suites**	◈◈◈	$116-$161 (SAVE)	270
50 p. 342	Hotel Brossard	◈◈◈	Rates not provided	270
51 p. 342	**Best Western Plus Brossard**	◈◈◈	$126-$180 (SAVE)	270
52 p. 342	Comfort Inn	◈◈	$90-$210	270
53 p. 342	Econo Lodge Montreal - Brossard	◈◈	$87-$200	270
54 p. 342	Alt Hotel Quartier Dix 30	◈◈◈	Rates not provided	270

Map Page	Restaurants	Diamond Rated	Cuisine	Meal Range	Page
82 p. 342	Restaurant Cumulus	◈◈◈	Canadian	$13-$29	271
83 p. 342	Les 3 Brasseurs	◈◈	Canadian	$9-$21	271
84 p. 342	L'Aurochs Angus Steakhouse	◈◈◈	Steak	$24-$95	270
85 p. 342	Rouge Bistro & Grill Oriental	◈◈◈	Asian	$12-$25	271

LACHINE

Map Page	Hotel	Diamond Rated	High Season	Page
57 p. 342	**Holiday Inn Express Hotel & Suites Montreal Aeroport**	◈◈◈	$140-$165 (SAVE)	295

Map Page	Restaurants	Diamond Rated	Cuisine	Meal Range	Page
100 p. 342	12 Bar Grill	◈◈	Canadian	$7-$28	295
101 p. 342	Restaurant Topaze	◈◈	Steak	$9-$28	295
102 p. 342	Ristorante Il Fornetto	◈◈◈	Italian	$12-$30	295

DORVAL

Map Page	Hotels	Diamond Rated	High Season	Page
60 p. 342	**Hampton Inn & Suites by Hilton Montreal (Dorval)**	◈◈◈	Rates not provided (SAVE)	279
61 p. 342	**Comfort Inn Dorval**	◈◈	$95-$225 (SAVE)	278
62 p. 342	**Montreal Airport Marriott** (See ad p. 279.)	◈◈◈◈	$149-$359 (SAVE)	281
63 p. 342	**The Sheraton Montreal Airport Hotel** (See ad p. 280.)	◈◈◈◈	$169-$249 (SAVE)	281
64 p. 342	**Aloft Montreal Airport** (See ad p. 278.)	◈◈◈	$99-$229 (SAVE)	278
65 p. 342	**Best Western Plus Montreal Airport Hotel**	◈◈◈	$130-$140 (SAVE)	278
66 p. 342	**Marriott Fairfield Inn & Suites Aeroport de Montreal Airport**	◈◈◈	$107-$143 (SAVE)	279
67 p. 342	**Quality Inn & Suites Aeroport Montreal-Trudeau**	◈◈	$80-$143 (SAVE)	281

Map Page	Restaurants	Diamond Rated	Cuisine	Meal Range	Page
(105) p. 342	Bijou Resto-Bar	▽▽▽	French	$15-$35	281
p. 342	Eclipse	▽▽▽	Continental	$16-$35	281

POINTE-CLAIRE

Map Page	Hotels	Diamond Rated	High Season	Page
(70) p. 342	**Quality Suites Montreal Aeroport, Pointe-Claire**	▽▽▽	$124-$169 SAVE	402
(71) p. 342	Holiday Inn Pointe-Claire Montreal Aeroport	▽▽▽	$139-$259	402
(72) p. 342	**Comfort Inn**	▽▽	$85-$135 SAVE	402

Map Page	Restaurants	Diamond Rated	Cuisine	Meal Range	Page
(112) p. 342	40 Westt Steakhouse	▽▽▽	Steak	$25-$60	403
(113) p. 342	Le Gourmand	▽▽▽	French	$17-$44	403
(114) p. 342	Le Chambertin	▽▽▽	French	$15-$40	403
(115) p. 342	Scarolies Pasta Emporium	▽▽	Italian	$10-$24	403
(116) p. 342	Moe's Deli & Bar	▽▽	Canadian	$9-$22	403

ST-EUSTACHE

Map Page	Restaurant	Diamond Rated	Cuisine	Meal Range	Page
(57) p. 342	Restaurant Château Lafitte	▽▽	Canadian	$7-$27	459

OUTREMONT

Map Page	Restaurants	Diamond Rated	Cuisine	Meal Range	Page
(60) p. 342	Restaurant Christophe	▽▽▽	French	$36-$58	399
(61) p. 342	Le Paris Beurre	▽▽	French	$12-$28	399
(62) p. 342	Restaurant Chez Léveque	▽▽▽	French	$17-$34	399
(63) p. 342	Restaurant Lemeac	▽▽▽	French	$19-$36	399

STE-DOROTHEE

Map Page	Restaurants	Diamond Rated	Cuisine	Meal Range	Page
(66) p. 342	Dunns Famous Delicatessen	▽▽	Deli	$7-$27	472
(67) p. 342	Le Mitoyen	▽▽▽▽	French	$24-$37	472

WESTMOUNT

Map Page	Restaurants	Diamond Rated	Cuisine	Meal Range	Page
(70) p. 342	Miso	▽▽	Japanese	$10-$30	487
(71) p. 342	Chine Toque	▽▽▽	Chinese	$10-$16	487
(72) p. 342	Kaizen Sushi Bar & Restaurant	▽▽	Japanese	$15-$32	487
(73) p. 342	Bistro on the Avenue	▽▽	French	$11-$26	486
(74) p. 342	Vago Cucina Italiana	▽▽▽	Italian	$18-$42	487
(75) p. 342	Taverne sur le Square	▽▽▽	Continental	$13-$38	487
(76) p. 342	Restaurant Wellhouse	▽▽	Canadian	$14-$33	487

COTE ST-LUC

Map Page	Restaurant	Diamond Rated	Cuisine	Meal Range	Page
(88) p. 342	Ernie & Ellie's Restaurant	▽▽	Kosher	$8-$25	276

VERDUN

Map Page	Restaurant	Diamond Rated	Cuisine	Meal Range	Page
(91) p. 342	Villa Wellington	▽▽	Peruvian	$9-$20	485

DOLLARD-DES-ORMEAUX

Map Page	Restaurants	Diamond Rated	Cuisine	Meal Range	Page
⑨④ p. 342	Dunns Famous Delicatessen	▽▽	Deli	$7-$27	277
⑨⑤ p. 342	Restaurant Aikawa	▽▽▽	Japanese	$12-$26	277
⑨⑥ p. 342	Madisons New York Grill & Bar	▽▽	Steak	$10-$30	277
⑨⑦ p. 342	Abie's Smoked Meat & Steak	▽▽	Deli	$8-$18	277

KIRKLAND

Map Page	Restaurants	Diamond Rated	Cuisine	Meal Range	Page
⑩⑧ p. 342	Le Steak frites St-Paul	▽▽	Steak	$21-$40	292
⑩⑨ p. 342	Madisons New York Grill & Bar	▽▽	Steak	$10-$30	292

STE-ANNE-DE-BELLEVUE

Map Page	Restaurant	Diamond Rated	Cuisine	Meal Range	Page
⑪⑨ p. 342	Le Surcouf	▽▽▽	French	$15-$38	470

L'ILE-PERROT

Map Page	Restaurant	Diamond Rated	Cuisine	Meal Range	Page
⑫② p. 342	Smoke Meat Pete	▽	Canadian	$8-$23	303

▼ *See AAA listing p. 365* ▼

DOWNTOWN MONTRÉAL

- Restaurants p. 375

ANNE MA SOEUR ANNE HOTEL-STUDIO
Phone: (514)281-3187 **1**

Hotel
$90-$155 6/1-10/31
$80-$140 11/1-5/31

Address: 4119 rue St-Denis H2W 2M7 **Location:** Just s of rue Rachel. **Facility:** 15 efficiencies. 3 stories (no elevator), interior/exterior corridors. **Parking:** street only. **Amenities:** high-speed Internet. **Free Special Amenities: continental breakfast and high-speed Internet.**

SAVE 📶 🛜 ✖ 🏢 🖥 💻

AUBERGE LE JARDIN D'ANTOINE
Phone: (514)843-4506 **6**

Hotel
$107-$172

Address: 2024 rue St-Denis H2X 3K7 **Location:** Just s of rue Sherbrooke. Located in the Latin Quarter. **Facility:** 25 units. 4 stories (no elevator), interior/exterior corridors. **Parking:** street only. **Terms:** 3 day cancellation notice-fee imposed. **Amenities:** high-speed Internet. **Free Special Amenities: expanded continental breakfast and high-speed Internet.**

SAVE 📶 BIZ 🛜 ✖ / SOME UNITS 🏢

AUBERGE LE POMEROL
Phone: (514)526-5511 **4**

Historic Hotel
$115-$200 6/1-10/31
$105-$180 11/1-5/31

Address: 819 de Maisonneuve est H2L 1Y7 **Location:** Just e of rue St-Hubert. **Facility:** Housed within a historic building, this small boutique hotel offers stylish guest rooms and many modern amenities. 27 units. 4 stories, interior corridors. **Parking:** on-site (fee). **Terms:** cancellation fee imposed. **Amenities:** high-speed Internet. *Some:* safes.

SAVE 📶 🛁 BIZ 🛜 ✖ 💻 / SOME UNITS 🏢

BEST WESTERN PLUS MONTREAL DOWNTOWN-HOTEL EUROPA
Phone: (514)866-6492 **49**

Hotel
$99-$189

AAA Benefit: Members save up to 20%, plus 10% bonus points with Best Western Rewards®.

Address: 1240 rue Drummond H3G 1V7 **Location:** Between rue Ste-Catherine and boul Rene-Levesque. **Facility:** 175 units, some two bedrooms, efficiencies and kitchens. 6 stories, interior corridors. **Parking:** on-site (fee) and street. **Dining:** Chez Cora, see separate listing. **Activities:** spa. *Fee:* saunas, whirlpool. **Guest Services:** valet laundry. **Free Special Amenities: local telephone calls and high-speed Internet.**

SAVE 📶 🍴 🍸 BIZ 🛜 ✖ 💻 / SOME UNITS 🏢

BEST WESTERN VILLE-MARIE HOTEL & SUITES
Phone: (514)288-4141 **40**

Hotel
$110-$426

AAA Benefit: Members save up to 20%, plus 10% bonus points with Best Western Rewards®.

Address: 3407 rue Peel H3A 1W7 **Location:** Corner of rue Peel and rue Sherbrooke. **Facility:** 170 units, some two bedrooms and kitchens. 21 stories, interior corridors. **Parking:** on-site and valet. **Amenities:** video games (fee), high-speed Internet. **Dining:** Zawedeh Restaurant, see separate listing. **Activities:** exercise room. **Guest Services:** valet laundry. **Free Special Amenities: local telephone calls and high-speed Internet.**

SAVE ECO 🍴 🍸 BIZ 🛜 FEE 🎮 🏢 💻 / SOME UNITS 🖥

▼ See AAA listing p. 353 ▼

Download eTourBook guides for ereaders and smartphones at AAA.com/ebooks

(See map & index p. 334.)

▼ See AAA listing p. 484 ▼

(See map & index p. 334.)

▼ See AAA listing p. 353 ▼

AAA/CAA MEMBER DISCOUNTS AHEAD

Consider your AAA/CAA card as the smallest, lowest tech GPS navigator
imaginable...it will take you right to the best deals in town,
wherever "town" is for you. Go to **AAA.com/discounts** to
find your way to the best deals.

Show Your Card & Save!

AAA.com/discounts

(See map & index p. 334.)

CANDLEWOOD SUITES

Phone: (514)667-5002 **12**

Extended Stay Hotel
$99-$169

Address: 191 boul Rene-Levesque est H2X 3Z9 **Location:** Corner of rue Hotel-de-ville. **Facility:** 145 kitchen units, some two bedrooms. 15 stories, interior corridors. **Parking:** valet and street only. **Terms:** cancellation fee imposed. **Amenities:** high-speed Internet. **Activities:** exercise room. **Guest Services:** valet and coin laundry. **Free Special Amenities: high-speed Internet and use of on-premises laundry facilities.** *(See ad p. 350.)*

SAVE ECO 🍴 BIZ 🛜 📶
📷 💻 / SOME UNITS FEE 🐾

CHÂTEAU VERSAILLES HOTEL

Phone: 514/933-3611 **54**

Historic Boutique Hotel
Rates not provided

Address: 1659 rue Sherbrooke ouest H3H 1E3 **Location:** Corner of rue St-Mathieu. **Facility:** In-room dining and evening turn-down service is offered at this stylish boutique hotel in a historic downtown graystone building. 65 units. 4 stories (no elevator), interior corridors. **Parking:** valet only. **Amenities:** video games (fee), high-speed Internet, safes, honor bars. **Activities:** sauna, limited exercise equipment. **Guest Services:** valet laundry. **Free Special Amenities: continental breakfast and high-speed Internet.** *(See ad opposite title page.)*

SAVE 🍴 📶 BIZ 🛜 ✕ FEE 📺 💻
/ SOME UNITS FEE 🐾

DAYS INN MONTREAL DOWNTOWN

Phone: (514)393-3388 **10**

Hotel
$81-$369

Address: 215 boul Rene-Levesque est H2X 1N7 **Location:** Corner of rue de l'Hotel de Ville. **Facility:** 123 units. 8 stories, interior corridors. **Parking:** valet only. **Terms:** check-in 4 pm, cancellation fee imposed. **Amenities:** *Some:* high-speed Internet, safes. **Guest Services:** valet laundry. **Free Special Amenities: newspaper and high-speed Internet.** *(See ad p. 352.)*

SAVE ECO 🍴 📺 BIZ 🛜
✕ 📶 💻 / SOME UNITS 📷

DELTA MONTREAL

Phone: (514)286-1986 **27**

Hotel
$175-$322 6/1-10/31
$145-$247 11/1-5/31

Address: 475 ave President-Kennedy H3A 1J7 **Location:** Corner of rue City Councillors. **Facility:** 456 units. 23 stories, interior corridors. **Parking:** on-site (fee) and valet. **Amenities:** high-speed Internet (fee). *Some:* honor bars. **Pool(s):** heated indoor. **Activities:** saunas, whirlpool, sports court, exercise room, spa. **Guest Services:** valet laundry.

SAVE ECO 🍴 📺 📶 🏊 BIZ 🛜 FEE 📺 💻
/ SOME UNITS FEE 🐾 FEE 📶 FEE 📷

Find valuable AAA/CAA
member savings
at AAA.com/discounts

EMBASSY SUITES MONTREAL PAR/BY HILTON

Phone: (514)288-8886 **28**

Extended Stay Hotel
$149-$579

AAA Benefit: Members save 5% or more everyday!

Address: 208 rue St-Antoine ouest H2Y 0A6 **Location:** Corner of rue St-Francois-Xavier. Across from Palais des Congres Convention Centre. **Facility:** 210 units, some two bedrooms, efficiencies and kitchens. 12 stories, interior corridors. **Parking:** on-site (fee). **Terms:** 1-7 night minimum stay, cancellation fee imposed. **Amenities:** *Fee:* video games, high-speed Internet. **Activities:** exercise room. **Guest Services:** valet and coin laundry. **Free Special Amenities: full breakfast and local telephone calls.** *(See ad p. 354.)*

SAVE ECO 🍴 📺 BIZ 🛜 FEE 📺 📶 📷
💻 / SOME UNITS FEE 🐾

FAIRMONT THE QUEEN ELIZABETH

Phone: 514/861-3511 **42**

Hotel
Rates not provided

Address: 900 boul Rene-Levesque ouest H3B 4A5 **Location:** Between rue University and Mansfield. **Facility:** This luxurious hotel, which features added amenities in its business-class units, has access to an underground mall. A few of the guest rooms are small. 1039 units, some two bedrooms. 21 stories, interior corridors. **Parking:** on-site (fee) and valet. **Terms:** check-in 4 pm. **Amenities:** honor bars. *Fee:* video games, high-speed Internet. *Some:* safes. **Dining:** 2 restaurants, also, The Beaver Club, see separate listing. **Pool(s):** heated indoor. **Activities:** whirlpool, steamrooms, spa. **Guest Services:** valet laundry.

SAVE ECO 🍴 📺 📺 📶 CALL 🛗 🏊 📶
BIZ 🛜 FEE 📺 💻
/ SOME UNITS FEE 🐾 FEE 📶 FEE 📷

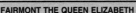

Fairmont
THE QUEEN ELIZABETH

A tradition of grandeur and intuitive service, ideal for business or leisure

HILTON GARDEN INN MONTREAL CENTRE-VILLE

Phone: (514)840-0010 **22**

Hotel
$209-$299 6/1-10/31
$149-$219 11/1-5/31

AAA Benefit: Unparalleled hospitality at a special Member rate.

Address: 380 rue Sherbrooke ouest H3A 0B1 **Location:** Corner of rue de Bleury. **Facility:** 221 units. 11 stories, interior corridors. **Parking:** on-site (fee) and valet. **Terms:** 1-7 night minimum stay, cancellation fee imposed. **Amenities:** high-speed Internet, safes. **Pool(s):** heated indoor. **Activities:** whirlpool, steamrooms, exercise room. **Guest Services:** valet and coin laundry. **Free Special Amenities: local telephone calls and high-speed Internet.**

SAVE ECO 🍴 📶 CALL 🛗 🏊 BIZ 🛜 ✕
FEE 📺 📶 📷 💻

Simply Reliable

The Diamond Ratings in this TourBook guide are backed by our expert, in-person evaluations, whether the hotel or restaurant is no-frills, moderate, or upscale.
Learn more at **AAA.com/Diamonds**

(See map & index p. 334.)

▼ *See AAA listing p. 356* ▼

TourBook Comments

Are we meeting your travel needs?

If your visit to an establishment listed in a AAA TourBook guide doesn't meet your expectations, tell us about it.

Complete an easy online form at
AAA.com/TourBookComments.

(See map & index p. 334.)

HILTON MONTRÉAL BONAVENTURE
Phone: (514)878-2332

Hotel
$190-$625

AAA Benefit: Members save 5% or more everyday!

Address: 900 rue de la Gauchetiere ouest H5A 1E4 **Location:** Corner of Mansfield. Located atop a major exhibition complex. **Facility:** All rooms in this downtown hotel, which sits atop a major convention center, have marble foyers, ergonomic desk chairs and marble bathroom counters. 395 units. 3 stories, interior corridors. **Parking:** on-site (fee) and valet. **Terms:** 1-7 night minimum stay, cancellation fee imposed. **Amenities:** safes. *Fee:* video games, high-speed Internet. **Dining:** Le Castillon, see separate listing. **Pool(s):** heated outdoor. **Activities:** exercise room, massage. **Guest Services:** valet laundry. **Free Special Amenities: newspaper and high-speed Internet.** *(See ad p. 355.)*

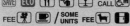

HOLIDAY INN EXPRESS HOTEL & SUITES MONTREAL CENTRE-VILLE
Phone: (514)448-7100 **13**

Hotel
$107-$300

Address: 155 boul Rene-Levesque est H2X 3Z8 **Location:** Corner of rue de Bullion. **Facility:** 161 units, some two bedrooms. 8 stories, interior corridors. **Parking:** valet and street only. **Amenities:** high-speed Internet. **Activities:** exercise room. **Guest Services:** valet and coin laundry. **Free Special Amenities: full breakfast and high-speed Internet.** *(See ad this page.)*

HOLIDAY INN MONTREAL-MIDTOWN
Phone: (514)842-6111 **25**

Hotel
$119-$149 6/1-10/31
$109-$139 11/1-5/31

Address: 420 rue Sherbrooke ouest H3A 1B4 **Location:** Between rue de Bleury and Aylmer. **Facility:** 488 units, some kitchens. 19 stories, interior corridors. **Parking:** valet and street only. **Terms:** 3 day cancellation notice. **Amenities:** *Some:* safes, honor bars. **Dining:** 2 restaurants. **Pool(s):** heated indoor. **Activities:** saunas, whirlpool, steamroom, exercise room. *Fee:* game room, massage. **Guest Services:** valet and coin laundry. **Free Special Amenities: newspaper and use of on-premises laundry facilities.**

HOLIDAY INN SELECT MONTREAL CENTRE-VILLE DOWNTOWN
Phone: (514)878-9888 **18**

Hotel
$119-$229 6/1-10/31
$109-$209 11/1-5/31

Address: 99 ave Viger ouest H2Z 1E9 **Location:** Corner of rue St-Urbain. Located in Chinatown, across from convention center. **Facility:** 235 units. 8 stories, interior corridors. **Parking:** on-site (fee). **Dining:** Chez Chine, see separate listing. **Pool(s):** heated indoor. **Activities:** sauna, whirlpool, exercise room, spa. **Guest Services:** valet and coin laundry. **Free Special Amenities: newspaper and high-speed Internet.** *(See ad p. 357.)*

Enjoy great savings on hotel rates at AAA.com or CAA.ca

▼ See AAA listing this page ▼

(See map & index p. 334.)

HOTEL DE LA MONTAGNE   Phone: (514)288-5656 51

Hotel

$179-$299 10/11-5/31
$189-$289 6/1-10/10

Address: 1430 rue de la Montagne H3G 1Z5 **Location:** Between rue Ste-Catherine and boul de Maisonneuve. **Facility:** 142 units, some two bedrooms. 22 stories, interior corridors. **Parking:** on-site (fee). **Terms:** 2 night minimum stay - weekends. **Amenities:** video games (fee), safes, honor bars. **Pool(s):** outdoor. **Activities:** Fee: massage. **Guest Services:** valet laundry. **Free Special Amenities:** continental breakfast and high-speed Internet.

[SAVE] [🍴] [🍸] [🏊] FEE[♨] [BIZ] [📶] FEE[🎥] [💻]
/SOME UNITS FEE[🐾] [🍱]

HOTEL DU FORT   Phone: (514)938-8333 59

Hotel

$105-$299

Address: 1390 rue du Fort H3H 2R7 **Location:** Corner of rue Ste-Catherine ouest. **Facility:** 124 units. 19 stories, interior corridors. **Terms:** check-in 4 pm. **Amenities:** safes. Some: high-speed Internet. **Activities:** exercise room. **Guest Services:** valet laundry. **Free Special Amenities:** local telephone calls and high-speed Internet.

(See ad p. 358.)

[SAVE] [ECO] [🍴] [🏊] [BIZ] [📶]
FEE[🎥] [🍱] [🖥] [💻]

HÔTEL ESPRESSO MONTRÉAL CENTRE-VILLE/DOWNTOWN
Phone: (514)938-4611 57

Hotel

$99-$169 11/1-5/31
$109-$159 6/1-10/31

Address: 1005 rue Guy H3H 2K4 **Location:** Just s of boul Rene-Levesque. **Facility:** 205 units. 7 stories, interior corridors. **Parking:** on-site (fee). **Terms:** cancellation fee imposed. **Amenities:** high-speed Internet. **Pool(s):** heated outdoor. **Activities:** sauna, exercise room, spa. **Guest Services:** valet laundry.

[🍴] [🍸] [🏊] [BIZ] [📶] [✕] [💻]
/SOME UNITS FEE[🐾] [🍱] [🖥]

HOTEL GAULT   Phone: (514)904-1616 36

Hotel

$300-$720 6/1-10/31
$240-$585 11/1-5/31

Address: 449 rue Ste-Helene H2Y 2K9 **Location:** Just s of rue Notre-Dame. Located in Old Montreal. **Facility:** 30 units, some efficiencies. 5 stories, interior corridors. **Parking:** valet only. **Terms:** check-in 4 pm. **Amenities:** high-speed Internet, safes, honor bars. **Activities:** exercise room. Fee: massage. **Guest Services:** valet laundry.

(See ad p. 359.)

[SAVE] [🍴] [🍸] [🏊] [BIZ]
[📶] [✕]
/SOME UNITS FEE[🐾] [🍱] [🖥]

HOTEL GOUVERNEUR PLACE DUPUIS
Phone: (514)842-4881 5

Hotel

$125-$399 6/1-10/31
$109-$179 11/1-5/31

Address: 1415 rue St-Hubert H2L 3Y9 **Location:** Between boul de Maisonneuve and rue Ste-Catherine. **Facility:** 352 units. 30 stories, interior corridors. **Parking:** on-site (fee). **Amenities:** high-speed Internet. Some: safes. **Pool(s):** heated indoor. **Activities:** saunas, exercise room. **Guest Services:** valet laundry.

(See ad p. 359.)

[SAVE] [ECO] [🍴] [🍸] [🏊] [🏊]
[BIZ] [📶] FEE[🎥] [💻]
/SOME UNITS FEE[🐾] FEE[🍱]

HOTEL KUTUMA   Phone: (514)844-0111 2

Hotel

$135-$400 6/1-8/31
$115-$350 9/1-5/31

Address: 3708 rue St-Denis H2X 3L7 **Location:** Just s of ave des Pins est. **Facility:** 9 units, some efficiencies and kitchens. 4 stories (no elevator), interior corridors. **Parking:** valet only. **Terms:** 2 night minimum stay - weekends, cancellation fee imposed. **Amenities:** high-speed Internet, safes. **Dining:** Le Nil Bleu Restaurant, see separate listing. **Guest Services:** valet laundry.

[🍴] [🍸] [📶] [✕] [🍱] [🖥] [💻]

▼ See AAA listing p. 356 ▼

▼ See AAA listing p. 357 ▼

EXCLUSIVE RATE FOR AAA/CAA MEMBERS

Our rooms and suites offer the luxury of space; they are among the largest in downtown Montreal.

All of our tastefully appointed rooms are equipped with: refrigerator, coffee maker and microwave.

Specialized in upscale and personalized service, we offer a unique experience that keeps our leisure guests returning again and again.

HÔTEL DU FORT

MONTRÉAL

1390 rue du Fort,
Montreal, Qc H3H 2R7
www.hoteldufort.com

CAA AAA
Approved

Eco-Rating Program

10% off the Best Available Rate

Including Indoor Parking, Wireless Internet & Local Calls

RESERVE TODAY !
(514) 938-8333 or 1-800-565-6333
reserve@hoteldufort.com

Scan this tag on your smartphone and start saving today!

Get the free mobile app at
http://gettag.mobi

(See map & index p. 334.)

Safety tip: Keep a current AAA/CAA Road Atlas in every vehicle

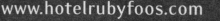

Share a New View on Travel at
AAATravelViews.com
Read stories, tips and trends from AAA insiders.
Post comments and get your questions answered by our travel experts.

▼ See AAA listing p. 362 ▼

(See map & index p. 334.)

HOTEL LE CANTLIE SUITES

Hotel
$139-$499 6/1-10/31
$109-$499 11/1-5/31

Phone: (514)842-2000 **44**

Address: 1110 rue Sherbrooke ouest H3A 1G9 **Location:** Between rue Stanley and Peel. **Facility:** 256 units, some two bedrooms, efficiencies and kitchens. 28 stories, interior corridors. **Parking:** valet and street only. **Terms:** check-in 4 pm, cancellation fee imposed. **Amenities:** high-speed Internet (fee). **Pool(s):** heated outdoor. **Activities:** exercise room. **Guest Services:** valet and coin laundry. **Free Special Amenities:** newspaper.
(See ad p. 361.)

HÔTEL LE CRYSTAL

Hotel
$209-$2499

Phone: (514)861-5550 **53**

Address: 1100 rue de la Montagne H3G 0A1 **Location:** Corner of boul Rene-Levesque. In the heart of downtown, this all-suite hotel offers stylish and ultra-comfortable guest units, each with luxurious bedding and excellent city views. 131 units, some two bedrooms and efficiencies. 12 stories, interior corridors. **Parking:** valet only. **Amenities:** high-speed Internet, safes, honor bars. **Dining:** 2 restaurants. **Pool(s):** heated indoor. **Activities:** saunas, whirlpool, exercise room, spa. **Guest Services:** valet laundry. **Free Special Amenities:** newspaper and high-speed internet.

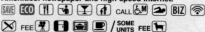

HOTEL LE DAUPHIN MONTREAL DOWNTOWN CONVENTION CENTRE   Phone: (514)788-3888 **29**

Hotel
$142-$295

Address: 1025 rue de Bleury H2Z 1M7 **Location:** Corner of rue de la Gauchetiere. Located near Montreal Convention Centre. **Facility:** 72 units. 10 stories, interior corridors. **Parking:** on-site (fee). **Amenities:** high-speed Internet, safes. **Activities:** exercise room. **Guest Services:** valet and coin laundry.

HÔTEL LE GERMAIN MONTRÉAL

Boutique Hotel
Rates not provided

Phone: 514/849-2050 **38**

Address: 2050 rue Mansfield H3A 1Y9 **Location:** Corner of ave President-Kennedy. **Facility:** This downtown boutique hotel offers spacious, stylish guest rooms with luxurious enhancements and convenient amenities for business travelers. Some luxury services are available. 101 units, some kitchens. 16 stories, interior corridors. **Parking:** valet and street only. **Amenities:** high-speed Internet, safes, honor bars. **Dining:** Laurie Raphaël/Montréal Restaurant/Boutique, see separate listing. **Activities:** exercise room. **Fee:** massage. **Guest Services:** valet laundry.

HOTEL LE ROBERVAL   Phone: (514)286-5215 **8**

Hotel
$119-$169 6/1-10/31
$90-$119 11/1-5/31

Address: 505 boul Rene-Levesque est H2L 5B6 **Location:** Corner of rue Berri. **Facility:** 76 units, some efficiencies and kitchens. 6 stories, interior corridors. **Parking:** on-site (fee). **Terms:** check-in 4 pm. **Amenities:** high-speed Internet. **Guest Services:** valet and coin laundry.

HOTEL LES SUITES LABELLE

Extended Stay Hotel
$129-$169 6/1-10/31
$109-$149 11/1-5/31

Phone: (514)840-1151 **9**

Address: 1205 rue Labelle H2L 4C1 **Location:** Just n of boul Rene-Levesque. **Facility:** 97 units, some two bedrooms, efficiencies and kitchens. 10 stories, interior corridors. **Parking:** on-site (fee). **Terms:** check-in 4 pm. **Activities:** exercise room. **Guest Services:** valet and coin laundry.

HÔTEL LE ST-JAMES   Phone: (514)841-3111 **33**

Historic Boutique Hotel
$320-$625

Address: 355 rue St-Jacques ouest H2Y 1N9 **Location:** Corner of rue St-Pierre. Located in Old Montreal. **Facility:** A private art collection and many imported and superbly crafted furnishings decorate the guest rooms, which feature oversize beds with Italian sheets and thick duvets. 60 units, some two bedrooms and kitchens. 12 stories, interior corridors. **Parking:** valet only. **Terms:** check-in 4 pm, cancellation fee imposed. **Amenities:** high-speed Internet, safes, honor bars. **Dining:** Restaurant XO, see separate listing. **Activities:** saunas, steamrooms, exercise room, spa. **Guest Services:** valet laundry.
(See ad p. 363.)

HOTEL LORD BERRI   Phone: (514)845-9236 **7**

Hotel
$119-$156 6/1-10/31
$99-$134 11/1-5/31

Address: 1199 rue Berri H2L 4C6 **Location:** Between boul Rene-Levesque and rue Ste-Catherine. **Facility:** 154 units. 10 stories, interior corridors. **Parking:** on-site (fee). **Amenities:** high-speed Internet. *Some:* safes. **Guest Services:** valet laundry.

HOTEL MANOIR DES ALPES

Hotel
$80-$130

Phone: (514)845-9803 **3**

Address: 1245 rue St-Andre H2L 3T1 **Location:** Just s of rue Ste-Catherine. **Facility:** 29 units. 3 stories (no elevator), interior corridors. **Terms:** cancellation fee imposed. **Amenities:** high-speed Internet.

HOTEL MARITIME PLAZA   Phone: (514)932-1411 **56**

Hotel
$100-$600

Address: 1155 rue Guy H3H 2K5 **Location:** Corner of boul Rene-Levesque; centre. **Facility:** 214 units, some efficiencies. 14 stories, interior corridors. **Parking:** on-site (fee). **Amenities:** safes. *Some:* high-speed Internet (fee). **Pool(s):** heated indoor. **Activities:** exercise room. **Guest Services:** valet laundry. **Free Special Amenities:** high-speed Internet.
(See ad opposite title page.)

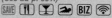

(See map & index p. 334.)

▼ See AAA listing p. 362 ▼

The ultimate luxury experience

MONTRÉAL

355, RUE SAINT-JACQUES, QUÉBEC, CANADA H2Y 1N9
T 514.841.3111   TOLL FREE 1 866.841.3111   HOTELLESTJAMES.COM

A member of
The Leading Hotels of the World

Plan. Map. Go.

TripTik® Travel Planner

Where premier mapping technology meets complete travel
information. Only on AAA.com and CAA.ca.

(See map & index p. 334.)

HÔTEL NELLIGAN

Hotel
$169-$1299

Phone: (514)788-2040 **23**

Address: 106 rue St-Paul ouest H2Y 1Z3 **Location:** Corner of rue St-Sulpice. **Facility:** Many luxury services are offered at this upscale Old Montreal hotel, which has large, stylish rooms with high-end furnishings, luxurious bedding and modern amenities. 105 units, some two bedrooms and efficiencies. 5 stories, interior corridors. **Parking:** valet and street only. **Terms:** cancellation fee imposed. **Amenities:** high-speed Internet, safes, honor bars. **Dining:** Méchant Boeuf Bar-Brasserie, Restaurant Verses, see separate listings. **Activities:** exercise room, massage. **Guest Services:** valet laundry, area transportation-downtown.

HÔTEL OMNI MONT-ROYAL

Hotel
$179-$279

Phone: (514)284-1110 **41**

Address: 1050 rue Sherbrooke ouest H3A 2R6 **Location:** Corner of rue Peel. **Facility:** Located in a fashionable area, this downtown hotel has an elegant lobby, large banquet halls and guest rooms with traditional décor and furnishings. 299 units. 31 stories, interior corridors. **Parking:** on-site and valet. **Terms:** cancellation fee imposed. **Amenities:** video games (fee), high-speed Internet, safes. **Pool(s):** heated outdoor. **Activities:** sauna, whirlpool, steamrooms, exercise room, spa. **Guest Services:** valet laundry.

HÔTEL PLACE D'ARMES

Historic Hotel
$199-$1500 6/1-10/31
$159-$600 11/1-5/31

Phone: (514)842-1887 **21**

Address: 55 rue St-Jacques Ouest H2Y 3X2 **Location:** Corner of Place d'Armes. Located in Old Montreal. **Facility:** Just a stone's throw from the Notre Dame Basilica, this restored hotel in scenic Old Montreal offers luxurious rooms, spacious suites and a posh spa. 133 units. 8 stories, interior corridors. **Parking:** valet only. **Terms:** cancellation fee imposed. **Amenities:** high-speed Internet, safes, honor bars. **Dining:** Aix Cuisine Du Terroir, see separate listing. **Activities:** steamroom, exercise room, spa. **Guest Services:** valet laundry, area transportation.

HOTEL ST-PAUL

Hotel
Rates not provided

Phone: 514/380-2222 **37**

Address: 355 rue St-Paul. **Location:** Corner of rue St-Paul. Located in Old Montreal. **Facility:** 120 units. 10 stories, interior corridors. **Parking:** valet and street only. **Amenities:** high-speed Internet. **Dining:** Restaurant Vauvert, see separate listing. **Activities:** exercise room. *Fee:* massage. **Guest Services:** valet laundry.

Get pet travel tips
and enter the photo contest
at AAA.com/PetBook

▼ See AAA listing p. 386 ▼

 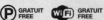

(See map & index p. 334.)

HOTEL TRAVELODGE MONTREAL CENTRE
Phone: (514)874-9090 **14**

Hotel
$76-$242

Address: 50 boul Rene-Levesque ouest H2Z 1A2 **Location:** Between rue Clark and St-Urbain. Located in Chinatown. **Facility:** 244 units, some efficiencies. 11 stories, interior corridors. **Parking:** on-site (fee). **Terms:** cancellation fee imposed. **Amenities:** high-speed Internet. *Some:* safes. **Guest Services:** valet laundry. **Free Special Amenities: expanded continental breakfast and high-speed Internet.**
(See ad opposite title page.)

HYATT REGENCY MONTREAL
Phone: (514)982-1234 **20**

Hotel
$89-$529

 **AAA Benefit:** Members save 10% or more everyday.

Address: 1255 Jeanne-Mance H5B 1E5 **Location:** Corner of rue Ste-Catherine. Adjacent to shopping mall. **Facility:** Well-appointed guest rooms range from standard units to business class to Regency class. Many overlook the Place des Arts concert hall and plaza. 605 units. 12 stories, interior corridors. **Parking:** on-site (fee) and valet. **Terms:** cancellation fee imposed. **Amenities:** video games (fee). *Some:* safes. **Pool(s):** heated indoor. **Activities:** sauna, steamroom, exercise room. *Fee:* massage. **Guest Services:** valet laundry. **Free Special Amenities: full breakfast.** *(See ad p. 349.)*

INTERCONTINENTAL MONTRÉAL
Phone: (514)987-9900 **32**

Hotel
$179-$289 6/1-10/25
$159-$229 10/26-5/31

Address: 360 rue St-Antoine ouest H2Y 3X4 **Location:** Corner of rue St-Pierre. Located in Old Montreal. **Facility:** This full-service hotel offers spacious guest rooms with custom-built furnishings, oversize flat-screen televisions and posh bedding. 357 units. 26 stories, interior corridors. **Parking:** on-site (fee) and valet. **Terms:** check-in 4 pm. **Amenities:** safes, honor bars. *Fee:* video games, high-speed Internet. **Dining:** Osco!, see separate listing. **Pool(s):** heated indoor. **Activities:** saunas, steamroom, exercise room. *Fee:* massage. **Guest Services:** valet laundry.
(See ad p. 366.)

L'APPARTEMENT HOTEL   **Phone:** (514)284-3634 **26**
Extended Stay Hotel
$127-$245 6/1-10/31
$115-$231 11/1-5/31

Address: 455 rue Sherbrooke ouest H3A 1B7 **Location:** Corner of rue Durocher. **Facility:** 126 kitchen units, some two bedrooms. 17 stories, interior corridors. **Parking:** on-site (fee). **Amenities:** high-speed Internet. **Pool(s):** heated indoor. **Activities:** saunas, exercise room. **Guest Services:** valet and coin laundry. **Free Special Amenities: expanded continental breakfast and high-speed Internet.**

LA TOUR BELVEDERE APARTMENT HOTEL
Phone: 514/935-9052 **60**

Extended Stay Hotel
Rates not provided

Address: 2175 boul de Maisonneuve ouest H3H 1L5 **Location:** Between Lambert-Closse and Chomedey. **Facility:** 150 kitchen units. 21 stories, interior corridors. **Parking:** on-site (fee) and street, winter plug-ins. **Amenities:** high-speed Internet (fee), safes. **Pool(s):** heated indoor. **Activities:** saunas, exercise room. **Guest Services:** valet and coin laundry.

LE CENTRE SHERATON
Phone: (514)878-2000 **48**

Hotel
$144-$699

⑤ Sheraton **AAA Benefit:** Members get up to 15% off, plus Starwood Preferred Guest® bonuses.

Address: 1201 boul Rene-Levesque ouest H3B 2L7 **Location:** Between rue Drummond and rue Stanley. **Facility:** This full-service high-rise hotel offers luxurious guest rooms, many with commanding views of the city; the conference facilities are extensive. 825 units. 37 stories, interior corridors. **Parking:** on-site (fee) and valet. **Terms:** cancellation fee imposed. **Amenities:** safes. *Fee:* video games, high-speed Internet. **Pool(s):** heated indoor. **Activities:** saunas, whirlpool, exercise room, spa. **Guest Services:** valet laundry. *(See ad p. 367.)*

LE MERIDIEN VERSAILLES-MONTREAL
Phone: (514)933-8111 **55**

Hotel
$149-$509

Le MERIDIEN **AAA Benefit:** Members get up to 15% off, plus Starwood Preferred Guest® bonuses.

Address: 1808 rue Sherbrooke ouest H3H 1E5 **Location:** Corner of rue St-Mathieu. **Facility:** 108 units. 14 stories, interior corridors. **Parking:** valet only. **Terms:** cancellation fee imposed. **Amenities:** video games (fee), high-speed Internet, safes, honor bars. **Activities:** exercise room. **Guest Services:** valet laundry. **Free Special Amenities: high-speed Internet.** *(See ad opposite title page.)*

LE NOUVEL HOTEL & SPA   **Phone:** (514)931-8841 **58**
Hotel
$109-$499

Address: 1740 boul Rene-Levesque ouest H3H 1R3 **Location:** Corner of rue St-Mathieu. **Facility:** 177 units, some efficiencies and kitchens. 8-12 stories, interior corridors. **Parking:** on-site (fee). **Terms:** cancellation fee imposed. **Amenities:** safes. **Pool(s):** heated outdoor. **Activities:** exercise room, spa. *Fee:* sauna, whirlpool, steamroom. **Guest Services:** valet and coin laundry, rental car service. **Free Special Amenities: high-speed Internet.**
(See ad opposite title page.)

▼ See AAA listing p. 365 ▼

▼ See AAA listing p. 365 ▼

Le Centre
Sheraton Montreal
HOTEL

Fun-Filled Getaways are Better when Shared

Sheraton is where families gather. Experience the completely renovated Le Centre Sheraton Montreal, located in the heart of downtown Montreal and just steps away from shopping, restaurants and the city's most popular attractions. AAA members enjoy up to 20% off published rates.

Scan with smartphone.
Save at Sheraton.

Book at Sheraton.com/lecentre or call 1 888 627 7102

Get the free mobile app at
http://gettag.mobi

spg.*
Starwood
Preferred
Guest

(See map & index p. 334.)

LE SAINT-SULPICE HÔTEL MONTRÉAL
Phone: (514)288-1000 **24**

Extended Stay
Hotel

$239-$539 6/1-10/31
$189-$349 11/1-5/31

Address: 414 rue St-Sulpice H2Y 2V5 **Location:** Just n of rue St-Paul. **Facility:** This hotel behind the Notre Dame Basilica offers studio and one- or two-bedroom suites as well as luxury services, an exercise room and fine dining. 108 efficiencies, some two bedrooms. 6 stories, interior corridors. **Parking:** valet and street only. **Terms:** cancellation fee imposed. **Amenities:** video games (fee), high-speed Internet, safes. **Activities:** *Fee:* massage. **Guest Services:** valet laundry. **Free Special Amenities: continental breakfast and high-speed Internet.**

SAVE ⊞ ⊞ ⊞ BIZ 🛜 ✕ FEE ⊞ ⊞ ⊞
⊞ / SOME UNITS FEE ⊞

LE SQUARE PHILLIPS HOTEL & SUITES
Phone: (514)393-1193 **34**

Extended Stay
Hotel

$145-$369

Address: 1193 Place Phillips H3B 3C9 **Location:** Between rue Ste-Catherine and boul Rene-Levesque. **Facility:** 160 kitchen units, some two bedrooms. 10 stories, interior corridors. **Parking:** valet only. **Terms:** cancellation fee imposed. **Amenities:** video games (fee), high-speed Internet. **Pool(s):** heated indoor. **Activities:** exercise room. **Guest Services:** valet and coin laundry. **Free Special Amenities: expanded continental breakfast and high-speed Internet.**
(See ad p. 369.)

SAVE ECO ⊞ ⊟ BIZ 🛜
FEE ⊞ ⊞ ⊞ ⊞ / SOME UNITS ⊞

LE ST-MARTIN CENTRE-VILLE HÔTEL PARTICULIER
Phone: (514)843-3000 **39**

Boutique Hotel

$175-$535

Address: 980 boul de Maisonneuve ouest H3A 1M5 **Location:** Corner of rue Metcalfe. **Facility:** This luxurious property features stylish rooms with impressive urban views, crown molding, excellent bedding and bathrooms with granite countertops. 123 units. 15 stories, interior corridors. **Parking:** valet only. **Amenities:** high-speed Internet, safes, honor bars. **Pool(s):** heated outdoor. **Activities:** exercise room. *Fee:* massage. **Guest Services:** valet laundry. **Free Special Amenities:** local telephone calls and high-speed Internet.
(See ad p. 370.)

SAVE ⊞ ⊞ CALL ⊞ ⊞ 🛜 ✕ FEE ⊞ ⊞
/ SOME UNITS ⊞

Learn about
AAA/CAA Diamond Ratings
at AAA.com/Diamonds

LE WESTIN MONTRÉAL
Phone: (514)380-3333 **31**

Hotel

$159-$329

WESTIN HOTELS & RESORTS **AAA Benefit:** Enjoy up to 15% off your next stay, plus Starwood Preferred Guest® bonuses.

Address: 270 rue St-Antoine ouest H2Y 0A3 **Location:** In Old Montreal. **Facility:** Overlooking the Palais des Congrès Convention Centre, the luxury hotel has stylish and spacious guest rooms with ultra-comfortable beds. 454 units, some two bedrooms. 8-22 stories, interior corridors. **Parking:** valet only. **Terms:** cancellation fee imposed. **Amenities:** high-speed Internet (fee), safes. **Dining:** Gazette, see separate listing. **Pool(s):** heated indoor. **Activities:** sauna, exercise room. *Fee:* massage. **Guest Services:** valet laundry. **Free Special Amenities: newspaper and high-speed Internet.**

SAVE ⊞ ⊞ CALL ⊞M ⊞ BIZ 🛜 ✕ FEE ⊞
⊞ ⊞ / SOME UNITS FEE ⊞ ⊞

LHOTEL
Phone: (514)985-0019 **30**

Hotel

$195-$485 6/1-10/31
$140-$305 11/1-5/31

Address: 262 rue St-Jacques ouest H2Y 1N1 **Location:** Between rue St-Jean and St-Pierre. Located in Old Montreal. **Facility:** 59 units. 4 stories, interior corridors. **Parking:** valet only. **Terms:** cancellation fee imposed. **Amenities:** safes. **Activities:** exercise room. *Fee:* massage. **Guest Services:** valet laundry.

⊞ BIZ 🛜 ✕ FEE ⊞ / SOME UNITS ⊞

LOEWS HÔTEL VOGUE
Phone: (514)285-5555 **50**

Hotel

$152-$764

Address: 1425 de la Montagne H3G 1Z3 **Location:** Between rue Ste-Catherine and boul de Maisonneuve. **Facility:** Marble-tiled bathrooms with a separate shower stall add an elegant touch to accommodations at this hotel in the heart of downtown. 142 units, some kitchens. 9 stories, interior corridors. **Parking:** valet and street only. **Terms:** cancellation fee imposed. **Amenities:** high-speed Internet (fee), safes, honor bars. **Activities:** exercise room. *Fee:* massage. **Guest Services:** valet laundry. **Free Special Amenities:** newspaper and high-speed Internet.
(See ad p. 371.)

SAVE ⊞ ⊞ ⊞ BIZ 🛜 FEE ⊞ ⊞
/ SOME UNITS FEE ⊞ ⊞ ⊞

MARRIOTT MONTRÉAL CHÂTEAU CHAMPLAIN
Phone: (514)878-9000 **47**

Hotel

$159-$599

Marriott HOTELS & RESORTS **AAA Benefit:** AAA hotel discounts of 5% or more.

Address: 1050 de la Gauchetiere W H3B 4C9 **Location:** Corner of rue Peel. **Facility:** Very good-size rooms feature upscale bedding and mattresses, and bathrooms with marble floors and tub walls. Some also feature a roll-out desk. 611 units, some two and three bedrooms. 36 stories, interior corridors. **Parking:** on-site and valet. **Amenities:** honor bars. *Some:* high-speed Internet. **Pool(s):** heated indoor. **Activities:** saunas, whirlpool, steamrooms, exercise room, spa. **Guest Services:** valet laundry. **Free Special Amenities:** newspaper and high-speed Internet.

SAVE ECO ⊞ ⊞ ⊞ ⊞ BIZ 🛜 ✕ FEE ⊞
⊞ / SOME UNITS ⊞

(See map & index p. 334.)

▼ See AAA listing p. 368 ▼

TourBook Comments

Are we meeting your travel needs?

If your visit to an establishment listed in a AAA TourBook guide doesn't meet your expectations, tell us about it.

Complete an easy online form at
AAA.com/TourBookComments.

(See map & index p. 334.)

MARRIOTT SPRINGHILL SUITES
Phone: (514)875-4333 16

Hotel
$134-$209

AAA Benefit:
AAA hotel discounts of 5% or more.

Address: 445 rue St-Jean-Baptiste H2Y 2Z7 **Location:** Jct St Laurent Blvd and Notre-Dame, just se. **Facility:** 124 units. 6 stories, interior corridors. **Parking:** valet only. **Amenities:** video games (fee), high-speed Internet. **Pool(s):** heated indoor. **Activities:** whirlpool, exercise room, spa. **Guest Services:** valet and coin laundry.

NEW RESIDENCE HALL/MCGILL UNIVERSITY
Phone: (514)398-5200 15

Hotel
$89-$149

Address: 3625 ave du Parc H2X 3P8 **Location:** Corner of rue Prince-Arthur. **Facility:** 421 units. 15 stories, interior corridors. **Parking:** on-site (fee). **Terms:** open 6/1-8/15 & 5/15-5/31, cancellation fee imposed. **Amenities:** high-speed Internet. **Guest Services:** coin laundry. **Free Special Amenities:** continental breakfast and local telephone calls.

NOVOTEL MONTREAL CENTRE
Phone: (514)861-6000 52

Hotel
$119-$499

Address: 1180 rue de la Montagne H3G 1Z1 **Location:** Between rue Ste-Catherine and boul Rene-Levesque. **Facility:** 227 units. 9 stories, interior corridors. **Parking:** on-site (fee). **Amenities:** video games (fee), high-speed Internet, safes, honor bars. **Dining:** L'Ô sur la Montagne, see separate listing. **Activities:** exercise room. **Guest Services:** valet laundry. (See ad p. 372.)

OPUS HOTEL MONTREAL
Phone: 514/843-6000 11

Hotel
Rates not provided

Address: 10 rue Sherbrooke ouest H2X 4C9 **Location:** Corner of boul St-Laurent. **Facility:** 136 units, some efficiencies. 5 stories, interior corridors. **Parking:** valet only. **Amenities:** safes, honor bars. **Fee:** video games, high-speed Internet. **Dining:** Koko Restaurant, see separate listing, nightclub. **Activities:** exercise room. **Fee:** massage. **Guest Services:** valet laundry.

PARC SUITES HOTEL
Phone: 514/985-5656 17

Extended Stay Hotel
Rates not provided

Address: 3463 ave du Parc H2X 2H6 **Location:** Between rue Sherbrooke and Milton. **Facility:** 8 kitchen units. 3 stories (no elevator), interior corridors. **Amenities:** high-speed Internet. **Guest Services:** valet laundry.

Simply Reliable

The Diamond Ratings in this TourBook guide are backed by our expert, in-person evaluations, whether the hotel or restaurant is no-frills, moderate or upscale.

Learn more at **AAA.com/Diamonds**

▼ See AAA listing p. 368 ▼

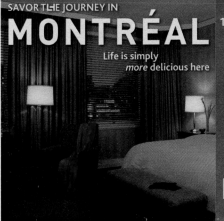

(See map & index p. 334.)

Share a New View on Travel at
AAATravelViews.com
Read stories, tips and trends from AAA insiders.
Post comments and get your questions answered by our
travel experts.

(See map & index p. 334.)

▼ See AAA listing p. 374 ▼

▼ See AAA listing p. 375 ▼

Explore the Travel Guides on AAA.com/Travel or CAA.ca/Travel

(See map & index p. 334.)

QUALITY HOTEL DOWNTOWN MONTREAL
Phone: (514)849-1413 **19**

Hotel
$89-$365

Address: 3440 ave du Parc H2X 2H5 **Location:** Between rue Sherbrooke and Milton. **Facility:** 138 units. 8 stories, interior corridors. **Parking:** on-site (fee). **Terms:** cancellation fee imposed. **Amenities:** high-speed Internet. **Guest Services:** valet laundry.

SAVE ECO [icons] FEE [icons]
/ SOME UNITS FEE [icons]

▼ See AAA listing this page ▼

RESIDENCE INN BY MARRIOTT MONTREAL-DOWNTOWN
Phone: (514)982-6064 **43**

Extended Stay
$169-$229

AAA Benefit: AAA hotel discounts of 5% or more.

Address: 2045 rue Peel H3A 1T6 **Location:** Between rue Sherbrooke and boul de Maisonneuve. **Facility:** 190 units, some efficiencies and kitchens. 24 stories, interior corridors. **Parking:** on-site (fee). **Amenities:** video games (fee), high-speed Internet. **Activities:** exercise room. **Guest Services:** valet and coin laundry. **Free Special Amenities: full breakfast and high-speed Internet.** *(See ad p. 373.)*

SAVE ECO [icons] BIZ [icons] FEE [icons]
[icons] / SOME UNITS FEE [icons]

RESIDENCE INN BY MARRIOTT MONTREAL WESTMOUNT
Phone: (514)935-9224 **61**

Extended Stay
Hotel
$179-$199

AAA Benefit: AAA hotel discounts of 5% or more.

Address: 2170 Lincoln Ave H3H 2N5 **Location:** Just e of rue Atwater. **Facility:** 220 units, some two bedrooms, efficiencies and kitchens. 19 stories, interior corridors. **Parking:** on-site (fee) and street. **Amenities:** high-speed Internet. **Pool(s):** heated indoor. **Activities:** saunas, exercise room. **Guest Services:** valet and coin laundry. **Free Special Amenities: full breakfast and high-speed Internet.**

SAVE ECO [icons] CALL [icons] BIZ [icons] FEE [icons]
[icons] / SOME UNITS FEE [icons]

THE RITZ-CARLTON MONTREAL   Phone: 514/842-4212

(fyi)
Classic Historic
Hotel
Rates not provided

Too new to rate, opening scheduled for February 2012. **Address:** 1228 rue Sherbrooke ouest H3G 1H6 **Location:** Corner de la Montagne. **Amenities:** 130 units, pets, restaurant, coffeemakers, pool, exercise facility.

SOFITEL MONTRÉAL LE CARRÉ DORÉ
Phone: (514)285-9000 **45**

Hotel
$180-$350

Address: 1155 rue Sherbrooke ouest H3A 2N3 **Location:** Corner of rue Stanley. **Facility:** Featuring a luxurious lobby, this contemporary hotel offers accommodations with excellent duvets, modern amenities and elegant bathrooms. 258 units. 16 stories, interior corridors. **Parking:** valet and street only. **Terms:** 3 day cancellation notice-fee imposed. **Amenities:** safes, honor bars. *Fee:* video games, high-speed Internet. **Dining:** Renoir, see separate listing. **Activities:** sauna, exercise room. **Guest Services:** valet laundry. **Free Special Amenities: early check-in/late check-out and high-speed Internet.** *(See ad this page.)*

SAVE ECO [icons] BIZ [icons] FEE [icons]
/ SOME UNITS [icons]

(See map & index p. 334.)

WHERE TO EAT

3 AMIGOS RESTO-BAR   Phone: 514/939-3329   [117]

Mexican
$7-$20

AAA Inspector Notes: The lively restaurant and pub specializes in affordable Mexican and Tex-Mex dishes, including burritos, tacos and fajitas in chicken, lamb, beef and vegetarian varieties. Daily specials also are prepared. Celebrity caricatures adorn a colorful wall mural. **Bar:** full bar. **Address:** 1657 Ste-Catherine ouest H3H 1L9 **Location:** Just e of rue St-Mathieu. **Parking:** street only. [L] [D]

AIX CUISINE DU TERROIR   Phone: 514/904-1201   [44]

French
$18-$39

AAA Inspector Notes: In a chic boutique hotel in Old Montreal, the fashionable restaurant specializes in "cuisine du terroir": dishes prepared with fresh regional produce such as salmon, foie gras, game and Angus beef. High-quality Quebec cheeses and desserts flavored with local maple syrup and Valrhona chocolate round out the menu. **Bar:** full bar. **Address:** 711 Cote de la Place d'Armes H2Y 2X6 **Location:** Corner of rue St-Jacques; in Hôtel Place d'Armes. **Parking:** valet and street only. [L] [D]

ALPENHAUS RESTAURANT
Phone: 514/935-2285   [119]

Swiss
$18-$35

AAA Inspector Notes: Swiss and European specialties include bourguignonne, Swiss cheese or Chinese fondue, sausage, Wiener schnitzel and veal dishes. The cozy mountain lodge decor, which incorporates a fireplace, adds to the ambience. A pianist performs most Friday to Sunday evenings. **Bar:** full bar. **Reservations:** suggested. **Address:** 1279 rue St-Marc H3H 2E8 **Location:** Corner of Ste-Catherine. **Parking:** street only. [D]

AU BISTRO GOURMET   Phone: 514/846-1553   [115]

French
$11-$35

AAA Inspector Notes: In a restored graystone building, the cozy and casual restaurant serves fine French cuisine at affordable prices. Among specialties are preparations of lamb, fresh fish, veal liver, poultry and kidneys. For those with a sweet tooth, a table of desserts awaits. **Bar:** full bar. **Address:** 2100 rue St-Mathieu H3H 2J4 **Location:** Between boul de Maisonneuve and ave Lincoln. **Parking:** street only. [L] [D]

BAR B BARN   Phone: 514/931-3811

Barbecue
$9-$25

AAA Inspector Notes: Rustic barn wood adorns the walls of the family restaurant. Specialties include slow-roasted chicken and pork ribs, as well as the popular ribs-and-chicken combination dish. **Bar:** full bar. **Address:** 1201 rue Guy H3H 2K5 **Location:** Between boul Rene-Levesque and rue Ste-Catherine. [L] [D]

BATON ROUGE   Phone: 514/931-9969

American
$11-$35

AAA Inspector Notes: This one offers an intimate setting with a casual steakhouse ambiance. Offerings include their signature BBQ pork ribs, fresh grilled fish, chicken, meal-sized salads, pasta, burgers and sandwiches. But the main attraction remains the aged AAA grade steaks and the slow-roasted prime rib of beef. **Bar:** full bar. **Reservations:** required. **Address:** 1050 rue de la Montagne H3G 1Y8 **Location:** Just s of boul Rene-Levesque. **Parking:** on-site (fee). [L] [D]

THE BEAVER CLUB
Menu on AAA.com   Phone: 514/861-3511   [79]

French
$28-$48

AAA Inspector Notes: This city landmark boasts an international menu that dabbles in Canadian and French cuisine. Enjoy such expertly prepared dishes as pan-seared foie gras, grilled game meats, beef Wellington, Dover sole, milk-fed veal, rack of piglet, Chateaubriand for two, beef Diane and roast prime rib. Service is professional and tableside preparations are available for a few dishes. **Bar:** full bar. **Reservations:** suggested. **Address:** 900 boul Rene-Levesque ouest H3B 4A5 **Location:** Between rue University and Mansfield; in Fairmont The Queen Elizabeth. **Parking:** on-site (fee) and valet. [D]

BICE RISTORANTE   Phone: 514/937-6009   [111]

Italian
$26-$48

AAA Inspector Notes: This fashionable restaurant prepares excellent pasta dishes, chicken and fresh seafood, including delicious octopus. Youthful servers are polite and refined. May be closed on Sundays after the summer. **Bar:** full bar. **Reservations:** suggested. **Address:** 1504 rue Sherbrooke ouest H3G 1L3 **Location:** Just e of rue Guy. **Parking:** valet only. [D]

BISHOKU JAPANESE RESTAURANT
Phone: 514/876-0056   [112]

Japanese
$10-$30

AAA Inspector Notes: Japanese cuisine can be savored at tables or at this sushi bar. Sushi specialties include sushi pizza, shrimp tempura, salmon with avocado and fried soft-shelled crab. Also offered are a dozen sashimi selections. Sushi-sashimi combination platters lay out a good variety. **Bar:** full bar. **Address:** 1184 rue Bishop H3G 2E3 **Location:** Between Ste-Catherine and boul Rene-Levesque. **Parking:** street only. [L] [D]

BONAPARTE   Phone: 514/844-4368   [51]

French
$16-$36

AAA Inspector Notes: This lively and sophisticated dining room presents a varied menu of innovative French-influenced dishes, including mushroom ravioli in butter cream sauce with sage, lobster stew flavored with vanilla, beef tartare, rack of lamb in a port wine sauce and wild boar marinated in red wine. The service is refined and the lemon meringue pie is divine. **Bar:** full bar. **Reservations:** suggested. **Address:** 447 rue St-Francois Xavier H2Y 2T1 **Location:** Just n of rue St-Paul; in Auberge Bonaparte. **Parking:** street only. **Historic** [L] [D]

(See map & index p. 334.)

BORIS BISTRO   Phone: 514/848-9575   69

French
$17-$24

AAA Inspector Notes: This bustling bistro features live Brazilian music some nights. The interesting menu includes the house specialty: duck (duck sandwich, duck confit, duck risotto), as well as grilled trout, cold beet soup, pasta, beef or tuna tartare, steak and fries. The seasonal terrace is a popular spot in summer. **Bar:** full bar. **Reservations:** required. **Address:** 465 rue McGill H2Y 2H1 **Location:** Just n of rue St-Paul. **Parking:** street only.

[L] [D]

BRASSERIE T!   Phone: 514/282-0808   43

French
$17-$25

AAA Inspector Notes: Diners can expect upscale bistro fare at this casual, sidewalk atrium eatery, adjacent to a museum and concert hall. This hopping spot during the summer festival season offers upscale bistro fare with a variety of excellent ingredients. The menu is music to your mouth-pan-fried foie gras, onion soup, beef or salmon tartar, venison terrine, fresh oysters, pork ribs, gourmet burger and fries, flank steak, croque monsieur and coquille St-Jacques. **Bar:** full bar. **Reservations:** required. **Address:** 1425 rue Jeanne-Mance H2X 2J4 **Location:** Corner of rue Ste-Catherine. **Parking:** street only.

[L] [D]

BRISKETS MONTREAL/SALON KRAUSMANN
          Phone: 514/878-3641   66

Canadian
$8-$17

AAA Inspector Notes: This lively, downtown restaurant and tavern offers something for everyone, including Montreal-style smoked meat on rye, pigs' knuckles, pasta, hamburgers, subs, chicken, beef liver, sausages, poutine, steaks, bagel and lox, club sandwiches, club rolls, soup and salad. **Bar:** full bar. **Address:** 1093 Beaver Hall Hill H2Z 1S5 **Location:** Just s of boul Rene-Levesque. **Parking:** street only. [B] [L] [D]

BRIT & CHIPS   Phone: 514/840-1001   70

English
$8-$15

AAA Inspector Notes: This casual diner is a great place to enjoy a golden and crispy fish and chips dinner. A variety of fish is available, including haddock, cod, salmon and hake. The fish batter varies from one selection to the next, including flavorings of beer, maple syrup, Guinness and orange Crush. The menu has other British favorites like steak and ale pie and pasties (a pastry turnover stuffed with meat and vegetables). Watch the chalkboard menu for the deep-fried anything specials. **Bar:** beer & wine. **Address:** 433 rue McGill H2Y 2H1 **Location:** Just n of rue St-Paul ouest. **Parking:** street only.

[L] [D]

BUONANOTTE   Phone: 514/848-0644   20

Italian
$17-$49

AAA Inspector Notes: This lively, upscale nightclub, lounge and restaurant is popular with locals and visiting celebrities. The menu of fine Italian cuisine is served at elegant tables, most of which overlook the vibrant St-Laurent boulevard. A live deejay spins dance tunes some evenings as the stylishly dressed, youthful clientele enjoy shimmering contemporary decor. **Bar:** full bar. **Address:** 3518 boul St-Laurent H2X 2V2 **Location:** Just n of rue Sherbrooke. **Parking:** valet and street only.

[L] [D]

CAFÉ HOLT   Phone: 514/282-3750   95

Coffee/Tea
$17-$22

AAA Inspector Notes: The stylish cafe and sandwich shop is at street level in the Holt-Renfrew luxury department store. The specialty is "tartine-style" open-faced sandwiches prepared with gourmet ingredients, including pricey imported Poilane bread baked daily in Paris and flown in. Patrons also enjoy tasty salads, specialty coffees, freshly squeezed juices, martinis and a choice of delicious desserts, a few of which are prepared with the gourmet Poilane bread. **Bar:** full bar. **Address:** 1300 rue Sherbrooke ouest H3G 1H9 **Location:** Corner of de la Montagne; in Holt-Renfrew. **Parking:** street only.

[L] [D]

CAFÉ REPUBLIQUE RESTAURANT BAR
          Phone: 514/875-1200   90

French
$13-$29

AAA Inspector Notes: This trendy, downtown bistro offers steak, salad, pasta, grilled sandwiches, fish and some seafood dishes. **Bar:** full bar. **Reservations:** suggested. **Address:** 1200 rue Peel H2B 2T6 **Location:** Between rue Ste-Catherine and boul Rene-Levesque. **Parking:** street only. [L] [D] [LATE]

CAFÉ SANTROPOL   Phone: 514/842-3110   17

Coffee/Tea
$8-$13

AAA Inspector Notes: This lively, eclectic café offers health-conscious meals, such as gourmet sandwiches, vegetarian chili, fruit juices, creative desserts and a wide variety of quality teas and fair-trade organic coffees. A seasonal garden terrace also is provided. **Address:** 3990 rue St-Urbain H2W 1T7 **Location:** Corner of rue Duluth. **Parking:** street only. [B] [L] [D]

CAGE AUX SPORTS   Phone: 514/878-2243

Canadian
$8-$22

AAA Inspector Notes: This popular Quebec chain of sports bars presents a menu of pub foods, including ribs, chicken, burgers, salads, crispy fries, pasta and tasty desserts. Guests might begin the meal with a basket of freshly popped popcorn as they check out the sports memorabilia. Children are welcomed. **Bar:** full bar. **Reservations:** suggested. **Address:** 1437 boul Rene-Levesque H3G 1T7 **Location:** Just w of rue Crescent.

[L] [D]

CARLOS AND PEPES   Phone: 514/288-3090   88

Mexican
$7-$19

AAA Inspector Notes: The lively restaurant and bar lures guests with inexpensive food and a popular happy hour. Daily specials are affordable. **Bar:** full bar. **Address:** 1420 rue Peel H3A 1S8 **Location:** Between boul de Maisonneuve and rue Ste-Catherine. **Parking:** street only.

[L] [D]

CASA DE MATEO   Phone: 514/844-7448   52

Mexican
$15-$23

AAA Inspector Notes: Ceramic suns and tiles, blown glassware and weekend live music lend to the restaurant's upbeat mood. Grilled fish and homemade enchiladas stand out on a menu of traditional Mexican fare. **Bar:** full bar. **Address:** 438 rue St-Francois Xavier H2Y 2T3 **Location:** Just s of rue Notre-Dame; in Old Montreal. **Parking:** street only. [L] [D]

(See map & index p. 334.)

CAVALLI RISTORANTE-BAR

Phone: 514/843-5100 (81)

Italian
$26-$44

AAA Inspector Notes: The popular and stylish bar area-back-lit with hot pink panels-sets the tone for this bustling and upscale Italian bistro. The youthful servers are well attired and proficient. The menu features fine Italian and Mediterranean cuisine with a strong focus on pasta and the freshest of fish and seafood. Dessert presentations are excellent. **Bar:** full bar. **Address:** 2042 rue Peel H3A 2R4 **Location:** Just n of boul de Maisonneuve. **Parking:** street only. [L] [D]

CHEZ CHINE

Phone: 514/878-9888 (38)

Chinese
$10-$45

AAA Inspector Notes: A full-size Chinese pagoda is the centerpiece of the elegant hotel dining room, set around a soothing goldfish pond. Fine Chinese cuisine is at the heart of a menu that also includes buffet, luncheons and a limited selection of Continental dishes. Smartly attired servers are attentive. **Bar:** full bar. **Address:** 99 ave Viger ouest H2Z 1E9 **Location:** Corner of rue St-Urbain; in Holiday Inn Select Montreal Centre-Ville Downtown. **Parking:** on-site (fee). [B] [L] [D]

CHEZ CORA

Phone: 514/286-6171

Canadian
$6-$13

AAA Inspector Notes: Eggs, omelets, waffles, crepes (sorry, no American-style pancakes here), French toast, fruit platters and all the breakfast meats--that's the specialty here, all day. However, at lunchtime the menu lists a selection of soups, salads, quiches, sandwiches and a dish called the grilled panini crepe. **Address:** 1240 rue Drummond H3A 1P4 **Location:** Between rue Ste-Catherine and boul Rene-Levesque; in Best Western Plus Europa-Downtown. **Parking:** street only. [B] [L]

CHEZ GAUTIER

Phone: 514/845-1245 (39)

French
$10-$35

AAA Inspector Notes: The lovely French bistro specializes in such classics as steak tartare, blood sausage ("boudin noir"), veal liver, "bavette" of beef, rib steak and fries, salads, burgers and fresh fish. After eating, guests can stroll into the Belgian-style bakery for take-out delicacies. **Bar:** full bar. **Reservations:** suggested. **Address:** 3487 ave du Parc H2X 2H6 **Location:** Corner of rue Milton. **Parking:** valet and street only.

[B] [L] [D]

CHEZ LA MERE MICHEL

Phone: 514/934-0473 (114)

Traditional French
$26-$40

AAA Inspector Notes: This long-established restaurant delivers fine, classic French cuisine served by a knowledgeable, tuxedoed staff. Country accents lend to the formality of the dining rooms. Food preparations are complex, creative and splashed with interesting color. **Bar:** full bar. **Reservations:** suggested. **Address:** 1209 rue Guy H3H 2K5 **Location:** Between boul Rene-Levesque and rue Ste-Catherine. **Parking:** street only. [D]

CHEZ L'ÉPICIER RESTAURANT BAR À VIN

Phone: 514/878-2232 (25)

French
$14-$40

AAA Inspector Notes: French and Asian influences give comfort foods a new twist at this casually elegant, stone-walled Old Montreal eatery and wine bar. Menus are printed on paper bags, and water is served from milk bottles. The menu of fine cuisine may include selections such as Arctic char, milk-fed veal carpaccio, snail shepherd's pie and Parmesan oil ravioli. Specialty gourmet items, cheeses, sauces, oils and sorbets can be purchased. The 2,000-bottle cellar includes many private imports and specialty wines. **Bar:** full bar. **Address:** 311 rue St-Paul est H2Y 1H3 **Location:** Just w of rue Bonsecours; facing Bonsecours Market in Old Montreal. **Parking:** street only. [L] [D]

CHEZ QUEUX

Phone: 514/866-5194 (31)

French
$25-$36

AAA Inspector Notes: In a historic 1862 stone building, the restaurant is quaint and sophisticated, with original stone walls, wood paneling and wood-beam ceilings. Flambés prepared tableside, rack of lamb, scampi, sweetbreads, fresh fish and seafood are representative of menu selections. Service is professional. **Bar:** full bar. **Reservations:** suggested. **Address:** 158 rue St-Paul est H2Y 1G6 **Location:** Corner of St-Paul est and Place Jacques-Cartier. **Parking:** street only. **Historic** [D]

COCO RICO

Phone: 514/849-5554 (15)

Portuguese
$6-$10

AAA Inspector Notes: Halfway down the block, the undeniable aroma of rotisserie-roasted chicken provides a strong hint that this simple diner is nearby. Patrons may also enjoy ribs, sandwiches and fries. **Address:** 3907 boul St-Laurent H2W 1X9 **Location:** Just n of rue Roy. **Parking:** street only. [B] [L] [D]

COMMENSAL VEGETARIAN RESTAURANT

Vegetarian
$8-$14

For additional information, visit AAA.com

AAA Inspector Notes: An upscale self-service buffet features an extensive selection of creative hot and cold items, such as leek pot pie, sweet potato kasha and lasagna, plus a variety of desserts, everything of which is exclusively vegetarian. The pleasant, contemporary surroundings change often as new paintings are displayed. **Bar:** beer & wine. [L] [D]

LOCATIONS:
Address: 1204 ave McGill College H3B 4J8 **Location:** Corner of rue Ste-Catherine. **Phone:** 514/871-1480

Address: 1720 rue St-Denis H2X 3K8 **Location:** Just s of rue Ontario. **Phone:** 514/845-2627 (13)

CRÊPERIE CHEZ SUZETTE

Phone: 514/874-1984 (41)

French
$9-$27

AAA Inspector Notes: This charming creperie overlooks a scenic Old Montreal street and serves a variety of 30 freshly prepared crepes, Chinese and cheese fondues, as well as sandwiches. For dessert, try a fruit crepe. The wine list is affordable as there is only a minimal mark-up above the restaurant's purchase price. **Bar:** full bar. **Reservations:** suggested. **Address:** 3 rue St-Paul est H2Y 1E9 **Location:** Just e of boul St-Laurent. **Parking:** street only. [L] [D]

DECCA 77 RESTAURANT

Phone: 514/934-1077 (100)

French
$18-$45

AAA Inspector Notes: A short walk from the Bell Centre arena, the stylish and upscale restaurant has a posh lounge area. The menu features market-fresh cuisine, including foie gras torchon, grilled beef strip, roasted guinea hen, pasta, lobster, fresh fish and game specialties. The wine list is impressive. **Bar:** full bar. **Reservations:** suggested. **Address:** 1077 rue Drummond H3B 4X4 **Location:** Corner of boul Rene-Levesque. **Parking:** valet and street only. [L] [D]

DEER GARDEN JARDIN DU CERF

Phone: 514/861-1056 (30)

Chinese
$7-$14

AAA Inspector Notes: Great food at low prices is what patrons of the simple Chinatown diner can expect. The menu lists Cantonese, Szechuan and Thai specialties. The wide variety of dishes includes noodles, rice, soups, seafood and poultry. Bring your own wine or beer. No credit cards accepted. **Address:** 1162 boul St-Laurent H2X 2S5 **Location:** Just n of boul Rene-Levesque. **Parking:** street only. [L] [D]

(See map & index p. 334.)

DUNNS FAMOUS DELICATESSEN
Phone: 514/395-1927 (84)

Deli
$11–$24

AAA Inspector Notes: This traditional deli specializes in Montreal-style smoked meat on rye, grilled steaks, latkes, chopped liver and club rolls. For dessert, try the cheesecake. **Bar:** full bar. **Reservations:** required. **Address:** 1249 rue Metcalfe H3B 2V5 **Location:** Just s of rue Ste-Catherine. **Parking:** street only.

B L D 24

EGGSPECTATION
Phone: 514/842-3447

Canadian
$7–$15

AAA Inspector Notes: The menu lists dozens of all-day breakfast possibilities, including eggs in a bagel, Bretonne-style crepes, eggs Benedict, pancakes, French toast and waffles. Salads, burgers, sandwiches, pasta, chicken, fish and steak, as well as specialty coffees and a variety of freshly squeezed juices, round out the offerings. **Bar:** full bar. **Address:** 1313 boul de Maisonneuve ouest H3G 2R9 **Location:** Corner of rue de la Montagne. **Parking:** street only. B L

EL GITANO
Phone: 514/843-8212 (37)

Spanish
$13–$32

AAA Inspector Notes: This informal Mediterranean-style restaurant specializes in Spanish and Portuguese food, including almost a dozen varieties of paella. Pasta, steak, seafood and fresh fish also are featured along with live Flamenco dancers on Saturday evenings beginning at 8:30 pm. **Bar:** full bar. **Address:** 3507 ave du Parc H2X 2H8 **Location:** Between rue Prince-Arthur and Milton. **Parking:** street only. L D

FERREIRA CAFÉ
Phone: 514/848-0988 (87)

Portuguese
$24–$40

AAA Inspector Notes: This upscale Portuguese bistro offers great food, a lively atmosphere and refined service. Menu specialties include grilled sardines, filet mignon, oysters, fresh fish, calamari, poached salmon and rack of lamb. An excellent variety of ports is featured. **Reservations:** suggested. **Address:** 1446 rue Peel H4K 1Y2 **Location:** Between boul de Maisonneuve and rue Ste-Catherine. **Parking:** street only. L D

FOURQUET FOURCHETTE DU PALAIS
Phone: 514/789-6370 (50)

Quebec
$12–$34

AAA Inspector Notes: This relaxed family restaurant, located in a contemporary steel and glass convention center, is furnished in decor typical of early settler dwellings. Traditional New France cuisine can be sampled from an a la carte menu that features seafood, game, meat and chicken delicacies. Micro-brewery beers are incorporated into some dishes. Restaurant hours may vary depending upon convention center events. **Bar:** full bar. **Address:** 265 rue St-Antoine ouest H2Z 1H5 **Location:** Corner of rue de Bleury. **Parking:** on-site (fee). L D

GALIANO'S PASTA & BAR
Phone: 514/861-5039 (32)

Italian
$11–$32

AAA Inspector Notes: Italian cuisine is served in the casual, stone-walled dining room in historic Old Montreal. **Bar:** full bar. **Address:** 410 rue St-Vincent H2Y 3A5 **Location:** Just n of rue St-Paul est. **Parking:** street only.

L D

GAZETTE
Phone: 514/380-3333 (53)

Continental
$16–$29

AAA Inspector Notes: This stylishly appointed restaurant and bar faces the Palais des Congrès Convention Centre. The restaurant takes its name from the Montreal daily newspaper that once occupied the hotel's main building. The menu features market-fresh cuisine with regional influences and just enough lighter pub fare, like a large steak sandwich, to satisfy the bar and lunch crowd. The dinner menu includes such items as Atlantic cod, lamb shank, Quebec pork, seafood pasta, Angus beef and duck confit. **Bar:** full bar. **Reservations:** suggested. **Address:** 270 rue St-Antoine ouest H2Y 0A3 **Location:** In Old Montreal; in Le Westin Montréal. **Parking:** valet only.

B L D CALL ⌂M

GIBBY'S
Phone: 514/282-1837 (62)

Steak
$28–$48

AAA Inspector Notes: Home-smoked salmon and rack of lamb stand out on a menu of mostly tried-and-true steak, fresh fish and other seafood preparations, which are served in ample portions. Desserts--such as tart Key lime pie, cheesecake and crème brûlée--are delightful. The garden terrace offers seasonal seating. **Reservations:** suggested. **Address:** 298 Place d'Youville H2Y 2B6 **Location:** Just e of rue McGill; in Old Montreal. **Parking:** valet and street only. **Historic** D

GLOBE RESTAURANT
Phone: 514/284-3823 (22)

International
$16–$38

AAA Inspector Notes: This glamorous restaurant supplies its youthful clientele with a steady diet of fine international cuisine. The diverse menu includes excellent seafood platters, duck confit, pasta, braised lamb burgers, beef short ribs, rib steak, sashimi, lobster salad and grilled quail. Pick up a cool vibe here on a hot summer night, but reserve early. **Bar:** full bar. **Reservations:** suggested. **Address:** 3455 boul St-Laurent H2X 2T6 **Location:** Just s of Prince-Arthur. **Parking:** valet and street only. D

GUIDO & ANGELINA
Phone: 514/393-3808 (68)

Italian
$11–$35

AAA Inspector Notes: Twenty choices of fresh pasta stand out among this restaurant's affordable choices, including seafood platters, steaks, pork, lamb chops, memorable strawberry cheesecake and 10 choices of thin-crust pizza. The lively, informal setting owes to the prime downtown location. A wide variety of specialty cocktails are offered along with a decent wine list offering several selections by the glass. **Bar:** full bar. **Address:** 690 rue Ste-Catherine ouest H3B 1B9 **Location:** Between ave McGill-College and rue University. **Parking:** street only. L D

HOLDER RESTAURANT-BAR
Phone: 514/849-0333 (71)

French
$16–$32

AAA Inspector Notes: The spirited Old Montreal bistro has high ceilings, copper-toned walls, tall pillars and colorful light fixtures. Guests dine casually on such choices as tartares, oxtail shepherd's pie, veal, liver, osso buco, fish and chips, clams, mussels and pasta. Sugar pie is a good dessert option. **Bar:** full bar. **Address:** 407 rue McGill H2Y 2G3 **Location:** Just n of rue St-Paul. **Parking:** street only. L D

(See map & index p. 334.)

HOUSE OF JAZZ/MAISON DE JAZZ
Phone: 514/842-8656   55

American
$10-$30

AAA Inspector Notes: Nightly live jazz has made this place a local landmark since 1980. Rib and chicken dishes are specialties on a menu that also lists potato skins, chicken wings and Caesar salad. Guests can choose from a variety of tasty treats, then pair it with a mug of temptingly aromatic amaretto coffee. **Bar:** full bar. **Reservations:** suggested. **Address:** 2060 rue Aylmer H3A 2E3 **Location:** Corner of ave President-Kennedy. **Parking:** on-site (fee) and street.   L   D   LATE

IL CAMPARI CENTRO
Phone: 514/868-1177   105

Italian
$17-$42

AAA Inspector Notes: Smartly attired servers deliver fine traditional dishes in the vintage downtown graystone. A varied menu lists fresh pasta, chicken parmigiana, tuna carpaccio, veal, fish and seafood, all accompanied by rich sauces. **Bar:** full bar. **Reservations:** suggested. **Address:** 1177 rue de la Montagne H3G 1Z2 **Location:** Just n of boul Rene-Levesque. **Parking:** on-site (fee) and street.

L   D

JARDIN SAKURA
Phone: 514/288-9122   97

Japanese
$15-$40

AAA Inspector Notes: This stylish dining room offers a variety of better-quality Japanese cuisine, including an impressive selection of sushi, sashimi and maki. Private sunken-floor Tatami dining rooms can be reserved for small groups. To watch the chef at work, reserve a seat at the sushi bar. **Bar:** full bar. **Address:** 2170 rue de la Montagne H3G 1Z7 **Location:** Between rue Sherbrooke and boul de Maisonneuve. **Parking:** street only.   L   D

KHYBER PASS CUISINE AFGHANE
Phone: 514/844-7131   4

Afghan
$14-$18

AAA Inspector Notes: The simple dining room has tightly-spaced tables with enchanting Afghanistan motifs and music. Inexpensive menu items include Afghan kebab brochettes--made with filet mignon, chicken, lamb or quail--as well as braised leg of lamb, basmati rice and mint coriander salad. Yogurt flavored with Afghan spices is a popular dessert. **Address:** 506 ave Duluth est H2L 1A7 **Location:** Corner of rue Berri. **Parking:** street only.   D

KOKO RESTAURANT
Phone: 514/657-5656   23

Mediterranean
$14-$32

AAA Inspector Notes: This stylishly decorated restaurant and nightclub has a youthful feel and funky furniture fabrics. It borders the lively St-Laurent strip and has a large and super-comfortable seasonal terrace. The menu features contemporary Mediterranean cuisine with preparations such as rack of lamb, chicken supreme, black Angus sirloin, sashimi, pasta, risotto and fresh fish and seafood. **Reservations:** suggested. **Address:** 8 rue Sherbrooke ouest H2X 4C9 **Location:** Corner of boul St-Laurent; in Hotel Opus Montreal. **Parking:** valet and street only.   B   L   D   CALL M

LA BAGUETTE D'IVOIRE
Phone: 514/932-7099   113

Asian
$10-$15

AAA Inspector Notes: Housed in a graystone duplex in a popular downtown neighborhood, the casual restaurant specializes in Vietnamese, Szechuan and Thai dishes. The menu includes Tonkinese soup, Cantonese-style spicy cuttlefish, basil beef, beef with black beans, sweet and sour pork, vegetables with greens, mango chicken, duck with ginger, General Tao chicken, Imperial chicken and lemongrass chicken. **Bar:** full bar. **Address:** 1242 rue Mackay H3G 2H4 **Location:** Between rue Ste-Catherine and boul Rene-Levesque. **Parking:** street only.   L   D

LA FONDERIE
Phone: 514-524-2100   1

Fondue
$22-$32

AAA Inspector Notes: For more than 20 years, this eatery has been satisfying the palates of Montrealers with its successful fondues. However, the menu offers steak, lamb, fish and seafood selections. **Bar:** full bar. **Reservations:** suggested. **Address:** 964 Rachel St est H2J 2J3 **Location:** Between Boyer and de Mentana sts. **Parking:** street only.   D

LALOUX
Phone: 514/287-9127   10

French
$22-$28

AAA Inspector Notes: Attentive service and innovative regional cuisine characterize the elegant yet informal dining room in a pleasant residential neighborhood. Menu options include snow crab flan, mussels with sweetbreads in orange-Pernod reduction, vanilla-flavored halibut, pan-seared yellowfin tuna, beef tournedos, Nunavut caribou, large shrimp in liqueur sauce and roasted veal chops. **Bar:** full bar. **Address:** 250 ave des Pins est H2W 1P3 **Location:** Corner of rue Laval. **Parking:** street only.

L   D

LA MAISON KAM FUNG
Phone: 514/878-2888   40

Chinese
$9-$18

AAA Inspector Notes: Diners can pick and choose from dishes that servers continually wheel past tables during dim sum, the Chinese equivalent of brunch. The food is authentic and the selection outstanding. House specialties include Peking duck, General Tao chicken and lobster served ginger- or Cantonese-style. **Bar:** full bar. **Reservations:** suggested. **Address:** 1111 rue St-Urbain H2Z 1X6 **Location:** Just s of boul Rene-Levesque. **Parking:** on-site (fee).   B   L   D

LA MAISON V.I.P.
Phone: 514/861-1943   35

Chinese
$9-$15

AAA Inspector Notes: This casual, modestly decorated restaurant is a popular spot for affordable Cantonese and Szechuan dishes. A 20-minute wait at the door is not uncommon on busy nights, even when reservations are made. **Bar:** full bar. **Address:** 1077 rue Clark H2Z 1K3 **Location:** Corner de la Gauchetiere; in Chinatown. **Parking:** street only.   L   D   LATE

LA MENARA
Phone: 514/861-1989   29

Moroccan
$40

AAA Inspector Notes: This restaurant transports guests downstairs from the cobbled streets of Old Montreal into a Moroccan oasis of spirited music, lively dancers, rich red fabrics and canopied ceilings. The menu features exotic Moroccan preparations of fish, lamb and quail, as well as Arabian spiced soup, couscous, and a tagine (stew) of chicken, meat or shrimp. A tasty dessert might center on a pastry with mint tea. **Bar:** full bar. **Reservations:** required. **Address:** 256 rue St-Paul est H2Y 1G9 **Location:** Just e of boul St-Laurent. **Parking:** street only.   D

L'AMÈRE À BOIRE
Phone: 514/282-7448   9

International
$10-$18

AAA Inspector Notes: This casual brew pub faces a lively street and features not only quality home-brewed beers but also international pub food, including beer-flavored fish and chips, tapas (Spanish appetizers), gravlax, spanakopita, moussaka, quesadillas, bar snacks, Quebec cheese and burgers (beef, lamb or vegetarian). **Bar:** beer & wine. **Address:** 2049 rue St-Denis H2X 3K8 **Location:** Just n of rue Ontario. **Parking:** street only.   D

(See map & index p. 334.)

LA QUEUE DE CHEVAL BAR & STEAKHOUSE
Phone: 514/390-0090 [101]

Steak
$27-$60

AAA Inspector Notes: An extensive variety of wines complements thoughtful preparations of dry-aged prime beef, veal and such seafood as jumbo shrimp, red snapper and swordfish. Service is gracious and refined at the downtown greystone facing the Bell Centre. **Bar:** full bar. **Reservations:** suggested. **Address:** 1221 boul Rene-Levesque ouest H3G 1T1 **Location:** Corner of Drummond St. **Parking:** valet and street only.

[L] [D]

LAURIE RAPHAËL/MONTRÉAL
RESTAURANT/BOUTIQUE   Phone: 514/985-6072 [76]

Quebec
$26-$35

AAA Inspector Notes: This youthful, stylish restaurant boasts haute Quebecoise cuisine served in smaller portions ideal for sharing. The presentations are artful and the ingredients market-fresh. Renowned Quebec City chef-owner Daniel Vezina has brought his culinary talents to Montreal, where a highly-skilled local team (including his son Raphael) offers cutting-edge cuisine that pleases food lovers. **Bar:** full bar. **Address:** 2050 rue Mansfield H3A 1Y9 **Location:** Corner of ave President-Kennedy; in Hotel Le Germain. **Parking:** valet and street only. [L] [D]

LE CASTILLON
Phone: 514/878-2992 [89]

Continental
$10-$34

AAA Inspector Notes: A waterfall and garden on the seasonal terrace lend to this restaurant's appeal. Inside, the posh, high-ceiling dining room features rich wood trim, elegant table settings and fully-upholstered, high-back chairs. The a la carte menu at Le Castillon offers such classic dishes as duck, rack of lamb, Angus beef, pasta, fresh fish and seafood, alongside a lighter bistro menu with burgers, sandwiches and salads. The breakfast and lunch buffet are popular. Smartly-attired career servers are helpful. **Bar:** full bar. **Reservations:** suggested. **Address:** 900 rue de la Gauchetiere H5A 1E4 **Location:** Corner of Mansfield; in Hilton Montréal Bonaventure. **Parking:** on-site (fee) and valet. [B] [L]

LE CLUB CHASSE ET PECHE
Phone: 514/861-1112 [24]

French
$15-$38

AAA Inspector Notes: The restaurant's name translates to "hunting and fishing club," and the decor evokes an elegant country hunting lodge, with rough wood beams and stone semi-basement walls. Table settings are refined. The sophisticated menu brings together creatively presented surf and turf items, such as lobster, veal, pork, duck, fresh fish, foie gras and scallops. **Bar:** full bar. **Address:** 423 rue St-Claude H2Y 3B6 **Location:** Just n of rue St-Paul. **Parking:** street only. [L] [D]

LE LATINI
Phone: 514/861-3166 [45]

Italian
$14-$40

AAA Inspector Notes: Fireplaces, a glassed atrium and a garden add to the informal elegance of the contemporary restaurant. The changing menu centers on seafood. An extensive selection of wine is displayed. Terrace seating is hard to come by in season. **Bar:** full bar. **Reservations:** suggested. **Address:** 1130 rue Jeanne Mance H2Z 1L7 **Location:** Corner of boul Rene-Levesque ouest. **Parking:** valet and street only.

[L] [D]

LE MILSA ROTISSERIE BRÉSILIENNE
Phone: 514/985-0777 [109]

Brazilian
$25-$30

AAA Inspector Notes: Near Concordia University, this lively downtown restaurant is memorable for its nightly Brazilian dancers and the all-you-can-eat grilled meat special. Meats-which include filet mignon, rib steak, Brazilian-cut strip loin, turkey, bacon, lamb and pork-are brought to the table on a spit and sliced onto diners' plates. Other main courses include poultry and fish. For dessert, try grilled pineapple. A limited a la carte menu of meat, fish or poultry is offered. **Bar:** full bar. **Address:** 1445A rue Bishop H3G 2E4 **Location:** Between boul de Maisonneuve and rue Ste-Catherine. **Parking:** street only. [D]

LE NIL BLEU RESTAURANT
Phone: 514/285-4628 [6]

Ethiopian
$10-$18

AAA Inspector Notes: Stylish seating, a waterfall and African-themed artwork provide an exotic appeal to this popular, slow-paced Ethiopian restaurant. The menu features stewed meat, seafood and vegetable dishes served with the traditional thin, stretchy ingera bread that guests use to pick up their food in lieu of the usual knife and fork (which are available upon request). Combination platters include four menu selections and are a popular way for guests to share a meal. **Bar:** full bar. **Address:** 3708 rue St-Denis H2X 3L7 **Location:** Just s of ave des Pins est; in Hotel Kutuma. **Parking:** street only. [D]

L'ENTRECÔTE SAINT-JEAN
Phone: 514/281-6492 [82]

French
$19-$24

AAA Inspector Notes: The casual, Paris-influenced bistro specializes in a table d'hote menu of rib steak served with flavorful Dijon mustard sauce, matchstick fries, soup, a walnut-garnished salad and delicious chocolate-drizzled profiteroles for dessert. **Bar:** full bar. **Address:** 2022 rue Peel H3A 2W5 **Location:** Just n of boul de Maisonneuve ouest. **Parking:** street only. [L] [D]

LE PIMENT ROUGE
Phone: 514/866-7816 [92]

Chinese
$20-$35

AAA Inspector Notes: The focus of this refined restaurant's menu is on fine Szechuan cuisine. Carefully prepared dishes include tasty General Tso's chicken, crispy duck, orange beef, Szechuan shrimp and beef with mango strips in Kahlua sauce. The comfortable dining room is appointed with attractive furnishings. The wine cellar brims with appropriate vintages. **Bar:** full bar. **Reservations:** suggested. **Address:** 1170 rue Peel H3B 4P2 **Location:** Between rue Ste-Catherine and boul Rene-Levesque. **Parking:** street only. [L] [D]

LE POIS PENCHÉ BRASSERIE PARISIENNE
Phone: 514/667-5050 [94]

French
$18-$40

AAA Inspector Notes: A chic Parisian bistro is the inspiration for this popular downtown restaurant and raw bar. Fresh seafood is displayed on ice at the main entrance, and patrons enjoy the elegant interior table settings and the seasonal sidewalk terrace. A long bar in the center of the restaurant is an ideal spot for sampling great wines by the glass or bottle. The menu features many upscale bistro classics such as tartares, salads, steak and fries, and fresh fish and other seafood. **Bar:** full bar. **Reservations:** suggested. **Address:** 1230 boul de Maisonneuve ouest H3G 1M2 **Location:** Corner of rue Drummond. **Parking:** street only. [L] [D]

(See map & index p. 334.)

LE RESTAURANT CLUB LOUNGE 737
Phone: 514/397-0737 (74)

French
$14-$46

AAA Inspector Notes: This elegant dining room and lounge sits atop Place Ville Marie, a modern 40-story skyscraper offering impressive downtown views, especially at night. One floor below is a popular nightclub. The menu features impressive appetizers, wild game, meats, fresh fish and seafood. **Bar:** full bar. **Address:** 1 Place Ville-Marie, Suite 4340 H3B 5E4 **Location:** Corner of boul de Maisonneuve and rue University. [L] [D]

LES 3 BRASSEURS Phone: 514/788-6100 (34)

Canadian
$9-$21

AAA Inspector Notes: The lively brew pub specializes in home-brewed beers, beer cocktails and a pizza-like dish called "flammekueche," which features a thin baked crust topped with gourmet ingredients including Quebec cheeses, bacon, onions, sour cream, feta cheese, smoked meat and pesto. The menu also lists salads, sandwich wraps, French onion soup, croque monsieur, baby back ribs, mussels with beer, game sausages, burgers, and steak. Patrons can view brewery equipment through a glass wall. **Bar:** full bar. **Address:** 105 Rue St-Paul est H2Y 1G7 **Location:** Just e of boul St-Laurent; in Old Montreal. **Parking:** street only. [L] [D] [LATE]

LES 3 BRASSEURS Phone: 514/788-6333 (73)

Canadian
$9-$21

AAA Inspector Notes: The lively brew pub specializes in home-brewed beers, beer cocktails and a pizza-like dish called flammekueche ("flamm," for short). Hailing from Alsace, France, this dish features a thin baked crust topped with such gourmet ingredients as Quebec cheeses, bacon, onions, sour cream, feta cheese, smoked meat and pesto. The menu also lists salads, sandwich wraps, French onion soup, croque monsieur, baby back ribs and steak. Patrons can view brewery equipment through a glass wall. **Bar:** full bar. **Address:** 732 rue Ste-Catherine ouest H3B 1B9 **Location:** Just e of McGill College. **Parking:** street only.

[L] [D] [LATE]

LES 3 BRASSEURS Phone: 514/845-1660 (108)

Canadian
$9-$21

AAA Inspector Notes: This lively pub specializes in home-brewed beers, beer cocktails and a pizza-like dish called "flammekueche," for short. This meal hails from Alsace, France, and features a thin, baked crust topped with gourmet ingredients such as Quebec cheeses, bacon, onions, sour cream, feta cheese, smoked meat and pesto. The menu also offers salads, sandwich wraps, French onion soup, croque monsieur, baby back ribs, mussels with beer, game sausages, burgers, bagel and cream cheese and steak. **Bar:** full bar. **Reservations:** required. **Address:** 1658 rue St-Denis H2X 3K6 **Location:** Corner of rue Emery. **Parking:** street only.

[L] [D] [LATE]

LES PYRENÉES RESTAURANT
Phone: 514/842-5566 (61)

Basque
$9-$37

AAA Inspector Notes: Bullfight prints and a traditional tapas stand out in the decor of this casually elegant Old Montreal restaurant. Representative of Catalonian dishes are Basque-style stuffed squid, Toulouse-style cassoulet, assorted tapas, breast of duck, seafood marmite and paella. **Bar:** full bar. **Address:** 320 rue St-Paul ouest H2Y 2A3 **Location:** Just e of rue St-Pierre. **Parking:** street only. [L] [D]

LE STEAK FRITES ST-PAUL
Phone: 514/842-0972 (42)

Steak
$12-$39

AAA Inspector Notes: The lively, informal bistro specializes in certified AAA-grade steak and all-you-can-eat, thin matchstick fries. Such classic entrees as duck confit, smoked salmon, escargot, fried calamari, grilled shrimp, salmon fillet and a surf and turf round out the menu. For dessert, try traditional creme brulee or chocolate-covered profiteroles. In typical French bistro fashion, the daily menu is written on a chalkboard. Alcohol is not sold on the premises, but guests can bring their own bottles. **Reservations:** suggested. **Address:** 12 rue St-Paul ouest H2Y 2Y3 **Location:** Corner of boul St-Laurent. **Parking:** street only. [L] [D]

LE STEAK FRITES ST-PAUL
Phone: 514/878-3553 (60)

Steak
$11-$39

AAA Inspector Notes: The lively, informal bistro specializes in certified AAA-grade steak and all-you-can-eat thin matchstick fries. Such classic entrees as duck confit, smoked salmon, escargot, fried calamari, grilled shrimp, salmon fillet and a surf and turf round out the menu. For dessert, try traditional crème brûlée or chocolate-covered profiteroles. Typical of a French bistro, the daily menu is written on a chalkboard. Alcohol is not sold on the premises, but guests can bring their own bottles. **Address:** 405 rue St-Antoine ouest H2Z 2A3 **Location:** Just w of rue St-Pierre. **Parking:** street only. [L] [D]

LE TAJ RESTAURANT Phone: 514/845-9015 (86)

Indian
$12-$25

AAA Inspector Notes: The tastefully decorated restaurant is a popular place for East Indian cuisine, including many vegetarian selections. A glass wall allows clients to see the chef in action in the kitchen. The entrance area is decorated with an ornate wall mural that was on display in the Indian pavilion at Montreal's Expo '67 World Fair. **Bar:** full bar. **Reservations:** suggested. **Address:** 2077 rue Stanley H3A 1R7 **Location:** Between rue Sherbrooke and boul de Maisonneuve. **Parking:** on-site (fee) and street.

[L] [D]

LE TOUR DE VILLE Phone: 514/879-4777 (80)

French
$36-$55

AAA Inspector Notes: Guests can enjoy breathtaking views of Montreal's major landmarks from every table in the revolving rooftop restaurant, which is decorated with sculptures and attractive artwork. The gourmet buffet delivers a tempting array of cold and hot choices, such as smoked salmon, duck and veal. Service, albeit limited, is attentive and professional, and a la carte menu items are delivered at an appropriate pace. A fee is charged for the mandatory coat check concession. **Bar:** full bar. **Reservations:** suggested. **Address:** 777 rue University H3C 3Z7 **Location:** Corner of rue St-Antoine; in Delta Centre-Ville. **Parking:** on-site (fee). [L] [D]

L'EXPRESS Phone: 514/845-5333 (5)

French
$14-$25

AAA Inspector Notes: This lively eatery-a Montreal favorite since 1980-is a must for lovers of a classic French bistro experience. Steak tartare and fresh seafood are specialties on a menu that also includes poultry, meat, salads, meat pies and caviar. Diners can select from an a la carte menu for lunch and dinner. An impressive wine list, by the bottle or glass, is available. Reservations are a must. **Bar:** full bar. **Reservations:** suggested. **Address:** 3927 rue St-Denis H2W 2M4 **Location:** Between ave Duluth and rue Roy. **Parking:** street only. [B] [L] [D]

(See map & index p. 334.)

L'ORCHIDEE CHINE RESTAURANT CHINOIS
Phone: 514/287-1878   (83)

Chinese
$13-$30

AAA Inspector Notes: In the downtown business core, this upscale, comfortable restaurant specializes in fine Chinese cuisine. **Address:** 2017 rue Peel H3A 1T6 **Location:** Corner of boul de Maisonneuve ouest. **Parking:** valet and street only.

L'Ô SUR LA MONTAGNE   Phone: 514/861-6000   (106)

Canadian
$12-$23

AAA Inspector Notes: This lively and stylish hotel bar and restaurant features upscale bistro favorites including nicely presented salads, tartars, Brome Lake duck, steak and classic French desserts including tarte tatin apple tarts and strawberries au poivre. There is an excellent selection of wines by the glass. **Bar:** full bar. **Reservations:** suggested. **Address:** 1180 rue de la Montagne H3G 1Z1 **Location:** Between rue Ste-Catherine and boul Rene-Levesque; in Novotel Montreal Centre.

L'USINE DE SPAGHETTI DU VIEUX-MONTREAL
Phone: 514/866-0963   (28)

Italian
$12-$25

AAA Inspector Notes: In a 19th-century stone-walled building that once housed the Rasco Hotel, the family restaurant prepares a great variety of inexpensive pasta dishes, including several spaghetti variations, fettuccine, cannelloni and lasagna. Also on the menu are broiled shrimp, sauteed mushrooms, grilled Italian sausage, crab cakes and daily specials. Legend has it that Charles Dickens, while visiting Montreal in 1842, wrote the liner notes to "A Tale of Two Cities" in a back room. **Bar:** full bar. **Address:** 273 rue St-Paul est H2Y 1H1 **Location:** Just e of Place Jacques-Cartier; in Old Montreal. **Parking:** street only.

MAESTRO S.V.P.   Phone: 514/842-6447   (18)

Seafood
$10-$45

AAA Inspector Notes: This stylish and lively restaurant is popular for its year-round oyster bar and variety of fresh fish and seafood entrees. Patrons may also choose from a tapas menu, which features a variety of small-portion dishes ideal for sharing at a table or for takeout. A real conversation piece, the walls are covered with oyster shells that have been autographed by celebrities. **Bar:** full bar. **Reservations:** suggested. **Address:** 3615 boul St-Laurent H2X 1V5 **Location:** Just n of rue Prince-Arthur. **Parking:** street only.

M:BRGR   Phone: 514/906-2747   (93)

Burgers
$14-$40

AAA Inspector Notes: While tuna and veggie burgers are available, beef lovers will like the variety of quality cheeses, salad and sauces available to spice up burgers made with AAA beef, certified organic beef or tender Kobe beef. For those more adventurous, top it off with white or black truffles. The ultimate burger experience is a $99 burger with Kobe beef, foie gras and all the fixings. Or try an Angus beef dog, chicken breast, truffle chip-crusted macaroni and cheese, steak sandwich or sweet potato fries. **Bar:** full bar. **Reservations:** required. **Address:** 2025 rue Drummond H3G 1W6 **Location:** Just n of boul de Maisonneuve. **Parking:** street only. L D LATE

MÉCHANT BOEUF BAR-BRASSERIE
Phone: 514/788-4020   (47)

French
$15-$25

AAA Inspector Notes: This chic restaurant and pub is located in a luxury hotel in Old Montreal. Enjoy a cocktail in the stylish bar area then sample the upscale comfort foods including gourmet burgers, Angus AAA beef, fried calamari, tartars, beer-can-roasted chicken and braised pork poutine. **Bar:** full bar. **Reservations:** required. **Address:** 112 rue St-Paul ouest H2Y 1Z3 **Location:** Corner of rue St-Sulpice; in Hotel Nelligan. **Parking:** valet only.

MESA 14   Phone: 514/284-0344   (110)

Mexican
$12-$25

AAA Inspector Notes: In the heart of Montreal's nightclub area, this casual eatery prepares affordable and authentic Mexican dishes, including burritos, tacos and sizzling fajita platters. **Bar:** full bar. **Address:** 1425 rue Bishop H3G 2E4 **Location:** Between rue Sherbrooke and boul de Maisonneuve. **Parking:** street only.

MIKE'S RESTAURANT   Phone: 514/395-2222

Canadian
$8-$14

AAA Inspector Notes: This popular family-friendly restaurant specializes in pizza and hot submarine sandwiches, along with fries, burgers, soup, salads, pasta, grilled meats and seafood. An excellent variety of colorful desserts rounds out the offerings. **Bar:** full bar. **Address:** 1348 rue Ste-Catherine ouest H3G 1P5 **Location:** Just e of rue Crescent. **Parking:** street only.

MISTER STEER   Phone: 514/866-3233   (96)

American
$8-$25

AAA Inspector Notes: In business since 1958, the family restaurant ages its steaks on the premises and prepares fresh steer burgers daily. Suzie Q curly fries and chargrilled chicken also please hungry patrons. For dessert, it's hard to beat the simple sundaes. **Bar:** full bar. **Reservations:** suggested. **Address:** 1198 Ste-Catherine ouest H3B 1K1 **Location:** Between Drummond and Stanley sts. **Parking:** street only.

MOISHE'S STEAK HOUSE   Phone: 514/845-1696   (14)

Steak
$28-$54

AAA Inspector Notes: Long a favorite of Montrealers, this established restaurant bustles with activity, especially on weekends. The atmosphere is upscale for a steakhouse, with quality table settings and dark-wood wine cabinets. For dessert, try a delicious French pastry. Service is friendly and attentive. **Bar:** full bar. **Reservations:** suggested. **Address:** 3961 boul St-Laurent H2W 1Y4 **Location:** Between rue Pine and ave Duluth.

NEWTOWN RESTAURANT
Phone: 514/284-6555   (104)

Mediterranean
$30-$42

AAA Inspector Notes: On a favorite nightlife strip, this trendy, upscale dining room, lounge and night club has a lively, youthful ambience. Mediterranean dishes feature excellent fresh meats and seafood, including cod, yellowfin tuna and scallops. Open only in the evening, the upstairs dining room has an intimate feel. A lighter lunch and dinner menu is presented in the lounge area, where a DJ often mixes the music. The wine list is comprehensive. Québec race car driver Jacques Villeneuve once co-owned this place. **Bar:** full bar. **Reservations:** suggested. **Address:** 1476 rue Crescent H3G 2B6 **Location:** Corner of boul de Maisonneuve. **Parking:** valet and street only.

(See map & index p. 334.)

OSCO!
Phone: 514/847-8729   (49)

French
$21-$39

AAA Inspector Notes: This Province-style brasserie serves upscale French-bistro cuisine in an elegant and comfortable brick-walled dining room. An adjacent stylish lounge is convenient for a before-dinner drink. The menu features daily specials along with a la carte selections including fresh fish and seafood, guinea fowl, steak, French onion soup and gourmet salads. **Bar:** full bar. **Reservations:** suggested. **Address:** 360 rue St-Antoine ouest H2Y 3X4 **Location:** Corner of rue St-Pierre; in InterContinental Montréal. **Parking:** valet only.

B L D CALL ☻M

OTTO RISTORANTE-BAR
Phone: 514/395-3180   (65)

Mediterranean
$25-$42

AAA Inspector Notes: Trendy decor and glamorous service is outshined by a menu of fine Mediterranean cuisine with intriguing flavors, including fresh fish, seasonal seafood, steak and lamb. Desserts are memorable. The atmosphere is chic, especially in the posh red booths in front of a wall decorated with shimmering seashells. **Reservations:** suggested. **Address:** 901 Square Victoria H2Z 1R1 **Location:** Corner of rue St-Antoine; in W Montreal. **Parking:** valet only. *(See ad p. 373.)* B L D

PHO CALI RESTAURANT
Phone: 514/876-1064   (33)

Vietnamese
$6-$10

AAA Inspector Notes: This simply decorated Vietnamese diner serves an excellent variety of affordable Tonkinese soups and freshly-prepared traditional dishes. **Address:** 1011 boul St-Laurent H2Z 1J4 **Location:** Just n of rue St-Antoine; in Chinatown. **Parking:** street only. L D

PINTXO CUISINE ESPAGNOLE
Phone: 514/844-0222   (8)

Basque
$16-$28

AAA Inspector Notes: Original wood floors, a brick wall, colorful artwork and an open kitchen provide the ideal backdrop for casual conversation and fine Basque cuisine. The restaurant specializes in pintxos, tapas-sized appetizers popular in Spain. Larger main courses also are served. Choose from such items as tartars, poached octopus, sardine fillets, crab, seared foie gras, Basque cod, risotto, blood sausage, seared pork chops, filet mignon and a selection of Spanish cheese. Lunch served Wednesday through Friday. **Bar:** full bar. **Address:** 256 rue Roy est H2W 1M6 **Location:** Just w of rue St-Denis. **Parking:** street only.

L D

RENOIR
Phone: 514/285-9000   (85)

French
$20-$48

AAA Inspector Notes: The stylish, elegant hotel dining room has a fresh, youthful feel. The decor includes some architectural relics from the renowned Van Horne mansion. Creative food preparations include grilled Maine lobster, Atlantic cod fish, Alberta sirloin beef, pastilla of duck and lemon- and herb-roasted chicken. Crème brûlée or chocolate cake is worth a try for dessert. **Reservations:** suggested. **Address:** 1155 rue Sherbrooke ouest H3A 2N3 **Location:** Corner of rue Stanley; in Sofitel Montréal Le Carré Doré. **Parking:** valet and street only.

B L D

RESTAURANT AU PIED DE COCHON
Phone: 514/281-1114   (3)

Quebec
$14-$46

AAA Inspector Notes: The casual eatery strips away traditional fine-cuisine formality. Fresh, high-quality ingredients factor into such dishes as duck with foie gras, which is cooked in a can and opened at the table; poutine (fries, curd cheese, foie gras and gravy); pied de cochon (pig's feet) stuffed with foie gras; and venison tartare. The fine wine list includes by-the-glass and bottle choices. Fresh seafood is kept on ice before cooking and then carefully prepared and served on multi-tiered dishes. **Bar:** full bar. **Reservations:** suggested. **Address:** 536 rue Duluth est H2L 1A9 **Location:** Just w of rue St-Hubert. **Parking:** street only.

D

RESTAURANT BOFINGER BARBEQUE SMOKEHOUSE
Phone: 514/750-9095   (67)

Barbecue
$7-$15

AAA Inspector Notes: Southern-style barbecue food is on the menu at this casual eatery in the shadows of business-district skyscrapers. Guests line up, place their order and pay before grabbing a seat at one of the black vinyl booths. Poor boys and Cuban pork sandwiches are specialties on a menu that also includes beef or pork ribs with a choice of hot sauce, smoked meat, sausages, hamburgers, roast chicken and side dishes such as baked beans, chili, poutine and macaroni and cheese. **Bar:** beer & wine. **Address:** 1250 rue University H3B 3B8 **Location:** Just s of rue Ste-Catherine. **Parking:** on-site (fee).

L D

RESTAURANT DE L'INSTITUT
Phone: 514/282-5161   (7)

Quebec
$15-$32

AAA Inspector Notes: This contemporary restaurant, facing lovely Carre St-Louis park, is operated by a hotel and culinary arts school. The dining room boasts hardwood floors, large shuttered windows and elegant table settings. Skilled staff and students collaborate to prepare and present a menu of fine regional cuisine with an abundant use of Quebec produce. The menu features Quebec veal, pork, poultry and game served impressively. **Bar:** full bar. **Reservations:** suggested. **Address:** 3535 rue St-Denis H2X 3P1 **Location:** Just n of rue Sherbrooke. **Parking:** street only. B L D

RESTAURANT EUROPÉA
Phone: 514/398-9229   (102)

French
$20-$45

AAA Inspector Notes: In a vintage greystone building, this intimate restaurant boasts a stylish decor and seasonal terrace. The menu offers beautifully garnished contemporary French dishes, including pan-seared foie gras, North Shore scallops, Stanstead-region rabbit, Kamouraska lamb, rack of deer, braised veal cheeks, Cornish hen, sea bass filet and poached lobster. Multi-course tasting menus and a la carte selections are available. The owners offer cooking classes and a chef's table to view foods being prepared. **Bar:** full bar. **Address:** 1227 rue de la Montagne H3G 1Z2 **Location:** Between rue Ste-Catherine and boul Rene-Levesque. **Parking:** street only. L D

RESTAURANT FOU D'ASIE
Phone: 514/281-0077   (11)

Asian
$10-$26

AAA Inspector Notes: This casual split-level dining room has many tables overlooking lively rue St-Denis, in addition to seating in a bright atrium area and on the seasonal terrace. The menu features Asian dishes, including sushi, noodles, spring rolls, chicken teriyaki, seafood, meats and several Vietnamese specialties. **Bar:** full bar. **Reservations:** suggested. **Address:** 1732 rue St-Denis H2X 3K6 **Location:** Just s of rue Ontario. **Parking:** street only.

L D

384 DOWNTOWN MONTRÉAL, QC

(See map & index p. 334.)

RESTAURANT JULIEN   Phone: 514/871-1581   63

French
$20-$36

AAA Inspector Notes: The elegant downtown bistro features some classic dishes, including steak and fries, chicken supreme, steak tartare, scallops, beef bavette, veal, liver, sweetbreads, magret of duck, tuna, salmon and pasta. A garden terrace opens seasonally. **Bar:** full bar. **Reservations:** suggested. **Address:** 1191 ave Union H3B 3C3 **Location:** Just s of rue Ste-Catherine. **Parking:** street only. L D

RESTAURANT LA GARGOTE   Phone: 514/844-1428   64

French
$16-$33

AAA Inspector Notes: Market-fresh ingredients go into preparations of French cuisine at this historic, stone-walled restaurant set in the heart of Old Montreal. Choose from classics such as escargot, filet mignon in a pepper sauce, fish soup, braised lamb shoulder, foie gras, Provencale-style roasted scampi, breast of duck or the daily pasta. **Bar:** full bar. **Address:** 351 Place d'Youville H2Y 2B7 **Location:** Corner of rue St-Pierre facing Place d'Youville. **Parking:** street only. L D

RESTAURANT LA PIZZELLA   Phone: 514/939-3030   116

Italian
$16-$45

AAA Inspector Notes: Tasty fettuccine primavera is representative of menu selections at the cozy restaurant, a favorite, upscale spot for fresh pasta, gourmet pizza and Mediterranean specialties. The interior features a large wood-burning pizza oven at the back of the main dining room. Knowledgeable servers in smart attire adeptly answer questions about the choices. **Bar:** full bar. **Reservations:** suggested. **Address:** 2080 rue St-Mathieu H3H 2J4 **Location:** Between boul de Maisonneuve and ave Lincoln. **Parking:** street only. L D

RESTAURANT L'AUTRE VERSION   Phone: 514/871-9135   27

Mediterranean
$15-$40

AAA Inspector Notes: This contemporary-styled restaurant is found on a memorable cobbled-stone street in Old Montreal. The menu features creatively presented Mediterranean-influenced cuisine such as fresh selections of fish and seafood, premium meats, pasta and creative desserts. Choose from such dishes as salmon terrine, deer burgers, wild boar ribs, seared foie gras or smoked duck filet lardons. **Bar:** full bar. **Reservations:** suggested. **Address:** 295 rue St-Paul est H2Y 1H3 **Location:** Corner of rue du Marche Bonsecours. **Parking:** street only. L D

RESTAURANT LE PIÉMONTAIS   Phone: 514/861-8122   26

Italian
$17-$42

AAA Inspector Notes: The elegant restaurant serves fine Italian cuisine in a relaxed dining room staffed by genuinely friendly and refined servers. **Bar:** full bar. **Address:** 1145A rue de Bullion H2X 2Z2 **Location:** Corner of boul Rene-Levesque. **Parking:** street only. L D

RESTAURANT LES FILLES DU ROY   Phone: 514/282-1725   19

French
$25-$55

AAA Inspector Notes: Fine French cuisine is served in the lavish dining room of a historic mansion/inn that dates back to 1725. Benjamin Franklin once visited the property. **Bar:** full bar. **Address:** 405 rue Bonsecours H2Y 3C3 **Location:** Corner of rue St-Paul; in Hostellerie Pierre de Calvet A.D. 1725. **Parking:** street only. **Historic** D

RESTAURANT SHO-DAN CONCEPT JAPONAIS   Phone: 514/987-9987   77

Japanese
$12-$28

AAA Inspector Notes: This stylish and comfortable sushi bar entices with an extensive choice of sushi, sashimi and sushi maki menu items and many flavorful eye-catching specialty dishes, including a chef's special and a few dessert sushi selections. **Bar:** full bar. **Address:** 2020 rue Metcalfe H3A 1X8 **Location:** Between rue Sherbrooke and boul de Maisonneuve. **Parking:** street only.

RESTAURANT TOQUÉ!   Phone: 514/499-2084   57

French
$25-$48

AAA Inspector Notes: This spacious and stylish dining room has an upscale feel that appeals to the professional crowd. Guest-oriented servers are knowledgeable and gracious. The food is exquisite-superb in preparation, presentation and taste. Chef Normand Laprise takes great care to use the highest quality regional meat, fish and seafood, including rack of pork, duck breast, Atlantic halibut, braised lamb, poached lobster, roasted sea snails and princess scallops. A multi-course surprise tasting menu is available. **Bar:** full bar. **Reservations:** suggested. **Address:** 900 Place Jean-Paul Riopelle H2Z 2B2 **Location:** Corner of rue Ste-Antoine. **Parking:** valet only. L D

RESTAURANT VAUVERT   Phone: 514/876-2823   72

French
$17-$42

AAA Inspector Notes: This upscale hotel bistro and bar has stylish decor and a menu of contemporary French cuisine that offers high-quality ingredients and beautiful presentations. Select from artfully-presented meat, fish and seafood dishes. Lunch is a popular time for young professionals to meet. **Bar:** full bar. **Address:** 355 rue McGill H2Y 2E8 **Location:** Corner of rue St-Paul; in Hotel St-Paul. **Parking:** valet and street only. L D

RESTAURANT VERSES   Phone: 514/788-4000   46

French
$14-$40

AAA Inspector Notes: In an elegant Old Montreal boutique hotel, this upscale, yet hip, bistro and bar features a lobby lounge with a narrow atrium ceiling between historic walls of exposed brick. The dining room is a stylish bistro offering seating in semi-circular booths, along with a cozy fireplace and a well-stocked wine cellar. The menu features contemporary, French-inspired regional cuisine, including pan-seared foie gras, Quebec lamb, breast of duck, deer, fresh fish and seafood. **Bar:** full bar. **Reservations:** suggested. **Address:** 106 rue St-Paul ouest H2Y 1Z3 **Location:** Corner of rue St-Sulpice; in Hotel Nelligan. **Parking:** valet only. B L D

RESTAURANT XO   Phone: 514/841-3111   58

French
$18-$40

AAA Inspector Notes: This luxuriously-appointed hotel dining room is in a historic former bank and once was known as Bankers' Hall. The opulent setting has private dining nooks, high ceilings with two mezzanine areas, large stained-glass windows and lavish crystal chandeliers. The menu of fine regional cuisine, updated seasonally, includes duck foie gras, oysters, Boileau-region Quebec venison, free-range guinea fowl, Atlantic scallops, Quebec lamb, milk-fed Alberta beef and high-quality Quebec cheese. **Bar:** full bar. **Address:** 355 rue St-Jacques ouest H2Y 1N9 **Location:** Corner of rue St-Pierre; in Hotel Le St-James. **Parking:** valet only. B L D

Innovative and fresh market cuisine

REUBEN'S DELI & STEAK   Phone: 514/866-1029   91

Deli
$7-$26

AAA Inspector Notes: This downtown delicatessen has comfortable, vinyl-padded booths and specializes in Montreal smoked meat, steak and pizza. For dessert, try a hearty slice of delicious cheesecake. **Bar:** full bar. **Address:** 1116 Ste-Catherine St W H3B 1H4 **Location:** Corner of rue Peel. **Parking:** street only.

B L D LATE

(See map & index p. 334.)

RISTORANTE LE MEDUSA Phone: 514/878-4499 98

Italian
$15-$35

AAA Inspector Notes: This casually upscale eatery focuses on Italian preparations of fresh pasta, fish, meat and seafood, which are served by the personable staff. **Bar:** full bar. **Reservations:** suggested. **Address:** 1224 rue Drummond H3G 1V7 **Location:** Just n of boul Rene-Levesque. **Parking:** street only. [L] [D]

ROSALIE RESTAURANT Phone: 514/392-1970 103

French
$14-$35

AAA Inspector Notes: Chic, contemporary decor complements an innovative menu of modern French cuisine, including roasted duck, fresh fish, beef fillets, pork, pasta, smoked or poached salmon, beef tartare and rabbit. Dessert favorites include apple pie, chocolate mousse, crème brûlée or chocolate torte cake. A seasonal terrace with stainless-steel tables is popular in the summer. **Bar:** full bar. **Reservations:** suggested. **Address:** 1232 rue de la Montagne H3G 1Z1 **Location:** Just s of rue Ste-Catherine. **Parking:** valet only. [L] [D]

ST-HUBERT Phone: 514/866-0500

Canadian
$8-$24

AAA Inspector Notes: The pleasantly decorated family-friendly restaurant serves affordable chicken dinners, ribs, club sandwiches, chicken wings, salads, soups and hot chicken sandwiches. The children's menu includes animal nuggets. **Bar:** full bar. **Reservations:** suggested. **Address:** 1180 rue de la Gauchetiere ouest H3B 2S2 **Location:** Corner of rue Stanley; in Gare Windsor Train Station. **Parking:** street only. [L] [D]

SANTOS CAFÉ & LOUNGE
Phone: 514/849-8881 54

Canadian
$15-$20

AAA Inspector Notes: The two-level casual bistro/lounge is situated in a historic Old Montreal building adorned with typical architectural details. Red walls and tasteful artwork create an inviting atmosphere. The menu features upscale, comfort foods like steak, burgers and popular bistro fare. **Bar:** full bar. **Address:** 191 rue St-Paul ouest H2Y 1Z5 **Location:** Corner of rue St-Francois-Xavier. **Parking:** street only. [D]

SCHWARTZ'S MONTREAL HEBREW DELICATESSEN
Phone: 514/842-4813 16

Deli
$6-$20

AAA Inspector Notes: The casual delicatessen-diner is a favorite with locals and visiting celebrities who come for Montreal-style smoked meat sandwiches and other deli standards, including smoked turkey, latkes, liver and kosher dills. Take-out service is available. **Address:** 3895 boul St-Laurent H2W 1X9 **Location:** Just n of rue Roy. **Parking:** street only.

[B] [L] [D] [LATE]

SOUPEBOL Phone: 514/282-8388 59

Asian
$7-$15

AAA Inspector Notes: This stylish downtown diner specializes in Asian cuisine. Menu items include Tonkinese soups, sushi, grilled meats, seafood and Cantonese chow mein. **Bar:** full bar. **Address:** 1245 rue du Square-Phillips H3B 3E9 **Location:** Just s of rue Ste-Catherine. **Parking:** street only. [L] [D]

STASH CAFÉ Phone: 514/845-6611 56

Polish
$12-$18

AAA Inspector Notes: In a historic stone building, this informal Old Montreal restaurant is appointed with colorful European publicity posters and oak church pews. The refreshing menu features authentic Polish specialties, including pierogi, placki (Polish pancakes), bigos (cabbage stew with meat, sausage and mushrooms), golabki (cabbage rolls), Polish sausages, potato salad and pork cutlets. A selection of imported and local beers is offered. For dessert, try nalesniki (a cheese-filled pancake). **Bar:** full bar. **Reservations:** required. **Address:** 200 rue St-Paul ouest H2Y 1Z9 **Location:** Corner of rue St-Francois-Xavier. **Parking:** street only. [L] [D]

TATAMI SUSHI BAR Phone: 514/845-5864 48

Asian
$12-$30

AAA Inspector Notes: An ornate graystone facade fronts the casually elegant Old Montreal dining room and sushi bar. The menu features freshly-prepared sushi, maki and sashimi, as well as a few popular Japanese dishes. Diners can either sit at a windowside aquarium-based table or at the sushi bar. A private tatami room is available where guests sit cross-legged at tables sunken into the floor. **Bar:** full bar. **Address:** 140 rue Notre-Dame ouest H2Y 1T1 **Location:** Corner of rue St-Francois-Xavier. **Parking:** street only. [L] [D]

TROIKA RESTAURANT Phone: 514/849-9333 99

Russian
$25-$40

AAA Inspector Notes: Chicken Kiev, beef stroganoff and wild boar are representative of Russian and Czarist cuisine on the elegant restaurant's tempting menu. A wide selection of imported caviars, imported Siberian teas and flavored vodkas is available. For dessert, crepes are a tasty choice. Live music is performed nightly. Beveled mirrors decorate the walls of the dining room, where tables are tightly spaced. The formally attired waitstaff carries out refined service. **Bar:** full bar. **Reservations:** suggested. **Address:** 2171 rue Crescent H3G 2C1 **Location:** Just below rue Sherbrooke; opposite Museum of Fine Arts. **Parking:** street only. [D]

VARGAS STEAKHOUSE BAR SUSHI
Phone: 514/875-4545 75

Sushi
$14-$50

AAA Inspector Notes: This upscale eatery is in the heart of the downtown business core and popular for its Canadian Angus beef steaks, which are aged at least 35 days to increase tenderness. Specialties include slow-cooked roast beef, Chateaubriand for two, cherry-glazed filet mignon, sushi and shrimp stuffed with lobster and black truffles. The varied menu also includes rock lobster tails, grilled sea bass, grilled salmon, surf and turf and a fisherman's platter. **Bar:** full bar. **Address:** 690 boul Rene-Levesque ouest H3B 1X8 **Location:** Corner of rue University. **Parking:** on-site (fee). [L] [D] [LATE]

VIEUX-PORT STEAKHOUSE
Phone: 514/866-3175 36

Steak
$14-$45

AAA Inspector Notes: Steaks, lobster, fresh fish and other seafood are served in the informal Old Montreal restaurant, which occupies a vintage building. Sunday brunch also is offered. **Bar:** full bar. **Address:** 39 rue St-Paul est H2Y 1G2 **Location:** Corner of St-Gabriel; in Old Port District. **Parking:** street only. **Historic**

[L] [D]

(See map & index p. 334.)

WIENSTEIN AND GAVINOS PASTA BAR FACTORY CO LTD
Phone: 514/288-2231 | 107

Italian
$11-$32

AAA Inspector Notes: The atmosphere is hopping in this trendy, bistro-style pasta bar, which sits on the downtown nightclub strip. Diners can choose from a wide selection of freshly prepared pizza and pasta, as well as meats and salads. The seasonal terrace is comfortable and breezy. **Bar:** full bar. **Address:** 1434 rue Crescent H3G 2B6 **Location:** Between rue Ste-Catherine and boul de Maisonneuve. **Parking:** on-site (fee) and street.

L D

WOOD 35 RESTAURANT & BAR
Phone: 514/844-0027 | 21

Italian
$17-$32

AAA Inspector Notes: Youthful servers deliver creatively prepared dishes of pasta, filet mignon, sea bass, rib-eye, seared tuna, braised short ribs, seared salmon, filet mignon, shrimp tempura, calamari or an arugula salad. The stylish environment bustles with energy and LED lighting adds colorful energy to the stylish dining room. **Reservations:** suggested. **Address:** 3500 boul St-Laurent H2X 2V1 **Location:** At Milton. **Parking:** valet and street only. D

ZAWEDEH RESTAURANT
Phone: 514/288-4141 | 78

Lebanese
$10-$35

AAA Inspector Notes: This cozy hotel dining room offers polite service and a menu of authentic Lebanese cuisine including hummus, tabbouleh, baba ghanoush, falafel, cheese rolls, Lebanese sausage, fatouche salad, stuffed vine leaves, shish taouk, brochettes of beef kafta or filet mignon. Regional menu items include poached salmon, chicken supreme, beef medallions and lamb. For dessert, try the sweet baklava. **Bar:** full bar. **Reservations:** suggested. **Address:** 3407 rue Peel H3A 1W7 **Location:** Corner of rue Sherbrooke; in Best Western Plus Ville-Marie Hotel & Suites. **Parking:** valet and street only. B L D

ZYNG NOUILLERIE
Phone: 514/284-2016 | 12

Asian
$9-$14

AAA Inspector Notes: This relaxed, stylish eatery serves Asian soups and fresh noodle dishes. Guests walk up to a glass refrigerator and choice their noodles, spices, vegetables and meat (or vegetarian alternative), and the chef then prepares the meal. **Bar:** full bar. **Address:** 1748 rue St-Denis H2X 3K6 **Location:** Just s of rue Ontario. **Parking:** street only. L D

MONTRÉAL

- **Restaurants p. 388**
- **Hotels & Restaurants map & index p. 342**

AUBERGE DE LA FONTAINE
Phone: (514)597-0166 | 4

Bed & Breakfast
$139-$193 6/1-10/31
$119-$153 11/1-5/31

Address: 1301 rue Rachel est H2J 2K1 **Location:** Corner of rue Chambord. Located in a residential area, across from Parc Lafontaine. **Facility:** Complimentary snacks are available in the shared kitchen of this inn-style B&B set in a pleasant residential district facing popular Parc Lafontaine. 21 units. 3 stories (no elevator), interior corridors. **Parking:** on-site and street. **Terms:** cancellation fee imposed. **Amenities:** high-speed Internet. **Guest Services:** valet laundry. **Free Special Amenities:** expanded continental breakfast and high-speed Internet.

SAVE ⟨†⟩ BIZ 🛜 ✕

AUBERGE ROYAL VERSAILLES HOTEL
Phone: (514)256-1613 | 2

Hotel
$110-$180 6/1-10/31
$99-$159 11/1-5/31

Address: 7200 rue Sherbrooke est H1N 1E7 **Location:** Rt 138, 0.3 mi (0.4 km) w of Hwy 25. Next to Radisson metro station. **Facility:** 132 units. 2 stories, interior/exterior corridors. **Parking:** winter plug-ins. **Terms:** cancellation fee imposed. **Pool(s):** heated outdoor. **Guest Services:** valet laundry. **Free Special Amenities:** full breakfast and high-speed Internet.

SAVE ⟨¶⟩ ⟨Y⟩ 🛏 BIZ 🛜 FEE ⟨⟩ 🔲 🔳 / SOME UNITS 🖼

HOTEL LE PRESTIGE
Phone: (514)640-5500 | 1

Hotel
$96-$150

Address: 12555 Sherbrooke St est H1B 1C8 **Location:** Hwy 40 exit 87, 0.6 mi (1 km) s on boul du Tricentenaire, then just w. Located in east end commercial/industrial area. **Facility:** 72 units. 3 stories, interior corridors. **Parking:** winter plug-ins. **Amenities:** high-speed Internet. **Pool(s):** outdoor. **Activities:** whirlpool, exercise room. **Guest Services:** valet laundry.

⟨¶+⟩ 🛏 BIZ 🛜 🔲 🔳 / SOME UNITS FEE 🖼

HOTEL RUBY FOO'S
Phone: (514)731-7701 | 6

Hotel
$149-$229

Address: 7655 boul Decarie H4P 2H2 **Location:** Hwy 15N exit 69; east side service road. **Facility:** 198 units, some efficiencies. 4 stories, interior corridors. **Terms:** cancellation fee imposed. **Amenities:** high-speed Internet. **Pool(s):** heated outdoor. **Activities:** saunas, whirlpool, exercise room, spa. **Guest Services:** valet laundry. **Free Special Amenities:** local telephone calls and high-speed Internet.
(See ad p. 360.)

SAVE ⟨¶⟩ ⟨Y⟩ 🛏 BIZ 🛜 ✕ FEE ⟨⟩ 🔲 🔳 / SOME UNITS 🖼

HOTEL TERRASSE ROYALE
Phone: 514/739-6391 | 5

Hotel
Rates not provided

Address: 5225 chemin Cote-des-Neiges H3T 1Y1 **Location:** Just n of chemin Queen Mary. **Facility:** 56 units, some efficiencies and kitchens. 6 stories, interior corridors. **Parking:** on-site (fee). **Amenities:** high-speed Internet, safes. **Activities:** exercise room. **Guest Services:** coin laundry.

⟨¶⟩ 🛜 / SOME UNITS 🐾 🔲 🖼 🔳

HOTEL UNIVERSEL MONTREAL
Phone: (514)253-3365 | 3

Hotel
$127-$149 6/1-10/20
$117-$139 10/21-5/31

Address: 5000 rue Sherbrooke est H1V 1A1 **Location:** Corner of rue Viau; just e of Botanical Garden and Olympic Stadium. **Facility:** 230 units. 7 stories, interior corridors. **Parking:** winter plug-ins. **Terms:** cancellation fee imposed. **Dining:** Le Stadium Club Restaurant & Bar, see separate listing. **Pool(s):** heated outdoor, heated indoor. **Activities:** sauna, whirlpool, exercise room. **Fee:** massage. **Guest Services:** valet laundry. **Free Special Amenities:** early check-in/late check-out and room upgrade (subject to availability with advance reservations).
(See ad p. 364.)

SAVE ⟨¶⟩ ⟨f⟩ 🛏 🛜 ✕ FEE ⟨⟩ 🔲 🔳 / SOME UNITS FEE 🖼

(See map & index p. 342.)

MARRIOTT COURTYARD MONTREAL AIRPORT
Phone: (514)339-5333   **9**

Hotel
$122-$199

AAA Benefit:
AAA hotel discounts of 5% or more.

Address: 7000 Place Robert-Joncas H4M 2Z5 **Location:** Hwy 40 exit 65 (boul Cavendish), 0.3 mi (0.5 km) w on north side service road, then just n on rue Beaulac. **Facility:** 160 units. 6 stories, interior corridors. **Terms:** check-in 4 pm. **Amenities:** video games (fee), high-speed Internet. **Pool(s):** heated indoor. **Activities:** whirlpool, game room, exercise room. **Guest Services:** valet and coin laundry, area transportation-within 3 mi (5 km).

MARRIOTT RESIDENCE INN MONTREAL AIRPORT
Phone: (514)336-9333   **8**

Extended Stay
Hotel
$128-$209

AAA Benefit:
AAA hotel discounts of 5% or more.

Address: 6500 Place Robert-Joncas H4M 2Z5 **Location:** Hwy 40 exit 65 (boul Cavendish), 0.3 mi (0.5 km) w on north side service road, then just n on rue Beaulac. **Facility:** 169 efficiencies, some two bedrooms. 6 stories, interior corridors. **Terms:** check-in 4 pm. **Amenities:** video games (fee), high-speed Internet. **Pool(s):** heated indoor. **Activities:** whirlpool, exercise room. **Fee:** game room. **Guest Services:** valet and coin laundry, area transportation-within 3 mi (5 km).

QUALITY HOTEL MIDTOWN
Phone: (514)739-3800   **7**

Hotel
$99-$159

Address: 6445 boul Decarie H3W 3E1 **Location:** Hwy 15 (Decarie Expwy), on east side service road; corner of ave Plamondon. **Facility:** 104 units. 4-6 stories, interior corridors. **Terms:** cancellation fee imposed. **Amenities:** high-speed Internet. **Dining:** Le Grill Midtown, see separate listing. **Pool(s):** heated indoor. **Activities:** saunas, whirlpool, exercise room. **Guest Services:** valet and coin laundry. **Free Special Amenities:** expanded continental breakfast and high-speed Internet.

▼ See AAA listing p. 465 ▼

(See map & index p. 342.)

WHERE TO EAT

ALEX H. RESTAURANT   **Phone:** 514/487-5444   38

Italian
$18-$30

AAA Inspector Notes: Italian and French food are the specialties at this affordable family-run restaurant in the suburban borough of Notre-Dame-de-Grace. A chalkboard announces daily specials, which may include stuffed chicken, pork, lamb brochettes, magret of duck, veal liver, kidneys Dijonnaise and pasta. No alcohol is sold on the premises, but guests may bring their own wine. **Reservations:** suggested. **Address:** 5862 rue Sherbrooke ouest H4A 1X5 **Location:** Just w of rue Draper. **Parking:** street only.

ARAHOVA SOUVLAKI   **Phone:** 514/274-7828

Greek
$8-$25

AAA Inspector Notes: Souvlaki and gyro pitas, as well as other Greek specialties, can be eaten in the casual eatery's dining room or taken out. **Bar:** full bar. **Address:** 256 St-Viateur ouest H2V 1X9 **Location:** Between ave du Parc and rue Jeanne-Mance. **Parking:** street only.

ASEAN GARDEN   **Phone:** 514/487-8868   36

Asian
$10-$19

AAA Inspector Notes: The popular Asian restaurant is known for its Szechuan, Thai and sushi dishes as well as its tasty dim sum. The dining area is comfortable and relaxed, with party rooms available for groups. Worth trying are peanut butter dumplings, hot and sour soup, chicken satay, General Tao chicken, crispy duck, Szechuan-style shrimp and curried lamb. **Bar:** full bar. **Address:** 5828 rue Sherbrooke ouest H4A 1X3 **Location:** Corner of Melrose. **Parking:** street only.

B & M RESTAURANT   **Phone:** 514/488-1555   39

Canadian
$8-$34

AAA Inspector Notes: This popular family restaurant offers a variety of foods, including pizza, burgers, rotisserie and fried chicken, veal cutlets, pasta, salads, submarine sandwiches, smoked meat, souvlaki, brochettes, steak and seafood, Chinese dishes, hamburgers and poutine, a meal of fries doused in cheese curds and gravy. **Bar:** full bar. **Address:** 6200 Somerled Ave H3X 2B3 **Location:** Corner of boul Grand. **Parking:** street only.

B & M RESTAURANT   **Phone:** 514/484-3717   35

Canadian
$8-$34

AAA Inspector Notes: This popular family restaurant offers a variety of foods, including pizza, burgers, rotisserie and fried chicken, veal cutlets, pasta, salads, submarine sandwiches, smoked meat, souvlaki, brochettes, steak and seafood, Chinese dishes, hamburgers and poutine, a meal of fries doused in cheese curds and gravy. **Bar:** full bar. **Address:** 5800 rue Sherbrooke ouest H4A 1X3 **Location:** Corner of ave Melrose. **Parking:** street only.

BEAUTY'S LUNCHEONETTE   **Phone:** 514/849-8883   14

Canadian
$10-$30

AAA Inspector Notes: In the Plateau Mont-Royal district, the well-known breakfast and lunch restaurant has earned a regular clientèle by offering wholesome food, such as omelets, bagels with lox or cream cheese, bacon with eggs, sausages and great fresh-pressed orange juice. On weekends, expect a 10- to 15-minute wait at the door, even with a reservation. **Bar:** beer & wine. **Address:** 93 rue Mont-Royal ouest H2T 2S5 **Location:** Corner of rue St-Urbain. **Parking:** street only.

CHALET BAR-B-Q ROTISSERIE   **Phone:** 514/489-7235   31

Barbecue
$6-$11

AAA Inspector Notes: The simply decorated family restaurant is a favorite for broiled chicken cooked on a rotisserie over hardwood coals. Meals are served with barbecue sauce, a toasted roll and freshly cut fries. **Bar:** beer & wine. **Address:** 5456 rue Sherbrooke ouest H4A 1V9 **Location:** Just w of boul Decarie.

CHEZ BENNY   **Phone:** 514/735-1836   24

Kosher
$6-$17

AAA Inspector Notes: This busy glatt kosher cafeteria focuses on Israeli-style fast food: schnitzel, smoked meat, shish taouk, hot dogs, burgers, mixed grill and a salad bar. Honey pastry tastes great for dessert. Patrons pick up a tray, order at the counter, move down the line to collect their order from the kitchen staff and then seat themselves. **Bar:** beer only. **Address:** 5071 chemin Queen Mary H3W 1X4 **Location:** Just e of boul Decarie. **Parking:** street only.

COTE ST-LUC BAR-B-Q   **Phone:** 514/488-4011   27

Chicken
$9-$23

AAA Inspector Notes: A city favorite since 1953, the family restaurant specializes in charcoal-broiled barbecue chicken. Takeout orders are welcomed. **Bar:** wine only. **Address:** 5403 Cote St-Luc Rd H3X 2X3 **Location:** Just w of boul Decarie. **Parking:** street only.

CRACOVIE RESTAURANT POLONAIS   **Phone:** 514/731-3388   16

Polish
$15-$25

AAA Inspector Notes: This comfortable diner offers a very good selection of traditional Polish dishes, including pirogies, sausage, schnitzels and soups. The owners provide friendly and attentive service. **Bar:** full bar. **Address:** 5349 ave Gatineau H3T 1X1 **Location:** Just s of ave Lacombe. **Parking:** street only.

DUNNS FAMOUS DELICATESSEN   **Phone:** 514/387-3555   6

Deli
$7-$27

AAA Inspector Notes: The suburban delicatessen specializes in Montreal-style smoked meat on rye, grilled steaks, latkes, matzo ball soup, chopped liver and club rolls. For dessert, cheesecake is hard to beat. **Bar:** full bar. **Address:** 1029 rue du Marche-Central H4N 1J8 **Location:** Hwy 40 exit boul L'Acadie, 0.6 mi (1 km) n; in Marche Central Shopping Centre.

GIBEAU ORANGE JULEP   **Phone:** 514/738-7486   21

Canadian
$6-$10

AAA Inspector Notes: In a three-story building shaped like an orange, the family-friendly fast-food restaurant is easy to spot from the Decarie expressway. Not surprisingly, the house specialty is frothy, fresh-squeezed, sweetened orange juice. This also is a good place to grab an inexpensive burger, hot dog and fries. On Wednesday and Thursday nights, vintage and custom cars drop by. **Address:** 7700 boul Decarie H4P 2H4 **Location:** Corner of rue Pare.

(See map & index p. 342.)

KITCHENETTE   Phone: 514/527-1016

French
$14-$35

AAA Inspector Notes: This tastefully decorated bistro offers quality, French-inspired servings in small dish servings ideal for multicourse sampling. Its menu relies on fresh, market-inspired ingredients, while the daily chalkboard menu on the wall may include such skillfully prepared dishes as duck breast, pan-seared foie gras, rack of lamb, seared tuna, tiger prawns, pasta, warm duck salad or scallops. The excellent selection of wines by the glass allows for ideal wine pairings. **Bar:** full bar. **Address:** 1353 boul Rene-Levesque est H2L 2M1 **Location:** Corner of rue Panet. **Parking:** street only.

LA BINERIE MONT-ROYAL   Phone: 514/285-9078   ⑤

Quebec
$5-$11

AAA Inspector Notes: The bustling little diner, in operation since 1940, sits in the heart of a trendy residential neighborhood. The focus is on such authentic French Canadian foods as the house specialty: baked beans, as well as pea soup, "tourtiere" meat pie, stews, wieners and baked beans with maple syrup, or pâté made from pork drippings. For dessert, try Quebec classics like sugar pie or "pouding chomeur" (unemployment pudding). The narrow diner has a tidy but modest decor with counter or table seating. **Bar:** beer only. **Address:** 367 rue Mont-Royal est H2T 1R1 **Location:** Just w of rue St-Denis. **Parking:** street only. **Classic** ⒷⓁⒹ

LA CHRONIQUE   Phone: 514/271-3095   ⑪

International
$25-$42

AAA Inspector Notes: Internationally influenced fine Quebec cuisine is served in this small stylish dining room. The exciting menu bursts with creative food pairings and eye-catching presentations. Some weekends feature only a multi-course prix fixe menu. A la carte menu items include fresh fish, pan-seared foie gras with duck confit brioche, stuffed rabbit with red onions and scalloped potatoes, deer with potato crepe and grilled portobellos, and blackened duck with grilled shrimp. The service is refined. **Bar:** full bar. **Reservations:** required. **Address:** 99 rue Laurier ouest H2T 2N6 **Location:** Between ave du Parc and rue St-Urbain. **Parking:** street only. ⓁⒹ

LA LOUISIANE   Phone: 514/369-3073   ㊲

Cajun
$13-$30

AAA Inspector Notes: The popular Cajun restaurant does not accept individual reservations, so a short wait is to be expected on busy nights. Among menu selections are hush puppies, sweet potato fries, chicken wings, coconut beer shrimp, barbecue shrimp, shrimp or crawfish etouffee, crab cakes, blackened catfish, jambalaya, red bean soup gumbo and Southern pasta dishes. **Bar:** full bar. **Address:** 5850 rue Sherbrooke ouest H4A 1X5 **Location:** 0.4 mi (0.6 km) w of the Decarie Expwy; corner of rue Regent. **Parking:** street only. Ⓓ

LAURIER GORDON RAMSAY   Phone: 514/273-3671   ⑮

Canadian
$13-$28

AAA Inspector Notes: The menu at this eatery, now owned by brash celebrity chef Gordon Ramsay, offers freshly prepared comfort foods, including the house specialty-grain-fed rotisserie chicken served with legendary Laurier sauce, coleslaw and fresh-cut seasoned fries. Also choose from fish and chips, chicken pot pies, French onion soup, burgers, steak and fries, baby back ribs, porchetta sandwich, salmon cooked on a wood plank, hot chicken sandwich and poutine. Desserts and an impressive wine menu are offered. **Bar:** full bar. **Address:** 381 ave Laurier ouest H2V 2K3 **Location:** Just w of ave du Parc. **Parking:** street only. **Classic** ⓁⒹ

LE COIN D'ASIE   Phone: 514/482-4035   ㊵

Asian
$8-$20

AAA Inspector Notes: Casually elegant surroundings make for cozy dining at the West End dining room, where the menu centers on Vietnamese and other Asian dishes. Among examples are Tonkinese soup, seafood and fish, grilled meats, imperial rolls, fried won tons, sizzling platters, ginger chicken, salt-and-pepper calamari, Vietnamese steak, beef chop suey, fried rice with barbecue pork, noodles and several shrimp dishes. **Bar:** full bar. **Reservations:** suggested. **Address:** 6020 rue Sherbrooke ouest H4A 1X9 **Location:** Just e of rue Hampton. **Parking:** street only. ⓁⒹ

LE GRILL MIDTOWN   Phone: 514/739-3800   ㉓

Kosher
$6-$16

AAA Inspector Notes: This Israeli-style cafeteria features glatt kosher comfort foods, including hamburgers, beef brochettes, hotdogs, mixed grill, onion rings, grilled vegetables and a wide selection of chicken dishes. Apple or cherry pie are available for dessert, and there is a children's menu. Order and pay at the counter and wait at your table for the order to arrive. **Bar:** beer only. **Address:** 6445 boul Decarie H3W 3E1 **Location:** Hwy 15 (Decarie Expwy), on east side service road; corner of ave Plamondon; in Quality Hotel Midtown. ⓁⒹ

LE MAISTRE   Phone: 514/481-2109   ㉜

French
$20-$26

AAA Inspector Notes: This residential townhouse offers a quaint dining room operated by a French couple. Menu offerings include duck confit, fresh fish, filet of beef, lamb, veal, pork, kidneys, sweetbreads and some game specialties. Desserts are delicious and creatively presented. **Bar:** full bar. **Reservations:** suggested. **Address:** 5700 ave Monkland H4A 1E6 **Location:** Corner of rue Harvard. **Parking:** street only. Ⓓ

LE STADIUM CLUB RESTAURANT & BAR   Phone: 514/253-5195   ②

Italian
$11-$32

AAA Inspector Notes: This casual and stylish hotel restaurant impresses patrons with its views of the nearby Olympic Stadium. The menu features a variety of fine Italian dishes, steak and seafood. Seating is offered at tables and in more comfortable and intimate booths. **Bar:** full bar. **Address:** 5000 rue Sherbrooke est H1V 1A1 **Location:** Corner of rue Viau; just e of Botanical Garden and Olympic Stadium; in Hotel Universel Montreal. ⒷⓁⒹ

LEZVOS WEST   Phone: 514/484-0400   ㉖

Mediterranean
$12-$22

AAA Inspector Notes: This stylish and comfortable restaurant near the popular Monkland village offers a menu of Mediterranean dishes, including grilled fresh seafood. **Bar:** full bar. **Address:** 4235A boul Decarie H4A 3K4 **Location:** Just s of ave Monkland. **Parking:** street only. Ⓓ

MILOS RESTAURANT   Phone: 514/272-3522   ⑬

Greek
$22-$35

AAA Inspector Notes: The trendy taverna features Mediterranean-style decor, comfortable surroundings and a lively atmosphere. At the heart of the menu are skillful preparations of an excellent variety of fresh fish. Grilled octopus salad with capers is superb. Smartly attired staffers provide refined and friendly service. **Bar:** full bar. **Reservations:** suggested. **Address:** 5357 ave du Parc H2V 4G9 **Location:** Between ave Fairmount and St-Viateur. **Parking:** valet and street only. ⓁⒹ

(See map & index p. 342.)

MONKLAND TAVERN   Phone: 514/486-5768   (29)

California
$10-$26

AAA Inspector Notes: The popular neighborhood bistro exudes a warm, lively aura. Fresh pasta and salmon are specialties on a menu of California-style dishes, including a variety of salads and gourmet sandwiches. A good selection of microbrewed beers is offered. Seating on the seasonal terrace is popular. **Bar:** full bar. **Address:** 5555 Monkland Ave H4A 1E1 **Location:** Corner of Old Orchard Ave. **Parking:** street only.

 L D

NICKELS RESTAURANT   Phone: 514/735-7622

Canadian
$9-$20

AAA Inspector Notes: The Quebec chain of delicatessens specializes in Montreal-style smoked meat sandwiches, as well as pasta, burgers, fish, salads and seafood. **Bar:** full bar. **Reservations:** required. **Address:** 5252 chemin Cote-des-Neiges H3T 1X8 **Location:** Just n of Queen Mary. **Parking:** street only. B L D

PIAZZETTA   Phone: 514/847-0184

Italian
$10-$23

AAA Inspector Notes: This contemporary eatery offers a variety of reasonably priced Italian dishes including pizza, focaccia, sauteed pasta, veal cutlets, Italian pizza rolls and salads. Ask about the daily specials. **Bar:** full bar. **Address:** 4097 rue St-Denis H2W 2M7 **Location:** Just s of rue Rachel. **Parking:** street only.

 L D

PIZZAFIORE   Phone: 514/735-1555   (17)

Italian
$8-$18

AAA Inspector Notes: This popular family pizzeria offers a variety of more than 30 types of oven-baked pizzas, as well as calzones, pasta, chicken parmigiana, lasagna, veal scaloppine and panini with Italian sausage. **Bar:** full bar. **Address:** 3518 Lacombe Ave H3T 1M1 **Location:** Just e of chemin Cote-des-Neiges. **Parking:** street only.

 L D

QUARTIER PERSE   Phone: 514/488-6367   (25)

Iranian
$16-$30

AAA Inspector Notes: This casual diner is an ideal place to sample inexpensive Persian cuisine including kebabs of chicken, filet mignon or lamb. A seasonal exterior terrace is available. **Bar:** full bar. **Address:** 4241 boul Decarie H4A 3K4 **Location:** Corner of ave Monkland. **Parking:** street only. L D

RESTAURANT & TAVERNE MAGNAN   Phone: 514/935-9647   (22)

Steak
$9-$31

AAA Inspector Notes: Roast beef, Angus rib steaks, pigs' knuckles and grilled seafood are specialties at the informal eatery, which includes a boisterous tavern and a separate casual dining room downstairs. **Bar:** full bar. **Address:** 2602 rue St-Patrick H3K 1B8 **Location:** Corner of Charlevoix. L D

RESTAURANT BOFINGER BARBEQUE SMOKEHOUSE   Phone: 514/315-5056   (33)

Barbecue
$8-$20

AAA Inspector Notes: Guests can sample no-frills Southern barbecue at this popular diner. Guests line up, place their order and pay cash, then seat themselves at a table or vinyl-padded booth. When the meal is ready, the guest's name is called out. Po' boys and Cuban pork sandwiches are the specialty on a menu that also includes beef or pork ribs with a choice of sauce, maple-smoked meat, hamburgers, roast chicken and a variety of side dishes such as baked beans or macaroni and cheese. **Bar:** beer & wine. **Address:** 5667 rue Sherbrooke ouest H4A 1W6 **Location:** Just w of rue Oxford. **Parking:** street only.

 L D

RESTAURANT CHEZ DOVAL   Phone: 514/843-3390   (10)

Portuguese
$9-$20

AAA Inspector Notes: Varied preparations of Portuguese-style fare cooked on a wood-burning grill are offered at this casual eatery. Highlights include grilled sardines, chicken, steak with eggs, calamari, shrimp and brochettes. **Bar:** full bar. **Reservations:** suggested. **Address:** 150 Marie-Anne est H2W 1A5 **Location:** Just e of boul St-Laurent. **Parking:** street only. L D

RESTAURANT GANGES   Phone: 514/488-8850   (41)

Indian
$8-$14

AAA Inspector Notes: Amid casually elegant surroundings on the western outskirts of Montreal, well-attired servers promptly deliver Indian dishes seasoned with fresh herbs and spices. The menu includes tender tandoori chicken, fish and shrimp courses, biryanis (rice with vegetables or chicken), naan bread and tasty lamb, beef and chicken curries. **Bar:** full bar. **Address:** 6079 rue Sherbrooke ouest H4A 1Y2 **Location:** Just e of rue Hingston. **Parking:** street only. L D

RESTAURANT JOE BEEF MONTREAL   Phone: 514/935-6504   (19)

French
$25-$50

AAA Inspector Notes: This restaurant resembles a modest neighborhood tavern with wood floors and pub chairs. But the fine china and cloth table coverings set an elegant tone for the fine food conceived by accomplished Montreal chefs David McMillan and Frederic Morin. The offerings may include such items as oysters on the half shell, superb fish flown in at great cost, Dover sole, beef bavette, filet mignon with bone marrow or lobster Parmentier. The 35-seat restaurant has developed a strong loyal following. **Bar:** full bar. **Reservations:** required. **Address:** 2491 rue Notre-Dame ouest H3J 1N6 **Location:** Just e of rue Atwater. **Parking:** street only. D

RESTAURANT JUNI   Phone: 514/276-5864   (12)

Japanese
$21-$35

AAA Inspector Notes: Artfully presented sushi stands out on a fine menu that also includes dishes inspired by French, Italian and Mediterranean flavors. Guests can sample California rolls, a Peking duck appetizer and tasty preparations of sea urchin, eel, salmon, yellowfin tuna, king crab and soft-shell crab. The service is attentive and the decor casual at this stylish restaurant. **Bar:** full bar. **Reservations:** suggested. **Address:** 156 rue Laurier ouest H2T 2N7 **Location:** Just w of rue St-Urbain. **Parking:** street only. L D

RESTAURANT MOMESSO   Phone: 514/484-0005   (34)

Deli
$5-$15

AAA Inspector Notes: The simple diner tops steak and sausage subs with just enough hot sauce to elicit a smile. Other popular items include veggie and chicken subs, pizza, hamburgers and poutine. Hearty breakfasts are served every day except Sunday. **Bar:** full bar. **Address:** 5562 Upper Lachine Rd H4A 2A7 **Location:** Just w of ave Girouard. **Parking:** street only.

 B L D

RIB 'N REEF STEAKHOUSE & CIGAR LOUNGE   Phone: 514/735-1601   (18)

Steak
$29-$62

AAA Inspector Notes: High-quality preparations of prime USDA steak, roast beef, lobster and fresh fish make up most of the menu at this posh steakhouse. Elegant table settings, rich wood paneling and comfortable leather armchairs characterize this dining room, a local landmark since 1961. Patrons may also enjoy the seasonal terrace, an indoor cigar lounge and a wine cellar dining room available for group bookings. **Bar:** full bar. **Reservations:** suggested. **Address:** 8105 boul Decarie H4P 2H5 **Location:** Hwy 15 exit Jean-Talon; on east side service road. **Parking:** valet only. L D

(See map & index p. 342.)

RISTORANTE LA DORA
Phone: 514/255-8841

Italian
$9-$23

AAA Inspector Notes: Near the Olympic stadium, the popular, casual restaurant, family-run since 1940, specializes in quality food. On the menu are many selections of pasta, as well as breaded veal, mussels, fish and other seafood. The walls are white plaster, the tables tightly spaced and the wood chairs unpadded, evoking the charm of a traditional trattoria. **Bar:** full bar. **Reservations:** suggested. **Address:** 6837 rue Sherbrooke est H1N 1C7 **Location:** Corner of rue Arcand; 1.5 mi (2.5 km) e of Olympic Stadium. L D

ST-HUBERT
Phone: 514/844-9521

Canadian
$8-$22

AAA Inspector Notes: The pleasantly decorated family-friendly restaurant serves affordable chicken dinners, ribs, club sandwiches, chicken wings, salads, soups and hot chicken sandwiches. The children's menu includes animal nuggets. **Bar:** full bar. **Address:** 4462 rue St-Denis H2J 2L1 **Location:** Just s of Mont-Royal.

L D

SAINT-VIATEUR BAGEL & CAFÉ
Phone: 514/487-8051 30

Deli
$7-$15

AAA Inspector Notes: The bustling, stylish cafe serves legendary Montreal bagels baked in a wood-burning oven, using the same recipe as the original St-Viateur Street bagel shop, in operation since 1957. The menu lists varied bagel sandwiches, salads, specialty coffees and tempting desserts. A popular outdoor terrace opens seasonally. **Bar:** full bar. **Address:** 5629 Monkland Ave H4A 1E2 **Location:** Corner of rue Oxford. **Parking:** street only.

B L D

SCORES ROTISSERIE
Phone: 514/255-6060

Barbecue
$7-$25

AAA Inspector Notes: Those for whom cholesterol isn't a concern should consider a side dish of poutine--a greasily good Quebec specialty of french fries, melted cheese curds and gravy--with their preference among Scores Rotisserie's favorites, which include rotisserie chicken dishes, baby back ribs, sandwiches and preparations from the all-you-can-eat soup and salad bar. Although lemon pie, cakes and brownies beckon for dessert, another Quebec staple, tarte au sucre ("sugar pie"), merits extra consideration. **Bar:** full bar. **Address:** 5350 rue Sherbrooke est H1V 1A1 **Location:** Just e of rue Viau; facing Olympic Village. L D

SOY
Phone: 514/499-9399 7

Asian
$10-$18

AAA Inspector Notes: Eclectic yet casual decor adorns the dining room, where patrons enjoy such Asian dishes as pork dumplings, won ton ravioli, Szechuan duck, beef kalbi, crispy shrimp, General Tao chicken, crispy teriyaki chicken spring rolls, grilled portobello mushrooms and hot-and-sour or spicy vermicelli soup. Affordable dishes, ideal for sharing, are brought to the table in Chinese tradition: when each is ready rather than all together. Lunch specials include soup, rice, an entree, biscuit and tea or coffee. **Bar:** full bar. **Address:** 5258 boul St-Laurent H2T 1S1 **Location:** Just n of ave Fairmount. **Parking:** street only. L D

TAPEO-BAR A TAPAS
Phone: 514/495-1999 3

Spanish
$6-$17

AAA Inspector Notes: This lively and contemporary European-style tapas bar has seating at tightly spaced tables or at the bar. Sample a variety of affordable appetizer-sized tapas from a menu that includes seared tuna, octopus salad, sardines, calamari, paella, braised ribs, matchstick fries and seasonal fish and seafood. For dessert, sample a classic crème brûlée. For a small group, ask about booking the chef's table. **Bar:** full bar. **Reservations:** suggested. **Address:** 511 de Villeray est H2R 1H5 **Location:** Just e of rue Berri. **Parking:** on-site and street. L D

TEHRAN RESTAURANT
Phone: 514/488-0400 28

Middle Eastern
$14-$23

AAA Inspector Notes: Varied Iranian dishes are prepared at the casual diner located in a residential neighborhood facing the Vendome subway station. Thick lentil soup, basmati rice with red currants and marinated chicken in tomato sauce are highlights on an affordable menu that also includes filet mignon and chicken brochettes. Yogurt soda and Iranian tea are good thirst-quenchers. **Address:** 5065 boul de Maisonneuve ouest H4A 1Y9 **Location:** Corner of ave Grey. **Parking:** street only.

L D

THAI GRILL
Phone: 514/270-5566 9

Thai
$16-$32

AAA Inspector Notes: This sophisticated, corner restaurant, located in a trendy neighborhood, offers comfortable seating and Thai-inspired decor. Stylish lighting and impressive decorative woodwork gives the space an exotic feel. The open kitchen offers a glimpse into the chefs at work. Diners can sample a wide variety of Thai dishes, ranging from spicy to mild. Seafood selections, such as bass and red snapper, and curried noodles are representative of menu choices. **Bar:** full bar. **Reservations:** suggested. **Address:** 5101 boul St-Laurent H2T 1R9 **Location:** Corner of ave Laurier. **Parking:** street only.

L D

WILENSKY'S LIGHT LUNCH INC
Phone: 514/271-0247 8

Deli
$5-$10

AAA Inspector Notes: Family run since 1932, this vintage corner delicatessen served as a location for the 1974 film The Apprenticeship of Duddy Kravitz, starring Richard Dreyfuss. The decor remains virtually untouched. Patrons can take a seat at the counter and enjoy a Wilensky special sandwich made with salami, bologna and a choice of cheese, or nosh on a chopped egg sandwich, half-sour dill pickles, karnatzel (Jewish-style beef sausage infused with garlic, assorted seasonings and hot spice) or an all-beef hot dog. **Address:** 34 ave Fairmount ouest H2T 2M1 **Location:** Just w of boul St-Laurent. **Parking:** street only. Classic B L

MONT-ST-HILAIRE pop. 15,720

• Restaurants p. 392
• Part of Montréal area — see map p. 312

MANOIR ROUVILLE-CAMPBELL
Phone: 450/446-6060

Classic Historic Country Inn
$180-$400 6/1-10/31
$160-$350 11/1-5/31

Address: 125 chemin des Patriotes sud J3H 3G5 **Location:** Hwy 20 exit 113, 2.1 mi (4.2 km) s on Rt 133. **Facility:** French and English gardens grace the grounds, and upscale appointments adorn the rooms of this Tudor-style inn on the Richelieu River. 26 units. 3 stories, interior corridors. **Parking:** winter plug-ins. **Terms:** 10 day cancellation notice-fee imposed. **Amenities:** safes. **Dining:** La Table du Manoir, see separate listing. **Pool(s):** heated outdoor. **Activities:** Fee: boat dock. **Guest Services:** valet laundry.

WHERE TO EAT

LA TABLE DU MANOIR   **Phone:** 450/446-6060

French
$16-$40

AAA Inspector Notes: Guinea fowl and smoked salmon are specialties at the small, intimate restaurant, a favorite romantic spot for couples. The dining room affords views of the gardens and the Richelieu River. Sunday brunch is especially popular. **Bar:** full bar. **Reservations:** suggested. **Address:** 125 chemin des Patriotes sud J3H 3G5 **Location:** Hwy 20 exit 113, 2.1 mi (4.2 km) s on Rt 133; in Manoir Rouville-Campbell. B L D

MONT-ST-PIERRE (B-8) pop. 230, elev. 8m/25'

Because of its high altitude, Mont-St-Pierre is among the few southern Canada locales with a tundra region and a herd of caribou. At the edge of town is 411-metre (1,555-ft.) Mont St-Pierre, one of the most challenging hang-gliding sites in eastern North America. A road travels to its summit, which offers outstanding views.

The town provides access to the Chic-Chocs' 1,268-metre (4,797-ft.) Mont Jacques-Cartier, the tallest mountain in southeast Canada.

The scenic portion of Hwy. 132 passes through Mont-St-Pierre on its tour of the Gaspé Peninsula. East of town, Hwy. 132 joins Hwy. 299, which enters Gaspésie National Park *(see attraction listing p. 470).*

MONT-TREMBLANT (E-4)

• Restaurants p. 396

Overshadowed by the 932-metre-high (3,058-ft.) peak of Mont Tremblant, the highest peak in the Laurentians region, the town of Mont-Tremblant is surrounded by the Laurentians' greatest concentration of resort areas. Just a little more than an hour's drive from Montréal and less than 2 hours from Ottawa, scenic Mont-Tremblant is a year-round recreation destination where visitors can indulge in favorite pastimes or learn new ones from professionals.

Spring through fall, hiking and bicycling opportunities are many and the settings are varied—flat or steep, open or wooded, inland or waterside. The 232-kilometre (144-mi.) Parc linéaire Le P'tit Train du Nord is Canada's longest linear park, and a favorite with bicyclists, cross-country skiers and snowmobilers. Mont-Tremblant National Park *(see attraction listing)* is forest wilderness with ample wildlife viewing opportunities. The more adventurous can climb rock faces. Six golf courses and numerous tennis courts round out the venue.

The area's streams, rivers and waterfalls as well as hundreds of lakes offer myriad chances for swimming, boating, sailing, kayaking, water skiing, canoeing and viewing experiences. Fishing aficionados can count among their catch speckled and brown trout and northern pike.

Winter recreation facilities include 94 alpine ski runs, tubing slopes and groomed trails for cross-country skiers. For snowmobilers, thousands of kilometres of trails lead to and through small towns and

through wilderness areas. Morning and noontime dog sledding trips are available. For the truly hardy, ice climbing lessons are available—along with the rental gear.

Special events, large and small, are held throughout the year. In the summer Circuit Mont-Tremblant holds international automobile races from mid-June through September 30; phone (819) 425-6363. In July the Tremblant International Blues Festival (Festival international du blues de Tremblant) attracts thousands—bands from across North and South America perform on outdoor stages and in bars and restaurants.

Mont-Tremblant Chamber of Commerce: 990 rue Lauzon, Mont-Tremblant, QC, Canada J8E 3J5. **Phone:** (819) 425-8441.

Mont-Tremblant Tourism Office: 5080 Montée Ryan, Mont-Tremblant, QC, Canada J8E 1S4. **Phone:** (877) 425-2434.

MONT-TREMBLANT CRUISES (Les Croisières Mont-Tremblant) departs from the Mont-Tremblant village wharf (Quai Fédéral) near jct. ch. du Village and Montée Ryan. Passengers aboard the 66-seat covered boat are afforded a 1-hour narrated cruise on lac Tremblant. Parking is available across the street at Parc des Chutes. Tickets can be purchased in advance but departures are on a first-come, first-served basis; phone ahead to check availability.

Hours: Cruises depart daily at 11, 12:30, 2, 3:30 and 5, mid-July to early Sept.; Mon.-Fri. at 2:30 and 3:30, Sat.-Sun. at 12:30, 2, 3:30 and 5, late June to mid-July; Mon.-Fri. at 2, Sat.-Sun. at 2 and 3:30, late May-late June; Mon.-Fri. at 2, Sat.-Sun. at 2 and 3:30, early Sept. to mid-Oct. Hours may vary. **Cost:** $18; $15 (ages 65+); $5 (ages 6-12). **Phone:** (819) 425-1045.

MONT-TREMBLANT NATIONAL PARK (Parc national du Mont-Tremblant), 23 km (14 mi.) e. of Hwy. 117N, comprises 1,510 square kilometres (583 sq. mi.) and is a year-round favorite for outdoor recreational activities in the Laurentians. Rounded hilltops alternating with high peaks, trees as far as you can see, 400 lakes, a network of rivers and streams, 196 species of birds and facilities for summer and winter activities make the park one of Québec's more popular vacation areas. *See Recreation Chart.*

Visitor centers are at 3824 ch. du Lac Supérieur in Lac-Supérieur; 1002 rue du Lac Caché in La Macaza; 5555 ch. du Parc in St-Côme; and 2954 Rte. 125N in St-Donat. Pets are not permitted. **Hours:** Open daily; hours vary with the season. **Cost:** $6; $2.75 (ages 6-17); $12 (family, two adults and children); $8.75 (family, one adult and children). **Phone:** (819) 688-2281 or (800) 665-6527.

GAMBLING ESTABLISHMENTS

• **Casino de Mont-Tremblant** is at 300 ch. des Pléiades. **Hours:** Mon.-Thurs. noon-midnight, Fri.

noon-3 a.m., Sat. 11 a.m.-3 a.m., Sun. 11 a.m.-midnight. Phone ahead to confirm schedule. **Phone:** (819) 429-4150.

AUBERGE LE LUPIN BED & BREAKFAST

Phone: (819)425-5474

Bed & Breakfast
$106-$190 11/16-5/31
$107-$155 6/1-11/15

Address: 127 rue Pinoteau J8E 1G2 **Location:** Centre. **Facility:** This welcoming log home has spacious rooms ideal for small families, is just 0.6 mi (1 km) from the ski hill and is within walking distance of public beaches. 9 units. 2 stories (no elevator), interior corridors. **Terms:** 2 night minimum stay - seasonal and/or weekends, 21 day cancellation notice-fee imposed. **Activities:** beach access, cross country skiing. **Guest Services:** complimentary laundry.

Plan. Map. Go.

TripTik® Travel Planner

Where premier mapping technology meets complete travel information. Only on AAA.com and CAA.ca.

CHÂTEAU BEAUVALLON

Phone: 819/681-6611

Condominium
$159-$449

Address: 6385 Montee-Ryan J8E 1S5 **Location:** Hwy 117 exit 119, 4 mi (6.4 km) e. **Facility:** Château Beauvallon, a vintage Mont-Tremblant lodging that once stood at this location, inspired this upscale project offering luxurious one-, two- and three-bedroom condos. 70 condominiums, some efficiencies and kitchens. 3 stories, interior corridors. **Parking:** on-site and valet, winter plug-ins. **Terms:** check-in 4 pm, 3 day cancellation notice-fee imposed. **Amenities:** high-speed Internet, safes. **Dining:** Bon Vivant Grill, see separate listing. **Pool(s):** heated outdoor, heated indoor. **Activities:** whirlpool, putting green, hiking trails, exercise room. *Fee:* massage. **Guest Services:** valet and coin laundry, area transportation-within 9 mi (15 km). **Free Special Amenities:** full breakfast and high-speed Internet.

(See ad this page.)

COMFORT INN & SUITES MONT-TREMBLANT

Phone: (819)429-6000

Hotel
$100-$150

Address: 860 rue LaLonde (CP 4598) J8E 1A1 **Location:** On Hwy 117, 0.5 mi (0.8 km) ne of St-Jovite village. **Facility:** 94 units. 3 stories, interior corridors. **Parking:** winter plug-ins. **Terms:** check-in 4 pm, 2 night minimum stay - seasonal and/or weekends, cancellation fee imposed. **Amenities:** high-speed Internet. **Pool(s):** heated indoor. **Activities:** whirlpools, snowmobiling. *Fee:* massage. **Guest Services:** coin laundry, area transportation (fee)-ski hills.

COUNTRY INN & SUITES BY CARLSON
Phone: 819/681-5555

Hotel

Rates not provided

Address: 160 chemin Cure-Deslauriers J8E 1T1 **Location:** In Mont-Tremblant Resort Centre. **Facility:** 140 units, some kitchens. 4 stories, interior corridors. **Parking:** on-site (fee). **Terms:** check-in 4 pm. **Amenities:** *Fee:* video games, high-speed Internet. **Pool(s):** heated outdoor. **Activities:** sauna, whirlpool, rental boats, rental canoes, rental paddleboats, rental sailboats, rental sailboards, fishing, cross country skiing, recreation programs, rental bicycles, hiking trails, jogging, playground, limited exercise equipment. *Fee:* waterskiing, charter fishing, golf-36 holes, 6 lighted tennis courts, downhill skiing, ice skating, massage. **Guest Services:** coin laundry, area transportation.

⊪ ⊉ 🛜 ✕ FEE 📺 🖥 🖵 / SOME UNITS 🖼

ERMITAGE DU LAC MONT TREMBLANT
Phone: 819/681-2222

Condominium

Rates not provided

Address: 150 chemin Cure-Deslauriers J8E 1T1 **Location:** In Mont-Tremblant Resort Centre. **Facility:** Most of these luxurious condos have a fireplace and balcony. All have either an efficiency or full kitchen area. 69 condominiums. 5 stories, interior corridors. **Parking:** on-site (fee). **Terms:** check-in 4 pm. **Amenities:** high-speed Internet (fee). **Pool(s):** heated outdoor. **Activities:** whirlpool, limited beach access, rental boats, rental canoes, rental paddleboats, rental sailboats, rental sailboards, fishing, cross country skiing, recreation programs, rental bicycles, hiking trails, jogging, playground, exercise room. *Fee:* waterskiing, charter fishing, golf-36 holes, 6 lighted tennis courts, downhill skiing, ice skating. **Guest Services:** valet and coin laundry.

⊪ ⊉ BIZ 🛜 ✕ FEE 📺 🖥 🖼 🖵

FAIRMONT TREMBLANT
Phone: (819)681-7000

Resort Hotel

$169-$599 12/21-5/31
$169-$359 6/1-12/20

Address: 3045 chemin de la Chapelle J8E 1E1 **Location:** In Mont-Tremblant Resort Centre. **Facility:** This full-service hotel and spa offers ski-in/ski-out facilities along with well-appointed meeting space and three restaurants. 314 units, some efficiencies and kitchens. 7 stories, interior corridors. **Parking:** valet only. **Terms:** check-in 4 pm, 7 day cancellation notice-fee imposed. **Amenities:** safes, honor bars. *Fee:* video games, high-speed Internet. **Dining:** 2 restaurants, also, Restaurant Le Windigo, see separate listing. **Pool(s):** heated outdoor, heated indoor. **Activities:** sauna, whirlpools, steamrooms, rental boats, rental canoes, rental paddleboats, rental sailboats, cross country skiing, rental bicycles, hiking trails, exercise room, spa. *Fee:* fishing, charter fishing, golf-36 holes, 8 lighted tennis courts, downhill skiing, ice skating. **Guest Services:** valet and coin laundry.

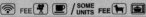

SAVE ECO ⊪ 🛖 Y 🕊 CALL 🔽 ⊉ BIZ
🛜 FEE 📺 🖵 / SOME UNITS FEE 🐾 🖼

A Full Service Luxury Resort. One of the closest locations to the Mt Tremblant Ski slopes.

Safety tip: Keep a current AAA/CAA Road Atlas in every vehicle

HOMEWOOD SUITES BY HILTON-MONT-TREMBLANT
Phone: 819/681-0808

Extended Stay Hotel

Rates not provided

AAA Benefit:
Contemporary luxury at a special Member rate.

Address: 3035 chemin de la Chapelle J8E 1E1 **Location:** In Mont-Tremblant Resort Centre. **Facility:** 100 kitchen units, some two bedrooms. 3-5 stories, interior corridors. **Parking:** on-site (fee). **Terms:** check-in 4 pm. **Amenities:** high-speed Internet. **Pool(s):** outdoor. **Activities:** sauna, whirlpool, rental boats, rental canoes, rental paddleboats, rental sailboats, rental sailboards, cross country skiing, recreation programs, rental bicycles, hiking trails, jogging, playground. *Fee:* waterskiing, fishing, charter fishing, golf-36 holes, 6 lighted tennis courts, downhill skiing, massage. **Guest Services:** valet and coin laundry, area transportation.

⊪ 🕊 ⊉ 🛜 🖥 🖼 🖵

HÔTEL QUINTESSENCE
Phone: (819)425-3400

Boutique Hotel

$350-$1735

Address: 3004 chemin de la Chapelle J8E 1E1 **Location:** Hwy 117 N exit 119 (Montee Ryan), 6 mi (10 km) e to Mont-Tremblant Resort Centre. **Facility:** This lakefront boutique hotel and spa, on three acres of private grounds in the resort village, has spacious, luxurious rooms and suites (of at least 700 square feet) with spacious marble bathrooms. 30 units, some cottages. 4 stories, interior corridors. **Parking:** valet only. **Terms:** check-in 4 pm, 2 night minimum stay - seasonal, 7 day cancellation notice-fee imposed. **Amenities:** high-speed Internet, safes, honor bars. **Dining:** Restaurant Quintessence & Winebar, see separate listing. **Pool(s):** heated outdoor. **Activities:** sauna, whirlpool, steamroom, beach access, canoeing, exercise room, spa. **Guest Services:** valet laundry, area transportation-ski hill & village.

SAVE ⊪ 🛖 Y 🕊 ⊉ BIZ 🛜 ✕ FEE 📺
🖵 / SOME UNITS 🖼

LA TOUR DES VOYAGEURS
Phone: 819/681-2000

Condominium

Rates not provided

Address: 151 chemin Cure-Deslauriers J8E 1T1 **Location:** In Mont-Tremblant Resort Centre. **Facility:** This property is in the center of the resort village and offers studios and one- and two-bedroom condos. 212 condominiums, some kitchens. 4 stories, interior corridors. **Parking:** on-site (fee). **Terms:** check-in 4 pm. **Amenities:** *Fee:* video games, high-speed Internet. **Pool(s):** heated outdoor. **Activities:** sauna, whirlpools, rental boats, rental canoes, rental paddleboats, rental sailboats, rental sailboards, fishing, ice skating, recreation programs, rental bicycles, hiking trails, jogging, playground, exercise room. *Fee:* waterskiing, golf-36 holes, miniature golf, 6 lighted tennis courts, downhill skiing, massage. **Guest Services:** valet and coin laundry, area transportation.

⊪ 🕊 ⊉ 🛜 FEE 📺 🖵 / SOME UNITS 🖥 🖼

LE BOISÉ DU RUISSEAU CLAIR
Phone: 514/429-6000

Condominium

Rates not provided

Address: 860 rue Lalonde CP 4598 J8E 1A1 **Location:** On Hwy 117 0.5 mi (0.8 km) ne of St-Village. **Facility:** These upscale condo-suites feature fully equipped kitchens, gas fireplaces, luxurious bedding and indoor heated parking in the basement. 25 condominiums. 3 stories, interior corridors. **Terms:** check-in 4 pm. **Amenities:** high-speed Internet. **Guest Services:** complimentary laundry.

🛜 ✕ 🖥 🖼

LE GRAND LODGE MONT-TREMBLANT
Phone: (819)425-2734

Resort Hotel
$134-$384 12/1-5/31
$134-$274 6/1-11/30

Address: 2396 rue Labelle J8E 1T8 **Location:** On Rt 327, 0.3 mi (0.4 km) s of Montee Ryan. **Facility:** This upscale lakefront hotel, in close proximity to a golf course and ski hill, features a log-beamed lobby and spacious guest rooms. 112 units, some two bedrooms and kitchens. 5 stories, interior corridors. **Parking:** winter plug-ins. **Terms:** check-in 4 pm, 2 night minimum stay - seasonal and/or weekends, 8 day cancellation notice-fee imposed. **Amenities:** video games (fee). **Pool(s):** heated indoor. **Activities:** sauna, whirlpool, steamrooms, canoeing, paddleboats, fishing, 4 tennis courts, cross country skiing, ice skating, rental bicycles, playground, game room, horseshoes, volleyball, exercise room, spa. *Fee:* downhill skiing. **Guest Services:** valet and coin laundry, area transportation-Tremblant ski area & village.

LE LODGE DE LA MONTAGNE
Phone: 819/681-2000

Condominium
Rates not provided

Address: 140 Au pied de la Montagne J8E 1T1 **Location:** In Mont-Tremblant Resort Centre. **Facility:** Many of these condo units have fireplaces and are convenient to ski hills, village shops and nightlife. 134 condominiums, some kitchens. 5 stories, interior corridors. **Parking:** on-site (fee). **Terms:** check-in 4 pm. **Amenities:** *Fee:* video games, high-speed Internet. **Pool(s):** heated outdoor. **Activities:** sauna, whirlpools, rental boats, rental canoes, rental paddleboats, rental sailboards, fishing, cross country skiing, recreation programs, rental bicycles, hiking trails, jogging, exercise room. *Fee:* waterskiing, charter fishing, golf-36 holes, 6 lighted tennis courts, downhill skiing, ice skating, massage. **Guest Services:** valet and coin laundry, area transportation.

LE SOMMET DES NEIGES
Phone: 819/681-2000

Hotel
Rates not provided

Address: 150 chemin au Pied de la Montagne J8E 1T1 **Location:** In Mont-Tremblant Resort Centre. **Facility:** 112 kitchen units, some two and three bedrooms. 4 stories, interior corridors. **Parking:** on-site (fee). **Terms:** check-in 4 pm. **Amenities:** *Fee:* video games, high-speed Internet. **Pool(s):** heated outdoor. **Activities:** sauna, whirlpool, rental boats, rental canoes, rental paddleboats, rental sailboats, rental sailboards, fishing, cross country skiing, recreation programs, rental bicycles, hiking trails, jogging, playground, game room, exercise room. *Fee:* waterskiing, charter fishing, golf-36 holes, miniature golf, 6 lighted tennis courts, downhill skiing, ice skating, massage. **Guest Services:** valet and coin laundry, area transportation.

LE WESTIN RESORT & SPA, TREMBLANT
Phone: (819)681-8000

Hotel
$199-$559

WESTIN HOTELS & RESORTS **AAA Benefit:** Enjoy up to 15% off your next stay, plus Starwood Preferred Guest® bonuses.

Address: 100 chemin Kandahar J8E 1E2 **Location:** Hwy 117 N exit 119 (Montee Ryan), 6 mi (10 km) e, follow signs. **Facility:** In the Mont-Tremblant ski village, the hotel offers luxuriously appointed, spacious accommodations as well as an oversize exterior four-season hot tub and a well-equipped exercise room. 123 units, some two bedrooms, efficiencies and kitchens. 6 stories, interior corridors. **Parking:** on-site (fee) and valet. **Terms:** check-in 4 pm. **Amenities:** safes. *Fee:* video games, high-speed Internet. **Dining:** Restaurant Yamada, see separate listing. **Pool(s):** heated outdoor. **Activities:** sauna, whirlpool, rental boats, rental canoes, rental paddleboats, rental sailboats, cross country skiing, rental bicycles, hiking trails, playground, exercise room, spa. *Fee:* fishing, charter fishing, golf-18 holes, 8 lighted tennis courts, downhill skiing, ice skating. **Guest Services:** valet and coin laundry, area transportation-area attractions. **Free Special Amenities:** newspaper.

PLACE ST-BERNARD
Phone: 819/681-2000

Condominium
Rates not provided

Address: 135 chemin Kandahar J8E 1T1 **Location:** In Mont-Tremblant Resort Centre. **Facility:** Most of these spacious studio, one- and two-bedroom units, in the center of the resort village, have fireplaces; a few units have a second-level loft. 105 condominiums, some kitchens. 3 stories, interior corridors. **Parking:** on-site (fee). **Terms:** off-site registration, check-in 4 pm. **Amenities:** *Fee:* video games, high-speed Internet. **Pool(s):** heated indoor. **Activities:** sauna, whirlpools, rental canoes, rental paddleboats, rental sailboats, rental sailboards, fishing, cross country skiing, recreation programs, rental bicycles, hiking trails, jogging, playground. *Fee:* boats, waterskiing, charter fishing, golf-36 holes, miniature golf, 6 lighted tennis courts, downhill skiing, ice skating. **Guest Services:** valet and coin laundry.

RESIDENCE INN MONT TREMBLANT MANOIR LABELLE
Phone: (819)681-4000

Extended Stay Hotel
$296-$398

AAA Benefit:
AAA hotel discounts of 5% or more.

Address: 170 chemin du Cure-Deslauriers J8E 1C9 **Location:** In Mont-Tremblant Resort Centre. **Facility:** 126 units, some efficiencies and kitchens. 3 stories, interior corridors. **Parking:** on-site (fee). **Terms:** check-in 4 pm. **Amenities:** video games (fee), high-speed Internet. **Pool(s):** heated outdoor. **Activities:** rental boats, rental canoes, rental paddleboats, rental sailboats, rental sailboards, fishing, cross country skiing, rental bicycles, hiking trails, jogging, exercise room. *Fee:* waterskiing, charter fishing, golf-36 holes, miniature golf, 6 lighted tennis courts, downhill skiing, ice skating, massage. **Guest Services:** valet and coin laundry.

WHERE TO EAT

AUX TRUFFES   Phone: 819/681-4544

French
$35-$46

AAA Inspector Notes: Chef/owner Martin Faucher, offers an innovative menu of quality ingredients that flavor such creatively presented dishes as foie gras, guinea fowl, scallops, sweetbreads, milk-fed veal, salmon, Boileau-region red deer, Angus filet mignon, beef tartar and breast of duck. An extensive selection of fine international wine is available as well as a six- or eight-course gastronomic menu. Service is knowledgeable and professional. A lighter lunch menu is served in summer and winter seasons. **Bar:** full bar. **Reservations:** suggested. **Address:** 3035 chemin de la Chapelle J8E 1B1 **Location:** In Mont-Tremblant Resort Centre. **Parking:** on-site (fee).

L D

BON VIVANT GRILL   Phone: 819/681-6488

French
$14-$48

AAA Inspector Notes: This casually elegant hotel restaurant serves pleasantly presented dishes of regional cuisine, including lamb, beef, pasta and seafood. Lighter menu items include fish and chips, burgers, pizza, club sandwiches and lunch salads topped with an optional grilled item. **Bar:** full bar. **Reservations:** suggested. **Address:** 6385 Montee-Ryan J8E 1S5 **Location:** Hwy 117 exit 119, 4 mi (6.4 km) e; in Chateau Beauvallon.

B L D

BULLSEYE   Phone: 819/681-2855

Steak
$11-$50

AAA Inspector Notes: At the foot of the ski slopes, this Western-themed steakhouse has a lively pub area for casual dining and an elegant evening dining room. The menu lists filet mignon, New York sirloin, rack of lamb, surf and turf, grilled salmon, Thai chicken, chicken quesadillas, burgers and salads, as well as children's fare. **Bar:** full bar. **Address:** 118 chemin Kandahar, CP 2609 J8E 1B1 **Location:** In Mont-Tremblant Resort Centre. **Parking:** street only. L D

CRÊPERIE CATHERINE   Phone: 819/681-4888

French
$10-$20

AAA Inspector Notes: In a cozy wood cottage in the heart of the resort village, the lovely creperie prepares crepes (thin pancakes) before guests' eyes in an open kitchen. Meal supplements include salad, escargots and French onion soup. **Bar:** full bar. **Address:** 113 chemin Kandahar J8E 1A1 **Location:** In Mont-Tremblant Resort Centre. B L D

FAT MARDIS   Phone: 819/681-2439

Cajun
$10-$30

AAA Inspector Notes: This popular restaurant and bar is at the foot of the ski slopes and focuses on Cajun fare, including Louisiana-style po' boy sandwiches, gumbo, crab cakes, burgers, chicken wings, beer-battered halibut fish and chips, ribs, sweet potato fries and AAA Angus steaks. The decor replicates the style of a vintage Bourbon Street burlesque nightclub and includes upholstered booths ideal for intimate dining. **Bar:** full bar. **Address:** 3035 ch de la Chapelle J8E 1E1 **Location:** In Mont-Tremblant Resort Centre. **Parking:** on-site (fee). L D

LA FORGE BAR & GRILL   Phone: 819/681-4900

Canadian
$10-$48

AAA Inspector Notes: Located at the foot of the ski hill, this restaurant has a casual pub-bistro downstairs and a finer dining room upstairs. The menu features meats, game and seafood cooked over a maplewood grill. The dining experience is bolstered by an impressive wine list. Salads, pub food and tasty desserts round out the menu. **Bar:** full bar. **Reservations:** suggested. **Address:** 3041 chemin de la Chapelle J8E 1B1 **Location:** In Mont-Tremblant Resort Centre. L D

MICROBRASSERIE LA DIABLE   Phone: 819/681-4546

International
$14-$24

AAA Inspector Notes: This jovial country pub features beers brewed on the premises and a menu of international dishes, including European sausages, chicken cordon bleu, Quebec poutine, grilled salmon, pasta, chicken. Youngsters can order from the children's menu. **Bar:** full bar. **Address:** 117 chemin Kandahar J8E 1B1 **Location:** In Mont-Tremblant Resort Centre.

L D K

MOE'S BAR & GRILL   Phone: 819/425-9821

Canadian
$10-$25

AAA Inspector Notes: In a rural mountain village, this outpost of the regional chain prepares such Canadian pub foods as Montreal-style smoked meat, steaks, fish, pizza, burgers, calamari and French onion soup. **Bar:** full bar. **Address:** 340 Rt 117 (CP 4687) J8E 2X3 **Location:** On Hwy 117; in St-Jovite Village; in Club de Vacances Tremblant. L D

PIZZATERIA TREMBLANT   Phone: 819/681-4522

Italian
$10-$16

AAA Inspector Notes: This casual family-friendly restaurant at the center of the resort village has a separate bar area and a seasonal terrace. The menu features a choice of 26 thin-crust pizzas, focaccia, Italian grilled sandwiches, calzones and pasta. **Bar:** full bar. **Address:** 118 chemin Kandahar J8E 1B1 **Location:** In Mont-Tremblant Resort Centre. **Parking:** no self-parking. L D

RESTAURANT BAR TERRASSE ANTIPASTO
                                                  Phone: 819/425-7580

Italian
$11-$35

AAA Inspector Notes: Housed in the town's original train station and bedecked in decor fitting of the location, the family restaurant delivers hearty food, from wood-oven pizzas and pasta dishes to preparations of veal and chicken. Food is inexpensive, and portions are generous. **Bar:** full bar. **Address:** 855 rue de St-Jovite J8E 3J8 **Location:** Centre; in St-Jovite sector. L D

RESTAURANT LE CHEVAL DE JADE
                                                  Phone: 819/425-5233

French
$25-$35

AAA Inspector Notes: Elegant country décor infuses this cozy rural cottage, a perfect spot in which enjoy fine French-influenced cuisine. In addition to the main menu, the six- and eight-course tasting menus are popular choices. Choices include pan-seared foie gras, bouillabaisse, scallops, tableside-flambéed tiger prawns, tilapia, red tuna, filet mignon, duck magret, red deer carpaccio and fish soup prepared with fresh fish imported from France. Service is refined. The seasonal terrace is popular in summer. **Bar:** full bar. **Reservations:** suggested. **Address:** 688 rue de St-Jovite J8E 3J8 **Location:** Just ne of Hwy 117 N; centre; in St-Jovite sector. D K

RESTAURANT LE WINDIGO   Phone: 819/681-7685

Canadian
$20-$54

AAA Inspector Notes: Choose from an a la carte menu of fine regional Canadian cuisine at this upscale restaurant or take advantage of the themed gourmet buffets, including the surf and turf along with a salad and dessert selection on the weekend. Breakfast, lunch and dinner are served and guests in the dining room may occasionally see deer walk right up to the restaurant windows. A stylish lounge area with lovely mountain views offers a light menu. Convenient valet parking is available. **Bar:** full bar. **Reservations:** suggested. **Address:** 3045 chemin de la Chapelle J8E 1E1 **Location:** In Mont-Tremblant Resort Centre; in Fairmont Tremblant. **Parking:** valet only.

B L D CALL M

RESTAURANT QUINTESSENCE & WINEBAR
Phone: 819/425-3400

French
$16-$48

AAA Inspector Notes: This luxurious boutique-hotel restaurant offers table seating in either the posh wine bar or the upscale dining room. There's also a chef's table off the kitchen for a unique culinary experience or a wine-sampling dining area in the wine cellar. The menu of innovative regional French cuisine may include pan-seared foie gras, truffle-flavored lobster bisque, warm oysters, halibut, red mullet, lobster tail, organic duck, rabbit, Angus beef, rack of lamb and quail. **Bar:** full bar. **Address:** 3004 chemin de la Chapelle J8E 1E1 **Location:** Hwy 117 N exit 119 (Montee Ryan), 6 mi (10 km) e to Mont-Tremblant Resort Centre; in Hôtel Quintessence. **Parking:** valet only.

[B] [L] [D]

RESTAURANT YAMADA
Phone: 819/681-4141

Japanese
$20-$35

AAA Inspector Notes: In the village, the upscale, stylish restaurant offers a variety of imported sakes to complement dozens of choices of freshly prepared sushi, sashimi and maki. **Bar:** full bar. **Reservations:** suggested. **Address:** 100 chemin Kandahar J8E 1E2 **Location:** Hwy 117 N exit 119 (Montee Ryan), 6 mi (10 km) e, follow signs; in Le Westin Resort & Spa, Tremblant. **Parking:** on-site (fee) and valet. [D]

MURDOCHVILLE (B-9) pop. 812

Since the early 1950s Murdochville has been the site of a prosperous copper mining industry. Local companies are known for their use of the room and pillar method of mining: thick pillars of rock are left to support the ceilings of dugout chambers.

Murdochville Tourist Bureau: 365 av. Miller, Murdochville, QC, Canada G0E 1W0. **Phone:** (418) 784-2242.

COPPER INTERPRETATION CENTRE OF MURDOCHVILLE (Centre d'interprétation du cuivre de Murdochville), 345 Rte. 198, features displays and interactive exhibits about the history of copper mining. A 1-hour tour of a copper mine and a 1-hour tour of a windmill site are offered. **Time:** Allow 2 hours minimum. **Hours:** Daily 9-5, early June-late Sept. **Cost:** Mine tour $16; $9 (ages 15+); $7 (ages 6-14). Windmill site tour $21; $11 (children). Combination ticket for both tours $27; $16 (children); $60 (family). Prices may vary; phone ahead. **Phone:** (418) 784-3335, or (800) 487-8601 in Québec.

NEW RICHMOND (C-8) pop. 7,760

THE GASPÉSIAN BRITISH HERITAGE VILLAGE (Village gaspésien de l'Héritage Britannique) is 3 km (1.9 mi.) n.w. to 351 boul. Perron Ouest. Celebrating the heritage of British settlers, the village comprises 24 typical Gaspésian buildings dating from the late 18th century to the early 20th century.

Visitors can see a tearoom and a forge, take a guided tour or stroll wooded paths that run down to the Baie des Chaleurs. Each Labour Day weekend, the village hosts the New Richmond Bluegrass Festival. **Time:** Allow 2 hours minimum. **Hours:** Mon.-Sat. 10-5, July-Sept. **Cost:** $8; $5 (ages 0-11 and 65+); $20 (family). **Phone:** (418) 392-4487.

HOTEL LE FRANCIS
Phone: (418)392-4485

Hotel
$115-$230

Address: 210 chemin Pardiac G0C 2B0 **Location:** Just s of Rt 132. **Facility:** 38 units. 2 stories (no elevator), interior/exterior corridors. **Parking:** winter plug-ins. **Terms:** cancellation fee imposed. **Amenities:** Some: high-speed Internet. **Pool(s):** heated outdoor. **Activities:** whirlpool, fishing, cross country skiing, snowmobiling, bicycles, hiking trails. **Guest Services:** valet laundry.

[icons] SOME UNITS

NORMANDIN (C-5) pop. 3,220

GARDENS OF NORMANDIN (Jardins de Normandin), 1515 av. du Rocher, comprises 17 hectares (42 acres). The lush site illustrates the evolution of gardening. Guided tours are conducted through such areas as an herb garden, an English garden, a flower path and an Oriental flower tapestry.

CLOSURE INFORMATION: The site is closed until sometime in 2012; phone ahead for updates and to confirm schedule and prices. **Time:** Allow 1 hour, 30 minutes minimum. **Hours:** Tours daily 9-6, June 22-Labour Day. **Cost:** $12; $10 (ages 66+); $6 (ages 7-22); $25 (family, two adults and children ages 0-11). **Phone:** (418) 274-1993.

NORTH HATLEY (F-9) pop. 722
• Restaurants p. 398

CAPELTON MINES (L' Épopée de Capelton), 8 km (5 mi.) e. to Rte. 108, is a journey through time. Visitors travel by wagon up the mountain to the copper mine's entrance. The temperature in the mine is 9 C (48 F). They then explore the shafts and galleries on foot for 2 hours accompanied by a guide who is as passionate about the site as the original miners were in the 1800s. Also on the 263-hectare (650-acre) site are nature trails, a physical fitness course and a mining museum.

Tour narration in English is available by reservation. Warm clothing and comfortable walking shoes are recommended. **Hours:** Tours are given daily on the hour 10-3, June-Aug. Phone ahead to confirm schedule. **Cost:** $22; $19 (students with ID); $15 (ages 6-15); $5 (ages 3-5); $50 (family, two adults and two children). Reservations are recommended. **Phone:** (819) 346-9545 or (888) 346-9545. [icons]

AUBERGE MANOIR LE TRICORNE
Phone: (819)842-4522

Historic Bed & Breakfast
$139-$250 6/1-10/31
$119-$229 11/1-5/31

Address: 50 chemin Gosselin J0B 2C0 **Location:** Rt 108, 1.3 mi (2 km) n on chemin McFarland, follow signs. Located in a quiet rural area. **Facility:** Surrounded by 90 acres of woodlands, this Bed and Breakfast offers fireplaces and whirlpools in many of its attractively decorated guest rooms. 17 units. 2 stories (no elevator), interior corridors. **Terms:** 2 night minimum stay - seasonal and/or weekends, 7 day cancellation notice-fee imposed. **Pool(s):** heated outdoor. **Activities:** sauna, cross country skiing, snowmobiling, hiking trails.

[icons] SOME UNITS

MANOIR HOVEY RELAIS & CHÂTEAUX

Phone: (819)842-2421

Classic Historic
Country Inn
$330-$970

Address: 575 chemin Hovey J0B 2C0 **Location:** Hwy 55 exit 29, 7.5 mi (12 km) e on Rt 108 E. **Facility:** On scenic lakefront grounds, this 1900 manor home features luxurious accommodations with stylish bathrooms. Two vista suites boast steam showers, a hot tub and share a heated swimming pool. 39 units, some efficiencies, kitchens and cottages. 3 stories (no elevator), interior/exterior corridors. **Parking:** winter plug-ins. **Terms:** check-in 4 pm, 14 day cancellation notice-fee imposed. **Amenities:** *Some:* safes. **Dining:** Le Hatley Relais & Châteaux, see separate listing. **Pool(s):** heated outdoor. **Activities:** boating, canoeing, paddleboats, boat dock, fishing, lighted tennis court, cross country skiing, ice skating, exercise room. *Fee:* massage. **Guest Services:** valet laundry. **Free Special Amenities:** local telephone calls and high-speed Internet.

WHERE TO EAT

LE HATLEY RELAIS & CHÂTEAUX

Phone: 819/842-2421

French
$15-$65

AAA Inspector Notes: The seasonally changing menu at this restaurant delivers innovative, contemporary French cuisine with either the a la carte selections or a multi-course tasting menu paired with wines. Choose from such regional and coastal delicacies as seared-duck breast, venison loin, striped sea bass, halibut, pan-seared foie gras, sea scallops or organic salmon gravlax. Views of the lake and gardens are sublime from the intimate dining room. **Bar:** full bar. **Reservations:** suggested. **Address:** 575 chemin Hovey J0B 2C0 **Location:** Hwy 55 exit 29, 7.5 mi (12 km) e on Rt 108 E; in Manoir Hovey Relais & Châteaux. B L D

PILSEN RESTAURANT & PUB

Phone: 819/842-2971

American
$11-$28

AAA Inspector Notes: Food is consistently good in the bright and airy, family-friendly restaurant and pub. A good selection of microbrewed and imported beers complements dishes on the table d'hote menu. The summer terrace overlooks the river, which is frequented by ducks. **Bar:** full bar. **Reservations:** suggested. **Address:** 55 rue Principale J0B 2C0 **Location:** Centre. L D

RESTAURANT CAFÉ MASSAWIPPI

Phone: 819/842-4528

French
$14-$36

AAA Inspector Notes: Chef Dominic Tremblay and his team serve fine cuisine in this sleepy Eastern Townships village. The decor is 1930 country elegant with hardwood floors and tables set with fine tablecloths and upscale dishes and glassware. The menu is punctuated with many fine selections, such as venison tartare, seared scallops, red tuna, AAA beef tenderloin, smoked duck carpaccio and pan-seared foie gras. An extensive wine list and gourmet coffee round out the menu. A popular gourmet brunch is served on Sunday. **Bar:** full bar. **Reservations:** suggested. **Address:** 3050 chemin Capelton J0B 2C0 **Location:** On Rt 108; centre. L D

ODANAK (E-5)

In the 17th century the French-allied Abenaki Indians moved to Odanak from New England. To convert and educate them, Jesuits established a mission in 1700.

ABÉNAKIS MUSEUM (Musée des Abénakis) is off Rte. 132 at 108 rue Waban-Aki, at the n. end of the Pierreville Bridge following signs. The museum's displays relate the history of the Abenaki Tribe of Odanak. **Hours:** Daily 10-5, July-Aug.; Mon.-Fri. 10-5, Sat.-Sun. 1-5, May-June. and Sept.-Oct.; Sat.-Sun. by appointment, rest of year. **Cost:** $8.50; $7.50 (ages 66+); $6.50 (students ages 13-24 with ID); $5.50 (ages 4-12); $20 (family). **Phone:** (450) 568-2600.

ORFORD (F-9) pop. 1,987

MONT-ORFORD NATIONAL PARK (Parc national du Mont-Orford) is off Autoroute 10 exit 118. The four-season recreation area boasts three impressive peaks: Mont Orford is the highest at 853 metres (2,799 ft.), Mont Alfred-DesRochers rises to 670 metres (2,198 ft.) and Mont Chauve is 600 metres (1,968 ft.) high. The provincial park offers a visitor center, 50 kilometres (31 mi.) of cross-country skiing and snowshoeing trails, 80 kilometres (50 mi.) of hiking trails, 475 camping sites, and hut and cabin lodgings. Such activities as kayaking, swimming and rock climbing also can be enjoyed. Various species, including white-tailed deer and great blue herons, may be observed in their natural habitat.

Nestled within the park is the Orford Arts Centre (Centre d'arts Orford), home to a world-class academy of music and the Orford Summer Festival. Founded in 1951, the center also features three exhibition spaces for visual artists as well as a sculpture garden. *See Recreation Chart.* Pets are not permitted. **Hours:** Daily 8 a.m.-9 p.m., June-Aug.; 8-4, rest of year. **Cost:** $6; $2.75 (ages 6-17); $12 (family, two adults and children); $8.75 (family, one adult and children). Prices may vary. **Parking:** $10. **Phone:** (819) 843-9855 for the park, or (800) 567-6155 for the Orford Arts Centre.

ESTRIMONT SUITES & SPA

Phone: (819)843-1616

Hotel
$149-$329

Address: 44 ave de L'Auberge J1X 6J3 **Location:** Hwy 10 exit 118, follow signs to Orford Park. **Facility:** 95 units. 3 stories, interior corridors. **Terms:** check-in 4 pm, 2 night minimum stay - weekends, cancellation fee imposed. **Amenities:** high-speed Internet, safes. **Pool(s):** heated outdoor, heated indoor. **Activities:** sauna, whirlpools, 2 lighted tennis courts, snowmobiling, bicycles, playground, exercise room, spa.

HOTEL CHERIBOURG

Phone: 819/843-3308

Hotel
$140-$260 1/1-5/31
$130-$260 6/1-12/31

Address: 2603 chemin du Parc J1X 8C8 **Location:** Hwy 10 exit 118, 1.9 mi (3 km) n on Hwy 141. **Facility:** 121 units, some kitchens and cottages. 2-3 stories (no elevator), interior/exterior corridors. **Parking:** winter plug-ins. **Terms:** check-in 4 pm, 2 night minimum stay - seasonal and/or weekends, cancellation fee imposed. **Amenities:** video games (fee), high-speed Internet. **Pool(s):** heated outdoor, heated indoor. **Activities:** saunas, whirlpool, 2 lighted tennis courts, playground, sports court, volleyball, exercise room, spa. **Guest Services:** valet laundry.

MANOIR DES SABLES HOTEL & GOLF
Phone: 819/847-4747

Resort Hotel
Rates not provided

Address: 90 ave des Jardins J1X 6M6 **Location:** Hwy 10 exit 118, 1.3 mi (2 km) n on Rt 141. **Facility:** Guests of the resort stay in tastefully furnished rooms, many of which have private balconies that afford views of the lake and nearby ski hills. 139 units. 3 stories, interior corridors. **Parking:** winter plug-ins. **Terms:** check-in 4 pm. **Amenities:** high-speed Internet. *Some:* safes, honor bars. **Dining:** 2 restaurants. **Pool(s):** heated outdoor, heated indoor. **Activities:** saunas, whirlpool, boating, canoeing, paddleboats, boat dock, fishing, 4 tennis courts (2 lighted), cross country skiing, ice skating, tobogganing, bicycles, hiking trails, playground, volleyball, exercise room, spa. *Fee:* golf-27 holes, game room. **Guest Services:** valet laundry.

ORMSTOWN (F-6) pop. 3,651

Ormstown began as a small settlement of farms in the late 1790s and early 1800s. Around 1810 the area's population began to shrink as speculators finagled local farmers out of their land, and American settlers left for the United States under the growing threat of war.

Ormstown was the site of the Battle of Châteauguay, an important clash in the War of 1812. After the war the town settled into quiet prosperity as a farming and cattle raising center.

BATTLE OF THE CHÂTEAUGUAY NATIONAL HISTORIC SITE (Lieu historique national de la Bataille-de-la-Châteauguay), 6 km (4 mi.) e. on Hwy. 138 at 2371 Rivière Châteauguay, commemorates the battle of Oct. 26, 1813, when Lt. Col. Charles-Michel de Salaberry and his force of 300 Canadians stopped 3,000 invading U.S. troops. Interpretation center exhibits analyze the background of the battle and the living conditions of its participants.

Time: Allow 1 hour, 30 minutes minimum. **Hours:** Daily 10-5, May 24-Sept. 4; Sat.-Sun. 10-5, Sept. 5-Oct. 9. **Cost:** $3.90; $3.40 (ages 66+ and students with ID); $1.90 (ages 6-16); $9.80 (family). **Phone:** (450) 829-2003 or (888) 773-8888.

OUTREMONT
• **Hotels & Restaurants map & index p. 342**
• **Part of Montréal area — see map p. 312**

LE PARIS BEURRE
Phone: 514/271-7502   61
French
$12-$28

AAA Inspector Notes: The chic, casual bistro is located on a trendy shopping street. The menu of southwestern French cuisine boasts a number of bistro classics like beef tartare, lamb chops, duck magret, duck confit, cassoulet, salmon and filet mignon. Desserts include a classic creme brulee. **Bar:** full bar. **Reservations:** suggested. **Address:** 1226 ave Van Home H2V 1K3 **Location:** Between ave Champagneur and Bloomfield. [L] [D]

RESTAURANT CHEZ LÉVEQUE
Phone: 514/279-7355   62
French
$17-$34

AAA Inspector Notes: The cosmopolitan bistro is a charming, lively spot for fine French cuisine and gracious service. The menu changes frequently to offer only the freshest of seasonal specialties, such as oysters, crab, lobster, shrimp and wild game. **Bar:** full bar. **Reservations:** suggested. **Address:** 1030 rue Laurier ouest H2V 2K8 **Location:** Between rue Hutchison and Durocher. **Parking:** street only. [D]

RESTAURANT CHRISTOPHE
Phone: 514/270-0850   60
French
$36-$58

AAA Inspector Notes: Modern French influences are evident on a menu of abundant fresh fish selections, including salmon and tuna. Veal, venison and some shellfish round out the choices. The restaurant founder was once a private chef for the late French President Francois Mitterrand. The lively dining room is swathed in youthful contemporary decor. If you desire a glass of wine with your meal, you're encouraged to bring your own bottle. **Reservations:** suggested. **Address:** 1187 Van Horne Ave H2V 1K1 **Location:** Between Bloomfield and de l'Epee aves. **Parking:** street only. [D]

RESTAURANT LEMEAC
Phone: 514/270-0999   63
French
$19-$36

AAA Inspector Notes: On a fashionable shopping street, the elegant bistro breathes new life into classic French-style recipes. Diners can enjoy braised short ribs, thick grilled pork chops, rack of lamb, rillettes pate, veal liver, asparagus risotto, magret of duck, black pudding and kidneys. Among dessert enticements are lemon pie, chocolate mousse or one of the house-prepared sorbets. In the summer, the outdoor terrace is the place to be. **Bar:** full bar. **Reservations:** suggested. **Address:** 1045 ave Laurier ouest H2V 2L1 **Location:** Just w of ave du Parc. **Parking:** street only. [L] [D]

PAPINEAUVILLE pop. 2,247

LA TABLE DE PIERRE DELAHAYE
Phone: 819/427-5027
French
$18-$36

AAA Inspector Notes: Guests can settle in to this quaint, country-style dining room to enjoy quality dishes of market-fresh food, such as perch served with whipped potatoes and parsnips. A small hallway separates two stylish dining rooms decorated with chandeliers and simple draperies. The restaurant is open for lunch on Sunday only. **Bar:** full bar. **Reservations:** suggested. **Address:** 247 rue Papineau J0V 1R0 **Location:** On Rt 148; centre. [D]

RESTAURANT LE LOUIS-JOSEPH
Phone: 819/427-5866
Canadian
$11-$31

AAA Inspector Notes: The service has been friendly and the comfort food very satisfying each time I have visited this rural restaurant. The wood-trimmed ceiling and walls, along with a cozy fireplace, evoke a rustic feel amid wood tables neatly set with white tablecloths. Fill up fast with some tasty Canadian-style comfort foods including steak, seafood, pasta, pizza, barbecue chicken (a specialty), lightly battered fries and hot chicken sandwiches. Ask about the freshly baked pies. **Bar:** full bar. **Reservations:** suggested. **Address:** 300 rue Papineau J0V 1R0 **Location:** On Rt 148; centre. **Parking:** street only. [L] [D]

PERCÉ (C-9) pop. 3,419
• **Hotels p. 400 • Restaurants p. 401**

Percé lies at the eastern extremity of the Gaspé Peninsula on the Gulf of St. Lawrence. During the 17th century the town was a favored port for ships traveling to Québec from France. Percé was later destroyed by British frigates in a 1690 attack on Québec.

Although dormant for a half-century, the site's sheltered location eventually drew enough fishermen to make Percé an important fishing port. While the wharves are still busy with lobster boats, the town also has become a popular destination for visitors to the Gaspé Peninsula.

Available in French and in English, Taxi Percé offers a 2-hour narrated tour of the mountains and towns aboard a four-wheel-drive vehicle; phone (418) 782-2102. Starting from behind the Church of St-Michel, the hiking trails of Mont-Ste-Anne *(see attraction listing p. 265)*, the grotto and the crevice allow walkers to explore the mountains of Percé and discover spectacular landscapes. A detailed map is available at the tourism bureau office.

The scenic drive around the mountains starts at the west end of the village, by turning north on Route des Failles. At the intersection where St. Paul's Anglican Church is located keep north and follow the very steep hill. You will then drive on a sinuous mountain road for about 5 kilometres (3 mi.) until you reach Route 132. You turn east to go back to Percé village. Along the 5 kilometre (3 mi.) drive back to Percé the road passes the Mont-Blanc, the Overlook, the Big Bowl, the Pic of Dawn, the Three Sisters Cliffs and a spectacular view of the natural Amphitheater of Percé.

For scuba-diving enthusiasts, the nautical center of Percé offers equipment rentals, a diving school and snorkeling and scuba sites. Rental sea kayaks also are available. For information about whale-watching tours contact the Percé Tourism Bureau.

Percé Tourism Bureau: 142 Rte. 132, Percé, QC, Canada G0C 2L0. **Phone:** (418) 782-5448 or (855) 782-5448.

ÎLE BONAVENTURE AND PERCÉ ROCK NATIONAL PARK (Parc national de l'Île-Bonaventure-et-du-Rocher-Percé) is 4.7 kilometres (3 mi.) offshore. The park, which includes Percé Rock *(see attraction listing)* and Île Bonaventure, is a migratory bird sanctuary for more than 200,000 seabirds. The island shelters a colony of gannets as well as several other species. Trails lead to cliffs overlooking the bird ledges. Various cruise operators offer narrated sightseeing excursions of the conservation area, with some tours featuring stopovers at Île Bonaventure.

Pets are not permitted. **Hours:** Information kiosk open daily 9-5, June 1 to mid-Oct. Sightseeing cruises generally depart Percé daily. **Cost:** (includes Discovery Centre) $6; $2.75 (ages 6-17); $12 (family, two adults and children); $8.75 (family, one adult and children). Fares for sightseeing cruises vary. **Phone:** (418) 782-2240 or (800) 665-6527.

Discovery Centre is in Le Chafaud at 4 rue du Quai. The center, within sight of Île Bonaventure, uses films and wildlife displays to explain the interaction of land and ocean. **Hours:** Daily 9-7, June 1 to mid-Oct. **Cost:** (includes admission to Île Bonaventure and Percé Rock National Park) $6; $2.75 (ages 6-17); $12 (family, two adults and children); $8.75 (family, one adult and children). **Phone:** (418) 782-2240.

Percé Rock (Rocher Percé), in the Gulf of St. Lawrence just off the tip of the Gaspé Peninsula, is one of the most recognized natural attractions in Canada. Rising abruptly from the sea and often dramatically changing color as light and weather conditions vary, the rock, which is pierced by a large arched opening, presents a spectacular sight. Measuring 433 metres (1,420 ft.) long by 88 metres (288 ft.) high, it is a tall calcareous block experts speculate was formed on the bottom of the sea during the Devonian geologic period.

Note: Visitors are strongly advised to refrain from walking alongside Percé Rock and Mont Joli; frequent rock slides and falling debris make these areas extremely dangerous. **Phone:** (418) 782-2240.

MUSEUM CHAFAUD (Musée le Chafaud) is at 145 Rte. 132. Housed in one of the oldest preserved structures in the region, the museum includes an art gallery and is devoted to the cultural heritage of the Percé region. **Hours:** Daily 10-8, mid-June to late Sept. **Cost:** $5; $3.50 (ages 66+ and students with ID); $2 (ages 0-12); $13 (family). **Phone:** (418) 782-5100.

AU PIC DE L'AURORE
Cottage
$117-$245 7/3-5/31
$65-$165 6/1-7/2
Phone: (418)782-2151
Address: 1 Rt 132 G0C 2L0. **Location:** 1.2 mi (2 km) e from village. **Facility:** 32 units, some houses and cottages. 1 story, exterior corridors. **Terms:** office hours 7:30 am-10 pm, check-in 4 pm, 3 day cancellation notice. **Activities:** playground. **Guest Services:** coin laundry.

HOTEL LA NORMANDIE
Hotel
$79-$259
Phone: 418/782-2112
Address: 221 Rt 132 ouest G0C 2L0. **Location:** Waterfront. Centre. **Facility:** 45 units. 3 stories (no elevator), interior corridors. **Terms:** open 6/1-10/13 & 5/19-5/31. **Dining:** restaurant, see separate listing.

HOTEL/MOTEL LE MIRAGE
Motel
$82-$198
Phone: (418)782-5151
Address: 288 Rt 132 ouest G0C 2L0. **Location:** On Rt 132. **Facility:** 67 units. 2 stories (no elevator), exterior corridors. **Terms:** open 6/1-10/10 & 5/28-5/31, cancellation fee imposed. **Pool(s):** heated outdoor. **Activities:** tennis court. **Guest Services:** valet laundry.

HOTEL MOTEL MANOIR DE PERCÉ
Phone: (418)782-2022

Hotel
$68-$178

Address: 212 Rt 132 G0C 2L0 **Location:** Centre. **Facility:** 39 units. 2 stories (no elevator), interior/exterior corridors. **Terms:** open 6/1-10/15 & 5/21-5/31. **Dining:** restaurant, see separate listing. **Activities:** *Fee:* charter fishing. **Guest Services:** coin laundry.

WHERE TO EAT

HOTEL MOTEL MANOIR DE PERCÉ DINING ROOM
Phone: 418/782-2022

Seafood
$19-$42

AAA Inspector Notes: In a village motel, the cozy, comfortable family-run dining room features a full array of fresh regional seafood, including salmon pie, fried cod tongues, poached cod, halibut, red deer, surf and turf, lobster and seafood bouillabaisse. During the low-season, the restaurant may be closed on some evenings. **Bar:** full bar. **Address:** 212 Rt 132 G0C 2L0 **Location:** Centre; in Hotel Motel Manoir de Perce. B D

LA NORMANDIE DINING ROOM   **Phone:** 418/782-2112

Regional French
$14-$38

AAA Inspector Notes: Tastefully furnished and decorated, the stylish dining room overlooks Perce Rock and Bonaventure Island. The atmosphere is upscale and comfortable. Tempting preparations include lobster, roasted stuffed quail, chicken supreme with maple glaze, braised pork, grilled beef sirloin, grilled breast of duck and guinea fowl. During the low-season, the restaurant may be closed on some evenings. **Bar:** full bar. **Reservations:** suggested. **Address:** 221 Rt 132 ouest G0C 2L0 **Location:** Centre; in Hotel La Normandie. B D

LE CAFÉ CHAMPETRE   **Phone:** 418/782-2036

Canadian
$7-$25

AAA Inspector Notes: This family-friendly diner near the Perce harbor offers a menu of fish, seafood and Canadian fast-food, including lobster rolls, cod pie, hot chicken, burgers, salads, all-day breakfasts and sandwiches. **Bar:** beer & wine. **Address:** 162-B Rt 132 G0C 2L0 **Location:** On Rt 132; in Place Charles-Robin. B L D

LE CAFÉ DES COULEURS   **Phone:** 418/645-2745

Coffee/Tea
$11-$16

AAA Inspector Notes: This cozy café and art gallery has its walls adorned with the works of several regional painters. The menu specialty is waffles with scallops in wine sauce or with a mousse of shrimp or smoked salmon. Also offered are soups, salads, shrimp salad, sandwiches, cheese bagels with smoked salmon, seafood pate and duck confit. For dessert, try an artfully garnished dessert waffle. Specialty coffees include espresso. **Bar:** beer & wine. **Address:** 1004 Rt 132 est G0C 1A0 **Location:** On Rt 132; 10.8 mi (18 km) ne of Perce Village. B L

LE FOURNAND BAKERY AND CAFÉ
Phone: 418/782-2211

Breads/Pastries
$5-$10

AAA Inspector Notes: The village cafe-bakery offers both a take-out counter and a casual seating area with a seasonal terrace. The affordable menu includes fresh breads, cheeses, sandwiches, salad, tourtiere meat pies, baked beans, quiches and pizza. Fresh desserts include French pastries, sugar pie, muffins, croissants, brioches and danishes, as well as specialty coffee and tea. **Address:** 194 Rt 132 ouest G0C 2L0 **Location:** Centre. **Parking:** street only. B L D

RESTAURANT LA MAISON DU PECHEUR/CAFÉ DE L'ATLANTIQUE
Phone: 418/782-5331

Seafood
$13-$45

AAA Inspector Notes: Next to the port area where tour boats depart, this waterfront restaurant focuses on local seafood, including the specialty cod tongues in sea urchin butter. Menu highlights include lobster, snails, salmon tartare, snow crab, grilled ocean perch or catfish, mussels, shrimp and delicious maplewood-oven pizza. Home-style pies and cakes are made on the premises. The owner maintains a caged reserve of fresh lobsters on the sea bottom off the shores of Perce. **Bar:** full bar. **Reservations:** suggested. **Address:** 155 Place du Quai G0C 2L0 **Location:** Centre; at wharf. B L D

RESTAURANT L'AUBERGE DU GARGANTUA
Phone: 418/782-2852

French
$29-$40

AAA Inspector Notes: This renowned mountaintop restaurant and inn, named after a fictitious giant monster, offers a comfortable, country-home feel and spectacular sunset views. Cuisine bourgeoisie centers on extremely generous portions of local seafood. Each meal begins with a hearty platter of salads, pates and snails. Hosts entertain diners with a collection of vintage LPs. **Bar:** full bar. **Reservations:** suggested. **Address:** 222 Rt des Failles G0C 2L0 **Location:** 1 mi (1.6 km) n on Rt des Failles from jct Hwy 132. D

RESTAURANT LE BASTION   **Phone:** 418/368-2281

Canadian
$20-$36

AAA Inspector Notes: A jazzy atmosphere punctuates the pleasant, bistro-style restaurant, which overlooks the scenic ocean. The focus is on gourmet meals prepared with market-fresh products, such as cod-liver pate, goat cheese, sweetbreads, scallops, cod tongues, seafood crepes, lobster, caribou, lamb and salmon smoked on the premises. The smartly attired servers are gracious and efficient. **Bar:** full bar. **Reservations:** suggested. **Address:** 2053 boul Douglas G0C 2X0 **Location:** On Rt 132; in Perce St-Georges de-Malbaie; in Auberge Fort Prevel. B D

PÉRIBONKA (C-5) pop. 541

French author Louis Hémon brought fame to Péribonka in 1912 when he used the remote agricultural locale on the north shore of lac St-Jean as the setting for his romantic novel "Maria Chapdelaine." The Louis-Hémon Museum (Musée Louis-Hémon), 700 Maria Chapdelaine, honors the novelist; phone (418) 374-2177.

Péribonka marks the departure point of the Lac St-Jean International Crossing (Traversée Internationale du lac St-Jean), held the last Sunday in July. This swimming competition dates from 1955, when Jacques Amyot swam across lac St-Jean from Péribonka to Roberval in 11 hours and 32 minutes. Contestants must swim the same passage, a distance of 40 kilometres (64 mi.); phone (418) 275-2851.

PETITE-RIVIÈRE-ST-FRANÇOIS (D-6)
pop. 703

RECREATIONAL ACTIVITIES
Skiing

- **Le Massif** is off Hwy. 138 at 1350 rue Principale. **Hours:** Mon.-Fri. 9-4, Sat.-Sun. and holidays 8:30-4, early Dec. to mid-Apr. Phone ahead to confirm schedule. **Phone:** (418) 632-5876 or (877) 536-2774.

PETIT-SAGUENAY pop. 780

AUBERGE DU JARDIN   Phone: (418)272-3444

Country Inn
$108-$172

Address: 71 boul Dumas G0V 1N0
Location: On Rt 170; centre. **Facility:** 12 units. 2 stories (no elevator), interior/exterior corridors. **Parking:** winter plug-ins. **Terms:** open 6/1-11/2 & 12/10-5/31, 7 day cancellation notice-fee imposed. **Activities:** snowmobiling, hiking trails. **Guest Services:** coin laundry. 🍴 🍸 BIZ 🛜 ✉ / SOME UNITS 🐾 💻

PLAISANCE (E-3) pop. 1,024

PLAISANCE FALLS PARK (Parc des Chutes de Plaisance) is 5 km (3 mi.) n. on rue Montée Papineau from jct. Hwy. 148, then just w. on ch. Malo; a heritage center is at 276 rue Desjardins. In the late 1800s a large sawmill powered by the falls operated here, but it was torn down in the early 20th century. Today the park encompasses observation points and a hiking trail for visitors lured by the natural beauty of 67-metre (188-ft.) Plaisance Falls. The Plaisance Heritage Center houses archeological displays and other exhibits that detail regional history.

Tours: Guided tours are available. **Time:** Allow 2 hours minimum. **Hours:** Park and heritage center daily 10-6, mid-June through Labour Day. **Cost:** (includes heritage center) $4; $3 (ages 65+); $2 (students with ID); free (ages 0-9). **Phone:** (819) 427-6400. 🏕

POINTE-À-LA-CROIX (C-8) pop. 1,587

BATTLE OF RESTIGOUCHE NATIONAL HISTORIC SITE OF CANADA (Lieu historique national du Canada de la Bataille-de-la-Restigouche), 40 boul. Pérron Ouest (Hwy. 132), was the location of the last naval battle fought in North America during the Seven Years' War, 1756-63. The interpretation center's exhibits include various artifacts as well as sections of an 18th-century French frigate recovered during underwater excavation of the site. A film explains the battle, while a re-creation of the ship's interior helps convey what life was like aboard the vessel.

Hours: Daily 9-5, first Sat. in June-Thanksgiving. **Cost:** $3.90; $3.40 (ages 65+); $1.90 (ages 6-16); $9.80 (family). **Phone:** (418) 788-5676 or (888) 773-8888.

POINTE-AU-PIC (D-6)

Pointe-au-Pic, a summer resort established in the 19th century, is noted for its cottage architecture and the stunning views across the St. Lawrence River afforded by its high cliffs.

CHARLEVOIX MUSEUM (Musée de Charlevoix), 10 ch. du Havre, presents changing exhibitions about the culture, history and arts of Charlevoix County. **Time:** Allow 30 minutes minimum. **Hours:** Daily 9-5, June 1 to mid-Oct.; Mon.-Fri. 10-5, Sat.-Sun. 1-5, rest of year. **Cost:** $7; $5 (ages 60+ and

students with ID); free (ages 0-11). **Phone:** (418) 665-4411.

POINTE-CALUMET (F-7) pop. 6,574
• Part of Montréal area — see map p. 312

SUPER AQUA CLUB is off Hwy. 640 exit 2, following signs to 322 Montée de la Baie. The water park offers more than 40 attractions, including waterslides, a lazy river, a beach area and a wave pool. Site highlights include The Storm, an interactive structure with water games and slides; The Castle, a water play area for children; and Pirate Island, an interactive jungle gym.

Pets are not permitted. **Time:** Allow 2 hours minimum. **Hours:** Daily 10-7, late June to mid-Aug.; 10-6, mid- to late Aug.; 10-5 , early to late June (weather permitting). **Cost:** $30.72; $22.82 (children 121-135 centimetres or 48-53 inches tall); $21 (children 107-120 centimetres or 42-47 inches tall); $17.56 (ages 55+). After 3 p.m. $22.82; $19.31 (children 121-135 centimetres or 48-53 inches tall); $18.43 (children 107-120 centimetres or 42-47 inches tall); $15.80 (ages 55+). After 5 p.m. $14.04. Under 12 must be with an adult. **Phone:** (450) 473-1013. 🍴 🏕

POINTE-CLAIRE pop. 30,161
• Hotels & Restaurants map & index p. 342
• Part of Montréal area — see map p. 312

COMFORT INN   Phone: (514)697-6210 **72**

Hotel
$85-$135

Address: 700 boul St-Jean H9R 3K2 **Location:** Hwy 40 exit 52, just s. Located in a suburban area. **Facility:** 99 units. 2 stories (no elevator), interior corridors. **Parking:** winter plug-ins. **Terms:** cancellation fee imposed. **Guest Services:** valet laundry.

SAVE ECO 🔌 🍴 BIZ 🛜 FEE 🎬 💻 / SOME UNITS 🛏 FEE 🐾 FEE 🍴

HOLIDAY INN POINTE-CLAIRE MONTREAL AEROPORT   Phone: (514)697-7110 **71**

Hotel
$139-$259

Address: 6700 Transcanadienne H9R 1C2 **Location:** Hwy 40 exit 52; south side service road. Located in a suburban area. **Facility:** 308 units. 15 stories, interior corridors. **Amenities:** high-speed Internet. **Pool(s):** heated indoor. **Activities:** saunas, whirlpool, exercise room. *Fee:* game room, massage. **Guest Services:** valet and coin laundry, area transportation-Dorval train station.

🔌 🍴 🍸 🍴 🛶 BIZ 🛜 💻 / SOME UNITS 🐾

QUALITY SUITES MONTREAL AEROPORT, POINTE-CLAIRE   Phone: (514)426-5060 **70**

Hotel
$124-$169

Address: 6300 Rt Transcanadienne H9R 1B9 **Location:** Hwy 40 exit 52 eastbound, south side service road; westbound, follow signs for boul St-Jean sud and Hwy 40 est to access south side service road. **Facility:** 161 units. 8 stories, interior corridors. **Parking:** winter plug-ins. **Terms:** cancellation fee imposed. **Amenities:** high-speed Internet. **Activities:** exercise room. **Guest Services:** valet and coin laundry.

SAVE ECO 🔌 🍴 🍸 CALL 🅼 🛜 FEE 🎬 💻 / SOME UNITS FEE 🐾 🐾 🍴

(See map & index p. 342.)

WHERE TO EAT

40 WESTT STEAKHOUSE

Steak
$25-$60

Phone: 514/428-9378 112

AAA Inspector Notes: Stone surfaces, rich wood moldings, high ceilings, elegant mirrors and etched glass highlight the decor of this upscale suburban steakhouse. The high-quality menu features prime cuts of steak, as well as an array of fresh fish and seafood. A butcher shop on the premises sells steaks for take-out. **Bar:** full bar. **Reservations:** suggested. **Address:** 2305 boul Transcanadienne H9R 5Z5 **Location:** Hwy 40 exit 55 (boul des Sources), just nw. L D

ARAHOVA SOUVLAKI

Greek
$6-$15

Phone: 514/695-1100

AAA Inspector Notes: Greek specialties, such as souvlaki, gyro pitas, moussaka and grilled fish and seafood, are served in a casual atmosphere. **Bar:** full bar. **Address:** 301 boul Brunswick H9R 4Y2 **Location:** Hwy 40 exit 52, 0.3 mi (0.5 km) n. L D

BAR B BARN

Barbecue
$9-$25

Phone: 514/683-0225

AAA Inspector Notes: Rustic barn wood adorns the walls of the family restaurant. Specialties include slow-roasted chicken and pork ribs, as well as the popular ribs-and-chicken combination dish. **Bar:** full bar. **Reservations:** required. **Address:** 3300 boul des Sources H9B 1Z7 **Location:** Hwy 40 exit 55 (boul des Sources), just n. L D

CHEZ CORA

Canadian
$7-$14

Phone: 514/630-8104

AAA Inspector Notes: Eggs, omelets, waffles, crepes (sorry, no American-style pancakes here), French toast, fruit platters and all the breakfast meats--that's the specialty here, all day. However, at lunchtime the menu lists a selection of soups, salads, quiches, sandwiches and a dish called the grilled panini crepe. **Address:** 183J boul Hymus H9R 1E9 **Location:** Hwy 40 exit 52, just se; in shopping mall. B L

LE CHAMBERTIN

French
$15-$40

Phone: 514/695-0620 114

AAA Inspector Notes: In operation since 1980, this romantic, upscale restaurant puts forth a menu of prime rib, fresh fish, other seafood and steaks. Social dinner and dancing evenings are held regularly. **Bar:** full bar. **Address:** 9 Place Frontenac H9R 4Z7 **Location:** Hwy 40 exit 52, 0.3 mi (0.5 km) n, then just e on boul Brunswick. **Parking:** on-site and valet. L D

LE GOURMAND

French
$17-$44

Phone: 514/695-9077 113

AAA Inspector Notes: This cozy restaurant is in a historic blacksmith shop built in 1848. The menu of French cuisine includes chicken breast, filet mignon, rack of lamb, smoked salmon, fresh fish, veal scaloppine, linguine with shrimp, duck magret and a mixed grill of lamb chops, shrimp and sausages. **Bar:** full bar. **Reservations:** suggested. **Address:** 42 rue Ste-Anne H9S 4P8 **Location:** Hwy 20 exit 49, 0.7 mi (1.1 km) s on ave Cartier, then just w on Bord-du-Lac/Lakeshore. **Parking:** street only. L D

MOE'S DELI & BAR

Canadian
$9-$22

Phone: 514/426-8247 116

AAA Inspector Notes: The atmosphere is busy and noisy in the energetic restaurant, especially during peak lunch times. The varied menu lists pasta, hamburgers, pizza, steaks and the house specialty smoked meat sandwiches. Portion sizes are generous. **Bar:** full bar. **Reservations:** required. **Address:** 940 boul St-Jean H9R 5N8 **Location:** Hwy 40 exit 52, 1.3 mi (2 km) n; in Colonades Pointe-Claire Shopping Centre. B L D

SCAROLIES PASTA EMPORIUM

Italian
$10-$24

Phone: 514/694-8611 115

AAA Inspector Notes: Italian dishes are the specialty at the casual, popular eatery in a suburban strip mall. Daily specials are offered along with such popular staples as freshly prepared pizza, veal scaloppine, linguine, ravioli, leg of lamb, Atlantic salmon and stuffed chicken. Fresh bread is served before the meal along with balsamic vinegar and olive oil. **Bar:** full bar. **Reservations:** suggested. **Address:** 950 boul St-Jean H9R 5N8 **Location:** Hwy 40 exit 52, just n. L D

PORTNEUF pop. 1,436

HOTEL LE PORTNEUVOIS

Hotel
Rates not provided

Phone: 418/286-6400

Address: 101 rue Simeon-Delisle G0A 2Y0 **Location:** Hwy 40 exit 261, 0.3 mi (0.5 km) s on rue Provencher. **Facility:** 22 units. 2 stories (no elevator), interior corridors. **Parking:** winter plug-ins. **Amenities:** high-speed Internet. **Guest Services:** valet laundry.

Québec

Then & Now

Québec, carved into the bluffs overlooking the St. Lawrence River by the forces of time and history, is a complex city. Capital of the province, it is the only walled city north of Mexico. It can almost be divided by a line into the old and the new. Modern-day Québec, extending up the hill beyond the Parliament Building, is shut off from the winding streets and 17th-century buildings of Upper and Lower Town by aging walls. A European bastion, it also is a profoundly French city.

In 1608 Samuel de Champlain, realizing the strategic importance of the site—not only would the cliffs provide an impregnable fortress for a settlement, but they also would protect ships anchored in the deep waters of the St. Lawrence River—built an *abitation,* or trading post, by the river at the foot of Cap Diamant. The city of Québec was established.

A growing base for trade and exploration of the interior continent, Québec expanded in the only direction possible—up the cliff. Lower Town,

or *Basse-Ville,* the city's mercantile district, was to be protected by *Haute-Ville,* the Upper Town, built on the cliff above it.

The French colony prospered in the 1600s, becoming the center of New France and enjoying a brisk trade with its mother country, which was at peace with rival England 1629-32. The tranquility ended in 1690 with a British attack on the city; it was the first of several to come.

Québec was successfully defended for 6 decades due to its natural defenses as well as the protective wall and fortifications built around Upper Town in 1720. In 1759, however, Québec fell to Britain.

Parliament Building Interior

The siege of the city culminated early on Sept. 13, when British general James Wolfe and his troops scaled sheer cliffs to reach the Plains of Abraham (known today as Battlefields Park or *Parc des Champs-de-Bataille*) above fortified Québec. They surprised and defeated the Marquis de Montcalm and his troops in about 20 minutes. With the peace treaty in 1763, France lost the province to Great Britain.

The French city became English, but in name only; in culture and tradition Québec remained French. Acceding to this fact, Britain passed the Québec Act in 1774, which allowed the French to worship in their native Roman Catholic Church rather than forcing them to attend the English Anglican Church.

A year later an American invasion challenged British troops to defend the city. The British were successful in defeating the attackers, whose New Year's Eve assault was spearheaded by generals Richard Montgomery and Benedict Arnold.

(Continued on p. 406.)

Destination Québec

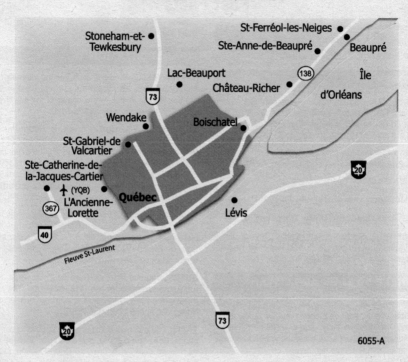

Stoneham-et-
Tewkesbury

St-Ferréol-les-Neiges

Ste-Anne-de-Beaupré

Beaupré

Lac-Beauport

Château-Richer

138

Île
d'Orléans

73

Wendake

Boischatel

St-Gabriel-de
Valcartier

Ste-Catherine-de-
la-Jacques-Cartier

✈ (YQB)

367

L'Ancienne-
Lorette

Québec

Lévis

20

40

Fleuve St-Laurent

20

73

6055-A

This map shows cities in the Québec vicinity where you will find attractions, hotels
and restaurants. Cities are listed alphabetically in this book on the following
pages.

Fast Facts

ABOUT THE CITY

POP: 525,376 ■ **ELEV:** 59 m/194ft.

MONEY

SALES TAX: Canada levies a 5 percent Goods and Service Tax. Québec's provincial sales tax is 8.5 percent on goods and services. The Québec City area has a 3 percent lodging surcharge.

WHOM TO CALL

EMERGENCY: 911

POLICE (non-emergency): (418) 310-4141

TIME AND TEMPERATURE: (418) 648-7766

HOSPITALS: St. Sacrament Hospital (Hôpital du St-Sacrement), (418) 682-7511 ■ Jeffery Hale Hospital (Hôpital Jeffery Hale), (418) 684-5333.

WHERE TO LOOK AND LISTEN

NEWSPAPERS: Both daily newspapers published in Québec, *Le Journal de Québec* and *Le Soleil*, are in French. An English daily, *The Gazette*, is printed in Montréal. *Voilà Québec* is a quarterly, bilingual guide to restaurants and entertainment.

RADIO: Québec radio station La Première Chaîne (106.3 FM) is programmed by Radio Canada ■ CBC Radio One (104.7 FM) is programmed by the Canadian Broadcasting Corp. ■ and la radio touristique de Québec broadcasts in English on 89.7 FM and in French on 90.3 FM.

VISITOR INFORMATION

Québec City Tourism, Borough of La Cité-Limoilou: 835 av. Wilfrid-Laurier, Québec, QC, Canada G1R 2L3. **Phone:** (418) 641-6290 .

Québec City Tourism, Borough of Ste-Foy-Sillery-Cap-Rouge: 3300 av. des Hôtels, Québec, QC, Canada G1W 5A8. **Phone:** (418) 641-6290 or (877) 783-1608.

TRANSPORTATION

AIR TRAVEL: Québec City Jean Lesage International Airport (YQB) is 16 kilometres (10 mi.) west in the Ste-Foy sector. A taxi to the center of the city averages $30, limousine service $65-$120.

RENTAL CARS: Hertz, offering discounts to AAA/CAA members, is in Old Québec, (418) 694-1224; in the Ste-Foy sector, (418) 658-6795; and at the Québec airport, (418) 871-1571. Phone (800) 263-0600 in Canada or (800) 654-3131 outside Canada. See the telephone directory for other companies.

RAIL SERVICE: Québec City area terminals of Via Rail Canada, serving U.S. and Canadian cities, are the Gare du Palais, 450 rue de la Gare-du-Palais, and Gare de Ste-Foy, 3255 ch. de la Gare in the Ste-Foy sector. Phone (888) 842-7245.

BUSES: The bus terminal, Gare du Palais, is at 320 rue Abraham-Martin; phone (418) 525-3000. The terminal in the Ste-Foy sector is at 3001 ch. des Quatre Bourgeois; phone (418) 650-0087.

TAXIS: You must get a taxi at a cab stand or order by phone. Base fare is $3.30, plus $1.60 per kilometre (.6 mi.). Major companies are Taxi Coop Québec, (418) 525-5191 ■ Taxi Québec, (418) 525-8123 ■ and Taxi Coop Ste-Foy and Sillery, (418) 653-7777.

PUBLIC TRANSPORTATION: Réseau de transport de la Capitale (RTC) buses run 5:30 a.m.-1 a.m. The fare is $2.60 (a ticket is $2.50); exact change is required. A daily pass is $6.70. Phone (418) 627-2511.

BOATS: Québec's harbor accommodates pleasure craft, ferries, sightseeing cruises and oceangoing vessels. The Port of Québec (Administration portuaire de Québec) is at 150 rue Dalhousie, C.P. 80, Station Haute-Ville, Québec, QC, Canada G1R 4M8; phone (418) 648-3640 or (418) 648-4956. The Québec-Lévis ferry docks at 10 rue des Traversiers; phone (418) 644-3704 or (418) 837-2408.

(Continued from p. 404.)

During the last of the 18th and most of the 19th centuries, Québec was a shipbuilding and wheat and lumber trading center. City walls and other defenses were refortified. By 1880 most English-speaking settlers had moved to Montréal, the United States or elsewhere, leaving Québec the predominantly French-speaking city it is today.

The turrets and verdigris copper roof of the luxe Fairmont Le Château Frontenac dominate Québec's skyline, provide a point of orientation and attest to the city's French heritage. The 1893 hotel's location atop that historic bluff overlooking the St. Lawrence River is in the heart of Old Québec (Vieux-Québec).

A perfect size to explore, Old Québec retains the feel of a centuries-old French village. The best way to fully appreciate this walled city is by foot, wandering along the narrow cobblestone streets, admiring the architecture of the 17th- and 18th-century stone buildings. The streets can be curvy and hilly, but it's worth the effort to experience the many historic sites, monuments and museums, not to mention the charming cafes, boutiques, art and antiques galleries and assortment of shops.

After the conquest in 1759, the British utilized the facilities to garrison their army. Numerous ancillary military installations were built during the 19th century. By 1871 the barracks were no longer needed and were converted into a munitions factory that was active until the end of World War II.

The interpretation center describes the evolution of the site over 3 centuries and displays a relief map of Québec City in 1808. The richly furnished Officers' Quarters have an 1830s atmosphere. The Dauphine Redoubt depicts scenes from the lives of the soldiers, officers and arsenal superintendent who once occupied it.

Guided tours are available; narration in English is offered. **Hours:** Daily 10-5, early May-second Sun. in Oct. **Cost:** $3.90; $3.40 (ages 65+); $1.90 (ages 6-16); $9.80 (family). **Phone:** (418) 648-4205 or (888) 773-8888.

THE CATHEDRAL OF THE HOLY TRINITY (Cathédrale Anglicane de la Ste-Trinité), 31 rue des Jardins, was the first Anglican cathedral built outside the British Isles. Completed in 1804 on the site of the Récollet monastery destroyed by fire in 1796, the church was designed by Capt. William Hall and Maj. William Robe, two British Army engineers who were inspired by London's St. Martin-in-the-Fields Church. Guided tours in English and French are given in summer. **Hours:** Daily 9-5, June-Oct. **Cost:** Free. **Phone:** (418) 692-2193.

THE CITADEL (La Citadelle) is on the Cap Diamant promontory; the entrance is off rue St-Louis at Porte St-Louis at Côte de la Citadelle. Constructed 1820-52 on the site of 17th-century French defenses, the fortification is one of the two official residences of the governor general of Canada. It remains the largest fortification in North America garrisoned by regular troops. A museum contains military items and documents.

Tour narration in English is available. **Hours:** Hour-long tours are given daily 9-5, May 1-late Sept.; 10-3, late Sept.-Oct. 31. A bilingual guided tour is given daily at 1:30, Nov. 1-late Mar. Ceremonial guard changes occur daily at 10 a.m., June 24-Labour Day (weather permitting). **Cost:** $10; $9 (ages 65+ and students with ID); $5.50 (ages 8-17); free (ages 0-7 and Canadian veterans and military with ID); $25 (family). **Phone:** (418) 694-2815.

DUFFERIN TERRACE (La terrasse Dufferin), next to Fairmont Le Château Frontenac, offers a spectacular view of Old Lower Town and the St. Lawrence River. An 1898 monument to Samuel de Champlain is at the north end of the terrace. From here one can descend the 55 metres (180 ft.) to Place-Royale, the center of Lower Town, via a stairway of 61 steps. A funicular also links upper and lower Québec.

The terrace is linked to Battlefields Park by the Promenade des Gouverneurs, a 670-metre-long (2,198-ft.) walk anchored by cliffs overlooking the river. **Hours:** Terrace and promenade open daily; promenade not maintained Dec.-Mar. Funicular operates daily 7:30 a.m.-11:30 p.m. (also 11:30 p.m.-midnight, in summer). **Cost:** Terrace and promenade free. Funicular $2; free (ages 0-4). **Phone:** (418) 692-1132.

FAIRMONT LE CHÂTEAU FRONTENAC, at 1 rue des Carrières next to Place d'Armes, was built in 1893 in the Medieval French style, with numerous turrets and copper roofs, and is an example of 19th-century Canadian Railway architecture. The painted ceilings and handsome metalwork of the banisters in the lobby recall its lavish past. The château was the meeting place for Winston Churchill, Franklin Roosevelt and leaders of other Allied nations during World War II; it is today part of the Fairmont Hotels & Resorts chain.

Tour narration in English is available. **Hours:** Fifty-minute tours are given daily on the hour 10-6, May 1 to mid-Oct.; Sat.-Sun. on the hour noon-5, rest of year. **Cost:** $9.50; $6 (ages 6-16). Reservations are required. **Phone:** (418) 691-2166.

FORTIFICATIONS OF QUÉBEC NATIONAL HISTORIC SITE (Lieu historique national des Fortifications-de-Québec) encircle Upper Town. Covering 4.6 kilometres (3 mi.), the ramparts (les remparts) are vestiges of the city's defense system, which evolved between the 17th and 19th centuries. In addition to heavy fortifications studded with iron cannons, the national historic site includes such components as gates, guard posts and barracks.

Guided 90-minute tours detailing the fortifications' history depart from the Frontenac kiosk on the Dufferin Terrace from June 1 to mid-October. The park's interpretation center is an addition to the Esplanade Powder Magazine (Poudrière de l'Esplanade), built in 1815 near the St-Louis Gate at 100 rue St-Louis.

Hours: Interpretation center daily 10-5, early May to mid-Oct.; by appointment rest of year. **Cost:** Interpretation center $3.90; $3.40 (ages 65+); $1.90 (ages 6-16); $9.80 (family). Guided tour $9.80; $7.30 (ages 65+); $4.90 (ages 6-16); $19.60 (family). **Phone:** (418) 648-7016.

THE FORT MUSEUM (Musée du Fort), opposite Fairmont Le Château Frontenac at 10 rue Ste-Anne, presents a sound and light show chronicling the military history of Québec City. A 37-square-metre (400-sq.-ft.) model depicts the city as it was in 1750. The sound and light shows are presented alternately in French (on the half-hour) and in English (on the hour). **Hours:** Daily 10-5, Apr.-Oct.; daily 11-4, day after Christmas-Jan. 8; Thurs.-Sun. 11-4, Jan. 27-Mar. 31 and in Nov. **Cost:** $8; $6 (students with ID and senior citizens). **Phone:** (418) 692-2175 or (418) 692-1759.

GOOD SHEPHERD MUSEUM (Musée Bon-Pasteur), 14 rue Couillard, recounts the history and ministries of the Congregation of the Servants of the Immaculate Heart of Mary—also known as the Good Shepherd Sisters of Québec—a religious order founded in 1850 by Marie-Josephte Fitzbach. Artifacts, historical documents, photographs and multimedia presentations are housed in a 19th-century neo-Gothic structure originally used as a hospital. Exhibits explain the order's work during the 19th and 20th centuries, which included caring for underprivileged women and orphaned children, and the Sisters' continuing humanitarian efforts.

Guided tours in French are available; narration in English is offered with advance notice. **Time:** Allow 1 hour minimum. **Hours:** Tues.-Sun. 1-5. **Cost:** $3; $2 (ages 65+ and students with ID); free (ages 0-12). Cash only. Reservations are recommended. **Phone:** (418) 694-0243.

LIBRARY OF THE LITERARY AND HISTORICAL SOCIETY OF QUÉBEC (Bibliothèque de la Société Historique et Littéraire de Québec), 44 rue chaussée des Ecossais, was founded in 1824 by British Governor General Lord Dalhousie. The library has evolved into the only English library in the city and its environs, becoming a repository for Canadiana and classic works. The library's collection of memorabilia includes a wooden statue of Gen. James Wolfe and Sir George-Étienne Cartier's desk.

Guided tours are available by appointment. **Hours:** Tues.-Fri. and Sun. noon-4 (also Tues. 4-9), Sat. 10-4. Closed major holidays. **Cost:** Free. **Phone:** (418) 694-9147.

MONTMORENCY PARK (Parc Montmorency), bounded by Côte de la Montagne and rues Port-Dauphin and des Remparts, occupies the site of the first Canadian Parliament building and affords a view of the St. Lawrence River. The park has monuments to Sir George-Étienne Cartier, one of the Fathers of Confederation, and Louis Hébert, one of Canada's earliest farmers. **Hours:** Daily 24 hours. **Cost:** Free.

MUSEUM OF FRENCH AMERICA (Musée de l'Amérique française) is at 2 Côte de la Fabrique. Housed in an old boarding school, the museum relates the establishment of French culture in the New World. ON THE ROAD: The Francophone Odyssey—a permanent gallery space featuring interactive exhibits, multimedia displays and relics—tells the story of the French-speaking immigrants who settled in North America between the 17th and 20th centuries.

Guided tours are available; phone ahead for schedule. Visitors must register at the reception pavilion for the tour. The language used (French or English) during each tour is determined by the preference of the first registered visitor for that tour. **Hours:** Daily 9:30-5, June 24-Labour Day; Tues.-Sun. 10-5, rest of year. Closed Christmas. **Cost:** $8; $7 (ages 65+); $5.50 (students with ID); $2 (ages 12-16). A combination ticket with Museum of Civilization and Place-Royale Interpretation Centre is available. **Phone:** (418) 692-2843 or (866) 710-8031.

NOTRE-DAME BASILICA-CATHEDRAL OF QUÉBEC (Basilique-Cathédrale Notre-Dame de Québec) is at 20 rue de Buade. The present church was erected in 1923 on the site where the city's first chapel—built in 1633 by Samuel de Champlain—once stood. It features magnificent stained-glass windows, a sanctuary lamp that was a gift from Louis XIV and three Casavant organs.

Under the cathedral, a crypt holds the remains of bishops, archbishops, cardinals and priests. Also of interest is the François-de-Laval Animation Centre, which offers exhibits about Québec's first bishop, who is buried in the cathedral's funeral chapel.

Time: Allow 1 hour minimum. **Hours:** Self-guiding tours are available Mon.-Fri. 9-6, Sat. 9:30-4:30, Sun. 12:30-4:30, late June-Labour Day; Mon.-Fri. 9-5, Sat. 9:30-4:30, Sun. 12:30-4:30, May 1-late June and day after Labour Day-Oct. 31; Mon.-Fri. 9-3:30, Sat. 9-4:30, Sun. 12:30-4:30, rest of year. Guided tours are given Mon.-Fri. 9-11:30 and 12:30-5:30, Sat. 9:30-4, Sun. 12:30-4, late June-Labour Day; Mon.-Fri. 9-11:30 and 12:30-4:30, Sat. 9:30-4, Sun. 12:30-4, rest of year. Animation center open Tues.-Sat. 10-11:30 and 2-4:30, Sun. 2-4:30.

Cost: Cathedral admission $2; $1 (ages 0-16). Crypt $5; $1 (ages 0-16). Animation center free. **Phone:** (418) 692-2533, or (418) 694-0665 for guided tours.

ST. ANDREW'S PRESBYTERIAN CHURCH (Église Presbytérienne de St-Andrew), 5 rue Cook, was built in 1810. The church has a high sidewall pulpit and an interesting arrangement of the pews and balcony. Marble tablets commemorating past ministers and benefactors adorn the walls, and documents and historic church-related objects are displayed in the vestry. Guided tours are available; narration in English is offered. **Hours:** Mon.-Sat. 10-4, Sun. noon-4, July-Aug. **Phone:** (418) 694-1347.

THE URSULINES MUSEUM (Musée des Ursulines), 12 rue Donnacona, displays such items as gilded sculptures, embroideries, documents and furniture from the 17th through the 19th centuries. Exhibits illustrate the daily life and the educational work of the Ursulines of Québec. **CLOSURE INFORMATION:** The museum is closed until sometime in 2012; phone ahead for updates and to confirm schedule and prices. **Hours:** Tues.-Sat. 10-5, Sun. 1-5, June-Sept.; Tues.-Sun. 1-5, rest of year. **Cost:** $6; $4 (students with ID); free (ages 0-11). **Phone:** (418) 694-0694.

WOLFE-MONTCALM MONUMENT (Monument Wolfe-Montcalm), in the Governor's Garden (Parc des Gouverneurs) behind Fairmont Le Château Frontenac at 1 rue des Carrières, is an 1827 obelisk honoring the generals who fought on the Plains of Abraham in 1759. **Hours:** Garden daily 24 hours. **Cost:** Free.

Outside the Fortifications

BATTLEFIELDS PARK (Parc des Champs-de-Bataille) is between rue Bougainville and the St-Louis Gate, with entrances on Grande Allée. The park encompasses the Plains of Abraham, where the armies of Gen. James Wolfe and the Marquis de Montcalm fought in 1759. The information and reception center is in the Discovery Pavilion of the Plains of Abraham.

The restored Martello Tower 1, vestige of the 19th century, offers an exhibit about the fortification's history and military engineering. The "Odyssey" is a multimedia exhibition, a virtual journey covering 400 years of history on the Plains of Abraham. In summer the park presents such horticultural displays as the Joan of Arc Garden, and the Edwin-Bélanger Bandstand offers a number of open-air concerts.

Hours: Martello Tower 1 daily 10-5, July 1-Labour Day. "Odyssey" is offered daily 10-5:30, July 1-Labour Day; 10-5, rest of year. English-narrated guided bus tours depart daily, July 2-Labour Day; phone ahead for schedule. Bandstand concerts are given Thurs.-Sun. at 8, mid-June to mid-Aug.

Cost: July 2-Labour Day (includes bus tour, Martello Tower 1 and "Odyssey") $14; $10 (ages 13-17 and 65+); $4 (ages 0-12). Rest of year (includes "Odyssey" only) $10; $8 (ages 13-17 and 65+). Garden and bandstand free. **Phone:** (418) 649-6157.

CAPITAL OBSERVATORY (Observatoire de la Capitale) is at 1037 rue de la Chevrotière at jct. boul. René-Lévesque, on the 31st floor of the Marie Guyart Building, the city's tallest edifice. Visitors ascend 221 metres (725 ft.) to the observation level, which affords excellent views of the city and its surroundings. Multimedia displays, including interactive touch screen terminals and sound booths, relate the history of the area. **Hours:** Daily 10-5, Feb. 1-second Sun. in Oct.; Tues.-Sun. 10-5, rest of year. **Cost:** $10; $8 (ages 65+ and students with ID); free (ages 0-12). **Phone:** (418) 644-9841 or (888) 497-4322.

CARTIER-BRÉBEUF NATIONAL HISTORIC SITE (Lieu historique national Cartier-Brébeuf) is 3.5 km (2 mi.) n. via Côte d'Abraham and rue de la Couronne at 175 rue de L'Espinay. The landscaped park on the St. Charles River commemorates the site where Jacques Cartier and his crew wintered during his second voyage to Canada in 1535.

The site also recalls the establishment of the first Jesuit residence in Québec by missionaries around 1625. An interpretation center is offered.

Guided tours are available; narration in English is offered. **Hours:** Tues.-Sun. 10-5, July-Aug.; Wed.-Sun. noon-4, mid-May through June 30 and Sept. 1 to mid-Oct. Phone ahead to confirm schedule. **Cost:** $3.90; $3.40 (ages 65+); $1.90 (ages 6-16); $9.80 (family). **Phone:** (418) 648-4038 or (888) 773-8888.

CHEVALIER HOUSE—see Museum of Civilization p. 416.

HAMEL-BRUNEAU HOUSE (Maison Hamel-Bruneau) is in the Ste-Foy sector at 2608 ch. St-Louis. This suburban cottage, built in 1857, now houses temporary art exhibits. Outdoor summer concerts are held in its splendid gardens. Guided tours are available in French or English by appointment. **Time:** Allow 1 hour minimum. **Hours:** Tues.-Sun. 11-5, June-Aug.; Wed.-Sun. 1-5, Mar.-May and Sept.-Dec. Phone ahead to confirm schedule. **Cost:** Free. **Phone:** (418) 641-6280.

ICE HOTEL (Hôtel de Glace) is off Hwy. 73 exit 154 in the sector of Charlesbourg at 9530 rue de la Faune. The structure is made entirely of ice and snow. It includes the Ice Bar, the Ice Café; 36 hotel rooms and themed suites for overnight guests, who have access to spas and a sauna; an ice chapel; and an ice slide.

Time: Allow 1 hour minimum. **Hours:** Open daily 10-midnight, Jan. 6-Mar. 25. Guided tours noon-5:30. **Cost:** $17.50; $15.50 (ages 55+ and students with ID); $8.75 (ages 6-12); $43.75 (family, two adults and three children). After 8 p.m. $13.50; $12 (ages 55+ and students with ID); $6.75 (ages 6-12). **Phone:** (418) 623-2888 or (877) 505-0423.

JACQUES-CARTIER NATIONAL PARK (Parc national de la Jacques-Cartier) is 40 km (25 mi.) n.w. via Hwy. 175. Encompassing 670 square kilometres (259 sq. mi.), this conservation area, surrounded by Laurentides Wildlife Reserve, centers on the Jacques-Cartier River and the surrounding wooded uplands and mountains. Atlantic salmon spawn in late September. The Discovery and Visitors Centre, 10 kilometres (6 mi.) from Hwy. 175, has exhibits and audiovisual presentations describing the park and its habitat. *See Recreation Chart.*

Pets are not permitted. **Hours:** Open daily, mid-May to late Oct. and mid-Dec. to early Mar. Hours vary; phone ahead. **Cost:** $6; $2.75 (ages 6-17); $12 (family, two adults and children); $8.75 (family, one adult and children). **Phone:** (418) 848-3599 in summer, (418) 528-8787 in winter or (800) 665-6527.

JESUIT HOUSE OF SILLERY (Maison des Jésuites de Sillery) is along the St. Lawrence River in the sector of Sillery at 2320 ch. du Foulon. Built about 1730, the house contains an archeological and historical museum, along with arts and crafts exhibits. **Hours:** Tues.-Sun. 11-5, June-Sept.; Wed.-Sun. 1-5, Apr.-May and Oct.-Dec.; Sat.-Sun. 1-5, in Mar. **Cost:** Free. **Phone:** (418) 654-0259.

KABIR KOUBA CLIFF AND WATERFALL PARK (Parc de la Falaise et de la chute Kabir Kouba), at 14 rue St-Amand in the sector of Loretteville, stretches 1.5 kilometres (1 mi.) along the St. Charles River. An interpretive center, an observation deck and walking trails highlight the 28-metre-high (92-ft.) waterfall as well as the canyon, which, at its highest point, reaches a height of 42 metres (138 ft.). Guided 75-minute tours discuss the site's geology, fossils (some more than 455 million years old), and flora and fauna.

Note: Visitors should wear comfortable walking shoes and use caution when navigating riverside paths. **Time:** Allow 1 hour minimum. **Hours:** Daily 10-4, mid-June to early Sept.; Sat.-Sun. 10-4, mid-May to mid-June and early Sept.-late Oct. **Cost:** Interpretation center free. Guided tour $5. **Phone:** (418) 842-0077.

LAURENTIDES WILDLIFE RESERVE (Réserve faunique des Laurentides), 60 km (37 mi.) n.w. via Hwy. 175, is in the Laurentian Mountains. The reserve covers 7,861 square kilometres (3,035 sq. mi.) of wooded uplands and contains more than 1,500 lakes and many rivers. Mountain peaks rise to elevations of 1,219 metres (4,000 ft.). Parts of the vast reserve are still unexplored. Its solitude offers refuge to various game, all protected by strict regulations.

The paved Québec-Chicoutimi Highway (Hwy. 175) traverses the reserve, shortening the distance between the two cities to 212 kilometres (132 mi.). Hwy. 169 (paved) branches north through the reserve to Hébertville. The road from Baie-St-Paul to Chicoutimi, which passes through St-Urbain, skirts the eastern boundary where the Laurentians are highest.

Bait fishing, except with minnows, and fly fishing are permitted. Guides always should be employed for trips into remote areas. Daily fishing permits can be obtained at the reserve entrance. *See Recreation Chart.*

For further information contact the Société des établissements de plein air du Québec (SÉPAQ), Reservations Office, 2640 boul. Laurier, Suite 250, Québec, QC, Canada G1V 5C2.

Outdoor activities, including seasonal hunting and fishing, are offered. **Hours:** Open year-round. **Cost:** Free. **Phone:** (800) 665-6527.

MONTMARTRE CANADIEN, in the sector of Sillery at 1669 ch. St-Louis, is a replica of the Paray-le-Monial in Paris, France. The sanctuary and grounds contain chapel stations, the Grotto of Lourdes and a monument to Our Lady of the Assumption. Guided tours are available for a fee. **Hours:** Grounds open daily. Hours vary; phone ahead. **Cost:** Grounds free. **Phone:** (418) 681-7357.

MONTMORENCY FALLS PARK (Parc de la Chute-Montmorency), 11.2 km (7 mi.) e. via Autoroute 440 in the sector of Beauport, is at the confluence of the Montmorency and St. Lawrence rivers. On the promontory, the park is reached via Hwy. 360 (avenue Royale), and offers a spectacular view of the 83-metre-high (270-ft.) falls, the St. Lawrence and the south shore of Québec. A suspension bridge spans the falls, which are 30 metres (98 ft.) higher than Niagara Falls.

A gondola lift provides rides to the promontory, where Montmorency Manor (Manoir Montmorency) offers an interpretation center and other facilities. The upper portion of the park also can be reached by climbing a panoramic, 487-step staircase. Winter activities include cross-country skiing and ice climbing (beginner's courses are available).

Hours: Daily 8:30-7:30, late June-late Aug.; daily 9-6, mid-Apr. to late June and late Aug.-Oct. 31; daily 10-4, late Dec.-early Jan.; Sat.-Sun. 10-4, late Jan. to mid-Apr. Phone ahead to confirm schedule. **Cost:** Grounds free. One-way gondola ride $7.99; $3.73 (ages 6-17). **Parking:** $9.75 maximum. **Phone:** (418) 663-3330.

MUSEUM OF CIVILIZATION (Musée de la civilisation), 85 rue Dalhousie across from the St. Lawrence River, is a landmark of architecture. A series of separate galleries presents permanent and temporary thematic exhibitions that illustrate the history and culture of Québec and other civilizations through ideas and inventions.

Exhibit presentations are in French and English. **Hours:** Daily 9:30-6:30, June 24-Labour Day; Tues.-Sun. 10-5, rest of year. **Cost:** $13; $12 (ages 65+); $9 (students with ID); $4 (ages 12-16). A combination ticket with Museum of French America and Place-Royale Interpretation Centre is available. **Phone:** (418) 643-2158.

Chevalier House (Maison Chevalier), 50 rue du Marché-Champlain, next to Place-Royale, was built for ship owner Jean-Baptiste Chevalier in 1752. Restored in 1959, the renovated structure today encompasses the neighboring Frérot and Chesnay Houses (Maisons Frérot and Chenay) and recreates the feel and atmosphere of the 18th and 19th centuries. On the ground floor, the Centre d'interprétation de la vie urbaine presents Vieux-Québec: Secrets and Stories; a self-guiding audio tour is included.

Guided tours are available in French or English; the language used is determined by the preference of the first registered participant for that tour. Visitors must register at the reception pavilion. **Hours:** Daily 9:30-5, June 24-Labour Day; Tues.-Sun. 10-5, day after Labour Day to mid-Oct., winter holiday season and May 1-June 23; Sat.-Sun. 10-5, rest of year. Closed Christmas. **Cost:** $2. **Phone:** (418) 646-3167 or (866) 710-8031.

NATIONAL MUSEUM OF FINE ARTS OF QUÉBEC (Musée national des beaux-arts du Québec), at 1 av. Wolfe-Montcalm in Battlefields Park, has three distinctive pavilions. The Grand Hall, which features large expanses of glass, connects the original 1933 Gérard-Morisset building and the 1871 Charles-Baillairgé building.

The museum, which chronicles Québec's art from the French Colonial period to the present, contains a large collection of fine arts, including paintings, sculptures and ceramics as well as articles fashioned of gold and silver. Features include traveling exhibitions, music recitals and films.

Hours: Daily 10-6 (also Wed. 6-9 p.m.), June 1-Labour Day; Tues.-Sun. 10-5 (also Wed. 5-9), rest of year. Closed Christmas. **Cost:** Permanent collection free. Special exhibits $15; $12 (ages 65+); $7 (students with ID); $4 (ages 12-17); $30 (family, two adults and three children). **Phone:** (418) 643-2150 or (866) 220-2150.

PARLIAMENT BUILDING (Hôtel du Parlement), at Grande Allée and av. Honoré-Mercier, is surrounded by statue-studded grounds. Inspired by the Second Empire-style Louvre, the 1886 Parliament Building is a monument commemorating significant national and provincial historical events. Guided tours are available in French and English, and, with an advance reservation, in Italian, Spanish or sign language (French). **Hours:** Mon.-Fri. 9-4:30, Sat.-Sun. 10-4:30, June 24-Labour Day; Mon.-Fri. 9-4:30, rest of year. **Cost:** Free. **Phone:** (418) 643-7239, or (866) 599-4999 in Canada.

PLACE-ROYALE, at the center of Lower Town, is the birthplace of Québec City, one of the first successful settlements in New France. Samuel de Champlain first established an *abitation*, or trading post, here in 1608. Despite a ruinous fire in 1682 and numerous attacks by the British, who finally captured the city in 1759, the area has been preserved virtually as it was during the 18th century.

Events and entertainment take place in the summer. Along the St. Lawrence are the docks for the Québec-Lévis ferry on rue des Traversiers and for the sightseeing boat MV *Louis Jolliet,* Quai Chouinard at 10 rue Dalhousie *(see Sightseeing p. 418).*

Guided tours of Place-Royale depart from the interpretation center at 27 rue Notre-Dame. Narration in English and French is offered; the language used during the tour is determined by the preference of the first registered participant for that tour. **Hours:** Tours are given daily at 10, 11:30, 1:15 and 3:30. Phone ahead to confirm schedule. **Cost:** Free. **Phone:** (418) 646-3167 or (866) 710-8031.

Our Lady of Victories Church (Église Notre-Dame-des-Victoires), jct. Notre-Dame and rue Sous-le-Fort, was restored after being destroyed by fire during the siege of Québec. The 1688 church, built on the foundations of Samuel de Champlain's trading post, has commemorative paintings and tablets. **Hours:** Daily 9-5, May-Oct. Mass is held Sun. at 10:30 and noon. **Cost:** Free. **Phone:** (418) 692-1650.

Place-Royale Interpretation Centre (Centre d'interprétation de Place-Royale), 27 rue Notre-Dame, relates the story of Place-Royale, cradle of French culture in the New World. A 3-D film, exhibitions, guided tours and a costume workshop are offered. **Time:** Allow 1 hour minimum. **Hours:** Daily 9:30-5, June 24-Labour Day; Tues.-Sun. 10-5, rest

of year. Closed Christmas. **Cost:** $7; $6 (ages 65+); $5 (students with ID); $2 (ages 12-16). A combination ticket with Museum of Civilization and Museum of French America is available. **Phone:** (418) 646-3167 or (866) 710-8031.

Quartier Petit Champlain is in Lower Town below Dufferin Terrace and is bounded by boul. Champlain, rue du Petit-Champlain, rue Sous-le Fort and rue du Cul-de-Sac. This area features many boutiques and restaurants on different street levels. The Louis Jolliet House is the lower station of the *funiculaire* that links Lower Town with Dufferin Terrace. The Théâtre Petit-Champlain, Maison de la Chanson at 68 rue Petit-Champlain regularly presents song recitals. **Phone:** (418) 692-2613.

Royal Battery (La Batterie Royale), rues St-Pierre and Sous-le-Fort, is part of the military defense system built in 1691. The battery was used to defend the city during the siege of 1759. It was completely rebuilt in 1977. **Hours:** Daily 10-5, mid-June through Labour Day. **Cost:** Free.

Unesco Park, at rues St-Pierre and du Porche, is a historical and maritime-themed playground for children.

PROMENADE DES GOUVERNEURS—see Dufferin Terrace p. 413.

QUÉBEC AQUARIUM (Aquarium du Québec) is in the sector of Ste-Foy at 1675 av. des Hôtels; from Hwy. 73S take exit 132 (last exit before accessing Pierre-Laporte Bridge), then just s.e. (loop around to av. des Hôtels, following signs). The 16-hectare (40-acre) outdoor park and the main pavilion enable visitors to explore marine life in carefully re-created indoor and outdoor environments.

Outside, habitats shelter such mammals as polar bears, walruses, seals and arctic foxes. The main pavilion houses 10,000 fish and invertebrates, 3,000 of which can be seen as visitors walk through an acrylic tunnel surrounded by 350,000 litres (92,470 U.S. gallons) of saltwater. Educational demonstrations and animal feedings are scheduled throughout the day.

Time: Allow 3 hours minimum. **Hours:** Daily 10-5, June 1-Labour Day; 10-4, rest of year. Closed Christmas. **Cost:** $15.50; $14.17 (ages 65+); $7.75 (ages 3-17). Family rates are available. **Phone:** (866) 659-5264.

ROGER-VAN DEN HENDE BOTANICAL GARDEN (Jardin botanique Roger-Van den Hende) is on the Laval University campus in the sector of Ste-Foy at 2460 boul. Hochelaga. The site is home to a dazzling array of plants—more than 4,000 species and cultivars arranged in order of botanical family. Along with flora native to Québec, ornamental plants from Asia, Europe and North America grace the grounds of this 6-hectare (15-acre) educational garden.

Visitors will appreciate the site's arboretum, idyllic water garden, collection of herbaceous plants and rhododendrons, and fragrant rose garden. **Time:** Allow 2 hours minimum. **Hours:** Daily 8-8, May-Oct. **Cost:** Free. **Phone:** (418) 656-3742.

ST. JOHN THE BAPTIST CHURCH (Église St-Jean-Baptiste) is at 480 rue St-Jean. Designed by architect Joseph-Ferdinand Peachy in the late 1800s, the ornate church features a large Louis XV-style baldaquin over the main altar, paintings by 19th-century Canadian artist Antoine Plamondon, 36 stained-glass windows and an 1885 organ that was enlarged by the Casavant brothers in 1921.

Time: Allow 1 hour minimum. **Hours:** Guided and self-guiding tours are available Mon.-Fri. 11-4, Sat.-Sun. 11-5, late June-Labour Day; Sat.-Sun. 11-5, day after Labour Day to mid-Oct. Mass is held Mon.-Fri. at 4:30, Sun. at 10:30. **Cost:** Donations. **Phone:** (418) 688-0350.

VILLA BAGATELLE, in the sector of Sillery at 1563 ch. St-Louis, with access by av. James LeMoine, is a restored neo-Gothic villa surrounded by a formal garden. Sillery—now part of Québec—was wooded wilderness when an English upper-class family built the villa as a country house in the 19th century. Impressive gardens display more than 350 varieties of native and exotic flowers. Art and history exhibits also are presented. **Hours:** Tues.-Sun. 11-5, June-Aug.; Wed.-Sun. 1-5, Mar.-May and Sept.-Dec. **Cost:** Free. **Phone:** (418) 654-0259.

VISITATION PARK HISTORIC SITE (Site Historique de la Visitation), in the sector of Ste-Foy at 2825 ch. Ste-Foy, comprises a public garden and the ruins of a church. A bell tower now functions as an observation tower and offers lovely views of Québec City and the distant Laurentian Mountains. A museum details the history of the Ste-Foy neighborhood.

Various cultural events are held on-site, including outdoor classical music concerts in summer.

A self-guiding audio tour is available. Guided tours are available in French by reservation. Guided tours in English may be available with advance notice. **Time:** Allow 1 hour minimum. **Hours:** Tues.-Sun. 11-5, June-Sept.; Wed.-Sun. 1-5, Apr.-May and Oct.-Dec.; Sun. 1-5, in Mar. Phone ahead to confirm schedule. **Cost:** Grounds free. Guided tour $3; free (ages 0-5). Cash only. Reservations are recommended. **Phone:** (418) 654-4576.

GAMBLING ESTABLISHMENTS

- **Salon de jeux de Québec** is at 250G boul. Wilfrid-Hamel. **Hours:** Daily 10 a.m.-3 a.m. **Phone:** (418) 529-7878. *(See ad this page.)*

Sightseeing
Boat Tours

COUDRIER CRUISES (Les Croisières le Coudrier) departs Pier 19 (close to the lock) in the Old Port of Québec at 180 rue Dalhousie at jct. St-André. The bilingual narrated sightseeing cruise takes visitors around Québec City aboard a 20-metre (65-ft.) vessel; the trip lasts 90 minutes. Also offered are daylong trips to Isle-aux-Coudres, Grosse Île, Isle-aux-Grues and Île d'Orléans, as well as dinner cruises.

Hours: Ninety-minute sightseeing cruises depart daily at 1:30, 3:30 and 8:30, May-Oct. Phone ahead to confirm schedule. **Cost:** Ninety-minute sightseeing cruise $32.99; $30.99 (ages 65+ and students with ID); $16.99 (ages 6-16); $65.99 (family, two adults and one child). Prices may vary. **Parking:** $6-$12. **Phone:** (418) 692-0107 or (888) 600-5554.

GEM SAVE **QUÉBEC CITY CRUISES** (Croisières AML), Quai Chouinard at 10 rue Dalhousie, offers 90-minute sightseeing cruises of the

▼ *See AAA listing this page* ▼

DOWNTOWN QUEBEC (cont'd)

Map Page	Hotels (cont'd)	Diamond Rated	High Season	Page
38 p. 425	Auberge du Quartier	◆◆	Rates not provided	432
39 p. 425	Appartements La Pergola	◆◆	Rates not provided	432

Map Page	Restaurants	Diamond Rated	Cuisine	Meal Range	Page
1 p. 425	**Restaurant Laurie Raphaël**	◆◆◆◆	Quebec	$18-$45	447
2 p. 425	Restaurant Le Café du Monde	◆◆	French	$14-$26	447
3 p. 425	Moss Bistro Belge	◆◆	Belgian	$15-$36	446
4 p. 425	**Restaurant l'Échaudé**	◆◆	French	$12-$40	447
5 p. 425	Charbon Steakhouse	◆◆◆	Steak	$14-$42	444
6 p. 425	Aviatic Club	◆◆◆	International	$13-$33	444
7 p. 425	Matto 71	◆◆	Italian	$13-$28	446
8 p. 425	**Panache Restaurant**	◆◆◆◆	Quebec	$15-$48	446
9 p. 425	**Restaurant Initiale**	◆◆◆◆	French	$18-$45	447
10 p. 425	Portofino Bistro Italiano	◆◆	Italian	$11-$30	446
11 p. 425	Pub St-Patrick	◆◆	Canadian	$11-$23	446
12 p. 425	D'Orsay Restaurant Pub	◆◆	International	$11-$38	445
14 p. 425	**Restaurant 1640**	◆◆◆	French	$10-$35	446
15 p. 425	**Restaurant Le Marie Clarisse**	◆◆◆	Seafood	$14-$38	447
16 p. 425	**Restaurant Le Patriarche**	◆◆◆	French	$28-$48	448
17 p. 425	Le Charles Baillairgé Resto Bar Lounge (See ad p. 439.)	◆◆◆	French	$7-$39	445
18 p. 425	**Saint Alexandre Pub**	◆◆	Canadian	$10-$20	448
19 p. 425	L'Entrecôte Saint-Jean	◆◆	French	$12-$27	445
20 p. 425	Le Lapin Saute	◆◆	French	$10-$31	445
21 p. 425	**Le Champlain**	◆◆◆◆	French	$38-$49	445
22 p. 425	**Restaurant La Cremaillere**	◆◆◆	Continental	$15-$44	447
23 p. 425	Au Petit Coin Breton Crêperie Restaurant	◆◆	Continental	$10-$20	444
24 p. 425	Café de la Paix	◆◆	French	$13-$42	444
25 p. 425	Pizzeria d'Youville	◆◆	Italian	$9-$18	446
26 p. 425	**Restaurant Le Continental**	◆◆◆	French	$13-$52	447
27 p. 425	**Crêperie Le Petit Château**	◆◆	French	$9-$23	444
28 p. 425	Restaurant Anh Le	◆◆	Vietnamese	$10-$20	446
29 p. 425	**Restaurant aux Anciens Canadiens**	◆◆	Quebec	$18-$45	447
30 p. 425	Restaurant au Parmesan	◆◆	Italian	$10-$30	446
31 p. 425	**Yuzu Resto + Club**	◆◆◆	Japanese	$12-$42	449
33 p. 425	Restaurant La Pointe Des Ameriques	◆◆	Italian	$12-$25	447
34 p. 425	Restaurant Le Saint Amour	◆◆◆	French	$16-$53	448
35 p. 425	Le Beffroi Steakhouse	◆◆◆	Steak	$12-$50	445
36 p. 425	**Restaurant L'Omelette**	◆◆	Canadian	$7-$19	448
37 p. 425	**Café de Paris**	◆◆	French	$11-$32	444
38 p. 425	**Restaurant Que Sera Sera**	◆◆◆	French	$12-$32	448
39 p. 425	Pizzeria Primavera Bistro Italiano	◆◆	Italian	$10-$25	446
40 p. 425	Le Postino Bistro-Bar	◆◆	French	$13-$28	445
41 p. 425	Apsara	◆◆	Asian	$11-$15	444

Map Page	Restaurants (cont'd)	Diamond Rated	Cuisine	Meal Range	Page
㊷ p. 425	**Le Veau d'or**	◆◆	Northern Italian	$11-$20	446
㊸ p. 425	Restaurant Le Parlementaire	◆◆◆	Regional French	$12-$28	447
㊹ p. 425	**Restaurant Louis Hébert**	◆◆◆	French	$14-$35	448
㊺ p. 425	**Savini resto-bar/vinotheque**	◆◆◆	Italian	$13-$29	448
㊻ p. 425	L'Astral	◆◆◆	French	$15-$41	445
㊼ p. 425	Trattoria La Scala	◆◆	Italian	$9-$22	448
㊽ p. 425	Le Graffiti Resto Cite	◆◆◆	French	$12-$35	445

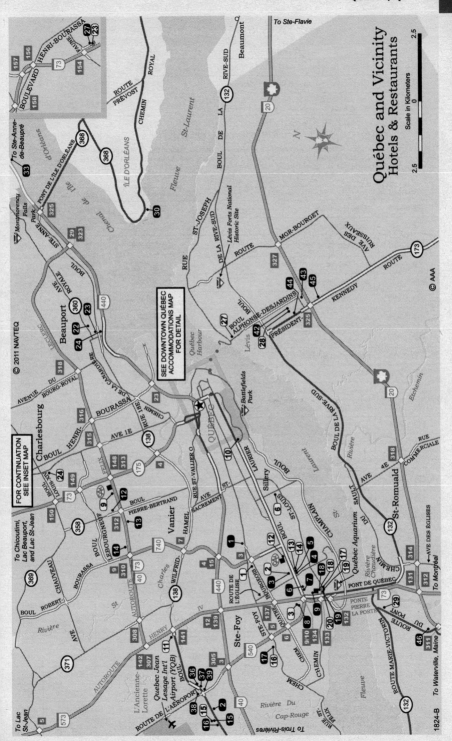

Québec and Vicinity
Hotels & Restaurants

✈ Airport Accommodations

Map Page	QUEBEC	Diamond Rated	High Season	Page
37 p. 429	Château Repotel, 1.1 mi (1.8 km) s of airport	▽▽	$93-$150	297
39 p. 429	Comfort Inn, 1.1 mi (1.8 km) s of airport	▽▽	$80-$120	297
16 p. 429	**Comfort Inn de l'Aeroport-Hamel, 3 mi (5 km) sw of airport**	▽▽	$86-$220 [SAVE]	449

Quebec and Vicinity

This index helps you "spot" where approved hotels and restaurants are located on the corresponding detailed maps. Hotel daily rate range is for comparison only and shows the property's high season. Restaurant rate range is a combination of lunch and/or dinner. Turn to the listing page for more detailed rate information and consult display ads for special promotions.

QUÉBEC

Map Page	Hotels	Diamond Rated	High Season	Page
1 p. 429	**Hotel Universel**	▽▽	$119-$229 [SAVE]	451
2 p. 429	Hotel Quebec Inn	▽▽▽	$114-$300	450
3 p. 429	ALT Hotel-Quebec	▽▽▽	Rates not provided	449
4 p. 429	Hotel Lindbergh	▽▽▽	$90-$225	450
5 p. 429	**Hotel Classique** (See ad p. 438.)	▽▽▽	$109-$289 [SAVE]	450
6 p. 429	Hotel Plaza Quebec	▽▽▽	$109-$209	450
7 p. 429	Sir Wilfrid	▽▽	$99-$250	451
8 p. 429	**Hotel Clarion Quebec** (See ad opposite title page.)	▽▽▽	$99-$229 [SAVE]	450
9 p. 429	**Holiday Inn Express Quebec** (See ad p. 428.)	▽▽▽	$119-$229 [SAVE]	450
12 p. 429	Hotel & Suites Normandin	▽▽▽	$120-$249	450
13 p. 429	Hotel Dauphin Quebec City	▽▽▽	$85-$152	450
14 p. 429	**Hotel Quality Suites Quebec**	▽▽	$115-$195 [SAVE]	450
15 p. 429	Hotel Super 8 Quebec Ste-Foy	▽▽▽	$72-$159	450
16 p. 429	**Comfort Inn de l'Aeroport-Hamel**	▽▽	$86-$220 [SAVE]	449
17 p. 429	**Château Bonne Entente** (See ad p. 433.)	▽▽▽▽	$159-$499 [SAVE]	449
18 p. 429	**Best Western Hotel L'Aristocrate** (See ad p. 424.)	▽▽▽	$109-$269 [SAVE]	449
19 p. 429	**Hôtel Sépia**	▽▽▽	$119-$229 [SAVE]	450
22 p. 429	Gite du Vieux-Bourg	▽▽	Rates not provided	449
23 p. 429	**Ambassadeur Hotel & Suites**	▽▽▽	$90-$240 [SAVE]	449
24 p. 429	Comfort Inn Beauport	▽▽	$86-$145	449
27 p. 429	**Four Points by Sheraton Quebec Resort**	▽▽▽	$100-$210 [SAVE]	449

Map Page	Restaurants	Diamond Rated	Cuisine	Meal Range	Page
1 p. 429	Café Pates a Tout	▽	Italian	$7-$10	451
2 p. 429	Bistango	▽▽▽	French	$12-$37	451
3 p. 429	Le Paris Grill	▽▽	French	$12-$25	452
6 p. 429	Paparazzi	▽▽	Italian	$14-$29	452
9 p. 429	Le Preben	▽▽	Canadian	$13-$34	452
10 p. 429	Restaurant du Musée	▽▽	Quebec	$10-$20	452
11 p. 429	Le Bif Steakhouse & Bar	▽▽	Steak	$9-$33	451
12 p. 429	Au Petit Coin Breton	▽▽	Continental	$10-$20	451

Map Page	Restaurants (cont'd)	Diamond Rated	Cuisine	Meal Range	Page
⑬ p. 429	Cosmos	▽▽▽	Continental	$10-$25	451
⑭ p. 429	Restaurant La Pointe des Ameriques	▽▽	Italian	$10-$25	452
⑮ p. 429	Jardin de Tang	▽▽	Chinese	$9-$20	451
⑯ p. 429	**Monte Cristo L'Original**	▽▽▽	Mediterranean	$39-$48	452
⑰ p. 429	Le Manoir du Spaghetti	▽▽	Italian	$9-$19	452
⑱ p. 429	**Restaurant La Fenouillière** (See ad p. 424.)	▽▽▽▽	French	$16-$38	452
⑲ p. 429	**Ristorante Michelangelo**	▽▽▽▽	Italian	$19-$45	453
⑳ p. 429	Restaurant Le Galopin	▽▽▽	Regional French	$16-$35	453
㉓ p. 429	Restaurant Le Dijon	▽▽▽	French	$11-$31	452
㉔ p. 429	Le Manoir du Spaghetti	▽▽	Italian	$9-$19	451

ÎLE D'ORLÉANS

Map Page	Hotel	Diamond Rated	High Season	Page
㉚ p. 429	Auberge La Goeliche	▽▽▽	$109-$279	290

BOISCHATEL

Map Page	Hotel	Diamond Rated	High Season	Page
㉝ p. 429	**Econo Lodge Montmorency**	▽▽	$75-$145 [SAVE]	267

L'ANCIENNE-LORETTE

Map Page	Hotels	Diamond Rated	High Season	Page
㊱ p. 429	Hotel & Suites Le Times	▽▽▽	$149-$169	297
㊲ p. 429	Château Repotel	▽▽	$93-$150	297
㊳ p. 429	Hotel Must	▽▽▽	$115-$305	297
㊴ p. 429	Comfort Inn	▽▽	$80-$120	297

LÉVIS

Map Page	Hotels	Diamond Rated	High Season	Page
㊷ p. 429	**Four Points by Sheraton Levis Convention Centre** (See ad p. 302.)	▽▽▽	$100-$210 [SAVE]	302
㊸ p. 429	Quality Inn & Suites Levis	▽▽▽	$109-$189	303
㊹ p. 429	Hotel Kennedy	▽▽	$90-$190	303
㊺ p. 429	**Comfort Inn**	▽▽	$85-$145 [SAVE]	302
㊻ p. 429	**Comfort Inn & Suites Rive-Sud Quebec**	▽▽▽	Rates not provided [SAVE]	302

Map Page	Restaurants	Diamond Rated	Cuisine	Meal Range	Page
㉗ p. 429	**Restaurant L'Intimiste**	▽▽▽	French	$10-$38	303
㉘ p. 429	Cosmos Café	▽▽▽	Continental	$9-$22	303
㉙ p. 429	**Restaurant Mustang Bill Pizza**	▽▽	Canadian	$6-$20	303

Simply Reliable

The Diamond Ratings in this TourBook guide are backed by our expert, in-person evaluations, whether the hotel or restaurant is no-frills, moderate or upscale.

Learn more at **AAA.com/Diamonds**

DOWNTOWN QUÉBEC

APPARTEMENTS LA PERGOLA

Phone: 418/681-1428 39

Condominium
Rates not provided

Address: 405 boul Rene-Levesque ouest G1S 1S2 **Location:** Between aves Moncton and des Erables. Located in a busy residential area. **Facility:** 6 units, some two bedrooms and kitchens. 2-3 stories (no elevator), interior corridors. **Parking:** winter plug-ins. **Guest Services:** coin laundry.

AUBERGE AUX DEUX LIONS

Phone: (418)780-8100 37

Classic Historic
Resort Hotel
$109-$209

Address: 25 boul Rene-Levesque est G1R 2A9 **Location:** Just e of ave de Salaberry. **Facility:** In an 1908 home, this intimate hotel offers small to good-size rooms with a mix of contemporary and vintage furnishings and small flat-screen televisions. 14 units. 3 stories (no elevator), interior/exterior corridors. **Parking:** on-site (fee), winter plug-ins. **Terms:** 2 night minimum stay - seasonal and/or weekends, 4 day cancellation notice-fee imposed. **Guest Services:** valet and coin laundry.

AUBERGE DU QUARTIER

Phone: 418/525-9726 38

Historic Bed
& Breakfast
Rates not provided

Address: 170 Grande Allee ouest G1R 2G9 **Location:** Between aves Bourlamaque and Cartier. **Facility:** Attractive rooms that range from small to spacious are offered at this restored 19th-century residence. 15 units. 3 stories (no elevator), interior corridors. **Parking:** on-site (fee) and street. **Guest Services:** valet laundry.

AUBERGE DU TRESOR

Phone: 418/694-1876 12

Historic Hotel
$135-$165 6/1-10/31
$100-$130 11/1-5/31

Address: 20 rue Ste-Anne G1R 3X2 **Location:** Corner of rue du Tresor. Located in Old Quebec. **Facility:** Overlooking the scenic Chateau Frontenac in the heart of Old Quebec, this red-roofed heritage inn stands on a property first inhabited in 1640. 23 units. 3 stories (no elevator), interior corridors. **Parking:** street only. **Terms:** check-in 3:30 pm. **Amenities:** *Some:* high-speed Internet. **Dining:** Restaurant 1640, see separate listing. **Guest Services:** valet laundry. *(See ad p. 433.)*

Enjoy great savings on hotel rates
at AAA.com or CAA.ca

▼ See AAA listing p. 449 ▼

▼ See AAA listing p. 432 ▼

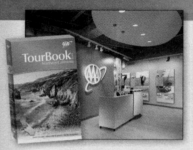

(See map & index p. 425.)

AUBERGE L'AUTRE JARDIN
Phone: (418)523-1790 **29**

Bed & Breakfast
$110-$250

Address: 365 boul Charest est G1K 3H3 **Location:** Between rue Dorchester and rue de la Couronne. **Facility:** Operated by a non-profit organization, this B&B has contemporary, stylish rooms in a prime neighborhood on the northwest cusp of downtown Quebec. A fair-trade gift shop is located in the lobby. 28 units. 3 stories (no elevator), interior corridors. **Parking:** street only. **Terms:** check-in 4 pm, cancellation fee imposed. **Guest Services:** valet laundry. **Free Special Amenities: expanded continental breakfast and high-speed Internet.**

BED & BREAKFAST MANOIR MON CALME
Phone: (418)523-2714 **35**

Historic Bed & Breakfast
$109-$149

Address: 549 Grande Allee est G1R 2J5 **Location:** Corner of Cours du Generale-De Montcalm. **Facility:** This handsome Victorian house offers spacious, tastefully decorated rooms within walking distance of restaurants and Old Quebec. 6 units. 3 stories (no elevator), interior corridors. **Terms:** check-in 4 pm, 4 day cancellation notice. **Guest Services:** coin laundry.

BEST WESTERN PLUS CITY CENTRE/CENTRE-VILLE
Phone: (418)649-1919 **19**

Hotel
$130-$410

AAA Benefit: Members save up to 20%, plus 10% bonus points with Best Western Rewards®.

Address: 330 rue de la Couronne G1K 6E6 **Location:** Corner of rue du Roi. **Facility:** 180 units. 6 stories, interior corridors. **Parking:** valet only. **Amenities:** safes. *Some:* high-speed Internet. **Pool(s):** heated indoor. **Activities:** whirlpool, limited exercise equipment. **Guest Services:** valet laundry. **Free Special Amenities:** local telephone calls and high-speed Internet.
(See ad p. 437.)

COURTYARD QUEBEC CITY
Phone: (418)694-4004 **25**

Hotel
$115-$219

AAA Benefit: AAA hotel discounts of 5% or more.

Address: 850 Place d'Youville G1R 3P6 **Location:** Corner of ave Honore-Mercier; in Old Quebec, facing Place d'Youville. **Facility:** 111 units. 8 stories, interior corridors. **Parking:** on-site (fee) and valet. **Terms:** check-in 4 pm. **Amenities:** high-speed Internet. **Dining:** Restaurant Que Sera Sera, see separate listing. **Activities:** whirlpool, exercise room. *Fee:* massage. **Guest Services:** valet and coin laundry.

DELTA QUEBEC
Phone: (418)647-1717 **31**

Hotel
$160-$299 6/1-10/31
$110-$250 11/1-5/31

Address: 690 boul Rene-Levesque est G1R 5A8 **Location:** Just w of boul Honore-Mercier. **Facility:** 377 units. 12 stories, interior corridors. **Parking:** on-site (fee) and valet. **Amenities:** *Fee:* video games, high-speed Internet. *Some:* honor bars. **Pool(s):** heated outdoor. **Activities:** saunas, exercise room. *Fee:* massage. **Guest Services:** valet laundry.

FAIRMONT LE CHÂTEAU FRONTENAC
Phone: (418)692-3861 **16**

Classic Historic Hotel
$179-$459

Address: 1 rue des Carrieres G1R 4P5 **Location:** In Old Quebec. **Facility:** Turrets and verdigris copper roofs distinguish this landmark 1893 château with its commanding view of the St. Lawrence River. Rooms, which range in size, are luxuriously appointed with upscale bedding. 618 units, some two bedrooms. 18 stories, interior corridors. **Parking:** on-site and valet. **Terms:** check-in 4 pm, cancellation fee imposed. **Amenities:** video games (fee), honor bars. *Some:* high-speed Internet (fee), safes. **Dining:** 3 restaurants, also, Le Champlain, see separate listing. **Pool(s):** heated indoor. **Activities:** whirlpool, steamrooms, exercise room, spa. *Fee:* bicycles. **Guest Services:** valet laundry.

Fairmont Le Chateau Frontenac in the heart of Old Québec, where magical moments turn into memories.

HILTON QUÉBEC
Phone: (418)647-2411 **30**

Hotel
$199-$299 10/16-5/31
$139-$179 6/1-10/15

AAA Benefit: Members save 5% or more everyday!

Address: 1100 boul Rene-Levesque est G1R 4P3 **Location:** Corner of ave Honore-Mercier. Located next to convention centre and shopping complex. **Facility:** This luxury high-rise hotel offers excellent city views and many luxury services. Some guest rooms are quite cozy. 571 units. 23 stories, interior corridors. **Parking:** on-site (fee) and valet. **Terms:** 1-7 night minimum stay, cancellation fee imposed. **Amenities:** *Fee:* video games, high-speed Internet. *Some:* safes. **Dining:** 2 restaurants. **Pool(s):** heated outdoor. **Activities:** sauna, exercise room. *Fee:* massage. **Guest Services:** valet laundry. *(See ad p. 436.)*

(See map & index p. 425.)

HOTEL 71 Phone: (418)692-1171 **6**

Historic Boutique Hotel

$275-$770 6/1-10/31
$224-$619 11/1-5/31

Address: 71 rue St-Pierre G1K 4A4 **Location:** Just e of Cote de la Montagne. **Facility:** Luxurious rooms at this stylish boutique hotel include high-quality bedding, granite-accented furniture, wireless Internet access and large showers. 60 units. 7 stories, interior corridors. **Parking:** valet only. **Terms:** cancellation fee imposed. **Amenities:** high-speed Internet, safes. **Dining:** Matto 71, see separate listing. **Activities:** bicycles, exercise room. *Fee:* massage. **Guest Services:** valet laundry. **Free Special Amenities:** high-speed Internet.

SAVE ｜ Y BIZ 🛜 ✕ / SOME UNITS FEE 🔌 FEE 🧳

HOTEL ACADIA Phone: 418/694-0280 **21**

Hotel

Rates not provided

Address: 43 rue Ste-Ursule G1R 4E4 **Location:** Just n of rue St-Louis; in Old Quebec. **Facility:** 40 units. 4 stories (no elevator), interior corridors. **Parking:** on-site (fee). **Terms:** check-in 4 pm. **Activities:** whirlpool. *Fee:* massage. **Guest Services:** valet laundry.

[📶] 🛜 ✕ 🖥 / SOME UNITS 🔌

▼ *See AAA listing p. 435* ▼

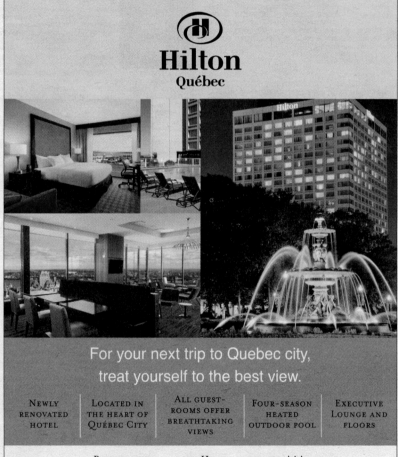

▼ *See AAA listing p. 435* ▼

WWW.HOTELQUEBEC.COM
INFO@HOTELQUEBEC.COM

Phone: 418 649-1919
Toll free: 1 877 625-7548
330, rue de la Couronne
Quebec (Quebec) Canada
G1K 6E6

Best Western
PLUS
Centre-ville Québec
City Centre Quebec

RESERVATIONS: 1-877-625-7548

PREFERRED RATES FOR AAA / CAA MEMBERS

- 1,9 km / 1.2 miles from cruise terminal
- Walking distance from Old Quebec
- Free: Wireless High Speed Internet Access
- 100% smoke-free and Pet Friendly
- Enjoy our indoor pool & hot tub
- Italian restaurant on site

CAA AAA
Approved
Lodging
♦ ♦ ♦

www.settimocielo.ca
Restaurant
Settimo Cielo!

Get the free mobile app at
http://gettag.mobi

(See map & index p. 425.)

HOTEL CHAMPLAIN VIEUX-QUEBEC
Phone: (418)694-0106

Hotel
$139-$279 6/1-10/31
$119-$229 11/1-5/31

Address: 115 rue Ste-Anne G1R 3X6 **Location:** Between rue Ste-Angele and St-Stanislas. Located in Old Quebec. **Facility:** 50 units, some kitchens. 5 stories, interior corridors. **Parking:** on-site (fee), winter plug-ins. **Terms:** cancellation fee imposed. **Guest Services:** valet laundry.

 / SOME UNITS FEE

HOTEL CHÂTEAU BELLEVUE
Phone: (418)692-2573 **23**

Historic Hotel
$115-$285 6/1-10/20
$99-$265 10/21-5/31

Address: 16 rue de la Porte G1R 4M9 **Location:** Corner of ave Ste-Genevieve. Located in Old Québec. **Facility:** This 1848 building overlooks Parc des Gouverneurs in Old Québec. The small to good-size rooms have attractive furnishings and luxurious bedding. 49 units. 4 stories, interior corridors. **Parking:** on-site (fee). **Terms:** check-in 4 pm. **Amenities:** high-speed Internet. **Guest Services:** valet laundry. **Free Special Amenities: expanded continental breakfast and high-speed Internet.**

 / SOME UNITS FEE

HOTEL CHÂTEAU LAURIER QUEBEC
Phone: (418)522-8108 **32**

Historic Hotel
$104-$379

Address: 1220 Place George-V ouest G1R 5B8 **Location:** Corner of Grande Allee est. **Facility:** Handsome guest rooms, available in a variety of sizes, are classically furnished at this well located downtown hotel. 289 units. 5 stories, interior corridors. **Parking:** on-site (fee) and valet. **Terms:** check-in 4 pm, 2 night minimum stay - seasonal and/or weekends, cancellation fee imposed. **Amenities:** safes. **Dining:** St-Hubert, see separate listing. **Pool(s):** heated indoor. **Activities:** sauna, whirlpools, exercise room, spa. **Guest Services:** valet laundry. **Free Special Amenities: newspaper.**

SAVE ECO / SOME UNITS

HOTEL CLARENDON
Phone: (418)692-2480 **14**

Historic Hotel
$159-$309 6/1-10/31
$109-$259 11/1-5/31

Address: 57 rue Ste-Anne G1R 3X4 **Location:** Corner of rue des Jardins. Located in Old Quebec. **Facility:** Within walking distance to many attractions in Old Quebec, the well-restored, historic hotel offers upscale rooms and a range of luxury services. 143 units. 8 stories, interior corridors. **Parking:** valet only. **Terms:** check-in 4 pm. **Amenities:** high-speed Internet. **Dining:** Le Charles Baillairgé Resto Bar Lounge, see separate listing. **Activities:** exercise room. *Fee:* massage. **Guest Services:** valet laundry. **Free Special Amenities: early check-in/late check-out and high-speed Internet.** (See ad p. 439.)

 / SOME UNITS

HOTEL DES COUTELLIER
Phone: 418/692-9696 **3**

Hotel
Rates not provided

Address: 253 rue St-Paul G1K 3W5 **Location:** Corner rue St-Andre; facing Marche du Vieux-Port. **Facility:** 24 units. 4 stories, interior corridors. **Parking:** street only. **Amenities:** honor bars. **Dining:** Moss Bistro Belge, see separate listing. **Activities:** *Fee:* massage. **Guest Services:** valet laundry.

HOTEL LE GERMAIN DOMINION
Phone: (418)692-2224 **2**

Historic Boutique Hotel
$229-$415 6/1-10/31
$209-$415 11/1-5/31

Address: 126 rue St-Pierre G1K 4A8 **Location:** Corner of rue St-Paul. **Facility:** Located in the Old Port district, this boutique hotel features luxurious furnishings and stylish bathrooms; some luxury services are offered. 60 units. 5-8 stories, interior corridors. **Parking:** on-site (fee) and valet. **Terms:** 2 night minimum stay - seasonal and/or weekends. **Amenities:** high-speed Internet, safes, honor bars. **Activities:** exercise room. *Fee:* massage. **Guest Services:** valet laundry.

▼ See AAA listing p. 450 ▼

(See map & index p. 425.)

HOTEL LE PRIORI
Phone: (418)692-3992 **8**

Historic Hotel

$199-$599 6/1-10/22
$129-$539 10/23-5/31

Address: 15 Sault-au-Matelot G1K 3Y7 **Location:** Between Cote de la Montagne and rue St-Antoine. Located in Old Port area. **Facility:** Decor with post-modern influences distinguishes this hotel, which is set in a restored 18th-century stone building. 26 units, some two bedrooms and kitchens. 3-4 stories, interior/exterior corridors. **Parking:** street only. **Terms:** 5 day cancellation notice. **Amenities:** safes. **Activities:** *Fee:* massage. **Guest Services:** valet laundry.

[SAVE] [Y] [fi] [BIZ] [📶] [X] [FEE🍴] [🖥️]
/[SOME UNITS] [🛏️] [🖼️]

HOTEL L'ERMITAGE
Phone: 418/694-0968 **27**

Historic Hotel

Rates not provided

Address: 60 rue Ste-Ursule G1R 4E6 **Location:** Corner of des Ursulines. Located in Old Quebec. **Facility:** Guest rooms have high ceilings; two have balconies. 10 units. 3 stories (no elevator), interior corridors. **Parking:** on-site (fee). **Terms:** off-site registration, check-in 4 pm. **Amenities:** high-speed Internet. **Guest Services:** valet laundry.

[🍴] [📶] [X] [🛏️] [🖥️]

HOTEL LE SAINT-PAUL
Phone: 418/694-4414 **4**

Hotel

Rates not provided

Address: 229 1/2 rue St-Paul G1K 3W3 **Location:** Corner of rue du Marche-du-Vieux Port. **Facility:** 27 units. 3 stories, interior corridors. **Guest Services:** valet laundry.

[🍴] [🥂] [📶] [X] [🖥️] /[SOME UNITS] [🛏️]

▼ *See AAA listing p. 438* ▼

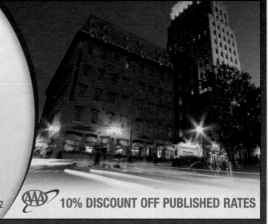

(See map & index p. 425.)

HOTEL MANOIR D'AUTEUIL

Phone: (418)694-1173 **24**

Historic Bed & Breakfast

$149-$289 6/1-10/31
$99-$249 11/1-5/31

Address: 49 rue d'Auteuil G1R 4C2 **Location:** Corner of rue Ste-Anne. Located in Old Quebec. **Facility:** Art Deco-style woodwork is featured in this 1835 inn, which is located near a park and the historic part of the city. 18 units. 4 stories (no elevator), interior corridors. **Parking:** street only. **Terms:** 2 night minimum stay - seasonal. **Amenities:** high-speed Internet. **Guest Services:** valet laundry. **Free Special Amenities:** continental breakfast and high-speed Internet.

`SAVE` `▯▮` `📶` `✕` / SOME UNITS `🔧`

HOTEL MANOIR DE LA TOUR

Phone: (418)525-6276 **36**

Hotel

$89-$169

Address: 385 rue Grande-Allee est G1R 2H8 **Location:** Corner of ave Tache. **Facility:** 13 units. 3 stories (no elevator), interior corridors. **Parking:** on-site (fee), winter plug-ins. **Terms:** 30 day cancellation notice-fee imposed. **Guest Services:** valet laundry. `📶` `✕` `▭` / SOME UNITS `🅆`

Enjoy great savings on hotel rates at AAA.com or CAA.ca

HOTEL MANOIR VICTORIA

Phone: (418)692-1030 **10**

Historic Hotel

$135-$299

Address: 44 Cote du Palais G1R 4H8 **Location:** Corner of rue St-Jean. Located in Old Quebec, across from hospital. **Facility:** This conveniently located hotel offers attractively furnished guest rooms and elegant common areas, including an upscale lobby with rich wood-trimmed walls. 156 units. 6 stories, interior corridors. **Parking:** valet and street only. **Terms:** cancellation fee imposed. **Amenities:** high-speed Internet, honor bars. *Some:* safes. **Dining:** 2 restaurants. **Pool(s):** heated indoor. **Activities:** sauna, exercise room, spa. **Guest Services:** valet laundry. **Free Special Amenities:** high-speed Internet.

(See ad this page.)

`SAVE` `▯▮` `Y` `🍽` `BIZ` `📶` `✕` FEE `🎥` `▭`

HOTEL MARIE-ROLLET

Phone: 418/694-9271 **15**

Historic Boutique Hotel

$95-$165

Address: 81 rue Ste-Anne G1R 3X4 **Location:** Corner of rue Pierre-Olivier-Chauveau. Located in Old Quebec. **Facility:** Vintage pieces and some antiques furnish this intimate 1876 hotel. 11 units. 4 stories (no elevator), interior corridors. **Parking:** street only. **Terms:** 2 night minimum stay - seasonal and/or weekends, 3 day cancellation notice-fee imposed. **Guest Services:** valet laundry. `▯+` `📶` `✕` `☎`

Safety tip: Keep a current AAA/CAA Road Atlas in every vehicle

(See map & index p. 425.)

HOTEL PALACE ROYAL   Phone: (418)694-2000   22

Hotel

$146-$496 6/1-10/15
$130-$400 10/16-5/31

Address: 775 ave Honore-Mercier G1R 6A5 **Location:** Corner of rue St-Jean. **Facility:** 234 units. 10 stories, interior corridors. **Parking:** on-site (fee) and valet. **Terms:** check-in 4 pm, 2 night minimum stay - seasonal and/or weekends, cancellation fee imposed. **Amenities:** high-speed Internet, safes. **Dining:** Le Beffroi Steakhouse, see separate listing. **Pool(s):** heated indoor. **Activities:** sauna, whirlpool, exercise room. *Fee:* massage. **Guest Services:** valet laundry.

ECO 🍴 🍷 🏋 🏊 BIZ 🛜 ✕ FEE🎬 🔌
🖨 💻

HOTEL PUR   Phone: 418/647-2611   20

Hotel

Rates not provided

Address: 395 rue de la Couronne G1K 7X4 **Location:** Corner of rue St-Joseph est. **Facility:** 242 units. 18 stories, interior corridors. **Parking:** valet only. **Amenities:** video games (fee), safes, honor bars. **Pool(s):** heated indoor. **Activities:** sauna, lifeguard on duty, exercise room. **Guest Services:** valet laundry.
(See ad this page.)

SAVE 🍴 🍷 CALL 🔌M 🏊
BIZ 🛜 FEE🎬 🔌 💻
/SOME UNITS 🛏 FEE🖨

HOTEL ROYAL WILLIAM, AN ASCEND COLLECTION HOTEL   Phone: (418)521-4488   28

Hotel

$111-$206

Address: 360 boul Charest est G1K 3H4 **Location:** On Rt 440. **Facility:** 44 units. 5 stories, interior corridors. **Parking:** on-site (fee) and street, winter plug-ins. **Terms:** check-in 4 pm, cancellation fee imposed. **Amenities:** high-speed Internet, safes, honor bars. **Activities:** limited exercise equipment. *Fee:* massage. **Guest Services:** valet laundry.

🍴 BIZ 🛜 ✕ 💻

HOTEL SAINTE-ANNE   Phone: 418/694-1455   13

Hotel

Rates not provided

Address: 32 rue Ste-Anne G1R 3X3 **Location:** Just w of rue du Tresor. Located in Old Quebec. **Facility:** 28 units. 4 stories, interior corridors. **Parking:** street only. **Terms:** office hours 7 am-11 pm. **Amenities:** high-speed Internet, honor bars. **Activities:** *Fee:* massage. **Guest Services:** valet laundry.

🍴 🍷 🛜 ✕ 🔌 💻

LE CHÂTEAU DE PIERRE   Phone: (418)694-0429   26

Historic Hotel

$140-$165 6/1-10/31
$102-$165 11/1-5/31

Address: 17 ave Ste-Genevieve G1R 4A8 **Location:** Between rue Laporte and des Grisons. Located in Old Quebec. **Facility:** This restored Victorian dwelling is near the parc des Gouverneurs in Old Quebec. Reserved parking sites are available off site for an extra charge. 15 units. 3 stories (no elevator), interior corridors. **Parking:** street only. **Terms:** 3 day cancellation notice. **Guest Services:** valet laundry. **Free Special Amenities:** local telephone calls and high-speed Internet.

SAVE 🍴 🛜 ✕ 💻 /SOME UNITS 🐾

LE GRANDE-ALLÉE HÔTEL ET SUITES   Phone: 418/647-4433   33

Historic Hotel

Rates not provided

Address: 601 rue Grande Allee est G1R 2K4 **Location:** Corner of de la Chevrotiere. **Facility:** A bustling district of sidewalk cafes surrounds this Victorian-era stone house. 38 units. 1-3 stories (no elevator), interior corridors. **Parking:** on-site (fee), winter plug-ins. **Guest Services:** valet laundry.

🍴 🍷 BIZ 🛜 ✕ FEE🎬 💻
/SOME UNITS 🔌 🖨

LE PORT-ROYAL HOTEL & SUITES   Phone: (418)692-2777   1

Extended Stay Hotel

$149-$388 6/1-10/15
$119-$228 10/16-5/31

Address: 144 rue St-Pierre G1K 8N8 **Location:** In Old Port district of Old Quebec. **Facility:** 45 units, some two bedrooms, efficiencies and kitchens. 4 stories, interior corridors. **Parking:** valet only. **Guest Services:** valet and coin laundry. **Free Special Amenities:** local telephone calls and high-speed Internet.

SAVE 🍴 🍷 BIZ 🛜 ✕ 🔌 🖨 💻

▼ See AAA listing this page ▼

(See map & index p. 425.)

LE SAINT-PIERRE AUBERGE DISTINCTIVE

Phone: (418)694-7981 **5**

▼▼▼▼
Historic Boutique
Hotel
$199-$325 6/1-10/31
$161-$249 11/1-5/31

Address: 79 rue St-Pierre G1K 4A3 **Location:** Between rue de la Barricade and St-Antoine. Located in Old Port area. **Facility:** Modern amenities and a full breakfast are among the draws at this upscale hotel, set in a restored 1821 building. Some luxury services are offered. 41 units. 4 stories, interior corridors. **Parking:** valet only. **Terms:** cancellation fee imposed. **Activities:** exercise room. *Fee:* massage. **Guest Services:** valet laundry. **Free Special Amenities:** high-speed Internet.

SAVE ﹝﹢﹞ BIZ 🛜 ⊠ 🖵 / SOME UNITS 🔲

L'HOTEL DU CAPITOLE Phone: (418)694-4040 **18**

▼▼▼▼
Hotel
$135-$295

Address: 972 rue St-Jean G1R 1R5 **Location:** Corner of des Glacis. Located in Old Quebec, facing Place d'Youville. **Facility:** 40 units. 4 stories, interior corridors. **Parking:** valet and street only. **Terms:** check-in 4 pm, cancellation fee imposed. **Amenities:** honor bars. **Dining:** Ristorante Il Teatro, see separate listing. **Activities:** *Fee:* massage. **Guest Services:** valet laundry. **Free Special Amenities:** local telephone calls and high-speed Internet.

SAVE ﹝﹢﹞ 🍽 🛜 ⊠ FEE 🔲

Visit AAA.com or CAA.ca for one-stop travel planning and reservations

---

▼ See AAA listing p. 443 ▼

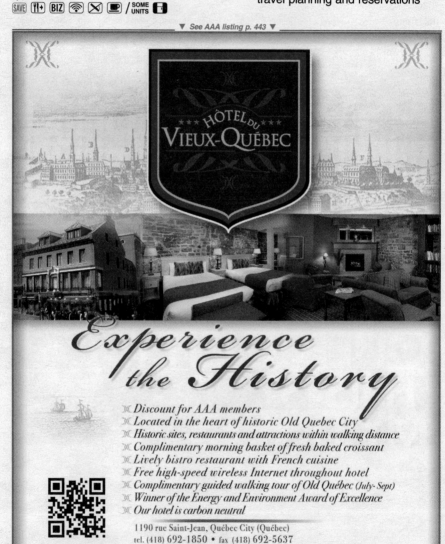

(See map & index p. 425.)

L'HOTEL DU VIEUX QUEBEC

Phone: (418)692-1850 **11**

Historic Boutique Hotel
$148-$328 6/1-10/23
$104-$268 10/24-5/31

Address: 1190 rue St-Jean G1R 1S6 **Location:** Corner of rue de l'Hotel-Dieu. Located in Old Quebec. **Facility:** This historic building houses small to very good-size rooms, including five with a stylish gas fireplace. Its location is ideal for exploring Old Quebec by foot. 45 units. 5 stories, interior corridors. **Parking:** street only. **Terms:** check-in 4 pm, 2-4 night minimum stay - seasonal and/or weekends. **Amenities:** high-speed Internet. *Some:* safes. **Activities:** exercise room. **Guest Services:** valet laundry. **Free Special Amenities:** continental breakfast and high-speed Internet.
(See ad p. 442.)

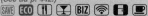

LOEWS HÔTEL LE CONCORDE

Phone: (418)647-2222 **34**

Hotel
$169-$299 6/1-10/31
$129-$239 11/1-5/31

Address: 1225 Cours du General-de-Montcalm G1R 4W6 **Location:** Corner of Grande Allee est. **Facility:** The hotel's spacious, luxurious rooms offer added amenities and commanding views. A revolving restaurant sits atop the building. 406 units, some two bedrooms. 29 stories, interior corridors. **Parking:** on-site (fee) and valet. **Terms:** check-in 4 pm, cancellation fee imposed. **Amenities:** safes, honor bars. *Some:* high-speed Internet (fee). **Dining:** L'Astral, see separate listing. **Pool(s):** heated outdoor. **Activities:** saunas, whirlpool, exercise room. *Fee:* massage. **Guest Services:** valet laundry.
(See ad this page.)

▼ See AAA listing this page ▼

(See map & index p. 425.)

RELAIS & CHATEAUX AUBERGE SAINT-ANTOINE
Phone: (418)692-2211 **7**

Historic Hotel
$169-$1500

Address: 8 rue St-Antoine G1K 4C9 **Location:** Corner of rue Dalhousie. Located in Old Port area. **Facility:** Old Québec artifacts decorate corridors at this restored 19th-century maritime warehouse. A variety of large, upscale guest rooms are available. 95 units, some efficiencies. 5 stories, interior corridors. **Parking:** valet only. **Terms:** check-in 4 pm, 3 day cancellation notice-fee imposed. **Amenities:** video games (fee), high-speed Internet, safes, honor bars. **Dining:** Panache Restaurant, see separate listing. **Activities:** saunas, exercise room, spa. **Guest Services:** valet laundry. **Free Special Amenities:** newspaper and high-speed Internet.

Auberge Saint-Antoine boasts 95 rooms, a unique contemporary and historical atmosphere to enjoy.

ROYAL DALHOUSIE
Phone: 418/575-1414 **9**

Vacation Rental Condominium
$275-$595

Address: 225 Cote de la Montagne G1K 4E6 **Location:** Just n of rue Dalhousie. Located in Old Port area. **Facility:** These spacious riverfront condo-style lofts feature high ceilings, hardwood floors, brick and stone accent walls, large floor-to-ceiling windows, stylish furnishings and impressive artwork. 6 condominiums. 6 stories, interior corridors. **Parking:** on-site (fee). **Terms:** 3 night minimum stay, 21 day cancellation notice-fee imposed. **Guest Services:** complimentary laundry. **Free Special Amenities:** high-speed Internet and use of on-premises laundry facilities.

WHERE TO EAT

APSARA
Phone: 418/694-0232 **41**

Asian
$11-$15

AAA Inspector Notes: In a historic stone building near St. Louis gate in Old Quebec, the eatery has attractive decor with an Asian feel, as do the servers, who dress in ethnic attire. The restaurant delivers authentic preparations of Cambodian, Vietnamese and Thai cuisine. For dessert, try the banana, apple or pineapple deep-fried beignets. **Bar:** full bar. **Address:** 71 rue d'Auteuil G1R 4C3 **Location:** Corner of rue St-Louis; in Old Quebec. **Parking:** street only. **Historic** [L] [D]

AU PETIT COIN BRETON CRÊPERIE RESTAURANT
Phone: 418/694-0758 **23**

Continental
$10-$20

AAA Inspector Notes: Eighty choices of French-style crepes line the menu at the charming family restaurant in Old Quebec. The servers' costumes and vintage decor reflect the style of Old France. The menu lists crepes bretonnes, stuffed crepes, French onion soup, salads and delicious dessert crepes, including crepes Suzette. **Bar:** full bar. **Reservations:** required. **Address:** 1029 rue St-Jean G1R 1R9 **Location:** Corner of rue Ste-Ursule; in Old Quebec. **Parking:** street only. [L] [D]

AVIATIC CLUB
Phone: 418/522-3555 **6**

International
$13-$33

AAA Inspector Notes: International specialties include lightly seared and thinly sliced salmon, served with mashed potatoes and freshly cooked vegetables. The diverse, seasonally updated menu lists an array of Asian dishes, such as sushi, tempura, sautéed spicy shrimp, chicken or beef, wok stir-fry, chicken teriyaki, General Tao chicken, orange beef and beef or salmon tartare. **Bar:** full bar. **Address:** 450 Gare du Palais G1K 3X2 **Location:** Just e of boul Jean-Lesage; in Gare du Palais Train Station. [L] [D]

CAFÉ DE LA PAIX
Phone: 418/692-1430 **24**

French
$13-$42

AAA Inspector Notes: The menu is built around preparations of seafood, veal, lamb, steak and house specialty seasonal game: quail, guinea fowl, duck, caribou and pheasant. Table d'hote specials are presented at lunch and dinner. The uniformed staff provides attentive service. Live music is featured most nights. **Bar:** full bar. **Reservations:** suggested, weekends. **Address:** 44 rue des Jardins G1R 4L7 **Location:** Corner of rue St-Louis; in Old Quebec. **Parking:** valet only. **Historic** [L] [D]

CAFÉ DE PARIS
Phone: 418/694-9626 **37**

French
$11-$32

AAA Inspector Notes: In the heart of Old Quebec, this restaurant is a tourist favorite for casual dining. Closely spaced tables make for a bustling experience. The menu outlines a variety of French and Italian dishes, including pasta. A strolling musician plays in the evening. **Bar:** full bar. **Reservations:** suggested. **Address:** 66 rue St-Louis G1R 3Z3 **Location:** Between rue des Jardins and Ste-Ursule; in Old Quebec. **Parking:** valet only. **Historic**
[L] [D]

CHARBON STEAKHOUSE
Phone: 418/522-0133 **5**

Steak
$14-$42

AAA Inspector Notes: This steakhouse focuses on steak and seafood cooked over charcoal. Among specialties are prime rib of beef, grilled shrimp, baby back ribs, surf-and-turf platters, Atlantic salmon and a variety of steaks, including filet mignon, New York cut, rib and porterhouse T-bone. The casual, comfortable dining room is in a vintage downtown train station. Free indoor parking for up to 2.5 hours is available. **Bar:** full bar. **Reservations:** suggested. **Address:** 450 Gare du Palais G1K 3X2 **Location:** Just e of boul Jean-Lesage; in Gare du Palais Train Station. [L] [D]

COMMENSAL VEGETARIAN RESTAURANT
Phone: 418/647-3733

Vegetarian
$8-$14

AAA Inspector Notes: An upscale self-service buffet features an extensive selection of creative hot and cold items, such as leek pot pie, sweet potato kasha and lasagna, plus a variety of desserts, everything of which is exclusively vegetarian. The pleasant, contemporary surroundings change often as new paintings are displayed. **Address:** 860 rue St-Jean G1R 1R3 **Location:** Between Saint-Augustin and Dufferin-Montmorency autoroute. **Parking:** street only. [L] [D]

CRÊPERIE LE PETIT CHÂTEAU
Phone: 418/694-1616 **27**

French
$9-$23

AAA Inspector Notes: Adjacent to the historic Chateau Frontenac, this casual creperie offers 60 affordable varieties of crepes as well fondues and raclette dishes. The seasonal terrace is a popular dining spot. Live music is featured some evenings. **Bar:** full bar. **Address:** 5 rue St-Louis G1R 3Y8 **Location:** Next to Fairmont Le Château Frontenac; in Old Quebec. **Parking:** street only.
[B] [L] [D]

(See map & index p. 425.)

D'ORSAY RESTAURANT PUB
Phone: 418/694-1582   (12)

International
$11-$38

AAA Inspector Notes: The eatery has a lively upscale bar area and an all-ages dining room in which patrons savor international preparations of steak, pasta, seafood and salads. **Bar:** full bar. **Reservations:** suggested. **Address:** 65 rue de Buade G1R 4A2 **Location:** Corner of rue des Jardins; in Old Quebec. **Parking:** street only.

L D

L'ASTRAL
Phone: 418/647-2222   (46)

French
$15-$41

AAA Inspector Notes: This revolving rooftop restaurant affords spectacular views of Quebec. International influences flavor preparations of such regional specialties as Charlevoix veal, Atlantic salmon and Quebec pork. A Sunday brunch is a splendid treat. **Bar:** full bar. **Reservations:** suggested. **Address:** 1225 Cours du General-de-Montcalm G1R 4W6 **Location:** Corner of Grande Allee est; in Loews Hôtel Le Concorde. **Parking:** on-site and valet. B L D

LE BEFFROI STEAKHOUSE
Phone: 418/380-2638   (35)

Steak
$12-$50

AAA Inspector Notes: This comfortable hotel dining room, just a short walk from the gates of Old Quebec, offers a menu of Alberta AAA steaks and seafood cooked over a maple wood grill. In addition to the grilled specialties, guests may enjoy daily lunch specials, salads, pasta and chicken. The large wine cellar stores an impressive selection of wines by the bottle or by the glass. A children's menu is available. **Bar:** full bar. **Reservations:** suggested. **Address:** 775 ave Honore-Mercier G1R 6A5 **Location:** Corner of rue St-Jean; in Hotel Palace Royal. **Parking:** on-site (fee) and valet. B L D

LE CHAMPLAIN
Menu on AAA.com
Phone: 418/692-3861   (21)

French
$38-$49

AAA Inspector Notes: A dining room staff attired in 17th-century costumes contributes to the Old World ambience of this historic landmark hotel. Menu highlights include foie gras, rack of lamb, salmon and game specialties. Beef Chateaubriand is just one of several dishes flambeed in dramatic fashion tableside. The multi-course tasting menu offers the chef a chance to dazzle guests with delicacies. For dessert, try one of the heavenly souffles. The wine list is superb. A popular Sunday gourmet brunch is served. Semi-formal attire. **Bar:** full bar. **Reservations:** suggested. **Address:** 1 rue des Carrieres G1R 4P5 **Location:** In Old Quebec; in Fairmont Le Château Frontenac. **Parking:** on-site and valet. **Historic** D

LE CHARLES BAILLAIRGÉ RESTO BAR LOUNGE
Phone: 418/692-2480   (17)

French
$7-$39

AAA Inspector Notes: On historic rue Ste-Anne in Old Quebec, the upscale hotel restaurant highlights French-inspired regional cuisine, including preparations of seafood, lamb, steaks and salads. **Bar:** full bar. **Reservations:** suggested. **Address:** 57 rue Ste-Anne G1R 3X4 **Location:** Corner of rue des Jardins; in Hotel Clarendon. **Parking:** valet only. *(See ad p. 439.)* B L D

LE COCHON DINGUE
Phone: 418/692-2013

French
$10-$19

AAA Inspector Notes: The lively Old Quebec bistro faces the ferry boat port and serves classic steak and fries, pasta, sandwiches, salads and mussels. The breakfast menu lists Canadian bacon and eggs, eggs Benedict, maple syrup with pancakes or French toast, a variety of omelets and fresh fruit plates and juices. Fine wines are available by the glass, and the seasonal terrace is in high demand during the summer months. **Bar:** full bar. **Reservations:** suggested. **Address:** 46 boul Champlain G1K 4H7 **Location:** In Old Quebec. **Parking:** street only.
B L D

LE COCHON DINGUE
Phone: 418/523-2013

French
$12-$26

AAA Inspector Notes: The lively bistro prepares more than 20 choices for breakfast, in addition to lunch and dinner menus. On the breakfast menu are Canadian bacon and eggs, eggs Benedict, maple syrup with pancakes or French toast, a variety of omelets and fresh fruit plates and juices. Breakfast is served until 3 pm on weekends. Lunch and dinner specialties include mussels, steak with fries, pasta, salad and sandwiches. **Bar:** full bar. **Reservations:** required. **Address:** 46 boul Rene-Levesque ouest G1R 2A4 **Location:** Just e of rue Cartier. **Parking:** street only.
B L D

LE GRAFFITI RESTO CITE   **Phone:** 418/529-4949   (48)

French
$12-$35

AAA Inspector Notes: In a charming and fashionable shopping district, this bistro-style restaurant offers market cuisine that proudly features Quebec lamb, duck and quail. Items such as pasta, tartare and venison reveal French and Italian influences. **Bar:** full bar. **Reservations:** suggested. **Address:** 1191 ave Cartier G1R 2S9 **Location:** Just n of Grande-Allee. **Parking:** on-site (fee).
L D

LE LAPIN SAUTE
Phone: 418/692-5325   (20)

French
$10-$31

AAA Inspector Notes: This lively cafe prepares a mix of French bistro cuisine and American fare. Menu items include croque monsieur, grilled salmon sandwiches, pasta, hamburgers, shoestring fries, rabbit cannelloni, rabbit liver and kidneys and steak. **Bar:** full bar. **Reservations:** suggested. **Address:** 52 rue du Petit Champlain G1K 4H4 **Location:** In Old Quebec. **Parking:** no self-parking. B L D

L'ENTRECÔTE SAINT-JEAN
Phone: 418/694-0234   (19)

French
$12-$27

AAA Inspector Notes: The casual bistro specializes in a table d'hote menu of rib steak served with flavorful Dijon mustard sauce, matchstick fries, soup, a walnut-garnished salad and delicious chocolate-drizzled profiteroles for dessert. The menu also includes croque monsieur, lamb, veal, chicken and fish. **Bar:** full bar. **Address:** 1080 rue St-Jean G1R 1R8 **Location:** Corner of rue d'Auteuil. **Parking:** street only. L D

LE POSTINO BISTRO-BAR   **Phone:** 418/647-0000   (40)

French
$13-$28

AAA Inspector Notes: In a historic graystone that once housed a post office, this chic bistro features a Mediterranean menu that includes a choice of pasta, Angus beef, braised lamb, salmon steaks, veal cutlets, tartars, chicken Parmigiana and duck confit salad. **Bar:** full bar. **Reservations:** required. **Address:** 296 rue St-Joseph est G1K 3A9 **Location:** Corner of rue Dorchester. **Parking:** street only. B L D

(See map & index p. 425.)

LE VEAU D'OR Phone: 418/525-7371 **42**

Northern Italian
$11-$20

AAA Inspector Notes: Overlooking a lively street just outside the walls of Old Quebec, the casual Italian restaurant prepares fresh veal as its specialty in variations to suit every taste: veal Marsala, Parmesan, Milanese, normande, cordon bleu, butter-lemon or a l'anglaise, in addition to veal brains and liver. A wide selection of pasta, fresh fish and seafood rounds out the menu of affordable items. **Bar:** full bar. **Address:** 801 rue St-Jean G1R 1R2 **Location:** Corner of Saint-Augustin. **Parking:** street only.

MATTO 71 Phone: 418/266-9444 **7**

Italian
$13-$28

AAA Inspector Notes: This stylish and casual dining room, located in a luxury boutique hotel, pleases patrons with carefully prepared Italian comfort food, including a variety of pizza and pasta dishes, along with Italian salads, lamb, veal, salmon and steak. Popular dishes include the wild mushroom pizza, osso buco and the oven-baked lasagna. Black and white framed photographs add a touch of nostalgia to the dining area, which also features an attractive bar back-lit in red. **Bar:** full bar. **Address:** 71 rue St-Pierre G1K 4A4 **Location:** Just e of Cote de la Montagne; in Hotel 71. **Parking:** valet only.

MOSS BISTRO BELGE Phone: 418/692-0233 **3**

Belgian
$15-$36

AAA Inspector Notes: The stylish bistro specializes in mussels prepared 14 ways and offers Belgian chocolate desserts and 40 varieties of imported and local beers. **Bar:** full bar. **Address:** 253 rue St-Paul G1K 3W5 **Location:** Corner rue St-Andre; facing Marche du Vieux-Port; in Hotel des Coutellier. **Parking:** street only.

PANACHE RESTAURANT Phone: 418/692-1022 **8**

Quebec
$15-$48

AAA Inspector Notes: In a historic stone-walled hotel in Old Quebec's Old Port area, this stylish dining room brings in diners for its fine Quebecois cuisine, which is prepared with panache. Main courses may be complemented by side dishes ordered separately. Exciting and skillfully prepared dishes include Mauricie region sweetbreads, Magdalen Islands lobster and scallops, Atlantic halibut, free-range chicken, Alberta beef, pan-seared foie gras, duckling and clams. **Bar:** full bar. **Reservations:** suggested. **Address:** 8 rue St-Antoine G1K 4C9 **Location:** Corner of rue Dalhousie; in Relais & Chateaux Auberge Saint-Antoine. **Parking:** valet only.

PIAZZETTA Phone: 418/529-7489

Italian
$10-$23

AAA Inspector Notes: This contemporary eatery offers a variety of reasonably priced Italian dishes including pizza, focaccia, sauteed pasta, veal cutlets, Italian pizza rolls and salads. Ask about the daily specials. **Bar:** full bar. **Reservations:** required. **Address:** 707 rue St-Jean G1R 1R1 **Location:** Just w of ave Honore-Mercier. **Parking:** street only.

PIZZERIA D'YOUVILLE Phone: 418/694-0299 **25**

Italian
$9-$18

AAA Inspector Notes: This cozy and lively family eatery serves Italian specialties, including pizza, pasta, meats and seafood. The decor incorporates the original stone and brick of this historic Old Quebec building. **Bar:** full bar. **Address:** 1014 rue St-Jean G1R 1R6 **Location:** Corner rue d'Auteuil; in Old Quebec. **Parking:** street only.

PIZZERIA PRIMAVERA BISTRO ITALIANO Phone: 418/694-0030 **39**

Italian
$10-$25

AAA Inspector Notes: Rich wood-beamed ceilings, a vintage stone wall, a brick wood-burning pizza oven and contemporary colors mark this bistro, which resides in the heart of Old Quebec. The light Italian menu lists a good selection of wood-oven pizza, in addition to meat, pasta and salads. Smartly attired staff members provide courteous and attentive service. The restaurant is closed in winter except for the weekends during the Quebec Winter Carnival. **Bar:** full bar. **Reservations:** suggested. **Address:** 73 rue St-Louis G1R 3Z2 **Location:** Corner rue Ste-Ursule; in Old Quebec. **Parking:** street only. **Historic**

PORTOFINO BISTRO ITALIANO Phone: 418/692-8888 **10**

Italian
$11-$30

AAA Inspector Notes: A lively feel punctuates the contemporary Italian bistro in Old Quebec. Menu highlights include pizza baked in a wood-burning oven, as well as homemade pasta, veal and fish dishes. Nightly live music lends to the atmosphere. Valet parking is available. **Bar:** full bar. **Reservations:** suggested. **Address:** 54 rue Couillard G1R 3T3 **Location:** In Place Livernois, at angle of rue St-Jean; in Old Quebec. **Parking:** on-site (fee) and valet.

PUB ST-PATRICK Phone: 418/694-0618 **11**

Canadian
$11-$23

AAA Inspector Notes: Ambience abounds as local and imported beer flows within the historic stone walls of the boisterous Old Quebec Irish pub and bistro. Live music is heard on some nights. Such standard pub foods as fish and chips, sandwiches, pasta and steak line the menu. The pub's vaulted ceilings date to 1749, and the wine cellar boasts 300 selections. Private rooms are available. **Bar:** full bar. **Address:** 1200 rue St-Jean G1R 1S8 **Location:** Corner of rue Cote de la Fabrique; in Old Quebec. **Parking:** street only.

RESTAURANT 1640 Phone: 418/694-1876 **14**

French
$10-$35

AAA Inspector Notes: On the ground floor of an historic 17th-century building, the restaurant combines the formality of a fine dining room, a more casual bistro and a seasonal terrace. Guests seeking upscale dining enjoy polished, friendly service. Valet parking is available most summer evenings. **Bar:** full bar. **Reservations:** suggested. **Address:** 20 rue Ste-Anne G1R 3X2 **Location:** Corner of rue du Tresor; in Auberge du Tresor. **Parking:** street only. **Historic**

RESTAURANT ANH LE Phone: 418/529-8881 **28**

Vietnamese
$10-$20

AAA Inspector Notes: In the St-Roch neighborhood, the casual diner serves affordably priced Vietnamese and Thai dishes, including Asian-style fondues, seafood, caribou, chicken, beef, noodles, fish, shrimp and beef Tonkinese soups. Diners may bring their own wine. No alcohol is sold on the premises. **Address:** 325 rue de la Couronne G1K 6E7 **Location:** Corner of rue de Lasalle. **Parking:** street only.

RESTAURANT AU PARMESAN Phone: 418/692-0341 **30**

Italian
$10-$30

AAA Inspector Notes: A favorite of locals, the established, bistro-style restaurant bustles with activity. A blend of French and Italian dishes, such as fettuccine Alfredo, characterize a varied menu that includes selections of steak and seafood. Service is friendly and attentive from start to finish. Nightly live music lends to the atmosphere. **Bar:** full bar. **Reservations:** suggested. **Address:** 38 rue St-Louis G1R 3Z1 **Location:** Between rue des Jardins and du Parloir; in Old Quebec. **Parking:** valet only.

(See map & index p. 425.)

YUZU RESTO + CLUB
Menu on AAA.com   Phone: 418/521-7253   [31]

▽▼▽▼▽
Japanese
$12-$42

AAA Inspector Notes: A youthful ambience permeates this chic sushi bar decorated with bonsai plants, contemporary seats and a glassed wine cellar. The menu features a variety of freshly prepared sushi and sashimi garnished with fresh ginger, wasabi and soy sauce. Dishes of chicken, shrimp and grilled salmon round out the menu, along with creatively garnished desserts. The seasonal terrace is ideal for people-watching in summer. **Bar:** full bar. **Address:** 438 rue du Parvis G1K 6H8 **Location:** Corner of boul Charest est. **Parking:** street only.

[L] [D]

QUÉBEC
- Restaurants p. 451
- Hotels & Restaurants map & index p. 429

ALT HOTEL-QUEBEC
Phone: 418/658-1224   [3]

▽▼▽▼▽
Hotel
Rates not provided

Address: 1200 ave Germain-des-Pres G1V 3M7 **Location:** Just n of boul Laurier; facing Place Laurier mall. **Facility:** 126 units. 9 stories, interior corridors. **Parking:** on-site and valet.
Amenities: honor bars. *Some:* high-speed Internet. **Dining:** Bistango, see separate listing. **Activities:** *Fee:* massage. **Guest Services:** valet laundry.

[YI] FEE[🛗] [🛜] [✕] FEE[🎿] / SOME UNITS FEE[🐾]

AMBASSADEUR HOTEL & SUITES
Phone: (418)666-2828   [23]

▽▼▽▼▽
Hotel
$90-$240

Address: 3401 boul Ste-Anne G1E 3L4 **Location:** Hwy 440 exit Francois-de-Laval, just e. **Facility:** 145 units. 4 stories, interior corridors. **Terms:** seasonal, check-in 4 pm. **Amenities:** *Some:* high-speed Internet. **Pool(s):** heated indoor. **Activities:** saunas, whirlpool, exercise room. **Guest Services:** valet laundry. **Free Special Amenities:** room upgrade (subject to availability with advance reservations) and high-speed Internet.

[SAVE] [YI] [Y] [🛜] [✕] [💻]
/ SOME UNITS FEE[🛗] FEE[🖥]

CHÂTEAU BONNE ENTENTE
Phone: (418)653-5221   [17]

▽▼▽▼▽
Hotel
$159-$499

Address: 3400 chemin Ste-Foy G1X 1S6 **Location:** Hwy 540 (Autoroute Duplessis) exit chemin Ste-Foy, just w. **Facility:** Common areas at this hotel include a lively lounge, elegant restaurant and luxury spa. Guest rooms are luxuriously appointed. 161 units. 3 stories, interior corridors. **Parking:** on-site (fee) and valet, winter plug-ins. **Terms:** check-in 4 pm, cancellation fee imposed. **Amenities:** safes, honor bars. *Some:* high-speed Internet. **Dining:** 2 restaurants, also, Monte Cristo L'Original, see separate listing. **Pool(s):** heated outdoor. **Activities:** sauna, whirlpools, jogging, exercise room, spa. **Guest Services:** valet laundry, area transportation-Old Quebec, golf course La Tempete. **Free Special Amenities:** full breakfast.
(See ad p. 433.)

[SAVE] [✈] [YI] [Y] [🎬] CALL[🔊] [🏊] [BIZ] [🛜]
[✕] FEE[🎿] [💻] / SOME UNITS FEE[🐾]

COMFORT INN BEAUPORT
Phone: (418)666-1226   [24]

▽▼▽▼▽
Hotel
$86-$145

Address: 3390 boul Ste-Anne G1E 3L7 **Location:** Hwy 440 exit Francois-de-Laval. **Facility:** 79 units. 2 stories, interior corridors. **Parking:** winter plug-ins. **Terms:** cancellation fee imposed. **Guest Services:** valet laundry.

[ECO] [YI] [🛜] [💻] / SOME UNITS FEE[🛗] FEE[🖥] FEE[🖥]

COMFORT INN DE L'AEROPORT-HAMEL
Phone: (418)872-5038   [16]

▽▼▽▼▽
Hotel
$86-$220

Address: 7320 boul Wilfrid-Hamel G2G 1C1 **Location:** Hwy 138, 0.9 mi (1.5 km) w of boul Duplessis. **Facility:** 79 units. 2 stories (no elevator), interior corridors. **Parking:** winter plug-ins. **Terms:** cancellation fee imposed. **Guest Services:** valet laundry.

[SAVE] [ECO] [YI] [BIZ] [🛜] [💻] / SOME UNITS FEE[🛗] [🖥]

FOUR POINTS BY SHERATON QUEBEC RESORT
Phone: (418)627-8008   [27]

▽▼▽▼▽
Hotel
$100-$210

FOUR ⇃ POINTS
BY SHERATON

AAA Benefit: Members get up to 15% off, plus Starwood Preferred Guest® bonuses.

Address: 7900 rue du Marigot G1G 6T8 **Location:** Hwy 73 exit 154, just e. **Facility:** 102 units. 4 stories, interior corridors. **Dining:** Restaurant Le Dijon, see separate listing. **Activities:** whirlpool, snowmobiling, exercise room, spa. *Fee:* golf-18 holes. **Guest Services:** valet laundry. **Free Special Amenities:** local telephone calls and newspaper.

[SAVE] [YI] CALL[🔊] [BIZ] [🛜] [✕] FEE[🎿] [💻]
/ SOME UNITS [🛗] [🖥]

GITE DU VIEUX-BOURG
Phone: 418/661-0116   [22]

▽▼▽▼▽
Bed & Breakfast
Rates not provided

Address: 492 ave Royale G1E 1Y1 **Location:** Hwy 440 exit Francois-de-Laval, just n, then 0.3 mi (0.5 km) e. **Facility:** 4 units. 2 stories (no elevator), interior corridors. *Bath:* some shared. **Terms:** check-in 4 pm. **Pool(s):** outdoor.

[YI] [🏊] [🛜] [✕] [W] / SOME UNITS [🅿] [✉] [💻]

(See map & index p. 429.)

HOLIDAY INN EXPRESS QUEBEC
Phone: (418)653-9321 **9**

Hotel
$119-$229 6/1-10/11
$119-$179 10/12-5/31

Address: 3145 ave des Hotels G1W 3Z7 **Location:** Jct Hwy 73 exit 133 (chemin St-Louis). **Facility:** 88 units. 4 stories, interior corridors. **Activities:** whirlpool, exercise room. **Guest Services:** valet laundry, area transportation-Old Quebec. **Free Special Amenities: full breakfast and high-speed Internet.**
(See ad p. 428.)

SAVE ECO (†|♦) BIZ 🛰 ⊠
FEE 🎥 📞 💻

HOTEL & SUITES NORMANDIN
Phone: (418)622-1611 **12**

Hotel
$120-$249 6/1-9/4
$116-$249 9/5-5/31

Address: 4700 boul Pierre-Bertrand G2J 1A4 **Location:** Hwy 40 exit 312N eastbound to boul Pierre-Bertrand, then n to rue Bouvier; exit 312N westbound, just w on rue Bouvier. **Facility:** 136 units. 4 stories, interior corridors. **Parking:** winter plug-ins. **Amenities:** high-speed Internet. **Dining:** Restaurant Normandin, see separate listing. **Activities:** exercise room. **Guest Services:** valet and coin laundry, area transportation-Old Quebec.

(†|♦) BIZ 🛰 ⊠ 📞 💻 / SOME UNITS 🛏

HOTEL CLARION QUEBEC
Phone: (418)653-4901 **8**

Hotel
$99-$229

Address: 3125 boul Hochelaga G1V 4A8 **Location:** Hwy 73 exit 136 (Hochelaga ouest). **Facility:** 231 units. 12 stories, interior corridors. **Parking:** winter plug-ins. **Pool(s):** heated indoor. **Activities:** sauna, exercise room, spa. **Guest Services:** valet and coin laundry. **Free Special Amenities: high-speed Internet.**
(See ad opposite title page.)

SAVE (†|♦) ⊤ 🛰 BIZ 🛰
FEE 📞 💻
/ SOME UNITS 🛏 📞 💻

HOTEL CLASSIQUE
Phone: (418)658-2793 **5**

Hotel
$109-$289

Address: 2815 boul Laurier G1V 4H3 **Location:** Corner of ave de Germain-des-Pres. **Facility:** 263 units, some two bedrooms and kitchens. 13 stories, interior corridors. **Terms:** check-in 4 pm, 2 night minimum stay - seasonal and/or weekends, 10 day cancellation notice. **Amenities:** high-speed Internet. **Dining:** Cosmos, Restaurant La Pointe des Ameriques, see separate listings. **Pool(s):** heated indoor. **Activities:** exercise room. **Guest Services:** valet and coin laundry. **Free Special Amenities: local telephone calls and high-speed Internet.**
(See ad p. 438.)

SAVE (†|♦) 🛰 BIZ 🛰 📞 💻 / SOME UNITS 🛏

HOTEL DAUPHIN QUEBEC CITY
Phone: (418)688-3888 **13**

Hotel
$85-$152

Address: 400 rue du Marais G1M 3R1 **Location:** Hwy 40 exit 312S (Pierre-Bertrand sud), just w of Rt 358. **Facility:** 83 units. 3 stories, interior corridors. **Parking:** winter plug-ins. **Amenities:** high-speed Internet, safes. **Activities:** exercise room. **Guest Services:** valet and coin laundry.

ECO (†|♦) CALL 🔊 BIZ 🛰 ⊠ FEE 🎥 📞 💻
/ SOME UNITS FEE 🛏 📞

HOTEL LINDBERGH
Phone: (418)653-4975 **4**

Hotel
$90-$225

Address: 2825 boul Laurier G1V 2L9 **Location:** Between rue d'Eglise and Germain Despres. **Facility:** 124 units. 4 stories, interior corridors. **Terms:** check-in 4 pm, 10 day cancellation notice-fee imposed. **Amenities:** high-speed Internet. **Pool(s):** heated outdoor. **Activities:** exercise room. **Guest Services:** valet and coin laundry.

(†|♦) 🛰 BIZ 🛰 ⊠ FEE 🎥 📞 💻

HOTEL PLAZA QUEBEC
Phone: (418)658-2727 **6**

Hotel
$109-$209

Address: 3031 boul Laurier G1V 2M2 **Location:** Hwy 73 nord exit boul Laurier, just e. **Facility:** 233 units. 7 stories, interior corridors. **Parking:** winter plug-ins. **Terms:** check-in 4 pm, cancellation fee imposed. **Amenities:** high-speed Internet, safes. **Pool(s):** heated indoor. **Activities:** sauna, whirlpool, exercise room. **Guest Services:** valet and coin laundry.

(†|♦) ⊤ 🛰 BIZ 🛰 ⊠ 📞 💻

HOTEL QUALITY SUITES QUEBEC
Phone: (418)622-4244 **14**

Hotel
$115-$195

Address: 1600 rue Bouvier G2K 1N8 **Location:** Hwy 40 exit 312N (Pierre-Bertrand nord), 1.3 mi (2 km) w of jct Rt 358. **Facility:** 119 units. 3 stories, interior corridors. **Parking:** winter plug-ins. **Terms:** cancellation fee imposed. **Guest Services:** valet and coin laundry.

SAVE ECO (†|♦) 🏃 FEE 🛏 BIZ 🛰 FEE 🎥 💻
/ SOME UNITS FEE 🛏 📞 💻

HOTEL QUEBEC INN
Phone: 418/872-9831 **2**

Hotel
$114-$300

Address: 7175 Wilfred-Hamel ouest G2G 1B6 **Location:** 0.6 mi (1 km) w of Hwy 540 (Autoroute Duplessis). **Facility:** 135 units. 2 stories (no elevator), interior/exterior corridors. **Terms:** check-in 4 pm, cancellation fee imposed. **Amenities:** high-speed Internet. **Dining:** nightclub. **Pool(s):** heated indoor. **Activities:** sauna, whirlpools, snowmobiling, exercise room, spa. **Guest Services:** valet and coin laundry.

(†|♦) ⊤ 🛰 BIZ 🛰 ⊠ FEE 🎥 💻
/ SOME UNITS 📞 💻

HÔTEL SÉPIA
Phone: (418)653-4941 **19**

Hotel
$119-$229 6/1-10/15
$99-$159 10/16-5/31

Address: 3135 chemin St-Louis G1W 1R9 **Location:** Hwy 73 exit 133 (chemin St-Louis). **Facility:** 81 units. 2 stories (no elevator), interior corridors. **Parking:** winter plug-ins. **Dining:** Restaurant Le Galopin, see separate listing. **Pool(s):** heated outdoor. **Activities:** exercise room. **Guest Services:** valet laundry.

SAVE ECO (†|♦) 🛰 BIZ 🛰 ⊠ FEE 🎥 📞 💻

HOTEL SUPER 8 QUEBEC STE-FOY
Phone: (418)877-6888 **15**

Hotel
$72-$159

Address: 7286 boul Wilfred Hamel G2G 1C1 **Location:** Hwy 138, 0.7 mi (1.1 km) w of boul Duplessis. **Facility:** 79 units. 4 stories, interior corridors. **Parking:** winter plug-ins. **Amenities:** high-speed Internet. *Some:* video games. **Pool(s):** heated indoor. **Activities:** whirlpool, waterslide, limited exercise equipment. **Guest Services:** valet and coin laundry.

ECO (†|♦) 🛰 BIZ 🛰 FEE 🎥 📞 💻
/ SOME UNITS FEE 🛏

(See map & index p. 429.)

HOTEL UNIVERSEL
Phone: 418/653-5250

Hotel

$119-$229 6/1-8/31
$99-$189 9/1-5/31

Address: 2300 chemin Ste-Foy G1V 1S5 **Location:** Hwy 73 exit 137, 1.4 mi (2.3 km) e on chemin des Quatre-Bourgeois. Across from university. **Facility:** 158 units, some kitchens. 4 stories, interior/exterior corridors. **Parking:** winter plug-ins. **Terms:** check-in 4 pm, cancellation fee imposed. **Pool(s):** heated indoor. **Activities:** saunas, whirlpools, exercise room. *Fee:* massage. **Guest Services:** valet laundry. **Free Special Amenities:** local telephone calls and room upgrade (subject to availability with advance reservations).

 / SOME UNITS

SIR WILFRID
Phone: 418/651-2440

Hotel

$99-$250

Address: 3055 boul Laurier G1V 4X2 **Location:** Hwy 73 nord exit boul Laurier, just e. **Facility:** 106 units, some two bedrooms and efficiencies. 3 stories, interior/exterior corridors. **Terms:** check-in 4 pm, 10 day cancellation notice. **Amenities:** *Some:* high-speed Internet. **Pool(s):** heated outdoor. **Guest Services:** valet and coin laundry.

 / SOME UNITS

WHERE TO EAT

AU PETIT COIN BRETON
Phone: 418/653-6051 (12)

Continental
$10-$20

AAA Inspector Notes: While this eatery is located in a suburban commercial building, the servers' costumes and the restaurant's decor evoke the style of Old France. Glass cases display European decorative dolls and model ships. Eighty varieties of French-style crepes are offered, including crepes bretonnes. Some are prepared tableside. The menu also features salads, French onion soup, omelets, pizza crepes, filet of sole, pasta and tasty dessert crepes. **Bar:** full bar. **Reservations:** suggested. **Address:** 2600 boul Laurier G1V 4T3 **Location:** Corner of rue de Quen, just n of boul Laurier. L D

BISTANGO
Phone: 418/658-8780 (2)

French
$12-$37

AAA Inspector Notes: A lively bistro atmosphere infuses this casual, stylish eatery. Representative of menu selections are salmon tartare, cannelloni and lamb shank with couscous and tomato sauce. Dessert choices are appealing in appearance. Service is gracious. The excellent wine list includes many selections by the glass or bottle. **Bar:** full bar. **Reservations:** suggested. **Address:** 1200 ave Germain-des-Pres G1V 3M7 **Location:** Just n of boul Laurier; facing Place Laurier mall; in ALT Hotel-Quebec. **Parking:** on-site and street. B L D

CAFÉ PATES A TOUT
Phone: 418/651-8284 (1)

Italian
$7-$10

AAA Inspector Notes: There's nothing pretentious about this place, a fast food counter in a small, indoor food market. Fresh pasta and sauces go into such dishes as linguine, fettuccine Alfredo and lasagna. The breakfast menu includes bacon, eggs, pancakes and French toast. **Address:** 2500 chemin des Quatre-Bourgeois G1V 4P9 **Location:** Jct Autoroute du Robert-Bourassa; in Les Halles de Ste-Foy. L D

CHEZ CORA

For additional information, visit AAA.com

Canadian
$8-$13

AAA Inspector Notes: Eggs, omelets, waffles, crepes (sorry, no American-style pancakes here), French toast, fruit platters and all the breakfast meats--that's the specialty here, all day. However, at lunchtime the menu lists a selection of soups, salads, quiches, sandwiches and a dish called the grilled panini crepe. B L

LOCATIONS:
Address: 1020 Rt de l'Eglise G1V 3V9 **Location:** 0.3 mi (0.5 km) n of boul Laurier. **Phone:** 418/650-5205

Address: 710 rue Bouvier G2J 1C2 **Location:** Hwy 40 exit 312 (Pierre-Bertrand nord), just e. **Phone:** 418/626-7955

Address: 3437 boul Ste-Anne G1E 3L4 **Location:** Hwy 440 exit Francois-de-Laval, just e. **Phone:** 418/663-6767

COSMOS
Phone: 418/652-2001 (13)

Continental
$10-$25

AAA Inspector Notes: This stylish hotel restaurant and bar features wholesome foods including twelve choices of pasta, French onion soup, poutine, burgers, smoked salmon, cheese platters, pizza, gourmet hot dogs, salads, grilled chicken, veal parmigiana and filet mignon. A large breakfast menu also is available. After dark, the fiber-optic lighting system continuously changes the room's color scheme. **Bar:** full bar. **Address:** 2815 boul Laurier G1V 4H3 **Location:** Corner of ave de Germain-des-Pres; in Hotel Classique. B L D LATE

JARDIN DE TANG
Phone: 418/877-8737 (15)

Chinese
$9-$20

AAA Inspector Notes: The family-friendly buffet displays a large selection of Canadian-style Chinese dishes, including won ton soup, noodles, egg rolls, seafood, chow mein, fried rice and frogs' legs. The a la carte menu lists additional Chinese dishes, such as Cantonese lobster, General Tao chicken and a sizzling seafood platter. Take-out and delivery service are available. **Bar:** full bar. **Address:** 7272 boul Wilfrid-Hamel G2C 1C1 **Location:** 0.5 mi (0.8 km) w of boul Duplessis (Rt 540). L D

LE BIF STEAKHOUSE & BAR
Phone: 418/871-1717 (11)

Steak
$9-$33

AAA Inspector Notes: The restaurant satisfies the cravings of folks in the mood for a sizzling steak. Huge portions of traditional steakhouse fare--including fine steaks, prime rib and seafood selections--keep locals coming back. Among starters are shrimp cocktail, French onion soup and escargots. Meals come with a tasty house salad and the ever-popular biftheque croutons. Diners should arrive with a hearty appetite. **Bar:** full bar. **Address:** 5050 boul Wilfrid-Hamel G2E 5X5 **Location:** Hwy 73 exit boul Wilfrid-Hamel. L D

LE COCHON DINGUE
Phone: 418/684-2013

French
$10-$25

AAA Inspector Notes: The menu at this lively eatery centers on French bistro cuisine and includes an impressive selection of wines by the glass as well as by the bottle. Steak and fries, mussels, croque monsieur sandwiches, panini, pasta and house-smoked maple ribs are among the specialties. A sunny seasonal terrace is a popular place for people-watching. **Bar:** full bar. **Address:** 1326 ave Maguire G1T 1Z3 **Location:** Between chemin St-Louis and boul Laurier. **Parking:** street only. B L D

LE MANOIR DU SPAGHETTI
Phone: 418/627-0161 (24)

Italian
$9-$19

AAA Inspector Notes: The comfortable family restaurant prepares varieties of spaghetti and other pastas. **Bar:** full bar. **Address:** 7685 1er Ave G1H 2Y1 **Location:** Corner of 76ieme rue; centre. L D

(See map & index p. 429.)

LE MANOIR DU SPAGHETTI

Phone: 418/659-5628 (17)

Italian
$9-$19

AAA Inspector Notes: This family restaurant, located in a vintage suburban cottage, specializes in multiple varieties of spaghetti and other Italian dishes. **Bar:** full bar. **Address:** 3077 chemin St-Louis G1W 1R6 **Location:** Just e of Pont Pierre-Laporte. [L] [D]

LE PARIS GRILL

Phone: 418/658-4415 (3)

French
$12-$25

AAA Inspector Notes: This French-style brasserie pub in suburban Quebec features a mix of pub foods and bistro favorites. The house specialty is Alsacian pie (a thin-crust pizza topped with fresh cream, small lardons, sweet onions and cheese). Also choose from Angus beef with fries, Toulouse sausage, chicken or lamb kebabs, calf's liver, pork chops, filet mignon tartare, sauteed tartare steak, fish casserole, croque monsieur, salmon cooked on a cedar plank, grilled tuna, mussels, duck confit rolls and poutine. **Bar:** full bar. **Address:** 3121 boul Laurier G1V 2M1 **Location:** Corner of Route-de-l'Eglise. [B] [L] [D]

LE PREBEN

Phone: 418/627-7766 (9)

Canadian
$13-$34

AAA Inspector Notes: This casual and lively eatery, located in a commercial complex, offers affordable selections that include AAA Alberta beef, grilled seafood, pasta, chicken, ribs and salads. In the evenings, guests can order Chateaubriand for two. The daily lunch menu offers very good value. **Bar:** full bar. **Reservations:** required. **Address:** 670 rue Bouvier, Suite 104 G2J 1A7 **Location:** Hwy 40 exit 312 N, just e of boul Pierre-Bertrand. [L] [D]

MONTE CRISTO L'ORIGINAL

Menu on AAA.com

Phone: 418/650-4550 (16)

Mediterranean
$39-$48

AAA Inspector Notes: Modern Mediterranean cuisine is served in an elegant, contemporary dining room and lounge. The menu lists preparations of lobster, salmon, rack of lamb, calf sweetbread, cod, duck, red tuna and pan-seared foie gras. The appetizer trio serves up a main preparation enhanced by three taste pairings. The smartly attired servers provide refined and friendly service. A lighter menu is served at lunch in the nearby lounge. Wood, marble and brass decorate the elegant, contemporary dining room and lounge. **Bar:** full bar. **Reservations:** suggested. **Address:** 3400 chemin Ste-Foy G1X 1S6 **Location:** Hwy 540 (Autoroute Duplessis) exit chemin Ste-Foy, just w; in Château Bonne Entente. [D]

PAPARAZZI

Phone: 418/683-8111 (6)

Italian
$14-$29

AAA Inspector Notes: This informal suburban restaurant entices guests with Italian dishes and a sushi bar. Representative of menu offerings are preparations of pasta, meat, shrimp and tuna, as well as salmon tartare, foie gras and veal ravioli. **Bar:** full bar. **Address:** 1363 ave Maguire G1T 1Z2 **Location:** Between chemin St-Louis and boul Laurier. **Parking:** street only. [L] [D]

PIAZZETTA

Phone: 418/650-6655

Italian
$10-$23

AAA Inspector Notes: This contemporary eatery offers a variety of reasonably priced Italian dishes including pizza, focaccia, sauteed pasta, veal cutlets, Italian pizza rolls and salads. Ask about the daily specials. **Bar:** full bar. **Reservations:** required. **Address:** 3100 rue de la Forest G1W 1L8 **Location:** Corner of chemin St-Louis. [L] [D]

RESTAURANT DU MUSÉE

Phone: 418/644-6780 (10)

Quebec
$10-$20

AAA Inspector Notes: The atmosphere is bright and contemporary in the simply decorated casual dining outlet within the Quebec Museum. The menu lists dishes with French and Quebecois influences, such as sweetbread in fruit sauce, mushrooms in puff pastry and Quebec roast pork. Lighter lunch fare includes grilled sandwiches and salads. For dessert, try créme brûlée with a specialty coffee. **Bar:** full bar. **Reservations:** suggested. **Address:** 1 rue Wolfe-Montcalm G1R 5H3 **Location:** Just s of Grande Allee rue Wolfe-Montcalm. **Parking:** on-site (fee). [L] [D]

RESTAURANT LA FENOUILLIÈRE

Phone: 418/653-3886 (18)

French
$16-$38

AAA Inspector Notes: A typical dinner at the upscale restaurant might include a choice of Atlantic salmon, red tuna, scallops, snow crab or pork filets. The overall dining experience is lively yet refined. **Bar:** full bar. **Reservations:** suggested. **Address:** 3100 chemin St-Louis G1W 1R8 **Location:** Hwy 73 exit 133 (chemin St-Louis); in Best Western Plus Hotel L'Aristocrate. *(See ad p. 424.)* [B] [L] [D]

RESTAURANT LA POINTE DES AMERIQUES

Phone: 418/658-2583 (14)

Italian
$10-$25

AAA Inspector Notes: Pizza, pasta, salads, filet mignon, fajitas and panini are among the varied menu items offered at this popular suburban restaurant and bar. **Bar:** full bar. **Reservations:** required. **Address:** 2815 boul Laurier G1V 4H3 **Location:** Corner of ave de Germain-des-Pres; in Hotel Classique. [L] [D]

RESTAURANT LA TANIÈRE

Phone: 418/872-4386

French
$69-$150

AAA Inspector Notes: In an elegant rural home overlooking a field of resident deer, this restaurant offers an experience centered around chef Laplante's impressive eight-, 14- or 20-course tasting menus, which showcase small portions of superb fresh game meats paired with artfully presented organic garnishes and sauces. Cutting-edge culinary techniques and flavorful specialties of wild game--including bison, elk, red deer, caribou, wild boar, ostrich, guinea hen and partridge--are what set the intimate spot apart. **Bar:** full bar. **Reservations:** suggested. **Address:** 2115 rang Ste-Ange G2E 3L9 **Location:** Jct Hwy 540, 2 mi (3.4 km) w on boul Wilfrid-Hamel, then 2.5 mi (4.1 km) n. [D]

RESTAURANT LE DIJON

Phone: 418/627-8008 (23)

French
$11-$31

AAA Inspector Notes: This stylish dining room has large windows that overlook a golf course. The menu features contemporary French bistro cuisine inspired by many Quebec regional products, including salmon or beef tartare, duck confit, French onion soup, chicken breast in Dijon mustard sauce, Angus beef, Quebec pork tenderloin, game specialties, fish and seafood. Tabletops are upscale, and the seating is comfortable, especially in the banquette seats. **Bar:** full bar. **Reservations:** required. **Address:** 7900 rue du Marigot G1G 6T8 **Location:** Hwy 73 exit 154, just e; in Four Points by Sheraton Quebec. [B] [L] [D]

(See map & index p. 429.)

RESTAURANT LE GALOPIN

Regional French
$16-$35

Phone: 418/652-0991 ⃞20

AAA Inspector Notes: A wide range of regional products, with a heavy focus on game, is used to create innovative, market-sensitive cuisine. Flavorful choices include fillet of pork, salmon tartare, sweetbreads, seafood stew, rabbit and beef mignon. The decor and table settings are upscale. Seating on the summer terrace is popular. **Bar:** full bar. **Reservations:** suggested. **Address:** 3135 chemin St-Louis G1W 1R9 **Location:** Hwy 73 exit 133 (chemin St-Louis); in Hôtel Sépia. B L D

RESTAURANT NORMANDIN

Canadian
$6-$14

For additional information, visit AAA.com

AAA Inspector Notes: The family restaurant prepares affordable comfort foods that include roasted chicken, hot chicken sandwiches, pasta, burgers and fries. Take-out service, a children's menu and cutely decorated desserts are among other offerings. **Bar:** full bar. B L D LATE

LOCATIONS:

Address: 2355 boul Bastien G2B 1B3 **Location:** On Hwy 369. **Phone:** 418/842-6601

Address: 709 boul Charest ouest G1K 3H4 **Location:** Jct Hwy 440 and 138. **Phone:** 418/681-0207

Address: 986 rue Bouvier G2J 1A3 **Location:** Hwy 40 exit 312N eastbound to boul Pierre-Bertrand, then n to rue Bouvier; exit 312N westbound, just w on rue Bouvier; in Hotel & Suites Normandin. **Phone:** 418/627-1265

Address: 2500 chemin Ste-Foy G1W 1R8 **Location:** Between Hwy 740 and rue Beauregard. **Phone:** 418/653-4844

RISTORANTE MICHELANGELO

Menu on AAA.com

Italian
$19-$45

Phone: 418/651-6262 ⃞19

AAA Inspector Notes: Art Deco-inspired style punctuates this inviting and stylish dining room. Service is superior in all aspects, including some dishes prepared tableside. The menu of fine Italian cuisine lists risotto, steak tartare, seafood platter, milk-fed veal and house-prepared pasta dishes, such as wonderful manicotti with tomato sauce. An excellent wine list is offered, including an outstanding selection of fine French and Italian vintages. The family-run restaurant features and Italian gourmet food shop. **Bar:** full bar. **Reservations:** suggested. **Address:** 3111 chemin St-Louis G1W 1R6 **Location:** Corner of ave des Hotels. **Parking:** on-site and valet. L D

ST-HUBERT

Canadian
$8-$22

Phone: 418/650-1234

AAA Inspector Notes: The pleasantly decorated family-friendly restaurant serves affordable chicken dinners, ribs, club sandwiches, chicken wings, salads, soups and hot chicken sandwiches. The children's menu includes animal nuggets. **Bar:** full bar. **Address:** 2905 boul Laurier G1V 2M2 **Location:** Hwy 73 exit boul Laurier. L D

RIGAUD pop. 6,552

AUBERGE DU MONT-RIGAUD

Hotel
$85-$145

Phone: 450/451-2202

Address: 20 rue Bourget J0P 1P0 **Location:** Jct Rt 342, 0.4 mi (0.6 km) w on rue St-Pierre, then just s. **Facility:** 15 units. 2 stories (no elevator), interior corridors. **Parking:** winter plug-ins. **Terms:** 7 day cancellation notice-fee imposed. **Pool(s):** heated outdoor. **Activities:** whirlpool. **Guest Services:** valet laundry.

HOWARD JOHNSON

Hotel
$62-$170

Phone: (450)458-7779

Address: 93 Montee Lavigne (Rt 201) J0P 1P0 **Location:** Hwy 40 exit 17, just ne. **Facility:** 31 units. 2 stories (no elevator), interior corridors. **Terms:** check-in 4 pm, cancellation fee imposed. **Amenities:** high-speed Internet. **Guest Services:** valet laundry.

WHERE TO EAT

RESTAURANT RUBE

Steak
$11-$44

Phone: 450/458-5369

AAA Inspector Notes: Steak and seafood top the menu of this lively pub and restaurant in a rural area. The atrium dining room affords pretty views of the forest. Patrons can sample filet mignon, New York steak, rack of lamb, surf and turf, Texas-style smoked ribs, Wiener schnitzel, chicken, cod, sandwiches and salads. **Bar:** full bar. **Reservations:** suggested. **Address:** 147 Rt 201 J0P 1P0 **Location:** Hwy 40 exit 17, 0.6 mi (1 km) s. L D

RIMOUSKI (C-7) pop. 31,305
• Hotels p. 454 • Restaurants p. 454

Rimouski is the administrative capital of eastern Québec, and an important educational and cultural center halfway between Québec City and Gaspé.

Rimouski Tourism & Information Bureau: 50 rue St-Germain Ouest, Rimouski, QC, Canada G5L 4B5. **Phone:** (418) 723-2322 or (800) 746-6875.

LAMONTAGNE HOUSE (Maison Lamontagne), 1.5 km (.9 mi.) e. of Rimouski Port via Hwy. 132 to 707 boul. du Rivage, is an 18th-century half-timbered house. Antique furniture, architectural and cultural exhibits, and a display about the conservation and preparation of food in the 18th century are featured. Free outdoor concerts take place on Sundays in July and August, and, on Fridays, batches of bread are prepared in an outdoor oven.

Guided tours are available; narration in English is offered. **Time:** Allow 1 hour minimum. **Hours:** Daily 9-6, late June-Labour Day; Thurs.-Sun. 9-6, day after Labour Day-second Sun. in Oct. **Cost:** $4; $3 (ages 65+); $2 (students with ID); free (ages 0-6). **Phone:** (418) 722-4038.

POINTE-AU-PÈRE MARITIME HISTORIC SITE—MUSEUM OF THE SEA (Site historique maritime de la Pointe-au-Père—Musée de la Mer) is at 1000 rue du Phare in the sector of Pointe-au-Père. The museum's exhibits describe regional history; marine life; and the shipwreck of the *Empress of Ireland,* a cruise ship which sank off Rimouski on May 29, 1914, with a loss of 1,012 lives. A 3-D projection re-creates the final moments of the ship's journey.

Also on-site is the *Onondaga,* a 90-metre (295-ft.) Canadian Navy submarine in service for 33 years. A 45-minute self-guiding audio tour relates the daily life of a submariner as well as the vessel's mechanical engineering.

Guided tours are available; narration in English is offered. **Time:** Allow 2 hours, 30 minutes minimum.

Hours: Daily 9-6, mid-June to mid-Oct. **Cost:** Museum $9; $6 (ages 8-15). *Onondaga* submarine $14.75; $8.75 (ages 8-15). Combination ticket $18.75; $13 (ages 8-15). Combination tickets with Pointe-au-Père Lighthouse also are available. **Phone:** (418) 724-6214.

Pointe-au-Père Lighthouse (Le phare de Pointe-au-Père) is at 1034 rue du Phare in the sector of Pointe-au-Père. This 33-metre-high (108-ft.) rare octagonal structure was completed in 1909. Exhibits are displayed in the lightkeeper's house. **Time:** Allow 1 hour minimum. **Hours:** Daily 9-6, mid-June through Aug. 31; 9-5, Sept. 1 to mid-Oct. **Cost:** $4; $2 (ages 6-17). A combination ticket with Pointe-au-Père Maritime Historic Site—Museum of the Sea is available. **Phone:** (418) 724-6214.

RIMOUSKI REGIONAL MUSEUM (Musée régional de Rimouski), 35 rue St-Germain Ouest, is in an 1824 stone church that has a modern interior. Exhibitions deal with local history, science and technology in the Bas St-Laurent and contemporary Canadian art. **Time:** Allow 30 minutes minimum. **Hours:** Wed.-Fri. 9:30-8, Sat.-Tues. 9:30-6, late June-early Sept.; Wed.-Sun. noon-5 (also Thurs. 5-9), rest of year. **Cost:** $4; $3 (ages 51+ and students with ID); $10 (family). **Phone:** (418) 724-2272.

AUBERGE LA MARÈE DOUCE   **Phone:** 418/722-0822

Historic Bed
& Breakfast
Rates not provided

Address: 1329 boul Ste-Anne G5M 1W2 **Location:** On Rt 132; in Pointe-au-Pere sector. **Facility:** This circa 1860 Victorian inn offers pleasantly decorated rooms. Accommodations are available also in a cottage or in the annex built in 1996. 9 units, some cottages and condominiums. 1-2 stories (no elevator), interior/exterior corridors. **Terms:** seasonal. **Guest Services:** complimentary laundry.

COMFORT INN   **Phone:** (418)724-2500

Hotel
$115-$125

Address: 455 boul St-Germain ouest G5L 3P2 **Location:** On Rt 132. **Facility:** 79 units. 2 stories (no elevator), interior corridors. **Parking:** winter plug-ins. **Guest Services:** valet laundry.

HOTEL GOUVERNEUR RIMOUSKI
          Phone: (418)723-4422

Hotel
$85-$149

Address: 155 boul Rene-Lepage E G5L 1P2 **Location:** On Rt 132. **Facility:** 163 units. 4 stories, interior corridors. **Parking:** winter plug-ins. **Amenities:** video games (fee). **Pool(s):** heated outdoor. **Activities:** lifeguard on duty, spa. **Guest Services:** valet laundry.

HOTEL L'EMPRESS   **Phone:** 418/723-6944

Hotel
$119-$425

Address: 360 Montee Industrielle & Commerciale G5M 1X1 **Location:** Hwy 20 exit 614, 2.1 mi (3.4 km) n. **Facility:** 62 units, some two bedrooms. 2 stories, interior corridors. **Parking:** winter plug-ins. **Terms:** 7 day cancellation notice. **Amenities:** high-speed Internet. **Dining:** Cage aux Sports, see separate listing. **Activities:** snowmobiling. **Guest Services:** coin laundry.

HOTEL RIMOUSKI   **Phone:** (418)725-5000

Hotel
$107-$149

Address: 225 boul Rene-Lepage est G5L 1P2 **Location:** On Rt 132; corner of rue Julien-Rehel. **Facility:** 185 units. 5 stories, interior corridors. **Parking:** winter plug-ins. **Terms:** 15 day cancellation notice. **Amenities:** *Some:* video games (fee), high-speed Internet, honor bars. **Pool(s):** heated indoor. **Activities:** sauna, whirlpool, waterslide, exercise room, spa. *Fee:* miniature golf. **Guest Services:** valet and coin laundry.

WHERE TO EAT

CAGE AUX SPORTS   **Phone:** 418/723-0121

Canadian
$8-$22

AAA Inspector Notes: This popular Quebec chain of sports bars presents a menu of pub foods, including ribs, chicken, burgers, salads, crispy fries, pasta and tasty desserts. Guests might begin the meal with a basket of freshly popped popcorn as they check out the sports memorabilia. Children are welcomed. **Bar:** full bar. **Address:** 360 Montee Industrielle & Commerciale G5M 1X1 **Location:** Hwy 20 exit 614, 2.1 mi (3.4 km) n. B L D

RESTAURANT NORMANDIN   **Phone:** 418/723-7233

Canadian
$6-$18

AAA Inspector Notes: The family restaurant prepares affordable comfort foods that include roasted chicken, hot chicken sandwiches, pasta, burgers and fries. Take-out service, a children's menu and other offerings. **Bar:** full bar. **Reservations:** required. **Address:** 405 boul Jessop G5L 1M9 **Location:** On Rt 132; corner of ave Leonidas. B L D

ST-HUBERT   **Phone:** 418/723-4419

Canadian
$8-$22

AAA Inspector Notes: The pleasantly decorated family-friendly restaurant serves affordable chicken dinners, ribs, club sandwiches, chicken wings, salads, soups and hot chicken sandwiches. The children's menu includes animal nuggets. **Bar:** full bar. **Address:** 185 boul Rene-Lepage est G5L 1P2 **Location:** On Rt 132; centre. L D

RIVIÈRE-DU-LOUP (C-6) pop. 18,586

According to local legend, Rivière-du-Loup owes its name to the sea lions, or *loups marins,* that once frequented the mouth of the river. Other tales suggest that it was named after the French ship *Le Loup,* which was stranded at the mouth of the river around 1660.

The area is noted for its eight beautiful waterfalls; the largest, at 30 metres (100 ft.), and most picturesque, is reached via rues de la Chute and Frontenac and highlights the center of the city. The Park of the Illuminated Cross (Parc de la Croix Lumineuse) affords an excellent view of the region and contains a large illuminated cross.

From June to mid-October large numbers of whales migrate through nearby waters. Up to seven different species, ranging from the relatively small beluga to the enormous blue whale, can be sighted. Whale-watching cruises are offered in late summer.

Rivière-du-Loup Tourism & Information Bureau: 189 boul. de l'Hôtel-de-Ville, Rivière-du-Loup, QC, Canada G5R 5C4. **Phone:** (418) 862-1981 or (888) 825-1981.

CHRISTMAS AT THE CASTLE (Noël au Château) is at 65 de l'Ancrage. Inspired by the Cinderella Castle at Disney's Magic Kingdom Park in Central Florida, the whimsical structure houses a variety of Christmas decorations. Highlights include a collection of miniature lighted houses, figurines depicting international holiday traditions, an assortment of decorated Christmas trees, and ornate Nativity sets from around the world.

Guided tours of the château are given in French; brochures describing the tour in English are available. **Time:** Allow 1 hour minimum. **Hours:** Daily 9-9, late June-Labour Day; Mon.-Sat. 9-5 (also Thurs.-Fri. 5-9), Sun. noon-5, Easter-late June and Labour Day-Dec. 31; otherwise varies. Phone ahead to confirm schedule. **Cost:** $6; $4 (students with ID); $3 (ages 4-12); $15 (family). **Phone:** (418) 863-6635 or (866) 865-6635.

LOWER ST. LAWRENCE ISLAND CRUISES (Croisières dans les Îles du Bas-St-Laurent) departs from the Rivière-du-Loup ferry service dock. La Société Duvetnor Ltd. offers a variety of naturalist guided sightseeing cruises of the lower St. Lawrence islands, ranging from 90 minutes to 3 hours. An overnight cruise to the lighthouse at Île du Pot à l'Eau-de-Vie also is offered.

Tour narration in English is offered. Inquire about weather policies and minimum number of passengers for departure. **Hours:** Cruise to Île aux Lièvres departs at varying times daily, mid-June to late Sept. Cruise to Île du Pot à l'Eau-de-Vie departs daily at 2, early June to mid-Sept. **Cost:** Three-hour cruise to Île du Pot à l'Eau-de-Vie or cruise to Île aux Lièvres $43.89; $21.95 (ages 0-12). Overnight lighthouse cruise $210. Reservations are required. **Phone:** (418) 867-1660.

LOWER ST. LAWRENCE MUSEUM (Musée du Bas-St-Laurent), 300 rue St-Pierre, includes contemporary artworks and photographs. **Hours:** Daily 9-6, June 24-Labour Day; daily 1-5, day after Labour Day to mid-Oct.; Wed.-Sun. 1-5, rest of year. Phone ahead to confirm schedule. **Cost:** $5; $3 (students with ID); free (ages 0-11 with adult); $12 (family). Cash only. **Phone:** (418) 862-7547.

WHALE-WATCHING CRUISES (Croisières d'observation aux baleines-Croisières AML) departs from the yacht club near the St-Siméon/Rivière-du-Loup ferry service. During a 3.5-hour cruise aboard the *Cavalier des Mers*, bilingual naturalists help passengers discover the whales, birds and lighthouses of the St. Lawrence River.

Inquire about weather policies and minimum number of passengers required for departure. **Hours:** Cruises depart daily at 9:30 and 1:30, mid-June to late Sept. **Cost:** $68; $63 (students with ID and senior citizens); $33 (ages 6-12); $160 (family).

Prices may vary. Reservations are required. **Phone:** (800) 563-4643.

COMFORT INN   **Phone:** (418)867-4162

Hotel
$93-$170
Address: 85 boul Cartier G5R 4X4 **Location:** Hwy 20 exit 507, just se; Hwy 85 exit 96 (Fraserville), follow signs. **Facility:** 67 units. 2 stories (no elevator), interior corridors. **Parking:** winter plug-ins. **Terms:** 3 night minimum stay - weekends, cancellation fee imposed. **Guest Services:** valet laundry.

DAYS INN RIVIERE-DU-LOUP   **Phone:** 418/862-6354
Hotel
Rates not provided
Address: 182 rue Fraser G5R 1C8 **Location:** Hwy 20 exit 503, 0.6 mi (1 km) e on Rt 132. **Facility:** 50 units, some kitchens and cottages. 2 stories (no elevator), interior/exterior corridors. **Parking:** winter plug-ins. **Amenities:** *Some:* safes. **Pool(s):** heated outdoor. **Activities:** playground. **Guest Services:** valet laundry.

HOTEL LEVESQUE   **Phone:** 418/862-6927
Hotel
Rates not provided
Address: 171 rue Fraser G5R 1E2 **Location:** Hwy 20 exit 503, 0.8 mi (1.2 km) e on Rt 132. **Facility:** 83 units. 2 stories (no elevator), interior corridors. **Parking:** winter plug-ins. **Amenities:** *Some:* high-speed Internet, safes. **Dining:** Restaurant Union Pacifique, see separate listing. **Pool(s):** heated outdoor. **Activities:** saunas, whirlpool, snowmobiling, bicycles, playground, spa. *Fee:* exercise room. **Guest Services:** valet laundry.

MOTEL AU VIEUX PILOTEUX   **Phone:** 418/867-2635
Motel
$78-$150
Address: 185 rue Fraser G5R 1E2 **Location:** Hwy 20 exit 503, 0.6 mi (1 km) e on Rt 132. **Facility:** 23 units. 1 story, exterior corridors. **Parking:** winter plug-ins. **Terms:** cancellation fee imposed. **Amenities:** *Some:* high-speed Internet. **Pool(s):** heated outdoor. **Activities:** snowmobiling, playground. **Guest Services:** valet laundry.

QUALITY INN RIVIERE-DU-LOUP   **Phone:** 418/867-8221
Hotel
Rates not provided
Address: 61 boul Cartier G5R 5Z3 **Location:** Hwy 20 exit 507, just se. **Facility:** 62 units. 3 stories, interior corridors. **Parking:** winter plug-ins. **Amenities:** high-speed Internet. **Pool(s):** heated indoor. **Activities:** whirlpool, hiking trails, exercise room. **Guest Services:** valet laundry.

WHERE TO EAT

RESTAURANT NORMANDIN   **Phone:** 418/867-1366
Canadian
$8-$18
AAA Inspector Notes: The family restaurant prepares affordable comfort foods that include roasted chicken, hot chicken sandwiches, pasta, burgers and fries. Take-out service, a children's menu and cutely decorated desserts are among other offerings. **Bar:** full bar. **Reservations:** required. **Address:** 83 boul Cartier G5R 2N1 **Location:** Hwy 20 exit 507, just s. [B] [L] [D]

RESTAURANT UNION PACIFIQUE   **Phone:** 418/862-6927

French
$15-$38

AAA Inspector Notes: This stylish bring-your-own-wine dining room overlooks the scenic riverfront so it is not surprising to find a menu focused on regional fish and seafood. Choose from shrimp, delectable seafood platters, salmon, cod and the popular surf-and-turf. From the bistro menu, try a steak and fries or mussels prepared to your liking. Alcohol may be ordered in the adjacent bar, but is not sold in the dining room. The atrium section is a nice spot to watch the sun set on the riverfront. **Reservations:** suggested. **Address:** 171 rue Fraser G5R 1E2 **Location:** Hwy 20 exit 503, 0.8 mi (1.2 km) e on Rt 132; in Hotel Levesque. B D

ST-HUBERT   **Phone:** 418/867-1830

Canadian
$8-$22

AAA Inspector Notes: The pleasantly decorated family-friendly restaurant serves affordable chicken dinners, ribs, club sandwiches, chicken wings, salads, soups and hot chicken sandwiches. The children's menu includes animal nuggets. **Bar:** full bar. **Address:** 80 boul Cartier G5R 2M9 **Location:** Hwy 20 exit 507. L D

RIVIÈRE-ÉTERNITÉ (C-6) pop. 557

SAGUENAY FJORD NATIONAL PARK (Parc national du Fjord-du-Saguenay), accessible via Hwy. 170, lies along each side of the Saguenay River. Managed by the provincial government, the 300 square kilometres (116 sq. mi.) of long, rugged and heavily forested valley stretch through the Saguenay-Lac-St-Jean, Charlevoix, Manicouagan and Haute-Côte-Nord tourism regions.

During the last ice age glaciers gouged a deep gash through the Laurentian Mountains to the St. Lawrence River, creating the steep-sided Saguenay Fjord—one of the biggest in the world. The park protects a sizable portion of this dramatic landscape. Although the Saguenay Fjord is its major feature, there are hiking trails along the river, and a short hike ascends Cap Trinité to a statue of the Virgin Mary.

Information is available at visitor centers and kiosks in Rivière-Éternité, L'Anse-St-Jean, Sacré-Coeur and Tadoussac. Primitive camping is permitted throughout the park; developed facilities are available in the Baie-Éternité sector. *See Recreation Chart.* **Phone:** (418) 272-1556, or (800) 665-6527 for camping information.

SAGUENAY-ST. LAWRENCE MARINE PARK (Parc marin du Saguenay-St-Laurent) is accessible via hwys. 138, 170, 172 and 132. Managed by both the provincial and the federal government, the 1,245-square-kilometre (480-sq.-mi.) marine park consists of most of the river bed of Saguenay Fjord and a part of the northern half of the St. Lawrence estuary.

Created in 1998, the park protects a biologically diverse ecosystem. More than fifteen species of marine mammals are known to frequent the area, including minke, fin, humpback and blue whales that migrate here in summer and beluga whales and harbor seals, both of which are year-round residents.

Such activities as sightseeing cruises, hiking, kayaking and scuba diving can be enjoyed in the park. Ferry service as well as exhibits and information about the area are available in Baie-Ste-Catherine, Les Escoumins, Rivière-du-Loup, Tadoussac and Trois-Pistoles. *See Recreation Chart.* **Phone:** (418) 235-4703 or (888) 773-8888.

ROBERVAL (C-5) pop. 10,544

Settled in 1855, Roberval was named for Jean François de la Roque, who served as the first lieutenant general of the king in New France. The town developed into a commercial center for the western portion of lac St-Jean County.

In late July the Lac St-Jean International Crossing (Traversée Internationale du lac St-Jean), a 40-kilometre (25-mi.) swimming marathon, takes place between Péribonka *(see place listing p. 401)* and Roberval. Swimmers from around the world compete in the event; phone (418) 275-2851 for information.

VAL-JALBERT HISTORIC VILLAGE (Village Historique de Val-Jalbert), 10 km (6 mi.) s. on Hwy. 169, preserves the remains of Val-Jalbert, a once thriving early 20th-century industrial village. Built to exploit the churning waters and 72-metre (235 ft.) falls of the Ouiatchouan River, the village was abandoned in 1927. Features include a school, a hotel, a bank and rows of workers' houses.

Hiking and bicycling paths are accessible, including the 30-kilometre (19-mi.) Ouiatchouan Trail. A cable car operating from early June to mid-October takes visitors to a scenic overlook above Ouiatchouan Falls. **Time:** Allow 3 hours minimum. **Hours:** The 2011 schedule was daily 9-6, mid-June to late Aug.; 10-5, early to mid-June and late Aug. to mid-Oct.; otherwise varies. Phone ahead for 2012 schedule. **Cost:** Admission in 2011 was $24; $12 (ages 6-13); $62.50 (family). Cable car fare $4; $2 (children); $10 (family). Phone ahead for 2012 prices. **Phone:** (418) 275-3132.

HOTEL CHÂTEAU ROBERVAL   **Phone:** 418/275-7511

Hotel
Rates not provided

Address: 1225 boul Marcotte G8H 2P1 **Location:** On Hwy 169; centre. **Facility:** 124 units. 3 stories, interior corridors. **Parking:** winter plug-ins. **Dining:** Restaurant L'Abordage, see separate listing. **Pool(s):** heated indoor. **Activities:** whirlpool, snowmobiling, exercise room. **Fee:** bicycles, massage. **Guest Services:** valet laundry.

WHERE TO EAT

RESTAURANT L'ABORDAGE   **Phone:** 418/275-7511

Quebec
$9-$40

AAA Inspector Notes: The informal hotel restaurant presents a menu of affordable regional cuisine, including Lac-St-Jean tourtiere (meat pie), ouananiche (a regional fish), salmon, scallops, shrimp, supreme chicken, Alberta filet mignon, sandwiches and children's dishes. Minaki, a popular blueberry-based aperitif, is a treat. **Bar:** full bar. **Reservations:** suggested. **Address:** 1225 boul Marcotte G8H 2P1 **Location:** On Hwy 169; centre; in Hotel Chateau Roberval. B L D

ROUYN-NORANDA pop. 28,270

BEST WESTERN PLUS ALBERT CENTRE-VILLE
Phone: (819)762-3545

Hotel
$115-$125

AAA Benefit: Members save up to 20%, plus 10% bonus points with Best Western Rewards®.

Address: 84 Ave Principale J9X 4P2 **Location:** Centre. **Facility:** 50 units. 3 stories, interior corridors. **Terms:** cancellation fee imposed. **Activities:** snowmobiling, bicycles, exercise room. **Guest Services:** valet laundry. **Free Special Amenities:** local telephone calls and high-speed Internet.

COMFORT INN   **Phone:** (819)797-1313

Hotel
$88-$135

Address: 1295 ave Lariviere J9X 6M6 **Location:** On Rt 117, 2.5 mi (4 km) s from town centre. **Facility:** 78 units. 2 stories (no elevator), interior corridors. **Parking:** winter plug-ins. **Terms:** cancellation fee imposed. **Guest Services:** valet laundry.

HOTEL GOUVERNEUR LE NORANDA
Phone: (819)762-2341

Hotel
$105-$125

Address: 41 6ieme rue J9X 1Y8 **Location:** Corner of rue Murdoch; centre. **Facility:** 71 units, some efficiencies. 4 stories, interior/exterior corridors. **Parking:** winter plug-ins. **Terms:** check-in 4 pm. **Activities:** bicycles, exercise room, spa. Fee: steamroom. **Guest Services:** valet laundry.

ST-AIMÉ-DES-LACS (D-6) pop. 1,076

HAUTES-GORGES-DE-LA-RIVIÈRE-MALBAIE NATIONAL PARK (Parc national des Hautes-Gorges-de-la-Rivière-Malbaie) is 26 km (16 mi.) n. on rue Principale, following signs. Named after a series of valleys, the 224-square-kilometre (86-sq.-mi.) park encompasses 1,000-metre-high (3,281-ft.) mountains; numerous lakes, rivers and waterfalls; and forests harboring American elms, ash and sugar maples. Recreational pursuits include canoeing, fishing, hiking, kayaking and bicycling.

The Félix-Antoine-Savard Discovery and Visitor Centre offers interpretive exhibits detailing the area's cultural and geological history. Departing from the Le Draveur Visitors Centre, 90-minute riverboat tours aboard Le Menaud explore the Rivière Malbaie. Both covered and outdoor viewing areas are available for passengers taking in the majestic wooded cliffs and serene waters along this 15-kilometre (9-mi.) cruise. See Recreation Chart.

Pets are not permitted. Reservations for the cruise are required; visitors also should arrive 1 hour prior to cruise departure time. **Time:** Allow 2 hours minimum. **Hours:** Shuttle buses to the park depart the main parking area daily, late June-Labour Day; Sat.-Sun., mid-May to late June and day after Labour Day-early Oct. Riverboat cruises depart three to five times daily, mid-May to early Oct. Shuttle and cruise departure times vary; phone ahead. **Cost:** Park admission $6; $2.75 (ages 6-17); $12 (family, two adults and children); $8.75 (family, one adult and children). Riverboat cruise $33.05; $24.79 (ages 6-17). **Phone:** (418) 439-1227 or (800) 665-6527.

ST-ANDRÉ-D'ARGENTEUIL (F-3)
pop. 3,097

In 2000 the formerly independent municipalities of Carillon and St-André-Est amalgamated with St-André-d'Argenteuil. The area's storied history is largely derived from its location on the banks of the Ottawa River some 85 kilometres (53 mi.) from Montréal. Initially a trading post, Carillon was the site of the Battle of Long Sault in May 1660, when 17 men saved New France from an Indian invasion.

In 1833 British Army engineers built the first Carillon Canal as part of the inland waterway system designed to link Montréal and Kingston as a defensive measure against invasion by the United States. At the Carillon Canal National Historic Site of Canada (Lieu historique national du Canada du Canal-de-Carillon), plaques at the entry lock, which is intact, detail the chronology of the site. The lock and dam are part of a 654,500-kilowatt power project. With a gradient of 24 metres (79 ft.), this is highest conventional lock in Canada; small craft pass through in 40 minutes. The collector's house presents an exhibit about the first two canal systems; phone (450) 447-4888.

The Carillon Barracks National Historic Site of Canada (Lieu historique national du Canada de la Caserne-de-Carillon), an early 19th-century stone military building, now houses the Argenteuil County Historical Museum (see attraction listing). Accessible near the museum is the Pointe-Fortune à Carillon Ferry, which crosses the Ottawa River April through November.

ARGENTEUIL REGIONAL MUSEUM (Musée régional d'Argenteuil) is at 44 Rte. du Long Sault. The museum is in a four-story stone barracks constructed 1834-37 to house soldiers building the first Carillon Canal. The barracks housed 108 men during the Rebellion of 1837. Displays include local history items, military artifacts and natural history specimens. **Hours:** Wed.-Sun. 10-5, June 24-Labour Day; Sun. 11-5, day after Labour Day-Oct. 31; Tues.-Fri. by appointment, rest of year. **Cost:** $3.50; $3 (ages 65+); $2.50 (students with ID); free (ages 0-11). **Phone:** (450) 537-3861.

CARILLON GENERATING STATION is just s. of Hwy. 344. Narrated tours of this generating station, built on the Ottawa River near the site of the 1660 Battle of Long Sault, last 75 minutes. The facility is operated by Hydro-Québec, a provincially owned electric utility corporation based in Montréal. Interpretive displays are on-site as is a lock at the dam site.

Note: Photo ID is required to tour the facility. **Time:** Allow 1 hour, 45 minutes minimum. **Hours:** Tours are given Mon.-Fri. at 9, 10:30, noon, 1:30 and 3, Victoria Day-late June; Wed.-Sun. at 9:30, 11, 12:30, 2 and 3:30, late June-late Aug. **Cost:** Free. **Phone:** (800) 365-5229.

ST-ANTOINE-DE-TILLY pop. 1,449

MANOIR DE TILLY   **Phone:** 418/886-2407

Country Inn
$115-$230
Address: 3854 chemin de Tilly G0S 2C0 **Location:** Jct Hwy 20 exit 291, 5.3 mi. (8.5 km) n on Rt 273; centre. Located in a quiet area. **Facility:** This contemporary inn, which overlooks the St. Lawrence River, includes a manor house built in 1786. 30 units. 3 stories (no elevator), interior corridors. **Parking:** winter plug-ins. **Terms:** check-in 4 pm, 3 day cancellation notice-fee imposed. **Activities:** spa. **Guest Services:** valet laundry. / SOME UNITS FEE

ST-BERNARD-DE-LACOLLE pop. 1,537

BEST WESTERN HOTEL ST. BERNARD
    Phone: (450)246-4000

Hotel
$90-$140
AAA Benefit: Members save up to 20%, plus 10% bonus points with Best Western Rewards®.

Address: 115 Chemin Guay J0J 1V0 **Location:** Hwy 15 exit 1, just se, follow signs. **Facility:** 39 units. 2 stories (no elevator), interior/exterior corridors. **Parking:** winter plug-ins. **Terms:** cancellation fee imposed. **Dining:** Premier Bistro, see separate listing. **Pool(s):** heated outdoor. **Activities:** cross country skiing, snowmobiling, exercise room. **Free Special Amenities:** continental breakfast and high-speed Internet.

WHERE TO EAT

PREMIER BISTRO   **Phone:** 450/246-4000

Canadian
$9-$24
AAA Inspector Notes: At the last exit before the U.S. border crossing and duty-free shop, this hotel/family bistro serves up a variety of popular comfort foods including rotisserie chicken, ribs, club sandwiches, steak and fries, crepes, burgers, duck confit, pasta, fish and chips, hot chicken sandwich, soup and salads. **Bar:** full bar. **Reservations:** required. **Address:** 115 Chemin Guay J0J 1V0 **Location:** Hwy 15 exit 1, just se, follow signs; in Best Western Hotel St. Bernard. [B] [L] [D]

ST-CONSTANT (F-7) pop. 23,957
• Part of Montréal area — see map p. 312

EXPORAIL, THE CANADIAN RAILWAY MUSEUM (Exporail, le Musée ferroviaire canadien), 110 rue St-Pierre, contains a collection of 250,000 railway objects and documents, including 162 pieces of rolling stock, an exhibit pavilion showcasing 44 of its best vehicles, a turntable and two train stations. Visitors can take a ride aboard a vintage streetcar and a miniature railroad.

Time: Allow 1 hour minimum. **Hours:** Daily 10-6, June 24-early Sept.; daily 10-5, mid-May through June 23; Wed.-Sun. 10-5, early Sept. to mid-Oct.; Sat.-Sun. 10-5, rest of year. **Cost:** $17; $14 (ages 65+); $11 (students ages 13-17 with ID); $8 (ages 4-12); $44 (family, two adults and two children). **Phone:** (450) 632-2410.

ST-DENIS-SUR-RICHELIEU pop. 2,243

LES CHANTERELLES DU RICHELIEU
    Phone: 450/787-1167

French
$20-$28
AAA Inspector Notes: Fine regional French cuisine is served in a 1905 Victorian-style home. Among specialties are guinea fowl, quail, Quebec veal, filet mignon, sweetbreads and fresh fish. An a la carte brunch is served on Sundays. **Bar:** full bar. **Reservations:** suggested. **Address:** 611 chemin des Patriotes J0H 1K0 **Location:** Hwy 20 exit 113, just s of jct Rt 137 on Rt 133 N. [D]

ST-EUSTACHE (E-7) pop. 42,062
• Hotels & Restaurants map & index p. 342
• Part of Montréal area — see map p. 312

EXOTARIUM: REPTILE FARM (Exotarium: Ferme de Reptiles) is off Autoroute 640 exit 11, w. on Hwy. 148 to boul. Industriel, 2 km (1.2 mi.) s. to ch. Fresnière, then 7 km (4 mi.) w. to 846 ch. Fresnière. This breeding farm and mini-zoo for reptiles displays 135 species, including boa constrictors, crocodiles, iguanas, pythons, turtles and insects.

Time: Allow 1 hour minimum. **Hours:** Daily 10-5, July-Aug.; Fri.-Sun. 10-5, Feb.-May and Sept.-Dec. Animal shows are given at 11:30, 1, 2:30 and 4. **Cost:** $12; $8 (ages 3-15); $34 (family). **Phone:** (450) 472-1827.

LÉGARÉ MILL (Moulin Légaré) is at 232 rue St-Eustache. Built in 1762, the flour mill is one of the oldest continually operating mills in North America. Visitors can explore the site via self-guiding or guided tours. Across from the historic structure is a cultural center housing exhibits about the mill and the surrounding area.

Time: Allow 1 hour minimum. **Hours:** Mill and cultural center daily 9-5, May 1 to mid-June; 10-7, mid-June through Oct. 31. Guided tours are given at 10:30, 11:30, 1:30 and 3. **Cost:** $5; $4.50 (ages 65+ and students with ID); free (ages 0-6). Reservations are required for guided tours. **Phone:** (450) 974-5170.

WINERIES
• **River of the Oak Vineyard** (Vignoble de la Rivière du Chêne) is at 807 ch. de la Rivière Nord. **Hours:** Tastings daily 10-5. Guided tours are given daily 10-5, late June-early Nov. **Cost:** Wine

(See map & index p. 342.)

tasting $5. Guided tour $5; free (ages 0-13). Reservations are required for guided tours. **Phone:** (450) 491-3997.

RESTAURANT CHÂTEAU LAFITTE

		Phone: 450/472-1414

Canadian
$7-$27

AAA Inspector Notes: The casual, family-friendly restaurant offers many Italian dishes, including pizza, lasagna, spaghetti, veal scaloppine, in addition to salads, club sandwiches, hot subs, hot chicken sandwiches, souvlaki, steak, barbecue chicken, seafood, Chinese food and burgers. **Bar:** full bar. **Address:** 106 rue St-Eustache J7R 2K9 **Location:** Centre. **Parking:** street only.

B   L   D

ST-FAUSTIN-LAC-CARRÉ (E-4) pop. 2,985

Settled in 1817 and incorporated in 1878, St-Faustin-Lac-Carré is a farming and lumber center on the Canadian Pacific Railway. The town is a country resort in the Laurentides, offering both winter and water sports as well as camping, fishing and hunting.

MOTEL TREMBLANT SUR LA COLLINE

                  Phone: 819/688-2102

Motel
$79-$109

Address: 357 Rt 117 J0T 1J2 **Location:** On Rt 117, 2.5 mi (4 km) n of exit for city. **Facility:** 27 units, some efficiencies. 1-2 stories, interior/exterior corridors. **Parking:** winter plug-ins. **Terms:** 7 day cancellation notice-fee imposed. **Amenities:** Some: high-speed Internet. **Pool(s):** heated outdoor. **Activities:** playground.

LE P'TIT STOP   **Phone:** 819/688-3111

Canadian
$5-$9

AAA Inspector Notes: The family-run, roadside diner serves hamburgers made from 100 percent fresh beef, as well as grilled cheese sandwiches, hot dogs and poutine (fries topped with curd cheese and gravy). Patrons place their order at the counter and then wait to have it brought to their table. For dessert, sugar pie made from a family recipe is tasty, and the house-prepared flat pastry treats, served with a choice of sweet toppings, are popular choices. **Address:** 1176 Rt 117 J0T 1J3 **Location:** On Rt 117.   L   D

ST-FÉLICIEN (C-5) pop. 10,477

St-Félicien, on the Ashuapmushuan River, is an important spawning area for ouananiche (landlocked salmon) as well as home to a paper mill.

St-Félicien Tourist Information Bureau: 1209 boul. Sacré Coeur, C.P. 7, St-Félicien, QC, Canada G8K 2P8. **Phone:** (418) 679-9888 or (877) 525-9888.

ASHUAPMUSHUAN WILDLIFE RESERVE (Réserve Faunique Ashuapmushuan), n.w. on Hwy. 167, contains approximately 4,487 square kilometres (1,732 sq. mi.) of virgin country, traversed by Hwy. 167. Hunting and fishing are permitted seasonally. Reservations are required for cottages. A special fishing permit is necessary in addition to a provincial fishing license.

For further information contact the Société des établissements de plein air du Québec (SÉPAQ), Reservations Office, 2640 boul. Laurier, Suite 250, Québec, QC, Canada G1V 5C2. *See Recreation Chart.* **Hours:** Grounds daily 24 hours. **Cost:** Grounds free. **Phone:** (418) 256-3806, or (800) 665-6527 to reserve a cottage.

ST-FÉLICIEN WILD ANIMAL ZOO (Zoo sauvage de St-Félicien) is 5 km (3 mi.) n.w. on Hwy. 167 toward Chibougamau, at 2230 boul. du Jardin. A river winds through 485 hectares (1,198 acres) of wooded and landscaped areas. Exhibits include about 1,000 specimens of more than 75 species of birds, mammals and reptiles of the Northern Hemisphere. Fauna roam freely in natural settings.

The visitor center contains two large movie theaters, one with a giant screen and another that shows special effects films. A train takes visitors through a North American habitat where there are re-creations of a lumberjack camp, a trading post, an Indian village and a 19th-century farmhouse. Other highlights include a children's farm and water games.

Time: Allow 3 hours, 30 minutes minimum. **Hours:** Daily 9-6, June-Aug.; 9-5 in May and Sept.-Oct. Last departure of Nature Trail Park train is at 3:30. Phone ahead to confirm schedule. **Cost:** $39; $32.50 (ages 65+ and students with ID); $25.50 (ages 6-14); $16 (ages 3-5). Family rates are available. Prices may vary. **Phone:** (418) 679-0543 or (800) 667-5687.

HOTEL DU JARDIN   **Phone:** (418)679-8422

Hotel
$150-$200 6/1-9/30
$109-$179 10/1-5/31

Address: 1400 boul du Jardin G8K 2N8 **Location:** Jct Hwy 167 and 169. **Facility:** 85 units. 6 stories, interior corridors. **Parking:** winter plug-ins. **Dining:** L'Oasis, see separate listing, nightclub. **Pool(s):** heated indoor. **Activities:** whirlpool, snowmobiling, exercise room, spa. **Guest Services:** valet laundry.

L'OASIS   **Phone:** 418/679-8422

French
$10-$30

AAA Inspector Notes: This comfortable hotel dining room offers fine regional cuisine, including a multicourse tasting menu. Dishes include three styles of mussels, escargot, filet mignon, Chateaubriand beef, salmon, scallops, scampis, smoked trout, Saguenay-style tourtiere meat pie, pasta and club sandwiches. In the off season, lunches may be served in the bar area. **Bar:** full bar. **Reservations:** suggested. **Address:** 1400 boul du Jardin G8K 2N8 **Location:** Jct Hwy 167 and 169; in Hotel du Jardin.   B   D

ST-FÉLIX-D'OTIS (C-6) pop. 1,007

THE NEW FRANCE SITE (Site de la Nouvelle-France), 370 Vieux Chemin, is a faithfully re-created

17th-century Québec settlement. During 90-minute tours, bilingual guides provide insight into the customs of a typical Montagnais family and details of the traditions of early French and Amerindian villagers. An equestrian show features trick riding and acrobatics.

Hours: Daily 9-4:30, early June-late Aug. Guided tours are given Tues.-Sun., with tours in English departing at 9:30 and 3:30. **Cost:** $15; $14 (senior citizens); $7 (ages 6-13). Prices may vary; phone ahead. **Phone:** (418) 544-8027.

ST-FERRÉOL-LES-NEIGES (A-2) pop. 2,546
• Part of Québec area — see map p. 405

THE SEVEN WATERFALLS (Les Sept-Chutes) is at 4520 av. Royale. Located beside the Ste-Anne-du-Nord River, the site offers a variety of hiking trails, 20 scenic lookout points and an interpretation center. Guided tours of one of Québec's oldest operational hydroelectric power plants are available. A water play area and a playground also are on-site.

Time: Allow 30 minutes minimum. **Hours:** Daily 9-5:45, late June to mid-Aug.; 10-4:30, mid-May to late June and mid-Aug. to mid-Oct. Last admission 1 hour before closing. Phone ahead to confirm schedule. **Cost:** $9.95; $8.95 (ages 65+ and students with ID); $6.95 (ages 6-17); $23.45 (family). **Phone:** (418) 826-3139 or (877) 724-8837. 🍴 ⛽

CHALETS MONTMORENCY CONDOMINIUMS
MONT-SAINTE-ANNE QUEBEC   **Phone:** (418)826-2600

Condominium
$89-$159
Address: 1768 ave Royale G0A 3R0 **Location:** On Hwy 360. **Facility:** 37 condominiums. 2 stories (no elevator), exterior corridors. **Parking:** winter plug-ins. **Terms:** check-in 4 pm, 30 day cancellation notice-fee imposed. **Pool(s):** outdoor, heated indoor. **Activities:** whirlpool, snowmobiling, hiking trails. **Fee:** downhill & cross country skiing. **Guest Services:** complimentary laundry, area transportation (fee)-ski hill.

🛏 🛗 🏊 📶 ❌ 🛏 🖥 🖨
/ SOME UNITS FEE 🐾 🎖

ST-GABRIEL-DE-VALCARTIER (A-1)
• Part of Québec area — see map p. 405

VALCARTIER VACATION VILLAGE (Village Vacances Valcartier), 1860 boul. Valcartier, is a summer and winter recreation complex 20 minutes from downtown Québec City. In the summer the water park offers more than 35 waterslides, two theme rivers, a wave pool, acrobatic diving shows, white-water rafting and hydrospeed (riverboarding). Winter fare includes 42 inner-tube slides, snow rafting, 17 mechanical lifts, skating paths and ice carting.

Hours: Opens daily at 10, early June-late Aug. and mid-Dec. to late Mar. **Cost:** The 2012 summer admission is $33.06; $26.09 (ages 65+ and under 132 centimetres or 52 inches tall). The 2011-12 winter season rates were $25.22-$30.44; $20-$25.22 (ages 5-11); $10.44 (ages 3-4). Phone ahead to confirm summer and winter rates as well as both schedules. **Phone:** (418) 844-2200 or (888) 384-5524. 🍴

ST-GEORGES (BEAUCE) pop. 29,616

COMFORT INN   Phone: 418/227-1227

Motel
Rates not provided
Address: 16525 boul Lacroix G5Y 2G2 **Location:** On Rt 173, just n of jct Rt 204 W. Located on busy thoroughfare. **Facility:** 51 units, some kitchens. 3 stories (no elevator), interior/exterior corridors. **Parking:** winter plug-ins. **Guest Services:** valet laundry.

🍴 🍷 📶 FEE 🏃 🖥 / SOME UNITS FEE 🛏 🖨

LA TABLE DU JUNIOR   Phone: 418/227-0888

Regional French
$12-$30
AAA Inspector Notes: An excellent variety of wines complements internationally inspired and creative presentations of calamari, mussels, lobster tails, Atlantic salmon, duck breast, filet mignon, milk-fed veal, Quebec pork and a tapas menu. **Bar:** full bar. **Reservations:** suggested. **Address:** 10735 1ere Ave G5Y 2B8 **Location:** Corner of 107th est rue, just w of jct Rt 173. Ⓛ Ⓓ

MONDO RESTO BAR   Phone: 418/228-4133
Italian
$8-$25
AAA Inspector Notes: The casual restaurant focuses its menu on light meals. Among offerings are delicious wood-oven pizzas, pasta, steaks, salads, stir-fries, scampi, shrimp, chicken supreme and veal. **Bar:** full bar. **Address:** 11615 1ere Ave G5Y 2C7 **Location:** Just w on 118ieme rue from Rt 173; centre; in Gouverneur Hotel St-Georges. **Parking:** street only. Ⓑ Ⓛ Ⓓ

ST-HUBERT   Phone: 418/227-0001

Canadian
$8-$22
AAA Inspector Notes: The pleasantly decorated family-friendly restaurant serves affordable chicken dinners, ribs, club sandwiches, chicken wings, salads, soups and hot chicken sandwiches. The children's menu includes animal nuggets. **Bar:** full bar. **Address:** 16505 boul Lacroix G5Y 2G2 **Location:** On Rt 173, just n of jct Rt 204 W. Ⓛ Ⓓ

ST-GERMAIN-DE-GRANTHAM pop. 3,993

HALTE CHEZ LEMAIRE   Phone: 819/395-5327

Canadian
$6-$10
AAA Inspector Notes: This roadside cafeteria and cheese shop offers a menu of fast foods, including an impressive variety of Quebec's popular comfort food, poutine (fries topped with gravy and curd cheese). Other menu items include burgers, fish 'n' chips and tasty desserts. There is also an excellent selection of high-quality Quebec and imported cheeses for sale. **Bar:** beer & wine. **Address:** 182 boul Industriel J0C 1K0 **Location:** Hwy 20 exit 170, just ne. Ⓑ Ⓛ Ⓓ

ST-HUBERT-DE-RIVERE-DU-LOUP
• Part of Montréal area — see map p. 312

ST-HUBERT   Phone: 450/443-8774
Canadian
$8-$22
AAA Inspector Notes: The pleasantly decorated family-friendly restaurant serves affordable chicken dinners, ribs, club sandwiches, chicken wings, salads, soups and hot chicken sandwiches. The children's menu includes animal nuggets. **Bar:** full bar. **Address:** 5885 boul Cousineau J3Y 7P5 **Location:** Centre. Ⓛ Ⓓ

ST-HYACINTHE (E-8) pop. 51,616
• Hotels p. 461 • Restaurants p. 462

Colonists arrived in St-Hyacinthe in 1757 and began clearing land for crops. Shortly after, a waterfall was discovered on the Yamaska River and a sawmill, a flour mill and a carding mill were built. Today it ranks among the 30 largest cities in the province and its rich soil and bountiful harvests have made the area the agribusiness capital of Québec. This bounty is celebrated the third Friday in July through the last Sunday of the month when more than 175,000 visitors attend the St-Hyacinthe Agriculture and Food Exposition, a celebration held annually since 1837; phone (450) 773-9307. Many other special events are offered throughout the year.

St-Hyacinthe has been the seat of a Roman Catholic diocese since 1852 and therefore has many churches and chapels worth a visit. The St-Hyacinthe Cathedral, 1900 rue Girouard Ouest, was built in 1878 and is noted for its chandeliers. The Our Lady of Fatima Sanctuary (Sanctuaire Notre-Dame de Fatima), 650 rue Girouard Ouest, is an eight-sided chapel. Our Lady of the Rosary Church (Église Notre-Dame-du-Rosaire), 2200 rue Girouard Ouest, is richly decorated.

May through September the domesticated animals and 300 species of perennial plants of Ferme la Rabouillère delight visitors; phone (514) 345-8521. Birds of prey are the subject of presentations given in French late June to early October at the Chouette à Voir—The Owl Sees site in nearby St-Jude; phone (450) 773-8521, ext. 18545.

In nearby St-Pie, Ferme Du Coq à l'Âne offers French narrated tours of a working farm by reservation; phone (450) 772-6512. For a hands-on agricultural experience, there are farms where you can pick your own blueberries, strawberries, tomatoes and apples—or you can always just purchase these fruits from the roadside stands.

St-Hyacinthe Chamber of Commerce and Tourism Bureau: 2090 rue Cherrier, St-Hyacinthe, QC, Canada J2S 8R3. **Phone:** (450) 774-7276 or (800) 849-7276.

Shopping areas: A public market built more than 100 years ago, Le vieux marché de St-Hyacinthe at 1555 rue Des Cascades Ouest dominates the old part of the town and continues to offer foodstuffs; it is open Mon.-Wed. 9-6, Thurs.-Fri. 8:30-9, Sat. 8:30-5 and Sun. 10-5. Galeries St-Hyacinthe, 3200 boul. Laframboise, houses more than 100 stores and restaurants and fast-food establishments.

DANIEL A. SÉGUIN GARDEN (Le Jardin Daniel A. Séguin) is off Hwy. 20 exit 130, then s. on rue Laframboise .4 km (.25 mi.), w. on rue Casavant, then 1 km (.6 mi.) s. on rue Choquette, then .8 km (.5 mi.) w. to 3215 rue Sicotte. Founded by a retired professor and affiliated with a school of agriculture, the 20 gardens and their landscaping and integration in this 4.5-hectare (11.25-acre) site are impressive.

Visitors can stroll through an herb garden, a French garden, a Zen garden, a Japanese garden, a Québec garden of yesteryear and through a rockery and past a waterfall. **Time:** Allow 1 hour, 30 minutes minimum. **Hours:** Daily 10-5, mid-June through Labour Day. **Cost:** $10; $8.50 (ages 65+ Wed.); $5 (students with ID); free (ages 0-5 with adult); $25 (family, two adults and two children). Prices may vary; phone ahead. **Phone:** (450) 778-0372 or (450) 778-6504, ext. 6215. 🎫

HOLIDAY INN EXPRESS & SUITES   **Phone:** 450/251-1111

Hotel
Rates not provided

Address: 1500 rue Johnson est J2S 8W5 **Location:** Hwy 20 exit 133, just sw on boul Casavant est. **Facility:** 94 units. 4 stories, interior corridors. **Parking:** winter plug-ins. **Amenities:** Some: safes. **Pool(s):** heated indoor. **Activities:** exercise room. **Guest Services:** valet and coin laundry. *(See ad this page.)*

▼ See AAA listing this page ▼

Explore the Travel Guides on AAA.com/Travel or CAA.ca/Travel

HOTEL DAUPHIN ST-HYACINTHE Phone: (450)774-4418

Hotel
$95-$139

Address: 1250 rue Johnson ouest J2S 7K7 **Location:** Hwy 20 exit 130S, 0.3 mi (0.5 km) s on boul Laframboise, then e on rue Gauvin. Next to convention centre. **Facility:** 98 units, some efficiencies and kitchens. 2-3 stories, interior corridors. **Parking:** winter plug-ins. **Amenities:** high-speed Internet, safes. **Activities:** exercise room. **Guest Services:** valet and coin laundry.

HOTEL DES SEIGNEURS SAINT-HYACINTHE
Phone: (450)774-3810

Hotel
$120-$240

Address: 1200 rue Johnson J2S 7K7 **Location:** Hwy 20 exit 130S, just e on rue Gauvin from boul Laframboise. **Facility:** 290 units, some efficiencies and kitchens. 2-13 stories, interior corridors. **Parking:** winter plug-ins. **Terms:** cancellation fee imposed. **Amenities:** Fee: video games, high-speed Internet. **Dining:** Restaurant Les Quatre Saisons, see separate listing. **Pool(s):** heated outdoor, heated indoor. **Activities:** sauna, whirlpool, racquetball court, snowmobiling, playground, exercise room, spa. **Guest Services:** valet laundry. **Free Special Amenities:** high-speed Internet and children's activities.

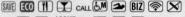

CHEZ CORA Phone: 450/778-2000

Canadian
$6-$13

AAA Inspector Notes: Eggs, omelets, waffles, crepes (sorry, no American-style pancakes here), French toast, fruit platters and all the breakfast meats-- that's the specialty here, all day. However, at lunchtime the menu lists a selection of soups, salads, quiches, sandwiches and a dish called the grilled panini crepe. **Address:** 1310 rue Johnson oust J2S 7E5 **Location:** Hwy 20 exit 130, just se on boul Laframboise, then just ne on rue Gauvin. B L

LE PARVIS DINING ROOM Phone: 450/774-2200

French
$11-$25

AAA Inspector Notes: The stylishly converted basement of an 1878 church is a quaint place in which to enjoy a romantic, intimate dining experience. Seafood pasta, cod fillets in butter-lemon sauce, sweetbreads, New York-cut pepper steak and raspberry duck are representative of menu selections. Dinner theater packages are available in the summer. This place is open only by reservation on Sunday. **Bar:** full bar. **Reservations:** suggested. **Address:** 1295 rue Girouard ouest J2S 2Z2 **Location:** Centre. L D

RESTAURANT LES QUATRE SAISONS
Phone: 450/774-3810

French
$19-$30

AAA Inspector Notes: This casually elegant dining room overlooks the interior atrium, which is lush with foliage. Representative of fine French cuisine are stuffed salmon, guinea fowl, breast of duck, sweetbreads, pork, beef and seafood. A buffet is set up at breakfast and lunch. **Bar:** full bar. **Reservations:** suggested. **Address:** 1200 rue Johnson J2S 7K7 **Location:** Hwy 20 exit 130S, just e on rue Gauvin from boul Laframboise; in Hotel des Seigneurs Saint-Hyacinthe. B L D

TI-PERE RESTAURANT Phone: 450/773-0415

Canadian
$6-$19

AAA Inspector Notes: The simple diner specializes in roasted chicken, spaghetti, sandwiches, chicken wings and salad. For dessert, try sugar or pecan pie. **Bar:** full bar. **Address:** 2995 boul Laframboise J2S 4Z3 **Location:** Hwy 20 exit 130S, 0.5 mi (0.8 km) s. B L D

ST-JEAN-PORT-JOLI (D-6) pop. 3,363

Founded in 1679, St-Jean-Port-Joli is a handicraft center known as the wood carving capital of Québec. It is noted for Bourgault woodcarvings and Leclerc miniature boats as well as for weavings and paintings. Most of the church of St-Jean-Baptiste on Hwy. 132 dates from 1779. The interior, designed by the Baillairgé brothers, remains intact, and a manger scene of 22 figures is displayed.

MUSEUM OF THE EARLY CANADIANS (Musée des Anciens Canadiens), 4 km (2.5 mi.) s. on Hwy. 132 at 332 av. de Gaspé Ouest, displays more than 250 carvings and handicrafts by local artisans, including works by the Bourgault brothers. Among the collection's highlights are a life-size sculpture of Parti Québécois founder René Lévesque and wood reproductions of Norman Rockwell illustrations.

Time: Allow 30 minutes minimum. **Hours:** Daily 8:30 a.m.-9 p.m., July-Aug.; 9-5:30, May-June and Sept.-Oct.; by appointment rest of year. **Cost:** $7; $6 (students with ID and senior citizens); $3 (ages 6-12); $17 (family). **Phone:** (418) 598-3392.

AUBERGE DU FAUBOURG Phone: 418/598-6455

Motel
$80-$275 6/1-10/9
$80-$220 5/1-5/31

Address: 280 ave de Gaspe ouest (Rt 132) G0R 3G0 **Location:** 1.4 mi (2.4 km) w on Rt 132 from jct Rt 204; Hwy 20 exit 414. **Facility:** 75 units, some cottages. 2 stories (no elevator), exterior corridors. **Terms:** open 6/1-10/9 & 5/1-5/31, 10 day cancellation notice-fee imposed. **Dining:** restaurant, see separate listing. **Pool(s):** heated outdoor. **Activities:** whirlpool, spa.

AUBERGE DU FAUBOURG DINING ROOM
Phone: 418/598-6455

Regional French
$12-$41

AAA Inspector Notes: Sunlight pours through many windows to give the riverfront dining room a bright, cheerful feel. The French-influenced menu features many regional products in dishes such as seafood fettuccine, salmon in beurre blanc sauce, duck breast, roasted lamb, beef mignon and a variety of fowl preparations. **Bar:** full bar. **Reservations:** suggested. **Address:** 280 ave de Gaspe ouest (Rt 132) G0R 3G0 **Location:** 1.4 mi (2.4 km) w on Rt 132 from jct Rt 204; Hwy 20 exit 414; in Auberge Du Faubourg. B L D

ST-JEAN-SUR-RICHELIEU (F-7)
pop. 87,492

St-Jean-sur-Richelieu, once a terminus of the first railway in Canada, opened traffic between St-Jean and La Prairie in 1836.

A boulder on rue Champlain beside the Richelieu River marks the site of Fort St-Jean, which played a crucial role in the 1775 American invasion of Canada. Also alongside the Richelieu River, the Chambly Canal was built in the mid-1800s to bypass the river's rapids. No longer a waterway for forest products, the 19-kilometre-long (12-mi.) canal connecting to Chambly now accommodates pleasure craft, and the towpath accommodates bikers and pedestrians. The lock operates daily from May to October.

Specialty items, produce and other items are available at the St-Jean Public Market (Marché public du Vieux St-Jean), held Wednesdays and Saturdays at 182 rue Jacques-Cartier Sud.

Haut-Richelieu Tourism Bureau: 31 rue Frontenac, St-Jean-sur-Richelieu, QC, Canada J3B 7X2. **Phone:** (450) 542-9090 or (888) 781-9999.

MUSEUM OF HAUT-RICHELIEU (Musée du Haut-Richelieu), 182 rue Jacques-Cartier Nord, contains exhibits about regional and military history, the first Canadian railroad in 1836, the opening of the Chambly Canal and locally crafted ceramics. **Time:** Allow 1 hour minimum. **Hours:** Tues.-Sat. 11-5, Sun. 1-5. **Cost:** $5; $4 (ages 65+); $3 (ages 6-12); $12 (family, two adults and two children). **Phone:** (450) 347-0649.

HOLIDAY INN EXPRESS
Phone: (450)359-4466

Hotel
$109-$199

Address: 700 rue Gadbois J3A 1V1 **Location:** Hwy 35 exit 45, e on rue Pierre-Caisse. **Facility:** 98 units. 2 stories, interior corridors. **Parking:** winter plug-ins. **Terms:** cancellation fee imposed. **Pool(s):** heated indoor. **Activities:** whirlpool, exercise room. **Guest Services:** valet and coin laundry.

HOTEL RELAIS GOUVERNEUR
ST-JEAN-SUR-RICHELIEU
Phone: 450/348-7376

Hotel
Rates not provided

Address: 725 boul du Seminaire nord J3B 8H1 **Location:** Hwy 35 exit 43. **Facility:** 111 units. 8 stories, interior corridors. **Parking:** winter plug-ins. **Terms:** check-in 4 pm. **Amenities:** *Some:* honor bars. **Pool(s):** heated indoor. **Guest Services:** valet laundry.

LE SAMUEL
Phone: 450/347-4353

New French
$20-$50

AAA Inspector Notes: This stylish, contemporary dining room lovely views of the river and countryside, especially from the seasonal rooftop terrace. The menu of French and Mediterranean dishes includes lamb loin, veal chops, Angus beef, barbecue guinea hen, scallops, breast of duckling, grilled fresh fish, house-smoked salmon and beef carpaccio. **Bar:** full bar. **Reservations:** suggested. **Address:** 291 rue Richelieu J3B 6Y3 **Location:** Between rue Foch and St-Charles; centre. L D

RESTAURANT L'IMPREVU
Phone: 450/346-2417

French
$10-$37

AAA Inspector Notes: In the city's historic district, this restaurant delivers imaginative dishes, including preparations of filet mignon, mussels, fish, veal liver, salmon, shrimp and pasta. The lively seasonal terrace offers comfortable, sunny seating. Service is attentive. **Bar:** full bar. **Reservations:** suggested. **Address:** 163 rue St-Jacques J3B 2K4 **Location:** Corner of rue Laurier; centre. L D

ST-JEROME   pop. 63,729
- Restaurants p. 464
- Part of Montréal area — see map p. 312

BEST WESTERN PLUS HOTEL ST. JEROME
Phone: (450)438-1155

Hotel
$125-$130

AAA Benefit: Members save up to 20%, plus 10% bonus points with Best Western Rewards®.

Address: 420 rue Mgr-Dubois J7Y 3L8 **Location:** Hwy 15 exit 43E (Centre-ville), just e on de Martigny. **Facility:** 50 units. 2 stories (no elevator), interior corridors. **Parking:** winter plug-ins. **Terms:** check-in 4 pm. **Amenities:** honor bars. **Pool(s):** heated outdoor. **Guest Services:** valet laundry. **Free Special Amenities:** full breakfast and high-speed Internet.

COMFORT INN & SUITES SAINT-JEROME
Phone: (450)438-8000

Hotel
$90-$130

Address: 255-8 de Martigny ouest J7Y 2G4 **Location:** Hwy 15 exit 43E (Centre-ville), just e to Carrefour St-Jerome. **Facility:** 85 units. 3 stories, interior corridors. **Parking:** winter plug-ins. **Terms:** cancellation fee imposed. **Amenities:** high-speed Internet. **Activities:** sauna, whirlpool, exercise room. **Guest Services:** valet laundry.

SUPER 8 ST-JEROME   **Phone:** (450)438-4388

Hotel
$79-$148

Address: 3 boul J. F. Kennedy J7Y 4B4 **Location:** Hwy 15 exit 41 southbound, just n; on west side of autoroute. **Facility:** 81 units. 4 stories, interior corridors. **Parking:** winter plug-ins. **Terms:** cancellation fee imposed. **Amenities:** high-speed Internet. **Pool(s):** heated indoor. **Activities:** whirlpool, waterslide, exercise room. **Guest Services:** coin laundry.

(ECO) CALL (&M) (🅿) (BIZ) (🛜) (✕) (🛈) (🖨) (💻)
/SOME UNITS FEE (🐕)

WHERE TO EAT

SCORES ROTISSERIE   **Phone:** 450/432-2060

Barbecue
$7-$25

AAA Inspector Notes: Those for whom cholesterol isn't a concern should consider a side dish of poutine--a greasily good Quebec specialty of french fries, melted cheese curds and gravy--with their preference among Scores Rotisserie's favorites, which include rotisserie chicken dishes, baby back ribs, sandwiches and preparations from the all-you-can-eat soup and salad bar. Although lemon pie, cakes and brownies beckon for dessert, another Quebec staple, tarte au sucre ("sugar pie"), merits extra consideration. **Bar:** full bar. **Address:** 255 de Martigny, Unite 7 J7Y 2G4 **Location:** Hwy 15 exit 43E (Centre-ville), just e to Carrefour St-Jerome. (L) (D)

ST-JOACHIM-DE-MONTMORENCY (A-2)

CAP TOURMENTE NATIONAL WILDLIFE AREA (Réserve nationale de faune du cap Tourmente), 10 km (6 mi.) n.e. of Beaupré off Hwy. 360, is a major habitat for migrating snow geese on their way from the Arctic to a winter home in the Carolinas. The 2,399 hectares (5,930 acres) of marshy plains along the St. Lawrence accommodate thousands of geese in April and May and from the last week of September to late October.

The changing foliage provides a vivid backdrop for viewing many bird species as well as other wild-life. Twenty kilometres (12 mi.) of nature trails wind through marsh, plain and forest. Nature activities and guided tours are available by reservation; narration in English is offered. **Hours:** Daily 8:30-5, May 1-late Oct.; 8:30-4, early Jan. to mid-Mar.; limited access rest of year. **Cost:** $6; $5 (students with ID); free (ages 0-11). **Phone:** (418) 827-4591.

WINERIES

• **Domaine Royarnois Vineyard** (Vignoble Domaine Royarnois) is off Hwy. 138; just s. on rue Prévost, then 5.2 km (3.3 mi.) s.e. on av. Royale, then follow signs to 146 ch. du Cap Tourmente. **Hours:** Daily 9-5. Closed Jan. 1, Christmas, day after Christmas and Dec. 31. **Phone:** (418) 827-4465.

ST-JOSEPH-DE-LA-RIVE (D-6)

On the St. Lawrence River, St-Joseph-de-la-Rive is the departure point for ferries to Isle-aux-Coudres *(see place listing p. 291).* A popular beach is near the ferry dock. Isle-aux-Coudres can be reached by a ferry that departs daily from 3 rue du Port; phone (418) 438-2743 for schedule and fare information.

The St-Joseph-de-la-Rive Church contains unusual decorations, including a giant seashell baptismal font.

CHARLEVOIX MARITIME MUSEUM (Le Musée Maritime de Charlevoix), in the village center at 305 rue de l'Église, depicts the traditional trading boat of the St. Lawrence River at a shipyard where generations of boatbuilders have worked. A small museum demonstrates the development of the schooner and displays three original boats and a restored carpentry shop.

Time: Allow 30 minutes minimum. **Hours:** Daily 9-5, June 24-Labour Day; Mon.-Fri. 9-4, Sat.-Sun. 11-4, mid-May through June 23 and day after Labour Day-second Mon. in Oct.; Mon.-Fri. 9-4, rest of year. **Cost:** $5; $2 (ages 12-17). **Phone:** (418) 635-1131.

ST. GILLES PAPER FACTORY (Papeterie St-Gilles Économusée), 304 rue Félix-Antoine-Savard, offers tours of its small mill, which uses 17th-century methods to produce acid-free, cotton paper. Comparable to the chiné papers of France, this high-quality paper contains the image of St. Gilles in its watermark. **Hours:** Daily 9-5, May-Oct.; Sat.-Sun. 9-5, rest of year. Phone ahead to confirm schedule. **Cost:** Free. **Phone:** (418) 635-2430 or (866) 635-2430.

ST-LAMBERT (F-7) pop. 21,599, elev. 15m/52'
• Part of Montréal area — see map p. 312

ST. LAWRENCE SEAWAY LOOKOUT (Observatoire extérieur de la Voie Maritime du St-Laurent) is reached via Hwy. 132 exit boul. Laurier, following signs to the e. end of Pont Victoria. An observation tower at St-Lambert Lock is accessible near the visitor parking area. The Seaway is open late March through December. **Hours:** Lookout open daily 6:30 a.m.-10 p.m., late Mar.-late Dec. Phone ahead to verify schedule and accessibility. **Cost:** Free. **Phone:** (450) 672-4115, ext. 2237.

ST-LAURENT (F-7)
• Hotels & Restaurants map & index p. 342
• Part of Montréal area — see map p. 312

(SAVE) **THE MUSEUM OF QUÉBEC MASTERS AND ARTISANS** (Le Musée des maîtres et artisans du Québec) is in an 1867 neo-Gothic church at 615 av. Ste-Croix, on the grounds of the College St-Laurent. Displaying furniture and other objects dating from 1650 to the present, the permanent exhibition, From Masters' Hands, details old crafts honed by centuries of use and carefully transmitted from generation to generation.

Time: Allow 30 minutes minimum. **Hours:** Wed.-Sun. noon-5. **Cost:** $7; $5 (ages 65+); $4 (students with ID); free (ages 0-5 and to all Wed.); $14 (family, two adults and children). **Phone:** (514) 747-7367.

(See map & index p. 342.)

CROWNE PLAZA MONTREAL AIRPORT
Phone: (514)344-1999 42

Hotel
$119-$189

Address: 6600 Cote-de-Liesse H4T 1E3 **Location:** Hwy 520 exit 5 eastbound on south side service road; exit westbound to rue Ness, follow signs for rue Hickmore and Hwy 520 E. **Facility:** 222 units. 9 stories, interior corridors. **Amenities:** video games (fee), high-speed Internet, safes, honor bars. **Pool(s):** heated indoor. **Activities:** saunas, waterslide, exercise room. **Guest Services:** valet laundry, area transportation-train station. **Free Special Amenities: high-speed Internet and airport transportation.**

SAVE ⊁ ⵏ 🍴 Y 🏊 BIZ 🛜 ✕ FEE 🎥 🖥 / SOME UNITS FEE 🛏 🔌 🖨

HILTON GARDEN INN MONTREAL AIRPORT
Phone: (514)788-5120 46

Hotel
$131-$176

AAA Benefit:
Unparalleled hospitality at a special Member rate.

Address: 7880 Cote-de-Liesse H4T 1E7 **Location:** Hwy 520 exit 4 eastbound, on south side service road; exit 4 (Montee de Liesse) westbound. **Facility:** 159 units. 4 stories, interior corridors. **Parking:** on-site (fee). **Terms:** 1-7 night minimum stay, cancellation fee imposed. **Amenities:** video games (fee), high-speed Internet, safes. **Pool(s):** heated indoor. **Activities:** whirlpool, exercise room. **Guest Services:** valet and coin laundry, area transportation-within 4 mi (7 km).

⊁ ⵏ Y 🏊 BIZ 🛜 FEE 🎥 🔌 🖨 🖥

HOLIDAY INN MONTREAL-AIRPORT
Phone: (514)739-3391 41

Hotel
$199-$229 6/1-6/9
$95-$145 6/10-5/31

Address: 6500 Cote-de-Liesse H4T 1E3 **Location:** Hwy 520 exit 5 eastbound on south side service road; exit westbound to rue Ness, follow signs for rue Hickmore and Hwy 520 E. **Facility:** 258 units, some kitchens. 2 stories, interior/exterior corridors. **Parking:** winter plug-ins. **Terms:** 3 day cancellation notice. **Amenities:** high-speed Internet, safes. **Dining:** entertainment. **Pool(s):** heated indoor. **Activities:** saunas, lifeguard on duty, exercise room, spa. Fee: game room. **Guest Services:** valet and coin laundry, area transportation-Dorval train station. **Free Special Amenities:** newspaper and high-speed Internet.

SAVE ⊁ ⵏ 🍴 Y CALL 🗺 🏊 BIZ 🛜 ✕ FEE 🎥 🔌 🖨 🖥 / SOME UNITS FEE 🛏

NOVOTEL MONTREAL AIRPORT
Phone: (514)337-3222 45

Hotel
$129-$329

Address: 2599 boul Alfred-Nobel H4S 2G1 **Location:** Hwy 40 exit 60 (boul Alfred-Nobel); just s of south side service road. **Facility:** 120 units. 5 stories, interior corridors. **Terms:** cancellation fee imposed. **Amenities:** safes. **Pool(s):** heated indoor. **Activities:** whirlpool, exercise room. **Guest Services:** valet laundry. (See ad p. 372.)

SAVE ECO ⊁ ⵏ 🍴 Y 🏊 BIZ 🛜 ✕ FEE 🎥 🔌 🖥 / SOME UNITS 🛏 🖨

PARK INN HOTEL & SUITES MONTREAL AIRPORT
Phone: (514)733-8818 43

Hotel
$89-$249 6/1-10/31
$79-$149 11/1-5/31

Address: 7300 Cote-de-Liesse H4T 1E7 **Location:** Hwy 520 exit 4 eastbound on south side service road; exit 4 (Montee-de-Liesse) westbound. **Facility:** 186 units. 2 stories, interior corridors. **Parking:** winter plug-ins. **Amenities:** video games (fee), high-speed Internet. **Dining:** Ristorante Venezia, see separate listing. **Pool(s):** outdoor. **Activities:** exercise room. **Guest Services:** valet and coin laundry, area transportation-Dorval train station. (See ad p. 387.)

SAVE ⊁ ⵏ 🍴 Y 🏊 BIZ 🛜 FEE 🎥 🖥 / SOME UNITS 🛏 FEE 🔌 FEE 🖨

On-site restaurant, meeting space access and free high-speed Internet.

QUALITY HOTEL DORVAL
Phone: (514)731-7821 44

Hotel
$127-$195

Address: 7700 Cote-de-Liesse H4T 1E7 **Location:** Hwy 520 exit 4 eastbound, on south side service road; exit 4 (Montee-de-Liesse) westbound. **Facility:** 159 units. 4 stories, interior corridors. **Parking:** on-site (fee). **Terms:** cancellation fee imposed. **Amenities:** high-speed Internet. Some: safes. **Pool(s):** heated outdoor. **Activities:** saunas, whirlpools, exercise room. **Guest Services:** valet and coin laundry, area transportation-within 3 mi (5 km).

⊁ ⵏ Y 🏊 BIZ 🛜 FEE 🎥 🔌 🖥 / SOME UNITS FEE 🛏 🖨

WHERE TO EAT

CAGE AUX SPORTS
Phone: 514/332-2243

Canadian
$8-$24

AAA Inspector Notes: This popular Quebec chain of sports bars presents a menu of pub foods, including ribs, chicken, burgers, salads, crispy fries, pasta and tasty desserts. Guests might begin the meal with a basket of freshly popped popcorn as they check out the sports memorabilia. Children are welcomed. **Bar:** full bar. **Address:** 3450 boul De la Cote-Vertu H4R 1P8 **Location:** Hwy 40 exit 65 (boul Cavendish), just w on north side service road, then just n on rue Beaulac. L D

RISTORANTE VENEZIA
Phone: 514/733-8818 79

Italian
$10-$34

AAA Inspector Notes: This popular Italian bistro has a casual ambience with a colorful decor of multicolored wood chairs and floor tiles and a hand-painted wall mural depicting a scene from Venezia. The menu features a wide selection of classic Italian meat, fish and seafood favorites as well as pizza, sandwiches and an array of pasta. A children's menu in offered. **Bar:** full bar. **Address:** 7300 Cote-de-Liesse H4T 1E7 **Location:** Hwy 520 exit 4 eastbound on south side service road; exit 4 (Montee-de-Liesse) westbound; in Park Inn Hotel & Suites Montreal Airport. B L D

Discover mobile travel solutions at AAA.com/mobile and CAA.ca/mobile

ST-LIN-LAURENTIDES (E-4)

St-Lin-Laurentides, originally called the Parish of St-Lin, was founded in 1828. Twenty-seven years later the village elected as its first mayor Carolus Laurier, father of Sir Wilfrid Laurier, Canada's prime minister 1896-1911. In 1883 the village of St-Lin was incorporated, and the name was changed to Ville des Laurentides. Near the Achigan River, it is in a tobacco farming and dairying region. At the heart of the village stands a magnificent Byzantine-style church, many historic ancestral houses and a national historic site.

SIR WILFRID LAURIER NATIONAL HISTORIC SITE (Lieu historique national de Sir-Wilfrid-Laurier) is at the jct. of hwys. 158 and 337 at 945 12th Ave. Born in St-Lin in 1841, Sir Wilfrid Laurier was the first French Canadian to head the federal government (1896-1911). The 1870 house is furnished in period, vividly re-creating the interior of a mid-19th-century rural home. Guided tours offer visitors a look at Sir Wilfrid Laurier's lifestyle when he was a child. Adjoining the house is an interpretation center with displays detailing Laurier's life.

Hours: Daily 9-5, mid-June through Sun. before Labour Day weekend; Wed.-Sun. 9-5, early May to mid-June. **Cost:** $3.90; $3.40 (ages 65+); $1.90 (ages 6-16); $9.80 (family). **Phone:** (450) 439-3702 or (888) 773-8888.

ST-MARC-SUR-RICHELIEU

HOSTELLERIE LES TROIS TILLEULS & SPA GIVENCHY
Phone: (514)856-7787

Hotel
$155-$500

Address: 290 rue Richelieu J0L 2E0 **Location:** Hwy 20 exit 112, 4.4 mi (7 km) n on Rt 223. **Facility:** 41 units. 3 stories (no elevator), interior corridors. **Terms:** check-in 4 pm, cancellation fee imposed. **Amenities:** safes. **Dining:** restaurant, see separate listing. **Pool(s):** heated indoor. **Activities:** saunas, 2 lighted tennis courts, exercise room, spa. **Guest Services:** valet laundry. / SOME UNITS

WHERE TO EAT

RESTAURANT LES TROIS TILLEULS
Phone: 514/856-7787

French
$32-$59

AAA Inspector Notes: On the Richelieu River, this elegant dining room has the sophisticated feel of a relaxed country inn. Highlights include rack of lamb, organic salmon, fresh fish of the day, grilled scallops, Angus rib steak, lobster and beef tenderloin flambeed tableside. Many diners visit to savor the sit-down Sunday brunch menu. **Bar:** full bar. **Reservations:** suggested. **Address:** 290 rue Richelieu J0L 2E0 **Location:** Hwy 20 exit 112, 4.4 mi (7 km) n on Rt 223; in Hostellerie Les Trois Tilleuls & Spa Givenchy.
B L D

ST-OURS (E-8) pop. 1,700

ST-OURS CANAL NATIONAL HISTORIC SITE (Lieu historique national du canal de St-Ours) is on Rte. 133, 2 km (1.2 mi.) s. at 2930 ch. des Patriotes. Visitors may view the operations of a functioning canal lock, used primarily by pleasure craft navigating the Richelieu River.

Boats are raised and lowered in the locks most days between 8:30 a.m. and 8 p.m. from late June to mid-August. The former superintendent's house on this 1849 canal contains an exhibit detailing the development of the Richelieu River Canal System. **Hours:** Canal site daily 10-4:30, mid-June to mid-Aug.; Sat.-Sun. 10-4:30, mid-May to mid-June and mid-Aug. through Labour Day. **Cost:** $2.90; $2.40 (ages 66+); $1.40 (ages 6-16); $7.30 (family). **Phone:** (450) 785-2212 or (888) 773-8888.

ST-PIERRE-DE-VERONNE-A-PIKE-RIVER

AUBERGE-INN LA SUISSE   Phone: (450)244-5870

Country Inn
$95

Address: 119 Rt 133 J0J 1P0 **Location:** 1.4 mi (2.2 km) n from town centre. **Facility:** 4 units. 2 stories (no elevator), interior corridors. **Bath:** shower only. **Parking:** winter plug-ins. **Terms:** 7 day cancellation notice-fee imposed. **Dining:** Restaurant La Suisse, see separate listing. **Free Special Amenities:** expanded continental breakfast and high-speed Internet.

WHERE TO EAT

RESTAURANT LA SUISSE   Phone: 450/244-5870

Swiss
$8-$30

AAA Inspector Notes: The atmosphere is far from hurried in this laid-back restaurant, which occupies a quaint, pleasant inn near Lake Champlain and area wineries. Raclette and fondues are specialties on a menu of Swiss-European cuisine. Eclectic, country-style pieces painted by the owner and her daughter adorn the walls. Fine Swiss chocolate bars and house-prepared jams are sold on the premises. **Bar:** full bar. **Address:** 119 Rt 133 J0J 1P0 **Location:** 1.4 mi (2.2 km) n from town centre; in Auberge-Inn La Suisse. L D

ST-ROCH-DES-AULNAIES (D-6) pop. 939

AULNAIES' MANOR AND MILL (Seigneurie des Aulnaies), 525 de la Seigneurie, dates from a 1656 seigneurial grant. The manor house was designed by Québec architect Charles Baillairgé between 1850 and 1853. The mill, which was built in 1842, continues to produce flour. Also on the wooded property are ornamental, rose and kitchen gardens. Available mid-May to mid-October, guided tours led by costumed guides describe the work of the mill and the social and historical background of the manor.

Hours: Daily 9:30-6, mid-June to mid-Sept.; Sat.-Sun. 10-6, mid-May to mid-June and mid-Sept. to mid-Oct. Phone ahead to confirm schedule. **Cost:** $12.50; $11.50 (ages 65+); $10 (students with ID); free (ages 0-12); $30 (family, two adults and two children). Prices may vary. **Phone:** (418) 354-2800, or (877) 354-2800 in Canada.

ST-SAUVEUR

AUBERGE SOUS L'EDREDON   Phone: (450)227-3131

Bed & Breakfast
$100-$160 6/1-11/1
$90-$150 11/2-5/31

Address: 777 rue Principale J0R 1R2 **Location:** Hwy 15 exit 60, 1.1 mi (1.8 km) w on Rt 364, then 0.8 mi (1.4 km) s. **Facility:** 6 units, some efficiencies. 2 stories (no elevator), interior corridors. **Parking:** winter plug-ins. **Pool(s):** heated outdoor. **Terms:** 7 day cancellation notice.
Activities: whirlpool.

HOTEL & SUITES LES LAURENTIDES   Phone: (450)227-4628

Hotel
$80-$160

Address: 190 chemin de la Gare J0R 1R3 **Location:** Hwy 15 exit 60, then just w of jct Rt 364. **Facility:** 40 units, some efficiencies and kitchens. 3 stories (no elevator), interior corridors. **Terms:** office hours 8 am-midnight, check-in 4 pm, 2 night minimum stay - seasonal and/or weekends, cancellation fee imposed. **Amenities:** high-speed Internet.

HOTEL LE VERSAILLES ST-SAUVEUR
Phone: (450)240-0808

Hotel
$99-$199

Address: 50 rue Principale J0R 1R6 **Location:** Hwy 15 exit 60, n on chemin du Lac-Millette, 2 km (1.3 mi) e on Rt 364 (rue Principale). **Facility:** 52 units. 3 stories, interior corridors. **Terms:** check-in 4 pm, cancellation fee imposed. **Amenities:** high-speed Internet. **Pool(s):** heated indoor. **Activities:** whirlpool, limited exercise equipment. **Guest Services:** valet laundry.

MANOIR SAINT-SAUVEUR   Phone: (450)227-1811

Resort Hotel
$149-$249

Address: 246 chemin du Lac Millette J0R 1R3 **Location:** Hwy 15 exit 60, just w. **Facility:** Quality furnishings enhance standard hotel rooms and condo units, some with wood-burning fireplaces, set in a scenic ski village. 250 units, some kitchens. 3-4 stories, interior corridors. **Terms:** check-in 4 pm, cancellation fee imposed. **Amenities:** high-speed Internet (fee), honor bars. *Some:* video games (fee), safes. **Dining:** 2 restaurants. **Pool(s):** heated outdoor, heated indoor. **Activities:** sauna, whirlpool, steamroom, 2 lighted tennis courts, spa. **Guest Services:** valet laundry, area transportation-ski hill.
(See ad p. 298.)

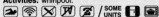

40 NORTHH STEAKHOUSE BAR   Phone: 450/227-6673

Steak
$28-$50

AAA Inspector Notes: Rich wood-beamed ceilings, a stone fireplace, elegant mirrors and an inviting bar area highlight the decor of this upscale village steakhouse. The high-quality menu features Canadian Prime beef that is dry-aged on the premises for three to four weeks, as well as an array of fresh fish and seafood. A butcher shop on the premises sells steaks for take-out. **Bar:** full bar. **Reservations:** suggested. **Address:** 235 rue Principale J0R 1R0 **Location:** Center.

CAGE AUX SPORTS   Phone: 450/227-8787

Canadian
$8-$22

AAA Inspector Notes: This popular Quebec chain of sports bars presents a menu of pub foods, including ribs, chicken, burgers, salads, crispy fries, pasta and tasty desserts. Guests might begin the meal with a basket of freshly popped popcorn as they check out the sports memorabilia. Children are welcomed. **Bar:** full bar. **Address:** 75 ave de la Gare J0R 1R6 **Location:** On Rt 364; centre.

CHEZ CORA   Phone: 450/227-1077

Canadian
$6-$13

AAA Inspector Notes: Eggs, omelets, waffles, crepes (sorry, no American-style pancakes here), French toast, fruit platters and all the breakfast meats--that's the specialty here, all day. However, at lunchtime the menu lists a selection of soups, salads, quiches, sandwiches and a dish called the grilled panini crepe. **Address:** 10 rue Filion J0R 1R0 **Location:** Hwy 15 exit 60; centre.

CRÊPERIE A LA GOURMANDISE BRETONNE
Phone: 450/227-5434

Canadian
$11-$23

AAA Inspector Notes: In the heart of St-Sauveur Village, the family-oriented restaurant specializes in crepes, which diners can fill with a wide array of ingredients, such as creamy bechamel sauce--a melted cheese. Excellent desserts are served in huge portions. Cozy dining areas feature elegant country decor. The terrace opens seasonally. Service is attentive and friendly. **Bar:** full bar. **Address:** 396 rue Principale J0R 1R0 **Location:** Centre.

GIBBYS   Phone: 450/227-2623

Steak
$23-$50

AAA Inspector Notes: Cultivated oysters, lobster and several hearty selections of fresh fish mingle with beef dishes on the traditional menu at this eatery. Several dining areas have cozy fireplaces, subtle lighting and beamed ceilings. **Bar:** full bar. **Reservations:** suggested. **Address:** 414 rue Principale J0R 1R4 **Location:** Jct Rt 364 and chemin Turcotte.

ST-SIMÉON   (C-6) pop. 1,360, elev. 43m/144'

MOUNTAIN ADVENTURE PARK OF THE PALISSADES (Parc d'aventure en Montagne Les Palissades) is 11 km (7 mi.) n.w. on Rte. 170. Visitors can enjoy rock climbing, rappelling and a zipline over a glacier-formed lake at this mountainous site. With more than 15 kilometres (9 mi.) of scenic trails, hiking is another popular activity at the park. A variety of challenging climbing routes are offered. For those with no previous climbing experience, the Via Ferrata courses feature a guided tour and safety harnesses.

Time: Allow 1 hour, 30 minutes minimum. **Hours:** Daily 9-5. **Cost:** $5; $3 (ages 7-17). Rock climbing $55-$95. Zipline $15. Reservations are required for Via Ferrata courses. **Phone:** (418) 638-3833 or (800) 762-4967.

ST-URBAIN   (D-6) pop. 1,448
• Hotels p. 468

GRANDS-JARDINS NATIONAL PARK (Parc national des Grands-Jardins), 20 km (12 mi.) n. via Hwy. 381, conserves 310 square kilometres (120 sq. mi.) of subarctic vegetation—black spruce, lichen and peat bogs known collectively as taiga. This vegetative cloak overlies a landscape of rivers, lakes and mountains that can be seen from the 4.2-kilometre (2.6 mi.) hiking trail that ascends Mont du lac des Cygnes. Backcountry skiing and snowshoeing are popular winter pastimes. Wildlife includes black bears, moose, reintroduced caribou and trout. *See Recreation Chart.*

Pets are not permitted. **Hours:** Thomas-Fortin Visitors Centre open late May to mid-Oct.; otherwise varies. **Cost:** $6; $2.75 (ages 6-17); $12 (family, two adults and children); $8.75 (family, one adult and children). **Phone:** (800) 665-6527.

AUBERGE DU RAVAGE Phone: 418/665-4400

Country Inn
Rates not provided

Address: CP 156 (Parc-des-Grands-Jardins) G0A 4K0 **Location:** Jct Rt 138, 35.3 mi (56.5 km) n on Rt 381, then 9.5 mi (15.2 km) e on rough gravel road. **Facility:** 12 units. 2 stories (no elevator), interior/exterior corridors. *Bath:* shower only. **Parking:** winter plug-ins. **Activities:** sauna, boating, rental canoes, snowmobiling, rental bicycles, hiking trails, exercise room. *Fee:* charter fishing, cross country skiing, massage. **Guest Services:** coin laundry, area transportation (fee).

STE-ADÈLE (E-4)

On the slopes of Mont Chantecler and the shores of lac Ste-Adèle, Ste-Adèle is a writers' and artists' colony and a popular ski resort.

Ste-Adèle Tourism Bureau: 1490 rue St-Joseph, Ste-Adèle, QC, Canada J8B 1G4. **Phone:** (450) 229-3729, or (800) 898-2127 in Québec.

THE WONDERLAND (Au Pays des Merveilles) is off Hwy. 15 exit 72 at 3795 ch. de la Savane. Inspired by fairy tales, the theme park features costumed characters as well as more than 45 activities for children. Included are playgrounds with inflatable structures, slides and a wading pool; a giant maze; eight mechanical rides; and an 18-hole miniature golf course. **Time:** Allow 2 hours minimum. **Hours:** The 2012 schedule is daily 10-6, mid-June to late Aug.; Sat.-Sun. 10-6, late Aug. to mid-Sept. Last admission is at 4. Phone ahead to confirm schedule. **Cost:** $18; free (ages 0-1). **Phone:** (450) 229-3141.

HOTEL L'EAU À LA BOUCHE Phone: (450)229-2991

Country Inn
$185-$330

Address: 3003 boul Ste-Adele J8B 2N6 **Location:** Hwy 15 exit 67, 2.8 mi (4.5 km) n on Rt 117. Located in a quiet area. **Facility:** In a picturesque mountain setting, this country inn features spacious rooms with luxurious bedding and superb mountain and garden views. 21 units. 3 stories (no elevator), interior corridors. **Terms:** check-in 4 pm, 14 day cancellation notice-fee imposed. **Dining:** Restaurant L'Eau à la Bouche, see separate listing. **Pool(s):** heated outdoor. **Activities:** hiking trails, spa. *Fee:* sauna, whirlpool, steamroom. **Guest Services:** valet laundry.

HOTEL MONT-GABRIEL Phone: (450)229-3547

Resort Hotel
$99-$209

Address: 1699 chemin Mont-Gabriel J8B 1A5 **Location:** Hwy 15 exit 64, 1.3 mi (2 km) w. **Facility:** Featuring well-sized guest rooms and cottages, the family resort offers facilities for downhill skiing, golf and tennis. 132 units, some cottages and condominiums. 3 stories (no elevator), interior/exterior corridors. **Terms:** check-in 4 pm, cancellation fee imposed. **Dining:** 2 restaurants. **Pool(s):** heated outdoor, heated indoor. **Activities:** sauna, whirlpools, 6 tennis courts (3 lighted), snowmobiling, ice skating, recreation programs, hiking trails, playground, exercise room, spa. *Fee:* golf-18 holes, downhill & cross country skiing, game room. **Guest Services:** valet laundry. **Free Special Amenities:** newspaper and manager's reception.
(See ad opposite title page.)

CHEZ MILOT Phone: 450/229-2838

French
$12-$39

AAA Inspector Notes: The country-elegant dining room of this eatery offers comfortable, well-spaced tables situated in an informal, cozy atmosphere. A good selection of wines complements such dishes as the specialty mussels-as well as rack of lamb, pasta, veal, steak, chicken and seafood. Waffles, cakes and crème brûlée beckon from the dessert menu. The charming terrace is covered and heated. **Bar:** full bar. **Reservations:** required. **Address:** 958 rue Valiquette J8B 2M3 **Location:** Corner of rue Notre-Dame. L D

NICKELS RESTAURANT Phone: 450/229-9553

Deli
$8-$20

AAA Inspector Notes: This family-friendly deli and bar serves Montreal-style smoked meat, sandwiches, steaks, fish and chips, burgers, salads, pasta and ribs. The dining room is modeled after a vintage '50s-style diner with comfortable vinyl-seat booths and walls adorned with pop memorabilia. The kids' menu offers several affordable smaller portion dishes. **Bar:** full bar. **Address:** 480 boul de Ste-Adele J8B 2N2 **Location:** Hwy 15 exit 67, 0.4 mi (0.6 km) nw on Rt 117. B L D

RESTAURANT LA CLEF DES CHAMPS Phone: 450/229-2857

French
$22-$36

AAA Inspector Notes: The cordial owner of this intimate, family-run restaurant overlooking a lovely Lautentian hillside, often can be found humming as he oversees the dining room. Gourmet, French-inspired cuisine features a noteworthy selection of fish and seafood including grilled or poached salmon, cod Meuniere, Dover sole, mussels, lobster Thermidor, lobster Newberg, scampi, frogs' legs, seafood salad, octopus, clam chowder and lobster bisque. A nightly, three-course tasting menu is offered. **Bar:** full bar. **Reservations:** suggested. **Address:** 875 chemin Pierre-Peladeau J8B 1Z3 **Location:** Hwy 15 exit 69, 0.6 mi (1 km) e. D

RESTAURANT L'EAU À LA BOUCHE Phone: 450/229-2991

French
$39-$48

AAA Inspector Notes: In an elegant country cottage separate from the main inn, this internationally recognized chef puts heart and soul into preparations of French-influenced regional cuisine. Notable dishes include pan-seared scallops, foie gras, giant shrimp, beef filet, roasted rack of lamb, venison and Quebec pork tenderloin. In summer, guests can enjoy a short but memorable walk from the main inn building over a small bridge through well-tended gardens. **Bar:** full bar. **Reservations:** suggested. **Address:** 3003 boul Ste-Adele J8B 2N6 **Location:** Hwy 15 exit 67, 2.8 mi (4.5 km) n on Rt 117; in Hotel L'Eau à la Bouche. D

STE-AGATHE-DES-MONTS (E-4) pop. 9,679

Ste-Agathe-des-Monts is a year-round recreation center. The town's centerpiece is lac des Sables, which creates three municipal beaches: Plage Major, Plage Ste-Lucie and Plage Tessier. In addition to providing the beaches, the lake is popular for a variety of water sports, including swimming, canoeing and sailing.

The surrounding Canadian Shield, covered with trees and laced with nature trails, is ideal for hiking. Bicyclists, fishing enthusiasts and golfers will find plenty to do in the town and its environs. Winter sports include ice-skating, snowmobiling and cross-country skiing.

A nature preserve with hiking trails is about 32 kilometres (20 mi.) north of the lake. Ste-Agathe-des-Monts also boasts a summer stock theater, Le Patriote. Village du Mont-Castor, about 1 kilometres (.6 mi.) north, is a re-creation of a turn-of-the-20th-century village of Québécois influence. The houses are private, but visitors are welcome to drive through and admire this unique community.

Ste-Agathe-des-Monts Tourist Information Bureau: 24 rue St-Paul Est, C.P. 323, Ste-Agathe-des-Monts, QC, Canada J8C 3C6. **Phone:** (819) 326-0457 or (888) 326-0457.

ALOUETTE CRUISES (Croisières Alouette) departs from the main street pier; take Autoroute 15N exit 86 to the n. end of rue Principale and Centre-Ville. The narration on the 50-minute cruises on lac des Sables is in French and/or English. **Hours:** Cruises depart daily at 10:30, 11:30, 1:30, 2:30 and 3:30, June 1-early Oct. (also at 5 and 7:30 p.m., late June to mid-Aug.). **Cost:** $16; $14 (ages 60+); $12 (students with ID); $6 (ages 5-14). Prices may vary; phone ahead. Reservations are recommended. **Phone:** (819) 326-3656 or (866) 326-3656.

SUPER 8 STE-AGATHE   **Phone:** (819)324-8880

Hotel
$83-$144

Address: 500 rue Leonard J8C 0A3 **Location:** Hwy 15 exit 86, just w on Rt 117 to rue Leonard, then 0.3 mi (0.5 km) s. **Facility:** 74 units. 4 stories, interior corridors. **Parking:** winter plug-ins. **Terms:** 2 night minimum stay - weekends, cancellation fee imposed. *Some:* video games. **Pool(s):** heated indoor. **Activities:** whirlpool, waterslide, snowmobiling. **Guest Services:** coin laundry.

[ECO] [icon] [BIZ] [icon] FEE[icon] [icon] [icon] [icon]
/ SOME UNITS FEE[icon]

STE-ANNE-DE-BEAUPRÉ (A-2) pop. 2,803
• Hotels p. 470 • Restaurants p. 470
• Part of Québec area — see map p. 405

On the north shore of the St. Lawrence River, Ste-Anne-de-Beaupré is the site of a shrine that annually attracts more than a million pilgrims and visitors. Soon after the first chapel was built in 1658, those who visited the shrine reported miraculous cures.

ATELIER PARÉ MUSEUM OF WOOD SCULPTURE (Atelier Paré économusée de la sculpture sur bois), 9269 av. Royale, features paintings and wood creations depicting Québec legends. Visitors can watch local artisans at work and take a self-guiding tour of a colorful outdoor sculpture garden. Guided tours are available in French and English. **Time:** Allow 30 minutes minimum. **Hours:** Daily 9-5, May-Sept.; Wed.-Sun. 1-4 or by appointment, rest of year. **Cost:** Free. **Phone:** (418) 827-3992. [icon]

CANYON STE-ANNE is 6 km (4 mi.) e. to 206 Hwy. 138. The Ste-Anne River cuts through narrow chasms and tumbles 74 metres (245 ft.) in a series of falls and whirlpools to the riverbed. A path through the woods leads to a network of trails, bridges and lookouts that follows the river's course. The falls can be crossed at three places by cable suspension bridges. On sunny days rainbows can be seen from the scenic overlooks.

The majesty of the canyon has long been admired. In September 1850 transcendental author and naturalist Henry David Thoreau wrote of the canyon "Take it altogether, it was a most wild and rugged and stupendous chasm, so deep and narrow where a river had worn itself a passage through a mountain of rock, and all around was the comparatively untrodden wilderness." **Time:** Allow 1 hour, 30 minutes minimum. **Hours:** Daily 9-5:45, June 24-Labour Day; 9-5, day after Labour Day-third Sun. in Oct. and May 1-June 23. **Cost:** $11.50; $8.50 (ages 13-17); $5.50 (ages 6-12). **Phone:** (418) 827-4057. [icon] [icon]

CYCLORAMA OF JERUSALEM (Cyclorama de Jérusalem), 8 rue du Sanctuaire, is a cylindrical painting, 14 metres (46 ft.) in height and 110 metres (361 ft.) in circumference. Painted in Munich, Germany, this work depicts events in Jerusalem, on Calvary and in the surrounding countryside at the time of Jesus' crucifixion. The panorama, exhibited since 1895, is viewed from a raised platform in the center of the painting; a bilingual narration is provided. **Hours:** Daily 9-5, mid-May to late Oct. **Cost:** $9; $8 (ages 65+); $5 (ages 6-16). **Phone:** (418) 827-3101.

EDISON PHONOGRAPH MUSEUM (Musée Edison du Phonographe), 9812 rue Royale, offers bilingual guided tours explaining the history of Thomas Alva Edison's invention of the cylinder phonograph. More than 200 of them are exhibited, including some of the rarest. Of particular interest is a display of talking dolls, the second commercial application of phonographic technology. **Hours:** Daily 10-6. **Cost:** $5; $4 (ages 65+ and students with ID); $2.50 (ages 6-12). **Phone:** (418) 827-5957.

STE-ANNE-DE-BEAUPRÉ SHRINE (Sanctuaire Ste-Anne-de-Beaupré), between av. Royale and boul. Ste-Anne (Hwy. 138), was built in 1923. It contains the Miraculous Statue of St. Anne and related relics. The basilica's architecture has neo-Romanesque features. On avenue Royale near the site of the first chapel, is the Memorial Chapel, remodeled in 1878.

Next to the chapel is the Scala Santa, a replica of the 28 steps Jesus ascended to meet Pontius Pilate. Life-size bronze statues depicting the stations of the cross are on the hillside. **Hours:** Basilica daily 7 a.m.-9 p.m., June-Sept.; 7-5, rest of year. **Cost:** Free. **Phone:** (418) 827-3781.

Museum of St. Anne (Musée de Ste-Anne), 9803 boul. Ste-Anne, features interactive exhibits relating to St. Anne, the history of the shrine, and the 350 years of pilgrimage at Ste-Anne-de-Beaupré. Guided tours are available by appointment. **Hours:** Daily 9:30-5, June-Aug.; 9:30-4:30 in May and Sept. 1 to mid-Oct. **Cost:** $3. **Phone:** (418) 827-3781, ext. 2700.

QUALITY SUITES MONT SAINTE-ANNE
Phone: 418/827-1570

Hotel
Rates not provided

Address: 9800 boul Ste-Anne G0A 3C0 **Location:** On Hwy 138. **Facility:** 47 efficiencies. 3 stories, interior corridors. **Parking:** winter plug-ins. **Guest Services:** coin laundry. **Free Special Amenities: full breakfast and high-speed Internet.**

WHERE TO EAT

RESTAURANT LE MARIE BEAUPRE
Phone: 418/827-3446

Canadian
$8-$20

AAA Inspector Notes: Near Ste-Anne-de-Beaupre shrine, the restaurant serves divine family food, including burgers, salads, rib steaks, club sandwiches, roasted chicken, hot chicken sandwiches and chicken pot pie. No meal is complete without dessert, and some winners here include coconut cream pie, sugar pie, apple turnovers and ice cream sundaes. **Bar:** full bar. **Address:** 9749 boul Ste-Anne G0A 3C0 **Location:** On Hwy 138.

B L D

RESTAURANT LE MONTAGNAIS   Phone: 418/827-3681

Canadian
$8-$20

AAA Inspector Notes: This family-friendly restaurant serves up affordable comfort food, including pizza, pasta, chicken, sandwiches and salads. The talented pastry chef prepares a variety of tarts, pies and pastries, including coconut cream pie and mille-feuilles. **Bar:** full bar. **Reservations:** required. **Address:** 9450 boul Ste-Anne G0A 3C0 **Location:** On Hwy 138.

B L D

STE-ANNE-DE-BELLEVUE (F-7) pop. 5,197
- **Hotels & Restaurants map & index p. 342**
- **Part of Montréal area — see map p. 312**

Ste-Anne-de-Bellevue Canal National Historic Site of Canada (Lieu historique national du Canada du Canal-de-Ste-Anne-de-Bellevue), 170 rue Ste-Anne, links lacs St-Louis and des Deux-Montagnes. When the canal opened in 1843 it was a crucial link in the Montréal-Ottawa-Kingston shipping route. Today the canal primarily is used by pleasure craft. From mid-May to mid-October, visitors can take advantage of the site's park area and enjoy watching boat traffic; phone (514) 457-5546.

LE SURCOUF
Phone: 514/457-6699 (119)

French
$15-$38

AAA Inspector Notes: Fine French cuisine is prepared in an elegant and charming vintage home near the shores of the St. Lawrence and adjacent to the John Abbott College campus. The dining room exudes romance, while the menu highlights rack of lamb, red deer, sweetbreads and fresh fish. **Bar:** full bar. **Reservations:** suggested. **Address:** 51 rue Ste-Anne H9X 1L5 **Location:** Centre of village. **Parking:** on-site (fee). L D

STE-ANNE-DES-MONTS (B-8) pop. 6,772

EXPLORAMER, DISCOVERING THE SEA (Exploramer, la mer à découvrir), 1 rue du Quai, offers innovative exhibits dedicated to exploring the wonders of the marine world. An aquarium park with touch-pools introduces species of the St. Lawrence River, while the *Exploramer* offers an ecological sea excursion. Also available is Explore the Underwater Shoreline, a 2-hour guided educational activity held at low tide.

Time: Allow 1 hour, 30 minutes minimum. **Hours:** Daily 9-5, mid-June to mid-Oct. **Cost:** Aquarium park $13.50; $11 (ages 65+ and students with ID); $8.25 (ages 6-17); $32.75 (family, two adults and children). Sea excursion $43; $36 (ages 65+ and students with ID); $25 (ages 6-17); $19 (ages 0-5); $111 (family, two adults and two children ages 0-17; each additional child $15). Explore the Underwater Shoreline $28.75; $23.75 (ages 65+ and students with ID); $17.25 (ages 6-17); $72.75 (family, two adults and two children ages 0-17; each additional child $10.35). Combination tickets are available. **Phone:** (418) 763-2500.

GASPÉSIE NATIONAL PARK (Parc national de la Gaspésie), 40 km (25 mi.) s. on Hwy. 299 on the Gaspé Peninsula, covers 802 square kilometres (310 sq. mi.). Encompassing the Chic-Chocs and McGerrigle mountains, the park is a sanctuary for a variety of animals, including caribou. Focal points include 1,154-metre (3,786-ft.) Mont Albert and 1,268-metre (4,160-ft.) Mont Jacques-Cartier.

The Discovery and Visitors Centre offers nature displays and exhibits detailing the ecology and layout of the park. For additional information contact the park at 1981 route du Parc, Ste-Anne-des-Monts, QC, Canada G4V 2E4. *See Recreation Chart.*

Hours: Discovery and Visitors Centre open daily, June 24 to mid-Oct. and late Dec. to mid-Apr. Hours vary; phone ahead. **Cost:** $6; $2.75 (ages 6-17); $12 (family, two adults and children); $8.75 (family, one adult and children). **Phone:** (866) 727-2427.

GITE DU MONT-ALBERT

Phone: (418)763-2288

Hotel
$158-$348

Address: 2001 Rt du Parc G4V 2E4 **Location:** On Rt 299; in Parc de la Gaspesie. **Facility:** 83 units, some cabins. 3 stories (no elevator), interior/exterior corridors. **Terms:** seasonal, check-in 4 pm, cancellation fee imposed. **Dining:** restaurant, see separate listing. **Pool(s):** heated outdoor. **Activities:** sauna, cross country skiing, hiking trails, playground. *Fee:* fishing, massage. **Guest Services:** coin laundry.

MOTEL BEAURIVAGE

Phone: (418)763-2291

Motel
$65-$160

Address: 245 1ere ave ouest G4V 1E3 **Location:** Just off Rt 132. **Facility:** 49 units, some efficiencies and cottages. 1 story, interior/exterior corridors. **Terms:** seasonal, office hours 7 am-11 pm, 3 day cancellation notice. **Amenities:** safes. **Activities:** playground. *Fee:* miniature golf. **Free Special Amenities:** local telephone calls and high-speed Internet.

RESTAURANT GITE DU MONT-ALBERT

Menu on AAA.com

Phone: 418/763-2288

Canadian
$17-$44

AAA Inspector Notes: The tranquil, forested surroundings set the scene for this romantic dining room overlooking Mont-Albert, a scenic mountain that loses its snow caps for a few weeks each summer. **Bar:** full bar. **Reservations:** suggested, for Sunday brunch. **Address:** 2001 Rt du Parc G4V 2E4 **Location:** On Rt 299; in Gite de la Gaspesie; in Gite du Mont-Albert. B L D

STE-CATHERINE-DE-LA-JACQUES-CARTIER

• Part of Québec area — see map p. 405

AUBERGE-STATION TOURISTIQUE DUCHESNAY

Phone: (418)875-2711

Resort Hotel
$99-$269

Address: 140 Montee de L'Auberge G3N 0J5 **Location:** On Rt 367. **Facility:** Recreational facilities at this vast resort include a heated indoor pool, beach, dock, game room and areas for boating, hiking and varied snow sports. 88 units. 2-3 stories (no elevator), interior/exterior corridors. **Terms:** check-in 4 pm, 2 night minimum stay - seasonal, cancellation fee imposed. **Amenities:** *Some:* high-speed Internet, honor bars. **Dining:** Le Quatre Temps, see separate listing. **Pool(s):** heated indoor. **Activities:** sauna, whirlpool, lifeguard on duty, limited beach access, rental canoes, rental paddleboats, boat dock, cross country skiing, snowmobiling, ice skating, recreation programs, rental bicycles, hiking trails, playground, game room, horseshoes, shuffleboard, volleyball, exercise room, spa. *Fee:* tobogganing. **Guest Services:** coin laundry.

LE QUATRE TEMPS

Phone: 418/875-2711

French
$8-$19

AAA Inspector Notes: The wood-beamed ceiling is as lofty as the forest of trees visible from every window at this upscale resort dining room. The elegant table settings and fine regional French cuisine lend a bit of refinement to a day spent enjoying the abundant outdoor activities. The menu features creatively presented dishes such as fish in an amandine sauce, breast of duck, filet of wapiti and fine soups, including the popular French onion soup. A lighter lunch menu as well as a breakfast buffet are offered. **Bar:** full bar. **Reservations:** suggested. **Address:** 140 Montee de l'Auberge G3N 0J5 **Location:** On Rt 367; in Auberge-Station Touristique Duchesnay. B L D CALL

RESTAURANT NORMANDIN

Phone: 418/875-1014

Canadian
$6-$12

AAA Inspector Notes: The family restaurant prepares affordable comfort foods that include roasted chicken, hot chicken sandwiches, pasta, burgers and fries. Take-out service, a children's menu and cutely decorated desserts are among other offerings. **Bar:** full bar. **Reservations:** required. **Address:** 4756 boul Fossambault G0A 3M0 **Location:** On Hwy 40, 1.9 mi (3 km) w of jct Hwy 540. B L D

STE-CROIX (E-5) pop. 2,390

JOLY-DE LOTBINIÈRE FIELD (Domaine Joly-De Lotbinière) is at 7015 rte. de Pointe Platon. The riverfront estate was once owned by Sir Henri-Gustave Joly de Lotbinière, the fourth premier of Québec (1878-79) who also later served as a federal cabinet minister and as a lieutenant governor of British Columbia. The residence was built in 1851 by his parents who sought out new techniques in landscaping and gardening; today, the results of their efforts can be seen at the lush site that many consider to be one of Canada's finest gardens.

Walking paths, ponds, rare varieties of trees (including towering black oaks), perennials and shrubs blend harmoniously on the impeccably manicured grounds. A visit includes a tour of the family's summer manor and access to more than 2 kilometres (1.2 mi.) of trails. In addition, a variety of cultural activities are offered during the summer, including concerts held Sundays at 11 from late June through Labour Day.

Time: Allow 1 hour, 30 minutes minimum. **Hours:** Grounds daily 10-5, mid-May to mid-Oct. Interpretive center daily 11-5, mid-June through Labour Day; Sat.-Sun. and holidays 11-5, day after Labour Day to mid-Oct.; by appointment mid-May to mid-June. **Cost:** $14; $13 (ages 65+); $8 (students with ID); free (ages 0-6); $33 (family, two adults and two children). **Phone:** (418) 926-2462.

STE-DOROTHEE

- Hotels & Restaurants map & index p. 342
- Part of Montréal area — see map p. 312

DUNNS FAMOUS DELICATESSEN   **Phone:** 450/689-2525   (66)

Deli
$7-$27

AAA Inspector Notes: This suburban delicatessen specializes in Montreal-style smoked meat on rye, grilled steaks, latkes, matzo ball soup, chopped liver and club rolls. For dessert, cheesecake is hard to beat. **Bar:** full bar. **Address:** 2260 Autoroute Chomedey H7X 4G8 **Location:** 0.6 mi (1 km) n of boul Samson, from Hwy 13; in Mega Centre Ste-Dorothee; off west side service road.

LE MITOYEN   **Phone:** 450/689-2977   (67)

French
$24-$37

AAA Inspector Notes: Seasonal and regional produce is emphasized in creative, artfully prepared specialties, including Atlantic salmon, deer, caribou, rack of lamb, ostrich and scallops. The eight-course degustation menu is a celebration of haute cuisine. The elegant country dining room is suitable for relaxed, intimate meals. **Bar:** full bar. **Reservations:** suggested. **Address:** 652 Place Publique H7X 1G1 **Location:** Hwy 15 exit 9, 5.1 mi (8.5 km) w on boul St-Martin, just off Rt 148; adjacent to Place Publique Park. (D)

STE-EULALIE   pop. 894

MOTEL MARIE-DAN   **Phone:** 819/225-4604

Motel
$50-$85

Address: 311 rue des Bouleaux (Rt 161) G0Z 1E0 **Location:** Hwy 20 exit 210, follow signs to Rt 161, then just s. **Facility:** 16 units. 2 stories (no elevator); exterior corridors. **Terms:** cancellation fee imposed. **Pool(s):** outdoor. **Activities:** snowmobiling. **Guest Services:** valet laundry.

STE-FLAVIE   pop. 943

CAPITAINE HOMARD   **Phone:** 418/775-8046

Seafood
$9-$30

AAA Inspector Notes: The casual, seafront restaurant delivers specialties of fresh boiled lobster, seafood bouillabaisse, seafood crepes, fried clams, mussels, surf 'n' turf, lobster club sandwiches and maplewood-smoked salmon. A red tin roof sits atop the white, wood-shingled exterior. The dining room decor is decidedly nautical, with fish nets and fishing apparel strung from the ceiling. After dining, guests may shop for a maritime souvenir in the gift shop or purchase fresh fish and seafood in the fish market. **Bar:** full bar. **Address:** 180 Rt de la Mer G0J 2L0 **Location:** On Rt 132, 1.5 mi (2.5 km) w of village.

STE-JULIE   pop. 29,079

- Part of Montréal area — see map p. 312

RESTAURANT NORMANDIN   **Phone:** 450/922-9221

Canadian
$6-$12

AAA Inspector Notes: The family restaurant prepares affordable comfort foods that include roasted chicken, hot chicken sandwiches, pasta, burgers and fries. Take-out service, a children's menu and cutely decorated desserts are among other offerings. **Bar:** full bar. **Address:** 2001 rue Nobel J3E 1W6 **Location:** Just s of Hwy 20.

(B) (L) (D)

STE-MARGUERITE-DU-LAC-MASSON

BISTRO À CHAMPLAIN
Menu on AAA.com   **Phone:** 450/228-4988

Regional French
$25-$48

AAA Inspector Notes: This restored general store now functions as an upscale traditional Quebec dining room, decorated with magnificent works of modern art by Riopelle and other local and international artists. Complex and eclectic dishes line a menu complemented by an exceptional wine list. Presentations are creative. Tours of the owner's vast wine cellar are offered. **Bar:** full bar. **Reservations:** suggested. **Address:** 75 chemin Masson J0T 1L0 **Location:** Hwy 15 exit 69, 7.8 mi (12.5 km) e on Rt 370. (D)

STE-MARIE   (E-6) pop. 11,584

The first Canadian cardinal, Elzéar Alexandre Cardinal Taschereau, was born in Ste-Marie in the early 1800s. The shrine of Ste-Anne-de-Beauce is next to the 1809 neoclassical Taschereau House (Maison Taschereau), the cardinal's boyhood home on rue Notre-Dame.

J.-A. VACHON HOUSE (Maison J.-A. Vachon) is at 383 av. de la Coopérative. A 1-hour guided tour takes visitors through this historic 1908 wood-frame structure, once the family home of Rose-Anna Giroux and Joseph-Arcade Vachon. The couple founded the bakery company Vachon Inc., now famous for its mass-produced, packaged snack cakes. **Hours:** Daily 9-4, June-Sept.; Mon.-Fri. 9-4, rest of year. **Cost:** $8; $4 (ages 6-17). Cash only. **Phone:** (418) 387-4052, or (866) 387-4052 in Québec.

STE-MARIE CHURCH (Église Ste-Marie), 62 rue Notre-Dame, is an 1856 neo-Gothic structure with a vaulted ceiling and 14 monochrome paintings on glass. **Hours:** Daily 9-4, June-Sept.; Mon.-Fri. 9-4, rest of year. **Phone:** (418) 387-5467.

RESTAURANT NORMANDIN   **Phone:** 418/387-3874

Canadian
$6-$12

AAA Inspector Notes: The family restaurant prepares affordable comfort foods that include roasted chicken, hot chicken sandwiches, pasta, burgers and fries. Take-out service, a children's menu and cutely decorated desserts are among other offerings. **Address:** 525 rue Cameron G6E 1B1 **Location:** Between Hwy 73 and 173.

(B) (L) (D) (LATE)

STE-MARTHE   pop. 1,080

AUBERGE DES GALLANT   **Phone:** (450)459-4241

Country Inn
$140-$250 1/18-5/31
$125-$250 6/1-1/2

Address: 1171 chemin St-Henri J0P 1W0 **Location:** From Hwy 201, 5.3 mi (8.5 km) w. **Facility:** A trout pond takes center stage in the lovely gardens surrounding this contemporary country inn, which offers many rooms with a balcony and fireplace. 24 units. 2 stories (no elevator); interior corridors. **Parking:** winter plug-ins. **Terms:** open 6/1-1/2 & 1/18-5/31, office hours 7 am-11 pm, 2 night minimum stay - seasonal and/or weekends, 7 day cancellation notice. **Amenities:** high-speed Internet. **Dining:** restaurant, see separate listing. **Pool(s):** heated outdoor. **Activities:** sauna, whirlpool, cross country skiing, bicycles, hiking trails, playground, volleyball, exercise room, spa. **Guest Services:** valet laundry.

WHERE TO EAT

AUBERGE DES GALLANT DINING ROOM

Phone: 450/459-4241

Regional French
$25-$55

AAA Inspector Notes: Regional menu selections include fresh fish, seafood, veal and lamb. The dining room has the cozy, quiet ambience of a casual country inn. Guests can enjoy unhurried relaxation and good food during the restaurant's Sunday brunch. **Bar:** full bar. **Reservations:** suggested. **Address:** 1171 chemin St-Henri J0P 1W0 **Location:** From Hwy 201, 5.3 mi (8.5 km) w; in Auberge des Gallant. [B] [L] [D]

STE-URSULE (E-4) pop. 1,419

STE-URSULE FALLS PARK (Parc des Chutes de Ste-Ursule) is at 2575 rang des Chutes. Bordering the Maskinongé River, the rural site offers access to Ste-Ursule Falls, which descend more than 270 metres (886 ft.) through a narrow gorge. A welcome center features interpretative panels describing the impressive cascade and area wildlife. The park also includes hiking paths, a suspension bridge, a campground and rental cabins. Snowshoe rentals are available in winter.

Note: Visitors should wear comfortable walking shoes and use caution when navigating hiking paths. **Time:** Allow 1 hour minimum. **Hours:** Daily 9-5 (also Sat.-Sun. 5-7). **Cost:** $6.25; $4.50 (ages 6-11 and 61+). **Phone:** (819) 228-3555.

SALABERRY-DE-VALLEYFIELD
pop. 26,170

HOTEL PLAZA VALLEYFIELD

Phone: (450)373-1990

Hotel
$109-$139

Address: 40 ave du Centenaire J6S 3L6 **Location:** Corner of rue St-Laurent; centre. **Facility:** 122 units. 9 stories, interior corridors. **Amenities:** video games (fee). **Pool(s):** heated indoor. **Activities:** saunas, whirlpools, steamrooms, exercise room, spa. **Guest Services:** valet and coin laundry.

WHERE TO EAT

ST-HUBERT

Phone: 450/371-9222

Canadian
$8-$22

AAA Inspector Notes: The pleasantly decorated family-friendly restaurant serves affordable chicken dinners, ribs, club sandwiches, chicken wings, salads, soups and hot chicken sandwiches. The children's menu includes animal nuggets. **Bar:** full bar. **Address:** 1370 boul Mgr-Langlois J6S 1E3 **Location:** Just s of Rt 201. [L] [D]

SEPT-ÎLES (A-8) pop. 25,514

Sept-Îles is named for the seven islands that protect the mouth of its almost circular bay. Tucked into the northwest corner of the Gulf of St. Lawrence, the bay has long been a refuge from the storms of the Atlantic and the Gulf of St. Lawrence.

Sept-Îles' location and nearness to the iron mines of northern Québec have made the city a major shipping port. From June to August the Parc du Vieux-Quai features fresh seafood and crafts along a boardwalk.

Sept-Îles Tourism Office: 1401 boul. Laure Ouest, Sept-Îles, QC, Canada G4R 4K1. **Phone:** (418) 962-1238, or (888) 880-1238 in Québec.

THE NORTH SHORE REGIONAL MUSEUM (Musée Régional de la Côte-Nord), 500 boul. Laure, presents a permanent exhibit devoted to the area's history. Also offered are changing displays of works by regional and well-known artists as well as exhibitions about the natural sciences, archeology and ethnology of the North Shore.

Time: Allow 1 hour minimum. **Hours:** Daily 9-5, June 25-Labour Day; Tues.-Fri. 10-noon and 1-5, Sat.-Sun. 1-5, rest of year. Closed Jan. 1-2, Christmas Eve and Christmas. **Cost:** $7; $6 (ages 60+ and students with ID). **Phone:** (418) 968-2070.

COMFORT INN

Phone: (418)968-6005

Hotel
$110-$138

Address: 854 boul Laure G4R 1Y7 **Location:** 2.8 mi (4.5 km) w on Rt 138. **Facility:** 61 units. 2 stories (no elevator), interior corridors. **Parking:** winter plug-ins. **Terms:** cancellation fee imposed. **Guest Services:** valet laundry.

HOTEL GOUVERNEUR SEPT-ILES

Phone: (418)962-7071

Hotel
$109-$169

Address: 666 boul Laure G4R 1X9 **Location:** On Rt 138. **Facility:** 120 units. 4 stories, interior corridors. **Parking:** winter plug-ins. **Amenities:** video games (fee). **Pool(s):** heated outdoor. **Activities:** exercise room. **Guest Services:** valet laundry.

WHERE TO EAT

CAGE AUX SPORTS

Phone: 418/962-2243

Canadian
$8-$22

AAA Inspector Notes: This popular Quebec chain of sports bars presents a menu of pub foods, including ribs, chicken, burgers, salads, crispy fries, pasta and tasty desserts. Guests might begin the meal with a basket of freshly popped popcorn as they check out the sports memorabilia. Children are welcomed. **Bar:** full bar. **Address:** 395 ave Arnaud G4R 3A8 **Location:** Rt 138, just sw on rue Maltais; facing harbor. [L] [D]

CHEZ CORA

Phone: 418/960-0226

Canadian
$6-$13

AAA Inspector Notes: Eggs, omelets, waffles, crepes (sorry, no American-style pancakes here), French toast, fruit platters and all the breakfast meats-- that's the specialty here, all day. However, at lunchtime the menu lists a selection of soups, salads, quiches, sandwiches and a dish called the grilled panini crepe. **Address:** 1006 boul Laure ouest G4R 5P1 **Location:** On Rt 138; centre. [B] [L]

ST-HUBERT

Canadian
$8-$22

Phone: 418/968-9191

AAA Inspector Notes: The pleasantly decorated family-friendly restaurant serves affordable chicken dinners, ribs, club sandwiches, chicken wings, salads, soups and hot chicken sandwiches. The children's menu includes animal nuggets. **Bar:** full bar. **Address:** 1005 boul Laure ouest G4R 4S6 **Location:** On Rt 138. [L] [D]

SHAWINIGAN (E-5) pop. 51,904

CITY OF ENERGY (La Cité de l'énergie), 1000 av. Melville, is a science- and technology-themed center located near Shawinigan Falls, an important source of hydroelectric power. State-of-the-art displays explore the themes of electricity, aluminum smelting, pulp and paper, and electrochemistry as well as these fields' relevance to the city of Shawinigan. Included are The Ages of Energy and Stories from our Lives exhibits and the multimedia presentation "The Spirit of the Earth."

In addition the center offers tours of the hydroelectric power plant Shawinigan-2, a river cruise and a city sightseeing tour. A panoramic view can be enjoyed from a 115-metre (377-ft.) observation tower.

Hours: Daily 10-6, mid-June to late Sept. Phone ahead to confirm schedule. **Cost:** $18; $17 (ages 65+); $16 (students with ID); $11 (ages 6-12); $40 (family, two adults and one child, $6 for each additional child). **Phone:** (819) 536-8516 or (866) 900-2483. [∏]

City of Energy Evening Show is at 1000 av. Melville. Presented in a revolving, heated and canopied amphitheater, the stage performance is a blend of circus skills, humor and suspense. **Note:** The show narration is in French. **Hours:** Performances are given Tues.-Sat. at dusk, early July-late Aug. **Cost:** $54.50; $22 (ages 0-12). **Phone:** (819) 536-8516 or (866) 900-2483.

City of Energy River Cruise, departing from the City of Energy's main building at 1000 av. Melville, travels upstream on the St. Maurice River to the foot of the des Hêtres rapids. During the 75-minute trip, passengers are afforded magnificent views of the city of Shawinigan. **Hours:** Departures require a minimum of 15 people. Cruises are offered late June-Labour Day; departure days and times vary. **Cost:** $12; $30 (family). Reservations are required. **Phone:** (819) 536-8516 or (866) 900-2483.

City of Energy Sightseeing Tour departs the City of Energy's main building at 1000 av. Melville. Narrated 75-minute trips aboard streetcar-style buses introduce visitors to the architecture, urban landscapes and history of the city of Shawinigan. **Note:** The tour narration is presented in French. **Hours:** Departures require a minimum of 15 people. Tours are offered late June-Labour Day; departure days and times vary. **Cost:** $12; $30 (family). Reservations are required. **Phone:** (819) 536-8516 or (866) 900-2483.

Museum of Canada in the World (Musée du Canada dans le Monde) is in Espace Shawinigan at 1882 rue Cascade. The site comprises North America's oldest existing aluminum smeltery, which cast its first aluminum ingot in 1901. **Note:** The complex is closed while it is being converted into an exhibition space dedicated to exploring Canada's role on the global stage. Opening is tentatively scheduled for summer 2012; phone ahead for updates as well as hours and prices. **Phone:** (819) 537-5300 or (866) 900-2483.

The Synergetic Gardens (Jardins de la Synergie) is at 1000 av. Melville. Inspired by English country gardens, the site contains more than 450 varieties of annuals, perennials, shrubs and trees. Thousands of Norway pine and white spruce enhance the site, which is accessible by foot paths. **Hours:** Daily dawn-dusk, in summer (weather permitting). **Cost:** Free. **Phone:** (819) 536-8516 or (866) 900-2483.

AUBERGE ESCAPADE INN

Hotel
Rates not provided

Phone: 819/539-6911

Address: 3383 rue Garnier G9N 6R4 **Location:** Hwy 55 exit 217, 0.3 mi (0.5 km) n on Rt 351. **Facility:** 40 units. 2 stories (no elevator), interior/exterior corridors. **Parking:** winter plug-ins. **Activities:** snowmobiling. **Guest Services:** valet laundry.

AUBERGE GOUVERNEUR & CENTRE DE CONGRÈS SHAWINIGAN

Hotel
Rates not provided

Phone: 819/537-6000

Address: 1100 Promenade-du-St-Maurice G9N 1L8 **Location:** Hwy 55 N exit 211, 2.8 mi (4.4 km) n on Hwy 153, follow signs. **Facility:** 106 units. 2 stories (no elevator), interior corridors. **Terms:** check-in 4 pm. **Amenities:** Some: safes. **Pool(s):** heated indoor. **Activities:** whirlpools, snowmobiling, rental bicycles, spa. Fee: game room. **Guest Services:** valet and coin laundry.

COMFORT INN & SUITES

Hotel
$81-$144

Phone: (819)536-2000

Address: 500 boul du Capitaine G9P 5J6 **Location:** Hwy 55 N exit 211, 2.8 mi (4.4 km) n on Hwy 153, then 1.3 mi (2 km) s on Rt 157. **Facility:** 71 units. 3 stories (no elevator), interior corridors. **Parking:** winter plug-ins. **Terms:** cancellation fee imposed. **Amenities:** high-speed Internet. **Activities:** snowmobiling, exercise room. **Guest Services:** valet and coin laundry.

[WHERE TO EAT]

LE RESTO-PUB 57

Canadian
$8-$30

Phone: 819/536-2657

AAA Inspector Notes: This family restaurant and pub features 1950s memorabilia and a menu of classic American comfort foods, including burgers, ribs, chicken and steaks. Your children will be thrilled if you are able to get a seat at one of the tables installed inside a vintage automobile or rail car. Or you can snap a photograph of yourself next a full-size replica of Marilyn Monroe. **Bar:** full bar. **Reservations:** required. **Address:** 880 Promenade-du-St-Maurice G9N 6V9 **Location:** Hwy 55 N exit 211, 2.8 mi (4.4 km) n on Hwy 153, then just s on Rt 157. **Parking:** street only. [L] [D]

MICRO-BRASSERIE LE TROU DU DIABLE

Phone: 819/537-9151

Quebec
$10-$27

AAA Inspector Notes: A menu of contemporary Quebec cuisine along with an excellent selection of house-brewed beers can be found here at this relaxed pub. Choose from a menu that includes bison steak, red deer, St-Alexis trout, slow-cooked ribs, sausage sandwiches, marinated trout, beef or lamb burgers, house-prepared terrines, Caesar salad and Quebec fine cheese. The bar opens at 3 pm; the kitchen two hours later. A window from the dining area allows you to view the brewing equipment. **Bar:** full bar. **Reservations:** required. **Address:** 412 ave Willow G9N 1X2 **Location:** Hwy 55 N exit 211, 2.8 mi (4.4 km) n on Hwy 153, then just s on Rt 157. **Parking:** street only. [D]

RESTAURANT LA PINATA

Phone: 819/537-7806

Mexican
$10-$23

AAA Inspector Notes: Facing a scenic riverfront park near the convention center, this lively bar and restaurant serves a variety of well-prepared Mexican dishes, including enchiladas, tortillas, Mexican-style chicken, tortilla-pizza, tacos and port-marinated steaks. Ask about the all-you-can-eat fajita nights. The seasonal terrace is a popular summer gathering spot. **Bar:** full bar. **Reservations:** required. **Address:** 902 Promenade du St-Maurice G9N 1L8 **Location:** Hwy 55 N exit 211, 2.8 mi (4.4 km) n on Hwy 153, then just s on Rt 157. **Parking:** street only. [L] [D]

SHERBROOKE (F-9) pop. 147,427
• Hotels p. 476 • Restaurants p. 477

This area was once a hunting and fishing ground of the Abenaki Indians who called it Ktineketole-kwac, which means "Grand Forks." The locale's prime geographic location also was not lost on Gilbert Hyatt, who, in 1801, chose this site at the confluence of the Magog and St. Francis river to build a flour mill and a sawmill. In 1818 the expanding settlement was named Sherbrooke to honor Sir John Coape Sherbrooke, then governor general of Canada.

Sherbrooke is now home to two universities: Bishop's University and the University of Sherbrooke. The latter school has six campuses, three of which are in Sherbrooke.

Stretching through downtown Sherbrooke is the Cité des Rivières, a network of pedestrian walkways connecting businesses, cultural sites and recreational centers. Visitors traversing the Esplanade Frontenac discover merchants and eateries. On rues Alexandre, Bowen, Dufferin, Frontenac and Wellington, passersby gaze at buildings adorned with vibrant murals depicting Sherbrooke's history. Also adding color to the city is a modern sculpture at Place des Moulins by Montréal artist and architect Melvin Charney.

A number of recreational activities are afforded in Sherbrooke, including canoeing, golf and hiking. Surrounding a picturesque lake is the 3.5-kilometre (2-mi.) Promenade du Lac-des-Nations. In summer visitors can walk, skate or bicycle along the path, past fountains and scenic lookout points. In winter an ice-skating rink is on the north end of the lake. Tubing as well as downhill and cross-country skiing also can be enjoyed in the area.

Next to the lake, a restored train station at 720 rue Minto houses the Station Market (Marché de la Gare). On weekends during the summer an outdoor farmers market is added.

Additionally Sherbrooke plays host to a number of annual summer events, including The Lac des Nations Festival (La Fête du Lac des Nations), a spectacular fireworks competition held in July. In August the Traditions of the World Festival (Festival des traditions du monde) offers a variety of activities and live entertainment. Throughout the summer, more than 100 free outdoor concerts are staged across Sherbrooke.

Sherbrooke Tourism Office: 785 rue King Ouest, Sherbrooke, QC, Canada J1H 1R8. **Phone:** (819) 821-1919 or (800) 561-8331.

Eastern Townships Tourism Association: 20 rue Don-Bosco Sud, Sherbrooke, QC, J1L 1W4 Canada. **Phone:** (819) 820-2020.

Shopping areas: Two major malls serving the Sherbrooke area are Carrefour de l'Estrie, 3050 boul. Portland, and Galeries Quatre Saisons, 930 13e av. Nord.

BEAUVOIR SHRINE (Sanctuaire de Beauvoir), Hwy. 10 exit 143 via boul. St-François to 675 Côte de Beauvoir, offers panoramic views from 366 metres (1,201 ft.) above the St. Francis Valley. **Hours:** Daily 8 a.m.-8:30 p.m., early May-late Oct. **Cost:** Donations. **Phone:** (819) 569-2535.

FRONTENAC POWER STATION is at 395 rue Frontenac. The hydroelectric power plant, said to be the province's oldest still in use, houses a museum displaying interactive and interpretive exhibits relating hydroelectric production and the history of electricity in Sherbrooke. Picnicking is permitted on an outdoor terrace overlooking the Magog River Gorge.

The exhibition is offered in French and English. **Tours:** Guided tours are available. **Time:** Allow 1 hour minimum. **Hours:** Mon.-Fri. 9:30-4:30, mid-June to early Sept.; by appointment rest of year. Phone ahead to confirm schedule. **Cost:** $6; $5 (ages 55+ and students with ID); $2 (ages 7-12); $10 (family). Guided tour free. **Phone:** (819) 821-5757 or (819) 821-5406.

HISTORICAL INTERPRETATION CENTRE OF SHERBROOKE (Centre d'interprétation de l'histoire de Sherbrooke) is at 275 rue Dufferin. A former postal office built in 1885 houses the city's archives as well as two exhibition halls featuring interactive historical displays.

Self-guiding iPad or iPod heritage tours are available through the interpretation center. Guided walks around the Magog River Gorge and tours of the Frontenac Power Station (see attraction listing) also can be arranged. **Time:** Allow 1 hour minimum. **Hours:** Mon.-Fri. 9-5, Sat.-Sun. 10-5, late June-early Sept.; Tues.-Fri. 9-noon and 1-5, Sat.-Sun.

1-5, rest of year. **Cost:** $6; $5 (ages 55+ and students with ID); $2 (ages 7-12); $10 (family). Reservations are required for guided tours. **Phone:** (819) 821-5406.

ORFORD EXPRESS TOURIST TRAIN (Train Touristique l'Orford Express) departs from the station at 806 rue Place de la Gare. During the 3.5-hour train ride, passengers learn about the history and culture of the region while enjoying the picturesque countryside that lies between Sherbrooke, Magog's Merry Point and Eastman.

Hours: Departure times vary for sightseeing trips without meals. Train rides with meals depart Wed.-Fri. at 1 and 6:30, Sat. at 10, 2 and 6:30, Sun. at 10 and 2, late June-early Sept.; Wed.-Fri. at 10, 1, 2 and 6:30, Sat. at 10, 2 and 6:30, Sun. at 10 and 2, mid-May to late June. Phone ahead to confirm all schedules. **Cost:** Sightseeing trip only (no meal) $50; $40 (ages 3-12). Prices for train rides with meals start at $69. Reservations are required. **Phone:** (819) 575-8081 or (866) 575-8081.

SHERBROOKE MUSEUM OF FINE ARTS (Le Musée des beaux-arts de Sherbrooke) is at 241 rue Dufferin. The museum highlights the work of artists from the Eastern Townships. Its collection of more than 4,000 pieces includes naïve art, sculpture, photography, contemporary art and works on paper.

Time: Allow 1 hour minimum. **Hours:** Daily 10-5, late June-early Sept.; Tues.-Sun. noon-5, rest of year. Guided tours conducted in French are given Tues. at 2; tours in English are available by appointment. **Cost:** $7.50; $6 (ages 65+); $5 (students with ID); free (ages 0-6); $15 (family). Guided tour free. **Phone:** (819) 821-2115.

SHERBROOKE NATURE AND SCIENCE MUSEUM (Musée de la nature et des sciences de Sherbrooke), 225 rue Frontenac, allows visitors to explore nature and the life sciences through educational exhibits, including Terra Mutantès. An interactive, multisensory show explaining the geological origins of Sherbrooke, the 25-minute presentation combines film footage with computer-driven special effects.

Hours: Daily 10-5, late June-Labour Day; Wed.-Sun. 10-5, rest of year. **Cost:** $7.50; $6.75 (ages 55+ and students with ID); $5 (ages 4-17); $20 (family, two adults and two children). **Phone:** (819) 564-3200 or (877) 434-3200.

THE SHERBROOKE UNIVERSITY CULTURAL CENTRE'S ART GALLERY (Galerie d'Art du Centre Culturel de l'Université) is at 2500 boul. de l'Université, next to the Maurice O'Bready Concert Hall, home of the Sherbrooke Symphony Orchestra (Orchestre symphonique de Sherbrooke). The contemporary art gallery showcases regional, national and international exhibits by professional multimedia artists.

Hours: Daily 1-5, with extended hours some evenings. Closed between exhibitions. Phone ahead to confirm schedule. **Cost:** Free. **Parking:** $4.25-$6.50. **Phone:** (819) 820-1000, ext. 63748. [🍴]

UPLANDS CULTURAL AND HERITAGE CENTRE is at 9 rue Speid. Contemporary artwork, antiques and temporary exhibits are displayed in a historic house surrounded by tranquil gardens. A re-created Victorian parlor, bedroom and bathroom are on the second floor, as is a display of Victorian-era household items.

Time: Allow 45 minutes minimum. **Hours:** Center Tues.-Sun. 10-4:30, June 25-Sept. 2; Wed.-Sun. 1-4:30, early Feb.-June 24 and Sept. 3-late Dec. Afternoon tea is offered Tues.-Sat., in summer; Sat.-Sun., rest of year. Closed major holidays. Phone ahead to confirm schedule. **Cost:** Admission by donation. Afternoon tea prices vary. **Phone:** (819) 564-0409.

COMFORT INN
Hotel
$98-$125
Phone: (819)564-4400
Address: 4295 boul Bourque J1N 1S4 **Location:** Hwy 410 exit 4 W, 0.9 mi (1.5 km) w on Rt 112. **Facility:** 59 units. 2 stories (no elevator), interior/exterior corridors. **Parking:** winter plug-ins. **Terms:** check-in 4 pm, cancellation fee imposed. **Guest Services:** valet laundry.
[ECO] [🍴] [📶] [🖥] / SOME UNITS FEE [🐾] FEE [🔧] FEE [🧳]

DELTA SHERBROOKE HOTEL AND CONFERENCE CENTRE
Hotel
$104-$279
Phone: (819)822-1989
Address: 2685 rue King ouest J1L 1C1 **Location:** Hwy 410 exit 4 W, 0.6 mi (1 km) e on Rt 112. **Facility:** 178 units. 10 stories, interior corridors. **Terms:** cancellation fee imposed. **Amenities:** video games (fee). **Pool(s):** heated indoor. **Activities:** sauna, whirlpool, exercise room, spa. **Guest Services:** valet laundry.
[ECO] [🍴] [🍸] [🛗] [🏊] [BIZ] [📶] [✕] FEE [🔧] [🖥] / SOME UNITS FEE [🐾] [🧳]

GRAND TIMES HOTEL
Boutique Hotel
$175-$185 6/1-12/31
$165-$175 1/1-5/31
Phone: (819)575-2222
Address: 1 rue Belvedere sud J1H 0G8 **Location:** Corner of rue King ouest; downtown. **Facility:** Mixing an industrial look with elegant touches, this stylish downtown lakeside hotel faces Lac des Nations and a scenic bike path. 120 units. 4 stories, interior corridors. **Parking:** winter plug-ins. **Terms:** cancellation fee imposed. **Amenities:** high-speed Internet. Some: safes. **Pool(s):** heated indoor. **Activities:** whirlpool, exercise room. Fee: massage. **Guest Services:** valet and coin laundry.
[🍴] [🍸] [🏊] [BIZ] [📶] [✕] FEE [🔧] / SOME UNITS [🧳] [🧳] [🖥]

HOTEL LE PRESIDENT
Hotel
$100-$150
Phone: (819)563-2941
Address: 3535 rue King ouest J1L 1P8 **Location:** Hwy 410 exit 4 E. **Facility:** 117 units. 3 stories, interior corridors. **Parking:** winter plug-ins. **Terms:** 7 day cancellation notice-fee imposed. **Pool(s):** heated indoor. **Activities:** whirlpool, lifeguard on duty, snowmobiling. **Guest Services:** valet and coin laundry. **Free Special Amenities:** local telephone calls and high-speed Internet.
[SAVE] [🍴] [🏊] [📶] [✕] FEE [🔧] [🧳] [🖥]

QUALITY HOTEL & SUITES SHERBROOKE
Phone: (819)563-4755

Hotel
$96-$134

Address: 4206 rue King ouest J1L 1V5 **Location:** Hwy 410 exit 4W, 0.4 mi (0.6 km) w. **Facility:** 44 units. 3 stories (no elevator), interior/exterior corridors. **Parking:** winter plug-ins. **Terms:** 3 night minimum stay - seasonal, cancellation fee imposed. **Pool(s):** outdoor. **Activities:** spa. **Guest Services:** valet laundry. **Free Special Amenities: local telephone calls and high-speed Internet.**

CHEZ CORA
Phone: 819/823-0781

Canadian
$6-$13

AAA Inspector Notes: Eggs, omelets, waffles, crepes (sorry, no American-style pancakes here), French toast, fruit platters and all the breakfast meats—that's the specialty here, all day. However, at lunchtime the menu lists a selection of soups, salads, quiches, sandwiches and a dish called the grilled panini crepe. **Address:** 3200 rue King ouest J1L 1C9 **Location:** On Rt 112; centre.

DA TONI
Phone: 819/346-8441

Italian
$13-$43

AAA Inspector Notes: This stylish, contemporary dining room features a glassed wine cellar and elegant table settings. The menu includes French and Italian preparations of pasta, seafood and steak. The impressive wine list incorporates selections to suit every budget. **Bar:** full bar. **Reservations:** suggested. **Address:** 15 rue Belvedere nord J1H 4A7 **Location:** Corner rue King ouest; downtown. **Parking:** on-site and valet.

LA TOQUADE
Phone: 819/569-9164

International
$9-$21

AAA Inspector Notes: The lively pub and restaurant serves better-quality bistro and pub foods, including main course salads, pasta, grilled chicken, steak and fries, salmon, thin-crust pizzas, calamari, beef carpaccio, tempura fish, European hot dogs and ribs as well as gourmet lamb, beef or vegetarian burgers. **Bar:** full bar. **Reservations:** required. **Address:** 196 rue Wellington nord J1H 5C6 **Location:** Corner rue Frontenac; facing city hall; downtown. **Parking:** street only.

LE CHOU DE BRUXELLES
Phone: 819/564-1848

Belgian
$15-$27

AAA Inspector Notes: This bring-your-own-wine spot specializes in mussels, including a preparation with garlic and Parmesan and mozzarella cheese. Among other menu highlights is veal sweetbread and kidneys served in cream sauce. Wall sconces provide subtle lighting in the upbeat dining room. Well-timed, attentive service satisfies from start to finish. **Reservations:** suggested, weekends. **Address:** 1461 rue Galt ouest J1H 2A9 **Location:** Rt 112 (rue King ouest), 0.7 mi (1.1 km) s on J Cartier to rue Galt ouest, then 0.3 mi (0.5 km) e.

RESTAURANT NORMANDIN
Phone: 819/822-0555

Canadian
$6-$12

AAA Inspector Notes: The family restaurant prepares affordable comfort foods that include roasted chicken, hot chicken sandwiches, pasta, burgers and fries. Take-out service, a children's menu and cutely decorated desserts are among other offerings. **Address:** 2707 rue King ouest J1L 1C1 **Location:** On Rt 112 (rue King ouest).

ST-HUBERT
Phone: 819/563-5112

Canadian
$8-$22

AAA Inspector Notes: The pleasantly decorated family-friendly restaurant serves affordable chicken dinners, ribs, club sandwiches, chicken wings, salads, soups and hot chicken sandwiches. The children's menu includes animal nuggets. **Bar:** full bar. **Address:** 3070 rue King ouest J1L 1C9 **Location:** Hwy 50 exit rue King ouest.

SCORES ROTISSERIE
Phone: 819/563-4444

Barbecue
$5-$18

AAA Inspector Notes: Those for whom cholesterol isn't a concern should consider a side dish of poutine--a greasily good Quebec specialty of french fries, melted cheese curds and gravy--with their preference among Scores Rotisserie's favorites, which include rotisserie chicken dishes, baby back ribs, sandwiches and preparations from the all-you-can-eat soup and salad bar. Although lemon pie, cakes and brownies beckon for dessert, another Quebec staple, tarte au sucre ("sugar pie"), merits extra consideration. **Bar:** full bar. **Reservations:** suggested. **Address:** 2800 rue King ouest J1L 1Y7 **Location:** On Rt 112 (rue King ouest); corner of rue Burlington.

SEBBY'S PUB & GRILL
Phone: 819/569-9755

Steak
$7-$30

AAA Inspector Notes: Lending to the feel of a vintage steakhouse are a country pub, red-checkered tablecloths and rustic, wood-trimmed walls. The straightforward menu pleases patrons with a selection of AA-AAA grade steaks, barbecue ribs, club sandwiches, chicken, salads and brochettes. **Bar:** full bar. **Reservations:** suggested. **Address:** 83 rue Queen J1M 1J3 **Location:** On Rt 143, just s of jct Rt 108.

SOREL-TRACY pop. 36,786

ST-HUBERT
Phone: 450/742-4574

Canadian
$8-$22

AAA Inspector Notes: The pleasantly decorated family-friendly restaurant serves affordable chicken dinners, ribs, club sandwiches, chicken wings, salads, soups and hot chicken sandwiches. The children's menu includes animal nuggets. **Bar:** full bar. **Address:** 381 boul Fiset J3P 3R4 **Location:** On Rt 132.

STANBRIDGE EAST (F-8) pop. 833

Stanbridge East, in the fertile farming and dairying region of the Eastern Townships (Cantons-de-l'Est), was settled in the early 1800s by British sympathizers, also known as Loyalists, who had fled the United States after the American Revolutionary War.

MISSISQUOI MUSEUM (Musée de Missisquoi), 2 rue River (Hwy. 202), is a rural complex of three buildings. The three-story main building, historic Cornell Mill in Stanbridge East, dates from 1830. It has displays and artifacts relating the history of the United Empire Loyalists, the Fenian Raids and Missisquoi County.

Near the mill is Hodge's General Store, furnished with the inventory of a typical country store from the World War II era. Eight kilometres (5 mi.) from Cornell Mill in the hamlet of Mystic is the 12-sided Walbridge Barn, which contains exhibits that trace the county's agricultural history. **Time:** Allow 1 hour, 30 minutes minimum. **Hours:** Daily 10-5, last Sun. in May-second Sun. in Oct. **Cost:** $10; $8 (senior citizens); $5 (students with ID); $3 (children); free (ages 0-5). **Phone:** (450) 248-3153.

STANSTEAD (F-5) pop. 2,957

In some homes in Stanstead meals prepared in the United States are eaten in Canada because slightly fewer than 60 buildings were constructed before the international boundary was established through the community in 1961. Referred to as "line houses," the structures include houses, factories, a hotel, a cocktail lounge and the historic Haskell Free Library and Opera House.

HASKELL FREE LIBRARY AND OPERA HOUSE (Bibliothèque et la Salle d'Opéra Haskell), 1 Church St., is on the international boundary. The stage is in Canada; half the 400 seats are in the United States. Many performances are staged in the Opera House during the summer. **Hours:** Library open Tues.-Fri. 10-5 (also Thurs. 5-6), Sat. 10-2. Opera House tours Tues.-Fri. 10-4, Sat. 10-1, May-Oct. Closed Jan. 1, day before Easter, Christmas and major holidays. **Cost:** Library free. Opera house tour $5. Performance ticket prices vary; phone ahead. **Phone:** (819) 876-2471, or (802) 873-3022 in the United States.

STOKE (F-9) pop. 2,475

LUNE DE MIEL HONEY HOUSE AND INTERPRETATION CENTRE (Miellerie Lune de Miel et centre d'interprétation) is 8.4 km (5.2 mi.) s.w. on Hwy. 216, then just s.e. to 252 rang 3 Est. Guided tours of this honey farm allow visitors to closely observe bees while learning about how honey is processed. The insects' behavior inside hives also is discussed. During the tour, a large replica of a beehive and an animated film relating the lives of bees may be seen. Bees at work may be watched from the safety of a protected area, and samples of various honeys are offered.

Time: Allow 1 hour, 30 minutes minimum. **Hours:** Tours depart Mon.-Fri. at 10, 11, 1, 2, 3 and 4, June 1 to mid-Oct.; by appointment rest of year. **Cost:** Center $8; $6 (ages 4-16). Guided tour free. **Phone:** (819) 346-2558. 🍴 🎫

STONEHAM-ET-TEWKESBURY (A-1)
elev. 191m/627'
• Part of Québec area — see map p. 405

THE MARSHES OF THE NORTH (Les Marais du Nord) is at 1100 ch. de la Grand-Ligne. Visitors to these marshes at the confluence of three waterways can walk through a natural environment rich in flora and fauna or explore the area on a narrated 90-minute canoe trip.

Narrated canoe trips require reservations and are subject to guide availability; departures require a minimum of eight people. Canoe rentals also are available. **Hours:** Grounds daily 8-5, May-Aug.;

Mon.-Fri. 9-4, Sat.-Sun. 8-5, Sept.-Oct.; Mon.-Fri. 9-4, Sat.-Sun. 9-4:30, rest of year. Closed Jan. 1, Christmas Eve and Christmas. **Cost:** $5; $4 (college students with ID and senior citizens); $3 (ages 6-17). Guided canoe trip $12; $6 (ages 6-17); $4 (ages 0-5). **Phone:** (418) 841-4629.

RECREATIONAL ACTIVITIES
Skiing and Snowboarding
• **Stoneham Mountain Resort** (La station touristique Stoneham) is at 600 ch. du Hibou, Stoneham-et-Tewkesbury, QC, Canada G3C 1T3. **Hours:** Daily 9 a.m.-9:30 p.m., mid-Nov. to early Apr. Other activities are available rest of year. **Phone:** (418) 848-2411 or (800) 463-6888.

TADOUSSAC (C-6) pop. 850

At the confluence of the St. Lawrence and Saguenay rivers, Tadoussac reigned as capital of the territory allotted to Pierre Chauvin for his trade with the Indians. A reconstruction of the Chauvin dwelling contains artifacts recovered from the area. A cross near the village church commemorates the visit of Jacques Cartier in 1535. Dominating the town's horizon is the red-roofed Hôtel Tadoussac, a popular summer resort.

Free ferry service is available between Tadoussac and Baie-Ste-Catherine; phone (418) 235-4395 or (877) 787-7483. Expeditions to watch whales that travel the St. Lawrence to the mouth of the Saguenay to feed from May to October can be arranged in Tadoussac and Les Bergeronnes *(see place listing p. 301)*, 22 kilometres (14 mi.) northeast. It is often very cold in the middle of the St. Lawrence, which is 16 kilometres (10 mi.) wide at this point, so warm clothing and dressing in layers is advisable. Although whales usually are sighted on trips, there is no guarantee they will be.

Some companies make pickups at the north end of the Saguenay at Baie-Ste-Catherine *(see place listing p. 265)* as well as at Tadoussac. Companies providing whale-watching cruises are Croisières AML, (800) 563-4643; Croisières Groupe Dufour, (418) 235-1584 or (800) 463-5250; Croisières 2001 Inc., (418) 235-3333 or (800) 694-5489; and Otis Excursions Inc. (418) 235-4197 or (877) 235-4197.

DUNES INTERPRETATION CENTER (La Maison des Dunes) is 5 km (3 mi.) e. of Hwy. 138 at 750 ch. du Moulin à Baude in Saguenay Fjord National Park *(see attraction listing p. 456)*. The center, in a restored 1922 stone house at the summit of the dunes, provides scenic views of the St. Lawrence and Saguenay rivers.

Exhibits interpret the history of the region and the sand dunes formed by glacial action in the last ice age. **Time:** Allow 30 minutes minimum. **Hours:** Thurs.-Mon. 10-5, mid-June to mid-Oct. **Cost:** $4.87; $11 (family, two adults and children). Prices may vary; phone ahead. **Phone:** (418) 235-4238 or (800) 665-6527.

THE MARINE MAMMAL INTERPRETATION CENTRE (Centre d'interprétation des mammifères marins), 108 de la Cale-Sèche, educates visitors about the world's largest mammal—the whale—through a variety of hands-on exhibits. Visitors can compare a whale's breathing patterns to their own, listen to the singing of the whales and see a model of the world's second-largest whale.

Bilingual guides are available to answer questions. **Time:** Allow 1 hour minimum. **Hours:** Daily 9-8, early June-late Sept.; noon-5, late Sept. to mid-Oct. **Cost:** $9; $6.75 (ages 66+); $4.50 (ages 6-12); $20.50 (family). **Phone:** (418) 235-4701.

THE OLD CHAPEL (Petite Chapelle), on the St. Lawrence riverfront off Hwy. 138, at 169 rue du Bord de l'Eau, is on the site of the oldest Indian mission in Canada. The original Jesuit chapel, built in 1642, was burned in 1665; the present structure dates from 1747. **Hours:** Daily 9-6, mid-June to early Sept. **Cost:** $3; $1 (ages 7-14). **Phone:** (418) 235-4324.

POINTE-NOIRE INTERPRETATION AND OBSER-VATION CENTRE—see Baie-Ste-Catherine p. 265.

 SAGUENAY FJORD NATIONAL PARK— see Rivière-Éternité p. 456.

 SAGUENAY-ST. LAWRENCE MARINE PARK—see Rivière-Éternité p. 456.

DOMAINE DES DUNES   **Phone:** 418/235-4843

▽▽▽▽
Cottage
$136-$170

Address: 585 chemin du Moulin a Baude G0T 2A0 **Location:** 1.6 mi (2.5 km) se of village via rue des Pionniers. **Facility:** 11 cottages. 2 stories (no elevator), interior corridors. **Parking:** winter plug-ins. **Terms:** 30 day cancellation notice-fee imposed. **Activities:** snowmobiling, playground, horseshoes, volleyball. *Fee:* bicycles. **Guest Services:** coin laundry.

HOTEL TADOUSSAC   **Phone:** (418)235-4421

▽▽▽▽▽
Classic Historic Hotel
$165-$304

Address: 165 rue Bord de l'Eau G0T 2A0 **Location:** Just off rue des Pionniers; centre. **Facility:** With upscale guest rooms, this landmark red-roofed hotel built in 1942 is located in the heart of a village famous for summer whale-watching tours. 149 units. 3 stories, interior corridors. **Terms:** open 6/1-10/8 & 5/11-5/31, check-in 4 pm, cancellation fee imposed. **Dining:** 2 restaurants, also, Restaurant William, see separate listing. **Pool(s):** heated outdoor. **Activities:** lifeguard on duty, tennis court, shuffleboard, spa. **Guest Services:** valet laundry, area transportation-cruise boats & golf. **Free Special Amenities:** high-speed Internet and children's activities.

 WHERE TO EAT

CAFÉ BOHEME   **Phone:** 418/235-1180

▽▽▽ ▽▽▽
Coffee/Tea
$8-$20

AAA Inspector Notes: This laid-back restaurant-cafe serves delicious soups, salads, pasta, fish, panini sandwiches, French-style pastries and only fair-trade coffees and chocolate bars. The upstairs book-exchange library, Internet cafe and book store offers the perfect retreat. The seasonal terrace is a popular place to gather and soak up the village charm. **Bar:** beer & wine. **Address:** 239 rue des Pionniers G0T 2A0 **Location:** Centre. **Parking:** street only. [B] [L] [D] [XC]

RESTAURANT WILLIAM   **Phone:** 418/235-4421

▽▽▽▽
French
$29-$42

AAA Inspector Notes: This small and intimate atrium dining room provides a fine dining option at this family-friendly hotel. The multi-course tasting menu is an excellent way to sample the fine regional cuisine, including sweetbreads, pan-seared foie gras, deer, breast of duck, scallops, lobster, crab and fresh fish. Service is proficient. **Bar:** full bar. **Reservations:** suggested. **Address:** 165 rue Bord de l'Eau G0T 2A0 **Location:** Just off rue des Pionniers; centre; in Hotel Tadoussac. [D]

TERREBONNE (E-7) pop. 43,149
• **Hotels & Restaurants map & index p. 342**
• **Part of Montréal area — see map p. 312**

ÎLE DES MOULINS (Mill Island) is in the Mille Îles River off Hwy. 25N exit 22E, then 2 km (1.6 mi.) following signs. An 1803 bakery, a 1725 wood mill, a 1721 flour mill, an 1850 office and a carding mill built about 1850 grace the island, which is a popular recreation center. Various walking tours, including a 60-minute guided tour recounting the development of the site, are available. Concerts, interactive historical presentations, exhibits and a pontoon boat tour also are offered.

Tour narration in English is available by reservation. **Hours:** Island accessible daily 7 a.m.-11 p.m. Interpretation center open daily 1-9, June 24-Labour Day. Guided site tours are given Wed.-Sun., late June-early Sept. Pontoon boat tours depart every 30 minutes Wed.-Sun. 1-9, late June-late Aug.

Cost: One exhibit $3; free (ages 0-10). All exhibits $5; free (ages 0-10). Guided site tours $3-$10; free (ages 0-10). Pontoon boat tour $5; free (ages 0-5). A combination ticket is available. **Phone:** (450) 471-0619.

SUPER 8 HOTEL LACHENAIE TERREBONNE
    Phone: (450)582-8288   **12**

▽▽▽▽
Hotel
$105-$162

Address: 1155 ave Yves-Blais J6V 0A9 **Location:** Hwy 640 exit 50, just s on Montee des Pionniers, then just e; in Lachenaie sector. **Facility:** 81 units. 4 stories, interior corridors. **Parking:** winter plug-ins. **Terms:** cancellation fee imposed. **Amenities:** high-speed Internet. *Some:* video games. **Pool(s):** heated indoor. **Activities:** whirlpool, waterslide, exercise room. **Guest Services:** coin laundry.

THETFORD MINES (E-5) pop. 16,628
• **Hotels p. 480** • **Restaurants p. 480**

SAVE **THETFORD MINES MINING AND MINERAL-OGICAL MUSEUM** (Musée Minéralogique et Minier de Thetford Mines), 711 boul. Frontenac Ouest, focuses on asbestos, mineralogy, geology and mining history. Collections include more than 15,000 mineral specimens from around the world, including one 3.8 billion years old. Five different exhibitions are presented each year.

A 2-hour guided tour of an asbestos mine departs the museum; narration in English is offered. **Hours:** Daily 9:30-6, mid-June to early Aug.; Mon.-Fri. 9:30-4:30, Sat.-Sun. 1-5, rest of year. Phone ahead to confirm schedule. **Cost:** Museum $9; $8 (senior citizens); $4.50 (students with ID); free (ages 0-6). Combination ticket (includes museum and mine tour) $21; $12.50 (ages 7-17). Prices may vary. **Phone:** (418) 335-2123.

COMFORT INN **Phone:** (418)338-0171

Hotel
$126-$132

Address: 123 boul Frontenac ouest G6G 7S7 **Location:** On Rt 112. **Facility:** 62 units. 2 stories, interior corridors. **Parking:** winter plug-ins. **Terms:** cancellation fee imposed.

Guest Services: valet laundry.

[ECO] [⬆️] [👪] [BIZ] [🛜] [▢]
/SOME UNITS [🐾] FEE [] FEE [📶]

WHERE TO EAT

LA PIZZERIA DU BOULEVARD **Phone:** 418/335-7531

Canadian
$8-$25

AAA Inspector Notes: The family-friendly diner serves hearty food, including pizza, pasta, hamburgers and fries. For dessert, try a slice of coconut cream pie. Breakfast is served daily. Delivery is available.

Bar: full bar. **Address:** 83 boul Frontenac est G6G 1N3 **Location:** On Rt 112; centre. [B] [L] [D]

ST-HUBERT **Phone:** 418/335-7557

Canadian
$8-$22

AAA Inspector Notes: The pleasantly decorated family-friendly restaurant serves affordable chicken dinners, ribs, club sandwiches, chicken wings, salads, soups and hot chicken sandwiches. The children's menu includes animal nuggets. **Bar:** full bar. **Address:** 203 boul Frontenac ouest G6G 6K2 **Location:** On Rt 112. [L] [D]

TROIS-PISTOLES (C-7) pop. 3,500, elev. 152m/501'

PARK OF THE BASQUE ADVENTURE IN AMERICA (Parc de l'aventure basque en Amérique) is at 66 rue du Parc. The riverfront museum describes the history of nearby Île-aux-Basques, frequented by Basque explorers and whalers in the 16th century. Originally from France and Spain, the fishermen set up seasonal camps along the St. Lawrence River. Interactive exhibits chart the movement of the fishermen and also detail archeological discoveries and early Basque settlements.

Guided tours in English are available by appointment. Interpretive displays are in French; however, an English translation is available. **Time:** Allow 1 hour minimum. **Hours:** Daily 10-6, mid-June to mid-Sept.; by appointment rest of year. Phone ahead to confirm schedule. **Cost:** $6; $4 (students with ID); $5 (senior citizens); $12 (family, two adults and two children). **Phone:** (418) 851-1556 or (877) 851-1556. [🍴] [🏕️]

TROIS-RIVIÈRES (E-5) pop. 126,323
• Hotels p. 482 • Restaurants p. 482

Founded in 1634, Trois-Rivières is the second oldest French city in the province. As a frontier post, it served as a sentinel protecting Québec City from the Iroquois and as a center for trade with the enemies of the Iroquois, the Algonquins, who brought

furs down the St. Maurice River from the Great Lakes region.

Trois-Rivières also was a departure point for a number of legendary explorers, or voyageurs: Pierre Gaultier de Varennes was one of the first to see the Rocky Mountains; Pierre Esprit Radisson and Médard Chouart Des Groseilliers traveled to Lake Superior and Hudson Bay; and Father Jacques Marquette explored the Mississippi River and the Midwest.

Trois-Rivières' early importance stemmed from its location. At the junction of the St. Lawrence and the three channels—hence its name—of the St. Maurice River, and halfway between Montréal and Québec, the settlement became a major crossroads for New France in the 1700s. Location continues to play a vital role, ensuring the city's status as one of the world's largest paper-manufacturing centers.

Harbourfront Park (Parc portuaire) is a riverfront park on the site of the old port. The Laviolette Bridge (pont Laviolette) is one of Canada's longest at 3,490 metres (11,450 ft.) and the only bridge between Québec and Montréal to span the St. Lawrence River.

Trois-Rivières' old section, the rue des Ursulines and its adjoining side streets, is characterized by 18th-century-style structures. Describing key events in Trois-Rivières' history, guided walking tours of the city are offered Saturdays and Sundays in summer. The 90-minute tour departs from the tourist information office; phone (819) 375-1122 for more information.

Trois-Rivières Tourist Information Bureau: 1457 rue Notre-Dame Centre, Trois-Rivières, QC, Canada G9A 4X4. **Phone:** (819) 375-1122 or (800) 313-1123.

Shopping areas: Two major shopping malls serve the Trois-Rivières area: Le Centre Commercial Les Rivières, with 117 stores at 4125 boul. des Forges, and Le Carrefour, with 123 stores at 4520 boul. des Récollets. Les Galeries du Cap, on Hwy. 40 at 300 rue Barkoff, offers some 40 stores.

ART GALLERY OF THE PARK/TONNANCOUR MANOR (Galerie d'art du Parc/Manoir de Tonnancour) is at 864 rue des Ursulines. Built in 1794, the restored building houses a contemporary art gallery. **Time:** Allow 45 minutes minimum. **Hours:** Tues.-Fri. 10-noon and 1:30-5, Sat.-Sun. 1-5. **Cost:** Donations. **Phone:** (819) 374-2355.

BORÉALIS: CENTRE FOR THE HISTORY OF THE PAPER INDUSTRY (Boréalis: Centre d'histoire de l'industrie papetière) is at 200 av. des Draveurs. Interactive exhibits, multimedia displays and manufacturing equipment are housed inside a former Canadian International Paper (CIP) water filtration plant. Available in either English or French, a guided tour explains the history of the local paper production industry and includes a walk through the basement's cavernous water storage vaults. For an additional fee, visitors also can participate in a paper-making workshop.

Note: This is an industrial building, so some areas may have steep stairs or low-hanging pipes. **Time:** Allow 1 hour, 30 minutes minimum. **Hours:** Daily 10-6, June-Oct.; Tues.-Sun. 10-5, rest of year. **Cost:** $9; $6 (ages 6-18); $25 (family). Paper-making workshop additional $4; $10 (family). **Phone:** (819) 372-4633. [⊤][⊼]

BOUCHER DE NIVERVILLE MANOR (Manoir Boucher de Niverville), 168 rue Bonaventure, is one of the oldest preserved examples of New France architecture in the Trois-Riviéres area. The 18th-century stone structure houses a permanent historical exhibition, along with temporary cultural displays. Guided tours in either English or French are available by appointment. **Time:** Allow 1 hour minimum. **Hours:** Daily 10-6, in summer; Mon.-Fri. 10-5, Sat.-Sun. noon-5, rest of year. Closed Christmas Eve-Jan. 4. **Cost:** Free. **Phone:** (819) 372-4531.

THE FLAMBEAU is in Place Pierre Boucher. This shaft of granite commemorates the city's tercentenary in 1934. Financed by the contributions of local schoolchildren, it is dedicated to those who contributed to the city's growth.

FORGES OF ST. MAURICE NATIONAL HISTORIC SITE OF CANADA (Lieu historique national du Canada des Forges-du-St-Maurice), 13 km (8 mi.) n. at 10000 boul. des Forges, is the 50-hectare (124-acre) site of Canada's first industrial community. From 1730 to 1883 the industrial village of Trois-Rivières influenced the economic, political and social climate of Canada. The forge mainly produced iron bars for shipbuilding, stoves, pots and pans, kettles, wagon wheels, axes and ammunition.

The two main interpretation centers, the Ironmaster's House and the Blast Furnace present the story of cast-iron making, charcoal making and the processes of treating such raw materials as iron ore. A multimedia show and various interpretative activities also are offered.

Tour narration in English is offered. **Time:** Allow 2 hours minimum. **Hours:** Daily 9:30-5:30, July 11-Sept. 5; Wed.-Sun. 9:30-5:30, mid-May through July 10; Wed.-Sun. 9:30-4:30, Sept. 6-Oct. 10. **Cost:** $3.90; $3.40 (ages 66+); $1.90 (ages 6-16); $9.80 (family). **Phone:** (819) 378-5116 or (888) 773-8888. [⊼]

PIERRE BOUCHER MUSEUM (Musée Pierre Boucher) is at 858 rue Laviolette. This living-heritage museum exhibits regional art and presents changing displays of artifacts and furnishings. **Hours:** Tues.-Sun. 1:30-4:30. **Cost:** Free. **Phone:** (819) 376-4459.

[SAVE] **QUÉBEC MUSEUM OF FOLK CULTURE** (Musée québécois de culture populaire) is at 200 rue Laviolette. This facility offers visitors a chance to explore six exhibit rooms detailing Québec's society and folk art. At the historic Trois-Rivières Old Prison, guides explain prison life in the interactive Go to Jail! exhibit.

Tour narration in English is offered. **Time:** Allow 1 hour, 30 minutes minimum. **Hours:** Daily 10-6, June 24-Labour Day; Tues.-Sun. 10-5, rest of year. Closed Jan. 1-2, Christmas Eve, Christmas, day after Christmas and Dec. 31. **Cost:** Museum $10; $9 (senior citizens); $8 (students with ID); $6 (ages 5-17); $25 (family, two adults and two children). Separate individual admission to the prison is available. Prices may vary; phone ahead. **Phone:** (819) 372-0406.

SEIGNEURIAL MILL OF POINTE-DU-LAC (Moulin seigneurial de Pointe-du-Lac) is at 11930 rue Notre-Dame Ouest. Guides recount the history and mechanics of this river-powered flour mill built on a seigneury during the 18th century. A saw mill, added to the site around 1945, also is operational. Exhibits and a scenic walking trail are offered. **Time:** Allow 1 hour minimum. **Hours:** Daily 10-5, late May-late Sept. **Cost:** $3.50; $2.50 (ages 8-17 and 65+). **Phone:** (819) 377-1396 or (877) 377-1396. [⊼]

SHRINE OF NOTRE-DAME-DU-CAP (Sanctuaire Notre-Dame-du-Cap) is at 626 rue Notre-Dame Est. Each year thousands of believers make their pilgrimages to Canada's national shrine to the Virgin Mary. The 1659 wooden chapel was replaced by a stone building inaugurated in 1720. The Basilica of Notre-Dame-du-Cap, inaugurated in 1964, is a modernistic octagonal structure that seats 1,660.

The Madonna of Notre-Dame-du-Cap within the chapel has been considered miraculous since 1888, when her eyes allegedly became momentarily animated. **Hours:** Daily 8 a.m.-9 p.m., May-Oct.; 9-5, rest of year. **Cost:** Free. **Phone:** (819) 374-2441.

TROIS-RIVIÈRES CATHEDRAL (Cathédrale de Trois-Rivières) is at 362 rue Bonaventure. This beautiful example of Westminster Gothic architecture was begun in 1858. The stained-glass windows by Guido Nincheri are some of the finest in North America. **Hours:** Mon.-Fri. 9-11:30 and 1:30-5:30, Sat. 9-11 and 1:30-5:15, Sun. 9:30-11:45. **Cost:** Free. **Phone:** (819) 374-2409.

URSULINE MONASTERY (Monastère des Ursulines), 734 rue des Ursulines near St. James' Anglican Church, dates from 1697 and houses a museum and an art collection. The architecture is typical of convents in Normandy, France. A sundial dating from 1860 is on the exterior wall of the monastery.

Ursuline Museum (Musée des Ursulines), 734 rue des Ursulines, has a large collection of textiles, books, silverware and decorative arts collected by the Ursuline nuns of Trois-Rivières since the late

17th century. Across the street, Ursulines Gardens (Jardin des Ursulines) provides scenic views of the St. Lawrence River.

Guided chapel tours are available; narration in English is offered. **Hours:** Daily 10-5, late June-early Sept.; Tues.-Sun. 10-5, May 1-late June and early Sept.-Oct. 31; Wed.-Sun. 1-5, Nov.-Feb.; by appointment rest of year. **Cost:** $4; $3 (ages 65+ and students with ID). **Phone:** (819) 375-7922.

GAMBLING ESTABLISHMENTS

• **Salon de jeux de Trois-Rivières** is at 1900 rue de l'Hippodrome. **Hours:** Daily 10 a.m.-3 a.m. **Phone:** (819) 693-4774.

COMFORT INN
Phone: (819)371-3566

Hotel
$101-$121

Address: 6255 rue Corbeil G8Z 4P9 **Location:** Hwy 55 exit 183 (boul Jean XXIII); 1.3 mi (2 km) n of Laviolette Bridge, then 0.3 mi (0.5 km) e. **Facility:** 80 units. 2 stories (no elevator), interior corridors. **Parking:** winter plug-ins. **Terms:** cancellation fee imposed. **Amenities:** high-speed Internet. **Guest Services:** valet laundry.

 / SOME UNITS FEE

DAYS INN
Phone: (819)377-4444

Hotel
$80-$135

Address: 3155 boul St-Jean G9B 2M4 **Location:** Hwy 55 exit 183 (boul Jean XXIII), 0.3 mi (0.5 km) w, then 0.3 mi (0.4 km) n. **Facility:** 74 units, some two bedrooms and kitchens. 2 stories (no elevator), interior corridors. **Terms:** check-in 4 pm, cancellation fee imposed. **Amenities:** Some: safes. **Guest Services:** valet and coin laundry. **Free Special Amenities:** continental breakfast and high-speed Internet.

 / SOME UNITS FEE

DELTA TROIS-RIVIERES HOTEL AND CONFERENCE CENTER
Phone: (819)376-1991

Hotel
$114-$275

Address: 1620 rue Notre-Dame Centre G9A 6E5 **Location:** Corner of rue St-Roch; centre. **Facility:** 159 units. 12 stories, interior corridors. **Parking:** on-site (fee). **Terms:** check-in 4 pm, 3 day cancellation notice. **Amenities:** video games (fee), honor bars. **Dining:** Le Troquet, see separate listing. **Pool(s):** heated indoor. **Activities:** sauna, whirlpool, steamroom, exercise room, spa. **Guest Services:** valet laundry.

 / SOME UNITS FEE FEE

HOTEL GOUVERNEUR TROIS-RIVIERES
Phone: (819)379-4550

Hotel
$98-$146

Address: 975 rue Hart G9A 4S3 **Location:** Corner of rue Laviolette; centre. **Facility:** 128 units. 6 stories, interior corridors. **Terms:** check-in 4 pm. **Amenities:** video games (fee), high-speed Internet. **Pool(s):** outdoor. **Activities:** whirlpool, exercise room. **Guest Services:** valet laundry.

 FEE

HOTEL LES SUITES DE LAVIOLETTE
Phone: (819)377-4747

Hotel
$109-$149 6/1-10/31
$99-$139 11/1-5/31

Address: 7201 rue Notre-Dame ouest G9B 1W2 **Location:** Hwy 55 exit 181; at north end of Laviolette Bridge. **Facility:** 104 units, some efficiencies. 2 stories (no elevator), interior/exterior corridors. **Parking:** winter plug-ins. **Terms:** 7 day cancellation notice-fee imposed. **Amenities:** high-speed Internet. Some: safes. **Pool(s):** heated outdoor. **Activities:** lighted tennis court, bicycles. **Guest Services:** valet and coin laundry.

 / SOME UNITS

SUPER 8 TROIS-RIVIERES
Phone: (819)377-5881

Hotel
$82-$163

Address: 3185 boul St-Jean G9B 2M4 **Location:** Hwy 55 exit 183 (boul Jean XXIII), just nw. **Facility:** 78 units. 3 stories, interior corridors. **Parking:** winter plug-ins. **Terms:** cancellation fee imposed. **Amenities:** high-speed Internet. Some: video games. **Pool(s):** heated indoor. **Activities:** whirlpool, waterslide, exercise room. **Guest Services:** valet and coin laundry.

 FEE / SOME UNITS FEE

WHERE TO EAT

AU FOUR A BOIS
Phone: 819/373-3686

Canadian
$10-$28

AAA Inspector Notes: The open dining room has the feel of a warm country home. A cozy fireplace and quaint, covered terrace lend to the informal atmosphere. The menu lays out a wide selection of pizzas prepared in a wood-burning oven, as well as steak, pasta and salad. **Bar:** full bar. **Address:** 329 rue Laviolette G9A 1V1 **Location:** Corner of rue Hart; centre. L D

CASTEL DES PRES RESTAURATION
Phone: 819/375-4921

French
$15-$39

AAA Inspector Notes: Smoked salmon is a flavorful choice on a varied menu that includes mussels, filet mignon, rack of lamb, sweetbreads, steak tartare, pasta, salads, sandwiches and steak with fries. Patrons can choose from seating in the lively bar-area bistro or in the more intimate adjacent dining room. The extensive wine list includes many by-the-glass selections. Terrace tables are popular during the summer. **Bar:** full bar. **Address:** 5800 boul Royal G9A 4P2 **Location:** Hwy 55 exit 181, 0.6 mi (1 km) e on Rt 138. L D

CHEZ CORA
Phone: 819/697-2662

Canadian
$6-$13

AAA Inspector Notes: Eggs, omelets, waffles, crepes (sorry, no American-style pancakes here), French toast, fruit platters and all the breakfast meats--that's the specialty here, all day. However, at lunchtime the menu lists a selection of soups, salads, quiches, sandwiches and a dish called the grilled panini crepe. **Address:** 4 rue des Ormeaux G9A 4J4 **Location:** Hwy 40 exit 202, 0.5 mi (0.8 km) ne. B L

LE TROQUET
Phone: 819/372-5979

Canadian
$9-$37

AAA Inspector Notes: Colorful art and cherry paneling exemplify the bright, contemporary bistro decor. Preparations of Quebec cuisine include varieties of smoked trout, bison, veal and lamb. The dessert table displays a good selection of temptations. **Bar:** full bar. **Reservations:** suggested. **Address:** 1620 rue Notre-Dame Centre G9A 6E5 **Location:** Corner of rue St-Roch; centre; in Delta Trois-Rivieres Hotel and Conference Center. B L D

RESTAURANT LE LUPIN
Phone: 819/370-4740

French
$10-$40

AAA Inspector Notes: In a vintage, two-story Victorian home, this restaurant is a nice spot for casual, comfortable dining. The ever-changing menu centers on traditional French dishes, crepes, mussels, fresh fish, game and fresh pasta. The beautifully presented stuffed crepe is delicious. The service is attentive and friendly. **Address:** 376 rue St-Georges G9A 2K6 **Location:** Corner of rue Champlain; centre. **Parking:** street only. L D

RESTAURANT NORMANDIN

Canadian
$6-$18

For additional information, visit AAA.com

AAA Inspector Notes: The family restaurant prepares affordable comfort foods that include roasted chicken, hot chicken sandwiches, pasta, burgers and fries. Take-out service, a children's menu and cutely decorated desserts are among other offerings. [B] [L] [D]

LOCATIONS:
Address: 1350 boul des Recollets G8Z 4L5 **Location:** Just ne of boul des Forges. **Phone:** 819/691-0507

Address: 580 boul Thibeau G8T 6Z4 **Location:** On Hwy 157. **Bar:** full bar. **Phone:** 819/372-0146

ST-HUBERT

Canadian
$8-$22

Phone: 819/375-7521

AAA Inspector Notes: The pleasantly decorated family-friendly restaurant serves affordable chicken dinners, ribs, club sandwiches, chicken wings, salads, soups and hot chicken sandwiches. The children's menu includes animal nuggets. **Bar:** full bar. **Address:** 5275 boul des Forges G8Y 4Z3 **Location:** Hwy 40 exit boul des Forges. [L] [D]

VAL-DAVID (E-4) pop. 4,216

Val-David is a Laurentian village of artists and artisans. For physical recreation the 22-metre-high (70-ft.) Mont Condor and the 23-metre-high (75-ft.) Condor Needle offer challenging climbs.

Québec Federation for Climbing and Mountaineering: 4545 av. Pierre-de-Coubertin, Succursale M, Montréal, QC, Canada H1V 3R2. **Phone:** (514) 252-3004, or (866) 204-3763 in Québec.

SANTA CLAUS' VILLAGE (Village du Père Noël) is 2 km (1.2 mi.) n. from Autoroute 15 exit 76; take Hwy. 117 n., then e. at the first traffic light to 987 rue Morin. This summer residence of Father Christmas offers 40 recreational facilities such as slides, an electric train, pedal boats, climbing nets and a 10-metre-high (32-ft.) decorated Christmas tree which spouts jets of water onto visitors frolicking in a wading pool. A petting zoo houses goats, pot-bellied pigs, small sheep, lamas and fallow deer.

Time: Allow 2 hours minimum. **Hours:** Daily 10-6, June-Aug.; Sat.-Sun. 10-6, Sept. 1-Labour Day. Winter holiday schedule varies. Phone ahead to confirm schedule. **Cost:** $15; $12.50 (ages 66+); free (ages 0-1). Prices may vary. **Phone:** (819) 322-2146, or (800) 287-6635 in Québec.

ROTISSERIE AU PETIT POUCET

Quebec
$9-$25

Phone: 819/322-2246

AAA Inspector Notes: Maple-smoked ham, baked beans, pigs' knuckles, chicken pot pie, rainbow trout and meat pie are representative of regional Québécois comfort foods. The log cabin is appointed with woodwork and rustic charm. Homemade fruit and sugar pies are tempting desserts-get a sugar pie to go. A supper buffet is available Saturday and Sunday. Meats and preserves are available at a take-out counter. The seasonal terrace brings you closer to the great outdoors. **Bar:** full bar. **Address:** 1030 Rt 117 J0T 2N0 **Location:** Hwy 15 N exit 76; in town centre. [B] [L]

VAL-D'OR (C-2) pop. 22,748

 THE CITY OF GOLD (La Cité de l'Or) is at 90 av. Perreault. Step into the boots of a gold miner and descend 91 metres (298 ft.) underground to visit the Old Lamaque Mine. A guide details extraction methods and miners' duties during the tour, which also includes a screening of the short film "The Miner's Symphony."

Back on the surface, a guided tour of five heritage buildings details the daily operations of the mining complex. Also offered is a self-guiding audio tour of the Bourlamaque Mining Village, featuring 60 log houses.

Note: The temperature in the mine is 8 C (46 F). Warm clothing and closed shoes are recommended. For those unable to visit the mine, a film version of the underground tour is presented on the surface. **Time:** Allow 4 hours minimum. **Hours:** Tours depart daily, late June-Labour Day; by reservation rest of year. Tour schedule varies; phone ahead.

Cost: Underground mine tour only $25.25; $20.25 (ages 60+ and students with ID); $12.25 (ages 6-11); $67.75 (family). Surface exhibits only $18.25; $15.25 (ages 60+ and students with ID); $12.25 (ages 6-11); $48.50 (family). Combination ticket $38; $30.25 (ages 60+ and students with ID); $18.25 (ages 6-11); $101.50 (family). Self-guiding mining village audio tour $7; $5 (ages 60+ and students with ID); $3 (ages 6-11); $18 (family). Prices may vary. Under 6 are not permitted on the underground tour. **Phone:** (819) 825-1274 or (877) 582-5367. [⫯]

COMFORT INN

Hotel
$115-$145

Phone: (819)825-9360

Address: 1665 3ieme Ave J9P 1V9 **Location:** In town centre. **Facility:** 80 units. 2 stories (no elevator), interior corridors. **Parking:** winter plug-ins. **Terms:** cancellation fee imposed.

Guest Services: valet laundry.
[ECO] [⫯] [⧉] [⊡] / SOME UNITS FEE [⛺] [⊟] [⊞]

L'ESCALE HOTEL MOTEL SUITE   **Phone:** 819/824-2711

Hotel
$125-$140

Address: 1100 rue L'Escale J9P 4G8 **Location:** In town centre. **Facility:** 70 units. 2 stories (no elevator), interior/exterior corridors. **Parking:** winter plug-ins. **Amenities:** *Some:* high-speed Internet, honor bars. **Dining:** Restaurant Le Canon, see separate listing. **Activities:** snowmobiling. **Guest Services:** valet laundry.

[⫯] [⌾] [⧉] [✕] FEE [⛺] [⊟] [⊞] [⊡] / SOME UNITS [⛺]

QUALITY INN & SUITES VAL-D'OR

Hotel
$103-$131

Phone: (819)874-8888

Address: 1111 rue de l'Escale J9P 4G8 **Location:** Corner of 3ieme ave; centre. **Facility:** 82 units, some two bedrooms. 3 stories, interior corridors. **Parking:** winter plug-ins. **Terms:** cancellation fee imposed. **Amenities:** high-speed Internet. **Activities:** exercise room. **Guest Services:** valet and coin laundry.

[⫯] [BIZ] [⧉] [✕] FEE [⛺] [⊟] [⊞] [⊡]

RESTAURANT LE CANON
Phone: 819/824-2711

Continental
$11-$40

AAA Inspector Notes: This cozy hotel restaurant has elegant country decor and is one of the best places in town for steak and seafood. Menu selections include St-Mathieu trout, beef brochettes, filet mignon, scallops, shrimp, rack of lamb, roast beef, Chinese fondue, walleye fillet, seafood linguine, grilled lobster tails, scampi, escargot and smoked salmon. For dessert, cheesecake or creme caramel are two tasty choices. **Bar:** full bar. **Reservations:** suggested. **Address:** 1100 rue L'Escale J9P 4G8 **Location:** In town centre; in L'Escale Hotel Motel Suite. [B] [L] [D]

RESTAURANT PIZZERIA VAL-D'OR
Phone: 819/825-7111

Canadian
$7-$14

AAA Inspector Notes: This popular family restaurant specializes in pizza, pasta, burgers, fries, poutine(a Québécois favorite of warm french fries, topped with fresh cheese curds and smothered with gravy), barbecue chicken and fish and chips. **Bar:** full bar. **Address:** 1272 3ieme ave J9P 1V4 **Location:** On Rt 117; centre. [L] [D]

VALLEE-JONCTION pop. 1,868

RESTAURANT FEUILLE D'ERABLE
Phone: 418/253-6133

Canadian
$9-$27

AAA Inspector Notes: A large, stained-glass maple leaf adorns the wall of the casual family-friendly eatery, which has a second, more upscale dining room where French cuisine is served. Among wholesome meals are hamburger steak with mashed potatoes, club sandwiches, chicken, steaks, seafood pasta, fish, pizza and poutine. Take-out service and a salad bar are available. **Bar:** full bar. **Address:** 242 rue Principale G0S 3J0 **Location:** On Rt 173, jct Rt 112 W; centre. [B] [L] [D]

VAL-MORIN pop. 2,756

CRÊPERIE BRETONNE AU TOURNESOL
Phone: 819/322-1401

French
$9-$20

AAA Inspector Notes: The beamed ceiling and varnished pine tables of this casual creperie provide the charm of a quaint ski lodge, where guests may enjoy a variety of freshly prepared Bretagne-style crepes (thin pancakes). Start a meal with a cheese-topped French onion soup and end it with a delicious fruit dessert crepe. The crepes are prepared in an open kitchen. **Reservations:** suggested. **Address:** 5825 Rt 117 J0T 2R0 **Location:** Hwy 15 exit 76, then just ne. [D]

VAUDREUIL-DORION (F-6) pop. 25,789
• Part of Montréal area — see map p. 312

Vaudreuil-Dorion, a country resort on the Ottawa River, dates back to the 1773 founding of the Parish of Vaudreuil. Established in 1850, the village changed from a predominantly farming and dairying center to a popular vacation spot with the construction of bridges connecting it to Île Perrot and Montréal.

VAUDREUIL-SOULANGES REGIONAL MUSEUM
(Musée Régional de Vaudreuil-Soulanges), 431 av. St-Charles, is in a 19th-century stone schoolhouse. The museum offers changing exhibits about the traditional and domestic arts of Québec. **Time:** Allow 1 hour minimum. **Hours:** Mon.-Fri. 9:30-noon and 1-4:30, Sat.-Sun. 1-4:30. Closed during Christmas holidays. Phone ahead to confirm schedule. **Cost:** $5; $3.50 (students with ID and senior citizens); $2 (children). **Phone:** (450) 455-2092.

CHÂTEAU VAUDREUIL SUITES HÔTEL
Phone: (450)455-0955

Hotel
$170-$185 6/1-10/31
$160-$175 11/1-5/31

Address: 21700 Trans-Canada Hwy 40 J7V 8P3 **Location:** Hwy 40 exit 36 westbound; exit 35 eastbound. **Facility:** On manicured grounds, this modern chateau-style hotel affords views of Lac des Deux Montagnes; guest rooms and public areas are luxuriously appointed. 116 units. 6 stories, interior corridors. **Parking:** winter plug-ins. **Terms:** cancellation fee imposed. **Amenities:** safes, honor bars. *Fee:* video games, high-speed Internet. **Dining:** Villa D'Este, see separate listing. **Pool(s):** heated indoor. **Activities:** whirlpool, steamroom, boating, canoeing, paddleboats, boat dock, fishing, 2 tennis courts, bicycles, playground, volleyball, exercise room, massage. **Guest Services:** valet laundry. **Free Special Amenities:** local telephone calls and high-speed Internet. *(See ad p. 351.)*

[SAVE] [ECO] [🍴] [🛎] [📺] [🛗] [🏊] [BIZ] [📶] [✕]
[FEE][🎮] [💻] /SOME UNITS [🔲] [📠]

SUPER 8
Phone: (450)424-8898

Hotel
$77-$149

Address: 3200 boul de la Gare J7V 8W5 **Location:** Hwy 40 exit 35, just s on ave St-Charles, 0.3 mi (0.4 km) w on boul de la Cite-des-Jeunes, then just w. **Facility:** 56 units. 4 stories, interior corridors. **Amenities:** high-speed Internet. **Pool(s):** heated indoor. **Activities:** whirlpool.

[ECO] [🍴] [🛋] [📶] [✕] [💻] /SOME UNITS [FEE][🐾] [📠]

CHEZ CORA
Phone: 450/424-2220

Canadian
$6-$13

AAA Inspector Notes: Eggs, omelets, waffles, crepes (sorry, no American-style pancakes here), French toast, fruit platters and all the breakfast meats--that's the specialty here, all day. However, at lunchtime the menu lists a selection of soups, salads, quiches, sandwiches and a dish called the grilled panini crepe. **Address:** 84 boul Harwood J7V 1X8 **Location:** On Hwy 20. [B] [L]

MADISONS NEW YORK GRILL & BAR
Phone: 450/424-1224

Steak
$10-$39

AAA Inspector Notes: This lively suburban pub and steakhouse has comfortable chairs and private leather-upholstered booths. The grill menu offers fresh seafood, filet mignon, rib steaks, milk-fed veal, roast beef, ribs, grilled chicken, burgers, giant shrimp, shrimp cocktail, salmon salad, Caesar salad and a choice of sandwiches, including club, crab or red tuna. **Bar:** full bar. **Address:** 48 boul Cite des Jeunes J7V 9L5 **Location:** Hwy 40 exit 35, just s on ave St-Charles, then just w; in shopping mall. [L] [D]

ST-HUBERT
Phone: 450/455-0409

Canadian
$8-$22

AAA Inspector Notes: The pleasantly decorated family-friendly restaurant serves affordable chicken dinners, ribs, club sandwiches, chicken wings, salads, soups and hot chicken sandwiches. The children's menu includes animal nuggets. **Bar:** full bar. **Address:** 601 ave St-Charles J7V 7H4 **Location:** Hwy 40 exit 35. [L] [D]

VILLA D'ESTE

Phone: 450/455-0955

▽▽▽▽
Italian
$12-$43

AAA Inspector Notes: Elegant decor and an exceptional lake view enhance the dining experience in this casually upscale restaurant. The menu focuses on fine Italian cuisine, which is backed by an impressive selection of imported wines. Live band entertainment accompanies dinner and dancing on Friday and Saturday evenings. Weekday lunch buffets and a popular Sunday brunch are other offerings. **Bar:** full bar. **Reservations:** suggested. **Address:** 21700 Trans-Canada Hwy 40 J7V 8P3 **Location:** Hwy 40 exit 36 westbound; exit 35 eastbound; in Chateau Vaudreuil Suites Hotel. **Parking:** on-site and valet. [B] [L] [D] [LATE]

VERDUN

- Hotels & Restaurants map & index p. 342
- Part of Montréal area — see map p. 312

VILLA WELLINGTON

Phone: 514/768-0102 [91]

▽▽ ▽▽
Peruvian
$9-$20

AAA Inspector Notes: South American handicrafts decorate the casual eatery, within walking distance of the de l'Eglise subway station in a vibrant blue-collar neighborhood. The menu boasts hearty portions of affordable Peruvian dishes, including steak, grilled fish, seasoned rice, seafood, stews, grilled chicken, calamari and marinated seafood salad. **Bar:** full bar. **Reservations:** required. **Address:** 4701 rue Wellington H4G 1X2 **Location:** Corner of 2nd Ave. **Parking:** street only. [L] [D]

VICTORIAVILLE (E-5) pop. 40,486

Victoriaville grew rapidly as its wood and metal industries developed. Now an economic center of the Bois-Francs region, the town is known for its Victorian houses.

LAURIER MUSEUM (Musée Laurier), 16 rue Laurier Ouest, was once the home of Sir Wilfrid Laurier, who held office as the first French-Canadian prime minister 1896-1911. Built in 1876, the Victorian mansion houses a collection of Laurier memorabilia and furniture, and temporary historical and political exhibits. The Pavillon Hôtel des Postes Museum, a striking Second-Empire-style post office built in 1910, presents fine arts exhibits.

Time: Allow 30 minutes minimum. **Hours:** Mon.-Fri. 10-noon and 1-5, Sat.-Sun. 1-5, July-Aug.; Tues.-Fri. 10-5, Sat.-Sun. 1-5, rest of year. **Cost:** $5; $4 (ages 66+); $3 (ages 13-18 and students with ID); $2 (ages 7-12). **Phone:** (819) 357-8655.

QUALITY INN & SUITES VICTORIAVILLE

Phone: 819/330-8888

[fyi]
Hotel
Rates not provided

Too new to rate, opening scheduled for December 2011. **Address:** 1 boul Arthabaska E G6P 4B8 **Location:** Hwy 20 exit 210. **Amenities:** 74 units, pets, coffeemakers, pool, exercise facility.

VILLE DE MONT-TREMBLANT—See
MONT-TREMBLANT p. 392.

VILLE-MARIE (D-1) pop. 2,696

BROTHER MOFFET'S HOUSE (Maison du Frère-Moffet), 2 blks. w. of Hwy. 101 at 7 rue Notre-Dame-de-Lourdes, was built in 1881 of interlocked logs and features period furniture and clothing. Guided tours are available; narration in English is offered. **Time:** Allow 1 hour minimum. **Hours:** Daily 10-6, mid-June through Labour Day; by appointment early May to mid-June and day after Labour Day-Oct. 31. **Cost:** Fees $2-$10; free (ages 0-5). **Phone:** (819) 629-3533.

WAKEFIELD

AUBERGE LE MOULIN WAKEFIELD MILL INN & SPA

Phone: 819/459-1838

▽▽▽▽
Historic
Country Inn
Rates not provided

Address: 60 chemin Mill J0X 3G0 **Location:** 0.6 mi (1 km) w of Riverside Dr; centre. **Facility:** This stone-walled inn, adjacent to Gatineau Park, offers upscale guest rooms in a scenic rural setting. An atrium dining room overlooks scenic waterfalls. 40 units. 5 stories, interior corridors. **Terms:** check-in 4 pm. **Activities:** whirlpool, cross country skiing, snowmobiling, tobogganing, hiking trails, spa. [ECO] [♦] [Y] [🛜] [✕] FEE[♦] [▣] /SOME UNITS FEE[🛍]

Safety tip: Keep a current AAA/CAA
Road Atlas in every vehicle

WENDAKE (A-1)
• Part of Québec area — see map p. 405

A thriving arts community, Wendake shelters several arts and crafts shops as well as an amphitheater that showcases First Nations cultural events. Also featured is a re-creation of a traditional Indian village. Recreational pursuits include hiking along the St. Charles River on the Parc linéaire de la rivière St-Charles, a scenic 32-kilometre (19-mi.) walking trail, and biking on the Corridor des Cheminots. Adorning the bicycle path are eight decorative plantings that represent the clans of the Huron-Wendat Nation.

Tourisme Wendake: 100 boul. Bastien, Wendake, QC, Canada G0A 4V0. **Phone:** (418) 847-1835 or (888) 936-3253.

HURON-WENDAT MUSEUM is at 15 Place de la Rencontre. Bilingual interactive displays, photographs and artifacts reveal the history of the Huron-Wendat First Nations community. The lower level of the museum houses temporary art exhibits.

During the 2-hour guided Discovery Tour, visitors explore such Old Wendake cultural sites as the Tsawenhohi House (Maison Tsawenhohi), built in the early 1800s for Grand Chief Nicolas Tsawenhohi Vincent; the 1730 Notre-Dame-de-Lorette Church; and the Kabir Kouba waterfall.

Time: Allow 1 hour minimum. **Hours:** Museum daily 9-4, late June-late Oct.; Wed.-Sun. 9-4, rest of year. Discovery Tour schedule varies; phone ahead. **Cost:** Museum only $10; $9 (ages 65+); $8 (students with ID); $5 (ages 7-16); $26 (family, two adults and two children). Discovery Tour (includes museum) $14; $13 (ages 65+); $12 (students with ID); $8 (ages 7-16); $35 (family, two adults and two children). Reservations are recommended. **Phone:** (418) 847-2260.

KABIR KOUBA CLIFF AND WATERFALL PARK—see Québec p. 415.

LA TRAITE LE RESTAURANT   **Phone:** 418/847-2222

Native American
$12-$38

AAA Inspector Notes: Located in a contemporary hotel on the Huron-Wendat Reserve, this comfortable dining room and lounge serves up a menu inspired by First Nations traditions, including organic regional spices and produce. Choose from flavorful preparations of game specialties, fish and chicken. An impressive selection of wine is available. For dessert, try the traditional sugar pie. **Bar:** full bar. **Reservations:** suggested. **Address:** 5 Place de la Rencontre Ekionkiestha G0A 4V0 **Location:** Hwy 73 exit 150, 9 km (5.6 mi) w on boul Louis-XIV, following signs; in Hotel-Musee Premieres Nations. B L D

WEST BROME

AUBERGE & SPA WEST BROME   **Phone:** 450/266-7552

Hotel
Rates not provided

Address: 128 Rt 139 J0E 2P0 **Location:** Jct Rt 104, 1.3 mi (2.1 km) s. **Facility:** 26 units, some kitchens. 3 stories (no elevator), interior corridors. **Parking:** winter plug-ins. **Terms:** office hours 7:30 am-11 pm. **Amenities:** high-speed Internet. **Dining:** restaurant, see separate listing. **Pool(s):** heated indoor. **Activities:** sauna, whirlpool, exercise room, spa. **Guest Services:** valet laundry.

[ECO] [icons] / SOME UNITS [icons]

WHERE TO EAT

AUBERGE WEST BROME RESTAURANT
     Phone: 450/266-7552

French
$23-$53

AAA Inspector Notes: The sommelier provides detailed information about wines to complement French-inspired choices using many regional ingredients, including of duck, seafood, Angus beef, fresh fish, Quebec veal and lamb, Atlantic salmon. Gracious servers tend to patrons in the charming and elegant country setting. The seafood and fish buffet served Friday nights is popular, along with the gourmet Sunday brunch. Open for lunch by reservation for six or more people. **Bar:** full bar. **Reservations:** suggested. **Address:** 128 Rt 139 J0E 2P0 **Location:** Jct Rt 104, 1.3 mi (2.1 km) s; in Auberge & Spa West Brome. B D

WESTMOUNT (F-7) pop. 20,494
• Hotels & Restaurants map & index p. 342
• Part of Montréal area — see map p. 312

SHAAR HASHOMAYIM SYNAGOGUE (Synagogue de Shaar Hashomayim), 450 Kensington Ave. (M: Atwater), dates from 1846 and is the second oldest synagogue in Canada. The size of the congregation, more than 1,600 families, and the 2,000-person seating capacity of the sanctuary make this among the largest synagogues in the country. Guided tours are available; narration in English is offered. **Hours:** Tours depart Mon.-Thurs. 9:30-4. **Cost:** Donations. Reservations are required. **Phone:** (514) 937-9471.

TEMPLE EMANU-EL BETH SHOLOM, 4100 Sherbrooke St. W. (M: Atwater), dates from 1882 and is known as the country's oldest Reform Jewish congregation. **Hours:** Mon.-Thurs. 8:30-5, Fri. 8:30-3. **Cost:** Donations. **Phone:** (514) 937-3575.

BISTRO ON THE AVENUE   **Phone:** 514/939-6451   (73)

French
$11-$26

AAA Inspector Notes: On a popular commercial strip in an upscale neighborhood, this chic bistro offers gourmet burgers and sandwiches, fresh grilled fish, chicken, pasta and a variety of salads. **Bar:** full bar. **Reservations:** suggested. **Address:** 1362 Greene Ave H3Z 2B1 **Location:** Between rue Sherbrooke and Ste-Catherine. **Parking:** street only. L D

Plan. Map. Go.

TripTik® Travel Planner

Where premier mapping technology meets complete travel information. Only on AAA.com and CAA.ca.

(See map & index p. 342.)

CHINE TOQUE
Phone: 514/989-5999 [71]

Chinese
$10-$16

AAA Inspector Notes: This downtown dining room offers fine Chinese cuisine in an appealing atmosphere. The menu includes Szechuan pork, Cantonese duck, crispy orange beef, General Tao chicken, shrimp in black bean sauce, chicken dumplings with peanut butter sauce and Singapore-style rice noodles. Take-out service is available. **Bar:** full bar. **Reservations:** suggested. **Address:** 4050 rue Ste-Catherine ouest H3Z 1P2 **Location:** Just w of ave Atwater. **Parking:** street only.

[L] [D]

KAIZEN SUSHI BAR & RESTAURANT
Phone: 514/707-8744 [72]

Japanese
$15-$32

AAA Inspector Notes: Guests can dine at a private table or join others at the Japanese-style sushi bar at this spot, just steps away from some of Westmount's poshest downtown residences. A talented chef prepares fresh sushi dishes and patrons can order a variety of sushi and sashimi dishes, in addition to teriyaki beef, chicken and shrimp, all served in a stylish decor. **Bar:** full bar. **Reservations:** suggested. **Address:** 4075 rue Ste-Catherine ouest H3Z 3J8 **Location:** Between Wood and Greene aves. **Parking:** street only. [L] [D]

MISO
Phone: 514/908-6476 [70]

Japanese
$10-$30

AAA Inspector Notes: This stylish Asian restaurant faces the old Montreal Forum Arena (now an entertainment complex) and features a vast selection of freshly prepared sushi and sashimi. **Bar:** full bar. **Address:** 4000 rue Ste-Catherine ouest H3Z 1P1 **Location:** Corner of ave Atwater. **Parking:** street only. [L] [D]

RESTAURANT WELLHOUSE
Phone: 514/482-2167 [76]

Canadian
$14-$33

AAA Inspector Notes: This casually upscale bistro in Westmount's Victoria village serves up market-fresh dishes such as lamb shepherd's pie, mussels, gnocchi with pesto, calamari, a penne surf and turf, mushroom roulade with fine herbs, gourmet burgers and club sandwiches. An impressive variety of fine wines is available by the glass or bottle. The semicircular banquette seats are popular for intimate dining. **Bar:** full bar. **Address:** 4858 rue Sherbrooke ouest H3Z 1H1 **Location:** Just w of rue Victoria. **Parking:** street only. [L] [D]

TAVERNE SUR LE SQUARE
Phone: 514/989-9779 [75]

Continental
$13-$38

AAA Inspector Notes: In Westmount Square shopping mall, the upscale bistro serves market-fresh cuisine, including a selection of lighter meals at lunchtime. Among menu offerings are steak and fries, fresh fish, meat chops, macaroni, grilled tuna sandwiches, salads, burgers and fish and chips. **Bar:** full bar. **Reservations:** suggested. **Address:** 1 Westmount Square H3Z 2P9 **Location:** Corner of rue Ste-Catherine and Westmount Square Shopping Mall. [L] [D]

VAGO CUCINA ITALIANA
Phone: 514/846-1414 [74]

Italian
$18-$42

AAA Inspector Notes: This upscale bistro, on fashionable Greene Avenue, offers seating in both the main dining room and in a bright atrium. The menu lines up a strong variety of pasta and veal dishes and several Italian specialties, such as chicken Marsala. Cherries jubilee is a tempting ender. **Bar:** full bar. **Address:** 1336 ave Greene H3Z 2B1 **Location:** Just s of rue Sherbrooke. **Parking:** street only. [L] [D]

ENJOY A MAGICAL DISNEY VACATION WITH

What's the best way to experience all the enchantment of a vacation to the *Walt Disney World*® Resort in Florida or the *Disneyland*® Resort in California? How do you squeeze the most magic out of the Theme Parks and the whimsically themed *Disney Resort* hotels? And how can you enjoy great savings and exclusive benefits not available anywhere else? By booking a *AAA Vacations*® package from AAA Travel, of course!

DISNEYLAND® RESORT, CALIFORNIA

- Stay just steps away from the magic at a *Disneyland*® Resort Hotel.

- Catch World of Color, a nighttime spectacular at *Disney California Adventure*™ Park.

Disneyland® Resort Hotels

World of Color

LET AAA BE YOUR GUIDE...

With a *AAA Vacations*® package, you can create the Disney vacation that fits your family, your taste and your budget. And not only will your AAA Travel professional help put everything (like accommodations, flights and tickets) together, you'll also get to enjoy great Disney benefits on top of the exclusive AAA benefits and savings once you get there! Then all you need to do is relax and have fun.

ENCHANTING AAA BENEFITS!

Disney Parks

WALT DISNEY WORLD RESORT, FLORIDA

- Enjoy amazing theming at a *Walt Disney World*® Resort hotel.

- Experience magical moments in all four Theme Parks.

Disney's *BoardWalk* Resort

Theme Park magic

READY TO START MAKING MAGIC?
Then contact your **AAA Travel professional** today!

490

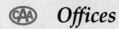 *Offices*

Cities with main offices are listed in **BOLD TYPE** and toll-free member service numbers in *ITALIC TYPE*.
All are closed Saturdays, Sundays and holidays unless otherwise indicated.
The addresses, phone numbers and hours for any AAA/CAA office are subject to change.
The type of service provided is designated below the name of the city where the office is located:

+ Auto travel services, including books and maps, and on-demand TripTik® routings.
● Auto travel services, including selected books and maps, and on-demand TripTik® routings.
■ Books/maps only, no marked maps or on-demand TripTik® routings.
▲ Travel Agency Services, cruise, tour, air, car and rail reservations; domestic and international hotel reservations; passport photo services; international and domestic travel guides and maps; travel money products; and International Driving Permits. In addition, assistance with travel related insurance products including trip cancellation, travel accident, lost luggage, trip delay and assistance products.
✪ Insurance services provided. If only this icon appears, only insurance services are provided at that office.
✖ Car Care Plus Facility provides car care services.

AAA NATIONAL OFFICE: 1000 AAA DRIVE, HEATHROW, FLORIDA 32746-5063, (407) 444-7000

NEW BRUNSWICK

FREDERICTON—CAA ATLANTIC, 418 YORK ST, E3B 3P7. WEEKDAYS (M-F) 8:30-5:30, THU 8:30-7:00, SAT 10:00-1:00. (506) 452-1987, *(800) 561-8807.* + ▲ ✪

MONCTON—CAA ATLANTIC, 500 MAPLETON RD STE140, E1G 0N3. WEEKDAYS (M-F) 8:30-5:30, THU 8:30-7:00, SAT 10:00-1:00. (506) 857-8225, *(800) 561-8807.* + ▲ ✪

SAINT JOHN—CAA ATLANTIC, 378 WESTMORLAND RD, E2J 2G4. WEEKDAYS (M-F) 8:30-5:30, THU 8:30-7:00, SAT 10:00-1:00. (506) 634-1400, *(800) 561-8807.* + ▲ ✪

NEWFOUNDLAND AND LABRADOR

ST. JOHN'S—CAA ATLANTIC, 55 KELSEY DR, A1B 5C8. WEEKDAYS (M-F) 8:30-5:30, THU 8:30-7:00, SAT 10:00-1:00. (709) 579-4222, *(800) 561-8807.* + ▲ ✪

NOVA SCOTIA

DARTMOUTH—CAA ATLANTIC, 133 ILSLEY AVE UNIT H, B3B 1S9. WEEKDAYS (M-F) 8:30-5:30, THU 8:30-7:00, SAT 10:00-1:00. (902) 468-6306, *(800) 561-8807.* + ▲ ✪

HALIFAX—CAA ATLANTIC, 3514 JOSEPH HOWE DR STE 5, B3L 4H7. WEEKDAYS (M-F) 8:30-5:30, THU 8:30-7:00, SAT 10:00-1:00. (902) 443-5530, *(800) 561-8807.* + ▲ ✪

PRINCE EDWARD ISLAND

CHARLOTTETOWN—CAA ATLANTIC, 193 MALPEQUE RD, C1E 0C4. WEEKDAYS (M-F) 8:30-5:30, SAT 10:00-1:00. (902) 892-1612, *(800) 561-8807.* + ▲ ✪

QUEBEC

BOISBRIAND—CAA QUEBEC, 2715 D'ANNEMASSE ST, J7H 0A5. WEEKDAYS (M-F) 10:00-6:00, THU 10:00-9:00, FRI 10:00-9:00, SAT 9:00-5:00. (450) 435-3636, *(800) 686-9243.* ● ▲ ✪

BROSSARD—CAA QUEBEC, 20-8940 LEDUC BLVD, J4Y 0G4. WEEKDAYS (M-F) 9:00-6:00, THU 9:00-9:00, FRI 9:00-9:00, SAT 9:00-5:00. (450) 465-0620, *(800) 686-9243.* ● ▲ ✪

CHICOUTIMI—CAA QUEBEC, 1100-1700 TALBOT BLVD, G7H 7Z4. WEEKDAYS (M-F) 9:00-5:30, THU 9:00-8:00, SAT 9:00-4:00. (418) 545-8686, *(800) 686-9243.* ● ▲ ✪

GATINEAU—CAA QUEBEC, 960 MALONEY BLVD W, J8T 3R6. WEEKDAYS (M-F) 9:30-5:30, THU 9:30-9:00, FRI 9:30-9:00, SAT 9:00-5:00. (819) 778-2225, *(800) 686-9243.* ● ▲ ✪

LAVAL—CAA QUEBEC, 100-3131 W ST-MARTIN BLVD, H7T 2Z5. WEEKDAYS (M-F) 9:00-6:00, THU 9:00-8:00, FRI 9:00-8:00, SAT 10:00-4:00. (450) 682-8100, *(800) 686-9243.* ● ▲ ✪

MONTREAL—CAA QUEBEC, 1180 DRUMMOND ST, H3G 2R7. WEEKDAYS (M-F) 8:30-6:00, THU 8:30-7:00, FRI 8:30-7:00, SAT 9:30-4:00. (514) 861-5111, *(800) 686-9243.* ● ▲ ✪

POINTE CLAIRE—CAA QUEBEC, 90-1000 ST JEAN BLVD, H9R 5P1. WEEKDAYS (M-F) 9:00-6:00, THU 9:00-8:00, FRI 9:00-8:00, SAT 9:00-4:00. (514) 426-2760, *(800) 686-9243.* ● ▲ ✪

QUEBEC—CAA QUEBEC, 133-2600 LAURIER BLVD, G1V 4T3. WEEKDAYS (M-F) 9:00-5:30, THU 9:00-8:00, FRI 9:00-8:00, SAT 9:00-4:00. (418) 653-9200, *(800) 686-9243.* ● ▲ ✪

QUEBEC—CAA QUEBEC, 202-500 BOUVIER ST, G2J 1E3. WEEKDAYS (M-F) 9:00-5:30, THU 9:00-8:00, FRI 9:00-8:00, SAT 10:00-4:00. (418) 624-8222, *(800) 686-9243.* + ▲ ✪

SHERBROOKE—CAA QUEBEC, 2990 KING W ST, J1L 1Y7. WEEKDAYS (M-F) 9:00-5:30, THU 9:00-8:00, FRI 9:00-8:00, SAT 10:00-4:00. (819) 566-5132, *(800) 686-9243.* ● ▲ ✪

ST-LEONARD—CAA QUEBEC, 7360 LANGELIER BLVD, H1S 3C4. WEEKDAYS (M-F) 9:00-6:00, THU 9:00-8:00, FRI 9:00-8:00, SAT 9:00-5:00. (514) 255-3560, *(800) 686-9243.* ● ▲ ✪

TERREBONNE—CAA QUEBEC, 302 MONTEE DES PIONNIERS, J6V 1S6. WEEKDAYS (M-F) 9:30-6:00, THU 9:30-8:00, FRI 9:30-8:00, SAT 9:30-5:00. (450) 585-9797, *(800) 686-9243.* ● ▲ ✪

TROIS RIVIERES—CAA QUEBEC, 4085 BOUL DES RECOLLETS, G9A 6M1. WEEKDAYS (M-F) 9:00-5:30, THU 9:00-8:00, FRI 9:00-8:00, SAT 9:00-4:00. (819) 376-9394, *(800) 686-9243.* ● ▲ ✪

Complete Vacation Planning

AAA.com/Travel and **CAA.ca/Travel** –
everything you need to plan and book your vacations, backed by the travel experts at local AAA/CAA offices.

Metric Equivalents Chart

TEMPERATURE

To convert Fahrenheit to Celsius, subtract 32 from the Fahrenheit temperature, multiply by 5 and divide by 9.
To convert Celsius to Fahrenheit, multiply by 9, divide by 5 and add 32.

ACRES

1 acre = 0.4 hectare (ha)   1 hectare = 2.47 acres

MILES AND KILOMETRES

Note: A kilometre is approximately 5/8 or 0.6 of a mile.
To convert kilometres to miles multiply by 0.6.

Miles/Kilometres		Kilometres/Miles	
15	24.1	30	18.6
20	32.2	35	21.7
25	40.2	40	24.8
30	48.3	45	27.9
35	56.3	50	31.0
40	64.4	55	34.1
45	72.4	60	37.2
50	80.5	65	40.3
55	88.5	70	43.4
60	96.6	75	46.6
65	104.6	80	49.7
70	112.7	85	52.8
75	120.7	90	55.9
80	128.7	95	59.0
85	136.8	100	62.1
90	144.8	105	65.2
95	152.9	110	68.3
100	160.9	115	71.4

Celsius °		Fahrenheit °
100	BOILING	212
37		100
35		95
32		90
29		85
27		80
24		75
21		70
18		65
16		60
13		55
10		50
7		45
4		40
2		35
0	FREEZING	32
-4		25
-7		20
-9		15
-12		10
-15		5
-18		0
-21		-5
-24		-10
-27		-15

LINEAR MEASURE

Customary	Metric
1 inch = 2.54 centimetres	1 centimetre = 0.4 inches
1 foot = 30 centimetres	1 metre = 3.3 feet
1 yard = 0.91 metres	1 metre = 1.09 yards
1 mile = 1.6 kilometres	1 kilometre = .62 miles

LIQUID MEASURE

Customary	Metric
1 fluid ounce = 30 millilitres	1 millilitre = .03 fluid ounces
1 cup = .24 litres	1 litre = 2.1 pints
1 pint = .47 litres	1 litre = 1.06 quarts
1 quart = .95 litres	1 litre = .26 gallons
1 gallon = 3.8 litres	

WEIGHT

If You Know:	Multiply By:	To Find:
Ounces	28	Grams
Pounds	0.45	Kilograms
Grams	0.035	Ounces
Kilograms	2.2	Pounds

PRESSURE

Air pressure in automobile tires is expressed
in kilopascals. Multiply pound-force per
square inch (psi) by 6.89 to find kilopascals
(kPa).

24 psi = 165 kPa   28 psi = 193 kPa
26 psi = 179 kPa   30 psi = 207 kPa

GALLON AND LITRES

Gallons/Litres				Litres/Gallons			
5	19.0	12	45.6	10	2.6	40	10.4
6	22.8	14	53.2	15	3.9	50	13.0
7	26.6	16	60.8	20	5.2	60	15.6
8	30.4	18	68.4	25	6.5	70	18.2
9	34.2	20	76.0	30	7.8	80	20.8
10	38.0	25	95.0	35	9.1	90	23.4

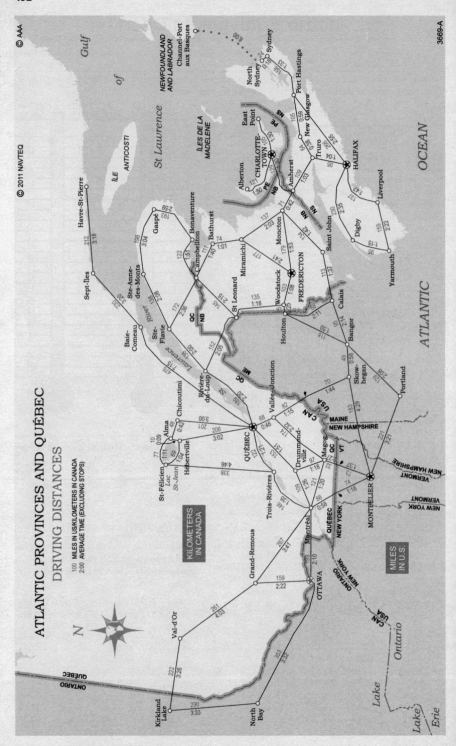

492

ATLANTIC PROVINCES AND QUÉBEC
DRIVING DISTANCES

100 MILES IN US/KILOMETERS IN CANADA
2:00 AVERAGE TIME (EXCLUDING STOPS)

KILOMETERS IN CANADA

MILES IN U.S.

© AAA
© 2011 NAVTEQ
3669-A

Border Information

U.S. Residents Traveling to Canada

Border crossing requirements: Travelers are required to present proper travel documents in order to enter Canada and return to the U.S.

Air travel: A U.S. passport is required.

Land or sea travel: Proof of citizenship and proof of identity are required. Approved documents include a passport or passport card, Enhanced Driver's License or NEXUS trusted traveler program card. Visit the U.S. Department of State website travel.state.gov for the most current information on these requirements. Canadian citizens should refer to the Canada Border Services Agency website www.cbsa-asfc.gc.ca.

U.S. resident aliens: An Alien Registration Receipt Card (Green Card) as well as a passport from the country of citizenship is required.

Children: All children must provide their own travel documents. In lieu of a U.S. passport or passport card, children under 16 traveling to Canada by land or sea may present an original or copy of their birth certificate, a Report of Birth Abroad obtained from a U.S. consulate or a Naturalization Certificate. Minors must be accompanied by parents, or have a notarized letter of consent from one or both absent parents giving permission to go on the trip.

Legal Issues: Persons with felony convictions, DUI convictions or other offenses may be denied entry into Canada.

Firearms: Canada has strict laws regarding the importing, exporting, possession, use, storage, display and transportation of firearms. These are federal laws that apply across the country. Firearms are divided into classes: non-restricted (most ordinary rifles and shotguns); restricted (mainly handguns) and prohibited (full and converted automatics and certain handguns, among others).

To bring a non-restricted or restricted firearm into Canada you must:
- Be 18 years of age or older
- Declare firearm(s) at the first point of entry
- Obtain an Authorization to Transport (ATT) from a provincial or territorial Chief Firearms Officer prior to arrival at the point of entry; contact the Canadian Firearms Centre at (800) 731-4000 for additional details.

Hunters may bring in, duty-free, 200 rounds of ammunition; a valid license or declaration to purchase ammunition is required. Those planning to hunt in multiple provinces or territories must obtain a hunting license from each one.

Firearms are forbidden in many of Canada's national and provincial parks, game reserves and adjacent areas. For additional information regarding the temporary importation and use of firearms consult the Canada Border Services Agency website.

Personal items: Clothing, personal items, sports and recreational equipment, automobiles, snowmobiles, cameras, personal computers and food products appropriate for the purpose and duration of the visit may be brought into Canada duty and tax-free. Customs may require a refundable security deposit at the time of entry.

Tobacco products: Those meeting age requirements (18 years in Alberta, Manitoba, Northwest Territories, Nunavut, Saskatchewan, Quebec and Yukon; 19 years in other provinces) may bring in up to 50 cigars, 200 cigarettes, 200 grams of tobacco and 200 tobacco sticks.

Alcohol: Those meeting age requirements (18 years in Alberta, Manitoba and Quebec;

19 years in other provinces and territories) may bring in limited alcoholic beverages: 40 ounces of liquor, 1.6 quarts of wine or 9 quarts of beer or ale (equivalent to 24 12-ounce bottles or cans).

- Amounts exceeding the allowable quantities are subject to federal duty and taxes, and provincial/territorial liquor fees.
- Provincial fees are paid at customs at the time of entry in all provinces and Yukon.
- It is illegal to bring more than the allowable alcohol quantity into the Northwest Territories or Nunavut.

Purchases: Articles purchased at Canadian duty-free shops are subject to U.S. Customs exemptions and restrictions; those purchased at U.S. duty-free shops before entering Canada are subject to duty if brought back into the United States.

Prescription drugs: Persons requiring medication while visiting Canada are permitted to bring it for their own use. Medication should be in the original packaging with a label listing the drug and its intended use. Bring a copy of the prescription and the prescribing doctor's phone number.

Gifts: Items not exceeding $60 (CAN) in value (excluding tobacco, alcoholic beverages and advertising matter) taken into or mailed to Canada are allowed free entry. Gifts valued at more than $60 are subject to regular duty and taxes on the excess amount.

Pets: You must have a certificate for a dog or cat 3 months and older. It must clearly describe the animal, declare that the animal is currently vaccinated against rabies and include a licensed veterinarian signature.

- Collar tags are not sufficient proof of immunization.
- Be sure the vaccination does not expire while traveling in Canada.
- The certificate is also required to bring the animal back into the U.S.

Exemptions: Service animals; healthy puppies and kittens under 3 months old with a health certificate signed by a licensed veterinarian indicating that the animal is too young to vaccinate.

Vehicles
- Vehicles entering Canada for leisure travel, including trailers not exceeding 8 feet 6 inches (2.6 m) in width, are

generally subject to quick and routine entry procedures.

- To temporarily leave or store a car, trailer or other goods in Canada if you must leave the country, you must pay an import duty and taxes or present a valid permit. Canadian Customs officials issue vehicle permits at the point of entry.
- You are required to carry your vehicle registration document when traveling in Canada.
- If driving a car other than your own, you must have written permission from the owner.
- If driving a rented car, you must provide a copy of the rental contract.
- A valid U.S. driver's license is valid in Canada.
- In all Canadian provinces and territories except Alberta, British Columbia and Saskatchewan, it is illegal to use radar detectors, even if unplugged.
- Seat belt use is required for the driver and all passengers.

Financial Responsibility Laws in Canada: When an accident involves death, injury or property damage, Canadian provinces and territories require evidence of financial responsibility.

U.S. motorists should check with their insurance company regarding whether they are required to obtain and carry a yellow Non-Resident Inter-Province Motor Vehicle Liability Insurance Card (accepted as evidence of financial responsibility throughout Canada). Those not carrying proper proof may be subject to a substantial fine. If renting a vehicle, check with the rental car company.

U.S. Residents Returning to the U.S.

U.S. citizens returning to the U.S. from Canada by air must have a valid passport. Those returning by land or sea are required to present the appropriate travel documents outlined above.

Every individual seeking entry into the United States—foreign visitors, U.S. citizens or lawful permanent residents—must be inspected at the point of entry. Random searches may be conducted by U.S. Customs and Border Protection agents.

U.S. Exemptions for a Stay in Canada of 48 Hours or More

- Each individual may bring back tax- and duty-free articles not exceeding $800 in retail value.
- Any amount over the $800 exemption is subject to duty.
- The exemption is allowed once every 30 days.
- A family (related persons living in the same household) may combine purchases to avoid exceeding individual exemption limits.
- Exemptions are based on fair retail value (keep receipts of all purchases as proof).
- Exemptions apply to articles acquired only for personal or household use or as gifts and not intended for sale.
- The exemption may include 100 cigars, 200 cigarettes and 1 liter of liquor per person over age 21 (state liquor laws are enforced).
- All articles must accompany you on your return.

U.S. Exemptions for a Stay in Canada Less Than 48 Hours

- Each individual may bring back tax- and duty-free articles not exceeding $200 in retail value.
- The exemption may include no more than 50 cigarettes, 10 cigars, 5 fluid ounces (150 milliliters) of alcoholic beverage or 150 milliliters of perfume containing alcohol.
- A family may not combine purchases.
- If purchases exceed the $200 exemption, you forfeit the exemption and all purchases become subject to duty.
- All articles must be declared and accompany you upon return.

Gifts

- Gifts up to $100 fair retail value may be sent to friends or relatives in the United States provided no recipient receives more than one gift per day (gifts do not have to be included in the $800 exemption).
- Gifts of tobacco products, alcoholic beverages or perfume containing alcohol valued at more than $5 retail are excluded from this provision.
- Mark the contents, retail value and "Unsolicited Gift" on the outside of the package.

Prohibited: Narcotics and dangerous drugs, drug paraphernalia, obscene articles and publications, seditious or treasonable matter, lottery tickets, hazardous items (fireworks, dangerous toys, toxic or poisonous substances) and switchblade knives. Also prohibited are any goods originating in embargoed countries.

Canadian Residents Traveling to the U.S.

Canadian citizens entering the U.S. by air must have a valid passport. Canadian citizens entering the U.S. by land or sea are required to present the appropriate travel documents; refer to the Canada Border Services Agency website www.cbsa-asfc.gc.ca for the most current information on these requirements.

If traveling to the United States with a minor, carry documentation proving your custodial rights. A person under age 18 traveling to the United States alone or with only one parent or another adult must carry certified documentation proving that the trip is permitted by both parents.

U.S. Customs permits Canadian residents to bring—duty-free for personal use and not intended for sale—the following: clothing, personal items and equipment appropriate to the trip, up to 200 cigarettes, 50 cigars or 2 kilograms of tobacco, and 1 liter of alcoholic beverage.

Canadian Residents Returning to Canada

Canadian residents may bring back, free of duty and taxes, goods valued up to $400

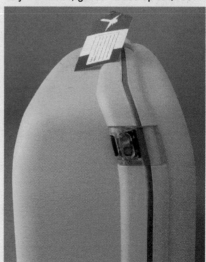

(CAN) any number of times a year, provided the visit to the United States is 48 hours or more and all goods accompany the purchaser (a written declaration may be required).

You may claim a $50 (CAN) exemption on goods, excluding alcoholic beverages and tobacco products, if returning after an absence of less than 48 hours and not using any other exemption. If bringing back more than $50 worth of goods, the regular duty and tax rate is levied on the entire value. This exemption may apply any number of times in a year. No tobacco or alcohol may be brought back if returning from a visit of less than 48 hours.

If returning after 7 days or more (not counting the departure day from Canada) you may claim up to a $750 (CAN)

exemption. Goods other than alcohol and tobacco products need not accompany you (a written declaration may be required).

Permitted within the $400 and $750 exemptions: up to 50 cigars, 200 cigarettes, 200 tobacco sticks and 6.4 ounces of tobacco, and up to 40 ounces of liquor or 1.6 quarts of wine or 9 quarts of beer or ale (the equivalent of 24 12-ounce bottles or cans). You must meet the minimum age requirement of the province or territory entered to claim alcohol or tobacco products.

While AAA makes every effort to provide accurate and complete information, AAA makes no warranty, express or implied, and assumes no legal liability or responsibility for the accuracy or completeness of any information contained herein.

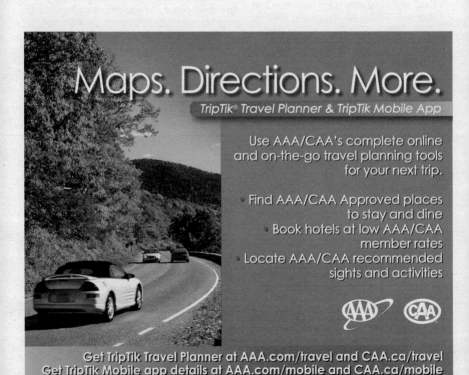

Points of Interest Index

Attractions appear at the top of each category
and offer a Great Experience for Members®.

Index Legend

CHILDREN'S ACTIVITIES

EVENTS & FESTIVALS

HISTORIC SITES & EXHIBITS

OUTDOORS & SCIENCE

SHOPPING

SPORTS & RECREATION

TOURS & SIGHTSEEING

Photo Credits

Page numbers are in bold type. Picture credit abbreviations are as follows:
■ (i) numeric sequence from top to bottom, left to right ■ (AAA) AAA Travel library.

514

(cont'd)

- **211** (iv) © John Sylvester / Alamy
- **211** (v) © Dan Leeth / Alamy
- **212** (i) © All Canada Photos / Alamy
- **212** (ii) © All Canada Photos / Alamy
- **212** (iii) © Stephen Saks Photography / Alamy
- **212** (iv) © John Sylvester / Alamy
- **242** (i) © Doug Plummer / Panoramic Images
- **242** (ii) © Perry Mastrovito / age fotostock
- **243** © Alan Marsh / age fotostock
- **244** (i) © Cephas / Wikimedia Commons
- **244** (ii) © Daily Mail/Rex / Alamy
- **247** (i) © nevio doz / age fotostock
- **247** (ii) © SIME / eStock Photo
- **247** (iii) © Dan Bannister / awl-images
- **247** (iv) © SIME / eStock Photo
- **247** (v) © Guylain Doyle / Lonely Planet Images
- **248** (i) © First Light / Alamy
- **248** (ii) © Andre Jenny / Alamy
- **248** (iii) © GFC Collection / Alamy
- **248** (iv) © SIME / eStock Photo

- **311** © SIME / eStock Photo
- **314** © Perry Mastrovito / age fotostock
- **315** © Richard Cummins / Robert Harding
- **316** © CORBIS / age fotostock
- **317** © Bill Brooks / Alamy
- **318** © Photononstop / Alamy
- **319** © pierre rochon / Alamy
- **320** © Perry Mastrovito / age fotostock
- **321** © All Canada Photos / Alamy
- **322** © Bruno Perousse / age fotostock
- **323** © Damian Siqueiros / Grand Canadian Ballet of Montréal
- **404** © RENAULT Philippe / age fotostock
- **407** © Stephen Saks / Lonely Planet Images
- **408** © Ed Lefkowicz / Alamy
- **409** © SIME / eStock Photo
- **410** © Mauritius / SuperStock
- **411** © Hemis / Alamy
- **493** © Garry Gay / Alamy
- **495** © image100 / age fotostock

KEEP YOUR CHILDREN SAFE IN THE CAR

AAA and the timeless characters of Richard Scarry, one of the best-selling children's authors of all time, have partnered to promote child passenger safety. To keep your child safe, use the right car seat and follow the guidelines at **AAA.com/SafeSeats4Kids**; in Canada visit Transport Canada at **www.tc.gc.ca**.

Remember, car seats save lives!

What do these items have in common?
AAA/CAA members spend less.

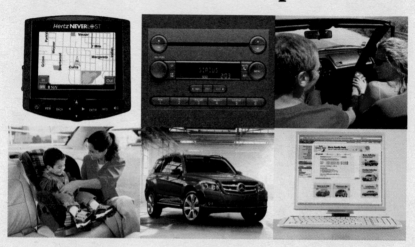

Hertz offers AAA/CAA members exclusive discounts and benefits including:

- $6.99 daily fee for Hertz NeverLost® GPS rental
- 50% off SIRIUS XM Radio® rental
- Additional authorized driver at no charge

- Free use of a child seat
- Special Internet pricing
- Member Satisfaction Guarantee
- 10% Off Fuel Purchase Option
- 10% Off U.S. prepaid rates

SHOW YOUR AAA/CAA CARD AND SAVE

THE ONLY CAR RENTAL COMPANY ENDORSED BY AAA/CAA

hertz.com/hertz.ca
For restrictions, visit your AAA/CAA office.
® Reg. U.S. Pat. Off. © 2011 Hertz System, Inc.

Visit	Over 1,100 AAA/CAA Offices		
Click	AAA.com/Hertz or CAA.ca/Hertz	Call	800-654-3080 or 888-333-3120